THE OXFORD HANDBOOK OF

MUSIC THERAPY

Jane Edwards is a qualified music therapist with extensive experience in medical, mental health, and child and family practice. Originally from Australia she has held academic and healthcare positions and affiliations in Ireland, the UK (Scotland and England), the USA, and Germany, as a presenter, academic, researcher, and consultant. She founded the Music & Health Research Group at the University of Limerick, Ireland. She is Editor-in-Chief of *The Arts in Psychotherapy*, and inaugural President of the International Association for Music & Medicine. Her previous edited book with OUP, *Music Therapy and Parent-Infant Bonding* (2011), was received enthusiastically by practitioners in music therapy and related fields across the world.

THE OXFORD HANDBOOK OF

MUSIC THERAPY

Edited by

JANE EDWARDS

OXFORD
UNIVERSITY PRESS

OXFORD

UNIVERSITY PRESS

Great Clarendon Street, Oxford, OX2 6DP,
United Kingdom

Oxford University Press is a department of the University of Oxford.
It furthers the University's objective of excellence in research, scholarship,
and education by publishing worldwide. Oxford is a registered trade mark of
Oxford University Press in the UK and in certain other countries

Published in the United States of America by Oxford University Press
198 Madison Avenue, New York, NY 10016, United States of America

British Library Cataloguing in Publication Data

Data available

Library of Congress Cataloging in Publication Data

Data available

ISBN 978–0–19–963975–5 (Hbk.)
ISBN 978–0–19–881714–7 (Pbk.)

Printed and bound by
CPI Group (UK) Ltd, Croydon, CR0 4YY

This book is dedicated to all students of music therapy;
past, present, and future.

Foreword

··

After the pleasures which arise from gratification of the bodily appetites, there seems to be none more natural to man than Music and Dancing. … Without any imitation, instrumental Music can produce very considerable effects … : by the sweetness of its sounds it awakens agreeably, and calls upon the attention; by their connection and affinity it naturally detains that attention, which follows easily a series of agreeable sounds, which have all a certain relation both to a common, fundamental, or leading note, called the key note; and to a certain succession or combination of notes, called the song or composition. … Time and measure are to instrumental Music what order and method are to discourse; they break it into proper parts and divisions, by which we are enabled both to remember better what has gone before, and frequently to forsee somewhat of what is to come after: …. the enjoyment of Music arises partly from memory and partly from foresight.

> Adam Smith (1777). Of the nature of that imitation which takes place
> in what are called the imitative arts. In: *Essays on Philosophical Subjects*
> (eds W.P.D Wightman and J.C. Bryce), Indianapolis: Liberty Fund, 1982.

THE psychiatrist Daniel Stern gave us a new scientific appreciation of the vital foundations of verbal or representational intelligence in the spontaneous impulses of human communication, including the imitative arts of music and dance. Stern studied the power of twins a few months old to share consciousness and feelings with a mother in play (Stern 1971), and he related this understanding to enrich psychoanalytic therapy for emotional distress in relationships (Stern 2000). He proposed that the source of our sense of relating emotionally with other persons is the unspoken "vitality dynamics" of our actions-with-awareness—the "how" we move, not the articulate "why" or "what" of our purpose or the object we choose (Stern 2010). Stern describes the expressive qualities of movement as "forms of feeling" engaged with emotional "attunement," and he draws special attention to the organization of movements through time in"proto-narrative envelopes." These powers need no words to engage hearts and minds in therapy for depressed emotions and to relieve suffering from social isolation (Trevarthen and Malloch 2000).

In the introduction to the second edition of his book *The Interpersonal World of the Infant*, Stern wrote, "One consequence of the book's application of a narrative perspective to the non-verbal has been the discovery of a language useful to many psychotherapies that rely on the non-verbal. I am thinking particularly of dance, music, body, and movement therapies, as well as existential psychotherapies. This observation came as a pleasant surprise to me since I did not originally have such therapists in mind; my thinking has been enriched by coming to know them better." (Stern 2000, p. xv).

Advances in movement psychology over the last century have brought to medical science the realization that prospective control of movements requires, not training to assemble thoughtless reflex reactions to stimulating events, but exploration of creative motor plans through consciously guided measures of time, with emotions that control economy of the energy required to sustain well-being in the body. Charles Sherrington (1906) discovered *proprioception*, the feelings of muscle action, which he called the "felt Me," and was led by exploration of the neural foundations of agency to a more humane medical concern for disorders of the will, which he presented in his Gifford Lectures entitled *Man on His Nature* (Sherrington 1955). In that book he articulated a rich conception of evolution and development of a human person from a fertilized ovum as an epigenetic creation of organic vitality, concluding: "It would be imagination rather than memory which we must assume for the ancestral cell; memory could not recall experience it never had."(Sherrington 1955, Chapter 4, *The Wisdom of the Body*, pp. 103–104). This remains as a firm reminder that our actions and experience, and our affective states and the expressions of our personality, cannot be attributed to a "gene code." They are inventive products of the processes of an effort of the whole organism to live in relations, which have powers to regulate how our genes are expressed.

Rigorous proof of the power of the brain to imagine consequences of motor action was obtained by Nikolai Aleksandrovich Bernstein, a Russian scientist in Moscow's Central Institute of Laborin the 1930s who developed microscopic analysis of films, of athletes running, of workers using tools and of young children mastering toddling, walking, and running, to prove that the remarkable efficiency of our powerful or delicate motor actions requires precise prospective planning by a dynamic and rhythmic "image" in the brain, which assembles complexes of muscle activity throughout the body to function adaptively (Bernstein 1967). Bernstein's work inspired the science of *kinesics*, how postures and gestures exchanged in live conversation "orchestrate" and "conduct" the meaning specified in words. Film studies of how movements of the whole body accompany conversational use of words, enriching meaning and resolving ambiguities of understanding (Condon and Ogston 1966; Birdwhistell 1970), inspired Stern's research with infants. Condon and Sander (1974) showed that hand gestures of a newborn infant can translate shared experience in synchrony with a spoken message of an adult. All the parameters of personal motor control—the *kinematics* or rhythm, the *energetics* or effort, and the *physiognomics* or form—are enhanced and coordinated in proto-conversations and games with babies as adult and child use face, hands, eyes, and voice (Trevarthen 1986). They are giving emotionally charged purpose to sensory-motor organs that are already formed in the human foetus for communicating states of mind (Trevarthen and Delafield-Butt 2013).Their expressive actions in proto-conversational engagements and games have natural properties of "communicative musicality" (Malloch 1999; Malloch and Trevarthen 2009).

Now, motion capture technology gives rich confirmation of the discoveries of Sherrington and Bernstein, supporting a mathematical model of the foresightful process by which the brain takes up or "assimilates" perceptions of being alive in the world by mastering well the resources of a heavy body (Lee 2005). This account of prospective motor control gives us a richer appreciation of how we sense feelings of life in other persons to share awareness and meaning, and it is inspiring a new brain science of intersubjective communication (Ammaniti and Gallese 2014). The power of language to make reference to goals for action and to tell stories depends upon using the musicality of movement in convivial ways, and instinctive concern for the experience of others with "affective attunement," and this ancient dependence is revealed to be an essential resource for all rational and technical mastery of collective work in ambitious modern culture, and for representation of its knowledge and conventions in artificial media (McGilchrist 2009).

Spoken language has evolved as a way of symbolizing the memory and imagination of precise experiences. It is a traditional cultural code learned to enrich the primary inter-subjective communication that comes to life in proto-conversations with infants (Bateson 1979; Trevarthen 1979). Music expresses a more ancient and more intimate way of sharing the meaning of life (Blacking 1976; Cross and Morley 2009; Trevarthen 2012). It has special power to enrich and sustain trusting relationships in large and busy human communities, to define personal identity, and to make calm understanding of stressful experiences and imagining (Brandt 2009). All human cultures depend on a fellowship of artful creativity that celebrates the pulse of life, with what Victor Turner calls "the human seriousness of play" (Turner 1982), and with the imaginative talents Jerome Bruner attributes to us as "story-making animals" (Bruner 1990). With music and dance we celebrate community in ritual ceremonies, and individuals who lead these in artful ways are responded to with admiration and their inventions are imitated and remembered as treasures of culture (Dissanayake 2009)

The grace and efficiency of any activity is determined by feelings for the rhythms of life, the dynamic transitions between serial projects of motor activity (Trevarthen 2013). Emotional states are primarily concerned with the anticipation of the risks and benefits of our actions. Stern related his theory of Vitality Dynamics to the process philosophy of Susan Langer who wrote of "forms of feeling," as in a melody, that combine physiological events of embodied experience and the compositions of narrative and thought. "There are certain aspects of the so-called 'inner life'—physical or mental—which have formal properties similar to those of music—patterns of motion and rest, of tension and release, of agreement and disagreement, preparation, fulfillment, excitation, sudden change, etc." (Langer 1942, p. 228). Music has power to influence the well-being of the self by directly engaging with the autonomic nervous system to relieve the damaged spirit of traumatized individuals (Osborne 2009).

Jaak Panksepp, a leading researcher on the emotional systems of the brain and their neurochemistry, applies his knowledge to develop "affective neuroscience" and "neuro-psychoanalysis." He interprets emotions in music as follows: "Through unfathomed neurochemical responses in the brain, the sounds of music can bring joy and dull the jab of pain, as endogenous opioids and many other affective chemistries are recruited in musically entrained minds." (Panksepp and Trevarthen 2009, p. 105). Thus music becomes a medium for engaging with "primary affective consciousness" (Solms and Panksepp 2012).There is a growing science of the deep consciousness of vitality in the body and of its sympathetic communication at all stages of life in community, from the prenatal relation of the fetus with the mother's vitality through all stages of companionship in learning how to live well through "higher level" consciousness of meaning and who to share it with. This attributes a more lively intelligence with its own measures of self-feeling consciousness and sense of relating to the mysterious "unconscious" of Freud, and leads to development of different, less explicit or more intuitive, methods of psychoanalysis and of therapy. The philosopher Barbara Goodrich, in an article entitled "We do, therefore we think: time, motility, and consciousness" reviews work of two leading scientists Rodolfo Llinás and GyörgyBuszáki who study motor control and rhythms of the brain, to support the conclusion that "playing music—one of the most cognitively and emotionally demanding of all human activities, arguably one of the most definitively 'human' of all activities—is founded in carefully, creatively guided movement —not thought alone" (Goodrich 2010, p. 339).

Jane Edwards' book offers us a rich review of current understanding how guided practice in sharing musical performance can relieve the shame of loss of self-confidence in relationships and the fear of acting in communication. As current President of the International Association for Music and Medicine, she has recruited an impressive group of experienced music therapists from many countries who review how music therapy has developed for work to help persons of all ages and with different needs for help with self-confidence, communication, social engagement, and expression of feelings. Different models of practice are compared and different levels of training and qualification are considered. Most importantly methods of research in music therapy are reviewed to explain the nature of the treatment and the beneficial effects it has.

As with the sciences of movement psychology and of communication in infancy, reliable knowledge of the natural process of music therapy has come from detailed case studies with special methods of observation, recording, and analysis, rather than from experimentation with large numbers of subjects using limited measures and statistical analysis. Both "validation" and "reliability" of descriptions of human behavior and experience, and of their emotional regulation between subjects and in groups, require open acceptance of the intrinsic dynamics of the motivation and regulation of agency and the movements that express them. Standardized clinical trials that measure effects of prescribed treatments may not be sufficiently sensitive to the essential causes and controls. This book is a major contribution to the rich and growing practice of music therapy for all ages.

Colwyn Trevarthen, 30 June, 2014

References

Ammaniti, M. and Gallese, V. (2014). *The Birth of Intersubjectivity: Psychodynamics, Neurobiology, and the Self*. New York: Norton.

Bateson, M.C. (1979). The epigenesis of conversational interaction: A personal account of research development. In: M. Bullowa (ed.), *Before Speech: The Beginning of Human Communication*, pp. 63–77. London: Cambridge University Press.

Bernstein, N. (1967). *Coordination and Regulation of Movements*. New York: Pergamon.

Birdwhistell, R. (1970). *Kinesics and Context*. Philadelphia: University of Pennsylvania Press.

Blacking, J. (1976). How Musical is Man? London: Faber and Faber.

Brandt, P.A. (2009). Music and how we became human—a view from cognitive semiotics: Exploring imaginative hypotheses. In: S. Malloch and C. Trevarthen (eds), *Communicative Musicality: Exploring the Basis of Human Companionship*, pp. 31–44. Oxford: Oxford University Press.

Bruner, J.S. (1990). *Acts of Meaning*. Cambridge, MA: Harvard University Press.

Condon, W.S. and Ogston, W.D. (1966). Sound film analysis of normal and pathological behavior patterns. *Journal of Nervous and Mental Diseases* 143(4): 338–457.

Condon, W.S. and Sander, L.S. (1974). Neonate movement is synchronized with adult speech: Interactional participation and language acquisition. *Science* 183: 99–101.

Cross, I. and Morley, I. (2009). The evolution of music: Theories, definitions and the nature of the evidence. In: S. Malloch and C. Trevarthen (eds), *Communicative Musicality: Exploring the Basis of Human Companionship*, pp. 61–81. Oxford: Oxford University Press.

Dissanayake, E. (2009). Bodies swayed to music: The temporal arts as integral to ceremonial ritual. In: S. Malloch and C. Trevarthen (eds), *Communicative Musicality: Exploring the Basis of Human Companionship*, pp. 533–544. Oxford: Oxford University Press.

Goodrich, B.G. (2010). We do, therefore we think: Time, motility, and consciousness. *Reviews in the Neurosciences* 21: 331–361.

Langer, S.K. (1942). *Philosophy in a New Key: A Study in the Symbolism of Reason, Rite, and Art.* Cambridge MA: Harvard University Press.

Lee, D.N. (2005).Tau in action in development. In: J.J. Rieser, J.J. Lockman, and C.A. Nelson (eds), *Action as an Organizer of Learning and Development*, pp. 3–49. Hillsdale, NJ: Erlbaum.

Malloch, S. (1999). Mother and infants and communicative musicality. In: I. Deliège (ed.), *Rhythms, Musical Narrative, and the Origins of Human Communication. Musicae Scientiae, Special Issue, 1999-2000*, pp. 29–57. Liège, Belgium: European Society for the Cognitive Sciences of Music.

Malloch, S. and Trevarthen, C. (eds). (2009). *Communicative Musicality: Exploring the Basis of Human Companionship*. Oxford: Oxford University Press.

McGilchrist, I. (2009). *The Master and His Emissary: The Divided Brain and the Making of he Western World*. New Haven and London: Yale University Press.

Merker, B. (2009). Ritual foundations of human uniqueness.In: S. Malloch and C. Trevarthen (eds), *Communicative Musicality: Exploring the Basis of Human Companionship*, pp. 45–60. Oxford: Oxford University Press.

Osborne, N. (2009). Music for children in zones of conflict and post-conflict: A psychobiological approach. In: S. Malloch and C. Trevarthen (eds), *Communicative Musicality: Exploring the Basis of Human Companionship*, pp. 331–356. Oxford: Oxford University Press.

Panksepp, J. and Trevarthen C. (2009).The neuroscience of emotion in music. In: S. Malloch and C. Trevarthen (eds), *Communicative Musicality: Exploring the Basis of Human Companionship*, pp. 105–146. Oxford: Oxford University Press;.

Sherrington, C.S. (1906). *The Integrative Action of the Nervous System*. New Haven: Yale University Press.

Sherrington, C.S. (1955). *Man on His Nature*. (The Gifford Lectures, 1937–1938). Harmondsworth: Penguin Books.

Smith, A. (1777). Of the nature of that imitation which takes place in what are called the imitative arts. In: W.P.D Wightman and J.C. Bryce (eds), *Essays on Philosophical Subjects*. Indianapolis: Liberty Fund, 1982.

Solms, M. and Panksepp, J. (2012). The "Id" knows more than the "Ego" admits: Neuropsychoanalytic and primal consciousness perspectives on the interface between affective and cognitive neuroscience. *Brain Sciences* 2: 147–175.

Stern, D.N. (1971). A micro-analysis of mother-infant interaction: Behaviors regulating social contact between a mother and her three-and-a-half-month-old twins. *Journal of American Academy of Child Psychiatry* 10: 501–517.

Stern, D.N. (2000).*The Interpersonal World of the Infant: A View From Psychoanalysis and Development Psychology*. 2nd Edn, with new Introduction. New York: Basic Books.

Stern, D.N. (2010). *Forms of Vitality: Exploring Dynamic Experience In Psychology, the Arts, Psychotheraphy, and Development*. Oxford: Oxford University Press.

Trevarthen, C. (1979). Communication and cooperation in early infancy. A description of primary intersubjectivity. In: M. Bullowa (ed.), *Before Speech: The Beginning of Human Communication*, pp. 321–347. London: Cambridge University Press.

Trevarthen, C. (1986). Development of intersubjective motor control in infants. In: M.G. Wade and H.T.A. Whiting (eds), *Motor Development in Children: Aspects of Coordination and Control*, pp. 209–261. Dordrecht: MartinusNijhof.

Trevarthen, C. (2012). Born for art, and the joyful companionship of fiction. In: D. Narvaez, J. Panksepp, A. Schore, and T. Gleason (eds), *Evolution, Early Experience and Human Development: From Research to Practice and Policy*, pp. 202–218. New York: Oxford University Press.

Trevarthen, C. (2013). Chronobiology or Biochronology. In: K. Kirkland (ed.), *International Dictionary of Music Therapy*, pp. 22–23. Hove/New York: Routledge.

Trevarthen, C. and Delafield-Butt, J. (2013). Biology of shared experience and language development: Regulations for the inter-subjective life of narratives. In: M. Legerstee, D. Haley, and M. Bornstein (eds), *The Infant Mind: Origins of the Social Brain*, pp. 167–199. New York: Guildford Press.

Trevarthen, C. and Malloch, S. (2000). The dance of wellbeing: Defining the musical therapeutic effect. *The Nordic Journal of Music Therapy* 9(2): 3–17.

Turner, V. (1982). *From Ritual to Theatre: The Human Seriousness of Play*. New York: Performing Arts Journal Publications.

ACKNOWLEDGEMENTS

This book was made possible with the support of two universities; the University of Limerick, Ireland and Deakin University, Victoria, Australia. Thanks are due to colleagues, friends, and family for their kindness and support. The book was devised and edited primarily while resident in Ireland and Australia but some parts were completed in Scotland, Germany, Italy, and England. The editorial team at OUP are due thanks for their support and advice, especially Martin Baum and Charlotte Green. Thanks also to Oonagh McMahon who contributed her expertise to an early round of editing. Special gratitude is due to the authors who contributed their time and expertise to the *Oxford Handbook of Music Therapy*.

CONTENTS

SECTION TWO: APPROACHES AND MODELS OF MUSIC THERAPY

SECTION THREE: MUSIC THERAPY METHODS

SECTION FOUR: MUSIC THERAPY RESEARCH

SECTION FIVE: MUSIC THERAPY TRAINING AND PROFESSIONAL ISSUES

LIST OF CONTRIBUTORS

Aasgaard, Trygve, Professor, Oslo and Akershus University College of Applied Sciences, Norwegian Academy of Music, Oslo, Norway.

Abad, Vicky, Lecturer, School of Music, University of Queensland, Brisbane, Australia.

Ahonen, Heidi, Professor of Music Therapy, Wilfrid Laurier University and Director of the Manfred and Penny Conrad Institute for Music Therapy Research, Waterloo, Ontario, Canada.

Ansdell, Gary, Director of Education, Nordoff Robbins Music Therapy, London, UK.

Austin, Diane, Director of the Music Psychotherapy Center, New York, USA.

Bergmann, Thomas, Music therapist, Ev. Krankenhaus Königin Elisabeth Herzberge; Lecturer, Centre for Music Therapy at Berlin University of Arts, Berlin, Germany.

Blichfeldt Ærø, Stine C., Music therapist, Oslo University Hospital, Rikshospitalet, Oslo, Norway.

Burns, Debra S., Associate Professor and Chair, Department of Music and Arts Technology, Purdue School of Engineering and Technology at IUPUI, Indiana University Simon Cancer Center, Indianapolis, Indiana, USA.

Clair, Alicia Ann, Professor Emeritus, University of Kansas, Lawrence, Kansas, USA.

Clark, John, Anthroposophical Music Therapist, Camphill Community Ballytobin, Callan, Co. Kilkenny, Ireland.

Colwell, Cynthia M., Professor, School of Music, University of Kansas, Lawrence, Kansas, USA.

Curtis, Sandra L., Professor and Music Therapy Graduate Program Coordinator, Creative Arts Therapies Department, Concordia University, Montreal, Canada.

Daveson, Barbara A., Cicely Saunders International Lecturer in Health Services Research, Cicely Saunders Institute, Department of Palliative Care, Policy and Rehabilitation, King's College London, London, UK.

Dearn, Trish, Clinical Director, Early Intervention Music Therapy Clinic, Melbourne, Australia.

Edwards, Jane, Professor, Deakin University, Victoria, Australia, and Music and Health Research Group, University of Limerick, Ireland.

Elefant, Cochavit, Associate Professor and Head of the Graduate School of Creative Arts Therapies, University of Haifa, Israel.

Erkkilä, Jaakko, Professor, University of Jyvaskyla, Finland.

Gfeller, Kate E., Professor, School of Music, Department of Communication Sciences and Disorders, University of Iowa, Iowa City, USA.

Ghetti, Claire M., Associate Professor, Grieg Academy of Music Therapy Research Centre, the Grieg Academy, University of Bergen, Bergen, Norway.

Gilbertson, Simon, Associate Professor, The Grieg Academy and Grieg Academy Music Therapy Research Centre,University of Bergen, Bergen, Norway.

Grocke, Denise, Emeritus Professor, Melbourne Conservatorium of Music, University of Melbourne, Victoria, Australia.

Guerrero, Nina, Nordoff-Robbins Center for Music Therapy, Steinhardt School of Culture, Education, and Human Development, New York University, New York, USA.

Hadley, Susan, Professor and Music Therapy Program Director, Slippery Rock University, Pennsylvania, USA.

Hahna, Nicole, Fellow, Association for Music and Imagery, Slippery Rock University, Pennsylvania, USA.

Hanser, Suzanne B., Chair, Music Therapy Department, Berklee College of Music, Boston, Massachusetts, USA.

Hayes, Tommy, Self-employed Music Therapist, Clare, Ireland.

Intveen, Andrea, Music Therapist, University Clinic Ulm, Child and Adolescent Psychiatry, Ulm, Germany.

Kennelly, Jeanette, Honorary Research Fellow, School of Music, University of Queensland, Brisbane, Australia.

Kenny, Carolyn, Professor Emerita, Antioch University, Yellow Springs, Ohio, USA.

Ledger, Alison, Lecturer, Leeds Institute of Medical Education, University of Leeds, UK.

Lee, Colin Andrew, Professor, Wilfrid Laurier University, Waterloo, Canada.

Loewy, Joanne, Director & Associate Professor, Louis Armstrong Music Therapy Department, Mount Sinai Beth Israel& Icahn School of Medicine, New York, USA.

Loth, Helen, Course Leader, MA Music Therapy, Department of Music and Performing Arts, Anglia Ruskin University, Cambridge, UK.

Magill, Lucanne, Manager, Creative Arts Therapy, MJHS Institute for Innovation in Palliative Care, MJHS Hospice and Palliative Care, New York, USA.

Marcus, David, Nordoff-Robbins Center for Music Therapy, Steinhardt School of Culture, Education, and Human Development, New York University, New York, USA.

McCaffrey, Tríona, Lecturer, Irish World Academy of Music and Dance, University of Limerick, Ireland.

Metzner, Susanne, Professor, Hochschule Magdeburg-Stendal, University of Applied Sciences, Faculty of Social and Health Sciences, Magdeburg, Germany.

Michael, Natasha, Associate Professor, Palliative Care Service, Cabrini Health, Melbourne, Australia.

Mondanaro, John, Clinical Director, Louis Armstrong Music Therapy Department, Mount Sinai Beth Israel Medical Center, New York, New York, USA.

Nöcker-Ribaupierre, Monika, Music Therapist DMtG, Head of Freies Musikzentrum, Munich, Germany.

Noone, Jason, Music and Health Research Group, University of Limerick, Ireland.

O'Callaghan, Clare, Music Therapist, Caritas Christi Hospice, St Vincent's Hospital; Palliative Care Service, Cabrini Health; Associate Professor, Department of Medicine, St Vincent's Hospital, The University of Melbourne, Australia.

Odell-Miller, Helen, Director of The Centre for Music Therapy Research, and Professor of Music Therapy, Anglia Ruskin University, UK. Honorary Therapist and Researcher Cambridge and Peterborough NHS Foundation Trust.

Oldfield, Amelia, Senior Professor of Music, Department of Music and Performing Arts, Anglia Ruskin University, Cambridge, UK.

Pavlicevic, Mercedes, Nordoff-Robbins Music Therapy, School of Oriental and African Studies, University of London, UK and University of Pretoria, South Africa.

Reid, Philippa, Department of Education and Training, Melbourne, Australia.

Robb, Sheri L., Associate Professor, Indiana University School of Nursing, Indianapolis, Indiana, USA.

Rolvsjord, Randi, Associate Professor, GAMUT – The Grieg Academy Music Therapy Research Centre, University of Bergen, Norway.

Shoemark, Helen, Associate Professor of Music Therapy, Temple University, Philadelphia, USA. Team Leader, Sensory Experience in Early Development, Murdoch Children's Research Institute, Melbourne, Australia.

Stige, Brynjulf, Professor, GAMUT – The Grieg Academy Music Therapy Research Centre, University of Bergen and Uni Research Health, Bergen, Norway.

Trondalen, Gro, Professor in Music Therapy Director of Centre for Music and Health Norwegian Academy of Music, Oslo, Norway.

Turry, Alan, Managing Director of the Nordoff-Robbins Center for Music Therapy, Steinhardt School of Culture, Education, and Human Development, New York University, New York, USA.

Twyford, Karen, Music Therapist, Occupational Therapy Department, Princess Margaret Hospital, Perth, Australia.

Watson, Tessa, Senior Lecturer, Department of Psychology, University of Roehampton, UK.

Wheeler, Barbara L., Professor Emerita, Montclair State University, New Jersey, USA.

···

CONCEPTUALIZING MUSIC THERAPY

Five Areas that Frame the Field

···

JANE EDWARDS

Everyone has the right freely to participate in the cultural life of the community, to enjoy the arts and to share in scientific advancement and its benefits.

Article 27 of the Universal Declaration of Human Rights, 1948

INTRODUCTION

···

ANSWERING the question "what is music therapy?" briefly and comprehensively can be challenging for new students entering training. Most seasoned practitioners can present a few short sentences to sum up their work but when starting out it can feel awkward and confronting having chosen a wonderful profession to encounter difficulty in explaining it to others. Loewy (2001) has advised that responding to questions is part of our everyday lives as music therapists. She wrote, "we have to explain and show rather than roll our eyes, hide or become introverted" (p. 4) reflecting that many practitioners learn how to explain music therapy to others by describing a recent event from their practice in which the use of music made a difference; supporting or helping a client in some way.

This chapter presents a discussion of definitions of music therapy, along with five constructs relevant to music therapy internationally that are represented in the *Oxford Handbook of Music Therapy*. These framing constructs are; music therapy contexts and populations across the lifespan, music therapy models and approaches, music therapy methods, music therapy research, and music therapy training and professional issues. These are discussed in turn with reference to chapters presented in the *Oxford Handbook of Music Therapy*.

THE OXFORD HANDBOOK OF MUSIC THERAPY

The music therapy profession is consolidating its role in education, community, and health care services internationally. The Oxford Handbook of Music Therapy has provided the opportunity to bring together some of the major practice, research, and training features and activities by which the profession of music therapy is known worldwide. This text seeks to provide twenty-first-century students and practitioners in music therapy with a snapshot of activities and practices that make up the field across a range of countries.

This book represents some of the major research, practice, and theory in music therapy, primarily in the English-speaking world but also more widely with further chapters from authors in Europe and Scandinavia. To gain a deeper understanding of the field it is important to observe practitioners, attend conferences, and read widely in the research literature. This text points the reader to key developments in music therapy across countries in the English-speaking world and beyond. The authors are based in nine countries: Australia, Canada, Finland, Germany, Ireland, Israel, Norway, the UK, and the USA. It would be impossible to read the book cover to cover in a single sitting so the chapter list and the index are useful to the reader in finding what they need. Students seeking further information are encouraged to use the reference list in each chapter to guide their reading.

Music therapy is increasingly a highly diverse community of practitioners, with many models and approaches, techniques, and methods. Summing up this breadth in a single text would be impossible, and has not been attempted. New practices emerge in response to new dilemmas and needs in communities, and new methods emerge as technologies change and develop. The ways people access music making, learning, and music listening in their lives is dependent on many factors, and this diversity and interdependence of factors influences music therapy practice.

MUSIC THERAPY PRACTICE DEFINITIONS

Music therapy is a relational therapy involving the use of music in therapeutic processes with individuals and groups by a qualified practitioner who has undertaken appropriate training and undertakes ongoing professional development. It is a unique way of working in which the dynamic capacities of music and musical relating are harnessed to serve the needs of the client, family, or group who is seeking help. Many people have observed responses to music by people who have for example, some kind of altered state of consciousness, a developmental difficulty, illness, or some kind of dementia. These responses to music can seem miraculous and astounding leading people to believe they have witnessed a music therapy process when instead they have observed a music response. More personally, almost every human being has been touched by music's emotional power. Remembering a favorite song of a loved one after they have passed can evoke tears. Hearing a romantic song, or *our song* meaningful to one's intimate relationship can bring a smile and feelings of tenderness. Relating these experiences of the wonder of music and everyday human experience to the practice of music therapy is easy, but explaining the differences between these observed effects of music's highly evocative capacities and the practice of music therapy can be challenging.

One of the reasons that music therapy can be difficult to define and explain to others is because music therapy is highly dependent on the context of practice and the needs or opportunities of the people attending programmes to rationalize what it is and how it works. For example, two children's hospitals may have completely different music therapy services. In one, the music therapists may have developed their services in response to the needs of hospitalized children who have a psychological disturbance related to illness, injury, or other events in their lives. Therefore the music therapy service provides one to one confidential sessions with the children in a designated music therapy space equipped with instruments. In another hospital music therapy is offered to support the needs of children who are in pain, or who are attending painful procedures. In this hospital music therapy is offered in medical treatment rooms and at bedside with no dedicated music therapy space for sessions and often with other professionals present along with family members. These examples reveal that every music therapy service is offered in a context in which the development of the service has been responsive to the needs of the people being served. With greater experience of the contexts in which music therapy is practiced, defining music therapy becomes easier.

Definitions of music therapy

Bruscia (1998) has located the problem with defining music therapy as relating to many complexities including that the agreed definitions for both of the words *therapy* and *music* are problematic. He devised a frequently cited definition as follows:

> Music therapy is a systematic process of intervention wherein the therapist helps the client to promote health, using music experiences and the relationships that develop through them as dynamic forces of change.

Bruscia 1998, p. 20

This definition emphasizes that the music therapist works in a systematic way, guided by foundational principles, using techniques for which training is required to ensure that these techniques are applied effectively, and working towards the development of a relational process between the group or client and the therapist. This relationship is built up through musical interactions that scaffold the formation of the client's trust, confidence, and agency.

Professional associations for music therapy around the world have each developed their own agreed definition, and these are regularly updated and refined. The World Federation for Music Therapy (WFMT), which is the international association for these professional bodies, has defined music therapy as follows:

> Music therapy is the professional use of music and its elements as an intervention in medical, educational, and everyday environments with individuals, groups, families, or communities who seek to optimize their quality of life and improve their physical, social, communicative, emotional, intellectual, and spiritual health and wellbeing. Research, practice, education, and clinical training in music therapy are based on professional standards according to cultural, social, and political contexts.

WFMT 2015: <http://www.wfmt.info/WFMT/About_WFMT.html>.

The WFMT definition includes reference to the cultural and localized aspects of working in music therapy, and the need for the music therapist to be trained and sensitive when working with people who are from cultural or social backgrounds that differ from their own. This definition also refers to professional standards which include a code of ethics, scope of practice guidelines, and standards of practice or competency to work in the field.

Is music therapy an intervention?

Some music therapists have indicated concern with the word *intervention* that is commonly used in therapeutics (for example Kenny this volume) and which appears in the definitions above. The word intervention can be helpful in explaining music therapy because it indicates that the therapy process is enacted with the intent to *do something* to change a client's state, and it references common terminology in health care. The word *intervention* can be perceived as problematic because it indicates the potential overriding of respectful collaboration between service users and therapists that is an essential part of relational therapy processes.

Using the word intervention implies that the therapeutic process is active rather than benign. This is important to remember when offering music because humans can close their eyes but hearing cannot be turned off. Some music therapists have recommended that this more contested aspect of practice, that is the potential intrusiveness of music therapy, should be better acknowledged (for example, Gardstrom 2008). Yet others have raised concerns that when music is promoted or perceived as only having potential for beneficence in music therapy and music education, practitioners can lose awareness of the ways in which music can be instrumentalized to serve political or social ends that might not be in the best interests of an individual or group (Edwards 2011). In acknowledging that music can also have disturbing or disruptive capacities, the music therapist helps colleagues to choose music thoughtfully, collaboratively, and respectfully when supporting music listening choices for clients.

The structure of music therapy

Music therapy work with clients is framed by the structure of the programme overall, and the processes within sessions. The structure of the programme usually involves a period during which assessment of the needs of the client or group is undertaken, followed by the implementation of the programme with reference to the aims and objectives for the client(s); that is, the intent of the programme in relation to meeting the needs of the individual or group. Evaluation of the aims and objectives can be undertaken as the programme progresses or towards the end. During the programme conclusion phase careful attention is paid to how the final sessions are advised, negotiated, and managed with the client. Most music therapy work is reported to colleagues or a team verbally or in writing, for example in the client's case notes on file. In some contexts reporting is required after each session, in others reporting by exception is the norm, and others can have feedback requirements at key points during the year, for example in some school-based services.

Processes within sessions can mirror the overall structure of the programme. At the start of a session the therapist tunes in to the client's current state and needs, then the work moves towards formulating how the session will meet those needs, followed by the working phase of the session with a conclusion that is neither too extended nor too brief, allowing the client to prepare for the conclusion of music therapy and to transition into the next part of their day.

During music therapy sessions the therapist uses deep reflective listening to try and understand the client's experiences. The therapist listens to and observes the client, the client's playing, and the music that the client and therapist co-create. This sensitive listening includes attention to the somatic experiences, or sensations in the body, of the therapist and to other thoughts and impressions that arise. These impressions are not censored in the way they might be in social interactions in everyday life but are allowed to be experienced and felt, coming into conscious awareness so they can be thought about and reflected upon in order to increase awareness of clients' experiences. With many clients these experiences of the therapist are not able to be relayed back to them in words because they may not be able to comprehend language, or these experiences are not able to be discussed because the client may not be able to understand or reflect on these impressions. Therefore these experiences are discussed in supervision sessions, and are used by the therapist to deepen their awareness of the life world of the client, and the thoughts, impressions, and experiences of that world.

Music therapy embraces multiple practices developed uniquely in each region of the world. The agreed definition of the field in one region or country might not be the same as that of another. Different authors writing about practice and research describe music therapy in ways that reflect their training context, their practice context, and the relevant region in which they practice. Although highly context dependent, a unifying characteristic of music therapy internationally is the application of music therapy across the lifespan. Music therapy practitioners can work with pregnant women, with infants and young children and their parents and carers, with older children and adolescents, and with people at all stages of adult life. Increasingly music therapists work with families (Edwards and Abad this volume; Oldfield this volume), within community practice contexts, as well as in hospitals, clinics, and schools.

Music therapy contexts and populations across the lifespan

When describing music therapy practice, relaying information about the populations music therapists serve can help build a picture of the work. Populations are groups who share similar characteristics or needs, for example, adults diagnosed with depression or teenagers who have eating disorders. Some client groups receive treatment in a specialized service therefore the music therapist's knowledge includes information about the relevant diagnosis and subsequent needs in general while learning about the individual client more specifically. Additionally, information about the contexts for practice can help to inform the listener about music therapy services. Contexts are the situations in which music therapy services are provided such as a community day programme or a hospital. Some contexts serve diverse populations, for example a special school which may have students with a range of needs and diagnoses, and others are highly specified, such as a neonatal intensive care unit (NICU).

Each practice context has its own culture which includes the principles and values, also described as the *ethos,* of the organization. This ethos has explicit and implicit dimensions. The explicit aspects can be found in public materials such as mission statements and strategic planning documents. Hidden features of the ethos of the organization can be difficult to uncover or understand until one has worked in the organization for some time. These might relate to how organizational policies are interpreted in practice, or the everyday processes by which work is conducted. These are only possible to know through observing others or being mentored by an experienced colleague within the organization.

Developing an understanding of both the context and the population served is key to effective implementation of music therapy programmes. It is also one of the ways in which translation of music therapy models and services between countries can be problematic. That is, an ethos consistent with a practice in one country may not be relevant or easily understood in another. For example, countries which have *socialized* or equal access to medical care for all may be able to develop services for refugee populations who have experienced trauma and who have no capacity to pay for the service, but these might not be typical service user populations in other countries where pay per service or through individualized or workplace health insurance is the norm. A further example is that one country might have extensive and highly developed services for children with disabilities and their families which are paid for by the government, while another country relies on families setting up support networks, and charity funding to receive such services.

References to workplace practices in music therapy must be contextualized otherwise they run the risk of producing research and techniques that when implemented elsewhere are either ineffective or run the risk of causing harm. The new music therapist, and the student must take care to ensure they understand as much as possible about the population, the services, and the wider political context of funding support before translating research findings or the techniques described in case studies or research reports into their own emergent practice. Learning how to concisely summarize the context of practice and the services offered when presenting music therapy practice accounts can help others to understand the work and appreciate its impact and effectiveness.

MUSIC THERAPY MODELS AND APPROACHES

It is highly beneficial to the development of the profession that so many music therapy models and approaches have been developed across the world. Most have distinctive sole founders or founding collaborators, and some models are named after these founders, such as Nordoff-Robbins music therapy (Guerrero et al. this volume). Many of the models were developed in specific locations and then were adapted and expanded as other regions and services engaged the model. The distinction between models and approaches is useful to the purposes of this chapter and the *Oxford Handbook of Music Therapy*, however in practice many music therapists use the terms *model* and *approach* interchangeably.

Music therapists undertake their work based on a model of practice where methods and techniques specific to music therapy are implemented such as in Nordoff-Robbins' Music Therapy, or they base their work on a music therapy approach in which music therapy methods and techniques are overlaid across a model or theoretical framework from another area, such as in the case of Developmental Music Therapy, or Analytical Music Therapy. Many of the founders of contemporary models of music therapy were influenced by existing theoretical or practice perspectives but then developed and refined their model to create a discrete music therapy approach. The 11 approaches and models presented in the *Oxford Handbook of Music Therapy* were chosen because they have an established literature base, and one or more training programmes exist that are based on the model. Four of the models and approaches are briefly described below to show the diversity of contemporary practices in the field.

Nordoff-Robbins music therapy

The Nordoff-Robbins music therapy model was founded through the experiences of Paul Nordoff and Clive Robbins providing music sessions in special education services (Nordoff-Robbins 1977; Guerrero et al. this volume). Paul Nordoff was a composer for 25 years before he became a pioneer in the field of music therapy (De'Ath 2013). Clive Robbins was a special educator working with children with disabilities when they began their collaboration (Hadley 2003). As Guerrero et al. this volume have explained, the co-work between them occurred over many years starting with a collaboration in special education:

> Their partnership began in 1959 at Sunfield Children's Homes in Worcestershire, England, and they worked together for approximately 16 years in Europe and the United States. In 1975, formal training in Nordoff-Robbins music therapy began at the newly opened Nordoff-Robbins Music Therapy Centre in London. In the same year, Clive Robbins formed a new music therapy team with his wife Carol Robbins (1942–1996). The Robbinses continued to develop and disseminate the Nordoff-Robbins approach to music therapy, and in 1990 established the Nordoff-Robbins Center for Music Therapy at New York University's Steinhardt School of Culture, Education, and Human Development.
>
> (p. x, this volume)

A feature of the model is that it is primarily *music-centred* (Aigen 2014). Aigen has explained that "in music-centered music therapy, the mechanisms of music therapy process are located in the forces, experiences, processes, and structures of music" (Aigen 2014, p. 18). Many countries offer training based on the Nordoff-Robbins model, and training workshops for qualified practitioners from other approaches are also offered internationally.

Feminist perspectives in music therapy

The feminist approach in music therapy (Hadley and Hahna this volume) has been elaborated by many practitioners and theorists (for example, Baines 2013; Curtis 2012; Edwards and Hadley 2007; Hadley 2006). In this approach the foundational principles of feminism are used to understand contexts of practice and the ways in which peoples' needs are defined and framed in such contexts. Because feminism arose from concerns about the social and political subjugation of women, there is a common misconception that only women can be feminists, but feminism is a way of perceiving the world and the needs of communities that can be productively shared and embraced by people of any gender (Edwards and Hadley 2007).

Although there are multiple perspectives within feminism, many theorists and activists are concerned with relations of power in social and political domains. A feminist sensibility promotes the idea that many groups in society, especially those marginalized by stigma relating to disease or disability, are severely disadvantaged in relation to dominant groups that conform to societal norms and have access to unseen privilege (McIntosh 1998). The music therapist working within the feminist approach is an activist and advocate for the groups with whom she or he works (Baines 2013). The role of music therapy is not simply to invite participation and to offer support to clients, but to also enable their emancipation (Hadley 2006).

Carolyn Kenny's field of play

The Field of Play is a model of music therapy developed by Carolyn Kenny (Kenny this volume), a practitioner and researcher in music therapy who is also well known for her contribution and research in the area of indigenous studies. She has described the field to which the title of the model refers as a:

> ... river that constantly flows beneath our various methods of practice, we can accept the grounded energy of the river, which flows without effort. Too often, we take the river for granted or forget about it entirely. This river of being holds the greatest gifts for our patients and clients because it is our presence, our being, and our very existence. If we accept this river, then we can do or try our work as part of a natural process in an ecology of being.
>
> Kenny this volume

This ecology of practice is reliant on the practitioner accepting the importance of self-awareness, not just of one's psychological state including feelings and moods, but of the cultural and social context in which one resides and to make effort to understand the values one holds because of that context. It is important that therapists suspend their judgement as to what a life should be like (Kenny 2003). Valuing the need of therapists to reach their own potential provides a pathway to journeying with clients as they reach theirs. As Carroll has indicated in her reflection on the applicability of the *Field of Play* in music therapy education:

> We all have an inner drive to know and reach our potential. I envision inner drive as a spark that needs to be fuelled through meaningful activity that is goal-oriented, resource-rich, culturally sensitive and socially-mediated.
>
> Carroll 2010, np

The *Field of Play* has applications for every music therapy practitioner even if they do not employ it as their primary model of practice. For the mature practitioner, revisiting the *Field of Play* every once in a while can offer further riches through prompting consideration of the self and other in interaction towards integration.

Community music therapy

Community Music Therapy has been described as *resisting* definition (Ansdell and Stige this volume; Pavlicevic and Ansdell 2004). Nonetheless a broad definition has been proposed by Stige and Aarø (2011), who wrote that "Community music therapy encourages musical participation and social inclusion, equitable access to resources, and collaborative efforts for health and wellbeing in contemporary societies" (p. 5).

Community Music Therapy represents dissatisfaction with some aspects of twentieth century music therapy traditions and practices, as well as one in which new or emergent practice is fostered (Stige 2002). Stige (2002) related the foundation of the model to multiple developments across four decades in Germany, Norway, and the UK. One of the founding reference points for Community Music Therapy is German music therapist Schwabe's Social Music Therapy (Stige 2002) which emphasizes the communal rather than individual nature of human experience in society. Some common misperceptions include that it is a model that refers to work in community or non-clinical contexts (Ansdell and Stige this volume). Stige has described *community* as conceptualized within Community Music Therapy as "no longer being just a context to work *in* but also a context to work *with*" (Stige 2002, np).

Some early proponents of Community Music Therapy anticipated an adversarial relationship between the model and what was described as the *consensus model* of music therapy. Minimal critique was afforded to the polarising of Community Music Therapy against the proclaimed *consensus model*. This perhaps slowed the understanding of Community Music Therapy as a unifying clarion call to music therapists navigating new healthcare service contexts where the music therapy models founded on an older institutional and pathology-treatment perspective were found wanting when new and dynamic perspectives entered mainstream healthcare. Community Music Therapy has agitated, excited, and infuriated many in the music therapy world. This has been immensely useful as a process by which further consideration of what it is we do in music therapy, and why, has been fostered.

MUSIC THERAPY METHODS

Music therapists use music in various ways depending on the context and the needs of the clients with whom they work. Music can be co-created between the therapist and the client, or the client or the therapist can be engaged in solo music making while the other listens. Known songs can be sung together, improvisations can be initiated and followed through, songs can be written by individuals or in group contexts, music soundscapes can be developed to accompany new or existing stories, and sometimes clients sing or accompany tunes on a keyboard or guitar. Music therapists also use music technology to support music making or composing, some music therapists' focus on learning music together as an opportunity for clients to build specific music based skills and capacities, and there are music therapists who perform music with their clients or encourage recordings and performances as part of the work.

Bruscia (1998) described four categories of methods in music therapy; improvisation, re-creation, composition, and receptive. The main improvisatory methods in his schema are instrumental play between the therapist and client but this can also include such techniques as vocal improvisation, and improvised songs. Re-creative techniques include song singing, or playing pre-composed music. Composition primarily refers to song writing, and receptive techniques focus on experiences of music listening.

The primary goal of music making in music therapy is to address the needs of the client or group. In some music therapy traditions certain techniques or methods are predominant, for example the British Association for Music Therapy defines practice as involving improvised music created between the therapist and client as follows:

> Attentive listening on the part of the therapist is combined with shared musical improvisation using instruments and voices so that people can communicate in their own musical language, whatever their level of ability.
>
> BAMT fact sheet 2015

By comparison the Australian Music Therapy Association described that "a range of music making methods" are used <http://www.austmta.org.au/content/what-music-therapy>. It is not clear why some traditions emphasize the use of all kinds of musical interactions in the work while others favor specific kinds of music making—further historical research about the development of music therapy could offer illumination on this issue. However, unless it is understood that certain traditions have a different view of the scope of music used in therapy then misunderstandings can occur when people from different regions try to collaborate and share knowledge.

Music therapy is offered in one to one sessions or in group configurations, including work with families, or small groups of people with similar issues and difficulties that are seeking support and change through music therapy services. Since music making is a potentially socially unifying experience, using music in group therapy processes can create highly dynamic and productive experiences for participants.

Historically some music therapists have categorized methods as either *active* or *passive* (for example, Montello and Coons 1998). This distinction is used less frequently in music therapy as contemporary knowledge of how the brain processes music indicates that music is a whole brain activity engaging large neural networks outside of the auditory area (Alluri et al. 2012). One can be sitting quietly listening to music and hence be perceived in behavioral observation terms as participating *passively,* but the process of listening is activating multiple brain regions. Therefore all music therapy methods are considered active, and are potentially activating for clients.

MUSIC THERAPY RESEARCH

Research is a process of making new discoveries through the systematic applications of rigorous methods. Music therapy research has involved the use of traditional methods of inquiry for health care practice including a range of controlled study methods such as the Randomized Controlled Trial, as well as case study methods, qualitative method studies using approaches such as Grounded Theory (Corbin and Strauss 2008), and mixed methods. At the training stage music therapy students need to know how to read and understand research papers and learn how the findings can be usefully and ethically applied in practice. Usually the music therapy course curriculum includes some attention to research skills training and a small research study is also completed. This helps the student to engage in the knowledge community in music therapy and to understand the processes of research.

Practitioners similarly need to use these skills of reading and understanding to remain up to date with the research in the field and to be able to apply key new findings in their practice. Many practitioners engage in regular evaluations of their programmes. Some service evaluations can be described as research, but not all. A research study must have ethical clearance from a relevant statutory body and it must be guided by an understanding of the system of knowledge creation to which its method refers, called *epistemology* (see further in Edwards 2012), whereas evaluation is an ethical imperative for every practitioner. Professional associations have a responsibility to support practitioner knowledge development through events such as conferences and seminars, and through providing journal publications funded through the membership dues.

Music therapy research is often urged to demonstrate the effectiveness of treatments but there are further responsibilities for research activities. Descriptive qualitative research can help us to understand client experiences, and reading these studies can increase practitioner empathy. Theoretical qualitative research in which theory building is the goal can help to promote an understanding of mechanisms of change in therapeutic processes, and support deeper knowledge of the music therapy experiences and effects for clients. Audits that determine how practitioners use techniques, or what types of work they are doing and with whom provide information about the scope of professional practice whether the audit is in a local setting or undertaken internationally. Research which includes the service user's voice is also needed in order that music therapy practice honours clients' experiences of music therapy services, and that research can demonstrate music therapists' commitment to client-centred practices.

Music therapy training and professional issues

In spite of the multiple training courses around the world and the many thousands of people practising there are relatively few studies of music therapists' professional experiences, and the experiences of students in training courses. In the *Oxford Handbook of Music Therapy* a range of topics relevant to this topic are explored including music therapists' work in developing new positions in healthcare facilities (Ledger this volume), self-care for music therapists (Trondalen this volume), as well as training requirements (Hanser this volume), and accreditation requirements (Nocke Ribeaupierre this volume).

Training is highly context-dependent. Each country has their own training systems and courses including procedures for recognition of courses. Some countries have undergraduate trainings while others, such as Ireland and the UK, only have postgraduate training programmes. Most music therapy courses are offered through universities or higher education systems of accreditation. Many countries have professional associations which accredit courses, and these associations also have professional development requirements that graduates must follow. Most music therapy ethical codes emphasize the necessity for personal development of the practitioner to ensure safe and efficacious professional practice.

However, the processes by which this development is encouraged for the individual student, and then the practitioner, is applied differently across the world.

Conclusion

According to Article 27 of the Universal Declaration of Human Rights "Everyone has the right freely to participate in the cultural life of the community, to enjoy the arts and to share in scientific advancement and its benefits." Music therapists around the world uphold human rights when they celebrate the human capacity for music making and music appreciation with their clients.

Music therapy as a twenty-first-century profession is constantly updating, upskilling, and refining its approaches and techniques. At the same time practicing music therapy involves the use of the dynamic medium of music which has been part of every culture and every community since ancient times, possibly even before the human era (Mithen 2005). Navigating the historical and future capacities of music to bring comfort, joy, enlightenment, and solace to those in distress, pain, or who are seeking further opportunities for growth is the wondrous task of every student and practitioner. Music therapy needs leaders, competent practitioners, innovators, and questioners. Bringing oneself fully and wholly into the profession requires a commitment to ongoing self-awareness, and insight about ones capacities and interests in order to grow and serve within the music therapy community internationally. A book such as the *Oxford Handbook of Music Therapy* can serve as a reference point for navigating new practice and research terrains to enhance the quality of music therapy internationally, but nothing can replace the value of everyday learning through spending time with clients and their families and discovering and relating within their musical world.

References

Aigen, K. (2014). Music-centered dimensions of Nordoff-Robbins Music Therapy. *Music Therapy Perspectives* 32(1): 18–29.

Alluri, V., Toiviainen, P., Jääskeläinenp, I.P., Glerean, E., Sams, M., and Brattico, E. (2012). Large-scale brain networks emerge from dynamic processing of musical timbre, key and rhythm. *Neuroimage* 59(4): 3677–3689.

Baines, S. (2013). Music therapy as an anti-oppressive practice. *The Arts in Psychotherapy* 40: 1–5.

Bruscia, K.E. (1998). *Defining Music Therapy*. Gilsum, NH: Barcelona Publishers.

Carroll, D. (2010). The Field of Play in music therapy education. *Voices: A World Forum for Music Therapy* 10(2).

Corbin, J. and Strauss, A. (2008). *Basics of qualitative research: Techniques and procedures for developing grounded theory*, 3rd ed. Los Angeles, CA: SAGE.

Curtis, S.L. (2012). Music therapy and social justice: A personal journey. *The Arts in Psychotherapy* 39: 209–213.

De'Ath, L. (2013). "A sun among men": The EE Cummings songs of Paul Nordoff. *Journal of Singing* 69: 307.

Edwards, J. (2011). A music and health perspective on music's perceived "goodness." *Nordic Journal of Music Therapy* 20: 90–101.

Edwards, J. (2012). We need to talk about epistemology: Orientations, meaning, and interpretation within music therapy research. *Journal of Music Therapy* 49: 372–394.

Edwards, J. and Hadley, S. (2007). Expanding music therapy practice: Incorporating the feminist frame. *The Arts in Psychotherapy* 34: 199–207.

Gardstrom, S.C. (2008). Music therapy as noninvasive treatment: Who says? *Nordic Journal of Music Therapy* 17(2): 142–154.

Hadley, S. (2003). Meaning making through Narrative Inquiry: Exploring the Life of Clive Robbins. *Nordic Journal of Music Therapy* 12(1): 33–53.

Hadley, S. (ed.) (2006). *Feminist Perspectives in Music Therapy*. Gilsum, NH: Barcelona Publishers.

Kenny, C.B. (2003). Beyond this point there be dragons: Developing general theory in music therapy. *Voices: A world forum for music therapy* 3(2).

Loewy, J.V. (2001). Building bridges in team centred care. *Australian Journal of Music Therapy* 12: 3–12.

McIntosh, P. (1998). White privilege: Unpacking the invisible knapsack. *Race, class, and gender in the United States: An integrated study* 4: 165–169.

Mithen, S.J. (2005). *The Singing Neanderthals: The Origins of Music, Language, Mind, and Body*. Harvard University Press.

Montello, L. and Coons, E.E. (1998). Effects of active versus passive group music therapy on preadolescents with emotional, learning, and behavioral disorders. *Journal of Music Therapy* 35(1): 49–67.

Nordoff, P. and Robbins, C. (1977). *Creative Music Therapy: Individualized Treatment for the Handicapped Child*. New York: John Day Company.

Pavlicevic, M. and Ansdell, G. (eds), (2004). *Community Music Therapy*. London: Jessica Kingsley Publishers.

Stige, B. (2002). The relentless roots of community music therapy. *Voices: a world forum for music therapy* 2(3). https://voices.no/index.php/voices/article/view/98

Stige, B. and Aarø, L.E. (2011). *Invitation to Community Music Therapy*. London: Routledge.

UN General Assembly, *Universal Declaration of Human Rights*, 10 December 1948, 217 A (III), available at: <http://www.refworld.org/docid/3ae6b3712c.html> [accessed 21 October 2014].

MUSIC THERAPY CONTEXTS AND POPULATIONS ACROSS THE LIFE SPAN

···

CHAPTER 1

MUSIC THERAPY
An Evidence-based Allied Health Service
Applicable Through the Life Span

···

JANE EDWARDS

Art shows us how to be more than we are. It is heightened, grand, an act of effrontery. It is a challenge to the confines of the spirit. It is a challenge to the comfortable
pleasures in everyday life .... Once encountered, art will get a response ...

Jeanette Winterson, *Art Objects: Essays on Ecstasy and Effrontery*, p. 94
London: Vintage, 1994

INTRODUCTION

···

IN music therapy the complexity of music meets the complexity of the patient or client with
fluidity, grace, and inspiration. The therapist plays many roles during music therapy including as a responder in music making, and as the person who reflects upon and processes what
is happening for themselves and between themselves and the client as the music therapy sessions evolve. The music therapist is responsible for devising the music therapy procedures in
consultation with the client where possible, engaging the process of therapy, and evaluating
and reporting the outcomes of the therapy to other members of the team, to the client, and
to the family and carers where applicable. The skills of the music therapist in communicating
and relating with the client in therapy practice, and advising and reporting the outcomes is
key to developing and maintaining practice competence.

This chapter considers how the context of music therapy practice, the place where the services are provided, as well as the population, that is the people who come to music therapy,
can be useful points of reference when communicating about music therapy. Descriptions of
the ways evidence are used to inform practice are provided.

Most accounts of music therapy are written by music therapists therefore the dominant
dialogic refers to music therapists' accounts of what occurred and their experience of the
therapy process. A music therapist might find it perfectly natural that a room or trolley full of
instruments should be provided to a person and then music making ensue as part of a music
therapy session. When people receiving health and education services who are referred for

music therapy enter a room containing many instruments for the first time, or are greeted by the arrival of a person wheeling a trolley of instruments into the space they occupy it can be an exciting, puzzling, or even daunting experience. Navigating and responding to the client's first impressions and then interacting and supporting with the evolving verbal and musical responses is part of the skilled repertory of the music therapy practitioner.

POPULATIONS AND CONTEXTS

Explaining music therapy eloquently to others is a requirement for all practitioners in the field. Describing the needs of the clients they seek to help along with a description of the service or context in which the music therapy programme is provided are useful starting points for conveying this information. This builds a picture for the listener as to where and how the work of music therapy is provided. In this chapter, *populations* are groups of people attending music therapy who share similar characteristics or needs, for example, adults who have cancer (O'Callaghan and Magill this volume), or infants with life-threatening medical conditions (Shoemark this volume). Some client groups receive treatment in a specialized service, therefore the music therapist's knowledge includes information about the relevant diagnosis and subsequent needs in general while learning about the individual client more specifically.

For the purposes of this chapter *contexts* are considered to be the situations in which music therapy services are provided, such as a community day programme, special education facility, or a residential service. Some contexts serve diverse populations, for example a special school may provide services for students with a range of needs, ages, and diagnoses. Other contexts are highly specified, such as a neonatal intensive care unit (NICU). The service always exists within a wider health care culture that requires attention and reflection. As Rolvsjord and Stige (2015) have advised:

> Any health care system, in turn, is situated in a larger context of society and culture, of social economy, and political systems. These broader social, cultural, and political contexts influence a person's health and the practice of therapy in complex ways (e.g. as contributing causes for illness and health, provision of health services, social support, stigmatization, and demoralization). p. 52

Information about the contexts for practice can help to inform the listener about music therapy services. Each practice context has its own culture which includes the *ethos* of the organization, comprising explicit and implicit dimensions. Mission statements and strategic planning documents provide information about the explicit ethos of the service or institution. Hidden features of the ethos of the organization can be difficult to uncover or understand until one has worked in the organization for some time. These might relate to how organizational policies are interpreted in practice, or the everyday processes by which work is conducted. Many of the idiosyncratic aspects of a service are only possible to know through observation of the ways in which people within the organization make decisions and negotiate, and through receiving mentoring from an experienced colleague within the organization.

Developing an understanding of the dynamics of the context, along with the needs of the population that can be addressed through music therapy, contributes to effective implementation of music therapy programmes. References to workplace practices in music therapy must be contextualized otherwise they run the risk of producing research and techniques that when implemented elsewhere can be ineffective or might result in harm. The new music therapist, and the student must take care to ensure they understand as much as possible about the population, the services, and the wider political context of funding support in the place where they are providing services before translating research findings or the techniques described in case studies or research reports to their own emergent practice.

Populations

The Oxford Handbook of Music Therapy (Edwards 2015) seeks to represent the life span age range served in music therapy providing examples of work with infants (see Edwards and Abad, this volume), children (Barry this volume), adults (McCaffrey this volume), and older adults (Clair this volume). One day in the future it is possible that each of the areas of practice outlined in this volume will have their own OUP handbook representing the diversity of approaches and techniques that are employed in the field.

While all people attending music therapy sessions have capacities that can be described using such terms as cognition, sensory, language, communication, mobility, psychosocial and so forth the main capacities with which the authors in this volume are concerned are with how people referred for music therapy can be provided with opportunities to use music's capacities in restorative and growth oriented ways. Working with the client to honor and support their strengths is a great privilege of the work of the music therapist.

Contexts

In the *Oxford Handbook of Music Therapy* (Edwards 2015) four contexts are considered: (1) medical, (2) developmental and educational, (3) mental health, and (4) community. The chapters in the contexts and populations section of the book are loosely grouped around these topics as they cannot be considered fixed settings for service delivery (see Figure 1.1). Some services provide support in some or all of these contexts. For example, a drug and alcohol service may provide medical treatment for symptoms of withdrawal, offer psycho-education and mental health supports, and be delivered in a community setting. Not every type of work situation would fit into these four broad categories, for example music therapy provided within prison services. Nonetheless these contexts are presented here as offering a way to consider how music therapy services are provided and to whom.

Services provided by hospitals and medical services can be offered to all age groups and a wide range of needs. *Medical contexts* have unique features and have sometimes been criticized as behaving within "silos of specialism" (James et al. 2013, p. 296). Specialism is important because highly trained, highly qualified medical personnel are needed to treat specific

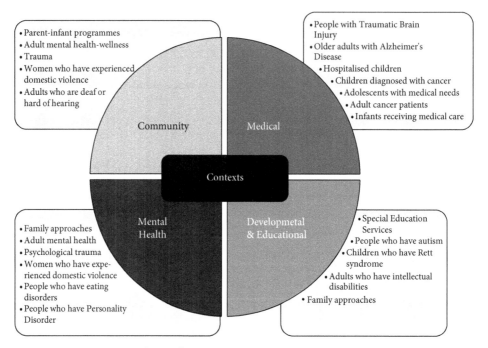

FIGURE 1.1 Contexts and populations.

conditions expertly. The salient point made by James et al. (2013) is that when a patient has complex needs, services can become disjointed and unhelpful. For example, if an orthopedic team keep expertly treating an older man who falls frequently by setting his broken arm, or repairing his fractured spine at what point will the reason for the fall be investigated? The music therapist has a role to play in such a specialized system. For example, if a child with autism (see Bergmann this volume) is admitted to hospital for a tonsillectomy, the music therapist can use their knowledge of working with families, alternative communication systems, and neuro-diversity to facilitate greater understandings for the child, the family, and the team, and to work with the patient's regular music therapist to help plan for the difficult parts of treatment which might involve planning and facilitating transitions between the ward and surgical area, and on awakening from anesthetic.

A description of how a music therapist can engage with the complexity encountered in hospital based music therapy practice is outlined in a case example by Dr Joanne Loewy. She described working with a drug dependent mother who gave birth to her son prematurely. The mother, Tasha was subsequently admitted to the psychiatric services because she advised that she intended to harm herself. Dr Loewy moved between Tasha, awaiting admission and Daniel, in the Neonatal Intensive Care Unit (NICU) whom Tasha did not yet feel she had the strength to visit. A lullaby song was composed by the mother with Dr Loewy's support and prompting. Dr Loewy was then able to sing to the baby in the NICU (Loewy 2011). She described this process as follows:

> Providing nurturance through favorite lullabies designed for parents is critical at this time. Initiating a point of contact using a lullaby is highly personal. Beginning from playing in a familiar meter and moving into a holding meter, and then to a rubato style, music's ability to

contain, and gradually withhold the need for a fixed predictable meter can assist in the creation of a relaxation effect, which can be achieved in a very short period of time.

Loewy 2011, p. 188

Developmental and educational contexts refer to services which are offered to support educational attainment, such as special schools (see Hayes this volume), and early intervention services (see Oldfield this volume). One example is provided by Kelly (2011) who described the development of a parent-infant programme in a school setting in one of the most socially disadvantaged regions of Ireland. Music therapy sessions were offered in a group format for children of three to four years of age and their caregivers over one academic year. Kelly presented a series of child and caregiver interactions that occurred during the programme. The music therapy sessions were perceived by teachers and caregivers to achieve greater cohesion and relating between caregivers and children. Children were reported by caregivers to have grown in confidence, and caregivers were perceived by teachers as being less anxious in engaging with the school during sessions but also at other times.

Mental health contexts include any services with the primary aim of promoting and supporting optimal mental health. These contexts can include services to adults with mental health diagnoses (see McCaffrey this volume), and to infants (see Edwards and Abad this volume). One example can be seen in the work of McCaffrey et al. (2011) where the music therapist (Tríona) worked with a 40-year-old service user "Kevin" supporting him to re-engage his musical interest that had been dormant since his diagnosis of schizophrenia in his mid-20s. Through the supportive relationship offered by the music therapist Kevin composed songs, and developed keyboard skills contributing to his sense of mastery and pride with positive effects for his self-concept and confidence.

Community contexts are settings in which music therapy services are provided to people in their own homes or in a community based context such as a community health center, or in a community based service that may move through different locations within a geographical location. Leaders in Community Music Therapy (see Ansdell and Stige this volume) caution against confusing community contexts of practice with the purposes of Community Music Therapy. One example of a community context where music therapy is provided is by Toni Day, a music therapist and Helen Bruderer, a social worker (2011). They developed a support service for women who were mothers or pregnant and had been abused as children. Music making opportunities were facilitated through song writing and recording the compositions in groups. The goal of the programme was to facilitate resolution of the past trauma and support safe and effective parenting. The women shared the song recordings with friends and family to educate them about their experiences, and to receive additional support. The women reported that participating in the programme gave them a stronger sense of pride and achievement about their lives.

THE DEVELOPING EVIDENCE BASE FOR MUSIC THERAPY SERVICES

Many authors in the *Oxford Handbook of Music Therapy* (Edwards 2015) have presented research evidence that indicates the value of music therapy to meet clients' needs. Evidence takes various forms and can include findings from randomized controlled trials, from controlled studies, from the findings of qualitative studies, or from case series, and expert opinion. Research studies provide an indicator of the likely outcomes that will be achieved in music therapy, and afford reassurance that no harmful effects will occur. The best place to find evidence for music therapy services is in the refereed journal literature. There are also useful collations of research findings available in the Cochrane library <http://www.cochranelibrary.com/>.

Some published studies undertaken in hospitals and community contexts where music is used as a therapeutic agent for some kind of change such as increased relaxation or pain relief, have not employed music therapists either as the service delivery expert or as an adviser. Therefore it is important when looking at studies how the music was conceptualized as part of the research. Sometimes music is studied as if it is similar to a pharmacological medication and the researchers have not adequately considered whether the participant has heard the music before, or whether they like the music (Vaajoki et al. 2012). Additionally some research studies have described the use of music listening as *music therapy* even when there is no qualified music therapist involved with the study (for example, Karagozoglu et al. 2013). Improving the ongoing dialogue between practitioners in music therapy and health and social care is the ideal way to address these issues. This has led to music therapy researchers advising reporting guidelines for the inclusion of music in research studies (Robb et al. 2011) which are now used by several journals in the field. Additionally, some researchers advise that *music medicine* should be the term used when medical practitioners and nurses provide music listening opportunities to health care recipients (for example Bradt et al. 2013). Students and new practitioners who are collating evidence should make sure these guidelines have been followed in the papers they present.

Conclusion

Music therapists' work involves consideration and reflection on the needs of individuals and groups with reference to the wider cultural and societal influences on the context in which the service is provided. Describing the needs of clients in relation to the context for service provision in which music therapy is offered is a useful way to communicate about work in the field. The *Oxford Handbook of Music Therapy* presents a range of populations with whom music therapists work and discusses the evidence base and the theoretical principles on which music therapy practice is based. Readers are encouraged to follow up their interest in chapters in the relevant sections through consulting the reference list, and following the author's additional contributions to the field.

References

Bradt, J., Dileo, C., and Shim, M. (2013). Can music interventions replace sedatives for reduction of preoperative anxiety? *PubMed Health*. Available at: <http://www.ncbi.nlm.nih.gov/pubmedhealth/PMH0056745/>.

Day, T. and Bruderer, H. (2011). Music therapy to support mothers who have experienced abuse in childhood. In: J. Edwards (ed.), *Music Therapy and Parent-infant Bonding*, pp. 141–158. Oxford: Oxford University Press.

Edwards, J. (ed.) (2015). *Oxford Handbook of Music Therapy*. Oxford: Oxford University Press.

James, D.M., Hall, A., Phillipson, J., McCrossan, G., and Falck, C. (2013). Creating a person-centred culture within the North East Autism Society: Preliminary findings. *British Journal of Learning Disabilities* 41(4): 296–303.

Karagozoglu, S., Tekyasar, F., and Yilmaz, F.A. (2013). Effects of music therapy and guided visual imagery on chemotherapy-induced anxiety and nausea/vomiting. *Journal of Clinical Nursing* 22(1–2): 39–50.

Kelly, K. (2011). Supporting attachments in vulnerable families through an early intervention school-based group music therapy programme. In: J. Edwards (ed.), *Music Therapy and Parent-infant Bonding*, pp. 101–114. Oxford: Oxford University Press.

Loewy, J.V. (2011). Music therapy for hospitalized infants and their parents. In: J. Edwards (ed.), *Music Therapy and Parent-infant Bonding*, pp. 179–192. Oxford: Oxford University Press.

McCaffrey, T., Edwards, J. and Fannon, D. (2011). Is there a role for music therapy in the recovery approach in mental health? *The Arts in Psychotherapy* 38: 185–189.

Robb, S.L., Burns, D.S., and Carpenter, J.S. (2011). Reporting guidelines for music-based interventions. *Music and Medicine* 3(4): 271–279.

Rolvsjord, R. and Stige, B. (2015). Concepts of context in music therapy. *Nordic Journal of Music Therapy* 24(1): 44–66.

Vaajoki, A., Pietilä, A.M., Kankkunen, P., and Vehviläinen-Julkunen, K. (2012). Effects of listening to music on pain intensity and pain distress after surgery: an intervention. *Journal of Clinical Nursing* 21(5–6): 708–717.

CHAPTER 2

....

MUSIC THERAPY
IN THE MEDICAL
CARE OF INFANTS

....

HELEN SHOEMARK AND TRISH DEARN

INTRODUCTION

....

THE expected gestational age for a healthy full-term infant is 40 weeks calculated from the mother's last menstrual period. As dates can sometimes be difficult to establish, full-term infants are considered those born from 37 weeks gestation onwards. Very preterm infants (<32 weeks) and extremely preterm (<28 weeks) have a range of medical complications associated with being born with immature physiological and neurological systems. Moderately or late preterm birth (33 to 36 completed weeks of gestation) is increasingly understood to bring its own unique set of problems (Bakewell-Sachs 2007). Post-term infants (<42 weeks) may also experience complex problems (Gardner and Hernandez 2011).

In the neonatology context the terms *low risk* and *high risk* refer to the complexity of the infant's medical condition and therefore indicate a possible clinical pathway or treatment. Low risk does not indicate an absence of risk but rather a more linear progression of problem, treatment, and recovery. High risk suggests that the recovery is marred by infection or other deterioration, and an escalating array of treatments which need to be introduced to address those changes. The term *medically complex* is sometimes used to refer to high risk infants who have chronic life threatening conditions which require complex medical care or dependency on technology (such as ventilators or respirators). These infants can be born with or develop a diverse range of medical complications which means that they are a heterogeneous group and are difficult to research.

Why is a baby hospitalized at birth? Preterm infants often have lungs that are not yet sufficiently developed to expand in air rather than amniotic fluid (Gardner et al. 2011). In the Neonatal Intensive Care Unit (NICU) they receive essential respiratory support from a ventilator (or respirator). Most will be unable to maintain adequate body temperature due to lack of body fat and will be cared for in a humidicrib (also known as an incubator or isolette) until sufficiently mature to do this for themselves (Brown and Landers 2011). Infants do not develop a coordinated breathe-suck-swallow action until at least 32 weeks gestation

(Mizuno and Ueda 2003) and therefore need supported feeding systems such as nasogastric feeding directly into the stomach. These key issues are likely to be part of the care of all preterm infants, including those considered to be low risk. If complications arise however, infants can move quickly from a low to high risk classification.

Full-term infants are hospitalized for a range of problems including congenital heart defects (CHD), lung conditions, congenital diaphragmatic hernia (CDH) and other abdominal wall conditions, Hypoxic Ischemic Encephalopathy (HIE), metabolic disorders, and medical issues associated with congenital anomalies. For many of these infants, surgery will be conducted on day one of life to reverse malformations or to provide temporary solutions, such as a gastrostomy tube to feed a baby directly to the infant's stomach. While the full term infant may have neurological and physiological maturity, their complex medical issues may also cause further issues which require a long hospitalization.

It is now understood that the while the medical and nursing teams attend to the medical issues of the infant, infant development and family well-being must be supported to ensure that trauma for all is minimized, and healthy development of the infant is maximized (Coppola et al. 2007; Laing et al. 2010).

NEURODEVELOPMENT OF THE
HOSPITALIZED INFANT

Even though survival for preterm infants has improved over the past few decades, they are at increased risk of neurodevelopmental impairments arising from the loss of typical brain development in utero and neonatal brain injury (Spittle et al. 2010; Zwicker and Harris 2008). Preterm infants have a significantly higher incidence of learning difficulties as children, including visual motor problems and attention difficulties including impaired memory, delayed language skills and executive dysfunction (Daily et al. 2011; Mathur and Inder 2009).

The generally accepted model of infant development is currently that of psychobiologist Robert Lickliter (2000) who used dynamics systems theory to propose that early development is co-actional or multidimensional, meaning that no one component will determine the developmental outcome. Early development is experience-dependent, context sensitive, and strongly influenced by the immediate surroundings. There is a "critical window" for sensory systems development and particularly that the early introduction of light or unusual vestibular stimulation can impact on auditory development (Lickliter and Bahrick 2001).

The key time points in the development of auditory processing (see Table 1.1) are vital to understanding the potential of music as a supportive experience for infant development.

It is understood that preterm infants are at greater risk of auditory processing deficits putting later language abilities at risk (Bisiacchi et al. 2009). Key et al. (2012) reported that there is a combined effect of gestational age and postnatal age on auditory processing in the temporal region of the brain where language and music are both processed. Such emergent research gives strength to the potential of music to preserve neural functioning in key areas of the brain.

Table 1.1 Key milestones in fetal auditory processing development

Gestational age in weeks	Auditory processing
19	Earliest response to sound in utero (Hall 2000)
28	Consistent response to sound (American Academy of Pediatrics 1997)
32	Afferent pathways to auditory cortex complete (Graven and Browne 2008)
33	Activation in the primary auditory cortex (Jardri et al. 2008)
36	Reliable response to sound of mother's voice (Moon and Fifer 2000)

HISTORICAL DEVELOPMENT INTERNATIONALLY

The idea that music can be used with newborn babies is something which most people easily understand. We can readily imagine parents humming lullabies or singing play songs. However, the hospital environment is highly technological and focused on medical treatment and music can seem out of place. While a few studies in the 1970s and 80s reported the application of music with newborn infants (Chapman 1978; Owens 1979), it was Professor Jayne Standley at Florida State University, USA who forged the speciality known as "NICU Music Therapy" where NICU stands for Neonatal Intensive Care Unit. The study undertaken by Standley's student Janel Caine in 1991 introduced a new context of practice for music therapy. Thus NICU music therapy can be understood as a relatively new practice area which parallels the development of the relatively new medical field of neonatology.

Music therapy in neonatology further developed in different parts of the world from the late 1990s onwards. In Germany, Dr Monika Nöcker-Ribaupierre from the University Children's Hospital, Munich championed the ways in which a music psychotherapy program could address the needs of the mother-infant dyad (Nöcker-Ribaupierre 1999), and Dr Joanne Loewy at the Louis Armstrong Centre for Music and Medicine at Beth Israel Hospital in New York honored the infant in the ecological world of the womb, the family and culture (Loewy 2000). Dr Helen Shoemark from The Royal Children's Hospital Melbourne Australia, broadened the application of music therapy to encompass work with medically complex full-term infants (Shoemark 2006). The subsequent expansion of this area of music therapy practice still includes the NICU but has moved into a wider range of medical contexts in which newborns are supported. In order to embrace music therapy practices with preterm and full-term infants, the broader term Newborn Music Therapy (NbMT) will be used in this chapter.

In most instances NbMT clinical work and research has been emerging in countries where the broader profession of music therapy is well established (USA, Australia, Germany, Switzerland, Sweden, United Kingdom, Canada, Israel). In countries such as China (including Taiwan), Japan, Singapore, Thailand, music therapy is not recognized by the government or families must pay for the service, there is obvious interest but little growth in services has been observed. However limited growth has occurred in places with nationalized health care such as the UK, and France, perhaps reflecting lack of congruence between the medical models and music therapy training.

The observed growth in NbMT research has been bolstered by many studies undertaken by non-music therapists who are often members of the nursing profession. The two landmark and most often quoted early studies (Caine 1991; Collins and Kuck 1991) reported that when compared to ambient noise, listening to recorded music improved weight gain, reduced length of stay and provided overall behavioral stability for the preterm infant. This was important evidence for music therapists to start NbMT programmes. Recorded music was shown to decrease agitation and minimize time spent in high arousal and promote improved behavioral regulation in preterm infants (Collins and Kuck 1991; Kaminski and Hall 1996; Lorch et al. 1994). Some studies have reported no effect of recorded music on infants (Calabro et al. 2003) however none have reported negative outcomes. This coincided at the time with research which indicated that many types of auditory stimuli resulted in better health outcomes for infants than silence (Coleman et al. 1997; Lorch et al. 1994; Standley and Moore 1995). Recent research has renewed this concern with the low auditory stimulation for preterm infants in single rooms responsible for poorer communication outcomes in preterm infants (Jobe 2014).

Variability in the cohorts, protocols, and measures between studies mean that they do not rate well when subjected to systematic review (Allen 2013; Hartling et al. 2009; Hodges and Wilson 2010; Neal and Lindeke 2008), but through meta-analyses and integrative reviews more meaning can be derived (Haslbeck 2012; Hodges and Wilson 2010; Standley 2002, 2012).

MEDICAL MUSIC THERAPY

While NbMT clinical practice encompasses family-centered practice (Shoemark 2011a), the research to date with newborn infants has usually been child focused because it is more straightforward. Recorded lullaby music has been the most common stimulus researched. This may be because it can be more easily defined as a research stimulus than live music, is cheap and easy to implement and does not require musical skills. Therefore it can be applied by nurses, some of whom have conducted a significant number of studies. There are few studies that report use of live music as a sole stimulus in the NICU and only two of these reported significant effects on the physiological or behavioral responses of the infant (Arnon et al. 2006; Teckenberg-Jansson et al. 2011). There is however an important stream of research where live singing or humming is used within a multimodal protocol and this will be discussed a little later in the chapter.

Recorded music

The majority of research with preterm and medically fragile infants to date has investigated the infant's immediate physiological and behavioral response to recorded lullaby music with sedative intent. Multiple studies examining the effect of sedative recorded music on stable preterm infant self regulation have reported positive outcomes for heart rate, oxygen saturation, and behavioral state response to sedative music. Several studies have reported a significant decrease in mean heart rate (more recently, Garunkstiene et al. 2014, Tramo et al. 2011) and a positive effect on oxygen saturation levels (Calabro et al. 2003; Cassidy and Standley 1995; Chou et al. 2003; Collins and Kuck 1991). In addition, several studies have reported a positive effect of recorded music on behavior, most often reported as an increase in quiet sleep states, or a decrease in arousal (more recently, Butt and Kisilevsky 2000; Keith et al. 2009; Lai et al. 2006; Tramo et al. 2011; Bo and Callaghan 2000; Whipple 2008).

Further studies have reported positive effects of recorded music on preterm infant weight gain and earlier discharge (Standley 2003), increased non nutritive sucking (Standley 2000, 2003; Standley et al. 2010; Cevasco and Grant 2005; Whipple 2008), faster recovery times and minimized arousal during painful procedures (Bo and Callaghan 2000; Butt and Kisilevsky 2000; Chou et al. 2003; Johnston et al. 2009; Johnston et al. 2007; Joyce et al. 2001), less crying (Keith et al. 2009), decreased energy expenditure (Lubetzky et al. 2010), and improved infant sleep cycles (Olischar et al. 2011).

Maternal voice

Newborn infants are sensitive to the characteristics of their own mother's voice (Kisilevsky et al. 2009) making it a relevant stimulus for NbMT. While studies have shown some mixed results, the renewed emphasis on using the maternal voice in practice means it is important to report here. While term newborns do not have the same ability to discriminate tones as adults do (Werner 2007), they can recognize their mothers' voice (DeCasper and Fifer 1980; Kisilevsky et al. 2009) and some characteristics of their native language as well (Bertoncini et al. 1989; Nazzi et al. 1998).

Bergeson and Trehub (2002) demonstrated that mothers' singing is more consistent in rendition than their speech, thus providing their infant with a predictable stimulus for establishing a safe and familiar experience.

In many studies the mother's recorded voice has often been compared to instrumental music, or a recording of the mother singing lullabies. Recorded spoken maternal voice has been compared to lullaby music (Chapman 1978; Standley and Moore 1995) and routine care (Bozzette 2008; Katz 1971) with infants of different gestational ages to account for the neurodevelopmental stage of the preterm infant (Cevasco 2008; Krueger 2010). Recorded spoken maternal voice has also been compared to a stranger's voice (deRegnier et al. 2000; Thieren et al. 2004) maternal singing (Cevasco 2008) and mother's voice filtered through amniotic fluid (Doheny et al. 2012; Johnston et al. 2007). Of these studies, positive effects on the infant include turning to hear the voice of their mother (Malloy 1979), weight gain (Chapman 1978), tolerance for stimulation (Katz 1971; Segall 1972), increase in stability behaviors and less movement (Bozzette 2008) and earlier discharge (Cevasco 2008).

Krueger (2010) suggested that the lack of statistically significant findings in many studies of maternal voice could be due to the wide age range of the preterm infant participants and the related neurodevelopmental variability over that time. She also suggested that had the mother actually been physically present, infants may have responded differently (Krueger 2010). Loewy et al. (2013) found that the intentional use of live sound, including soft musical instruments and parent-preferred lullabies, provided a range of significant physiological and behavioral changes for the infant and lowered parental stress. In a study of first exposure to recorded music, Dearn and Shoemark (2014) reported that infants exhibited significantly higher oxygen saturation in the presence of the mother even when the mother spent 65 percent of the time not actively make noise or touching her infant.

Recorded music and pain

Recorded music has been examined as a strategy to ameliorate the response of preterm infants to painful procedure or intervention. Pain can cause elevated heart rate, respiratory rate, and increased oxygen consumption, which consume calories needed for growth and healing (Gardner et al. 2011). Most studies investigating the impact of recorded music on pain response have examined the preterm infant's physiological and behavioral response after a heel prick (also known as heel stick or lance). Studies comparing recorded music to ambient sound reported significantly decreased heart rate (Bo and Callaghan 2000; Butt and Kisilevsky 2000; Tramo et al. 2011). Other research has examined the infant's response to recorded music after suctioning (Chou et al. 2003) and during circumcision (Joyce et al. 2001; Marchette et al. 1989, 1991) with no negative outcomes reported and positive physiological outcomes including lowered heart rate, improved oxygen saturation and improved stress behaviors.

Recorded music within the Developmental Care framework

Recognition that sensory stimulation can overwhelm preterm infants and increase physiologic signs of stress has led to attempts to reduce noise and lighting in NICUs as part of the Developmental Care strategy (Gardner and Goldson 2011). More recently, developmentally appropriate soothing sensory input has been recommended to avoid sensory deprivation (Graven and Browne 2008; McMahon et al. 2012). While clinical work is being undertaken in this field, to the knowledge of the authors there are no studies to date that have examined the adapted and layered use of recorded music as a neurodevelopmental strategy for the hospitalized infant.

Recorded music combined with Kangaroo Care

Kangaroo Care (KC) emerged from the Developmental Care framework because close physical contact with the mother encourages physiological and behavioral stability in the preterm infant (Ludington-Hoe and Hosseini 2005; Westrup 2005). Recorded music has been combined with Kangaroo Care in an attempt to improve attachment and enhance physiological and behavioral stability (see Family during hospitalization section below). The comparison of KC alone to KC combined with recorded music has reported no significant differences in physiological or behavioral outcomes (Lai et al. 2006; Johnston et al. 2007, 2009). A recent study by music therapist Teckenberg-Johannsen et al. (2011) investigated the addition of live female voice and lyre (stringed instrument) to KC rather than recorded music, over a series of six sessions. They found a significant improvement in mean and systolic blood pressure and positive improvements in respiration, calmer infants and positive parental response in infants who had received KC and live music combined when compared to KC alone.

Recorded music for non-nutritive sucking

Several studies have utilized recorded music as a reinforcement for learning. A key component in a preterm infant's development is the suck-swallow reflex (Gardner and Hernandez 2011). If the preterm infant is still having difficulty feeding by 35 weeks gestation, interventions such as physical manipulation of the baby's mouth and posture are used to encourage feeding (Standley and Walworth 2010). Standley (2000, 2003, Standley et al. 2010) devised a Pacifier Activated Lullaby system (PAL). This is a system by which a plastic teat or nipple is placed in the baby's mouth and the baby is rewarded with a short burst of recorded music when sucking rates are at a certain rate and pressure. In order to continue to listen to the music the infant must continue to suck. Standley reported that non nutritive sucking significantly increased with the PAL and concluded that at 35 weeks, preterm infants seemed to be capable of learning and therefore the PAL was a potential clinically useful tool to promote weight gain (Standley 2000). In a second study evaluating this device, Standley assessed feeding rate instead of sucking rate and found a significant increase in oral feeding rates (Standley 2003). The most recent study (Standley et al. 2010) reported improved feeding length and faster nipple feeding transition. In two other studies using the PAL, authors also reported an increase in non nutritive sucking (Cevasco and Grant 2005; Whipple 2008) and significantly fewer stress behaviors when used as a supportive strategy during a heel prick (Whipple 2008).

Recorded music and breastfeeding

Mothers of hospitalized infants experience stress and fatigue, separation from their infant, and shortened pregnancy in the case of preterm infants, all of which can cause decreased breast milk volumes. In a study of mothers using an electric pump to express breast milk, Keith et al. (2012) compared standard support to initiate and maintain breast milk production with a recorded spoken relaxation and guided imagery protocol, and the same protocol with the addition of recorded guitar lullabies or photos of the infant. Results showed a significant increase in milk volume and fat content over six days for all three versions of the relaxation and imagery protocol, with the best results for the protocol combined with guitar lullabies and photos of the participant's own infant.

Vianna et al. (2011) measured breastfeeding rates at the time of discharge and follow-up 60 days later for mothers of preterm infants. They reported a significantly higher breastfeeding rates for the experimental group which had received a combination of improvisational and receptive music therapy provided three times a week during the admission.

Live singing/humming

Early intervention can improve the neurobehavioral development of preterm infants (Spittle et al. 2010; Vanderveen et al. 2009). Making live music may establish and reinforce neural pathways integral for communication and social interaction (Malloch et al. 2012). McMahon et al. (2012) suggested that vocal music is a suitable stimulus for newborn infants because it contains a large spectrum of intonations which are both rhythmic and melodic (Trehub 2001) which serves the infant well when the mother's voice is not available live (Loewy 2000).

Live singing and humming must be structured to safely stimulate the post 32 week gestation infant with full attention to infant cues of engagement and disengagement. Founded in mother-infant attachment theory, singing for the full-term infant provides core experience for the primary infant-adult relationship (de l'Etoile 2006; Loewy 2000; O'Gorman 2006; Stewart 2009).

The inclusion of live singing within the multi-modal stimulation was established by Standley and others in a series of seminal studies with preterm infants (Standley 1998; Whipple 2000). The original protocol known as the Audio Tactile Visual Vestibular (ATVV) protocol was developed by Rosemary White-Traut and her team as a neurodevelopmental strategy in which sensory stimulation was progressively layered to increase tolerance for stimulation (Burns et al. 1994; White-Traut et al. 1987). The results indicated a positive trend towards improved weight gain and shorter hospital stay for the preterm participants. Standley (1998) included humming instead of the unspecified talking because sung voice had been found to be more predictable and consistent than the spoken voice (Coleman et al. 1997; Standley and Moore 1995). This resulted in significantly earlier discharge from hospital compared to standard care. Whipple (2000, 2005) employed the modified multi-modal stimulation protocol to facilitate infant parent bonding by teaching the parents the steps involved and reported decreased length of stay and improved weight gain per day, although this was not statistically significant.

Shoemark adapted this protocol to safely stimulate reciprocal interaction for medically complex newborn infants rather than preterm infants (Shoemark 1999). Shoemark used the decision tree strategy from the multi-modal stimulation to safely layer improvized singing (or contingent singing, see Methods section) to stimulate active interplay while maintaining physiologic and behavioral parameters within safe ranges. The infants who received contingent singing, framed by the ATVV protocol, showed significantly better neurobehavioral development than infants who received standard care (Malloch et al. 2012). Shoemark's subsequent microanalysis of the interplay (Shoemark and Grocke 2010) produced a taxonomy of infant and therapist behaviors which has stimulated further categorization of infant-therapist interplay (Haslbeck 2012, 2013).

MUSIC IN THE NICU AUDITORY ENVIRONMENT

A review of research in medical music therapy with hospitalized infants would not be complete without a discussion regarding the parallel significant body of research examining noise in the NICU and the impact of noxious sound on the preterm infant. This is a critical first step when adding another form of stimulation to the environment of the preterm infant.

Without the attenuation of sound provided by the uterus, the preterm infant is exposed to a much wider range of frequencies than their ears are ready to process (Graven and Browne 2008). The NICU environment contains unpredictable and sudden noise sources, fluctuations in sound levels and constant noise (Bremmer et al. 2003; Lasky and Williams 2009). Immediate behavioral changes in response to noise can include state transition from alertness, quietness or sleep to fussing and crying (Wachman and Lahav 2011). Negative short term physiological changes can include apnoea and bradycardia, elevated heart rate, blood pressure, and respiratory pattern, gastrointestinal motility, oxygenation, intestinal peristalsis and glucose consumption, increased intracranial pressure, and interference with sleep (Gardner and Goldson 2011; Wachman and Lahav 2011; Gray and Philbin 2004; Maschke et al. 2000). Longitudinal studies of preterm infants exposed to constant noise in the NICU have reported long-term interference with development of frequency discrimination including problems with sound pattern recognition (Bamiou et al. 2001), sound localization and speech intelligibility (Gray and Philbin 2004; Luoma et al. 1998), deficits in auditory discrimination and temporal processing (Lister et al. 2002) and potential hearing loss (Williams et al. 2007).

There are key historical precedents for the use of music in NICU which are now generating further investigation. Because of the positive findings of early music therapy studies, music therapy and nursing researchers concentrated on comparing recorded music to the ambient sound or to other sounds with the underlying assumption that music provided a stable sound, which was preferable to the unpredictable NICU sounds. Standley and Walworth (2010) stated the accepted construct that "recorded music can be used to provide auditory respite from noise induced stress" (p. 84). This assumption comes from the understanding that that attention to music can cause the other sound (background noise) to fade from the infant's immediate sense of perception (Standley and Walworth 2010). The other premise was that music has different acoustical properties to noise; the sound waves of music are regular with consonant frequency and harmonic overlay compared to irregular patterns of dissonant harmonies (Jourdain 2002). Music contains a range of sounds combined to form a larger organized context creating expectations, resolutions and predictability (Zatorre et al. 2007).

Importantly and perhaps a key argument for adding recorded music into the environment of the preterm infant is that music and noise are processed differently in the brain (Peretz and Zatorre 2005). Over the last decade, several studies investigating music processing in the brain have illustrated that music is not processed in the same part of the brain as noise and that different elements of music such as pitch and rhythm, are processed in separate parts of the auditory cortex (Griffiths 2003; Patterson et al. 2002; Peretz and Zatorre 2005). A detailed review of music psychology and cognitive neuroscience studies is beyond the scope of this chapter however, the discoveries made in these music psychology studies could potentially explain why preterm infants do not respond in the same way to noise and music.

While there is evidence to illustrate that music is processed differently from noise, we also now understand that an infant has less capability to differentiate one tone from another in an ambient environment (Werner 2007; Werner and Boike 2001) and therefore may find it difficult to discriminate music from the ambient background noise. If this is the case, why then are there many studies which have shown positive and no negative effect to recorded music on the preterm infant? This question has not been answered unequivocably with large randomized control trial studies and further multi-disciplinary research needs to be done in collaboration with neuroscience and auditory specialists. Despite this debate, the practice of using recorded music by both nurses and music therapists continues because positive physiological and behavioral results have been reported along with no negative responses.

THE FAMILY DURING HOSPITALIZATION

A meta-synthesis by Aargaard and Hall (2008) revealed five metaphors that captured the mothers' experiences of their newborn's hospitalization. These metaphors centered on reciprocal relationships that consisted of mother-baby relationship (from "their baby" to "my baby"), maternal development (striving to be a real, normal mother), the turbulent neonatal environment (from foreground to background), maternal care giving and role reclaiming strategies (from silent vigilance to advocacy), and mother-nurse relationship (from continuously answering questions through chatting to sharing of knowledge). Families need support to sustain role as primary nurturer and advocate; acknowledgement of the complex situation they face, and strategies to cope (Harris 2005; Peebles-Kleiger 2000).

Family centered care (FCC) is defined as "an approach to the planning, delivery, and evaluation of health care that is grounded in mutually beneficial partnerships among health care providers, patients, and families" (Institute for Family-Centered Care 2007). Instead of the professional staff making decisions and then informing families, or therapists working with infant and then explaining progress to the families, in FCC families are in active partnership with staff to confirm plans and actions in a timely fashion. FCC not only informs the way in which the therapist interacts with the family but in how he/she thinks about the infant. The simple framework of ecological theory (Bronfenbrenner 1979) helps to understand infant in the context of family. The infant is "nested" into the family which provides an inner circle of safety (Dunst et al. 1988). Outside that family circle, are the extended family and other community support for the family. Therefore all interventions while in hospital should seek to preserve the family's capacity to nurture and bond with their baby. However, in hospital that inner circle can be easily disrupted as healthcare teams provide medical care to the infant. The full-term infant's relationship with parents is compromised (Laing et al. 2010) and the infant can become wary of adults and interaction (Malloch et al. 2012). In a family centered care setting, the healthcare teams can work with the family to make all decisions and promote a routine of care which honors the family role.

Whipple (2000) found that parents taught to use music modified multi-modal stimulation (N = 10) displayed significantly fewer stress behaviors, appropriateness of parents actions and responses were significantly greater, and that parents spent significantly more time visiting their infants. However Shoemark (2013) observed that parents may feel exposed by being asked to sing aloud. Therefore, singing may be an additional stressor rather than something which empowers them to engage meaningfully with their baby. In a study to investigate the contingent effect of maternal singing on feeding, Blumenfeld and Eisenfeld (2006) found that fewer than 20 percent of mothers who had agreed to sing to their infants as part of the study were actually able to complete the task. Mothers reported feeling "excessive anxiousness" (p. 68) and shyness or inhibition about singing in the hospital. By preparing mothers to sing and use their voice in recording, Cevasco (2008) found that mothers of full-term and preterm infants were able to understand and value the importance of music for their babies' well-being.

In a survey of 60 mothers in a newborn surgical unit, Shoemark and Arnup (2014) found that of the mothers who reported they had not sung to their infant in the NICU, 54 percent (13) were too embarrassed, 42 percent (10) felt too obvious, 33 percent (8) said they could not sing, and 25 percent (6) felt too strange. However 60 percent (36) had actually sung to their infant. Previous experience of learning a musical instrument or making music in a choir or band had a weak association with singing. This association reflected other research showing a significant association between American mothers' and fathers' experience of learning and playing music and singing to their healthy infants (Custodero and Johnson Green 2008).

PRACTICAL ISSUES IN PROVIDING CLINICAL SERVICES

Models of service delivery

There is a direct relationship between the models of practice that music therapists use, the care team to which they belong, the reasons for referral and the goals and objectives of the music therapy service. When a music therapist is employed to work in a NICU or other medical unit caring for sick newborn infants, it is most likely that they will or should seek to be aligned with one of the care teams. In a perinatal center in a maternity or general hospital that includes nurseries the most likely team will be a *Developmental Care* team which focuses on optimising all care for the infant based on the infant's demonstrated capacities to cope with stimulation, including physical care and interpersonal contact. Usually a team will include other allied health practitioners such as physical therapy, occupational therapy, speech therapy or pathology, psychology, a nursing care manager, and a member of the medical staff. In this team, the music therapist is likely to receive referrals from other team members to either provide direct services to help an infant regulate their state and therefore to improve sleep and minimize irritability, or work with family to maximize attachment and thereby improve neurodevelopment. In a pediatric hospital setting the music therapist might be involved in a neurodevelopment team which is concerned with the long-term consequence of complex medical conditions and long-term hospitalization. This team might include neurologists, neuropsychologists, and allied health clinicians who assess the infant's developmental status, treat any immediate concerns which may have long-term consequences, and refer infants for early intervention or follow up in outpatient clinics. The music therapist might receive a referral from within this team to create appropriate opportunities for healthy development, and to help to educate families about how to safely and productively meet the infant's needs for interaction.

Despite the logistical difficulties involved in providing individualized infant-centered care at all times, the culture in the NICU and Special Care Nurseries in hospitals in the developed world has largely adopted the principals of Developmental Care for preterm infants (Als et al. 2004). Developmental Care strategies aim to optimize neurological, physiological, behavioral, and psychological development in the preterm infant. Developmental Care promotes reduced handling, adapted positioning to optimize physical development, reduced environmental stimuli to minimize overstimulation, and minimized interruption of sleep to promote self-habituation and growth (Gardner and Goldson 2011). Music therapy services are highly congruent with Developmental Care principles (Hanson-Abromeit 2003), which is perhaps why many of the studies involving music and preterm infants have been conducted by nurses.

In wards operating without a team structure or service delivery model, bedside nurses and doctors may refer directly to the music therapy service. The music therapist should provide regular education for these staff to ensure referrals are appropriate to the service the music therapist is skilled to provide. Families who value music or have heard about music therapy may self-refer and this provides an optimal starting point as music already has an intrinsic value for the family.

FOUNDATIONS OF PRACTICE FOR ALL METHODS

Before treatment begins, there are some key issues that need to be considered regarding the context of the infant.

Ambient sound environment

NICU music therapists have a responsibility to measure the sound environment of the infant before adding any other kind of stimulation. Sound level meters are relatively affordable and easy to use. The better quality devices with data logging capacity are connected to software programs which analyse levels over time. Given that many NICUs exceed the recommended sound levels (American Academy of Pediatrics 1997; White et al. 2013) it is preferable to establish a general overall sound level of the infant's environment at different times of the day. It is important to remember that different beds in the same NICU can have different sound levels due to variation in equipment provided such as number of staff, ventilation and pumps, and proximity to doors, telephone, nursing desk, etc. It is therefore important to monitor the sound level at the individual bed to make a decision about suitable times for music or music therapy. The optimal time is when it is quiet, and times which are busy with human activity (medical rounds, nursing hand-over) should be avoided.

Age to commence service

While music was thought to be a safe stimulus for infant 26 weeks gestation and beyond in the early 1990s, more recent evidence of neurological processing (see Table 2.1) and capabilities in the preterm infant issues caution about the potential long-term damage of early over-stimulation (Aucott et al. 2002; Graven and Browne 2008). It is the opinion of these authors that prior to 28 weeks gestation, only a trained and experienced clinician should apply any auditory stimulation as a treatment. Services which require the infant to use cortical processing (multi-modal stimulation, PAL) should wait until the infant is 33 weeks gestation when the preterm infant may be sufficiently mature to recognize and learn auditory information (Krueger et al. 2004) and regulate the heart rate in response to an external stimulus (Gardner and Goldson 2011; Groome et al. 1999; White-Traut et al. 2009). At any point the music therapist can use her extensive knowledge of music, auditory processing and infant development to educate and support the parents to understand their infant's cues, and use their own voices to nurture their infant.

Physical context

In addition to considerations of the ambient sound environment, the music therapist must attend to the type of bed and the infant's position in the bed. The preterm or medically fragile infant may be placed into an incubator which is an enclosed environment in which sound reverberates and therefore the volume of the music needs to be checked and decreased as needed. In any type of bed, the infant may be surrounded by a nest of towels and blankets to help the infant feel secure and promote self-regulation. Prone positioning decreases heart rate variability, improves oxygenation, and decreases energy expenditure resulting in more quiet sleep (Kassim et al. 2007; Kurlak et al. 1999). Positioning therefore needs to be taken into consideration when evaluating physiological and behavioral response during music.

Timing

Timing of the intervention can be critical to the infant's capacity to respond. If the infant has had a change in ventilatory support it can take several hours to adapt and music risks over-stimulation. Music should only be considered if it is already a standard part of that infant's care regime. The infant may not respond to the music as he/she had previously done, and therefore the music therapist should closely monitor the effect of the music on the infant. If the infant has had a procedure or other intervention his/her responses might be different from other times. He/she may be fatigued and not able to tolerate as much stimulation as other times, or conversely may be unsettled and need additional support to facilitate sleep. Handling such as diaper change, a wash or bath, assessments, feeding, or procedures can fatigue the infant therefore during and afterwards the infant may have less tolerance for musical stimulation.

Cautions

There are some phenomena which indicate that music therapy is contraindicated or should be delayed:

- Extra Corporeal Membrane Oxygenation (ECMO) and oscillating ventilators produce noise which is already louder than the recommended sound level. To make the music audible to the infant it would need to be played at a much louder level than is safe and therefore music is contraindicated.
- The introduction of music to infants who have had a significant number of apnea or bradycardia episodes on that day should be carefully assessed and cautiously applied or left until another time.

- Infants with some conditions should not have music therapy unless the clinician is part of a treating team and has consent from medical team. This includes infants with grade 3 or 4 intra-ventricular hemorrhages, or hypoxic ischemic encephalopathy (HIE) because of the infant's altered capabilities to respond, temporary hearing loss, and because it is not yet understood how music will be processed neurologically in infants with brain injury.
- Caution is needed in interpreting responses from infants receiving sedatives, caffeine citrate, or antibiotics which can impact physiological state and/or auditory processing.
- When an infant is born to a drug-addicted mother, he/she is likely to have Neonatal Abstinence Syndrome which requires the music therapist to be educated in specific considerations.
- When a mother has a significant mental health issue or is drug addicted, the music therapist will only commence work in collaboration with the mental health team.

Treatment methods

The preterm infant's main task of achieving homeostasis can be assessed through their capacity to experience good quality sleep. Sleep interruption and disturbance can affect the development of the neurosensory and motor systems, the creation of memory and long-term memory circuits, and the maintenance of brain plasticity (Arditi-Babchuk et al. 2009; Graven and Browne 2008; Graven 2006). Recorded music may be cautiously used to ameliorate the environment and potentially facilitate improved sleep outcomes and physiological and behavioral stability.

If recorded music is used with this population, it is imperative that the music therapist considers the current guidelines regarding duration and frequency of presentation (Standley and Walworth 2010), frequency spectrum of musical elements and appropriate sound levels (Cassidy and Ditty 1998), and understanding that recorded music played free field will not completely mask the ambient noise.

Despite the many different types of music being compared, including maternal heart beat, womb sounds, recorded mother's voice, and live music, no one clear stimulus has risen above the others consistently to achieve both behavioral and physiological organization. Given this, it is difficult then to state definitively which music is best for preterm infants and under which conditions.

Recommendations for music selections for preterm infants include simplicity, gentle rhythms, flowing and lyrical melodies, simple harmonies, and a soft tone color. The tempo should be slow (60 to 82 beats per minute) regular, monotonous, and repetitive, while a lower pitch promotes relaxation (Standley and Walworth 2010; Schwartz 2003). Standley and Walworth (2010) recommended using soothing, constant, stable, and relatively unchanging sounds with a light and constant rhythm sung by a female voice alone or only one accompanying instrument to reduce alerting responses of the infant.

Choosing music in the lower frequency range best heard by the preterm infants (500–1000 Hz) can maximize the potential for the preterm infant to differentiate the auditory stimulus from the background noise (Cassidy and Ditty 1998; Wightman et al. 2003).

Recorded music to lower arousal and facilitate Quiet Sleep

The research evidence is as yet unable to fully support any practical proven steps to provide recorded music to promote sleep. Olischar et al. (2011) reported a trend towards more mature sleep-wake cycling in healthy infants at 32 weeks or more gestational age exposed to a recording of Brahms' Lullaby, suggesting that there might be a small effect of music on quiet sleep in newborns.

Beyond the music itself, it is also important to establish a presentation protocol. The music therapist should conduct a baseline assessment of the infant's behavioral and physiological status including heart rate, oxygen saturation, and behavioral state both with and without music. The music therapist should include results of the assessment and the recommended presentation protocol in the infant's medical file so staff can confirm this for parents. When nurses use the recorded music in the absence of the music therapist, usage and response should be documented in the medical record. This allows the music therapist to make adaptations to the program, including length of exposure as the infant gets older.

Where possible, the initial use of music to support sleep should be implemented by parents as primary carers to support their "normal" role as parents and for which they value the opportunity to feel useful (Dearn 2005).

Recorded music for learning

As infants approach term age, recorded music can be used to provide supplementary opportunities for stimulation or interaction with infants in a Quiet Alert state. The music therapist can work with the family to create a music listening library of simple familiar songs or new songs they find enjoyable. Music selections can be drawn from the family's own collection particularly when they are beyond the music therapist's own resources. Selections honor the family's own experience, and may acknowledge the cultural background.

The music library can be used as a framework for interaction. With the music playing, family and staff can be encouraged to sing along with lyrics, add some playful touch or even add traditional actions, for example twinkling fingers for *Twinkle Twinkle Little Star*.

The music library becomes an extension of familiar experience for the infant when families are absent from the NICU because they have other children, work, or live a long distance from the hospital. Given that infants have a preference for maternal language at birth (Granier-Deferre et al. 2011), vocal music may also provide a source of familiarity and exposure to the family's language when it is different from the staff in the NICU.

Recorded music to support the mother during Kangaroo Care

Kangaroo Care is the opportunity for a parent to hold the baby in skin-to-skin contact on their chest. While this is a cherished time, transferring baby from bed to chair can be stressful. The parent may fear they will hurt or over-tax her fragile baby and can therefore struggle to relax and enjoy the experience. In collaboration with the bedside nurse, pre-chosen relaxing music may be played once they are settled to assist in relaxation. The music is played quietly so it does not increase stimulation to the infant or intrude on the dyad's experience of each other.

Recorded music for pain

While there are no published clinical protocols for using recorded music for pain, there is a body of research that supports the use of music for pain management. The music therapist can create a programmed music list for use after a procedure to support the infant's effort to recover. This needs to be done in collaboration with the bedside nurse and needs to be followed up regularly to ensure that it continues to be effective. This would not be suitable for infants less than 33–34 weeks gestation because of immature auditory processing and autonomic nervous system.

There is legitimate concern that over time the infant may learn to associate the music with the painful procedure but at this stage there is no research to suggest this association. In clinical practice, music therapists recommend that music is introduced when an infant is in a Quiet Alert, Transition, or sleep state (Thoman and Ingersoll 1999) to build a positive association between music and state. This positive association should be maintained so that the application of music to ameliorate pain or distress is the smaller experience of music in an otherwise positive association.

Recorded maternal voice for infant stability and parent connectedness

Recent evidence has shown that maternal voice can facilitate short-term physiological stability (Doheny et al. 2012, Picciolini et al. 2014). Often parents in the NICU find it hard to leave the baby when it is time to go home and feel they would like to leave something of themselves with the baby. Recorded parental voice is a strategy where the music therapist provides an opportunity for parents to record their voice for their baby. Parents can be supported to sing some favorite simple songs/lullabies, or if this is not viable, they can read, say nursery rhymes or simply talk to their baby. This resource is then used in a similar way to recorded music.

Contingent interaction to support neurodevelopment

Live singing is perhaps the most obvious and readily implemented music therapy program in a clinical program and can influence the infant's neurodevelopment (Malloch et al. 2012). Songs represent a range of cultural phenomena which can be replicated by anyone who is part of, or who has access to, that culture. Underpinned by sociological models of attachment and dynamics systems theory, the songs that families know and love, "songs of kin" are a celebration of their culture (Loewy 2000). Depending on gestational age at birth, the infant may have heard the mother's song preferences while in utero, which may now also be useful as familiar song repertoire. This use of pre-existing experience may draw on the strengths of the family into this time of crisis.

Contingent singing (Shoemark 2008) is a therapeutic method derived from the naturally occurring patterns of successful adult-infant communication. Contingent singing is guided by the infant's availability for social engagement and is therefore not appropriate with pre-term infants less than 36 weeks gestation. During wakeful periods around feed time, the infant may be sufficiently alert to engage with the parent or therapist. Most commonly used with medically complex newborn infants, this method requires the music therapist to pri-marily use voice, but also facial expression, posture and gesture to entice, respond to and direct the infant (Shoemark 2011b). Before 12 weeks of age, the infant will primarily use facial expression, gesture and posture in combinations that are quiet or active, to show whether he is available or not (for a full exposition of these behaviors see Shoemark and Grocke 2010). Around 12 weeks the infant will also begin to use voice, however the vocal cords may be tem-porarily weakened by long-term ventilation, or other airway and muscular problems, and this should be confirmed before setting up an expectation in parents.

The critical feature of contingent singing is the smooth transition between infant-directed speech and singing. The music therapist can teach the parent or others involved in the infant's care a procedure for contingent singing (Shoemark and Grocke 2010; Shoemark 2013) as follows. The adult partner uses a time of silence to observe the infant's state and readiness to respond in the interaction. Such a "space" allows the infant time to formulate a response or even initiate something new for the interplay. Between silence and singing there are several possible steps. The attuned partner can use the highly intonated infant-directed speech or "half-singing" to entice the infant into the interplay. A type of chanting such as repeating a single word like "sh-sh" or "there there" can be used to soothe or provide mod-est stimulation. The next slightly more active step is "sing and wait" in which the adult sings just a phrase or line of melodic motif and waits for the infant to demonstrate a response of acceptance or rejection before repeating or extending it. Finally if the infant has shown acceptance or enjoyment of some of the modest singing steps, the adult partner might sing a song (or half a song) to provide an ongoing context for interaction. This step-wise progres-sion from silence to speech to singing provides a bridge for the infant to take the first tenta-tive steps of communication and extend these attempts all the while being supported by the adult. The resulting nuanced interaction acknowledges and supports the infant to extend his or her capabilities safely.

Multi-modal stimulation

In multi-modal stimulation, the therapist uses a sequence of carefully structured sensory experiences to expose the infant to a progressively more demanding series of stimulation, without over-stimulating. The premise for multi-modal stimulation is that systematically layered sensory stimulation at the infant's threshold for coping promotes an increasing capacity to cope with stimulation. The use of a decision tree mechanism enables the therapist to explicitly assess the infant's response and constantly modify what they offer according to the infant's status. The intention is to safely arouse the infant and help them to organize their behaviors so they can more easily engage in social interaction (White-Traut and Hutchens Pate 1987).

The therapist holds the infant in her arms thereby providing tactile stimulation. Just allowing oneself to be held can be taxing for an infant. If the infant is awake there may also be visual stimulation at this point. Systematically the therapist adds stroking (see Burns et al. 1994 for the full sequence) and introduces humming or singing. The therapist carefully watches for the infant's cues of disengagement and removes sensory modalities in response. That is, in response to the infant's subtle changes in physiologic signs, within the individual's safe limits, or cues of behavioral disengagement such as hiccupping or yawning, the therapist pauses the stimulation for 15 seconds. If the infant cue abates, the stimulus is recommenced and the prescribed routine continued. If, however, the cue remains the same, that portion of the stimulus is immediately concluded and the next step is commenced. If the infant cue becomes more potent, such as crying, whining, fussing, cry face, spitting/vomiting, or hand held up in stop-like gesture, or a physiologic sign such as heart rate or oxygen saturation moves outside the infant's safe range, each modality is withdrawn, and containing care is offered until the infant is again stable (Burns et al. 1994). The infant's progress and any adverse events during the multi-modal stimulation protocol should be documented in the medical file. The method has been tested with medically fragile infants (Malloch et al. 2012) and with neurologically compromised infants (White-Traut et al. 1999). When working with infants who have had surgery or have major medical care such as intravenous drips or a central line, the stroking component may not be acceptable to the infant. It is likely there will be continuing discomfort and tissue tenderness, and the possibility that touch in these areas threatens rather than reassures. Nutrition via intravenous lines inserted into veins in the back of hands, feet, arms, or head means that stroking of limbs and head could also be unwelcome.

Family musicality to support attachment and early development

The intention of family-centered intervention is to support and facilitate the family's capability to provide their infant with a stable and nurturing context during the hospital admission. Shoemark and Dearn (2008) championed the significance of the parents' experience in family-centered music therapy in hospital. They highlighted the pivotal role of the music therapist as partner with parents in understanding their infant as a "baby" and not a patient. The music therapist can stimulate and facilitate family music making to generate an expanded sense of each other.

Shoemark and Dearn (2008) proposed seven characteristics for an effective clinical service:

1. The music therapist must be poised so the family can have confidence in her capacity to help them. For new practitioners this may seem daunting but is really only a matter of respecting the family in this extraordinary time. The key to poise is preparation. Before meeting a family, the therapist must think through what she can bring to the family. This does not need to include everything, but some touchpoints of likely knowledge she will need, and the skills she can bring. She should discuss with other staff a suitable time to approach the family to minimize over-taxing them or experiencing

refusal of service. The family may not be ready to consider music therapy because they are fatigued and stressed and may not have the reserve to consider a new service. Arrangements can be made to return at a more suitable time. The music therapist should be prepared to ask the family about their needs, and to be ready for respond to any cues of fatigue or stress by making a decision to continue or schedule a return visit at another time.

2. Music therapy is a triadic relationship which acknowledges that the music therapist works with the infant and the family.
3. The hospital admission may be one of endurance involving steps of relapse and recovery. The music therapist ensures continuity of service to the family through each stage of this journey. That continuity may mean more or less direct service, but should assure the family that the music therapist remains available to them.
4. Parents experience joy watching their baby enjoying him/herself during music therapy.
5. Music therapy acknowledges the "whole" developing child—we are not trying to "fix" something but rather to enjoy and celebrate the infant's capacities.
6. The contingent relationship between the infant and the parents is supported.
7. A whole life—it is important to honor this phase of the baby's life so that parents do not feel that this time has been "lost." The music therapist helps to create moments of joy which can be cherished and remembered in counter-balance to the medical journey of the infant.

In family-centered music therapy, the music therapist works firstly with the parents to determine the acceptability and usefulness of music as a medium for their family and their child within the family. In music therapy sessions, family-centered practice means relinquishing the role of being the primary music-provider, and taking up the role as facilitator and music modeller for the parents as needed. The music therapist brings to the family's consciousness their own musical potential, re-engaging them with their uses of music with their other children or calling on their own childhood experiences of song-singing and playing music. Then the resulting music is shared with the infant to co-create a new and meaningful dimension to their relationship (Tronick 2007).

Family-centered practice is suited to infants of all ages and regardless of the medical condition. The focus of the work can be to sustain the family's experience of their infant as a baby, and can also lay the foundation for the infant's future development.

Mothers' singing/presence

Mothers in the NICU often feel disempowered to nurture or do something for their child. For high risk infants, mothers may not be able to hold or rock their baby and therefore it is vital that other opportunities to feel connected to their infant are provided. By engaging a mother in her own existing musicality, the music therapist can help the mother understand her own capabilities and the value she has to her baby's sense of safety and wellbeing. Mothers value this information as it allows them to be *normal* in this abnormal situation and promotes a sense of doing something *helpful* for their baby at a time when they may feel disempowered. It is also helpful for the music therapist to explain that there is evidence to show that the infant benefits simply from the mother's presence beside the bed even if she feels that she does not know what to do (Dearn and Shoemark 2014).

Individual songbooks/recorded music library

The music therapist is only available to families for relatively brief periods of time during the day while conducting sessions. Therefore providing the family with resources to enhance their opportunities for interaction with the baby between sessions can be important. A recorded music library can be generated within the safe parameters described in previously. The music therapist can work with the parents to determine their music style preferences, and then combine this with knowledge about the dimensions of music needed to make it a safe modality.

A songbook can be made by identifying key songs of the family's culture in collaboration with the parents, including lullabies, and play songs, and printing these into a songbook with the baby's name on it to keep at the bedside. These ongoing resources assure the family that the therapist holds them in mind beyond the moments they are there, sustaining the sense of support particularly in the evenings and weekends.

Supporting the family transitioning home

A music therapy service can also assist families with the transition home. When families go home, sometimes a music therapist will provide a follow up consultation discussing the use of music at home. Often families return to the hospital for medical follow up and music therapy may be provided as an outpatient service to provide developmentally appropriate recorded music or other required resources and links with music services in the community. In the event that an infant dies, sometimes a music therapist will provide music services for the funeral. This is dependent on a number of issues which may be specific to the hospital. Most commonly this would only be offered where a relationship between the music therapist and the family had been developed during the admission. The participation in the funeral is a continuation of the service previously established. Further consideration are funding issues, and number hours per week of music therapy paid for by the hospital as time away from the hospital to attend means other families miss out.

EVALUATION AND REPORTING

Evaluating the effectiveness of a music therapy program is a key responsibility. This can be done in many ways and is dependent on the intention of the services provided. If the intention is to facilitate more stable physiological and behavioral state, an assessment form completed after the first session can be re-done at regular intervals to assess infant response or tolerance for recorded music. This is particularly important in the case where the recorded music is being used in the absence of the music therapist by the family or the bedside nurse.

Evaluation of the program may be required when the treatment has been proposed by the team of specialists, be it psychosocial or neurodevelopmental and it is important to report all considerations in infant response. The ability to describe the intention of the program is critical when discussing the progress within non music therapy teams. It is recommended that NICU music therapists consider additional training in standardized scales of infant development in order to be able to evaluate the development of the infant in terms understood by the neonatal team.

The reporting required is usually determined by the funding body paying for the service whether a philanthropic trust or a healthcare provider. It is sometimes difficult to explain the intricacies of a music therapy program and it is recommended that the music therapist in this setting should regularly document case studies, and with permission collects other artifacts such as photographs and videos. As a part of the clinical program, the music therapist should adopt the larger scale requirements of other allied health or appropriate professionals to create evidence which is valued by the hospital. Small pilot studies to monitor the effect of clinical protocols will provide simple but effective evidence to argue for continuing or expanding services. Larger studies are needed with this population but require significant funding and therefore smaller studies are easier to conduct within regular clinical work. Necessary cautions are required regarding clinical intention versus research when working with families, it is nonetheless possible to do both within a clinical program.

CONCLUSION

Clinical work with hospitalized infants is an intricate and complicated dance. Music therapists need to attend to the complexities of an infant's medical status, the infant's behavioral state, and the family dynamics in order to be able to effectively assist both the infant and the family within the acute medical context of the NICU or other type of care service for newborns. An understanding of the hospital environment is required alongside the ability to articulate music therapy protocols within a team of allied health and medical specialists to facilitate opportunities for the infant during this critical time. As this work expands across the world, there will be many instances where music therapy will be introduced by a music therapist working in the area for the first time. As experienced practitioners who have developed programmes in hospital settings, the authors' advice is to align the program with an appropriate team such as the neurodevelopment or psychosocial team. Belonging to such a team will provide a theoretical under-pinning, secure a stream of referrals, focus the intention of the program, and guide the knowledge and skills required to provide the service.

More research is required to substantiate the clinical protocols being used around the world and standardized music therapy protocols need to be further researched and developed around recorded music presentation, particularly type of music, duration, frequency, and volume. Clinical music therapy in the NICU has developed in parallel with other fields including neuroscience, auditory processing, and music psychology and needs to continue to address newfound knowledge when evaluating effectiveness or appropriateness of clinical/research protocols.

References

Aargaard, A. and Hall, E. (2008). Mothers' experiences of having a preterm infant in the neonatal care unit: A meta-synthesis. *Journal of Pediatric Nursing* 23(3): e26–e36.

Allen, K. (2013). Music therapy in the NICU: Is there evidence to support integration for procedural support? *Advances in Neonatal Care* 13(5): 349–352.

Als, H., Duffy, F.H., McAnulty, G.B. et al. (2004). Early experience alters brain function and structure. *Pediatrics* 113: 846–857.

American Academy of Pediatrics (1997). Noise: A hazard for the fetus and newborn. *Pediatrics* 100(4): 724–726.

Arditi-Babchuk, H., Feldman, R., and Eidelman, A.I. (2009). Rapid eye movement (REM) in premature neonates and developmental outcome at 6 months. *Infant Behavior and Development* 32(1): 27–32.

Arnon, S., Shapsa, A., Forman, L. et al. (2006). Live music is beneficial to preterm infants in the Neonatal Intensive Care Unit Environment. *Birth* 33: 131–136.

Aucott, S., Donohue, P.K., Atkins, E. et al. (2002). Neurodevelopmental care in the NICU. *Mental Retardation and Developmental Disabilities Research Reviews* 8: 298–308.

Bakewell-Sachs, S. (2007). Near-term/late preterm infants. *Newborn and Infant Nursing Reviews* 7(2): 68–71.

Bamiou, D., Musiek, F., and Luxon, L. (2001). Etiology and clinical presentation of auditory processing disorders: A review. *Archives of Diseases in Childhood* 85: 361–365.

Bergeson, T. and Trehub, S. (2002). Absolute pitch and tempo in mothers' songs to infants. *Psychological Science* 13(1): 72–75.

Bertoncini, J., Morais, J., Bijeljac-Babic, R. et al. (1989). Dichotic perception and laterality in newborns. *Brain and Language* 37: s591–s605.

Bisiacchi, P., Mento, G., and Suppiej, A. (2009). Cortical auditory processing in preterm newborns: An ERP study. *Biological Psychology* 82: 176–185.

Blumenfeld, H. and Eisenfeld, L. (2006). Does a mother singing to her premature baby affect feeding in the neonatal intensive care unit? *Clinical Pediatrics* 45(1): 65–70.

Bo, L.K. and Callaghan, P. (2000). Soothing pain-elicited distress in Chinese neonates. *Pediatrics* 105: E49.

Bozzette, M. (2008). Healthy preterm infant responses to taped maternal voice. *Journal of Perinatal and Neonatal Nursing* 22(4): 307–316.

Bremmer, P., Byers, J.F., and Kiehl, E. (2003). Noise and the premature infant: physiological effects and practice implications. *Journal of Obstetric, Gynecologic, and Neonatal Nursing* 32: 447–454.

Bronfenbrenner, U. (1979). *The Ecology of Human Development: Experiments by Nature and Design*. Cambridge, MA: Harvard.

Brown, V.D. and Landers, S. (2011). Heat balance. In: S. Gardner, B. Carter, M. Enzam-Hines, and J. Hernandez (eds), *Merenstein And Gardner's Handbook of Neonatal Intensive Care*, 7th edn., pp. 113–133. St. Louis: Mosby.

Burns, K., Cunningham, N., White-Traut, R. et al. (1994). Infant stimulation: Modification of an intervention based on physiologic and behavioral cues. *Journal of Obstetric, Gynecologic, and Neonatal Nursing* 23(7): 581–589.

Butt, M.L. and Kisilevsky, B.S. (2000). Music modulates behaviour of premature infants following heel lance. *Canadian Journal of Nursing Research* 31(4): 17–39.

Caine, J. (1991). The effects of music on the selected stress behaviors, weight, caloric and formula intake, and length of hospital stay of preterm and low birth weight neonates in a newborn intensive care unit. *Journal of Music Therapy* 28(4): 180–192.

Calabro, J., Wolfe, R., and Shoemark, H. (2003). The effects of recorded sedative music on the physiology and behaviour of premature infants with a respiratory disorder. *Australian Journal of Music Therapy* 14: 3–19.

Cassidy, J.W. and Ditty, K.M. (1998). Presentation of aural stimuli to newborns and premature infants: an audiological perspective. *Journal of Music Therapy* 35: 70–87.

Cassidy, J.W. and Standley, J.M. (1995). The effect of music listening on physiological responses of premature infants in the NICU. *Journal of Music Therapy* 32(4): 208–227.

Cevasco, A. (2008). The effect of mothers' singing on fullterm and preterm infants and maternal and emotional responses. *Journal of Music Therapy* 45(3): 273–306.

Cevasco, A.M. and Grant, R.E. (2005). Effects of the pacifier activated lullaby on weight gain on premature infants. *Journal of Music Therapy* 42(2): 123–139.

Chapman, J.S. (1978). Influence of varied stimuli on development of motor patterns in the preterm infant. *Birth Defects: Original Article Series* 15(7): 61–80.

Chou, L., Wang, R., Chen, S., and Pai, L. (2003). Effects of music therapy on oxygen saturation in premature infants receiving endotracheal suctioning. *Journal of Nursing Research* 11(3): 209–215.

Coleman, J.M., Pratt, R.R., Stoddard, A., Gerstmann, D.R., and Abel, H.H. (1997). The effects of the male and female singing and speaking voices on selected physiological and behavioral measures of premature infants in the intensive care unit. *International Journal of Arts Medicine* 5(2): 4–11.

Collins, S. and Kuck, K. (1991). Music therapy in the neonatal intensive care unit. *Neonatal Network* 9(6): 23–26.

Coppola, G., Cassibba, G., and Costantini, A. (2007). What can make a difference? Premature birth and maternal sensitivity at 3 monts of age: The role of attachment organization, traumatic reaction and baby's medical risk. *Infant Behavior and Development* 30: 679–684.

Custodero, L.A. and Johnson-Green, E.A. (2008). Caregiving in counterpoint: reciprocal influences in the musical parenting of younger and older infants. *Early Child Development and Care* 178(1): 15–39.

Daily, D.K., Carter, A., and Carter, B.S. (2011). Discharge and follow-up of the neonatal intensive care unit infant. In: S. Gardner, B. Carter, M. Enzam-Hines, and J. Hernandez (eds), *Merenstein And Gardner's Handbook of Neonatal Intensive Care*, 7th edn., pp. 938–961. St. Louis: Mosby.

de l'Etoile, S. (2006). Infant-directed singing: A theory for intervention. *Music Therapy Perspectives* 24(1): 22–29.

Dearn, T. (2005). *Music therapy in the NICU: pilot program*. Mercy Hospital for Women. Melbourne. Unpublished report.

Dearn, T. and Shoemark, H. (2014). The effect of maternal presence on premature infant response to recorded music. *Journal of Obstetric, Gynecological, and Neonatal Nursing* 43: 341–350.

DeCasper, A.J. and Fifer, W.P. (1980). Of human bonding: Newborns prefer their mothers voices. *Science* 208: 1174–1176.

deRegnier, R.A., Nelson, C.A., Thomas, K.M., Wewerka, S., and Georgieff, M.K. (2000). Neurophysiologic evaluation of auditory recognition memory in healthy newborn infants and infants of diabetic mothers. *Journal of Pediatrics* 137: 777–784.

Doheny, L., Hurwitz, S., Insoft, R., Ringer, S., and Lahav, A. (2012). Exposure to biological maternal sounds improves cardiorespiratory regulation in extremely preterm infants. *Journal of Maternal-Fetal and Neonatal Medicine* 25: 1591–1594.

Dunst, C., Trivette, C., and Deal, A. (1988). *Enabling and Empowering Families: Principles and Guidelines for Practice.* Cambridge, MA: Brookline Books.

Gardner, S.L. and Goldson, E. (2011). The neonate and the environment: impact on development. In: S. Gardner, B. Carter, M. Enzam-Hines, and J. Hernandez (eds), *Merenstein And Gardner's Handbook of Neonatal Intensive Care*, 7th edn., pp. 270–332. St. Louis: Mosby.

Gardner, S.L. and Hernandez, J.A. (2011). Initial nursery care. In: S. Gardner, B. Carter, M. Enzam-Hines, and J. Hernandez (eds), *Merenstein And Gardner's Handbook of Neonatal Intensive Care*, 7th edn., pp. 78–112. St. Louis: Mosby.

Gardner, S., Enzam-Hines, M., and Dickey, L.A. (2011). Pain and pain relief. In: S. Gardner, B. Carter, M. Enzam-Hines, and J. Hernandez (eds), *Merenstein And Gardner's Handbook of Neonatal Intensive Care*, 7th edn., pp. 223–269. St. Louis: Mosby.

Garunkstiene, R., Buinauskiene, J., Uloziene, I., and Markuniene, E. (2014). Controlled trial of live versus recorded lullabies in preterm infants. *Nordic Journal of Music Therapy* 23(1): 71–88.

Granier-Deferre, C., Bassereau, S., Ribeiro, A., Jacquet, A-Y., and DeCasper, A.J. (2011). A melodic contour repeatedly experienced by human near-term fetuses elicits a profound cardiac reaction one month after birth. *PLoS ONE* 6(2): e17304.

Graven, S.N. (2006). Sleep and brain development. *Clinics in Perinatology* 33: 693–706.

Graven, S.N. and Browne, J. (2008). Auditory development in the fetus and infant. *Newborn and Infant Nursing Review* 8(4): 187–193.

Gray, L. and Philbin, M.K. (2004). Effects of the neonatal intensive care unit on auditory attention and distraction. *Clinics in Perinatology* 31: 243–260.

Griffiths, T.D. (2003). Functional imaging of pitch analysis. *Annals of the New York Academy of Sciences* 999: 40–49.

Groome, L.J., Mooney, D.M., Holland, S.B., Sith, L.A., Attenbury, J.L., and Dykman, R.A. (1999). Behavioral state affects heart rate response to low-intensity sound in human foetuses. *Early Human Development* 54: 39–54.

Hall, J.W. (2000). Development of the ear and hearing. *Journal of Perinatology* 20(8 Pt 2): S12–S20.

Hanson-Abromeit, D. (2003). The Newborn Individualized Developmental Care and Assessment Program (NIDCAP) as a model for clinical music therapy interventions with premature infants. *Music Therapy Perspectives* 21: 60–68.

Harris, J. (2005). Critically ill babies in hospital—Considering the experience of mothers. *Infant Observation* 8(3): 247–258.

Hartling, L., Shaik, M. S., Tjosvold, L. et al. (2009). Music for medical indication in the neonatal period: a systematic review of randomized controlled trials. *Archives of Disease in Childhood-Fetal and Neonatal Edition* 94: F349–F354.

Haslbeck, F.B. (2012). Music therapy for premature infants and their parents: an integrative review, *Nordic Journal of Music Therapy* 21(3): 203–226.

Haslbeck, F. (2013). Creative music therapy with premature infants: An analysis of video footage. *Nordic Journal of Music Therapy*, DOI:10.1080/08098131.2013.780091.

Hodges, A.L. and Wilson, L.L. (2010). Preterm infants' responses to music: An integrative literature review. *Southern Online Journal of Nursing Research* 10(3): 72–73.

Institute for Family-Centred Care (2007). Available at <http://www.ipfcc.org/>.

Jardri, R., Pins, D., Houfflin-Debarge, V. et al. (2008). Fetal cortical activation to sound at 33 weeks of gestation: A functional MRI study. *NeuroImage* 42: 10–18.

Jobe, A. (2014). A risk of sensory deprivation in the Neonatal Intensive Care Unit. *Journal of Pediatrics* 164: 1265–1267.

Johnston, C.C., Filion, F., and Nuyt, A.M. (2007). Recorded maternal voice for preterm neonates undergoing heel lance. *Advances in Neonatal Care* 7(5): 258–266.

Johnston, C.C., Filion, F., Campbell-Yeo, M. et al. (2009). Enhanced kangaroo mother care for heel lance in preterm neonates: a crossover trial. *Journal of Perinatology* 29: 51–56.

Jourdain, R. (2002). *Music, the Brain, and Ecstasy*. New York: Harper Collins Publishers.

Joyce, B.A., Keck, J.F., and Gerkensmeyer, J. (2001). Evaluation of pain management interventions for neonatal circumcision pain. *Journal of Pediatric Health Care* 15: 105–114.

Kaminski, J. and Hall, W. (1996). The effect of soothing music on neonatal behavioral states in the hospital newborn nursery. *Neonatal Network* 15(1): 45–54.

Kassim, Z., Donaldson, N., Khetriwal, B. et al. (2007). Sleeping position, oxygen saturation and lung volume in convalescent, prematurely born infants. *Archives of Disease in Childhood—Fetal and Neonatal Edition* 92: 347–350.

Katz, V. (1971). Auditory stimulation and developmental behavior of the premature infant. *Nursing Research* 20: 196–201.

Keith, D.R., Russell, K., and Weaver, B.S. (2009). The effects of music listening on inconsolable crying in premature infants. *Journal of Music Therapy* 46(3): 191–203.

Keith, D.R., Weaver, B.S., and Vogel, R.B. (2012). The effect of music-based listening interventions on the volume, fat content, and caloric content of breast milk produced by mothers of premature and critically ill infants. *Advances in Neonatal Care* 12(2): 112–119.

Key, A., Lambert, W., Aschner, J., and Maitre, N. (2012). Influence of gestational age and postnatal age on speech sound processing in NICU infants. *Psychophysiology* 49: 720–731.

Kisilevsky, B.S., Hains, S.M., Brown, C.A. et al. (2009). Fetal sensitivity to properties of maternal speech and language. *Infant Behavior and Developmental Psychobiology* 32: 59–71.

Krueger, C. (2010). Exposure to maternal voice in preterm infants: A review. *Advances in Neonatal Care* 10(1): 13–18.

Krueger, C., Holditch-Davis, D., Quint, S., and DeCasper, A. (2004). Recurring auditory experience in the 28- to 34-week-old foetus. *Infant Behavior and Development* 27: 537–543.

Kurlak, L.O., Ruggins, N.R., and Stephenson, T.J. (1999). Effects of nursing position on incidence, type and duration of clinically significant apnoea in preterm infants. *Archives of Disease in Childhood—Fetal and Neonatal Edition* 71: F16–F19.

Lai, H.L., Chen, C.J., Peng, T.C. et al. (2006). Randomized controlled trial of music during kangaroo care on maternal state anxiety and preterm infants' responses. *International Journal of Nursing Studies* 43: 139–146.

Laing, S., McMahon, C., Ungerer, J., Taylor, A., Badawi, N., and Spence K. (2010). Mother–child interaction and child developmental capacities in toddlers with major birth defects requiring newborn surgery. *Early Human Development* 86: 793–800.

Lasky, R.E. and Williams, A.L. (2009). Noise and light exposures for extremely low birth weight newborns during their stay in the neonatal intensive care unit. *Pediatrics* 123: 540–546.

Lickliter, R. (2000). Atypical perinatal sensory stimulation and early perceptual development: Insights from developmental psychobiology. *Journal of Perinatology* 20: S45–S54.

Lickliter, R. and Bahrick, L. (2001). The salience of multimodal sensory stimulation in early development: Implications for the issue of ecological validity. *Infancy* 2(4): 451–467.

Lister, J., Graven S., and Graven, M. (2002). *Auditory processing and effects associated with preterm birth*. Paper presented at the Physical and Developmental Environment of the High-Risk Infant, Clearwater, FL.

Loewy. J. (ed.) (2000). *Music Therapy in the Neonatal Intensive Care Unit*. New York: Satchnote.

Loewy, J., Stewart, K., Dassler, A-M., Telsey, A., and Homel, P. (2013). The effects of music therapy on vital signs, feeding, and sleep in premature infants. *Pediatrics* 131(5): 902–918.

Lorch, C.A., Lorch, V., Diefendorf, A.O., and Earl, P.W. (1994). Effect of stimulative and sedative music on systolic blood pressure, heart rate, and respiratory rate in premature infants. *Journal of Music Therapy* 31(2): 105–118.

Lubetzky, R., Mimouni, F.B., Dollberg, S., Reifen, R., Ashbel, G., and Mandel, D. (2010). Effect of music by Mozart on energy expenditure in growing preterm infants. *Pediatrics* 125(1): e24–e28.

Ludington-Hoe, S.M. and Hosseini, R.B. (2005). Skin-to-skin contact analgesia for preterm infant heel stick. *AACN Clinical Issues* 16(3): 373–387.

Luoma, L., Herrgard, E., Martikainen, A., and Ahonen, T. (1998). Speech and language development of children born at < or = 32 weeks' gestation: A 5-year prospective follow-up study. *Developmental Medicine and Child Neurology* 40(6): 380–387.

Malloch, S., Shoemark, H., Črnčec, R. et al. (2012). Music therapy with hospitalised infants—the art and science of intersubjectivity. *Infant Mental Health Journal* 33: 386–399.

Malloy, G.B. (1979). The relationship between maternal and musical auditory stimulation and the developmental behavior of premature infants. *Birth Defects Original Article Series* 15: 81–98.

Marchette, L., Main, R., and Redick, E. (1989). Pain reduction during neonatal circumcision. *Pediatric Nursing Research* 15: 207–208.

Marchette, L., Main, R., Redick, E., Bagg, A., and Leatherland, J. (1991). Pain reduction interventions during neonatal circumcision. *Nursing Research* 40: 241–244.

Maschke, C., Rupp, T., and Hech, K. (2000). The influence of stressors on biochemical reactions—a review of present scientific findings with noise. *International Journal of Hygiene And Environmental Health* 203: 45–53.

Mathur, A. and Inder, I. (2009). Magnetic resonance imaging—Insights into brain injury and outcomes in premature infants. *Journal of Communication Disorders* 42: 248–255.

McMahon, E., Wintermark, P., and Lahav, A. (2012). Auditory brain development in preterm infants: The importance of early experience. *Annals New York Academy of Science* 1252: 17–24.

Mizuno, K. and Ueda, A. (2003). The maturation and coordination of sucking, swallowing, and respiration in preterm infants. *Journal of Pediatrics* 142: 36–40.

Moon, C. and Fifer, W. (2000). Evidence of transnatal auditory learning. *Journal of Perinatology* 20: 37–44.

Nazzi, T., Bertoncini, J., and Mehler, J. (1998). Language discrimination by newborns: Toward an understanding of the role of rhythm. *Journal of Experimental Psychology: Human Perception and Performance* 24: 756–766.

Neal, D.O. and Lindeke, L.L. (2008). Music as a nursing intervention for preterm infants in the NICU. *Neonatal Network* 27(5): 319–327.

Nöcker-Ribaupierre, M. (1999). Short and long-term effects of the maternal voice on the behaviours of very low birth weight infants and their mothers as a basis for the bonding process. In: R. Rebollo-Pratt and D. Erdonmez (eds), *MusicMedicine* 3, pp. 153–161. Melbourne: University of Melbourne.

O'Gorman, S. (2006). Theoretical interfaces in the acute pediatric context: A psychothera-peutic understanding of the application of infant-directed singing. *American Journal of Psychotherapy* 60: 271–283.

Olischar, M., Shoemark, H., Holton, T., Weninger, M., and Hunt, R.W. (2011). The influence of music on aEEG activity in neurologically healthy newborns >32 weeks' gestational age. *Acta Pædiatrica* 100: 670–675.

Owens, L. (1979). The effects of music on the weight loss, crying, and physical movement of newborns. *Journal of Music Therapy* 16(2): 83–90.

Patterson, R.D., Uppenkamp, S., Johnsrude, I.S., and Griffiths, T.D. (2002). The processing of temporal pitch and melody information in auditory cortex. *Neuron* 36: 767–776.

Peebles-Kleiger, M. (2000). Pediatric and neonatal intensive care hospitalization as traumatic stressor: Implications for intervention. *Bulletin of the Menninger Clinic* 6(2): 257–280.

Peretz, I. and Zatorre, R.J. (2005). Brain organization for music processing. *Annual Review of Psychology* 56: 89–114.

Picciolini, O., Matteo Porro, M., Meazza, A. et al. (2014). Early exposure to maternal voice: Effects on preterm infants development. *Early Human Development* 90: 287–292.

Schwartz, F.J. (2003). Music and sound effect on perinatal brain development and the prema-ture baby. In: J.V. Loewy (ed.), *Music Therapy in the Neonatal Intensive Care Unit*, 2nd edn., pp. 9–19. New York: Satchnote.

Segall, M.E. (1972). Cardiac responsivity to auditory stimulation in premature infants. *Nursing Research* 21(1): 15–19.

Shoemark, H. (1999). Indicators for the inclusion of music therapy in the care of infants with Bronchopulmonary Dysplasia. In: T. Wigram and J. De Backer (eds), *Clinical applications of music therapy in developmental disability, paediatrics and neurology*, Vol. 1, pp. 32–46. London: Jessica Kingsley.

Shoemark, H. (2006). Infant-directed singing as a vehicle for regulation rehearsal in the medi-cally fragile full-term infant. *Australian Journal of Music Therapy* 17: 54–63.

Shoemark, H. (2008, July). Infant-directed singing as a vehicle for regulation rehearsal in the medically fragile full-term infant. In *Voices: A world forum for music therapy* 8(2).

Shoemark, H. (2011a). Translating "infant-directed singing" into a strategy for the hospital-ised family. In: J. Edwards (ed.) *Music therapy and parent-infant bonding*, pp. 162–178. London: OUP.

Shoemark, H. (2011b). Contingent singing: The musicality of companionship with the hos-pitalized newborn infant. In: Baker, F. and S. Uhlig (eds), *Therapeutic Voicework in Music Therapy*, pp. 229–249. London: Jessica Kingsley Publishers.

Shoemark, H. (2013). Working with full-term hospitalized infants. In: J. Bradt (ed.), *Guidelines for Music Therapy Practice: Pediatric Care*, pp. 116–151. Philadelphia: Barcelona Publishers.

Shoemark, H. and Arnup, S. (2014). A survey of how mothers think about and use voice with their hospitalized newborn infant. *Journal of Neonatal Nursing* 20: 115–121.

Shoemark, H. and Dearn, T. (2008). Keeping parents at the centre of family centred music ther-apy with hospitalised infants. *Australian Journal of Music Therapy* 19: 3–24.

Shoemark, H. and Grocke, D. (2010). The markers of interplay between the music therapist and the medically fragile newborn infant. *Journal of Music Therapy* 47: 306–334.

Spittle, A.J., Anderson, P.J., Lee, K.J. et al. (2010). Preventive care at home for very preterm infants improves infant and caregiver outcomes at 2 Years. *Pediatrics* 126(1): e171–e178.

Standley, J.M. (1998). The effect of music and multimodal stimulation on response of prema-ture infants in neonatal intensive care. *Pediatric Nursing* 24(6): 532–538.

Standley, J.M. (2000). The effect of contingent music to increase non-nutritive sucking of premature infants. *Pediatric Nursing* 26(5): 493–499.

Standley, J.M. (2002). A meta-analysis of the efficacy of music therapy for premature infants. *Journal of Pediatric Nursing* 11: 107–113.

Standley, J.M. (2003). The effect of music-reinforced nonnutritive sucking on feeding rate of premature infants. *Journal of Pediatric Nursing* 18(3): 169–173.

Standley, J. (2012). Music Therapy Research in the NICU: An updated meta-analysis. *Neonatal Network* 31(5): 311–316.

Standley, J.M. and Moore, R.S. (1995). Therapeutic effects of music and mother's voice on premature infants. *Pediatric Nursing* 21(6): 509–512.

Standley, J.M. and Walworth, D. (2010). *Music Therapy with Premature Infants*, 2nd edn. Silver Spring: American Music Therapy Association, Inc.

Standley, J.M., Cassidy, J., Grant, R. et al. (2010). The effect of music reinforcement for non-nutritive sucking on nipple feeding of premature infants. *Pediatric Nursing* 36(3): 138–145.

Stewart, K. (2009). Patterns: A model for evaluating trauma in NICU music therapy: Part 1—Theory and design. *Music and Medicine* 1(1): 29–40.

Teckenberg-Jansson, P., Huotilainen, M., Pölkki, T., Lipsanen, J., and Järvenpääf, A.L. (2011). Rapid effects of neonatal music therapy combined with kangaroo care on prematurely-born infants. *Nordic Journal of Music Therapy* 20(1): 22–42.

Thieren, J., Worwa, C., Mattia, F., and deRegnier, R. (2004). Altered pathways for auditory discrimination and recognition memory in preterm infants. *Developmental Medicine and Child Neurology* 46: 816–824.

Thoman, E. B., and Ingersoll, E. W. (1999). Sleep/wake states of preterm infants: stability, developmental change, diurnal variation, and relation with caregiving activity. *Child Development* 70(1): 1–10.

Tramo, M. J., Lense, M., Van Ness, C., Kagan, J., Settle, M. D., and Cronin, J. H. (2011). Effects of Music on Physiological and Behavioral Indices of Acute Pain and Stress in Premature Infants Clinical Trial and Literature Review. *Music and Medicine* 3(2): 72–83.

Trehub, S.E. (2001). Musical predispositions in infancy. *Annals of the New York Academy of Science* 930: 1–16.

Tronick, E. (2007). *The Neurobehavioral and Social-Emotional Development of Infants and Children*. New York: W.W. Norton and Co.

Vanderveen, J.A., Bassler, D., Robertson, C.M., and Kirpalani, H. (2009). Early interventions involving parents to improve neurodevelopmental outcomes of premature infants: A meta-analysis. *Journal of Perinatology* 29: 343–351.

Vianna, M., Barbosda, A., Carvalhaes, A., and Cuinha, A. (2011). Music therapy may increase breastfeeding rates among mothers of premature newborns: a randomized controlled trial. *Jornal de Pediatria* 87(3): 206–212.

Wachman, E.L. and Lahav, A. (2011). The effects of noise on preterm infants in the NICU. *Archives of Disease in Childhood—Fetal and Neonatal Edition* 96: F305–F309.

Werner, L.A. (2007). Issues in human auditory development. *Journal of Communication Disorders* 40(4): 275–283.

Werner, L.A. and Boike, K. (2001). Infants' sensitivity to broadband noise. *Journal of the Acoustical Society of America* 109: 2101–2111.

Westrup, B. (2005). Newborn individualized developmental care and assessment program (NIDCAP) family-centered developmentally supportive care. *NeoReviews* 6(3): e115–e122.

Whipple, J. (2000). The effect of parent training in music and multimodal stimulation on parent-neonate interactions in the neonatal intensive care unit. *Journal of Music Therapy* 37(4): 250–268.

Whipple, J. (2005). The effect of parent training in music and multimodal stimulation on parent-neonate interactions in the Neonatal Intensive Care Unit. *Journal of Music Therapy* 37(4): 250–268.

Whipple, J. (2008). The effect of music-reinforced nonnutritive sucking on state of preterm, low birthweight infants experiencing heel prick. *Journal of Music Therapy* 45(3): 227–272.

White, R., Smith, J., and Shepley, M. (2013). Recommended standards for newborn ICU design, eighth edition. *Journal of Perinatology* 33: S2–S16.

White-Traut, R. and Hutchens Pate, C. (1987). Modulating infant state in premature infants. *Journal of Pediatric Nursing* 2: 96–101.

White-Traut, R., Nelson, M., Silvestri, J. et al. (1999). Developmental intervention for preterm infants diagnosed with periventricular leukomalcia. *Research in Nursing and Health* 22: 131–143.

White-Traut, R.C., Nelson, M.N., Silvestri, J.M. et al. (2009). Maturation of the cardiac response to sound in high-risk preterm infants. *Newborn and Infant Nursing Reviews* 9(4): 193–199.

Wightman, F.L., Callahan, M.R., Lutfi, R.A., Kistler, D.J., and Oh, E. (2003). Children's detection of pure-tone signals: informational masking with contralateral maskers. *Journal of the Acoustical Society of America* 113(6): 3297–3305.

Williams, A., Drongelen, W., and Lasky, R. (2007). Noise in contemporary neonatal intensive care. *Journal of the Acoustical Society of America* 121(5): 2681–2690.

Zatorre, R.J., Chen, J.L., and Penhune, V.B. (2007). When the brain plays music: auditory–motor interactions in music perception and production. *Nature Reviews Neuroscience* 8: 547–558.

Zwicker, J.G. and Harris, S.R. (2008). Quality of Life of formerly preterm and very low birthweight infants from preschool age to adulthood: a systematic review. *Pediatrics* 121: e366–e376.

CHAPTER 3

MUSIC THERAPY FOR HOSPITALIZED CHILDREN

JANE EDWARDS AND JEANETTE KENNELLY

INTRODUCTION

MUSIC therapy is a relational therapy in which the development of rapport and relationship can be facilitated quickly through musical interactions with children and their families in a hospital setting. Once this rapport is established the therapist can then support the child and family, meeting a child's needs relating to rehabilitation, pain management, psychosocial care, or family issues. Music therapists use musical improvisation, music listening, musical composition such as song stories, or writing of songs, and any other music interactions initiated by the child to support and attain positive changes in mood, psychological state, pain report, or social interaction with others (Bradt 2013; Edwards 2005; Edwards and Kennelly 2011; Loewy 1997; Robb 2003). The music therapist works with the child and family at bedside, in a specialist treatment room, or in a group context, depending on the needs of the child and family, and the type of work required.

Music therapy is provided to hospitalized children to support the treatment goals of all team members including those in the medical team and the psychosocial team. Along with the work of the music therapist, and the cooperation and participation of the child and their family, these goals support the attainment of optimal well-being of the child.

Although children's hospitals at one time used to keep family members away except for special visiting hours, better knowledge about children's needs has placed the family at the center of treatment and care in pediatric medical contexts (Jolley and Shields 2009). Music therapy is regularly offered within a family centered care model of services. Where it is possible and appropriate, family members are included in sessions and encouraged to take an interest in their child or sibling's music making and music listening needs outside of sessions.

THE CHILD IN HOSPITAL

When a child is admitted to a hospital it is a challenging time, for them and also for their family. If they are seriously ill they may not be able to understand everything that they are hearing or seeing. If they have been injured they may be in pain and facing an uncertain future in relation to their physical functioning or mobility. If they have a chronic illness their admission to hospital may mark some difficulties in their current treatment, leading to uncertainty about whether or when they will be able to normalize their routines and how quickly they can return home. In all cases the child's everyday life will have been disrupted, along with those of their families. This means the music therapist must take special care to observe and understand the child's experience, and explore the child's understanding of their hospitalization in order to support them to cope and adjust to these changed circumstances.

In times past children in hospital were not permitted to be visited regularly by their parents. It took a long time to change this practice. It needed to be shown that in hospitals where infants were not cuddled or held because of fears of infection there were higher mortality rates, and that by changing practices, lower mortality rates could be proven to occur (van der Horst and van der Veer 2009). In UK hospitals during the 1940s parents were only permitted minimal contact with their child in hospital because:

> … parents were seen as ignorant and noisy intruders who only criticized the staff and disturbed the quiet and disciplined course of events in the ward. Meanwhile, the parents themselves had few possibilities to change the existing situation. Even if they had been eloquent and knowledgeable enough and realized that something was awry, there was little that they could do to oppose the medical doctors who had allegedly introduced all those rules to the benefit of their child. In sum, the emotional problems of isolated children in hospital were not appreciated or considered serious enough.
>
> van der Horst and van der Veer 2009, p. 124

Nowadays the problems that can be caused by separating children, especially very young children, from their parents or primary care giver are much better understood. In order to offer support to the child throughout their stay many hospitals have facilities for parents to sleep in the child's room or beside their bed on the ward.

Family-centered care for hospitalized children is ethical and appropriate (Jolley and Shields 2009). Music therapy's theoretical basis is strengthened by the discovery of *communicative musicality* (Malloch and Trevarthen 2009) which provides a basis for the relevance of musical work with families. The earliest interactions between parents and their infants are highly musical, contributing to the bonds of lifelong attachment (Edwards 2011).

THE MUSIC THERAPY TREATMENT PROCESS

In this section the referral and assessment process is described, and the ways in which the music therapist works with different groups of patients is presented. Depending on the environment, and the agreed role for the music therapist, the way in which music therapy is provided can vary with the general tenet that music therapy sessions are usually child led. This means that the therapist provides sensitive and responsive musical interactions. For example, when introducing song singing the therapist will ask whether the child has any song preferences, or favorite performers and will use the child's response to direct the choices made.

Robb (2003) demonstrated how a contextual model of support helps music therapists to structure treatment processes across a range of environments. Using theories of stress and coping she showed that that music can provide support and assist coping when the music therapist focuses on the ways in which music can provide: (1) Structure, (2) opportunities for the child to demonstrate autonomy, and (3) facilitate involvement, including enjoyment and interest (Robb 2003). These three aspects are important in facilitating the child's adjustment to hospital and their ability to cope.

The techniques used by the music therapist are attentive to the child and family and their interests, preference, and needs. Use of electronic music technology is expanding in music therapy practice (Whitehead-Pleaux et al. 2011). Students and practitioners need to be able to use a range of these technologies along with being able to sing, compose, accompany, and improvise using portable instruments such as guitar or keyboard. The process of assessment is important for understanding the needs and capacities of the child, and discovering how a music therapy process might best help them. Being open to all musical possibilities can be challenging in a busy ward environment, or when there are many children on the referral list for music therapy. However, it is important to keep in mind that the child will benefit when the music therapist makes time to focus on finding a useful way to collaborate meaningfully with the child and family in the music therapy process.

Although they demonstrated the capabilities of electronic music technology to provide multiple options for supporting a child's therapeutic needs in music therapy programmes, nonetheless Whitehead-Pleaux et al. (2011) also advised that:

> … traditional music therapy interventions provide human-to-human connection that is so vital in treating trauma and providing reality orientation. Electronic music technologies can be less flexible, create a barrier between the music therapist and the patient, and have elements that can be disorienting.

> p. 157

This does not mean that electronic media should not be used but there are cautions when using any type of technology whether a musical instrument or a music technology device. Sometimes children in a hospital can be highly fatigued and confused. Therefore, understanding instructions, or explanations, can be difficult for them. It is important to monitor musical interactions carefully, and be watchful for signs of exhaustion and stress.

Referral and assessment

Pediatric music therapy practice, whether individual or group focused, begins with a referral and assessment process. Patients can be referred to music therapy by professional healthcare staff, the child's family, or by the child; known as *self-referral*. The referral process may be formal such as by using a music therapy specific referral form, or communicated to the music therapist via ward rounds or multidisciplinary meetings. Criteria for referral to music therapy are based on the needs of the child which can be divided into the following areas: anxiety reduction and pain management; psychosocial care; rehabilitation, developmental skill attainment, and palliative care (Kennelly and Brien-Elliot 2002). This chapter provides a general overview of the music therapy role in addressing needs for children in medical settings. Bradt (2013) has provided specific guidelines for music therapy practice in pediatric care, and therefore is recommended for further reading.

Music therapy assessment procedures vary depending on the needs of the child and their degree/type of injury or illness. For example, assessment of a child with burns in the acute stages of their injury may be complicated by the child's ability to communicate with the therapist whilst medicated for pain relief, therefore assessment may involve several sessions before programme goals are identified (Whitehead-Pleaux 2013). Assessment of a child receiving palliative care requires careful consideration of their emotional, physical, and spiritual states in order to understand their needs and determine goals and objectives (Lindenfelser 2013). The reasons for hospitalization, ranging from an initial admission, repeated multiple admissions or relapse during illness must also be considered by the therapist in order to conduct a comprehensive assessment process.

Reporting of programme outcomes is an important component of the music therapy treatment process. It allows for the communication of these outcomes to non-music therapy staff who are involved in the care of the child and contributes towards the multidisciplinary management of the child's needs. This reporting takes place through team meetings where the therapist verbally reports on the child's progress during music therapy sessions, and can also be documented in medical chart entries where specific written detail is provided in relation to the outcomes from each session.

Music therapy for anxiety reduction and pain management

When providing music therapy for pain management or anxiety reduction it is important to remember that children in pain are often highly anxious, and many ways in which children indicate distress are indistinguishable between pain and anxiety reactions (Edwards 2005). Therefore it is important to consider and address stress, anxiety, and pain issues when referred children who are in pain, or who need support during potentially painful procedures such as having injections, or having wound dressings changed.

Many practitioners in the children's hospital context offer music to manage pain and anxiety, not just music therapists. Studies have shown that recorded music played in the background or provided through headphones assists children to reduce their pain (Klassen et al. 2008). Some studies have distinguished between music provided by music therapists and the music provided by non-music therapists, such as a nurse providing music listening through headphones, by calling music therapy *active* music therapy, and music listening *passive* music therapy (Klassen et al. 2008). Although this is not a distinction used in the pediatric music therapy literature, it can be helpful to try to find ways to differentiate between music therapy practices and the uses of music by other therapy and medical practitioners in the hospital setting. Some researchers have used the term *music stimulation* to refer to other types of musical support provided for pain reduction and management other than music therapy (Bernatzky et al. 2011).

One criticism of the use of music by non-music therapy personnel is that music is often presented as useful to *distract* the child from their pain. Increasingly music therapists have turned away from this conceptualization of the function of music. One reason is given by Bradt (2013) as follows:

Distraction implies a quick diversion, one that can be easily interrupted by another distraction. When using music listening for pain management, it is important that the child's attention to the music can be sustained.

Bradt 2013, np.

If the pain experience is relatively brief such as when a needle-stick is being performed,
music can be used to hold the child's attention while encouraging deep and slow breathing to assist anxiety reduction. When pain is present over a longer time either because of a
longer procedure, or because of the presence of chronic pain, the music therapist must pay
close attention to the child's capacity to be held musically. This is where the use of live music
provided by the music therapist has its greatest potency. The music therapist's capacity to
alter musical parameters such as tempo, volume, and accompaniment, allows flexibility in
providing music as a procedural support.

Children who are supported during procedures are better able to cope with subsequent
procedures. One of the main factors that improves outcomes for children is to be able to
reduce "exaggerated negative memories of pain and anxiety" (Noel et al. 2010, p. 626).
Presenting the findings of a study of children's experience of procedures and subsequent
coping, Noel et al. (2010) suggested that "once exaggerated memories develop, they become
a powerful predictor of children's pain and distress during subsequent exposures to the
same painful experience" (p. 633). They have also indicated that poorly managed procedural
pain in childhood can have lifelong effects such as medical treatment avoidance as an adult.
Therefore it is important for the child to be appropriately supported during treatment procedures to reduce their pain experience, to promote coping, and to prevent long-term difficulties relating to treatment pain.

Although many music therapists have described how live music provided by the therapist
during painful procedures can provide comfort and support (e.g. Edwards 1994; Edwards
and Kennelly 2011) increasingly music therapy practitioners are also successfully using
active music-making techniques to address pain (Bradt 2013).

Music therapy to promote psychosocial care of children
in a hospital setting

Psychosocial care of children and their families includes minimising the psychological
impact of hospitalization, and promoting well-being and coping, paying attention to the
social context of the child's life experience to date. Where do they feel safe? Who cares for
them? Who do they play and have fun with? Music therapy is used to strengthen connections between family members, and to support the child's coping by providing opportunities
for expressing emotional states, reducing the stress response, and engaging in normal, every
day fun and play.

When experiencing *stress* the human being uses *coping* to maintain equilibrium via a process of self-regulation. As Sajaniemi (2013) has explained:

The mobilization of the body's resources starts when emotional or physical threat destabilizes
internal equilibrium. The mobilization of resources is always arousing, and is experienced as

a shift toward increasing stress. When equilibrium is regained, this is experienced as a shift toward decreasing stress.

p. 44

When children are sick and in pain their resources for coping can be compromised. When the stress system is "chronically activated" (Sajaniemi 2013, p. 44) the capacity to achieve equilibrium is no longer available and it can be difficult to turn off the stress response (Sajaniemi 2013). A constantly activated stress response impacts on behavior in multiple ways, and longer term effects also occur. As Sajaniemi (2013) has described, there is:

> … growing evidence that the inability to regulate stress responses harms brain development in various areas, including the hippocampus and prefrontal cortex, both of which are known to be fundamentally important in learning, memory, and executive functions.

p. 45

Edwards and Kennelly (2011) have described a stress and coping framework for music therapy practice with children in hospital. Their framework involves consideration of four theoretical areas: (1) Theories of stress, coping, and adjustment, (2) transactional models of stress, (3) developmental theories, and (4) family-centered care. Integrating these aspects allows the widest consideration of the ways in which the stress of hospitalization and treatments may be compromising coping for children and their families. Providing music therapy to manage stress for hospitalized children must be culturally sensitive, musically appropriate, and family centered.

Music therapy and rehabilitation

The role of music therapy in pediatric rehabilitation is supported by a range of descriptive practice reports and research studies (Kennelly 2013). It is important for the student music therapist or new practitioner to source research evidence and descriptive reports when preparing to work within this field (Gilbertson 2009). Music therapy research in pediatric rehabilitation demonstrates the usefulness of receptive and re-creative processes to support, encourage, or change behaviors following posttraumatic amnesia (Bower 2010); the ability for creative music therapy techniques to promote communication (Gilbertson and Aldridge, 2008), and the consideration of age-related and developmental factors when using song writing with this population (Baker et al. 2005a,b,c). Non-music therapy techniques such as orientation, feedback, and humor are used by the music therapist during sessions to assist the attainment of clinical goals (Edwards and Kennelly 2004).

Music therapy programs in pediatric rehabilitation begin for many children in the intensive care unit (ICU). Children who sustain severe acquired brain injuries may initially present with various levels of consciousness and it is imperative that the therapist consult with the medical team before commencing any form of music therapy assessment. Depending on the child's awareness state and assessment outcomes, program goals and methods during this stage of recovery may include music listening to promote arousal, entrainment of physiological functions and the encouragement of communication; and improvisation, song writing and song singing to promote family support and involvement (Townsend 2013; Kennelly and Edwards 1997).

As the child's awareness state improves and he or she becomes more oriented to the environment, programme goals will change and develop according to his needs. Moving from the acute phase of rehabilitation to the subacute phase requires reassessment of music therapy goals and methods (Kennelly 2013; Kennelly and Brien-Elliot 2001). During intensive rehabilitation, program goals can be divided into two broad areas: functional and psychosocial. Functional goals include areas of: (a) Communication such as improved intonation and articulation; (b) physical needs including improved gait, posture, balance, and muscle relaxation; and (c) cognition and behavior such as improved orientation, attention, and learning. Goals related to psychosocial needs include adjustment to the hospital environment and the injury, emotional support including feelings of anger, sadness, and frustration concerning the injury and time spent away from family, friends, and the home environment (Kennelly 2013). Music therapy methods used to address functional and psychosocial goals will depend on the age of the child and the extent of their injuries and resulting impairments. Receptive music therapy methods may be used to increase orientation and arousal, promote physical functioning, assist pain management, and aid relaxation. Instrumental improvisation can be used to reduce a child's verbal and behavioral perseverations and promote direction following. Song singing may be used to improve articulation and rate of speech and also gait rehabilitation while song writing can provide emotional support, opportunities for self-expression, and promote learning in relation to physical and cognitive tasks (Kennelly 2013).

The final phase of rehabilitation is the chronic phase where the child is prepared for discharge (Anderson et al. 2001). The previously described physical and psychosocial needs may be similar in this phase however the focus of discharge to home or a different rehabilitation setting will guide the music therapy goals and methods. The child may require support in relation to his communicative abilities within school and peer group settings. Additionally the thought of returning to the school and family home environment may create stressful feelings for the child and music therapy may be used effectively to address these concerns. Similarly to the subacute phase, song writing methods may be used to promote conversational skills and support the child emotionally as he prepares to re-engage with family and peers (Kennelly 2013).

Evaluation of music therapy programs will depend on the needs of the child, the goals and methods used within each session, the level of acquired brain injury and resulting impairment and the child's developmental age. Therefore it is beyond the scope of this chapter to include specific detail relating to the evaluation of all program goals. The music therapist may use a variety of formal and informal tools to measure and record responses as they relate to the program goals. Guidelines for music therapy evaluation specific to pediatric rehabilitation (Kennelly 2013), and medically fragile children in low awareness states (Townsend 2013) are recommended for further reading.

Music therapy and developmental skills attainment

When a child is hospitalized, care is taken by professional staff to assist the patient and family members in their adjustment towards the new environment and the child's illness/injury. However, the impact of these factors is known to affect the child's growth and development. Lengthy periods of hospitalization which take place during vital developmental growth stages, such as when children first learn to walk or communicate can significantly affect the attainment of these milestones. Children who are receiving care while in ICU or in an isolation room because of their immunosuppressed state may also be subjected to environments with either little or excessive sensory stimulation (Kennelly and Edwards 1997; Kennelly 2001; Ghetti 2013). Therefore a planned approach towards the management of these developmental concerns is important in order for children to attain normal developmental milestones whilst living in hospital.

Children can benefit from a multidisciplinary approach which addresses the maintenance and improvement of developmental competencies. The music therapist can work individually or together with other allied therapists such as physiotherapists, occupational therapists, and speech pathologists to create developmental programs. These programs can focus on all areas of development, including motor, communication, behavioral, emotional, cognitive, and social skills (Kennelly 2000; Neugebauer 2013). Musical elements such as rhythm, timbre, melody, tempo, and dynamics can evoke and stimulate developmental functioning and thereby engage a child using more normalized tasks and activities (Kennelly 2000).

Music therapy goals differ according to the area of developmental need. The methods used to address these goals will also differ according to the developmental age of the child and their current skills, their illness/injury and the context of their hospitalization. Further reading specific to pediatric clinical guidelines which address developmental delay is recommended (Ghetti 2013; Neugebauer 2013). It is beyond the scope of this chapter to comprehensively cover all possible goal areas, however the following four developmental domains provide examples of suggested goals and music therapy methods:

1. Cognitive: cause and effect—improvised song such as an "in and out" song to engage the child with a game using small hand held percussion instruments to reinforce the concept (Neugebauer 2013).
2. Communication/Motor: oromotor stimulation—improvised song or song parody prompts a carer to use gentle tapping actions near the child's mouth in preparation for songs which reinforce kissing or blowing actions (Kennelly 2000).
3. Motor: bringing hands to mid-line—improvised songs, known songs or song parodies to promote bilateral hand movement in order to grasp an instrument or perform an action such as clapping (Kennelly 2000; Neugebauer 2013).
4. Social: listening and following instructions—song parody where the lyrics reinforce and cue the child to recall and perform a particular action, for example a "good talking tips" song for school aged-children (Kennelly 2000).

Evaluation of the child's responses during developmental sessions may involve the use of checklists which detail the number of times the child successfully demonstrates/initiates the required skill. Video footage of each session could also assist the therapist in their evaluation post-therapy and be useful in demonstrating the progress of a child's developmental skill attainment using music therapy to non-music therapy staff.

Music therapy and palliative care

Music therapy practice for children receiving palliative care is based on a family-centered model which supports the needs of the child, as well as carers and siblings (Lindenfelser et al.

2012; Daveson and Kennelly 2000). The role of music therapy in this setting is to support and extend family interactions (Daveson and Kennelly 2000; Pavlicevic 2005); provide choice and control opportunities (Sheridan and McFerran 2004), emotional support and quality of life experiences (Hilliard 2003; Daveson and Kennelly 2000). Research to support music therapy practice in pediatric palliative care is slowly expanding. Findings have explored the experiences and perceptions of participants such as parents and carers (Lindenfelser et al. 2008, 2012; Knapp et al. 2009). Qualitative research supports the value and applicability of music therapy for bereaved parents including the importance of creative engagement during a time of stress and sadness (Lindenfelser et al. 2008, 2012).

Goals addressed within this setting predominantly focus on supporting psychosocial needs. These include providing opportunities for self-expression and alleviating fear and anxiety. An example of goals and methods used with this population include:

1. Supporting feelings and emotions in relation to illness and isolation from family/friends/home environment: music listening, improvisation, song singing, and composition (Lindenfelser 2013; Daveson and Kennelly 2000).
2. Providing opportunities for relaxation: music-guided imagery/music listening (Lindenfelser 2013).
3. Providing opportunities for choice and control (Sheridan and McFerran 2004).
4. Creating a legacy in memory of the child: composition/song writing (Lindenfelser 2013: Hilliard 2003; Aasgaard 2002).

Music therapy guidelines in relation to pediatric palliative care, end-of-life or hospice care, and children with life-limiting conditions have been developed (Lindenfelser 2013). Evaluation of music therapy programs in palliative settings include descriptive accounts of the child, carer's, and sibling's responses and interactions according to the session goals. Particular regard should be made to any medication used by the child to manage palliative needs and its potential influence on participation and the processing of musical stimuli (Lindenfelser 2013).

DEVELOPING MUSIC THERAPY SERVICES
FOR HOSPITALIZED CHILDREN

Music therapy service development in children's hospitals requires special skills and strategies for successful and sustained programmes to be established (e.g. Edwards 2005; Loewy 2001; 2007), with a particular emphasis on entrepreneurship and creativity (Ledger et al. 2013). The services provided through music therapy are relevant to some areas of need in a hospital setting more than others, and music therapy resources are not always able to be stretched across every area of a hospital. The music therapist educates, informs, and supports other members of the team as they seek to discover the value and role of music therapy within the hospital context.

In a reflection on her work founding and then developing a music therapy service at a children's hospital in Australia, Edwards (2005) indicated that encouragement from staff through frequent meetings with them about the needs on the ward was an important starting point in developing an effective service. She noted the way that her writing about the service was always much more logical and organized than the day-to-day reality of delivering the service in a complex and busy care environment. Even in her reflection written more than ten years after the service was developed she described the role of the music therapist as "emergent" (Edwards 2005, p. 43). It is difficult to predict the factors that show that music therapy has become *established* in any setting, although markers such as the programme continuing after the founders have left can be indicative. Continuing to publish and research about the need for music therapy in hospital environments contributes to the clearer identity of the music therapy role, and indicates the needs of children which can be met effectively.

The evidence base for music therapy with children in hospitals is increasing (Bradt 2013). Providing summaries of the available recent literature, building rapport with key figures in the hospital, ward, or unit, and explaining and demonstrating music therapy is key to building programmes and maintaining them over time (Ledger 2010). Loewy has shown how collaboration with key staff, use of staff in promotional films as advocates of music therapy, training music therapy students, and using music as part of the staff wellness programme can all be useful strategies in building the identity and value of the music therapy programme (Loewy 2001; 2007).

Ledger (2010) undertook an ethnographic study of music therapy service development following a new music therapy service being established in a large hospital. She observed the sole music therapist for three months during the implementation phase of the music therapy service. She identified five strategies that the music therapist used in her successful service development work. The first was *educating* where the therapist demonstrated, explained, and presented about her work. The second was *interprofessional working*. The music therapist worked collaboratively in many sessions with other allied health practitioners giving colleagues the opportunity to observe the work which increased their perception of its value. The further strategies she observed were *remaining flexible, generating evidence,* and *investing time and energy.* This research shows that the music therapist developing a new service has to be skilled in the entrepreneurial and development skills as well as in the skills of clinical music therapy service provision. Choosing successful mentors, building peer networks, and keeping track of the contemporary literature in the field are all essential to effectual programme building.

Conclusion

Music therapy for children hospitalized for injury or illness provides therapeutic support within a family centered and holistic approach individualized for each referral. Music therapy can be provided during treatment procedures such as dressing changes, or debridement, and can be used at bedside, in small groups, or as an interprofessional process supporting the work of other members of the care team. Music therapists need expertise in flexibly using music in a range of contexts and for an array of purposes. Live music making is the hallmark of the music therapist's repertory of skills, although increasingly music technology is an added resource.

REFERENCES

Aasgaard, T. (2002). *Song creations by children with cancer: Process and meaning.* Doctoral dissertation. Retrieved from: vbn.aau.dk/files/195251818/trygve_aasgaard_thesis_150909.pdf.

Anderson, V., Northam, E., Hendy, J., and Wrennall, J. (2001). *Developmental Neuropsychology: A Clinical Approach.* Hove, East Sussex: Psychology Press.

Baker, F., Kennelly, J., and Tamplin, J. (2005a). Song writing to explore identity change and sense of self/self concept following traumatic brain injury. In: F. Baker and T. Wigram (eds), *Song Writing Methods, Techniques and Clinical Applications for Music Therapy Clinicians, Educators and Students*, pp. 116–133. London: Jessica Kingsley Publishers.

Baker, F., Kennelly, J., and Tamplin, J. (2005b). Adjusting to change through song: Themes in songs written by clients with TBI. *Brain Impairment* 6(3): 205–211.

Baker, F., Kennelly, J., and Tamplin, J. (2005c). Themes in songs written by clients with traumatic brain injury: Differences across the lifespan. *Australian Journal of Music Therapy* 16: 25–42.

Bernatzky, G., Presch, M., Anderson, M., and Panksepp, J. (2011). Emotional foundations of music as a non-pharmacological pain management tool in modern medicine. *Neuroscience & Biobehavioral Reviews* 35(9): 1989–1999.

Bower, J. (2010). Music therapy for a 10-year-old child experiencing agitation during posttraumatic amnesia: An intrinsic mixed methods study. Master's thesis. Retrieved from: <http://repository.unimelb.edu.au/10187/8949>.

Bradt, J. (2013). Pain management with children. In: J. Bradt (ed). (2013). *Guidelines for Music Therapy Practice in Pediatric Care*, Chapter 2, pp. 15–65. Gilsum, NH: Barcelona Publishers.

Daveson, B.A. and Kennelly, J. (2000). Music therapy in palliative care for hospitalised children and adolescents. *Journal of Palliative Care* 16(1): 35–38.

Edwards, J. (1994). The use of music therapy to assist children who have severe burns. *Australian Journal of Music Therapy* 5: 3–6.

Edwards, J. (2005). A reflection on the music therapist's role in developing a program in a children's hospital. *Music Therapy Perspectives* 23(1): 36–44.

Edwards, J. (2011). Music therapy and parent-infant bonding. In: J. Edwards (ed.), *Music Therapy and Parent-infant Bonding*, pp. 4–20. Oxford: Oxford University Press.

Edwards, J. and Kennelly, J. (2004). Music therapy in paediatric rehabilitation: The application of modified grounded theory to identify techniques used by a music therapist. *Nordic Journal of Music Therapy* 13(2): 112–126.

Edwards, J. and Kennelly, J. (2011). Music Therapy for children in hospital care: A stress and coping framework for practice. In: A. Meadows (ed). *Developments in Music Therapy Practice: Case Study Perspectives*, pp. 150–165. Gilsum, NH: Barcelona.

Ghetti, C. (2013). Pediatric Intensive Care. In: J. Bradt (ed.), *Guidelines for Music Therapy Practice in Pediatric Care*, pp. 152–204. Gilsum, NH: Barcelona Publishers.

Gilbertson, S. (2009). A reference standard bibliography: Music therapy with children who have experienced traumatic brain injury. *Music and Medicine* 1(2): 129–139.

Gilbertson. S. and Aldridge, D. (2008). *Music Therapy and Traumatic Brain Injury: A Light on a Dark Night.* London: Jessica Kingsley Publishers.

Hilliard, R. (2003). Music therapy in pediatric palliative care: Complimenting an interdisciplinary approach. *Journal of Palliative Care* 19(2): 127–132.

Jolley, J. and Shields, L. (2009). The evolution of family-centered care. *Journal of Pediatric Nursing* 24(2): 164–170.

Kennelly, J. (2000). The specialist role of the music therapist in developmental programs for hospitalized children. *Journal of Paediatric Health Care* 14(2): 56–59.

Kennelly, J. (2001). Music therapy in the bone marrow transplant unit: Providing emotional support during adolescence. *Music Therapy Perspectives* 19: 104–108.

Kennelly, J. (2013). Brain injuries and rehabilitation in children. In: J. Bradt (ed.), *Guidelines for Music Therapy Practice in Pediatric Care*, pp. 356–402. Gilsum, NH: Barcelona Publishers.

Kennelly, J and Brien-Elliott, K. (2001). The role of music therapy in paediatric rehabilitation. *Paediatric Rehabilitation* 4(3): 137–143.

Kennelly, J. and Brien-Elliott, K. (2002). Music therapy for children in hospital. *Educating Young Children—Learning & Teaching in the Early Childhood Years* 8(3): 37–40.

Kennelly, J. and Edwards, J. (1997). Providing music therapy to the unconscious child in the paediatric intensive care unit. *The Australian Journal of Music Therapy* 8: 18–29.

Klassen, J.A., Liang, Y., Tjosvold, L., Klassen, T.P., and Hartling, L. (2008). Music for pain and anxiety in children undergoing medical procedures: a systematic review of randomized controlled trials. *Ambulatory Pediatrics* 8(2): 117–128.

Knapp, C., Madden, V., Wang, H., Curtis, C., Sloyer, P., and Shenkman, E. (2009). Music therapy in an integrated pediatric palliative care program. *American Journal of Palliative Medicine* 26(6): 449–455.

Ledger, A. (2010). Am I a founder or am I a fraud? Music therapists' experiences of developing services in healthcare organizations. PhD dissertation, University of Limerick <http://ulir.ul.ie/handle/10344/1131>.

Ledger, A., Edwards, J., and Morley, M. (2013). A change management perspective on the introduction of music therapy to interprofessional teams. *Journal of Health Organization and Management* 27(6): 714–732.

Lindenfelser, K. (2013). Palliative and end-of-life care for children. In: J. Bradt (ed)., *Guidelines for Music Therapy Practice in Pediatric Care*, pp. 324–355. Gilsum, NH: Barcelona Publishers.

Lindenfelser, K., Grocke, D., and McFerran, K. (2008). Bereaved parents' experiences of music therapy with their terminally ill child. *Journal of Music Therapy* 45(3): 330–348.

Lindenfelser, K., Hense, C., and McFerran, K. (2012). Music therapy in pediatric palliative care: Family-centered care to enhance quality of life. *American Journal of Hospice and Palliative Medicine* 29(3): 219–226.

Loewy, J.V. (ed.) (1997). *Music Therapy and Pediatric Pain*. Cherry Hill, NJ: Jeffrey Books.

Loewy, J.V. (2001). Building bridges in team centred care. *Australian Journal of Music Therapy* 12: 3–12.

Loewy, J.V. (2007). Developing music therapy programs in medical practice and healthcare communities. In: J. Edwards (ed.), *Music: Promoting Health and Creating Community in Healthcare Contexts*, pp. 17–28. Newcastle Upon Tyne: Cambridge Scholars Publishing.

Malloch, S. and Trevarthen, C. (2009). *Communicative musicality: Exploring the basis of human companionship*. New York: Oxford University Press.

Neugebauer, C. (2013). Children in general in patient care. In: J. Bradt (ed.), *Guidelines for Music Therapy Practice in Pediatric Care*, pp. 477–512. Gilsum, NH: Barcelona Publishers.

Noel, M., McMurtry, C.M., Chambers, C.T., and McGrath, P.J. (2010). Children's memory for painful procedures: The relationship of pain intensity, anxiety, and adult behaviors to subsequent recall. *Journal of pediatric psychology* 35(6): 626–636.

Pavlicevic, M. (ed.) (2005). *Music Therapy in Children's Hospices: Jessie's Fund in Action*. Philadelphia, PA: Jessica Kingsley.

Robb, S.L. (2003). Designing music therapy interventions for hospitalized children and adolescents using a contextual support model of music therapy. *Music Therapy Perspectives* 21(1): 27–40.

Sajaniemi, N. (2013). Brain development and the everlasting process of self-regulation. In: R. Laaksonen and M. Ranta (eds), *Introduction to Neuropsychotherapy: Guidelines for Rehabilitation of Neurological and Neuropsychiatric Patients throughout the Lifespan*, pp. 39–64. Psychology Press.

Sheridan, J. and McFerran, K. (2004). Exploring the value of opportunities for choice and control in music therapy within a paediatric hospice setting. *Australian Journal of Music Therapy* 15: 18–32.

Townsend, J. (2013). Medically fragile children in low awareness states. In: J. Bradt (ed.), *Guidelines for Music Therapy Practice in Pediatric Care*, pp. 442–476. Gilsum, NH: Barcelona Publishers.

van der Horst, F. and van der Veer, R. (2009). Changing attitudes towards the care of children in hospital: a new assessment of the influence of the work of Bowlby and Robertson in the UK, 1940–1970, *Attachment & Human Development* 11: 119–142. DOI: 10.1080/14616730802503655.

Whitehead-Pleaux, A. (2013). Burn care for children. In: J. Bradt (ed.), *Guidelines for Music Therapy Practice in Pediatric Care*, pp. 252–89. Gilsum, NH: Barcelona Publishers.

Whitehead-Pleaux, A.M., Clark, S.L., and Spall, L.E. (2011). Indications and counterindications for electronic music technologies in a pediatric medical setting. *Music and Medicine* 3(3): 154–162.

CHAPTER 4

MUSIC THERAPY FOR CHILDREN AND ADOLESCENTS DIAGNOSED WITH CANCER

PHILIPPA REID

CHILDREN AND ADOLESCENTS WITH CANCER

Cancer types, treatments, and effects

CANCER is the term used to describe a broad group of diseases that involve abnormal cell growth. Cells divide and grow uncontrollably, forming tumors or spreading to different parts of the body. Each child or adolescent's cancer, treatment, and response to treatment is different. The most common types of pediatric cancers include: (a) Leukemia, (b) lymphoma, (c) solid tumors, and (d) central nervous system (CNS) tumors (Tomlinson and Kline 2010).

The primary types of cancer treatment include: (a) Chemotherapy, which is cytotoxic (cell-killing) drug therapy used to prevent malignant (cancerous) cell division and spread; (b) radiotherapy, the use of high-energy radiation to destroy cancer cells; (c) surgery, to take a biopsy (sample), remove a tumor mass, determine the location and extent of cancer, insert supportive care devices, or provide palliative surgery (to relieve symptoms, including pain, caused by tumors that have been unresponsive to treatment; Tomlinson and Kline 2010); and (d) hematopoietic stem cell transplantation (HSCT), to replace diseased, damaged, or absent stem cells with healthy stem cells.

Acute side-effects from cancer treatments may include nausea, vomiting, oral mucositis (inflammation and ulceration in the mouth), diarrhoea, constipation, hair loss, rashes, tiredness, fatigue, febrile episodes (fever), infection, weight gain or loss, and changes in bloods (Tomlinson and Kline 2010). Additionally, the treatments that help children to survive their cancer can cause subsequent health problems, known as late effects. Late effects of treatments may include infertility, neurocognitive deficits, weakness, secondary malignancies, high-frequency hearing loss and tinnitus (noises or ringing in the ears), and sensory changes (Tomlinson and Kline 2010). About 50–60 percent of children treated for cancer will have some risk of neurocognitive impairment resulting from the cancer and/or its treatment (Simone et al. 2003). Cognitive late effects may include impairments in short-term memory, processing speed, and attention and concentration, which can affect school performance, learning, and social function (Simone et al. 2003).

Incidence of childhood cancer

Childhood cancers are rare and survival rates have been improving over the last few decades. Comparisons in international incidence rates can be problematic because of different population standards and disease classifications (Baade et al. 2010). Public health infrastructure, which enables children to rapidly receive a diagnosis and treatment, differs between low and high income countries. In high income countries (such as Australia, Canada, Denmark, Norway, UK, and USA) the five-year event-free survival for children with cancer is high. However, low cure rates occur in middle- and low-income countries (such as India, Nigeria, Papua New Guinea, Vietnam, and Zimbabwe) and children under the age of five years have high mortality rates (Howard et al. 2008).

In Australia, childhood cancer is rare. There are approximately 620 new cases (approximately 158 per million) of children under the age of fifteen years diagnosed with cancer in Australia each year (Baade et al. 2010; Youlden 2012). After injuries, cancer is the second leading cause of death in Australian children. However, the five-year survival for all childhood cancers in Australia has increased from 67 percent (1982–1986) to 79 percent (1998–2004; Momber 2010). This increase over the last three decades highlights the significant and ongoing advancements in treatment and international research efforts to improve childhood cancer outcomes.

The causes of childhood cancers are largely unknown. Only a small percentage of cases can be explained, which include cases of children with genetic abnormalities and Down syndrome (Seewald et al. 2012). Parents of children diagnosed with cancer often create theories to understand the cause of their child's illness, and largely believe the cause may be from environmental factors such as pollution or radiation (Bernardi and Badon 2008). Their beliefs are often unresolved after initial discussions with medical staff that the cause of the cancer is unknown.

Adolescents and Young Adults with cancer (AYA) are a specific group requiring special attention and support when receiving medical treatment and associated care. In Australia, there are approximately 419 cases of cancer per million diagnosed among AYA (15–29 years; Australian Institute of Health and Welfare 2011). AYA account for approximately less than two percent of all cancer cases diagnosed in Australia (Australian Institute of Health and Welfare 2011). However, cancer is the leading cause of non accidental death in AYA and the incidence of cancer in young people in Australia increased by 30 percent between 1993–2001 (Mitchell et al. 2004). Although there is a higher and increased incidence of cancer in this age group, survival rates have not improved or benefited from improvements in childhood cancer outcomes (Haggar 2012). There is growing research indicating that cancer may have a different biology in adolescents and young adults than in younger or older people with cancer (Bleyer 2009; Thomas et al. 2006).

Worldwide it is recognized that AYA have distinct needs which may not be met in pediatric or adult systems (D'Agostino et al. 2011; Palmer et al. 2007; Thomas 2007). Children and adolescents with cancer have higher survival rates if treated in clinical trials at specialized centers (Mitchell et al. 2004). This poses a challenge to health systems. For example, within the state of Victoria in Australia, with a population of over five million, most AYA will have their cancer treated in any of 67 different adult institutions (Palmer et al. 2007) with only ten percent receiving treatment in dedicated pediatric institutions (Thomas 2007). It is acknowledged that the distinct medical, psychosocial, and information needs of AYA are often unmet in cancer care (Palmer et al. 2007).

Music therapy in pediatric oncology

A cancer diagnosis for a child or adolescent can have ongoing problematic effects for the young person and their family. Time in hospital separates children from their home, friends, family, school, and community. Children's reactions to time in hospital can often include anxiety, withdrawal, regression, and defiance (Brodsky 1989). Cancer treatments and procedures can become the overwhelming focus, which can disrupt normal development and can leave a child or adolescent feeling like a patient rather than a *normal* person. It is important to ensure that psychosocial care is integrated with medical care (Noll and Kazak 2004) and that a holistic approach is taken to providing comprehensive services to children with cancer and their families. Music therapy can provide adjunct support to medical treatments, to reduce distress, improve coping, provide comfort, and offer opportunities for children/ adolescents and their families to share positive musical experiences alongside their illness experience.

CURRENT RESEARCH IN PEDIATRIC ONCOLOGY MUSIC THERAPY

A range of research studies provide evidence for music therapy's beneficial effects in pediatric oncology treatment contexts (Hilliard 2006; Standley and Hanser 1995). Pediatric oncology research literature highlights the usefulness of music therapy to address the physical, psychological and social needs, and to enhance the care and quality of life for pediatric patients (Standley and Hanser 1995). Seven pediatric oncology research studies using quantitative or mixed methods designs were conducted in a 25-year period up until 2013 in the USA, Canada, Norway, and Australia (O'Callaghan et al. 2013). In addition to these, a number of qualitative studies, case reports, and clinical reflections provide descriptions of music therapy's usefulness with this population. The use of methods from quantitative and qualitative traditions are important as they offer clinicians different types of information about music therapy in this context (Hilliard 2006; O'Callaghan et al. 2013). Controlled and descriptive studies of music therapy in pediatric oncology will be presented in the next part of the chapter focussed in six areas: Music therapy's relevance in pediatric cancer centers; music therapy provision in isolation rooms; music therapy during radiation therapy; music and music therapy during procedures; music therapy with adolescents and young adults; and palliative care music therapy.

Music therapy's relevance in pediatric oncology settings

Research studies highlight how children with cancer and their families benefit from music therapy programs in hospital settings. In Australia, multisite qualitative research investigated music and music therapy's relevance for children with cancer and their parents (O'Callaghan et al. 2011). Interviews with children (n = 26, <15 years old; median age 5.7 years) and parents (n = 28) revealed that children's cancer experiences can be helped by (a) their own music, (b) musical interactions within their families, social networks, and electronic (online) connections, and (c) hospital music therapy programs. Findings from this research were integrated with focus group research examining four registered music therapists' perceptions about music's role for children with cancer (O'Callaghan et al. 2013). The focus group research found that: (a) Music is imperative in children's attachment, adjustment, enculturation, identity formation, and social adjustment; (b) psychosocial and health factors affect young cancer patients' interactions with music and therapists in oncology hospital settings; and (c) positive transformation, including dissipation of distress, can occur through young cancer patients' observing musical instruments and engaging in music therapy. The findings from the two studies were comparable and informed the following abridged statement of combined findings:

> Children's adverse cancer experiences are often alleviated by music usages. Broader family, social, and electronic musical interactions also promote children's resilience and "normal" development. Music therapy and associated programs often, but not always, alleviate children's distress. Positive effects can carry over into children's home, social, and school lives, and vicariously support families.
>
> O'Callaghan et al. 2011

The authors suggested that this statement constitutes a substantive grounded theory, and may be generalized to comparable contexts, including where children have the choice of receiving similar music therapy services during their cancer treatment and follow-up care.

A multisite randomized controlled trial in the USA supports the use of music therapy to reduce the impact of hospital and treatment stressors and enhance positive coping behaviors in children with cancer (Robb et al. 2008). An active music engagement (AME) protocol was designed to change stressful qualities of the in-patient hospital environment. The AME intervention involved a music therapist offering opportunities for the child to experience mastery, make choices, and interact through a variety of age-appropriate music-based activities. The results indicate that children (n = 83, aged four to seven) in the AME group had a significantly higher frequency of coping-related behaviors compared with the music listening or audio storybook control conditions. Positive facial affect (smiling or laughter) and active engagement were significantly higher, and initiation (verbal or gestural) was significantly higher during AME than the audio storybooks. These areas are indicators of improved mood, positive coping strategies and children's exploring and interacting with their environment in hospital.

In Canada, the effects of active music therapy to support hospitalized young patients with cancer (n = 65, six months to seventeen years) has been explored (Barrera et al. 2002). Interactive music therapy sessions focused on age-appropriate music-making with the child (and family if present). Typically patients were engaged in the following: Adolescents and school-age children participated in singing, songwriting, instrumental improvisation, and listening to self-selected pre-recorded music; preschoolers and toddlers participated in animated play songs, rhymes, and playing instruments; and infants and toddlers participated in vocal play, play songs, lullabies, rhymes, and playing instruments. The results suggest a significant improvement in children's self ratings of their feelings from pre- to post-music therapy ($p < 0.01$). Responses from the satisfaction questionnaires by children, parents and staff were grouped into the themes of enjoyment of music, change in mood and comfort, and general comments/suggestions, and all produced positive comments about music therapy.

Descriptive studies have highlighted the use of music therapy to foster the healthy aspects of a child when in an oncology hospital environment, through supporting the child's creative side in a socially active way. Case examples illustrate the usefulness of music therapy on the pediatric oncology ward environment, including enhancing the child's role in various relationships in their social environment through writing and performing their own songs (Aasgaard 2001; 2005). Music therapy initiatives, and the creation of songs, can enable children or adolescents with a life-threatening illness to be something other than "just a patient" (Aasgaard 2001, p. 177). Case studies highlight how the performance of an individual's song compositions in the hospital setting can increase feelings of self-esteem and empowerment, and increase social interaction (Abad 2003) and allow the young person to be seen as a normal, creative young individual, not primarily a patient with cancer (Aasgaard 2001; 2005).

A range of music therapy goals and methods are required to suit the varied stages and contexts that the children present with in hospital through their cancer trajectory (Daveson 2001). Musical instruments or methods that are flexible, age appropriate, engaging, and that do not require musical skill are essential, so that patients do not become frustrated with being unable to play or participate (Brodsky 1989). "Bricolage," that is using strategies and methods available in the immediate setting, has been presented as a framework for working as a music therapy clinician in a pediatric oncology setting (Dun 2007). Case study highlights how the flexible music therapist can recognize and embrace the healthy aspects of a child in various areas of the hospital (Dun 2007).

Music therapy provision in isolation rooms

Children and adolescents may be placed in isolation rooms during their treatment in order to prevent infection. In the isolation rooms children may experience separation from friends and family, decreased social interaction, reduced stimulation, and fewer physical activities. Young patients' emotional responses to being placed in isolation can often include loneliness, depression, rejection, anger, confusion, and lowered self-esteem (Brodsky 1989). Staff entering these rooms are often required to wear hospital gowns and surgical masks to protect children who have a reduced or absent immune system. Little is known about the psychological impact of wearing masks when working with children. However, when entering an isolation room it is important to consider that masks could be intimidating or frightening to young children new to the hospital environment and/or who have not met the staff member outside of the room.

Pilot research provides support for the use of music therapy song writing to reduce anxiety for pediatric patients (nine to seventeen years) undergoing bone marrow transplant (Robb and Ebberts 2003). Case studies describe the use of music therapy, including the use of instruments and song activities, with children in isolation rooms in an Israeli pediatric oncology center (Brodsky 1989). Music therapy offered these children opportunities for interpersonal interaction, shared musical experiences, increased control, self expression, and the development of more adaptive coping. Environmental stressors and the effects of hospitalization, such as anxiety, withdrawal, and loss of control, can be addressed in music therapy (Brodsky 1989).

Music therapy and pediatric radiation therapy

The benefits of music therapy for pediatric radiotherapy outpatients attending an adult cancer center providing radiotherapy have been reported in Melbourne, Australia (O'Callaghan et al. 2007). Case studies illustrate the usefulness of music therapy to reduce anxiety, stress, and fears of children, and to facilitate creative, positive experiences which may be shared between pediatric radiation therapy out-patients and their families. Following these descriptive findings, research was undertaken to explore the usefulness of music therapy to support pediatric patients during their initial radiotherapy treatment (Barry et al. 2010). The music therapy procedures involved children creating a music CD using interactive computer-based music software to listen to whilst isolated during radiotherapy. The mixed methods research recruited outpatients (n = 11, aged six to thirteen), whom were randomly assigned to either the music or standard care group. An outstanding difference was that 67 percent of the children in the standard care group used social withdrawal as a coping strategy, compared to zero percent of the children in the music therapy group. The music therapy process is perceived to have offered a medium for enhanced communication and interaction between the children and the radiation therapy staff, when in the treatment room separated from parents. Overall, the music therapy CD creation was fun, engaging, and developmentally appropriate, which helped to prevent distress and support children's use of effective coping strategies to meet the demands of their initial radiotherapy (Barry et al. 2010).

This research and advancements in technology enabled the extension of music's supportive qualities for children during the administration of their radiotherapy. Clinical audio-visual opportunities were implemented to avoid the use of general anesthesia with children undergoing treatment (Willis and Barry 2010). A simple, inexpensive audio-visual system was established by radiation therapists using commercially available equipment, which enabled isolated children to see and hear their parents or staff including the music therapist during their treatment. Over a two-year period (March 2007–May 2009), children (n = 24, two to six years) participated in audio-visual interventions, and 92 percent (n = 22) of these children did not require the use of general anesthesia for some or all of their treatment. Case study descriptions illustrate how the audio-visual system allowed a young child and the music therapist to continue to maintain visual contact whilst the child was isolated in the treatment room. Music therapy could be flexibly delivered during treatment, which without the audio-visual set-up, would otherwise be impossible. The benefits of music therapy as a nonpharmacological anxiolytic for children in the out-patient waiting areas (O'Callaghan et al. 2007) were extended, and as this study suggests, helped to reduce the need to anesthetize children undergoing radiotherapy treatment (Willis and Barry 2010).

MUSIC AND MUSIC THERAPY
DURING PROCEDURES

Music therapy may support children during invasive procedures, such as dressing changes, line changes, injections, medication administration, chemotherapy, and induction of anesthesia. Qualitative document analysis was used to critically examine the literature (n = 19) where music therapy has provided procedural support during invasive medical procedures (Ghetti 2012). A working model of music therapy as procedural support was developed. It conceptualizes that the music therapist engages in a reflexive process of continually assessing the patient's responses in order to refocus the process to positively influence outcomes. Music techniques used may change from moment to moment based on the patient's responses and changing needs. The music therapist is required to make ongoing assessments and relevant adjustments to interventions used (Ghetti 2012).

The use of music-assisted relaxation for children (n = 6, six to fifteen years) during bone marrow aspirations without sedation was evaluated (Pfaff et al. 1989). Relaxation music on cassette tape was played during the bone marrow procedure with the music therapist coaching the child in relaxation exercises. Reductions in anticipatory and experienced fear, experienced pain, and anticipatory behavioral distress were found. Similarly, in Vietnam a randomized clinical trial explored the impact of listening to music through headphones on pain and anxiety in children undergoing lumbar punctures (Nguyen et al. 2010). Children with leukemia (n = 40, seven to twelve years) were randomly assigned to the music listening or control group. Children's choices of music included traditional Vietnamese and children's songs. No local anesthetics or other analgesics were administered during the procedure, as is standard care in most Vietnamese hospitals. The music group reported lower pain scores and heart and respiratory rates during and after the lumbar puncture, and anxiety scores were lower both before and after the procedure. Interviews with the children supported the numeric findings through descriptions of positive experiences listening to music, including less pain and fear.

A randomized controlled trial in the USA examined the effect of interactive music therapy on pre-induction anxiety for children undergoing outpatient surgery (Kain et al. 2004). Children were randomized to one of three groups: Interactive music therapy ($n = 51$), oral midazolam ($n = 34$), or control ($n = 38$). The results showed that children who received midazolam (inducing sedation and amnesia) were significantly less anxious during the induction of anesthesia than children in the music therapy and control groups. The research revealed a significant therapist effect; i.e. during separation from parents and on entrance to the theatre, children treated by one of the therapists were significantly less anxious than children in the other therapist group and the control group. The researchers concluded that music therapy may be helpful on separation from parents and entrance to the surgery room, depending on the therapist. However, preoperative interactive music therapy does not appear to relieve children's anxiety during the induction of anesthesia. Separation anxiety from parents, anxiety post surgery, and the interpersonal elements of the music therapists are not described limiting understandings and explanation of the therapist effect.

MUSIC THERAPY WITH ADOLESCENTS AND YOUNG ADULTS

Music can enhance important areas of an adolescent's health, including identity formation, resilience, competence, and connectedness (McFerran 2010). However, a cancer diagnosis, treatments, and required time in hospital can have adverse consequences on normal development. Music can have calming, supportive, and relaxing effects that can promote endurance and identity adjustment through treatment (O'Callaghan et al. 2012).

In the USA, a randomized controlled trial was conducted across eight sites with AYAs (n = 113; 11–24 years old) undergoing hematopoietic stem cell transplant (Robb et al. 2014). Participants were randomized to either a therapeutic music video (TMV) intervention or an audiobooks group, completing six sessions over three weeks with a music therapist. The multisite study measured illness-related distress, social integration, spiritual perspective, family environment, coping, hope-derived meaning, and resilience, at baseline, post-intervention, and 100 days post-transplant. The TMV group reported significantly better courageous coping post-treatment, and significantly better social integration and family environment 100 days post-transplant. The results indicate that the TMV approach positively supported AYAs to use protective factors to buffer adverse cancer effects during and after treatment (Robb et al. 2014).

Music therapy groups can provide AYA with the opportunity to connect with other young people with cancer from different treatment centers (O'Callaghan and Barry 2009). A music group for AYA (n = 8, 19–25 years) co-facilitated by a music therapist and social worker included song sharing with discussion and group song writing. Thematic analysis from participant responses revealed benefits of music therapy group work with AYA, including: (a) Connecting and expressing themselves with a group who understands the cancer experience; (b) reducing loneliness, isolation, and risk of depression; and (c) using songwriting and music allowed it to be a group not focusing on cancer (O'Callaghan and Barry 2009). Music can be used in therapeutic group work with AYA to enable young people to comfortably express their experiences of cancer and connect with supportive peers who are undergoing comparable treatments.

Music and music therapy's relevance for AYA was explored in a grounded theory informed study (O'Callaghan et al. 2012). Twelve people (16–24 years old, mean age 21) with cancer diagnoses in Victoria participated in a semi-structured interview, providing their perspectives about their music usage and what it offered them. The research revealed five themes: (a) AYAs' music backgrounds affect their musical experiences and reflections about their lived lives when living with cancer; (b) AYAs' *normal* development alongside cancer's biopsychosocial impact changes their *musicking* mildly to profoundly; (c) *musicking* signifies and promotes AYAs' endurance and identity adjustment through treatment and recovery; (d) some AYA find that time with flexible music therapists promotes normality, fun, and/or support; and (e) wisdom: Sound and music-based support strategies are recommended for health care providers and other AYA which include flexibility and choice.

Participants reported that a music therapy group for AYA (as discussed above) connected people without the therapy stigma, felt normal and fun, and the group songwriting enabled closure. Perceptions of individual music therapy were that it was not desired by everyone, but can be fun, loved, and promote normality when offered by a flexible, conversational, and friendly music therapist. AYA sometimes described involvement with music therapists yet report that they had not *received* music therapy. Additionally one participant, who had spent time with two music therapists, reported that one therapist was more helpful than the other because she allowed him to feel *normal* through friendly conversations and spontaneous and flexible sessions, rather than pre-determined times which made him feel more like a cancer patient (O'Callaghan et al. 2012). Consideration needs to be taken by music therapists working with young cancer patients to ensure that their approach is not stigmatizing, including through use of formal treatment times and assessments. Rather, music therapists should aim to develop flexible and friendly approaches to these young patients, to establish normalizing therapeutic relationships that promote creativity, abilities, normality, and fun (O'Callaghan et al. 2012).

Music therapy and life-limiting cancer

Moments of play, fun, and laughter enabled by music therapy can be invaluable for families when a child's cancer is life-limiting (O'Callaghan et al. 2013). Creative experiences in the hospital environment that promote healthy aspects of the child or adolescent (Fagen 1982) are important. Opportunities for peer group identification and normalcy are limited when an adolescent is coping with life-limiting cancer in hospital. Friends may be overwhelmed by their peer's cancer illness and compromised abilities, yet when friends are available, music and playing instruments can be a normal activity that can be shared (Callaghan 2007).

The music therapist can sensitively and flexibly offer children and adolescents and their families the opportunity to keep living whilst receiving palliative care. Understandings of death vary depending on developmental age and stage. For example, preschoolers (three to five years) may have a limited understanding of death and see it as reversible or temporary, whereas an adolescent (twelve to nineteen years) may understand death as much as adults do, yet may tend to think they will not die as a young person (Tomlinson and Kline 2010). It is the author's experience that children, adolescents, and families appreciate the normalized and personalized music-based interactions and support that the music therapist can provide during end-stage care.

Theoretical frameworks

A variety of theoretical models can be used to guide and consider practice in pediatric oncology. In this setting, practice is not prescriptive. Theories can support music therapists to explore and understand how music functions to benefit the child or adolescent with cancer. In Victoria, Australia, the Pediatric Integrative Cancer Service (PICS) developed a model for providing art, music, and play therapies to children and adolescents with cancer and their families. It is a three-tiered model in which level of intervention is based on need (Figure 4.1).

The child or adolescent may move up or down the levels as they go through their cancer experience, based on assessed changing needs (PICS 2007). For example, a child identified as level one low risk, may have a change in diagnosis, treatment, or prognosis that may cause acute distress and require level three care. The ongoing assessment and flexibility of the music therapist is essential to meeting the fluctuating needs of the child or adolescent and their family.

The Children's Hospital of Philadelphia undertook research to develop a *blueprint* to help assure that children with cancer and their families have access to evidence-based care (Kazak et al. 2007). The two theoretical models developed were: The Pediatric Psychosocial Preventative Health Model (PPPHM) and the Pediatric Medical Traumatic Stress Model (PMTS, Kazak et al. 2006). The PPPHM is reflective of the PICS model. The three tiers are labelled: (a) Universal: Children and families are distressed but resilient; (b) Targeted: Acute distress and risk factors are present; and (c) Clinical/Treatment: Persistent/escalating distress and high risk factors. Similarly to the PICS model, level of intervention moves from general support to specialized interventions across the three levels. The PMTS model was developed to guide psychosocial assessment and intervention with children with illness or injury in medical settings across the various phases of care to reduce symptoms of post-traumatic stress (Kazak et al. 2006). The researchers propose that the PPPHM and PMTS models may be integrated to guide evidence-based psychosocial practice with children and their families across the spectrum of their cancer treatment (Kazak et al. 2007).

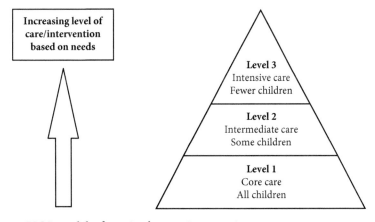

FIGURE 4.1 PICS model of music therapy intervention.

The PMTS model provides a useful guide for music therapists understanding short and long-term consequences of cancer treatment for children and their parents (Robb 2012). Traditional outcome-focused research in music therapy provides information about whether an intervention was effective for a given demographic. However, often information about how and why an intervention worked in this style of research often cannot be answered. The identification of variables (such as child and family demographics and individual cancer treatment characteristics) and measurement of potential mediating factors (such as perceived family normalcy and parental self-efficacy) can allow for a more comprehensive evaluation of intervention outcomes. Theory-based research can advance understandings of the diverse and complex interactions in music therapy between music, patients, and the health care environment (Robb 2012).

A cancer diagnosis and associated treatments in childhood is recognized as a potentially traumatic event for the child and their family members. Parents of children diagnosed with cancer may experience acute stress disorder (ASD) or post-traumatic stress symptoms (PTSS; Kazak et al. 2007; McCarthy et al. 2012). However, positive outcomes can develop from a traumatic event, which can be known as post-traumatic growth. Adolescents and young adults often report that their cancer experience influences positive self changes, improvements in relationships with others, and new or changed future plans. Researchers encourage that music therapy approaches with children and families should have a sustained focus on processes of growth and development (Kazak et al. 2006; O'Callaghan et al. 2012).

Clinical practice in children's oncology music therapy

Music therapists practicing in pediatric oncology centers are required to be flexible in their music therapy approaches to meet the fluctuating demands of the service and the changing needs of children and their families. Music therapy support may be requested by staff, families, or children who are newly diagnosed, undergoing procedures/treatments, or hospitalized. Music therapy referrals, assessment, methods, and evaluation and reporting will now be discussed.

Referrals

Referrals can come from a variety of sources within the oncology medical setting. Multidisciplinary staff members, including medical, nursing, and allied health, may notify the music therapist of a child who would potentially benefit from music therapy. Referrals may be received verbally, including in meetings or handovers, or written, via e-mail, paging messaging systems, or in a specific referral form. Children, adolescents, and their families may also self-refer to music therapy, by either approaching the music therapist directly, or by asking other staff members. However, parents may often be reluctant to initiate music therapy referrals because they perceive that their child is too unwell to "play music"

(Horne-Thompson et al. 2007). It is important that staff can advocate for the child or adolescent to ensure they can maintain normal activities alongside cancer treatments.

Reasons for referral vary depending on the referral source, yet may include support during hospitalization, assistance before, during or after a medical procedure, to improve mood, reduce stress, or support coping. It is important that staff have knowledge about what a music therapy service may offer so that appropriate referrals are received. The music therapist can work with the multidisciplinary team to determine the appropriateness and urgency of referrals. The music therapist gathers information to determine the urgency and priority level of the referral. In the case of medical procedural support, often the referral is to see the child on that day or at that moment. Yet staff may also inform the music therapist of a child to be met during their next hospital admission which may be days or weeks away. In some centers, the ideal model indicates that all children diagnosed with cancer should have access to music therapy (PICS 2007). The music therapist's task is to effectively prioritize patients.

Fun and positive emotional experiences facilitated by music therapists with children during their initial treatments for cancer may prevent distress responses, support their use of effective coping strategies and enhance their overall treatment experiences (Barry et al. 2010). It is important to educate referral sources about the role of music therapy, to avoid delayed referrals that limit music therapy's intervention (Horne-Thompson et al. 2007). Music therapists may aim to incorporate supportive care interventions into children's initial medical procedures to support their adjustment to new hospital and cancer treatment experiences.

Assessment

Most children and adolescents have pre-existing musical preferences, backgrounds, and positive experiences with music when they arrive at the hospital. The child or adolescent's existing experience with music can be used by the music therapist as the foundation for building a therapeutic relationship (Edwards 2005) and used in conducting assessments. Three main types of assessment used by music therapists with children in hospital include: (a) Initial assessment, to determine the child's strengths and weaknesses and to develop goals; (b) comprehensive assessment, to examine multiple aspects of functioning; and (c) ongoing assessment throughout the treatment process (Douglass 2006). The assessment process with children with cancer continues informally throughout their treatment journey. The needs of children and their family vary depending on the stage and outcomes of their treatment.

Assessment areas, based on those from the Pediatric Inpatient Music Therapy Assessment Form (PIMTAF; Douglass 2006) developed for use with hospitalized children, include: (a) Background information, including patient and family details, cancer diagnosis, and types of treatment; (b) referral information, such as reason for referral; (c) physiological information, including side-effects from treatments, infection control precautions, and medical equipment precautions (attached to monitors, IVs, incubated, immobilized); (d) physical skills, including ambulation, gross/fine motor and hearing and vision; (e) cognitive skills, including development or a known developmental delay; (f) social and emotional behaviors, including areas of need (coping skills, socialization, expression of emotions), mood, and attitude towards medical procedures; (g) communication skills, such as the child's communication style and language/s spoken; and (h) musical behaviors, including responses to music, musical background, and favorite songs/artists/types of music.

Assessment with AYA varies from those with younger children with cancer. The initial task of the music therapist is to develop rapport with the young person, which can be achieved through discussion about their music background and behaviors. Discussions may reveal areas of changed *musicking* (O'Callaghan et al. 2012) where a music therapist can listen and provide validation, support, intervention or resources. It helps if the music therapist is authentic and has knowledge of their own way of working and being with adolescents (McFerran 2010). Initial assessments with AYA may function as a one-off session, or provide the starting point for an ongoing therapeutic relationship. Findings from research examining music's relevance for AYA with cancer (O'Callaghan et al. 2012) can guide the informal assessments conducted with young people, which may include discussions of:

(a) Music backgrounds: The importance of music to AYA prior to cancer diagnosis, music preferences, listening behaviors, access to music and listening devices, and effects of music.
(b) Changed *musicking*: Physical, emotional, financial, and environmental impact of cancer and treatments on music background, alterations to music preferences and listening behaviors, and changes in *musicking* (performing, listening, rehearsing, practicing, composing, dancing, and imagery).
(c) Endurance and adjustment: Helpfulness of music during cancer diagnosis and treatments, cognitive, emotional, physical, and imagery responses to music, and use of music to integrate cancer's effects into identity adjustment and development.
(d) Wisdom: Sound and music-based support strategies suggested by AYA can be offered to other AYA patients.

Goals and objectives

Goals and objectives are individual for each child and their family, because no two children's musical life and cancer experience is the same and each music therapist will have a different effect (O'Callaghan et al. 2013). Research and theoretical literature can be useful in informing practice, however, in this field they cannot be used to establish a prescriptive way of practicing. It is essential to listen to patients and their families, to understand their stories and to carefully determine their individual needs and the best response to make (Edwards 2005). Overall, there are some goals and objectives that are common to children and adolescents with cancer. They can be divided into cancer treatment and hospital, social and emotional, and musical goals:

(a) Cancer treatment and hospital goals: Prevent distress, reduce stress and anxiety, improve coping, provide comfort, motivate physical movement and rehabilitation, relax, distract, or support during procedures, and motivate approach to hospital and treatments.

(b) Social and emotional goals: Provide shared positive musical experiences, foster/support healthy aspects of child, improve/change mood, increase social interaction, increase control, foster independence/autonomy, enhance self-expression, reduce separation anxiety, reduce isolation/loneliness, provide normality, promote fun, support identity and normal development, and support adjustment to cancer and treatments.
(c) Musical goals: Support regular musical development, enable access to music and musical instruments, promote creativity, enable fun and enjoyment, support musical skills, develop new music skills, and enable self-expression.

Music therapy methods

A variety of music therapy methods can be applied with children and adolescents with cancer in hospital or community contexts to meet these goals. The five primary areas of practice are: (a) Song creation, (b) active music therapy, (c) receptive music therapy, (d) improvisation, and (e) technology. These music therapy methods will now be described.

Song creation

In pediatric oncology settings, song creation is a flexible process that can be adapted to the needs of the individual child and their family. Song creation can provide pediatric patients and their families with expressive and enjoyable opportunities, enhance their social support both inside and outside the hospital (Aasgaard 2005), allow musical expressions of feelings, messages, and stories (O'Callaghan 2005), and promote coping strategies (Robb 2003). With advancements in technology, songs can be created and recorded instantly, and some children and families send these recordings electronically to family members, school, and extended social supports, or keep the video on a personal device to be watched individually. Song creation is different across the developmental age range. The content of songs may often be about animals/pets, friends/family, favorite things, or messages to others. Songs can be written with a music therapist about the hospital or about upcoming procedures.

> A ten-year-old girl with Ewing's Sarcoma of the pelvis was hospitalized and lying on her back, awaiting surgery for the removal of the tumor, reconstruction of the bone, and application of a hip spica; a cast used to immobilize the hip. The child, diagnosed on the autistic spectrum, was reportedly highly anxious about the surgery and there were difficulties in her understanding of waking up with the immobilization cast on. The music therapist had a pre-existing therapeutic relationship with the girl. Together they discussed the hip spica, and in particular how exciting it was that she would have a cast on that would not fit anyone other than her. They wrote and recorded a song on the spot:
>
> **My Cast**
>
> My plaster cast, It won't fit anyone else.
> My plaster cast, It won't fit anyone else.
> Not Dad! Not Mum!

> Not the Nurses! Nobody!
> Not even Pip!
> Because it's my plaster cast!

The child, whilst lying on her back, played the maracas and a rain stick creatively during the song, which was instantly recorded on the child's portable tablet. She giggled and smiled during the creation of the song and enthusiastically gave a performance for a nurse, and shared the recording with her parents at a later time. Over the weeks after this, the child wrote many more spontaneous and silly songs. She initiated telling the music therapist that if she wanted to share her songs with other children in the hospital to help them, that she could.

Active music therapy

Active music therapy interventions are age-appropriate, music-based activities, offering opportunities for choice of materials and flexibility of live music, with the child's decisions and actions supported and central to the activity (Robb et al. 2008). A variety of musical instruments can be offered for infants, children, and adolescents of all ages and abilities. A standard session involves the music therapist flexibly offering the patient choices and control in selecting instruments and songs that they would like to listen to and play and/or sing along to.

> The music therapist arrived to hear an eighteen-month-old boy loudly crying as nursing staff were commencing a procedure on the central line (a tube that goes into the chest and directly into one of the major blood vessels) and changing the dressing. The music therapist had only met the child once in the week prior and recalled that he showed interest in yellow castanets that are shaped like ducks. The mum sat her crying child on her lap and the music therapist produced her guitar and the ducks and began to sing, "five little ducks." The child ceased crying, said "duck," and reached for a castanet. Over the next fifteen minutes, his mum, nursing staff, and the music therapist sang a medley of familiar children's songs during the line change, and the child was easily distracted and engaged by the toy animals during "Old MacDonald had a farm" the frog castanets during "five little speckled frogs," and shakers during other known children's songs. The initially distressing procedure was transformed through the music and music therapist into an enjoyable experience for the child, mum, and nursing staff.

When children and adolescents are undergoing long hospital admissions, they may be invited to play or borrow a musical instrument, such as a guitar, ukulele, or keyboard. Therapeutic music lessons may be offered, to support the young person to learn the basics of the instrument, so they can learn favorite songs, create their own, or improvise. Often receiving the loan of a musical instrument can be helpful for adolescents. The music therapist can encourage the young person to play the instrument whilst in hospital, for leisure, diversion, and to pass the time. Young people often can continue to develop their playing outside of the hospital, and on subsequent visits to the hospital for appointments or admissions, the young person can share what they have been working on at home. In turn, the music therapist may share new songs that they have learnt, and provide the music and lyrics if the child desires.

Receptive music therapy

When working with withdrawn pediatric patients, music listening has been anecdotally reported to be an effective shared experience that can enhance the patient-therapist relationship and subsequently allow for the discussion of thoughts and feelings (Fagen 1982). Receptive music therapy methods can be used for a wide range of therapeutic purposes with children in the hospital context. The musical style preferred by and/or familiar to the child is the most effective music to use for receptive experiences (Grocke and Wigram 2007). Music therapists may also suggest new music which they feel the child or adolescent may like. Receptive musical experiences may be live or recorded improvisations, performances, or compositions by the client or therapist, or other recordings that a client can listen to and respond to in a silent, verbal, or other manner (Bruscia 1998).

> A thirteen-year-old boy with very high risk leukemia was experiencing ongoing pain, weakness, and discomfort in hospital. Since his diagnosis, he required support from his parents to toilet, shower, and carry out other activities of daily living, during a time when he had been developing his own identity and independence. The music therapist had seen the young man for one to two sessions per week for a month, each session including members of his family. Initially, his response to choices of live songs offered by the music therapist was "I don't mind." The music therapist assessed that it was important to gently encourage him to make choices about the types of music he wished to hear, given his rapid dependence on his parents. The music therapist told him that her homework was to create a book of songs that she thought he might like. He appeared indifferent to this suggestion. On returning for their next session, he asked, "Did you do your homework?" The music therapist produced various songs and he indicated yes, no and maybe to each. Over the next few sessions, he requested new songs for the music therapist to learn and play and indicated clear music preferences, which were discussed and shared with his family. A few sessions later the therapist arrived and a live music session was offered. He was out of bed and in a wheelchair and his mum laid down on his bed. A range of his selected favorite songs were played, however, they were all modified and played at a moderate tempo, using finger picking on the guitar, and a gentle vocal tone. He and his mum both had closed their eyes during the live music, and afterwards reported feeling very relaxed. A week later he significantly deteriorated on the hospital ward and was admitted to ICU where he was intubated. After four days, his parents were bedside, awaiting the medical team to come to discuss withdrawing treatment. Whilst they waited, the music therapist offered to play a song that he liked. The parents held their son's hand during the live music. At the end of the first song, the Mum requested another favorite song they had shared together in the weeks prior. The following day he was transferred to the ward and extubated and died shortly afterwards with his family present. They played recorded music of favorite songs during this time, and played songs shared together in music therapy sessions at his funeral.

Improvisation

Children with cancer can creatively engage in improvisational music therapy experiences. Improvisational methods are when a child can experience making-up music using musical mediums within his/her capabilities, with help and guidance from the music therapist (Bruscia 1998). Music therapists can use improvisational techniques such as matching, involving the therapist producing music that matches the client's style of playing to confirm and validate their emotional expression, and mirroring, doing exactly what the child is doing musically, expressively and through body language in unison, to reflect back the child's own behavior through the therapist's behavior (Wigram 2004). In hospital settings, creative improvisation can be used in varied areas with children of different ages and energy levels. Improvisation can often occur through spontaneously created free-flowing lyrics/ singing, or creative play on musical instruments.

An eight-year-old girl with a cancer diagnosis and developmental delay was admitted to hospital with febrile neutropenia (fever and low white blood cell counts). The child was known to the music therapist since their initial diagnosis six months prior, and the child had enthusiastically engaged in active music making sessions to favorite popular music. Over the next three weeks the child was extremely tired and unwell. She began medically improving, however, was not eating, was socially withdrawn and showing limited interest in her usual favored activities. The music therapist came and asked the child if she would like the therapist to bring in her guitar and have music. The child said no. The therapist turned to the child's favorite teddy "Janet" and asked her about the child's new dog toy that was also on the bed. The child picked up Janet and sang in a country and western style "that's Spotty." The free creative musical play that unfolded involved the child and therapist singing and playing through the four toys on the bed. The child gave each toy its own musical style: Janet the teddy sang country, Spotty the dog sang rock, Dolly the doll sang pop, and a toy elephant Eddie sang rap. The therapist and child interchangeably provided the voices for the toys, and the child created a free-flowing musical story of love between Janet and Spotty, and the fight from Dolly for Spotty, whilst Eddie narrated. The giggles and smiles from the girl during this free creative play was the first time her mum had seen her have fun in weeks. Her mum recorded a video of the musical drama that they continued to play back and enjoy after the session.

Technology: iPads/tablets

Advancements in technological devices have revolutionized the way that music therapists can work in acute pediatric cancer settings. iPads and other tablets (touch screen computers) are portable, lightweight devices that can play music, make sound and video recordings, store sheet music, take photos, and provide online internet access. In the moment, children and adolescents can create their own music, listen to pre-recorded music, watch music videos, read lyrics, access popular music and artist/band news and information, play educational, fun, and distracting musical games, and take photos in music therapy in any area of the hospital. These technology devices have enhanced the potential for music therapists to incorporate supportive music interventions in all areas with pediatric patients to improve their treatment and hospital experiences.

Previously, music therapists did not readily have the potential to access music instantaneously in sessions, even though there was a demand for implementing music interventions instantly to support children through adverse procedures (Barry et al. 2010). Rapid improvements in technology now allows children to create their own music, playlists, or other supportive applications of music, that can be used to help them manage the demands of their cancer treatments and procedures. Currently, there are limited reports in the literature about the usefulness of iPads/tablets in music therapy. However, many music therapists are utilizing these in their daily sessions. Music therapists have demonstrated how embracing technology can allow for treatment experiences to be enhanced through reducing the need for general anesthesia during radiotherapy with young children with cancer (Willis and Barry 2010). A program at a children's hospital in New York, USA, uses iPads and iPods as a distraction method for children during medical procedures (Borges et al. 2011). Staff have noted that the digital devices are effective in distracting and offering mastery and control to children during invasive procedures, as well as being the preferred medium for children whom are part of the digital culture.

An iPad/tablet is an effective way of storing hundreds of popular music lyrics and chords. Hard copy song books can be heavy to carry, can pose issues with infection control, and can be difficult to manually update with the latest popular music requests of children and adolescents. The portable tablets are lightweight and easy to carry, easily cleaned to maintain infection control, and offer easy instant access to sheet and recorded music. Tablets are also essential in providing music that the music therapist may be unable to successfully reproduce. For example, the music preferences of many teenage males that the author has worked with, include metal, R & B, hip-hop, dance, electronic, and drum and bass, which cannot be effectively replicated on acoustic guitar and female voice. The tablet allows for instant access to YouTube music videos in various areas of the hospital, which facilitates authentic song sharing and music discussion.

Musical games and apps can support children, including when they may not have the ability to engage in discussion, music making, or interact directly with the music therapist.

> An energetic six-year-old boy was undergoing a bone marrow transplant and the music therapist visited him twice weekly in his isolation room. The first two weeks the boy enthusiastically engaged in active music making sessions, which included playing the drum machine, percussion instruments, and singing with great enthusiasm and energy. However, he experienced side-effects from treatment including decreased blood counts and mucositis, leaving him tired, unwell, withdrawn, and unable to verbally communicate or sing. The music therapist made a quick assessment on seeing the child curled up looking very sad under the bed sheets through the door, to bring in her iPad. Initially when she entered the room the mum commented that he wasn't happy or well enough for music today. The music therapist said she'd just say hello, then sat bedside and gently asked if he would like to see her Singing Monsters. He nodded, and she shared a music app that allows you to create monsters that sing together. After a brief demonstration of the app the music therapist invited the child to play. His hand appeared from under the sheets and he actively and quietly engaged in the app with the therapist. During the next two weeks, the child was very unwell, and the therapist visited three times per week, each time offering musical instruments or the Singing Monsters. Each time the child chose the singing monsters, and in-between visits would eagerly ask his mother when the music therapist was coming. He was so excited to see his new monsters, giggle at their funny singing, and keep them happy. The child renamed all of the singing monsters to be those of his family members, and named two after himself. For a very sick child, the moments of smiles and giggles at the funny singing of the monsters were special. Post-transplant, the child would attend the hospital for weekly medical appointments. He would ask the staff to send the music therapist a message to come and see him. His family had placed the app on his own iPad at home and each week he wanted to compare singing monsters, and continue to giggle about their funny singing.

Reporting

In the hospital context, a summary of the music therapy session is documented in the medical file in the progress notes. Every hospital has varied protocols for the structure of the notes and which details need to be documented. Details of a progress note may include the: (a) Date, time, and name of service; (b) reason for the contact and the type of intervention/s offered; (c) outcomes of the session, such as the child's participation, mood, and engagement; (d) any areas of concern that arose during the session, including medical, social, and/or emotional, that the music therapist will follow-up with a member of the treating team; (e) the plan for ongoing contact with the patient; and (f) the music therapist signs and prints their name along with a contact number. In the case of out-patient hospital music therapy groups, or community music therapy programs, correspondence of the patient outcomes can be provided to the young person's primary hospital treatment team or to the referral source if appropriate.

Often issues may arise in the music therapy session that the therapist may need to discuss with other members of the child's multidisciplinary team. Often, the therapist will seek permission from the child or the child's caregiver, to discuss the matter with a specific staff member or the nursing, medical or allied health team. Examples of these areas of concern may include negative treatment experiences, newly impaired/decreased movement, pain, anxiety or distress, social/family issues, personal/family events or celebrations, existential or spiritual distress, or other negative hospital experiences.

Parents often report that children are eager to return to the hospital, including on weekend non-treatment days, when supportive care initiatives are offered (Willis and Barry 2010). The music therapist can regularly receive feedback from children's caregivers, such as "you are more important than any of the doctors and nurses to our child," "never underestimate what you do," and "our child wants to come back to the hospital to see you." Music therapy programs can often promote resilience in young patients and their families. Positive effects from music therapy may carry over into children's home lives (O'Callaghan et al. 2011) and may motivate children's approach towards the hospital (Barry et al. 2010).

Future recommendations

The role of the music therapist working in a hospital is emergent and responsive, and is required to adapt and change in response to transformations in hospitals and treatments (Edwards 2005). Similarly, the music therapist is required to keep up-to-date with new technology (such as tablets) and where appropriate incorporate these into practice.

Research offers support for the usefulness of music therapy in pediatric oncology settings. Ongoing research is necessary, however, to support the use of music therapy in this context (Hilliard 2006). Music therapists are encouraged to use theory-based research to advance understanding of the complex interactions between music, clients, and the healthcare environment and how these interactions benefit clients (Robb 2012). Collaborations with staff from medical, nursing, and allied health disciplines may increase the relevance and integration of music supportive care strategies into standard care practices in the hospital. Children's cancer centers can be busy and music therapists may have large caseloads and limited hours to meet the demand for the service. Evidence from other medical settings has shown that staff are typically welcoming to music therapy services (Bouhairie et al. 2005). Creative ways to support other staff, empower parents/caregivers, and support the children during treatments and procedures when the music therapist may not be able to attend, should be considered.

Standard protocols for assessing and delivering music therapy services with children and adolescents with cancer do not exist. Perhaps this is because flexibility of practice is essential to address the individual and changeable music and therapeutic needs of each child and family. Clinical decisions made by the music therapist are in response to the informal assessments made in the moment. Detailed descriptions of music therapy methods/interventions and their theoretical underpinnings provide understandings for the efficacy of music. Further research and descriptions of practice will support music therapists to develop their own authentic music therapy approach to best support young people with cancer and their families.

References

Aasgaard, T. (2001). An ecology of love: Aspects of music therapy in the pediatric oncology environment. *Journal of Palliative Care* 17(3): 177–182.

Aasgaard, T (2005). Assisting children with malignant blood diseases to create and perform their own songs. In: F. Baker and T. Wigram (eds), *Songwriting: Methods, Techniques and Clinical Applications for Music Therapy Clinicians, Educators and Students*. London: Jessica Kingsley Publishers.

Abad, V. (2003). A time of turmoil: Music therapy interventions for adolescents in a paediatric oncology ward. *The Australian Journal of Music Therapy* 14: 20–37.

Australian Institute of Health and Welfare (2011). Cancer in adolescents and young adults in Australia. Cancer series no. 62. Cat. no. CAN 59. Canberra: AIHW.

Baade, P., Youlden, D., Valery, P., Hassall, T., Ward, L., Green, A. et al. (2010). Trends in incidence of childhood cancer in Australia, 1983–2006. *British Journal of Cancer* 102: 620–626.

Barrera, M.E., Rykov, M.H., and Doyle, S.L. (2002). The effects of interactive music therapy on hospitalized children with cancer: A pilot study. *Psycho-Oncology* 11: 379–388.

Barry, P., O'Callaghan, C., Wheeler, G., and Grocke, D. (2010). Music Therapy CD Creation for Initial Pediatric Radiation Therapy: A Mixed Methods Analysis. *Journal of Music Therapy* 47(3): 233–263.

Bernardi, M. and Badon, P. (2008). Descriptive survey about causes of illness given by the parents of children with cancer. *European Journal of Oncology Nursing* 12: 134–141.

Bleyer, A. (2009). Adolescent and young adult (AYA) cancers: distinct biology, different therapy? *Cancer Forum* 33(1): 4.

Borges, L., Huber, D., and Lugo, S. (2011). Harnessing the power of digital devices. *Pediatric Nursing* 37(2): 88.

Bouhairie, A., Kemper, K.J., Martin, K., and Woods, C. (2005). Staff attitudes and expectations about music therapy: Pediatric oncology versus neonatal intensive care unit. *Journal of the Society for Integrative Oncology* 4(2): 71–74.

Brodsky, W. (1989). Music therapy as an intervention for children with cancer in isolation rooms. *Music Therapy* 8(1): 17–34.

Bruscia, K.E. (1998). *Defining Music Therapy*, 2nd edn. Gilsum, NH: Barcelona Publishers.

Callaghan, E.E. (2007). Achieving balance: A case study examination of an adolescent coping with life-limiting cancer. *Journal of Pediatric Oncology Nursing* 24: 334–339.

D'Agostino, N.M., Penney, A., and Zebrack, B. (2011). Providing developmentally appropriate psychosocial care to adolescent and young adult cancer survivors. *Cancer* (May 15): 2329–2334.

Daveson, B.A. (2001). Music therapy and childhood cancer: Goals, methods, patient choice and control during diagnosis, intensive treatment, transplant and palliative care. *Music Therapy Perspectives* 19: 114–120.

Douglass, E.T. (2006). The development of a music therapy assessment tool for hospitalized children. *Music Therapy Perspectives* 24(2): 73–79.

Dun, B. (2007). Journeying with Olivia: Bricolage as a framework for understanding music therapy in paediatric oncology. *Voices: A World Forum for Music Therapy*. Retrieved April 20 2007, from: <http://www.voices.no/mainissues/mi40007000229.php>.

Edwards, J. (2005). A reflection on the music therapist's role in developing a program in a children's hospital. *Music Therapy Perspectives* 23(1): 36–44.

Fagen, T. (1982). Music therapy in the treatment of anxiety and fear in terminal pediatric patients. *Music Therapy* 2(1): 13–24.

Ghetti, C.M. (2012). Music therapy as procedural support for invasive medical procedures: Toward the development of music therapy theory. *Nordic Journal of Music Therapy* 21(1): 3–35.

Grocke, D. and Wigram, T. (2007). *Receptive Methods In Music Therapy: Techniques and Clinical Applications for Music Therapy Clinicians, Educators and Students*. London: Jessica Kingsley Publishers.

Haggar, F., Preen, D., Pereira, G., Holman, C., and Einarsdottir, K. (2012). Cancer incidence and mortality trends in Australian adolescents and young adults, 1982–2007. *BMC Cancer* 12(151).

Hilliard, R.E. (2006). Music therapy in pediatric oncology: A review of the literature. *Journal of the Society for Integrative Oncology* 4(2): 75–78.

Horne-Thompson, A., Daveson, B., and Hogan, B. (2007). A project investigating music therapy referral trends within palliative care: An Australian perspective. *Journal of Music Therapy* 44(2): 139–155.

Howard, S.C., Metzger, M.L., Wilimas, J.A., Quintana, Y., Pui, C.-H., Robison, L.L. et al. (2008). Childhood cancer epidemiology in low-income countries. *Cancer* 112(3): 461–472.

Kain, Z.N., Caldwell-Andrews, A.A., Krivutza, D.M., Weinberg, M.E., Gaal, D., Wang, S. et al. (2004). Interactive music therapy as a treatment for preoperative anxiety in children: a randomized controlled trial. *Anesthesia and Analgesia* 98: 1260–1266.

Kazak, A. E., Kassam-Adams, N., Schneider, S., Zelikovsky, N., Alderfer, M. A., and Rourke, M. (2006). An integrative model of pediatric medical traumatic stress. *Journal of Pediatric Psychology* 31(4): 343–355.

Kazak, A. E., Rourke, M. T., Alderfer, M. A., Pai, A., Reilly, A. F., and Meadows, A. T. (2007). Evidence-based assessment, intervention and psychosocial care in pediatric oncology: A blueprint for comprehensive services across treatment. *Journal of Pediatric Psychology* 32(9): 1099–1110.

McCarthy, M.C., Ashley, D.M., Lee, K.J., and Anderson, V.A. (2012). Predictors of acute and posttraumatic stress symptoms in parents following their child's cancer diagnosis. *Journal of Traumatic Stress* 25: 1–9.

McFerran, K. (2010). *Adolescents, Music and Music Therapy: Methods and Techniques for Clinicians, Educators and Students*. London: Jessica Kingsley Publishers.

Mitchell, A., Scarcella, D., Rigutto, G., Thursfield, V., Giles, G., Sexton, M. et al. (2004). Cancer in adolescents and young adults: Treatment and outcome in Victoria. *Medical Journal of Australia* 180: 59–62.

Momber, S. (2010). Childhood cancer in Australia. *The Australian Journal of Cancer Nursing* 11(2): 12–15.

Nguyen, T.N., Nilsson, S., Hellström, A.-L., and Bengtson, A. (2010). Music therapy to reduce pain and anxiety in children with cancer undergoing lumbar puncture: A randomized clinical trial. *Journal of Pediatric Oncology Nursing* 27(3): 146–155.

Noll, R.B. and Kazak, A.E. (2004). Psychosocial care. In: A.J. Altman (ed.), *Supportive Care of Children with Cancer: Current Therapy and Guidelines from the Children's Oncology Group*, 3rd edn., pp. 337–353. Baltimore: Johns Hopkins University Press.

O'Callaghan, C. (2005). Song writing in threatened lives. In: C. Dileo and J. Loewy (eds), *Music Therapy at the End of Life*, pp. 117–127. Cherry Hill, NJ: Jeffrey Press.

O'Callaghan, C. and Barry, P. (2009). Music therapists' practice-based research in cancer and palliative care: Creative methods and situated findings. *Voices: A World Forum for Music Therapy* 9(3). https://voices.no/index.php/voices/article/viewArticle/53

O'Callaghan, C., Sexton, M., and Wheeler, G. (2007). Music therapy as a non-pharmacological anxiolytic for paediatric radiotherapy patients. *Australasian Radiology* 51: 159–162.

O'Callaghan, C., Baron, A., Barry, P., and Dun, B. (2011). Music's relevance for pediatric cancer patients: a constructivist and mosaic research approach. *Supportive Care in Cancer* 19(6): 779–788.

O'Callaghan, C., Barry, P., and Thompson, K. (2012). Music's relevance for adolescents and young adults with cancer: a constructivist research approach. *Supportive Care in Cancer* 20: 687–697.

O'Callaghan, C., Dun, B., Baron, A., and Barry, P. (2013). Music's relevance for children with cancer: Music therapists' qualitative clinical data-mining research. *Social Work in Health Care* 52: 1–19.

Palmer, S., Mitchell, A., Thompson, K., and Sexton, M. (2007). Unmet needs among adolescent cancer patients: a pilot study. *Palliative and Supportive Care* 5(2): 127–134.

Pfaff, V.K., Smith, K.E., and Gowan, D. (1989). The effects of music-assisted relaxation on the distress of pediatric cancer patients undergoing bone marrow aspirations. *Child Health Care* 18: 232–236.

PICS (2007). *Art, Music and Play Therapy: A Service Model for the Future*. Melbourne: Pediatric Integrative Cancer Service.

Robb, S.L. (2003). Designing music therapy interventions for hospitalised children and adolescents using a contextual support model of music therapy. *Music Therapy Perspectives* 21: 27–39.

Robb, S.L. (2012). Gratitude for a complex profession: The importance of theory-based research in music therapy. *Journal of Music Therapy* 49(1): 2–6.

Robb, S.L., and Ebberts, A.G. (2003). Songwriting and digital video production interventions for pediatric patients undergoing bone marrow transplantation, Part I: An analysis of depression and anxiety levels according to phase of treatment. *Journal of Pediatric Oncology Nursing* 20(1): 2–15.

Robb, S. L., Clair, A. A., Watanabe, M., Monahan, P. O., Azzouz, F., Stouffer, J. W., ... and Hannan, A. (2008). Randomized controlled trial of the active music engagement (AME) intervention on children with cancer. *Psycho-Oncology*, 17(7): 699–708.

Robb, S.L., Burns, D.S., Stegenga, K.A., Haut, P.R., Monahan, P.O., Meza, J. et al. (2014), Randomized clinical trial of therapeutic music video intervention for resilience outcomes in adolescents/young adults undergoing hematopoietic stem cell transplant: A report from the Children's Oncology Group. *Cancer* 120(6): 909–917.

Seewald, L., Taub, J., Maloney, K., and McCabe, E. (2012). Acute leukemias in children with Down syndrome. *Molecular Genetics And Metabolism* 107(1/2): 25–30.

Simone, J.V., Weiner, S.L., & Hewitt, M. (eds). (2003). *Childhood Cancer Survivorship: Improving Care and Quality of Life*. National Academies Press.

Standley, J.M. and Hanser, S.B. (1995). Music therapy research and applications in pediatric oncology treatment. *Journal of Pediatric Oncology Nursing* 12(1): 3–8.

Thomas, D. (2007). Adolescents and young adults with cancer: The challenge. *Palliative and Supportive Care* 5: 173–174.

Thomas, D., Seymour, J., O'Brien, T., Sawyer, S., and Ashley, D. (2006). Adolescent and young adult cancer: a revolution in evolution? *Internal Medicine Journal* 36: 302–307.

Tomlinson, D. and Kline, N.E. (eds). (2010). *Pediatric Oncology Nursing: Advanced Clinical Handbook*, 2nd edn, Heildelberg: Springer.

Wigram, T. (2004). *Improvisation: Methods and Techniques for Music Therapy Clinicians, Educators and Students*. London: Jessica Kingsley Publishers.

Willis, D. and Barry, P. (2010). Audiovisual Interventions to Reduce the Use of General Anaesthesia with Paediatric Patients during Radiation Therapy. *Journal of Medical Imaging and Radiation Oncology* 54: 249–255.

Youlden, D.R., Baade, P., Valery, P., Ward, L., Green, A., and Aitken, J. (2012). Childhood cancer mortality in Australia. *Cancer Epidemiology* 36: 476–480.

CHAPTER 5

MUSIC THERAPY WITH ADOLESCENTS IN MEDICAL SETTINGS

JOHN MONDANARO AND JOANNE LOEWY

Introduction

DURING adolescence, growth changes across biophysical, cognitive, and psychosocial domains accelerate to a pace that challenge not only the adolescent, but in many circumstances the adolescent's care givers as well. The seemingly sudden shifts that occur in adolescence can seem tumultuous. This notable time has been reflected upon both philosophically and scientifically, but perhaps it is the poets who best capture the unbridled spirit in opposition with convention that defines this period. In the words of the English Romantic poet, John Keats (1795–1821), " … there is a space of life … in which the soul is in a ferment, the character undecided, the way of life uncertain, the ambition thick-sighted". Indeed the adolescent period resounds with a myriad of challenges typically confronting teenagers. This can be particularly confounded when this stage of development is interrupted by illness, injury, and ensuing hospitalizations.

The complexity of changes being reconciled and negotiated by the optimally developing adolescent provides a context for understanding the impact of hospitalization due to both traumatic circumstances, and acute or chronic diagnoses. Understanding the challenges associated with the domains of biophysical, cognitive, and psychosocial development provides a necessary context for understanding music therapy not only as a non-pharmacological treatment option for physical symptoms of pain but also as an accessible and potent means of psychotherapy to address associated anxiety.

THE ADOLESCENT IN HEALTH AND DISEASE

The changes occurring during puberty often mean that teenagers become more adult in size and appearance. As a result, some teens seem more mature than their actual cognitive capacity. The body's growth spurt expressed in physical maturation exceeds the actual cognitive and physical realm of the teen's own perception of self. The rate of a child's cognitive development upon emerging through adolescence into adulthood challenges the capacity for not only decision-making strategies, but the application of comprehensible moral rationale as well. Egocentricity poses a distinct risk to the adolescent (Berger 1998), and particularly the adolescent living with illness. Without fully developed organizational skills, the adolescent may tend towards ideation of immortality or invincibility, creating a distorted sense of reality which in turn may give rise to life-threatening risk-taking behaviors (Suris et al. 2008b).

A developing child at the age of twelve or thirteen experiences increased hormone levels that render a host of physical changes. He or she is often burdened with additional stress when such changes disrupt normal constructs that have served important positioning within various social groups and amongst peers. Advancement into puberty, and the variation in rate at which this occurs can be problematic for some adolescents facing yet another possible cause of social isolation. Such separation from social desirability is further compounded when chronic illness is diagnosed (Alvin et al. 2003; Blum 1992; Boice 1998; Brown 1982; Compas et al. 2012; Gunther 1985; Hatherill 2007).

Living with a diagnosis of chronic illness is challenging, most particularly in adolescence. Epilepsy (Baker et al. 2005; Buchanan 1988; Cengel-Kultur et al. 2009; Gagliardi et al. 2011; Rossi et al. 1997; Viberg et al. 1987), diabetes (Wysocki and Greco 2006; Sperling 1994; Pelicand et al. 2012; Court et al. 2009), asthma (de Benedictis and Bush 2007; Henriksen 2009; Komatsu et al. 2009; Kurukulaaratchy et al. 2012; Merrick and Merrick 2005), Crohn's Disease (Whittington et al. 1977; Wengrower et al. 1997), sickle cell anemia (Begue and Castello-Herbreteau 2001; Midence et al. 1993), and a myriad of other chronic and acute diagnoses place many adolescents in a state of high vulnerability (Pittet et al. 2010). These, and other conditions may not be easily managed when cognitive development precludes full comprehension of the importance, indeed at times life sustaining necessity, for medical adherence (Taylor et al. 2008; Suris et al. 2004; Suris 2002). Further complicating the issues of adherence for some adolescents are multiple side-effects that can occur as a result of pharmacological intervention. Body-image consciousness, so crucial to social positioning at this time, can be sabotaged if weight gain resulting in obesity occurs (Nathan and Moran 2008; Gunther 1985; Domine et al. 2009; Baker et al. 2005). Additionally risk-taking behaviors such as substance abuse, smoking, (Tager 2008), and promiscuity (Suris and Parera 2005; Suris et al. 2008b), may be triggered by feelings of hopelessness.

The cognitive development of the child emerging through adolescence into adulthood, can challenge the capacity for application of a comprehensible rationale in decision-making. While some adolescents are beginning to think hypothetically, deductively, and theoretically, the prevalence of residual egocentricity poses a threat to agency and decision making (Berger 1998) for the adolescent living with illness. Consequently, the adolescent may exhibit a propensity for ideation of immortality or invincibility, which can give rise to risk-taking behaviors (Suris et al. 2008b), further reinforced by the notion that one is immune to the effects of illness. The impact on coping and adherence of this distorted thinking can place the chronically ill adolescent at risk of harm.

The psychosocial domain is perhaps most profoundly important to the adolescent because of the multiplicity of role definition and individuation toward the formation of identity (Orr et al. 1984). This process, impacted by parenting style and involvement, social and cultural norms, and economic status, collectively contribute to the adolescent's sense of self or lack thereof. This is further complicated by the emergence of a changing, or new, body type that one must accept even if contradictory to the adolescent's desire or expectations, and moreover to by what society has deemed desirable (Berger 1998). Here, peer support and acceptance is of paramount importance in the transition from teen to adult (Erikson 1975). However, this evolution may pose significant challenges and threats within the parental bond particularly when a teen becomes ill (Blankenburg et al. 2008; Anderson et al. 2009). The psychosocial well-being of the adolescent is determined ultimately by how the challenges described above are negotiated, especially within the context of the typical stressors experienced in, but not limited to, school, society, and family. The risks associated with the developmental interruption brought on by illness and hospitalization need to be navigated carefully.

MUSIC THERAPY FOR THE ADOLESCENT: FROM REFERRAL TO TREATMENT

Depending on the treatment context, music therapy referrals can be received from social workers, nurses, doctors, chaplains, child life, physical therapists, and family members. At Mount Sinai Beth Israel Hospital in New York City where the authors work, patients may also refer themselves to music therapy. Additionally, the music therapists are able to refer any patient within any of the Mount Sinai Healthcare System's many hospital sites. Therefore, therapists must be trained to inform medical team partners of not only *who* is seen and why, but furthermore why one patient has priority to be seen over another. To this end, referrals for music therapy as a form of psychotherapy result from the identification of existential themes for the patient such as isolation, separation, abandonment, betrayal, the many layers of loss, non-adherence, and family stress, while referrals focusing on physical symptoms such a pain, anxiety, dyspnea (labored breath), and tension may also occur (Loewy 2000, 2015).

The referral process within The Louis Armstrong Music Therapy Department of the Mount Sinai Health System in New York is a collaborative process that may be the result of initiation through music therapists' attendance at *Interdisciplinary Rounds*, which are meetings of all the team members who have responsibility for the person being discussed. At these meetings the music therapist is often an educator about the efficacy of music therapy by identifying to medical staff the potential referrals and explaining the rationale during the medical teams' discussion of a case. Referrals are also made directly to the department by informed staff via phone call or email, or via a referral form that is completed and placed in the unit mailbox available at most of the in-patient units. Upon referral, a patient is seen within 24 hours and an assessment is written and filed in the patient's chart.

Annual in-services which define and describe the criteria for referrals (Appendix 5.1) and weekly round discussions of clinical examples well-timed to meet the need, for instance, of an unserved aspect of care is critical to ensuring the flow of communication from therapist to doctor, nurse to social worker, family to patient, etc. This ultimately provides the optimal integrative care that can be offered. The Louis Armstrong music therapy team has a strong reputation for not only follow up on referrals, but the sensitivity and clinical acuity for the identification of patients at risk. Teenagers with chronic conditions frequently experience unique threats medically and psychosocially, and may therefore be referred to music therapy. In all treatment populations, it is critical to approach the patient within a family/society context, but when providing therapy with a teenager, further issues must be considered in order to provide care that is patient centered. Parents and care givers can be involved if deemed appropriate, but the first step is to check with the teenage patient to become aware of what his/her desires are; recognizing his or her voice as a powerful agent of treatment focus. This may be best achieved through a private assessment with the teen. If desired, a section of the assessment that is inclusive of the care giver or sibling can be undertaken, but only if and when desired by the teen. In best practice this would not be presented as a requirement to the teen, however, it may prove useful, if permitted, to the therapist, in order to assess roles, and authority/independence/dependence dynamics of the family system which offer cues for subsequent treatment decisions.

Music therapy as a treatment modality can occur at the bedside, treatment room, or public space such as a playroom or family room, and may include staff, family members, or peers. Peer support among hospitalized adolescents can offer a rich forum for emotional support and normalization within the parameters of illness and required treatment. Improvisation, (Mondanaro and Needleman 2011), songwriting, song development techniques such as Joanne Loewy's *Song Sensation* (Loewy 2002), Story Song (Rubin-Bosco 2002; Loewy and Stewart 2004), and freestyle songwriting facilitated within genres such as pop or hip-hop (Mondanaro 2013; Frisch-Hara 2012; Steele 2012) can provide desirable therapeutic entry points through which adolescents may be inclined to accept music therapy services, and by which music therapists choosing to work with this population can facilitate meaningful and purposeful therapeutic processes.

Treatment sessions that focus on identifying and reinforcing the sense of self that is in process of definition during adolescence, are most effective when the adolescent's right to choose and set the pace for integration is supported by the therapist. Accepting and validating the adolescent's preferred genre even if outside the therapist's realm of comfort can dignify the individual and facilitate active participation in the therapy process. Provisions for the treatment of physical symptoms and how they connect with stressors and trauma (Loewy et al. 2009) can be addressed directly with music therapy interventions, as in the treatment of teens in extreme pain (Loewy 1999), resulting from diseases such as sickle cell anemia, or in teens with asthma where music meditations and/or wind play can enhance lung volume capacity and enhance a relaxation response (Loewy 2012). One of the most common reasons for missed school days in adolescents is asthma exacerbation. Protocols for music therapy enhancing breath capacity can serve other areas of disease process as an initial de-stressor activity. The role of live music play and tonal intervallic synthesis (Loewy 2011) in deepening the breath and treating aspects of trauma should not be overlooked in treating teens with medical conditions (Loewy et al. 2008). The provision of aesthetic distance from the traumatic qualities of hospitalization might be indicated as well, and can be addressed, for instance, through Storysong (Rubin-Bosco 2002; Loewy and Stewart 2004); or through the introspective metaphoric mechanisms of Song Sensation (Loewy 2002); or within the free-associative and expressive qualities inherent to musical genres such as rap (Frisch-Hara 2012) and hip-hop (Steele 2012). Each of these interventions provide opportunities by which songwriting and expression at both the verbal and non-verbal levels can support the adolescent whose already turbulent life is further intensified during hospitalization. Examples of such procedures will be contextualized within diagnosis-specific case vignettes below.

CONFIDENTIALITY AND ETHICS

The laws generated around health care in the US allow a certain latitude to providers to support clinical experience and wisdom (Campbell and English 2011; Michaud et al. 2004). Still the decision to uphold confidentiality for the individual adolescent patient when prescribing life-protecting measures such as contraception can contrast greatly with other decisions, such as keeping their HIV status confidential. It is this latter point that marks the integration of psychotherapy and family-centered care that carefully balances the needs of the adolescent with the role of family, and society.

The clinician advocating for "alone time" must do so with sensitivity and intelligence, because in most hospital settings the patient's stay is temporary. Unless there is abuse in the household, the adolescent will leave the hospital to return to the usual routines of home and family. The therapist may be the one who is peripheral to the family structure, and what is in place at home will remain intact after discharge. Here it may become challenging for the therapist to negotiate the earned trust of the patient with the law. Mandatory reporting of child abuse, as well as legal and ethical requirements to report suicidal ideation with reasonable grounds for follow through (a detailed plan), and other direct threats to child safety may further complicate issues of confidentiality (Campbell and English 2011; Lothen-Kline et al. 2003; Suris et al. 2008a). The inclusion or exclusion of parents and other family members can ensue from astute assessment by the therapist as well as the interdisciplinary team, and may be indicated if there is a sense that the adolescent's comfort level with being authentic in the presence of family members is hindered. The decision to include others may also be influenced by other criteria such as circumstances where a parent is over-protective or abusive. The latter scenario is generally addressed through social work who may collaborate closely with music therapists with recognition of the importance of non-verbal process offered within a music experience.

Vital themes and issues can be undertaken with families and especially parents through the modeling of authenticity. The adolescent who is avoidant and uncomfortable with honesty may be engendering patterns of parental behavior encountered at home. The therapist's support of honesty within the family unit can be modeled and supported by assessing the value of honesty in the home. Generally most parents will provide space for therapy to occur, if the end result is greater authentic sharing with their teen. Parents who can practice honesty with their adolescent in terms of diagnosis, treatment, and other medical information will be establishing a level of authenticity that their adolescent will be more prone to practice with the parent in return as he or she moves through the changes of adolescence.

Modeled by the therapist both verbally and non-verbally, this level of authenticity can be reinforced through such music therapy methods as improvisation and songwriting (Mondanaro 2013). Through both of these musical techniques, the adolescent's expression and processing of themes can be given aesthetic form within the music. Songwriting (Mondanaro and Needleman 2011) can offer profound catharsis to the adolescent living with physical and emotional pain, as it places value upon the creative expression of the individual. The patient whose self-esteem has been shattered by the reality of illness and treatment can reignite the process of identity development so often interrupted by the onslaught of illness and the family's response to it (Loewy 2015).

DIAGNOSIS-SPECIFIC CASE VIGNETTES

A primary concern in the treatment of adolescents living with illness and the interruption in development caused by hospitalization is the psychosocial impact that is inevitable. Care givers are justifiably challenged to treat the individual rather than the illness (Taylor et al. 2008), yet research (Abraham et al. 1999; Boice 1998; Brown 1982; Compas et al. 2012) indicates that adherence with treatment is more promisingly ensured when psychoeducational measures and clear communication about illness, treatment outcomes, and the importance of adherence are all a part of an active dialogue. Thus the importance of psychotherapeutic support in both individual and group is strongly indicated. Music therapy (Diephouse 1968; Magee et al. 2011; Tervo 2001; Avers et al. 2007), as an adjunct to medical treatment provides an important forum for such themes as universality and altruism to emerge and for the important developmental work of adolescence to be supported (Berger 1998). Songwriting can be particularly useful as a means of psychotherapy, where the adolescent's expression and processing of meaningful life themes can be given aesthetic form within the music. Songwriting (Mondanaro and Needleman 2011) can offer profound catharsis to the adolescent living with physical and emotional pain, as it places value upon the creative expression of the individual. Song Sensation (Loewy 2002) may provide a safe means in a group context for the teen in turmoil to align his/her inner fear with a viable symbol in the outside world—a favorite song that perhaps is related to significant history, culture, or referentially, another moment in time.

Erikson's classification of adolescence as a time in which one must achieve a sense of identity in occupation, gender roles, politics, and religion (Loewy 2015; Erikson 1975) is important, particularly as we think about the role that music might have for a teen at risk of illness. Understanding the teen's interest, whether it is pizza, cars, math, make-up, sleep, sports, or skateboarding, can provide a context for the therapeutic relationship to begin. As sexuality expressed through gender role is so prominently emerging, the therapist's assignment of role unconsciously or directly by the teen, may be well understood as a transference that emerges naturally through a musical play relationship. Such adherence to assignment might uncover aspects of inter-relatedness whereby the teen will grow to trust or take on authority leading toward his/her own empowerment outside of the music relationship as well. The therapist may represent a mother, father, or authority figure; a peer or even an alter ego, where the teen may see the therapist as an extension of him or her self. Each of these transferences are optimal and all have potential as healing processes in the therapy.

Discussion about politics and religion might stem from the beliefs within the teen's home or community. Resistance to such authorities may reveal the sources of anger or frustration tolerance that the teen is facing at that moment in time. Music can capture each of the integral essences Erikson suggests we consider in adolescent work, and does so without confrontation and at times with no words at all, but mere sound, play, solo, duet, ensemble where the musical experiences involve both playing and listening in the moment of exchange, or as a moment of silence, or resistance to play (Erikson 1975).

The following case examples illustrate the efficacy of music therapy across a myriad of diagnoses and contexts. These examples are not meant to be seen as "how to's" or "exemplars," per se, but more as possibilities that might be the result of a music psychotherapy assessment, inspired by a particular adolescent or group of adolescents creative expression, accessed during the music therapy evaluation. As music psychotherapists, we make no assumptions and carry no recipes for "no-fail" activities. Rather, through our combined decades of clinical experience with adolescents, we have memories and actual case histories of individuals and groups where music psychotherapy has served unique aspects of adolescent function where other approaches and therapies may have limited or failed the adolescent patient. We are thrilled to be able to share these clinical options and hope they will be viewed within a psychotherapeutic construct, rather than as "activities" to simply be reused by others. And yet, the activities presented have provided flow of access to the lifeworld of the teens because they are process-oriented. We firmly believe that music psychotherapy warrants an assessment (Appendix 5.2) that takes into account the diagnosis (and/or previous diagnoses and past hospitalizations), personal preferences, idiosyncrasies, culture, and family context of each individual adolescent patient assessed in music psychotherapy.

Automobile accidents

According to National Center for Injury Prevention and Control (Faul et al. 2010), car accidents are the leading cause of death among teens This is due to the combination and independent occurrence of the following three variables: Speeding, drinking and driving, and/or a lack of seat belt use. Any in-hospital music therapist with experience will have treated a multitude of teenagers who were drivers or passengers in a car accident and who as a result are in coma with TBI (traumatic brain injury), or at the other more fortunate end of the spectrum, may have broken ribs or limbs, or perhaps a concussion or broken jaw or teeth.

Whether mild or severe, the automobile accident and the music therapy referral as a result of a teen car accident will have layers of treatment aspect potentials and the experienced therapist must first ascertain which level to come into and this is based upon the referral directly, or taken from attending rounds and learning about the level of physical and psychological input of nurses and doctors who have information on admitting, the trauma itself and the physical/cognitive impact. A music psychotherapist will often likely be working with aspects of each of these areas. The level of impact will vary and the music therapist must be open to the possibilities that present themselves upon assessment. For instance, whereas the referral for a patient in coma with likely TBI and uncertain outcome as far as brain function capacity, the music therapist may have received a referral from an MD for "stimulation"—at rounds the team might ask for the MT to find the teen's favorite melody and to see if this might illicit neural pathway function.

Upon arrival at the bedside, the MT may find the father of the teen, who is weeping and who presents as having guilt for being on a business trip when the teen used his car on graduation weekend. Suddenly, music psychotherapy is beginning with the father ... this was unexpected and social work had not yet met the father. However, in the meeting with the patient's father, and having the opportunity to help him sort out feelings, and to privately release his shame and guilt in the context of music therapy and in the presence of a therapist who can hold and comfort and then work with the issues, perhaps even involving the father in the music stimulation—through singing a song from the teen's youth, might be well indicated. This is one example of thousands, where MT is recommended in one way, and the recovery process is achieved through another way—within a family context, or for a family member, rather than directly with the patient referred, or under the circumstance that the team referral was offered.

Traumatic brain injury (TBI)

TBI is often the result of a potentially fatal accident. It may be mild or severe. It can be "closed," which involves a blow to the head, such as a fall or car accident or "penetrating"— where an object enters the skull. "Closed" TBI affects thinking and memory, or feeling and sensation. Thirty-two percent of all TBI cases that result from traffic injuries and motor vehicle crashes end in death. Almost half of all the cases hospitalized for TBI after a year have a related disability. At any level of diagnosis, great care must be taken for if and how music therapy can be offered (Faul et al. 2010).

Case example

Neurologic music therapy (NMT) developed by Michael Thaut (Thaut 2005; Thaut et al. 1999; Thaut et al. 2001), most often involves the use of music in the recovery of movement and in the context of cognitive function. The human ability to perceive and engage in music, even when the central nervous system has been compromised, renders music therapy as a viable integrative treatment. Thaut's work speaks to the tremendous possibilities for neuro-rehabilitation through the use of music therapy to improve gait training, speech retrieval, and spatial orientation. For the adolescent patient, the promise of reconnection to any of these primary areas of functioning can provide the impetus for greater motivation and participation.

In any accident but in particular where there is human error involved, there are layers to the associated impact. It is critical for the teen and/or family to have a safe place to sort out the feelings associated with the accident, particularly because the unresolved and expressed guilt can harbor resentment and guilt which are hot beds for the triggering of anxiety and will contribute in negative ways to the festering of "tension holding." This can foster pain and put a hold on healing. The effects can be subtle. A teenager who has been the driver of a car full of teens with others who die or are injured, for instance, will need a space to release tears and a place to put him/herself back together.

Music provides non-confrontational means for addressing any or all of the feelings a teen might be having. Simply playing music with another can provide a visceral experience of release and support. Clinical music improvisatory experiences such as drumming may relieve tension in teens who have anger, particularly if the music therapist can use African rhythms marked to build and release. Release drum rolls where toning is invited can offer an emotion–personal sound connected expression–confession without words. This experience might then lead to some rap, which may give the teen a means of contextualizing and reconstructing as described by Gestalt music therapist Frank Bosco (Loewy 2002). Rapping about an experience makes for a way to have intention be expressed. Rap is in between a poem, speaking, and song, and has elements of each.

It is helpful for the music therapist to have training in trauma, particularly to understand what kind of trauma is being endured, and at what level emotionally and physically the trauma is being endured by the teen him/herself and within the family and the teen's social community. It is therefore recommended that the music therapist who works with a teen, particularly a teen involved in a traumatic accident, has had significant training in trauma. This is not necessarily the kind of therapy an entry-level therapist should be undertaking.

Depression

Depression is the most common mental health disorder in the US among teens and adults. It affects teens of both sexes, though occurs more frequently in girls than in boys. Twenty percent of all teens are prone to experience depressed episodes before reaching their adult years <http://www.teenhelp.com/teen-depression/depression-statistics.html>.

Dysthymia, is the descriptor used by the American Psychiatric Association's DSM V (2013) for defining the symptoms of depression. Its effects are generally long-lasting, affecting nearly two percent of teens, many of whom will face a bipolar disorder by age eighteen. SAD (seasonal affective disorder) may be part of teen depression and develops most often during the winter months. Teen depression can affect an adolescent regardless of gender, income level of the teen's family, and its onset can occur regardless of what the teen has achieved. Teenaged girls may have onset of depression that is triggered by a perceived loss of friend ties. Girls are more likely to seek help for their depression than are their boy teen counterparts. Onset for these episodes might include:

- Previous episodes of depression.
- Experiencing trauma, abuse, or a long-term illness or disability.
- A family history of depression; between 20 to 50 percent of teens who suffer from depression have a family member with depression or other mental disorders.
- Other untreated problems; about two-thirds of teens with major depression also suffer from another mental disorder, such drug addictions and/or alcohol consumption antisocial behaviors.

Teens with depression often report spending time alone and may alienate themselves from participating in extra-curricular activity and partaking in opportunities that might lead toward the building of a career. They may take sexual risks or try to commit suicide—the third leading cause of death among teenagers. Ninety percent of suicide victims suffer from a mental illness, and suffering from depression can make a teenager as much as twelve times more likely to attempt suicide. Unfortunately, less than 33 percent of teens with depression get help yet 80 percent of teens with depression can be successfully treated <http://www.teenhelp.com/teen-depression/depression-statistics.html>.

Eating disorders

Adolescent eating disorders are quite common in males and females, particularly in American and Hispanic populations. According to the DSM III (R) (American Psychiatric Association 2000), 0.3 percent of youth have been affected by anorexia, 0.9 percent by bulimia, and 1.6 percent by binge-eating disorder.

Research has also tracked the rate of some forms of eating disorders not otherwise specified (ED-NOS), which is a general term signifying symptoms grouped together in a non-specific way, that do not meet full criteria for specific disorders but nevertheless can have a grave influence in a teenager's functional daily living. ED-NOS is the attributed to the most frequent of eating disorder diagnoses with 0.8 percent having "subthreshold anorexia" (Caucasions have highest anorexia), and 2.5 percent showing symptoms of "subthreshold binge-eating disorder" (Hispanics show highest bulimia).

The prevalence of these disorders and their association with coexisting disorders, role impairment, and suicidal thinking suggest that eating disorders represent a major public health concern. In addition, the significant rates of subthreshold eating conditions support the notion that eating disorders tend to exist along a spectrum and may be better recognized by doctors if they included a broader range of symptoms. In addition, the findings clearly underscore the need for better access to treatment specifically for eating disorders (Swanson et al. 2011)." As eating disorders are so frequent among teens and can be associated with some aspect of comorbid depression and/or suicide, the following group case will meld the two together.

Case example: Group-Song Sensation

In an out-patient clinic where teens are treated for depression, particularly post-hospitalization, a song sharing may be a non-confrontational way for group members to share their problems, feelings, or issues with one another.

A group of five fifteen to seventeen-year-old female teens gathered for music psychotherapy on a weekly basis. Most often they had been drawn to the drums and for the most part after sporadic attendance through the summer months, attendance and commitment to the group was notably growing. Sarah, the group's eldest member of seventeen years came into the group for a recent session mentioning a song she could "not get out of her (sic) head."

Rather than simply listen to the song, or play it all together, I made a decision to inquire about a "Song Sensation" (Loewy 2002) experience to see if the group would be interested. I explained that we would be using the song in therapy, and as part of the therapy. I asked if we could table it until next week so that I could prepare for it … and find a recording of it for us to use. Sarah agreed and relayed to me her preferred rendition of the song. It was critical that in seeking out the song for my learning and preparation, that I would find the exact arrangement and recording that Sarah was familiar with. She named the song by Demi Lavato: "Unbroken."

I prepared with the lyrics and music for the song looking carefully at the lyrics, considering how they might be applicable to Sarah's life from what little I knew of her history and her recent hospitalization.

First, I learned that the singer who composed and sang this song, Demi Lavato, had wrestled with her own bout of bulimia. My patient, Sarah, had struggled with anorexia on and off since she was ten years old. Identification with the singer, was indeed something to consider, and how Sarah reported her love of Ms Lavato's voice and singing was significant, though she did not communicate that she herself had had an eating disorder, she did disclose to the group what the lyrics meant to her during the citation and feedback stage of the "Song Sensitation" experiential.

The lyrics that another quieter member of the group had felt were significant to some of this member's own issues were:

> "Locked up tight. Like I would never feel again. Stuck in some kind of love prison. And threw away the key. Ooh ooh, terrified."

This younger member shared feelings about her own older sister being better at everything than she was, and wondered through verbal inquiry if Sarah had ever felt "less than" … a third member brought up another song she stated was by a singer named Pink entitled "Less than Perfect" and the group discussed, each in their own way, the pressures incurred by family and friends to be more than what each of them could bear.

Sarah then discussed feelings of self-hate and disclosed to the group her own self cutting … The intimacy born through the symbolized shared song led to each members' self-reflection. In the final step of the Song Sensation experience, Sarah assigned musical support to the song, which she chose to sing with a chime recitative and a very slow, hard rock feel. The group recorded the song—which unconsciously in some ways and directly at other moments disclosed extremely fragile information about each member. They bonded in sharing other favorite songs, which led to further disclosing, self-expression and self-reflection in the safe space of what was created through the favorite tunes and Song Sensation experience.

HIV

Teen girls and minorities have been particularly affected by HIV. In recent years, the national average of reported cases has diminished with better available treatments and adherence with prevention strategies has increased. Even so, in 2006, teen girls represented 39 percent of AIDS cases reported among 13–19 year olds. Black teens represented 69 percent of cases reported among 13–19 year olds; Latino teens represented 19 percent (Center for AIDS Research, 2012). The disease, first identified in the early 1980s, still carries much of the same stigma generated at its onset, and this point, driven by ignorance, contributes to the conspiracy of silence sustained by those infected. Compounded by the adolescent's principal quest for identity and acceptance, HIV status often contributes to painful isolation, that can, at times, be ameliorated through a range of music therapy methods (Mondanaro and Vaskas 2013).

Case example

John's recent hospitalization caught him and his medical team by surprise. Since the death of his mother seven years prior and the disappearance of his father, at birth, John had managed exceedingly well. Vice President of his student government and second lead trumpeter in the jazz band with a 3.6 average were among a few of the activities that characterized John as a leader among his community of family and peers. Three weeks before his college of choice interview, at seventeen years old, John contracted pneumonia and had not wanted visitors during his long hospital stay. His uncle was the only visitor John had willingly accepted into his hospital room. Contracting HIV through transmission from his mother, John had been fortunate to have very few hospitalizations in his lifetime and was considered to have no evidence of disease since his last course of treatment five years prior.

Suddenly, his breathing was labored and his platelets were at a recorded low. As John did not want psyche or counseling, the music therapist made careful entry into his room and, surprisingly, after his second week of isolation John accepted. He chose not to play any of the wind instruments, but pointed to an African d'jembe drum. The male music therapy intern, about six years his elder laid down a basic beat and soon the two young men were drumming. The drumming ensued for approximately 30 minutes non-stop. There were rolls, repartes, and different beat patterns explored. Each time the music therapy intern sought to bring the music down to a softer cadence would be just the moment that John would add a new kind of rhythm: merengue, tango, funk, and finally full physical release. There were no reports from weekly clinic notes from seven years prior or in any of his follow up out-patient appointments that relayed any discussion or grief expressions. John did attend his mother's funeral, but had not reportedly dealt with the tension and anger of his own contracting of HIV. John's role in growing up was one of keeping compliant and staying healthy—and he did this exceedingly well. In becoming very ill, so unexpectedly, years of unexpressed anger and unresolved sadness seemed to find a place in the voice of physical release through drumming. When the drumming finally ended, as the music therapy intern caught his breath, John expressed two words after several moments of silence: "wow ... thanks!"

Pelvic inflammatory disease

It is estimated that more than 750,000 women in America have an episode of acute PID and as many as 15 percent of these women may become infertile when PID goes untreated. A large proportion of the ectopic pregnancies occurring every year are due to the consequences of PID (Westrom and Eschenbach 1999).

Case example

Jessica selected the marimba and did not want to talk. She only wanted to play. She came from a woman's shelter where she lived with her mother and baby sister. In the assessment she shared the song "Hero" when her i-pod was mounted in the i-pod compound. After we listened, she asked if I could play the song and I nodded. Slowly, I began to play it after she had selected the piano as her desired accompaniment. "You sing" she said. As I sang the words, I thought to myself how the text reflected the tendency to assign power to someone else: "Then a hero comes along, with the strength to carry on ... and you cast your fears aside and you know you will survive..."

I made a long mid-section, where Jessica could create her own melodies, without depending on my singing. Risk, strength, and improvisation: Teens cannot have enough experiences of healthy risk with frames of musical support that provide the canvas for safe expression. Additionally, we forget at times, that singing to and for teens might be quite nurturing and a way to hold and support. Jessica loved my singing. She would curl up under her blankets. I knew that singing for Jessica was the right activity. Her mother, a mere fifteen years her senior, was often caring for her younger sister. She was often reportedly on the street selling drugs. Jessica herself was in and out of school and trying to become an "emancipated minor" and was seen by the shelter as a child prostitute. She had had numerous sexual partners, not sure of how, who, or when her last time was, according to the chart. I was certain singing was the right thing to do, particularly because Jessica had asked this of me. In many future sessions as I would sing songs she selected, always relating to love and/or abandonment, she would fall into a deep sleep reflecting the safety of musical nurturance that was provided.

Suicide

Suicide is the leading cause of death among teens. Suicide classification is generally comprised of two categories: Attemptors and completors. Three times as many men succeed compared with women, but more women make attempts. Suicide is often the result of depression or unresolved guilt.

Individual session

There are no recommended common activities for teens who have tried to take their own lives. The one rule of thumb is to show up. No matter how many times rejection has occurred, the offering of another session is a must. And then, after the tenth offering, when the teen finally lets you in the door, you face the silence. It may be a prolonged, pregnant pause. Silence is part of teen music, and so is control. Give the control of the session over to them. Use short sentences that say what might happen if they would like it to … or not. "I can play for you…" "We can listen to something you would like to hear…" "what are you thinking about today and how can I help?…" It can be amazing what evolves when we have no agenda but to support, serve and anchor the patient through music.

Crohn's disease

Crohn's disease (Whittington et al. 1977; Wengrower et al. 1997) is a gastrointestinal disease which impacts the development of adolescents in a most debilitating way. The visibility of symptoms and infringement upon healthy social development has a critical impact in the teen years. Symptoms impacting psychosocial life include dietary limitation, abdominal pain, and frequent restroom visits, which for teenagers at the height of body awareness can be demoralizing. Feelings of isolation are common amongst teenagers living with the disease, and thus the importance of support groups focusing on normalization through social contact and expression. One such group focused on the provision of a separate support group for parents, which brought emphasis to the unique emotional needs of not only the adolescents living with Crohn's but their care givers as well.

Case example: Crohn's support group

A music therapy group developed over a three-year period and included a core group of four regularly attending teenage girls and an extended contingent of more sporadic attendees.

The group members were most receptive to improvisational exercises that allowed them to transcend the degree of illness they shared, and to experience themselves as alert vital human beings. The therapist introduced several constructs that facilitated creative expression including a type of musical charades which became a group favorite. The members would identify various emotions they felt, and then non-verbally recreate the emotional quality of a given piece on various instruments. The re-enactment could be heard and seen by the other members.

A second interaction was based on an improvisational game called "Home and Traveler," which involved the group members formation of a circle and home base in the form of a commonly held drum beat. Individually each member would move to the center of the circle to improvise on another instrument, in a counter melody or rhythm. This free expression would develop and contrast with the held rhythm, and extend until the improviser wished to join the home beat. As each member moved to the center of the circle to improvise against the home beat, a sense of elation would fill the room as each teenager felt the strength to be an individual. The visible effects of this intervention on the self-esteem of the members were meaningful enough that they elected to call the game "Dare to Be Different."

Adolescent grief

By adolescence, the developmental understanding of death is emerging as a reconciliation of one's own mortality (Mondanaro 2005). Acceptance that death happens to everyone is no more comforting however, and often sits in juxtaposition to the previously referenced propensity toward thoughts of invincibility common to adolescence. The universality of the experience is central to the grief process and group work in music therapy is a natural therapeutic entry point.

Grief support group

A support group for teenage siblings of Sudden Infant Death Syndrome (SIDS) and Sudden Unexpected Death Syndrome (SUDS), organized annually through a regional organization, specifically targeted the use of creative arts therapies to support expression and process. Music therapy offered a forum that not only connected to a vital emotional outlet for the age group, but offered creative opportunity to express feelings that are not easily accessed otherwise.

A form of free-associative songwriting that drew upon hip-hop and rap structures (Frisch-Hara 2012; Steele 2012) provided rich forum for the adolescents to reflect, verbally share, and bear witness to the experience of growing up in a family where loss was a familiar experience. Each member had a unique experience that warranted being told, and the creation of a song form that included space for both verbal and non-verbal process proved rich. The choice of instruments and sounds (including body percussion and vocal sound effects, known as beat-boxing) was maintained as that of the members, with the therapist providing occasional guidance as to structure and arrangement. What emerged was a piece of music that would cycle through a harmonic structure with richly added layers of sounds until stopping at the cadence to render a space for silence. The silence was established for either quiet reflection on a spoken name or a shared memory of the deceased sibling. Following, the music would resume the repeated cycle until the next cadence and break, with the piece continuing as long as necessary to allow each member to take a space.

The familiarity and safety of music in this form provided the dichotomy of structure and looseness that allowed the adolescents to connect authentically to the loss that they too had been living not only as a family member but as an individual.

Epilepsy

The diagnosis of epilepsy begins with varying degrees of diagnostic testing for seizure activity, ranging from ambulatory electroencephalogram (EEG) to 24-hour video-electroencephalogram (VEEG). Relatively simple, these versions of the EEG pose pronounced interruption to the developmental trajectory of adolescence. When diagnosed, epilepsy is generally treated pharmacologically or through various other interventions singularly or simultaneously, such as a special dietary monitoring known as the ketogenic diet or the surgical placement of a vagus nerve stimulator. Additionally, surgical intervention can be an option for a relatively small number of patients presenting with focal seizures.

A range of necessary treatments can visibly impact the psychosocial well-being of the adolescent because of the potential side-effects that can occur (Baker et al. 2005; Buchanan 1988; Cengel-Kultur et al. 2009). The physical presentation of any given seizure type as well as the side-effects of many anti-epileptic drugs (AEDs), which can include weight gain, lethargy, and a range of mood disorder s including depression can place the vulnerable teen in greater danger of social isolation or bullying. Additionally concerning is that successful seizure management can render the diagnosis invisible, which can perpetuate a conspiracy of silence among families believing that such stigmatization will hinder their child's social functioning. To the adolescent who enjoys the feelings of normalcy under effective pharmacologic management, there may exist the issue of non-adherence, which can be life threatening when the brain is neurochemically dependant upon psychotropic drugs.

The clearest psychosocial support given the myriad of clinical outcomes and stressors, is psychotherapeutic support with strong psychoeducational intervention to ensure openness and understanding (Mondanaro 2008). This support is strongest when originating within the family, and has even greater impact when established among peers. Music therapy offers a range of therapeutic possibilities (Mondanaro 2013). Procedural support, psychoeduction, and psychotherapeutic support on an individual basis may be offered during diagnostic testing, and continue through treatment, and even when surgical intervention is indicated.

Individual case: JME

The importance of psychotherapeutic support (Mondanaro and Needleman 2011) at all junctures of treatment is reflected in the following case of a sixteen-year-old male diagnosed with Juvenile Myoclonic Epilepsy (JME) at the age of thirteen. Music therapy as both a forum in which the patient could ask questions and express feelings pertaining to his developing understanding of his diagnosis, and as procedural support in the form of refocusing interventions during the placement of electrodes (leads) was offered during the initial stages of diagnostic testing. Frequent admissions to the epilepsy monitoring unit were necessary in order to eventually manage the patient's seizures, which resulted in numerous interruptions of routine and school activities. Individual psychotherapy involving both verbal and non-verbal intervention provided the patient with a solid foundation of understanding and confidence to educate his peers about what it would mean to "do the right thing" if they witnessed him having a seizure.

The patient eventually agreed to attend a music therapy support group (Rossi et al. 1997) for other adolescents living with JME and other types of epilepsy. The group offered an altruistic environment in which sharing occurred through such normal social constructs as listening to each members' favorite song or artist and discussing the significance of lyrics, as well as music improvisation on various emotional themes (abandonment, isolation, betrayal, and loss) listed as important by the group members. The provision of drums, chimes, guitars, keyboards, synthesizers, and miscellaneous world percussion allowed for richly expressive improvisations.

The strong support system that this young man was able to create in both his personal life through the support group and his public life with friends and school were easily integrated with honesty, understanding, and authenticity providing impetus.

End-stage renal disease

The treatment of ESRD is arduous and imposes profound interruption to structure and normalcy in the trajectory of adolescent development (Snethen et al. 2004; Aase 2010). Frequent blood analyses, dietary restriction, and immanently dialysis pose tremendous interruption to the normal tasks of adolescent development outlined earlier.

Individual case

The individual work done with a twelve-year-old boy living with end-stage renal disease (ESRD), spanned almost two years while he awaited a kidney transplant. Complicating this case was the reality of an impoverished family background, including an incarcerated father, as a perpetrator of physical abuse on the patient, his mother, and his older and younger siblings. Extreme financial stress and other adversity culminated in the separation of the family, as the children were placed in various facilities while the mother received assistance to reorganize her resources.

The music therapy relationship served as a forum in which to process themes of uncertainty, loss, isolation, treatment adherence, hygiene, and of course, separation. The latter was exacerbated by the transitions to and from the hospital that were inherent to the teen's dialysis schedule. The presence and consistency of music therapy sessions during dialysis provided opportunities for valuable reinforcement of the idea that while there was uncertainty as to the duration of his waiting for a transplant, the time and space was transitional and that his life would eventually move forward. Music therapy provided a structure through which the therapist supported the necessary developmental tasks of organization and maintenance of identity through an approach that dignified the boy's sense of pride and autonomy as a young man. Improvisation and songwriting focusing on the earlier identified themes as they ensued from the daily routines of the hospital and staff, provided the structure and continuity that were otherwise missing from this boy's life. Through the verbal and non-verbal processes of music therapy, resolution, and reconciliation became resources, which allowed this boy to effectively cope with months of waiting.

Diabetes

The diagnosis of diabetes during school age generally results in a child's solid foundational understanding of the disease and its treatment. This understanding is rudimentary to good management of the disease, due in part to early psychosocial intervention recognizing the importance of supporting a child's understanding of diabetes and its effects on the body. Patterns of adherence established early on have an optimal chance of continuing into adolescence when other obstacles, such as peer pressure, identity, and body image emerge.

The most common form of diabetes in childhood and adolescence is type 1, which results from the body's underproduction of insulin needed to metabolize sugar. Type 1 is detectable at its onset with several weeks of visible symptoms inclusive of fatigue, frequent thirst, hunger, hyperclycemia, weight loss, and renal difficulty to name a few. While type 1 is more prevalent in adolescence, type 2 diabetes, generally attributable to aging and obesity, is on the increase due to the rise of obesity in childhood and adolescence (Nathan and Moran 2008).

Psychosocial support service negotiating the balance of the adolescent's need for autonomy and individuation with appropriate parental involvement (Silverstein et al. 2005), may appropriately integrate music therapy in this endeavor due again to its clinical adaptability. That an adolescent should be solely responsible for management of the disease is a misconception given the combined challenges of dietary adherence, monitoring of insulin levels, and the normal trajectory of developmental tasks. Given the stress of managing the disease music therapy can offer a forum for peer support and normalization.

Psychosocial support groups

One particular group of teenagers participating in music therapy created a play in which each player, using an instrument of choice, personified an emotional state that was commonly felt among the group's members. Anger was matched with a bodhrán (Irish drum), embarrassment was played on a recorder, and determination played on a trumpet. This play provided aesthetic meaning about what it meant for the group to be living with diabetes. Creating music together provided a tolerable forum in which the members could be authentic in their feelings about diagnosis and the daily negotiation of checking blood level and insulin injections with an active teen lifestyle.

CONCLUSION

The course of adolescence can be arduous, and yet, under optimal circumstances, it may provide tremendous reward on multiple levels. No other age group seemingly elicits as much trepidation on the part of care givers as the teen years. Perhaps this is because under stress we are all prone to perpetrate adolescent behaviors to some small degree, for example, the way in which professional envy echoes sibling rivalry. For many care givers, the visible emotional duress of adolescent patients can reactivate unresolved issues originating in their own adolescence, and this truth does not rest comfortably within a medical paradigm where staff are expected to engender the qualities of authority and paternalism to be considered credible. The irony here is that while most adolescents experience turmoil in their search for their own identity and authenticity, they have an innate ability to recognize what isn't authentic, and in having this ability often show diminished tolerance when pretense is suspected. One need not be a rapper to access rap music, nor must one have all of the answers to the question about how to survive adolescence. One must simply be willing to be *in the moment* with adolescents whose primary task is to make sense of what is happening to them. The combined qualities of defensiveness, vulnerability, cynicism, and self-admonishment define the adolescent's world that care givers must infiltrate in order to extend care. Patience, respect, and nurturance from a respectable distance are the attributes of the care giver who comes to the adolescent world with a key to their heart; music.

References

Aase, S. (2010). Kidney friendly: what the National Kidney Disease Education Program strategic plan means for dietetic practice. *Journal of the American Dietetic Association* 110: 346–351.

Abraham, A., Silber, T.J., and Lyon, M. (1999). Psychosocial aspects of chronic illness in adolescence. *Indian Journal of Pediatrics* 66: 447–453.

Alvin, P., De Tournemire, R., Anjot, M.N., and Vuillemin, L. (2003). Chronic illness in adolescence: ten pertinent questions. *Archives de pédiatrie: organe officiel de la Société française de pédiatrie Société française de pédiatrie* 10: 360–366.

Anderson, B.J., Holmbeck, G., Iannotti, R.J., Mckay, S.V., Lochrie, A., Volkening, L. K., and Laffel, L. (2009). Dyadic measures of the parent-child relationship during the transition to adolescence and glycemic control in children with type 1 diabetes. *Families, Systems, & Health* 27: 141–152.

American Psychiatric Association (2013). *Diagnostic and statistical manual of mental disorders* (5th ed.). Washington D.C.: American Psychiatric Association.

Avers, L., Mathur, A., and Kamat, D. (2007). Music therapy in pediatrics. *Clinical Pediatrics* 46: 575–579.

Baker, G.A., Spector, S., McGrath, Y., and Soteriou, H. (2005). Impact of epilepsy in adolescence: a UK controlled study. *Epilepsy & Behavior* 6: 556–562.

Begue, P. and Castello-Herbreteau, B. (2001). Sickle cell disease: from childhood to adolescence. Management in 2001. *Bulletin de la Société de pathologie exotique* 94: 85–89.

Berger, K.S. (1998). *The Developing Person Through the Life Span*, 4th edn. New York: Worth Publishers.

Blankenburg, B., Kolch, M., and Mehler-Wex, C. (2008). A need for independent adolescence psychiatry and psychotherapy. *Psychiatrische Praxis* 35: 216–218.

Blum, R.W. (1992). Chronic illness and disability in adolescence. *Journal of Adolescent Health* 13: 364–368.

Boice, M.M. (1998). Chronic illness in adolescence. *Adolescence* 33: 927–939.

Brown, C.J. (1982). Hospital management of chronic illness in adolescence: a development model. *Journal of Chronic Diseases* 35: 659–667.

Buchanan, N. (1988). Social aspects of epilepsy in childhood and adolescence. *Australian Paediatric Journal* 24: 220–221.

Campbell, A.T. and English, A. (2011). Law, ethics, and clinical discretion: recurring and emerging issues in adolescent health care. *Adolescent Medicine: State of the Art Reviews* 22: 321–334, xi.

Cengel-Kultur, S.E., Ulay, H.T., and Erdag, G. (2009). Ways of coping with epilepsy and related factors in adolescence. *Turkish Journal of Pediatrics* 51: 238–247.

Center for AIDS Research, E.S. (2012). National HIV/AIDS Statistics. Sacramento, CA: The Center for AIDS Research, Education and Services.

Compas, B.E., Jaser, S.S., Dunn, M.J., and Rodriguez, E.M. (2012). Coping with chronic illness in childhood and adolescence. *Annual Review of Clinical Psychology* 8: 455–480.

Court, J.M., Cameron, F.J., Berg-Kelly, K., and Swift, P.G. (2009). Diabetes in adolescence. *Pediatric Diabetes* 10 Suppl 12: 185–194.

De Benedictis, D. and Bush, A. (2007). The challenge of asthma in adolescence. *Pediatric Pulmonology* 42: 683–692.

Diephouse, J.W. (1968). Music therapy: a valuable adjunct to psychotherapy with children. *Psychiatric Quarterly Supplement* 42 Pt 1: 75–85.

Domine, F., Berchtold, A., Akre, C., Michaud, P.A., and Suris, J.C. (2009). Disordered eating behaviors: what about boys? *Journal of Adolescent Health* 44: 111–117.

Erikson, E. (1975). *Life History and the Historical Moment*. New York: Norton.

Faul, M., Xu, L., Wald, M., and Coronado, V. (2010). Traumatic Brain Injury in the United States: Emergency department visits, hospitalizations, and deaths 2002–2006. Atlanta (GA): Centers for Disease Control and Prevention, National Center for Injury Prevention and Control.

Frisch-Hara, A. (2012). RAP (requisite, ally, protector) and the desperate contemporary adolescent. In: S. Hadley and G. Yancy (eds), *Therapeutic Uses of Rap and Hip-hop*. New York: Routledge Taylor & Francis Group.

Gagliardi, I. C., Guimaraes, C.A., Souza, E.A., Schmutzler, K.M., and Guerreiro, M.M. (2011). Quality of life and epilepsy surgery in childhood and adolescence. *Arquivos de Neuro-Psiquiatria* 69: 23–26.

Gunther, M.S. (1985). Acute-onset serious chronic organic illness in adolescence: some critical issues. *Adolescent Psychiatry* 12: 59–76.

Hatherill, S. (2007). Psychatric aspects of chronic physical illness in adolescents. *Continuing Medical Education* 25: 212–214.

Henriksen, J.M. (2009). Adolescence asthma and transition. *Clinical Respiratory Journal* 3: 67–68.

Komatsu, Y., Fujimoto, K., Yasuo, M., Urushihata, K., Hanaoka, M., Koizumi, T., and Kubo, K. (2009). Airway hyper-responsiveness in young adults with asthma that remitted either during or before adolescence. *Respirology* 14: 217–223.

Kurukulaaratchy, R. J., Raza, A., Scott, M., Williams, P., Ewart, S., Matthews, S. et al. (2012). Characterisation of asthma that develops during adolescence; findings from the Isle of Wight Birth Cohort. *Respiratory Medicine* 106: 329–337.

Loewy, J.V. (1999). Music psychotherapy assessment in pediatric pain. In: C. Dileo (ed.), *Applications of music in medicine vol. II: Theoretical and clinical perspectives,* pp. 189–206. Silver Spring, Maryland: AMTA.

Loewy, J. (1999). The quiet soldier: Pain and sickle-cell anemia. In J. Hibben (ed.), *Inside music therapy: Client experiences.* Gilsum, NH: Barcelona Publishers.

Loewy, J.V. (2000). Music psychotherapy assessment. *Music Therapy Perspectives,* 18(1): 47–58.

Loewy, J.V. (2002). Song Sensation: How fragile we are. In: J.V. Loewy and Frisch-Hara, A. (eds), *Caring for the Caregiver: The Use of Music and Music Therapy in Grief and Trauma.* Silver Spring, MD: AMTA.

Loewy, J. (2011). Tonal intervallic synthesis in medical music therapy. In: F. Baker and S. Ulig (eds), *Voicework in Music Therapy,* pp. 242–263. London: Jessica Kingsley Publishers.

Loewy, J. (2012). Manage your stress and pain through music. *Journal of Music Therapy* 49(4): 453–455.

Loewy, J. (2015). Medical music therapy for children. In B. Wheeler (ed.), *Music therapy handbook.* (pp. 425–440). ISBN9781462518036.

Loewy, J.V. and Stewart, K. (2004). Music therapy to help traumatized children and caregivers. In: N. B. Webb (ed.). *Mass trauma and violence: Helping families and children cope,* pp. 191–215. Guilford Press.

Loewy, J.V., Azoulay, R., Harris, B., and Rondina, E. (2008). Clinical improvisation with winds: Enhancing breath in music therapy. In: R. Azoulay and J.V. Loewy (eds), *Music, the Breath and Health: Advances in Integrative Music Therapy,* pp. 87–102. New York: Satchnote Press.

Loewy, J., Rubin-Bosco, J., Fleetwood, R., and Kabayashi, T. (2009). The impact of creative arts therapies on children who have experienced trauma. In: K. Stewart (ed.), *Bridging Theory and Clinical Practice,* pp. 59–87. NY: Satchnote Press.

Lothen-Kline, C., Howard, D.E., Hamburger, E.K., Worrell, K.D., and Boekeloo, B.O. (2003). Truth and consequences: ethics, confidentiality, and disclosure in adolescent longitudinal prevention research. *Journal of Adolescent Health* 33: 385–394.

Magee, W.L., Baker, F., Daveson, B., Hitchen, H., Kennelly, J., Leung, M., and Tamplin, J. (2011). Music therapy methods with children, adolescents, and adults with severe neurobehavioral discorders due to brain injury. *Music Therapy Perspectives* 29: 5–13.

Merrick, E. and Merrick, J. (2005). Asthma in adolescence. *International Journal of Adolescent Medicine and Health* 17: 313–314.

Michaud, P.A., Suris, J.C., and Viner, R. (2004). The adolescent with a chronic condition. Part II: healthcare provision. *Archives of Disease in Childhood* 89: 943–949.

Midence, K., Fuggle, P., and Davies, S.C. (1993). Psychosocial aspects of sickle cell disease (SCD) in childhood and adolescence: a review. *British Journal of Clinical Psychology* 32 (Pt 3): 271–280.

Mondanaro, J. (2005). Interfacing music therapy with other creative arts modalities to address anticipatory grief and bereavements in pediatrics. In: C. Dileo and J. Loewy (eds), *Music Therapy at the End of Life,* pp. 25–32. Cherry Hill, NJ: Jeffrey Books.

Mondanaro, J. (2008). Music therapy in the psychosocial care of pediatric patients living with epilepsy. *Music Therapy Perspectives* 26: 102–109.

Mondanaro, J. (2013). Surgical and procedural support for children. In: Bradt, J. (ed.), *Guidelines for Music Therapy Practice in Pediatric Care,* pp. 205–259. Gilsum, NH: Barcelona Publishers.

Mondanaro, J. and Needleman, S. (2011). Social work and creative arts therapy services. In: T. Altilio and S. Otis-Green (eds), *The Oxford Textbook of Palliative Social Work,* pp. 465–469. New York: Oxford University Press.

Mondanaro, J. and Vaskas, C. (2013). Music therapy and HIV/AIDS related pain. In: J. Mondanaro and G. Sara (eds), *Music and Medicine: Integrative Models in the Treatment of Pain,* pp. 373–402. New York: Satchnot Press.

Nathan, B.M. and Moran, A. (2008). Metabolic complications of obesity in childhood and adolescence: more than just diabetes. *Current Opinion in Endocrinology, Diabetes and Obesity* 15: 21–29.

Orr, D.P., Weller, S.C., Satterwhite, B. and Pless, I.B. (1984). Psychosocial implications of chronic illness in adolescence. *Journal of Pediatrics* 104: 152–157.

Pelicand, J., Maes, M., Charlier, D. and Aujoulat, I. (2012). [Adolescence and type 1 diabetes: Self-care and glycemic control]. *Archives de pédiatrie: organe officiel de la Sociéte française de pédiatrie* 19: 585–592.

Pittet, I., Berchtold, A., Akre, C., Michaud, P.A., and Suris, J.C. (2010). Are adolescents with chronic conditions particularly at risk for bullying? *Archives of Disease in Childhood* 95: 711–716.

Rossi, G., Bonfiglio, S., Veggiotti, P., and Lanzi, G. (1997). Epilepsy: a study of adolescence and groups. *Seizure* 6: 289–295.

Rubin-Bosco, J. (2002). Resolution vs. reenactment: A story song approach to working with trauma. In: Loewy, J.V. and Frisch-Hara, A. (eds), *Caring for the caregiver: The use of music and music therapy in grief and trauma*. Silver Spring, MD: AMTA.

Silverstein, J., Klingensmith, G., Copeland, K., Plotnick, L., Kaufman, F., Laffel, L. et al. (2005). Care of Children and Adolescents with Type I Diabetes: A statement of the American Diabetes Association. *Diabetes Care* 28: 186–212.

Snethen, J., Broome, E., Kelber, S., and Warady, B.A. (2004). *Coping Strategies Utilized by Adolescents with End Stage Renal Disease*. Jennetti Publications, Inc.: The CBS Interactive Business Network.

Sperling, M.A. (1994). Diabetes in Adolescence. *Adolescent Medicine* 5: 87–96.

Steele, N. (2012). Beat it: The effects of rap music on adolescents in the pediatric medical setting. In: S. Hadley and G. Yancy (eds), *Therapeutic Uses of Rap and Hip-Hop*. New York: Routledge Taylor & Francis Group, LLC.

Stewart, K. (ed.). (2010). *Music therapy & trauma: Bridging theory and clinical practice*. New York, NY: Satchnote Press.

Suris, J.C. (2002). Chronically ill but still adolescent. *Minerva Pediatrica* 54: 507–510.

Suris, J.C. and Parera, N. (2005). Sex, drugs and chronic illness: health behaviours among chronically ill youth. *European Journal of Public Health* 15: 484–488.

Suris, J.C., Michaud, P.A., and Viner, R. (2004). The adolescent with a chronic condition. Part I: developmental issues. *Archives of Disease in Childhood* 89: 938–942.

Suris, J.C., Domine, F., and Akre, C. (2008a). The transition from pediatric to adult care of chronically ill adolescents. *Revue Médicale Suisse* 4: 1441–1444.

Suris, J.C., Michaud, P.A., Akre, C., and Sawyer, S.M. (2008b). Health risk behaviors in adolescents with chronic conditions. *Pediatrics* 122: e1113–e1118.

Swanson, S., Crow, S., Legrange, D., Swendsen, J., and Merikangas, K. (2011). Prevalence and correlates of eating disorders in adolescents: Results from the National Comorbidity Survey Replication Adolescent Supplement. *Archives of General Psychiatry* 68(7): 714–723.

Tager, I.B. (2008). The effects of second-hand and direct exposure to tobacco smoke on asthma and lung function in adolescence. *Paediatric Respiratory Reviews* 9: 29–37.

Taylor, R.M., Gibson, F., and Franck, L.S. 2008. The experience of living with a chronic illness during adolescence: a critical review of the literature. *Journal of Clinical Nursing* 17: 3083–3091.

Tervo, J. (2001). Music therapy for adolescents. *Clinical Psychology and Psychiatry* 6: 79–91.

Thaut, M.H. (2005). The future of music in therapy and medicine. *Annals of the New York Academy of Sciences* 1060: 303–308.

Thaut, M.H., Kenyon, G.P., Schauer, M.L., and Mcintosh, G.C. (1999). The connection between rhythmicity and brain function. *IEEE Engineering in Medicine and Biology Magazine* 18: 101–108.

Thaut, M.H., Mcintosh, K.W., Mcintosh, G.C., and Hoemberg, V. (2001). Auditory rhythmicity enhances movement and speech motor control in patients with Parkinson's disease. *Functional Neurology* 16: 163–172.

Viberg, M., Blennow, G., and Polski, B. (1987). Epilepsy in adolescence: implications for the development of personality. *Epilepsia* 28: 542–546.

Wengrower, D., Goldin, E., Fich, A., and Granot, E. (1997). Crohn's disease in late adolescence: acute onset or long-standing disease? *Journal of Clinical Gastroenterology* 24: 224–226.

Westrom, L. and Eschenbach, D. (1999). Pelvic Inflamimatory Disease. In: K. Holmes, P. Sparling, and P. Mardh (eds), *Sexually Transmitted Diseases*, 3rd edn, pp. 1017–1050. New York: McGraw-Hill.

Whittington, P.F., Barnes, H.V., and Bayless, T.M. (1977). Medical management of Crohn's disease in adolescence. *Gastroenterology* 72: 1338–1344.

Wysocki, T. and Greco, P. (2006). Social support and diabetes management in childhood and adolescence: influence of parents and friends. *Current Diabetes Reports* 6: 117–122.

APPENDIX 5.1

REFERRAL

MOUNT SINAI BETH ISRAEL
Louis and Lucille Armstrong Music Therapy Program
Name of PT: _____

Diagnosis:_____

Floor and Room:_____

Primary Language of Patient:_____ English:_____ yes _____ no

Caretaker(s) Name: _____

Primary Language of Caretaker:_____ English: _____ yes _____ no

Relationship to patient: _____ mother _____ father _____ sibling
_____ foster parent _____ relative _____ friend

Reason (s) of patient's Referral for Music Therapy (definitions on reverse side)
Check areas that apply:

Anxiety/Fear: ( ) Separation Anxiety   ( ) Pre or post operative Anxiety
                       ( ) General Anxiety

Pain/Stress: ( ) Breathing Difficulties ( ) In need of tension release

Expressive Difficulties: ( ) Depression or   ( ) Acting out or hyperactive
                         Non-Verbal

Coping: ( ) In Facing the Illness   ( ) Self Esteem   ( ) Communication/
                                                                           Socialization

In Loss of Consciousness: ( ) Increase awareness ( ) Increase stimulation or use of imagery

Other Specify:

_____

Comments:

_____

_____

Person Referring: _____ Ext: _____ Date: _____

MUSIC THERAPY REFERRAL CRITERIA

I. **Anxiety/Fear**

Music Therapy soothes, familiarizes, and/or activates:

A. Separation anxiety Chanting, musical holding and collaborative musical experiences create
                       a feeling of safety in the hospital.

B. Pre/Post operative Making music relaxes and eases the mind and body of tension and fear
   anxiety   stimulated by hospital procedures.

C. General anxiety   Musical experiences help patients make sense of their fears through a
                       non-threatening medium.

II. **Pain/Stress**

Clinical improvisation provides an alternative, non-verbal means of release for a patient in
discomfort:

| A. Breathing & Vocalizing | Life rhythms and tonal intervallic synthesis help a patient synchronize and deepen the breathing process. Toning stimulates the connection between the body breath and feeling states. |
| B. Tension release | Opening channels of musical creativity stimulates the body's need to release tension. |

III. Expressivity

| A. Depression, non-verbal/inactivity | Structured and unstructured therapies help elicit feelings that may be "muted" or "blocked". |
| B. Acting out or hyperactivity | The implicit structure music therapy techniques such as African drumming song sensation, and instrumental composition offer patients a safe means of channeling their excessive amounts of energy. |

IV. Ego strength/Coping

A. Facing the illness	The metaphoric use of music in song selection and composition offer patients a safe way into understanding and adjusting to their illness.
B. Self esteem	Performing and tape creating strengthen a patient's feeling of worth during this fragile time.
C. Communication/Socialization	Community singing, drumming circles, and collaborative free improvisations foster communications between patients and within families.

V. Loss of Consciousness/Coma/ICU

| A. Awareness | The use of familiar melodies help patients become oriented or tuned in to a state grounded, familiarized awareness. |
| B. Stimulation | The use of music and guided imagery stimulates the healing process. |

APPENDIX 5.2

MUSIC THERAPY ASSESSMENT

Mount Sinai Beth Israel

The Louis and Lucille Armstrong Music Therapy Program

_____Individual _____Family _____Group

Referred by:_____

Reason for Referral:

_____

_____

Instruments/Activity:

Voice:

Description of the music:

Significant issues

Follow-up plan:

Music Therapist: _____Ext. Beeper: _____Date: _____

Time:_____

CHAPTER 6

MUSIC THERAPY WITH ADULTS DIAGNOSED WITH CANCER AND THEIR FAMILIES

CLARE O'CALLAGHAN AND LUCANNE MAGILL

CANCER is one of the leading causes of death in the world, accounting for 7.6 million deaths in 2008 (WHO), with numbers increasing annually. In Australia, UK, and USA (Cancer Council Australia 2011; CDC, n.d.; Office for National Statistics, n.d.), where cancer is a leading cause of mortality, between 33 and 50 percent of these countries' populations are expected to be diagnosed with cancer in their lifetimes, and most are diagnosed after 55 years of age. In Australia, more than 60 percent will be effectively treated (Cancer Council Australia 2011). In South, East, and Southeast Asia, the incidence of cancer is on the rise. Cancer prevalence in India is estimated to be around 2.5 million, with over 800,000 new cases and 550,000 deaths occurring each year due to this disease (Dinshaw et al. 1999). More than 70 percent of the cases report for diagnostic and treatment services in the advanced stages of the disease, which has led to a poor survival and high mortality rate. In 2002, 4.2 million new cancer cases—39 percent of new cases worldwide—were diagnosed among 3.2 billion persons (48 percent of the world population) living in the fifteen most highly developed countries in Asia (Pfizer 2008). Uncertainties often associated with cancer prognoses and aversive treatment effects can render living with a cancer diagnosis extremely challenging, both for those diagnosed and those significant in their lives (sometimes called "care givers" but called family here). This chapter presents ways in which music therapists may support cancer patients, their families, and oncology staff, and describes evidence justifying music therapy's role in cancer care.

WHAT IS CANCER?

Cancer refers to a malignant neoplasm (new growth) or tumor (abnormal swelling) comprising an abnormal growth of cells which invade and spread in the body. They are distinguished from benign tumors which grow slowly and do not invade surrounding tissue. There are many types of cancer because they arise from different types of cells found throughout the body (Underwood 2009). In adults malignant cells most commonly originate in the skin, lung, breast, prostate, rectum, and colon (Rosenthal 2001). Malignant cancers invade and destroy adjacent tissues, and can also detach from the primary tumor site and invade arteries and the lymphatic system, leading to metastases (secondary tumors) in other parts of the body (Underwood 2009).

Types of conditions and etiology

Cancers can be classified histologically, that is, according to cell type, with major categories being epithelial, such as, bladder, bowel, breast, skin, brain, connective tissue, such as bone, muscle, fat, lymphoid, such as lymphomas gland, and hemopoietic, that is leukemias. Subdivisions within each category allow the exact classification of all tumors and help doctors select treatments. The incidence of cancer types varies across countries. In the UK and USA lung cancer is the most frequent (Underwood 2009).

Carcinogens are environmental agents that contribute to cancer development and are considered to be involved in 85 percent of cancer risk. Suspected agents include specific chemicals, for example in the link between smoking and lung cancer, and viruses, such as human papilloma virus causing cervical cancer. Radiation energy is also implicated, for example ultraviolet light is a contributing factor in skin cancer. Extrinsic factors associated with cancer risk also include skin color, for example fair skinned people and skin cancer risk, diet which is exemplified by evidence that a high fat diet can cause breast and colorectal cancer. Inherited predispositions and increasing age are also causal factors (Underwood 2009). In spite of prevailing views about cancer causes, psychosocial factors, such as personality traits, depressions and stress "do not appear to play a major role in cancer causation" (Johansen 2010, p. 60).

Cancer treatments

Cancer treatment options vary depending on the nature and extent of disease. Three main treatments include (Rosenthal 2001):

Surgery. Cancers may be cured through complete primary tumor removal, for example, an early detected breast cancer. Surgery may also reduce tumor size and this may enhance the effectiveness of radiotherapy or chemotherapy. Surgery may also be used palliatively to alleviate symptoms and diminish suffering, for example, to remove a bowel obstruction to prevent fecal vomiting.

External beam radiation therapy (radiotherapy). High energy x-rays are delivered via linear accelerators to destroy cancer cells. They may cure localized tumors including unresectable cancers, for example, isolated brain tumor, while minimizing damage to surrounding normal tissues. Palliative radiotherapy may reduce symptoms, for example, pain from bone metastases. Neoadjuvant radiation therapy uses less than curative doses for reducing tumor size and is used to improve other treatments outcomes, such as surgery. When cancer cells are spread widely through the body, total body irradiation (TBI) is also sometimes administered.

Chemotherapy. Chemical agents are made from plants, such as vincristine, and other sources to kill tumors by selectively destroying multiplying cells and inhibiting cell division. Most chemotherapy drugs are administered through a series of treatments over time as treatments are a balance between killing tumor cells and not killing healthy cells. Neoadjuvent chemotherapy may reduce tumor size with the aim of curing the disease through follow-up radiotherapy or surgery. While its toxic effects usually limit the amount of chemotherapy that can be given, marrow or stem cell transplantation (TP) has enabled much higher chemotherapy dosages and has thus improved cure rates for some cancers, including lymphomas and leukemias. Marrow or stem cell transplantation involves the use of donor (allogenic TP) or one's own (autologous TP) marrow or peripheral blood stem cells to replace destroyed marrow cells after high dose chemotherapy. It is used to treat various hematological diseases which are cancers of blood forming cells, such as leukemia and Hodgkin's disease.

Recent treatment advances also include:

Immunotherapies. Antibodies are produced to target specific cancer cell antigens located on the cellular walls. When injected into the body they bind to the antigen and result in cell death.

Biological agents. Naturally occurring compounds can be manufactured and when injected into the body either suppress cancer growth or enhance the body's ability to produce normal blood cells thus enabling recovery from high dose chemo-radiotherapy.

Effects of cancer and its treatments

The considerable impairment and life threatening nature of metastatic cancer can be due to pressure on tissues and their destruction, blood loss from ulceration, obstructions of flow such as bowel obstruction, abnormal hormone secretion, and paraneoplastic effects in the peripheral or central nervous system causing debility and weight loss, and pain and anxiety (Underwood 2009).

Chemotherapy and radiotherapy treatments can have a variety of both short-term and longer term side-effects. These vary according to the type and amount of drugs administered, the body parts which receive radiotherapy, and the individual's idiosyncratic response to treatment. Some patients report few side-effects, although fatigue is common. Radiation to the brain and some cancer drugs may also cause cognitive problems, the effects of which may reduce over time (American Cancer Society 2011). The following example of treatment side-effects for breast cancer illustrates how some patients with other kinds of cancers may also react to treatment. Chemotherapy for breast cancer treatment can result in short-term side-effects including: Nausea; vomiting; bone marrow suppression which can cause anemia, bruising and bleeding, increased infection risk; hair loss; fatigue; and nerve damage which can cause numbness, weakness, or loss of function. Longer term effects may include cognitive dysfunction, infertility, heart and lung damage, and chemotherapy induced tumors (Shapiro 2012). Radiotherapy for breast cancer can cause acute side-effects including fatigue and skin changes and longer term complications may include lymphodema, nerve injury, lung inflammation, rib fractures, and radiation induced tumors (El-Ghamry and Taghian 2012). Surgical side-effects may include wound breakdown, infection, blood clots, chest infections, etc.

Psychosocial and emotional factors

When cancer is diagnosed, patients and their family members may experience shock, panic, and feelings of helplessness. Degrees of denial may range from a naturally protective response as one assimilates the new reality, to pathological responses which have the potential to interfere with treatment decisions. Patients may also feel guilt, have reduced clarity of thinking, and experience a range of fears including worry about being burdensome to family and friends, fear of abandoning loved ones, disfigurement, pain, or death. Anger is a common response resulting in communication difficulties with loved ones, reducing the patients' and family members' capacity to support each other. Existential issues may include a sense of isolation and despair and one's spiritual beliefs may be challenged (Breitbart 2002; Wells and Turney 2001). Ongoing emotional reactions to the illness and treatment may include anxiety, depression, disillusionment, and grief when the illness affects plans and hopes. Lifestyle and role changes in the patient's family system may be needed as they endeavor to adust to treatment demands. Being a cancer survivor is sometimes likened to living with a chronic illness; as one adjusts to possible late effects which can arise years after treatment ends, for example cataracts, osteoporosis, lymphedema (Mayo Clinic Staff 2011), illness relapses, or possible palliative care. Financial strains are also common when the illness affects the capacity to work. Cognitive effects related to tumor or treatment side-effects may be mild or extreme. When patients are severely brain impaired, families may grieve for the person they once knew while adjusting to the person's altered self. Dealing with the sometimes fickle and unpredictable cancer trajectory can involve relentless and exhausting highs and lows. For example, as one faces the prospect of end-of-life care, an unexpected positive reaction or remission may allow positive prognostic readjustments and plans for the future, but then the illness may recur (O'Callaghan and Jordan 2011). Intensified distress is associated with harsh treatment and side-effects, subsequent disfigurement and disability, vulnerable pre-morbid functioning, and poor prognosis (Wells and Turney 2001).

While many report that cancer is a negative life changing experience, other cancer patients and their families may gain strength from their spiritual lives, and some also report finding meaning and changed life priorities. One's biopsychosocial context can affect their response to cancer, with the adverse impact being buffered by good social support and family presence (Holland and Weiss 2010). Further information about cancer illness, common cancer treatments and their side-effects can be found in reputable oncology websites including the American Cancer Society, Mayo Clinic, Cancer Council Australia, and also in McDougal Miller and O'Callaghan (2010).

MUSIC THERAPY

In oncology, music therapy is the skilled and professionally informed use of music-based interventions within a therapeutic relationship to address biopsychosocial and/or spiritual concerns to alleviate discomfort, support coping, restore function, and improve life quality. The application of music therapy in cancer care can be traced back to 1973 when Lucanne Magill sang, accompanied by guitar, for patients and families waiting for diagnostic procedures in the Diagnostic Radiology Department at Memorial Sloan Kettering Cancer Center, New York. With the support of the Hospital's Pain and Psychiatry Services, she eventually developed the first music therapy program and, while working over the next three decades, trained countless music therapy interns to enable music therapy in oncology settings throughout the world (Magill and O'Callaghan 2011). Lucanne's recent pioneering efforts to establish oncology music therapy in India and Nepal are described in a further section of this chapter. The following will delineate examples of how adult music therapy is provided in western oncology hospitals and private clinics.

Needs that music therapists may alleviate in cancer care

Music therapists aim to help patients, families, and staff find ways to integrate music into their lives to ameliorate suffering, grief (Bradt et al. 2011; Magill 2001, 2010), and improve comfort, coping skills, and personal well-being (Magill 2010). Other issues and symptoms that music therapy may address relate to: Agitation, confusion and cognitive impairment, anxiety, pain, depression, spiritual concerns, lack of social support, and isolation. Music therapy offers distraction through aversive procedures, physical rehabilitation, and opportunities to celebrate an event (Dougall Miller and O'Callaghan 2010). Music therapy participation can also address issues of low self-esteem, assist communication between patients and their families, and enable a refuge from arduous experiences. A patient and family-centered approach encompasses therapists endeavoring to address what participants regard as meaningful.

Referral, assessment, and approaching patients

Music therapists assess the specific and idiosyncratic concerns of each patient or family member who accepts music therapy. They may be referred by members of the multidisciplinary team, verbally, or through written documentation (Hilliard 2005), or they may also self-refer. Referral patterns vary across clinical settings and tend to evolve into what "fits" the context (O'Callaghan 2006).

Assessment is an evolving procedure in cancer care; the music therapist may be alerted to concerns amenable to music therapy when given the referral, when hearing about the patient in a team meeting, when meeting the patient, or when reading the case history. As music therapy proceeds, therapists may continue gently questioning and evaluating participants' strengths and vulnerabilities, offer methods which may help, and may refer problems to other team members for additional psychosocial support. The assessment may encompass the patient's disease status, mood, cognitive function, abilities, musical background and preferences, cultural and spiritual issues, family and social issues, and coping skills (Magill 2001; O'Callaghan 2001).

When offering music therapy to patients in an oncology hospital CO states something like: "Hello … my name is Clare and I work here as a music therapist. I offer to bring music to only those people interested … Do you like music? (or) This can involve live music or CDs and players you can borrow free of charge, or other music techniques, for example writing a song or playing instruments…" The introduction is an art, tailored to the patients' needs and according to how the patients respond verbally and non-verbally. Engaging the patient in a conversation about music is associated with increased likelihood of them accepting music therapy (O'Callaghan and Colegrove 1998). Research examining cancer and cardiac patients' expectations of music therapy benefits informed suggestions that music therapists may have greater success when inviting patients to participate in music therapy by learning about patients' individual challenges, explaining music therapy's potential benefits, finding out about patients' background and preferences; and to start with listening experiences incorporating patients' music preferences (Bruscia et al. 2009).

Therapists offer music therapy techniques based on their assessments of need. Patients and families choose whether and how they become involved in music therapy. Therapists may provide single sessions or develop more enduring therapeutic relationships, in accordance with the participants' wishes and the scope for service provision. Many music therapists have indicated that flexibility is a key ingredient due to patients' sometimes rapidly changing conditions, unexpected procedures, and visitors (for example, Barry and O'Callaghan 2008; Magill 2011).

Music therapy contexts

Music therapists use their singing voices and large or portable musical instruments such as electric piano, guitar, harp, autoharp, omnichord, metallophones, and hand held percussive instruments, for example, djembe drum. Music software can also be used for music composition and arranging. At Peter Mac, where CO worked for fifteen years, and at Caritas Christi Hospice, CO often visited patients at their bedside with a 6.5 octave electric piano and books containing over 6000 songs and classical piano works. LM commonly uses voice and guitar and an eclectic assortment of musical resources, including improvised melodies and songs, the patient's favorite songs, and songs and chants from around the world.

In-patient settings

Music therapy sessions are held with individuals or groups, which can include both patients and their families. Group work may be preplanned or spontaneously arise in inpatient rooms, homes, or in clinic settings. When planning music therapy for a patient in a shared room, the therapist needs to ask other patients for permission to conduct the audible session. Patients' neighbors seldom refuse permission and quite often make positive comments, or may become involved in the session when that is acceptable to the patient receiving music therapy. If patients do state that they would prefer that music therapy is not conducted in their shared room, however, the therapist may need to try and conduct the session elsewhere. In the authors' experience objecting patients mostly relent if the therapist states that they will keep the session quiet and give a specific time when the session will end. Hesitant patients may also appreciate being asked to state what songs they do not want the music therapist to play.

Group sessions may enable patients and sometimes their families to share memories, stories, illness-related concerns, and share and receive support. Pleasurable and congenial atmospheres can also emerge with staff sometimes singing along, helping a patient to record a song composition, or dancing with a patient. As Aasgaard recommends, when music therapy is directed at both individual and environmental care in cancer settings, people can mutually help "one another to experience hope, joy and beauty" (Aasgaard 1999, p. 34). Music can transform these settings, where attention may be focused on cell counts, beeping IV pump occlusions, and physical symptoms, into *transient ward communities* (O'Callaghan 2007). Oncology staff also report that witnessing the positive effects of music therapy in the wards also helps them cope with their work, and relate to patients as people (O'Callaghan and Magill 2009).

Immunosuppressed patients may also need to be treated in isolated rooms where staff must enter with gowns and gloves, and clean with alcohol wipes anything taken from the room. Music therapy sessions can still be held in these rooms if one is prepared to clean everything when leaving the room. Alternately, sessions can proceed through doorways. "Hallway" music therapy sessions in these contexts may proceed whereby a therapist takes "requests" from patients in isolation and their families. Some patients may be able to put on a surgical gown and gloves and leave their isolation room and come and sit with the therapist, sing and play instruments. When the therapist plays their requests in this context, the authors often then witness memories and shared loving gestures amongst patients and families.

Out-patient settings

Patients may attend out-patient music therapy after receiving inpatient sessions, or for support while undergoing out-patient treatments and adjusting back in the community. Sessions may be held in homes when continuity of care is provided. It may also be offered in day chemotherapy settings, which are usually in large public waiting room contexts. Therapists may improvise or offer live music requests in these contexts. While some choose to ignore it, preferring to sleep or to use their own iPods, CDs, DVDs or books, others may request songs, sing along, and start to plan extended one-to-one music therapy sessions with the therapist; some of these extended sessions may involve creating a special song. Therapists need to assess these public contexts as music is played, and be wary of playing themes that have overt lyrics about death such as Danny Boy or Amazing Grace. The authors usually play improvised music or instrumental music in such public areas, watchful of patients' and families' reactions. When the music is complete, the authors may visit patients to invite conversation about the music, and offer support if needed.

Table 6.1 Common Music Therapy Techniques in Oncology

Replaying music from one's life, chosen by patient/family or therapist
   Therapist and/or patient plays familiar songs
   Listening to familiar songs (live or recorded)
   Lyric analysis
   Music-based reminiscence
   Word substitution in known songs

Exploring "new" music
   Music improvisation
   Songwriting
   Therapeutic music lessons
   Unfamiliar precomposed music (recorded or live)
   Chanting and toning

Music relaxation and supportive imagery (with live or recorded music)
   Strategies alongside music focus on breathing, muscle relaxation, imagined altered states

Music-based gift or legacy creation
   Formalizing one of the above methods to give to someone else or personal expression or
   legacy, e.g., making a song recording

Similarly, music therapists may also provide therapeutic services to patients with cancer in private settings. For example, a patient, Maria Logis, diagnosed with stage IV non-Hodgkins lymphoma in 1994, has described how her improvisations in music therapy, accompanied by her music therapist, helped her to express her sadness and realize a joyful and music-enriched ongoing life (Logis 2011).

Music therapy techniques and ways in which they may help

Music therapy provides opportunities for patients and families to re-experience music from their lives, to create music that reflects times of meaning and significance in their lives, and to experience the therapist's music, in order to "get through" cancer treatments and progress to living the best quality life possible. A brief description of common music therapy techniques (Table 6.1) and the ways in which they may help cancer patients and their families follows. Further detailed presentation of how music therapy can be used across the cancer continuum is elsewhere (McDougal Miller and O'Callaghan 2010).

Replaying music from one's life, chosen by patient/family or therapist

Patients and family members tend to choose music that reflects feelings or thoughts they may have and for which they desire to gain support, or to connect with special memories and people in their lives: Individuals tend to project into and take from music what is needed. Patients and families may choose songs that reflect inner feelings and themes of meaning. Thus, they may identify with song lyrics and singers, a process that can enable them to feel part of a wider human experience and feel validated and less alone (Magill Bailey 1984). This was possible for one cancer patient who improvised the music backing for her requested "(I was) Born to Try," which was sung and recorded by a popular singer diagnosed with a similar cancer (Goodrem and Mtawarira 2002). Lyric messages may also soothe, including spiritual songs that may affirm faith, or songs with messages that one needs to hear (Magill 2005). Patients and families may also choose songs with lyrics or memories that can affirm the significance of each other in their lives. While memories inspired by the music can affirm personal contributions and be enjoyable, unresolved issues may also arise and can be discussed in the supportive therapeutic relationship. In palliative care, musical life reviews can also be more formally created in music therapy, as the music therapist can compile the patient's significant music from his or her life onto an audio recording (O'Callaghan 1984). This may include patients' verbal reflections. Audio-visual recordings may also include the patients' musical performance and life review interview (Beggs 1991). While these can be interesting and affirming for the patients to create, and be helpful legacies for family members, music therapists need to carefully assess when using this intervention. Reminiscence can remind one of disappointments which cannot be resolved, thus at times it may be contraindicated (Coleman 1994). In general, however, the therapist-supported music therapy session environments often provide the space and time through which patients and families may acknowledge losses and accomplishments, reducing feelings of guilt and remorse and leading to improved coping and sense of fulfilment.

Listeners can engage with familiar music in creative ways in music therapy, even if the music has been heard before, because each time a listener engages with music it is heard anew.

Musical listening is:

> ... a creative act on the part of the participant ... Perceiving is an act of composition, and perceiving a work of art can involve conscious and wilful acts of composition. What this proposes to the artist is the creation of forms that contain many possibilities of realization by the perceiver ... (and) ... allows the perceiver to compose a new work within that form at each encounter. This proposes a relation to art that demands of perception that it be creative in essence.
>
> McAdams 1984, p. 319

As such, music listening can creatively expand the way one views his/her world, and the process can potentially help one find more adaptive ways of being within it. While lyric analyses may help to increase insight, lyrics do not need to be present in order for music to move and support one's way of being. For example, after listening to the therapist play classical music on an electric piano, including Chopin Nocturne in E flat Major which she asked to be repeated, a newly admitted cancer patient stated: "That music makes me think I can deal with anything coming my way now." Patients may also change the lyrics of known songs. Their improvised lyrics serve to help them creatively articulate and express thoughts of importance. For example, one patient changed the lyrics of "White Christmas" to state his dream of having a "White Cell Christmas when all my neutrophils are up," i.e., raised white blood cell counts signifying for him that he would have improved health.

Music is also a life interest that music therapists can make more accessible to patients when they do not have the energy or cognitive capacity to keep up hobbies such as reading or watching movies. As patients become unwell their musical interests may also shift, temporarily or permanently, and therapists can help them to explore unfamiliar genres which they may find interesting and helpful. For example, one young patient who had always enjoyed heavy metal music found that she did not want to listen to this genre as her condition deteriorated, and welcomed live piano classical music and hymns. Another young patient who always loved classical music found it difficult to listen to this music as she felt overwhelmed by the fearful images it was eliciting in her. While the therapist supported her in talking about her fears, she also offered suggestions to her for using lyrical music during times of stress and insomnia which would gently guide her thoughts into images and words of comfort and support. When resources and copyright laws allow, therapists can also help patients to develop playlists or favorite music CDs, and electronic libraries for patient and family usage.

If patients are experiencing cognitive impairment as a result of cancer or treatments affecting the brain, familiar music may be something that they can still enjoy, relate to, and share with family members. Neural pathways that are responsible for language and music are separate, therefore, when a therapist is using music and language with a person with brain impairment they have the capacity to access what is still preserved neurally, more so than when using language alone. Patients can sometimes sing despite word finding difficulties, and well-known lyrics can be relatively preserved when one experiences memory impairment (O'Callaghan 1999). Family singing in music therapy, including the sharing of elicited memories, can be a source of delight, affirmation, and strength for all participants (Magill 2009a).

Music therapists need to learn a variety of well-known multicultural songs, especially those of the significant minority groups receiving cancer care. For example, CO regularly witnesses smiles and joyful surprise when playing Chinese songs for people from Chinese backgrounds, such as Jasmine Flower, and many will sing along. Also, therapists can use culturally-centered song writing techniques with patients and families from diverse ethnic backgrounds by incorporating specific modes and rhythms (Dileo and Magill 2005). Hearing a song of "kin to (their) cultural realm" (Loewy et al. 2006, p. 347) in an unfamiliar environment can possibly reduce these patients' feelings of isolation if unable to speak English and increase their feelings of dignity and support. Local elders may help therapists to develop this kind of song repertoire, and understandings about sensitivities possibly related to song usages.

Exploring 'new' music

Music improvisation can be used in a varied of ways with patients with cancer, ranging from single sessions at bedside to long-term therapeutic relationships over many years (Logis and Turry 1999). Lending instruments to patients to share musical play with their children in hospitals can offer fun and enjoyable interactions which can help children feel more comfortable visiting the hospital. In music improvisation, the therapist musically mirrors and "plays" with patients' musical expressions, potentially inspiring them to extend their musical creativity. This process can transduce into imaginings of ways to cope and adapt with situations. It may also enable insights and the feeling of being healthily transported, such as to a "walk through Paris" (Aldridge 2008), and improved ways of dealing with illness uncertainties and living an enriched life (Logis 2011).

Therapeutic song writing is an approach that patients and families may use to express what is important in a contained, often quick, and powerful way, and the music can extend the therapeutic impact of the lyrics (O'Callaghan 1997). Song writing can allow participants to creatively express what may be difficult to verbalize, and can also help instill pleasure and pride, support personal and spiritual affirmations, or promote cathartic relief (Magill 2005; O'Callaghan 2005a). Parents' song compositions for their children can be helpful for children when the parent is separated from them, either because of hospitalization or if sadly the parent dies, as the children can hear that they are or were in their parents' thoughts. Knowing that their parents are (and have been) thinking about them can be especially important for younger children's healthy development (Winnicott 1971). Patients may write songs about their journey with cancer, for a significant other, for the general community, or in honor of their faith, and thereby experience relationship closure, self-expression, spiritual enhancement, and fulfillment through life review (Dileo and Magill 2005). O'Brien (2006) has also used song writing with four cancer patients in order to create an opera which helped them to feel calmed, healed, proud, and soothed, and to express fears and grief.

Varying therapeutic song writing procedures used in cancer care have been outlined by Dileo, Magill, O'Brien, and O'Callaghan (Dileo and Magill 2005; O'Callaghan 1996, 2005a; O'Brien 2005). Comparable elements within these music therapists' song writing paradigms include:

(a) Brainstorming, where the patients' ideas are collected through free association, and possibly extended through therapist reflective prompts and questions.
(b) The therapist and patient then group and transform the ideas into a song structure.
(c) The therapist invites the patients' suggestions for melodies, rhythms, and harmonies, and the therapist may encourage this through offering choices of musical elements or suggestions.
(d) The therapist, patient, or an extended group record the completed song (O'Callaghan et al. 2009, p. 1151).

Other music therapy work such as O'Brien (2003, 2012), Dileo and Magill (2005), and Magill (2001) also illustrates how the patients' songs can span broad genres.

Therapeutic music lessons may also be offered to patients who have more time, such as when cancer affects work-life, they can no longer pursue high energy hobbies, or because re-evaluation of life goals, including the aim to finally get around to learning an instrument. For example, one anxious and tense young patient learned to play the guitar in music therapy as per his deep wish. He consequently became more relaxed with an improved sense of control, and thus felt more comfortable talking about his fears with the music therapist through improvised songs (Magill 2010).

CHANTING AND TONING

Chanting and toning have been used for centuries as ways to achieve spiritual enlightenment, to commune in fellowship, and to gain feelings of comfort or inner strength. Toning, the use of vocalized vowel sounds at various pitches (Keyes 1973), has been used as a method in spiritual practices to improve spiritual and physical well-being. Likewise, chants are common to every culture and are used as ways to focus intention and unite in purpose.

These methods are useful in oncologic practices in order to enhance mindfulness and promote comfort and relaxation, concentration and an improved focus on affirmations. Toning is used in music therapy to reduce tension, enhance energy flow, and to center attention. Music therapists work closely with patients in pain to engage cognitive processes, i.e., to actively vocalize and "breathe" sound "to," "in," "around", and "away from" the pain (Magill 2010). The technique of toning also offers the patient a tool that he or she can use during pain episodes, such as vocalizing with exhalations to redirect thoughts onto a mantra or an inspirational image.

Chanting is similar in that vocalizations are repetitive, however it also includes the dynamic of tempo and the presence of purposely selected words (Gass and Brehony 1999). Music therapists establish a rhythmic pattern that is suitable to the needs of the patient, for example, matching the patient's rate of respiration, and then adapting the tempo to positively affect mood and feelings of comfort. This use of rhythm follows the familiar music therapy method of entrainment, wherein sound stimuli "lock in" and can influence the flow of the physiological responses, such as heart rate and breath rate (Dileo and Bradt 1999; Rider 1985). The repetitive nature of chanting tends to be soothing and lulling, and the words can help affirm personal strengths and can inspire hope and faith. Chanting often results in improved feelings of self-efficacy.

Toning and chanting are beneficial to those patients seeking techniques to regain sense of control and/or improve ability to cope with pain or illness-related stress. These strategies have been used to bring patients and families together, for example in "circles of love" (Magill 2009a), where individuals hold hands and share words and tones in close circles. Toning may not be suitable, however, for patients who are emotionally fragile, who may need the direction and guidance of structured rhythms and melodies, such as songs or formal compositions, to help assuage hyper reactions or to placate frightening images and feelings of apprehension (Magill 2010). Toning and chanting can provide support and symptom relief for many patients and families.

Music relaxation and supportive imagery

When hospitalized for treatment or end-of-life care, people with cancer can find it difficult to concentrate for extended periods but may benefit from short relaxation or imagery sessions to reduce tension or enable some imagined respite from their illness situation. When patients feel very unwell, are drowsy, have breathing difficulties or mild pain, therapists may invite them to focus their attention on live or recorded music which should be steady, and without extremes of volume or rapid pitch changes. Patients may be invited to "sample" the therapists' live improvisations or performances of varied musical genres, or other recorded music selections. Patients' relaxing sound preferences can inform the music that therapists use in these sessions. Therapists may draw on the iso principal to help patients relax, initially presenting music that reflects the patients' breathing, movements, and emotions, then slowing the pace to a calmer level. Live improvised music can be adapted easily according to this principle.

When the patient does not have substantial breathing or coughing difficulties, inviting the patient to experience a short induction may be helpful, for example, "Try and move yourself into a comfortable position. Feel your body supported by your bed/chair. You may like to close your eyes. You may take slightly deeper breaths than usual; whatever is comfortable for you. And now listen to the music." Patients may be invited to listen to the music or imagine a peaceful place and allow the images to change as the music suggests. Between five to fifteen minutes of music may be played after this induction. For example, CO may play on the electric piano improvised music, or a selection like Beethoven's Moonlight Sonata (1st Movement), Saint-Saen's The Swan (piano version), Enya's Watermark, Meyers Cavatina Deer Hunter, Mozart's Piano Concerto Theme, No 21, and a Chopin Nocturne; or LM may offer to play improvised music or an improvised simple folk or jazz melody instrumentally, setting the tempo to suit the patient's symptoms and needs. Shorter music segments may be presented when introducing the method to the patients for the first time, and when the therapist elects to not invite the patient to allow the imagery to change. Imagery-based or gentle progressive muscle relaxation inductions may also be used. Further helpful inductions may be found in various texts including Boog and Tester (2008) and Grocke and Wigram (2007). Individuals without distressing symptoms, including those living in the community, may find lengthier inductions and music presentations more helpful. Teaching and helping cancer patients and their family members to use music listening (Clark et al. 2006; Magill 2009a) and imagery (Burns et al. 2008) may also help to reduce stress and anxiety during and following cancer treatments. The Bonny Method of Guided Imagery and Music (BMGIM) by trained therapists can also be helpful when survivors are exploring ways of living with the cancer diagnosis (Bonde 2007).

Music therapists are encouraged to develop their own repertoire of music which can be used to promote patients' and families' relaxation and supportive imagery. Ultimately when using music to promote relaxation and supportive imagery it is important to understand what music they prefer, find helpful, and satisfying. This pertains to types of music, inductions, and all musical dynamics, such as rhythm, tempos, pitches, and volume. As musical preference is very personal, depending on associations with selections and genres, music that is relaxing for some people may lead to agitation and feelings of stress in another person. CO was once told by a patient that her improvised xylophone sounds reminded him of bombs being dropped when his country was at war. Another patient with whom LM was working found his favorite requested selection to be suddenly overwhelming to him due to his feelings of loss associated with the elicited memories. Some patients also find up-beat and fast tempos, or heavy metal music relaxing. Music therapists must always seek to understand patient preferences and support emerging needs.

Music therapy in cancer care in India and Nepal

In developing countries, such as India and Nepal, the use of music therapy in clinical practice is relatively new, even though music has been valued and honored in traditional customs as a healing medium since the beginning of recorded history. In Indian culture esthetic experiences in music are known to help transport individuals into higher states of transcendental consciousness and awareness. Raga chikitsa, an ancient manuscript which deals with the therapeutic effects of raga, has been commonly used throughout time in

India and also in Nepal to promote healing and influence mood and physiological parameters (Sundar 2007; Popley 1966). Vedic traditions, dating back approximately 5000 years, had a great understanding about the power of sound and intonation. The Vedic chants and music were used as a source of healing and upliftment and reflected the intuition that each intonation and inflection of the voice could have effects on an individual; beneficially or adversely (Sundar 2007).

In developing countries, patients commonly present with advanced stages of cancer, as they tend to seek treatment when their disease has metastasized; thus care of the physical condition becomes the major focus. Early detection of cancer and its timely treatment are still obscure for the large populace; however simultaneous, physical and emotional or holistic care is gradually becoming more available in larger metropolitan communities. Lack of education and inadequate financial and health resources for a major portion of society contribute to the prevalence of advanced disease in these countries, and adequate psychosocial support for cancer is lacking in most places.

Although the clinical use of music therapy is new, there has been some work-to-date. The focus of music therapy in these cultures is patient and family centered. As these societies are pluralistic in nature, it has been LM's recent experience working in India that it is common for three generations to be actively participating at the bedside of the patient. The unit of care is the patient and family system as a whole, including the extended families and all individuals involved with the patient. While the needs of the patient are central, the family is closely engaged and participates openly in the singing and instrument playing, including the use of madals, dholaks, sarangi, guitar, wooden flutes, tabla and simple hand instruments, such as egg shakers.

There is also an emphasis on faith in the music therapy sessions. It has been LM's experience that patients and families seek to incorporate their beloved chants, bhajans, kirtans, devotional songs or hymns, all of which are normally lyrical, expressing love for the Divine. The music in sessions is mainly vocal and all participate enthusiastically, including welcoming improvised lyrics as guided by the music therapist. For example, in one family, the children gathered around the grandmother who had advanced cancer. They all offered words of meaning in familiar bhajan melodies. One day when the grandmother was actively dying in her home, during a home visit, the youngest granddaughter—who was very close to her throughout her illness—held her grandmother's hands and sang her favorite Hindi words while the music therapist encouraged her to sing gently near her so that her grandmother would hear her and feel her support. The other family members sat on the floor near the bed, including the sons and daughters, aunts, uncles, and friends.

Music therapy in these countries tends to be readily accepted and intuitively understood, especially due to the familiar role that music has played over time in health and healing regimens. Its role as a specialized health profession within multidisciplinary teams is new and in its infancy, and has been practiced in New Delhi at CanSupport by LM and her students, and in Chennai by Dr Sumathy Sundar (2007), who has also conducted research in music therapy in cancer care; and it has also been introduced in Kathmandu by LM and her colleagues in Nepal. As also noted by Dr Sundar, music therapy is an emerging complementary therapy in this part of the world and there is a need for more research; however the multidimensional nature of music lends itself naturally in interdisciplinary settings and can in time play an even more important role in oncology and palliative care practices (Magill 2011; Sundar 2007).

Contraindications

While music therapy can be adapted to meet most of the presenting needs of patients and families, there are times it may not be appropriate. The significance of the stimulus of music in the care of patients with serious and life-threatening illnesses must not be overlooked. The potential that music has to stimulate neurological centers is remarkable, as it is observed to have ameliorating effects on pain and symptoms of fear, anxiety, depression, frustration, and loneliness. It is paramount, however, that thorough and ongoing, moment-to-moment assessments guide the music therapist at all times so that interventions are used that will best suit overall needs. As music evokes emotions, there may be times when the presence of music may not be indicated, such as with acutely distressed and/or emotionally fragile patients who may not be able to manage any surfacing of emotions. Also when there are crises, or acute episodes of emotional stress or severe pain, patients may be in a state of sensory overload during which the addition of the stimulus of music would create increased and difficult-to-manage stress. There are times, too, for example, when cultural morays and traditions determine the inappropriateness of the presence of music. The therapist must be skilled and well trained so as to astutely assess the emotional needs of patients and families, to determine, in collaboration with the patient and family as much as possible, if, when, how, and what kinds of music may best suit the overall status. Nevertheless, music has the unique potential to operate multi-dimensionally and holistically and can serve a range of symptoms and issues faced by patients and families across the continuum of illness.

Research in music therapy in oncology

Research about music therapy in oncology includes a range of approaches; objectivist (quantitative), constructivist (qualitative) (Kuper et al. 2008), and mixed methods (Lingard et al. 2008). Before selectively summarizing this work it is important to mention the Cochrane review on the effect of music interventions on physical and psychological outcomes in cancer patients. Bradt et al. (2011) examined 30 trials which included 1891 participants. Findings suggested that the music interventions may have helped to reduce anxiety and pain, and improve life quality and mood in people with cancer. The authors, however, warned that the findings need to be viewed cautiously, as most of the studies included high bias risks. Discussion of the comparable merits of findings emergent from well conducted studies informed by the different methodologies, and further descriptions of palliative care research, is found elsewhere (O'Callaghan 2008).

Objectivist research

Randomized controlled trials (RCTs) which achieved significant positive findings indicated that varied kinds of music therapy methods improved cancer patients' mood (Burns 2001; Cassileth et al. 2003; Magill Bailey 1983), life quality (Burns 2001; Hanser et al. 2006; Hilliard 2003), relaxation (Chuang et al. 2010; Chuang et al. 2011; Ferrer 2007), coping, social integration (Robb et al. 2014) and diastolic blood pressure (Ferrer 2007), and reduced heart rate (Hanser et al. 2006), anxiety (Ferrer 2007; Lin et al. 2011; Burns et al. 2008), fear, (Ferrer 2007), and pain (Gutsgell et al. 2013; Li et al. 2011). In a non-randomized pre-post test study, music therapy improved patients' mood (Waldon 2001). Music therapy also reduced patients' pain and nausea (Sahler et al. 2002). Other quantitative studies indicated that music therapy reduced isolation (Magill Bailey 1983) and boredom (O'Brien 1999), and improved mood (Magill Bailey 1983; Burns 2001), communication (Magill Bailey 1983), treatment tolerance (O'Brien 1999), endurance, cooperation, participation (Boldt 1996), life quality (Burns 2001), and was satisfying (Weber et al. 1997). Relaxation exercises were also preferred (Boldt 1996), as was classical music in a chemotherapy study (Weber et al. 1997). Seventy per cent of American music therapists also preferred to use live music interventions in cancer care (Kruse 2003). Many cancer patients are also interested in experiencing music therapy (Burns et al. 2005).

Constructivist research

Constructivist (qualitative) research found that varied music therapy methods can reduce cancer patients' preoccupation with adversity, help to enable their positive self-expression (Bunt and Marston-Wyld 1995) and emotional experience (O'Callaghan and McDermott 2004), affirm their aliveness, expand awareness (O'Callaghan and McDermott 2004), and provide opportunities for creativity, choice, enrichment, freedom, release, healing, balance, esthetic, meaning, expanded identity, and/or empowerment (Magill 2009a; Daykin et al. 2007), spiritual connectedness (Magill 2009b; McClean et al. 2012), peer support, improved confidence, and relaxation (Pothoulaki et al. 2012). Music therapists perceived that music therapy can help to expand a patient's sense of identity (Aldridge and Aldridge 2008), and also help oncology patients, hospital visitors, and staff to encounter intra-awareness and community participation (O'Callaghan and McDermott 2004). Staff bystanders also found it personally helpful to witness oncologic music therapy's effects (O'Callaghan and Magill 2009) and parents who witnessed adolescents and young adults receiving music therapy during stem cell transplantation also indirectly benefitted through improved insight into their children's cancer experiences and relief because of the program's beneficial effect on their children (Docherty et al. et al. 2013). Journal writing and analysis were helpful for a music therapy student's practice development (Barry and O'Callaghan 2008) and also understandings about how music therapy elicits hospital ward communities (O'Callaghan 2005b).

Cancer patients found song writing to be pleasurable, unique, calming, helpful and easy, and it enabled them to record significant life events and express themselves (Magill 2005; O'Brien 2005). Song writing is a forum where parents can express important messages to their children including love, their children's meaning for them, hopes, compliments, suggestions about who they can turn to, and existential beliefs (O'Callaghan et al. 2009).

Mixed methods research

Mixed methods research indicated that music therapy increased patients' faith, hope, and well-being (Magill et al. 2008), decreased their tension (Burns et al. 2001) and distress

(Magill et al. 2008), and was linked with survivors' transcendence and empowerment (Magill 2009b; Rykov 2008). The Bonney Method of Guided Imagery and Music (BMGIM improved cancer survivors' life quality (Bonde 2005), including through reducing their anxiety, and enhancing mood, coping, and dealing with existential issues (Bonde 2007). Finally, United Kingdom cancer care managers characterized music therapy as: Enjoyment, communication, healing, background, entertainment, and an expressive exploratory and release tool (Daykin et al. 2007).

CONCLUSION

Music therapy with adults in oncology and palliative care settings addresses a wide range of cancer-related symptoms promotes improved well-being and quality of life in patients and family members. Music therapists maintain access to a wide variety of techniques and strategies that may be adapted to specific patient requests and multiple biopsychosocial and spiritual needs. Music therapists must assess patients and families on an ongoing basis and consider the patients' personal wishes and hopes and their ethnic and spiritual preferences, while at all times affirming their unique strengths and gifts.

As the needs of those facing the challenges of cancer are prevalent, music therapists need to be compassionate, maintaining well developed listening and attention skills and displaying a calm and accepting demeanor. It is also paramount that the therapist has astute self-awareness skills so as to be able to be fully present to the needs of patients and families. Music therapists must also be flexible and innovative in their approaches, so as to be able to adapt to the changing needs in and between sessions.

The role of the music therapist within an interdisciplinary team still needs to be clarified, and the specific contributions that this modality can offer needs to be better understood and to be continually researched. There are some common misunderstandings: The role of the music therapist must not be confused with the role of the recreational therapist or *arts healers*, who also fulfill essential but different needs; and they must not be seen as solely providing a specialized activity for musically or artistically talented patients.

In general, through the clinical experiences of the authors and an analysis of the literature in this field, music therapists seem to be particularly effective in five areas: (a) In the enhancement of positive feelings of calmness, relaxation, and of personal well-being; (b) in offering safe cathartic expressions and transformations; (c) in facilitating the elaboration of existential and spiritual issues and improving sense of meaning; (d) in facilitating communication between patients, family members, and staff; and (e) improving overall quality of life. Thus, music therapy serves a range of significant benefits and plays a meaningful and important role in multidisciplinary patient care.

REFERENCES

Aasgaard, A. (1999). Music therapy as milieu in the hospice and paediatric oncology ward. In: D. Aldridge (ed.), *Music Therapy in Palliative Care: New Voices*, pp. 29–42. London: Jessica Kingsley Publishers.

Aldridge, G. (2008). *Melody in music therapy*. Jessica Kingsley Publishers.

Aldridge, G. and Aldridge, D. (2008). *Melody in Music Therapy: A Therapeutic Narrative Analysis*. London: Jessica Kingsley Publishers.

American Cancer Society (2011). Find support and treatment. Available at: <http://www.cancer.org/Treatment/TreatmentsandSideEffects/PhysicalSideEffects/ChemotherapyEffects/chemo-brain>. Accessed on 14 March 2012.

Barry, P. and O'Callaghan, C. (2008). Reflexive journal writing: A tool for music therapy student clinical practice development. *Nordic Journal of Music Therapy* 17: 55–66.

Beggs, C. (1991). Life review with a palliative care patient. In: K Bruscia (ed.), *Case Studies in Music Therapy*, pp. 611–616. Gilsum, NH: Barcelona Publishers.

Boldt, S. (1996). The effect of music therapy on the psychological well-being, physical comfort, and exercise endurance of bone marrow transplant patients. *Journal of Music Therapy*, 33: 164–188.

Bonde, L.O. (2005). "Finding a new place..." Metaphor and narrative in one cancer survivor's BMGIM Therapy. *Nordic Journal of Music Therapy* 14: 137–154.

Bonde, L.O. (2007). Imagery, metaphor, and perceived outcome in six cancer survivors Bonny Method of Guided Imagery and Music (BMGIM) Therapy. In: A. Meadows (ed.), *Qualitative Inquiries in Music Therapy: A monograph series*, 3, pp. 132–164. Gilsum NH: Barcelona Publishers.

Boog, K.M. and Tester, C.Y. (2008). *Palliative Care: A Practical Guide for the Health Professional*. Edinburgh: Churchill Livingstone.

Bradt, J., Dileo, C., Grocke, D., and Magill, L. (2011). Music interventions for improving psychological and physical outcomes in cancer patients. *Cochrane Database of Systematic Reviews*, Issue 8. Art. No.: CD006911. DOI: 10.1002/14651858.CD006911.pub2.

Breitbart, W. (2002). Spirituality and meaning in supportive care: spirituality- and meaning-centered group psychotherapy interventions in advanced cancer. *Supportive Care in Cancer* 10(4): 272–280.

Bruscia, K.E., Dileo, C., Shultis, C., and Dennery, K. (2009). Expectations of hospitalized cancer and cardiac patients regarding the medical and psychotherapeutic benefits of music therapy. *The Arts in Psychotherapy* 36: 229–234.

Bunt, L. and Marston-Wyld, J. (1995). Where words fail, music takes over: A collaborative study by a music therapist and a counselor in the context of cancer care. *Music Therapy Perspectives* 13: 46–50.

Burns, D.S. (2001). The effect of the bonny method of guided imagery and music on the mood and life quality of cancer patients, *Journal of Music Therapy* 38: 51–65.

Burns, S.J., Harbuz, M.S., Hucklebridge, F., and Bunt, L. (2001). A pilot study into the therapeutic effects of music therapy at a cancer help center. *Alternative Therapies* 7(1): 48–56.

Burns, D.S., Sledge, R.B., Fuller, L.A., Daggy, J.K., and Monahan, P.O. (2005). Cancer patients' interest and preferences for music therapy. *Journal of Music Therapy* 42: 185–199.

Burns, D.S., Azzouz, F., Sledge, R., Rutledge C., Hincher, K., Monahan P.O., and Cripe, L.D. (2008). Music imagery for adults with acute leukemia in protective environments: a feasibility study. *Supportive Care in Cancer* 16: 507–513.

Cassileth, B., Vickers, A., and Magill, L. (2003). Music therapy for mood disturbance during hospitalization for autologous stem cell transplantation. *Cancer* 98: 2723–2729.

Clark, M., Isaacks-Downton, G., Wells, N., Redlin-Frazier, S., Eck, C., Hepworth, J. T., and Chakravarthy, B. (2006). Use of preferred music to reduce emotional distress and symptom activity during radiation therapy. *Journal of Music Therapy* 43(3): 247–265.

Cancer Council Australia (2011). Frequently Asked Questions. Available at: <http://www.cancer.org.au/aboutcancer/FAQ.htm#3007>. Accessed 14 March, 2012.

CDC. (n.d.). Centres for Disease Control and Prevention. National Centre for Health Statistics, USA. Available at: <http://www.cdc.gov/nchs/fastats/lcod.htm>. Accessed 14 March 2012.

Chuang, C., Han, W., Li, P., and Young, S. (2010). Effects of music therapy on subjective sensations and heart rate variability in treated cancer survivors: A pilot study. *Complementary Therapies in Medicine* 18: 224–226.

Chuang, C., Han, W., Li, P., Song, M., and Young, S. (2011). Effect of long-term music therapy intervention on autonomic function in anthracycline-treated breast cancer patients. *Integrative Cancer Therapies* 10: 312–316.

Coleman, P. (1994). Reminiscence within the study of ageing. In: J. Bornat (ed.), *Reminiscence Reviewed*, pp. 8–20. Buckingham: Open University Press.

Daykin, N., McClean, S., and Bunt, L. (2007). Creativity, identity and healing: participants' accounts of music therapy in cancer care. *Health* 11(3): 349–370.

Dileo, C. and Bradt, J. (1999). Entrainment, resonance and pain-related suffering. In: C. Dileo, *Music Therapy and Medicine: Theoretical and Clinical Applications*, pp. 181–188. Silver Spring, MD: American Music Therapy Association.

Dileo, C. and Magill, L. (2005). Songwriting with oncology and hospice adult patients from a multicultural perspective. In: F. Baker and T. Wigram (eds), *Songwriting: Methods and Clinical Applications for Music Therapy Clinicians, Educators and Students*, pp. 226–245. London: Jessica Kingsley Publishers.

Dinshaw, K.A., Rao, D.N., and Ganesh, B. (1999). Tata Memorial Hospital Cancer Registry Annual Report. Mumbai, India.

Docherty, S.L, Robb, S.L., Phillips-Salimi, C., Cherven, B., Stegenga, K, Hendricks-Ferguson, V. et al. (2013). Parental perspectives on a behavioral health music intervention for adolescent/young adult resilience during cancer treatment: report from the children's oncology group. *Journal of Adolescent Health* 52: 170–178.

Dougal Miller, D. and O'Callaghan, C. (2010). Music therapy in adult oncology. In: D. Hanson-Abromeit and C. Colwell (eds), *AMTA Monograph Series: Effective Clinical Practice in Music Therapy: Medical Music Therapy for Adults in the Hospital Setting*, pp. 217–307. Silver Spring, MD: American Music Therapy Association.

El-Ghamry, M.N. and Taghian, A. (2012). Radiation techniques for locally advanced breast cancer. Up to Date Marketing Professional. Available at: <http://www.uptodate.com/contents/radiation-techniques-for-locally-advanced-breast-cancer?source = search_result&selectedTitle = 2%7E150&view = outline>. Accessed 14 March 2012.

Ferrer, A.J. (2007). The effect of live music on decreasing anxiety in patients undergoing chemotherapy treatment. *Journal of Music Therapy* 44: 242–245.

Gass, R. and Brehony, K. (1999), *Chanting: Discovering Spirit in Sound*. New York: Random House.

Goodrem, D. and Mtawarira, A. (2002). *Born to Try* [CD]. Epic label.

Grocke, D. and Wigram, T. (2007). *Receptive Methods in Music Therapy*. London: Jessica Kingsley Publishers.

Gutgsell, K.J., Schluchter, M., Margevicius, S., DeGolia, P.A., McLaughlin, B., Harris, M. et al. (2013). Music therapy reduces pain in palliative care patients: a randomized controlled trial. *Journal of Pain and Symptom Management* 45: 822–831.

Hanser, S.B., Bauer-Wu, S., Kubicek, L., Healy, M., Manola, J., Hernandez, M., and Bunnell, C. (2006). Effects of a music therapy intervention on quality of life and distress in women with metastatic breast cancer. *Journal of the Society of Integrative Oncology* 4: 116–124.

Hilliard, R. E. (2003). The effects of music therapy on the quality and length of life of people diagnosed with terminal cancer. *Journal of Music therapy* 40(2): 113–137.

Hilliard, R. (2005). *Hospice and Palliative Care Music Therapy: A Guide to Program Development and Clinical Care.* Cherry Hill: Jeffrey Books.

Holland, J.C. and Weiss, T.R. (2010). Introduction. In: J.C. Holland, W.S. Breitbart, P.B. Jacobsen, M.S. Lederberg, M.J. Loscalzo, and R. McCorkle (eds), *Psycho-oncology,* 2nd edn., pp. 1–12. Oxford: Oxford University Press.

Johansen, C. (2010). Psychosocial factors. In: J.C. Holland, W.S. Breitbart, P.B. Jacobsen, M.S. Lederberg, M.J. Loscalzo, and R. McCorkle (eds), *Psycho-oncology,* 2nd edn., pp. 57–61. Oxford: Oxford University Press.

Keyes, L.E. (1973). *Toning: The Creative Power of the Voice.* Camarillo, CA: DeVorss.

Kruse, J. (2003). Music therapy in United States cancer Settings: Recent trends in practice. *Music Therapy Perspectives* 21: 89–98.

Kuper, A., Reeves, S., and Levinson, W. (2008). Qualitative research: An introduction to reading and appraising qualitative research. *British Medical Journal* 337: 404–407.

Li, X., Yan, H., Zhou, K., Dang, S., Wang, D.L., and Zhang, Y.P. (2011). Effects of music therapy on pain among female breast cancer patients after radical mastectomy: results from a randomized controlled trial. *Breast Cancer Research and Treatmet* 128: 411–419.

Lin, M., Hsieh, Y., Hsu, Y., Fetzer, S., and Hsu, M. (2011). A randomised controlled trial of the effect of music therapy and verbal relaxation on chemotherapy-induced anxiety. *Journal of Clinical Nursing* 20: 988–999.

Lingard, L., Albert, M., and Levinson, W. (2008). Grounded theory, mixed methods, and action research. *British Medical Journal* 337: 459–461.

Loewy, J. V., Hallan, C., Freidman, E., and Martinez, C. (2006). Sleep/sedation in children undergoing EEG testing: A comparison of chloral hydrate and music therapy. *American Journal of Electroneurodiagnositc Technology* 46: 343–355.

Logis, M. (2011). Facing the dread and desolation of cancer through music therapy: A client's perspective. *Music and Medicine* 3: 27–30.

Logis, M. and Turry, A. (1999). Singing my way through it: facing the cancer, darkness and fear. In: J. Hibben (ed.), *Inside Music Therapy: Client Experiences,* pp. 97–119. Gilsum, NH: Barcelona Publishers.

Magill Bailey, L. (1983). The effects of live versus tape recorded music on hospitalized cancer patients. *Music Therapy* 3(1): 17–28.

Magill Bailey, L. (1984). The use of songs in music therapy with cancer patients and families. *Music Therapy* 4(1): 5–17.

Magill L. (2001). The use of music therapy to address the suffering in advanced cancer pain. *Journal of Palliative Care* 17(3): 167–172.

Magill L. (2005). Music therapy: Enhancing spirituality at the end-of-life. In: C. Dileo and J. Loewy. *Music Therapy and End-of-life,* pp. 3–18. Cherry Hills, NJ: Jeffrey Books.

Magill, L. (2009a). Caregiver empowerment in music therapy: Through the eyes of bereaved caregivers. *Journal of Palliative Care* 25(1): 68–75.

Magill, L. (2009b). The spiritual meaning of pre-loss music therapy to bereaved caregivers of advanced cancer patients. *Journal of Palliative and Supportive Care* 7: 97–108.

Magill, L. (2010). Art therapy and music therapy. In: J.C. Holland, W.S. Breitbart, P.B. Jacobsen, M.S. Lederberg, M.J. Loscalzo, and R. McCorkle. *Psycho-oncology*, 2nd edn., pp. 22–28. Oxford: Oxford University Press.

Magill, L. (2011). Bereaved family caregivers' reflections on the role of the music therapist. *Music and Medicine* 3: 56–63, first published on October 25, 2010. DOI: 10.1177/1943862110386233.

Magill, L. and O'Callaghan, C. (2011). Guest Editors. Music therapy in supportive cancer care. *Music and Medicine (Special Issue)* 3(10): 7–8.

Magill, L., Levin, T., and Spodek, L. (2008). One-session music therapy and CBT for critically ill cancer patients. *Psychiatric services (Washington, DC)*, 59(10): 1216.

Mayo Clinic Staff (2011). Cancer survivors: Late effects of cancer treatment. <http://www.mayoclinic.com/health/cancer-survivor/CA00073>. Accessed 14 March 2014.

McAdams, S. (1984). The auditory image: A metaphor for musical and psychological research on auditory organization. In: W.R. Crozier and A.J. Chapman (eds), *Cognitive Processes in the Perception of Art*, pp. 289–323. Amsterdam: North-Holland, Elsevier Science.

McClean, S., Bunt, L., and Daykin, N. (2012). The healing and spiritual properties of music therapy at a cancer care centre. *Journal of Alternative and Complementary Medicine* 18: 402–407.

McDougal Miller, D. & O'Callaghan, C. (2010). Music therapy in adult oncology. In D. Hanson-Abromeit and C. Colwell (eds), *AMTA Monograph Series: Effective Clinical Practice in Music Therapy: Medical Music Therapy for Adults in the Hospital Setting*, pp. 217–307. Silver Spring, MD: American Music Therapy Association.

McDougal Miller, D. and O'Callaghan, C. (2010). Music therapy in adult cancer care: Across the cancer continuum. In: D. Hanson-Abromeit and C. Cowell (eds), *Medical Music Therapy for Adults in Hospital Settings*, pp. 217–306. Silver Spring, Maryland: American Music Therapy Association.

O'Brien, E. (1999). Cancer patients' evaluation of a music therapy program. In: R. Rebollo Pratt and D. Erdonmez Grocke (eds), *MusicMedicine* 3: 285–300. Melbourne: Faculty of Music, University of Melbourne.

O'Brien, E. (2003). *Living Soul* [CD]. Crystal Mastering, Melbourne.

O'Brien, E. (2005). Songwriting with adult patients in oncology and clinical haematology. In: F. Bakerand T. Wigram (eds), *Songwriting Methods, Techniques and Clinical Applications for Music Therapy Clinicians, Educators and Students*, pp. 185–205. London: Jessica Kingsley Publishers.

O'Brien, E. (2006). Opera therapy: Creating and performing a new work with cancer patients. *Nordic Journal of Music Therapy* 15(1): 89–103.

O'Brien, E. (2012). "Morphine mamma": Creating original songs using rap with women with cancer. In: S. Hadley and S.G. Yancy (eds), *Therapeutic uses of Rap and Hip-hop*, pp. 337–352. New York: Routledge.

O'Callaghan, C. (1984). Musical profiles of dying patients. *Australian Music Therapy Association Bulletin* 7(2): 5–11.

O'Callaghan, C. (1996). Lyrical themes in songs written by palliative care patients. *Journal of Music Therapy* 33: 74–92.

O'Callaghan, C. (1997). Therapeutic opportunities associated with the music when using song writing in palliative care. *Music Therapy Perspectives* 15(1): 32–38.

O'Callaghan, C. (1999). Recent findings about neural correlates of music pertinent to music therapy across the life span. *Music Therapy Perspectives* 17: 32–36.

O'Callaghan, C. (2001). Bringing music to life: Music therapy and palliative care experiences in a cancer hospital. *Journal of Palliative Care* 13: 155–160.

O'Callaghan, C. (2005a). Song writing in threatened lives. In: C. Dileo and J. Loewy (eds), *Music Therapy in End of Life Care*, pp. 117–128. Cherry Hill, NJ: Jeffrey Publications.

O'Callaghan, C. (2005b). Qualitative data-mining through reflexive journal analysis: Implications for music therapy practice development. *Journal of Social Work Research and Evaluation* 6: 219–231.

O'Callaghan, C. (2006). Clinical Issues: Music therapy in an adult cancer inpatient treatment setting. *Journal of the Society of Integrative Oncology* 4(2): 57–61.

O'Callaghan, C. (2007). Music therapy inspired transient ward communities in oncology. In: J. Edwards (ed.), *Music: Promoting Health and Creating Community in Healthcare Contexts*, pp. 1–16. Newcastle-upon-Tyne: Cambridge Scholars.

O'Callaghan, C. (2008). Lullament: Lullaby and lament therapeutic qualities actualized through music therapy. *American Journal of Hospice and Palliative Medicine* 25: 93–99.

O'Callaghan, C. and Colegrove, V. (1998). Effect of the music therapy introduction when engaging hospitalised cancer patents. *Music Therapy Perspectives* 16(2): 67–74.

O'Callaghan, C. and Jordan, B. (2011). Music therapy supports parent-infant attachments affected by life threatening cancer. In J. Edwards (ed.), *Music Therapy in Parent-infant Bonding*, pp. 191–207. Oxford: Oxford University Press.

O'Callaghan, C. and Magill, L. (2009). Effect of music therapy on oncologic staff bystanders: A substantive grounded theory. *Journal of Palliative and Supportive Care* 7: 219–228.

O'Callaghan, C. and McDermott, F. (2004). Music therapy's relevance in a cancer hospital researched through a constructivist lens. *Journal of Music Therapy* 41: 151–185.

O'Callaghan, C., O'Brien, E., Magill, L., and Ballinger, E. (2009). Resounding attachment: Cancer inpatients' song lyrics for their children in music therapy. *Supportive Care in Cancer* 17: 1149–1157.

Pfizer (2008). The burden of cancer in asia. USA: Pfizer, Inc. Available at: <http://www.pfizer.com/files/products/cancer_in_asia.pdf>.

Popley, H.A. (1966). *The Music of India. The Heritage of India Series*. New Delhi: YMCA Publishing House.

Pothoulaki, M., MacDonald, R., and Flowers, P. (2012). An interpretative phenomenological analysis of an improvisational music therapy program for cancer patients. *Journal of Music Therapy* 49: 45–67.

Rider, M.S. (1985). Entrainment mechanisms are involved in pain reduction, muscle relaxation, and music-mediated imagery. *Journal of Music Therapy* 22(4): 183–192.

Robb, S.L., Burns, D.S., Stegenga, K.A., Haut, P.R., Monahan, P.O., Meza, J. et al. (2014). Randomized clinical trial of therapeutic music video intervention for resilience outcomes in adolescents/young adults undergoing hematopoietic stem cell transplant: A report from the Children's Oncology Group. *Cancer* 120: 909–917.

Rosenthal, D.S. (2001). The nature of adult cancer: Medical diagnosis and treatment. In: M.M. Lauria, E.J. Clark, J.F. Hermann, and N.M. Stearns (eds), *Social Work in Oncology: Supporting Survivors, Families, and Caregivers*, pp. 1–26. Atlanta, Georgia: American Cancer Society.

Rykov, M. H. (2008). Experiencing music therapy cancer support. *Journal of Health Psychology* 13(2): 190–200.

Sahler, O.J., Hunter, B.C., and Liesveld, J.L. (2002). The effect of using music therapy with relaxation imagery in the management of patients undergoing bone marrow transplantation: a pilot feasibility study. *Alternative Therapies in Health and Medicine* 9(6): 70–74.

Shapiro, C.L. (2012). Side effects of adjuvant chemotherapy for early stage breast cancer. <ttp://www.uptodate.com/contents/side-effects-of-adjuvant-chemotherapy-for-early-stage-breast-cancer?source=search_result&selectedTitle=1%7E150&view=outline>. Accessed 14 March 2012.

Sundar, S. (2007). Traditional healing systems and modern music therapy in India. *Music Therapy Today* [Online] Vol. VIII (3). Available at: <http://musictherapyworld.net>.

Underwood, J.C.E. (2009). Carcenogenesis and neoplasia. In: J.C.E. Underwood and S.S. Cross (eds), *General and Systematic Pathology*, 5th edn., pp. 183–219. Edinburgh: Churchill Livingston.

Waldon, E. (2001). The effects of group music therapy on mood states and cohesiveness in adult oncology patients. *Journal of Music Therapy* 38: 212–238.

Weber, S., Nuessler, V. and Wilmanns, W. (1997). A pilot study on the influence of receptive music listening on cancer patients during chemotherapy. *International Journal of Arts Medicine* 5(2): 27–36.

Wells, N.L. and Turney, M.E. (2001). Common issues facing adults with cancer. In: M.M. Lauria, E.J. Clark, J.F. Hermann, and N.M. Stearns (eds), *Social Work in Oncology: Supporting Survivors, Families, and Caregivers*, pp. 27–44. Atlanta, Georgia: American Cancer Society.

Winnicott, D.W. (1971). *Playing and Reality*. London: Routledge.

CHAPTER 7

··

MUSIC THERAPY AND PARENT-INFANT PROGRAMMES

··

JANE EDWARDS AND VICKY ABAD

INTRODUCTION

EVERY day around the world parents and care givers vocalize playfully with their infants and children. They sing songs together, join in chants and rhymes, play recorded music in the car, and perhaps as a special treat put on a favorite CD before bed and listen together or dance. This use of music in family life provides a basis for understanding why it is proposed that music and music therapy can be helpful for children and their care givers who need support and help in their relationship.

For many parents the birth of their baby represents a joyous, much anticipated milestone, but for other parents' additional support and help is needed in order for them to feel competent and satisfied with their parenting role and tasks. Postnatal depression is a condition that some parents can experience following the birth of a child and is a serious mental health issue warranting its own classification. Parental depression during the early years of a baby's life has negative impacts on many domains of development, especially if occurring during the first twelve months after birth (Field 2010). Although incidence and prevalence have been difficult to determine accurately (Mann et al. 2010) the Australian resource *Beyondblue* estimates that as many as one in ten women will experience depression in the postnatal period (<www.beyondblue.org.au>) while the DSM V indicates a lower rate of between three and six percent (American Psychiatric Association 2013).

The incidence of postpartum depression in fathers is estimated as lower than for women, but having a female partner with postpartum depression increases men's risk of becoming depressed (Goodman 2004). Although there are calls for further research about same sex couples' experience of postpartum depression (for example, Goldberg and Smith 2011) there is no available information as yet about incidence and prevalence of depression within same sex parental constellations. Prenatal depression is predictive of postnatal depression, and is considered to occur more frequently than postnatal mood disorders (Field 2010). Given that the most recent annual audit of live births in Australia indicates that more than 300,000 births were recorded (Australian Bureau of Statistics 2012), even accounting for multiple births, the incidence of parents who are depressed and need help and support is likely to be in the thousands every year.

The birth of a baby can be considered a maturational stressor involving major adjustment and coping for new parents. Other stressors can include being a member of a cultural minority, or another contextual factor which adds to risks arising from marginalization such as poverty or disability. In developing her system of the four care giving dimensions; sensitivity vs. insensitivity, acceptance vs. rejection, cooperation vs. interference, and accessibility vs. ignoring (Ainsworth et al. 1974), Ainsworth cautioned that cultural norms and historical context must be referenced in assessments of the sensitivity and quality of care-giving (Ainsworth 1977). A large body of research has shown differences in maternal responsiveness across different cultural groups (for example, Richman et al. 1992). Therefore an understanding of cultural norms is needed to assess care giver sensitivity.

Birth trauma usually refers to some kind of injurious physical event for the infant during birth, but it is also understood that other kinds of events during the birth can be traumatizing for mother, other parent, and/or the newborn including preterm delivery, separation soon after birth, and onset of illness following birth, leading in some cases to the development of post-traumatic stress disorder (Beck 2011; Garthus-Niegel et al. 2013). It is therefore important that practitioners working therapeutically with infants and care givers seek out information from families as to their experience of childbirth, as well as their psychological and emotional states before and immediately after the birth of the baby. Some clinicians refer to this information as the *birth history*.

This chapter describes how music therapy can contribute to the development of healthy, positive, and mutually satisfying communication between parents and their infants. The theoretical basis for this work is first elaborated followed by information about music therapy based parenting programmes. The family support programme *Sing & Grow* is described extensively as it is the most extensive and developed programme in music therapy to date. Techniques in developing and delivering programmes are presented and described.

MUSIC THERAPY FOR INFANTS AND THEIR CARE GIVERS

Music therapy with care givers and infants has been described as:

> ... a process of developing a relationship with a care giver/dyad in order to support, develop and extend their skills in using musical and music like interactions including vocal improvisation, chants, lullabies, songs, and rhymes, to promote and enhance the sensitivity and mutual co-regulation between infant and care giver, in order to create the optimal environment for secure attachment to be fostered.
>
> Edwards 2011, p. 6

Music therapy shares the premise promoted by many contemporary infancy researchers that rather than emphasizing the pre-linguistic features of vocal expressions in infancy, exploring the infant's vocalizations, and the shared vocal interplay between parent and infant as *musical* or music-like provides a broader framework through which to understand how and why the baby vocalizes (Malloch and Trevarthen 2009; Trevarthen 2001). Humans are evolutionarily driven to use music to engage and interact with infants, and infants are biologically hardwired to hear us (Dissanayake 2008; Mithen 2005). In infancy, music in the form of songs, chants, lullabies, and improvised vocal play is not referenced to high art cultural symbols; instead, spontaneous music making is a social, relational resource available to all regardless of musical skill, knowledge, or training. From a developmental psychology perspective "Music is not communicative in the sense of sharing information. Instead, it is concerned with sharing feelings and experiences and the regulation of social behavior" (Trehub 2003, p. 672).

Musical exchanges such as singing nursery songs or lullabies, or engaging in highly creative and expressive vocal interplay, offer a means to convey feeling states as well as to experience mutually satisfying and meaningful interactions between the care giver and infant. It is therefore highly relevant to use music or music-like techniques in order to facilitate and promote attachment between parents and infants in music therapy. While examples of this musical and music-like interplay are readily heard, when the infant's vocal play is considered as *inherently* musical an important focal point is provided to examine what occurs in parent-infant interactions. *Communicative musicality* is a term that is used to describe the intuitive musicality of parenting (Malloch and Trevarthan 2009). This communication relies firstly on the innate musicality of the child, and secondly on the care givers' capacity to be a sensitive and intuitive listener and responder.

PARENT-INFANT ATTACHMENT

In a healthy relationship the care giver " ... affords emotional access to the child and responds appropriately and promptly to his or her positive and negative states." (Schore 2001, p. 205). This supports the adaptation of the infant towards internal regulation functions which relate to "the regulation of arousal, the maintenance of alertness, the capacity to dampen arousal in the face of overstimulation, the capacity to inhibit behavioral expression, and the capacity to develop predictable behavioral cycles." (Beebe and Lachmann 1998, p. 485). This interpersonal and intrapsychic regulation within the parent-infant dyad is considered "interactive regulation" (Beebe 2000, p. 425). "Interactive regulation flows in both directions, on a moment-to-moment basis, so that each experiences influencing, as well as being influenced by, the other's behavior." (Beebe and Lachmann, p. 500).

Throughout the second half of the twentieth century many influential figures gave credence to the necessity for a secure carer, or parent-infant base to support the development of lifelong capacities for psychological stability and the capacity to form intimate relationships successfully with others (Beebe and Lachmann 1998; Robertson and Bowlby 1952; Ainsworth 1979; Trevarthen 2001; Winnicott 1965). The development of the infant's ability to relate and communicate is described as a series of building blocks or developmental phases of intrapsychic and interpersonal capacity (Stern 2000). At each stage of development the infant needs a communicating partner who is sensitive and responsive to their relating needs. Papoušek has proposed that the success of interactions for the communicating parental partner requires: "(a) the presence or absence as well as the liveliness and expression of infant-directed qualities (e.g. the qualities of infant-directed speech) and (b) the sensitive attunement of this behavior to the infant's signals." (Papoušek 2011, p. 35).

In healthy parent-child relationships musicality is present and observable. Vocal musical interactions through animated call-and-response games demonstrate the capacity for musical play. When the ability to seek or maintain this communication is absent or impaired in the relationship support and help is needed. A qualified music therapist works in gentle non-intrusive ways to help parents and their infants discover and strengthen their capacity for relating through encouraging a range of musical play that supports, and is derived from, the usual repertory of parent-infant interactions (Edwards 2014).

Parent-infant programmes in music therapy

Parent-infant work in music therapy has developed as a professional specialism with recognized leaders (for example Abad and Williams 2007; Loewy 2011; Flower and Oldfield 2008; Dearn and Shoemark 2014). Music therapy practitioners working with vulnerable parents and infants, especially in early intervention community based settings have demonstrated a consistent and developing practice base (Abad and Williams 2007; Bargiel 2004; Edwards et al. 2007; Jonsdottir 2002).

Music therapy programmes with parents and their infants have shown benefits in the quality of interaction observed, and self-reported satisfaction with participation in the sessions (Oldfield and Bunce 2001; Oldfield et al. 2003). Observations during music therapy sessions held over several months with mothers and their infants from the asylum seeker community revealed that interactions and interpersonal engagement improved for these vulnerable, *preoccupied* mothers and their children (Edwards et al. 2007). In a report of a music therapy group programme with self-referred well families it was shown that benefits included parents reporting that they had enhanced their learning about ways to deal with parental challenges (Mackenzie and Hamlett 2005). Additionally, a series of case reports on the uses of music therapy in a range of group and other programmes with parent-infant dyads has demonstrated the values of music therapy in providing effective support to promote attachment (Edwards 2011).

Music therapy programmes that specifically aim to support attachment behaviors between vulnerable parents and their infants have been founded, notably the Australian programme *Sing & Grow* (Abad and Edwards 2004; Abad and Williams 2007). *Sing & Grow* aims to "strengthen parent-child relationships through increasing developmentally conducive interactions, by assisting parents to bond with their children, and by extending the repertory of parenting skills in relating to their child through interactive play" (Abad and Williams 2007, p. 52).

Sing & Grow began in the Australian state of Queensland in 2001 after a successful bid for national funding prepared and submitted by Jane Edwards provided a funding base from which to establish and evaluate a two-year pilot with parents and their infants experiencing a range of vulnerabilities (Abad and Edwards 2004). The success of the two-year pilot led by Vicky Abad as the inaugural *Sing & Grow* Director initiated a further year of funding followed by a national roll out of *Sing & Grow* in every state and territory of Australia (Abad and Williams 2007). *Sing & Grow* became an international music therapy project in 2010 with the implementation of *Sing & Grow* UK. To date over 1000 standard programmes have taken place across Australia and in the UK <http://singandgrow.org/about-sing-grow/>.

Sing & Grow is described as a community based music therapy project because it provides services in communities where families reside, and because the project works to "promote the strength of family and community as participants experience for themselves the value of connectedness" (website). This is achieved through several programme models, including weekly group music therapy sessions, group workshops for families and workers, and/or intensive one to one music therapy services.

The standard *Sing & Grow* programme is provided through short-term weekly sessions for groups of families referred because of difficulties of vulnerabilities between infant and care givers (Abad and Williams 2007). These sessions are held in accessible community venues and operate on the basis of a sole music therapist providing a group based music therapy programme to up to ten referred families for ten consecutive weeks. Each family receives a CD of age-appropriate songs for use at home, and evaluation of changes of interactions is conducted through parental self-report and therapist observations of the group program.

The first study to evaluate a short-term early intervention music therapy parent-infant programme using validated measures found that for 358 parents and infants, a number of significant benefits impacted the parent and child in a range of areas including education in the home and parental mental health (Nicholson et al. 2008).

Sing & Grow also offer community placements and facility-based music therapy programmes for targeted families requiring a more intensive level of music therapy work. Based within an accessible community venue, a *Sing & Grow* clinician collaborates with existing family-focused agencies to provide music therapy services designed to better engage families who, for a range of reasons, may otherwise not participate in community programs. Service delivery can include home visits, 1:1 sessions, workshops, and group programmes that extend beyond the traditional ten week timeframe. *Sing & Grow* facility-based placements enable the delivery of intensive music therapy programmes that specifically cater for parents and children with complex needs in facilities including early parenting centers, early intervention centers, and mental health in-patient units that cater for women experiencing depression and their infants. *Sing & Grow* works to complement existing parenting supports offered within the relevant facility and implements both group and individual family music therapy services that address a range of early childhood and parenting issues.

CONSIDERATIONS FOR STARTING PROGRAMMES

Funding

Initially in developing a parent-infant programme (PIP) the source of funding needs to be decided and secured. Government and not-for-profit funding is the most commonly accessed stream of funding for programmes to date (Abad and Williams 2009). While current global economic conditions may impact negatively on funding opportunities (Abad and Williams 2009; Abad and Thomas 2013), experience shows that governments are more likely to fund programmes that have an evidence base to support their expenditure (Abad and Williams 2009; Williams et al. 2011). There is now an established and growing evidence base that supports the use of music therapy with care givers and their infants, as outlined above. Using this as a basis for justifying funding for a parent-infant programme is the first step when introducing a new service.

Referrals

Once funding has been procured, referrals need to be sourced. The basis of referrals will depend on the reason the programme is being offered and the clinical setting in which it is being held, and it will be influenced by the service delivery model.

Why refer to a parent-infant music therapy programme?

A music therapist may be referred parent-infant dyads for support where the relationship between the infant and their carer is compromised or at risk of not developing. The reason for referral may be as a result of a child-oriented issue or a parent concern. A child who has a disability and lives in the community with their family may be referred as the experience of living with a child with a disability has been shown to increase the risk of depression and isolation for the child's parent (Williams et al. 2012). A parent who experiences a mental health issue, drug or alcohol addiction, social, economic or cultural experience that impacts on their ability to parent, and in particular to be emotionally available to their child, may be referred to the program.

It is important to remember that it is the dyad that have been referred to music therapy. Whether the reason for referral originated from the needs of the child or the needs of the parent, the usual reason for the referral is an identified risk or compromise of the parent-child relationship. In a parent-infant programme there are potentially three clients. These include the child as client, thus focusing on the developmental and emotional needs of the child; the parent as client, focusing on the parents' mental health and support needs, using music therapy to validate and support their parenting role; and the parent-infant dyad, that is, the relationship that exists between the two. In dyadic work music allows a space for the pair to explore, connect, and share.

A well-informed parent-infant programme will usually incorporate the three concepts above, and the methods used will overlap. Parent-infant programmes most often focus on the relationship between the parent and child, and how music can bolster, support and strengthen this relationship. By doing this, the music therapy programme will support the parent in their parenting role and provide them with hands-on practical parenting strategies that will empower them as parents, and encourage the development and growth of the infant in a developmentally appropriate way.

Who is referred to a parent-infant music therapy programme?

People are referred to a PIP when there is concern about, or potential for compromise within, the relationship between a care giver and child. This is because optimal child development is achieved when parents or care givers and their children share a secure and loving relationship (Bowlby 2005). A range of issues and events can impact on a parent's ability to be available to their child. For this reason, clients are referred to a PIP with a wide range of backgrounds and needs. This includes, but is not limited to, families where a young parent, or a single parent is head of the family; where the family has recently immigrated to a new country, are refugees, or identify from a cultural minority, including indigenous families; a parent has an addiction issue; one or both parents are in prison, or have been in prison; one or both parents has a mental health issue; the parent or child has a disability or learning difficulty; foster families; adoptive families; and families where the child has experienced abuse or trauma; women who are survivors of domestic violence with their children; families under economic pressure.

Who makes the referral to the parent-infant music therapy programme?

Most parent-infant music therapy programmes are based in the community sector, and referrals will come from professionals who work with families identified as at-risk in community outreach programmes. This includes, but is not limited to: (1) Community workers, (2) allied health professionals including social workers, occupational therapists, speech and language pathologists, physiotherapists and psychologists, and (3) medical professionals including child and maternal health nurses, general practitioners, pediatricians, community nurses, and psychiatrists.

It is important that the music therapist establishes and maintains excellent community networks early in the development of the PIP to ensure families know about the programme and in fact access it. The reason for this is families who are considered at-risk of experiencing parenting issues that impact on their relationship with their child are usually hard to reach (Cortis et al. 2009; Coren and Barlow 2004), thus requiring the music therapist to work closely with community organizations who know the families to gain access to and trust from these families.

Attending community meetings, getting to know the community services available in the areas the PIP will service and ensuring community staff have information and a clear understanding of the PIP will ensure appropriate referrals are received seamlessly. A key way of achieving this is to hold regular community in-services and inviting a range of community and health workers to these.

Abad and Edwards (2004) reported how providing community in-services were a key means by which the *Sing & Grow* programme was promoted when it was first founded in the community sector. In the first six months of the programme a total of 30 in-services were delivered to 200 people from various community organizations that supported parents identified as at risk. Child health nurses were also targeted in geographic regions where the *Sing & Grow* programme was being rolled out (Abad and Williams 2007). Another way of building community networks and therefore ensuring referral networks are seamless is to attend staff meetings of community organizations, to firstly make connections and learn how the organization supports families, and secondly to provide information at the meetings about the PIP. The information should be presented in a short and relatively informal way. Producing an easy to read yet informative brochure that staff can hand out to families is another useful device and these can be handed out at both in-services and staff meetings.

Another referral pathway is that of family, friend, or self-referral to the programme. An interview based qualitative study of 20 parents experiencing financial hardship and not engaged with formal services revealed that they preferred to access non-agency based supports, which they perceived as *normal* and non-stigmatizing rather than agency based social services which they described as leading them to feel as if they are being judged and placed under surveillance (Winkworth et al. 2010). The researchers recommended playgroups as a way that parents could find a pathway into receiving more formal supports. If a friend has attended the PIP and enjoyed it, they may tell other friends who in turn may invite family members. It is therefore important to have an open door policy to allow access for friends and families who may attend. This may be encouraged in particular, with groups of young women and those living in residential or shared living settings.

Methods and techniques

A parent and child are referred to a PIP when there is concern for the relationship between the parent and child, and therefore the ongoing welfare of that child. The music therapist implements a music therapy programme aimed at meeting the needs of the parent and the child as a dyad. In order to do this they use music to support non-musical outcomes, by choosing methods and techniques that support the interaction between the dyad, nurture the relationship between the dyad, encourage physical closeness and empower the parent to use music for interacting in positive and loving ways with their infant.

Music therapy methods

Music therapy methods are the approaches chosen by the therapist to achieve therapeutic change. Generally speaking, these are usually categorized as receptive, improvisatory, recreative, or creative. The music therapist then employs a range of musical and therapeutic techniques within these methods to ensure their use meets the outlined needs of the client. It is important to note that methods and techniques, while explained separately in this text, often overlap and intertwine in their delivery to provide a supportive contained environment that allows parents the opportunity to safely explore, play and connect with their child, and different techniques may be employed to achieve the same outcome. Certainly, in both research and practice music therapy methods and techniques are used flexibly and in a blended, intertwined manner (Schwartz 2013).

Music therapy techniques and therapeutic outcome

Receptive music therapy techniques

Receptive music therapy involves techniques where the client is an active recipient of the music experience, rather than an active music maker (Grocke and Wigram 2007). In a PIP there may be times when a parent and child listen to the music therapist make music, or are listening to resources developed by the music therapist. The most common receptive music therapy techniques employed in a PIP are listening to live music in a session, listening to recorded music from the PIP outside of the session, and using music for relaxation. It is important to remember that auditory stimulation involves complex neurological processes (Skoe and Kraus 2010). Therefore it is not correct to describe receptive experiences as *passive*.

Listening to live music in a session

There may be occasions when the music therapist sings songs, while the parent and infant listen. In the experience of the authors however, the parent and or child often engage and respond musically during such musical experiences. The music therapist may be leading an activity where parents are encouraged to hold and rock their babies while the music therapist sings known children's songs and lullabies. Often, while gently rocking the parent is observed humming and interacting musically with her child. This should not be considered a receptive music therapy technique, and will be further discussed below.

Listening to live music in a session is used when the therapist wants to create a calm and contained environment for the dyad to be present in, to experience the here and now, and share a special quiet time together. Parents may be encouraged to hold their babies facing them, or rock their babies gently while paying attention to their breathing, facial expression and body movements. This technique provides a container for safe exploration of feelings associated with togetherness.

Listening to recorded music outside of a session

A music therapist may design a CD of songs to accompany a PIP so that parents can take home the music and listen to the songs with their child. Abad and Williams (2007) reported on the production of a CD that was given to each participating family. The CD concludes with quiet lullaby songs that were written and recorded with the intention of encourage parents and children to sit together and share a quiet time (p. 54).

Listening to recorded music outside of a session is used when the therapist wants to provide resources for families to use at home to extend the experience of shared togetherness in the home environment.

Music for relaxation

A music therapist may use music during a session for relaxation, particularly if they are focusing on providing a quiet and nurturing environment for parents and infants to experience closeness. This may involve the music therapist singing lullaby like songs while encouraging parents to massage their babies, or rub their infant's back to the music. Parents can also be encouraged to use music to assist children to relax and sleep, by using song recordings from sessions at home at sleep time (Abad and Williams 2007).

Music for relaxation is used when the music therapist wants to provide the parent with some strategies to assist their infant to relax and sleep, thus empowering them in their role as parents and encouraging the use of music in all of their parenting tasks.

Improvisation

Clinical improvisation is "the use of musical improvisation in an environment of trust and support established to meet the needs of clients" (Wigram 2004, p. 37). In a PIP, it is important that the environment created is one where families feel supported. Certain improvisatory techniques can be used to contain and support families in a musical space. A PIP will generally follow an established session plan (see below) but should include space to allow for free musical expression within the session. Improvisatory techniques that will allow and support this include structured improvisation, free improvisation, spontaneous improvisation, improvised song material; and music improvisation for containment.

Structured improvisation

The music therapist may provide space in a session to improvise that is structured and therefore supported. For example the music therapist may improvise a repeated harmonic structure and accompaniment, such as repeating two different suspended chords, while improvising a melody that reflects the mood of the group, the play currently underway or a concept or theme that the group has been exploring. By using this set harmonic series of two chords in a repetitive manner the parent-child dyad is able to explore musically on their instruments and with their voices within a supportive environment.

This technique is used when the music therapist wishes to provide a space for parent-child dyads to explore but at the same time feel safe and supported.

Free improvisation

During the PIP the music therapist may provide space for the parent and infant to explore musically and have fun. This can be achieved in a free improvisation where there are no musical *rules* that have to be followed. This technique may be introduced during the course of a PIP rather than in the first few sessions, in order to build trust with families so they feel confident to in fact explore musically without guidance. This section of a session may be accompanied by the music therapist on guitar, voice or the music therapist may participate in the improvisation on a percussion instrument. The element of "play" is central to this technique during a PIP.

Spontaneous improvisation

Abad and Williams (2006) described how spontaneous improvisation is used in *Sing & Grow* sessions with adolescent mothers and their children. Improvisation is used to respond in the moment to a child or to engage with a parent and/or child that have disengaged from a group. This technique is used when the music therapist wants to respond in the moment, engage or regain the attention of a parent, capture the attention of a child, or draw the parent's attention to the child's interactions. An example of this is singing the child's name and also what they are dong (playing the bells, bopping to music) and thereby drawing the parent's attention back to the group and focusing the parent on the child's participation and successes (Abad and Williams 2006). The music therapist can then include in the improvisation appropriate ways of praising the child's participation and educational messages to the parents about the child's actions.

Improvised song

This technique involves the music therapist taking a known song that is familiar to the families and embellishing it musically and harmonically to reflect the mood of the group. This technique is used when the music therapist wishes to connect to and engage with families using a song they know but adapting it to suit a specific therapeutic situation. For example, if children are very active, and lively, a known song can be adapted to meet the energy levels and then entrainment techniques can be used to transition the children into a quieter state, that allows for sensitive interactions between the parents and the children (Abad and Williams 2006). The beat, tempo, or pacing of the song can be changed from a livelier up beat to a slow triple time to achieve this. The creation of a song during the session to reflect a mood, action, or moment should be considered a creative technique, and will be discussed in the next section.

Creative music therapy techniques

Creative music therapy involves the creation, or composition of music, namely songs. Song writing is a common music therapy technique used in a variety of clinical settings (O'Callaghan et al. 2013). Songs can be written for clients, and with clients, or created spontaneously. While there is clinical evidence to support the use of song writing and creation in parent-infant music therapy work, it is a technique that has been reported more commonly in 1:1 work rather than group work. Oldfield and Franke (2005) provided an overview of their use of spontaneous song writing to support children in individual sessions in a mental health treatment setting. This chapter, however, focuses on PIP for groups in community settings, thus the creative music therapy techniques explored here are the more commonly used ones of writing songs for clients.

Songs written for a client

In a PIP the music therapist may write songs for use in sessions that encourage certain outcomes. For example, they might write lullabies and songs that are gentle and nurturing to encourage physical touch and closeness, or they might write songs that focus on particular developmental outcome. They may also write songs for use outside of the session to encourage the transition of skills learnt in the therapy space to the home environment. This can be seen in the *Sing & Grow* Together CD discussed earlier in this chapter. A song may be composed to promote interactions such as cuddling, or to provide instructions that prompt parents to interact in meaningful ways. Songs may also accompany dyadic play that involves physical touch and/or facilitation. Songs can be composed to facilitate a particular developmental milestone of the child such as sounding certain words, or for songs to support infants' tummy time. A song can be composed to carry a message or provide information for the parent about developmental milestones and/or care. Specifically composed songs can also help transition families from one activity to another during a session.

Recreative music therapy techniques

Recreative techniques are those that involve the recreation or performance of music (Bruscia 1998). In a PIP these are often the most common techniques used (Schwartz 2013). This is because the music therapist uses the familiarity of such songs to create a safe and supportive environment for parents and infants to come together, and the repetitious nature of these early childhood songs allows opportunities for practice and rehearsal of parenting interaction skills. Singing songs in a group is an integral part of human culture (Levintin 2011) and is therefore something familiar that the music therapist can draw upon to encourage great adult input. Recreative techniques used in PIP include singing traditional songs, interacting through musical games, singing popular children's songs, structured movement songs, and adapting children's songs, including adapting songs for transitional purposes.

Singing traditional children's songs

While this seems obvious, singing familiar songs lays the foundation for the group work to occur in a safe and supportive environment. Drawing on the familiarity of music provides the safety net for families to explore deeper emotions and interactions within the group, and to practice interactions that naturally occur in most children's songs. The music therapist needs to ensure the songs they choose as "traditional" are in fact traditional to the culture of the families in the group. It is also important to remember that some parents who have experienced deprived childhoods may not know many traditional children's songs. For this reason, the music therapist also takes on the role of educator and "teaches" these songs to parents so that they can add them to their repertory of play skills for use outside of the therapy space.

Interacting through musical games

Many children's songs are presented as musical games, where two people are required to interact with each other to achieve the desired outcome. Such games provide the music therapist with an excellent technique for encouraging interactions between parents and their infants, to highlight how parents can take delight in their infant's interactions, and empower the parent to interact and "play" with their infant at home in a way that is healthy and conducive to the child's development. For example, Incy Wincy Spider has actions that a parent can co-facilitate thus providing opportunity for touch and learning. Round and round the garden requires a parent to hold their infant's hand, gently touch it and then move up their arm to tickle them at the climax of the song. Song like this also provide opportunities for the child to practice anticipation and take delight in the tickle, touch, and cuddles often shared with a parent at the end of the song.

Singing popular/familiar children's songs

While this may seem the same or very similar to singing traditional children's songs, there is a greater focus here on social and cultural awareness when using this technique. For example, in Australia many children are familiar with the songs of the *Wiggles, Hi 5*, and *Justine Clarke*, but this may not be the case in other countries. While some music therapists do not like to use commercially popular songs, they can provide a bridge to accessing families who do not have a wealth of traditional songs to draw from, but are familiar with popular culture due to the use of TV, computers, commercial musical toys, and media in their ecological environments. For this reason, the music therapist should be aware of the social backgrounds of families, and aware of current popular trends in children's music and toys.

Adapting children's songs

Many children's songs can be adapted by a music therapist to provide opportunities for positive interactions between parents and their infants in a PIP. Again, this provides a non-threatening way for parents to explore the emotions and feelings associated with interacting with their infants. For example, the popular children's songs can have verses added that instructs parents to tickle tummies, thus encouraging physical touch and laughter. A further addition can be to "have a cuddle." Similarly, lullabies and play songs can be adapted to increase opportunities for touch, eye contact, and co-facilitated play.

Adapting children's songs for transitional purposes

Transitions between activities, places, or events can be extremely challenging for young children, and music has been used in many settings to assist children with smooth transitioning (Register and Humpal 2007). For this technique the music therapist may adapt a well-known song to act as a transitional song between sections of the session.

Structured movement songs

Structured movement songs are ubiquitous in early childhood music (Schwartz 2013). It is often impossible to separate the movement from the music in young children. Songs that focus on movement and coordination are an important and fun part of a session and can be used in a PIP to encourage physical closeness, parent facilitated play and to encourage fun interactions between dyads.

STARTING A MUSIC THERAPY PROGRAMME: PIECING IT TOGETHER

The music therapist chooses methods and techniques to use in a PIP that will support and therefore meet the needs of the family. To do this, the music therapist must devise a well-structured yet flexible session plan. There are well established session plans that have been evaluated as effective in meeting the needs of vulnerable families in parent-infant programmes, namely the *Sing & Grow* session plan (Abad and Edwards 2004). This session plan has been successfully implemented for families with different social and cultural backgrounds within the *Sing & Grow* project (Nicholson et al. 2008; Williams et al. 2005), and also by music therapists working with families in other contexts (Drake 2011). It is therefore a session plan that has been effectively used with a range of families in a range of settings and may be one worth consideration to use in a start-up programme, and one that is available for you to use.

Table 7.1 below provides an overview of this session plan, along with the methods, techniques, and songs for use in the sessions. Session plans, and further reference information is available on the *Sing & Grow* website: <http://static.squarespace.com/static/512176bee4b0b5151b73112a/t/51535941e4b029068f6f08b4/1364416833706/SnG%20Music%20and%20Child%20Development%20Colour%20Border.pdf>.

Table 7.1 Parent infant groups' structure and process

Activity	Method	Technique	Desired outcome	Song ideas
Greeting	Recreative	Singing popular/familiar song	Marks the start of music, reinforces appropriate social skills, strengthens listening skills, encourages looking, waving, sitting, responding	Greeting song Known, or adaptation. *What do you think my name is?*
	Creative	Song written for a client	Song composed to focus on social and attending skills at the start of the session	Original composition
Action songs	Recreative	Singing traditional children's songs Interacting through musical game	Therapist modelling to parents interactive and facilitative play strategies Parent facilitation via hand over hand and co-facilitated actions to songs, and parent modelling to children, resulting in increased opportunities for eye contact, touch, interaction between parent and child. Child also develops fine motor and hand coordination skills	*Twinkle Twinkle Little Star* *Incy Wincy* *Open Shut Them* Tickle songs or Peek a boo songs that encourage interaction through actions and touch
	Creative	Song written for a client	Songs written to encourage particular outcomes such as concept comprehension, or fine motor development	*Where's your nose?* (V. Abad)
Hand percussion instruments	Recreative	Playing instruments to popular/ familiar song Interacting through musical games	Therapist modelling to parents interactive and facilitative play strategies Parent facilitation via hand over hand and co-facilitated playing of instruments, and parent modelling to children, resulting in increased opportunities for eye contact, touch, interaction between parent and child. Child also develops fine motor and eye hand coordination skills, bilateral hand coordination and concept comprehension skills	*Old Macdonald* *Five Little Ducks* Original composition
	Creative	Song written for a client	Songs written to encourage particular outcomes such as concept comprehension, or fine motor development	Original composition

	Improvisatory	Music Therapist improvises musical material to support free play between parent and child with hand percussion instruments, such as animal castanets or bells Music therapist improvises spontaneously in response to interactions, words, feelings that are observed between parents and their children Music Therapist provides structured improvisation around a repeated harmonic structure to accompany interactive play with the hand percussion	Parent and child interact freely in a musical environment that is not restricting or directive Music therapist sees child do something interesting and integrates this into a spontaneous improvisation, and by doing so draws the parent into the musical interaction and reinforces the child's ability and the importance of the parent's response to their actions Parent and child interactions are still free but are supported in a more structured musical environment, thus providing support in cases where free improvisation and therefore exploration are considered to be too overwhelming for participants	
Dancing	Recreative	Dancing to popular/familiar songs Interacting through musical games Structured movement song	Therapist modelling to parents interactive and facilitative play strategies in both group and individual contexts. The music therapist can lead a group dance that requires all participants to work together as a team. They can also model 1:1 dances that encourage physical closeness and touch, including hand holding and synchronised body movements. Parents facilitate their child's participation in many dances, thus increasing physical contact as well as opportunities to share in successful and fun experiences. The child also develops coordination and balance skills, strength and awareness of body parts and its ability.	*Hokey Pokey* *Dingle Dangle Scarecrow* *Row Row Row Your Boat*

(continued)

Table 7.1 Continued

Activity	Method	Technique	Desired outcome	Song ideas
	Creative	Song written for a client	Song written to encourage certain physical interactions and concepts such as following two step instructions, listening before doing and responding to the cues of an adult.	*Who can listen to the music?* (V. Abad)
Drumming	Recreative	Drumming to well-known songs Interacting through musical games	Drumming activities provide opportunities for the therapist to again demonstrate co-facilitated and hand over hand interactive play techniques. Parents can assist children and therefore share in their success as they master drumming skills. These skills will encourage gross and fine motor coordination, bi-lateral hand control, crossing of the mid-line, eye hand coordination and listening skills. Drumming games can also be used to help children learn about self-regulation, as they wait for a turn, regulate their anticipation and control their input, as directed by the therapist (loud, soft, fast slow)	*We can play on the big bass drum* *Leo the Lion*
	Creative	Write your own drum songs for clients to encourage certain interactions or skills, such as concept comprehension or regulation songs	The therapist writes songs specifically to achieve certain outcomes, either to increase parent facilitation, involvement, understanding, or child development	*We are in a band* (V. Abad)
	Improvisatory	Improvise freely and spontaneously to support group drumming and reflect group mood Structured improvisation is provided around a set harmonic and rhythmic motive to provide freedom to play and explore but support so that the experience is not overwhelming	The therapist improvises music to support group drumming, providing a container for the group to explore freely. The therapist improvises music in a harmonically and rhythmically structured way so that the experience of drumming is not overwhelming. This provides great containment and support to clients to then explore together.	

Movement with props	Recreative	Known songs Musical games Structured movement songs	Moving together promotes closeness and creativity. Parents can support their child's creative play, and the therapist can model nurturing interactions. This can be achieved with props like ribbons, bubbles, or the use of puppets, scarves, parachutes etc	*I Can Sing a Rainbow*
	Creative	Original songs composed for a specific purpose	The therapist writes songs specifically to achieve certain outcomes	*Let's make a rainbow (V. Abad)*
	Improvisatory	The music therapist improvises freely to match the group dynamic, feel and participation in movement, using kinesthetic, visual and auditory cues to guide the improvisation Structured improvisation can be used if families are not moving "freely" but require additional musical support	The music therapist responds in the moment to the movement patterns, mood, interactions between and physical cues provided by the parents and the children The music therapist uses rhythm and repeated harmonic motives, possibly even based on a song known to families, to provide containment and safety to physically explore the environment and to support movement together.	
Cuddle time/relaxation	Recreative	Known songs	The therapist provides a time in the session for parents to be physically close and calm with their child. They may encourage nurturing behaviors such as rocking, holding, massaging or rubbing of backs. This also provides a time for children to regulate their bodies and emotions and calm down after the excitement of the music, and to share a special time with their parent	*It's so nice to have a cuddle*

(continued)

Table 7.1 Continued

Activity	Method	Technique	Desired outcome	Song ideas
	Creative	Original songs composed for a specific purpose	Music therapist writes a song that provides explicit instruction on holding, rocking, cuddling, being close, being in the here and now and with the child	*Sing and Grow Together (B. Walker)*
	Improvisatory	Improvised music to support closeness	The music therapist may choose to improvise music at this point that supports the group to be close in the "here and now" and experience each other. The music acts as a container.	
	Receptive	Listening to live music in a session	During quiet time some parents may choose to listen to the music with their child, or while gentle holding their child	*Lullaby like song, Hush Little Baby*
		Music for relaxation	During quiet time the music therapist may use music to encourage relaxation in parent and child	
Goodbye song	Recreative	Known songs	The goodbye song marks the end of music and helps prepare the children to leave the therapeutic space. The therapist can model appropriate social greetings to parents and children. Parents can support their child in closure and in responding in a socially appropriate way	*Good bye song*
	Creative	Original songs composed for a specific purpose		*Thanks for coming to music (V. Abad)*

Implementation

Further to a session plan, the music therapist needs to consider how the session plan will be implemented. There are some key points to remember when implementing the PIP session plan outlined above. One of the main issues is how to include the parents in the session in a way that they can feel comfortable, engaged but not overwhelmed by the expectation that they will need to do something musical or performance based. Therefore parents should be encouraged to sit with their children, on the floor preferably, with either children on laps or immediately in front of the parent; within arm's length. This will allow for parent facilitation, physical touch, and closeness during the session. Encouraging parents to sit in circle formation allows them to see each other, and this promotes learning and support between them throughout the sessions.

When playing songs, it is important to choose keys that are developmentally appropriate to the children such as C or D major, but will also be attractive to parents to sing along, who will generally have a lower range, for example A major. Therefore, some songs will need to be transposed down a few keys to suit both parents and children.

Singing songs through twice encouraged the learning of words so that parents feel confident to sing along; remembering that when infants are enjoying themselves they have a high tolerance for repetition.

Since a key goal of this work is interaction between parents and infants providing encouragement to parents through verbal and non-verbal prompts about interacting with their child through musical play, facilitated play, eye contact, physical touch, and smiles is crucial. For example, the music therapist might sing *Incy Wincy Spider* once, and then when repeating the song may suggest that parents turn their infants around, or lie them on the floor in front of them, so that the child can see the actions, see their parent's face, and consequently interact through eye contact and touch.

The music therapist provides gentle cues throughout sessions and uses music in any way possible to encourage positive play. For example, during a peek-a-boo game the music therapist might say to a parent "Look how your child is anticipating you finding them, isn't that lovely how she waits for you to lift the scarf and say boo!" a further learning cue would be for the music therapist to say to parents "you know this game can be played on the change table, or in the bath with a face washer" thus providing parents with suggestions for interactive play in the home environment.

Musical interludes are used by the music therapist as gentle teaching points. For example, in an action song the music therapist can sing the song once, and then the second time say "come on parents, let's sing it again and this time you can do the actions for your bubs."

CONCLUSION

Many of the ways that adults and/or parents and very young children interact vocally is highly musical. This interactive responsiveness is a building block for creating and supporting attachment between parents and their infants. Music therapists working with parents and infants where some vulnerability exists can support and scaffold the development of a wider repertory of skills and capacities from the existing or innate musical base of the parent infant pair.

Music therapy for parents and infants is a developing resource internationally. As the available expertise increases, the development of greater research resources to more closely examine the effectiveness of techniques and approaches is assured.

REFERENCES

Abad, V. and Edwards, J. (2004). Strengthening families: A role for music therapy in contributing to family centred care. *Australian Journal of Music Therapy* 15: 3–17.

Abad, V. and Thomas, D. (2013, September). The economics of therapy—Building a financially healthy and sustainable future in music therapy in the 21st Century: Exploring current economic trends and future funding possibilities for our profession. Australian Music Therapy National Conference, Melbourne.

Abad, V. and Williams, K. (2006). Early intervention music therapy for adolescent mothers and their children. *British Journal of Music Therapy* 20: 31–38.

Abad, V. and Williams, K. (2007). Early intervention music therapy: Reporting on a 3-year project to address needs with at-risk families. *Music Therapy Perspectives* 25(1): 52–58.

Abad, V. and Williams, K (2009). Funding and employment conditions: Critical issues for Australian music therapy beyond 2009. *Australian Journal of Music Therapy* 20: 56–62.

Ainsworth, M.D.S. (1977). Attachment theory and its utility in cross-cultural research. *Culture and infancy* 49–67.

Ainsworth, M.D.S. (1979). Infant–mother attachment. *American psychologist* 34(10): 932.

Ainsworth, M.D.S., Bell, S.M., and Stayton, D.J. (1974). Infant-mother attachment and social development: "Socialization" as a product of reciprocal responsiveness to signals. In: M. Richards (ed.), *The Integration of the Child into a Social World*, pp. 99–135. Cambridge: Cambridge University Press.

American Psychiatric Association. (2013). *Diagnostic and statistical manual of mental disorders* (5th ed.). Washington, DC: Author.

Australian Bureau of Statistics (2012). *2012 Year Book Australia*, cat no. 1301.0. ABS, Canberra.

Bargiel, M. (2004). Lullabies and play songs: Theoretical considerations for an early attachment music therapy intervention through parental singing for developmentally at-risk infants. *Voices: A World Forum for Music Therapy* 4(1).

Beck, C.T. (2011). A metaethnography of traumatic childbirth and its aftermath: Amplifying causal looping. *Qualitative Health Research* 21(3): 301–311.

Beebe, B. (2000). Coconstructing mother–infant distress: The microsynchrony of maternal impingement and infant avoidance in the face-to-face encounter. *Psychoanalytic Inquiry* 20(3): 421–440.

Beebe, B. and Lachmann, F. M. (1998). Co-constructing inner and relational processes: Self-and mutual regulation in infant research and adult treatment. *Psychoanalytic Psychology* 15(4): 480.

Bowlby, J. (2005). *A Secure Base: Clinical Applications of Attachment Theory*, Vol. 393. London: Taylor and Francis.

Bruscia, K.E. (1998). *Defining Music Therapy*. Gilsum, NH: Barcelona Publishers.

Coren, E. and Barlow, J. (2004). Individual and group-based parenting programmes for improving psychosocial outcomes for teenage parents and their children (Cochrane Review). *The Cochrane Library*, 2. Chichester, UK: John Wiley.

Cortis, N., Katz, I., and Patulny, T. (2009). *Engaging hard-to-reach families and children Strong Families and Communities Strategy 2004–2009.* Canberra: Department of Families, Housing and Community Services and Indigenous Affairs.

Dissanayake, E. (2008). If music is the food of love, what about survival and reproductive success? *Musicae Scientiae* 12(1 suppl): 169–195.

Dearn, T. and Shoemark, H. (2014). The effect of maternal presence on premature infant response to recorded music. *Journal of Obstetric, Gynecologic, & Neonatal Nursing* 43: 341–350.

Drake, T. (2011). Becoming in tune: The use of music therapy to assist the developing bond between traumatized children and their new adoptive parents. In: J. Edwards (ed.), *Music therapy and parent-infant bonding*, pp. 22–41. Oxford: Oxford University Press.

Edwards, J. (2011). Music therapy and parent-infant bonding. In: J. Edwards (ed.), *Music Therapy and Parent-infant Bonding*, pp. 5–21. Oxford: Oxford University Press.

Edwards, J. (2014). The role of the music therapist in promoting parent infant attachment. *Canadian Journal of Music Therapy* 20(1): 41–51.

Edwards, J., Scahill, M., and Phelan, H. (2007). Music therapy: Promoting healthy mother-infant relations in the vulnerable refugee and asylum seeker community. In: J. Edwards (ed.), *Music: Promoting Health and Creating Community.* Newcastle Upon Tyne: Cambridge Scholars.

Field, T. (2010). Postpartum depression effects on early interactions, parenting, and safety practices: A review. *Infant Behavior and Development* 33(1): 1–6.

Flower, C. and Oldfield, A. (2008). *Music Therapy with Children and their Families.* London: Jessica Kingsley Publishers.

Garthus-Niegel, S., von Soest, T., Vollrath, M.E., and Eberhard-Gran, M. (2013). The impact of subjective birth experiences on post-traumatic stress symptoms: a longitudinal study. *Archives of Women's Mental Health* 16(1): 1–10.

Goldberg, A.E. and Smith, J.Z. (2011). Stigma, social context, and mental health: lesbian and gay couples across the transition to adoptive parenthood. *Journal of Counseling Psychology* 58(1): 139.

Goodman, J.H. (2004). Paternal postpartum depression, its relationship to maternal postpartum depression, and implications for family health. *Journal of Advanced Nursing* 45: 26–35. DOI: 10.1046/j.1365-2648.2003.02857.x.

Grocke, D. and Wigram, T. (2007). *Receptive Methods in Music Therapy: Techniques and Clinical Applications for Music Therapy Clinicians, Educators and Students.* London: Jessica Kingsley Publishers.

Jonsdottir, V. (2002). Musicking in early intervention. *Voices: A World Forum for Music Therapy* 2(2).

Levitin, D.J. (2011). *This is your brain on music: Understanding a human obsession.* Bloomsbury, UK Atlantic Books Ltd.

Loewy, J.V. (2011). Music therapy for hospitalized infants and their parents. In: J. Edwards (ed.), *Music therapy and parent–infant bonding*, pp. 179–190. Oxford: Oxford University Press.

Mackenzie, J. and Hamlett, K. (2005). The Music Together program: Addressing the needs of "well" families with young children. *Australian Journal of Music Therapy* 16: 43–59.

Malloch, S. and Trevarthen, C. (eds). (2009). *Communicative musicality: Exploring the basis of human companionship.* Oxford University Press, USA.

Mann, R., Gilbody, S., and Adamson, J. (2010). Prevalence and incidence of postnatal depression: what can systematic reviews tell us? *Archives of Women's Mental Health* 13(4): 295–305.

Mithen, S. J. (2005). *The singing Neanderthals: The origins of music, language, mind, and body.* Harvard University Press.

Nicholson, J.M., Berthelsen, D., Abad, V., Williams, K., and Bradley, J. (2008). Impact of music therapy to promote positive parenting and child development. *Journal of Health Psychology* 13 (2): 226–238.

O'Callaghan, C. C., McDermott, F., Hudson, P., and Zalcberg, J. R. (2013). Sound continuing bonds with the deceased: the relevance of music, including preloss music therapy, for eight bereaved caregivers. *Death Studies* 37(2): 101–125.

Oldfield, A. and Bunce, L. (2001). Mummy can play too ... Short-term music therapy with mothers and young children. *British Journal of Music Therapy* 15(1): 27–36.

Oldfield, A., Adams, M., and Bunce, L. (2003). An investigation into short-term music therapy with mothers and young children. *British Journal of Music Therapy* 17(1): 26–45.

Oldfield, A. and Franke, C. (2005). Improvised songs and stories in music therapy diagnostic assessments at a unit for child and family psychiatry: A music therapist's and a psychotherapist's perspective. In: F. Baker and T. Wigram, *Songwriting: Methods, techniques and clinical applications for music therapy clinicians, educators and students*, pp. 24–44. London: Jessica Kingsley Publishers.

Papoušek, M. (2011). Resilience, strengths, and regulatory capacities: hidden resources in developmental disorders of infant mental health. *Infant Mental Health Journal* 32(1): 29–46.

Register, D. and Humpal, M. (2007). Using musical transitions in early childhood classrooms: Three case examples. *Music Therapy Perspectives* 25(1): 25–31. Retrieved from: <http://search.proquest.com/docview/199553554?accountid=14723>.

Richman, A.L., Miller, P.M., and LeVine, R.A. (1992). Cultural and educational variations in maternal responsiveness. *Developmental Psychology* 28(4): 614.

Robertson, J. and Bowlby, J. (1952). Responses of young children to separation from their mothers. *Courrier of the International Children's Centre, Paris, II*, 131–140.

Schore, A. N. (2001). The effects of early relational trauma on right brain development, affect regulation, and infant mental health. *Infant mental health journal* 22(1–2): 201–269.

Schwartz, E. (2013). Guidelines for music therapy practice in developmental care. In: Bradt J. (ed.), *Guidelines for Music Therapy Practice in Pediatric Care*. Gilsum, NH: Barcelona Publishers.

Skoe, E. and Kraus, N. (2010). Auditory brainstem response to complex sounds: a tutorial. *Ear and Hearing* 31(3): 302.

Stern, D.N. (2000). *The Interpersonal World of the Infant a View From Psychoanalysis and Developmental Psychology: A View from Psychoanalysis and Developmental Psychology*. New York: Basic books.

Trehub, S.E. (2003). The developmental origins of musicality. *Nature neuroscience* 6(7): 669–673.

Trevarthen, C. (2001). Intrinsic motives for companionship in understanding: Their origin, development, and significance for infant mental health. *Infant Mental health journal* 22(1–2): 95–131.

Wigram, T. (2004). *Improvisation: Methods and Techniques for Music Therapy Clinicians, Educators and Students*. New York: J. Kingsley Publishers.

Winkworth, G., McArthur, M., Layton, M., Thomsom, M., and Wilson, F. (2010). Opportunities lost—why some parents of young children are not well-connected to the service systems designed to assist them. *Australian Social Work* 63(4): 431–444.

Williams, K.E. and Abad, V. (2005). Reflections on music therapy with Indigenous families: cultural learning put into practice. *Australian Journal of Music Therapy* 16: 60–69.

Williams, K., Nicholson, J., Abad, V., Docherty, L., and Berthelsen, D. (2011). Evaluating parent-child group music therapy programmes: challenges and successes for *Sing & Grow*.

In: J. Edwards (ed.), *Music Therapy and Parent-infant Bonding*, pp. 73–92. Oxford: Oxford University Press.

Williams, K., Berthelsen, D., Nicholson, J., Walker, S., and Abad, V. (2012). The effectiveness of a short-term group music therapy intervention for parents who have a child with a disability. *Journal of Music Therapy* 49(1): 23–44.

Winnicott, D.W. (1965). *The maturational processes and the facilitation environment: Studies in the theory of emotional development*. London: Hogarth Press.

....

CHAPTER 8

FAMILY APPROACHES IN MUSIC THERAPY PRACTICE WITH YOUNG CHILDREN

....

AMELIA OLDFIELD

INTRODUCTION

....

IN April 1992, heavily pregnant with twins, I presented a paper entitled: *Music therapy with families, initial reflections* at the conference: Music Therapy in Health and Education in the European Community (Oldfield 1993). This was an international event held at Kings College at the University of Cambridge in England in which 300 music therapists from 23 countries gathered together. Amongst many fascinating papers and presentations mine was the only one at the conference about working simultaneously with children and parents. My paper was well attended, and there were a few enthusiastic listeners who clearly thought, as I did, that this was the way we should direct our work with many young children in the future. However, there were also those who questioned the validity of including parents in sessions. They observed that "this is not the way we have been taught how to work;" questioning "how will working with families in the room affect the all important therapist-client relationship?," and asked "how can the therapist simultaneously meet the needs of both the child and the parent?" I fielded the questions as best I could, feeling slightly detached, my lively and kicking babies distracting me and reminding me of my own feelings of attachment to my children. Although music therapists who felt it was important to work jointly with young children and parents seemed to be very much in the minority at that time, I remember already being convinced both by my clinical work in addition to my own experience of being a mother to a three year old and a one year old, as well as by my feelings for the baby twins dancing around inside me, that we had to develop this way of working as music therapists.

Since that time, more and more music therapists all around the world have worked with families, and the burgeoning literature shows the developments in practice and research that have occurred subsequently.

In some ways it is difficult to understand why it has taken so long for family music therapy to develop. In the UK certainly no other out-patient treatment for preschool children would normally take place without the parent or carer being present, with the possible exception of some forms of play therapy or psychotherapy. One could perhaps argue that if the attachment between the parent and child is unhealthy, the therapist needs to enable the child to experience a healthy relationship with an adult, before it is possible to *repair* the unhealthy attachment between the parent and the child. Nevertheless, although there might be occasions when it may be important or useful to separate a young child and a parent in music therapy, the advantages of working with either parent or carer in the room seem to outweigh these disadvantages.

Perhaps another reason is that the Nordoff-Robbins music therapy approach (1971, 1977) has strongly influenced the way some music therapists work with children. Initially this way of working was developed in special schools with the composer, Paul Nordoff, improvising at the piano while the educational specialist, Robbins, physically guided and supported the child. As it was a school setting parents were not usually present. However, even in school settings music therapy with families is now developing.

This chapter provides an overview of this emerging literature and considers the different ways of grouping a wide range of practices with children and families. Two vignettes of my music therapy practice with families are presented. Both the literature review and the case material will be used to briefly reflect on the rationale for the uses of music therapy with families and young children.

LITERATURE REVIEW

Initial publications

Up until 2001, very little music therapy work with families was documented or published (Sobey 2008, p. 13). Streeter (1993) published a guide for parents, which encouraged parents to use music with their children at home. While she didn't include parents in her music therapy sessions herself at that time, her book aimed to help families consider the benefits of interactive music making at home. Two further important investigations that should be mentioned from this period are Muller and Warwick's (1993) research into the role of mothers in music therapy sessions with children with autism, and an MA thesis (Heal 1994) about working with groups of families with children who have Down's syndrome. In addition Nocker-Ribaupierre (1999) was writing about music therapy with premature babies and their parents.

A review of four textbooks

In the first book Oldfield (2006a) described her music therapy approach at a child development center. Eleven case studies of different children and their families were presented in the first five chapters and many of these included reports from the parents themselves. Later in the book a research project investigating ten preschool children with autistic spectrum disorder and their parents who received weekly individual music therapy over a period of 18 to 26 weeks each, was described. The sessions were videotaped and the videos analyzed in detail. The parents were interviewed and asked to fill in questionnaires both pre- and post-treatment. Nine out of the ten dyads achieved some or all of the treatment aims set out before treatment began. All the parents indicated their view that music therapy had been effective.

The second book, Oldfield (2006b), described the author's music therapy approach at the Croft Unit for Child and Family Psychiatry, the only psychiatric unit in the UK to admit groups of families with children with complex difficulties, residentially. In this book a variety of music therapy cases with primary age children and their families were described and considered, as well as several music therapy groups with families with younger children where there were attachment difficulties. Further music therapy family work is described in Holmes et al. (2011), a book entirely devoted to describing the Croft multidisciplinary approach to families and children with complex needs.

The other two textbooks, Oldfield and Flower (2008), and Edwards (2011) are edited texts which present the work of music therapists working in different ways with children and families with a wide range of difficulties. In the first of these, ten contributors described their work in a variety of UK settings such as schools, child development centers, and hospices, and include work with families with children with learning disabilities, autism, and adopted children (Oldfield and Flower 2008). The ages of the children vary from toddlers to teenagers. The second book presents work with families and younger children, but again work takes place in a wide range of settings by music therapists with different backgrounds from Ireland, the UK, Australia and the USA (Edwards 2011). These texts provide ample evidence that around the world many music therapists work with families, and consider a family oriented approach important.

The next section is an overview of the literature ranging from toddlers to primary age children. Once this material has been examined, other ways of grouping publications and clinical approaches will be considered.

MUSIC THERAPY WITH CHILDREN WITH LIFE-THREATENING ILLNESSES AND THEIR CARERS/FAMILIES

Work with children with life-threatening illnesses and their parents varies depending in particular on the nature of the child's illness and the age of the child. Many children may have severe learning difficulties and be physically disabled. In these cases the focus in music therapy can be on reflecting a child's mood or movements, setting up momentary improvised musical dialogues or eliciting small responses from the child. Unlike in the hospital environment where premature babies are primarily the responsibility of the medical staff, if music therapy is taking place in an out-patient center, a hospice, or in the home, the parent is the "specialist" and will advise the therapist on what the child can and can't do and how to best position the child, for example. However, in addition to working in partnership with the parent to best meet the needs of the child, the music therapist will be providing support for the parent, and possibly offering new ideas about how the family may communicate or play together.

When working with children with acute illnesses such as terminal cancer, each family will have different needs and the music therapist may have to adapt to primarily supporting the child, the parents or siblings depending not only on how ill the child is but also on how the family is managing on that particular day. This is evident in Flower's (2008) chapter where she shows how the music therapist in one case might primarily connect with the child while the mother mainly listens and provides support for the child; how in another case it is mainly the siblings and the parents who are connecting with the child and with each other, while the music therapist provides "holding" music; and in a third case the music therapist directly supports a parent to sing and play to the child.

When children are too ill to leave home, music therapists can provide treatment in the home, which was the case for the work described above by Flower (2008). This home based care via music therapy has also been explored by Nall and Everitt (2005) and by Mitchell et al. (2012). The music therapist has then not only to adapt to the needs of each of the families, but also to working in an unfamiliar space. Musical instruments will have to be transported and fitted into whatever room might be available in the home.

In a similar way music therapists working on pediatric wards also often have to transport instruments and adapt to the space available next to a child's bed. Work sometimes takes place individually with children, but in other cases parents or whole families will also be involved in the sessions. In her music therapy guide to pediatrics, Lorenzato (2005) devoted a chapter to "The Art of the Family." She wrote that "the important thing is to set up opportunities for families to have a wonderful time being a family together" (p. 102). (Griessmeier and Bossinger 1994 and 2012) described case studies from her work in which children who were dying made recordings of themselves singing and playing which they knew their parents would be able to keep. Both Lorenzato and Griessmeier mention how important it is for the music therapist who has been working with families to grieve with the family after the child has died, and in some cases attend and take part in funerals.

Although much of the work described so far involves working with individual children and their families, some group work with children and parents in hospitals or hospices has also been described. Casey (2010), described a parent and toddler group in a children's hospice, and many music therapists working on children's wards run open groups for parents and young children (Lorenzato 2005 and Griessmeier and Bossinger 1994). These groups have some similarities to music therapy groups which have been established in social or community centers, schools, out-patient clinics, or sometimes at child development centers for preschool children and their parents.

MUSIC THERAPY GROUPS FOR PRESCHOOL CHILDREN AND THEIR PARENTS

In all the work described so far, the children who are being treated have had special needs or difficulties either because they have been unwell or because they are not developing in usual ways. This does not mean that the therapeutic objectives have always been centered on the child—in some case the main focus of the therapy has been to aid, support, or treat the parent—but the family would not have been referred had it not been for the child's needs. In this next section, however, the child may not be the primary reason for referral so this is why I will first look at groups where the child has a special need (clinical music therapy groups) and then at groups where the family or the parent might be in need of support (community music therapy groups).

CLINICAL MUSIC THERAPY GROUPS

Oldfield (2006a, pp. 146–154) described two groups she ran with children and parents at a child development center. The first of these groups was a multidisciplinary group run jointly with a physiotherapist and a speech therapist for families with a preschool child with special needs. Some children had Down's syndrome, some had cerebral palsy and others were on the autistic spectrum. Between four and ten families attended every week, some families coming every week, others only managing to attend fortnightly. Younger siblings might attend with their older brother or sister, and during the school holidays, siblings who normally attended school would be enlisted as "helpers." The children were referred to the group because it was felt that they would benefit from the social experience, as well as giving the therapists a chance to work on their individual specific difficulties within the group. For the parents and siblings, the group provided a chance to get to know other families experiencing similar difficulties which could be particularly supportive for young parents who were only just coming to terms with the fact that their child had special needs.

The other group was for three children in wheelchairs with severe physical difficulties and learning disabilities, and their mothers. In many ways the group was similar to the preceding one, but the activities were more specifically geared to the physical needs of these children. Time had to be given for each child to respond, and creative ways of adapting instruments and activities had to be explored. Although this group was run by the music therapist on her own the physiotherapist would regularly visit to give advice on seating or equipment. Groups similar to this second one for children with specific difficulties have been described by Woodward (2004) working with families with children with autistic spectrum disorder and Loth (2008) working with families with toddlers who had a learning disability. Results from a questionnaire given to parents attending the Loth's group (p. 61) showed that:

> … all the mothers felt their child benefitted from attending the group in terms of developing communication and social skills, learning to be with other children, waiting for their turn, taking initiative and improving their listening skills and self expression.

In addition many mothers emphasized how much pleasure they had in watching their child enjoying themselves.

Oldfield and Bunce (2001) described groups of parents and babies, and parents and toddlers on an out-patient psychiatric ward. Here it is the parents who have the identified difficulties rather than the children, but this work is described under the "clinical" heading because it is funded by the National Health Service and occurs on a psychiatric ward. Parents were referred to these groups for a variety of social and medical reasons including, a history of post-natal depression, attachment difficulties, extreme social poverty, or previous drug dependency. Music therapy group interventions would take place once every six weeks with the mothers and babies and be videoed. The following week parents would review video excerpts from the previous week focusing on excerpts chosen by the music therapist to reveal strengths in the relationship between the parent and the child, and thereby addressing the particular difficulties facing each parent. A research investigation (Oldfield et al. 2003) into this work was able to show that while both children of "clinical" families and children of non-clinical families at a local nursery all were very engaged in music making during music groups, the non-clinical parents were excited and enthusiastic about their children's participation, whereas the parents in the clinical group did not feel that what their children were doing was special in any way. This finding indicated that families who are at risk need help and support to recognize and value their children's enjoyment and capacity to play.

COMMUNITY-BASED MUSIC THERAPY GROUPS

Other music therapists have worked with mixed groups of families where some but not all of the children have special needs. Typically these groups take place in deprived areas for families who may be seen as being vulnerable or at risk. Davies and Rosscornes (2012) describe a "drop-in" music therapy group held at a children's center in Cambridge. They described how the group provides an opportunity to strengthen the bond between the parent and the child within a safe and structured environment. Kelly (2011) wrote about a series of eight to ten week music therapy groups in preschools within the socially vulnerable areas of Limerick city, Ireland. Comments that care givers made in evaluation forms included mentioning the importance of spending one-to-one time with their children, watching their child's confidence grow and seeing the children smiling and happy (Kelly 2011, p. 112). She concluded that the programme offered social support to families and opportunities for care givers to play an active role in their children's education.

Burrell (2011) described open music based groups she runs at the Coram Community Centre in London for children under three and their parents. She wrote:

> Parents bring their children in the hope of giving their child a head start in future education, high achievement and well being. They bring their child to have fun and to be entertained, or to establish a firm foundation for any musical talents. However, the added benefit is that music can become an inspirational part of daily life, giving parents permission to "play" with their child.
>
> Burrell 2011, p. 97

Here then, the group is not directly seen as therapeutic but has important therapeutic by-products. However, Burrell may then refer some of the families on for individual music therapy with one of her colleagues.

Sing & Grow is a music therapy programme for parents and young children which started in 2001, in Australia (Williams et al. 2011).

> Sing & Grow is an early intervention music therapy programme for families with infants from birth to 3 years of age, who are socially, economically or physically disadvantaged. It aims to improve parenting skills and confidence, promote positive parent-child interactions, stimulate child development and provide social networking opportunities.
>
> Williams et al. 2011, p. 76

Sing & Grow programmes are evaluated through parental feedback. Data was collected from 683 families attending 63 programmes between 2002–2005. The results indicated high levels of parental satisfaction and a positive perception of the programme's impact on parent-child relationships (Williams et al. 2011, p. 76). Williams (2010) investigated *Sing & Grow* groups for families with young children with disabilities. Her findings indicated that music therapy had a positive impact on participants' mental health, parenting behaviors and child development. In 2010, *Sing & Grow UK* was established (Thomas 2012). Throughout 2012, 29 programmes were delivered across all of the UK.

A question that sometimes arises regarding these types of groups is one raised by Ledger (2011) who described group music therapy for families of slightly older children in schools, namely whether or not these groups should be considered music therapy groups or "music for fun." Teachers in the schools where she worked were concerned that if the group was called "therapy" parents wouldn't come. Ledger, however, felt it was important to be clear to parents that these groups were designed to give families an opportunity to spend quality time together and support and in some cases improve relationships. A similar issue that arises for music therapists running these types of groups in the UK is that many parents initially assume that these groups are similar to other preschool action song groups that may be run by music teachers or by a parent who plays the guitar or the piano. Again it is important to be clear with families why the groups have been set up and what the aims might be, even if the most obvious characteristic is that the children are engaged in music making and having fun.

As well as this increase in interest in working with groups of young children and their parents there has been an increase in individual work with young children and their parents, in child development centers, in some primary schools and in child and family psychiatric centers.

INDIVIDUAL FAMILY MUSIC THERAPY IN CHILD DEVELOPMENT CENTERS AND SCHOOLS

Family work in child development centers

In addition to the work mentioned earlier in Oldfield (2006a), Loombe (2012) described a successful working partnership between herself and the father of a three-year-old boy, Taylor, with autistic spectrum disorder. Taylor's father was a musician himself and became so enthusiastic about music therapy that he decided to train as a music therapist himself. Another partnership between a father and music therapist is described in the training DVD entitled: "Joshua and Barry; music therapy with a partially sighted little boy with cerebral palsy." During eighteen months of music therapy, vocalizations, and singing exchanges between the music therapist, Barry (Joshua's father), and Joshua, eventually led to Joshua developing speech (Oldfield and Nudds 2002).

Thompson (2012) reported on a randomized control trial investigation where young children with autism and their parents had music therapy for sixteen weekly sessions in their homes. The children receiving music therapy showed significant improvement in interpersonal relationships and play-skills and the parents participating in music therapy showed a significant increase in self-reports of involvement with their children. Drake (2008 and 2011) wrote moving accounts of her music therapy work with individual traumatized families and families adopting children, at the Coram Community Centre in London. Many of her referrals came from the music group run by Burrell (2011) described earlier in this chapter.

Family work in schools

When children start school, this can often be a good moment to stop the preschool music therapy family work and in some cases refer the child on to the music therapist working at the school either for individual work or for group work. Some parents and children will need help preparing for this separation and these issues may be addressed in the music therapy sessions. The independence that children develop in school is important and it may therefore not always be appropriate for parents to come to music therapy sessions with their children within the school setting. However, many music therapists working in special schools have found that it has been very beneficial to include parents in the work. Bull (2008) was able to address attachment issues for families with young children with autistic spectrum disorder by inviting three mothers to attend a music therapy group in a London primary school for children with severe learning difficulties. Kaenampornpan (2012) worked in a special school in Thailand where parents and carers take part in all their children's school activities. She ran individual music therapy sessions with six families and then followed these sessions up with home visits to encourage families to continue using music in the home. Both these authors emphasize that the special schools they are working in have a tradition of supporting and including the families of their pupils.

Howden (2008) worked in several different primary schools in areas of socioeconomic deprivation in North London, where many of the children had been traumatized by witnessing violence. She described how, with some of the children, she progressed from one-to-one sessions to inviting the parents to attend with the children, mainly because the child's difficulties lay within the family's relationships.

Family work in psychiatric centers, or with children with emotional difficulties

When families such as those described by Howden (2008) are in crisis, help available on an out-patient basis might no longer suffice to meet their needs. Subsequently, the family might be admitted to a psychiatric unit. In addition to the two text books mentioned earlier (Oldfield 2006b and Holmes et al. 2011), Davies (2008) and O'Hanrahan (2012) have reported on music therapy case studies within a psychiatric unit where the relationship between a father and a child, and a grandmother and a child was enhanced by family music therapy treatment. In Oldfield et al. (2012) the authors noticed from their clinical observations that at the start of treatment, the child's difficulties were the main focus of the work, but that later on in treatment, it is the relationship with the parents that become the primary consideration. They also ask questions about whether the gender of the therapist could be an important consideration in certain types of family music therapy work. In one case, a young mother who was very socially isolated and reticent to engage in therapy with her sons, was able to be convinced to try when she discovered that the female music therapist had children of a similar age. In another case a father who had been through a traumatic divorce was not willing to accept support from a female therapist, but was able to use improvised "jamming" with a male therapist to help him to become more playful with his son.

Tuomi (2010) combines the use of voice and theraplay ideas (Booth and Jernberg 2009) to explore new ways of enabling parents and young children with emotional difficulties and attachment issues to communicate with one another. She and Jacobsen (2012) often find they model "good parenting" in their sessions and in her PhD investigation Jacobsen developed and trialed a parenting assessment tool that can be used by music therapists. Oldfield (2012) reports on a case where the music therapist was able to provide evidence of good parenting in music therapy sessions. Sadly, the child still had to be taken away from the mother. Nevertheless, the mother was able to be provided with video evidence that at times she was able to be a good parent and have positive times with her child.

Reflections

This overview of the literature which started with children with life threatening illnesses and ended with children in psychiatric centers has also to some extent considered work according to the place in which it is carried out, hospitals, hospices, in people's homes, community family centers, primary schools, and psychiatric family units. This might be a useful way of dividing up music therapy with young children and their families, as the work will be heavily influenced by the setting in which it is taking place. Nevertheless it must be remembered that there are overlaps between the settings, e.g., work in the home could be with families who would normally be seen in a hospice. Similarly, families with children with emotional difficulties might be treated in a psychiatric center or in a school, and in some cases at home.

One distinction that it is useful for the music therapist to make when planning the work, is whether it is primarily the child who has been referred, the parent who has been referred, or whether the music therapist is being specifically asked to address difficulties in the relationship between the child and the parent. In many cases this is clearly outlined before treatment begins, but in others it may not be clear and the focus of the work may change as treatment evolves as was shown in the afore mentioned article (Oldfield et al. 2012). Sometimes this distinction is specific to a particular client group, for example, when working with families with young children with autistic spectrum disorder, the initial reason for referral might be the child's isolation and communication difficulties, even if a part of the work becomes working with and supporting the parent. When working in child psychiatry, a family may be referred to boost the confidence of a parent who has previously suffered from post-natal depression. However, even within one client group, the focus may be more on the child or the family depending on each family's specific circumstances. This was well illustrated in Flower's (2008) chapter regarding working with terminally ill children and their families in their homes.

CASE VIGNETTES

For confidential reasons, names and details have been changed.

Becky and Jenny

As I prepare the room for Becky and her mother, Jenny, I overhear Jenny chatting and laughing with the receptionist. I know the administrative staff on the unit enjoy seeing Jenny and Becky every week. They exchange general news about how they are and how the week has gone. I go to the reception area to meet them and my music therapy colleague, Andrew, is sitting next to Jenny and they are both facing Becky in her wheelchair. He and Becky are smiling and laughing together and I tease them by saying: "Don't get any ideas, Andrew, she's mine—you can't have her…" they all laugh. Jenny is proud of the fact that her daughter is so popular, and Becky senses that the adults are relaxed and at ease together. Not all my out-patients know the staff on the unit so well, but Becky and Jenny have been coming to see me on a weekly basis (with some breaks when Becky has been unwell) for just over two years. The fact that the unit is a friendly and welcoming place to come to is very important. The receptionists know and recognize all the families I see and will be sensitive to their needs, talking to some but remaining quiet with those families who prefer to be more private.

Four-year-old Becky has severe learning difficulties and is physically disabled. She also suffers from epilepsy and over the two years I have seen her, the doctors have been adjusting her medication to try to control her seizures. She has to work very hard to control the use of her arms and hands. She can vocalize but doesn't say any words. In music therapy sessions we have been encouraging her to direct her hands towards the instruments and play independently, give her a chance to use her vocalizations as a means of expression and help her to develop interactive exchanges through her playing and vocalizing.

Becky clearly recognizes the music space as she is wheeled into the room by her mother, and smiles broadly as soon as I start to sing the familiar "Hello song," accompanying myself on the guitar. Jenny looks fondly at her daughter saying "you do love your music don't you?" I then put the guitar in front of Becky balancing it on the sides of the wheelchair. Becky lifts her right arm and directs it towards the guitar, her fingers strumming the open strings as she does this. I improvise a tune based on the pentatonic scale of the guitar's strings. I vocalize freely so that Becky's random strums will fit into the music, sometimes I sing "la, la, la…" at other times I insert words such as: "Becky can play" or "Mummy is watching." We then move on to playing a large tambour covered with quite rough skin, which is placed on Becky's lap where the three of us can play it. Becky can quite easily scratch this drum independently with her fingers and produce a clear sound. Occasionally she will also tap it. Again I sing to accompany our playing, sometimes freely as previously to accommodate unpredictable beats, but sometimes I incorporate a short rhythmic phrase which is often repeated and becomes a recognizable theme which gives Jenny and me a chance to take turns and can motivate Becky to remain on task. Jenny joins in with our playing, using one hand to tap the tambour and the other to gently wipe Becky's mouth to stop her dribbling onto the instrument. Sometimes I will put my mouth very near the drum and my singing will echo into the drum, making the skin vibrate. Becky can feel this when her hands are on the drum and this will further encourage her to make music with us. At times the music making is slow and gentle and there might be pauses while we give Becky time to respond to our musical suggestions. At other times we might both play quite energetically, and Becky will enjoy being helped to play by her mother.

I then give Jenny a set of wind chimes to hold for Becky to play and I reach for my clarinet. Jenny says: "oooh ... Becky's favorite...." She is proud of the fact that Becky particularly responds to this instrument. Sure enough, as soon as I play, Becky smiles and looks toward the instrument and very soon starts vocalizing at the same time as playing the wind chimes with her hands. I alternate between singing and playing, bending the notes to try and match her vocal sounds. Becky also starts vocalizing with us and I become very quiet allowing Jenny and Becky to have a brief babbling exchange. Later Jenny tells me that they have started having more of these babbling exchanges at home and that her husband has a special repertoire of sounds he uses with Becky that she responds well to. I respond with enthusiasm and encourage her to continue whenever possible. We reflect on how much more Becky is vocalizing now, and on how much more engaged she is than a year ago.

The following week is Becky's last music therapy session with me. She has started attending a special school on a part-time basis, and will now be attending full-time. I have already liaised with my music therapy colleague at the school who will be seeing her for music therapy sessions there. However, Jenny will not be present at these sessions and while we have both decided it is now the right time for these family sessions to finish and for Becky to be a little more independent of Jenny, we're both sad about this ending. As it is half-term, Becky older brother, Tony, who is six, has come to join us. He has come before during the holidays, and I know he loves playing the instruments and is very musical.

After the greeting I give Tony a guitar to strum while we improvise in our usual way with occasional strums from Becky. This time I incorporate Tony's name when I sing and Becky looks over at him and smiles, clearly pleased that he is there. During the tambour playing I give Tony his own drum and a chorus line develops:

Tony, Jenny, and I all three play energetically together to accompany the singing. Then I improvise in a more fluid way in the same key to give Becky a chance to play. I prepare a repeat of our chorus by saying: "ready..." pausing dramatically and then doing a vocal glissandi up to the first note. At the end I thank Tony for listening so well and helping with the rhythm. He appears pleased to be joining in and doing an activity with his sister. Jenny looks proud of both of them. During the clarinet and chime playing I give Tony two reed horns which he plays with me during my improvising on the clarinet, sometimes I follow his playing, at other times I leave gaps for him to complete the musical phrases. In between the wind instrument playing, Jenny and Becky vocalize, and I sing that we are making music together and that Jenny's brother, Tony has come along to play the horns. Becky is unusually free in her singing, but I sense that Jenny is fighting back tears, she is moved to see the two children playing together and sad because it is our last session.

We do our usual goodbyes on the bongo drums, and Tony presents me with a beautiful bunch of flowers and a card. Now I have to hold on to my emotions. Jenny is also sad that she can't say goodbye to one of the receptionists who is on holiday that week. We promise to pass on messages, and Jenny says she will stay in touch.

There are many reasons why it was essential for Jenny to be being present in the room with Becky. Initially I needed Jenny to tell me what Becky could and couldn't do, and also to advise me on how much I should push her and when to stop encouraging her. Jenny also would often hold instruments while I played the clarinet or the piano. When I started the work Becky was only two and would have been scared to be with a stranger without her mother being present. Once Becky started becoming involved in playing and vocalizing it was essential for Jenny to see this so that she could then carry on with these ideas at home and expect the same from Becky in other settings. It was also very valuable for Jenny to know that every week she would have a good experience with her daughter in music therapy sessions. This was particularly important as Becky had many health problems, was often in and out of hospital and had great difficulties sleeping, which meant that Jenny was almost always up with her for much of the night. In this context, having a positive and supportive experience on a weekly basis was as important for Jenny as it was for Becky.

Judy and Rachel

Judy and her eight-year-old daughter, Rachel came to the psychiatric assessment unit to accompany Judy's twelve-year-old son, Craig, who had Asperger's syndrome as well as severe emotional and behavior problems. Judy, a single mother, had been suffering from depression for many years. She was very overweight, and spoke very little and slowly, as though everything was too much effort. Both she and Rachel were frightened by Craig's violent outbursts. Rachel was also very quiet, would only speak when spoken to, and like her mother did not seem motivated to take part in activities or engage in conversations. The team felt that music therapy might be a good way to engage this family and to allow them to communicate in some way and express themselves non-verbally. The first music therapy session was completely dominated by Craig who was reluctant to come to the music room. Once in the room he made a point of refusing to take part in any way and would shout and complain when we tried to ignore him, making it impossible for anyone else in the room to engage in music making either. After about fifteen minutes he walked out. It was then decided that I would offer Judy and Rachel four sessions together to give them both an opportunity to play together without having to worry about Craig.

Judy was less reluctant to take up this offer than I expected, saying she liked music and had played the trumpet as a child, but unlike her sister who had played the violin, she was no good at it. Since Judy did not usually speak or initiate much conversation it was encouraging that she had volunteered this information. It seemed that in spite of the difficulties with Craig in our first session, she had enjoyed playing the instruments.

After a welcoming song on the guitar I explained to Judy and Rachel that we would be playing instruments together in the session and would take it in turns to choose the instruments.

I chose a xylophone, a metallophone, and a glockenspiel for the three of us, thinking that such quiet, slow moving people might need a gentle introduction to music making. Judy immediately said she didn't know how to play and I tried to reassure her, saying that it didn't matter. She was still uncertain, and Rachel was taking her cues from her mother, unwilling to try if Judy was hesitant. I suggested we play with our eyes closed, and this worked. Judy started hitting the xylophone randomly, giggling when she missed the notes. Rachel immediately followed suit, not smiling, but at least playing quite spontaneously.

Judy chose next, surprising me by immediately selecting the drum kit for herself, and then after a little reflection, two large drums and a cymbal for Rachel, and the piano for me. I initiated a solid 4/4 rhythmic pattern on the keyboard and within a few seconds Judy was playing the drum kit loudly and furiously. I tried to match and hold her playing, and noticed that Rachel was also playing forcefully and energetically. We continued to play at this intense volume for about fifteen minutes. There was a grim determination about the playing and there was nothing light or playful about it. Occasionally the music slowed a little and it became slightly less fierce, but this didn't last long before Judy again picked up the volume. I felt as though the playing was a way for Judy and Rachel to express inner frustration and turmoil. Our playing slowed and we came to a common ending. I asked Judy whether the piece had finished and she replied: "yes." I left some space in case Judy or Rachel wanted to say anything about this astounding music making, but they both wore unexpressive masks—in complete contrast to the music that had just been played. Rachel was then unwilling to make a choice of instruments herself so I suggested we all share the rainbow bells as I had noticed that she seemed to like playing these the previous week. We took turns and played together, but I think we were all still overwhelmed by the amount of energy and emotion that had gone into our previous improvisation. At the end of the session, I asked them both what they thought about the session. After a few moments Judy said in an expressionless voice that she had enjoyed it, and Rachel nodded. I asked whether they would mind if we videoed next week's session, so that we could look at it together and they could have a record of their music making to take home with them. They agreed to this.

The following three sessions continued in much the same vein in that most of the time was taken up by forceful loud drumming by Judy and Rachel. However, the music gradually ebbed and flowed more, with each of us taking on leadership roles, either in a structured pre-determined way, or in more spontaneous exchanges. Rachel smiled occasionally and acknowledged that she liked playing and there was some spontaneous eye contact between Judy and Rachel during the improvisations. They seemed pleased to see the videos of themselves playing, but this viewing didn't prompt any conversation or reflections from Judy as I had hoped. It appeared that the therapeutic nature of this work at this stage was predominantly through the action of playing and improvising together. With their permission I showed excerpts of the videos to the psychiatric team who were as amazed as I had initially been by this completely uncharacteristic spontaneity and energy shown by Judy in her playing. I wrote a report emphasizing that Judy and Rachel would greatly benefit from continued longer term music therapy treatment after they left the unit. Sadly, I knew this was unlikely to take place, as they lived in a remote area of the UK where no music therapy was available.

These two cases are very different. In the first longer case it was the child, Becky, who was referred. In the second, the work was short-term and it was the mother, Judy, who was the main focus of the treatment. However, in both cases music therapy was effective and the work could not have taken place without the other member of the family being present. In the last section of this chapter I will examine why music therapy is useful with families.

RATIONALE FOR MUSIC THERAPY
WITH FAMILIES AND YOUNG CHILDREN

For both Becky and Judy the first reason that music therapy helped was because they both liked music and enjoyed playing the instruments and (in Becky's case) vocalizing. If they hadn't been motivated by the music it would have been very difficult to engage Becky and Judy would not have come into the room. Enjoyment of the music making is mentioned by nearly all the authors I have cited earlier but particularly by those working with groups of parents and young children (Williams 2010, Loth 2008). This motivation to be involved in playing enabled Becky to overcome her physical difficulties and Judy to break through the lethargy caused by her depression. Spontaneous involvement in shared and creative music making allows parents and children to express themselves and communicate. In musical improvisation and playful exchanges they are equal partners. There are many parallels here with Winnicott's (1986 and 1997) thoughts about play and families, it is useful to remember his thought that "playing is itself a therapy" (1997, p. 50).

Another key factor for both the previous cases is that music became a non-verbal means of communicating and exchanging. Becky was not using language yet, and both Judy and Rachel spoke very little, however, they were all three able to exchange and communicate through the music they made. When working with pre-verbal or non-verbal young children, improvised musical exchanges can be similar to vocal babbling exchanges between mothers and babies. Daniel Stern (1985) studied these early vocal dialogues and showed that mothers don't just copy the babies' sounds, but tune into the babies' emotional states to initiate subtle changes in their own vocalizing, and in this way keep the exchange alive and interesting. Trevarthen (1993) underlines the importance of these early dialogues, suggesting that they provide the foundation necessary to develop language. Trehub (2001) emphasizes that these babbling exchanges are musical in nature with rhythmic patterns and melodic contours specific to each dyad. Music therapists can enable parents and children to use music making to dialogue in similar ways, creating a way for babbling exchanges to occur (as in the case of Becky and Jenny) or enabling a mother and a child to rediscover the possibility of exchanging (as in the case of Judy and Rachel).

An underlying assumption that exists in most music therapy work with parents and young children is that both the child and the parent benefit from having a healthy relationship with one another. Bowlby (1997 and 2000) writes extensively about the attachment between the child and the primary care giver, emphasizing the importance of a "secure base" for the healthy emotional development of the child. With families such as Becky and Jenny's the secure base already exists, but because of the severity of Becky's difficulties, Jenny needs support to maintain this healthy attachment, and benefits from the experience of communicating in a positive way with her daughter on a regular basis. For Judy, the experience of engaging in music making allows her to discover more healthy ways of playing and being with her daughter. Rachel can use the improvised playing to find herself and interact more independently with her mother, rather than simply mirroring her and living in her shadow.

I am not alone in referring to these authors' to explore the reasons why music therapy is important for families. In fact when looking at Edward's (2011) book I found that out of thirteen authors, eight had cited Winnicott and Bowlby; seven had cited Stern, four had cited Trevarthan, and three had cited Trehub. These and many other music therapists working with families have explored in much more depth than I have space for here the literature regarding (for example) early music between mothers and children and the musicality of pre-verbal interactions. What is important is that the authors feel that this parallel body of research provides additional evidence to justify family-based music therapy. It is also interesting to note that a number of music therapists working with families have been influenced by similar authors and theories.

Conclusion

It is personally fulfilling to see how much the field of music therapy with families has grown, and how many music therapists now work in this area. It is clear that there are a number of different types of work with families and young children, and that the music therapy interventions will be different depending on the types of difficulties presented by the children and the families, and the settings in which the work takes place. Sometimes it is the child who is the main reason for the referral and sometimes it is the parent. At other times the music therapist might be asked specifically to work on the relationship between the child and the parent. In some instances, however, it may not be exactly defined which member of the family the treatment is primarily aimed at, and, in addition, the focus of the work may shift from one family member to another. The music therapist has to remain flexible and not only open to the needs both of the individual people in the room, but also to those of the family as a whole. In this chapter I have already given many reasons why music therapy is effective with families, but perhaps one of the simplest and most important is that through playing together the family can just "be," exist, and be valued as a unit. After eighteen months of working together, Barry, the father of a little boy with cerebral palsy was interviewed about the music therapy sessions and said:

> I wouldn't have missed it for the world ... just generally being his Dad in the music therapy sessions

> Oldfield and Nudds 2002

References

Bowlby, J. (1997). *Attachment.* [1969.] London: Pimlico.
Bowlby, J. (2000). A *Secure Aase: Clinical Applications of Attachment Theory.* [1988.] London: Routledge.

Booth, P.B. and Jernberg, A.M. (2009). *Theraplay: Helping Parents and Children Build Better Relationships Through Attachment-based Play*. Chichester: John Wiley & Sons.

Bull, R. (2008). Autism and the family: Group music therapy with mothers and children. In: A. Oldfield and C. Flower (eds), *Music Therapy with Children and their Families*, pp. 71–88. London: Jessica Kingsley Publishers.

Burrell, M. (2011). The benefits of music sessions for very young children with their parents or carers through the eyes of a music therapist. In: J. Edwards (ed.), *Music Therapy and Parent-Infant Bonding*, pp. 93–100. Oxford: Oxford University Press.

Casey, O. (2010). Issues of attachment and separation within parent-toddler groups in a children's hospice. Paper presented at the Eigth European Music Therapy Congress, Cadiz, Spain 5–9 May, 2010.

Davies, E. (2008). It's a family affair: music therapy for children and families at a psychiatric unit. In: A. Oldfield and C. Flower (eds), Music *Therapy with Children and their Families*, pp. 121–140. London: Jessica Kingsley Publishers.

Davies, E. and Rosscornes, C. (2012). Setting up and developing music therapy at a children's centre, for pre-school children and their families and carers. In: J. Tomlinson, P. Derrington, and A. Oldfield (eds), *Music Therapy in Schools; Working with Children of all Ages in Mainstream and Special Education*, pp. 19–32. London: Jessica Kingsley Publishers.

Drake, T. (2008). Back to Basics: Community-based music therapy for vulnerable young children and their parents. In: A. Oldfield and C. Flower (eds), Music *Therapy with Children and their Families*, pp. 37–52. London: Jessica Kingsley Publishers.

Drake, T. (2011). Becoming in tune: the use of music therapy to assist the developing bond between traumatized children and their new adoptive parents. In: J. Edwards (ed.), *Music Therapy and Parent-Infant Bonding*, pp. 22–41. Oxford: Oxford University Press.

Edwards, J. (ed.) (2011). *Music Therapy and Parent-Infant Bonding*. Oxford: Oxford University Press.

Flower, C. (2008): Living with dying: reflections on family music therapy with children near the end of life. In: A. Oldfield and C. Flower (eds), *Music Therapy with Children and their Families*, pp. 177–189. London: Jessica Kingsley Publishers.

Griessmeier, B. and Bossinger, W. (1994). *Musiktherapie mit Krebskranken Kindern. Transl. Music therapy with children who have cancer*. Studtgard: Gustav Fischer Verlag.

Griessmeier, B. (2012). Forever young—music therapy with a young adolescent and his mother during stem cell transportation. Paper presented at the Music Therapy with Families Symposium, during the Seventh Nordic Music Therapy Congress, Jyvaskyla, Finland, June 13–16, 2012.

Heal, M. (1994). An exploration of the emotional impact on co-therapists of running a music therapy group for mothers, their toddlers with Down's syndrome and accompanying siblings. MA thesis, University of East London.

Holmes, J., Oldfield, A., and Polichroniadis, M. (2011). *Creating Change for Complex Children and their Families—a Multi-disciplinary Approach to Multi-Family Work*. London: Jessica Kingsley Publishers.

Howden, S. (2008). Music therapy with traumatised children and their families in mainstream schools: a case study with a six-year-old girl and her mother. In: A. Oldfield and C. Flower (eds), Music *Therapy with Children and their Families*, pp. 103–119. London: Jessica Kingsley Publishers.

Jacobsen, S. (2012). Working with parents and their emotionally neglected children. Being a facilitator and a role model. Paper presented at the Seventh Nordic Music Therapy Conference, Jyvaskyla, Finland, June 13–16, 2012.

Kaenampornpan, P. (2012). Working collaboratively with parents and their children with special needs: my role as a music therapist. Paper presented at the Music Therapy and Dramatherapy Conference at Anglia Ruskin University, 30th November–1st December, 2012.

Kelly, K. (2011). Supporting attachments in vulnerable families through an early intervention school-based group music therapy programme. In: J. Edwards (ed.), *Music Therapy and Parent-Infant Bonding*, pp. 101–114. Oxford: Oxford University Press.

Ledger, A. (2011). Extending group music therapy to families in schools: a reflection on practical and professional aspects. In: Edwards, J. (ed.), *Music Therapy and Parent-Infant Bonding*, pp. 53–70. Oxford: Oxford University Press.

Loombe, D. (2012). Music therapy sessions with a boy and his father. Paper presented at the Music Therapy and Dramatherapy Conference at Anglia Ruskin University, 30th November–1st December, 2012.

Lorenzato, K.I. (2005). *Filling a need while making a noise*. London: Jessica Kingsley Publishers.

Loth, H. (2008). Music therapy groups for families with a learning disabled toddler: bridging some gaps. In: A. Oldfield and C. Flower (eds), Music *Therapy with Children and their Families*, pp. 214–234. London: Jessica Kingsley Publishers.

Mitchell, E. Melia, J., and Stevens, A. (2012). Music therapy with Thomas's fund: the pros and cons of working with children and young people in their homes. Paper presented at the Music Therapy and Dramatherapy Conference at Anglia Ruskin University, 30th November–1st December, 2012.

Muller, P. and Warwick, A. (1993). Autistic children and music therapy: the effects of maternal involvement in therapy. In: M. Heal and T. Wigram (eds), *Music Therapy in Health and Education*, pp. 147–158. London: Jessica Kingsley Publishers.

Nall, K. and Everitt, E. (2005). From hospice to home: music therapy outreach. In: M. Pavlicevic (ed.), *Music Therapy in Children's Hospices: Jessie's Fund in Action*. London: Jessica Kingsley Publishers.

Nocker-Ribaupierre, M. (1999). Premature birth and music therapy. In: T. Wigram and J. de Backer (eds), *Clinical Applications of Music Therapy in Developmental Disability, Paediatrics and Neurology*, pp. 47–65. London: Jessica Kingsley Publishers.

Nordoff, P. and Robbins, C. (1971). *Therapy in Music for Handicapped Children*. London: Victor Gollancz Ltd.

Nordoff, P. and Robbins, C. (1977). *Creative Music Therapy*. New York: The John Day Company.

O'Hanrahan, A. (2012). Combining skills as a music therapist and a social worker when working with families. Paper presented at the Music Therapy with Families Symposium, during the Seventh Nordic Music Therapy Congress, Jyvaskyla, Finland, June 13–16, 2012.

Oldfield, A. (1993). Music therapy with families. In: M. Heal and T. Wigram (eds), *Music Therapy in Health and Education*, pp. 46–54. London: Jessica Kingsley Publishers.

Oldfield, A. (2006a). *Interactive Music Therapy—a Positive Approach: Music Therapy at a Child Development Centre*. London: Jessica Kingsley Publishers.

Oldfield, A. (2006b). *Interactive Music Therapy in Child and Family Psychiatry: Clinical Practice, Research and Teaching*. London: Jessica Kingsley Publishers.

Oldfield, A. (2012). Positive moments in a desperate situation. Paper presented at the Music Therapy with Families Symposium, during the Seventh Nordic Music Therapy Congress, Jyvaskyla, Finland, June 13–16, 2012.

Oldfield, A. and Bunce, L. (2001) "Mummy can play too &" short-term music therapy with mothers and young children. *British Journal of Music Therapy* 15(1): 27–36.

Oldfield, A. and Flower, C. (eds). (2008). *Music Therapy with Children and their Families.* London, Jessica Kingsley Publishers.

Oldfield, A. and Nudds, J. (2002). Joshua and Barry: Music Therapy with a partially-sighted little boy with cerebral palsy. Video, Anglia Polytechnic University.

Oldfield, A., Bunce, L., and Adams, M. (2003). An investigation into short-term music therapy with mothers and young children. *British Journal of Music Therapy* 17(1): 26–45.

Oldfield, A., Bell, K., and Poole, J.A. (2012). Three families and three music therapists; reflections on short-term music therapy in child and family psychiatry. *Nordic Journal of Music Therapy* 21(3): 250–267.

Sobey, K. (2008). Introduction. In: A. Oldfield & C. Flower (eds), *Music therapy with children and their families*, pp. 11–17. London: Jessica Kingsley Publishers.

Stern, D. (1985). *The Interpersonal World of the Infant.* New York: Basic Books.

Streeter, E. (1993). *Making music with the young child with special needs: A guide for parents.* Jessica Kingsley Publisher.

Thompson, G. (2012). Family-centred music therapy and young children with ASD-results from a randomised controlled trial. Paper presented at theSeventh Nordic Music Therapy Congress: Music Therapy Models, Methods and Techniques, Jyvaskyla, Finland, June 13–16, 2010.

Thomas, D. (2012). Sing & Grow UK—An early intervention approach for families and pre-school children. Paper presented at the 7th Nordic Music Therapy Conference, Jyvaskyla, Finland, June 13–16, 2012.

Trehub, S.E. (2001). Musical predispositions in infancy. *Annals of the New York Academy of Sciences* 930: 1–16.

Trevarthen, C. (1993). The function of emotions in early infant communication and development. In: J. Nadel and L. Camioni (eds), *New Perspectives in Early Communicative Development*, pp. 48–81. London: Routledge.

Tuomi, K. (2010). When individual therapy is not enough; dyadic interaction treatment for traumatized children. Paper presented at the Eigth European Music Therapy Congress, Cadiz, Spain, 5–9th of May, 2010.

Williams, K. (2010). The effectiveness of short-term group music therapy intervention. Research MA, Queensland University, Australia.

Williams, K., Nicholson, J., Abad, V., Docherty, L., and Berthelsen, D. (2011). Evaluating parent-child group music therapy programmes: Challenges and successes for Sing & Grow. In: J. Edwards (ed.), *Music Therapy and Parent-Infant Bonding*, pp. 73–92. Oxford: Oxford University Press.

Winnicott, D.W. (1986). *Home is where we start from: essays by a psychoanalyst, DW Winnicott.* Penguin Books.

Winnicott, D.W. (1997). Thinking about children. Da Capo Press.

Woodward, A. (2004). Music therapy for autistic children and their families: a creative spectrum. *British Journal of Music Therapy* 18(1): 8–14.

CHAPTER 9

....

MUSIC THERAPY IN
THE CONTEXT OF THE
SPECIAL SCHOOL

....

TOMMY HAYES

SPECIAL EDUCATION

....

SPECIAL education is the term used for the education and training of children who have additional needs because of a developmental difficulty or disorder in one or more areas of functioning. Although from the 1990s through to the present day the philosophy of inclusion and integration has flourished based on the aspirations of the Salamanca statement (UNESCO 1994), nonetheless special education service provision continues to be provided separately in some contexts (Graham and Jahnukainen 2011). Special education services are provided in specialist schools or units, while other services are embedded within what is described as *mainstream* school provision where students who have disabilities are integrated into schools alongside students who do not have disabilities. In this chapter music therapy in special education will describe work in specialist schools that provide services to children who have additional needs. The term *disability* will be used rather than other terms such as *handicap*.

Each country has their own policy regarding education provision for students with disabilities, and some types of service provision can vary between regions within countries. The terminology used in the sector can be different from country to country. Therefore, students starting placement or writing assignments about music therapy in the area of special education services are encouraged to explore special education with reference to the relevant cultural and social context.

The provision of education to children with disabilities has historically been poorly provided with not all people with disabilities receiving an education. It was only in the 1970s that many countries began to regulate requirements for the education of people with disabilities. In the USA the Individuals with Disabilities Education Act (IDEA) was enacted in 1975, requiring the provision of free and appropriate education to children and youth between 3 and 21 years of age deemed eligible (Aud and Wilkinson-Flicker 2013). The Education Act of 1970 in the UK heralded the right of children with disabilities to an education, and in Ireland it was only with the passing of the Disability Act in

2004 that the right to education for children with disabilities was enshrined. The passing of the Act in Ireland resulted from intense campaigning by interest groups, mainly parents of children with a disability, and many campaigners remain disappointed that the right to education stops at age 18 for people who have a disability (De Wispelaere and Walsh 2007).

Through much of the twentieth century the view prevailed in many countries that people with disabilities required *care* rather than education, and this care was considered to be best provided in large institutions out of sight of the general public. Most of these institutions have now been disbanded through changes in the way disabilities are viewed; changes were made in line with the imperative of *normalization* (Wolfensberger and Tullman 1982). The gradual deinstitutionalization of residents occurred over the middle decades of the twentieth century. The history of the development of institutions for people with disabilities has been recorded (Wright and Jackson 2001) along with the experiences of institutional life for some former residents (e.g. Brown et al. 2010).

As educational rights were gained for people with disabilities, the area of *disability studies* challenged the concept of a disability as a medical condition made up of deficits (Ferguson and Nusbaum 2012). Disability studies has provided a way to think about disability as having a primarily socially constructed dimension; that is, people with disabilities are *excluded* because of human prejudices against difference. The inability of society—government, policy, practice—to remove the hindrances and barriers for full participation by all people creates and maintains the notion of *disability*. Although there have been tensions between the disability studies field and the field of special education (e.g., Anastasiou and Kauffman 2011), nonetheless some special education services have continued to be provided in special schools in many countries, especially to students with high support needs. These services benefit from ethical reflection on their provision of education. Additionally, students and practitioners entering the area of special education can learn about the tensions and contributions of the disability studies field in order to further their thinking and extend their ethical scope of practice.

As the field of disability studies has grown the honoring of first person accounts of what it is like to live with a disability has occurred. For example, many people diagnosed with autism have shared their lived experience of their world, and these can give professionals, carers, and family a close insight into their experiences (Higashida 2013; Lipsky 2011; Nazeer 2007). Parents have also offered perspectives on life with a child who has a disability (e.g. Resch et al. 2010). Students and practitioners are encouraged to read these stories to increase their sensitivity and empathy in their work.

Special education services vary from country to country in their historical development and current delivery but there are common factors internationally (Daveson and Edwards 1998). In many countries assessment generally follows these steps:

- The screening and identification of any suspected learning difficulties or delays.
- Diagnosis of a particular condition and the pupil's eligibility for additional resource support.
- The development of an Individual Education Plan (IEP).
- The consideration of programme planning and placement.
- An evaluation of the pupil's strengths, areas for growth and general progress.

Shevlin et al. 2013, pp. 124–125

Usually by the time a student is referred for music therapy the above steps have been completed, and the IEP will be available for consultation and reference.

MUSIC THERAPY AND SPECIAL EDUCATION

Music therapy has a long history of being part of special education services. Solomon found evidence of the use of music in special education through the nineteenth century (Solomon 1980). Music making is a natural part of early life, especially in the period before speech develops when the vocalizations of the infant are scaffolded by the parent or care giver in what is increasingly understood to be a highly musical way (Trevarthen and Malloch 2002; Rochat et al. 1999).

Music therapy services rely on the ability of music to support creative interactions between the therapist and the child, often eliciting new responses and behaviors. As McFerran and Shanahan (2011) have observed: "Music therapy can reveal a creative and communicative capacity in the child that is often not evident in other settings" (p. 109). In music therapy the music therapist observes the student closely, while listening and responding musically. This special way of listening has been shown through research to assist in non-musical gains. For example, in a study by Kim et al. (2008) it was found that previously published research studies indicated:

> … superior gains in joint attention, language development and social communication skills when the adult's behavior remains either contingent, or imitative of the child's behavior showing high level of synchronization and matching during play interaction.
>
> Kim et al. 2008, p. 1759

More specifically, for children who have autism spectrum disorder (ASD) evidence from music therapy research but also evaluations of other music-based interactions shows that: "… novel, embodied rhythm-based, multisystem interventions grounded in singing, music making, joint action, and social synchrony can be used to alleviate the core social communication deficits and perceptuo-motor and behavioral comorbidities of children with ASDs." (Srinivasan and Bhat 2013, p. 11). However, Srinivasan and Bhat (2013) have also pointed out that some research studies about music and ASD have lacked systematic rigor. Therefore they have offered a range of suggestions for improving future research in this area. These include researching active music making rather than music listening, small group music processes for children who have autism, and the application of music based activities in the natural environment rather than a laboratory or other unfamiliar space.

Music therapy researchers and practitioners have developed assessments that assist in ensuring that the goals of music therapy are suited to the capacities and potential of the student. For example, the Special Education Music Therapy Assessment Process (Brunk and Coleman 2000) is a standardized procedure (rather than a standardized test) that was developed from the authors' professional work over two decades. It directly references the student's IEP and is mapped onto the legal requirements for special education services in the USA. New practitioners or training students working in special education services should always examine the existing assessment procedures and consider those published in the literature when beginning work with new clients.

Music therapy to support
communication goals

Every student in special education services has their own unique way of communicating. In many special education settings a majority of children will be non-verbal. Where children have multiple disabilities and have not developed language skills, their skills may be at an early stage of pre-verbal development. They may not yet have developed intentional communication but rather be functioning at a *pre-intentional* stage of interaction (Perry 2003). This references Rowland's communication matrix in which there are seven levels of communication through early development: pre-intentional behavior; intentional behavior; unconventional pre-symbolic communication; conventional pre-symbolic communication; concrete symbols; abstract symbols and language (Rowland and Fried-Oken 2010).

A goal of music therapy sessions is to work out how the therapist and the student can communicate together. Working out how it is possible to communicate takes time and patience. Many students will vocalize, perhaps to indicate they are in pain, or bored, are hungry, or want something that only the caregiver can reach or provide. Responses to vocalizations are a common way to develop communicative potentials through music therapy. Firstly the music therapist must rule out localized sources of pain or distress that could be alleviated before responding to a vocalization that sounds distressed. Pitch is a useful starting point for tuning into the sounds the student is making. The therapist can match the sounds with their own voice, and augment the sounds, finding melodic and rhythmic possibilities in the sounds. If using known songs the music therapist can play the song in a key that is relevant to the pitch of vocalizations of the student.

Example:
Donal is aged 13 and has a severe and profound disability with multiple needs. He has no specified diagnosis. He lives in a care home. He is independently mobile and he doesn't speak. He refuses to use his hands and instead his mouth and his feet are used to pick up or explore objects. He has developed a habit of engaging in self-injurious behavior.

Donal vocalizes with a few unique sounds all in the tonality of E. When he uses a medium pitch in low register this means he is hungry. When he growls or roars, this means he is upset. Usually when he makes this sound he follows it by making a self-injurious action. Additionally he has a sound he makes when he is feeling happy. This is higher pitched and can be written as ning, ning, ning. *Vocalizing with him in music therapy can be calming, and supportive for both the therapist and Donal.*

The goal of the team is to encourage Donal to use his hands. The goal in music therapy is to lessen his agitation, and to encourage his intentionality. At an earlier stage of music therapy he was playing with his hands on the piano but recently chooses not to do this. When Donal is upset he will calm down if the music therapist plays in the key of E, and sometimes he can calm down enough to go to sleep.

Many students in special education services who cannot speak have some capacity to use Augmented and/or Alternative Communication (AAC) such as Picture Exchange Communication (PECS). The music therapist must learn the system that the student uses to communicate, and then use it consistently in consultation with teachers, the Speech and

Language specialist staff, and parents (McCarthy et al. 2008). PECS can be used to offer choices of instruments, and choices of participatory actions such as singing or instrument playing. The music therapist can develop a visual representation of a song using PECS. This is especially relevant for children who have autism. The music therapist can also learn to use the signs for the words in songs.

Where children do have some capacity to communicate using language the music therapy goals can be targeted towards increasing vocabulary and improving speech articulation. Singing can be a positive way to support this goal. A microphone can be used to encourage singing. A loop pedal can be connected to an amp and laptop connected to a speaker. With this set-up it is possible to sing along to songs on the internet. These can be recorded and played back to the student. It is a highly pleasurable process and results in feelings of satisfaction and pride. There is an observable increase in articulation of words in songs when singing is offered consistently.

Music therapy to support social goals

Group sessions are vital to supporting social goals. An identity can be created for the group by focussing on each child at a time, while at the same time working on the group cohesion. Because some children are at different stages and have different music interests the music therapist must find ways to engage all students while encouraging each child. To facilitate group cohesion and interaction some students in the group can play an instrument to provide an accompaniment to someone else's song being sung.

Music therapy to support emotional goals

Working within a relational frame allows a therapeutic alliance to be developed. This relationship can be important to the students' well-being, especially when developmental stages of change are encountered, for example the onset of puberty. The therapeutic relationship builds through working with the student regularly and tuning in sensitively to how they are feeling and interacting on the day of the session, especially for students who cannot relate this to the therapist in words. The therapist is often viewed differently to the teacher by the student, and the type of relationship that is formed is one of emotional interaction and support via musical interaction.

Music therapy to support cognitive goals

The PECS system of communication can be used to support skills such as recognition of objects. Counting songs and games, songwriting, and memorizing song lyrics require cognitive skills that students may transfer across to other areas of their learning.

Music therapy to support physical goals

Students can often reach out to strum the guitar while it is being held by the therapist who changes the chords during a song. Alternatively the guitar can be modified using an open D tuning so that the student can hold and strum the guitar during a song. If the pitch is not quite right a capo can be used to modify the register so it is an easier singing key for the student or group. Drumming and using shakers during songs or improvisation provides opportunities to strengthen skills in grasping and coordination.

Methods and techniques

Songs

Songs can be used in many ways in special education. Songs can be created or improvised in the moment to respond to something that is happening between the student and the therapist. The therapist can compose songs that are about what a child likes to eat or drink or enjoys doing; such as eating chocolate or dancing. While singing songs the therapist can pause and wait for the student to sing or vocalize the next word. Some clients repeat language, such as words or sentences that they have heard. Singing these words in a song can provide a context for the language the student is using.

It can be difficult to provide age-appropriate experiences when clients have learned and liked children's songs which they request in sessions. Although providing age-appropriate materials is important it must be remembered that the songs that students learned as children may symbolize comfort and safety to them.

Example:
One client I was working with would only sing children's songs. One day he leaned towards me and mentioned the name of a Dubliner's song. I quickly learned that he knew many songs appropriate to his age, and so brought these in to sessions from then on.

Sometimes playing the first few bars of a song will quickly indicate a student's interest or familiarity with that song. Where students have strong preferences for songs they learned as infants or young children and seem reluctant to engage with new repertory, it is important to remember that as they were able to learn and enjoy these nursery songs, it stands to reason that they have the capacity to learn new song repertory. Music therapy can be a place where this new learning is facilitated.

Vibrational work

For many students, engaging their optimal capacity to reveal their strengths in music making requires more than auditory stimulation. Vibrational work seeks to access the sense of touch as well as rhythm stimulation through other sense than hearing. The music therapist can use rattles and shakers and run them gently along the client's arms. The music therapist can lay the guitar across the students' legs and co-actively strum. The vibration of the Tibetan bowl can be created while moving around students' physical space. For students who cannot grasp objects easily small Velcro straps can be used to attach bells or other small instruments on to their wrist, ankle or feet ensuring that every movement is captured in sound.

In each of the above uses of sound and music the response of each student music can be observed closely. If a student puts their hands over their ears, the sound must be changed immediately. Additionally working with students who do not speak requires the therapist to tune into the feeling state of the student, and the capacities they bring on the day. This requires *sensitive responding* like that of a parent responding to the baby's coos and cries.

Providing music therapy for groups

One of the issues in providing music therapy services in special schools is that students often are grouped according to age rather than their needs. Therefore group programmes in music therapy where a classroom of students are referred to music therapy can be challenging for students or new practitioners seeking to understand varied and complex needs across a group of individuals. It is important to find out from those who understand the needs of the children best, such as the parent, classroom teacher or the special needs assistant, how each child participates in a group context, and to then use this information in planning how the group can provide opportunities for developing skills and increasing competence.

PROFESSIONAL ISSUES

Working with teachers and special needs assistants

Staff working at the school can help with information about what is happening at home for students. This is important for the music therapist as changes in a student's demeanor or behavior during music therapy might be able to be referenced to tensions at home.

It can sometimes be challenging to describe the therapeutic process to someone such as a teacher who is trying to help through *doing* their work as an educator. This can create tensions with the role of someone who is *being* with another person in music as a therapist. The music therapist must be sensitive when aligning these different agenda. The connection with the student, and the inter-responsiveness able to be elicited through music is sometimes easier to demonstrate to the education team, including through replaying recordings of sessions, rather than explained in words.

When reporting back to teachers, it is important to focus on what the individuals are able to do in music therapy that might not be happening in class. Sometimes teachers notice higher levels of cooperation and participation in music therapy than in regular classes. This observation can be difficult to manage at times because the music therapist can be popular with the students and this might create envy. It can be important to work with this dynamic, rather than to feel wounded by the ways in which this envy might manifest.

Working with families

Family members of the student with a disability usually receive regular progress reports from the school across all programs. Additionally the music therapist may send home suggestions for use of music during the evenings, or at times when the student might become stressed such as when coping with self-care routines.

Children with disabilities are more vulnerable to all types of abuse than non-disabled peers

It is important to be aware that children and adolescents with disabilities are at risk for abuse at a higher rate than for the general population. In particular, child sexual abuse in the general population remains high (Johnson 2004) even though more is known about how abusers operate, and how such abuse might be curtailed. Music therapists must therefore keep in mind that significant changes in behavior, or regression to earlier stages of functioning, may be linked to abuse.

Svensson et al. (2011) showing that children with disabilities are more vulnerable to all types of abuse than children who do not have a disability. Although the study by Brunnberg et al. (2012) was conducted in a mainstream school setting, nonetheless the relevance to the special school population is evident with their results indicating that: " ... force at sexual debut (intercourse) is more common among adolescents with a disability (4.0%) than those not reporting any disability (1.6%), and is most common among those reporting multiple disabilities (10.4%)." (p. 292). In an overview study of the incidence of child sexual abuse, having a disability which impaired credibility of reporting increased risk of abuse and especially for males (Putnam 2003).

As difficult as it can be, reporting suspicions is an important part of being a responsible therapist. Music therapists must therefore be aware of the reporting requirements in the jurisdiction where they work, even if they only spend a few hours in the school each week. Upholding the rights of the child is a responsibility of all music therapists, and advocacy for children's well-being is part and parcel of professional practice.

CONCLUSION

Working as a music therapist in the special education sector can be highly rewarding. One dimension is the experience of enjoyment and satisfaction when children are able to overcome some of the limitations that their disability and the restrictions of society in relation to disability affords. Wheeler (1999) noted that in her own experience she found working with children with severe disabilities pleasurable especially when she could link the goals of the therapy with her own life goals.

The skilled practitioner must be flexible, able to work with a range of musical and non-musical techniques, and be able to devise programs that challenge students while not overwhelming them. The music therapist has to work cooperatively with colleagues.

Negotiation skills are often needed in creating suitable physical places for the music therapy program in resource challenged services. Additionally since many students do not speak or have access to narrative communication processes, the ability to be calm and to avoid stressful reactions when with students is helpful to working optimally. A personal meditation practice can aid in achieving this.

References

Anastasiou, D. and Kauffman, J.M. (2011). A social constructionist approach to disability: Implications for special education. *Exceptional Children* 77(3): 367–384.

Aud, S. and Wilkinson-Flicker, S. (2013). *The Condition of Education*. USA: Government Printing Office.

Brown, J., Dodd, K., and Vetere, A. (2010). "I am a normal man": A narrative analysis of the accounts of older people with Down's syndrome who lived in institutionalised settings. *British Journal of Learning Disabilities* 38(3): 217–224.

Brunk, B.K. and Coleman, K.A. (2000). Development of a special education music therapy assessment process. *Music Therapy Perspectives* 18(1): 59–68.

Brunnberg, E., Boström, M.L., and Berglund, M. (2012). Sexual force at sexual debut. Swedish adolescents with disabilities at higher risk than adolescents without disabilities. *Child Abuse and Neglect* 36(4): 285–295.

Daveson, B. and Edwards, J. (1998). A role for music therapy in special education. *International Journal of Disability, Development and Education* 45(4): 449–457.

De Wispelaere, J. and Walsh, J. (2007). Disability rights in Ireland: Chronicle of a missed opportunity. *Irish Political Studies* 22(4): 517–543.

Ferguson, P.M. and Nusbaum, E. (2012). Disability studies: What is it and what difference does it make? *Research and Practice for Persons with Severe Disabilities* 37(2): 70–80.

Graham, L.J. and Jahnukainen, M. (2011). Wherefore art thou, inclusion? Analysing the development of inclusive education in New South Wales, Alberta and Finland. *Journal of Education Policy* 26(2): 263–288.

Higashida, N. (2013). *The reason I Jump*. London: Hodder and Stoughton.

Johnson, C.F. (2004). Child sexual abuse. *The Lancet* 364(9432): 462–470.

Kim, J., Wigram, T., and Gold, C. (2008). The effects of improvisational music therapy on joint attention behaviors in autistic children: a randomized controlled study. *Journal of Autism and Developmental Disorders* 38(9): 1758–1766.

Lipsky, D. (2011). *From Anxiety to Meltdown: How Individuals on the Autism Spectrum Deal with Anxiety, Experience Meltdowns, Manifest Tantrums, and How You Can Intervene Effectively*. London: Jessica Kingsley Publishers.

McCarthy, J., Geist, K., Zojwala, R., and Schock, M.Z. (2008). A survey of music therapists' work with speech-language pathologists and experiences with augmentative and alternative communication. *Journal of Music Therapy* 45(4): 405–426.

McFerran, K. and Shanahan, E. (2011). Music therapy practice in special education and children's hospice: A systematic comparison of two music therapists' strategies with three pre-adolescent boys. *Music Therapy Perspectives* 29(2): 103–111.

Nazeer, K. (2007). *Send in the Idiots: Stories from the Other Side of Autism*. New York: Bloomsbury Publishing.

Perry, M.M.R. (2003). Relating improvisational music therapy with severely and multiply disabled children to communication development. *Journal of Music Therapy* 40(3): 227–246.

Putnam, F.W. (2003). Ten-year research update review: Child sexual abuse. *Journal of the American Academy of Child and Adolescent Psychiatry* 42(3): 269–278.

Resch, J.A., Mireles, G., Benz, M.R., Grenwelge, C., Peterson, R., and Zhang, D. (2010). Giving parents a voice: A qualitative study of the challenges experienced by parents of children with disabilities. *Rehabilitation Psychology* 55(2): 139.

Rochat, P., Querido, J.G., and Striano, T. (1999). Emerging sensitivity to the timing and structure of protoconversation in early infancy. *Developmental Psychology* 35(4): 950.

Rowland, C. and Fried-Oken, M. (2010). Communication matrix: A clinical and research assessment tool targeting children with severe communication disorders. *Journal of Pediatric Rehabilitation Medicine* 3(4): 319–329.

Shevlin, M., Winter, E., Rose, R., and O'Raw, P. (2013). Investigating perceptions of the assessment process for pupils with special educational needs within an Irish context. *Irish Educational Studies* 32(2): 121–137.

Solomon, A.L. (1980). Music in special education before 1930: Hearing and speech development. *Journal of Research in Music Education* 28(4): 236–242.

Srinivasan, S.M. and Bhat, A.N. (2013). A review of "music and movement" therapies for children with autism: embodied interventions for multisystem development. *Frontiers in Integrative Neuroscience* 7: 1–15.

Svensson, B., Bornehag, C.G., and Janson, S. (2011). Chronic conditions in children increase the risk for physical abuse–but vary with socio-economic circumstances. *Acta Paediatrica* 100(3): 407–412.

Trevarthen, C. and Malloch, S. (2002). Musicality and music before three: Human vitality and invention shared with pride. *Zero to Three* 23(1): 10–18.

UNESCO (1994). *The Salamanca Statement and Framework for Action on Special Needs Education*. Paris: UNESCO.

Wheeler, B.L. (1999). Experiencing pleasure in working with severely disabled children. *Journal of Music Therapy* 36(1): 56–80.

Wolfensberger, W. and Tullman, S. (1982). A brief outline of the principle of normalization. *Rehabilitation Psychology* 27(3): 131.

Wright, D. and Jackson, M. (2001). *Mental disability in Victorian England: The Earlswood Asylum*. Oxford: Clarendon.

....

CHAPTER 10

MUSIC THERAPY FOR PEOPLE WITH AUTISM SPECTRUM DISORDER

....

THOMAS BERGMANN

> Music is one of those mood stabilizers, a grounding force that helps me to bring my mind back in to focus […]. It's akin to being scattered from one end of the room to the other and the music brings all the pieces back into one cohesive unit. It allows me to focus and function. It is the background noise that provides rhythm and pace and gives my restless mind something to grab onto.
>
> Murphy, 2011

AUTISM and music are closely linked with each other, as the above words by an affected woman from an internet blog of people with Asperger's syndrome suggest. Leo Kanner's publication of a case series of three girls and eight boys was the first description of the contemporary autistic phenotype (Kanner 1943). In this report, Kanner repeatedly mentioned the musical abilities and interests of six of the children who were included. Since then, music therapy has developed in parallel with the research, diagnosis, and changing understanding of autism. Nowadays, music therapy is regarded as an option with high potential in the treatment of autism (Gold et al. 2006). Current research on music processing in autism provides models for understanding the role and function of music for people with autism, either in a therapeutic context or in everyday life for recreational and other purposes, such as learning a musical instrument, or enjoying concerts, and making music with others (Khetrapal 2009; Molnar-Szakacs and Heaton 2012; Srinivasan and Bhat 2013).

AUTISM SPECTRUM DISORDER

....

Autism is a pervasive developmental disorder marked by qualitative impairments in social interaction and communication as well as restricted and repetitive patterns of behavior and interests with early onset (World Health Organization 2008). Autism Spectrum Disorder (ASD) is the umbrella term used in the current diagnostic manual DSM-5 (American Psychiatric Association 2013) to describe a continuum of neurodevelopmental conditions, including infantile autism, Asperger's syndrome, and pervasive developmental disorders not otherwise specified (PDD-NOS). The concept behind this term is a dimensional view of a broader autistic phenotype, i.e. certain conditions belonging to the individual's personality that have a strong impact on their behavior and social functioning along a continuum of varying severity across the lifespan (Howlin and Moss 2012).

People with ASD have communication deficits, such as responding inappropriately in conversations or misreading non-verbal interactions, or having difficulty building friendships appropriate to their age. Language development is delayed or abnormal, the language often seems strange and does not serve primarily for two-way communication, or speech is missing completely. In addition, people with ASD are overly dependent on routines, highly sensitive to changes in their environment, or intensely focused on inappropriate items.

In addition to social and behavioral features, affective deregulation and anxiety-like psychomotor tension are described in the ICD-10 diagnostic manual as *other nonspecific problems*. Motor clumsiness and coordination deficits belong to *Gillbergs' criteria for Asperger's syndrome* (Gillberg and Gillberg 1989) and are discussed as cardinal features of ASD over the entire spectrum as well (Fournier et al. 2010; Heasley 2012). Impairments in the emotional system are evident, as first described by Leo Kanner, who conceptualized autism as a lack of "affective contact" (Kanner 1943). Meanwhile, multiple studies have shown deficiencies in various aspects of emotional development, e.g. perception, recognition, understanding, expression, and regulation of emotions (Kasari et al. 2012). Specifically, perceptual difficulties in processing facial features (Hobson 1986), altered eye-gaze processing (Klin et al. 2002), impaired recognition of emotions (Bölte and Poustka 2003), and deficits in cognitive empathy (Dziobek and Köhne 2011) are described. However, emotional empathy is not limited, i.e. people with ASD respond by feeling pain when perceiving other's distress (Fan et al. 2013). The conflict between heightened empathic arousal and a lack of social understanding may be revealed in the most frequent co-morbidities of depression and anxiety disorders in higher functioning individuals (Caamaño et al. 2013; Strang et al. 2012) and challenging behaviors, particular self-injury and affective deregulation, in individuals with ASD and intellectual disability (McTiernan et al. 2011; Rojahn et al. 2010). These often chronic conditions may lead to social isolation, frequent temper tantrums, and psychotropic long-term medication, as well as unemployment in higher functioning individuals, and require appropriate treatment and support.

VIGNETTE 1

Vignettes 1–3 are taken from author's own practice

Anna is in her early twenties, is studying biostatistics, and lives alone with her two cats. Even as a baby, she was different from her siblings; she appeared to be indifferent to the members of her family, cried a lot, and was almost wholly inconsolable. Anna played for hours alone in the sand or ripped paper into small shreds, which she then collected. She did not start to talk until she was two-and-a-half years old, although then already in short sentences. Her parents were relieved to see that she also began to play with other children, although the play had to follow fixed rules. She was already fascinated by mathematics and numbers as a child, a magical cosmos of classification systems to which she felt more closely connected than to the real world. She was also extremely interested in the dulcimer, first due to the bright sound, and second, due to the clear structure of the instrument. At school, she was an outsider and was regarded as being odd and a "know-it-all." She was never able to immediately comprehend ironic comments or jokes with a double meaning, and today, she still dislikes having her leg pulled in this way. Anna has always felt extremely uncomfortable looking other people in the eye or shaking hands. She avoids small talk and coffee-break chats, while by contrast, becoming very animated during discussions on statistical issues, frequently not noticing that the people she is talking to can no longer follow her. Her style of language is very specific, with little modulation, and she says what she thinks in a direct way, which many people find impolite. She is very sensitive to noise: For example, when a fellow student is rustling a plastic bag, she can no longer follow what the lecturer is saying. Under increasing stress and confusion, she has the feeling that her head is bursting, and what she would most like to do would be to scream and bang her head against the wall. When the pressure gets too high, a "shutdown" occurs in which she falls into a state of rigidity, and it takes days for her to recover. Since her youth, she has also suffered from phases of a depression-like lethargy, with a loss of appetite and drive. During these periods, she can neither work nor go to university. Several attempts at therapy failed, since she was utterly overwhelmed by the psychodynamic group concept. Following this experience, she searched for the cause of her problems herself, and found many aspects of her biography and her personal idiosyncrasies reflected in a self-help group for people with autism. Following the clinical diagnosis of Asperger's syndrome, she can now claim her right to suitable conditions for people with autism at university. For two years, she has been seeing a music therapist for individual sessions every week, and this has become an anchor in her life. She rediscovered the dulcimer, composing short repetitive melodies to give her feelings a musical form. The music therapist supports her in decrypting, organizing, and communicating them.

ASD is a lifelong condition that is currently estimated to affect around 1:100 individuals (Centers for Disease Control and Prevention 2012). Thus, it is a major social and health concern within society (Ganz 2007). Males are affected at a higher frequency than females, with average estimates suggesting a 4:1 ratio for the spectrum as a whole (Fombonne 2009). ASD and intellectual disabilities (ID) are frequently co-occurring neurodevelopmental conditions with an increasing prevalence of ASD being linked to the increasing severity of ID (Charman et al. 2011). Within the ID group, every fourth person has an additional diagnosis of ASD (Bryson et al. 2008; Sappok et al. 2010). This underlines the special educational and treatment needs of this subgroup.

VIGNETTE 2

Paul is in his early 50s and lives in a shared flat for people with a mental handicap. Little is known about his childhood, since his parents have died and contact with the rest of his family has been broken off. He is regarded as a loner and almost never seeks contact with the others in his group, but focuses instead on the care staff. Usually, he is motivated to make contact when he wants to have or know something, while appearing to have no understanding of the needs of the other person. He has perfected rituals of complex sequences of activity, although he needs a great deal of time to complete daily tasks and is completely incapable of acting when he is interrupted. He reacts to changes in the daily and weekly routine with a high degree of agitation: Stamping, screaming, biting himself, and ripping his clothing. He enjoys travelling or going on day trips, but these must be well planned in advance with his involvement. He reacts with panic to dogs and the subject of death. His favorite color is red and he usually wears red clothes. He has an abrupt, peculiar way of moving, and sometimes turns around on his own axis before sitting down. His facial expression is either rigid, or his eyes are focused in the distance; direct eye contact seldom occurs. He has a good understanding of language, but only talks in broken sentences of two to three words. His language is monotonous, like a robot, and is characterized by strange expressions such as "you know without" instead of "I don't know," swapping the pronouns, or avoiding the "I" form by referring to himself as "Paul." Although autistic patterns of behavior and stress-related restlessness have been known for a long time, he was diagnosed with ASD only a few years ago. On the one hand, medication with typical neuroleptica was reduced, while on the other, it has been possible to minimize his challenging behaviors through structure, the friendly behavior of the people in his immediate environment, and an understanding of his idiosyncrasies. He has also received individual music therapy sessions for several years. Here, he insists on a ritualized sequence, which he determines. Within the musical stations which are "worked through", he is creative and develops social competencies, such as joint attention, or practical skills, such as single-note piano playing with a guided hand. Through repeated singing of the German song "Ein Mops kam in die Küche," in which a pug dog is beaten and is buried by another dog, he regularly brings the subject of his phobia of dogs and the subject of death and mourning to the fore.

What causes ASD?

ASD can be caused by many different disorders or conditions. "Idiopathic" ASD is assumed to result from polygenetic alterations (Abrahams and Geschwind 2008), which, in turn, affect brain functions. On a neurobiological level, a hypothesis of aberrant network connectivity has increasingly been favored over one of focal brain dysfunction (Courchesne et al. 2011; Dziobek and Köhne 2011). According to this hypothesis, the brains of individuals with ASD are characterized by short-range over-connectivity and long-range under-connectivity, the latter being thought to be associated with the social-emotional and communication impairments of autism. Various further hypotheses aim to explain the neuropsychological deficits in ASD: Atypical *Theory of Mind* development (Baron-Cohen et al. 1985), which results in problems in attributing mental states to oneself and others and in understanding that others have beliefs, desires, and intentions that are different from one's own; weak *central coherence* (Frith and Happé 1994), which describes the limited ability to understand the situational context or to "see the big picture" in favor of a detail-oriented perception; limited *executive functions* (Ozonoff and Pennington 1991), which relate to planning, goal-directed action, self-monitoring, attention, response inhibition, and coordination of complex cognition and motor control; reduced *social drive* (Kohls et al. 2012), with a preferred interest in the material world; and *sensory perceptual* issues (Ben-Sasson et al. 2009; Bogdashina 2003), such as reduced filter functions and cross-modality matching, synesthesia, and hyper- or hypo-sensitivity to certain stimuli. None of these theories explains all aspects of ASD, but they provide a basis for an understanding of the condition and thus for music therapy treatment concepts and interventions (Geretsegger 2005).

The diagnosis of ASD

Given the lack of defined biological markers specific for ASD, diagnosis is based on medical history and behavioral assessment. The diagnosis of ASD has evolved since Kanner's first descriptions of the disorder. In the fifth edition of the Diagnostic and Statistical Manual of Mental Disorders (American Psychiatric Association 2013) the *triad of impairments* (Wing 1981) in interaction, communication, and stereotyped behaviors is divided into two domains. The first encompasses deficits in social communication and interaction, such as a lack of social-emotional reciprocity, reduced sharing of interests and emotions, and difficulties with using or understanding non-verbal communicative behaviors, such as eye contact, pointing, or gesturing. The second domain consists of fixated interests and repetitive, stereotyped behaviors including repetitive speech abnormalities. This domain was extended from previous diagnostic criteria to include sensory aspects, such as hyper- or hypo-reactivity to certain stimuli or unusual interests in sensory aspects of the environment, for example, the smell or color of a musical instrument. The former domain of verbal communication merges with the DSM-5 ASD dyad, which includes non-verbal individuals on the lower functioning end of the spectrum.

In order to diagnose ASD, the person's behaviors must have been present in childhood, even if the person is diagnosed later, for example, as a teenager or adult (American Psychiatric Association 2013). Early diagnosis is essential to make targeted early intervention possible to support speech and language development and to promote contact and relationship ability as well as to regulate emotional states as a basis for further psychosocial development. Later diagnosis in adulthood may explain psychosocial and biographical particularities and problems and can be a significant relief for the affected individual. In the treatment of co-morbid conditions, such as chronic depression or challenging behavior, it offers an explanatory model concerning the underlying disorder and serves to initiate appropriate treatment and support. A diagnostic standard exists in children and adolescents suspected of having ASD, including questionnaires, parental interview, and structured behavioral observation (Kim and Lord 2012). There is a lack of valid instruments to clarify suspected ASD in adults, particularly for non-verbal individuals (Matson and Shoemaker 2009; Sappok et al. 2014).

Living with ASD

The characteristics and symptoms of ASD influence the relationship to the self, to other people, and to objects, and thus the impact is experienced in all areas of life (Reddy et al. 2010; Schumacher and Calvet 2008a; Williams 2008). Wing introduced the idea of four prototypic social manifestations within ASD (Wing 1996). The *aloof* type of social manifestation means that the person shows almost complete indifference to other people and behaves as though other people did not exist; the *passive and friendly* type is indicated where the person will accept social approaches but does not initiate social interaction; the *active but odd* type describes a person who will initiate interactions with others but in an odd, repetitive, and often inappropriate way; and the *stilted* type refers to a person with ASD who is overly formal, trying hard to behave well and cope by sticking rigidly to the rules of social interaction. Wing suggested that these social manifestations are ways that people with ASD compensate for their deficits. Recognizing different compensation mechanisms and phenotypes in the context of ASD may be of importance for both diagnosis and therapy.

A diagnosis of ASD means that a person will have a specific cognitive and sensory perceptual style. This distinctive mode of being, feeling, thinking, and acting challenges normative assumptions about neuro-homogeneity. Apart from fundamental social restrictions, most of the functions and dysfunctions mentioned above have advantages and disadvantages. The ability to focus on details could be advantageous in some contexts, such as checking for errors in a data list, whereas problems in capturing the overall context in the field of central coherence could be challenging when trying to understand what is happening in a complex social situation, such as a competitive professional relationship. At the high functioning end of the spectrum, many affected people have problems with complex social demands, either in their families, at school, or at work, and may be preferred targets for bullying and mobbing (Zablotsky et al. 2014). At the other end of the spectrum, coping strategies to navigate through the social world are limited due to cognitive impairments. In particular, this group is dependent on stable environmental factors in order to lead a healthy and content life (Van Bourgondien et al. 2003). In the autobiographical literature of people on the autism spectrum, many authors describe the feeling of being cut off from the world or living on the wrong planet. As Temple Grandin stated: "I'm an anthropologist from Mars" (Cohen 2005). Could music bridge the distance between the planets?

MUSIC AND AUTISM

Music is one area within which some individuals with ASD demonstrate exceptional skills. The jazz pianist and composer Matt Savage, for example, learned classical piano at the age of six and started his international career aged eight (Pine 2005). Brilliant technique, perfect pitch, and an excellent musical memory in terms of structured music are general characteristics of musical savants, i.e. people with exceptional musical talents in combination with sensory, cognitive, and/or neurodevelopmental impairments. In particular, perfect pitch, i.e. the ability to classify a note within a tonal system precisely without reference, has been extensively studied in connection with autism. Around five percent of individuals with ASD have this rare ability regardless of musical training, and in musicians with absolute pitch memory, autistic traits could be observed (Dohn et al. 2012). In addition, significantly improved intonation and melody memory was found in children with ASD compared to typically developed controls (Stanutz et al. 2012). This is in contrast to the usually impaired speech and language development among individuals with ASD. Reduced filter functions and a predominantly local, detail-focused cognitive processing style are assumed to explain this discrepancy in overlapping neural networks of music and speech processing (DePape et al. 2012). This connection, together with a preference for musical stimuli, has been used to develop promising music-based programs for targeted language training in children with ASD (Lim 2010; Wan et al. 2011). Furthermore, in a study of 199 children diagnosed with ASD, eighteen percent were shown to have hyperacousis, a type of hypersensitivity regarding certain acoustic stimuli (Rosenhall et al. 1999).

Limitations in detecting and sharing emotions and mental states are a central feature of ASD (Baron-Cohen 1995; Bons et al. 2013). In various studies on emotion recognition, individuals with ASD have been shown to be able to assign different emotional states in passages of music just as well as the control group without ASD (Heaton et al. 2008; Heaton et al. 1999; Quintin et al. 2011). However, in a more complex task, adolescents with ASD with average intelligence were not equally able to recognize the communication of emotion in music when the parameters of temporal and amplitude expressivity were altered in excerpts of Chopin's Nocturnes (Bhatara et al. 2010). Regarding the potential improvement of emotion recognition among people with ASD, music may be a channel to communicate, experience, and differentiate emotions for this group.

MUSIC THERAPY

History of music therapy as a treatment modality for people with ASD

The definition of music therapy as a treatment method and as a profession emerged alongside the first case reports concerning children with autism by Kanner and Asperger during the 1940s (Davis et al. 2008). In the following decades, many music therapists used adapted music education elements, such as singing, dancing, improvisation, and rhythm activities for the purpose of self-expression, recreation, and rehabilitation (Gilliland 1955; Scheerenberger 1953) and in order to integrate children with disabilities into groups with other children (Harbert 1955). During this early period, much of the literature emphasized autistic children's unusual interest and outstanding abilities in music, such as the accurate reproduction of familiar pieces (Euper 1966; Sherwin 1953).

When Nordoff and Robbins published their book on *Creative Music Therapy* (1977), the improvisational music therapy approach in the treatment of developmentally disabled children gained a theoretical foundation. Their work pre-dated the DSM-III (American Psychiatric Association 1980), in which autism was first internationally classified as a distinct disorder, with six defined symptoms separated by schizophrenic type disorders, such as *infantile autism*. Thaut later presented a developmentally-based music therapy treatment model alongside diagnostic criteria and opened the window to future decades, which were characterized by evidence-based treatment and the question of efficacy (Thaut 1984). In her historical review of music therapy for people with ASD, Reschke-Hernández (2011) described the period from 1940–1989 as being characterized by trial and error, with innovative approaches but a lack of scientific research.

Together with the development of standards in autism diagnostics, the increase in discussions about autism in the media and among the general public, very active parent organizations of autistic children, and an autism community of highly functioning people, may have contributed to the considerable increase in the numbers of people being officially diagnosed with autism in recent years (King and Bearman 2009). Autism has changed from being a peripheral phenomenon to a social fact, with a huge variety of more or less relevant and effective methods of treatment. In music therapy, increasing numbers of empirical studies have focused on the measurable effects of clearly defined interventions. For instance, when analyzing effects on joint attention, Kim found significantly more and longer eye contact and turn-taking in the improvisational music therapy group compared to play therapy (Kim et al. 2008). As anecdotal reports outside her study design suggest, some non-verbal children developed initial language skills. In a meta-analysis of nine quantitative studies conducted with children and adolescents with ASD, Whipple found a significant average effect strength of $d = 0.77$ (Whipple 2004). She concluded that all musical intervention was effective, regardless of the purpose or the form of implementation. Another meta-analysis with more stringent inclusion criteria noted the short-term effects of music therapy on communication, but not on behavior problems (Gold et al. 2006). In a recent update of this, the Cochrane review provided evidence that music therapy may help children with ASD to improve their skills in primary outcome areas that constitute the core of the condition, including social interaction, verbal communication, initiating behavior, and social-emotional reciprocity. Furthermore, in secondary outcome areas, music therapy may contribute to increasing social adaptation skills in children with ASD and to promoting the quality of parent-child relationships (Geretsegger et al. 2014a). In a review of "novel and emerging treatments" in ASD, music therapy is the only psychosocial method among the most favorably assessed procedures in an evidence-based grading system (Rossignol 2009). Compared to an empirical standard, the conclusiveness is still limited due to small sample sizes, the methodological weakness of the underlying studies, and a lack of records regarding sustainability. However, much substantial work has been done and is currently being carried out to verify the evidence regarding the role music therapy might play in the treatment of ASD (Geretsegger et al. 2012). Together with a huge amount of case reports and research concerning music perception, the high potentials of music in the treatment and education of this group are underlined.

Music therapy potential and practice in the treatment of ASD

As indicated above, core features of ASD in the area of social interaction and communication; restricted behaviors; and sensory, motor, and emotional issues, can be matched to certain musical and perceptual qualities. Table 10.1 shows these correspondences in detail in order to highlight the potential of music for treating and educating individuals on the autistic spectrum.

Table 10.1 provides the potential to create multisystem interventions based on music in the treatment of the widespread symptomalogy of ASD with a focus on qualitative impairments in social interaction. Depending on the method, the framework, and individual indication, the ASD features mentioned in Table 10.1 can be seen as potential treatment goals. Outcomes supported by research in the treatment of ASD are increased socialization and attention, improved verbal and sensory-motor skills, decreased self-stimulation and agitation, as well as successful and safe self-expression (American Music Therapy Association 2010). Music-based therapies form about twelve percent of all autism interventions and 45 percent of alternate treatment strategies used within school settings (Hess et al. 2008; Simpson 2005). In the therapeutic context, the individual setting is preferred due to lower social demands and reduced stress in case of high irritability and sensory-perceptual sensitivity. In education, the group setting prevails; in this context, music and movement interventions are mostly components of superordinate, exercise-based concepts. In terms of method, active improvisational music therapy (IMT) dominates, which is based on active, spontaneous music-making, with the therapist generally following the client's focus of attention, behaviors, and interests (Carpente 2011; Green et al. 2010; Kim et al. 2008, 2009; Schumacher 1999; Wigram 2002). This also includes receptive interventions, such as singing and improvising for the client or listening to recorded music. According to the upcoming IMT treatment guide for children with ASD (Geretsegger et al. 2014b), unique principles are as follows:

- facilitating musical and emotional attunement (by responding to and synchronization with musical, vocal and motor expression with holding, mirroring and matching technique).

Table 10.1 Potential of music in the treatment of individuals with ASD

ASD characteristics	Musical/perceptual qualities
1. Social interaction and communication	
Joint attention deficits	• General musical interests in people with ASD • Instrument and song/music as third object to relate to within an interaction
Limited socio-emotional reciprocity	• Intersubjective quality of playing or improvising together; musical dialogue • Activation of multiple brain regions during music making and perception fostering long-range connectivity
Deficits in social cognition	• Potentially improved emotion recognition in music
Isolation, reduced social drive	• Undemanding relationship formation in music (e.g. playing for the client, no eye contact required)
Deficits in social awareness	• Joint singing, music making, and movement (e.g. hand clapping)
(Verbal) communication deficits	• Non-verbal interaction in music-making with shared neuronal networks of music and speech processing • Audio-motor integration in singing
2. Stereotyped behaviors and imagination	
Restricted and repetitive behaviors	• Structure and variability in musical form and development
Deficits in imagination and play	• Imagination in music perception (sounds, dynamics, mood, melody/songs) • Creativity in musical improvisation • Music as an age-independent form of play (→ adults)
Reduced exploratory behavior	• High inviting character and multisensory quality of musical instruments
Deficit in task planning and goal directed activity	• Song structure and content to organize/sequence activities • Rhythmic impulses to initiate motor activity
3. Sensory and motor issues	
Sensory issues, deficits in cross-modality matching	• Multisensory quality of instruments • Multimodal perceptual experience during active music making (perception-action linkage) • participation of the motor cortex in music processing
Motor clumsiness, coordination and motor sequencing/praxis problems	• Music and dance, whole body rhythmic actions (gross motor) • Quality of movement when playing an instrument (fine motor)
4. Affect and emotion	
Affective deregulation	• Tension in musical dynamics, dynamic attunement in joint play, possibility to control dynamics in play • Psychomotoric action with sensory feedback in playing loud (e.g. beating a drum) • Calming effect of music/sound on autonomic nervous system
Anxiety, need for sameness	• Repetitive structure of songs providing security
Disturbance of the sense of self	• Perception of a simple core self in musically coordinated atmosphere • Experience of self-efficacy through auditory and sensory feedback • Experience of "self with another" in playing together

- scaffolding interactions dynamically (by meeting the client's initiatives/behaviors as communicatively intended and creating a musical form of recognizable patterns or motifs with rhythmic grounding, shaping, exaggerating, and frameworking technique).
- tapping into a shared history of (musical) interaction (by jointly creating musical/social patterns and routines but also creating moments where musical expectations are playfully violated with unexpected pauses and/or sudden dynamic variations, redirecting technique).
- facilitating enjoyment (by creating a pleasant and joyful atmosphere incorporating the client's interests).

Basic principles that are essential in the treatment of ASD, but are not unique to music, are providing a secure environment, building and maintaining a positive therapeutic relationship, employing a non-directive approach, and setting treatment goals.

As social impairments are so prominent in ASD, in many music therapy approaches, relationship formation is both the basis and the content of therapeutic access. Issues such as high irritability with social demands, inappropriate proximity and distance, and functionalizing or ignoring others, are reflected in interactions in the therapeutic processes. In a relationship-based context, the music therapist offers unique opportunities for creating contact and progressively building trust and communication. This can start with playing live music, allowing the client to relate to the atmosphere in the room. The therapist can mirror the perceived emotional states and physical movements of the client, thus creating togetherness without introducing themselves as a person or requesting dialogue or imitation. In this case, music or song could be seen as an intermediary object that surrounds the client. An instrument as a third object played by both partners may facilitate the development of the relationship. The exchange of motifs and the development of a common musical form in free improvisation is a highly communicative process, requiring social skills and flexibility, and in many cases, is accompanied by shared joy in social reciprocity.

Music therapy approaches to assist people with ASD

Several music therapy approaches to working with people with ASD have been developed. Many of these draw on a theoretical foundation outside of music therapy, with corresponding assessments to allow therapy evaluation and structured intervention planning.

Paul Nordoff and Clive Robbins pursued a child-centered improvisational approach in the development of their *Creative Music Therapy* (Nordoff and Robbins 1965). They used music to engage children with developmental disorders, including autism, in a musical experience. Juliette Alvin, pioneering music therapist and founder of the British Society of Music Therapy, has also pursued a child-directed approach based on sound, improvisation, and movement to recorded music in the treatment of autism. She considers establishing communication to be a primary treatment goal. The case described below demonstrates this approach using receptive techniques at the beginning of the music therapy process with an eight-year-old boy named Oliver, diagnosed as mute autistic and suffering from noise phobia.

VIGNETTE 3

At first there was no communication, he did not look at me and seemed to be unaware of the environment. During the first sessions I assessed Oliver's negative or positive reactions to various musical experiences. I made him see and hear a number of musical instruments: Chime bars, piano, drums, cymbals, flutes, maracas, cello. He showed no reaction to rhythm, and drums did not attract him. He showed no inclination towards any instrument. He refused to open his mouth to sing. But he reacted positively to beautiful sustained, resonant sounds, especially on the cello. When he heard them he looked up and followed the sounds attentively, until they had died out. The vibrations seemed to create for him a protective environment which made no demands on him. [...] From the beginning I used receptive and active techniques to establish communication. Oliver's response to resonant sounds was already a form of communication which had to be transformed into a pleasurable and purposeful experience during which he would hear and create music himself.

For several months he started the session by sitting in an armchair looking quite lost and vulnerable. I did not use words but played for him on my cello, facing him. [...] He listened well, closing his eyes. When he had enough he just whispered "no more." He never showed any motivation to touch the cello, his pleasure was in listening to it, although the motivation came later.

Alvin and Warwick 1992, pp. 30–31

Dorita S. Berger has developed a method oriented to sensory perceptual features and brain and motor functions in individuals with pervasive developmental disorders, including autism (Berger 2002). The elements of music as well as the selection of instruments are interpreted in the sense of sensory adaptation. Her main treatment goals are rhythm internalization, adaptive responses to the environment, auditory integration and discrimination, sequencing, pacing of body movement and breath, creativity, self-initiative and task organization, behavioral redirection, speech and language, etc. These objectives demonstrate an approach that is less focused on the social behavior items that are formulated as diagnostic criteria and more on possible causes in terms of atypical brain functions. The following case study demonstrates music therapy based on sensory integration with a thirteen-year-old boy diagnosed with Asperger's Syndrome, characterized as extremely verbal and well-developed for his age, and with an abundance of high energy:

VIGNETTE 4

David's behaviors are erratic, non-conventional, demanding, bordering on Oppositional Defiance Disorder. [...] David has been on and off cocktails of medications including psychotropic drugs, tranquilizers, "uppers," "downers," and others. David personifies pure fear. That is the basic core emotion to which his system has adapted and for which it is attempting to compensate. All of his behaviors point to his visceral fear responses. David is in continuous survival mode. [...] He wants to play every instrument, but cannot seem to "organize" and stay with the task before darting off in some other request. He wants to write a song, but cannot seem to sequence words and thoughts well enough. [...] My understanding of basic adaption and sensory systems led me to the conviction that, before anything else, I must help this child to slow down his body rhythm. Unless his brain learns to slow his body down before installing a response to stimulus, David's erratic behaviors will never cease. [...] We begin every session with the lights turned down, sitting on the floor, blowing into our recorders, with pure American Indian flute music in the background. David found this to be excruciatingly difficult for the first few times [...], and interrupted the activity with constant caustic remarks and questions. [...] My response to David's queries was non-verbal. I simply continued to play. He eventually became quiet and, although he did not blow into the recorder, he did become less restless. In each session, any conversation and activity that follows the preliminary quieting time is usually executed with better-paced thoughts and movement.

> We have been working together for over a year, only one hour a week, but exciting adaptions are already evident. His "fear" still predominates his actions, but he is often less fearful with directives and has less of a need to control. He is beginning to trust his body.
>
> Berger 2002, pp. 166–168

Although autism is the main item covered by the term "pervasive developmental disorders" as defined in the DSM-IV (American Psychiatric Association 2000), developmental approaches in therapy are rare. During decades of work with autistic children, Schumacher and Calvet have created a music therapy approach based on recent findings of infant research (Schumacher 1999). The central element is the phenomenon of synchronization (Schumacher and Calvet 2008b), referring to the coordination of perception, motion, and emotion on the individual and interpersonal level. The *Assessment of the Quality of Relationship* (AQR, Schumacher and Calvet 2007) has been developed as a structuring aid for treatment planning and as an assessment tool for therapy evaluation. The scale is based on the self-development concepts of Daniel Stern (2000) and consists of eight graded modes that mainly relate to the pre-verbal development period. Three subscales assess the client's instrumental, vocal, and physical-emotional behavior and expression while one scale assesses the therapist and his

Table 10.2 Assessment of the Quality of Relationship (AQR): Developmental matching of client and therapist

AQR mode	Client characteristics	Therapist interventions
Modus 0 Lack of contact/ contact refusal/ pause	No awareness of musical instruments (does not play) Restriction of social interaction (no eye contact, no directed vocalization) Stereotyped behaviors	Musical space—surrounding Creating a musical atmosphere without forcing direct contact Playing for the client, for the room, or for oneself Therapist is unacknowledged
Modus 1 Contact-reaction Functional- sensory-contact	Short awareness of musical instruments (plays "by chance") Vocal expression stimulated by movement Short contact to others in situation of sensory	Perception—connecting Making movements audible by synchronous moments in musical improvisation Therapist is mobilized by short positive reactions of the client
Modus 2 Functional- sensory-contact	Handling of instruments in a sensory, destructive, or stereotyped way Unmodulated vocalizations expressing inner tension Hyperactivity, restlessness, high body-tension, controlling eye-contact	Affect attuning Physical, musical, and vocal matching of tension and dynamics Providing secure framework for destructive and aggressive impulses Therapist is functionalized
Modus 3 Contact to oneself/sense of a subjective self	Exploration, recognising objects as "musical" instruments Motifs in vocalization Curiosity in exploring the body of the other, physical contact looking for self effectiveness	Aiding awareness Accompaniment of client's exploration Fostering awareness and the feeling of authorship of activities Therapist considers himself as supportive

(continued)

Table 10.2 Continued

AQR mode	Client characteristics	Therapist interventions
Modus 4 Contact to others/ intersubjectivity	Instrument is played according to its function, sound is socially referenced Tonal attuning in vocalization, connection to gestures, joint phrases Joint attention and social referencing. Eye contact with expression of confirmation	Social referencing Confirmation of the client's perception and feelings Introducing own ideas without wanting to bring about any dialogue Therapist is included as a person
Modus 5 Relationship to others/ Interactivity	Musical turn-taking, the instrument is played in form of a dialogue Imitation, motifs, and joint creating of form Eye contact regulates social interaction	Musically answering and questioning Initiation of ideas independent from each other Therapist interacts as a person separate from the client
Modus 6 Joint experience/ Interaffectivity	In musical dialogue, the instrument is played in consistently positive state of affect The voice is expressed in enjoyable games (i.e. nonsense songs or rhymes) Expression of pleasure and fun is expressed in eye contact	Having fun in dialogue Role swapping and flexible exchange of ideas Therapist is as a partner in dialogue
Modus 7 Verbal-music space	The instrument sets off emotional changes and/or imaginary contents Imaginative ideas become verbalized	Reflecting Connecting emotional experience and speech Providing introspection verbally or by song texts Therapist's emotions reflect serious interest in the client's topic

Note: Adapted from "The AQR-Instrument: An observation instrument to assess the quality of a relationship", by Schumacher and Calvet (2007).
To measure the client characteristics, the AQR provides three subscales relating to the instrumental quality (IQR), vocal pre-speech quality (VQR), and physical-emotional quality (PEQR) of the relationship. Items of each subscale have been strongly condensed to provide a concise overview.

interventions. Matching with the client's needs and socio-emotional capacities is seen as fundamental for a therapeutic relationship and for progress. Table 10.2 gives a condensed overview of the client-therapist matching within the particular AQR modes.

Modus 1 to modus 4 provide unique musical interventions, like playing for the client in various ways without expectation of dialogue, that are integral to therapy for people with ASD mainly characterized by qualitative impairments of social interactive capacities and high irritability (Bergmann et al. 2011). The following example demonstrates this developmental approach to: first, support the client without intersubjective demands in musical exploration (AQR modus 3); second, achieve social referencing and affective attunement in joint play (AQR modus 4); and finally, achieve a perspective including turn taking and musical dialogue (AQR modus 5). It shows a 30-year-old woman with moderate ID, diagnosed with ASD, self-injurious behavior, and suspected traumatization during childhood:

VIGNETTE 5

Using simple words, she described an incident that started with a breakdown of the workshop's bus followed by a temper tantrum during which she completely lost control. Sitting on the therapist's right-hand side at the piano, she began to play up and down, with both hands, within a clearly limited range of notes. The therapist supported her playing with a rhythmic and harmonic accompaniment and picked up the "bus theme" in song. Slight irregularities in her playing made the clear accompaniment become unsteady, without however destroying its structure. Further small variations and irregularities on both sides made the music more lively; it became faster and more dramatic. For the first time, B looked directly at her caregiver and the therapist, who returned the glance in a friendly and affirmative manner. Thereafter, the music developed to a furious finale played alternately with the left and right hand, with the greatest possible acceleration and complete dissolution of the form. The concluding exchange of glances and simultaneous exhalation conveyed the sensation that both players have experienced, and shared, something exciting.

Clearly, the client had succeeded in experiencing a high degree of affective intensity in a manner that was pleasurable and musically productive. The increasingly uncontrolled, dramatic and furious playing had the character of a catharsis, a re-enactment of a dramatic situation in a different, playful, interpretative context. Later, in the context of other stabilising factors in her living and working environment, she attained an increasing degree of autonomy and self-control. In the music-therapeutic context, it proved possible to accompany this development by the dissolution of a ritualized sequence of events, by independently playing on loud instruments (drum set, large gong) and the resulting experience of autonomy, and by the chance to play in a manner with an increasing component of dialogue and partnership.

In addition to approaches based on musical improvisation, there are also education-orientated song-based concepts. To allow children with ASD to manage daily transitions and routines successfully, songs could help by providing structure, predictability, and consistency. In combination with music and sound cues to convey a message or to sequence the steps of an activity, it is recommended this concept be implemented by parents and teachers by making up new lyrics to familiar tunes (Kern 2012). In an inclusive approach, the use of songs individually composed by a music therapist and sung by the teacher was able to help two young children with entering the classroom, greeting the teacher and/or peers, and engaging in play (Kern et al. 2007). A similar concept has been used in a community-based approach to support the outdoor play of young children with ASD (Kern and Aldridge 2006).

Several attempts are being made to add music therapy intervention to established child treatment programmes. Lim has incorporated music into the Applied Behavior Analysis Verbal Behavior (ABA VB), a widespread early-intervention training method (Barbera and Rasmussen 2007). Musical stimuli have been successfully used to enhance the functional verbal production in 22 children with ASD who were verbal or pre-verbal with immediate echolalia (Lim and Draper 2011). Social stories are a means of teaching social behavior in children with ASD and of strengthening the cognitive skills needed for social interaction. Brownell has combined this technique successfully with music by composing original songs for students of an elementary school using the text of the individual social story as lyrics (Brownell 2002). Similarly, music therapy has been used within the SCERTS model, i.e. a comprehensive curriculum designed to assess and identify treatment goals within a multidisciplinary team of clinicians and educators for children with ASD (Walworth et al. 2009). This can be seen as an interdisciplinary approach to integrate and evaluate music therapy within a context of multisystem interventions correlating to the multisystem nature of impairments in ASD (Srinivasan and Bhat 2013).

Alongside active or receptive music therapy methods based on musical improvisation, song, and movement, there are also medical approaches based on the functional use of music. Auditory Integration Therapy (AIT) typically involves twenty half-hour sessions over ten days listening to specially filtered and modulated music (Bérard 1993). This addresses sensory processing problems, such as hyperacousis. The emotional and intersubjective qualities of music are left out. Currently, there is no evidence that AIT or other sound therapies are effective as treatments for ASD (Sinha et al. 2011).

Considerations for the treatment setting

Individuals with ASD have a range of special needs regarding which the therapist must show sensitivity and respect. The therapist should understand the client's need for sameness and particular sensory-perceptual characteristics, such as hypo- or hyper-reactivity to sensory input. Alvin recommended the use of a room specially designed for children with ASD, with suitable furniture and equipment. The room should allow freedom of movement and provide a sense of security (Alvin and Warwick 1992). To avoid panic, tantrums, and withdrawal, the arrangement and the order of the instruments should be kept the same from session to session, with an allowance to be made for small changes. This principle may also be taken into account when planning interventions, by working through a course of instruments in a structured way and providing certain qualities and opportunities with regard to contact and relationship formation, with a predictable beginning and end (Bergmann et al. 2009). On the one hand, sensory overstimulation should be avoided by ensuring good ventilation, warm room acoustics, and the possibility of regulating direct sunlight, while the room and the instruments should provide sufficient sensory stimulation to encourage curiosity and exploratory behavior. This may not only be the sound of an instrument, but also its color, form, smell, or surface texture, in order to appeal to a wide range of sensory modalities. Some additional features are proposed, such as an armchair as a safe place (Alvin and Warwick 1992), a hammock to stimulate proprioceptive perception (Schumacher and Calvet 2008b), and/or a drum table as a central structuring element (Bergmann et al. 2009).

Assessment tools and music therapy diagnostic instruments

Music therapy plays a relevant role in diagnostic and clinical assessment by providing a tool for evaluating strengths and weaknesses in many areas of development (Wigram and Gold 2006). Besides the AQR already described above, there are further approaches to assess the client's musical behavior to facilitate therapy evaluation and intervention planning working in the field of ASD. Nordoff and Robbins designed two scales, the first to assess the *child-therapist relationship* in musical activity, the second to assess *musical communicativeness* (Nordoff and Robbins 1977). This assessment is widely used today in the context of the Nordoff-Robbins *Creative Music Therapy* approach (Nordoff and Robbins 1965) for the documentation, evaluation, and training of music therapists. Against the background of the Nordoff-Robbins approach, John A. Carpente developed the *Individual Music-Centered Assessment Profile for Neurodevelopmental Disorders* (IMCAP-ND; Carpente 2014). Within a musical-play and developmental and relationship-based framework, this assessment is a method for observing and rating musical emotional responses, cognition and perception, preferences, perceptual efficiency, and self-regulation. The IMCAP-ND is applicable to individuals at various developmental levels and chronological ages and serves to support the therapist in formulating clinical goals and strategies for working with the client.

Wigram has focused much of his work on the development of assessments in arts therapies (Wigram 1999a, 2000). In diagnosing autism in a music therapy setting, he selected the two subscales of autonomy and variability of Bruscia's *Improvisation Assessment Profiles* (IAP) (Bruscia 1987). In reporting the case of a five-year-old boy, Wigram has demonstrated the qualities of the *Harper House Music Therapy Assessment* to study autistic core features for the purpose of differentiating between communicative disorders and ASD (Wigram 1999b). Oldfield has developed the *Music Therapy Diagnostic Assessment* (Oldfield 2006), modelled after the *Autism Diagnostic Observation Schedule* (Lord et al. 1989), an established play-based diagnostic instrument. Referring to borderline autistic children, Oldfield concludes that "the MTDA has given us useful information even with the most difficult group of children to diagnose [...]" (Oldfield 2004). In the field of adults with intellectual disability with suspected ASD, Bergmann has developed the *Musical Scale for Autism Diagnostics* (Bergmann et al. 2012). Due to the lack of diagnostic instruments specifically designed for this group, he used the age-independent, non-verbal quality of musical play to assess adults with a low level of functioning in a structured diagnostic setting. The assessment was well accepted among 91 participants, and a preliminary study suggests positive records of its objectivity, reliability, and validity (Bergmann et al. 2015a; Bergmann et al. 2015b). Despite positive indications regarding the music therapy setting as an ideal framework for the identification of autistic symptomatology, work still needs to be done before these approaches can fulfil the criteria for test's quality required to support clinicians and researchers in diagnosing ASD with valid tools based on musical interaction.

CONCLUSION AND FUTURE DIRECTIONS

Most research concerning music and the brain has focused on special abilities, such as absolute pitch detection in individuals with ASD, thus underlining the link between ASD and music on a neurocognitive level. The field concerning emotionality, empathy, and affective regulation in connection with music reception and active music playing seems to be more relevant for the music therapy practice. Research on the efficacy of music therapy in the treatment of ASD is dominated by case reports and studies with small sample sizes. To provide evidence, more random controlled studies are needed, which should be possible as a result of the increasing "academization" of music therapy and the potential financial support of governmental and non-governmental organizations for ASD research projects. One promising example is the ongoing international multi-site TIME-A study (Geretsegger et al. 2012), which analyzes the effectiveness of improvisational music therapy for children with ASD. The aim is to overcome the methodological limitations of previous studies, e.g. by using a larger sample size and by examining the effects over longer periods of time. More activities of this kind could potentially emphasize and provide evidence for the appropriateness of music therapy for ASD and move it away from the orbit of complementary and alternative methods and in the direction of established procedures and best practice.

Music therapy approaches are well established in the treatment of ASD and have been developed against a behavioral, creative, sensory-perceptional, developmental, and educational background. Guidelines are needed in order to set standards in practice and research, as well as in the training of music therapists. Goals, settings, basic principles, and interventions should be further defined. Currently, a treatment guide for improvisational music therapy for children with ASD is being developed (Geretsegger et al. 2014).

Music therapy is used in the treatment of children with ASD, as reflected by the huge number of studies and case reports. Since ASD is a lifelong condition, and music is a highly interactive and age-independent medium, the possibilities of using musical interventions in the treatment of adults should also be considered (Boso et al. 2007). Music therapy has great potential, particularly for use with adults with cognitive impairments and limited language skills (Bergmann et al. 2011), and this should be further investigated.

Assessments in music therapy are needed as a basis for therapeutic practice. This concerns the treatment goals, intervention planning, therapy evaluation, and education of music therapists. In the field of therapy, the AQR (Schumacher and Calvet 2007) provides unique qualities through its developmental foundation correlating to ASD as a pervasive developmental disorder, while the IMCAP-ND (Carpente 2014) supports the formulation of clinical goals and strategies against a Nordoff and Robbins background. In the field of education, the SCERTS model makes it possible to assess music therapy within an interdisciplinary and multimodal approach (Walworth et al. 2009).

In diagnosing ASD, the music therapy setting is an appropriate framework for behavioral observation, since the multisystem and non-verbal character of music correlates with widespread autistic features. Various music-based assessments provide diagnostic hints, but until now, they have lacked a test-theoretical verification. A closer orientation to the criteria for test quality would be desirable in order to achieve valid results and to establish music-based diagnostic procedures in the clinical context.

The close connection between autism and music on many levels; the intertwined, parallel history of music therapy and autism; and the high potential of music-based interventions, as well as many open questions, suggest a common future.

REFERENCES

Abrahams, B.S. and Geschwind, D.H. (2008). Advances in autism genetics: On the threshold of a new neurobiology. *Nature Reviews Genetics* 9(5): 341–355. doi: 10.1038/nrg2346.
Alvin, J. and Warwick, A. (1992). *Music therapy for the autistic child.* Oxford, New York: Oxford University Press.

American Music Therapy Association. (2010). *Autism spectrum disorders: Music therapy research and evidence based practice support.* Retrieved from: <http://www.musictherapy. org/assets/1/7/bib_autism10.pdf>.

American Psychiatric Association. (1980). *Diagnostic and statistical manual of mental disorders: DSM-3*, 3rd edn., Washington, DC: American Psychiatric Association.

American Psychiatric Association. (2000). *Diagnostic and statistical manual of mental disorders: DSM-IV-TR*, 4th edn., text revision. Washington, DC: American Psychiatric Association.

American Psychiatric Association. (2013). *Diagnostic and statistical manual of mental disorders*, 5th edn., Arlington, VA: American Psychiatric Publishing.

Barbera, M.L. and Rasmussen, T. (2007). *The verbal behavior approach: How to teach children with autism and related disorders.* London, Philadelphia: Jessica Kingsley.

Baron-Cohen, S. (1995). *Mindblindness: An essay on autism and theory of mind. Learning, development, and conceptual change.* Cambridge, MA: MIT Press.

Baron-Cohen, S., Leslie, A.M., and Frith, U. (1985). Does the autistic child have a "theory of mind"? *Cognition* 21(1): 37–46. doi:10.1016/0010-0277(85)90022-8.

Ben-Sasson, A., Hen, L., Fluss, R., Cermak, S.A., Engel-Yeger, B., and Gal, E. (2009). A meta-analysis of sensory modulation symptoms in individuals with autism spectrum disorders. *Journal of Autism and Developmental Disorders* 39(1): 1–11. doi:10.1007/ s10803-008-0593-3.

Bérard, G. (1993). *Hearing equals behavior.* New Cannan, CT: Keats Pub.

Berger, D.S. (2002). *Music therapy, sensory integration and the autistic child.* London, New York: Jessica Kingsley.

Bergmann, T., Sappok, T., Schumacher, K., and Diefenbacher, A. (2009). Musiktherapeutischer Ansatz in der Behandlung von Erwachsenen mit Autismus und geistiger Behinderung [Music-therapeutic aproach in the treatment of adults with autism and intellectual disability]. In: F. Schneider and M. Groezinger (eds), *Psychische Erkrankungen in der Lebensspanne: Abstractband zum DGPPN Kongress 2009*, p. 26. Berlin: Deutsche Gesellschaft für Psychiatrie, Psychotherapie und Nervenheilkunde.

Bergmann, T., Dziobek, I., Reimer, S., Schumacher, K., Diefenbacher, A., and Sappok, T. (2011). Jenseits des Dialogs: Beziehungsqualität in der Musiktherapie bei Menschen mit Autismus und Intelligenzminderung [Beyond the dialogue: Quality of relationship in music therapy for individuals with autism and intellectual disability]. *Me Men Geist Mehrf Beh (Medizin für Menschen mit Geistiger und Mehrfacher Behinderung)* 8(1): 14–20.

Bergmann, T., Sappok, T., Diefenbacher, A., and Dziobek, I. (2012). Musikbasierte Autismusdiagnostik (MUSAD): Entwicklung eines Untersuchungsverfahrens für erwachsene Menschen mit Intelligenzminderung und Autismusverdacht [Music-based autism diagnostics: Designing an assessment tool for adults with intellectual disability and suspected autism]. *Musiktherapeutische Umschau* 33(2): 126–140. doi: 10.13109/ muum.2012.33.2.126

Bergmann, T., Sappok, T., Diefenbacher, A., Dames, S., Heinrich, M., Ziegler, M., & Dziobek, I. (2015a). Music-based Autism Diagnostics (MUSAD): A newly developed diagnostic measure for adults with intellectual developmental disabilities suspected of autism. *Research in Developmental Disabilities*, (43–44), 123–135. doi:10.1016/j.ridd.2015.05.011

Bergmann, T., Sappok, T., Diefenbacher, A., & Dziobek, I. (2015b). Music in diagnostics: Using musical interactional settings for diagnosing autism in adults with intellectual developmental disabilities. *Nordic Journal of Music Therapy*, 1–33. doi:10.1080/08098131.2015.103956

Bergmann, T., Sappok, T., Diefenbacher, A., Dames, S., Heinrich, M., Ziegler, M., and Dziobek, I. (2014a). *Music-based Autism Diagnostics (MUSAD): A newly developed diagnostic measure for adults with intellectual developmental disabilities suspected of autism.* In *Journal of applied research in intellectual disabilities*, Vol. 27, no. 4, 303.

Bhatara, A., Quintin, E.-M., Levy, B., Bellugi, U., Frombonne, E., and Levitin, D.J. (2010). Perception of emotion in musical performance in adolescents with autism spectrum disorders. *Autism Research* 3(5): 214–225. doi:10.1002/aur.147.

Bogdashina, O. (2003). *Sensory perceptual issues in autism and asperger syndrome: Different sensory experiences, different perceptual worlds.* London, New York: Jessica Kingsley.

Bölte, S. and Poustka, F. (2003). The recognition of facial affect in autistic and schizophrenic subjects and their first-degree relatives. *Psychological Medicine* 33(5): 907–915.

Bons, D., van den Broek, E., Scheepers, F., Herpers, P., Rommelse, N., and Buitelaaar, J.K. (2013). Motor, emotional, and cognitive empathy in children and adolescents with autism spectrum disorder and conduct disorder. *Journal of Abnormal Child Psychology* 41(3): 425–443.

Boso, M., Emanuele, E., Minazzi, V., Abbamonte, M., and Politi, P. (2007). Effect of long-term interactive music therapy on behavior profile and musical skills in young adults with severe autism. *The Journal of Alternative and Complementary Medicine* 13(7): 709–712. doi:10.1089/acm.2006.6334.

Brownell, M.D. (2002). Musically adapted social stories to modify behaviors in students with autism: four case studies. *Journal of Music Therapy*, 39(2), 117–144.

Bruscia, K.E. (1987). *Improvisational Models of Music Therapy.* Springfield, IL: C.C. Thomas.

Bryson, S.E., Bradley, E.A., Thompson, A., and Wainwright, A. (2008). Prevalence of autism among adolescents with intellectual disabilities. *Canadian Journal of Psychiatry* 53(7): 449–459.

Caamaño, M., Boada, L., Naranjo, J., Moreno, C., Llorente, C., Moreno, D. (2013). Psychopathology in children and adolescents with ASD without mental retardation. *Journal of Autism and Developmental Disorders*, 43(10), 2442-2449. doi:10.1007/s10803-013-1792-0.

Carpente, J.A. (2011). Addressing core features of autism: Integrating Nordoff-Robbins music therapy within the Developmental, Individual-Difference, Relationship-based (DIR)/Floortime™ model. In: A.N. Meadows (ed.), *Developments in music therapy practice. Case study perspectives*, pp. 134–149. Gilsum: Barcelona Publishers.

Centers for Disease Control and Prevention (2012). Prevalence of autism spectrum disorders: Autism and developmental disabilities monitoring network, 14 sites, United States, 2008. MMWR Surveillance Summaries, 61(3).

Carpente, J.A. (2014). Individual Music-Centered Assessment Profile for Neurodevelopmental Disorders (IMCAP-ND): New developments in music-centered evaluation. *Music Therapy Perspectives.* 32(1), 56–60.

Charman, T., Pickles, A., Simonoff, E., Chandler, S., Loucas, T., and Baird, G. (2011). IQ in children with autism spectrum disorders: Data from the Special Needs and Autism Project (SNAP). *Psychological Medicine* 41(03): 619–627. doi:10.1017/S0033291710000991.

Cohen, D. (2005, October 25). Temple Grandin: "I'm an anthropologist from Mars." *The Guardian.* Retrieved from: <http://www.theguardian.com/education/2005/oct/25/higher-educationprofile.academicexperts.>

Courchesne, E., Webb, J. S., and Schumann, C.M. (2011). From toddlers to adults: The changing landscape of the brain in autism. In: D. Amaral, D. Geschwind, and G. Dawson (eds), *Autism Spectrum Disorders*, pp. 611–631. Oxford, New York: Oxford University Press.

Davis, W.B., Gfeller, K.E., and Thaut, M.H. (2008). *An Introduction to Music Therapy: Theory and Practice*, 3rd edn. Silver Spring, MD: American Music Therapy Association.

DePape, A.-M.R., Hall, Geoffrey, B.C., Tillmann, B., and Trainor, L.J. (2012). Auditory processing in high-functioning adolescents with autism spectrum disorder. *PLoS ONE* 7(9): e44084.

Dohn, A., Garza-Villarreal, E.A., Heaton, P., and Vuust, P. (2012). Do musicians with perfect pitch have more autism traits than musicians without perfect pitch? An empirical study. *PLoS ONE* 7(5): e37961.

Dziobek, I. and Köhne, S. (2011). Bildgebung bei Autismusspektrumstörungen [Brain imaging in autism spectrum disorders. A review]. *Der Nervenarzt* 82(5): 564–572.

Euper, J.A. (1966). *A study of musicality in early infantile autism* (Thesis). University of Kansas, Kansas.

Fan, Y.-T., Chen, C., Chen, S.-C., Decety, J., and Cheng, Y. (2013). Empathic arousal and social understanding in individuals with autism: Evidence from fMRI and ERP measurements. *Social Cognitive and Affective Neuroscience*, 9(8), 1203–1213.

Fombonne, E. (2009). Epidemiology of pervasive developmental disorders. *Pediatric Research* 65(6): 591–598. doi:10.1203/PDR.0b013e31819e7203.

Fournier, K.A., Hass, C.J., Naik, S.K., Lodha, N., and Cauraugh, J.H. (2010). Motor coordination in autism spectrum disorders: A synthesis and meta-analysis. *Journal of Autism and Developmental Disorders* 40(10): 1227–1240. doi:10.1007/s10803-010-0981-3.

Frith, U. and Happé, F. (1994). Autism: Beyond "theory of mind." *Cognition* 50(1–3): 115–132.

Ganz, M.L. (2007). The lifetime distribution of the incremental societal costs of autism. *Archives of Pediatrics and Adolescent Medicine* 161(4): 343–349. doi:10.1001/archpedi.161.4.343

Geretsegger, M. (2005). *Was die Neuropsychologie der Musiktherapie zu berichten hat: Kognitive Modelle in musiktherapeutischer Arbeit mit Kindern mit Autismus* [What neuropsychology has to tell to music therapy: Cognitive models in music therapy with children with autism]. Retrieved from: <http://www.oebm.org/files/jf_geretsegger_2005.pdf>.

Geretsegger, M., Holck, U., and Gold, C. (2012). Randomised controlled trial of improvisational music therapy's effectiveness for children with autism spectrum disorders (TIME-A): Study protocol. *BMC Pediatrics* 12(1), 2-9. doi:10.1186/1471-2431-12-2.

Geretsegger, M., Elefant, C., Kim, J., and Gold, C. (2014a). Music therapy for people with autism spectrum disorder. *The Cochrane Database of Systematic Reviews* 6: CD004381. doi:10.1002/14651858.CD004381.pub3

Geretsegger, M., Holck, U., Carpente, J., and Elefant, C. (2014b). *Defining improvisational music therapy: Development of a treatment guide for children with autism spectrum disorders*. Manuscript submitted for publication

Gillberg, I.C. and Gillberg, C. (1989). Asperger Syndrome? Some epidemiological considerations: A research note. *Journal of Child Psychology and Psychiatry* 30(4): 631–638. doi:10.1111/j.1469-7610.1989.tb00275.x.

Gilliland, E.G. (1955). Functional music for the exceptional child in the special schools of Chicago. In: P.W. Dykema and H.M. Cundiff (eds), *School Music Handbook. A Guide for Music Educators, Designed to Meet the Needs of Classroom Teachers and Special Music Teachers in the Grades and Junior High School*, pp. 585–591. Boston: C.C. Birchard.

Gold, C., Wigram, T., and Elefant, C. (2006). Music therapy for autistic spectrum disorder. *The Cochrane Database of Systematic Reviews* (2), CD004381.

Green, J., Charman, T., McConachie, H., Aldred, C., Slonims, V., Howlin, P., et al. (2010). Parent-mediated communication-focused treatment in children with autism

(PACT): A randomised controlled trial. *The Lancet* 375(9732): 2152–2160. doi:10.1016/S0140-6736(10)60587-9.

Harbert, W.K. (1955). Music education for exceptional children. In: H.N. Morgan (ed.), *Music in American Education. Music Education Source Book Number Two*, pp. 263–271. Chicago: Music Education National Conference.

Heasley, S. (2012). *Motor impairments core feature of autism—disability scoop*. Retrieved from: <http://www.disabilityscoop.com/2012/02/21/motor-impairments-autism/15022/>.

Heaton, P., Hermelin, B., and Pring, L. (1999). Can children with autistic spectrum disorders perceive affect in music? An experimental investigation. *Psychological Medicine* 29(6): 1405–1410.

Heaton, P., Allen, R., Williams, K., Cummins, O., and Happé, F. (2008). Do social and cognitive deficits curtail musical understanding? Evidence from autism and Down syndrome. *British Journal of Developmental Psychology* 26(2): 171–182. doi:10.1348/026151007X206776.

Hess, K.L., Morrier, M.J., Heflin, L.J., and Ivey, M.L. (2008). Autism treatment survey: Services received by children with autism spectrum disorders in public school classrooms. *Journal of Autism and Developmental Disorders* 38(5): 961–971. doi:10.1007/s10803-007-0470-5.

Hobson, R.P. (1986). The autistic child's appraisal of expressions of emotion. *Journal of Child Psychology and Psychiatry* 27(3): 321–342. doi:10.1111/j.1469-7610.1986.tb01836.x.

Howlin, P. and Moss, P. (2012). Adults with autism spectrum disorders. *Canadian Journal of Psychiatry* 57(5): 275–283.

Kanner, L. (1943). Autistic disturbance of affective contact. *Nervous Child* 2: 217–250.

Kasari, C.L., Jahromi, L.B., and Gulsrud, A.C. (2012). Emotional development in children with developmental disabilities. In: J.A. Burack (ed.), *Oxford Library of Psychology. The Oxford handbook of intellectual disability and development*, 2nd edn., New York: Oxford University Press.

Kern, P. (2012). *Using music for children's learning and growth*. Retrieved from: <http://www.ectacenter.org/~pdfs/meetings/inclusionMtg2012/Kern_Handout_UsingMusicfor ChildrensLearningandGrowth2012.pdf>.

Kern, P. and Aldridge, D. (2006). Using embedded music therapy interventions to support outdoor play of young children with autism in an inclusive community-based child care program. *Journal of Music Therapy* 43(4): 270–294.

Kern, P., Wolery, M., and Aldridge, D. (2007). Use of songs to promote independence in morning greeting routines for young children with autism. *Journal of Autism and Developmental Disorders* 37(7): 1264–1271. doi:10.1007/s10803-006-0272-1.

Khetrapal, N. (2009). Why does music therapy help in autism? *Empirical Musicology Review* 4(1): 11–18.

Kim, S.H. and Lord, C. (2012). Combining information from multiple sources for the diagnosis of autism spectrum disorders for toddlers and young preschoolers from 12 to 47 months of age. *Journal of Child Psychology and Psychiatry* 53(2): 143–151. doi:10.1111/j.1469-7610.2011.02458.x.

Kim, J., Wigram, T., and Gold, C. (2008). The effects of improvisational music therapy on joint attention behaviors in autistic children: A randomized controlled study. *Journal of Autism and Developmental Disorders* 38(9): 1758–1766.

Kim, J., Wigram, T., and Gold, C. (2009). Emotional, motivational and interpersonal responsiveness of children with autism in improvisational music therapy. *Autism* 13(4): 389–409. doi:10.1177/1362361309105660.

King, M. and Bearman, P. (2009). Diagnostic change and the increased prevalence of autism. *International Journal of Epidemiology* 38(5): 1224–1234. doi:10.1093/ije/dyp261.

Klin, A., Jones, W., Schultz, R., Volkmar, F., and Cohen, D. (2002). Visual fixation patterns during viewing of naturalistic social situations as predictors of social competence in individuals
with autism. *Archives of General Psychiatry* 59(9): 809–816.

Kohls, G., Chevallier, C., Troiani, V., and Schultz, R. T. (2012). Social "wanting" dysfunction in autism: neurobiological underpinnings and treatment implications. *Journal of
Neurodevelopmental Disorders* 4(1): 10. doi:10.1186/1866-1955-4-10.

Lim, H.A. (2010). Effect of "developmental speech and language training through music" on
speech production in children with autism spectrum disorders. *Journal of Music Therapy*
47(1): 2–26.

Lim, H.A. and Draper, E. (2011). The effects of music therapy incorporated with applied behavior analysis verbal behavior approach for children with autism spectrum disorders. *Journal
of Music Therapy* 48(4): 532–550.

Lord, C., Rutter, M., Goode, S., Heemsbergen, J., Jordan, H., Mawhood, L., and Schopler, E.
(1989). Austism Diagnostic Observation Schedule: A standardized observation of communicative and social behavior. *Journal of Autism and Developmental Disorders* 19(2): 185–212.
doi:10.1007/BF02211841.

McTiernan, A., Leader, G., Healy, O., and Mannion, A. (2011). Analysis of risk factors and early
predictors of challenging behavior for children with autism spectrum disorder. *Research in
Autism Spectrum Disorders* 5(3): 1215–1222. doi:10.1016/j.rasd.2011.01.009.

Matson, J.L., and Shoemaker, M. (2009). Intellectual disability and its relationship to autism
spectrum disorders. *Research in developmental disabilities* 30(6): 1107–1114.

Molnar-Szakacs, I., and Heaton, P. (2012). Music: A unique window into the
world of autism. *Annals of the New York Academy of Sciences* 1252(1): 318–324.
doi:10.1111/j.1749-6632.2012.06465.x.

Murphy, A. (2011). *Aspergers and the alien: The importance of music*. Retrieved from: <http://
aspergersthealien.blogspot.de/2011/05/importance-of-musicautism-aspergers.html>.

Nordoff, P. and Robbins, C. (1965). *Music therapy for handicapped children: Investigations and
experiences, St George books*, 1st edn. New York: R. Steiner Pub.

Nordoff, P. and Robbins, C. (1977). *Creative Music Therapy: Individualized Treatment for the
Handicapped Child*. New York: John Day Co.

Oldfield, A. (2004). *Music therapy with children on the autistic spectrum: Approaches derived
from clinical practice and research*. PhD thesis, Anglia Ruskin University, Cambridge.

Oldfield, A. (2006). *Interactive Music Therapy in Child and Family Psychiatry: Clinical Practice,
Research, and Teaching*. London, Philadelphia: Jessica Kingsley.

Ozonoff, S. and Pennington, B.F.R.S. (1991). Executive function deficits in high-functioning
autistic individuals: Relationship to theory of mind. *Journal of Child Psychology and
Psychiatry* 32(7): 1081–1105.

Pine, D. (2005, September 16). Autistic jazz prodigy already playing with greats. *The Jewish
News Weekly of Northern California*.

Quintin, E.-M., Bhatara, A., Poissant, H., Fombonne, E., and Levitin, D.J. (2011). Emotion perception in music in high-functioning adolescents with autism spectrum disorders. *Journal
of Autism and Developmental Disorders* 41(9): 1240–1255.

Reddy, V., Williams, E., Costantini, C., and Lan, B. (2010). Engaging with the self: Mirror
behaviour in autism, Down syndrome and typical development. *Autism* 14(5): 531–546.
doi:10.1177/1362361310370397.

Reschke-Hernández, A.E. (2011). History of music therapy treatment interventions for children with autism. *Journal of Music Therapy* 48(2): 169–207.

Rojahn, J., Wilkins, J., Matson, J.L., and Boisjoli, J. (2010). A Comparison of adults with intel-lectual disabilities with and without ASD on parallel measures of challenging behaviour: The Behavior Problems Inventory-01 (BPI-01) and Autism Spectrum Disorders-Behavior Problems for intellectually disabled Adults (ASD-BPA). *Journal of Applied Research in Intellectual Disabilities* 23(2): 179–185. doi:10.1111/j.1468-3148.2009.00519.x.

Rosenhall, U., Nordin, V., Sandstrom, M., Ahlsen, G., and Gillberg, C. (1999). Autism and hear-ing loss. *Journal of Autism and Developmental Disorders* 29(5): 349–357.

Rossignol, D.A. (2009). Novel and emerging treatments for autism spectrum disorders: A sys-tematic review. *Annals of Clinical Psychiatry* 21(4): 213–236.

Sappok, T., Bergmann, T., Kaiser, H., and Diefenbacher, A. (2010). Autismus bei erwachsenen Menschen mit geistiger Behinderung [Autism in adults with intellectual disabilities]. *Der Nervenarzt* 81(11): 1333–1345. doi:10.1007/s00115-010-3098-1

Sappok, T., Gaul, I., Bergmann, T., Dziobek, I., Bölte, S., Diefenbacher, A., and Heinrich, M. (2014). The Diagnostic Behavioral Assessment for autism spectrum disorder—Revised: A screening instrument for adults with intellectual disability suspected of autism spectrum disorders. *Research in Autism Spectrum Disorders*, 8(4), 362–375.

Scheerenberger, R. (1953). Description of a music program at a residential school for man-mtally handicapped. *American Journal of Mental Deficiency* 57: 573–579.

Schumacher, K. (1999). *Musiktherapie und Säuglingsforschung [Music therapy and infant research]*. Frankfurt am Main: Peter Lang.

Schumacher, K. and Calvet, C. (2007). The "AQR-instrument" (Assessment of the Quality of Relationship): An observation instrument to assess the quality of a relationship. In: T. Wosch and T. Wigram (eds), *Microanalysis in Music Therapy. Methods, Techniques and Applications for Clinicians, Researchers, Educators and Students*, pp. 79–91. London, Philadelphia: Jessica Kingsley.

Schumacher, K. and Calvet, C. (2008a). Music therapy with children based on devel-opmental psychology, using the example of "synchronization" as a relevant moment. *Synchronisation—Music Therapy with Children on the Autistic Spectrum, DVD supplement.* Göttingen: Vanderhoeck and Ruprecht.

Schumacher, K. and Calvet, C. (2008b). *Synchronisation, 1 DVD: Musiktherapie bei Kindern mit Autismus.* Göttingen: Vandenhoeck and Ruprecht.

Sherwin, A.C. (1953). Reactions to music of autistic (schizophrenic) children. *American Journal of Psychiatry* 109: 823–831.

Simpson, R.L. (2005). *Autism spectrum disorders: Interventions and treatments for children and youth.* Thousand Oaks, CA: Corwin Press.

Sinha, Y., Silove, N., Hayen, A., and Williams, K. (2011). Auditory integration training and other sound therapies for autism spectrum disorders (ASD). *The Cochrane Database of Systematic Reviews* 12: CD003681.

Srinivasan, S.M. and Bhat, A.N. (2013). A review of "music and movement" therapies for children with autism: Embodied interventions for multisystem development. *Frontiers in Integrative Neuroscience* 7: 22. doi:10.3389/fnint.2013.00022.

Stanutz, S., Wapnick, J., and Burack, J. (2012). Pitch discrimination and melodic memory in children with autism spectrum disorder. *Autism.* Retrieved from: <http://www.gopubmed.org/search?q = 23150888andt = endnote>.

Stern, D. (2000). *The Interpersonal World of the Infant: A View from Psychoanalysis and Developmental Psychology: with a new Introduction by the Author*, 1st edn. New York: Basic Books.

Strang, J.F., Kenworthy, L., Daniolos, P., Case, L., Wills, M.C., Martin, A., and Wallace, G.L. (2012). Depression and anxiety symptoms in children and adolescents with autism spectrum disorders without intellectual disability. *Research in Autism Spectrum Disorders* 6(1): 406–412. doi:10.1016/j.rasd.2011.06.015.

Thaut, M.H. (1984). A music therapy treatment model for autistic children. *Music Therapy Perspectives* 1: 7–13.

Van Bourgondien, M.E., Reichle, N.C., and Schopler, E. (2003). Effects of a model treatment approach on adults with autism. *Journal of Autism and Developmental Disorders* 33(2): 131–140.

Walworth, D.D., Register, D., and Engel, J.N. (2009). Using the SCERTS model assessment tool to identify music therapy goals for clients with autism spectrum disorder. *Journal of Music Therapy* 46(3): 204–216.

Wan, C.Y., Bazen, L., Baars, R., Libenson, A., Zipse, L., Zuk, J., Norton, A., and Schlaug, G. (2011). Auditory-motor mapping training as an intervention to facilitate speech output in non-verbal children with autism: a proof of concept study. *PLoS ONE* 6(9): e25505.

Whipple, J. (2004). Music in intervention for children and adolescents with autism: A meta-analysis. *Journal of Music Therapy* 41(2): 90–106.

Wigram, T. (1999a). Assessment methods in music therapy: A humanistic or natural science framework? *Nordic Journal of Music Therapy* 8(1): 6–24. doi:10.1080/08098139909477950.

Wigram, T. (1999b). Contact in music: The analysis of musical behaviour in children with communication disorder and pervasive developmental disability for differential diagnosis. In: T. Wigram and J. de Backer (eds), *Clinical Applications of Music Therapy in Developmental Disability, Paediatrics and Neurology*, pp. 69–118. London: Jessica Kingsley.

Wigram, T. (2000). *Assessment and Evaluation in the Arts Therapies: Art Therapy, Music Therapy and Dramatherapy*. Radlett: Harper House.

Wigram, T. (2002). *Indications in music therapy: Evidence from assessment that can identfy the expectations of music therapy as a treatment for autistic spectrum disorder (ASD): Meeting the challenge of evidence based practice*. British Journal of Music Therapy, 16, 11–28.

Wigram, T. and Gold, C. (2006). Music therapy in the assessment and treatment of autistic spectrum disorder: clinical application and research evidence. *Child: Care, Health and Development* 32(5): 535–542.

Williams, J.H. (2008). Self–other relations in social development and autism: multiple roles for mirror neurons and other brain bases. *Autism Research* 1(2): 73–90. doi:10.1002/aur.15.

Wing, L. (1981). Language, social, and cognitive impairments in autism and severe mental retardation. *Journal of Autism and Developmental Disorders* 11(1): 31–44. doi:10.1007/BF01531339.

Wing, L. (1996). *The autistic spectrum*. London: Robinson.

World Health Organization. (2008). *ICD-10: International statistical classification of diseases and related health problems* (10th Rev. ed.). New York: Author.

Zablotsky, B., Bradshaw, C.P., Anderson, C.M., and Law, P. (2014). Risk factors for bullying among children with autism spectrum disorders. *Autism* 18(4): 419–427.

....

CHAPTER 11

MUSIC THERAPY
AND RETT SYNDROME

....

COCHAVIT ELEFANT

INTRODUCTION

....

WHEN I first began working with children with Rett syndrome (RTT) over twenty years ago not much had been written on what they needed or how a music therapist could work with them. In retrospect this informational void made me work very hard to find my own way into the world of each individual, precious girl with Rett syndrome. Rather than reading books or articles about Rett syndrome and music therapy I had to learn to read those deep expressive eyes and to look for signs and meanings in them. I did know that life used to be totally different for them before this debilitating syndrome had taken over their lives, leaving them locked and isolated from the world. I believed that there was a human being ready for communication with others, and with me. This belief has helped me keep working with them to this day. Let me illustrate my connection with these girls with an event that happened recently.

> A couple of weeks ago, I met Talia (a young woman with RTT) at a party in her home. We had not seen each other for several years. I went over and said hello to her, telling her how excited I was to see her and how much I had missed her. People around us looked as if I was talking to the chair, but I knew that Talia would recognize my voice and turn her head towards me, so I waited and waited. Sure enough, after almost one minute, she turned her head towards me looked at me straight in the eyes with a big smile. I started talking to her quietly; asking her if she remembered the songs we used to sing together and then I began singing to her. During these precious moments, Talia became lively and people around us became speechless. The following day, I received a text message from Talia's mother which said: "Dear Cookie, you have no idea how important you are to our family. Thank you for your eyes that see the beauty in her. We especially thank you for being attuned to Talia and turning every meeting with her into a moving event that stirs us with excitement and happiness. It keeps reminding us that this unique life with Talia is really special and that there is nothing in this world that can substitute it."

The musical interaction Talia and I had made during our short meeting that evening made her vital and revealed parts of herself that others do not see very often. To be part of Talia's story is a touching experience, and I am grateful for each and every girl that has given me the opportunity to tell such beautiful and meaningful stories.

In this chapter, I will attempt to describe some of what I have learned from years of musical and personal encounters with individuals with RTT and their families. The aim is to help understand what lies behind those deep and penetrating eyes and behind the "screaming silence." Through short vignettes, I hope to shed light on these girls' inner capacity and to show how music with its various forms can help to bring them to life as well as motivate their families. There is a unique personality behind each person with RTT; however, I have not yet met one individual with RTT that does not respond to live music.

It was important for me right from the beginning of this chapter to reveal to the reader some of the resources we can expect to find in each individual with RTT, however, in the next section, I will describe the harsher side of this disorder.

Rett syndrome disorder

Rett syndrome (RTT) is a genetic disorder resulting from an X-linked dominant mutation in MECP2 gene (Amir et al. 1999, 2000). It primarily affects females and is found in a variety of racial and ethnic groups worldwide with a versatile clinical phenotype (Hagberg and Hagberg 1997). The syndrome is named after an Austrian physician, Andreas Rett, who was the first to identify the syndrome in 1966 (Rett 1966). Since the discovery of the genetic cause for RTT (Amir et al. 2000), the genetic diagnosis of RTT is found to be positive in 95 % of individuals showing the classical clinical characteristics and in 75 % of individuals showing atypical characteristics of RTT. Despite the high specificity and sensitivity regarding genetic diagnosis, clinicians still rely primarily on a clinical diagnosis The estimated incidence of RTT is 10:100,000 females (Leonard et al. 1997), although higher incidence rates have been reported (Fombonne et al. 2003; Pini et al, 1996; Skesedel et al. 1997). It is considered to be the second most common cause of multi-disabling genetic disorders in females after Down's syndrome (Ellaway and Christodoulou 2001; Hagberg 1995).

RTT is a severe neurodevelopmental disorder characterized by the loss of intellectual functioning; fine and gross motor skills, and communicative abilities; deceleration of head growth; and the development of stereotypic hand movements, occurring after a period of apparently normal development. Individuals with RTT often develop seizures, a disturbed breathing pattern with hyperventilation, and periodic apnea, scoliosis, growth retardation, and gait apraxia (Hagberg 1993; Engerstrom and Kerr 1998; Lotan 2006). To date, mutations in this gene can be found in about 90 % of females with the classical phenotype of this disorder (Neul and Zoghbi 2004). Despite the genetic high specificity and sensitivity, RTT is still considered a clinical diagnosis characterized by a specific developmental profile that should meet certain clinical diagnostic criteria (Trevethan and Moser 1998; Hagberg et al. 2001).

Stages of Rett Syndrome

Individuals with RTT show a pre- and perinatal period with apparently normal developmental progress for the first five to six months of life. The birth head circumference is within the norm, with subsequent deceleration of head growth, usually leading to microcephaly, emerging at around four months postnatally (Naidu 2000; Schults et al. 2001). At this stage, minor developmental abnormalities are evident in the majority of these children, such as mild hypotonia, poor suck, a weak cry, and a calm disposition. Such minor signs are difficult to detect even by developmental disabilities experts (Burford 2005, Einspieler et al. 2005). The development of RTT is usually described in four stages (Hagberg 1993):

Stage I: *Early Onset Stage*—Between three months and three years, there is reduction or loss of acquired skills such as purposeful hand function, vocalization, and communication skills. The girls then enter a short period of developmental stagnation.

Stage II: *Rapid Destructive Stage*—This stage is detected when the child is around the age one to four years. This stage is usually short; from weeks to several months in length. It is characterized by rapid regression in language and motor skills. One of the characteristics of this stage is extreme screaming and crying episodes by 18–24 months of age (Coleman, et al. 1988). Additional characteristics include autistic-like features, panic-like attacks, bruxism, episodic apnea and/or hyperpnea, seizures, gait ataxia and apraxia, tremors, and acquired microcephaly. The emergence of hand stereotypical mannerisms is the prominent feature of this stage. After this period of rapid deterioration, RTT becomes relatively stable.

Stage III: *Plateau Stage*—This stage is usually apparent at preschool age to adulthood. Apraxia, motor problems are more prominent during this long stage. They will show less irritability and enhanced awareness of her surrounding. This stage usually can last for decades and enables the person to gain achievements in various fields.

Stage IV: *Late Motor Deterioration Stage*—This stage is characterized by reduced mobility; those who were never ambulant move from Stage II to IV. Despite the motor deterioration at this stage, there is no decline in cognition, communication, or hand skills.

Apraxia in Rett Syndrome

Individuals with RTT may have changes in mood and in functional level. Such changes can sometimes be linked to her medical state or they may be completely unexplainable. These changes may appear abruptly or gradually; they may be present for a few month or change within the time frame of hours (Lindberg 2006). Some of the difficulties presented by individuals with RTT are limited hand function, stereotypic hand movements, a chaotic dysfunctional sensory system, and difficulties in planning and executing motor acts (apraxia). These are issues that music therapists need to take into consideration in planning sessions.

While individuals with RTT are defined as apraxic, this definition does not stand well with the fact that apraxia is usually associated with some form of head trauma and in the case of RTT, no damage can be found in their brains. It is therefore suggested to amalgamate two different terms "apraxia" and "developmental dyspraxia" in order to characterize the type of difficulty experienced by them, and thereby suggest a form of therapy through sensory integration intervention as suggested by Jean Ayres.

When Ayres first related to this issue in 1972 she referred to it as developmental dyspraxia (DD). To distinguish this term from the term *Apraxia*, associated with people with brain injury (Clark and Allen 1985), Ayres claimed that the term apraxic is more suitable for someone who can learn to perform a task yet both the learning period as well as his task performance are slow and do not reach high efficiency (Clark and Allen 1985). In Ayres' terminology, the term DD means a problem in brain function that stems from the person's difficulty in processing sensory information from the tactile, proprioceptive, and vestibular systems, thereby harming motor planning. The term "developmental" points to that the problem is initiated at the early stages of the child's life, and affects his development (Ayres 1982).

Since learning is a process in which we cognitively internalize repeated information until it becomes automated, a child with an impaired body scheme will be unable to transfer motor patterns from the cortical level to an automated level. This inability will require long and repeated planning by the child for each task she is asked to perform. Since no motor patterns are being built, the child will relate to each new action as it has never happened before and with every new task she will have to assess her position and the way she is requested to act. These types of difficulties are very consistent with the description of the dyspraxtic child by Fisher et al. (1991).

A dysfunctional sensory system is a most baffling state. The uncontrolled and unexplained incoming sensory messages leave the child in a state of chaos that is very typical of stage II of RTT (Lindberg 2006). This might explain why most individuals with RTT withdraw into what is usually perceived by the outside observer as *autistic-like* behavior. If your own sensory system has crushed and can no longer be trusted, then the most logical thing to do would be to separate your self from the outer world to reduce the number of stimuli. We will come back to this point when I later on discuss music therapy.

As one can see, RTT is a constellation of complex difficulties. It is somewhat easy to focus on the diagnosis and the severe symptoms and lost skills. The losses are brutal and difficult to comprehend and can naturally lead to view them in a hopeless and a pessimistic manner. This in turn, can easily affect the individual and could result in their state of depression or apathy. These pessimistic and helpless views can close the options to help individuals with RTT to feel better, even to the point that they will be able to retrieve some of their lost skills.

Despite their severe developmental disabilities, most children with RTT during their early development had normal emotional, communicative, cognitive, and motor development (Burford 2005; Einspieler et al. 2005), with the appearance of abnormality between six months and two years of age (Hagberg 1993). Today we are witnessing that people with RTT are able to regain some skills such as walking (Lotan 2008) and hand use (Downs et al. 2013). Improvements in communicative and cognitive abilities have also been shown (Elefant 2002, 2005, 2009, 2011; Elefant and Wigram 2005; Wigram and Elefant 2009). Recent research using eye-tracking devices, has opened up possibilities in studying brain processing in the area of cognition, attention, and recognition memory. The results of these studies show that individuals with RTT have similar performance in some areas of recognition and memory while in other areas they show less maturity than that of typically developing comparison groups (Berger-Sweeney 2011; Rose et al. 2013).

Individuals with RTT seem motivated and eager to further explore the world as these remarkable positive changes take place. This leads to the questions; How could the contrast between their external physical disabilities and their internal abilities be so misleading? How is it possible that these "silent angels" with deep and penetrating expressive eyes seemingly don't perceive what is happening to them and around them? The theoretical perspective of Daniel Stern (1985/2000) and Malloch and Trevarthen (2009) is relevant when thinking about these questions regarding the emotional and communicative development of individuals with RTT.

THEORETICAL FOUNDATION

If we take the point of reference that an infant with RTT usually experiences normal development at the beginning of her life, we can presume that her early interactions with primary caregivers were similar to an infant with normal development (Elefant 2009, 2011). There was nothing that interrupted this early parent-infant interaction during the early development which means that both the child and the primary caregiver had meaningful emotional interactive experiences through pre-verbal communicative dialogues. The infant and the parent identify with each other's facial expressions, gestures, explore different vocal interactions through *affect attunement* (Stern 1985/2000) and find pleasure in the experience of interacting within the frame of *communicative musicality* (Malloch 1999; Malloch and Trevarthen 2009; Trevarthen and Malloch 2002). Holck (2002) explains that "in mutual interplay, both partners participate in turn-organisation, and therefore an analysis of cues indicating turn-taking and turn-yielding can give information on the participants' social skills, whether or not the dialogue is verbal" (p. 402). Parents of children with RTT have reported that they have had these enriching experiences with their daughters until the onset of the disorder (Burford 2005).

If we look at the developmental condition of RTT and compare it to Stern's (1985/2000) account of the development of "the five senses of self" in infancy, it seems that most girls with RTT developed through an *emergent self*, the *core self with others*, the *inter-subjective self*, and many have even begun to develop the *verbal self* around the age of 12 months, acquiring spoken language and expressing themselves verbally. As a result of the drastic change in Stage II, the destructive stage, which occurs between 6–24 months, the girl's interactions with others starts to change. She becomes agitated, cries constantly, and at the same time doesn't want anyone to get close to her. These behaviors may change the response and expression towards her by the surrounding and may lead to misdiagnosis of autism. The stormy period, troubling for both the girl and her family (Kerr and Witt Engerström 2001), interrupts the flow in emotional communication that mediates inter-subjectivity (Elefant 2011; Wigram and Elefant 2009). It isn't difficult then for the child and her family to be situated in a feeling of "total loss" and the inevitable belief that what had been lost may never be retrieved or reclaimed again. After this stormy period the girl enters Stage III, a Plateau stage. The third stage is usually apparent at preschool age to adulthood and is a stable stage which enables her to open up again to her surroundings. Although apraxia and motor problems are more prominent during this long stage the girl will show less irritability and is eager to have contact with others.

MUSIC THERAPY AND RETT SYNDROME

The theoretical perspective outlined above has a direct implication on music therapy work with individuals with RTT. Each unique individual enters music therapy carrying the emotional grief of her loss; she may feel dysfunctional, helpless and in a state of disarray and confusion. The music therapist may choose to work through these emotional hurdles with her, but should also remember and remind the girl of the many meaningful experiences of her past. In other words, the therapist can express that "this is an extremely difficult condition to be in, but I know you have an array of possibilities waiting to emerge whenever you are ready." When the therapist manages to sincerely communicate this and the girl begins to trust the therapist, a therapeutic dialogue can take place. When she feels understood, her motivation and willingness to communicate is enhanced.

The music therapist should remember how the girl must have been before she experienced these great losses. At the same time the therapist needs to understand the emotional difficulties and frustrations that she may be experiencing with the limited use of hands or the difficulty accomplishing an activity because of apraxia. Let me illustrate this by an example:

> Maya is a beautiful young girl with RTT who came to individual music therapy session twice a week. Using picture communication symbols she used to choose the instruments she wanted to play or wanted me to play as well as the songs she wanted me to sing. She progressed by playing more and more instruments and by expanding her song repertoire, choosing a song from 8 different song choices. During one of the sessions, I suggested to Maya that she could hold a mallet with her hand in order to play the xylophone. Almost instantly, she let go of the mallet. I tried a couple of times to put the mallet in her hand but with no success. At the end of the session I improvised a song summarizing in words what we had done during the session. Maya was very attentive and excited as I sang the song; she was laughing, came close to my face and tried to join in by strumming on the guitar. Towards the end of the second verse I sang: "And you tried unsuccessfully to play the xylophone with the mallet and maybe we could try it again next time." Just when I sang this line, Maya stopped laughing, her face became serious and she went towards the exit door and tried to get out of the room.

There are many lessons to be learnt from the above vignette. First of all, it seems that Maya understood the song text and secondly, she reacted quite adversely by trying to leave the room when I pointed out that she didn't succeed playing the xylophone with the mallet. She may have been frustrated by this and especially when I had *rubbed it in*. I find her behavior to be quite well suited to her situation. In fact, I see this type of reaction often with children and adolescence with no developmental disabilities in my private clinic. No one chooses to do something they can't succeed in it; and if they fail they may either deny their failure, avoid certain difficulties or say that they don't want to come back to music therapy. These turning points are critical and can be opportunities to be carefully discussed and worked through with the clients through musical or verbal dialogue. In the case of Maya, I continued the song:

"I can imagine that it is not easy for you to hold the mallet with your hand and you can choose whether you want to try it next time or not." Maya returned to the center of the room with a big smile on her face.

It is important to see that the goals we set need to consider the desire and motivation our clients may express and we, the therapists have to become better at reading them without involving our own desires. This is not an easy task, especially when working with individuals with no language. Trevarthen and Malloch have emphasized the need for the therapists to become better aware and attuned to the other. They refer to individuals with developmental delay or disabilities and suggest that the therapist can use musical communication as interactive play where both partners can engage in mutual interaction (Malloch 1999; Trevarthen and Malloch 2002; Wigram and Elefant 2009). The therapist can develop awareness for the client's physical, facial gestures and vocalizations as an indication of her relatedness and express them in a musical form. This *communicative musicality* (Malloch 1999; Malloch and

Trevarthen 2009; Trevarthen and Malloch 2002) is shared as a therapeutic dialogue. These communicative forms are unique to each individual and need to be created in each therapeutic encounter. For Maya, playing the xylophone with a mallet was a goal I had set and obviously there was no space for mutual engagement.

When interacting musically while attuning to the person's emotional state, improvisation and pre-composed songs can be used (Elefant 2005; Wigram and Elefant 2009). These interactions provide an opportunity to discover hidden resources that may not be readily accessed because of the disability. With each such positive shift in musical interactions, the person can become empowered and driven towards new challenges that enhance growth.

Musical Conversation

Although the individuals with RTT I have worked with are usually non-verbal, I still choose to talk to them. I describe elsewhere (Elefant 2011) a case study with Ella in which I explain this method of *musical conversation* in which improvisation and verbal expressions are used simultaneously, conversing on a certain topic that relates to and address some of her concerns and desires. It is similar to what was described above in Maya's vignette; however in musical conversation the client chooses the topic of conversation. I gathered topics from either reading her daily log book in which her parents and staff members write or by debriefing with the staff. Such topics could be about different feelings she may be encountering; events such as a birth of a sibling, birthdays, moving, a wedding or death of a close family member, becoming a teenager, and so on. She chose the topic with *yes* and *no* communication cards or by looking at me when the right topic comes along. To work out this type of communication and choice making the she and I had to develop a common emotional and communicative understanding. We had to create a space where she could express herself in a way that she felt understood. This was a delicate issue because the "conversations" were limited by the fact that only I have spoken language, while she doesn't. It is similar to a parent–infant conversation; however the content is on a different level, with the assumption that she understands the content of what is said, not only the emotional intent as with parent-infant communication. The intent of these *narratives of the experiencing self* is an attempt to reflect and attune to her internal world in order to confirm her inner emotions and intentions (Stern 1985/2000). This is a partnership in which I become the *voice*, attempting to give meaning to the girl's thoughts and feelings, but also helping her finding solutions and taking responsibilities. The music always supports the narrative so the intent is conveyed either by the music, the narrative, or both.

These musical conversations are not always easy as sometimes difficult issues may arise and the girl may not want to deal with intense emotions. I accept that I may not really know what she wants to express, but I find that this type of musical-verbal conversations provide a useful way of interacting in comparison to other musical interactions such as: improvisation, pre-composed songs or playing the instruments.

Vocalization

Vocalization is one of the first forms of expression in young infants. Through vocalization the young child communicates with his surroundings and it is an important aspect of the development of the self. Most individuals with RTT do not speak and may not always vocalize. It is crucial to help them to regain the vocalization as most of them have previously used and explored their voices and may have even used a few words and short sentences. Intentional vocal sounds may initially appear very gentle with soft quality, while with time they can develop a stronger sound. The sounds become varied and it seems that she will have more control over her own vocalization. The development of vocalization can be seen as an extension of her development of self-confidence, motivation and follows along the developments in her play (Hill 1997) within the vocal interaction with others (Burford and Trevarthen 1997). The vocalization becomes interactive and communicative. Wigram and Cass (1996) described one girl who during assessment session vocalized to a familiar tune with much joy and once the music was stopped the vocalization changed to sounds of dissatisfaction and unhappiness. Once the music began, the girl began to smile and contented vocal sounds were heard.

From my own clinical experience, I have witnessed several girls who not only began to vocalize but who also began to express single words when interacting vocally; repetitively using the words in musical games. These were words they had used previously but seemed to have vanished from their repertory. In many accounts the individual with RTT vocalized in an echolalic manner, as if trying to repeat a word that had been spoken. These incidences need to be captured by the music therapist and used as a lever to enhance vocal expression (Wigram 1991). These interactive vocal dialogues enable her to regain her voice and give her the opportunity to express her intimate inner emotional feelings (Elefant 2009). Moreover the act of vocalizing for a silent person can enables her to bring herself forth and to become present.

Choices and Learning in Music Therapy

> I recently presented in a World Congress for Rett Syndrome in New Orleans, USA. During one of the coffee breaks, a mother of a teenager with RTT approached me and said very excitingly that she had heard my keynote presentation 12 years ago in a conference where I had first presented my PhD research results on communication and music therapy with girls with RTT. My message and plea then to the audience was that individuals with RTT have intentional communication and are able to learn, if only provided the means to do so. This mother wanted to tell me that she had followed my advice and that her daughter was about to finish high school. She had felt, as many other parents of RTT children do, that her daughter could learn, but research in music therapy had helped to fight for her daughter's rights to learn.

In my PhD study "Enhancing communication in girls with Rett syndrome through songs in music therapy," seven girls with RTT participated for the purpose of finding out whether they have intentional choice making (Elefant 2001, 2002, 2005). The results of this study showed that all seven girls had intentional choice making, with the capacity to learn and to maintain this learning. The findings showed that they have individual song preference and their response time decreases with each experience of choosing songs. What this study showed was that through familiar and unfamiliar songs the girls in the study were showing abilities in a measurable way.

Musical Preference

Individuals with RTT have musical preferences and favorites (Elefant 2002; Elefant and Wigram 2005; Holdsworth 1999; Merker et al. 2001). In a survey by Holdsworth (1999) music is described as a means to a positive mood change if familiar, and negative reactions are sometimes observed to unfamiliar music. When unfamiliar music is introduced diminishing responsiveness is viewed when one compares levels of responsiveness to those found when familiar music is presented.

In the previously mentioned research study (Elefant 2001, 2002; Elefant and Lotan 2004), all seven girls with RTT showed clear song preferences. The girls intentionally chose songs through eye pointing or by touching picture symbols of familiar and unfamiliar songs. In this study I asked each girl to choose between either two to four songs that were represented by picture symbols or orthography. After the intentional choice of a song was made, the song was immediately sung to her. The results indicated that each girl had her own song preference. They preferred familiar songs to unfamiliar ones, which tended to be age appropriate. All the girls who participated in this study preferred songs with faster tempo, with musical elements such as tension and release, rhythmical accents and various vocal plays (Elefant 2001, 2002).

When using songs it is important to consider age appropriate choices, and the cultural, familial and social context. Since the girls in my study were young, I used age appropriate children's songs. The songs were short, repetitive with a clear structure. The songs included musical elements such dynamic and rhythmic changes, sustention, accents, and vocal sounds. These helped in creating tension and release, anticipation and humor in the songs. The girls in the study enjoyed the musical nuances created in the songs and seemed to pay less attention to the songs' content. On the other hand, this seems to be different with teenagers with RTT. I ask several parents of teenagers about their daughters' musical preferences. Many of them I asked indicated that they like to listen to pop or rock music (similarly to their parents), while others at that age seem to prefer musicals such as: *The Sound of Music, My Fair Lady, Mary Poppins, Fiddler on the Roof*, etc. These types of choices could help indicate that the teenagers not only enjoy the music but may also understand the content of the musical.

Music Therapy in Different Settings

Individual music therapy

Individual music therapy sessions can focus and relate to individual needs of a client. These sessions are typically less structured and tend to change according to individual needs at the time of the session. Individuals with RTT have many complex physical issues that contribute to their emotional state and the music therapist can identify the difficulties the girls might undergo and help them understand them by musical interactions. There are times when she comes to the session and cries in grief. The therapist can then put words, supported by musical improvisation, into what she sees and feels is happening. The client will usually connect and relate to the content of songs reflecting her emotions. This can partially fulfill her emotional and communicative needs, helping her to develop vitality and well-being. During such sessions, the therapist tries to help the client to find solutions to or acceptance of some of her difficulties. These types of sessions are usually quite profound for both the therapist and the client. It can also be plain fun and emotionally rewarding and she might express herself by laughing, vocalizing, singing, and dancing.

It is recommended to have music therapy with clients with RTT twice a week, or even more frequently when they are in distress.

Music therapy groups

Individuals with RTT have social need which benefit from interactions that occur in group situations. Group music therapy takes into account interrelationships between individuals in the group. They flourish within such a frame and express their emotions in group music therapy, especially when some of the participants are active and vocal. Because a girl with RTT will benefit from a group situation it is highly recommended to integrate her in a music group with verbal children. The child tends to make contact with other children, observe them, imitate and make progress due to their social interest. They show interest in the music group by smiling, swaying back and forth, moving their legs or wringing their hands to the music's tempo. Group music therapy contains typically musical activities that are structured. All children, whether with RTT or others can benefit from structured activities; they are predictable and give organization, resulting in a feeling of security both on an individual and group basis. The music can function as a containing structure by which the children can connect and build relationships.

The girls I have worked with are usually quite attentive during music groups, but at times when the attention is not directed towards them or when there is only talking in the group, it could be very easy to "lose" them during the group activities, or at least it may seem so as they tend to be passive. It is therefore important that the music therapist stays attuned in order to help them engage during the group activities. They also are non-initiators, but with motivating activities they could be encouraged to initiate.

The therapist needs to give them ample time to respond during the activities as their response time is typically delayed. They can participate in almost all activities, choose a song or a game, play an instrument or move to the music similarly to the other participants; however they almost always need this little extra time. Here is a short vignette that will illustrate this issue:

> During group music therapy with children with developmental disabilities, I walked around with the guitar, greeting each child, inviting the child to strum the guitar while singing the child's name. Most children eagerly waited for their turn and usually managed to strum the guitar with a basic beat. When I approached Hanna, a girl with RTT she smiled, then laughed and swayed her body from side to side. I stopped playing the guitar and waited for Hanna to strum it. Hanna stopped swaying, began hand wringing, hyperventilated, pushed her body forwards, brought her face towards the guitar (almost touching the guitar), lifted up her head, looked at me, smiled, swayed her hand forwards and finally managed to strum the guitar one time. She had a big smile of achievement in her face.

Hanna needed ample time to respond, to plan and then execute the action. She also needed to have trust in the therapist who waited patiently for her response. An additional way of dealing with this type of delayed response (due to apraxia) could be to prolong and to slow down the greeting song, thus giving her enough time to organize herself for the task. This whole process could take up to a few minutes if the child is motivated yet inexperienced. It is not easy for the other children to be kept waiting, but the response time could be reduced after she has had many opportunities and becomes familiar with the activity. Another way to shorten reaction time is to start the greeting song with the child with RTT thereby getting her in an active mode that could sustain for the rest of the session.

Bringing the girls together and forming a group for only individuals with RTT is an important experience. I have visited several family summer holidays in different resorts all over the world where year after year family's of RTT meet as well as in conferences. It is a very moving experience to watch their meetings. They seem to identify with one another by physically touching and emotionally connecting to each other. In such a music therapy group sessions the therapist can identify issues that the girls may be occupied with and aid them in dealing with these issues. It is important to help them realize that they are not "alone" and that there are other people with the same needs. During these types of groups different relevant topics to the girls' emotional needs could be explored. They should be age relevant as well as coincide with topics that occupy normally developed girls. The music therapist could reflect in singing while the girls can respond by vocalization or by the use of Alternative Augmentative Communication (AAC). Song writing is a successful technique for dealing with some of the topics. During these groups a combination of structured and familiar activities and more improvised are recommended. The variety in musical activities can help the group develop as a group but also in taking care of individual needs.

Inclusion through music therapy

Individuals with RTT seek interaction and social attention with other children; this tendency results in children wanting to get closer to them. However, because they lack language, children are not always certain how to approach a child with RTT. In a four year community music inclusion project (Elefant 2010), children with severe developmental disorders, including several girls with RTT were integrated into a regular neighboring elementary school during music activities. The project was initiated for the purpose of making social change in a community in a middle class city in Israel where children with special needs were segregated from the community. Through the development of the music group the children learnt to know and to relate to each other through musical activities as mutual interest. The children without special needs asked many questions concerning some of the difficulties of the children with special needs, but as these were answered and the difficult barriers were lifted they gradually became closer. The children with RTT showed affection and compassion towards the other children.

The project had a positive effect on the children, staff, parents, and the community and lasted for many years. The music project was extended to other activities outside the music room and was moved into extensive integration activities in the community. The girls with RTT who participated in the project became less dependent during the music group activities, they made new friends and were empowered by this experience. The following is an excerpt from the music integration project which can describe the relationships the children had built. It took place towards the end of the project and the elementary school children did not want to terminate the project. They decided to initiate a summer camp for all the children.

> Sharon, Nina, Amy, Abigail and Mira were sitting on the bench in the schoolyard when the cameraman and a reporter from the Israeli Public Television approached them. "We are here to ask you a few questions about your inclusion project. We heard that this group is planning a summer camp. How is it possible that out of all the summer camps there are in this town you chose to initiate one in the special education center?
> Sharon answered: "Most friends go together to summer camps, and now that we have Amy and Mira (and others) as our friends it is only natural that we would spend the summer together." Nina looked at Amy (while holding Amy's hand) and said: "Do you have any idea how much I have learned from this girl?" "How is this possible, she doesn't even talk?" asked the reporter. "We can't even begin to explain this. You won't understand" replied Sharon.
>
> Elefant 2010, p. 87

Through integration we can see that it isn't only individuals with RTT who can benefit from the experience but also the other children. This type of music integration group was a group empowerment.

Conclusion

The purpose of this chapter was to introduce and recognize individual with RTT in a different light and also attempted to convey possibilities of how to engage in music therapy with them. Although RTT is a severe neurological developmental disorder we must remember that there is a sensitive human being beyond the symptoms. They respond emotionally and cognitively to musical interactions which helps them open up and expand new venues for communication and learning.

Individuals with RTT can benefit from individual or group music therapy sessions, however these have different purposes. Group work can be in the form of integration with typically developed children or in groups with people with special needs as well as in groups with only individuals with RTT. Another area that music therapy can be valuable for individuals with RTT and the family is assessment and evaluation through multi-disciplinary team. The Israeli Rett Centre has developed a multi-disciplinary assessment model that consists of educational/therapeutic team (Lotan et al. 2006). In this model the music therapist is leading the assessment while other team members enter the arena as needed. The music and the personal relationship can motivate the girl and help her to bring forth resources that otherwise may be difficult to detect. Her communicative, cognitive, learning, and motor abilities can be brought to higher levels through the accompaniment and the support of the music therapist. This is extremely beneficial when the duration of an assessment is very short.

In the past few years we see more and more males with RTT syndrome. The difference is that they are born quite disabled whereas the girls seem to develop normally until the disorder comes upon them. The few boys that I have met also have the characteristic of deeply communicative eyes. I believe this is an area that more is needed to be done in order to explore the possibilities in music therapy.

Author note: "Silent Angels" was a term first by a mother of a girl Rett syndrome with reference to the beautiful facial features of these children, and their inability to speak. "Silent Angels" has since become a commonly encountered description of individuals with RTT.

References

Amir, R.E., Van den Veyver, I.B., Wan, M., Tran, C.Q., Francke, U., and Zoghbi, H.Y. (1999). Rett syndrome is caused by mutations in X-linked MECP2, encoding methyl-CpG-binding protein 2. *Nature and Genetics* 23(2): 185–188.

Amir, R.E., Van Den Veyve, I.B., Schultz, R., Malicki, D.M., Tran, C.Q., and Dahle, E.J. (2000). Influence of mutation type and X chromosome inactivation on Rett syndrome phenotypes. *Annals of Neurology* 47: 670–679.

Ayres, J.A. (1982). *Sensory Integration and the Child*, 5th ed. Los Angeles: Western Psychological Services.

Berger-Sweeney, J. (2011). Cognitive deficits in Rett syndrome: What we know and what we need to know to treat them. *Neurobiology of Learning and Memory* 96: 637–646.

Burford, B. (2005). Perturbations in the development of infants with Rett disorder and the implications for early diagnosis. *Brain & Development* 27(Suppl. 1): S3–S7.

Burford, B. and Trevarthen, C. (1997). Evoking communication in Rett syndrome: Comparisons with conversations and games in mother-infant interaction. *European Child Adolescents Psychiatry* 6(Suppl. 1): 26–30.

Coleman, M., Brubaker, J., Hunter, K., and Smith, G. (1988). Rett syndrome: a survey of North American patients. *Journal of Mental Deficiency Research* 32: 117–124.

Clark, P.N. and Allen, A.S. (1985). *Occupational Therapy for Children*. St Louis, MO: CV Mosby.

Downs, J., Parkinson, S., Ranell, S., Leonard, H., Diener, P., and Lotan, M. (2013). Perspectives on hand function in girls and women with Rett Syndrome. *Developmental Neurorehabilitation* 1–8, Early Online.

Ellaway, C. and Christodoulou, J. (2001). Rett syndrome: clinical characteristics and recent genetic advances. *Disability and Rehabilitation* 23: 98–106.

Einspieler, C., Kerr, A.M., and Prechtl, H.F. (2005). "Abnormal general movements in girls with Rett disorder: the first four months of life." *Brain & Development* 27(Suppl. 1): S8–S13.

Elefant, C. (2001). Speechless yet Communicative: Revealing the Person behind the Disability of Rett Syndrome through Clinical Research on Songs in Music Therapy. In: D. Aldridge; G. Di Franco; E. Ruud, and T. Wigram (eds), *Music Therapy in Europe*, pp. 113–28. Rome: ISMEZ.

Elefant, C. (2002). *Enhancing communication in girls with Rett syndrome though songs in music therapy*. Unpublished PhD Thesis. Aalborg University, Aalborg, Denmark.

Elefant, C. (2005). The use of single case designs in testing a specific hypothesis. In: D. Aldridge (ed.), *Case Study Designs in Music Therapy*, pp. 145–162. London: Jessica Kingsley.

Elefant, C. (2009). Rett syndrome and music therapy. *International Journal of Disability and Human Development* 8(4): 359–368.

Elefant, C. (2010). Musical Inclusion, Intergroup Relations, and Community Development. In: B. Stige, G. Ansdell, C. Elefant, and M. Pavlicevic (eds), *Where Music Helps. Community Music Therapy in Action and Reflection*, pp. 65–90. Aldershot, UK: Ashgate.

Elefant, C. (2011). Music Therapy and Rett Syndrome: Unveiling Resources in Persons with Rett Syndrome. In: A. Meadows (ed.), *Developments in Music Therapy Practice: Case Study Perspectives*, pp. 86–103. Gilsum, NH: Barcelona Publishers.

Elefant, C. and Lotan, M. (2004). Rett Syndrome: Dual Intervention—Music and Physical Therapy. *Nordic Journal of Music Therapy* 13(2): 172–182.

Elefant, C. and Wigram, T. (2005). Learning ability in children with Rett syndrome. *Journal of Brain & Development* 27: 97–101.

Engerstrom, I.W. and Kerr, A. (1998). Workshop on autonomic function in Rett Syndrome, Swedish Rett center, Frösön, Sweden. *Brain and Development* 20: 323–326.

Fisher, A.G., Murray. E.A., and Bundy A.C. (1991). *Sensory Integration Theory and Practice*. Philadelphia, PA: FA Davis Company.

Fombonne, E., Simmons, H., Ford, T., Meltzer, H., and Goodman, R. (2003). Prevalence of pervasive developmental disorders in the British nationwide survey of child mental health. *International Reviews of Psychiatry* 15(1–2): 158–165.

Hagberg, B. (1993). *Rett Syndrome: Clinical and Biological Aspects*. London: Mac Keith Press.

Hagberg, B. (1995). Rett syndrome: clinical peculiarities and biological mysteries. *Acta Paediatrica* 84: 971–976.

Hagberg, B. and Hagberg, G. (1997). Rett syndrome: epidemiology and geographical variability. *European Child and Adolescents Psychiatry* 1: 5–7.

Hagberg, B., Hanefield, F., Percy, A., and Skjeldal, O. (2001). An update on clinically applicable diagnostic criteria in Rett syndrome. Comments to Rett Syndrome Clinical Criteria Consensus Panel Satellite to European Paediatric Neurology Society Meeting, Baden Baden, Germany, 11 September 2001. *European Journal of Paediatric Neurology* 6: 293–297.

Hill, S.A. (1997). The relevance and value of music therapy for children with Rett syndrome. *British Journal of Special Education* 24(3): 124–128.

Holck, U. (2002). "Kommunikalsk" Samspil i Musikterapi ["Commusical" Interplay in Music Therapy. Qualitative Video Analyses of Musical and Gestural Interactions with Children with Severe Functional Limitations, including Children with Autism]. Unpublished PhD thesis, Aalborg University.

Holdsworth, J. (1999). *Responsiveness to music in 21 girls and women with Rett syndrome*. Unpublished paper, Department of Psychology, University of Hull.

Kerr, A. and Witt Engerström, I. (eds). (2001). *Rett Disorder and the Developing Brain*, Oxford: Oxford University Press.

Leonard, H., Bower, C., and English, D. (1997). The prevalence and incidence of Rett syndrome in Australia. *European Child and Adolescents Psychiatry* 1: 8–10.

Lindberg, B. (2006). *Understanding Rett Syndrome: A Practice Guide for Parents, Teachers and Therapists*, 2nd rev. ed. Toronto: Hogrefe Huber.

Lotan, M. (2006). *Management for Rett syndrome*. Tel Aviv, IL: Rotem Pubisher. [Hebrew].

Lotan, M. (Nov. 2008). *The time is now—appropriate therapeutic intervention for individuals with Rett Syndrome*. Key note presentation: National Conference of the Irish Rett Syndrome Association. Limerick, Ireland.

Lotan, M., Manor-Binyamini, I., Elefant, C., Wine, J., Saraf, E., and Yoshei, T. (2006). The Israeli Rett Syndrome Center. Evaluation and transdisciplinary play-based assessment. *Scientific World Journal* 6: 1302–1313.

Malloch, S.N. (1999). Mother and infants and communicative musicality. In: Rhythms, musical narrative, and the origins of human communication. *Musicae Scientiae*, Special Issue, 1999–2000, pp. 29–57. LiÃ¨ge: European Society for the Cognitive Sciences of Music.

Malloch, S. and Trevarthen, C. (eds). (2009). *Communicative musicality: Exploring the Basis of Human Companionship*. Oxford: Oxford University Press.

Merker, B., Bergstrom-Isacsson, M., and Witt Engerstrom, I. (2001). Music and the Rett disorder: The Swedish Rett Center survey. *Nordic Journal of Music Therapy* 10(1): 42–53.

Naidu, S. (2000). Research Findings on Rett Syndrome. IRSA Annual Conference, May, Las Vegas, Nevada.

Neul, J.L. and Zoghbi, H.Y. (2004). Rett syndrome: a prototypical neurodevelopmental disorder. *Neuroscientist* 10(2): 118–128.

Pini, G., Milan, M. and Loppella, M. (1996). Rett syndrome in northern Tuscany (Italy): family tree studies. *Clinical Genetics* 50: 486–490.

Rett, A. (1966). Uber ein eigartiges hirnatrophisches Syndrom bei Hyperammoniamie in Kindesalter. *Wien Med Wochenschr* 116: 723–738.

Rose, S.A., Djukic, A., Jankowski, J.J., Feldman, J.F., Fishman, I., and Valicenti-Mcdermott, M. (2013). Rett syndrome: an eye-tracking study of attention and recognition memory. *Developmental Medicine & Child Neurology* 55(4): 364–371.

Schults, R.R., Glaze, D.G., Motil, K.J., Armstrong, D.D., Del-Junco, D.J., Hubbard, C.R. (2001). Rett syndrome in a boy with a 47, XXY karyotype confirmed by a rare mutation in the MECP2 gene. *Neuropediatrics* 32: 162–164.

Skesedel, O.H., Von-Tetzchner, S., Aspelund, F., Herder, G.A., and Lofterld, B. (1997). Rett syndrome: geographic variation in prevalence in Norway. *Brain and Development* 19: 258–261.

Stern, D.N. (1985/2000). *The Interpersonal World of the Infant*. New York: Basic Books.

Trevarthen, C. and Burford, B. (2001). Early communication and the Rett disorder. In: A. Kerr and I. Witt Engerström, (eds), *Rett Disorder and the Developing Brain*, pp. 303–326. Oxford: Oxford University Press.

Trevarthen, C. and Malloch, S. (2002). Musicality and music before three: Human vitality and invention shared with pride. *Zero to Three* 25(1): 10–18.

Trevethan, E. and Moser, H. (1998). Diagnostic criteria for Rett syndrome. The Rett Syndrome Diagnostic Criteria Work Group. *Annals Neurology* 23: 425–428.

Wigram, T. (1991). Music therapy for a girl with Rett's syndrome: Balancing structure and freedom. In: K. Bruscia, (ed.), *Case Studies in Music Therapy*, pp. 39–55. Gilsum, NH: Barcelona Publisher.

Wigram, T. and Cass, H. (1996). Music therapy within the assessment process for a therapy clinic for people with Rett syndrome. Paper presented at the Rett Syndrome World Conference in Sweden.

Wigram, T. and Elefant, C. (2009). Therapeutic dialogues in music: Nurturing musicality of communication in children with autistic spectrum disorder and Rett syndrome. In: S. Malloch and C. Trevarthen (eds), *Communicative Musicality: Exploring the Basis of Human Companionship*, pp. 423–445. Oxford: Oxford University Press.

CHAPTER 12

MUSIC THERAPY FOR CHILDREN AND ADULTS WHO ARE DEAF OR HARD OF HEARING

KATE E. GFELLER

HISTORICAL PRECEDENCE

As music is primarily an auditory art form, it is easy to assume that it is an inappropriate therapeutic medium for persons with hearing losses. However, advocacy of music for the deaf appeared in print as early as 1848 (Darrow and Heller 1985). William Wolcott Turner and David Ely Bartlett, who were teachers in the first US school for the deaf, stated that expressive qualities of music could be perceived through the senses of sight and touch (Turner and Bartlett 1848). Since that time, a growing body of clinical resources in many countries has recommended singing, playing instruments, movement, and listening exercises for improving language development, speech production, auditory acuity, socialization, and the development of musicality (e.g. Amir and Schuchman 1985; Bang 1971, 1980; Darrow and Cohen 1991; Darrow et al. 2000; Darrow and Starmer 1986; Edwards 1974; Epley 1972; Fahey and Birkenshaw 1972; Flanders 1928; Ford 1985; Galloway and Bean 1974; Gfeller 1987, 2000, 2001, 2007; Gfeller and Darrow 1987, 2008; Hsiao and Gfeller 2011; Hummel 1971; Jordan 1900; McDermott 1971; Riordan 1971; Robbins and Robbins 1980; Sheldon 1997; Stern 1975; Thornton 1926; Vettese 1974; Wecker 1939). Therapeutic uses of music have been refined by research documenting the variability among this population with regard to music perception and appreciation as a function of auditory profile and other influential factors (e.g. Darrow 1979, 1990a,b, 1984, 1987, 2006; Darrow and Novak 2007; Darrow and Starmer 1986; Edmonds 1984; Epley 1972; Fahey and Birkenshaw 1972; Ford 1985; Gfeller 1986, 2007; Gfeller and Darrow 2008; Hsiao and Gfeller, 2012; Klajman et al. 1982; Korduba 1975; Madsen and Mears 1965; Raleigh and Odom 1972; Stern 1975). Because goals and musical materials chosen for music therapy should take into account a client's auditory profile, the following sections provide foundational information regarding hearing, particularly in relation to musical and speech sounds.[1]

SOUND ENERGY AND HEARING

Acoustic properties of musical and speech sounds

Sound sources such as the human speaking or singing voice, musical instruments, and sound equipment, such as stereos, or iPods, vibrate and create sound waves that travel through mediums such as air, water, or solids (e.g. metal) (Gfeller and Darrow 2008). Musical and speech sounds are largely quasi-periodic auditory signals in which frequency, timbral, temporal, and intensity components are presented in an organized manner (Looi 2008).

Frequency. The term frequency describes the number of cycles per second at which a sound source (voice, instrument, etc.) is vibrating. The unit of measurement for frequency is called Hertz (abbreviated as Hz, e.g. 440 Hz.). If a sound source vibrates slowly, it produces a low-frequency sound (e.g. 20 Hz); quick vibrations result in high-frequency sounds (e.g. 10,000 Hz). The term *pitch* is used to describe the *perception* of frequency—that is, how high or low it sounds to the listener (Gillam et al. 2000; Gfeller and Darrow 2008).

Human beings with a healthy hearing mechanism are able to hear sounds ranging from approximately 20 to 20,000 Hz. Though human speech generates sounds as low as 50 Hz and upwards of 8000 Hz, the majority of energy for human speech falls between approximately 300 and 3400 Hz. The fundamental frequencies produced by musical instruments range from a lower limit of 20 Hz to an upper limit of about 7000 Hz. However, the harmonics (see Timbre, below), associated with these complex tones extend the range further still (see Figure 12.1).

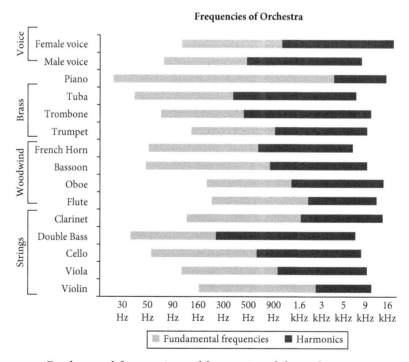

FIGURE 12.1 Fundamental frequencies and harmonics of the orchestra.

Timbre. Most spoken and musical sounds in everyday life are complex tones, which are composites of simultaneous sounds called harmonics (Gillam et al. 2000). A complex tone includes the fundamental frequency, which is the first harmonic, plus whole-number multiples of the fundamental. Timbre, often called tone quality, is "that attribute of auditory sensation in terms of which a listener can judge that two sounds similarly presented and having the same loudness and pitch are dissimilar" (Acoustical Society of America 1960). The distribution of acoustic energy in the harmonics at the onset, steady state, and decay of each sound wave contribute to the distinctive tone quality (e.g. nasal, breathy, brilliant, hollow, etc.) of a given voice or instrument.

Temporal and intensity (amplitude) characteristics. Speech and musical sounds are also characterized by the temporal (durational) elements of sound. Accurate perception of rapidly changing temporal fluctuations in the amplitude envelope of speech conveys much of the linguistic meaning (Shannon et al. 1995; Zatorre et al. 2002). In music, temporal fluctuations can occur in at least two distinct time scales. Rapid fluctuations (in the order of milliseconds) contribute to the perception of timbre in the form of the attack, decay, sustain and release times and the tremolo of individual notes. Longer time-scale fluctuations (from hundreds of milliseconds to tens of seconds), contribute to what the listener perceives as rhythm and tempo.

Intensity (amplitude) (measured in decibels, dB), is perceived by the listener as loudness. In spoken communication, the amplitude of a whisper is around 20 dB while conversational speech is around 50 to 60 dB (Gillam et al. 2000). The intensity of music can vary enormously, from sounds that are barely audible, to large orchestral or electronic sounds that measure 120 dB or louder. Figure 12.2 illustrates the amplitude as well as frequency range of a

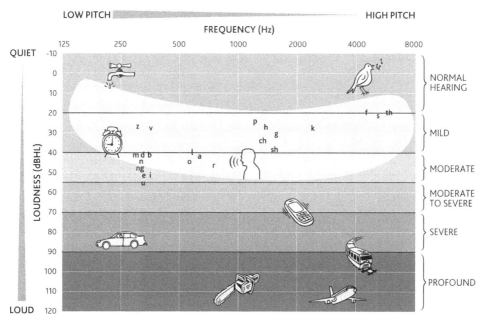

FIGURE 12.2 Audiogram of environmental and speech sounds. Printed with permission from Cochlear Corporation.

number of speech, musical, and environmental sounds in relation to different levels of hearing acuity.

THE HEARING MECHANISM

Figure 12.3 illustrates the parts of the human ear. The ear is made up of three primary parts: The outer, middle, and inner ear. Sound waves are collected and encoded in different parts of the ear. The outer ear, which includes the pinna (ear lobe), funnels sound waves into the ear canal. The mechanical energy of the sound wave is transmitted to the middle ear, which includes the tympanic membrane and ossicles. These ossicles act as levers to conduct the mechanical energy to the cochlea, which is part of the inner ear. The cochlea houses a gelatinous fluid and the basilar membrane, which holds in place thousands of fine hair cells known as cilia. Mechanical energy transmitted from the middle ear moves across the cilia. As these hair cells are stimulated, the mechanical energy is converted to electrochemical energy. This energy is sent via the auditory nerve to the brain, where the sound is processed and interpreted (Gillam et al. 2000; Gfeller and Darrow 2008).

Complex combinations of pitch, timbre, duration, and intensity are analyzed and encoded with remarkable speed and sensitivity by the healthy hearing mechanism. Disease, anatomical anomalies, or malfunction can impair hearing at any point along this auditory pathway, and thus affect perceptual acuity and quality of sound that an individual hears (American Speech-Language-Hearing Association 2011; Gillam et al. 2000). Different terms used to describe the anatomical origins of different types of hearing losses are described below.

Diagram of the Ear

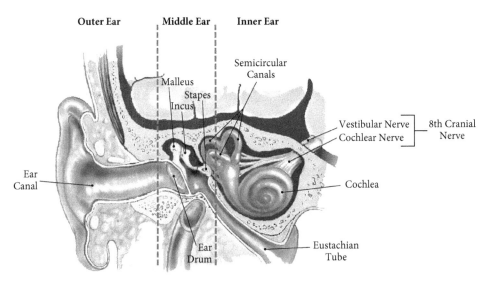

FIGURE 12.3 Parts of the ear. Printed with permission from the American Speech-Language Hearing Association.

Hearing losses

Types of hearing loss

A conductive hearing loss. This is caused by disease, malformation, or obstruction in the outer or middle ear, which impedes transmission of mechanical sound energy. Conductive hearing losses often impair hearing acuity across a wide range of frequencies (American Speech-Language-Hearing Association 2011; Gillam et al. 2000; Gfeller and Darrow 2008). Devices such as hearing aids (see below) that amplify sounds are often helpful for this type of loss.

A sensorineural hearing loss. This is the result of damage to or absence of the delicate hair cells of the inner ear. This impedes conversion of sound waves from mechanical to electrochemical energy. The extent of damage at various locations within the inner ear influences perceptual accuracy for difference frequencies (see section below on Configuration of hearing loss). Persons with more severe sensorineural losses receive less benefit from conventional hearing aids, and may qualify for an auditory prosthesis called a cochlear implant, (see below). A mixed hearing loss is a combination of conductive and sensorineural losses in one ear (American Speech-Language-Hearing Association 2011; Gillam et al. 2000; Gfeller and Darrow 2008).

A central hearing loss. This involves damage or impairment to the central nervous system. Interventions for this type of loss, which interferes with understanding the sound signal, is more closely related to neurological disorders than hearing loss, and is beyond the scope of this chapter.

Degree of hearing loss

Hearing losses vary in degree or severity, as well as in the type and cause. The continuum of severity is described as slight, mild, moderate, severe, and profound (American Speech-Language-Hearing Association 2011; Gfeller and Darrow 2008). At one end of the continuum, people with slight hearing losses may have difficulty hearing very quiet or distant speech or music; in contrast, people with profound losses can hear only very loud sounds and have considerable difficulty hearing normal conversational speech. The impact of degree of hearing loss in relation to different speech, musical, and environmental sounds is illustrated in Figure 12.2. With a profound loss, sounds may be experienced as a tactile (vibration) sensation rather than having distinct pitch or timbre. Profound or total deafness is rare. Instead, usually people with hearing loss have some usable hearing, called residual hearing. In general, the greater the severity of loss, the greater the impact on spoken communication and music perception, and the greater the need for some form of (re)habilitation (Davis and Hardick 1981; Gillam et al. 2000; Gfeller and Darrow 2008).

People with less severe losses who retain more residual hearing can perceive and enjoy the pitch and timbre components of music more easily than those persons with severe or profound hearing losses, especially with sufficient sound intensity (loudness) (Darrow 1979,

1984, 1987). Though large pitch changes are more easily perceived than small changes (i.e. stepwise changes such as C to D), some children with severe hearing losses have been trained to recognize pitch changes as small as a minor third (Ford 1985). Research indicates that persons with hearing losses can perform at least as effectively or more so than normal-hearing persons on some types of rhythmic tasks (e.g. imitating a beat), especially if tactile or visual cues are available (Darrow 1979, 1984, 1987; Gfeller et al. 2008).

Configuration of hearing loss

According to the American Speech-Language Hearing Association, "configuration or shape of a hearing loss refers to the extent of hearing loss at each frequency and the overall profile of hearing that results" (American Speech-Language-Hearing Association [ASHA] 2008).). For example, many people with sensorineural losses have more residual (usable) hearing for lower pitches than for higher pitches. A person with more low-frequency hearing would hear male talkers more easily than female talkers; low-frequency instrumental sounds (i.e. trombone or contrabassoon) would be easier to hear than high pitched instruments (e.g. flute, violin).

Other hearing problems related to configuration include the course of the loss over time (e.g. sudden onset, progressive, stable, fluctuating) and unilateral (one ear) or bilateral (both ears) losses. Because localization of the origin of a sound source requires the use of both ears, localization would be an unsuitable therapy goal for an individual who has unilateral hearing (Gfeller and Darrow 2008).

Onset of hearing loss

Hearing loss is also categorized by onset, or when the hearing loss first occurred. A pre-lingual loss occurs before the acquisition of spoken language (approximately 0–2 years of age), a peri-lingual loss occurs as spoken language is developing (approximately 2–4 years), and a post-lingual loss occurs after the acquisition of language (approximately age 4 and up). Losses that occur before the acquisition of speech and language have a greater impact on the development of oral communication (Davis and Hardick 1981; Gfeller and Darrow 2008).

When a child is deprived of auditory stimulation such as speech, music, or environmental sounds, as a result of pre- or peri-lingual hearing loss, this deprivation has a negative impact on the neural development of the entire auditory system (Boothroyd 2010; Ryugo and Limb 2009). When hearing is lost well into adulthood, the auditory system will already have developed responses to auditory stimulation up to the point of significant hearing loss; thus, post-lingually-deafened adults have established neural connections for perceiving and deriving meaning from spoken or musical sounds. Consequently, the listener will have a mental representation (memory) for speech and musical sounds, which can provide contextual cues during listening. However, the strength of auditory neural connections of adults with hearing loss will eventually decay due to sensory deprivation unless sufficient stimulation is restored through an intervention such as medical treatment, hearing aids, or cochlear implants.

Differences in auditory development in relation to onset of hearing loss have important implications for prioritization of therapy goals. Music therapy goals for post-lingually deaf adults are typically quite different from those suitable for pre and peri-lingually deaf children.

Overall auditory profile

The interaction of type, degree, configuration, and onset of hearing loss results in an auditory profile that impacts functionality. For example, a person with a moderate post-lingual conductive hearing loss may function quite well with hearing aids and only a few minor lifestyle changes (e.g. closed captioning on TV). In contrast, a pre-lingual profound loss will likely require habilitation, alternative modes of communication, or possibly acoustic prosthetics (e.g. cochlear implants), in order to function effectively in hearing society. The following section describes some of the most common types of hearing devices, and outlines their effectiveness in conveying spoken and musical sounds.

HEARING DEVICES

Hearing aids and cochlear implants are two forms of hearing devices commonly used by persons who are deaf or hard of hearing. The following sections describe each device, and their effectiveness in conveying spoken and musical sounds.

Hearing aids

Personal hearing aids, which are usually worn within the ear canal, do not cure hearing losses. Rather, they aid sound detection by making some incoming sounds louder (amplification). In comparison with speech, musical sounds are made up of more variable and rapidly fluctuating frequencies, timbres, and intensities. These rapidly changing acoustical parameters are problematic for hearing aid technology (Chasin and Russo 2004), consequently, hearing aids are technically better suited for speech than for music. Many hearing aid users report that music has an unnatural or distorted sound quality through hearing aids (Franks 1982; Chasin and Russo 2004; Gabrielsson and Sjögren 1979).

Hearing aids are most helpful for people who have slight to moderate conductive losses. Persons with more severe sensorineural losses may receive partial or minimal benefit from hearing aids; some experience distortion in sound quality, especially with loud or complex sounds. Further, persons with more severe losses may have difficulty perceiving small pitch changes or subtleties of timbre, even in their best aided condition (Looi et al. 2008; Gfeller and Darrow 2008).

Cochlear implants

The Cochlear implant (CI) is a prosthetic hearing device for persons with severe to profound hearing losses who receive little benefit from conventional hearing aids. CIs are

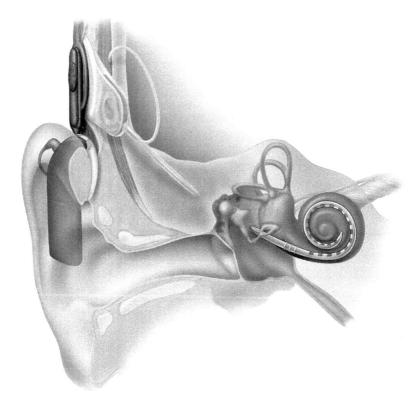

FIGURE 12.4 Diagram and parts of a cochlear implant. Printed with permission from Cochlear Corporation.

surgically implanted in the cochlea. Rather than amplifying sound (as occurs with a hearing aid), sound waves are picked up by a microphone worn at ear level and converted by a small externally-worn processor to an electrical signal. The electrical signal is transmitted to a small electrode array implanted in the cochlea, which stimulates the auditory nerve. The signal travels via the auditory nerve to the brain, where sound is interpreted for meaning (Wilson 2000; Looi 2008). Figure 12.4 illustrates the components of a cochlear implant in relation to the anatomy of the human ear.

A cochlear implant does not cure deafness, nor does it transmit a replica of sound as heard through normal hearing. Rather, the implant extracts and transmits specific parts of the auditory signal considered salient to speech perception. Some CI users enjoy greater benefit than others, depending upon various factors (e.g. age when implanted, etiology, etc.). However, most CI recipients find the CI quite helpful in understanding speech, especially in quiet listening environments (Wilson 2000).

CIs are less effective in conveying musical sounds. While most implant recipients are able to perceive longer time-scale temporal features of music (e.g. rhythm patterns, beat) with relative accuracy, many implant recipients have poor perception of pitch, melody and timbre. Many describe the timbre (tone quality) of music as sounding mechanical, harsh, or noisy (Galvin et al. 2007; Gfeller et al. 2000; Gfeller et al. 2008; Gfeller et al. 2007; Gfeller et al. 2002b; Gfeller et al. 2001b; Hsiao 2008; Hsiao and Gfeller 2012; McDermott 2004). CI recipients are clearly different from normal-hearing people when it comes to music perception and enjoyment. Interestingly, there is also considerable difference from one CI recipient to the next when it comes to music perception and enjoyment. Some implant recipients find music unpleasant to hear, while others enjoy listening to or making music (Gfeller et al. 2000a,2000b; Hsiao and Gfeller 2012).

The manufacturers of cochlear implants are making efforts to improve the technical features of the CI. Hopefully, future implants may provide a more satisfactory quality of sound for music listening (Gfeller 2007). In the meantime, some CI recipients have improved their music perception and enjoyment as a result of focused music training (e.g. Chen et al. 2010; Driscoll et al. 2009; Gfeller et al. 2002a; Gfeller et al. 2001a; Gfeller et al. 2001b; Gfeller et al. 2007; Hsiao and Gfeller 2011; Limb and Rubinstein 2012; McDermott 2004).

The technical limitations of the CI with regard to music perception and enjoyment have several implications for music therapy. On one hand, some CI recipients may find musical sounds unpleasant or less enjoyable than they did prior to acquiring a hearing loss. In such cases, these individuals may no longer find music a meaningful or motivating art form in everyday life or in music therapy for conditions not related to their hearing loss (e.g. music therapy as part of physical rehabilitation or pain management). However, music therapy may be helpful to CI recipients who would like to improve music perception and enjoyment through auditory training (Driscoll et al. 2009; Gfeller 2001a; Gfeller et al. 2001b).

In summary, because hearing aids and cochlear implants convey a sub-par or degraded representation of music, music therapists will need to take into account the type of prosthetic device in selecting music materials and prioritizing therapy goals. Music therapy approaches can also be beneficial in a therapy process called auditory training, (see below), which may help some persons to attain optimal benefit from the auditory signal they receive. The auditory profile (including benefit of hearing devices) of different clients influences not only perception of speech and music, but also the client's mode of communication, which is the focus of the following section.

MODES OF COMMUNICATION

People with hearing losses vary in their mode of communication. Some rely on spoken communication (oral), some rely on sign language (manual communication), while others use a combination of oral and manual communication. The combined impact of type, severity, onset of hearing loss, and benefit of hearing aid/CI is likely to influence an individual's choice of communication mode. For example, people with mild losses and greater residual hearing can generally communicate by speaking and speechreading (often referred to informally as lipreading) in conjunction with careful listening. This is known as an oral communication system.

Some people with more severe losses (especially those with early onset) who receive limited benefits from hearing aids or cochlear implants may have great difficulty forming clear, intelligible speech sounds, or understanding other people's verbal communication. Some of these individuals prefer to communicate manually. A manual approach includes the use of signs (symbolic representations of language made with the hands) and fingerspelling (hand shapes corresponding to the letters of the written alphabet). Some forms of manual com-munication are independent languages with a community of users (e.g. American Sign Language, British Sign Language, French Sign Language). Other manual approaches are sign systems in which the vocabulary and syntax from a spoken language is displayed through hand gestures (e.g. Signed English).

Historically, mode of communication has been the topic of considerable dissention and debate (Armstrong 1999; Baynton 1996; Gfeller and Darrow 2008; Marschark 2007). Factors besides the degree of hearing loss influence the preferred mode of communication, includ-ing philosophies of those personnel serving a child, community, regional or national mores or policies, and the family's form of communication. For example, a child with only a mild loss may be capable of oral communication but may elect to use manual communication if his parents, siblings, and extended family use sign language.

A client's chosen mode of communication is an important consideration in facilitating a music therapy session (e.g. establishing rapport, delivering instructions, conveying vocabu-lary, etc.). The music therapist should ascertain from the treatment team, family members, or client records the most appropriate mode of communication for therapy sessions (Gfeller and Darrow 2008). If manual communication is used, and the music therapist cannot com-municate fluently (both receptively and expressively) in sign, an interpreter should accom-pany the client to all music therapy sessions.

As the information in this chapter indicates, there is no singular profile that character-izes people who are deaf or hard of hearing. Individuals vary with regard to their audiologi-cal profile as well as chosen mode of communication. These and other societal policies and beliefs contribute to the use of different terms used to describe this population, which are discussed in the following section.

TERMS CONVEYING AUDITORY STATUS
AND CULTURAL AFFILIATION

A number of different terms have been and continue to be used in describing persons with hearing losses (Hardman et al. 2002; Heward 2003, Turnbull et al. 2001). Some terms reflect primarily auditory status. For example, individuals who are described as hard-of-hearing generally respond to speech and other auditory sounds through the use of their resid-ual hearing or hearing devices. Their primary and preferred mode of communication is speech. Individuals who are deaf and do not have sufficient hearing (residual or through prosthetic devices) necessary to process speech are more likely to use some form of manual communication.

Other terms associated with hearing loss may reflect educational or regulatory policies of a given country. For example, in the United States, the term, "hearing impairment," is used in regulatory language related to the provision of special education services. Hearing impair-ment is a general term that describes all hearing losses, regardless of type, severity, classifica-tion, or onset. This term is also used commonly by hearing people in everyday conversations when they discuss hearing losses (Darrow 2005; Gfeller and Darrow 2008).

From a cultural perspective, there are individuals who find the term *hearing impaired* offensive because they believe the word *impaired* implies "broken" or "defective." The use of upper case "D" for the word, Deaf, suggests cultural affiliation with a linguistic minority within the hearing world, as opposed to auditory status (Darrow 1993; Padden and Humphries 1988; Padden 1996). Persons with strong affiliation to Deaf culture are likely to consider oral communication and auditory experiences (including music) of lesser personal priority; sign language is their primary language. Some Deaf individuals reject music as a hearing value and find no use for it in their lives (Darrow 1993).

Given the variability in the deaf and hard of hearing population with regard to auditory status and cultural values, music therapists should determine individual attitudes regarding usage of these terms as well as attitudes toward music therapy. For example, some culturally Deaf individuals may have less interest in social uses of music than is typical among hearing persons (Darrow 1993, 2006; Darrow and Loomis 1999) and therapy goals of enhanced hearing and spoken communication may be a low personal priority.

Keeping in mind that there is no singular profile that characterizes the functional abilities and attitudes of persons who are deaf or hard of hearing, there are, nevertheless, some commonly-observed problems associated with significant hearing losses. The following section outlines problems associated with early onset, and then difficulties associated with onset well into adulthood.

PROBLEMS ASSOCIATED WITH HEARING LOSS

Losses in childhood (pre- and peri-lingual losses)

Unless a hearing loss exists in conjunction with other disabilities or health problems, the primary problem associated with pre- or peri-lingual hearing loss is in the development of spoken and written forms of language. The term, language refers to a standardized set of symbols and conventions for combining symbols into words, phrases, sentences, and texts in order to communicate thoughts and feelings (Gillam et al. 2000). Language is usually conveyed in a spoken or written form. The earlier the onset and the more severe the loss, the greater the impact on oral (spoken) and written communication (Gfeller and Darrow 2008).

Children with severe hearing losses may have speech with an improper pitch level (i.e. too high or low for age and gender), omitted or improperly formed speech, unusual prosody (inflection and rhythm) and less intelligible speech. Children who miss out on robust models of their native language in everyday life are likely to experience delays in language development, including spoken language (limited and poor speech quality), internal language (the mental processes associated with language), slow or reduced acquisition of vocabulary and syntax, and written forms.[2] Direct instruction is typically necessary in order for children with significant hearing losses to acquire competence in spoken and written language. Problems with speech and language also have a negative impact on academic skills that require reading, writing, or verbal communication (e.g. history, literature, etc.) and on spoken communication and socialization (Davis and Hardick 1981; Meadow 1980a).

Music therapists contribute to the habilitation of children with significant hearing losses in four primary goal areas: (1) Language development, (2) speech production, (3) auditory training, and (4) social skill attainment (Darrow et al. 2000; Gfeller and Darrow 2008; Schum and Gfeller 1994). These goal areas are likely to be the focus during the preschool, elementary, or middle school years. As the child enters adolescence and young adulthood, the music therapist may begin to emphasize the social and emotional aspects of music, such as participation in music ensembles as a leisure-time activity and art form.

Children who receive habilitation as part of their educational services may receive music therapy as part of an individual education plan. Some children may receive music therapy services as part of early childhood programs or in conjunction with community-based clinical programs. Therapy goals should be coordinated with those selected by the child's speech and language therapy professional and audiologist.

Hearing loss acquired in adulthood

Adults with acquired hearing losses have typically grown up using oral communication, and thus, will not require direct habilitation for speech and language. They are also less likely to have a strong affiliation with Deaf culture. The primary problem for post-lingually deaf persons is understanding the spoken communication of others, especially in noisy listening environments.

This can result in social isolation (i.e. difficulty understanding others in conversation, etc.), vocational disabilities (i.e. understanding the instructions of supervisors, etc.), depression in relation to social competency, and loss of enjoyable entertainment and cultural enrichment (i.e. difficulty hearing concerts, etc.), all which result in reduced quality of life. For individuals who derive considerable pleasure from music listening or participation, a significant hearing loss can result in the loss of a valued source of personal enjoyment (Gfeller et al. 2000a).

For persons who affiliate with hearing culture, adjusting to the loss of sensory input, and optimizing the benefits of hearing devices may require counseling or rehabilitation. Adults with acquired hearing loss are less likely to seek or be referred for formal rehabilitation. However, the psychosocial problems accompanying adult-onset hearing loss are well documented (Gfeller et al. 2000a; Gfeller and Darrow 2008), and some adults may benefit from participation in social-support groups or rehabilitative audiology in order to learn coping strategies. Recently, there has been increasing documentation that structured auditory training programs can also optimize the benefits of hearing aids and cochlear implants (Gfeller 2001; Gfeller et al. 2001b; Looi and She 2010). Music therapists can contribute to training and support programs for adults, usually as a consultant to a support group or through clinical research programs utilizing training programs for speech and music. Taking into account typical problems associated with hearing loss in childhood or adulthood, the following section describes music therapy goals most typical for children and for adults.

MUSIC THERAPY WITH PERSONS WHO HAVE HEARING LOSSES

Selection of appropriate music therapy goals for each client will be influenced by the following interactive factors: Chronological and developmental age, age of onset, auditory profile (type, severity, configuration of loss), hearing devices (if used), mode of communication, and educational, social, and cultural values and demands (see Figure 12.5). Therapy that focuses on the initial development of skills is referred to as habilitation. Children with pre- and peri-lingual onset will typically require habilitation in order to develop language, speech, and auditory skills. Music therapy for habilitation is likely to take place in an educational setting or clinical program, and may be considered a part of the individual education plan or treatment plan, depending upon the local procedural requirements for referral and treatment implementation.

Therapy designed to re-establish skills, as in auditory training for adults, is referred to as rehabilitation. Persons with onset of hearing loss well into adulthood have already developed speech, language, and auditory skills, and have to re-establish functional skills and social integration. An adult may be self-referring, or utilize music therapy as part of a more

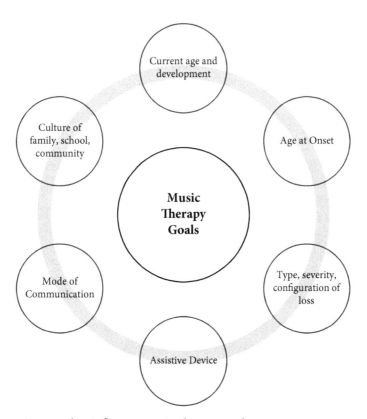

FIGURE 12.5 Factors that influence music therapy goals.

comprehensive rehabilitation program. The following section focuses on common music therapy goals and examples of interventions and accommodations that can support an effective music therapy session.

Common music therapy goals and interventions

Goals related to language and speech development

Language development

Language development goals in music therapy typically focus on one or more of the following: (1) Increased and appropriate use of vocabulary, (2) increased spontaneous or topic-related interaction, (3) sentence structure, (4) more sophisticated language structures and usage (e.g. metaphors, figures of speech, etc.), and (5) pragmatics, which concerns the use of language its use with a social context (Darrow et al. 2000; Gfeller 1990; Gfeller and Baumann 1988; Gfeller and Darrow 2008; Gfeller et al. 2011). Goals and objectives should reflect the language goals established by the speech-language pathologist, who has in-depth professional training regarding language development.

The lyrics of songs can be selected or revised to introduce and practice target vocabulary words and syntax. For example, many preschool songs are filled with vocabulary such as numbers, colors, animals, and other words that children need to learn (Gfeller 1990; Gfeller et al. 2011). As children mature, they will need to learn more complex and symbolic usage of language. More sophisticated lyrics may include more abstract language usage such as metaphors, figures of speech, humor, and symbolism, which are commonly used within creative art forms.

Activities such as writing songs or pairing sign language with music provide motivating ways to introduce or practice new vocabulary words (Gfeller 1987; Gfeller and Darrow 1987; Schum and Gfeller 1994). During the process of constructing a song, clients are encouraged to generate and express ideas using language skills. As group members discuss their ideas and formulate the lyrics and music, the music therapist encourages topic-related interaction among group members.

Interactive use of vocabulary and syntax can be practiced during instrument playing or movement to music. Because music making occurs over time, directives and discussions regarding music making can address temporal concepts (e.g. "Who plays first?", "John is playing fast/slow"). Moving to music can incorporate spacial concepts (e.g. reaching high, moving to the left, behind, etc.). Musical instruments can be used to represent categories such as shapes (round, rectangle, triangle) and sizes (big, little) (Gfeller 1990; Gfeller et al. 2011). Within the context of music making, social rules such as turn taking and following rules of engagement can be emphasized.

Language assessment is complex and requires fluent communication in the child's mode of communication. Furthermore, interpretation of a language sample requires an understanding of normal, delayed, and deviant language patterns. Therefore, unless the music therapist has had extensive training in this area, he or she would always collaborate with the speech and language specialist to establish short-term objectives, long-term goals, and to select measures for monitoring progress (Gfeller and Baumann 1988).

Speech production

Speech production is a common habilitative goal for children with pre- or peri-lingual hearing losses.

Assessing and correcting articulation errors fall within the professional scope of practice of practitioners within the speech and language area, but music therapy programs can reinforce goals established by the speech and language therapy professional, including: (1) Increased vocalization; (2) increased production of more natural speech rhythms, pitch, and inflections (speech prosody); and (3) increased production of target speech sounds in commonly-used vocabulary (Bang 1971, 1980; Darrow 1990a,b; Darrow and Cohen 1991; Darrow and Starmer 1986; Gfeller 1990; Gfeller and Darrow 2008; Gfeller et al. 2011; Robbins and Robbins 1980).

Singing offers many opportunities for vocalization and has several advantages over conventional speech production as a therapeutic medium. With regard to vocalization, singing requires a more sustained and rhythmic respiration and phonation. It is acceptable to sing at a slower and more consistent tempo than would occur in natural spoken conversation (Wan et al. 2010; Schlaug et al. 2008). Thus, singing provides opportunities for more controlled production of, and clear feedback on, speech sounds. Further, many songs naturally include repetitions of words within verses and choruses. For example, in the children's song, "Old MacDonald Had a Farm," the vowels, "e-i-e-i-o" are repeated many times in a predictable, controlled tempo. It is important to remember, however, that a significant hearing loss may result in difficulty with singing in tune (Xu et al. 2009; Hsiao and Gfeller 2012). Consequently, singing in music therapy should focus to a greater extent on increased production and clear articulation as opposed to the achievement of tonal accuracy.

Many lyrics in children's songs include speech sounds that develop in early childhood (Gfeller 1990; Gfeller et al. 2011). For example, the animal sounds of cows and sheep in the song, "Old MacDonald Had a Farm" provide opportunities to produce the sounds of "mmmooo" and "bah," speech sounds.

Group music making provides opportunities for speech production. For example, in instrumental play, a child can be required to use their voice (e.g. saying "my turn," or "I want the shaker") in order to request the use of instruments, or to discuss their experiences in music making. The music therapist should collaborate with the speech-language professional in determining which speech sounds are developmentally most appropriate and suitable targets for an individual child at different stages in the therapy process, as well as the use of specific prompts or cues (e.g. hand gesture) that may assist a child in using better articulation.

Progress in correct articulation should be assessed by the relevant speech and language professional. However, a music therapist can measure length or number of free vocalizations or uses of particular speech sounds within a session as an indicator of therapy progress.

Improved listening skills: Auditory training

Auditory training promotes optimal usage of the auditory signal, be it residual (usable) acoustic hearing or the electrical stimulation provided by a cochlear implant. Even though improved speech perception is typically the target goal for auditory training, music listening can contribute to this process. Music and speech share common structural characteristics (e.g. pitch, tone quality, duration), and studies from cognitive neuroscience suggest an overlap in neural resources used in processing of speech and musical sounds (Patel 2011; Shahin 2011).

However, acoustic properties of music that are sufficiently different from speech and require different neural processing may offer particular therapeutic benefits. For example, music often includes a wider frequency and intensity range than speech. Consequently some musical sounds may be more readily accessible to the listener's residual hearing (Gfeller and Darrow 2008), which can be useful in early sound detection exercises. In other instances, the acoustic parameters of music place greater demands on the auditory system than speech. Music is made up of diverse timbres that are acoustically richer and a present a more challenging stimulus than speech (Limb and Rubinstein 2012; Patel 2011; Shahin 2011). The listener must attend to acoustic sounds that require more careful listening, thus pushing the auditory system toward more efficient processing. This can, in turn, benefit perception of complex speech sounds, such as speech in background noise or differences in voice quality (Patel 2011; Limb and Rubinstein 2012, etc.).

In comparison with speech production, active music making (e.g. playing percussion instruments) often presents more overt visual cues of sound production. This can help children in making associations between the sound source and the subsequent sound (Boothroyd 2010). Participation in making music can be engaging and motivating, which motivates sustained, attentive listening (Amir and Schuchman 1985; Bang 1980; Gfeller et al. 2011; Patel 2011; Robbins and Robbins 1980).

Auditory training involves a hierarchy of simple to complex listening tasks. This hierarchy includes: (1) Sound detection (absence or presence of sound), (2) sound discrimination (same or different), (3) sound identification (recognizing the sound source), and (4) the comprehension (understanding) of sound (Erber and Hirsh 1978; Gfeller and Darrow 2008). The music therapist initially chooses sounds most accessible to the client, taking into account their auditory profile and hearing device, and gradually increases the difficulty of the listening tasks. Auditory training may also include compensatory skills, through which the listener learns to reduce environmental factors that impeded listening and increase the likelihood of satisfactory listening (Gfeller et al. 2001a).

For younger children, auditory training activities often take the form of interactive music making through playing instruments, singing, games, and movement to music. Interactive music making fosters engaged listening. In a sound detection exercise, a child can move to the sound of a rhythm instrument, and stop when the sound discontinues. Sound discrimination can include listening games such as determining if two instruments sound the same or different. An example of a comprehension task would be having the child move in response to the instructions heard in song lyrics (Gfeller and Darrow 2008). These are only a few possible examples.

Music sounds are highly suitable for auditory training as musical instruments are pitched in a wide range of frequencies, can be played relatively loudly, and may have vibrotactile elements, for example the vibration felt from a drum beat. Additionally, some instruments may be perceived more readily than speech sounds, which have a more limited frequency (pitch) and intensity (loudness) range. These musical sounds can provide successful experiences during the early stages of sound detection.

Adult clients can also benefit from auditory training, but therapists need to ensure that their engagement is age appropriate and personally meaningful (Gfeller 2001). Adults may engage in sound exploration by playing and listening to different instruments such as a piano keyboard or xylophone. Listening to previously familiar recordings can encourage careful listening to song lyrics and the melodic and rhythmic elements. Adults may also enjoy computerized training programs that can be accessed at one's convenience.

The music therapist assesses progress in auditory training through informal testing and through the use of standardized assessment procedures (Darrow et al. 2000; Gfeller and Baumann 1988). Formal tests of auditory comprehension are available (Darrow et al. 2000). Some of these tests require the test administrator to have specialized training in a speech pathology or audiology field.

In addition to active music making, children or adults music therapy interventions can involve computerized listening "games." Computerized auditory training may improve the efficiency of peripheral auditory processing, or improve the efficiency of central processing, which is how the brain processes and assigns meaning to sound. For example, active listening strategies, such as attending to specific cues can be promoted (Fu and Galvin 2007; Moore and Amitay 2007). Sometimes training programs employ an adaptive format, starting with easy sound contrasts, and gradually increasing complexity and difficulty. The music therapist's presence is not required throughout computerized training, but he or she may have a role in (a) developing computer training programs, (b) in identifying on-line resources, (c) motivational and instructional support to during program completion, and (d) to assist the individual in analyzing future strategies/therapy needs once the outcome of the training has been assessed.

While the primary goal of auditory training is likely to be enhanced speech perception, auditory training can also be used to improve music listening enjoyment (Driscoll et al. 2009; Gfeller et al. 2001a). This may be of particular importance for some post-lingually deaf adults for whom music was an important source of pleasure and social connection prior to their hearing loss. Auditory training for music enjoyment may include exercises intended to enhance perceptual acuity as well as counseling to assist in control of environmental circumstances that impact music enjoyment, for example the use of FM systems, and other assistive devices.

Music therapy for social skills development or reintegration

Social skill development for children

Children with pre- and peri-lingual hearing loss often have delayed language development and speech production problems, and consequently may have compromised interactions with others. Difficulty understanding instructions, asking questions, and expressing concerns or frustration can contribute to problems in social adjustment, such as immature behaviors or socially unacceptable forms of expression (Meadow 1980a; Schum and Gfeller 1994; Gfeller and Darrow 2008).

Because music can be structured as a cooperative group event, music activity offers a splendid opportunity to practice social skills, such as taking turns, paying attention, following directions, sharing, working cooperatively, and expressing feelings appropriately (Bang 1980; Darrow et al. 2000; Gfeller and Darrow 2008; Schum and Gfeller 1994). For some individuals, music making (i.e. playing instruments, writing songs, etc.) can be a satisfying leisure time activity and opportunity for personal achievement.

One convenient way to measure improvement in social skills is through changes over time in the occurrence of specific problem behaviors (e.g. interruptions, outbursts). The therapist can also use a specially designed scale, such as the Meadow/Kendall Social-Emotional Assessment Inventory for Deaf Students (Meadow 1980b), to assess social/emotional competency.

Social reintegration for adults

As noted previously, a hearing loss in adulthood can have a deleterious impact on social interaction. Music therapy services may be beneficial in helping adults to learn compensatory strategies for coping with a hearing loss, particularly in relation to social events that involve music. Likely goals would be the development of strategies to enhance music listening (e.g. use of FM units or other assistive devices in concert halls), establishing realistic expectations for listening in the home or community, and social support of others who have learned to cope with similar circumstances.

In summary, music therapy can enhance perceptual acuity for speech and music, music enjoyment, speech production, language development, and social integration. It is important to note that goals commonly addressed in music therapy (listening, spoken communication, music listening) may not be a high priority or culturally-suitable intervention for some individuals whose daily life revolves around manual communication and other life experiences associated with Deaf culture (Darrow 1993; Gfeller and Darrow 2008).

Accommodations in music therapy

Successful participation in music therapy requires a suitable acoustic environment and communication modes that support that facilitate clear and effective interaction. The music therapy environment should have minimum background noise and good lighting. Some persons get particular benefit from an FM system or other sort of assistive listening device that provides more direct input of sound. (Darrow et al. 2000). The client's auditory profile (hearing history, hearing device) should be taken into account when selecting musical instruments and other musical materials that will be more accessible and engaging (Hsiao and Gfeller 2011).

Because of language deficiencies commonly experienced by children with serious hearing losses, poor hearing acuity, or uses of manual communication, careful attention must be given to verbal as well as musical communication throughout music therapy sessions (Darrow et al. 2000; Ford 1985). In general, the music therapist needs to communicate in the child's mode of communication with language that is within the present developmental level of the child (Gfeller and Baumann 1988). If the child uses manual communication (i.e. ASL, Signed English, etc.), the therapist either should be able to engage in two-way communication through sign, or should ensure that a qualified interpreter is available for each session.

Summary

In summary, there is no single profile that characterizes all persons with hearing losses. A significant hearing loss can have a serious impact on a person's ability to understand speech and environmental sounds, speech production, language development, and social interaction. The type, severity, and onset of loss, the impact of hearing devices, and the family and community environment will all influence therapeutic needs and priorities. The acoustic characteristics and social nature of making music can offer rich opportunities for music therapy goals intended to enhance language and speech development, optimal listening skills, and social integration.

Notes

1. The scope of this chapter does not include educational goals and accommodations associated with music education, performance arts for persons who are Deaf, or hearing loss as a secondary condition for multicategorical diseases or disabilities.
2. Patterns of language acquisition for deaf children of deaf parents differ from those of deaf children raised in families that use predominately oral communication.

References

Acoustical Society of America (1960). *American Standards Acoustic Terminology*. New York: Author.

American Speech-Language-Hearing Association (2011). *Type, Degree, and Configuration of Hearing Loss*. [Online] Available at: <http://asha.org/public/hearing/disorders/types.htm>. [Accessed 12 May 2008].

Amir, D. and Schuchman, G. (1985). Auditory training through music with hearing impaired preschool children. *Volta Review* 87: 333–343.

Armstrong, D.F. (1999). *Original Signs: Gesture, Sign and the Sources of Language*. Washington (DC): Gallaudet University Press.

Bang, C. (1971). Music therapy for multiply handicapped deaf children. *Contact* 1, Aalborg, Denmark: Døveskolernes Materialelaboratorium.

Bang, C. (1980). A work of sound and music. *Journal of the British Association for Teachers of the Deaf* 4: 1–10.

Baynton, D.C. (1996). *Forbidden Signs: American Culture and the Campaign against Sign Language*. Chicago: University of Chicago Press.

Boothroyd, A. (2010) Adapting to changed hearing: the potential role of formal training. *Journal of the American Academy of Audiology* 21: 601–611.

Chasin, M. and Russo, F. (2004). Hearing Aids and Music. *Trends in Amplification* 8: 35–47.

Chen, J.K., Chuang, A.Y., McMahon, C., Hsieh, J.C., Tung, T., and Li, L. P. (2010). Music training improves pitch perception in prelingually deafened children with cochlear implants. *Pediatrics* 125: 793–800.

Darrow, A.A. (1979). The beat reproduction response of subjects with normal and impaired hearing: an empirical comparison. *Journal of Music Therapy* 16: 6–11.

Darrow, A.A. (1984). A comparison of the rhythmic responsiveness in normal hearing and hearing-impaired children and an investigation of the relationship of the rhythmic responsiveness to the suprasegmental aspects of speech perception. *Journal of Music Therapy* 21: 48–66.

Darrow, A.A. (1987). An investigative study: the effect of hearing impairment on musical aptitude. *Journal of Music Therapy* 24: 88–96.

Darrow, A.A. (1990a). The effect of frequency adjustment on the vocal reproduction accuracy of hearing impaired children. *Journal of Music Therapy* 27: 24–33.

Darrow, A.A. (1990b). The role of hearing in understanding music. *Music Educators Journal* 77: 24–27.

Darrow, A.A. (1993). The role of music in deaf culture: Implications for music educators. *Journal of Research in Music Education* 43(1): 2–15.

Darrow, A.A. (2005). Students with hearing loss. In: M. Adamek and A.A Darrow (eds), *Music in Special Education*, pp. 233–253, Silver Spring, MD: AMTA.

Darrow, A.A. (2006). The role of music in deaf culture: deaf students' perception of emotion in music. *Journal of Music Therapy* 43: 2–15.

Darrow, A.A. and Cohen, N. (1991). The effect of programmed pitch practice and private instruction on the vocal reproduction accuracy of hearing impaired children: two case studies. *Music Therapy Perspectives* 9: 61–65.

Darrow, A.A. and Heller, G.N. (1985). William Wolcott Turner and David Ely Bartlett: early advocates of music education for the hearing impaired. *Journal of Research in Music Education* 33: 269–279.

Darrow, A.A. and Loomis, D. (1999). Music and Deaf culture: images from the media and their interpretation by Deaf and hearing students. *Journal of Music Therapy* 36: 88–109.

Darrow, A.A. and Novak, J. (2007). The effect of vision and hearing loss on listener's perception of referential meaning in music. *Journal of Music Therapy* 44: 57–73.

Darrow, A.A. and Starmer, G.J. (1986). The effect of vocal training on the intonation and rate of hearing-impaired children's speech: a pilot study. *Journal of Music Therapy* 23: 194–201.

Darrow, A.A., Gfeller, K.E., Gorusch, A., and Thomas, K. (2000). Music therapy with children who are Deaf and hard-of-hearing. In: *Effectiveness of Music Therapy Procedures: Documentation of Research and Clinical Practice*, 3rd edn, pp. 135–157. Silver Spring (MD): American Music Therapy Association.

Davis, J. and Hardick, E.J. (1981). *Rehabilitative Audiology for Children and Adults*. New York: John Wiley and Sons.

Driscoll, V., Oleson, J., Jiang, D., and Gfeller, K. (2009). The effects of training on recognition of musical instruments presented through cochlear implant simulations. *Journal of the American Academy of Audiology* 20: 71–82.

Edmonds, K. (1984). Is there a valid place for music in the education of Deaf children? *ACEHI Journal* 10: 164–169.

Edwards, E. (1974). *Music Education for the Deaf*. South Waterford Maine: Meriam Eddy, Co.

Epley, C. (1972). In a soundless world of musical enjoyment. *Music Educators Journal* 58: 55.

Erber, N.P. and Hirsh, I.J. (1978). Auditory training. In: H. Davis and S.R. Silverman (eds), *Hearing and Deafness*, pp. 358–374. Chicago: Holt, Rinehart and Winston.

Fahey, J.D. and Birkenshaw, L. (1972). Bypassing the ear: the perception of music by feeling and touch. *Music Educators Journal* 58: 44–49.

Flanders, G.A. (September 1928). Rhythm for Deaf children in ungraded schools. *The Volta Review* 30: 487.

Ford, T.A. (1985). *The Effect of Musical Experiences and Age on the Ability of Deaf Children to Discriminate Pitch of Complex Tones*. Chapel Hill, NC: University of North Carolina.

Franks, J.R. (1982). Judgment of hearing aid processed music. *Ear and Hearing* 3: 18–23.

Fu, Q. and Galvin, J.J. (2007). Perceptual learning and auditory training in cochlear implant recipients. *Trends in Amplification* 11: 193–205.

Gabrielsson, A. and Sjögren, H. (1979). Perceived sound quality of hearing aids. *Scandinavian Audiology* 8: 159–169.

Galloway, H.F. and Bean, M.F. (1974). The effects of action songs on the development of body-image and body-part identification in hearing-impaired preschool children. *Journal of Music Therapy* 11: 124–134.

Galvin, J.J., Fu, Q., and Nogaki, G. (2007). Melody contour identification by cochlear implant listeners. *Ear & Hearing* 28: 302–319.

Gfeller, K.E. (1986). Music as a remedial tool for improving speech rhythm in the hearing-impaired: Clinical and research considerations. *MEH Bulletin* 2: 3–19.

Gfeller, K.E. (1987). Songwriting as a tool for reading and language remediation. *Music Therapy* 6: 28–38.

Gfeller, K.E. (1990). A cognitive linguistic approach to language development for the preschool child with hearing impairment. *Music Therapy Perspectives* 8: 47–51.

Gfeller, K. (2000). Accommodating children who use cochlear implants in the music therapy or educational setting. *Music Therapy Perspectives* 18: 122–130.

Gfeller, K. (2001). Aural rehabilitation of music listening for adult cochlear implant recipients: Addressing learner characteristics. *Music Therapy Perspectives* 19: 88–95.

Gfeller, K.E. (2007). Music therapy and hearing loss: A 30-year retrospective. *Music Therapy Perspectives* 20: 100–107.

Gfeller, K.E. and Baumann, A.A. (1988). Assessment procedures for music therapy with hearing-impaired children: language development. *Journal of Music Therapy* 25: 192–205.

Gfeller, K.E. and Darrow, A.A. (1987). Music as a remedial tool in the language education of hearing-impaired children. *The Arts in Psychotherapy* 14: 229–235.

Gfeller, K.E. and Darrow, A.A. (2008). Music therapy in the treatment of sensory disorders. In: W.B. Davis, K.E. Gfeller, and M.H. Thaut (eds), *An Introduction to Music Therapy Theory and Practice*, 3rd edn, pp. 365–404. Silver Spring, MD: American Music Therapy Association, Inc.

Gfeller, K., Christ, A., Knutson, J.F., Witt, S., Murray, K.T., and Tyler, R.S. (2000a). Musical backgrounds, listening habits, and aesthetic enjoyment of adult cochlear implant recipients. *Journal of the American Academy of Audiology* 11: 390–406.

Gfeller, K.E., Witt, S.A., Spencer, L. Stordahl, J., and Tomblin, J.B. (2000b). Musical involvement and enjoyment of children using cochlear implants. *Volta Review* 100: 213–233.

Gfeller, K., Witt, S., Stordahl, J., Mehr, M., and Woodworth, G. (2001a). The effects of training on melody recognition and appraisal by adult cochlear implant recipients. *Journal of the Academy of Rehabilitative Audiology* 33: 115–138.

Gfeller, K., Mehr, M., and Witt, S. (2001b). Aural rehabilitation of music perception and enjoyment of adult cochlear implant users. *Journal of the Academy of Rehabilitative Audiology* 34: 17–27.

Gfeller, K.E., Turner, C., Woodworth, G., et al. (2002a). Recognition of familiar melodies by adult cochlear implant recipients and normal hearing adults. *Cochlear Implants International* 3: 29–53.

Gfeller, K., Witt, S., Adamek, M., et al. (2002b). Effects of training on timbre recognition and appraisal by postlingually deafened cochlear implant recipients. *Journal of the American Academy of Audiology* 13: 132–145.

Gfeller, K., Turner, C., Oleson, J., et al. (2007). Accuracy of cochlear implant recipients on pitch perception, melody recognition and speech reception in noise. *Ear and Hearing* 28: 412.

Gfeller, K., Oleson, J., Knutson, J. F., Breheny, P., Driscoll, V., and Olszewski, C. (2008). Multivariate predictors of music perception and appraisal by adult cochlear implant users. *Journal of the American Academy of Audiology* 19: 120–134.

Gfeller, K. Driscoll, V., Kenworthy, M., and Van Voorst, T. (2011). Music therapy for preschool cochlear implant recipients. *Music Therapy Perspectives* 29: 39–49.

Gillam, R.B., Marquardt, T.P., and Martin, F.N. (2000). *Communication Sciences and Disorders*, pp. 57–61. San Diego, CA: Singular Publishing Group.

Hardman, M.L., Drew, C.J. and Egan, M.W. (2002). *Human Exceptionality: Society, School and Family*. Boston: Allyn and Bacon.

Heward, W.L. (2003). *Exceptional Children: An Introduction to Special Education*. Upper Saddle River (NJ): Merrill/Prentice Hall.

Hsiao, F. (2008). Mandarin melody recognition by pediatric cochlear implant patients. *Journal of Music Therapy* 45: 390–404.

Hsiao, F-L. and Gfeller, K.E. (2011). How we do it: adaptation of music instruction for pediatric cochlear implant recipients. *Cochlear Implants International* 12: 205–208.

Hsiao, F-L. and Gfeller, K.E. (2012). Music perception of cochlear implant recipients with implications for music instruction: a review of literature. *UPDATE* 30: 5–10.

Hummel, C.J. (1971). The value of music in teaching Deaf students. *Volta Review* 73: 224–228.

Jordan, S.A. (February 1900). Rhythm as an aid to voice training. *The Association Review* (now *The Volta Review*) 2: 16–19.

Klajman, S., Koldeg, E., and Kowalska, A. (1982). Investigation of musical abilities in hearing-impaired and normal-hearing children. *Folia Phoniatrica* 34: 229–233.

Korduba, O.M. (1975). Duplicated rhythmic patterns between Deaf and normal-hearing children. *Journal of Music Therapy* 12: 136–146.

Limb, C.J. and Rubinstein, J.T. (2012). Current research on music perception in cochlear implant users. *Otolaryngology Clinics of North America* 45: 129–140.

Looi, V. (2008). The effect of cochlear implantation on music perception: a review. *Otorhinolaryngology* 58: 169–190.

Looi, V., McDermott, H., McKay, C., and Hickson, L. (2008). Music perception of cochlear implant users compared with that of hearing aid users. *Ear and Hearing* 29: 421–434.

Looi, V. and She, J. (2010) Music perception of cochlear implant users: a questionnaire, and its implications for a music training program. *International Journal of Audiology* 49(2): 116–128.

Madsen, C.K. and Mears, W.G. (1965). The effect of sound upon the tactile threshold of deaf subjects. *Journal of Music Therapy* 2: 64–68.

Marschark, M. (2007). *Raising and Educating a Deaf Child: A Comprehensive Guide to the Choices, Controversies and Decisions Faced by Parents and Educators*. London: Oxford University Press.

McDermott, E.G. (1971). Music and rhythms—From movement to lipreading and speech. *Volta Review* 73: 224–228, 243–249.

McDermott, H.J. (2004). Music perception with cochlear implants: A review. *Trends in Amplification 8*: 49–81.

Meadow, K. (1980a). *Deafness and Child Development*. Los Angeles: University of California Press.

Meadow, K. (1980b). *Meadow/Kendall Social-Emotional Assessment Inventory for Deaf Students*. Washington (DC): Gallaudet College.

Moore, D.R. and Amitay, S. (2007). Auditory training: Rules and applications. *Seminars in Hearing 28*: 99–109.

Padden, C. (1996). *From the Cultural to the Bicultural: The Modern Deaf Community*. New York: Cambridge University Press.

Padden, C. and Humphries, T. (1988). *Deaf in America: Voices from a Culture*. Cambridge (MA): Harvard University Press.

Patel, A. (2011). Why would musical training benefit the neural encoding of speech? The OPERA hypothesis. *Frontiers in Psychology 2*. doi: 10.3389/fpsyg.2011.00142.

Raleigh, K.K. and Odom, P.B. (1972). Perception of rhythm by subjects with normal and deficient hearing. *Developmental Psychology 7*: 54–61.

Riordan, J.T. (1971). *They Can Sing Too: Rhythm for the Deaf*. Springfield (VA): Jenrich Associates.

Robbins, C. and Robbins, C. (1980). *Music for the Hearing Impaired & Other Special Groups: A Resource Manual and Curriculum Guide*. St. Louis: Magnamusic-Baton.

Ryugo, D.K., and Limb, C.J. (2009). Brain plasticity: The impact of the environment on the brain as it relates to hearing and deafness. In: J.K. Niparko (ed.), *Cochlear implants: Principles & practices*, 2nd edn, pp. 19–37. Philadelphia: Lippincott Williams & Wilkins.

Schum, R. and Gfeller, K. (1994). Engendering Social Skills. In: N. Tye-Murray (ed.), *Let's Converse: A "how-to" Guide to Develop and Expand Conversational Skills of Children and Teenagers Who are Hearing Impaired*. Washington (DC): Alexander Graham Bell Association.

Schlaug, G., Marchina, S., and Norton, D. (2008). From singing to speaking: why singing may lead to recovery of expressive language function in patients with Brocoa's aphasia. *Music Perception 25*: 315–323.

Shahin, A. (2011). Neurophysiological influence of musical training on speech perception. *Frontiers in Psychology 2*. doi: 10.3389/fpsyg.2011.00126.

Shannon, R.V., Zeng, F.G., Kamath, V., Wygonski, J., and Ekelid, M. (1995). Speech recognition with primarily temporal cues. *Science 270*: 303–304.

Sheldon, D.A. (1997). The Illinois school for the Deaf band: A historical perspective. *Journal of Research in Music Education 45*: 580–600.

Stern, V. (1975). They shall have music. *Volta Review 77*: 495–500.

Thornton, M. (1926). An outline of rhythm work and its application to schoolroom work. *American Annals of the Deaf 71*: 361–386.

Turnbull, R., Turnbull, A., Shank, M., Smith, S., and Leal, D. (2001). *Exceptional Lives: Special Education in Today's Schools*. Upper Saddle River (NJ): Prentice Hall.

Turner, W.W. and Bartlett, D.E. (October 1848). Music among the Deaf and Dumb. *American Annals of the Deaf and Dumb 2*: 1–6.

Vettese, J. (1974). Instrumental lessons for Deaf children. *Volta Review 76*: 19–22.

Wan, C., Rüber, T., Hohmann, A., and Schlaug, G. (2010). The therapeutic effects of singing in neurological disorders. *Music Perception 27*: 287–295.

Wecker, K. (1939). Music for deaf children. *American Annals of the Deaf* 84: 151–155.

Wilson, B. (2000). Cochlear implant technology. In: J.K. Niparko, K.I. Kirk, N.K. Mellon, A.M. Robbins, D.L. Tucci, and B.S. Wilson (eds), pp. 109–118. *Cochlear Implants: Principles and Practices*. New York: Lippincott, Williams & Wilkins.

Xu, L., Zhou, N., Chen, X., et al. (2009). Vocal singing by prelingually deafened children with cochlear implants. *Hearing Research* 225: 129–134.

Zatorre, R.J., Belin, P., and Penhune, V.B. (2002). Structure and function of auditory cortex: Music and speech. *Trends in Cognitive Science* 6: 37–46.

CHAPTER 13

··

MUSIC THERAPY IN MENTAL HEALTH CARE FOR ADULTS

··

TRÍONA MCCAFFREY

Music may offer the only bridge from inner world to outer reality. It may provide the only means to give expression, in a safe way, to inner feelings…. It is important that the music therapist's sphere of interest be the inner life of the patient—that the main concern be with the use of music as a vehicle by which this inner reality can be brought to the surface, to be heard, experienced, and examined in the presence of another.

Tyson 1981, p. 24

INTRODUCTION

THE promotion of mental well-being is an overarching aim of music therapy as a psychosocial practice. Music therapists work with the principle that central to a person's well-being is their need for meaningful relating (Odell-Miller 1995). Music therapy can offer the individual an alternative pathway of expression and connection with others that can help develop one's capacity to engage with and maintain relationships outside of the therapeutic work. Therefore music therapy is characterized by its relational and social capacities that foster improved mental well-being and quality of life of service users. Music therapy may be offered as a stand-alone therapeutic process or alternatively as an adjunct to standard pharmacological mental health treatment. As music therapy developed as a profession in Europe, Australia, and the US through the mid-twentieth century to the present day, it was initially introduced in large institutions through programmes that primarily focused on the treatment of mental illness (Davis 2003; Kramer 2000; Tyler 2000). Today, music therapy has become a diverse practice that encompasses preventative care through community based models, wellness programmes, as well as continuing to provide services within mental health care contexts (Meadows 2011).

MENTAL HEALTH

When introducing the topic of mental health diagnoses such as "depression," "schizophrenia," "psychosis," "anxiety" are often mentioned. These terms refer to mental disorders as described in the Diagnostic and Statistical Manual of Mental Disorders (DSM V) and in the ICD-10 classification of mental and behavioral disorders (ICD 10). Yet health is described as "a state of complete physical, mental and social well-being, and not merely the absence of disease" (WHO 1978, p. 1). Therefore, the aim of this chapter is to consider music therapy's capacity to promote mental well-being for people receiving mental health services in ways that exceed the limitations of psychiatric diagnosis and symptomatology.

Mental health care is an umbrella term that is used to define a multitude of health practices and models of care that are designed to address the needs of people experiencing psychological distress. Healthcare practice can be situated within an illness-wellness paradigm where healthcare professionals' area of practice, training, and personal philosophy influence how such distress is conceptualized and addressed. Reviewing the terminology employed in the mental health literature is a starting point from which to contextualize music therapy service provision. The term "mental disorder" (American Psychiatric Association 2013) is sometimes used instead of related medical terms such as "mental illness" (Anthony 1993). Other terminology includes "mental ill health" (Kai and Crosland 2001) or "mental health difficulty" (Lau and Cheung 1999). Similarly, the term "patient" (Mental Health Commission 2012) may be replaced with that of "client" (Clark et al. 1999), "customer" (McDonald 2006), "consumer" (Chinman et al. 2006) or "expert by experience" (Shepherd et al. 2008), "survivor" (Sweeney et al. 2009) or simply "person with a mental health difficulty" as employed by the *National Institute for Mental Health* (UK). The term "service user" will be employed in this chapter as it is consistent with a mandate from consumerist and democratic traditions that emphasize the development of participation within health services (McLaughlin 2009).

Psychiatry is a discipline that has specific way of understanding mental health problems and is concerned with the assessment, diagnosis and treatment of disorders of the mind (College of Psychiatry of Ireland 2013). In psychiatric care mental disorders are considered to belong to the patient who is treated by a mental health expert, or treatment team, with a focus upon identifying the symptoms that can be treated when targeted within a specific intervention, resulting in curing the disease or ailment (Wampold 2001).

A number of developments during the twentieth century contributed to the burgeoning of the field of psychiatry in partnership with the pharmacological industry, along with neuro-scientific discoveries, and behavior-based therapy interventions which have primarily focused on symptomatic management of mental disorders (Unkefer and Thaut 2005). These factors have propelled psychiatry and ultimately, its underlying medical model, to become the dominant discourse within mental health care. Yet, this model has been subject to much criticism for its' scientific underpinnings, which can overlook personal, social, and economic factors impacting upon a person's mental health (Wallcraft et al. 2009). Further discussion of this in relation to music therapy practice will be pursued later on in this chapter.

Music therapy in mental health

The promotion of mental well-being is an overarching aim of music therapy as a psychosocial practice. Music has the potential to mirror cultural, relational, and historical aspects of the self in therapy. It additionally affords access to thoughts and feelings that can be inaccessible via the spoken word, providing a process by which the individual is guided through personal difficulty or distress in a supportive and non-judgmental environment. Music's capacity to offer a means of "working through" beyond verbal media is often reason for referral to music therapy in the first instance as, for some people, words may be inaccessible or simply too difficult to voice. The "sounding" of a person's narrative may be drawn from a range of methods and techniques that gently and gradually build participants' confidence and capacities in regular supportive sessions over time (McCaffrey et al. 2011). Music is regarded as "the glue" that creates form and structure to such a relationship (DeNora 2002), where new avenues for self-expression and interpersonal connection may be found.

Such opportunities for non-verbal relating can offer an alternative means of communication for those who find words to be inadequate. By offering such therapeutic opportunities there is acknowledgement that more fruitful means of relating may be found outside the dominant verbal discourse. This is particularly important as growing emphasis is placed upon the nurturance of meaningful relationships between service users and providers while embracing the notion that meaning can not only be fostered through words but also through creative pathways such as those offered in music therapy.

Identifying people that may benefit optimally from music therapy is an ethical imperative for music therapy practice (Burton 2009). Mental distress can impact upon emotional and social domains of functioning that in turn can lead to disturbances in interpersonal and intrapersonal relating (Mössler et al. 2012). This may result in "low motivation" for verbal therapies such as psychotherapy or psychological counselling. This has resulted in an increasing focus on process and outcome measures with such client groups (Gold et al. 2005b; Mössler et al. 2012). While efforts continue to ascertain suitable candidates for referral to music therapy it is proposed that the term "low motivation" for verbal therapies is somewhat problematic and limiting about clients. Alternative terminology might consider that music therapy is suitable for those with higher incentive for expressive or arts based therapies than other treatments.

Theoretical orientations in music therapy for mental health

The therapeutic and theoretical orientation of the therapist influences the methods and techniques used, and the ways in which their purposes are conceptualized. Some therapeutic approaches favor cognitive methods, where the client is perceived as having difficulties arising from distorted thinking, while others aim to develop capacities for positive interpersonal relating, or resolving intra-psychic conflicts. Choi's (2008) survey of five hundred board-certified music therapists identified that diverse traditions including cognitive-behavioral, humanistic, medical, analytic, and eclectic orientations can be found across the profession in the USA. This suite of approaches reflects a range of foundational principles, and contrasting underpinnings. Results from another survey of music therapists showed that approaches such as behavioral, psychodynamic, and eclectic are most commonly used in mental health practice in the USA (Silverman 2007).

METHODS IN MUSIC THERAPY

There is increased interest in the relationship between process and outcome in music therapy (Burton 2009). Some music therapy literature identifies music processes in sessions as belonging to one of two categories; in active music therapy service users are actively involved in the music making process by playing instruments or singing (Vink et al. 2003) while in receptive music therapy there is an emphasis upon listening and attending to live or pre-recorded music played by the therapist (Grocke and Wigram 2007). Mössler and colleagues (2012) have further nuanced music therapy methods as follows: (a) "Production techniques" that encourage emotional expression and the creation of the therapeutic relationship through musical improvisation between client and therapist where something new is produced; (b) "reproduction techniques" that involve both parties playing or singing recomposed pieces of music, such techniques can also involve learning or practising musical skills and; (c) reception techniques that involve listening to live or recorded music. Programmes may be exclusively feature one or indeed a combination of such techniques depending upon the aims of therapy and orientation of the therapist. The following section will discuss some of the most commonly used methods in mental health practice namely: (a) improvisation as a production technique; (b) songwriting as a reproduction technique and: (c) music listening and discussion as a receptive technique. These discussions are certainly not exhaustive of the possible methods and reception techniques that can be employed in mental health practice.

IMPROVISATION

Music is a discourse that can be used as a means of human expression beyond the economy of words (McCaffrey 2013). Improvising in music therapy involves "playing live and extemporaneous music where a multitude of musical media may be employed including voice, body sounds, percussion and instruments" (McCaffrey 2013, p. 307). Pavlicevic (2000) proposed that the purpose of improvisation is not to make *good* music but rather to create an intimate personal relationship between client and therapist. This is built up gradually over time through regular and supportive play. Maratos et al. (2011) reported that such shared play has esthetic, physical, and relational dimensions.

In mental health care, the non-verbal nature of improvisation can open up alternate avenues of relating and new ways of experiencing oneself and others. Pavlicevic et al. (2000) showed that improvisation can be used to establish one-to-one interaction between therapist and person, in which a dialogue can develop that is based in the here and now. The aim of such shared play is to draw inner experiences and emotions to the musical surface so as to facilitate recognition of one's own capacities and to engage personal awareness and growth. These may exclusively stay within musical parameters or be reflected upon through verbal dialogue that promotes the service user's insight and awareness around difficulties that impact their everyday living. This mirrors the view of improvisation operating on a proto-symbolic level by triggering unconscious processes beyond pathology and, in a way, prepares the individual for fully symbolic expression and eventual verbalizing (Erkkilä et al. 2011).

De Backer and Van Camp (1999) have written that the provision of choice is fundamental when introducing instruments for improvisation in therapy. Being presented with a variety of instruments is required so that as one seeks to find a medium for musical expression one can sound one's voice in musical dialogue with others. It is advised that the therapist only introduce an instrument once they themselves have had extensive experience with it and thereafter that the value of individual instruments is judged for its usefulness in therapy on a case by case basis (De Backer and Van Camp 1999). Of course in some cases there may be reason for introducing fewer instruments in sessions so as not to overwhelm service users or where a service user has expressed a desire to play or learn certain instruments. The strength and robustness of instruments need to be considered ensuring that they can bear intensive expressions of human emotion (De Backer and Van Camp 1999).

Improvisation in Practice

Pedersen (2003) described a tentative first session in music therapy during which the client was introduced to piano improvisation. The therapist wrote "I instructed him to start to play by striking a key and listening to that sound and to let this sound lead him to the next sound, listen to it and so on" (p. 379). This description of early moments in music therapy reminds us of the uncertainty and perhaps even the demands that service users can encounter as they engage in improvisation for the first time. The leap between solitary experience of an internal world of thoughts, emotions, and impressions, and the expression of such a world with others through symbolic representation in music and sound can be challenging. Therefore, music therapists must be thoughtful and respectful when introducing improvisation.

Odell-Miller (1999) has provided case vignettes describing the way in which the music and the person are inextricably bound up in ways that cannot be separated. This is mirrored in the case study of music therapy with a young man with schizophrenia who appears to be disconnected from the world around him (Jensen 1999). The man's piano playing is initially described as being absent of excitement, agitation, and movement and reflective of the solitude that he experiences. Here Jensen realizes that it will take time to be allowed to enter this man's world, an entry that is eventually gained through holding and anchoring the client's music so as to reach a point in therapy where both individuals acknowledge and connect with each other within shared musical dialogue. This case study provides an example of the connection that can be made with reality through the physical process of playing instruments; firmly rooted within the present moment.

Kaser writes that within a group context improvisation can "address multiple symptoms of … illness while at the same time helping to develop … ability to focus, tolerate others and interact more successfully" (2011, p. 403). It is not surprising that perhaps for those same reasons, that group therapy is a frequently used modality in mental health practice (Silverman 2007). Improvising music with others not only facilitates social interaction and emotional expression but also promotes insight, a psychodynamic term, so that participants can understand more about themselves. This may be facilitated in the music itself, or through group discussion and reflection following instrumental play.

Stewart (2002) discussed the importance of enabling a sense of inclusion and belonging as core aspects of group work with people who have chronic mental health difficulties. Winnicott's (1965) concept of the "facilitating environment" is regarded as fundamental to the group developmental process. Through "M"'s experience of improvising within group therapy, it is explained how for some participants "having a good experience and enjoying it proves as challenging as exploring difficult feelings" (2002, p. 35). Stewart describes his awareness of how the musical parameters of play are vital to holding the group improvisatory process such as; playing a strong group pulse when other's playing seems dissimilar to the underlying tempo or, tuning into the dynamics of the music as emotionally engaged contributions are made by group members. These events illustrate how the group can communicate within the music while at the same time individuals can experience personal spontaneous "play," free from the constraints of musical rules and regulations. Ruud (1998) has proposed that group improvisations that lead from a sense of chaos to some consensus around common code or structure can be regarded as examples of the art of social organization, platforms that are particularly poignant for people who find social relating to be challenging. Thus, opportunities to experience such "miniature social systems" can be found in improvisation in group music therapy.

SONGWRITING

Songwriting is increasingly used in music therapy practice in many countries. It is "the process of creating, notating, and/or recording lyrics and music by the client or clients and therapist within a therapeutic relationship to address psychosocial, emotional, cognitive, and communicative needs of the client" (Baker and Wigram 2005, p. 16). Motives for using songwriting in working with service users in mental health care can be attributed to the tangible end-product it offers but also and even more importantly to the therapeutic process that can be engendered. Multiple reasons for choosing to employ this method in practice have been proposed such as experiencing mastery, developing insight, providing emotional support, improving coping and social skills, increasing self-esteem, in addition to reducing anxiety, anger, and tension (Baker and Wigram 2005). Survey results showed that songwriting is used for a number of different purposes by a large number of practitioners working in psychiatric services whereby the endorsed goals in songwriting are: (a) Choice and decision making; (b) developing a sense of self; (c) telling the individual's story; (d) clarifying thoughts and feelings and; (e) externalizing thoughts, fantasies, and emotions (Baker et al. 2008).

The songwriting process can be used as a means of promoting expression and exploration of thoughts and feelings around personally relevant topics to the individual where recapitulation of this journey may be found in the final song or product created. Songwriting can offer opportunities to express hopes, dreams, desires, and losses that can be framed within personal narratives that are related to the past, present, or future. As externalized self-expression, songs have the ability to contain and hold feelings that validate human experience in a highly personal manner.

The ways in which songwriting can be introduced to sessions vary from structured to unstructured (Baker and Wigram 2005). Techniques can range from filling in the blanks of pre-composed songs with lyrics offered by service users as described by Robb (1996), or, freely composing a song whereby melody, harmony, lyrics, genre and structured are considered anew as described by O'Callaghan (1997). Another commonly used technique in songwriting is that of song parody where original lyrics of a popular song are replaced with those of the individual while keeping the melodic and harmonic structure of the chosen song as illustrated by Ledger (2001), Edwards (1998) and McCaffrey et al. (2011). It is the experience of the author that sometimes service users in mental health programmes explicitly request their desire to write a song whereas in other instances songwriting comes about by suggestion of either service user or therapist at a point where exploration of a specific topic is prompted in therapy.

Baker (2013) interviewed 43 music therapists about environmental factors that support or constrain the therapeutic songwriting process and found that organizational structures, the physical space, the private space and the organizational culture individually and collectively can either support or constrain their practice. Of particular interest in this study is the voluntary and involuntary status of service users attending music therapy in mental health settings. This means that some people elect to be in care but others are required by law to be receiving care in such a context. One music therapist cited compulsory attendance as exacerbating *resistance* and voluntary attendance was viewed to fortify engagement in the songwriting process. Environmental factors that can impact upon the songwriting process such as interruptions, privacy, and staff culture (Baker 2013); factors that practitioners may have capacity to reduce and be cognisant of as they consider using this method in music therapy.

Songwriting in practice

McCaffrey et al. (2011) described the steps involved in introducing songwriting in sessions with "Kevin," an individual with enduring mental health needs. He chose to write his own lyrics to the song *No woman no cry* (1974) and the therapist outlines how the use of song parody served as a springboard to discussion between Kevin and therapist about his past experiences and the losses that occurred therein.

Improvements in quality of life have been found as a result of group sessions with people who have severe and enduring mental illness living in the community in which songwriting featured as a primary method of working (Grocke et al. 2008). Pre- and post-intervention measures on a Quality of Life scale indicated significant changes in general quality of life, health and support from friends. Focus groups with those participating in this study relayed that producing a positive outcome such as a song was surprising as well as the recognition of creativity that songwriting encouraged and the sense of achievement in producing recordings of the songs that could be shared with others. Analysis of songs written in sessions produced themes relating to; the difficulty of living with mental illness, the strength that is required to cope with mental illness, the healing sense of living in the present, religion and spirituality, concern for the world and, enjoyment in team-working. Vander Kooij (2009) also conducted a thematic analysis of songs written by people with mental health difficulties and writes that despite diversity in cultural and socioeconomic backgrounds, many similarities are to be found therein. Analysis of seventeen songs written by three participants of music therapy offered insight into the needs and experiences of those living with mental illness as well as discoveries into catalysts that promote recovery.

Similarly to the processes reported in the Grocke et al. (2008) study, there was a sense of achievement on behalf of participants in sharing recordings of their songs with others. This is reminiscent of Turry's (2005) view of recordings as something that can be held onto. Recordings can *live on* beyond the music therapy sessions and serve as a reminder of the therapeutic journey.

Music listening

Receptive methods in music therapy have varying degrees of use by practitioners and are most commonly described in practice accounts from the USA and Australia whereas in the UK receptive methods have been described as used rarely (Grocke and Wigram 2007; Maratos et al. 2008). "Receptive music therapy encompasses techniques in which the client is a recipient of the music experience, as distinct from being an active music maker" (Grocke and Wigram 2007, p. 15). Bruscia (1998) outlined a number of receptive techniques such as; music for relaxation, imaginal listening, song (lyric) discussion, song reminiscence, listening to music preferences, music appreciation, music collage, somatic listening, and eurhythmic listening. In-depth descriptions of each of these techniques are beyond the scope of this chapter but for the overall purposes of providing a supportive framework for broader contexts of music listening in mental health practice, the following section will consider related research findings.

Hsu and Lai's (2004) controlled clinical trial found that greater improvements can be achieved when music listening is combined with standard care for depression. Participants in the music group listened to soft music of their choice for 30 minutes daily for two weeks and showed improved scores on a self-rated depression scale when compared to the control group that were assigned bed rest for the same daily period. Lin et al. (2011) put forward an explanation of the neuroscience of music and suggested that this medium has positive psychophysiological effects in people who have depression. Field et al. (1998) showed attenuation in frontal EEG asymmetry in people with depression, both during and after listening to popular songs. Positive results have also been shown in a meta-analysis of 19 studies in relation to music listening upon the symptoms of psychosis (Silverman 2003). Of particular relevance to music therapists are the findings of a review of almost 100 studies of music and music therapy in mental health which concluded that:

> Music as used by music therapists results in clinical improvement. We found no demonstrable evidence that simply listening to music had the same type of result. Therefore, it may be that a purposeful and professional design for delivering music, coupled with other factors (such as

actually making music as part of therapy, or the interaction with a therapist), will potentiate the therapeutic effectiveness of music.

Lin et al. 2011, p. 43

Having briefly discussed some of the evidence that supports the use of music listening techniques in promoting mental wellness, the general practical implications of following receptive approaches in therapy will be considered. It is widely acknowledged in music therapy that the most effective music style and genre to use in practice is that of the service user's preferred genre (Grocke and Wigram 2007). This resonates with a person-centered model of music therapy that places the interest, desires and capacities of each individual at the heart of the decision-making process (Noone 2008). Employing music that is familiar to adult service users can be particularly helpful in the introductory sessions of therapy as such material can act as a shared common ground that may aid the establishment of rapport between client and therapist. Amir (2012) shared Musical Presentation (MP) as a therapeutic tool she developed to increase self-knowledge and share one's identity through listening to other's music selection in group therapy. This concept is closely linked to the notion of identity in music, the expression of personhood and the sounding of one's narrative through music (Procter 2004; Ruud 1997, 1998). Shared listening of the service user's selected songs that is conceptualized within an identity framework, has immense potential for therapeutic exploration of self that in turn may facilitate verbal discussion and reflection. Of course, in some instances the individual's selections may not be suitable for certain purposes in therapy, but reasonable solutions may be found in offering alternative presentations of selected music or indeed providing alternative music choices (Grocke and Wigram 2007).

Music listening in practice

The possibilities that music listening can offer service users in music therapy should not be underestimated. The literature provides us with some striking accounts of how music listening experiences can provide service users with valuable opportunities for connection in therapy. Eyre (2011) recounted her work with Julie, a young woman diagnosed with psychosis who had experienced multiple traumas. In the early stages of music therapy Julie was withdrawn, made minimal verbal communication and did not sing or play an instrument. In this case the therapist liaised with Julie's mother as to ascertain Julie's song preferences and this information informed the therapist's use of pre-composed songs that were sung to the client during bedside sessions. Eyre also described other music listening experiences that were provided for Julie such as vocal improvisation with guitar accompaniment to match her mood, singing songs to help her access soothing feeling states and encourage awareness of self and the other. This is similar to the case of "Ann" who expressed her wish to "just listen" to songs during weekly group sessions in which she often become visibly emotional and would sometimes leave the group (McCaffrey et al. 2011). This suggests that although sometimes brief, such receptive experiences were meaningful to her in some way. This case reminds us of music's capacity to engage the individual even within fragile circumstances when a more active role in music making is not tenable.

Baines' (2003) description of music therapy group work within a community mental health setting is based on consumers personal connection to music rather than focusing on a diagnostic problem that needs to be addressed. Program evaluation by service users yielded positive accounts of participation that were set within a therapeutic intervention where people had the choice to listen to personally significant songs if they so wished. Such consumer-directed and partnered programs may prove to be more manageable for those who wish to be amongst others in a social context but prefer to assume a more receptive role therein.

METHODS IN SUMMARY

The above presentation of various music therapy methods is by no means exhaustive and is written with the intention to provide a basic overview of some of the possible ways of working with people who have mental health difficulties. Other factors may impact upon the outcome of the intervention employed such as the relationship between therapist and service user and the theoretical orientation of the therapist. Therefore, there are multiple considerations to be taken into account before choosing to pursue a particular method in music therapy. These all begin and end with the person with whom the therapy is for and it is the role of the qualified therapist to identify indications and contraindications for employing certain methods in practice. Furthermore, the methods section above is presented in a manner that encourages the music therapist to consider the idiosyncratic nature of the individual in therapy rather than embracing a more pathological framework where the choice of method is related to diagnosis. This re-echoes the call to move away from treating service users as "discrete bundles of physiological and psychological functions which can be assessed and treated in isolation" (Procter 2004, p. 215). It also compliments the notion that music therapy is not usually targeted at a specific diagnosis but is rather broad in its aims and methods that aim to address the needs of the individual (Gold et al. 2009).

MUSIC THERAPY EVIDENCE

As an established allied health profession, music therapy is required to produce evidence to justify its role within health care (Edwards 2005). Quantitative research studies, primarily randomized controlled trails (RCTs) that examine efficacy and effectiveness have been increasing since the profession was first founded. In 2005 the first systematic review of music therapy in mental health appeared in the *Cochrane Library*, a database that is dedicated to disseminating high-quality research evidence to healthcare practitioners. Gold et al.'s review (2005a) was in relation to the treatment of schizophrenia and schizophrenia-like illness which has subsequently been updated by Mössler et al. (2011). These feature alongside an additional systematic review of music therapy in the treatment of depression (Maratos et al. 2008).

The findings above have established music therapy as an evidence-based intervention, a term that carries a significant degree of standing among Western health care providers.

Generating high-quality studies to produce reliable evidence that informs decision-making in healthcare is crucial in the establishment of "best practice" in music therapy. Equally important when reviewing main findings is the consideration of the processes and manner of enquiry employed in order to discern the growing trends that are informing music therapy practice in psychiatry and indeed, mental health care.

The majority of music therapy studies that are rooted in psychiatry focus upon music therapy as an intervention used to treat various types of mental disorders. Grocke et al. (2008) concluded that music therapy has demonstrated benefits for people with enduring mental disorders to improve social functioning, global state and mental state. In a review of the findings of such studies that relate to adults who have mental disorders, it was concluded that music therapy is "a structured interaction that patients are able to use to participate successfully, manage some of their symptoms, and express feelings relating to their experiences" (Edwards 2006, p. 33).

The focus upon music therapy as a form of treatment in psychiatry has also been accompanied by the creation of distinct categories of studies that relate to various types of mental disorder. This may be influenced by psychiatry's use of taxonomies that provide a common language and standardized criteria to psychiatrists in the diagnoses of a mental disorder. In May 2013, the American Psychiatric Association published the fifth edition of the Diagnostic and Statistical Manual of Mental Disorders (DSM-5). This most recent classification system provides mental health professionals with detailed descriptions of diagnostic criteria. It is used by clinicians and researchers from many different orientations across a multitude of mental health settings (American Psychiatric Association 2013). The following section will apply such categorization and highlight relevant studies that focus upon the outcomes of using music therapy to treat such disorders.

A systematic review of eight music therapy RCTs for patients who have schizophrenia or schizophrenia-like illnesses concluded that the music therapy intervention, in addition to standard care, improved patients' global state, mental state and social functioning (Mössler et al. 2011). The authors also highlighted the use of music therapy in addressing negative symptoms of schizophrenia. These results support those of Tang et al. (1994) who found that music therapy reduces the negative symptoms of schizophrenia by increasing patients' ability to converse with others, reducing their social isolation, and increasing their level of interest in external events. General symptom scores have also been shown to improve in those that were randomized to an improvisational music therapy group in study that compared music therapy and standard care to standard care alone (Talwar et al. 2006). These results suggest that music therapy may be a viable option in the treatment of those with schizophrenia. This has been recommended by the National Institute for Clinical Excellence (NICE) who state that in the treatment of schizophrenia, arts therapies are "the only interventions both psychological and pharmacological, to demonstrate consistent efficacy in the reduction of negative symptoms" (NICE 2009, p. 205).

Maratos et al. (2008) conducted a review that examined the efficacy of music therapy with standard care compared to standard care alone in the treatment of depression. A reduction in symptoms of depression was reported in those who were randomized to music therapy in four of the five studies reviewed and low levels of attrition were noted this group. In the first RCT on improvisational music therapy for working-age people with depression, improved symptom scores of depression, anxiety and general functioning were found in those assigned to the treatment group (Erkkilä et al. 2011). Significant variation in the effects of music therapy was not indicated across therapists involved in the study and it is suggested that the overall positive effects are related to the improvisation method employed.

Dose-response relationship in music therapy for people with serious mental disorders has been examined using a mixed-effects meta-analysis model (Gold et al. 2009). Music therapy, when added to standard care, was concluded to have significant effects on global state, general symptoms, negative symptoms, depression, anxiety, functioning, and musical engagement. Significant dose-effect relationships were found for general, negative, and depressive symptoms in addition to functioning when longer therapy programmes or more frequent sessions were provided.

The studies described above exemplify the efforts that have been made to firmly root music therapy within such practice where quantitative methodologies and laws of natural science apply. Silverman (2010) discusses the "psychiatric music therapy" literature base in relation to established levels and evidence concluding that there is a lack of RCTS and an overall low level of evidence therein, adding that such findings are similar with levels of evidence in other psychological treatments in psychiatry.

Cassity (2007) conducted a Delphi poll in relation to the future of psychiatric music therapy. The third most likely scenario rated by the panel was the call for evidence-based music therapy by health care providers. These findings resulted in explicit recommendations being made to the Certification Board for Music Therapists, USA, to continue examination of practitioners' knowledge of evidence-based music therapy and quantitative clinical research applications. Undoubtedly, there are possibilities in further embedding music therapy in evidence-based practice but it is equally important to reflect upon some of the challenges that arise in using the RCT, as a "gold standard" (Chalmers 1994; Sackett et al. 1996) that informs this mode of practice. The diversity of the music therapy population, the standardization of treatment in relation to person-centered care, and the measurement of outcomes have been raised as concerning issues when employing the RCT in music therapy research (Edwards 2005; O'Callaghan 2003).

As the RCT remains as the gold standard of evidence-based practice there is risk that the controlled and manipulated conditions it features fail to capture real-world music therapy settings and the complex phenomena that emerge between patient and therapist. The RCT method may easily lend itself to statistical evaluation but this does not apply so easily to measuring music therapy interventions. As music therapy research develops in psychiatry it is crucial that methodological tools are chosen based on their suitability towards the phenomenon under investigation, otherwise the profession will be placed in a situation as described by Richards who said that "when the only tool you have is a hammer everything else looks like a nail" (2002, p. 259).

The concept of manualizing therapy has increasingly featured in professional realms in mental health practice (Odell-Miller 2007; Rolvsjord et al. 2005). This involves the therapy process following a structured set of guidelines and techniques that aim to ensure treatment fidelity. However, concern has been raised in music therapy about the potential loss of therapeutic integrity, and the danger of overlooking the individual service user perspective when employing such standardized manuals that are in keeping with the requirements of some forms of research in healthcare. This presents mental health practitioners with "a dilemma between the demand for validity and replicability in relation to research on one side and the need for clinical flexibility on the other" (Rolvsjord et al. 2005, p. 23).

The tension that exists around the manualization debate is fuelled by the long-standing recognition of music therapy as a person-centered intervention, where service users' individual and unique needs, resources, and strengths directly inform the course of therapy and ultimately the ways in which music is presented in sessions by the qualified practitioner. The rationale for music therapy's identity as a person-centered and relational healthcare profession lies in its employment of the medium of music which has long been acknowledged as a cultural phenomenon that has the capacity to narrate one's life story and validate life experience of its listener. As Kramer wrote:

> The efficacy of music therapy is a result not of the music but of its apprehension in experience. Due to this dependency on experience, the therapeutic influence of music is necessarily governed by an extant phenomenal framework organizing the music experience for its participants. That is to say that some cultural conditions which legitimate certain therapeutic practices also render the target audience susceptible to the influence of those practices.
>
> Kramer 2000, p. 16

An individual's music narrative is deeply embedded within personal experience and cultural practice. This is a complex affair that impacts upon musical engagement in the present. Therefore it is the role of the therapist to skilfully find musical ways of tapping into such experiences so as to support the sounding of one's music narrative within a therapeutic context.

Burton (2009) recognized the challenge that music therapy confronts by being increasingly asked to produce "hard evidence" in the form of quantitative data but questions whose needs this really fulfils. Such evidence aids the growth and validity of the profession but these are within a governance of a model that has different epistemological roots to those of music therapy. It is imperative that therapists are aware of the influences of psychiatry, and its adherence to the medical model, within the practice of music therapy. Likewise, future research must not narrow its focus to simply adhere to the boundaries of conventional medicine as in doing so there may be risk of losing some of the quintessential features of music therapy in translation.

POSSIBILITIES FOR AND IN PRACTICE

Recovery in mental health is an approach or indeed movement that places listening to service user voices at the heart of its philosophy, first emerging in the 1980s at a time when people began to voice their experiences of using mental health services that were situated within a medical model. Thus recovery narratives began to appear of people who taught themselves how to live a meaningful life beyond a diagnosis and a "system" that was viewed to limit potential for growth and possibility for wellness (Deegan 1988). Key concepts of this paradigm are hope, positive self image and identity, spiritual connection, relationships, trust in self, self-determination, meaning, confidence and control, personal resourcefulness, and voice (Mental Health Commission 2008).

Recalling a famous logo of the *Zanussi* electrical company, Patrick McGowan, Expert by Experience said that the recovery approach could be regarded as a response to the "appliance of science" (2012, personal communication). The medical model's appliance of science in psychiatry and mental health has been the subject of much criticism that has in turn, fortified the recovery movement. Fervent interest in chemical imbalances and neurology has left many people with a mental health diagnosis feeling lost within a dominant and powerful model that fails to acknowledge individuality and personal resourcefulness (Fisher 2009). Opportunities for personal growth and overcoming mental health difficulties are seen to be constrained within such a model that fails to recognize the impact of social relating upon the individual (Campbell 2009).

Central to the recovery movement is the participation and involvement of "service users" at each and every stage of healthcare planning and delivery. The slogan "nothing about us without us" is one that has been adopted by recovery from the disability movement (Walmsley 2004). This promotes collaboration between those who use and provide services so as to enhance the delivery of healthcare provision that is grounded upon an equal footing where the voices of all parties concerned are respectfully listened to and heard.

Recovery in mental health is an area of practice that is slowly beginning to emerge in the music therapy literature (Grocke et al. 2008; McCaffrey et al. 2011; Solli 2012; Vander Kooij 2009). It places the client or service user at the helm of the therapy process where their lead and direction is followed. This of course resonates with music therapy practice as a whole where meaningful connection and collaboration between both parties is fundamental. However, the recovery approach may also conflict with some of the practices in music therapy that are akin to those of the medical model, particularly those that assume a powerful or dominant position towards the service user. Such challenges are not only faced by music therapists but indeed all those who are deemed to be providers of mental health services (Borg and Kristiansen 2004). Thought-provoking suggestions may be found in policy documents such as those featured in Shepherd et al. (2008).

The recovery movement's call to shift from an illness to wellness paradigm, focusing on capacities rather than limitations, resonates with recent models that have been developed in music therapy. Ansdell and Meehan (2010) point out that "resource-oriented music therapy" (Rolvsjord 2004) and "community music therapy" (Pavlicevic and Ansdell 2004) utilize music as a health promoting resource for people in times of illness. Such models are founded from a sociocultural view of music, health, and illness, and as a consequence, may help to create a possible path for the profession of psychiatry as it deliberates over possible future trajectories (Priebe et al. 2013).

Music therapy has a unique capacity to offer people ways in which to sound their personal narratives in a supportive environment that is centered upon shared human experience in music. It can offer meaningful connections with others in times of distress in esthetically inspired ways that are tailored to meet individual needs, hopes, and aspirations. Such creative pathways towards wellness, as guided by the qualified music therapist, can bridge inner and outer realities while fostering growth and possibility for change.

References

American Psychiatric Association (2013). *Diagnostic and Statistical Manual of Mental Disorders*, 5th edn. Arlington, VA: American Psychiatric Publishing.

Amir, D. (2012). "My music is me": Musical Presentation as a way of forming and sharing identity in music therapy group. *Nordic Journal of Music Therapy* 21(2): 176–193.

Ansdell, G. and Meehan, J. (2010). "Some light at the end of the tunnel" exploring users' evidence for the effectiveness of music therapy in adult mental health settings. *Music and Medicine* 2(1): 29–40.

Anthony, W.A. (1993). Recovery from mental illness: The guiding vision of the mental health service system in the 1990s. *Psychosocial Rehabilitation Journal* 16(4): 11–23.

Baines, S. (2003). A consumer-directed and partnered community mental health music therapy progam: Program development and evaluation. *Voices: A World Forum for Music Therapy*, 3(3). <https://voices.no/index.php/voices/article/view/137/113>. Accessed 29 May 2013.

Baker, F.A. (2013). The environmental conditions that support or constrain the therapeutic songwriting process. *Arts in Psychotherapy* 40(2): 230–238.

Baker, F. and Wigram, T. (2005). *Songwriting: Methods, Techniques and Clinical Applications for Music Therapy Clinicians, Educators and Students*. London: Jessica Kingsley.

Baker, F., Wigram, T., Stott, D., and McFerran, K. (2008). Therapeutic songwriting in music therapy: Part I: Who are the therapists, who are the clients, and why is songwriting used? *Nordic Journal of Music Therapy* 17(2): 105–123.

Bruscia, K.E. (1998). *Defining Music Therapy*. Gilsum, NH: Barcelona.

Borg, M. and Kristiansen, K. (2004). Recovery-oriented professionals: Helping relationships in mental health services. *Journal of Mental Health* 13(5): 493–505.

Burton, A. (2009). Bringing arts-based therapies in from the scientific cold. *The Lancet Neurology* 8(9): 784–785.

Campbell, J. (2009). We are the evidence: An examination of service user research involvement as voice. In: J. Wallcraft, B. Schrank, and M. Amering (eds), *Handbook of Service User Involvement in Mental Health Research*, pp. 113–137. Chichester, West Sussex: Wiley.

Cassity, M.D. (2007). Psychiatric music therapy in 2016: A Delphi poll of the future. *Music Therapy Perspectives* 25(2): 86.

Chalmers, T.C. (1994). Clinical trials of treatment. In: J.A. Barondess and S. Lock (eds), *The Oxford Medical Companion*, pp. 147–150. Oxford: Oxford University Press.

Chinman, M., Young, A. S., Hassell, J., and Davidson, L. (2006). Toward the implementation of mental health consumer provider services. *The Journal of Behavioral Health Services and Research* 33(2): 176–195.

Choi, B.C. (2008). Awareness of music therapy practices and factors influencing specific theoretical approaches. *Journal of music therapy* 45(1): 93.

Clark, C.C., Scott, E.A., Boydell, K.M., and Goering, P. (1999). Effects of client interviewers on client-reported satisfaction with mental health services. *Psychiatric Services* 50(7): 961–963.

College of Psychiatry of Ireland (2013). What is psychiatry? <http://www.irishpsychiatry.ie/Helpful_Info/whatispsychiatry.aspx>. Accessed 1 January 2013.

Davis, W.B. (2003). Ira Maxmillian Altshuler: Psychiatrist and pioneer music therapist. *Journal of Music Therapy* 40(3): 247–263.

Deegan, P.E. (1988). Recovery: The lived experience of rehabilitation. *Psychosocial Rehabilitation Journal* 11(4): 11–19.

De Backer J. and Van Camp, J. (1999). Specific aspects of the music therapy relationship to psychiatry. In: T. Wigram and J. De Backer (eds) *Clinical Applications of Music Therapy in Psychiatry*, pp. 11–23. London: Jessica Kingsley Publishers.

De Nora, T. (2002). *Music in Everyday Life*. Cambridge, UK: Cambridge University Press.

Edwards, J. (1998). Music therapy for children with severe burn injury. *Music Therapy Perspectives* 16: 21–26.

Edwards, J. (2005). Possibilities and problems for evidence-based practice in music therapy. *Arts in Psychotherapy* 32(4): 293–301.

Edwards, J. (2006). Music therapy in the treatment and management of mental disorders. *Irish Journal of Psychological Medicine* 23(6): 33–35.

Erkkilä, J., Punkanen, M., Fachner, J., Ala-Ruona, E., Pöntiö, I., Tervaniemi, M. et al. (2011). Individual music therapy for depression: randomised controlled trial. *The British Journal of Psychiatry* 199(2): 132–139.

Eyre, L. (2011). From ego disintegration to recovery of self. In: A. Meadows, (ed.), *Developments in Music Therapy Practice: Case Study Perspectives*, pp. 385–399. Gilsum, NH: Barcelona.

Field, T., Martinez, A., Nawrocki, T., Pickens, J., Fox, N.A., and Schanberg, S. (1998). Music shifts frontal EEG in depressed adolescents. *Adolescence* 33(129): 109–116.

Fisher, D. (2009). Politics. In: J. Wallcraft, B. Schrank, and M. Amering (eds), *Handbook of Service User Involvement in Mental Health Research*, pp. 227–242. Chichester, West Sussex: Wiley.

Gold, C., Heldal, T., Dahle, T., and Wigram, T. (2005a). Music therapy for schizophrenia or schizophrenia-like illnesses. *Cochrane Database of Systematic Reviews*. Art no.: CD004025. doi: 10.1002/14651858.

Gold, C., Rolvsjord, R., Aaro, L., Aarre, T., Tjemsland, L., and Stige, B. (2005b). Resource-oriented music therapy for psychiatric patients with low therapy motivation: Protocol for a randomised controlled trial [NCT00137189]. *BMC psychiatry* 5(1): 39.

Gold, C., Solli, H.P., Krüger, V., and Lie, S.A. (2009). Dose–response relationship in music therapy for people with serious mental disorders: Systematic review and meta-analysis. *Clinical Psychology Review* 29(3): 193–207.

Grocke, D. and Wigram, T. (2007). *Receptive Methods in Music Therapy: Techniques and Clinical Applications for Music Therapy Clinicians, Educators and Students*. London: Jessica Kingsley.

Grocke, D., Bloch, S., and Castle, D. (2008). Is there a role for music therapy in the care of the severely mentally ill? *Australasian Psychiatry* 16: 442–445.

Hsu, W.C. and Lai, H.L. (2004). Effects of music on major depression in psychiatric inpatients. *Archives of Psychiatric Nursing* 18(5): 193–199.

Jensen, B. (1999). Music therapy with psychiatric in-patients: A case study with a young schizophrenic man. In: T. Wigram and J. De Backer (eds), *Clinical Applications of Music Therapy in Psychiatry*, pp. 44–60. London: Jessica Kingsley.

Kai, J. and Crosland, A. (2001). Perspectives of people with enduring mental ill health from a community-based qualitative study. *The British Journal of General Practice* 51(470): 730–736.

Kaser, V. (2011). Singing in the recovery model. In: A. Meadows (ed.), *Developments in Music Therapy Practice: Case Study Perspectives*, pp. 400–413. Gilsum, NH: Barcelona Publishers.

Kramer, C. (2000). Soul music as exemplified in nineteenth-century German psychiatry. In: P. Gouk (ed.), *Musical Healing in Cultural Contexts*, pp. 137–148. Aldershot: Ashgate.

Lau, J.T.F., and Cheung, C.K. (1999). Discriminatory attitudes to people with intellectual disability or mental health difficulty. *International Social Work* 42(4): 431–444.

Ledger, A. (2001). Song parody for adolescents with cancer. *Australian Journal of Music Therapy* 12: 21–27.

Lin, S.T., Yang, P., Lai, C.Y., Su, Y.Y., Yeh, Y.C., Huang, M.F., and Chen, C.C. (2011). Mental health implications of music: insight from neuroscientific and clinical studies. *Harvard Review of Psychiatry* 19(1): 34–46.

McCaffrey, T. (2013). Music therapists' experience of self in clinical improvisation in music therapy: A phenomenological investigation. *The Arts in Psychotherapy* 40(3): 306–311.

McCaffrey, T., Edwards, J., and Fannon, D. (2011). Is there a role for music therapy in the recovery approach in mental health? *Arts in Psychotherapy* 38(3): 185–189.

McDonald, C. (2006). *Challenging Social Work: The Context of Practice.* Basingstoke: Palgrave Macmillan.

McLaughlin, H. (2009). What's in a name: "client patient," "customer," "consumer," "expert by experience," "service user"—what's next? *British Journal of Social Work* 39(6): 1101–1117.

Maratos, A.S., Gold, C., Wang, X., and Crawford, M.J. (2008). Music therapy for depression. *Cochrane Database of Systematic Reviews.* Art. No.: CD004517. doi: 10.1002/14651858.

Maratos, A., Crawford, M.J., and Procter, S. (2011). Music therapy for depression: it seems to work, but how? *The British Journal of Psychiatry* 199(2): 92–93.

Meadows, A. (Ed.). (2011). *Developments in Music Therapy Practice: Case Study Perspectives*, pp. 385–399. Gilsum, NH: Barcelona.

Mental Health Commission. (2008). *A recovery approach within the Irish mental health service: A framework for development.* Dublin: Mental Health Commission.

Mental Health Commission. (2012). *Your views of mental health inpatient services: Inpatient survey 2011.* Dublin: Mental Health Commission.

Mössler, K., Chen, X., Heldal, T.O., and Gold, C. (2011). Music therapy for people with schizophrenia and schizophrenia-like disorders. *The Cochrane Database Systematic Reviews.* Art. No.: CD004025. doi: 10.1002/14651858.

Mössler, K., Assmus, J., Heldal, T. O., Fuchs, K., and Gold, C. (2012). Music therapy techniques as predictors of change in mental health care. *Arts in Psychotherapy* 39(4): 333–341.

National Institute for Health and Clinical Excellence (2009). *Schizophrenia: Core interventions in the treatment and management of Schizophrenia in primary and secondary care (update).* London: National Institute for Health and Clinical Excellence.

Noone, J. (2008). Developing a music therapy programme within a person centred planning framework. *Voices: A world forum for Music Therapy* 8(3). <https://voices.no/index.php/voices/article/view/420/344>. Accessed 29 May 2013.

O'Callaghan, C.C. (1997). Therapeutic opportunities associated with the music when using song writing in palliative care. *Music Therapy Perspectives* 15(1): 32–38.

O'Callaghan, C. (2003). Music therapy. In: D. Doyle, G. Hanks, N. Cherny, and K. Calman (eds), *Oxford Textbook of Palliative Medicine*, 3rd edn., pp. 1041–1046. Oxford: Oxford University Press.

Odell-Miller H. (1995). Why provide music therapy in the community for adults with mental health problems? *British Journal of Music Therapy* 9: 4–11.

Odell-Miller, H. (1999). Investigating the value of music therapy in psychiatry. In: T. Wigram and J. De Backer (eds), *Clinical Applications of Music Therapy in Psychiatry*, pp. 119–140. London: Jessica Kinsley.

Odell-Miller H. (2007). *The practice of music therapy for adults with mental health problems: the relationship between diagnisis and clincial method.* Doctoral thesis, Aalborg University, Denmark. <http://vbn.aau.dk/files/41635432/odell_miller.pdf>. Accessed 20 May 2013.

Pavlicevic, M. (2000). Improvisation in music therapy: Human communication in sound. *Journal of Music Therapy* 37(4): 269–285.

Pavlicevic, M. and Ansdell, G. (2004). *Community Music Therapy.* London: Jessica Kinsley.

Pavlicevic, M., Trevarthen, C., and Duncan, J. (2000). Improvisational music therapy and the rehabilitation of persons suffering from chronic schizophrenia. In: J.Z. Robarts (ed.),

Music Therapy Research: Growing perspectives in theory and practice, Vol. 1, pp. 44–54. Hertfordshire: British Society for Music Therapy.

Pedersen, I.N. (2003). The revival of the frozen Sea Urchin: Music Therapy with a Psychiatric Patient. *Psychodynamic Music Therapy. Case Studies*, pp. 375–389. Gilsum, NH: Barcelona Publishers.

Priebe, S., Burns, T., and Craig, T.K. (2013). The future of academic psychiatry may be social. *The British Journal of Psychiatry* 202(5): 319–320.

Procter, S. (2004). Playing politics: Community music therapy and the therapeutic redistribution of musical capital for mental health. In: M. Pavlicevic and G. Ansdell (eds), *Community Music Therapy*, pp. 214–232. London: Jessica Kingsley.

Richards, G. (2002). Some problems with measurement. In: G. Richards (ed.), *Putting Psychology in its Place*, 2nd edn., pp. 251–262. New York: Routledge.

Robb, S. (1996). Techniques in song writing: Restoring emotional and physical well being in adolescents who have been traumatically injured. *Music Therapy Perspectives* 14: 30–37.

Rolvsjord, R. (2004). Therapy as Empowerment: Clinical and Political Implications of Empowerment Philosophy in Mental Health Practises of Music Therapy. *Nordic Journal of Music Therapy* 13(2): 99–111.

Rolvsjord, R., Gold, C., and Stige, B. (2005). Research rigour and therapeutic flexibility: Rationale for a therapy manual developed for a randomised controlled trial. *Nordic Journal of Music Therapy* 14(1): 15–32.

Ruud, E. (1997). Music and identity. *Nordic Journal of Music Therapy* 6(1): 3–13.

Ruud, E. (1998). *Music Therapy: Improvisation, Communication and Culture*. Gilsum, NH: Barcelona.

Sackett, D.L., Rosenberg, W., Gray, J.A., Haynes, R.B., and Richardson, W.S. (1996). Evidence based medicine: what it is and what it isn't. *British Medical Journal* 312: 71–72.

Shepherd, G., Boardman, J., and Slade, M. (2008). *Making Recovery a Reality*. London: Sainsbury Centre for Mental Health.

Silverman, M.J. (2003). The influence of music on the symptoms of psychosis: a meta- analysis. *Journal of Music Therapy* 40(1): 27.

Silverman, M.J. (2007). Evaluating current trends in psychiatric music therapy: a descriptive analysis. *Journal of Music Therapy* 44(4): 388.

Silverman, M. (2010). Perceptions of music therapy interventions from inpatients with severe mental illness: A mixed methods approach. *Arts in Psychotherapy* 37(3): 264–268.

Solli, H.P. (2012). Med pasienten i førersetet: Recovery-perspektivets implikasjoner for musikkterapi I psykisk helsearbeid. *Musikterapi i Psykiatrien Online*, 7(2).

Stewart, D. (2002). Sound company: psychodynamic group music therapy as facilitating environment, transformational object and therapeutic playground. In: A. Davies and E. Richards (eds), *Music Therapy and Group Work: Sound Company*, pp. 27–42. London: Jessica Kingsley.

Sweeney, A., Beresford, P., Faulkner, A., Nettle, M., and Rose, D. (2009). *This is Survivor Research*. Ross-on-Wye, UK: PCCS Books.

Talwar, N., Crawford, M., Maratos, A., Nur, U., McDermott, O. and Procter, S. (2006). Music therapy for in-patients with schizophrenia. *British Journal of Psychiatry* 189: 405–409.

Tang, W., Yao, X., and Zheng, Z. (1994). Rehabilitative effect of music therapy for residual schizophrenia: a one-month randomised controlled trail in Shanghai. *British Journal of Psychiatry Suppl.* Aug (24): 38–44.

Turry, A. (2005). Music psychotherapy and community music therapy: Questions and considerations. *Voices: A World Forum for Music Therapy* 5(1). <https://voices.no/index.php/voices/article/view/208/152>. Accessed 28 May 2013.

Tyler, H. (2000). The music therapy profession in modern Britain. In: P. Horden (ed.), *Music as Medicine*, pp. 375–393. Aldershot: Ashgate.

Tyson, F. (1981). *Psychiatric Music Therapy: Origins and Development*. New York: Creative Arts Rehabilitation Centre.

Unkefer, R. and Thaut, M. (2005). *Music Therapy in the Treatment of Adults with Mental Disorders: Theoretical Bases and Clinical Interventions*. Gilsum, NH: Barcelona.

Vander Kooij, C. (2009). Recovery themes in songs written by adults living with serious Mental illnesses. *Canadian Journal of Music Therapy* 15(1): 37–58.

Vink, A.C., Birks, J.S., Bruinsma, M.S., and Scholten, R.J.P.M. (2003). Music therapy for people with dementia. *Cochrane Database of Systematic Reviews*. Art. No.: CD003477. doi: 10.1002/14651858.CD003477.

Wallcraft, J., Schrank, B., and Amering, M. (2009). *A Handbook of Service User Involvement in Mental Health Services*. West Sussex, UK: Wiley.

Wampold, B. (2001). *The Great Psychotherapy Debate: Models, Methods, and findings*. Mahwah, NJ: Erlbaum.

Walmsley, J. (2004). Involving users with learning difficulties in health improvement: lessons from inclusive learning disability research. *Nursing Inquiry* 11(1): 54–64.

Winnicott, D.W. (1965). *The Maturational Processes and the Facilitation Environment: Studies in the Theory of Emotional Development*. London: Hogarth Press.

WHO. (1978). *Primary Health Care: Report of the International Conference of Primary Health Care Alma-Ata, USSR, September 6-12 1978*. World Health Organization: Geneva.

CHAPTER 14

ADULT TRAUMA WORK
IN MUSIC THERAPY

HEIDI AHONEN

Session 24 brought a stunning musical image of a gorgeous, freshly painted, yellow cottage. Mary goes inside and understands that this is her house (not the childhood house). She is not the prisoner of her childhood anymore. She looks out from her window (without shame) and notices that there are other houses too, many houses, with bright colors. There are people in the gardens. Someone waves to her and she waves back. In this dream, Mary made contact with other people. To become visible, you have to be seen by others and look at them, too…

Mary was home. What kind of house was that? It was not a medieval castle or a cave in a haunted forest. It was not her wicked childhood house. No, her home was a lovely cottage, freshly painted, yellow—on the mountains, with a window and door, in a village surrounded by other houses with bright colors and waving people with gardens. She lived in the house with the girl who had a porcelain doll that said "Mommy." Living in this "metaphoric" home, it was safe for her to continue her therapeutic journey…

Ahonen-Eerikainen 2007, p. 274

INTRODUCTION

....

ADULT trauma work in music therapy is well established globally, and various approaches presented in the literature reveal the positive impact of using music as part of a therapeutic process. The main music psychotherapy techniques in adult trauma work include improvisation and music listening. *Clinical improvisation with instruments* (Priestley 1975, 1994; Scheiby 2002; Hadley 1998; Dvorkin 1998; Montello 1998; Turry 1998; Trondalen 2011; Haase and Reinhardt 2011; Sutton 2011; Sekeles 2011) can be referential or non-referential. When *referential (titled) improvisation* (Bruscia 1987) is used in adult trauma work, client's improvisations can be stimulated by their memories, images, feelings, body sensations, artwork, etc. (Bruscia 1987; 1998a,b; Pavlicevic 1997; Priestley 1975, 1994). Referential improvisations are sound projections of a verbalized experience and are useful in exploring unconscious or conscious aspects of client's life (Bruscia 1987). *Non-referential improvisation* refers to the music itself, where the improvisation is built around the sounds without trying to portray anything else (Bruscia 1998b). Feelings and images that arise during the improvisations are discussed afterwards between the therapist and client (Bruscia 1987). *Analytical Music Therapy* (AMT) (Priestley 1975, 1994; Scheiby 2002; Hadley 1998) is a well-recognized approach that has excellent results when working with adult trauma. Other approaches and methods in which trauma has been treated with music therapy are vocal improvisation (for example, Austin 2002, 2008; Bosco 2011; Chumaceiro 2002a, 2002b; Kaser 2011; Loewy and Quentzel 2011), as well as *songwriting* (i.e. Nolan 2002; Baker 2005). There is a body of literature that describes the ways in which *music listening* in a safe relating space of music therapy offers a variety of emotional components for adult trauma survivors (Bonny 1975, 1986, 2002; Bruscia and Grocke 2002; Bunt 2011; Isenberg-Grzeda 1998; Pellitteri 1998; Summer 1998). Music allows clients to experience their feelings and to communicate these within a safe symbolic distance. Therapeutic music listening in adult trauma work may include listening to recorded music, and to the client's own improvisations. Drawing, painting, creative writing, clay work, or creative movement during or after music listening can be used. The therapist can also select music that will enable the client to re-experience their past, for example by using song regression (Bruscia 1998a). Both directed and unguided music imaging can be used (Bruscia 1998a). Additionally, *The Bonny Method of Guided Imagery and Music* (BMGIM) (Bonny 1975, 1986, 2002) is a well-established approach that has indicated good results when working with some types of adult trauma (Bonny 1975, 1986, 2002; Bruscia and Grocke 2002; Meadows 2002; Summer 1990).

GROUP ANALYTIC MUSIC THERAPY

Group Analytic Music Therapy (GAMT) was developed by the author (Ahonen-Eerikainen 2002, 2003, 2007). GAMT is a combination of *group analysis, interpersonal theories,* and *intersubjectivity.* The therapy group is observed and analyzed from three different perspectives responding to: (1) The individual in the group (the intersubjective window); (2) the members with one another (the interpersonal window); and (3) the group-as-a-whole (the group matrix window) (Ashbach and Schermer 1987; Salminen 1997; Foulkes 1964). In therapy situations these individual, interpersonal, and group-as-a-whole processes are closely related. According to the principle of isomorphism, all group-as-a-whole processes mirror individual-level processes, and the individual processes are reflected in group-as-a-whole phenomena (Ettin 1999). The levels of group matrix imply that the group can be discussed and understood as relating to different levels of consciousness: The conscious and the unconscious. *The conscious level* includes *the conscious level of social interactions.* The *three unconscious levels* include *the transference level* (Foulkes 1964, p. 115; Kutter 1982; Salminen 1997; Fiumara 1983, p. 119), *level of projection,* (Fiumara 1983; Salminen 1997; Foulkes 1964; Brown and Zinkin 2000), and *collective unconscious level* (Fiumara 1983; Salminen 1997; Foulkes 1964; Brown and Zinkin 2000). The levels of the group matrix and levels of consciousness become visible in different musical images and dreams that clients experience during GAMT. Musical images may have certain characteristics. The conscious social inter-action includes *music as communication*. The unconscious transference can include musical images as transferences of past experiences and trauma reconstruction, for example when a client says "*That music reminds me of my mother…*" The unconscious projections may include musical images as hidden wishes and fears, projections, containers, self-objects, self-representations, and the self-state images such as "*This music sounds as my feelings feel.*" The collective unconscious includes archetypal and transformative group images that touch the entire group (Ahonen-Eerikainen 2002, 2003, 2007).

The typical time structure of GAMT can vary from 80 minutes to three hours. From my experience, the most effective process will occur when the longer session time and a closed group format is available; that is, where the members of the group are fixed from week to week and there are processes for entering and exiting the group that minimize disruption. During the *warm-up discussion*, clients may speak of their immediate feelings, though this is not obligatory. This is followed by *therapeutic music listening* or *clinical improvisation* dur-ing or after which clients play, paint, draw, write, and/or listen to music. This is followed by verbal group analysis centered on *free-floating spontaneous discussion* and *further improvisa-tions*. The observations, emotions, and images that occur during the musical interventions are discussed. During clinical improvisations clients utilize the same operational strategies and emotional patterns they use in everyday life. The sound world creates projections and transference figures into which clients can place their emotions and thoughts.

TRAUMA DEFINED

Prior to the occurrence of a traumatic event we have certain basic assumptions that guide our life. We may believe that the world is kind, there is meaning in our life, that things make sense, or that we are worthy of having good things happen to us (Janoff-Bulman 1992). Then trauma strikes, sometimes suddenly like a tornado, bringing fear, pain, insecurity, destruc-tion, and many questions. Just as it takes time to clean the hideous destruction of a tornado, it sometimes is even more time consuming to heal the psychological damage of trauma. Sometimes healing is a long process, because during the acute trauma, the old wounds of earlier psychological trauma may have opened at the same time.

Adults seeking music psychotherapy have often been both traumatized and deprived. Being *traumatized* means experiencing something unbearably bad, alongside feelings of helplessness that were experienced too early in life. Being *deprived* means that at some criti-cal developmental age, good enough care was not received. In both situations inadequate empathy and support was available (Ahonen-Eerikainen 2007).

Some authors and practitioners refer to two distinct types of trauma, Type I and Type II (Terr 1994). *Type I trauma* is a single event, catastrophic, and unanticipated incidence/experience (for example, a sexual assault, a serious car crash, a natural disaster, a sudden loss of loved one). *Type II trauma* includes early traumatization, continuous trauma, or psychological trauma that makes a person vulnerable should the Type I trauma occur to them. According to Van der Kolk (1997), trauma is "the result of exposure to an inescapably stressful event that overwhelms a person's coping mechanisms" (cited in Klein and Schermer 2000, p. 4). Different variations of trauma definitions can be found throughout other trauma literature (e.g. Spiers 2001; Young and Blake 1999; McCann and Pearlman 1990; Gold 2000; Schwarz 2002). For example *psychological trauma* is "a sudden, overwhelming disruption of ego functions, imposed by an outside force and comparable to a wounding or crushing of the body by a physical force…. Whether the effect is immediate or delayed, the mind has a limited capacity to sustain itself as a coherent entity in the face of an attack from outside…." (Dowling 1987, p. 48).

During a traumatic event we lose our sense of empowerment, and we are suddenly no longer in control of what happened. We begin to feel vulnerable, suddenly our world no longer feels safe, and surreal feelings of what is happened occur. The meaning of life that held so securely just a short while before may be gone and everything feels strange and unfair. A traumatic event has many possible impacts, and it affects our feelings, thoughts, relationships, behaviors, attitudes, even our dreams. It can impact or cause *Acute Stress Disorder* (ASD), *Post Traumatic Stress Disorder* (PTSD), or *Complex PTSD*.

Remembering trauma includes both short-term and long-term memory, explicit/declarative memory, including facts, concepts, ability to recall the traumatic event, and implicit/nondeclaritive memory such as acts, descriptions, operations based on automatic internal states (Baranowsky 2011; Williams and Poijula 2002; Schwarz 2002; Spiers 2001; Gold 2000; Young and Blake 1999). The traumatic events are recorded in implicit memory (Rothschild 2000) which includes experience of various stimuli, and behaviors that have been learned through conditioning. During a traumatic event, visual sights, auditory sounds, smells, or kinesthetic cues become associated with that event in our mind. These cues easily become triggers that can lead us to have a similar reaction to them that we had during the original trauma event. Because PTSD is a disorder of memory (Rothschild 2000), it is sometimes difficult to make sense of PTSD symptoms and their triggers.

The task of a therapist is to encourage the client to tell their story, and to listen, witness, and validate what the client conveys. Some traumatized memories may be repressed but others may be remembered in detail. Remembering trauma is always a reconstructive process, and it is easily influenced and distorted over time. It is typical that people forget more than what they remember, and that the details are not always accurate. Sometimes we believe our own inaccurate memories. During therapy, it is important to help the client to recover enough information so that they can process the memory and put it into their past (Meichenbaum 1994). Remembering decreases the fear associated with the traumatic events. It is important to understand that memories themselves are not dangerous but they may sometimes feel dangerous. Continuously avoiding trauma memories keeps them in the present, with all their associated emotions, pain, fear, rage, depression, shame, and self-blame (Austin and Rothbaum 2000). The process of remembering helps traumatized clients to understand what happened to them even though the process often includes a painful reactive phase with variety of feelings of anger or grief. However, remembering safely will give the client a sense of empowerment over the experience and the horror they once felt. Music psychotherapy techniques such as clinical improvisation, or music listening such as BMGIM, can help a traumatized client to work through or process their traumatic history. Music can help them to integrate their trauma into their past.

Body memories include the nervous system that communicates the somatic trauma memories between brain and all other parts of the body. When trauma memories are stored as sensations, similar sensations can trigger the memories. Sometimes our body can remember a trauma that our conscious mind cannot. It is possible to experience an implicit (body) memory of trauma without the explicit (thought) memory that is often needed to make sense of it (Rothschild 2000). Emotions that are connected to trauma may also be carried in the body. According to Rothschild (2000) "Emotions, though interpreted and named by the mind, are integrally an experience of the body" (p. 56).

When a person undergoes trauma, there are often three experiential elements; the first, can be described as a devastating physical and/or emotional pain (Winnicott 1986). Secondly, a horrifying experience of total helplessness can occur (Winnicott 1986), and thirdly, a lack of empathy (Sanford 1990; Harwood and Pines 1998). Some therapists have suggested that it is not so much what the clients experienced in their lives that injured them, but the *lack of empathy* shown by important people in their lives during the time when bad things happened (Ahonen-Eerikainen 2007). According to Sanford "Trauma is the absence of healing responses, what *didn't* happen afterward" (1990, p. 22).

The damage trauma causes to the self has been described as a *soul murder* (Shengold 1989) because of the ultimate helplessness and injury that occurs. Sometimes clients describe that they feel as if they are forever damaged, and that they will never be able to have a healthy relationship again, or that they feel as if a part of themselves has been killed off (Klein and Schermer 2000). Sometimes clients simply describe that they have no feeling, that they are numb, as if their hearts were frozen. Some clients simply "do fine when they are not provoked to feel much" (Sanford 1990, p. 27).

GROUP ANALYTIC MUSIC THERAPY
AND TRAUMA WORK

During the last twenty years I have been conducting Group Analytic Music Therapy with traumatized adults including abused women living in a shelter, and women who have migrated through the refugee process. During those therapy groups clients have experienced Herman's (1997) trauma recovery stages which include: (1) Empowerment of the survivor; (2) remembrance and mourning; and (3) reconstructing the trauma story. The participant's lived experiences and shared stories witnessed during typical therapy sessions have included many traumatizing and painful memories. There have been several or multiple losses described including loss of loved ones (husbands, parents, and children); loss of security, finances, health, and home country. Traumatic events such as accidents, abuse, political terror, and human rights abuses have been described. There have also been painfully beautiful memories of lost loved ones, pets, hobbies, and with refugee women, the loss of the physical landscape of the country of origin. During the therapeutic process, each group member's journey has allowed them to explore various difficult emotions such as fear, grief, anxiety, and pain. As the process has emerged, there also have been feelings of hope, peace, and freedom; and a new narrative has started to materialize. The different levels of group analytic group matrix (group-as-a-whole) include *the conscious social interaction level* (music as a form of communication), and *the unconscious projective, transference, and collective unconscious levels.* On the projective level, participants' music often sounds as their feelings feel; their feelings are projected onto the music. On the transference level, images created during musical activities represent meaningful transferential object relations linking them to parents, siblings, loved ones, but also to the perpetrators of abuse. On the collective unconscious level, music activates archetypal images that can be shared by the entire group. The healing factors of the trauma group introduced by Klein and Schermer (2000) also take place during the Group Analytic Music Therapy processes. These include in the beginning telling and witnessing the trauma, then grieving over the trauma and its consequences. After that, little by little, the restructuring of the assumptive world that was damaged during the trauma is undertaken, restoring trust and the sense of reality, which was also damaged during the trauma. Finally, reintegrating the personality occurs.

As a group analyst, I believe that trauma often happens in a group context. If trauma happens between two people, there may be a silent witness who observes but does not help. For example, incest in the family can be overlooked and somehow swept under the carpet. Victims of trauma often repeat their traumas throughout their lives. Once rejected, the victim finds her–or himself again rejected or rejecting. Once bullied, the victim finds her–or himself being bullied again. It is as if people try to look for something different but can only find themselves in a situation that is familiar (Ahonen-Eerikainen 2007).

TRAUMA RECONSTRUCTION

> I first had images about an outer space war—some kind of catastrophe ... strange-looking characters hunting each other.... Then I was back on the Earth ... people fighting against people and mothers trying to protect their children ... people hiding. Violence and hiding ... it was scary. I wanted to stop it but my hands wouldn't obey. Then I remembered how it was when I was a child: Mother and Father drunk ... fighting in the middle of the night. I am scared. I am frozen. I would like to run, but my legs don`t obey. I think I am hiding under my blanket. I cannot breathe. There is nothing I can do. I try not to hear ... I am scared my Dad will kill my Mom. I don`t know how old I am ... maybe five or six.
>
> Ahonen-Eerikainen 2007, p. 145

This example was Samantha's image during a five minutes long *non-referential clinical improvisation* with two pianos. It took place during *Group Analytic Music Therapy* with an adult traumatized as a child, and it illustrates how musical images have an exceptional place in the process of trauma reconstruction. This image, like typical fairy tales, begins in the safe symbolic distance, in a faraway country, as far away as possible. *Once upon a time, there was this ... outer space war ... and a catastrophe somewhere. There were strange-looking characters hunting each other* (not even human beings). In the beginning of the improvisation there is nothing familiar, nothing to do with "me." The improvisation lasts around five minutes, and yet at the end it is all happening in the client's own childhood, in her bedroom. However, it is not a fairy tale but trauma reconstruction (Ahonen-Eerikainen 2007).

If psychological trauma is "an experience of meaning which results in a sense of total helplessness" (Dowling 1987, p. 49), then trauma reconstruction is the re-creation of an affective–cognitive experience of helplessness. It is also the re-creation of an external or internal event of the client at the time of the experience. Trauma reconstruction works if it allows clients to identify in *what way* and *why* they felt helpless. Trauma reconstruction includes true-life details of the event, emotional state of the individual, their id-ego-superego status, and the meaning that is somehow attributed to the event (Dowling 1987).

Images created during music, clinical improvisation or *music listening* can be a source of material for the reconstruction of trauma. During Samantha's clinical improvisation, there are all elements of trauma reconstruction. Her emotional imagery includes sensory/somatic, perceptual/schematic, and cognitive/conceptual, and meaning levels. First, there are the *true-life* details of the event (childhood home; drunken parents; her age, around five to six; hiding under her blanket in the middle of the night; parents fighting; etc.). Second, the client's *emotional state* at the time of the event can be described (fear, bodily symptoms, hiding). Finally, there are several *outcomes* of the *constructive activity of the mind,* the *unique meanings* that are somehow *attributed to this event.* In Samantha's case, she explained having serious difficulties with close relationships all her life but *never really understanding why.* After this improvisation, her insights are better and she begins to work through her trauma. Just like dreams, these images created during music became a unique source of clinical information providing information about Samantha's archaic ego states and trauma. Music as an auditive image provided a window to past memories and material that otherwise may have been unavailable and out of memory (Ahonen-Eerikainen 2007).

The next case vignette also illustrates a musical trauma reconstruction in the supportive GAMT milieu. It indicates how music can bring up past memories and help integrate them into current life:

> The clients have chosen different band instruments (two electric guitars, bass guitar, drum set, keyboard, and two bongo drums) and have begun to improvise. The therapist asks them to play anything that comes to mind. They play for approximately fifteen minutes. After that, the therapist asks the group what kind of observations they have made about themselves while playing.
>
> Bob, who played the drums, looked distressed, and afterward told the therapist he had felt uncomfortable while playing. When the therapist asked the reason, he said he had felt anxious because of the argument between the two electric guitar players sitting on either side of him and that he didn't want to get involved in their dialogue. The therapist asked him how that feeling manifested itself in his playing. He said he had tried to play as quietly as possible so that he wouldn't be dragged into the guitarists' quarrel. "I have always been a peace-loving person," he says, "and I can't stand it if people around me quarrel. When that happens, I always try to be as invisible as possible so that no one will notice me." While trying to play his drums as softly as he could, he had also been holding his breath.
>
> Later, Bob had a recollection of a time when he was less than three years old and cowered in a closet in the entrance hall, holding his breath and trying to be as quiet as possible so that his parents, who were drunk and fighting violently, wouldn't notice him, and he wouldn't be dragged into the fight. "I remember now that I sat in that closet often. I remember the smell of the damp clothes and how rough the woolen fabric felt on my skin."
>
> The auditive sound-world of the music during the playing and listening happened to be much the same as the emotional atmosphere of Bob's childhood. For the therapy process this recollection was of vital importance, since he was able to integrate it into his own present time and history. "I now understand that all my life I have lived as though sitting in a closet," he said during the discussion time. "I haven't dared to do anything more than peep through the crack occasionally to see how other people form relationships and take risks in their life. I haven't dared because I have been too afraid. It has been safer to avoid intimacy." Later in the therapy process, with support from the group, he was able to form relationships outside the group.
>
> Ahonen-Eerikainen 2007, p. 1247–1248

SELF-REPRESENTATION

When working with traumatized adults, images created during music listening or clinical improvisation can also be seen as a form of *self-representation*. In music, just like "in every dream there is a representation, often manifest, of the dreamer himself." (Eisnitz 1987, p. 72.) Self-representation may contain unconscious wishes, fears, values, and inner conflicts. During music therapy with traumatized adults, the connection between traumatizing past experiences and current problems may suddenly begin to make more sense. When clients begin to feel empowered over their paralyzing experiences it means new coping mechanisms and strategies are being developed, and the shadow of shame may diminish. Clients, perhaps for the first time in their lives, experience that they are good enough as they are. Music therapy groups could be compared to a hall of mirrors where each client is confronted with aspects of their psychological, social, or body image (Foulkes and Anthony 1990). The therapy group "acts as a mirror, reflecting how they appear in relating to others" (Chazan 2001, p. 76), and clients discover themselves, seeing who they are in a new light through their experiences in the group mirror. For many clients this is critical, as their family may not have provided that "magical" or good mirror we all need to see ourselves in a healthy light (Ahonen-Eerikainen 2007, p. 7). Their childhood mirror may have been "a grotesquely distorting mirror, reflecting ugly images, freezing images in time, imposing the features of the dead on those of the living, turning the young into the old, the old into the young, or, like a vampire, failing to reflect an image at all (Behr 1988, p. 315). The next example is John's visual image during music listening:

> There is a coffin in the middle of the sea. It must have been thrown there a long time ago from a ship. ... Someone is there, in it. It's already almost full of water. There are people on the beach ... sand and palm trees ... children, puppies, birds, and laughter ... but no one can see the coffin. ... They can only see the Sun ... the water looks so peaceful.
>
> Ahonen-Eerikainen 2007, p. 179

During discussion in the music therapy group, John explains that in this image he felt lonely, shameful, and worthless. Later, he improvises his feelings with the group. His image led the group into a discussion of being isolated, lonely, and how nobody else may see how we feel. As in dreams, in this image there is some level of *manifest representation* of the "dreamer," John himself (Eisnitz 1987, p. 72). There is also the *latent, associative content*. As an outcome, John's self-image says to him: "*Here I am sad*," "*Here I feel lost*," "*Here I feel lonely*," "*No one sees my pain*." During Group Analytic Music therapy with traumatized adults, it is typical that they discover their new identity, perhaps for the first time in their lives. It is like voiding the spell of an old grotesque image of something that made them freeze, preventing them from being visible, audible, livable, or loved. It is like giving them permission to be different, to be themselves, to show their true self, to become visible and audible (Ahonen-Eerikainen 2007, pp. 179–180). According to Singer (1983), "I can only become aware of myself if I am also aware of something that is not myself" (p. 57). In Group Analytic Music Therapy, clients have different ways of dealing with their issues and expressing their feelings. It becomes acceptable to be different, "to be one's own person" (Chazan 2001, p. 55)—to be individual. The goal of therapy is to bring isolated people together and set them free. According to Herman

(1997) "Creating a protected space where survivors can speak the truth is an act of liberation" (p. 247). In the next example, Peter's image during music listening, tells him: "*I'm lonely
because I'm scared and won't let anyone come near.*" (Ahonen-Eerikainen 2007, p. 181.)

> There was a lonely mountain in the middle of the desert, somewhere in Arizona. There was
> nothing else but a mountain in a desert ... only sand ... and a mountain. The mountain was
> full of army equipment and weapons. I was the only person on the mountain. The weapons
> were aimed in all directions. My duty on that mountain was to take care of the weapons ... to
> make sure they were in excellent condition. If I saw an airplane, helicopter, or cars come near,
> it was my duty to shoot them down.
>
> Ahonen-Eerikainen 2007, p. 181

When improvising, musical images and metaphors can integrate different personality traits
and feelings together. In Peter's case, it was his loneliness and isolation as well as elements of
his capabilities and inner resources that were hidden. The images activated in music represented Peter's thoughts about himself. The level of projection, was also activated in the group
following Peter's image. The topic of discussion became: *Is it safe in this group? Do I have to
be strong here? If I talk about my needs, is there anyone listening?* (Ahonen-Eerikainen 2007,
p. 182.)

Self-representation images created during music send messages to the client—"*You experience yourself as*" or how "*You wish to be.*" They enhance the therapy process and provide
new perspectives and tools to reflect clinical material. Just like dreams, musical images may
have either a manifest or a latent nature. The music therapist can focus on either the manifest
content of the client's music or the latent content, that is, the associations that emerge for the
client. Samantha's and Bob's images were manifest. However, John's and Peter's images with
regard to the coffin in the sea and the mountain in Arizona, needed their associations in
order to find the latent thoughts behind the image (Ahonen-Eerikainen 2007).

When I am working with traumatized adults as a therapist, it is important to know
when the client needs verbalization to integrate the musical self-representation experience
into their current life. A ten-minute improvisation can easily lead into a long discussion.
Similarly a ten-minute discussion can lead to a long improvisation. After the improvisation,
I may ask questions or reflect comments that show my interest in areas such as: How was it?
How did it feel? What did you find? What kind of images did you have? What happened in
your body? What did you think about it?

My task as a therapist is to assist the client in making sense of the unconscious processes
being activated during music, and to elevate the unconscious material into the conscious.
An improvisation however superficial can include important unconscious messages.
Without insightful, therapeutic discussion, it may remain concealed. As a therapist, I also
need to know how to allow free association of images to surface. Of course, this isn't meant
to imply that a therapeutic process would not occur without words. Indeed, we can never
translate everything into words. The manifest use of music and the musical process itself
is therapeutic, whether verbalized or not. "Music *is* the Royal Road to the Unconscious"
(Ahonen-Eerikainen 2007, pp. 81–90). As a therapist, it is my choice whether I travel the
manifest lane or the latent association lane as both lead to the unconscious. Music contains
unconscious projections and transferences. Sometimes the client may perceive the therapy
group as a repetition of earlier important people who disappointed them, or traumatized
their vulnerable self. When the client's subjective experience is accepted, validated, and

worked through, it allows for reinstallation and restoration of self-object bonds. It also allows the building of new psychological structures and identities (Harwood and Pines 1998). This reintegration of the personality is the ultimate goal of all psychotherapeutic processes. The goal of Group Analytic Music Therapy with traumatized adults is to link client's past with their present life, to bring their conflicts and symptoms up-to-date, and to achieve a more effective personality integration (Foulkes 1991).

Turning visible

When working with traumatized adults in a group setting, it is typical that one client's image becomes a group image as well and may articulate something about the developmental stage of the entire group. It may allow everyone to grasp something deeper. This means the collective unconscious level of the group has activated (Foulkes 1990). The next example illustrates a group image, a moment containing pain, a common experience for many in this group:

> After an improvisation, and while the group is listening back, Max, who came to therapy group because of burnout and depression, paints a "picture of a baby." Later, he explains that his mother became seriously ill when he was six months old. His twin sisters were born when he was fourteen months old. He felt rejected and worthless. Lately, he has begun to express these feeling of sadness. The therapist began by discussing Max's associations of his picture. She then improvised the picture with him. After this, the therapist raised the image with the group. In earlier sessions, there had been profound sharing about early relationships, particularly relationships with mothers. Max's image deeply touched the group, and everyone wondered how this baby might protect itself from psychological pain. The ultimate topics of the group were: Do I really want to see this neglected and deprived child in me, and how should I take care of him/her? What will happen if I begin to show different aspects of myself here in this group—in my current life? What if I show my weaknesses? Am I going to be accepted or rejected—as so many times before? What kind of "mother" is this group? Is this group experience similar to that of my mother, or is it new? Is it safe to be seen by the others in the group? Do I want to see me?
>
> Ahonen-Eerikainen 2007, p. 199

Music therapy makes it possible for lonely and isolated people to reconnect with their sense of togetherness. For a traumatized person this means: "Together we constitute the healing matrix of compassion and empowerment from which, individually, we have become isolated" (Klein and Schermer 2000, p. 17). The group allows differentiation but still retains a distinguishing wholeness (Pines 1998). This is the nature of an adult trauma work in music therapy. During trauma reconstruction processes, the client can experience all kinds of feelings. Even the most shameful sentiments, secretly carried for decades can be shared. It is therapeutic to be seen and heard—to accept oneself without guilt and shame.

When using music as a tool for symbolic distance, the process is, perhaps surprisingly, quicker and safer. Feelings are brought up sooner so that the process of integration can take place. As the process is always occurring within the safe symbolic distance of music, it is clients who choose how and what to verbalize. In Group Analytic Music Therapy, each interaction occurs in an intersubjective field, with each client experiencing each situation from their own viewpoint (Ahonen-Eerikainen 2007). When clients bring their subjective perspectives into the group, they create an intersubjective field (Harwood and Pines 1998). Working with traumatized people, this intersubjective experience is crucially therapeutic. Everyone's experience must be validated.

Since 1994, I have conducted many GAMT groups with traumatized adults. Analyzing some of them qualitatively (Ahonen-Eerikainen 2007), I discovered certain common features. Most of the cases included a process during which clients symbolically began to "turn more visible" and to "find their lost voices." According to Cattanach (1992), there are two ways to become invisible: To disappear, or to make the loudest noise (p. 17). In both of these situations, "the child is *lost, out of sight* in the *silence* or the screaming (p. 17). The abused child is often an invisible child. "To have your rights disregarded is to become invisible, not to count, so the sense of self is eroded" (Cattanach 1992, p. 17). Miller (1985), Terr (1990), Wohl and Kaufman (1985), Dale (1999), and McCann and Pearlman (1990) all note the significance of process in using art to explore feelings associated with the experiences of traumatized childhood. "Repressed feelings resulting from early childhood trauma take form in the works of artists and poets. For children who have been abused or have witnessed violence in their homes are often *silent in their suffering.* Art expression can be a way for what is secret or confusing to become tangible." (Malchiodi 1990, p. 5). Miller (1985) wrote about her artistic process, "I didn't want to be given psychoanalytic interpretations, didn't want to hear explanations offered in terms of Jungian symbols. I wanted only to let *the child in me speak and paint* long enough for me to *understand her language*" (p. 7).

During the therapy process of Mary, presented in my book, *Group Analytic Music Therapy* (2007), the group of traumatized women first began to recognize their needs and express them. The dreams and musical images presented by individual clients also began to address the same issues. For example, the typical metaphors and symbols included babies (who were born, had needs, were growing, were taken care of) and nature (birds, flying, sea, sailing, diving, growing, seasons changing, mountains, storms, undergrounds, caves, tunnels, wars). The next case vignette explores a typical Group Analytic Music Therapy process with traumatized individuals:

> Mary begins with a projective image during therapeutic music listening: "The scenario is of an old town with heavy strong walls surrounding it. It is a medieval town. Everything that is needed for living is inside the walls." Later on, she says: "This town is like me…. I am determined … have always been the strong one in my family." During the discussion of the painting, the other group members notice that there is no door and that the windows are high.
>
> Pauline has an image in which she is rowing a boat on a large lake. Suddenly she notices that her mother is swimming after her and, instead of coming aboard, she begins to rock the boat. She paints a picture of her mother trying to pull her into the water. In this picture, she is a little girl, about nine years old. During the same session Sara has an image of "freedom." She paints two swans flying in the sky. During the discussion, she recounts her previous dream in which she was first swimming and then, for some unknown reason, began to drown … as if someone were pulling her leg and trying to take her to the bottom of the sea. She didn't feel pain but was scared. In her dream, she was saved by an oil tanker. Someone extended a hand and lifted her from the water to the oil tanker.
>
> The topic of the group discussion was: May I ask for help? Do I have to be strong here? If I express my needs, is there anyone listening? Just like Mary in her castle, clients may feel protected by the "magic circle" of the group, "just like a city dweller inside the walls of a city" (Scategni 1996, p. 29). At the same time, there may be feelings of isolation and fear. Pauline's

image was activated at the level of transference. The theme of the "mother" was raised to the level of social interaction. The group was encouraged to speak about the following topics: What kind of "mother" could this group be? Is it a demanding, swallowing, or nurturing group? How do I behave here in order not to be rejected?

Sara's dream and Pauline's image bring their unconscious fears and hopes that were representative of the group. Images, such as a swan, drowning, oil tanker, medieval castle without doors, etc., were collective in nature. These images returned in further sessions. The conflictual, repetitive, and resistive dimension of transference was activated in Pauline's image. The self-object transference was present in Sara's dream. The group hoped for self-object experiences that were missing during their formative years. At the same time, the group expected and feared the repetition of early experiences of empathic failure. (See Shapiro 1991). In Mary's image, the internal object was used for the projection of intolerable psychic conflicts. The musical image was an effort to make use of a "not me" personification: This is not my feeling or my pain, but that of the music that attacks or stimulates me (Pines 2002, p. 27).

Pauline's image and Sara's dream illustrated the fears and wishes of the group. Also, they may have illustrated fear of dealing with one's feelings. It is common for clients, often in the early phases of therapy, to dream a typical dream in which something threatening appears (Eisnitz 1987, pp. 72–73). In these dreams or musical images, clients demonstrate that they are scared of their feelings and fantasies. They begin to investigate aspects of the unconscious that are frightening and that they wish to avoid. These dreams and images of Mary, Sara, and Pauline collectively illustrate how dreams and musical images can express the hidden fears, hopes, and object representations of the whole group.

During the Session 2 there are several varied images during music listening in the group. For example: Irene has a level of transference image regarding "her mother screaming with her mouth open." She paints and it resembles Edvard Munch's "The Scream." Later, during the discussion, she identifies with her mother: "My mother had a nervous breakdown.... I am scared it will happen to me, too."

Sara again has a powerful projective image of two large birds "flying and being scared of falling down." During the discussion, she speaks about "how difficult it is to jump into relationships, feelings.... It is difficult to trust other people.... It is difficult to trust that others won't begin to dislike me as soon they have met me."

The level of transference represents the group's fear of throwing oneself into the process, while the level of projection elicits previous shocking experiences and fears of falling down: Is it safe in this group? Can I trust this process? If I become more visible here, am I going to be disparaged and hurt or accepted and supported? New, healthier thoughts arise as the group gives support to Pauline: "The childhood traumas don't necessarily have to repeat themselves in my present life and my future. I can make different choices than I made as a child or than my mother made. I can choose!"

During Session 6 Pauline explains that she has ended her abusive relationship with her boyfriend. Immediately after the break-up, she had a dream that moves the group: "I was in my home country ... the mountains.... It was a peaceful day ... it was beautiful. Suddenly I began to feel the earth trembling. I became scared and thought it must be an earthquake. I looked around and noticed that it was a volcano. I was walking on a volcano. Suddenly I woke up."

During music listening, Mary has an image, which brings hope. Mary first draws four pictures, which she then titles: (1) "The Abused One"—a picture of a small girl crying. (2) "The Deluge. The Sky Is Crying"—a picture of a storm. (3) "Saved"—a picture of a large boat that looks like an oil tanker. (4) "The War Is Over"—a picture of a pregnant woman in the middle of the paper with a gun in her hand. It looks like there has been a war ... bodies lying in the ground.... The sky is gray.... There is a red flower on the left side of the paper.

Two polarities are felt strongly: Feelings of fear and of courage. The collective level activates within Pauline's dream. Something that is beautiful and relaxing turns into something threatening and frightening. Mary's image of the oil tanker has two faces. The tanker is a safe place, as it is huge, but it also can be exploitative and life-threatening. The group articulates their fears, their childhoods, and the battles they had to win in order to survive. The therapist brings these themes to the here and now: "How can I be sure that this positive experience in therapy won't turn into something negative as has happened before?"

At the same time, transformation begins to happen. In Mary's image, there was a red flower. This concrete image gives hope for the group. The grieving over the trauma and its consequences continued but some level of restructuring the assumptive world had also begun. It is typical that trauma overwhelmingly challenges our thinking and gives us a sense of continuation (Winnicott 1958, p. 303). The individual's fundamental values are brought into question when trauma happens, such as: Incest, a parent's or parents' death, a parent's or the parents' alcoholism, severe psychiatric illness, or somatic illness (Klein and Schermer 2000, pp. 21–21). These are all true for the clients in this group.

To survive, a trauma victim needs a "good internal holding group" and a mental representation of significant others. The group experience can help to reconstruct each client's damaged "internal holding group" or, in some cases, build a new one over the ashes of the old (Klein and Schermer 2000, pp. 21). The last picture of Mary symbolizes this. Something new is about to be born over the dead bodies of something old that was damaged in past wars. Pauline's dream is her unconscious scenario of her fears. After bringing them to the group, it is possible to discuss her fears and find trust. Her dream is also a group one; it articulates the fears of the group–as–a–whole. The therapist's role is to assist in the integration of dissimilar experiences and contain the strong affects and destructive energies. The therapist, in addition, must help the group to form connections between the fragmented and lost pieces of the inner self. It is like a puzzle in which some pieces are lost. Musical images as well as dreams will normally have a common thematic line, one which points to the shared fundamental issues with which the group is carpet (Schlachet 2002, p. 88).

During Session 7 Mary has a projective image during music listening. She draws a picture in which there is a little girl crying. She then improvises this feeling. It sounds lonely and sad. She also shares a dream she had the previous week … : ""I'm driving my car in the country. There are no houses … no people … just forest. Suddenly I see some kind of package on the pavement. I know I need to stop. It's a swaddled baby. She doesn't cry, but her enormous eyes are open. I take her into my car." This dream brings into the conscious level of the group matrix something profound that is happening in the group-as-a-whole. The group begins to discuss early relationships and the helplessness of the swaddled baby who cannot move her arms or legs, run, or fight back. The enormous open eyes of the baby and the fact the baby does not cry—not anymore, as a group member articulates—touches everyone in the group.

Mary's improvisation of the crying girl is like a corrective and compensative experience for the quietness of the swaddled baby. The image of the hidden cries and the silent screams (Wohl and Kaufman 1985) is moving. All of the clients had experienced this in their past. Even though Mary's image was about her past, there were also collective unconscious-level images that awake everyone in the group. There is a lively discussion about past experiences and the here and now: What kind of "mother" is this group? Is it similar to how my mother was? Is it a new kind of experience about a new kind of mother? What will happen if I begin to show different parts of myself? What will happen if I show my weaknesses? Am I going to accepted or rejected as has happened before? Do I want to be seen by the others? Do I really want to see myself? Do I want to take care of that neglected child in me?

That image of the baby who was about to be born after the war was over, the baby who had been badly neglected in her past, who had many needs, enormous eyes, a hidden cry. This was Mary's image. It was Mary's image about Mary—her inner child, her past, and her traumatized history. It was also the group image of the collective unconscious—something the group was able to share. They all shared the baby, the same traumatic experiences and memories, the fear and shame. The neglected baby was an image of a traumatized person, someone who was helpless, without hands and legs, unable to run away (swaddled baby), who was only able to observe everything that happened around her (enormous open eyes), and who did not cry (any more), and who had been left on the pavement next to the forest (deprived). This is the baby discovered by the group—the baby for whom the group was now providing shelter and a container.

Reflecting on the process, Sessions 6 and 7 were turning points. Metaphorically speaking, the baby was now safe. Now the images can grow. The atmosphere in these two sessions was emotionally charged. The group processed shared feelings and experiences—many babies were about to be born into the group matrix. Clients had become responsible for their own needs.

Ahonen-Eerikainen 2007, pp. 224–274

Externalization–internalization process

When working with traumatized adults in music therapy, both *externalization*[1] and *internalization*[2] are needed. Clients bring to therapy "a complete set of *introjects* of themselves and significant objects from their past, along with characteristic ways of projecting aspects of themselves onto the external world" (Bruscia 1998b, p. 37). As clients interact with the therapist and each other, they unconsciously refer back to these introjections and explore them on the therapist, also projecting them onto music (Bruscia 1998b, p. 37). Music can be viewed both as a transitional object and self-object (Winnicott 1958, 1960, 1964, 1965, 1971a,b,c, 1986; Kohut 1977; Lehtonen 1986, 1989, 1993), and it creates the safety zone and makes it possible to deal with difficult emotions and experiences in the symbolic distance. For instance, in the moment when clients first listen to recorded music, it is heard as something "external" in relation to them. They may feel that it is something abstract and that it does not make sense (Ahonen-Eerikainen 2007, pp. 91–96). As the process develops, clients will have feelings, that is the experience that: *This music sounds just like my feelings feel* (Langer 1953; Pratt 1952a,b). It is important that a music psychotherapy process with traumatized individuals begins from a safe symbolic distance. Clients should be allowed to speak about the feeling of music rather than their own feelings. For example: "This music is very sad … " or "This music is full of anxiety." The next step in the therapeutic process is when the feeling of the music becomes more personal. The client begins to understand that "It's not only the music that is sad … it's me who is sad, too." This is followed by the expression of feelings and communication embedded in the musical dialogue (Ahonen-Eerikainen 2007, p. 96). Musical image-work takes place in what Winnicott (1971c) calls the intermediate third area of experience, the "in between," a space for curiosity, exploration, discovery, the playground of experience (Pines 2003, pp. 30–31).

During the music psychotherapy process with traumatized adults, *external, abstract* music becomes an *internalized, concrete*, personal experience. It touches emotions at a deep level, and it may help them gain an understanding of themselves and their trauma. There may also be some level of cathartic emotional release (Ahonen-Eerikainen 2007).

During the improvisation process, the *internal* feeling of the individual is *externalized*. When clients begin to play, their inner feelings become *externalized*, audible. Using the language of music when working with traumatized adults is effective, because with music we are able to express more complicated feelings than through words. Music is the language of the feelings. Clinical improvisations occur either by the client improvising with the therapist while other clients listen or by the group improvising together (Ahonen-Eerikainen 2007, p. 94).

A typical Group Analytic Music Therapy session with traumatized adults includes:

1. Group improvisation *(externalization)*, recorded.
2. Group listening to recorded clinical improvisation. Images, feelings, and body sensations are observed by clients *(internalization)*.
3. Concrete representations. Sometimes images/feelings/ body sensations are modeled in clay or painted, or creative writing is encouraged *(externalization)*.
4. Individual-in-a-group improvisation (one client improvising and the other group members supporting). Once the writing, painting, etc., is ready, it can be taken to the piano or another instrument and serve as an inspiration for improvisation. I usually ask the improviser first to "Look at the painting and have an inner dialogue with it, and then play how it would sound in music" *(internalization–externalization)*.
5. Free-flowing group analytic discussion about images and feelings and the overall process to end the session *(internalization–externalization)*. (Ahonen-Eerikainen 2007, pp. 94–95).

As an outcome of the externalization–internalization or internalization–externalization process, traumatized clients may work through their trauma, learn about themselves and find new perspectives. Ferenczi (1995) sees dreams as attempts at mastery and settling of traumatic experiences. Images created during music listening or improvisation have the same function, and can be compared to children's play and drama. All musical image work can be considered as self-revealing projections of self. Images created during music therapy interventions are transitional spaces (Winnicott 1971c) in which a child grows through the creative staging of inner plays. They have a psychic cover that provides a safe boundary (Ahonen-Eerikainen 2007). Additionally, the musical image, just like a dream, can be considered a coping process by which the imager tries to expel unacceptable or intolerable feelings (Flanders 1993). Images created during music psychotherapy process when working with traumatized adults are equal to dreams and should be treated no differently than other associative material in psychotherapy processes (Ahonen-Eerikainen 2007). Bonny (2002), in GIM, uses music and imagery that may "provide materials for a client's history, diagnosis, and prognosis simultaneously" (p. 97).

GAMT groups work with auditory and pictorial collages that represent the perceptions of clients. One way to begin a dialogue with images that appear in music is to let the associations appear spontaneously. I usually ask: What do you feel about this image? What ideas, thoughts or words come to your mind when you look or think about it? What part of you is represented in the image? (Ahonen-Eerikainen 2007). When working with traumatized adults, the settings have implications for transference and countertransference (Bruscia 1998b, pp. 5–6; Turry 1998; Scheiby 2002; Montello 1998; Austin 1998; Dvorkin 1998; Bruscia 1987; Priestley 1975, 1994), and it is crucial that the therapist takes care his/her own issues at a personal psychotherapeutic process.

VICARIOUS TRAUMA: THE RISK FOR THE THERAPIST

When working with traumatized individuals, the position of the music therapist position in being an emotional receiver is difficult because professional defence mechanisms may not be always available. We easily become skinless and vulnerable to being absorbed into the client's helpless world. The continual onslaught of emotions and disturbing material from clients may create compassion fatigue, vicarious traumatization, and burn out.

The trauma work that we do as therapists slowly contributes to the changes of our inner self. When we listen to someone's trauma story, we witness a glimpse of their dark world. If we are open emotionally, as empathetic helpers need to be, we will be impacted (Pearlman and MacIan 1995). Vicarious traumatization is what happens to therapists' neurological, cognitive, physical, psychological, emotional, and spiritual health when we repeatedly listen to traumatic stories while having to control our reaction, as we have to, as therapists (Izzo and Carpel Miller 2011). Vicarious traumatization is a process similar to secondary traumatic stress disorder and compassion fatigue (Figley 1995, 2002), and it includes symptoms parallel to the post traumatic stress disorder (PTSD) experiences by survivors (Stamm 1999). It also has an all-encompassing impact of our self-image, world view, relationships, cognitive, emotional and spiritual functioning, and it disrupts our sense of trust and hope (Pearlman and Saakvitne 1995a,b). To take care of oneself continuous, regular clinical supervision with a suitably qualified therapist is crucial when working with traumatized adults. It is also important to have enough personal psychotherapy, as well as trauma therapy training so that the typical processes of trauma work can be understood and effectively worked with in music therapy.

Acknowledgement

All material reprinted from Ahonen-Eerikainen, H. *Group Analytic Music Therapy*, 2007 is reprinted with the permission of Barcelona Publishers LLC.

Notes

1. *Externalization*: "The process by which a mental image is imagined to be outside the self, by which an 'internal object' is projected onto some figure in the external world. In this sense, synonymous with projection and the opposite of introjection not internalization. Fairbairn, however, uses externalization and internalization in a somewhat individual sense to describe the location of objects outside and inside the self during his transitional stage of development." (Rycroft 1995, p. 52).

2. *Internalization*: "Although sometimes used synonymously with introjection, it is best used only to describe that process by which objects in the external world acquire permanent mental representation, i.e., by which percepts are converted into images forming part of our mental furniture and structure" (Rycroft 1995, pp. 84–85).

References

Ahonen-Eerikäinen, H. (2002). Group-analytic music therapy—using dreams and musical images as a pathway to the unconscious levels of the group matrix. *Nordic Journal of Music Therapy* 11(1): 48–53.

Ahonen-Eerikäinen, H. (2003). Unet ja musiikin herättämät mielikuvat kliinisenä materiaal-ina [Dreams and Images created by music as clinical Material]. In E. Ala-Ruona, J. Erkkilä, R. Jukkola, and K. Lehtonen (eds), Muistoissa Petri Lehikoinen 1940–2001. Jyväskylä, Suomen musiikkiterapiayhdistys, pp. 249–265.

Ahonen-Eerikainen, H. (2007). *Group Analytic Music Therapy*. Gilsum. NH: Barcelona Publishers.

Ashbach, C. and Schermer, V. (1987). *Object Relations, the Self, and the Group: A Conceptual Paradigm*. London: Routledge.

Austin, D. (1998/2002). When the psyche sings: transference and countertransference in improvised singing with individual adults. In: K. Bruscia (ed.), *The Dynamics of Music Psychotherapy*, pp. 315–334. Gilsum, NH: Barcelona Publishers.

Austin, D. (2008). *The Theory and Practice of Vocal Pschotherapy: Songs of the Self*. London: Jessica Kingsley Publishers.

Baker, F. (2005). *Songwriting: Methods, Techniques and Clinical Applications for Music Therapy Clinicians, Educators and Students*. Google eBook.

Baranowsky, A. (2011). *Trauma Practice. Tools for Stabilization and Recovery*. Cambridge, MA: Hogrefe Publishing.

Behr, H. L. (1988). A group analytic contribution to family therapy. *Journal of Family Therapy* 10(3): 307–321.

Bonny, H. (1975). Music and Consciousness. *Journal of Music Therapy* 12(3): 121–135.

Bonny, H. (1986). Music and healing. *Music Therapy* 6A(1): 3–12.

Bonny, H. (2002). Guided Imagery and Music (GIM): Mirror of consciousness. In: L. Summer (ed.), *Music Consciousness: The Evolution of Guided Imagery and Music*, pp. 93–102. Gilsum, NH: Barcelona Publishers.

Brown, D. and Zinkin, L. (eds). (2000). *The psyche and the social world: developments in group-analytic theory*. London: Jessica Kingsley Publishers.

Bruscia, K. (1987). *Improvisational Models of Music Therapy*. Springfield, Illinois: Charles C. Thomas.

Bruscia, K. (1998a). *Defining Music Therapy*. Phoenixville: Barcelona Publishers.

Bruscia, K. (1998b). *The Dynamics of Music Psychotherapy*. Gilsum, NH: Barcelona Publishers.

Bruscia, K. and Grocke, D. (2002). *Guided Imagery and Music: The Bonny Method and Beyond*. Gilsum, NH: Barcelona Publishers.

Bosco, F. (2011). The use of elemental music alignment in the journey from singer to healer/therapist. In: A. Meadows (ed.), *Developments in Music Therapy Practice: Case Study Perspectives*, pp. 470–485. Gilsum, NH: Barcelona Publishers.

Bunt, L. (2011). Bringing light into darkness: guided imagery and music, bereavement, loss and working through trauma. In: A. Meadows (ed.), *Developments in Music Therapy Practice: Case Study Perspectives*, pp. 501–517. Gilsum, NH: Barcelona Publishers.

Cattanach, A. (1992). *Play Therapy with Abused Children*. London: Jessica Kingsley Publishers.

Chazan, R. (2001). *The Group as Therapist*. London: Jessica Kingsley Publishers.

Chumaceiro, C.L. de. (2002a). Unconsciously induced song recall: a historical perspec-tive. In: K. Bruscia (ed.), *The Dynamics of Music Psychotherapy*, pp. 335–364. Gilsum, NH: Barcelona Publishers.

Chumaceiro, C.L. de. (2002b). Consciously induced song recall: transference-countertransference implications. In: K. Bruscia (ed.), *The Dynamics of Music Psychotherapy*, pp. 365–386. Gilsum, NH: Barcelona Publishers.

Dale, G., Kendall, J.C., Humber, K., and Sheehan, L. (1999). Screening young foster child for posttraumatic stress disorder and responding to their needs for treatment. *APSAC Advisor* 12(2): 6–9.

Dowling, S. (1987). The Interpretation of Dreams in the Reconstruction of Trauma. In: A. Rothstein (ed.), *The Interpretation of Dreams in Clinical Work*, pp. 44–56. New York: IUP.

Dvorkin, J.M. (1998). Transference and countertransference in group improvisation therapy. In: K. Bruscia (ed.), *The Dynamics of Music Psychotherapy*, pp. 287–298. Gilsum, NH: Barcelona Publishers.

Eisnitz, A.J. (1987). The Perspective of the Self Representation in Dreams. In: A. Rothstein (ed.), *The Interpretations of Dreams in Clinical Work*, pp. 69–85.

Ettin, M. (1999). *Foundations and Applications of Group Psychotherapy. International Library of Group Analysis 10*. London: Jessica Kingsley Publishers.

Ferenczi, S. (1995). *The Clinical Diary of Sandor Ferenczi*. Harvard University Press.

Figley C.R. (1995). Compassion Fatigue as Secondary Traumatic Stress Disorder: An Overview. In: Figley C.R. (ed.), *Compassion Fatigue: Coping with Secondary Traumatic Stress Disorder in Those Who Treat the Traumatized*, pp. 1–20. New York: Brunner/Mazel.

Figley, C.R. (ed.) (2002). *Treating Compassion Fatigue*. New York: Brunner/Routledge.

Fiumara, R. (1983). Analytical psychology and group analytic psycho-therapy: convergences. In: M. Pines (ed.), *The Evolution of Group Analysis*, pp. 109–127. London: Routledge & Kegan Paul.

Flanders, S. (1993). *The Dream Discourse Today*. London: Routledge.

Foulkes, D. (1991). Why study dreaming: One researcher's perspective. *Dreaming* 1(3): 245.

Foulkes, S.H. (1964). *Therapeutic Group Analysis*. London: GA and Unwin Ltd.

Foulkes, S. H., and Anthony, E. J. (1990). *Group psychotherapy. The psychoanalytic approach* (2nd ed.). London: Karnac Books.

Foulkes, S.H. (1990). Access to unconscious processes in the group analytic group. In: S.H. Foulkes and M. Pines (eds), *Selected Papers: Psychoanalysis and Group Analysis*. London: Karnac.

Gold, S.N. (2000). *Not Trauma Alone. Therapy for Child Abuse Survivors in Family and Social Context*. New York: Brunner-Routledge.

Haase, U. and Reinhardt, A. (2011). "Taking a close look": emotional awareness as a core principle in the music therapy treatment of a patient with an anxious-avoidant personality disorder. In: A. Meadows (ed.), *Developments in Music Therapy Practice: Case Study Perspectives*, pp. 453–469. Gilsum, NH: Barcelona Publishers.

Hadley, S. (1998). Transference experiences in two forms of improvisational music therapy. In: K. Bruscia (ed.), *The Dynamics of Music Psychotherapy*, pp. 249–286. Gilsum, NH: Barcelona Publishers.

Harwood, I. and Pines, M. (1998). *Self-Experiences in Group: Intersubjective and Self-Psychological Pathways to Human Understanding. International Library of Group Analysis, 4*. London: Jessica Kingsley Publishers.

Herman, J. (1997). *Trauma and Recovery*. New York: Basic Books.

Isenberg-Grzeda, C. (1998). Transference structures in guided imagery and music. In: K. Bruscia (ed.), *The Dynamics of Music Psychotherapy*, pp. 461–480. Gilsum, NH: Barcelona Publishers.

Izzo, E. and Carpel Miller, V. (2011). *Second-hand Shock: Surviving and Overcoming Vicarious Trauma*. San Diego, CA: High Conflict Institute Press.

Janoff-Bulman, R. (1992). *Shattered Assumptions: Towards a New Psychology of Trauma*. New York: Free Press.

Kaser, V. (2011). Singing in the recovery model with a chronic mentally ill offender. In: A. Meadows (ed.), *Developments in Music Therapy Practice: Case Study Perspectives*, pp. 400–415. Gilsum, NH: Barcelona Publishers.

Klein, R.H. and Schermer, V.L. (2000). *Group Psychotherapy for Psychological Trauma*. New York: The Gilford Press.

Kohut, H. (1977). *The Restoration of the Self*. New York: International Universities Press.

Kutter, P. (1982). *Basic Aspects of Psychoanalytic Group Therapy*. London: Karnac.

Langer, S. (1953). *Feeling and Form*. London: Routledge & Kegan Paul.

Lehtonen, K. (1986). Musiikki Psyykkisen Tyoskentelyn Edistäjänä. Doctoral Dissertation. Annales Universtatis Turkuensis. Serie C: 56. Finland: University of Turku.

Lehtonen, K. (1989). Musiikki Terveyden Edistäjänä. Porvoo-Helsinki-Juva: WSOY.

Lehtonen, K. (1993). Musiikki Sitomisen Välineenä. Reports of Psychiatria Fennica. Report No. 106. Finland: Foundation for psychiatric research.

Loewy, J. and Quentzel, S. (2011). The case of Paula: music psychotherapy with a musician. In: A. Meadows (ed.), *Developments in Music Therapy Practice: Case Study Perspectives*, pp. 297–312. Gilsum, NH: Barcelona Publishers.

Malchiodi, C. (1990). *Breaking the Silence*. New York: Brunner and Mazel.

McCann, L. and Pearlman L.A. (1990). *Psychological Trauma and the Adult Survivor. Theory, Therapy and Transformation*. New York: Brunner and Mazel.

Meadows, A. (2002). Distinctions between the Bonny Method of Guided Imagery and Music (BMGIM) and other imagery techniques. In: K. Bruscia and D. Grocke (eds), *Guided Imagery and Music: The Bonny Method and Beyond*, pp. 63–83. Gilsum, NH: Barcelona Publishers.

Meichenbaum, D. (1994). *A Clinical Handbook/Practical Therapist Manual for Assessing and Treating Adults with Post-Traumatic Stress Disorder*. Ontario, Canada: Institute Press.

Miller, K.A. (1985). *Emigrants and Exiles*. New York: Oxford University Press.

Montello, L. (1998). Relational issues in psychoanalytic music therapy with traumatized individuals. In: K. Bruscia (ed.), *The Dynamics of Music Psychotherapy*, pp. 299–314. Gilsum, NH: Barcelona Publishers.

Nolan, P. (1998/2002). Countertransference in clinical song-writing. In: K. Bruscia (ed.), *The Dynamics of Music Psychotherapy*, pp. 387–406. Gilsum, NH: Barcelona Publishers.

Pavlicevic, M. (1997). *Music Therapy in Context. Music, Meaning and Relationships*. London: Jessica Kingsley Publishers.

Pearlman, L.A. and MacIan, P.S. (1995). Vicarious traumatization: An empirical study of the effects of trauma work on trauma therapists. *Professional Psychology: Research and Practice* 26: 558–565.

Pearlman, L.A. and Saakvitne, K.W. (1995a). Treating therapists with vicarious traumatization and secondary traumatic stress disorders. In: C. R. Figley (ed.), *Compassion Fatigue: Coping with Secondary Traumatic Stress Disorder in Those Who Treat the Traumatized*. New York: Brunner/Mazel.

Pearlman, L.A. and Saakvitne, K.W. (1995b). *Trauma and the Therapist: Countertransference and Vicarious Traumatization in Psychotherapy with Incest Survivors*. New York: Norton.

Pellitteri, J. (1998). A self-analysis of transference in guided imagery and music. In: K. Bruscia (ed.), *The Dynamics of Music Psychotherapy*, pp. 481–490. Gilsum, NH: Barcelona Publishers.

Pines, M. (1998). What should a psychotherapist know? In: M. Pines (ed.), *Circular Reflections*. London: Jessica Kingsely Publishers.

Pines, M. (2002). The Illumination of Dreams. In: C. Neri, R. Friedman, and M. Pines (eds), *Dreams in Group Psychotherapy*, pp. 25–36. London: Jessica Kingsley Publishers.

Pines, M. (2003). The Time Unlimited Group. *Group Analysis* 36/2.224–227.

Pratt, C.C. (1952a). Music as the Language of Emotion. Lecture delivered in the Whittall Pavilion of the Library of Congress, December 21, 1950. Washington, DC: U.S. Government Printing Office.

Pratt, C.C. (1952b). *Music as the language of emotion: a lecture delivered in the Whittall Pavilion of the Library of Congress, December 21, 1950*. US Govt. Printing Office.

Priestley, M. (1975). *Music Therapy in Action*. London: Constable and Company Limited.

Priestley, M. (1994). *Essays on Analytical Music Therapy*. Gilsum, NH: Barcelona Publishers.

Rothschild, B. (2000). The body remembers: the psychophysiology of trauma and trauma treatment. New York: W.W. Norton and Company, Inc.

Rycroft, C. (1995). *A Critical Dictionary of Psychoanalysis*, new edn. London: Penguin Books.

Salminen, H. (1997). Ryhmäanalyysin Perusteet. [Basics of Group Analysis.] Jyväskylä: Gummerus kirjapaino Oy.

Sanford, L.T. (1990). *Strong at the Broken Places*. New York: Random House.

Scategni, W. (1996). *Psychodrama, Group Processes and Dreams: Archetypal Images of Inidividuation*. New York: Taylor & Francis.

Scheiby, B.B. (2002). Improvisation as a musical healing tool and life approach theoretical and clinical applications of analytical music therapy (AMT) in a short and long term rehabilitation facility. In: J.Th. Eschen (ed.), *Analytical Music Therapy*. London: Jessica Kingsley Publishers.

Schlachet, P. (2002). Sharing dreams in group therapy. In: C. Neri, R. Friedman, and M. Pines (eds), *Dreams in Group Psychotherapy*, pp. 79–97. London: Jessica Kingsley Publishers.

Schwarz, R. (2002). *Tools for Transforming Trauma*. New York: Brunner & Routledge.

Sekeles, C. (2011). From the highest height to the lowest depth: music therapy with a paraplegic soldier. In: A. Meadows (ed.), *Developments in Music Therapy Practice: Case Study Perspectives*, pp. 313–333. Gilsum, NH: Barcelona Publishers.

Shapiro, E. (1991). Empathy and safety in group: a self-psychology perspective. *Behavioral Science* 15(41): 219–224.

Shengold, L. (1989). *Soul Murder: The effects of Childhood Abuse and Deprivation*. New Haven, CT: Yale University Press.

Singer, P. (1983). *Hegel*. Oxford: Oxford University Press.

Spiers, T. (2001). *Trauma—A Practitioner's Guide to Counselling*. New York: Taylor & Francis.

Stamm, B.H. (ed.) (1999). *Secondary Traumatic Stress: Self-care Issues for Clinicians, Researchers, and Educators*, 2nd edn. Lutherville, MD: Sidran Press.

Summer, L. (1990). *Guided Imagery and Music in the Institutional Setting*. St. Louis: MMB Music.

Summer, L. (1998). The pure music transference in guided imagery and music. In: K. Bruscia (ed.), *The Dynamics of Music Psychotherapy*, pp. 431–460. Gilsum, NH: Barcelona Publishers.

Sutton, J. (2011). A flash of the obvious: music therapy and trauma. In: A. Meadows (ed.), *Developments in Music Therapy Practice: Case Study Perspectives*, pp. 368–384. Gilsum, NH: Barcelona Publishers.

Terr, L.C. (1990). Too Scared to Cry: Psychic Trauma in Childhood. New York: Harper & Row.

Terr, L.C. (1994). *Unchained Memories: True Stories of Traumatic Memories, Lost and Found.* New York: HarperCollins Publishers.

Trondalen, G. (2011). Music is about feelings: music therapy with a young man suffering from anorexia nervosa. In: A. Meadows (ed.), *Developments in Music Therapy Practice: Case Study Perspectives*, pp. 434–452. Gilsum, NH: Barcelona Publishers.

Turry, A. (1998). Transference and countertransference in Nordoff-Robbins music therapy. In K. Bruscia (ed.), *The Dynamics of Music Psychotherapy*, pp. 161–212. Gilsum, NH: Barcelona Publishers.

Van der Kolk, B.A. (1997). The psychobiology of post-traumatic stress disorder. *Journal of Clinical Psychiatry* 58: 16–24.

Williams, M.B. and Poijula, S. (2002). *The PTSD workbook: Simple, effective techniques for overcoming traumatic stress symptoms.* Oakland, CA: New Harbinger Publications.

Winnicott, D.W. (1958). Primary maternal preoccupation. In: D. Winnicott, *Collected Papers: Through Paediatrics to Psychoanalysis*, pp. 300–305. New York: Basic Books.

Winnicott, D.W. (1960). The theory of the parent-child relationship. *International Journal of Psycho-Analysis* 41: 585–595.

Winnicott, D.W. (1964). *The Baby as a Person. In The Child, the Family, and the Outside World.* London: Penguin Books.

Winnicott, D.W. (1965). Ego distortion in terms of true and false self. In: D. Winnicott, *The Maturational Processes and the Facilitating Environment: Studies in the Theory of Emotional Development*, pp. 140–152. New York: International Universities Press.

Winnicott, D.W. (1971a). *Playing and Reality.* London: Routledge. [Original work published in 1951.]

Winnicott, D.W. (1971b). Mirror role of mother and family in child development. In: D. Winnicott, *Playing and Reality*, pp. 111–118. London: Routledge.

Winnicott, D.W. (1971c). Transitional objects and transitional phenomena. In: D. Winnicott, *Playing and Reality*, pp. 1–25. London: Routledge.

Winnicott, D.W. (1986). *Holding and Interpretation: Fragment of an Analysis.* New York: Grove Press.

Wohl, A. and Kaufman, B. (1985). *Silent screams and hidden Cries: An interpretation of Artwork by Children from Violent Homes.* New York: Brunner Mazel.

Young, B.H. and Blake, D.D. (1999). *Group Treatments for Post-Traumatic Stress Disorder.* Philadelphia, PA: Brunner and Mazel.

CHAPTER 15

MUSIC THERAPY FOR WOMEN WHO HAVE EXPERIENCED DOMESTIC VIOLENCE

SANDRA L. CURTIS

MUSIC therapists working in the area of domestic violence represent an emergent, but growing practice (Cassity and Theobold 1990; Curtis 2000, 2006, 2008, 2013; Curtis and Harrison 2006; Fesler 2007; Hahna 2004; Hahna and Borling 2004; Hernández-Ruiz 2005; Laswell 2001; Lee 2007; Rinker 1991; Slotoroff 1994; Teague et al. 2006; Whipple and Lindsey 1999; York 2006; York and Curtis, 2015). The scope and the nature of this practice will be explored in this chapter, however prior to doing so attention must first be directed to issues surrounding the term "domestic violence."

Domestic violence is currently the most popularly-used and widely-recognized term for this phenomenon. It is for this reason it was chosen for use in this chapter's title. There has, however, been longstanding contention around the use of this term, as with the naming of all forms of violence against women (Brown 2008; Curtis, 2013). The term serves to mask the dimensions of gender and power involved, as well as individualizing the problem and effectively ignoring its sociopolitical underpinnings. It also masks the connection between this type of violence and all forms of male violence against women. In reality, women are overwhelmingly the victims of violence in intimate relationships (whether from husbands, ex-husbands, or boyfriends) and this violence is rooted in a sociopolitical context which supports it and connects it with such other forms of male violence against women as sexual assault and childhood sexual abuse (Curtis 1996, 2000; Sinha 2013). As a result to ensure a better understanding, the preferred term for all types of this violence is woman abuse, with intimate male partner violence (IMPV) the preferred term for violence against women in their intimate relationships. It should be noted that men can be victims of violence, but this violence is different in its nature, its scope, and its impact, and should therefore be addressed separately.

Having looked at the important issues surrounding the naming and understanding of this violence, attention will be directed to its incidence, followed by women's experiences of it. This shall include both the challenges they face and the great strengths they demonstrate. The chapter will then turn to the ways in which music therapy—when informed by the latest understanding of woman abuse and by a multicultural approach of cultural humility—can be effectively used to free women from the harm of such violence and to ultimately empower them as they reclaim their lives.

INTIMATE MALE PARTNER VIOLENCE: INCIDENCE

The incidence rate of IMPV is difficult to accurately determine because sociopolitical factors render it difficult to report and unlikely, until recently, to be counted (Curtis 2008, 2013; Sinha 2013; York and Curtis 2015). Historically, public awareness has ebbed and waned, remaining relatively minimal until a specific incident makes the headlines; it generates much discussion at the time—although typically in terms of an individual love story gone wrong—and then it drops from public consciousness, replaced by the next headliner. There is, however, some increasing understanding that IMPV is a serious and pervasive phenomenon facing many women (Sinha 2013). Internationally, it is identified as one of the most common forms of violence against women (Sinha 2013). Of those who do report intimate partner violence in the US, women account for 85 percent, with an average of three women per day killed by their intimate male partner and one in four women experiencing IMPV at some point in their lifetime (Black et al. 2011; National Coalition against Domestic Violence 2012). Incidence rates are similar in other countries, showing IMPV to take not only a personal toll but also a social and economic toll with such costs as health care, legal services, and productivity loss (Curtis 2008; Kanani 2012; Sinha 2013; Teague et al. 2006). In Canada, the total cost of IMPV has been estimated at 4.8 billion (Sinha 2013). Ultimately, with women reluctant to report abuse (and understandably so), music therapists can expect to see an increasing number of women survivors of IMPV—whether or not they work at agencies specifically providing services for them and whether or not the women have identified themselves as abuse survivors.

WOMEN'S EXPERIENCES OF IMPV

In discussing women and their experiences of IMPV, it is important to be careful in identifying certain parameters. Historically, abused women have been blamed for the abuse in looking to identify individual characteristics which result in their seeking out and/or remaining in abusive relationships. In contrast, what follows is a discussion of women's experiences in terms of the *results* of harmful and longstanding violence with an understanding that individual women's experiences can vary dramatically depending on: The nature of the violence and the relationship; available personal, interpersonal, and societal resources; coping skills; and the presence or absence of children. These can be further influenced by any intersection of such other sources of oppression as racism, classism, sexism, ableism, etc. Ultimately in describing women's experiences, beyond focusing on effects rather than causes, it is important also to move past defining women solely as victims or even solely as survivors. As one woman emphasized—her life is about so much more.

IMPV involves both physical and emotional impact. The physical impact can be severe and includes immediate impact as well as a negative impact on the physical health across the lifespan. The immediate physical impact includes: Physical injury (affecting four in ten women victims of IMPV) often requiring medical attention, treatment in hospitals, and time off work. It can involve physical and sexual assault (Sinha 2013).

Despite the considerable severity of the physical impact, it is the emotional impact of IMPV that women report as the most challenging to overcome (Curtis 2000). The emotional impact varies considerably from woman to woman and can include: Anxiety, fear, depression, sleep problems, stress, psychological distress, decreased self-esteem, and subsequent feelings of self-blame and shame (Curtis 2013; Sinha 2013; York and Curtis, 2015). These feelings of self-blame and shame are not merited, but reflect internalization of their experiences of violence. Women can also experience such diametrically-opposed responses as hypervigilance and denial, flooding, and numbing (Burstow 2003; Curtis 2013).

In looking at the negative impact of IMPV, it is important not to overlook the great strength and resilience women exhibit in their efforts to escape and recover from their experiences of violence (Burstow 2003; Curtis 2013; Curtis and Harrison 2006). They demonstrate many strong survival skills and effective coping strategies—within the abusive relationship, in seeking to escape from it, and in recovering afterwards. They are diligent in their care for their children and in their efforts to secure their safety.

Any consideration of the diversity of women and their experiences of IMPV must also be taken in conjunction with the manner in which that interacts with the diversity of music therapists and within the therapeutic process. In discussing diversity considerations for therapists, Brown (2008) identifies a variety of social locations which can give rise to differing experiences of oppression and privilege, and which can include: "Age, disability, religion, ethnicity, social class, sexual orientation, indigenous heritage, national origin, and gender/sex, as well as vocation, body size, health, experiences of colonization, and choices concerning partnership and parenting" (Curtis 2013, p. 6). Therapists must keep in mind the impact of their clients' social locations as well as their own if they hope to provide effective and sensitive therapy. Yet this poses considerable challenges, requiring more than an intellectual understanding of this intersectionality. Most recent recommendations to assist in this involve "cultural humility" (Brown 2008; Juarez et al. 2005; Schachter et al. 2008; Tervalon and Murray-Garcia 1998). This lifelong process of self-reflection requires therapists to act as allies and advocates for their clients while recognizing their individual skills and perspectives, to acknowledge the therapists' own limitations while demonstrating a willingness to learn, and to respect the diversity of the human experience.

With an understanding of the nature of woman abuse in general and IMPV in particular, a recognition of the diversity of the lives of clients and therapists alike, and a review of the importance of an approach of cultural humility, it is appropriate to turn in the section which follows to an examination of the specific use of music therapy to empower women who have experienced IMPV.

Music therapy to empower women who have experienced IMPV

Of the recently emerging practice of music therapy with abused women, an increasing segment involves Feminist Music Therapy (Curtis 2000, 2013; Hadley 2006; Purdon 2006; York

2006; York and Curtis, 2015). This makes sense since this particular approach adheres to the most recent and best informed conceptualization of male violence against women with a sociopolitical understanding of its nature. It also involves a broader understanding of women's lives and experiences which encompasses not only the influences of sex/gender, but the complex intersection of the full array of possible sources of oppression discussed earlier in the cultural humility approach: Age, ability, religion, ethnicity, social class, sexual orientation, indigenous heritage, national origin, and gender/sex, as well as vocation, body size, health, experiences of colonization, and choices concerning partnership and parenting. Given this, Feminist Music Therapy, while applicable for work with any client population, is particularly well suited for work with women survivors of violence. Given this particular suitability of Feminist Music Therapy and given that this approach is being increasingly embraced in the music therapy practice with survivors of IMPV, it is this approach which will be the focus of this chapter in the section which follows.

Feminist music therapy with abused women

Feminist Music Therapy evolved, like feminist therapy and like feminism itself, as a grass-roots movement and subsequently it reflects some diversity—a diversity which is embraced by its practitioners as both enriching and essential. Each practitioner brings to it their own understanding of feminism and the way this informs their therapy within the context of their own particular social locations and experiences. Yet underlying this diversity is a foundation common to all which is rooted in a "feminist belief system with its sociopolitical understanding of men's and women's lives as they are constructed within a patriarchal culture" (Curtis 2007, p. 199).

Given the commonalities and diversities within Feminist Music Therapy and among Feminist Music Therapists, it is important to be aware that what follows is a description of Feminist Music Therapy practice with abused women framed within my own particular context and experiences of intersectionality. These experiences started in 1996 with my development of the first model of Feminist Music Therapy (Curtis 2000) and evolved from my ongoing work with abused women and girls in the United States and Canada over the intervening years. The unique feminist understanding that underpins Feminist Music Therapy is reflected in its signature goals: To facilitate a sociopolitical understanding of women's experiences—of life in general and of abuse in particular; to empower women—personally, interpersonally, and politically; to foster recovery from the harm of violence; and to bring about personal and social change (Curtis, 2000, 2007, 2008). These goals make it explicit that work within therapy alone is insufficient; change on the sociopolitical level is also required—both on the part of the therapist and the client. This social activism component will be looked at later in the chapter. Attention will be turned first to the techniques used within Feminist Music Therapy.

Feminist Music Therapy techniques, although small in number, are a powerful reflection of its hallmark goals. Although unique in their philosophical framework and their application, they translate into some music experiences seen used for other purposes in other music therapy approaches. These techniques include: Feminist analysis of power and gender; women's empowerment; and the valuing of women and women's perspectives.

Feminist analysis of power and gender is accomplished through such music experiences as lyric analysis, songwriting, and recording/performance. Lyric analysis allows an opportunity to explore a diversity of issues surrounding power and gender role socialization that impact women and men—not just abuse, but a full spectrum including love, relationships, gender-role socialization throughout the life span, change, control, anger, self-nurturing, strength and empowerment, and witnessing (Curtis 2000, 2013). In lyric analysis, it is important to move from listening to pre-recorded music to performing live in the group under the music therapist's leadership. Listening to pre-recorded music allows the clients to hear similar stories from others (including well-known singer-songwriters), thus breaking the social isolation and countering the message from abusers (and at times society) that it is their fault and that it happens only to them. Performing the music live allows the clients to internalize the song, to make it their own. The music therapist can provide a good selection of diverse music from which the clients can choose; clients may also bring in their own and this can be a particularly effective way of empowering them and of addressing multicultural issues, as clients can be experts of their own music, their own culture, and their own lives. There is a wide selection of music available and the collection will vary for each music therapist depending on client makeup and interests. Music written by and/or at least performed by women is highly recommended as this allows the clients to more readily identify with the song lyrics. A partial listing of appropriate songs by theme can be found in Women Survivors of Abuse and Developmental Trauma, Chapter 8 in Eyre's *Guidelines for Music Therapy Practice: Mental health* (Curtis, 2013, pp. 11–12). Songwriting and recording serve as excellent follow ups to Lyric Analysis and are effective therapeutic experiences in which to accomplish Feminist Analysis. They are also effective tools for facilitating women's empowerment and so they shall be looked at next.

Women's empowerment is accomplished through a variety of music experiences—in addition to songwriting and recording, this can include improvisation in general, and drumming in particular in its use for body work and fostering self-esteem. In looking at each of these, it is important to remember that women's empowerment should be accomplished at the personal, interpersonal, and sociopolitical levels. Music therapists must focus with their clients on all levels as they move from work within the private sphere (in therapy, in their lives, and in their interpersonal relationships) to work in the public sphere (in social activism).

Songwriting and recording, when carefully introduced by the music therapist, provide a wonderful opportunity for women to give voice to their own experiences—a voice that is long silenced by abusers and an unresponsive (or at least inappropriately responding) community health and legal system. Telling their stories and letting them be heard through song—or witnessing—validates their experiences while allowing them to challenge the status quo, taking the feminist analysis from the impersonal level of lyric analysis to the very personal level of their own lived experiences. The subsequent recording of these original compositions can ultimately foster their sense of self-worth sometimes in a very profound way. Women have the choice of recording the song with themselves singing or having the music therapist perform it for them. In either case, the recording must be of the highest quality; and in either case the result is a powerful, esthetic reflection of the woman's own creativity and a testimony of her resilience.

Improvisation and drumming can also provide wonderful empowerment opportunities. Improvisation permits self-expression which bypasses the verbal; as such it allows intimacy and honesty without fear of judgement. Drumming which makes use of large powerful instruments and large powerful sounds provides unparalleled opportunities to address the important issues surrounding body and power that face abused women. Both body and spirit are attacked by abusive intimate partners who accompany their physical assaults with relentless messages that the women are worthless, deserve the violence, and indeed have asked for it; this is exacerbated by the social isolation abusers maintain over the women, thus removing possible sources of support that might contradict these messages (Curtis 2000). In taking control of such large, physically-demanding instruments as Japanese Taiko, abused women can reclaim their physical and spiritual strength and confidence.

Valuing of women is accomplished through such music experiences as lyric analysis, songwriting, and music-centered relaxation. Having already looked at the processes of lyric analysis and songwriting, attention will be directed here to the use of music-centered relaxation. Certainly abused women face considerable stress—before or after they have left—and music-centered relaxation can readily address this in the hands of a skilled music therapist. Beyond this, however, the issue of self-nurturance must be addressed. It is important to counter pop culture messages of a mother's selflessness—a selflessness that exists at the expense of themselves, their souls. Often women do not leave abusive situations until their children become the targets of the violence. It is important to understand that the children's wellbeing is compromised simply in witnessing their mothers' abuse. For the well-being of mother and child alike, women must leave—and must learn to value their own self-nurturance.

The role of Feminist Music Therapy with its sociopolitical understanding of violence has been examined with particular attention to its signature techniques of feminist analysis, empowerment, and the honoring of women's perspectives. Any examination, however, of women's experiences in Feminist Music Therapy would be incomplete without turning to the words of the women themselves. The positive outcomes for abused women in music therapy have been identified in terms of standardized tests (Curtis 2000; Curtis and Harrison 2006), but it is in their original songs that their true stories of resilience, power, and recovery truly resonate. Their power in word and music cannot be ignored. And so it is to one woman's song that attention is focused now—both the words (in the printed lyrics below) and the music (in the audio file available here)—and to her journey to be free.

> To Be Free
> *Verse one*
> The words in the paper were plain and simple no apparent emotions attached
> The headline stated starkly Crime Digest, December 1st, 1995.
> Underneath, laid out in neat little columns countless stories of other people's lives
> But one woman's story, not much different from the rest caught my eye
>
> *Verse two*
> It said a man was arrested Tuesday
> A woman said he tried to pull her in his car
> She said they struggled, she resisted
> He grabbed her purse and punched her in the eye
> The facts were told so cold, the names we must withhold
> To protect the innocent
> It simply mentioned his relationship—her ex-boyfriend—in a brief aside
>
> *Chorus*
> All I ask is that you hear my voice
> And listen to my story

Like all other women seeking safety
We want to be free

Verse three
She said he punched her in the face
Her eye was swollen and bruised
The facts were told as given, nothing inferred, no judgements made
Why does this story haunt me so? Why does it stay with me night and day?
Why do I feel there's so much more to be read between the lines?
I'll tell you my secret, I've told others, none have heard
That woman was me

Chorus
All I ask is that you hear my voice
And listen to my story
Like all other women seeking safety
We want to be free

Verse four
The papers tell our stories in terms of love
Is it love gone wrong or simply hate?
Some people look at me, they shake their heads
With words no different than what he said
The words trap my heart like clipped wings do a bird
More harmful than any blow
Some say, "Stand by your man," others ask, "Why don't you leave him?"
I ask, "Why won't he let me go?"

Chorus
All I ask is that you hear my voice
And listen to my story
Like all other women seeking safety
We want to be free
All we ask is that you hear our voices
And listen to our stories
Like all other women seeking safety
We want to be free

Curtis 1996, pp. 418–419

Before closing this chapter, it is important to return to the issue of work with abused women requiring change at not only the personal and interpersonal levels of the private sphere, but also at the political level in the public sphere. This is an explicit requirement of Feminist Music Therapy, but its importance is also now explicitly acknowledged by experts in the broader field of violence against women such as Statistics Canada:

> Violence against women has been recognized, at both the national and international levels, as a serious and ongoing impediment to gender equality and women's human rights and fundamental freedoms

Sinha, 2013, p. 4

Not only is violence against women an impediment to gender equity and women's human rights; it also will only be eliminated with a focus in the public sphere on actively ensuring these rights for women. In this regard, Feminist Music Therapists are already well situated as their approach, unique among music therapy approaches, has a twofold purpose—"to accomplish personal transformation by individuals within their own lives and sociopolitical change within the community" (Curtis 2007, p. 199). Feminist Music Therapists then work specifically and directly with their clients as they move into the public sphere, becoming advocates for themselves and for other women. Indeed, this is one of the great strengths of women survivors: They "demonstrate an understanding of others who have been traumatized, along with a strong commitment to social justice and much-needed activism" (Curtis, 2013, p. 5). In my work, women have moved out of the therapy room to speak for themselves in giving their family members and even their abusers copies of the songs they have recorded; they have also taken their music and their voices to the streets in participating in community walks against violence.

CONCLUSION

In this chapter, an examination has been provided of the emergent practice of music therapy with women who have experienced violence at the hands of their intimate male partner. The particular nature of this violence, the challenges faced by these women, and their remarkable strengths and resilience have been identified. Best practices for music therapy with this population have also been outlined. Because of the nature of violence against women, music therapists may expect to see abused women in their practice regardless of the particular population in which they work. As result, it behooves all music therapists to become familiar with the nature of this work so that they can provide sensitive and well-informed music therapy services. The women deserve nothing less.

It seems, subsequently, only fitting to close with women's own voices (Curtis, 1996, p. 419):

> All we ask is that you hear our voices
> And listen to our stories
> Like all other women seeking safety
> We want to be free

REFERENCES

Black, M.C., Basile, K.C., Breiding, M.J., Smith, S.G., Walters, M.L., Merrick, M.T. et al. (2011). *The national intimate partner and sexual violence survey (NISVS): 2010 summary report*. Atlanta, GA: National Center for Injury Prevention and Control, Centers for Disease Control and Prevention.

Brown, LS. (2008). *Cultural Competence in Trauma Therapy: Beyond the Flashback*. Washington, DC: American Psychological Association.

Burstow, B. (2003). Toward a radical understanding of trauma and trauma work. *Violence Against Women* 9: 1293–1317. DOI: 10.1177/1077801203255555.

Cassity, M. and Theobold, K. (1990). Domestic violence: Assessments and treatments employed by music therapists. *Journal of Music Therapy* 27: 179–194.

Curtis, S.L. (1996). *Singing subversion, singing soul: Women's voices in feminist music therapy* (Doctoral dissertation, Concordia University).

Curtis, S.L. (2000). *Singing subversion, singing soul: Women's voices in feminist music therapy.* Doctoral dissertation, Concordia University, 1997. *Dissertation Abstracts International* 60(12-A): 4240.

Curtis, S.L. (2006). Feminist music therapy: Transforming theory, transforming lives. In: S. Hadley (ed.), *Feminist Perspectives in Music Therapy*, pp. 227–244. Gilsum, NH: Barcelona Publishers.

Curtis, S. (2007). Claiming voice: Music therapy for childhood sexual abuse survivors. In: S. Brooke (ed.). *The use of creative arts therapies with sexual abuse survivors*, pp. 196–206. Springfield, IL: Charles C Thomas Publisher, Ltd.

Curtis, S.L. (2008). Gathering voices: Music therapy for abused women. In: S.L. Brooke (ed.), *Creative Arts Therapies and Domestic Violence*, pp. 121–135. Springfield, IL: C.C. Thomas.

Curtis, S.L. (2013). Women survivors of abuse and developmental trauma. In: L. Eyre (ed.), Guidelines for Music Therapy Practice: Mental Health, pp. 263–268. Philadelphia, PA: Barcelona Publishers.

Curtis, S.L. and Harrison, G. (2006). Empowering women survivors of violence: A collaborative music therapy-social work approach. In: S.L. Brooke (ed.), *Creative Modalities for Therapy with Children and Adults*, pp. 195–204. Springfield, IL: Charles C. Thomas.

Fesler, M.M. (2007). *The effect of music therapy on depression and post-traumatic disorder in a shelter for victims of domestic violence.* Unpublished manuscript. Radford University.

Hadley, S. (Ed.). (2006). *Feminist perspectives in music therapy.* Gilsum, NH: Barcelona Publishers.

Hahna, N.D. (2004). *Empowering women: A feminist perspective of the Bonny Method of Guided imagery and Music and intimate partner violence.* Unpublished master's thesis. Radford University, Radford, VA.

Hahna, N.D. and Borling, J.E. (2004). The Bonny Method of Guided Imagery and Music (BMGIM) with intimate partner violence (IPV). *Journal of the Association for Music and Imagery* 9: 41–57.

Hernández-Ruiz, E. (2005). Effect of music therapy on the anxiety levels and sleep patterns of abused women in shelters. *Journal of Music Therapy* 42(2): 140–158.

Juarez, J.A., Marvel, K., Brezinski, K.L., Glaznen, C., Towbin, M.M., and Lawton, S. (2005). Bridging the gap: A curriculum to teach residents cultural humility. *Family Medicine* 38(2): 9–102.

Kanani, R. (2012). DOJ director on violence against women in the United States. Retrieved from <http://www.forbes.com/sites/rahimkanani/2012/03/08/doj-director-on-violence-against-women-in-the-united-states/>.

Laswell, A. (2001). *The effects of music-assisted relaxation on the relaxation, sleep quality, and daytime sleepiness of sheltered, abused women.* Unpublished master's thesis. Florida State University, Tallahassee, FL.

Lee, J. (2007). Music therapy with a woman who was hurt by a cowboy. *Canadian Journal of Music Therapy* 13(1): 30–37.

National Coalition against Domestic Violence (2012). Domestic violence facts. Retrieved from <http://www.ncadv.org>.

Purdon, C. (2006). Feminist music therapy with abused teen girls. In: S. Hadley (ed.), *Feminist Perspectives in Music Therapy*, pp. 205–226. Gilsum, NH: Barcelona Publishers.

Rinker, R.L. (1991). Guided imagery and music (GIM): Healing the wounded healer. In: K.E. Bruscia (ed.), *Case Studies in Music Therapy*, pp. 309–319. Gilsum, NH: Barcelona Publishers.

Schachter, C.L., Stalker, C.A., Teram, E., Lasiuk, G.C., Danilkewich, A. (2008). *Handbook on sensitive practice for health care practitioner: Lessons from adult survivors of childhood sexual abuse.* Ottawa: Public Health Agency of Canada.

Sinha, M. (ed.). (2013). *Measuring violence against women: Statistical trends 2013.* Commissioned by the federal/provincial/territorial ministries responsible for the status of women. Ottawa, Canada: Statistics Canada.

Slotoroff, C. (1994). Drumming technique for assertiveness and anger management in the short-term psychiatric setting for adult and adolescent survivors of trauma. *Music Therapy Perspectives. Special Issue. Psychiatric Music Therapy* 12(2): 111–116.

Teague, A.K., Hahna, N.D., and McKinney, C.H. (2006). Group music therapy with women who have experienced intimate partner violence. *Music Therapy Perspectives* 24(2): 80–86.

Tervalon, M. and Murray-García, J. (1998). Cultural humility versus cultural competence: A critical distinction in defining physician training outcomes in multicultural education. *Journal of Health Care for the Poor and Underserved* 9(2): 117–125. DOI: 10.1353/hpu.2010.0233.

Whipple, J. and Lindsey, R.S. (1999). Music for the soul: A music therapy program for battered women. *Music Therapy Perspectives* 17(2): 61–68.

York, E. (2006). Finding voice. In: S. Hadley (ed.), *Feminist Perspectives in Music Therapy: Empowering Women's Voices,* pp. 245–265. Gilsum, NH: Barcelona Publishers.

York, E., and Curtis, S.L. (2015). Music therapy with women survivors of domestic violence. In: Barbara Wheeler (ed.), *Music Therapy Handbook,* pp. 379–389. New York: Guilford Press.

CHAPTER 16

....

MUSIC THERAPY
WITH PEOPLE WHO
HAVE EATING DISORDERS

....

HELEN LOTH

I couldn't say the music therapy conquered my eating disorders, but it helped me
to come to terms with my emotions. And that's vital if you're going to recover.

THIS chapter provides an overview of approaches to using music therapy with people who
have eating disorders; mainly work with adults and older teenagers. Eating disorders are now
generally understood to be complex psychological disorders; the restriction of food intake
and control of body weight serve to meet a psychological or emotional need. Music therapy can help people to explore and understand the psychological issues that may have led
them to using eating as a way of controlling their feelings and emotions. Music therapy offers
unique and powerful ways to address specific characteristics of eating disorder pathology.

ABOUT EATING DISORDERS
....

THERE is not thought to be a single cause responsible for the development of an eating disorder, rather a combination of factors including psychological, interpersonal, family, cultural,
and biological. Some research shows that genetic disposition may also play a role in predis-
posing someone to developing an eating disorder (Institute of Psychiatry).

   Until 2013, the three main definitions of eating disorders given in the DSM-IV (American
Psychiatric Association 1994) were for Anorexia Nervosa, Bulimia Nervosa and "Eating
Disorder Not Otherwise Specified," (EDNOS). In the DSM-V (2013) Binge Eating Disorder
was added as a separate category in recognition of its prevalence; this had previously
been grouped within the category of EDNOS. Anorexia Nervosa is defined as a refusal to
maintain a body weight within normal parameters, severe weight loss and intense fear of

gaining weight, disturbed body image perception and amenorrhea. Two types are identified; restricting and binge eating/purging. Bulimia Nervosa is defined as recurrent episodes of binge eating accompanied by a sense of lack of control over the eating period, compensatory inappropriate behaviors to prevent weight gain such as vomiting, excessive use of laxatives and diuretics, and over-exercising. In Binge Eating Disorder, the recurrent episodes of binge eating, accompanied by a lack of sense of control are not followed by compensatory behaviours. Episodes cause marked distress to the individual and it may be associated with being overweight or obesity. The category of "Other Specified Feeding or Eating Disorder" is used for people with a range of eating behaviors which whilst clinically severe, do not meet the exact criteria for Anorexia Nervosa, Bulimia Nervosa or Binge Eating Disorder. Cooper and Fairburn (2012) suggested that eating disorders are more variable than the criteria in DSM allow, and that most eating disorders are not stable illnesses. They change over time and with age and duration. Patients can experience periods of anorexia followed by periods of bulimia or their eating disorder may be of a mixed state. Persistent anorexia of the restricting kind is the exception to this and remains a small minority of cases.

People of all ages, gender, and cultural background can develop an eating disorder. Younger women are most likely to be affected, but older women and men of all ages also develop eating disorders. Bulimia tends to have a later onset than anorexia; children as young as seven can develop anorexia. There is a greater proportion of boys in this younger age group, whilst adolescent boys with anorexia tend to over-exercise rather than restrict their food (Institute of Psychiatry).

Estimates for the prevalence of eating disorders in the population vary. The UK National Institute for Health and Clinical Excellence (NICE) states that about 1 in 250 females and 1 in 2000 males will experience anorexia nervosa, about five times as many will suffer from bulimia, and an even greater number will have an atypical eating disorder (NICE 2004). A survey by the NHS Information Centre, (2007) found that overall 6.4% of the population of England, 9.2% of women and 3.2% of men screened positive for an eating disorder in the preceding year. The UK charity "Men Get Eating Disorders Too" believes that men are underrepresented in national figures and estimates that between 10% and 25% of people who have eating disorders are male. (<http://mengetedstoo.co.uk>).

Eating disorders can be extremely serious illnesses, with anorexia having the highest mortality rate of any psychiatric disorder. Bulimia and binge eating disorder sufferers also frequently experience severe medical complications from the consequences of their eating behaviors.

WAYS OF UNDERSTANDING EATING DISORDERS

As stated in the introduction, eating disorders can develop through a combination of a range of factors. The UK eating disorders organisation *beat* (Beating Eating Disorders) describes anorexia nervosa as stemming from "low self esteem and an inability to cope safely with worries and problems" and bulimia as linked with "low self esteem, emotional problems and stress" ("beat" information leaflet). Eating disorders can completely dominate a person's life, severely affecting their quality of life. Often, a person will say that the eating disorder is the only way they feel they can stay in control of their life, but as it develops, the eating disorder in fact controls the person.

Hughes warns us to remember that "for the patient, the anorexia is a solution to another, more alarming problem." (Hughes 1997, p. 261) An eating disorder can be understood in psychodynamic terms as a defence against need and dependency which are experienced as unmanageable and cannot be tolerated. Sands (1991) describes eating disorders as disorders of the self that develop "due to chronic disturbance in the empathic interplay between the growing child and the care-giving environment." (p. 35). The anorexic patient has not been able to separate healthily from the family, and the conflicts of adolescence are kept alive in the refusal to eat and acknowledge an adult, separate self. The concept of the "no-entry" system of defence (Williams 1997) in which the anorexic child is attempting to prevent the projection of the parent's undigested anxieties entering them, is also made use of by music therapists in conceptualizing their work with some patients (Frank-Schwebel 2001; Loth 2002). In this way of thinking about what is happening, refusing food can be a way for a child to refuse to take in their parent's pain. Bulimia can also be seen as an attempt to control the inner world of the sufferer.

General treatment approaches

Treatment for eating disorders usually consists of two parts. The disordered eating behavior needs to be addressed, through weight restoration, the management of purging behaviors and the regulation of eating patterns, and the emotional and psychological difficulties underpinning and maintaining the disorder need to be engaged with.

Patients with an eating disorder are generally managed in the community, through specialist out-patient or day services, with in-patient treatment mainly being reserved for the more severely ill and extremely underweight patients (Cooper and Fairburn 2012). As a complex disorder, several different treatment approaches can be required, such as combining a behavioral approach to weight restoration and normalization of eating, family therapy to help understand the place of the disorder within the family system, psycho-education relating to food and nutrition, and individual or group psychological therapies to address the emotional difficulties that both underlie and result from the eating disorder. Music therapists usually work within specialist services or in private practice.

Arts therapies and eating disorders

Whilst there is very little empirical research into the efficacy of arts therapies in the treatment of eating disorders, arts therapies are increasingly being included in in-patient treatment programmes. Several music therapists have written about their work and discussed its validity. A survey conducted in the US (Frisch et al. 2006) identified specific reasons for including arts-based therapies in treatment programmes, which in addition to self-discovery, exploration, and self-expression, could provide a "healthy outlet for expression of emotions and

development of positive coping skills" (p. 138). For patients who found talking-based therapies difficult, arts therapies were felt to be particularly effective.

Hornyak and Baker (1989) have proposed that experiential therapies are particularly
appropriate for clients with eating disorders given the specific nature of their problems which
have a physical, somatic component; many clients are "cut off from their affective and cognitive internal experiences" (p. 2) and they are often reluctant to show their real selves when
interacting with others, as this engenders feelings of shame and self-hatred. Experiential
therapies can offer a way to "be with" clients and understand and engage with their difficult
behaviors and expressions of disturbance in a different and more hopeful way; patients can
learn new ways of expressing themselves and interacting with others. As treatments which
use some form of action, clients can use the "in-the-moment experience" to increase their
awareness and understanding of their feelings, thoughts, beliefs, and sensations and discover new ways of being and relating to others (Hornyak and Baker 1989).

Music therapy, can be thought of as an *action-oriented* treatment approach, and thus is
well suited to people who use action and embodiment to express their difficulties. Nolan
(1989) discusses how for bulimic patients, group improvising can develop their awareness of
thoughts and feelings in the here and now which can continue to be explored through further improvisations in which new ways of behaving can be tried out.

The relevance of music therapy being an experiential action-based therapy is also identified by Trondalen (2004). She explains that one of the key reasons for her research into
Significant Moments in music therapy with young people suffering from eating disorders was
the amount of requests for music therapy she received from parents despairing over their
adolescent children who were exhausted with talking to professionals and wanted to *do
something* instead of just using words.

MUSIC THERAPY AND EATING DISORDERS

Music therapy can help patients to better understand and address their psychological problems. Therapists work with groups and individuals often as part of a multi-disciplinary team.
As different aspects of the disorder need to be thought about simultaneously, weight, eating
behaviors, and emotional state, team work is very necessary with this client group. This is
most relevant in the inpatient setting but therapy may also take place within specialist teams
working in out-patient and community settings. The type of approach to music therapy will
be modified by where it is taking place, and thus, at what stage of the patient's treatment it
is situated within. When a patient with anorexia is severely underweight and experiencing
the effects of starvations, cognitive processes are impaired and insight oriented work is less
possible; a more supportive approach may be needed. At the other end of the continuum,
patients may have found a way to survive with their eating disorder in the community, and
choose to attend music therapy to gain a better understanding of their problems as they are
motivated to change.

Characteristics of people who have an eating disorder may include low self-esteem;
self-loathing; difficulties with intimacy, identity, and lack of sense of self; feelings of emptiness; inability to recognize and process feelings; and an extreme need for control. Music

therapy can address and engage with these characteristics in different ways, according to the music therapy approach and the framework for understanding the illness used.

Methods of music therapy generally used are improvisation, songwriting, and receptive methods. With the exception of Hilliard (2001) who uses a unique form of cognitive-behavioral music therapy, theoretical approaches can be defined as broadly psychodynamic, focusing on the meaning of the eating disorder within the patient's inner world and interpersonal relationships.

Research conducted by Odell-Miller (2007) found music therapy approaches considered most useful in work with eating disordered clients were a supportive psychotherapy approach, particularly for encouraging the development of a sense of self, and a psychoanalytically informed approach to enable development of insight into the symbolic functions of the illness. The need for caution in the timing of interpretations is noted, which should be related to the stage of illness and the patient's ability to work with interpretation. Free improvisation, with varying amounts of talking and interpretation was widely used "to help with self-expression and integration of thoughts and emotions" (Odell-Miller 2007, p. 260).

Although group music therapy is increasingly being undertaken with this client group, the majority of the literature refers to individual work. Group therapy affords particular possibilities for work, such as enabling aspects of family dynamics, competition, and rivalry to be explored (Loth 2002). McFerran (2005) discusses the arguments for and against group work for adolescents suffering from anorexia. In some treatment settings young anorexic patients are kept separately from each other so that they cannot share strategies and behaviors which help hide and maintain their restrictive practices, and so that competitive aspects, such as comparing weight loss, cannot be so clearly enacted. However, as McFerran notes, there is increasing support for group psychotherapy, and in adult services, group therapy is considered to be a very effective way of working with this client group (Harper-Guiffre and MacKenzie 1992).

Motivation is a key issue in treatment for people with eating disorders who are frequently highly ambivalent about changing their eating behaviors. Whilst on the one hand they may be desperate to live a normal life without the relentless preoccupation with food and eating, on the other hand, if the disorder is the solution to the problem, then attempts to question and change it can be terrifying and need to be strenuously resisted. As Land (2004) points out: "Patients who have dedicated themselves to abusing their hunger to avoid the worse pain of psychic reality have to face some losses if they decide to accept treatment fully." (p. 401). This is particularly apparent in the in-patient setting, where patients may be in semi-compulsory treatment, and feel that therapy is being forced upon them. In the music therapy session, the therapist can be experienced as persecutory, demanding that patients play (eat), become aware of feelings they have been deliberately repressing, and making them feel "bad" (Loth 2002). There can be attacks on the therapist for "making them" feel like this. In the counter-transference, the therapist can experience a real assault on her competency. Frank-Schwebel (2001) describes how patients can create "a characteristic counter-transference of failure in their care-takers, and engage them in a dynamic that is rich with anger, potential counter-aggression, guilt and hopelessness." (p. 261). It is important therefore to not only find ways to develop a therapeutic alliance with the patient, but also to be able to withstand the projections coming from them.

MUSICAL IMPROVISATION

One of the most powerful aspects of using music therapy with clients who have an eating disorder is that it can offer a way to "be with" the client, to hear and acknowledge them and their distress, and for the client to experience this being acknowledged without necessarily needing to do something about it, at least initially. This is something very unique or specific to the experience of playing together. Sands (1991) referring to psychotherapy and the dissociative aspects of bulimia writes:

> To try to talk the bulimic self out of bingeing or purging is like telling a cat stalking a bird to stop its carnivorous pursuit. What the bulimic self is able to hear is, first, an acknowledgement of its deeper needs in the present, and then, later on, an explanation of its genetic roots.

> (p. 40)

Improvising in music can be an opportunity for the acknowledgment of needs in the present, the "here and now" of jointly created sound. The "explanation" may form part of the musical relationship; it may be explored through talking about the music, or if working within a multidisciplinary team, may be pursued further in psychotherapy or other verbal therapy. Improvisation is used by many music therapists in this work in different ways, with varying degrees of structure and verbal reflection incorporated.

Improvisation can also be an interactive experience that enables patients to connect with parts of themselves and with others. Research conducted by Trondalen (2004) showed how musical improvisation could help link the inner and outer worlds as well as the mind and body of patients. The patient felt recognized and was able to experience the music as being able to "'fill" her emptiness, bear her ambivalence, and promote "peace of mind"' (Trondalen 2004, p. 6). It seems that the musical experience supported an experience of being connected in time and space. Trondalen further proposes that for people with anorexia the music therapy approach should include both musical and verbal dialogue, as, verbalizing the experience of the improvisation with the therapist involved in the playing enables a deeper understanding of it.

Some people who have eating disorders can talk with ease about their disorder, often in quite an intellectualised manner. This can be a way of distancing themselves from their feelings. Sloboda (1993) shows how, in contrast to the experience of talking about being ill, "the experience of improvising musically was a much more spontaneous and immediate one" enabling patients to "link the quality of their own improvisations with aspects of their internal world and everyday relationships" (Sloboda 1993, p. 105). Sloboda's approach includes discussion of the music with the client following their improvisation to support the client in experiencing and understanding their feelings better.

The contrast between verbal and musical interactions was highlighted for the author in the case of Hayley, a young anorexic woman seen for individual counselling whilst on an in-patient eating disorders unit. In counselling sessions Hayley would talk freely, in very chatty manner, telling me stories and being quite dramatic in a "typical teenage" manner. Her appearance was quite "tough" with slightly "punk" make-up and clothing. This all functioned successfully as a defence which it was very difficult to get past. She could not let herself be in a position of not-knowing, be vulnerable and really consider her feelings in our counselling sessions. I suggested that we take her sessions into the music therapy room instead, where we could use the instruments and playing as another way of talking together. In this setting I began to see much more of the real Hayley, and in our playing experienced her as very fragile and lacking in confidence. She could not interact with me in the same socially skilled way as she did through talking. Her playing was very quiet and lacking in conviction, she would quickly give up and criticize it as being "no good" and she seemed to find any contact in my musical interactions disturbing. It became evident that without the "false self" of her tough confident "punk" identity, she had little sense of who she was. Using music in addition to talking enabled us to work through her defences and begin to work at a deeper level.

Robarts and Sloboda (1994) suggest that improvisation in music is particularly relevant as a way for people to express their feelings and gain access to unconscious material: "When people play spontaneously together in musical improvisation, they reveal essential aspects of themselves: 'the way they *are*'" (Robarts and Sloboda 1994, p. 8). They link eating disorders to disturbances in infancy and early attachment relationships, resulting in a lack of development of the "child's sense of self as a basis for ego functioning" (Robarts and Sloboda 1994, p. 8). Improvisational music therapy which uses the concepts of Stern's affect attunement in mother-infant interaction and the musicality of early infant interactions can therefore activate the unconscious, early infant states and pre-verbal experiences in the client, making the available to be worked with.

Improvisations can also be recorded, listened back to and reflected upon with the therapist. The method of "self-listening" (Bruscia 1998) is used by several music therapists, (Nolan 1989; Trondalen 2003). It can be a way for patients to connect to themselves and their experience in the past, and to relive emotions at a slight distance. It may give them a different perspective on their experience. Trondalen (2003) uses self-listening in her work with anorectics, and suggests that "such an interpersonal sharing of experiences may contribute to increasing the capability to describe, identify and tolerate feeling states without being overwhelmed, which often happens with people suffering from anorexia." (Trondalen 2003, p. 4). Nolan (1989) describes how listening to recordings of group improvisations can give bulimic patients a more objective view of themselves. Their mainly negative perspectives of their playing reflected on after the improvisation can be contrasted with a more realistic view of its effect when heard in the recording. In particular, this offers the possibility of verbal feedback from other group members as a form of "reality testing."

STRUCTURE

Free improvisation is a commonly used method in many music therapy models, but when used with people who have eating disorders this can be particularly terrifying; exposing patients to their feelings of inadequacy, humiliation at not "getting it right", and their sense of internal emptiness, feelings which may form part of their pathology. Therefore the use of structure in the playing may be important, particularly at the beginning of work with a client or a group. The desire for control and fear of losing this is a fundamental feature of clients with eating disorders, who may feel their bodies are the only thing they can control. When improvising in music, patients may be fearful of their lack of the control due to lack of experience or skill, but they can also use the musical interaction to explore feeling in control in a healthy way. The inherent structure of music can offer the client a way to experiment with control. Parente (1989) suggests that this unique structure of musical experience, means the client is "free to 'let go' to the music only as much as she chooses and only for the length of time she desires." (Parente 1989, p. 308) Music can provide the structure, so the client does not have to. Predictability in the musical form, rhythm, and harmony can also be important in enabling connectedness (Trondalen 2003). In analyzing the shared musical improvisations of a client with bulimia nervosa Bauer (2010) notes that use of structure was an important element of this work, without which the client found it very difficult to self-regulate; she needed some playing rules in order not to feel lost and unseen in the improvisations. The use of structure in improvisation is further discussed by Odell-Miller (2007). Music therapists participating in her research used play rules and structures such as turn-taking and themes to improvise around. Musical role-play was also found to be particularly useful.

ROLE-PLAY

Musical role-play may be helpful to explore family dynamics. Relationships within the family can often play a part in the development of the eating disorder, and the eating disorder itself can greatly affect the family, particularly with young clients. In improvisations, different instruments can be assigned to different family members, with the qualities of an instrument representing the characteristics of the family member, as experienced by the client. For example, Sloboda (1993) describes a client choosing and playing different instruments to illustrate each family member, such as using a large drum to represent a domineering brother, and thereby understand better how he experienced them, and related to them. Patients can experiment with taking on the roles of their family members with the therapist taking on the role of the patient to re-enact their relationship patterns. In addition to representing other people, musical role-play can also be used to enable a person to represent and explore different aspects of themselves and their personality.

In an example from the author's clinical practice of group music therapy, Joan talked about how no-one heard her in her family. She was reminded of this experience in the group's improvisations, in which she felt "drowned out," yet she would usually play very quietly and without conviction. The group discussed this and suggested they would play the parts of a loud, talkative family, fully engaged with each other, whilst Joan would attempt to be heard. She found this extremely difficult, and began to recognise her own part in not expressing her needs "audibly" and yet expecting them to be seen, heard, and responded to. With support, she was able to bring the dynamic and quality of the xylophone she chose to play up to a level that was heard within the group music, and spontaneously the group gave it space and incorporated it within their music. Of real importance here was that Joan did not annihilate the others, or express herself loudly by shutting everyone else out. She was able engage and interact with the other group members whilst being heard, a type of intimacy which was a real challenge for her.

SONGWRITING

A specific form of structure useful for this client group is songwriting. McFerran (McFerran et al. 2006, 2008) proposed that songwriting is useful with adolescents who have acute anorexia for whom it has a particular appeal and relevance. It can provide "fresh insights about the nature of their predicament … especially in relation to individuation and identity formation." (McFerran et al. 2006, p. 402) She proposed that songwriting "has been particularly effective in freeing patients to express themselves in a creative way that also articulates important aspects of their being." (p. 402). Analysis of the song lyrics identified that issues to do with identity formation were the most prevalent, followed by family dynamics.

Songwriting can also be a way for adolescents to share difficult feelings with their family and friends. Lejonclou and Trondalen (2009) include poem and song-writing, together with improvisation in their approach to working with adults, which they describe as being based on the clients' personal interests and sensitive to their needs and wishes. This client-centered attitude they suggest "may promote internal healing, empower the client's strengths and allow for confirmation of personal identity" (Lejonclou and Trondalen 2009, p. 87).

ACTING OUT

As a psychological disorder in which distress and emotional conflicts are "acted out" through the body and eating disorder behaviors, a therapeutic intervention in which distress can be acted out through the artistic medium can be very relevant. Many patients feel out of control, or that they are overly controlled by others. These issues are acted out through the body. However, as Dokter (1994) emphasizes, it is important that this acting out is transformed into a therapeutic form of action which enables some kind of internal change.

In this context art therapist Schaverien (1994) sees the making of art as offering a way of enacting and symbolizing inner conflict She views the picture in art therapy as being a transactional object "an object through which unconscious transactions may be acted out and channelled" (Schaverien 1994, p. 35) and points out the need for a progression from acting out a feeling, which may be an unconscious process, to the deliberate enactment of a feeling, which has meaning and can be thought about. A similar process is possible in improvisational music therapy in which unconscious pain can be "played out" in the music, and later the music may be used deliberately in an enactment to consciously explore the issue.

Music gives a distance to the problem or conflict; it is "out there" in the room, a third object mediating between the client and the therapist. This distance can enable difficult feelings to be heard and experienced. However the immediacy of music can also be overwhelming, as the client receives instant feedback of their feeling state, which they have been attempting, through their eating disorder, to remain cut off from. This tendency to dissociate can continue in the music; clients sometimes say to me after an improvisation that they did not notice what I was playing or that they thought I had just been accompanying their playing, when in fact I had been doing something very different, such as challenging, or leaving spaces, which had gone unnoticed.

IDENTIFYING AND EXPRESSING FEELINGS

A salient feature of eating disorders is the difficulty with experiencing and tolerating feelings and emotions. Music therapy can enable these to be found and identified, expressed, but more importantly, to be borne and reintegrated into their sense of self. Improvisational methods are very powerful ways of addressing this, and as already discussed, allow for different amounts of structure to be used. Robarts (2000) discusses the anorexic adolescent's diminished capacity for realistic thinking and self-reflection, using the concept of alexithymia to describe the inability to identify feelings "as if having lost feeling connections between body and mind." (Robarts 2000, p. 5).

Several studies have investigated the relevance of alexithymia to eating disorder diagnoses. Alexithymia is defined as a syndrome or personality trait characterized by a difficulty or inability to identify and express feelings, and to distinguish between emotions and bodily sensations. People with these traits tend to lack words for feelings, lack a connection between soma and psyche, and have difficulties with symbolizing.

A study by Schmidt et al. (1993) of alexithymia in eating disorders concluded that eating disordered patients (both anorexic and bulimic) are considerably more alexithymic than normal controls; and that for patients with bulimia nervosa, the trait of alexithymia is only affected though the use of psychological treatment which facilitates emotional expression. Similarly, a study by Beales and Dolton (2000) which analyzed character traits of women with eating disorders also found that that alexithymia is a common feature and that it is linked to considerable deficits in social skills. This research indicates the relevance of using a therapeutic approach which helps such patients identify and express feelings, in the context of relating to others.

The linking of thoughts and feelings to the body through music therapy is also noted by Trondalen (2003) who suggests that inter-relating through music as a non-verbal medium, can lead to closer connections between soma and psyche. Movement is used in some music therapy approaches; the patients of Frank-Schwebel's music therapy group also dance, (2001), whilst Lejonclou and Trondalen (2009) describe the use music and movement in their work, in which patients used their "living bodies in a sounding relationship" through which was created a "living bridge between body and mind." (Lejonclou and Trondalen 2009, p. 88–89).

CHARACTERISTIC WAYS OF PLAYING

Some music therapists have identified specific ways of playing that people with eating disorders tend to use, which reflect something of their condition and ways of relating. Robarts and Sloboda (1994) list "musical emotional symptoms" for people with anorexia which can be summarized as a lack of structure or tight rhythmic structures, rapid playing and difficulty in slowing down, avoidance of phrasing and space, preference for high-pitched sounds over low, a lack of intense emotions and warmth, lack of flexibility, and difficulties in empathic interaction with the therapist, or over-empathizing with the therapist, following their playing symbiotically (Robarts and Sloboda 1994, pp. 8–9). In the author's clinical experience, types of playing characteristic of patients with bulimia include a tendency to play in a loud and chaotic manner, frequent crescendos and explosions, and long improvisations of continuous playing with no spaces left for the sounds of anyone else. The large hanging gong was favored by some bulimic clients who would begin by tapping it rapidly and quietly at the edges, gradually bring the sound up in a rolling crescendo and then strike it forcefully in the center for a deafening climax. This could effectively silence the group, who would all then listen as the reverberations diminished. The relationship to a binge and purge process were obvious and striking; music was being used as an emotional and tension release.

Self and autonomy

Music therapy can help clients with eating disorders develop a sense of autonomy and individuation, areas in which they are frequently lacking. Robarts and Sloboda (1994) describe how music therapy processes "'manifest some of the phenomena of self-organisational processes of infancy'" enabling patients to build up a sense of self and of self in relation to others, and move towards individuality and autonomy" (Robarts and Sloboda 1994, p. 13). Smeijsters (1996) sees improvisation as offering "the possibility of experiencing independence, autonomy and influence" (Smeijsters 1996, p. 9) and Trondalen (2004) describes how her patient found that being able to influence how he related to another through music showed him that he had the capacity to affect other areas of his life. The possibilities for music therapy experiences to help with development of self-regulation (Trondalen 2004) and self-esteem (Parente 1989) are also noted.

Receptive methods

Receptive music therapy methods may be used for specific aims; listening to pre-composed music can be used for relaxation purposes and to develop the capacity to self-soothe, a quality often lacking in clients with eating disorders (Frank-Schwebel 2001, Nolan 1989, Parente 1989). Nolan (1989) developed a variation on Bonny's Guided Imagery and Music technique (Bonny 1978), in which groups of patients with bulimia listening to self-improvised music whilst the therapist guided them through a relaxation procedure. Through this clients learnt that they were able to relax themselves and that they could provide their own self-soothing, rather than using binge eating for this purpose.

Conclusion

This chapter has described the breadth of approaches, theoretical ideas, and techniques which music therapists have developed to work with clients who have eating disorders. Through using musically interactive methods such as free and structured improvisation, creating songs, and listening to pre-composed music, clients with eating disorders can begin to recognize and tolerate their feelings, connect with others, and make links between their thoughts, feelings, and bodies. By providing a non-verbal, action-based, and creative medium, the music therapist offers the client a very particular experience in which they can feel heard and recognized, experience their emotions in the "here and now," and begin to integrate their thoughts and feelings. Music therapy can have a significant role within the treatment of eating disorders, and can help people in their journey to overcome or find a more healthy way to live with their difficulties.

AUTHOR NOTE

The opening quotation is by a former patient of the author, interviewed in an article "The rhythm of life", *Sunday Mirror*, "Personal" magazine, May 30, 1999.

REFERENCES

American Psychiatric Association: Diagnostic and Statistical Manual of Mental Disorders, Fourth Edition (1994) (DSM-IV). Washington DC: American Psychiatric Association.

American Psychiatric Association: Diagnostic and Statistical Manual of Mental Disorders, Fifth Edition (2013) (DSM-V). Arlington, VA: American Psychiatric Association.

Bauer, S. (2010). Music Therapy and Eating Disorders. A Single Case Study about the Sound of Human Needs. *Voices: A World Forum for Music Therapy* 10(2). Accessed online: <https://normt.uib.no/index.php/voices/article/view/258/214>.

Beales, D.L. and Dolton, R. (2000). Eating disordered patients: personality, alexithymia, and implications for primary care. *British Journal of General Practitioners* 50(450): 21–26.

"beat" Beating Eating Disorders: <http://www.b-eat.co.uk/about-beat/media-centre/facts-and-figures/>.

Bonny, H.L. (1978). *Facilitating GIM sessions: GIM monograph no.1.* Baltimore, MD: ICM Books.

Bruscia, K.E. (1998). *Defining Music Therapy.* Gilsum NH: Barcelona Publishers.

Cooper, Z., and Fairburn, C.G. (2012). Cognitive behavior therapy for bulimia nervosa. *Treatment of Eating Disorders* 243.

Dokter, D., (ed.) (1994). *Arts Therapies and Clients with Eating Disorders.* London: Jessica Kingsley.

Frank-Schwebel, A. (2001). The sound-object in anorexia nervosa. 5th European Music Therapy Congress, Naples. Conference Proceedings: Accessed online: <www.wfmt.info/Musictherapyworld/index.html>.

Frisch, M.J., Franko, D.L., and Herzog, D.B. (2006). Arts-Based Therapies in the Treatment of Eating Disovrders. *Eating Disorders* 14: 131–142.

Harper-Guiffre, H. and MacKenzie, K. (eds). (1992). *Group Psychotherapy for Eating Disorders.* Washington: American Psychiatric Press.

Hilliard, R. E. (2001). The use of cognitive-behavioral music therapy in the treatment of women with eating disorders. *Music Therapy Perspectives* 19(2): 109–113.

Hornyak, L.M. and Baker, E.K. (eds). (1989). *Experiential Therapies for Eating Disorders.* New York: The Guildford Press.

Hughes, P. (1997). The use of the countertransference in the therapy of patients with anorexia nervosa. *European Eating Disorders Review* 5(4): 258–269.

Institute of Psychiatry, Eating Disorders Research Group: <http://www.kcl.ac.uk/iop/depts/pm/research/eatingdisorders/>.

Land, P. (2004) Thinking about feelings: Working with the staff of an eating disorders unit. *Psychoanalytic Psychotherapy* 18(4): 390–403.

Lejonclou, A. and Trondalen, G. (2009). "I've started to move into my own body": Music Therapy with Women with Eating Disorders. *Nordic Journal of Music Therapy* 18(1): 79–92. doi: 10.1080/08098130802610924.

Loth. H. (2002) "There's no getting away from anything in here": A music therapy group within and inpatient programme for adults with eating disorders. In: A. Davies and E. Richards (eds), *Music Therapy and Group Work*, pp. 90–104. London: Jessica Kingsley.

McFerran, K. (2005). "Dangerous Liaisons": Group Work for Adolescent Girls who have Anorexia Nervosa. *Voices: A World Forum for Music Therapy* 5(1): Accessed online: <https://normt.uib.no/index.php/voices/article/view/215/159>.

McFerran, K., Baker, F., Kildea, C., Patton, G., and Sawyer, S.M. (2008). Avoiding Conflict. What do adolescents with disordered eating say about their Mothers in Music therapy? *British Journal of Music Therapy* 22(1): 16–23.

McFerran, K., Baker, F., Patton, G.C., and Sawyer, S.M. (2006). A Retrospective Lyrical Analysis of Songs Written by Adolescents with Anorexia Nervosa. *European Eating Disorders Review* 14: 397–403. doi: 10.1002/erv.746.

"Men Get Eating Disorders Too": <http://mengetedstoo.co.uk>.

NHS Information Centre, Adult Psychiatric Morbidity in England (2007). "Results of a Household Survey." Published by Health and Social Care Information Centre: <http://www.hscic.gov.uk>.

NICE (2004). Eating Disorders. Core interventions in the treatment and management of anorexia nervosa, bulimia nervosa and related eating disorders. Clinical Guideline 9. London: National Institute for Health and Care Excellence: <www.nice.org.uk>.

Nolan, P. (1989). Music Therapy Improvisation Techniques with Bulimic Patients. In: L.M. Hornyak and E.K. Baker (eds), *Experiential Therapies for Eating Disorders,* pp. 167–187. New York: The Guildford Press.

Odell-Miller, H. (2007). The Practice of Music Therapy for Adults with Mental Health Problems: the Relationship between Diagnosis and Clinical Method. Unpublished PhD thesis. Aalborg University.

Parente, A. (1989). Music as a Therapeutic Tool in Treating Anorexia Nervosa. In: L.M. Hornyak and E.K. Baker (eds), *Experiential Therapies for Eating Disorders*, pp. 305–328. New York: The Guildford Press.

Robarts, J.Z. (2000). Music Therapy and Adolescents with Anorexia Nervosa. *Nordic Journal of Music Therapy* 9(1): 3–12. doi: 10.1080/08098130009477981.

Robarts, J.Z. and Sloboda, A. (1994). Perspectives on music therapy with people suffering from anorexia nervosa. *Journal of British Music Therapy* 8(1): 7–14.

Sands, S. (1991). Bulimia, Dissociation and Empathy: a Self-Psychological View. In: C. Johnson (ed.), *Psychodynamic Treatment of Anorexia and Bulimia*, pp. 34–50. New York: The Guildford Press.

Schaverien, J. (1994). The transactional object: Art psychotherapy in the treatment of anorexia. *British Journal of Psychotherapy* 11(1): 46–61.

Schmidt, U., Jiwany, A., Treasure, J. (1993). A controlled study of alexithymia in eating disorders. *Comprehensive Psychiatry* 34(1): 54–58. Accessed online: <http://dx.doi.org/10.1016/0010-440X(93)90036-4>.

Sloboda, A. (1993). Individual therapy with a man who has an eating disorder. In: M. Heal and T. Wigram (eds), *Music Therapy in Health and Education*, pp. 103–111. London: Jessica Kingsley.

Smeijsters, H. (1996). Music Therapy with Anorexia Nervosa: an integrative theoretical and methodological perspective. *British Journal of Music Therapy* 10(2): 3–13.

Trondalen, G. (2003). Self-listening in Music Therapy with a Young Person Suffering from Anorexia Nervosa. *Nordic Journal of Music Therapy* 12(1): 3–17. doi: 10.1080/08098130309478069.

Trondalen, G. (2004). "Significant moments" in music therapy with young persons suffering from Anorexia Nervosa. Keynote presentation at The Sixth European Music Therapy Congress University of Jyväsklä, Finland July 19th, 2004 in *Music Therapy Today* V1(3): 396–425. Accessed online: <http://www.wfmt.info/Musictherapyworld/index.html>.

Williams, G. (1997). *Internal Landscapes and Foreign Bodies*. London: Duckworth.

CHAPTER 17

....

MUSIC THERAPY FOR PEOPLE WITH A DIAGNOSIS OF PERSONALITY DISORDER
Considerations of Thinking and Feeling

....

HELEN ODELL-MILLER

TOWARDS the end of the twentieth century the focus of thinking about people with a diagnosis of personality disorder began to change. Previously, people with personality disorders experienced marginalization within mental health services. They were perceived as a group of people hard to treat, who were unresponsive to medication, and for whom at that time there was no body of research directing practitioners towards effective treatments (Pickersgill 2013). More recently, this population has also been instrumental in speaking out about being misunderstood, through user movements such as Emergence[1] and the user-focused Royal College of Psychiatrists' website[2] in the UK, and through similar organizations across the world.

> Veronica is a 21-year-old woman diagnosed with a borderline personality disorder. In a music therapy group, she struck a large orchestral gong as part of an improvisation.
>   As she played, the therapist accompanied her by improvising harmonic piano music in response to her playing. This therapeutic incident took place shortly after the death of Veronica's mother, with whom she had begun to form a loving relationship, but who she had experienced as unloving and as someone who had failed to protect her against a man who sexually abused her.
>
> Odell-Miller 2011, p. 34[3]

Overwhelming, angry and raging feelings were expressed in Veronica's music therapy session, and she often referred back to that single "gong striking" as the most therapeutic moment for her in group music therapy. From this point, enabled by the therapist's verbal interpretations towards further meaning, and through shared music making, she began to find a means of expression and new understanding about relationships in her life. Hitherto she had been unable to do this. She also brought composed songs with hopeful and sometimes depressing suicidal themes to listen to with others in the group in order to help her link her thinking and feeling and to try to find strategies to manage her life.

In some countries, and the UK in particular, attention has more recently been drawn to people with personality disorder, and resources channeled into setting up specialist services specifically for people with the diagnosis. Now, it is easier for people with similar problems to Veronica, to access specialist psychological services, including music therapy. In this chapter the unique potential for music therapy to help people with this diagnosis is considered, drawing upon the small amount of music therapy research currently available, and music therapy case reports.

WHAT IS A PERSONALITY DISORDER?

On first encounter, the term personality disorder may sound like an unpleasant term, implying an actual deficit in character perhaps, and which some have found offensive (for example, Denman 2011). However, with increasing involvement of people diagnosed with this disorder involved in research and decisions on treatment models, it has been clear that understanding what it means to have this diagnosis outweighs the name itself. People with this diagnosis are often relieved to be diagnosed and to realise that there is some understanding and meaning given to the difficulties they have encountered, such as feeling misunderstood or being over sensitive to others. The main experience of people with this disorder is that their problems are associated with ways of thinking and feeling about others, and themselves, which significantly and adversely affect their functioning in everyday life. They encounter enduring patterns of inner disturbance leading to behavior and experiences that often deviate from cultural expectations. Usually personality disorder has an onset in adolescence or early childhood, and the condition is pervasive and inflexible, leading to distress and impairment.

The symptoms experienced by people with personality disorder are grouped into clusters. Recently new terminology has evolved[4] which the Royal College of Psychiatrists views as more "user friendly." These three traditional clusters: A, B, and C (American Psychiatric Association 2013) will be discussed with reference to what is known through the literature about the key role music therapy might play for people with these disorders.

Cluster A: The odd, eccentric cluster

Cluster A includes paranoid personality disorder, schizoid personality disorder, and schizotypal personality disorders. The common features of the personality disorders in this cluster are social awkwardness and social withdrawal, pervasive lack of trust in others, and for some, a feeling that others are out to get them. This can lead to distorted thinking and hostility. Many of the unique aspects for music therapy delivery for this group are similar to those for schizophrenia which is well served by existing music therapy literature and evidence (for example, Mössler et al. 2011). This chapter will therefore concentrate on clusters B and C.

Cluster B: The dramatic, emotional, erratic cluster

This cluster includes borderline personality disorder, narcissistic personality disorder, histrionic personality disorder, and antisocial personality disorder. Disorders in this cluster share problems with impulse control and emotional regulation being key to people's difficulties. Crucially, music therapy offers something specific in this realm, being flexible to matching and expression of different mood and impulse, and through rhythm, providing possibility for the experience of regulation, especially when musical improvisation is used interactively. Other main features for people with this disorder include identity disturbance and unstable self-image, with rapid changes in mood, intense unstable interpersonal relationships, marked impulsivity related to self-harm (spending, substance abuse, sex, reckless driving, binge eating, cutting, overdosing) instability in affect and in self-image, recurrent suicidal gestures, chronic feelings of emptiness, intense anger and difficulty in controlling this. There can also be transient stress-related paranoid ideation or severe dissociative symptoms.

For the group of people suffering from anti-social-type personality disorder, music therapy has a specific role of encouraging empathy (Compton-Dickinson et al. 2013) owing to the reciprocal nature of music making, and also an emphasis upon attuning to another in order to share a creative musical event. In their book *Forensic Music Therapy* Compton-Dickinson et al. (2013) include several case examples where violent destructive behavior is acknowledged and explored, and sometimes alleviated through music therapy, for people in high secure environments who have committed violent acts and who have a diagnosis of personality disorder. The role for music therapy could be through improvised or pre-composed music, but involves listening and adjusting musically, which can lead to increased appreciation of another's mood, point of view, and way of being.

Cluster C: The anxious, fearful cluster

This includes the avoidant, dependent, and obsessive compulsive disorders and these three groups of people share a high level of anxiety, a chronic sense of inadequacy, feelings of rejection and self-criticism, including a constant state of feeling judged by others. They share an avoidance of social situations and prefer to live in an isolated way, desiring more contact but avoiding and fearing it to such an extent that their life can be totally narrow in focus. Paradoxically, at the same time for someone with a dependent personality disorder, being alone is extremely difficult.[5] As clingy and compliant people, this group find group work very difficult but music therapy groups potentially enable a new way of relating through hearing, sharing, and having to appreciate and cooperate with others in order to make music, composed or improvised. Cluster C also includes people with obsessive compulsive personality disorder, who tend to be rigid and inflexible in their approach to anything, and musically may be highly accomplished but unable to feel or express emotion through music, or in relationships generally. Music therapy can be both frightening owing to its potential for order and also releasing in the sense that sometimes freedom to improvise simultaneously by creating an esthetic object (piece of music) with the therapist or group, can help shift patterns. Patients striving for perfection at the expense of their mental health, can, for example, become more able to allow chaos and messy cacophonous music which in turn can enable them to live more full lives (Pool and Odell-Miller 2011; Odell-Miller 2001).

An overview of literature
and research studies

The evidence base

Reasons for the paucity of literature and research in this field is in part owing to the fact that until recently the diagnostic group was not thought to warrant special attention in the field of psychiatry. There was a lack of evidence that medical (drug) intervention was successful. A body of general literature emerged in the early part of this century which began to highlight the importance and success of psychological interventions with this disorder (Bateman and Fonagy 2004).

Some case reports, anecdotal evidence, and systematic research has shown positive outcomes for people with different types of personality disorders who attend music therapy (Pedersen 2003; Hannibal 2003; Pedersen and Hannibal 2013; Odell-Miller 2007; Pool and Odell-Miller 2011). Below are more detailed examples taken from relevant literature.

Pool and Odell-Miller (2011) presented a case study of music therapy work with a man with personality disorders, in a context they describe as informed by The National Institute for Clinical Excellence (NICE 2014) consultation guidelines. NICE is an organization in the UK that validates effective treatments, and recommends which treatments and therapies the government should fund according to systematic reviews and expert advice. The multidisciplinary team of the unit where the work took place, contributed to the guidelines at the time of the study. The inclusion of arts therapies demonstrates the change in attitude towards music therapy as a more mainstream treatment for personality disorder (NICE 2014).

Arts therapies in the NICE guidelines are referred to generically, rather than music therapy being listed separately, and include art therapy, dance movement therapy, dramatherapy and music therapy, all of which use arts media as the primary mode of communication. Weekly therapy is described as the norm, and group or individual work is listed, with groups of no more than four to six recommended. "The primary concern is to effect change and growth through the use of the art form in a safe and facilitating environment in the presence of a therapist. Arts therapies can help those who find it hard to express thoughts and feelings verbally." (NICE 2014).

Further, the guideline states that traditionally, these therapies are thought of as:

> working with primitive emotional material that is "preverbal" in nature, and thus made available to exploration and rational thought. The nature of the therapist's work can thus be similar to the interpretations of psychoanalysis, or less interpretative and more supportive, to enable patients to understand what they want to understand from the work. For people with more severe borderline personality disorder, it is generally accepted that "plunging interpretations" without sufficient support are unlikely to be helpful.
>
> Meares and Hobson 1977

Arts therapies are summarized in the NICE guideline as:

> more concerned with the process of creating something, and the emotional response to this and/or the group dynamics of this. This can be very active (involving the physical

characteristics of the art work and movement), playful, symbolic, metaphorical or lead directly to emotions that need to be understood. Such understanding may be achieved through subsequent discussion, and the use of the art materials when helpful.

(NICE 2014)

In a recent report as part of the European collaboration network for research on music therapy and personality disorder, Pedersen and Hannibal (2013) reported that music therapists in Denmark have provided services to people with personality disorders over the last twenty years, mainly in psychiatric treatment settings. Music therapy has been applied as the primary intervention or as a combined intervention in cooperation with daycare treatment for this population. Music therapists working in this field have developed a treatment philosophy initially derived from a psychodynamic orientation based on work with transference (Hannibal 2000) and counter transference (Pedersen 2007). Currently, their approach has developed so that currently the underlying more modern theoretical orientation integrates developmental psychology (Hannibal 2007), attachment theory, mentalization-based treatment and neuro-psychology (Hannibal et al. 2012a).

In Odell-Miller's research (2007, 2014) findings concluded from a thematic analysis of a purposive survey across five large music therapy centers in Europe incorporating 23 experienced music therapists confirmed an agreed awareness of the characteristics and symptoms likely to be present for personality disorder, and recognition of their foundation, also therefore what types of music therapy approaches may be indicated. Other relevant literature (Hannibal 2003; Pedersen 2003) has also indicated the potential for improvisation in music therapy to provide access to the inner world of the patient when words may not be accessible. Odell-Miller's (2007) research showed that music therapists prioritized people in this diagnostic group in the same way as for schizophrenia, which was a shift from earlier findings where this population had not been prioritized by music therapists (Odell-Miller et al. 2006). In addition findings suggested that for people with non-psychotic disorders, including personality disorders, music therapy techniques that require symbolic thinking such as theme-based improvisation, musical role play, and use of other media are indicated. Structured and free improvisation using play rules, were prioritized for this population by expert music therapy respondents. Table 17.1 shows some examples taken from the qualitative data gathered from music therapists about this population and appropriate music therapy techniques.

The same study showed agreement that a psychoanalytically informed model with music making through improvisation, and interpretation is indicated for this group who need to address meaning and understand psychological frameworks for their mental state in order to progress. There is agreement that this population can tolerate an analytic approach working symbolically, and with unconscious material through music and talking. This was the diagnosis in the study where an analytical approach was most frequently used.

Further, considering techniques involving structures such as themes, music therapist participants in Odell-Miller's (2007) study agreed that these are only useful if the themes come from the patients. It is the very aspect of creative control linked to relevant themes of character, emotions, or life events that makes this method so useful. However, results from the study were not conclusive. Some respondents reported that composed music could act as a defense mechanism for people with personality disorder; whilst providing a holding function, it may

Table 17.1 Examples of techniques used in music therapy from Odell–Miller's
(2007) research, and comments by music therapists about their specific
use for people with personality disorders

Singing composed songs	"This might be part of the way that an interaction happens if desired by the patient, particularly at the beginning of the therapy. It MIGHT also be a goal or focus if it seemed as if this was the only way to start a relationship or if it seemed to help with overall therapeutic goals. Performance helps some overcome or explore feelings of shame, and builds up feelings of self-worth if handled in the right way with a music therapist." "People often bring songs they have written. The therapists' role includes composing an accompaniment, e.g. a patient who had been violently sexually assaulted never talked about it but began to bring songs describing this horror in a metaphorical way. This seemed to have been a safe way for her to begin to tackle this. Processing it musically and creating a satisfying *esthetic* seemed to enable her to take some power back from the abuser, and begin to mourn."
Activity-based music therapy	"This might be an important part and there might be an emphasis upon achievement at some stages in the therapy where a group would work on respect and trust of others by a shared activity for example. Sometimes the group might develop more esthetic desire, as more self-worth develops".
Free improvisation (without talking)	(One respondent links the importance of music-making to pathology in that music is affect-based like the illness.) "Music helps at the level of affect. The pathology (of personality disorders) is affect based—there is more of a mentalization problem. If a person cannot 'digest' (mentally) they project it to the therapist. The therapist is often 'affected' at a physical level (projective identification). Patients often who have been abused cannot understand at first what improvisation is for. This implies that the music therapist's task is to help the person understand the meaning of the affect."
Free improvisation (with talking, role play, or play rules)	"This is the main way of working with this population. The very central aim of the work is to use music to help integrate thoughts and feelings and to allow access to some emotional expression which is either kept hidden or often expressed inappropriately".

also prevent patients working on their own issues. Others reported that when people bring songs they have written, the therapists' role may include providing an accompaniment, and performance can help some patients explore or overcome feelings of shame, as in the case of Anna discussed later in this chapter. This can in turn build up feelings of self-worth if handled in the right way with a music therapist. This viewpoint is also supported by literature specializing in the use of the voice in song, improvised, and composed music, for people suffering from trauma, neglect, and abuse (Austin 1998; Montello 1998).

Robarts and Sloboda (1994) discussed role-play in music therapy for people with non-psychotic disorders, and Smeijsters (1996) described a range of more symbolic possibilities for people with eating disorders; eating disorders are commonly found amongst people diagnosed with personality disorder. Smeijsters (2005) also discussed the importance of reflection on past experiences through a combination of music making and talking.

FINDING MODELS OF WORK

The roots of personality disorder can arise from early trauma and difficulty, and literature in the psychological therapies supports working through meaning and understanding how to deal with present roles and emotions in the light of reflecting about this through role play, reciprocal roles (Ryle et al. 1997), and "mentalization"[6] (Bateman and Fonagy 2004). Mentalization was referred to by three centers in Odell-Miller's research (2007, 2014), revealing an emerging interest in this approach in the field of music therapy, developed more recently through the innovation of arts therapies mentalization based training in the UK run by the International Centre for Arts Therapies Training in the Central and Northwest London NHS Trust (ICAPT 2014), in collaboration with Professor Peter Fonagy (Roth and Fonagy 2004).

In seeking a model of music therapy for people with personality disorders, in this case borderline personality disorder, a crucial factor is that this group have no overt problems with cognition, or speaking. Observations from recent clinical work show that they may feel distressed, frightened, and in psychic pain on a daily basis, as well as having emotional and relationship difficulties, including problems of self-harm which are difficult to alleviate and can sometimes be hidden. In music therapy, therapists can play music with patients, or listen to and experience music created by patients, to better understand their emotions and how they interact with the world. These experiences and the emotions associated with them can then be made more meaningful through subsequent discussions, and in groupwork as we see later in this chapter, can help group members take care of themselves and develop concern for others. Patients involved in music therapy can more easily explore feelings that they otherwise find difficult to talk about and begin to turn away from their preoccupations with self-harm.

Hannibal (2003) emphasized the link between the capacity for music therapy to work with people who are driven by impulsivity, a specific issue for people with borderline personality disorder. Elsewhere in Europe, Danish research has documented that music therapy recruits 40 percent of its client population from this group, and that the adherence to treatment seems high, and participant attendance is stable (Hannibal and Pedersen 2000; Hannibal 2005; Hannibal et al. 2011; Hannibal et al. 2012b). Odell-Miller's (2007) research found similar priority being given to the treatment of personality disorder within the case loads of 23 music therapists in European psychiatric settings.

Although high level music therapy attendance has been reported for this population with drop outs as low as 11 percent (Hanibal et al. 2012b), in the wider treatment literature non completion of therapy programmes by people who have personality disorders has been reported as high as 37 percent (McMurran et al. 2010). This suggests that leaving services prematurely, or having difficulty engaging with services is one aspect that a new practitioner may wish to anticipate when starting out work in this area. Addressing this topic in supervision and treatment planning is recommended.

The clinical process has been documented and investigated through qualitative single case studies (Hannibal 2000; Pedersen 2003, 2005, 2014). Similarly to Odell-Miller's findings, this literature points to careful use of improvised music, and a focus upon linking emotion and thought (Pool and Odell-Miller 2011), drawing upon the ability of music to engage with underlying emotion when hidden, often self-destructive feelings, are hard to put into words.

Music therapy has been offered as both individual and group treatment (Hannibal 2000, 2003, 2008, Hannibal et al. 2011). The length of treatments in Denmark has been for shorter periods for groups (around 20 group sessions) and longer periods for individual treatment (up to three years), whilst in the UK and Belgium, group work and individual work have tended to be longer term (Odell-Miller 2001, 2007, 2011).

Primary aims of music therapy are focused on establishing an alliance, reducing symptoms, and developing personal skills and relational competences. Explicit and implicit mentalizing ability is the focus of treatment and of research (Hannibal 2013, 2014). Hannibal and Pedersen have sought to find out how to provide an environment where the patient can raise implicit mentalization capabilities through music therapy, understood as the ability to engage, manage, regulate, initiate, and separate relational processes. This can be through active and receptive music therapy and verbal interventions, with "here and now" work being the focus. When treating patients with personality disorders, keeping an optimal arousal level is considered essential, although this is sometimes most psychologically painful. The treatment must always try to provide an environment in which the patient has optimal conditions for growth and development. This process, or model, has recently been named as process orientated music therapy (PROMT) (Hannibal et al. 2012a). Research has primarily been single cased based at the Music Therapy Clinic at Aalborg University Hospital. A multicenter European RCT study with this population is planned since there is an immediate demand for delivering evidence that music therapy is an effective treatment for this population. Currently a pilot study is in progress, based on the treatment system of PROMT.

Strehlow (2011) examined individual music therapy sessions in a clinical setting in Germany with 20 female patients diagnosed with borderline personality disorder (BPD). Short- and long-term session plans involving a psychoanalytic perspective were investigated. The aim of the research was to look for typical features of how BPD patients deal with music in music therapy. The methodological basis used was systematic qualitative psychotherapy research using the concept of "forming types by comprehension." It is based on the systematic analysis of similarities and differences. The method offers the advantage of developing categories as well as transparency and comprehensiveness in the abstraction process. Four individual stages show how to get from the complex single case to generalizing ideal types.

The classification of a total of 80 sessions resulted in ten ideal-typical interaction patterns. Each of these is characterized by a specific use of music and its unconscious significance for the patient. The ten interaction patterns give examples for typical situations when working in music therapy with borderline personality disordered patients, so that the single case is much easier to understand. Studying these patterns can help the music therapist to be better prepared for "stormy" sessions that are typical when working with these patients. The ten interaction patterns defined by Strehlow are included in Box 17.1.

Strehlow states that the ten typical interaction patterns are an important help to maintain and reconstruct the therapist's capacity to play, to improvise, and to mentalize. Ultimately this will lead to better support for the patient. This research was validated reliably by a group of five external expert music therapists using an investigator-triangulation model.

Box 17.1 Strehlow's common patterns for music therapy
sessions with borderline personality disorder

1. Music as magical hope
2. Music goes beyond borders
3. Music makes everything worse
4. Music as a place of withdrawal
5. Music as a way of not being alone
6. Music for triangulation
7. Music allows disharmony
8. Music as a voice of dissent
9. Music gives structure
10. Music for integrating the excluded

FURTHER CLINICAL CONSIDERATIONS

Hannibal (2003) emphasized how free improvisation was helpful for one woman for whom there is an absent sense of self, common in this disorder. He described how the phenomenon of musical improvisation, owing to its immediate "sounding," enables the patient to feel more "present" through playing music. Hannibal's musical interactions and his way of listening gave the patient a sense of respect she did not seem to have prior to this, which was enabled, in his view, though the concrete act of playing music. In turn the patient experienced respect for her music and therefore her self-respect increased. Further, using free improvisation amongst other things enabled her to cut down her judging of herself, which diminished as she experienced Hannibal's acceptance and did not therefore fear rejection. For this person spoken language was a weak way to communicate and establish an alliance.

Pedersen (2003) similarly illustrates in "The revival of the frozen sea urchin," how a 41-year-old man with a personality disorder with obsessive compulsive and anhedonic features, used music therapy as part of an in-depth process to free up his "frozen" emotional world, through improvisation with the therapist holding certain changing positions and thinking within the countertransference, as he changed through the therapy from over intellectualizing, to being able to bring dreams and understand his internal world. This enabled him to get in touch with hidden trauma and work through some of this material musically and verbally. In the music therapy treatment he built up a more confident sense of self-worth, developed a stable sense of identity. He was able to eventually work with dreams symbolically, and with unconscious material which appeared to be unlocked and accessed as a result of musical flow, engagement, and gradual interpretative work with the therapist. In the patient's words in a moving quotation at the end of the chapter, he continued to use the sensations he had encountered through sound, after the therapy had ended: "just to sense how I feel inside myself ... This gives me a tool to loosen up the psychological knots and tensions building up." (Pedersen 2003, p. 386.)

Other authors argue against consideration of a specific approach linked to diagnosis. Stige (1999) has suggested that the focus of music therapy should be upon the meaning of music from the client's perspective. He has provided a detailed account of working with a man with a personality disorder (emotionally unstable borderline type). In this description, Stige puts forward an argument for holding the meaning of the music for the patient as a focus, rather than making too many assumptions as a therapist. For example he discovers with this particular client, that at certain times the use of improvisation provided a connection to the life history of the patient but at others it provided a disconnection. In contrast, Stige (1999) finds that at other times use of composed or more task-orientated music therapy techniques were important: "He would for instance engage himself in different activities, including playing music on the stereo or on the organ." (Stige 1999, p. 74.)

Furthermore Stige speculates upon which technique to use when, and his questions are related to the particular diagnosis of the patient, or to a desirable move away from a more traditional psychotherapeutic music therapy approach. He almost starts to put forward an argument about music therapy technique and personality disorder, but moves, as demonstrated in this example below, to a view that the client's history and the relationship between music, meaning and the understanding of this between therapist and client, is what should drive the therapy, rather than the diagnosis.

> In any case, Harold used music as a connection to his life history only a few times. He rarely explored his inner life but he seemed to be successful in his use of music as a disconnection. What importance should then be given to either? This question is related to some clinical considerations that must be explored by any therapist working with a patient with a personality disorder. Is the client ready for explorative therapy or is a more supportive strategy necessary?... ... Some of my questions about my own work with Harold were: How much should he be challenged to go in an explorative direction? If he should be challenged, how and when? And how and when could such challenge have a negative function, giving him a feeling of not being accepted and respected in the relationship? Working with Harold made it very clear to me that the clinical aspects of such questions could not be separated from the differences in the value systems of the two partners. Connected to this are differences in ideas on the meaning of music. I felt I needed to know more about Harold's relationship to music.
>
> Stige 1999, pp. 74–75

There is a sense in which the need for more specific guidelines about when to do what, and why, is described but no substantial conclusions are provided. The therapist is challenged by the fact that the client has a totally different meaning arising from the improvising together than the therapist, which causes the therapist to wonder about the techniques and frameworks he is using.

Van den Hurk and Smeijsters (1991) from the Netherlands described music therapy sessions with a 31-year-old man with obsessive compulsive personality disorder. He had music therapy for one year, and had previously been undergoing psychotherapy for feelings of doubt, panic, and unrest. Similarly to Pedersen's patient, this person had emotional and interpersonal blocks and was referred to music therapy where music improvisation was the primary method used. His psychotherapist at the time of referral had felt that music could help the patient "work through his rationalizations and emotional armors." Methods reported in this study are quite prescriptive, following the Dutch models at the time of a combination of active and receptive methods, clearly moving through stages which are described in detail but which move through using musical instruments in a specific order to match the patient's need for order. Within this, once musical engagement had started, there were possibilites for varying the degree of freedom and also intimacy within the relationship—both areas identified as needing exploration, and for which musical improvisation naturally lent itself.

Moving through the stages, one can see a clear development where the patient could acknowledge the importance of emotions, following musical and social-type interactions in the therapy sessions where eventually pleasure in social interactions was experienced. Subsequently feelings of grief were "allowed" to surface during the second stage of the therapy. The music therapist's role is characteristically described as leading and then following, and fluctuating between reciprocal roles, akin to Cognitive Analytic Therapy (CAT), increasingly used for people with this diagnosis in conjunction with music therapy (Odell-Miller 2007; Sleight and Compton-Dickenson 2013). Van den Hurk and Smeijsters describe the therapist's role as offering several 'several gradations of activity' and this could also be thought of as regulation of affect, which is a key concept emerging in the literature for personality disorder and music therapy.

By contrast Dvorkin (1991) has described individual music therapy drawing on object-relations theory with an adolescent female with borderline personality disorder. Separation disruption meant that individuation was impaired and she was unable to complete the separation process. Dvorkin described music therapy, using song writing, and she agrees that the patient's feelings can be projected into songs. The creation of music together in this way can help develop trust and intimacy. For a patient who had not been able to form close trusting relationships for fear of abandonment, "music was able to reflect her moods in a way which words could not" (p. 264). Songs were sung, with the therapist encouraging the use of different emotional tones through joint singing and music making in the therapy sessions. The song is likened to a *transitional object*; for example a child's blanket that is used of safety and comfort to keep them connected to a parent or care giver when they are going to sleep. So, after working through material and internalization of ideas was completed; through verbal and musical exploration with the therapists' supportive interpretation; the songs were no longer needed. This psychoanalytically-informed approach is very different to Stige's and Van den Hurk and Smeijsters' approach. However, most reported case studies suggest that patients seem to arrive at a specific point of recognition or change, which is related to the special and unique musical relationship, developed over time, in music therapy. Notwithstanding, as already stated, so far there are as yet no substantial scientific outcome studies that provide stronger evidence to support these reports.

THE FORENSIC FIELD, AGGRESSION, MUSIC THERAPY, AND PERSONALITY DISORDER

Violent impulse and aggression is common for many people with personality disorder. Pool and Odell-Miller (2011) investigated aggression, which was described as a common reason for referral to arts therapies services (Odell-Miller 1995, 2007). Forty percent of referrals given by mental health care professionals in Odell-Miller's survey were aggression-related or cited aggression as the reason for referral. Other articles have focused on treatment of aggression and anger in music therapy (Bensimon et al. 2008), in the arts therapies (Smeijsters and Cleven 2006), and in psychodynamic psychotherapy combined with movement (Twemlow et al. 2008).

Further, more recently Compton-Dickenson et al. (2013) include examples of music therapy for people who have exhibited violent destructive impulses and are diagnosed with anti-social personality disorder, culminating in having to live for many years in a high secure setting. Hervey and Odell-Miller (2013) carried out a research project investigating multidisciplinary attitude towards music therapy treatment programmes, and found that the aggressive tendencies of patients affected the staff team's capacity to be comfortable with some music therapy approaches using a psychoanalytically-informed music therapy approach, and concluded the following guidelines are important when considering music therapy in these settings. Further, Hervey and Odell-Miller (2013) summarize emergent suggested benefits from the literature about personality disorders music therapy and the forensic setting as fourfold:

- Partial reintegration of emotional states from which the patient formerly dissociated.
- Increased emotional connections with therapist, peers and/or self-history.
- Improved ability to recognize and tolerate difficult emotions (such as anger).
- Increased awareness of links between thoughts, emotions, and physical sensations. Hervey and Odell-Miller (2013, p. 210).

Hervey and Odell-Miller's survey used interpretative phenomenological analysis (IPA) to analyze semi-structured interviews with the multidisciplinary team (MDT). Their results revealed the following five areas for further research and consideration:

1. An awareness of the specific elements of psychoanalytically-informed music therapy likely to present challenges to forensic teams (and patients) is valuable in designing effective training for staff, within which such elements may be openly explored.
2. Creative solutions to the likely anxieties in teams may not be immediately apparent, but may be identified through discussion in clinical supervision and with more experienced colleagues and managers.
3. Multidisciplinary supervision groups should be established.
4. Allocation of adequate time for communication with forensic MDT's and careful structuring of the music therapist's cross-ward timetable.
5. Music therapists should recognize the particular likelihood of patient pathology having an impact upon staff and be aware of potential conflicts in the therapy work and in the team.

The latter conclusions are also supported in the music therapy literature as summarize also by Hervey and Odell-Miller (2013) under five salient points for music therapy in the forensic field and with people with borderline and anti-social personality disorder.

- Institutions may resist positive changes in patients due to high anxiety (Glyn 2002).
- Music therapy may evoke resistance from teams due to the formation of a "separate" therapeutic relationship (Roberts 2001).
- Music is often perceived by teams as a powerful, potentially overwhelming therapeutic tool (Roberts 2001; Sloboda 1997).
- MDT's may be concerned about music's capacity to trigger memories of early trauma in patients (Pool and Odell-Miller 2011).

- Music therapists may develop unrealistically optimistic perspectives of their ability to effect change in patients, because of their emergent and often marginalized work role (Sloboda 1997).

Authors indicate that where they occur, the phenomena listed above are likely to have an adverse effect on professionals' capacity to conduct meaningful therapeutic work. Clinical supervision and regular, open MDT discussions are emphasized as important means for recognizing and working with patients' projections on to team members, thereby minimizing acting out of the patient's inner conflicts. Such models indicate an acknowledgement of the potential for defensive social systems to develop, and a move towards more supportive, self-reflective systems. These combined findings lead to further attention upon the connections between creativity, aggressive impulses, and the role of music therapy, and Pool and Odell-Miller (2011) draw attention to the following important theoretical considerations.

Further theoretical considerations: Aggression, mastery, and the dynamics of the clinical environment

The relationship between a developing sense of identity and creativity as discussed by Storr (1972) and Winnicott (1971, 1950), and music therapy, enables people to experience themselves in a safe environment, by providing a psychological and musical (creative) space and another mind (the therapist's), to increase the capacity for insight into themselves and their behavior. Music and other arts therapies focus strongly on emotions and behavior (Smeijsters and Cleven 2006) and psychological treatments which enable aggressive expression by the patient, especially when aggression is suppressed or presented inappropriately, are therefore crucial for this population.

One emergent theme for populations diagnosed with personality disorder is the intention to harm, which can be linked to the aggressor's need for mastery, omnipotence, control of the object, or self-preservation (Pool and Odell-Miller 2011). Freud (1920) saw aggressiveness as a sign of resistance and implied that the arousal of aggression; including locating, uncovering, and getting hold of it; was an important part of treatment. Geen (2001) suggested that affective aggression is motivated mainly by the intention to harm, and can be linked to patterns of activity in the central nervous system, and this physiological link suggests a bodily arousal and explains why strong affective states may be aroused by playing music, which can activate the music-maker at physical, emotional, and expressive levels.

Mastering aggression and emotions through an omnipotent relationship and repetitive experiences may be explored through music making, as apparent in Odell-Miller's (2001) case study of Malcolm with personality disorder and bipolar disorder. Here, an acknowledgment of omnipotence through loud cymbal playing led to insight into problems of aggression in external relationships, which in turn as reported by the patient and multidisciplinary team, impacted positively on these relationships. Drawing on psychoanalytic theory, John (1995) has drawn attention to the process of sublimation by describing the process where the patient uses pre-verbal exchange to deal with rage and overwhelming emotions and can communicate and discharge into a containing holding object. Here, rage can be mastered and brought under conscious control. Patient's defense mechanisms may be seen through a rigid perseverative style of playing when a patient defends against pain brought to the surface in therapy, as in the case example described by Pool and Odell-Miller (2011).

Compton-Dickinson et al. (2013) focus upon the capacity for music therapy to increase empathy, and also upon the potential for the music therapy process to work with aggressive tendencies. Compton-Dickinson (2006, 2013) suggested that music has the potential to be the most intimately interactive of the arts therapies. This is owing to the active engagement of the therapist who can choose to match and bring to the surface the patient's inner world, helping him to express subtle aspects of this through shared musical expression. The skill of the music therapist lies in supporting the personality disordered patient to access and express enough, but not too much emotion through jointly-created music (Compton-Dickinson 2006).

Through case study research and substantiated systematic research into Group Cognitive Analytic Therapy (G-CAMT) Compton-Dickinson vividly describes work which shows how group music making can symbolize the real capacity to kill and be killed, and how new insights can be gained by participants through this process. In articulating the process she indicated:

> If during the creative process there is an uncontainable and distressing flood of emotions, the situation risks becoming overwhelming and unmanageable. In the forensic setting, music therapy in all its variations is associated with particular kinds of risk. There is the potential that emotional arousal and therefore dangerousness could be heightened or reduced through music. The instruments are themselves sometimes perceived as potential weapons, which could be secreted and honed, thrown or used as barricades. To ensure the safety of all, high security procedures therefore insist on rigorous equipment inventories for music therapy sessions.
>
> Sleight and Compton-Dickinson 2013, pp. 170–171

What emerges for this population is that the very nature of the potency and power of the music making situation in music therapy for this group is both its risk and its strength. Therefore the music therapist must be trained both psychotherapeutically, musically, and psychologically in order to achieve effective work in this setting. Additionally the music therapist must be able to negotiate with managers and funders as to the necessary support and equipment needed to provide effective services.

In an open day-center for people with personality disorders, Pool and Odell-Miller (2011) examined aggression and music therapy for people with personality disorders. An excerpt is shown below illustrating a main finding. Through a mixed methods study, which combined an in-depth case study and a thematic analysis of interviews of three experienced music therapists using a purposive sample, the data analysis draws on thematic analytic methods using interpretative phenomenological analysis (IPA) (Smith and Osborn 2003). The case study was of a young man with a personality disorder diagnosis and a forensic history of violence. Destructive aggression had featured strongly in his life and the music therapy work focused on channeling his aggression and experiencing it constructively. The case-work fell into three stages which are relatively common in music therapy casework of this kind:

- Phase 1: Establishing boundaries, safety, and identity.
- Phase 2: Holding, containment, and learning to master aggression.
- Phase 3: Separation, ending, and loss.

Charles began to explore difficult feelings he had about significant and longstanding rela-tionships as his music therapy progressed and he became more able to use music to express himself. He used music to discharge his aggression primitively in loud drumming and also to resist emotional expression by playing repetitively. By expressing aggression, he started to gain insight and became more able to show vulnerability and sublimate his aggression. Giving meaning to aggressive behavior is fundamental in promoting psychological growth (Twemlow et al. 2008). All interviewees emphasized the adaptability of the therapist's music to enable experience of aggression as manageable and meaningful. Insight into behavior is often achieved verbally. However, the patient may not be able to express a painful experience or feeling verbally in early stages of treatment. Therefore, musical interaction is a very suitable medium for working at a non-verbal, emotional level.

Pool and Odell-Miller 2011, pp. 173–174

Wigram (2004) indicated that working musically at a non-verbal level through the use of techniques including matching, synchronizing, reflecting, and grounding can provide the foundations for the verbal aspect in gaining insight. The interviews and case study suggested that giving the patient control in music therapy was indicated in order to empower and encourage confidence. The results of the study support this notion through the emergence of themes of self-reliance, meaning, and constructive use of aggression in becoming assertive. Charles's increasing ability to express aggression and to assert his wishes beyond the sessions suggests that he was developing his sense of self through music therapy. He seemed to gain a sense of empowerment through taking responsibility for his treatment.

The authors further conclude that Charles's sense of persecution arose from suppressing his emotions, which he had become accustomed to doing as a result of an abusive childhood. Through music therapy he began to experience that his own destructiveness and, hence, his feelings could be held and adapted to by another person. In particular, through express-ing aggression musically, without losing control he was able to express deeper more hidden emotional states such as shame. The making of a CD of some chosen parts of his improvisa-tions, with the music therapist, helped to counteract feelings of shame and humiliation. The success of his creative ability was embodied in this process.

SPECIFIC CONSIDERATIONS
OF GROUP MUSIC THERAPY

Individual work features prominantly in the literature described already, but group music therapy has certain unique benefits for people suffering from psychological trauma, a feature prevalent for this population. A long-term music therapy group was run for two years and a referral system was established for people with severe personality disorders (Cluster B type mainly), some of whom have an additional diagnosis such as depression, and often more than one type of personality disorder (Odell-Miller 2007, 2013). The group was therefore complex, as is usual for such a unit (Bateman and Fonagy 2004, Gunderson 2005). Complex difficulties included personality disorders such as narcissism, obsessive compulsive disor-der, anti-social, and depressive paranoid. There was a high risk of self-harm, including regu-lar severe cutting, or overdosing, and a difficulty in dealing with high levels of emotion often so intensely felt that strong cognitive processes or physical rituals or self-harm had developed to counter the feelings, or to express deep hurt in another way.

In the music therapy group there were clear boundaries between the beginnings and endings of music, manifest in often very controlled playing, and an avoidance of "letting go." There was a conscious avoidance of playing loud music, or playing freely with no structure. The therapist therefore had to use musical structures to provide a containing function and to lessen the re-experience of trauma. Improvisation in groups provides opportunities to work with empathy, because often patients have difficulty coping with another's playing, and improvisation can help through seeing, hearing, or sensing an atmosphere.

Furthermore the initial experience of patients in a music therapy group is often of a fear and dread of playing music. This is particularly the case for people who have been sexually abused, which is a very common feature in borderline personality disorder. Fear and dread may be present because of the heightened emotions that come to the fore through music. This point is also one of Strehlow's ten patterns listed above (Strehlow 2011). Reasons for this may include, in Western culture particularly, that the room and instruments can bring vivid early memories of school or nursery to mind. Similarly to Sleight and Compton-Dickinson (2013) quoted above, I have suggested that patients might even experience fear and dread of impulsive self-harming or harming of others in the presence of many objects that can be seen as potential weapons (Odell-Miller 2007). In addition to this, the relationship with the therapist and other group members, all of whom suggest potential for intimacy and contact, which for a group of abused clients can often bring back painful memories of abusive (physical, sexual, or emotional) relationships, and can be immediately uncomfortable. This view is supported by Hannibal (2005).

Group case example: Borderline personality disorder

The emotional processing of music can link thought and feeling, and for people with this condition, music therapy can be useful because making music involves collaboration. It can also allow raw expression of emotion, also important for in a safe therapeutic space. Listening back to group music therapy examples, the ability to reflect, to play music creatively, with the therapist is important, and the musical structures evolve naturally and through people listening and moderating their pace and meter, including an esthetic element. Participants report a physicality and a self-soothing component within music which is hard to describe in words and certainly hard to research scientifically.

Anna is a young mother, with two small children, and attended the music therapy group for two years. Prior to this she spent many years extremely ill, depressed, and lacking in self-worth, and benefitted from group psychotherapy and individual therapy, and was hospitalized for long periods, and at one point had electroconvulsive therapy (ECT). She has now ended music therapy, has not self-harmed for over three years and is living an independent life. She had an abusive childhood, in that her alcoholic father maltreated both her and her sister. She worked with me on the written material used here, and gave full consent for her story to be used, as long as she did not have to listen carefully to her own musical recordings. This is an example of her degree of low self-esteem—she is happy for others to hear her but cannot bear to face herself easily although enjoyed the process of preparation of this material. Our work started when she joined a music therapy group in a specific National Health

Service (NHS) for people with personality disorders, which used a multitude of musical ways of looking at relationships particularly that between the inner and outer worlds of members. The rationale that the nature of the group is powerful and forces between group members can be heard in the musical improvisations was crucial to this approach.

Anna often chose bongo drums to help herself think about her mood and affect, and also to connect with others in a way which she said relaxed her as she did not have to always talk.

Towards the end of therapy, Anna moved to wanting to work on producing a satisfying piece of music. Music can also focus on esthetics, which is important in building confidence and self-esteem, a facet substantiated through systematic research (Odell-Miller 2007, 2013). A focus on esthetics can help develop respect for a healthy unscarred body rather than one cut or burned.

Anna had joined a community choir during her time as an out- patient on the unit, and sometimes she talked longingly about wanting to improve her skills as a singer. At the end of the group therapy, she asked to start singing lessons and was put in touch with an excellent sensitive singing teacher. In two follow-up appointments after the ending of group therapy, she brought songs to show me her progress and I accompanied her on the piano, reflecting her movement and journey into her much higher sense of worth and esteem, and towards expanding her performances to solo work within her choir. If readers could hear the musical example of her rendering of a well-known song from West Side Story by Leonard Bernstein *There's a place for us*, the integrated expressive, dynamically changing, appropriately sometimes holding-back style of singing would be evident. It is what I would term an "improvised performance" using her full resources, but the relationship with the therapist and previous two years of psychoanalytically informed individual work was crucial to the process and outcome for her at the of the treatment. Anna subsequently ceased therapy and managed well in the community, attending the choir regularly but making use of the internalized process of therapy preceding this.

In summary the importance of music making links to the pathology of personality disorders because music, like the illness, is affect based. This implies that the music therapist's task for people with personality disorders is to help the person understand the meaning of the affect. This was suggested by Hannibal (2003) and is supported by Pedersen (2003). A group provides a supportive place for this to be possible, as illustrated in both Anna and Veronica's cases.

Conclusions

Generally people diagnosed with personality disorders who are attending music therapy services need less structure as therapy progresses. This is demonstrated in the case study of Anna above, who moved to a self-help model in her recovery and rehabilitation, through singing, but for whom previous music therapy using a psychoanlyatically-informed approach in a group had been useful. In comparison with the majority of seriously ill people suffering from psychotic illness, this group can tolerate interpretation and musical improvisation that moves between thinking and feeling, in order to understand meaning. Free improvisation is very useful in allowing people to be in touch with their difficult emotions and can provide links to meaning and words that might not otherwise have been available as evidenced above through the study findings, clinical experience, and the support of a very small body of music therapy literature.

The comparison with the population with schizoprehnia shows in particular a more careful use of music in improvisations, for personality disordered people, whereas those with schizophrenia and schizophrenia-like illness are more likely to disregard collaboration with others, through group music making for example. This can be seen through examining points of synchronicity for endings or beginnings of pieces of music. Odell-Miller's summary of specific ways in which people with personality disorder use music in music therapy. Odell-Miller (2007) follows:

- Music provides a link between emotion and thought.
- Music is used to heighten understanding of expression of emotion and the meaning of this.
- Reciprocal roles can be explored musically.
- Links between memory of abuse and childhood music making can be powerful.
- Music making links to the pathology of personality disorders because music, like the illness, is affect based.
- Esthetic qualities of music are particularly important for this group who are prone to self-harm.

People with personality disorders can work psychoanalytically but the approach might need to be adapted, to provide more structure. This could be, for example, by combining music therapy with CAT (Ryle et al. 1997; Compton-Dickinson 2013), where reciprocal roles can be explored through playing music in improvised and pre-composed structures, and through talking and reflection. Relationships and intimacy are difficult, emotional communication is problematic, and people may deal with inner pain by inflicting self-harm, often as a way of deflecting their emotional/psychic pain, or actually in order to communicate to others something about their inner pain.

Borderline personality disorder is characterized by unstable mood, instability of interpersonal relationships and self-image, self-harm, and marked impulsivity. Clinical and research experience substantiates this view that music can be both challenging for people who have been abused or who are psychologically fragile, as well as helpful in linking thoughts and feelings. The need for allowing a balance between structure and space for a person to feel they can "be themselves," supported and valued, before then moving to more challenging insight-orientated work, is indicated strongly in the literature. Many patients report that being in music therapy groups helps them understand their thoughts and emotions in new ways, and this leads them to better manage unbearable feelings.

Acknowledgements

My thanks go to all patients and colleagues involved in the work, and the following who contributed to the preparation towards this chapter: Niels Hannibal, Inge Nygaard Pedersen, Hayley Hind, Jonathan Pool, Stella Compton-Dickenson, and Gitta Strehlow.

NOTES

1. <http://www.emergenceplus.org.uk/>.
2. <http://www.rcpsych.ac.uk/healthadvice/problemsdisorders/personalitydisorder.aspx>.
3. With the exception of the case of Anna (pseudonym) who gave written consent for her story to be used in publications, other examples are not real but compilations of different elements which may be found in this work.
4. <http://www.sanp.ch/docs/2012/07/en/sanp-00110.pdf>.
5. For more information on diagnosis readers should consult the diagnostic manual DSMV (American Psychiatric Association 2013), Gundersen (2005), Bateman and Fonagy (2004), and *The Oxford Textbook of Psychotherapy* (Gabbard et al. 2005).
6. "Mentalization, the capacity to think about mental states as separate from, yet potentially causing actions, is assumed by us to arise as part of an integration of the pretend and psychic equivalent modes of functioning. This happens optimally in the contxt of a playful parent-child relationship. In such a relationship feelings and thoughts, wishes, and beliefs can be experienced by the child as significant and respected, on the one hand, but on the other as not being of the same order as physical reality" (Bateman and Fonagy 2004, pp. 70–71).

REFERENCES

American Psychiatric Association (2013). *Diagnostic and Statistical Manual of Mental Disorders*, 5th edn. Arlington, VA: American Psychiatric Publishing.

Austin, D. (1998). When the psyche sings: transference and countertransference in improvised singing with individual adults. In: K.E. Bruscia (ed.), *The Dynamics of Music Psychotherapy*, pp. 315–334. Gilsum, NH: Barcelona Publishers.

Bateman, A. and Fonagy, P. (2004). *Psychotherapy for Borderline Personality Disorders: Mentalisation Based Treatment*. Oxford: Oxford University Press.

Bensimon, M., Amir, D., and Wolf, Y. (2008). Drumming through trauma: Music therapy with post-traumatic soldiers. *The Arts in Psychotherapy* 35(1): 34–48.

Compton-Dickinson, S. (2006). Beyond Body, Beyond Words: Cognitive analytic music therapy in forensic psychiatry—New approaches in the treatment of Personality Disordered Offenders. *Music Therapy Today* (Online 22nd December) Vol. VII(4): 839–875. <http://musictherapyworld.net>.

Compton-Dickinson, S., Odell-Miller, H., and Adlam, J. (2013). *Forensic Music Therapy*. London: Jessica Kingsley Publishers.

Denman, C. (2011). *Personality Disorder*. Leaflets produced by Complex Cases Service Cambridge and Peterborough Foundation Trust for users and referrers.

Dvorkin, J. (1991). Individual music therapy for an adolescent with borderline personality disorder: an object relations approach In: K. Bruscia (ed.), *Case Studies in Music Therapy*, pp. 251–268. Gilsum, NH: Barcelona Publishers.

Freud, S. (1920). Beyond the pleasure principle. In: S. Freud (ed.), *The Essentials of Psycho-analysis*, pp. 218–268. London: Penguin.

Gabbard, G., Beck, J., and Holmes, J. (2005). *Oxford Textbook of Psychotherapy*. Oxford: Oxford University Press.

Geen, R. (2001). *Human Aggression*. Buckingham: Open University Press.

Glyn, J. (2002). Drummed Out of Mind—A Music Therapy Group with Forensic Patients. In: A. Davies and E. Richardson (eds), *Music Therapy and Group Work*. London: Jessica Kingsley Publishers.

Gunderson, J.G. (2005). *Understanding and Treating Borderline Personlity Disorder: A Guide for Professionals and Families*. Washington DC: American Psychiatric Publications.

Hannibal N. (2000). Preverbal transference in music therapy—A qualitative investigation of transference process in the musical interaction. Ph.D. dissertation, Institute for Music and Music Therapy, Aalborg University, December 2000.

Hannibal, N. (2003). A Woman's change from being nobody to somebody: music therapy with a middle-aged, speechless and self-destructive woman. In: S. Hadley (ed.), *Music Therapy: Case Studies*. Gilsum, NH: Barcelona Publishers.

Hannibal, N. (2005). Beskrivelse af patientpopulationen i klinisk musikterapi på fem psykiatriske institutioner i Danmark i perioden august 2003–juli 2004. I Ridder, H.M.O. (red.), *Musikterapi i psykiatrien. Årsskrift 4*. (s. 64–75). Aalborg: Aalborg Psykiatriske Sygehus, Aalborg Universitet.

Hannibal, N. (2007). Relevansen af nyere psykodynamisk teori for det klinisk musikterapeutiske arbejde med psykiatriske patienter med personlighedsforstyrrelser. *Psyke & Logos* 28(1): 385–407.

Hannibal, N. (2008). Gruppemusikterapi med patienter med borderline-personlighedsforstyrrelse i dagbehandlingsregi. *Musikterapi i Psykiatrien: Årsskrift* (5): 76–101.

Hannibal, N. (2013). Mentaliseringsbaseret behandling og musikterapi. *Musikterapi i Psykiatrien online (MIPO)* 8(1). http://journals.aau.dk/index.php/MIPO/article/view/255

Hannibal, N. (2014). Implicit and explicit mentalization in music therapy in psychiatric treatment of people with Borderline personality disorder. In: J. de Backer and J. Sutton (eds), *The Music in Music Therapy, European Psychodynamic Music Therapy: Clinical, Theoretical and Research Approaches*. London: Jessica Kingsley Publishers.

Hannibal, N. and Pedersen, I.N. (2000). Opgørelse af fremmøde-stabilitet for patienter i musikterapi 1997. I *Den musikterapeutiske behandling—teoretiske og kliniske refleksioner*. (s. 141–143). Aalborg: Aalborg Psykiatriske Sygehus, Aalborg Universitet.

Hannibal, N., Petersen, B., Windfelt, M., and Skadhede, S. (2011). Gruppemusikterapi i Dagbehandlingsregi: Opsamling på perioden 2003 til 2010. *Musikterapi i Psykiatrien: Årsskrift*, 6.

Hannibal, N., Pedersen, I.N., Bonde, L.O., Bertelsen, L.R., Dammeyer, C., and Nystrup Lund, H. (2012a). Manual for procesorienteret musikterapi med personer med BPD. *Musikterapi i Psykiatrien online (MIPO)* 7(2): 64–80. DOI: 10.5278/ojs/mipo/401ctlm2.

Hannibal, N., Pedersen, I.N., Hestbæk, T.L., Egelund, T., and Munk Jørgensen, P. (2012b). Schizophrenia and personality disorder patients' adherence to music therapy. *Nordic Journal of Psychiatry* 66(6): 376–379. DOI: 10.3109/08039488.2012.655775.

Hervey, P. and Odell-Miller, H. (2013) Containment or contamination? Music therapy, personality disorder and the forensic mental health team. In: S. Compton-Dickinson, H. Odell-Miller, and J. Adlam (eds), *Forensic Music Therapy*, pp. 205–229. London: Jessica Kingsley Publishers.

International Centre for Arts Psychotherapies Training (ICAPT) (2014). <http://www.cnwl.nhs.uk/health-professionals/icapt/>. Accessed 13 January 2014.

John, D. (1995). The therapeutic relationship in music therapy as a tool in the treatment of psychosis. In: T. Wigram, B. Saperston, and R. West (eds), *The Art and Science of Music Therapy: A Handbook*, pp. 157–166. Chur, Switzerland: Harwood Academic Publishers.

Meares, R. and Hobson, R. (1977). The persecutory therapist. *British Journal of Medical Psychology* 50: 349–359.

Montello, L. (1998) Relational issues in psychoanalytic music therapy with traumatised individuals. In: K.E. Bruscia (ed.), *The Dynamics of Music Psychotherapy*, pp. 229–314. Gilsum, NH: Barcelona Publishers.

Mössler, K., Chen, X., Heldal, T.O., and Gold, C. (2011). Music therapy for people with schizophrenia and schizophrenia-like disorders. *Cochrane Database of Systematic Reviews* 12.

McMurran, M., Huband, N., and Overton, E. (2010). Non-completion of personality disorder treatments: A systematic review of correlates, consequences, and interventions. *Clinical Psychology Review* 30(3): 277–287.

NICE Guidelines (2014) <http://www.nice.org.uk/nicemedia/live/12125/43045/43045.pdf>. Accessed 3 January 2014.

Odell-Miller, H. (1995). Why provide music therapy in the community for adults with mental health problems? *British Journal of Music Therapy* 9(1): 4–10.

Odell-Miller, H (2001). Music Therapy and Psychoanalysis. In: I. Streng and Y Searle (eds), *Where Analysis Meets the Arts*, pp. 127–152. London: Karnac Books.

Odell-Miller, H. (2007). The practice of music therapy for adults with mental health problems: the relationship between diagnosis and clinical method. PhD Thesis, Aalborg University, Denmark.

Odell-Miller, H. (2011). The value of music therapy for people with personality disorder. *Mental Health Practice Vol.* 14, Number 10.

Odell-Miller, H. (2014) The development of clinical music therapy in adult mental health practice: music, health and therapy. In: V. Bates, A. Bleakley, and S. Goodman (eds), *Medicine, Health and the Arts: Approaches to the Medical Humanities*, pp. 264–280. London: Routledge.

Odell-Miller, H., Hughes, P., and Westacott, M. (2006). An investigation into the effectiveness of the arts therapies for adults with continuing mental health problems. *Pscyhotherapy Research* 16(1): 122–139.

Pedersen, I.N. (2003). The revival of the frozen sea urchin: music therapy with a psychiatric patient. In: S. Hadley (ed.), *Psychodynamic Music Therapy: Case Studies*, pp. 375–389. Gilsum, NH: Barcelona Publishers.

Pedersen, I.N. (2005). At bruge musik til at håndtere modoverføring I individual musikterapi I hospitalspsykiatrien [Using music to cope with counter transference in individual music therapy in hospital psychiatry]. In: H.M. Ridder (ed.), Årsskrift 4, Musikterapi i Psykiatrien. Musikterapiklinikken. Aalborg Psykiatriske Sygehus og Aalborg Universitet, pp. 40–64.

Pedersen, I.N. (2007). Counter transference in music therapy: A phenomenological study on counter transference used as a clinical concept by music therapists working with musical improvisation in adult psychiatry. Department of Communication, Doctoral Dissertation, Faculty of the Humanities, Aalborg University.

Pedersen, I. and Hannibal, N. (2013). Report about European Personality Disorder Research. Personal communication through International Consortium for Research in Music Therapy.

Pedersen, I.N. (2014). Music therapy in psychiatry today: Do we need to specialize in the reduction of diagnosis-specific symptoms or on the overall development of resources. Or do we need both? *Nordic Journal of Music Therapy* 23(2): 73–194.

Pickersgill, M. (2013). How personality became treatable: The mutual constitution of clinical knowledge and mental health law. *Social Studies of Science* 43(1): 30–53.

Pool, J. and Odell-Miller, H. (2011). Aggression in music therapy and its role in creativity with reference to personality disorder. *The Arts in Psychotherapy* 38: 169–177.

Robarts, J. and Sloboda, A. (1994). Perspectives in music therapy with people suffering from anorexia nervosa. *Journal of British Music Therapy* 8(1): 7–14.

Roberts, C (2001). *An Exploration of the Relationship Between Music Therapy and the Forensic Environment*. MA dissertation, Anglia Ruskin University website.

Roth, A. and Fonagy, P. (2004). *What Works for Whom? A Critical Review of Psychotherapy Research*, 2nd edn. New York: Guilford Publications.

Ryle, A., Leighton, T., and Pollock, P. (1997). *Cognitive Analytic Therapy of Borderline Personality Disorders*. Chichester: John Wiley and Sons.

Sleight, V. and Compton-Dickinson S. (2013). Risks, ruptures and the role of the co-therapist in group cognitive analytic music therapy (G-CAMT): a pilot group at a secure hospital. In: S. Compton-Dickinson, H. Odell-Miller, and J. Adlam (eds), *Forensic Music Therapy*, pp. 169–183. London: Jessica Kingsley Publishers.

Sloboda, A. (1997). Music therapy and psychotic violence. In: *A Practical Guide to Forensic Psychotherapy*, pp. 121–130. London: Jessica Kingsley Publishers.

Smeijsters, H. (1996). Music therapy with anorexia nervosa: an integrative theoretical and methodological perspective. *British Journal of Music Therapy* 10(2): 3–13.

Smeijsters, H. (2005) *Sounding the Self: Analogy in Improvisational Music Therapy*. Gilsum, NH: Barcelona Publishers.

Smeijsters, H. and Cleven, G. (2006). The treatment of aggression using arts therapies in forensic psychiatry: results of a qualitative inquiry. *The Arts in Psychotherapy* 33: 37–58.

Smith, J. and Osborn, M. (2003). *Interpretative Phenomenological Analysis, from, Qualitative Psychology—A Practical Guide to Research Methods*, pp. 51–80. London: Sage Publications.

Stige, B. (1999). The meaning of music—from the client's perspective. In: T. Wigram and J. De Backer (eds), *Clinical Applications of Music Therapy in Psychiatry*, pp. 61–83. London: Jessica Kingsley Publishers.

Storr, A. (1972). *The Dynamics of Creation*. London: Secker and Warburg.

Strehlow, G. (2011). *Sounds on the border (Töne an der Grenze)*: Music therapy for patients with borderline personality disorder. PhD thesis, University of Hamburg. <http://www.sub.uni-hamburg.de/opus/volltexte/2011/4968>.

Twemlow, S., Sacco, F., and Fonagy, P. (2008). Embodying the Mind: Movement as a Container for Destructive Aggression. *American Journal of Psychotherapy* 62(1): 1–33.

Van den Hurk, J. and Smeijsters, H. (1991). Musical improvisation in the treatment of a man with obsessive compulsive disorder In: K. Bruscia (ed.), *Case Studies in Music Therapy*, pp. 387–402. Gilsum, NH: Barcelona Publishers.

Wigram, T. (2004). *Improvisation: Methods and Techniques for Music Therapy Clinicians, Educators, and Students*. London: Jessica Kingsley Publishers.

Winnicott, D. (1950). Aggression in relation to emotional development. In: D. Winnicott, *Through Paediatrics to Psychoanalysis: Collected Papers, (1958)*. London: Karnac.

Winnicott, D. (1971). *Playing and Reality*. Oxford: Routledge.

CHAPTER 18

···

THE WORLD IS ALIVE! MUSIC THERAPY WITH ADULTS WITH LEARNING DISABILITIES

···

TESSA WATSON

INTRODUCTION

···

> "If I didn't have a learning disability I would have my own life and it would be easy to do normal things." Emma, who in the future would like a job, a flat, a husband and three children.
>
> Manners and Carruthers 2006, p. 207

THIS chapter describes music therapy work with adults with learning disabilities. This group of people have a cognitive disability that will not change, bringing challenges to living a fulfilled and satisfying life and often associated health issues. A wide range of issues, from severe communication problems, bereavement, mental health problems, challenging behavior, to end-of-life issues require music therapists to bring a wide range of skills and approaches to their work. Really getting to know and listening to people with complex disabilities and challenges is challenging; it can be hard to remain open to such different experiences and lives (Steele 1988). Music therapy is a unique way of listening to and supporting a group of people who have much to contribute to society.

Terminology

In this chapter, several different words will be used to describe this group of people. Firstly, the term people with learning disabilities, used in the UK. The term learning difficulties, preferred by some, often describes specific difficulties in learning such as dyslexia or dyspraxia, and does not describe the main group of people considered in this chapter. In Europe and USA, the terms intellectual disabilities and developmental disabilities are synonymous with the term learning disabilities. The terms client and service user will also be used in the chapter, to describe a person with learning disabilities who is using a music therapy service. Terminology is an important issue in this field; Blackman states that "favored labels become outdated faster and faster, and often end up as words used to insult or hurt, as a process of euphemism" (2003, p. 20). There is more reflection on the idea of labelling as this chapter unfolds.

A life being lived

> People should not pity us, be afraid of us or ignore us. This is because we want to be a part of our community because we should not be on our own. In this way, other people will get to know us better and learn that we are like everyone else.

> Deguara et al. 2012, p. 127

Conceptualizing and diagnosing learning disability

Talbot et al. (2010) write about differing perspectives on learning disability. One of their concepts is of "a life being lived" (2010, p. 2). An article written by people with learning disabilities in Malta advises that "not everyone needs help in the same things. Some people need much help and others need a little." (Deguara et al. 2012, p. 125). Whatever support is needed, each person is living their own life.

Traditionally defined by medical diagnosis, the idea of learning disability is now influenced by broader thinking, including the social model of disability. Harris writes that intellectual disability is a "dynamic condition with a variable course that depends on its etiology and the available environment supports" (2006, p. 12). The interaction between the person and their environment is now considered as important as IQ in assessing disability. Living and working in a familiar, predictable environment will lead someone to have greater coping skills.

A definition of a learning disability includes the presence of; a significant intellectual impairment, deficits in social functioning or adaptive behavior (or basic everyday skills), which are present from childhood (Emerson et al. 2001). In order to ascertain that a person has a significant intellectual impairment, it is still usual to refer to intelligence quotient (IQ). An IQ of below 70 is the current score used to indicate a learning disability (measured with the Wechler Adult Intelligence Scale). The World Health Organization International Classification of Diseases (WHO 1992) currently details four categories of IQ; mild, moderate, severe, and profound. The USA Diagnostic and Statistical Manual of Mental Disorders uses similar categories (American Psychiatric Association 2000). To reflect changing terminology and thinking, the International Classification of Diseases is likely to update their terminology to "intellectual developmental disorder" (Carulla et al. 2011).

Biological, environmental, and social factors are all involved in the etiology a learning disability. The most common diagnoses are Down's Syndrome, Fragile X syndrome, and Autistic Spectrum Disorder. The reader is directed towards Talbot et al. 2010, Harris 2006, and Grant et al. 2005 for a comprehensive study of different diagnoses.

Most people with learning disabilities have some form of communication difficulty, which in its turn may cause emotional and behavioral difficulties (see Kevan 2003). About half of these people also have a sensory impairment such as vision or hearing loss, and many have an additional physical disability. Some people may use behavior which challenges services, often considered to be a response to a situation or experience. In addition to their primary disability, this population is 30 percent more likely to experience other health problems such as epilepsy. Approximately 40 percent of people with learning disabilities experience a mental health problem, including anxiety, self injury, mood disorders, psychotic disorders, and dementia (Watchman 2003). Sinason (1992) describes the burden of handicap and unmet needs as depleting the resources of the individual, making a mental health problem more likely.

From "put him away and forget all about him" to "disability isn't an end, it's a beginning"

(Harris 2005, p. 49 and Russell 1998, p. 93, respectively)

> I had my son in 1955. I was just told that he was a "Mongol," as they were called in those days, and there would be no future for him, and that he'd probably not live longer than five. They said the best thing for us to do was to put him in an institution. Needless to say my husband and I were so horrified we just picked up our bags and left. I had a good weep, of course. I think I spent the first two years crying.

Nickson 2005, p. 77

The history of this population has been well documented (Brown and Smith 1992; Dumbleton 1998; Thomas and Woods 2003; Walmsley and Rolph 2002). People with learning disabilities were accepted as part of society until the 1600s, but with the age of enlightenment having a learning disability became a stigma and often meant life in the workhouse. Later, institutions were education based, with some ideas of rehabilitation across Europe and the USA (e.g. Itard, Seguin, and Guggenbuhl) but there was general ill treatment. Families were blamed and individuals were segregated from their communities. People with learning disabilities were considered to have a negative influence on those around them, and as a result led limited, regimented lives. Ideas from eugenics were widespread, and we gain an insight into the extremes of thinking of this time from Tredgold's statement: "it would be an economical and humane procedure were their existence to be painlessly terminated" (cited in Race 2002, p. 33). Bicknell describes this cultural group as having been "threatened with eradication" several times in history, and this striking phrase helps us to realise how a history of oppression may have echoes in the present (Bicknell 1997).

Brave new words

Sinason articulates the idea of the euphemism treadmill that arises for a population who have been negatively labelled. She traces the history of terms from blockhead, cretin, imbecile, retard, subnormal, to disability and reminds us that:

> Nearly every book on mental handicap written in the last hundred years begins with a chapter on definitions and words chosen. Each such chapter praises itself for its hopeful new term. It is therefore doing a grave disservice to past pioneers to point contemptuously to their chosen

terms. Within another five years the process of euphemism will already be affecting the brave new words.

Sinason 1992, p. 40

With the beginning of the National Health Service in the UK in 1948, and ideas of rehabilitation across Europe and the USA, asylums became hospitals, bringing the "clear footprint of the medical model" (Race 2002, p. 36). Gradual change occurred as theorists such as John Tizard (1960) suggested hospital should be a place of development and rehabilitation. At this time most people with learning disabilities were living in large hospitals, excluded from society, with little control over their lives. For many, this was their whole life experience. Rolph et al. movingly document the stories of people with learning disabilities in the UK from a family perspective, providing illuminating timelines (2005).

NORMALIZATION AND INCLUSION

Across Europe in the 1960s and 1970s the writing of Wolfensberger (1972) and the concepts of normalization and inclusion began to change services. O'Brien wrote on the "principles of ordinary life" (1987), and community care began to see hospitals closed and residents resettled into the community (see Department of Health 1990). In Europe and the USA today, most people with learning disabilities live in community residential houses or family homes. In parallel with changes in thinking and service delivery, terminology changed; firstly to mental handicap or mental retardation, then to learning disability in the UK, with intellectual or developmental disabilities being adopted in the USA (Rolph et al. 2005; Farnan 2007). Alongside these developments, the idea of a social model of disability was growing. This model encourages a socially aware, inclusive culture, and brings attention to the barriers to full living faced by people with disabilities. In the USA in particular the civil rights movement in the 1960s promoted these issues, and in the UK in 1998 the Human Rights Act further promoted the idea of rights for all (HMSO 1998).

Alongside these changes, the support given to parents at birth and in the early years has changed significantly. Furneaux has described the painful experiences of parents when their child's disability was explained, and the impact of this on relationships and family life: "we blamed each other and almost split up ... we never went out or visited or had visitors ... " (1988, p. 30; also Marvin and Pianta 1996; Blackman 2003). Whilst families still take on a great deal of unpaid caring responsibility, more support is given to manage the impact that a learning disability can have on family life.

VALUING PEOPLE—CURRENT FRAMEWORKS

In the UK in 2001 a white paper had significant impact upon learning disability services. It set out four main principles; rights, independence, choice, and inclusion (Department of Health 2001; and see Department of Health 2007; 2009), and stated that "it is no longer acceptable for organizations to view people with learning disabilities as passive recipients of services; they must instead be seen as active partners" (2001, p. 51). There has been some criticism of this legislation, with Burton and Kagan (2006) describing it as a utopian picture, with choice simplistically promoted as having central importance, and new initiatives under resourced (see also Holland 2007). In the US, the President's Committee on Mental Retardation was formed in 1999, and the Developmental Disabilities Assistance and Bill of Rights Act was passed in 2000 to improve services for this group of people.

PERSON CENTERED THINKING AND QUALITY OF LIFE

New mechanisms have been introduced to ensure that people with learning disabilities can strive for an active and full life. Person centered planning encourages workers to keep the service user at the heart of thinking and planning: "a way of assisting people to work out what they want, the support they require and helping them get it" (Towell and Sanderson 2004 p. 12; and see Noone 2008). In the UK this concept has now developed further into personalization; though some pressure groups note that this kind of provision may in fact lead to a lower level of service (Simpson and Price 2010; Mencap 2012). Supported employment opportunities are highly valued by service users, but there are still too few jobs (Jahoda et al. 2009).

Advocacy has been central in supporting people with learning disabilities to move towards greater independence. Sometimes advocacy is a formal process, but health professionals can take an advocacy role when appropriate (Chapman et al. 2011). Better physical and mental health is encouraged through engagement with mainstream health services, and equity in health services is promoted (Cooper et al. 2004; Chaplin et al. 2009). Consideration is given to engaging minority ethnic communities who may have particular cultural and religious needs, as people with learning disabilities in these groups are further disadvantaged (Caton et al. 2007). Taboo issues such as sexuality are beginning to be addressed (McClimens and Combes 2005), and people with learning disabilities are also having their own families, though they may find it hard to care for their children (JARID 2008; Conder et al. 2010; MacIntyre and Stewart 2011). The overarching theme that embraces all these initiatives is quality of life: "valued outcomes for individuals" (Grant et al. 2005, p. 129); being able to pursue that which is important to us.

AN AMBITION TO BE HAPPY

Some people take up these opportunities with relish and inspire us, for example Jayne Burnett who writes in her blog:

> I reckon I want the same things from life as anyone else. I'm only 17, so I've not got everything I want from life figured out just yet—I don't know if I ever will, but I know the basics. I think I want to be a hairdresser—not sure. I want to have my own house. I want to have a laugh with my friends. I want to get married and have kids—but not yet…. Actually, my ambition is to be happy. Whatever that means.

Burnett 2008

However new opportunities can also be challenges, and one of the roles of music therapy is to support people as they take up new experiences. It is important that we can engage with service users' authentic responses to these new opportunities, bearing in mind the "painful external realities and painful internal worlds" of which Hodges (2003) speaks.

THE HISTORY OF MUSIC THERAPY IN THIS CLINICAL AREA

There is a thorough consideration of the music therapy literature in this clinical area from 1943–2006 by Hooper et al. (2008a,b). These authors describe three types of approach; active music therapy improvisation, music therapy activities and receptive interventions. McFerran provides another comprehensive review from 1990–2006, noting that active techniques are used predominantly and goals are adjusted depending upon the disability of the user (2009). Most early music therapy work in this clinical area took place in large hospitals, evolving from experiences of music performance and education (Tyler 2000). Pioneer Juliette Alvin (1975) provided examples of her directive style, and Wing stated that in music therapy, even with the most disabled clients "a thin link of communication has been forged" (1968, p. 8). Odell described a developing model of music therapy in Britain, where the music therapist worked "always from the spontaneous music [the client] produced, taking up ideas in an improvisatory way, until he eventually made eye contact, and dialogue was possible" (1979, p. 13). As work developed, it was documented through descriptive case studies (Blackburn 1992; Clough 1992; Cowan 1989; Davies and Mitchell 1990; Gale 1989; Heal 1994; Ritchie 1991 and 1993; Zallik 1987; Fischer 1991; Clarkson 1991).

MAKING RELATIONSHIPS AND MEETING EMOTIONAL NEEDS

Wigram's pioneering work is well documented, including a discussion in which Wigram looks back on his work and stresses the importance of engaging staff and carers (Bonde and Nygaard 2001). Wigram explained how music therapy services developed in this clinical area: "the therapist is required to provide weekly sessions for groups and individuals who receive very little else," and how although "referrals have often been made for all the wrong reasons," this enabled music therapists to develop specific skills and expertise in working with clients. A useful description of the function of music therapy at that time is provided:

> Seeking to create or develop an alternative means of interaction is one of the primary functions in music therapy. The effect of providing this new means for a person to make contact and be understood has a profound value in satisfying emotional needs, and in building relationships with other staff and particularly with other mentally handicapped people.
>
> Wigram 1988, p. 44

DOCUMENTING THE WORK

A growing body of literature documents clinical work and the development of theory, with several writers introducing psychoanalytic concepts (e.g. Heal-Hughes 1995). Gale's article captures the changes in the field at the time, considering the idea of normalization and integration (1989), and Margetts writes about the impact of institutionalization (2010). Kowski writes about analytical music therapy with a non-verbal woman (1998), and Rafieyan of an object relations approach (2003). Richards and Hind; Watson and Vickers (both 2002) and McFerran (undated) write about group sessions. Work with people with profound and multiple learning disabilities is documented (Agrotou 1994; Usher 1998; Graham 2004) including a consideration of bereavement (Tyas 2010). Two pieces of literature consider the ending of therapy (Atkinson 2003; Ruck 2010). Much of this literature begins to outline what Ansdell has termed the consensus model; psychodynamic music therapy (Sobey and Woodcock 1999; Ansdell 2002; Karkou and Sanderson 2006). The first UK text book to focus on this clinical area was published in 2007 (Watson 2007a).

AUTISTIC SPECTRUM DISORDER

Wager (2000), Raglio et al. (2001), Atkinson (2003), and Dimitriadis and Smeijesters (2011) write about music therapy with people with autistic spectrum disorder and there is also consideration of the link between music therapy and sensory integration (Berger 2002; Hooper et al. 2004). Berger studies the way in which music therapy can adapt the feedback control system and re-pattern brain circuits and cognitive processes to work on physiological function (2002; Schneck and Berger 2006). The Cochrane Review by Gold et al. is important to note, although only children are included in the studies to which the authors refer. They state that music therapy helps people with autistic spectrum disorder "to develop communicative skills and their capacity for social interaction" (2010).

DIVERSE APPROACHES

Other approaches are also described in the literature. For example, Hooper and Lindsay look at the alleviation of physical symptoms, measuring pulse rate and behavior in order to ascertain the effect of music on anxiety (1990), and Hooper, Lindsay, and Richardson consider the effect of recorded music (1991). Grocke and Wigram write about receptive methods such as relaxation, song discussion, music appreciation, and vibroacoustic therapy (2007). Wigram (1989), Skille (1989), and Hooper (2001) describe the effects of vibroacoustic therapy. Other music technology is also used; a survey by Hahna et al. of music therapists working in the USA, Canada, Australia, and the UK found that music technology was most frequently used with people with developmental or learning disabilities, with soundbeam the most frequently used equipment (2012).

Aigen has indicated that "music therapy for developmentally-disabled individuals involves meeting their most pressing life needs and providing situations in which they can experience themselves as more fully human" (1995, p. 44). Wigram et al. summarized the principles of work in Europe, stating that "the primary therapeutic goals ... involve working with contact, communication and sensory stimulation. Music and musicality as a tool can evoke the expression of feelings and emotions in people with physical and developmental delay" (2002, p. 169). Other models include Orff Music Therapy (or developmental music therapy, see Voight 2003) and anthroposophical music therapy (Intveen 2010). Schalkwijk described how, in the Netherlands, making distinctions between music therapy and remedial music, and product and process oriented work (1994). Ruud describes music therapy in Norway as being "concerned with special educational processes and their activities seen within a larger cultural or communal process," and gives examples of this (2010, p. 130). In the USA, more structured behavioral and directive approaches are often used. Pre-composed and receptive techniques are used as well as active improvisation (Grocke and Wigram 2007; Farnan 2003; Hanser 1999). Targets may be to increase physical skills, attention, or to change behavior (Farnan 2007).

The model of community music therapy (Ansdell 2002) is linked with the idea of community engagement to provide a therapeutic milieu for performance (Curtis and Mercado 2004). Stige describes a weekend festival project for adults with intellectual disabilities that culminates in a closing ceremony performance (2010). More thought is given to the idea of boundaries and collaboration later in this chapter.

Matching needs with approach

The diversity of need in this clinical area is clear from this summary of the literature. Therapists may work with an independent, verbal, and physically able client in one session, and with a profoundly and multiply disabled group the next. This clinical diversity can perhaps be linked with Aigen's idea of a situationally determined approach. He suggests that practitioners could choose "to inhabit a music-centered stance when it was clinically warranted and a psychodynamic stance when it was clinically warranted" (2005, p. xx). This idea seems to fit music therapy learning disability work, where practitioners have needed, in order to meet the diverse needs of their caseload, to conceptualize, frame, and practice their work in multiple ways.

Research in this area

Music therapy research

There is a small amount of research into music therapy with this client group. Aigen (2008a,b) found little doctoral research or published writing on qualitative music therapy research between 1987–2006 in this field. Wigram writes about several research projects; firstly measuring positive and negative behaviors during sessions (1993a), and secondly studying the effects of low frequency sound on anxiety for clients with challenging behavior (1993b). In this writing Wigram reflects on the ethical and methodological challenges of researching the work. Hooper and Lindsay (1990) study the effect of music on anxiety, and Hooper (1993) describes a research project using music therapy and control sessions. Oldfield and Adams (1990, 1995) compare music therapy and play activities in achieving behavioral objectives for people with profound disabilities, and Toolan and Coleman (1995) study levels of engagement and avoidance in music therapy sessions. Woodcock and Lawes document a project concerned with self injurious behavior (1995), likewise Ford (1999). Graham's research with pre-verbal adults uses transcription to analyse the musical therapeutic relationship (2004). More recently of interest is the study by Hooper et al. looking at responses to music (2010).

There are likely to be several reasons for the small amount of music therapy research in this area. It can be hard to gain consent to involve people with learning disabilities in research, and difficulty in self-reporting makes some types of research less accessible. Hays et al. provide thoughts on gaining approval for projects within the area of learning disability (2003). Kiernan notes that research by non-disabled interviewers "runs the serious risk of people with learning disabilities giving answers which they feel are required of them rather than their true views" (1999, p. 47). He has suggested that participatory research can still result in the exclusion of a proportion of clients who have severe or profound disabilities. Other writers have considered the difficulty of researching given the sometimes complex communication needs of this client group (Boxall and Ralph 2011).

Despite these challenges, people with learning disabilities are beginning to engage with the process of research (Burke et al. 2003; Walmsley 2004). Williams and Simons (2005), McClimens (2008) and White and Morgan (2012) consider how people with learning disabilities can work in partnership with non-disabled researchers, acting as role models and empowering others. White (a researcher who has learning disabilities) says "I know how to do research and I can do it by myself. I am confident and proud of myself" (White and Morgan 2012, p. 102).

THE PROCESS OF THERAPY

Referrals

Much of the music therapy work in this clinical area takes place within a framework of health or social care. Referrals can come from multidisciplinary team colleagues, parents or carers, or clients may self refer. In the following paragraphs some of the frequent reasons for referral are described.

Psychological distress including mental health problems can be addressed through music therapy (Richards 2007). Arthur (2003) has provided information about the neglect of emotional support for people with learning disabilities. Music therapy provides a supportive and creative environment for the expression and exploration of psychological distress.

Relating and communicating with others is a fundamental human need which can be difficult to meet for people with learning disabilities. Music therapy assists in the development of skills in making, maintaining and ending relationships. Restricted social networks are apparent for this client group from childhood and relationships reduce during the life span (Arthur 2003; Bane et al. 2012). Talbot et al. noted that "the skills required to develop and maintain friendships are acquired in childhood and include language development, cooperative play, the ability to have an empathic understanding of the perspective of another and to be able to label and recognize emotions" (2010, p. 119). To this list Grant et al. have added the need for confidence, interpersonal skills, and the ability to resolve conflict, and also note the issue of bullying (2005, p. 476). These can all be areas of focus in music therapy work (see Fillingham 2007).

Music therapy can be offered as a way to manage the challenges of living with, or working with people who are on the autistic spectrum disorder. Work undertaken with people with autism often focuses on communication and social interaction (see Raglio et al. 2001; Dimitriadis and Smeijesters 2011). Saville (2007) has described the importance of also using structure and working with physical movement in this work.

Summers and Witts provided information about the importance of theories of the grief process being applied to loss for people with learning disabilities (2003; see also Mappin and Hanlon 2005; Ryan et al. 2010). Tyas writes about the use of different arts modalities (including music therapy) where "the communication of these losses may be heard, named, held and assisted" (2010, p. 22).

The work done in music therapy helps people to manage the challenges that living more fully in the community can bring (Watson 2007b). Johnson et al. write of their therapy client Mary that "she has little chance of feeling good about her difference until society develops positive constructs of people with learning disabilities" (2003, p. 35).

Challenging behavior is a term describes the kind of behavior (often a way of communicating) that is severe enough to cause injury to the person or others, and to exclude the person from everyday opportunities (Twist and Montgomery 2010). Music therapy is an acceptable way of communicating, building relationships, and working in groups when usual ways of relating are too difficult (Warner 2007).

Growing into adulthood can be difficult for people with learning disabilities; this phase of life can bring struggles relating to identity and dependence/independence (Grant et al. 2005; Murphy et al. 2011). Music therapy gives support at times of transition to allow the expression of difficult feelings, and to help the development of skills and abilities needed for the next phase of life. At the end of life, or when facing the changes brought about by dementia, music therapy can help to process psychological distress as well as enliven, reduce isolation, and stimulate memory.

Working with physiological development of the client is important. Behavioral techniques can target specific areas of physiological development, and programmes are written in order to address specific needs (Berger 2002; Schneck and Berger 2006).

TREATMENT METHODS

> Fundamental to the practice of music therapy is the idea that the emotional world of patients is complex, full of good and bad experiences and is intact, regardless of the degree of intellectual difficulties or handicap.
>
> Toolan and Coleman 1995, p. 17

Referring to people with learning disabilities, Karkou and Sanderson have stated that "due to the wide diversity of needs of this client group, a wide diversity of therapeutic models is followed" (2006, p. 101). The range of treatment models used includes psychodynamic, developmental, music-centered, and behavioral models. Methods include improvisation, structured playing, songwriting and singing, listening, relaxation, and music and movement (McFerran 2010). Clinical improvisation, with the client producing music, is frequently used; a flexible approach is required, employing a continuum from tightly structured music to free improvisation (Darnley-Smith 2002, p. 82). Improvised songs, pre-composed themes and songs, and pre-recorded music are all used, to give structure and shape to sessions. Structure is also used to provide boundaries in and out of sessions and to facilitate transitions between sections where appropriate. Words, both speech and song, are used as part of sessions where appropriate (Pelham and Stacy 1999). Baker et al. note that song writing is common, most often with the client choosing the lyrics and the therapist responsible for the music (2009, p. 50) and McFerran suggests songwriting is particularly effective with young adults (2010). Collaborative work may also require the Music Therapist to adapt their approach to encompass different activities, such as physiotherapy exercises, communication activities or the use of other arts therapies media (Twyford and Watson 2008). In all approaches there should be a consideration of culture (Stige 2002; Grant et al. 2005).

COMMUNICATING ABOUT MUSIC THERAPY

Communication issues are likely to be present for most of this population (Fraser 1997). Thurman's writing helps us to think about communication in a detailed way:

> Communication is important in enjoying life, in expressing what you want and don't want, in expressing who you are and in making relationships. Communication is vital to being able to have the kind of life you want and being in control of what happens to you.
>
> (2011, p. 8).

The use of accessible information assists Music Therapists in conveying to the client how music therapy could help them. Information will usually involve pictures of the setting, the instruments and the therapist as well as the use of formal systems of communication (e.g. Makaton symbols), to give information in a form that can be understood. Within music therapy sessions, the Books Beyond Words series (Hollins and Sinason; Hollins et al. 2003) can be useful in focusing the process of therapy.

At the start of the therapy process, issues relating to consent and confidentiality should be considered. The idea of consent is complex for adults with learning disabilities. Mitchell states that "for people with learning disabilities, it can take time, consultation and imagination to help with understanding and agreement" (2012, p. 154). Again, here accessible information may be useful.

EVALUATING AND ENDING

There are currently no evaluation tools specifically developed to measure outcomes of music therapy with adults with learning disabilities (Grant 1995; Wigram et al. 2002). Standardized music therapy assessment tools relating to behavior are used in the USA (Gregory 2000); in many other countries evaluation tools are still being developed (Sabbatella 2004; Streeter 2010). Wosch and Wigram's book about microanalysis gives tools for analysing different levels of process in the music therapy session, including measuring pre-verbal communication and work with children with development disorders and ASD (2007).

As with research, some of the issues around evaluation are to do with the difficulty in service users using self-reporting methods, and the variables that are present when working with carers to evaluate therapy. As there are often other colleagues and services working in partnership with people with learning disabilities, it can be hard to isolate the benefits of music therapy. Evaluation could usefully measure the way in which music therapy supports the person to develop life skills; the "competencies necessary for adult independent living, successful community integration and quality living" (Talbot et al. 2010, p. 144). Life skills can include "problem solving skills, decision-making skills, communication (including developing joint attention, intention, participation) and interpersonal skills, self-awareness, empathy, coping with stress" (ibid. p. 144). Two evaluation tools currently being adapted are the outcomes star (MacKeith 2011) and CORE OM (Clinical Outcomes in Routine Evaluation Outcomes Measure; Marshall and Willoughby-Booth 2007; Brooks and Davies 2007).

Despite the lack of standardized evaluation tools, goals and outcomes are measured through both multidisciplinary and music therapy systems. Feedback about outcomes is frequently discussed with the person using the therapy, and then shared, with that person's permission, or in their best interests, with the team involved in the person's care and family or carers. Ruck gives useful guidelines for considering the ending of music therapy, including holding aims and goals at the center of the work, considering the impact of the ending on the client and thinking carefully about how the ending is communicated (Ruck 2010).

EXAMPLES OF CLINICAL WORK

Three case studies follow, from the author's practice, illustrative of the wide breadth of music therapy work in partnership with people with learning disabilities.

The world is alive!

Sarah came to music therapy through a referral made by her care worker, Natalie. Sarah, 32 years old, was living in a small residential group home where she had been settled and happy; she had recently stopped attending a two-day college placement. Sarah had a learning disability and a diagnosis of autism. Natalie and her colleagues were worried about Sarah because she had not seemed to recover from her grief since the death of her grandmother, over a year ago. She had become isolated and would not talk to her carers or family about how she was. Sarah found talking anxiety provoking and it was hard for her to talk about this painful experience. She could be heard crying in her room sometimes and the staff team felt she was distressed. This referral was discussed at the team's allocation meeting to bring together thoughts about Sarah's needs at this time. The team agreed that a referral to music therapy was helpful, and I invited Sarah and Natalie to meet with me in the music therapy room. Sarah found it hard to meet someone new and initially could not look at me or talk with me. In fact, she struggled to stay in the room; she was anxious, resistant, and withdrawn and there was a strong feeling of tension. But as I began to play the metallophone and other percussion to introduce the instruments to Sarah, and then used the guitar to sing to her, she began to relax. We had found a medium that could allow us to be together.

Naming and sharing feelings

After this first meeting, to her keyworker's surprise, Sarah was clear that she wanted to come back to the music therapy room and we began to meet weekly for 40 minutes. In the following months, we built up a musical relationship that was able to contain the painful feelings that Sarah had been experiencing. Sarah wanted to use the instruments and found a release in sharing her feelings in an expressive way that did not require her to talk. We used pictures related to grief and bereavement from the Books Without Words series (Hollins and Sinason various) to focus the work and to enable Sarah to identify specific experiences and feelings. The use of these in combination with our music helped Sarah to communicate expressively about her sad and then angry feelings. Sarah initially chose to use the glockenspiel, making very soft, fragile sounds. I used the guitar to support these tentative expressions, and we began to sing about Sarah's sadness. It was also important for Sarah to use bell like sounds such as the metallophone and gong, as these linked to her experience of her grandmother's funeral. Sarah grew in confidence and talked more, and we wrote down some of the most important ideas and feelings from her therapy. Sarah was able to understand that her feelings were part of the grief process. We often taped our music and listened back to it, and this process was important in validating Sarah's feelings. She asked to call one piece 'the world is alive!' saying that the music had helped her to feel alive and energetic.

Through my reflection on the transference relationship we were also able to think about Sarah's fear of making new relationships and of losing existing attachments. As we continued our work, Sarah was also able to identify some anger and bewilderment about her life. She began to describe others (particularly her siblings) as overtaking her. Her music here was louder and it was important that Sarah had a musical voice to safely share these feelings of anger. After six months in individual music therapy, Sarah and I decided the aims of the original referral had been met and we began to think about her moving into a community music therapy group. This would meet Sarah's need for greater community involvement and peer group interaction, and allow her to explore her experiences with others with learning disabilities.

Our music therapy family—a community group

To provide some context for this group, it is useful to refer to Sinason's thoughts about society, learning disability and the lack of community reciprocity. She writes:

> our society, which so privileges mental cognitive ability, is only just beginning to value its citizens with a learning disability. Having a mind that cannot perform at the same level as others of the same chronological age evokes guilt and fear. We disown our learning disabled citizens by either placing them out of the reach of the rest of society, or by bringing them into an area we choose to call 'community' without adequately enabling empowerment and inclusion

> (2003, p. xii).

Living a full life in the community can be difficult (Watson 2007b). People with learning disabilities frequently have limited social relationships, and their relationship circle often diminishes as they leave school and move into adult life; they may not value their peers or maintain relationships (Paterson et al. 2012). They can therefore be isolated in adult life. In addition, they may have to confront the difference between their lives and others' lives. For example, whilst some people with learning disabilities may find a job, a life partner and have a family, for most, these are wishes or dreams that will remain unfulfilled.

This music therapy group provides a supportive environment where Hodges "painful realities" can be uncovered and shared (2003). The group is for six people with learning disabilities who are living fairly independently in their own homes or in supported housing, who have little contact with other health or social care services. The group runs continuously, with members leaving as their work in the group is finished, and new members joining as a place becomes free.

The boundaries of the group provide a therapeutic container with particular qualities; active listening, freedom of expression, concern and care, and having ideas to move on with. Freedom of expression is greatly valued. This includes saying how you really feel and what you really want; particularly important for people with learning disabilities who can be sensitive to the expectations of society. The idea of learned helplessness has been of relevance to the group, and supporting the group to use their own ideas (including musical ideas), to help themselves and each other has been important for their sense of independence. The group music is a creative way of being together, a way to externalize and process emotions, and also symbolizes a place of retreat when thoughts and feelings are too raw. Group theory is used to inform this work (Bion 1961; Foulkes and Anthony 1984). Two vignettes from the group now follow.

Keep strong, don't cry

As Tom came into the session, he said he had something to tell us. His grandfather had died. The group was concerned; and there was some anxiety around talking about this. Some people in the group remembered other losses they had experienced and one began to cry. "Be strong" said Tom, "don't cry—there's no point." The group then wanted to play music, and we thought about trying to include the different feelings in the group in our music. Plaintive horn sounds and slow metallophone beats started the music. I accompanied with the piano, singing as well to include some of the phrases from our talking. Tom began to cry silently, and to play overwhelmingly loud, slow beats on the drum. After the improvisation had finished, one of the group members asked Tom about his drum music. He covered his face: "I had forgotten. I'm so angry. I wasn't allowed to go to the funeral, because I might, I might do something wrong or…." He began to cry. This was a dreadful moment, as Tom appeared to tell the group that he wasn't allowed to go to the funeral because he had a learning disability. In our group, Tom had reconnected with the feelings that had been initially too painful to remember, and was able to share them with us. We played together again to manage this painful truth; thrashing, raw and powerful music with shouting and smashing on the cymbal and drums.

Playtime

The group members crowded into the room for the start of the session. Everyone was present—unusual at this stage of the group as group members struggled with their own problems and their attendance. There was a sense of pleasure at seeing each other again. The group were keen to play and as we started our first improvized piece, the sense of fun continued. Laughter and musical jokes were shared, as were instruments. The music was light and lively, and I picked up the recorder to support this feeling of lightness and fun with my music. After the piece ended there was more laughter and we listened back to the piece, which had been recorded. Sandra suggested "let's call it 'playtime.' It reminds me of being at school." She talked about her memories of school, saying "I remember it as a happy time, I was so carefree, and I had good friends." She went on to talk about the worries that she now has as an adult. "I didn't know it would be like this when I grew up." Others joined in, with Alex talking about her wish for a job in a bank. "I always wanted to work in a bank, but don't think I would be allowed to," she muttered. These darker feelings were also brought to our music.

Our "playtime" music allowed the group to regress to a retreat, perhaps away from the weight of adult responsibility and disappointment. In future groups the playtime music was referred to and listened to again, a memory of a valuable group experience, and also a reminder of the possibility of being able to create a playful and joyful environment. Sandra seemed to internalize something about a nurturing family group, in later sessions describing the group as my "music therapy family," and giving the title to this case example.

Being hidden, being found

> Human beings have an inner world as well as an outer one, an unconscious as well as a conscious, and therefore those with a handicap need just as much attention to these aspects of life as others.
>
> Sinason 1992, p. 74

This case study describes the structure and content of a specialist music therapy group for people with profound and multiple learning disabilities run by two music therapists with care staff. These clients have a combination of the following challenges to accessing a normal life; profound learning disability, barriers to communication, sensory/physical disabilities, complex health needs, mental health needs and behavioral challenges. The following authors have written about music therapy groups with these clients; Graham 2004; Agrotou 1994, 1999; Watson 2007c, 2008.

Theories of development and attachment have been used to design a group environment where containment and attachment can be developed (Watson 2011). The session is planned to allow a process through initial engagement, active involvement, to an ending, with the music providing boundary and guiding functions through the session.

A space for communication

We listen to the same CD as we set the group up each week. This provides an aural boundary into the session, important for this group, who may not see clearly, or understand a verbal prompt. As the group begins, we encourage the members to indicate to us their wish or readiness to be sung to, by calling out, moving or gesturing, or by looking or waking up. We think of these as intentional communications to the group. The lead therapist moves with guitar to sit close to the person to whom we are going to sing, and the member of care staff also comes to sit close. All staff sing, with harmony, providing a thick musical texture. We use a well-known English folk song tune with altered harmonies and words, which helps care staff to feel confident to sing along. The song style is altered to match the communication of each person. Here, we are thinking about reverie and containment (Alvarez 1992). We are establishing a space into which communications can come, be heard and sensitively responded to, and are drawing group members into the work of the group. After the song has been sung once, the member of care staff invites the group member to begin moving and stretching, as the therapists continue to sing and echo the movements and sounds that the person is making. They work together, the member of care staff using physiotherapy exercises specifically designed for each person. By assisting the people in the group with stretching and moving, we start a process of physical self-awareness (Grocke and Wigram 2007, Chapter 10).

The idea of silence, timing, and pace, is important in this group (Sutton 2007). Interactive gestures are carefully offered and time given to take in what is happening. People with profound disabilities need time to process experiences and to make a response, and waiting is important. We must judge, through sensitive observation, the right moment to interact, or our contact may feel intrusive.

The liberation of music

The opening sections are thought of as creating a sense of containment and motivation, in order that the group can begin to playfully explore. Now we move from individual contact into group play, taking time to help each person find an instrument. We encourage free improvisation with instruments and singing. We have a selection of usual tuned and untuned music therapy percussion instruments, and also use a soundbeam and soundbeam switches. The soundbeam is an electronic instrument with an onboard sampler that uses sensor technology to translate body movement into digitally generated sound (Swingler 1995; Magee and Burland 2009). The soundbeam has been liberating for the group, allowing independent playing. Our group improvisation lasts for up to 30 minutes, and might have several "movements" as the style and quality of the music changes and different group members take different roles. This section of the group is often exciting with subtle new developments and interactions.

Ending and reflecting

As the session draws to a close, we use pre-recorded CDs whilst the instruments are slowly removed and put away. A wide variety of styles and genres of music are introduced to the group. We observe the responses of the group to the music that we play, and take ideas back into the next session in our improvisation.

As we end, we talk openly and respectfully about developments in the group, noticing changes such as; interest in the group and in others, less sensory dominated behavior, eye contact, new vocalizations, deliberate use of instruments, and links between group members. The regular provision of this group, encouraging the development of attachment and interaction, enables service users to make greater use of staff and environmental resources in their wider context. Thinking and working with care staff in this group over a long period helps to engender a process of containment for staff, enabling them to think in a more psychologically minded way about the people they support.

Broader roles and collaborations

Music Therapists working in this field have extended the scope of their work and have collaborated with others in a number of ways (Watson and Vickers 2002; Watson 2008). In working directly with service users they may adapt their clinical approach; the flexible use of methods, instruments and equipment, space and boundaries will all be considered in order to make best use of the music therapy milieu for those concerned.

Collaborating with colleagues and carers

Multidisciplinary and multi-agency working is important in this area of clinical work. Due to the communication difficulties that people with learning disabilities often experience, the progress and learning that results from therapy may need to be thought about and communicated in ways other than self-reporting. For example it may be helpful for a staff team to hear something about the therapy in order to adapt new strategies or responses to support the client. Issues relating to confidentiality and sharing are therefore important to consider.

Music therapists also use collaboration and creative approaches within sessions with staff and carers. Hooper states that "as music therapists working with clients who have a developmental disability, we need to broaden our conception of music therapy and acknowledge the significant role that it can play when joined in therapeutic work with other modalities" (Hooper et al. 2004). Other workers or carers may be an integral part of sessions, or may be involved in regular feedback sessions (particularly where a client cannot talk). Watson (2011) writes about a music therapy and sensory interaction group involving carers and a range of approaches including music therapy and physiotherapy techniques. Tyas (2010) writes about the innovative use of music and other arts therapies to help service users and staff to address bereavement. In some settings choirs or singing groups are run and music therapists may support the general use of music, advising on the soundscape of the environment (Kittay 2008). The concepts of person-centered planning and circles of support have also linked music therapists with the client's wider environment. In these ways we bring people with learning disabilities into greater participation with their wider environment and thus develop social capital (Stige 2006; Ruud 2010).

Training and supervision

Staff training, consultation, and supervision are frequently part of the music therapist's role. Training topics include the use of music, intensive interaction (Nind and Hewett 2001; Hewett 2012), communication skills, bereavement (McEvoy et al. 2010) and staff development workshops and consultation sessions. Storey et al. suggest that care staff working with people with learning disabilities benefit from support to use their personal feelings as therapeutic tools in their work (2012). Containing staff emotions can in turn allow staff to contain the emotions and projections of service users, helping to develop greater understanding of behavior and emotions and psychological mindedness in their work.

CONCLUSION

> If you talked to us more, you would know that disabled people are real people with things to say. Please hear us!
>
> Russell 1998, p. 93

This chapter has presented an overview of the diagnoses and needs of this client population, and a consideration of their history. A summary of music therapy literature and treatment models and methods is given, and illustrative case studies reveal a picture of the varied work that takes place in this area of music therapy. The thread that runs through the chapter is the importance of finding flexible, diverse, and collaborative ways of listening and working with each person. Music therapy provides creative spaces in which to meet needs, understand experiences and support people in finding the best way of living their lives.

NOTE

Parts of this chapter are adapted from Watson, T. (2007). *Music Therapy with Adults with Learning Disabilities*, pp. 1–9 and pp. 13–17, Routledge, with permission. The case studies in this chapter are composite case studies and draw on clinical work over a number of years. Details and names have been changed and the work anonymized.

REFERENCES

Administration on Developmental Disabilities. (2000). *Developmental Disabilities Assistance and Bill of Rights Act*. Washington.

Agrotou, A. (1994). Isolation and the multi-handicapped patient: an analysis of the music therapist-patient affects and processes. *The Arts in Psychotherapy* 21(5): 359–365.

Agrotou, A. (1999). *Sounds and Meaning. Group Music Therapy with People with Profound Learning Difficulties and their Carers*. London: Lumiere (Video).

Aigen, K. (1995). Cognitive and affective processes in music therapy with individuals with developmental delays: a preliminary model for contemporary Nordoff-Robbins practice. *Music Therapy* 13(1): 13–46.

Aigen, K. (2005). *Music-Centred Music Therapy*. Gilsum NH: Barcelona Publishers.

Aigen, K. (2008a). An analysis of qualitative music therapy research reports 1987–2006: doctoral studies. *The Arts in Psychotherapy* 35(5): 307–319.

Aigen, K. (2008b). An analysis of qualitative music therapy research reports 1987–2006: articles and book chapters. *The Arts in Psychotherapy* 35(4): 251–261.

Alvarez, A. (1992). *Live Company*. London: Routledge.

Alvin, J. (1975). *Music Therapy*. England: Hutchinson and Company Publishers Ltd.

American Psychiatric Association. (2000). *Diagnostic and Statistical Manual of Mental Disorders*, 4th edn. Washington: APA.

Ansdell, A. (2002). Community music therapy and the winds of change—a discussion paper. In: C. Kenny and B. Stige (eds), *Contemporary Voices in Music Therapy*, pp. 109–142. Oslo: Unipubforlag.

Arthur, R.A. (2003). The emotional lives of people with learning disability. *British Journal of Learning Disability* 31(1): 25–31.

Atkinson, C. (2003). The longest goodbye: a case study. *British Journal of Music Therapy* 17(2): 90–96.

Baker, F., Wigram, T., Stott, D., and McFerran, K. (2009). Therapeutic songwriting in music therapy, part II: comparing the literature with practice across diverse clinical populations. *Nordic Journal of Music Therapy* 18(1): 32–56.

Bane, G., Dooher, M., Flaherty, J., Mahon, A., McDonagh, P., Wolfe, M. et al. (2012). Relationships of people with learning disabilities in Ireland. *British Journal of Learning Disabilities* 40: 109–122.

Berger, D. (2002). *Music Therapy, Sensory Integration and the Autistic Child.* London: Jessica Kingsley.

Bicknell, J. (1997). Philosophical and ethical issues. In: O. Russell (ed.), *The Psychiatry of Learning Disabilities*, pp. 190–204. London: The Royal College of Psychiatrists.

Bion, W.R. (1961). *Experiences in Groups.* London: Tavistock.

Blackburn, R. (1992). On music therapy, fairy tales and endings. *Journal of British Music Therapy* 6(1): 5–9.

Blackman, N. (2003). *Loss and Learning Disability.* London: Worth Publishing.

Bonde, L.O. and Nygaard, I.N. (2001). Tony Wigram—the early years: interview with Tony Wigram January 12, 2011. *Voices: A World Forum for Music Therapy*, 11, 3. Available at: <https://normt.uib.no/index.php/voices/article/view/600/474> [Accessed 3 September 2012].

Boxall, K., and Ralph, S. (2011). Research ethics committees and the benefits of involving people with profound and multiple learning disabilities in research. *British Journal of Learning Disabilities* 39(3): 173–180.

Brooks, M. and Davies, S. (2007). Pathways to participatory research in developing a tool to measure feelings. *British Journal of Learning Disabilities* 36: 128–133.

Brown, H. and Smith, H. (1992). Inside out; a psychodynamic approach to normalisation. In: H. Brown and H. Smith (eds), *Normalisation, A Reader for the Nineties*, pp. 84–99. London: Routledge.

Burke, A., McMillan, J., Cummins, L., Thompson, A., Forsyth, W., McLellan, J. et al. (2003). Setting up participatory research: a discussion of the initial stages. *British Journal of Learning Disabilities* 31: 65–69.

Burnett, J. (2008). *Sunday Mail* blog. Available at: <http://blogs.sundaymail.co.uk/jayneburnett/2008/11/> [Accessed 12 September 2012].

Burton, M. and Kagan, C. (2006). Decoding Valuing People. *Disability and Society* 21: 229–313.

Carulla, L.S., Reed, G.M., Vaez-Azizi, L.M., Cooper, S-A., Leal, R.M., Bertelli, M. et al. (2011). Intellectual developmental disorders: towards a new name, definition and framework for "mental retardation/intellectual disability" in ICD-11. *World Psychiatry* 10(3): 175–180.

Caton, S., Starling, S., Burton, M., Azmi, S., and Chapman, M. (2007). Responsive services for people with learning disabilities from minority ethnic communities. *British Journal of Learning Disabilities* 35(4): 229–235.

Chaplin, E., O'Hara, J., Holt, G., and Bouras, N. (2009). Mental health services for people with intellectual disability: challenges to care delivery. *British Journal of Learning Disabilities* 37(1): 157–164.

Chapman, M., Bannister, S., Davies, J., Fleming, S., Graham, C., McMaster, A. et al. (2011). Speaking up about advocacy: finding from a partnership research project. *British Journal of Learning Disabilities* 40(1): 71–80.

Clarkson, G. (1991). Music therapy for a nonverbal autistic adult. In: K.E. Bruscia (ed.), *Case Studies in Music Therapy*, pp. 373–385. Gilsum, NH: Barcelona Publishers.

Clough, J. (1992). Music therapy; a description of work with a mentally handicapped young man. *Journal of British Music Therapy* 6(2): 16–23.

Conder, J., Mirfin-Veitch, B., Sanders, J., and Munford, R. (2010). Planned pregnancy, planned parenting: enabling choice for adults with a learning disability. *British Journal of Learning Disabilities* 39(2): 105–112.

Cooper, S.A., Melville, C., and Morrison, J. (2004). People with intellectual disabilities. Their health needs differ and need to be recognised and met. *British Medical Journal* 329(7463): 414–415.

Cowan, J., (1989). Role limits in music therapy. *Journal of British Music Therapy* 3(1): 5–9.

Curtis, S.L. and Mercado, C.S. (2004). Community music therapy for citizens with developmental disabilities. *Voices: A World Forum for Music Therapy*, 4, 3. Available at: <https://normt.uib.no/index.php/voices/article/view/185/144> [Accessed 3 September 2012].

Darnley-Smith, R. (2002). Music Therapy with Elderly Adults. In: A. Davies and E. Richards (eds), *Music Therapy and Group Work. Sound Company*, pp. 77–89. London: Jessica Kingsley.

Davies, A. and Mitchell A.R.K. (1990). Music therapy and elective mutism: a case discussion. *Journal of British Music Therapy* 4(2): 10–14.

Deguara, M., Jelassi, O., Micallef, B, and Callus, A. (2012). How we like to live when we have the chance. *British Journal of Learning Disabilities* 40: 123–127.

Department of Health. (1990). *NHS and Community Care Act*. London: HMSO.

Department of Health. (2001). *Valuing People: A New Strategy for Learning Disability for the 21st Century*. London: Department of Health.

Department of Health. (2007). *Valuing People now: from progress to transformation—a consultation on the next three years of learning disability policy*. London: Department of Health.

Department of Health. (2009). *Valuing People Now: A New Three-year Strategy for People with Learning Disabilities*. London: Department of Health.

Dimitriadis, T and Smeijesters, H. (2011). Autistic spectrum disorder and music therapy: theory underpinning practice. *Nordic Journal of Music Therapy* 20(2): 108–122.

Dumbleton, P. (1998). Words and numbers. *British Journal of Learning Disability* 26: 151–153.

Emerson, E. Hatton, C., Felce, D., and Murphy, G. (2001). *Learning Disabilities. The Fundamental Facts*. London: The Foundation for People with Learning Disabilities.

Farnan, L. (2003). Music therapy at Central Wisconsin Center for the Developmentally Disabled. *Voices: A World Forum for Music Therapy*, 3, 2. Available at: <https://normt.uib.no/index.php/voices/article/view/127/103> [Accessed 21 September 2012].

Farnan, L.A. (2007). Music Therapy and developmental disabilities: a glance back and a look forward. *Music Therapy Perspectives* 25(2): 80–85.

Fillingham, C. (2007). Friendship and group work. In: T. Watson (ed.), *Music Therapy with Adults with Learning Disabilities*, pp. 71–84. London: Routledge.

Fischer, R. (1991). Original song drawings in the treatment of a developmentally disabled autistic adult. In: K.E. Bruscia (ed.), *Case Studies in Music Therapy*, pp. 359–371. Gilsum, NH: Barcelona Publishers.

Ford, S.E. (1999) The effect of music on the self-injurious behaviour of an adult female with severe developmental disabilities. *Journal of Music Therapy* XXXVI(4): 293–313.

Foulkes, S.H. and Anthony, E.J. (1984). *Group Psychotherapy: The Psychoanalytic Approach.* London: Karnac.

Fraser, B. (1997). Communicating with people with learning disabilities. In: O. Russell (ed.), *The Psychiatry of Learning Disabilities*, pp. 47–53. London: The Royal College of Psychiatrists.

Furneaux, B. (1988). *Special Parents.* Oxford: Oxford University Press.

Gale, C.P. (1989). The question of music therapy with mentally handicapped adults. *Journal of British Music Therapy* 3(2): 20–30.

Gold, C., Wigram, T., and Cochavit, E. (2010). *Music Therapy for Autistic Spectrum Disorder. Cochrane Review.* Available at: <http://onlinelibrary.wiley.com/doi/10.1002/14651858. CD004381.pub2/full> [Accessed 22 September 2012].

Graham, J. (2004). Communicating with the uncommunicative: music therapy with pre-verbal adults. *British Journal of Learning Disabilities* 32(1): 24–29.

Grant, R.E. (1995). Music therapy assessment for developmentally disabled clients. In: T. Wigram, B. Saperston, and R. West (eds), *The Art and Science of Music Therapy: A Handbook*, pp. 273–287. The Netherlands: Harwood Academic Publishers.

Grant, G., Goward, P., Richardson, M., and Ramcharan, P. (2005). *A Life Cycle Approach to Valuing People.* England: Oxford: Oxford University Press.

Gregory, D. (2000). Test instruments used by the Journal of Music Therapy authors 1984-1997. *Journal of Music Therapy* 37(2): 79–94.

Grocke, D.E. and Wigram, T. (2007) *Receptive Methods in Music Therapy: Techniques and Clinical Applications for Music Therapy Clinicians, Educators and Students.* London: Jessica Kingsley.

Hahna, N.D., Hadley, S., Miller, V.H., and Bonaventura, M. (2012). Music technology usage in music therapy: a survey of practice. *The Arts in Psychotherapy* 39(5): 456–464.

Hanser, S. (1999). *The New Music Therapist's Handbook.* Boston: Berklee Press.

Harris, R. (2005). I don't think I'll ever give up till I die. In: S. Rolph, D. Atkinson, M. Nind, J. Welshman, L. Brigham, R. Chapman, et al. (eds), *Witnesses to Change. Families, Learning Difficulties and History.* Worcestershire: BILD.

Harris, J. (2006). *Intellectual Disability: Understanding its Development, Causes, Classification, Evaluation and Treatment.* New York: Oxford University Press.

Hays, S.J., Murphy, G., and Sinclair, N. (2003). Gaining ethical approval for research into sensitive topics: "two strikes and you're out?" *British Journal of Learning Disabilities* 31(3): 181–189.

Heal, M. (1994). The development of symbolic function in a young woman with down's syndrome. In: D. Dokter (ed.), *Arts Therapies and Clients with Eating Disorders. Fragile Board*, pp. 279–294. London: Jessica Kingsley.

Heal-Hughes, M. (1995). A comparison of mother-infant interactions and the client-therapist relationship in music therapy sessions. In: T. Wigram, B. Saperston, and R. West (eds), *The Art and Science of Music Therapy: A Handbook*, pp. 296–306. London: Harwood Academic Press.

Hewett, D. (2012). *Intensive Interaction Theoretical Perspectives.* London: Sage.

HMSO (1998). *Human Rights Act.* London: HMSO.

Hodges, S. (2003). *Counselling Adults with Learning Disabilities.* Basingstoke: Palgrave MacMillan.

Holland, K. (2007). So much policy, so little change! *Advances in Mental Health and Learning Disabilities* 1(1): 3–6.

Hollins, S. and Sinason, V. (various). *Books Without Words series*. London: Beyond Words. Available at: <http://www.booksbeyondwords.co.uk/> [Accessed 29 September 2012].

Hollins, S., Dowling, S., and Blackman, N. (2003). *When Somebody Dies*. London; Beyond Words.

Hooper, J. (1993). Developing interaction through shared musical experiences: a strategy to enhance and validate the descriptive approach. In: M. Heal and T. Wigram (eds), *Music Therapy in Health and Education*, pp. 208–213. London: Jessica Kingsley.

Hooper, J. (2001). An introduction to vibroacoustic therapy and an examination of its place in music therapy practice. *British Journal of Music Therapy* 15(2): 69–77.

Hooper, J. and Lindsay, B. (1990). Music and the mentally handicapped—the effect of music on anxiety. *British Journal of Music Therapy* 4(2): 19–26.

Hooper, J. Lindsay, B., and Richardson, I. (1991). Recreation and music therapy: an experimental study. *British Journal of Music Therapy* 15(2): 11.

Hooper, J., McManus, A., and McIntyre, A. (2004). Exploring the link between music therapy and sensory integration: an individual case study. *British Journal of Music Therapy* 18(1): 15–23.

Hooper, J., Wigram, T., Carson, D., and Lindsay, B (2008a). A review of the music and intellectual disability literature (1943-2006). Part one—descriptive and philosophical writing. *Music Therapy Perspectives* 26: 63–76.

Hooper, J., Wigram, T., Carson, D., and Lindsay, B (2008b). A review of the music and intellectual disability literature (1943-2006). Part two—experimental writing. *Music Therapy Perspectives* 26: 77–93.

Hooper, J., Wigram, T., Carson, D., and Lindsay, B. (2010). The practical implication of comparing how adults with and without intellectual disability respond to music. *British Journal of Learning Disabilities* 39: 22–28.

Intveen, A. (2010). "The piano is a wooden box with false teeth"—perspectives in anthroposophical music therapy as revealed through interviews with two expert practitioners. *The Arts in Psychotherapy* 37(5): 370–377.

Jahoda, A., Banks, P., Dagnan, D., Kemp, J., Kerr, W., and Williams, V. (2009). Starting a new job: the social and emotional experience of people with intellectual disabilities. *Journal of Applied Research in Intellectual Disabilities* 22(5): 421–425.

JARID (2008). *Journal of Applied Research in Intellectual Disabilities*, 21, 4. Issue focusing on people with learning disabilities as parents.

Johnson, A., Mason, H., and Withers, P. (2003). I might not know what you know but it doesn't mean you can be awful to me. *British Journal of Learning Disabilities*, 31(1): 31–36.

Karkou, V. and Sanderson, P. (2006). *Arts Therapies. A Research-based Map of the Field*. London: Elsevier Churchill Livingstone.

Kevan, F. (2003). Challenging behaviour and communication difficulties. *British Journal of Learning Disabilities* 31: 75–80.

Kiernan, C. (1999). Participation in research by people with learning disability: origins and issues. *British Journal of Learning Disabilities* 27(2): 43–47.

Kittay, J. (2008). The sound surround. Exploring how one might design the everyday soundscape for the truly captive audience. *Nordic Journal of Music Therapy* 17(1): 41–54.

Kowski, J. (1998). The sound of silence—the use of analytical music therapy techniques with a nonverbal client. In: J.T. Eschen (ed.), *Analytical Music Therapy*, pp. 85–94. London: Jessica Kingsley.

MacKeith, J. (2011). The development of the outcomes star: a participatory approach to assessment and outcome measurement. *Housing Care and Support* 14(3): 98–106.

MacIntyre, G. and Stewart, C. (2011). For the record: the lived experience of parents with a learning disability—a pilot study examining the Scottish perspective. *British Journal of Learning Disabilities* 40(1): 5–14.

Magee, W.L. and Burland, K. (2009). An exploratory study of the use of electronic music technologies in clinical music therapy. *Nordic Journal of Music Therapy* 17(2): 124–141.

Manners, P.J. and Carruthers, E. (2006). Living with learning disabilities: Emma's story. *British Journal of Learning Disabilities* 34(4): 206–210.

Margetts, L. (2010). Hansel and Gretel—meaning and relevance in a therapeutic journey: an exploration of the relevance of fairy tales with older learning disabled adults who have been institutionalised. *British Journal of Music Therapy* 24: 12–22.

Marshall, K. and Willoughby-Booth, S. (2007). Modifying the clinical outcomes in routine evaluation measure for use with people who have a learning disability. *British Journal of Learning Disabilities* 35(2): 107–112.

Marvin, R.S. and Pianta, R.C. (1996). Mothers' reactions to their child's diagnosis: relations with security of attachment. *Journal of Clinical Child Psychology* 25(4): 436–445.

Mappin, R. and Hanlon, D. (2005). Description and evaluation of a bereavement group for people with learning disabilities. *British Journal of Learning Disabilities* 33: 106–112.

McClimens, A. (2008). This is my truth, tell me yours: exploring the internal tensions within collaborative learning disability research. *British Journal of Learning Disabilities* 36(4): 271–276.

McClimens, A and Combes, H. (2005). (Almost) everything you ever wanted to know about sexuality and learning disability but were always too afraid to ask. In: G. Grant, P. Goward, R. Richardson, and P. Ramcharan (eds), *Learning Disability. A Life Cycle Approach to Valuing People*, pp. 361–379. England: Oxford University Press.

McEvoy, J., Guerin, S., Dodd, P., and Hillery, J. (2010). Supporting adults with an intellectual disability during experiences of loss and bereavement: staff views, experiences and suggestions for training. *Journal of Applied Research in Intellectual Disabilities* 23(6): 585–596.

McFerran, K. (2009). A descriptive review of the literature (1990–2006) addressing music therapy with people who have disabilities. *Musica Humana* 1(1): 45–80.

McFerran, K. (2010). *Adolescents, Music and Music Therapy. Methods and Techniques for Clinicians, Educators and Students.* London: Jessica Kingsley.

McFerran, K. (undated). *Who says I can't sing? Musical justice for people with intellectual disabilities.* Salvation Army. Available at: <http://www.salvationarmy.org.au/salvwr/_assets/main/documents/reports/who_says_i_cant_sing.pdf> [Accessed 23 September 2012].

Mencap (2012). *Stuck at Home: the Impact of Day Service Cuts on People with a Learning Disability.* London: Mencap.

Mitchell, D. (2012). Editorial. *British Journal of Learning Disabilities* 40(3): 165.

Murphy, E., Clegg, J., and Almack, K. (2011). Constructing adulthood in discussions about the futures of young people with moderate-profound intellectual disabilities. *Journal of Applied Research in Intellectual Disabilities* 24(1): 61–73.

Nickson, B. (2005). Never take no for an answer. In: S. Rolph, D. Atkinson, M. Nind, J. Welshman, L. Brigham, R. Chapman, et al. (eds), *Witnesses to Change. Families, Learning Difficulties and History.* Worcestershire: BILD.

Nind, M. and Hewett, D. (2001). *A Practical Guide to Intensive Interaction.* Kidderminster: BILD.

Noone, J. (2008). Developing a music therapy programme within a person centred planning framework. *Voices: A World Forum for Music Therapy,* 8, 3. Available at: <https://normt.uib.no/index.php/voices/article/view/420/344>. [Accessed on 3 September 2012].

O'Brien, J. (1987). A guide to lifestyle planning: using the activities catalogue to integrate services and natural support systems. In: B. Wilcox and G.T. Bellamy (eds), *A Comprehensive Guide to the Activities Catalogue: Alternative Curriculum for Youth Adults with Severe Disabilities*, pp. 175–189. Baltimore: Paul H. Brookes.

Odell, H. (1979). Music therapy in SSN hospitals, report of BSMT meeting. *British Journal of Music Therapy* 10(4): 12–15.

Oldfield, A. and Adams, M. (1990). The effects of music therapy on a group of profoundly mentally handicapped adults. *Journal of Mental Deficiency Research* 34(2): 107–125.

Oldfield, A. and Adams, M. (1995). The effects of music therapy on a group of adults with profound learning difficulties. In: A. Gilroy and C. Lee (eds), *Art and Music: Therapy and Research*, pp. 164–182. London: Routledge.

Paterson, L., McKenzie, K., and Lindsay, B. (2012). Stigma, social comparison and self-esteem in adults with an intellectual disability. *Journal of Applied Research in Intellectual Disabilities* 25(2): 166–176.

Pelham, G. and Stacy, J. (1999). *Counselling Skills and Creative Arts Therapists.* London: Worth Publishing Ltd.

President's Committee on Mental Retardation Administration for Children and Families US Department of Health and Human Services. (1999). The Forgotten Generation. Available at: <http://www.acf.hhs.gov/programs/pcpid/docs/mr_1999_final.pdf> [Accessed 24 September 2012].

Race, D.G. (2002). *Learning Disability A Social Approach.* London: Routledge.

Rafieyan, R. (2003). Meeting Rich. Individual music therapy with a man who has severe disabilities. In: S. Hadley (ed.), *Psychodynamic Music Therapy: Case Studies*, pp. 339–355. Gilsum NH: Barcelona.

Raglio, A., Traficante, D., and Oasi, O. (2001). Autism and music therapy. Intersubjective approach and music therapy assessment. *Nordic Journal of Music Therapy* 20(2): 123–141.

Richards, E. (2007). "Which bit of my head is talking now?" Music therapy with people with learning disabilities and mental illness. In: T. Watson (ed.), *Music Therapy with Adults with Learning Disabilities*, pp. 58–70. London: Routledge.

Richards, E. and Hind, H. (2002). Finding a space to play: a music therapy group for adults with learning disabilities. In: A. Davies and E. Richards (eds), *Music Therapy and Group Work. Sound Company*, pp. 120–132. London: Jessica Kingsley Publishers.

Ritchie, F. (1991). Behind closed doors; a case study. *Journal of British Music Therapy* 5(2): 4–10.

Ritchie, F. (1993). Opening doors. The effects of music therapy with people who have severe learning difficulties and display challenging behaviour. In: M. Heal and T. Wigram (eds), *Music Therapy in Health and Education*, pp. 91–102. London: Jessica Kingsley Publishers.

Rolph, S., Atkinson, D., Nind, M., Welshman, J., Brigham, L., Chapman, R. et al. (eds) (2005). *Witnesses to Change. Families, Learning Difficulties and History.* Worcestershire: BILD.

Ruck, W. (2010). "In my beginning is my end" A preliminary exploration into the framework and efficacy of endings in the music therapy process when working with adults with a learning disability. *British Journal of Music Therapy* 24: 30–41.

Russell, P. (1998). *Having a Say! Disabled Children and Effective Partnership in Decision Making.* London: Council for Disabled Children.

Ruud, E. (2010). *Music Therapy: A Perspective from the Humanities.* New Hampshire: Barcelona Publishers.

Ryan, K., Guerin, S., Dodd, P. and McEvoy, J. (2010). Exploring the experiences of people with intellectual disabilities when service users die. *British Journal of Learning Disabilities* 39(4): 259–265.

Sabbatella, P.E. (2004). Assessment and clinical evaluation in music therapy: an overview from literature and clinical practice. *Music Therapy Today* V(1): 1–32.

Saville, R. (2007). Music therapy and autistic spectrum disorder. In: T. Watson (ed.), *Music Therapy with Adults with Learning Disabilities*, pp. 33–46. London: Routledge.

Schalkwijk, F.W. (1994). *Music and People with Developmental Disabilities. Music Therapy, Remedial Music Making and Musical Activities.* London: Jessica Kingsley.

Schneck, D.J. and Berger, D.S. (2006). *The Music Effect. Music Physiology and Clinical Applications.* London: Jessica Kingsley Publishers.

Simpson, G. and Price, V. (2010). From inclusion to exclusion: some unintended consequences for valuing people. *British Journal of Learning Disabilities* 38(3): 180–186.

Sinason, V. (1992). *Mental Handicap and the Human Condition.* London: Free Association Books.

Sinason, V. (2003). Foreword. In: N. Blackman. *Loss and Learning Disability.* London: Worth Publishing Ltd.

Skille, O. (1989). VibroAcoustic therapy. *Music Therapy* 8(1): 61–77.

Sobey, K. and Woodcock, J. (1999). Psychodynamic Music Therapy. Considerations in Training. In: A. Cattanach (ed.), *Process in the Arts Therapies*, pp. 132–154. London: Jessica Kingsley.

Steele, P. (1988). Foreword. *Journal of British Music Therapy* 3.

Stige, B. (2002). *Culture Centred Music Therapy.* Gilsum NH: Barcelona.

Stige, B. (2006). On a notion of participation in music therapy. *Nordic Journal of Music Therapy* 15(2): 121–139.

Stige, B. (2010). Action: A society for all? The cultural festival in Sogn og Fjordance, Norway. In: B. Stige, G. Ansdell, C. Elefant, and M. Pavlicevic (eds), *Where Music Helps. Community Music Therapy in Action and Reflection*, pp. 115–124. England: Ashgate Publishing.

Storey, J., Collis, M.A., and Clegg, J (2012). A psychodynamic interpretation of staff accounts of working with people who have learning disabilities and complex needs. *British Journal of Learning Disabilities* 40(3): 229–235.

Streeter, E. (2010). *Computer aided music therapy evaluation: Investigating and testing the music therapy logbook prototype 1 system.* PhD Thesis, Department of Music, University of York. Available at: <http://etheses.whiterose.ac.uk/1201/> [Accessed 12 September 2012].

Summers, S.J. and Witts, P. (2003). Psychological intervention for people with learning disabilities who have experienced bereavement: a case study intervention. *British Journal of Learning Disabilities* 31(1): 37–41.

Sutton, J. (2007). The air between two hands: silence, music and communication. In: N. Losseff and J. Doctor (eds), *Silence, Music, Silent Music*, pp. 169–186. London: Ashgate.

Swingler, T. (1995). The drum is not the only weapon. *Nordic Journal of Music Therapy*: 4(2): 103–106.

Talbot, P., Astbury, G., and T. Mason (2010). *Key Concepts in Learning Disabilities.* London: Sage.

Thomas, D. and Woods, H. (2003). *Working with People with Learning Disabilities.* London: Jessica Kingsley Publishers.

Thurman, S. (2011). *Communicating Effectively with People with a Learning Disability: Supporting the Level 2 and 3 Diplomas in Health and Social Care (Learning Disability Pathway) and the Common Induction Standards.* Exeter: British Institute of Learning Disabilities.

Tizard, J. (1960). Public Health Aspects of Severe Mental Subnormality. *The Journal of the Royal Society for the Promotion of Health* 80(4): 327–331.

Toolan, P. and Coleman, S. (1995). Music therapy, a description of process: engagement and avoidance in five people with learning disabilities. *British Journal of Music Therapy* 9(1): 17–24.

Towell, D. and Sanderson, H. (2004). Person-Centred planning in its strategic context: reframing the Mansell/Beadle-Brown critique. *Journal of Applied Research in Intellectual Disabilities* 17: 17–21.

Twist, S. and Montgomery, A (2010) Promoting healthy lifestyles—challenging behaviour. In: G. Grant, P. Goward, M. Richardson, and P. Ramcharan (eds), *Learning Disability. A Life Cycle Approach to Valuing People*, pp. 340–360. Oxford: Oxford University Press.

Twyford, T. and Watson, T. (eds). (2008). *Integrated Team Working. Music Therapy as Part of Transdisciplinary and Collaborative Approaches.* London: Jessica Kingsley Publishers.

Tyas, R. (2010). A death in the family. *British Journal of Music Therapy* 24: 22–29.

Tyler, H.M. (2000). The music therapy profession in modern Britain. In: P. Horden (ed.), *Music and Medicine. The History of Music Therapy Since Antiquity*, pp. 375–393. England: Ashgate Publishing Limited.

Usher, J. (1998). Lighting up the mind—evolving a model of consciousness and its application to improvisation in music therapy. *British Journal of Music Therapy* 12(1): 4–19.

Voight, M. (2003). Orff music therapy. An overview. *Voices: A World Forum for Music Therapy*, 3, 3. Available at: <https://normt.uib.no/index.php/voices/article/view/134/110> [Accessed on 3 September 2012].

Wager, K.M. (2000). The effects of music therapy upon an adult male with autism and mental retardation: A four-year case study. *Music Therapy Perspectives* 18(2): 131–140.

Walmsley, J. and Rolph, S. (2002). The history of community care for people with learning difficulties. In: B. Bytheway, V. Bacigalupo, J. Bornat, J. Johnson, and S. Spurr (eds), *Understanding Care, Welfare and Community: A Reader*, pp. 28–41. London: Routledge.

Walmsley, J. (2004). Inclusive learning disability research: the (nondisabled) researcher's role. *British Journal of Learning Disabilities* 32: 65–71.

Warner, C. (2007). Challenging behaviour: working with the blindingly obvious. In: T. Watson (ed.), *Music Therapy with Adults with Learning Disabilities*, pp. 47–57. London: Routledge.

Watchman, K. (2003). Critical issues for service planning and providers of care for people with down's syndrome and dementia. *British Journal of Learning Disabilities* 31: 81–84.

Watson, T. (ed.) (2007a). *Music Therapy with Adults with Learning Disabilities.* London: Routledge.

Watson, T. (2007b). Community, culture and group work. In: T. Watson (ed.), *Music Therapy with Adults with Learning Disabilities*, pp. 85–97. London: Routledge.

Watson, T. (2007c). Working with people with profound and multiple learning disabilities in music therapy. In: T. Watson (ed.), *Music Therapy with Adults with Learning Disabilities*, pp. 98–111. London: Routledge.

Watson, T. (2008). Collaboration in music therapy with adults with learning disabilities. In: K. Twyford and T. Watson (eds), *Integrated Team Working. Music Therapy as Part of Transdisciplinary and Collaborative Approaches*, pp. 91–123. London: Jessica Kingsley Publishers.

Watson, T. (2011). *It is a joy to be hidden but a disaster not to be found.* Unpublished conference presentation.

Watson, T. and Vickers, L. (2002). A music and art therapy group for people with learning disabilities. In: A. Davies and E. Richards (eds), *Music Therapy and Groupwork. Sound Company*, pp. 133–148. London: Jessica Kingsley Publishers.

White, E., and Morgan, M. F. (2012). Yes! I am a researcher. The research story of a young adult with Down syndrome. *British Journal of Learning Disabilities* 40(2): 87–93.

Wigram, T. (1988). Music therapy—developments in mental handicap. *Psychology of Music* 16(1): 42–51.

Wigram, T. (1989). Vibroacoustic therapy: the therapeutic effect of low frequency sound on specific physical disorders and disabilities. *British Journal of Music Therapy* 3(3): 6.

Wigram, T. (1993a) Observational techniques in the analysis of both active and receptive music therapy with disturbed and self injurious clients. In: M. Heal and T. Wigram (eds), *Music Therapy in
Health and Education*, pp. 273–283. London: Jessica Kingsley.

Wigram, T. (1993b) The feeling of sound. The effect of music and low frequency sound in reducing
anxiety and challenging behaviour in clients with learning difficulties. In: H. Payne (ed.), *Handbook
of Inquiry in the Arts Therapies. One River, Many Currents*, pp. 177–197. London: Jessica
Kingsley Publishers.

Wigram, A.L., Pederson, I.N., and Bonde, L.O. (eds). (2002). *A Comprehensive Guide to Music
Therapy: Theory, Clinical Practice, Research and Training*. London: Jessica Kingsley.

Williams, V. and Simons, K. (2005). More researching together; the role of nondisabled researchers in
working with people first members. *British Journal of Learning Disabilities* 33(1): 6–14.

Wing, C. (1968). Music therapy in a hospital for subnormal adults. *British Journal of Music Therapy
Newsletter*, pp. 8–11. London: British Society for Music Therapy.

Wolfensberger, W. (1972). *Normalization. The principles of normalization in human services*.
National Institute on Mental Retardation, Toronto.

Woodcock, J. and Lawes, C. (1995). Music therapy and people with severe learning difficulties who
exhibit self-injurious behaviour. In: T. Wigram, B. Saperston, and R. West (eds), *The Art and
Science of Music Therapy: A Handbook*, pp. 288–295. London: Harwood Academic.

World Health Organisation (1992). *The ICD-10 Classification of Mental and Behavioural
Disorders: Clinical Descriptions and Diagnostic Guidelines*. Geneva: WHO.

Wosch, T. and Wigram, T. (2007). *Microanalysis in Music Therapy. Methods, Techniques and
Applications for Clinicians, Researchers, Educators and Students*. London: Jessica Kingsley.

Zallik, S. (1987). In search of the face—an approach to mental handicap. *Journal of British Music
Therapy* 1(1): 13–15.

CHAPTER 19

MUSIC THERAPY AND TRAUMATIC BRAIN INJURY

SIMON GILBERTSON

INTRODUCTION

Lives affected by traumatic brain injury

THE initial traumatic event leading to traumatic brain injury is characteristically catastrophic, lasting for a matter of only seconds. Typical events include accidental injury such as road traffic incidents, falls, play and sport incidents, and non-accidental injury including violence, war, and abuse. Road traffic incidents are the leading cause of traumatic brain injuries (Peden et al. 2004).

The diagnosis of the effects of traumatic brain injury occurs over a span of time, and the consequences often impact the remainder of the injured individual's life. The most common effects of traumatic brain injury include changes in consciousness, motor disturbances, memory impairments, speech/language disorders, disorders of cognition, behavioral changes, and disorders of physiological functions (Winkler 2014). For children who have experienced traumatic brain injuries the consequences of the initial seconds of trauma, when not fatal, ultimately affects the entirety of their lives both in time and scope. For adults, their biographies and life plans are marked permanently and altered radically.

Although perhaps logical, published literature often focuses on the injured individual. By doing so, authors miss the opportunity of uncovering an extended range of other individuals and processes affected by the initial trauma. From this extended stance, the context of the injured person forms not only the frame of understanding, but is the actual phenomenon that requires attention in itself. It is a complex, at times unfathomable process that encompasses the traumatic and severe nature of individual and social injury.

Traumatic brain injury: A relational trauma

For those affected by traumatic brain injury, including siblings, parents, grandparents, uncles and aunties, nephews, cousins, distant relations, closest friends, members of the emergency services, teachers, sport coaches, and many more recreational relationships, the effect of traumatic brain injury in terms of trauma-related processes may extend in time beyond the life of the injured person.

Although traumatic brain injury is classified as an injury of sole organic cause, the child or adult infrequently experiences the event of the injury alone. During the eight years of my clinical work in an early neurosurgical rehabilitation clinic in Germany, children admitted to the clinic included those who were the sole survivors of road traffic incidents with multiple fatalities, and surviving siblings who lost their parents. Some parents were admitted to the clinic in a serious post-coma state following road vehicle incidents without the knowledge of the deaths of their children. Some children and adolescents arrived in the accompaniment of a parent or family member who witnessed the event, or have been visited during their stay in the clinic by a friend and peer who witnessed the traumatic event or had heard about it from their own parent or teacher. Some visitors heard about the traumatic event in which their family member or friend were involved via radio or television. It was clear in the context of practice that traumatic brain injury not only involves the injured person, but that many others who are affected by traumatic brain injury may remain hidden and forgotten (see Gilbertson 2007).

Kennelly and Edwards (1997) provide an example of the relational and complex nature of traumatic injury in their writing about music therapy on the pediatric intensive care unit: "Sally (aged 10) and her brother Chris (aged 7) were involved in a motor vehicle accident, which caused each of them to sustain severe multiple injuries. Their younger sister died in the accident and a carer received minor injuries" (p. 20). This narrative highlights the devastating nature of traumatic injury for families. For each of the children, their injuries were not isolated to the head and brain, but "Sally" also experienced "a fractured right femur, cerebral edema, ruptured bladder, and multiple pelvic fractures and facial lacerations" (Kennelly and Edwards 1997, p. 21). Chris's injuries are described as including "a closed head injury with cerebral hemorrhage, a left frontal lobe hematoma, left occipital hematomas and a midline shift, bilateral lung contusions, ruptured left hemidiaphragm, ruptured spleen (removed), retroperitonal hemorrhage, pelvic fractures and a fractured left femur resulting in a through knee amputation" (Kennelly and Edwards 1997, p. 21).

From this reality, traumatic brain injury must be considered from a relational stance. By extending a perception of the individual injured child further to include those in relation to the child, from closest to indirect relationships, it is clear that a societal response to the effects of pediatric traumatic brain injury may be usefully formulated through relational and ecological frameworks of reference.

Traumatic brain injury or nervous system injury: A consideration of terminology

There are a small number of different terms that are used to describe injurious damage to structures of the brain. The differences in the terms are related to the way in which the brain is understood structurally and functionally in the human. Whereby the term "traumatic brain injury" defines the phenomena as injury to the structure of the brain, the term, cerebro-cranial trauma clearly identifies the involvement of both the brain ("cerebro") and the skull ("cranial"). However, both of these terms do not acknowledge the embodied nature of the brain, and oversimplify the complex, central, peripheral, and social nervous system in which humans exist.

Contemporary literature suggests the need to consider the brain as a situated and embodied brain, a structure that is an integral part of the whole nervous system, both central and peripheral, and thus stretching the conceptualization of lived experienced throughout the body's extremities (Clark 2011). No longer confined to the sharp and hard inner confines of the skull, it has been suggested that the brain can no longer be considered as an isolated, individual entity, but one part of a social structure determining cognition and perception which demands to be recognized as a social brain (Clark 1998). This conceptualization provides a rational for the material basis of the "social nervous system," the collection of brains and bodies through which humans live. As a result, the injury and trauma to the structure of an individual brain may be considered as "traumatic social nervous system injury" with all the consequences for therapy, education, research, and politics that might follow as a result.

Etiology, severity and recovery: A lifespan perspective from childhood to adulthood

Childhood traumatic brain injury

Globally, the number of deaths related to childhood traumatic brain injury is reducing (Bruns and Hauser 2003; Parslow et al. 2005). In a similarly positive trend, the number of children admitted to hospital following mild and moderate traumatic brain injuries has also reduced during the past 30 years (Thurman and Guerrero 1999; Peden et al. 2004).

However, the number of children surviving severe traumatic brain injuries is rising and has been projected to continue to do so in the future in studies of long-term trends up to 2020 (Carney et al. 1999; Peden et al. 2004). In terms of age distribution, some research has shown that children between zero and four years and adolescents between fifteen to eighteen years of age are at increased risk of experiencing traumatic brain injury (Langlois et al. 2006). This is of particular significance in regard to the familial context of the child during these developmental phases.

From this epidemiological viewpoint, there has been a change in quantity (reduced) that has been accompanied by a change in severity (increased). The enormous challenge that remains for the development of caring societies is the conception and provision of effective health care for children who have survived traumatic brain injuries and their families. Pediatric traumatic brain injury does not solely affect the injured child. Long-term outcome studies on pediatric traumatic brain injury (Anderson et al. 2011) show that during acute and short-term phases impairments in core neuropsychological, psychological, and social skills, affect process of interaction with conspecifics and the environment. These altered developmental processes commonly delay, inhibit, and prevent development during and beyond childhood into adulthood.

Adult traumatic brain injury

Traumatic brain injuries in adults are a major concern worldwide. In the US, it has been recently estimated that 1.7 million people suffer a traumatic brain injury each year (Faul et al. 2010). In an earlier study of the causes of head injury leading to treatment for 1005 patients at neurotrauma centers in twelve European countries 52 percent of the injuries were related to road traffic incidents, the major cause of head injuries worldwide (Murray ct al. 1999). The remaining 48 percent of causes were related to work incidents (6 percent), assault (5 percent), domestic incidents (12 percent), sport (3 percent), fall under the influence of alcohol (12 percent), or others (10 percent) (Murray et al. 1999). It should be noted that much of the available major statistical data regarding the incidence and prevalence of traumatic brain injury is inaccurate due to the lack of centralized national registries of traumatic brain injury and also because of the large differences in health care existence and provision around the world.

One aspect of adult traumatic brain injury that should be considered by music therapists in the future is a family perspective. Many adult patients are parents of children of all ages, and music therapy may offer yet unexplored possibilities for the rehabilitation of parents within a relational rehabilitative perspective for families.

Recovery over the lifespan

At one time, it was believed that children recover from traumatic brain injury better than adults because of the young brain's ability to generate new neuronal connections. However, this theory, known as the *Lennard Doctrine*, is now considered to be incorrect as research suggests that the outcome for children is far worse than for their adult counterparts (Carney et al. 1999; Thompson et al. 1994). This is because processes of the localization of functions in the brain may not be concluded at time of injury, and therefore are interrupted in the child's development. Of greater significance however, are those processes of localization that have not yet begun. Injury at this time may lead to a prevention of developmentally significant neuronal connections. The concept of critical periods as developmental windows of opportunity is central to this theory (Carney et al. 1999). In considering recovery and music therapy for children and adults, Baker and Roth (2004) reviewed recovery and music therapy in terms of how the injured brain adjusts following traumatic injury. In their discussion of neuroplasticity and functional recovery, Baker and Roth (2004) emphasize the significance of considering the changes in the pattern and location of neural activity and recommend the development of compensatory skills must be carried out as part of a consideration about the environmental influences and optimal timing of therapeutic responses during the process of rehabilitation. This perspective is crucial in gaining a comprehensive understanding of the situation of the child following traumatic brain injury. In contemporary neuroscience, neural recovery, and neurological reorganization has been understood within the paradigm of functional reorganization of neural activity within the central nervous system. Though once a matter of contention, neural change in adults is now commonly used as a model in conceptualizing neurological recovery following trauma or illness (Cramer et al. 2011).

Considering interrelatedness and music therapy

There are identifiable patterns of making explicit the ways individuals and processes are joined and interrelated. Abad and Edwards (2004) highlighted the significance of considering infant-parent work in music therapy based on theoretical constructs of attachment initially developed by Mary Ainsworth and John Bowlby in the 1960s (Ainsworth and Bowlby 1965). In infant-parent work, the lives of the infant and parent are considered to be inseparably fused by psychological and neurobiological substrates of relating and by way of early experience-dependent brain maturation (Schore and Schore 2008). In highlighting child-family interrelatedness as experienced in music therapy, Oldfield and Flower (2010) have brought together many voices of music therapists who have worked for many years with children and their families in the therapy process. The conceptualization and implementation of the practice and research of family therapy for those affected by traumatic brain injury is an important agenda for the music therapy profession in the future.

Assessment of traumatic brain injury

There are very many different assessment and referral procedures within institutions reflecting local and national practices, guidelines, and regulations. It is common in designated rehabilitation centers that the assessment of patients with traumatic brain injury is multidisciplinary and will include specialist assessment of the major symptoms and characteristics of the form of injury.

It is important that assessment of the brain injured patient includes the areas of consciousness, visual activity, paralysis, motor activity in the upper and lower extremities, sensory perception, language and speech capacity, dysarthria, and visual spatial neglect or anosognosia (lack of awareness of illness). Common standardized assessment tools in the field of neurorehabilitation include the Glasgow Coma Scale (Teasdale and Jennett 1974; Jennett 2002), Glasgow Outcome Scale (Jenett and Bond 1975), and the Rancho Los Amigos Levels of Cognitive Functioning Scale (Hagen et al. 1987) or the Rappaport Disability Rating Scale (Rappaport et al. 1982).

Jeong and Lesiuk (2011) have developed and field-tested a music-based assessment of attention which generates data in relation to sustained, selective, and divided attention for patients with traumatic brain injury. The assessment has demonstrated promising results in the early trials and will be further studied in relation to internal and external validity and correlations with existing assessment of attention in neuropsychology.

The team of music therapy clinicians and researchers at the Royal Hospital for Neurodisability in London have developed the standardized assessment tool MATADOC for the assessment of patients in neurorehabilitation (Magee et al. 2013; O'Kelly and Magee 2013). The acronym MATADOC stands for music therapy assessment tool for disorders of consciousness. The original version of the scale which was known as MATLAS, has been validated and:

> contains 14 items covering the five behavioral domains consistently included in other assessment formats; motor responses, communication, arousal, auditory and visual responsiveness. Each item is categorized hierarchically into levels of observed behavioral responses with a numerical grading. Each level specifies an observable behavior with definitions of behaviors provided in an accompanying instruction manual.
>
> Magee 2007, p. 321

The use of this scale should be an integral part of the assessment of patients with disorders of consciousness receiving treatment in neurological rehabilitation. Specialist training is required for the application of the scale to ensure the best possible quality of assessment.

MUSIC THERAPY AND REHABILITATION
FOLLOWING TRAUMATIC BRAIN INJURY

The word, rehabilitation comes from the Latin term, *rehabilitare*, which means "to restore to a previous condition; to set up again in proper condition" (Friedrischsen 1980). More recently rehabilitation is defined as the aim to "restore to health or normal life by training and therapy after imprisonment, addiction, or illness" (Soanes and Stevenson 2003). This, in the light of the devastating nature of traumatic brain injury may be misleading as restoration to a previous state is biographically, and in most cases, neurofunctionally not possible. The World Health Organization defined the term *rehabilitation* as "the combined and coordinated use of medical, social, educational and vocational measures for training or retraining the individual to the highest possible level of functional ability" (WHO 1969, cited in Glanville 1982, p. 7).

Wilson (1999) has described rehabilitation as a "two way process." She states:

> Unlike treatment, which is given *to* a patient, rehabilitation is a process in which the patient, client or disabled person takes an active part. Professional staff work together with the disabled person to achieve the optimum level of physical, social, psychological, and vocational functioning. The ultimate goal of rehabilitation is to enable the person with a disability to function as adequately as possible in his or her most appropriate environment.
>
> Wilson 1999, p. 13

From this description, rehabilitation is understood as a collection of activities that rely on the recognition of the patient's needs, wishes, and environmental context.

A historical perspective on the development of music therapy with individuals affected by traumatic brain injury

The initial application of music therapy in the area of neurology in general took place in the 1980s. There had been earlier single reports of the use of music in the therapy of motor ability in the setting of neurological rehabilitation (Fields 1954, Rauhe 1977). Other pioneers later published reports of their experiences gained with people with neurological disorders during the 1970's (Grocke 2003). An increase in the number of publications related to neurological disease/trauma took place in the 1980s and early years of the 1990s (Emich 1980; Oepen and Berthold 1983; Ojakangas 1984; Oepen and Berthold 1985; Brodsky and Niedorf 1986; Gadomski and Jochims 1986; Lucia 1987; O'Callaghan and Turnbull 1987; Cohen 1988; Goldberg et al. 1988; Claeys et al. 1989; Hiller 1989; Aldridge et al. 1990). Many more clinicians joined the pioneers of the 1980s and early 1990s to work in this area during the second half of the decade (see Gilbertson 2005a for an overview).

As an example, in Germany at the beginning of 1990s there were a handful of therapists employed in the area of neurological rehabilitation during the 1990s and Weymann and Przybilla in 1997 provided an impression of the variety of music therapy approaches found in neurology (Weymann and Przybilla 1997). In 2001, a survey of 139 German rehabilitation clinics reported the employment of music therapists in 40 clinics (Pöppel et al. 2002). During the following decade there has been a reduction in the number of music therapists working in neurorehabilitation. Though the 2001 survey has not be repeated, this reduction may be related to general reduction in financing within the health sector, music therapists who have changed their area of practice or work, or leaving clinical practice to enter into education and research positions. Already in 1996, the demand for music therapy in neurorehabilitation was becoming noticeable as Aldridge pointed out stating, "My music therapy colleagues have been so successful in their work with post-comatose patients in neurological rehabilitation that they simply cannot provide enough music therapists for the hospital positions" (Aldridge 1996, p. 273).

In the thirty years between 1980 and 2010 there have been many advances in understanding music, the brain, and traumatic brain injuries. Alongside perspectives of neurological illness in terms of situated and relational individuals (Aldridge 2001; Gilbertson 2005b), and the role music therapists can perform in rehabilitation (Kennelly 2000; Livingston 1996) there have been ground breaking advances in the area of cognitive neurosciences and music (see Levitin and Tirovolas 2009 for an introduction) and many music-based practices related to music therapy in neurorehabilitation (Altenmüller et al. 2009; Fujioka et al. 2012; Thaut and Abiru 2010).

However, within published music therapy literature there has been a disparity of between clinical work and published material regarding clinical work with children and adults with traumatic brain injuries. Anecdotally, many music therapists tell of a larger diversity of methods, a wider variety of symptoms and disorders, and different levels of integration within the treatment context than is reported in the literature.

As an example, only 46 clearly identifiable cases of children can be found in the literature related to music therapy and traumatic brain injury (see Table 18.1). Within an age range of zero to eighteen years, not all ages are represented. These publications have been published by a small number of music therapists during a period of over thirty years (see Gilbertson 2010 for a reference standard bibliography of these publications). Considering that a conventional music therapist case load can include up to 35 patients per week, with some treatment plans extending for as long as six months, the publication of fewer than 50 cases is surprising. No global survey of music therapy with either children or adults has been completed to date and this would contribute a great deal to understanding the use of music therapy as a treatment strategy.

THE MUSIC THERAPY PROCESS: REFERRALS, ASSESSMENT, AIMS AND OBJECTIVES, TREATMENT METHODS, EVALUATION AND REPORTING

The best possible treatment of a patient following traumatic brain injury is an integrated music therapy process within an interdisciplinary treatment context. The main aspects of the music therapy process, referral, assessment, goal and objective choice, treatment method, evaluation, and reporting are interlinked and often interdependant. The following section portrays common music therapy processes when working with people with traumatic brain injuries as summarized in tabular form (see Table 18.2). It is important to note that all music

Table 18.1 Reported cases of children and adolescents with traumatic brain injury who have received music therapy

Author(s)	Year	Case name	Age (years)	Gender	Traumatic event
Kennelly, Hamilton, and Cross	2001	Cathy	3	Female	MVA as pedestrian
Hurt-Thaut and Johnson	2003	"C"	4	Male	-
Baker, Kennelly, and Tamplin	2005a	"Children" (3)	5 to 8	Male = 3	-
Kennelly and Edwards	1997	Chris (brother of Sally)	7	Male	MVA, as car passenger
Rosenfeld and Dun	1999	David	7	Male	MVA as pedestrian
Gustorff and Hannich	2000	Andreas	7	Male	Fall from a carousel
Bischof	2001	René	8	Male	MVA
Baker, Kennelly, and Tamplin	2005a	"Early adolescents" (2)	9 to 12	Male = 1, Female = 1	-
Gilbertson	1999	Michael	9	Male	MVA
Gilbertson and Aldridge	2008	Neil	9	Male	MVA
Rosenfeld and Dun	1999	Matthew	9	Male	Fall from tree
Kennelly and Brien-Elliot	2001	Taylor	9	Male	MVA as passenger
Kennelly and Edwards	1997	Sally (sister of Chris)	10	Female	MVA, as car passenger
Bischof	2001	Emanuel	10	Male	MVA as car passenger
Bower et al.	2013	Evelyn	10	Female	MVA
Bischof	2001	Nina	11	Female	MVA as pedestrian
Kennelly and Brien-Elliot	2001	Nathan	12	Male	MVA as pedestrian
Kennelly, Hamilton, and Cross	2001	Tracey	12	Female	MVA as pedestrian
Wit et al.	1994	4 treatment, 1 control	13 to 17	3 female, 2 male	-
Gervin	1991	S.	14	Female	MVA
Baker, Kennelly, and Tamplin	2005a	"Mid Adolescents" (5)	14 to 16	Male = 0, Female = 5	-
Burke et al.	2000	A.T.	15	Female	MVA as pedestrian
Gilbertson and Aldridge	2008	Bert	15	Male	MVA
Jochims	1990	N.N.	15	Female	-

(Continued)

Table 18.1 Continued

Author(s)	Year	Case name	Age (years)	Gender	Traumatic event
Robb	1996	D.	16	Female	-
Robb	1996	B.	16	Male	-
Hiller	1989	A.B.	16	Male	-
Schinner et al.	1995	Patient #12	17	Male	MVA
Baker, Kennelly, and Tamplin	2005b	"Late Adolescents" (10)	17 to 21	Male = 5	-
Emich	1980	No specific cases mentioned	Children and adolescents	-	-
Glassman	1991	N.N.	Young woman	Female	MVA

(MVA = motor vehicle accident)

therapy processes must reflect the individual needs and wishes of the patient and be flexible in the setting of goals and objectives, the selection of treatment method and the timing and duration of the therapy.

Referrals

Following multidisciplinary assessment of the patient with traumatic brain injury as described earlier in this chapter, referrals are commonly made by the ward doctor in the hospital setting, or through discussion and agreement with the multidisciplinary team. In my experience as a music therapist in an early neurosurgical neurorehabilitation clinic in Germany between 1994–2002 (Gilbertson and Ischebeck 2001), the team that provided for patients with traumatic brain injuries had expertise in the following areas: art therapy, balneotherapy, music therapy, neuro-imaging consultation, neuropsychology, neurosurgical consultation, occupational therapy, physiotherapy, psychotherapy, rehabilitation medicine, rehabilitative nursing, speech and language therapy, sport therapy, and therapeutic gardening.

This scope and range of expertise provided for the assessment and referral possibilities for a wide range of diversity in the severity of symptoms, symptom complexes, and changes in rehabilitative progression on a case-to-case basis. The diversity of the multidisciplinary team also reflected the core areas of individual and social capacities and functioning often affected by traumatic brain injury.

Goals and objectives

In addition to the examples of goals and objectives that have been generated for patients following traumatic brain injury as shown in Table 18.2, it is important that the individual nature of traumatic brain injury and its effects are considered. When considering the development of goals and objectives for patients who have experience a traumatic brain injury it

Table 18.2 An overview of music therapy techniques, clinical symptoms, aims and goals, effect/change, and related sources in the literature

Music therapy methods/techniques	Clinical symptoms	Aims and goals	Effect/Change	Sources in the literature
Combined methods	Depression, social isolation; aphasia; anxiety-depression; disorders of executive function	Involvement in therapy, improvement of mood and motivation; increase in speech/language capacity	Increase in social interaction, motivation and active involvement in therapy; positive change in relation to capacity of verbalization, verbal repertoire and intelligibility	Nayak et al. 2000; Kennelly and Brien-Elliot 2001; Kennelly, Hamilton, and Cross 2001; Guetin et al. 2009; Bower and Shoemark 2009; Thaut et al. 2009
Improvised singing/song	Disorders of orientation	Development of chronological and contextual orientation	Greater awareness of time and space, improvements of orientation and level of awareness	Bischof 2001; Claeys et al. 1989; Kennelly and Edwards 1997; Bower and Shoemark 2009
Instructional song	Apraxia, cognitive disorders of executive function	Reduction of time needed to dress, to affect risk assessment behaviour	Reduction in time needed to dress and increase in level of independence, increase risk assessment and use of habilitative equipment safely	Gervin 1991
Instrumental improvisation	Disorders of consciousness, Organic Brain Syndrome	Exploration of patient's awareness, perception and communicative ability, establishment of patterns of relating in musical and non-musical domains, development of identity and social interaction	Diagnostically significant observations of stimulus–reaction patterns, development of patterns of relating in dynamic forms, re-establishment of personal identity	Bright and Signorelli 1999; Gadomski and Jochims 1986; Gilbertson 1999; Gilbertson and Aldridge 2008; Herkenrath 2002; Jochims 1994; Magee 1999; Tamplin 2000; Bower et al. 2013
Melodic Intonation Therapy and Modified Melodic Intonation Therapy	Broca's aphasia	Develop speech fluency and promote hemispherical neural activity	Increase in word retrieval, fluency and intelligibility, computer tomographic evidence of bi-hemispherical activation	Cohen 1992; Lucia 1987; Belin et al. 1995; Baker, Wigram, and Gold 2005; Thaut 2008

(Continued)

Table 18.2 Continued

Music therapy methods/techniques	Clinical symptoms	Aims and goals	Effect/Change	Sources in the literature
Motor skills rehabilitation, comprehensive battery of research-based intervention strategies	Hemiparesis	Increase range and temporal control of large motor skills	Significant re-training of gait and arm movement towards a physiological patterns of movement and reduction of pathological restrictions	Thaut 2008; Thaut and Abiru 2010
Music listening	Coma, post-coma	Initial reactions to auditory sources, increase in relaxation	Patients may respond in diffuse ways to known music during coma phases, increase in relaxation level, initiation of initial contact. Caution is expressed in relation to the use of music listening with patients in coma (see Shinner et al. 1995).	Hohmann 1997; Jones 1990; Knox and Jutai 1996, Schinner et al. 1995
Music-based attention training	Disorders of attention	Increase in general processes of attention	Improvements in paced and rhythmically organized exercises in attention. Increase in motivation to participate in attention-related therapies	Wit et al. 1994; Knox and Jutai 1996
Re-creating pre-composed music	Loss of social role and identity	Development of active role taking and re-definition of identity	Increase in involvement of music-based social activities and possibilities for performing a new identity	Price-Lackey and Cashman 1996
Rhythmic auditory stimulation	Hemiparesis	Increase in effective gait patterns	Significant change in gait symmetry	Hurt et al. 1998; Thaut 2008
Song composition	Psychological trauma, lack of social relating	Awareness of self-expression and development of interpersonal relating	Development of self-acceptance, increase in motivation to participate	Barker and Brunk 1991; Baker, Kennelly and Tamplin 2005

Technique	Condition	Goal	Outcome	References
Song reminiscing	Motor dysfunction and dyspraxia	Support the development of expression of emotion through song selection	Increase in the communication of emotional state and thoughts	Glassman 1991
Song singing	Coma, dysarthria, aphasia,	Support patient emerging from coma during developing vocalizations, development of functional speech, improve mood state	Wide range of vocal and motor responses elicited, increase in eye contact, awareness and orientation, Increase in speech intelligibility, motivation and enjoyment and improvement in mood state	Lucia 1987; Kennelly and Edwards 1997; Rosenfeld and Dun 1999; Kennelly, Hamilton and Cross 2001; Magee and Davidson 2002); Baker, Kennelly and Tamplin 2005; Tamplin 2008; Bower and Shoemark 2009
Song text writing, song creation	Loss of writing ability, aphasia, hospitalization	Development of functional language capacity and formulation of future personal goals	Development of word-retrieval, communication of gratitude for the help received during rehabilitation, achieving closure at the time of discharge from hospital	Robb 1996, Baker, Kennelly and Tamplin 2005
Traditional Oriental Music Therapy	Disorders of consciousness	Increase general awareness, interpersonal interaction and motivation	Increased awareness, interpersonal interaction and motivation towards participation	Tucek et al. 2001
Vocal exercises, including breathing	Expressive speech disorders	Development of fundamental speech frequency, variation of vocal intensity, rate of speech and intelligibility	Changes in fundamental frequency variability and rate of speech and intelligibility	Cohen 1992, Bower and Shoemark 2009, Thaut 2008
Vocal intonation	Aphasia	Development of the verbalization of common communicative phrases	Increased used of capacity to verbalized thoughts and wishes	Emich 1980, Cohen 1992, Thaut 2008

is important to consider the recommendations of national organizations and also the local practices of each treatment context.

In their recommendations for rehabilitation practice the National Institute for Health Development Panel (1999) have recommend that:
- Rehabilitation services should be matched to the needs, strengths, and capacities of each person with TBI and modified as those needs change over time.
- Rehabilitation programs for persons with moderate or severe TBI should be interdisciplinary and comprehensive.
- Rehabilitation of persons with TBI should include cognitive and behavioral assessment and intervention (p. 980).
Goals and objectives for patients with traumatic brain injuries should be developed in accordance with the results of the assessments carried out in accordance with usual practice in the treatment institution.

Treatment methods

A diversity of music therapy methods and techniques are used in rehabilitation following traumatic brain injury. These include improvised singing/song, instructional song, instrumental improvisation, Melodic Intonation Therapy and Modified Melodic Intonation Therapy, music listening, music-based attention training, recreating pre-composed music, rhythmic auditory stimulation, song composition, song reminiscing, song singing, song story, song text writing, song creation, Traditional Oriental Music Therapy, vocal exercises including breathing exercises and vocal intonation.

Although these methods received much individual attention during the past 30 years, it is most common in clinical practice that methods are selected and combined according to the needs of the patient, treatment concepts of the different institutions and also the therapist's level and scope of training and education.

Evaluation

The evaluation of music therapy with people with traumatic brain injury is a complex and often challenging task that is shared within the professions of the multidisciplinary team. The challenges in determining the effects of rehabilitation and evaluating patient progress and change comprise of: the dynamic nature of the neural and hormonal readjustment and recovery over time, the cross-effects of concurrent therapies, the effects and side-effects of essential medication which is also changed over time. Often, conventional rating scales found in other clinical areas of practice may provide useful evaluation criteria. Also, it is common that admission assessment routines are used to evaluate progress and change during the treatment phase. It is suggested that a systematic consideration of the use of a comprehensive evaluation catalogue such as the one provided as the Individualized Music Therapy Assessment Profile by Baxter and colleagues (2007) should be carried out in relation to this area of clinical application. The MATADOC assessment scale (Magee et al. 2013) will be increasingly implemented as an increasing number of therapists complete the specialized training required to administer the assessment.

Alongside these factors, differences in access to rehabilitative services makes the identi-fication of representative groups of patients for the generation of comparative data near to impossible and decision making processes within institutions about the provision of therapy services may not be permanently consistent. One proposed solution for some of the chal-lenging factors in determining the effect of rehabilitation in the future could be clinical prac-tice improvement models (Horn 2001, p. 10).

When carrying out an evaluation of the outcome evaluation of music therapy it is impor-tant to gather information about pre-injury factors that are described as directly affecting outcome. These factors include any pre-morbid illnesses (for example: cardio-pulmonary disorders, epilepsy, alcoholism, depression), educational level, and socioeconomic status as described by High and colleagues (2005).

Reporting

The reporting of the evaluation of outcomes is most commonly carried out within institution-specific database solutions with the effects of each therapy session and course of therapy being entered by all therapists working with the patient. Commonly, these computer-based systems combine pre-defined characteristics of change together with the possibility for the documentation of narrative descriptions of the therapy process.

To ensure a successful reporting of change observed in therapy, the music therapist work-ing in a multidisciplinary team must ensure that they are able to communicate their assess-ment and evaluation of the therapeutic process using the shared language of the team. This will mean that generic terminology related to traumatic brain injury and neurorehabilita-tion must be learnt, alongside the verbal conventions for describing symptoms, process of change and rational for continuation or suspension of therapy.

Though much reporting of music therapy will be carried out via written documentation, it is imperative that the music therapist is able to succinctly and coherently verbally describe individual developments within single sessions as well as developing their skills in providing a short summary of the patient's progress to date. This is not only important for communi-cating with colleagues and funding agencies, but also to create an open and clear channel of communication with the patient's family members who will be interested but often not well informed of the potential that music and music therapy holds for their relative with trau-matic brain injuries.

FUTURE PERSPECTIVES

Traumatic brain injury is catastrophic

Essentially, each individual sustaining a traumatic brain injury is isolated within nanosec-onds of emerging from the world of fragility following injury. The individual isolation sends traumatic waves of impact through those close to the individual spatially and relationally. It is a point in history, biography, and ecology that may be constructed and reframed, but not removed. Though its permanence may be covered and hidden by the healing power of nature and the art of human mastery of science, the construct of recovery must never be used as ignorance of the magnitude of impact.

Addressing trauma in the light of the day

Although most publications on music therapy practice and research commonly focus on the recovery of clearly described capacities such as speech or movement, as a profession music therapy is challenged to engage with the full range of trauma caused by traumatic brain injury. Traumatic brain injury is reflected in the human experience through which it is perceived.

The use of music in therapy with people affected by traumatic brain injury has developed extensively during the past 30 years both in terms of diversity and also in the depth of knowledge surrounding complex issues of recovery and rehabilitation. Looking into the future it will certainly be important that music therapy clinicians and researchers look beyond individual studies and consider traumatic brain injury within an ecological framework that reaches beyond common methods or specific effect studies.

Global inequality and access to music therapy

The geographical distribution of the sources of publications about the use of music in therapy with people affected by traumatic brain injury does not reflect the geographical distribution of the occurrence and prevalence of the group of individuals at a global level. Surely, many of the techniques identified in this chapter can, with the provision of necessary training fused with local expertise, contribute to the care of people affected by traumatic brain injury worldwide. There may be an uneven global distribution of funds for research in this field, but I feel that the distribution of findings of that research could be better disseminated into those places in the world where the prevalence of people affected by traumatic brain injury is high.

Misrepresentative literature

Though there may be existing, unpublished but ongoing clinical work that is not reported, the involvement of parents, extended family and friends in music therapy must be an area that is researched and practiced in the future. As a sensitivity to the relational effects of traumatic brain injury continue to emerge and be brought to light, so will the significance of the inclusion, not just consultation, of parents, family, and friends become clearer. Patterns of interpersonal neural activity are perhaps one of the most significant resources currently under-represented in music therapy by clinicians and researchers alike and this must be remedied in the future.

Advanced training

The implications of traumatic brain injury for the individual music therapist include the need for a self-driven impulse for continuing education both in the form of recognized training (see Thaut 2008 for an excellent example) and also personal or group study. The nature of traumatic brain injury, particularly when considered as a social trauma, makes great demands on the knowledge and expertise of the music therapy. There is a wide range and diverse scope of areas of proficiency that might be called upon at any one time in the therapeutic process. "Music therapists need to have knowledge of the psychological, social, and emotional stages of development across the lifespan in order to understand the wide range of needs presented by patients at any given time, particularly when faced with trauma, e.g. TBI" (Baker et al. 2005b, p. 28).

Clinical supervision

Finally, professional supervision for the music therapist working with people affected by traumatic brain injury is an area of specialization that needs expansion in relation to availability and training. The intense nature of traumatic brain injury demands that music therapists at all stages of their professional and personal development require consistent professional supervision to ensure safe and ethical practice while at the same time monitoring the effectiveness of the therapist's coping mechanisms.

The imminence of a promising future

Music therapy has a great deal to offer people affected by traumatic brain injury and the future shows much promise. As neuroscience continues to evolve, a balance between studies on individual functional ability will extend to include research on relational socio-functional aspects of recovery. In an earlier paper (Gilbertson 2013) I have addressed the possibilities of long-term repeated immersion research into the meaning of rehabilitation in music therapy when considered from three diverse research strategies including a musicological and personal construct theory perspective, a creative writing consideration of the role of music therapy for a parent of an injured child and the inseparable nature of the perceptive, active, cognitive, and embodied existence of the patient, their family, and the music therapist. It is at the intersection of individual neural and social trauma that neurorehabilitation exercises its greatest potential and it is hoped that the provision of therapy and research incentives supports the development of this promising future.

REFERENCES

Abad, V. and Edwards, J. (2004). Strengthening families: A role for music therapy in contributing to family-centred care. *Australian Journal of Music Therapy* 15: 3–16.

Altenmüller, E., Marco-Pallares, J., Münte, T.F., and Schneider, S. (2009). Neural reorganization underlies improvement in stroke-induced motor dysfunction by music-supported therapy. *Annals of the New York Academy of Sciences* 1169: 395–405.

Ainsworth, M. and Bowlby, J. (1965). *Child Care and the Growth of Love.* London: Penguin Books.

Aldridge, D. (1996). *Music Therapy Research and Practice in Medicine: From Out of the Silence.* London: Jessica Kingsley Publishers.

Aldridge, D. (2001). Music therapy and neurological rehabilitation: Recognition and the per-formed body in an ecological niche. *Music Therapy Today (online)*. Retrieved January 15, 2003, from: <www.musictherapyworld.net>.

Aldridge, D., Gustorff, D., and Hannich, H.J. (1990). Where am I? Music therapy applied to coma patients. *Journal of the Royal Society of Medicine* 83(6): 345–346.

Anderson, V., Brown, S., Newitt, H., and Hoile, H. (2011). Long-term outcome from childhood traumatic brain injury: intellectual ability, personality, and quality of life. *Neuropsychology* 25(2): 176–184.

Baker, F. and Roth, E. (2004). Neuroplasticity and functional recovery: Training models and compensatory strategies in music therapy. *Nordic Journal of Music Therapy* 13(1): 20–32.

Baker F., Wigram T., and Gold C. (2005). The effects of a song-singing programme on the affec-tive speaking intonation of people with traumatic brain injury. *Brain Injury* 19: 519–528.

Baker, F., Kennelly, J., and Tamplin, J. (2005a). Adjusting to change through song: Themes in songs written by clients with traumatic brain injury. *Brain Impairment* 6(3): 205–211.

Baker, F., Kennelly, J., and Tamplin, J. (2005b). Themes in songs written by patients with trau-matic brain injury: Differences across the lifespan. *Australian Journal of Music Therapy* 17: 25–43.

Barker, V.L. and Brunk, B. (1991). The role of a creative arts group in the treatment of clients with traumatic brain injury. *Music Therapy Perspectives* 9: 26–31.

Baxter, H., Berghofer, J.A., MacEwan, L., Nelson, J., Peters, K., and Roberts, P. (2007). *The Individualized Music Therapy Assessment Profile*. London: Jessica Kingsley.

Belin, P., Van Eeckhout, P., Zilbovicius, M., Remy, P., Francois, C., Guillaume, S., et al. (1995). Recovery from aphasia with the music and rhythm method: PET shows the reactivation of hypoperfused language structures in the left hemisphere. *Circulation et Metabolisme du Cerveau* 12(3): 210–211.

Bischof, S. (2001). Musiktherapie mit apallischen Kindern. In: D. Aldridge (ed.), *Kairos V: Musiktherapie mit Kindern*, pp. 58–66. Bern: Hans Huber Verlag.

Bower, J. and Shoemark, H. (2009). Music therapy to promote interpersonal interactions in early paediatric neurorehabilitation. *Australian Journal of Music Therapy* 20: 59–75.

Bower, J., Catroppa, C., Grocke, D., and Shoemark, H. (2013). Music therapy for early cognitive rehabilitation post-childhood TBI: An intrinsic mixed methods case study. *Developmental Neurorehabilitation, Early online* 1–8, DOI: 10.3109/17518423.2013.778910.

Bright, R. and Signorelli, R. (1999). Improving quality of life for profoundly brain-impaired clients: The role of music therapy. In: R. Rebollo Pratt and D. Erdonmez Grocke (eds), *MusicMedicine* 3, pp. 255–263. Parkville: University of Melbourne.

Brodsky, W. and Niedorf, H. (1986). Songs from the heart: New paths to greater maturity. *Arts in Psychotherapy* 13(4): 333–341.

Bruns, J. and Hauser, W.A. (2003). The epidemiology of traumatic brain injury: A review. *Epilepsia* 44(10): 2–10.

Burke, D., Alexander, K., Baxter, et al. (2000). Rehabilitation of a person with severe traumatic brain injury. *Brain Injury* 14(5): 463–471.

Carney, N., du Coudray, H., Davis-O'Reilly, C., et al. (1999). *Rehabilitation for traumatic brain injury in children and adolescents*. Evidence report no. 2, supplement (Contract 290-97-0018 to Oregon Health Sciences University). Rockville, MD: Agency for Health Care Policy and Research.

Claeys, M.S., Miller, A.C., Dalloul-Rampersad, R., and Kollar, M. (1989). The role of music and music therapy in the rehabilitation of traumatically brain injured clients. *Music Therapy Perspectives* 6: 71–77.

Clark, A. (1998). *Being There: Putting Brain, Body and World Together Again*. Bradford: Bradford Books.

Clark, A. (2011). *Supersizing the Mind: Embodiment, Action, and Cognitive Extension*. Oxford: Oxford University Press.

Cohen, N.S. (1988). The use of superimposed rhythm to decrease the rate of speech in a brain-damaged adolescent. *Journal of Music Therapy* 25(2): 85–93.

Cohen, N.S. (1992). The effect of singing instruction on the speech production of neurologically impaired persons. *Journal of Music Therapy* 29(2): 87–102.

Cramer, S.C., Sur, M., Dobkin, B.H., et al. (2011). Harnessing neuroplasticity for clinical applications. *Brain* 134(6): 1591–1609.

Emich, I.F. (1980). Rehabilitative potentialities and successes of aphasia therapy in children and young people after cerebrotraumatic lesions. *Rehabilitation* 19(3): 151–159.

Faul M., Xu L., Wald M.M., and Coronado V.G. (2010). *Traumatic brain injury in the United States: emergency department visits, hospitalizations, and deaths*. Atlanta (GA): Centers for Disease Control and Prevention, National Center for Injury Prevention and Control.

Fields, B. (1954). Music as an adjunct in the treatment of brain-damaged patients. American. *Journal of Physical Medicine* 33: 273–283.

Friedrischsen, G. (1980). *The Shorter Oxford English Dictionary*. Oxford: Oxford University Press.

Fujioka, T., Ween, J.E., Jamali, S., Stuss, D.T., and Ross, B. (2012). Changes in neuromagnetic beta-band oscillation after music-supported stroke rehabilitation. *Annals of the New York Academy of Sciences* 1252: 294–304.

Gadomski, M. and Jochims, S. (1986). Musiktherapie bei schweren Schaedel-Hirn-Traumen [Music therapy for severe craniocerebral trauma]. *Musiktherapeutische-Umschau* 7(2): 103–110.

Gervin, A.P. (1991). Music therapy compensatory technique utilizing song lyrics during dressing to promote independence in the patient with a brain injury. *Music Therapy Perspectives* 9: 87–90.

Gilbertson, S. (1999). Music therapy in neurosurgical rehabilitation. In: T. Wigram and J. de Backer (eds), *The Application of Music Therapy in Development Disability, Paediatrics and Neurology*, pp. 224–245. London: Jessica Kingsley Publications.

Gilbertson, S. (2005a). Music therapy with people who have experienced traumatic brain injury: A literature review. In: D. Aldridge (ed.), *Music therapy in Neurological Rehabilitation*, pp. 83–138. London: Jessica Kingsley Publishers.

Gilbertson, S. (2005b). *Music therapy in early neurorehabilitation with people who have experienced traumatic brain injury*. Unpublished Doctoral Thesis, University Witten/Herdecke, Witten.

Gilbertson, S. (2007). The silent epidemic of road traffic incidents: What can music therapists do about it? *Voices: An international forum for music therapy*, Online, 8. https://scholar.google.com.au/scholar?cluster = 17311112718178196614&hl = en&as_sdt = 0,5&sciodt = 0,5.

Gilbertson, S. (2010). A reference standard bibliography: Music therapy with children who have experienced traumatic brain injury. *Music & Medicine* 1(2): 129–139.

Gilbertson, S. (2013). Improvisation and Meaning. *International Journal of Qualitative Studies on Health and Well-being* 8: 65–74.

Gilbertson, S. and Aldridge, D. (2008). *Music Therapy and Traumatic Brain Injury: A Light on a Dark Night*. London: Jessica Kingsley Publishers.

Gilbertson, S. and Ischebeck, W. (2001). Merging pathways: Music therapy in neurosurgical rehabilitation. *Acta Neurochirurgica*, Suppl. 79: 41–42.

Glanville, H.J. (1982). What is Rehabilitation? In: L. Illis (ed.), *Neurological rehabilitation*, pp. 7–13. Oxford: Blackwell Scientific Publications.

Glassman, L.R. (1991). Music therapy and bibliotherapy in the rehabilitation of traumatic brain injury: A case study. *Arts in Psychotherapy* 18(2): 149–156.

Goldberg, F.S., Hoss, T.M., and Chesna, T. (1988). Music and imagery as psychotherapy with a brain damaged patient: A case study. *Music Therapy Perspectives* 5: 41–45.

Grocke, D. (2003). Music therapy. In: G. Triase and P. del Campo (eds), *Music Therapy and Art Therapy in Neurodegenerative Diseases*, pp. 9–24. Barcelona: Fundacó "la Caixa."

Guetin S., Soua B., Voiriot G., Picot M.C., and Herisson C. (2009). The effect of music therapy on mood and anxiety-depression: An observational study in institutionalized patients with traumatic brain injury. *Annals of Physical Rehabilitation Medicine* 52: 30–40.

Gustorff, D. and Hannich, H.-J. (2000). *Jenseits des Wortes: Musiktherapie mit komatoesen Patienten auf der Intensivstation* [Beyond Words: Music Therapy with Coma Patients at Intensive-care Units]. Goettingen: Hans Huber Verlag.

Hagen, C., Malkmus, D., and Durham, P. (1987). Levels of cognitive functioning. Professional Staff Association of Rancho Los Amigos Hospital. *Rehabilitation of the head injured adult: comprehensive physical management*. C.A. Downey, Rancho Los Amigos Hospital Inc.

Herkenrath, A. (2002). Musiktherapie und Wahrnehmung: Ein Beitrag der Musiktherapie zur Evalierung der Wahrnehmungsfähigkeit bei Patienten mit schweren Hirnverletzungen. In: D. Aldridge and M. Dembski (eds), *Music Therapy World: Musiktherapie, Diagnostik und Wahrnehmung*, pp. 122–131. Witten: University Witten Herdecke.

High, W.M., Sander, A.M., Struchen, M.A., and Hart, K.A. (eds). (2005). *Rehabilitation for Traumatic Brain Injury*. Oxford: Oxford University Press.

Hiller, P.U. (1989). Song story: A potent tool for cognitive and affective relearning in head injury. *Cognitive Rehabilitation* 7(2): 20–23.

Hohmann, W. (1997). Erfahrungen in der Auditiven Musiktherapie mit Hirngeschaedigten [Experiences with auditive music therapy with brain-damaged patients]. *Musiktherapeutische-Umschau* 18(3): 178–192.

Horn, S.D. (2001). Quality, clinical practice improvement, and the episode of care. *Managed Care Quarterly* 9(3): 10–24.

Hurt-Thaut, C. and Johnson, S. (2003). Neurologic music therapy with children: Scientific foundations and clinical application. In: S. Robb (ed.), *Music Therapy in Pediatric Healthcare: Research and Evidence-based Practice*. Silver Spring: AMTA Inc.

Hurt, C.P., Rice, R.R., McIntosh, G.C., and Thaut, M.H. (1998). Rhythmic auditory stimulation in gait training for patients with traumatic brain injury. *Journal of Music Therapy* 35(4): 228–241.

Jennett, B. (2002). The Glasgow Coma Scale: History and current practice. *Trauma* 4: 91–103.

Jennett, B. and Bond, M. (1975). Assessment of outcome after severe brain damage. *Lancet* 1: 480–484.

Jeong, E. and Lesiuk, T.L. (2011). Development and preliminary evaluation of a music-based attention assessment for patients with traumatic brain injury. *Journal of Music Therapy* 48(4): 551–572.

Jochims, S. (1990). Coping with illness in the early phase of severe neurologic diseases. A contribution of music therapy to psychological management in selected neurologic disease pictures. *Psychotherapie, Psychosomatik, Medizinische Psychologie* 40(3–4): 115–122.

Jochims, S. (1994). Kontaktaufnahme im Fruehstadium schwerer Schaedel-Hirn-Traumen: Klang als Brucke zum verstummten Menschen. *Krankengymnastik: Zeitschrift fur Physiotherapeuten* 46(10): 1316–1324.

Jones, C.P. (1990). Spark of life. *Geriatric Nursing* 11(4): 194–196.

Kennelly, J. (2000). The specialist role of the music therapist in developmental programs for hospitalized children. *Journal of Pediatric Health Care* 14(2): 56–59.

Kennelly, J. and Brien-Elliott, K. (2001). The role of music therapy in paediatric rehabilitation. *Pediatric Rehabilitation* 4(3): 137–143.

Kennelly, J. and Edwards, J. (1997). Providing music therapy to the unconscious child in the paediatric intensive care unit. *Australian Journal of Music Therapy* 8: 18–29.

Kennelly, J., Hamilton, L., and Cross, J. (2001). The interface of music therapy and speech pathology in the rehabilitation of children with acquired brain injury. *Australian Journal of Music Therapy* 12: 13–20.

Knox, R. and Jutai, J. (1996). Music-based rehabilitation of attention following brain injury. *Canadian Journal of Rehabilitation* 9(3): 169–181.

Langlois, J. A., Rutland-Brown, W., and Wald, M. M. (2006). The epidemiology and impact of traumatic brain injury. *Journal of Head Trauma Rehabilitation* 21: 375–378.

Levitin, D.J. and Tirovolas, A.K. (2009). Current advances in the cognitive neuroscience of music. *Annals of New York Academy of Sciences* 1156: 221–231.

Livingston, F. (1996). "Can rock music really be therapy?" music therapy programs for the rehabilitation of clients with acquired brain injury. *Australasian Journal of Neuroscience* 9(1): 12–14.

Lucia, C.M. (1987). Toward developing a model of music therapy intervention in the rehabilitation of head trauma patients. *Music Therapy Perspectives* 4: 34–39.

Magee, W.L. (1999). Music therapy within brain injury rehabilitation: To what extent is our clinical practice influenced by the search for outcomes? *Music Therapy Perspectives* 17(1): 20–26.

Magee, W (2007). Development of a music therapy assessment tool for patients in low awareness states. *NeuroRehabilitation* 22(4): 319–324.

Magee, W.L. and Davidson, J.W. (2002). The effect of music therapy on mood states in neurological patients: A pilot study. *Journal of Music Therapy* 39(1): 20–29.

Magee, W.L., Siegert, R.J., Daveson, B.A., Lenton-Smith, G., and Taylor, S.M. (2013). Music Therapy Assessment Tool for Awareness in Disorders of Consciousness (MATADOC): Standardisation of the principal subscale to assess awareness in patients with disorders of consciousness. *Neuropsychological Rehabilitation*, DOI: 10.1080/09602011.2013.844174.

Murray, G.D., Teasdale, G.M., Braakman, R., Cohadon, F., Dearden, M., Iannotti, F., et al. (1999). The European Brain Injury Consortium Survey of Head Injuries. *Acta Neurochirurgica* 141(3): 223–236.

National Institute of Health Consensus Development Panel on Rehabilitation of Persons with Traumatic Brain Injury (1999). Rehabilitation of persons with traumatic brain injury. *Journal of the American Medical Association* 282(10): 974–983.

Nayak, S., Wheeler, B.L., Shiflett, S.C., and Agostinelli. (2000). Effect of music therapy on mood and social interaction among individuals with acute traumatic brain injury and stroke. *Rehabilitation Psychology* 45(3): 274–283.

O'Callaghan, C. and Turnbull, G. (1987). The application of a neuropsychological knowledge base in the use of music therapy with severely brain damaged adynamic multiple sclerosis patients. Paper presented at the Australian Music Therapy Association Conference Proceedings, Australia.

O'Kelly, J. and Magee, W.L. (2013). Music therapy with disorders of consciousness and neuroscience: The need for dialogue. *Nordic Journal of Music Therapy* 22(2): 93–106.

Oepen, G. and Berthold, H. (1983). Rhythm as an essential part of music and speech abilities: Conclusions of a clinical experimental study in 34 patients. *Revue Roumaine de
Neurologie et de Psychiatrie* 21(3): 168–172.

Oepen, G. and Berthold, H. (1985). Haeufigkeit und Art amusischer Stoerungen nach unter-
schiedlichen Hirnlaesionen [Frequency and type of amusia following different cerebral
lesions]. In: R. Spintge and R. Droh (eds), *Musik in der Medizin—Music in medicine*, pp.
177–187. Paper presented at the 2nd International Symposium Sportkrankenhaus Hellersen.

Oldfield, A. and Flower, C. (2010). *Music therapy with children and their families.*
London: Jessica Kingsley Publishers.

Ojakangas, C. (1984). Courage residence: A unique transitional brain injury program.
Cognitive Rehabilitation 2(6): 4–10.

Parslow, R.C., Morris, K.P., Tasker, R.C., Forsyth, R.J., and Hawley, C.A. (2005). Epidemiology
of traumatic brain injury in children receiving intensive care in the UK. *Archives of Disease
in Childhood* 90: 1182–1187.

Peden M., Scurfield R., Sleet D., Mohan D., Hyder A.A., et al. (2004). World Report on Road
Traffic Injury Prevention. Geneva: World Health Organization.

Pöppel, A., Jochims, S., van Kampen, N., and Grehl, H. (2002). Evaluation of music therapy
in German neurorehabilitation—Starting point for European comparability. *Music Therapy
Today* (*online*). Retrieved August 5, 2002, from: <http://www.musictherapyworld.net>.

Price-Lackey, P. and Cashman, J. (1996). Jenny's story: Reinventing oneself through occupation
and narrative configuration. *American Journal of Occupational Therapy* 50(4): 306–314.

Rappaport, M., Hall, K.M., Hopkins, H.K., Belleza, T., and Cope, D.N. (1982). Disability rating scale for severe head trauma: Coma to community. *Archives Physical Medicine and
Rehabilitation* 63: 118–123.

Rauhe, H. (1977). Antriebsförderung durch Musik: ein Ansatz zur rezeptiven Musiktherapie in
der neurologischen Rehabilitation. *Die Therapie der Gegenwart* 116: 1789–1814.

Robb, S.L. (1996). Techniques in song writing: Restoring emotional and physical well-being in
adolescents who have been traumatically injured. *Music Therapy Perspectives* 14(1): 30–37.

Rosenfeld, J. V. and Dun, B. (1999). Music therapy in children with severe traumatic brain
injury. In R.R. Pratt and D.E. Grocke (eds), *Music Medicine 3. Music Medicine and music
therapy: Expanding Horizons*, pp. 35–46. Melbourne: University of Melbourne.

Schinner, K.M., Chisholm, A.H., Grap, M.J., et al. (1995). Effects of auditory stimuli on
intracranial pressure and cerebral perfusion pressure in traumatic brain injury. *Journal of
Neuroscience Nursing* 27(6): 348–354.

Schore, J.R. and Schore, A.N. (2008). Modern attachment theory: The central role of affect regulation in development and treatment. *Clinical Social Work Journal* 36: 9–20. DOI: 10.1007/
s10615-007-0111-7.

Soanes, C. and Stevenson, A. (eds). (2003). *Oxford Dictionary of English.* Oxford: Oxford
University Press.

Tamplin, J. (2000). Improvisational music therapy approaches to coma arousal. *Australian
Journal of Music Therapy* 11: 38–51.

Tamplin, J. (2008). A pilot study into the effect of vocal exercises and singing on dysarthric
speech. *NeuroRehabilitation* 23(3): 207–216.

Teasdale, G. and Jennett, B. (1974). Assessment of coma and impaired consciousness. *Lancet*
2: 81–84.

Thaut, M. (2008). *Rhythm, Music, and the Brain: Scientific Foundations and Clinical
Applications.* New York: Routledge.

Thaut, M.H. and Abiru, M. (2010) Rhythmic auditory stimulation in rehabilitation of movement disorders: A review of current research. *Music Perception* 27(4): 263–269.

Thaut M.H., Gardiner J.C., Holmberg D., Horwitz J., Kent L., Andrews G., Donelan B., and McIntosh G.R. (2009). Neurologic music therapy improves executive function and emotional adjustment in traumatic brain injury rehabilitation. *Annals of New York Academy of Sciences* 1169: 406–416.

Thompson, N.M., Francis, D.J., Stuebing, K.K., et al. (1994). Motor, visual-spatial, somatosensory skills after closed head injury in children and adolescents: A study of change. *Neuropsychology* 8: 333–342.

Thurman, D. and Guerrero, J. (1999). Trends in hospitalization associated with traumatic brain injury. *Journal of the American Medical Association* 282(101): 954–957.

Tucek, G., Auer-Pekarsky, A.-M., and Stepansky, R. (2001). Altorientalische Musiktherapie bei Schaedel-Hirn-Trauma [Traditional oriental music therapy for traumatic brain injury patients]. *Musik-, Tanz- und -Kunsttherapie* 12(1): 1–12.

Weymann, E. and Przybilla. (1997). Musiktherapie und Neurologie. In: F. Welter and P. Schönle (eds), *Neurologische Rehabilitation*, pp. 177–186. Stuttgart: Gustav Fisher Verlag.

Winkler, P. (2014). Traumatic brain injury. In: D.A. Umphred (ed.), *Neurological Rehabilitation*, 6th edition, pp. 753–790. St Louis: C.V. Mosby Company.

Wilson, B.A. (1999). *Case Studies in Neuropsychological Rehabilitation*. Oxford: Oxford University Press.

Wit, V., Knox, R., Jutai, J., and Loveszy, R. (1994). Music therapy and rehabilitation of attention in brain injury. *Canadian Journal of Music Therapy* 2(1): 72–89.

World Health Organization (1969). *Technical Report* No. 419, 1.2.1: World Health Organization.

CHAPTER 20

···

MUSIC THERAPY FOR PEOPLE WHO HAVE ALZHEIMER'S DISEASE

···

ALICIA ANN CLAIR

INTRODUCTION

THIS chapter will offer: (a) A review of selected clinical research studies I have conducted into music therapy and dementia care, (b) updated dementia information that has implications for current music therapy practice, (c) a theoretical framework for music therapy, and (d) the theoretical principles that guide clinical music therapy practice with care receivers and caregivers. The chapter concludes with a description of the current state of music therapy research with those who have dementia and the future of music therapy in dementia care. I would now like to take a moment to describe how I became interested in the field of dementia care.

THE AUTHOR'S PERSONAL PERSPECTIVE

Many persons who choose to work with those who have dementia arrive at such a choice through personal experience. Professional care givers very often have a story that involves a member of the family or a close friend with the disease. My fascination with Alzheimer's disease began quite early in my life. From my birth to age six, my parents, younger sister, and I lived with my paternal grandparents in a rather isolated, rural farmhouse in the middle of Kansas, USA. My first memories of my grandfather were at the age of three. At this time, the family physician recommended that my *Gran,* as we called him, who had dementia, be put in an institution so he could not hurt either my sister or me. Memories of him are limited to his tyrannical reactions to children and others in the household. As a very young child I found his behaviors frightening yet fascinating when I realized my abilities to trigger his outbursts and then run away from his grasp. My parents were clearly distraught with my behavior and his reactions; yet, neither my grandfather nor I had the cognitive capacity to understand one another. My impulses led me to provocation and he responded to the antagonist I had become.

As time went on my grandfather's behaviors became increasingly difficult to manage. His safety, and the safety of those who lived with him, were both threatened. He went into rages when his routines were disturbed. He was frustrated by his inabilities to perform daily tasks, and he wandered away from the house whenever vigilance dropped for a moment. The time had come for something to be done and there was only one alternative.

My grieving father took my grandfather to the county court. Gran stood before a judge, and was proclaimed mentally incompetent. He was legally committed to a state psychiatric hospital for the remainder of his life. When asked by the judge if he had anything to say, he replied, "This is my son, Rees. He will not let anything bad happen to me." In tears, my father led him away from the courtroom and drove him to the psychiatric hospital where he died four months later. At the time, dementia was called senility psychosis. There were no treatments and psychiatric hospitals were the only facilities where placements could be made when homes were no longer safe. Sadness and grief about my grandfather's hospitalization haunted my father the rest of his days.

Specialized care for those with dementia was developed many years after my grandfather's death. Early care efforts in the Midwest United States began in the 1980s, occurring shortly before I joined a dementia care team as a board-certified music therapist and clinical researcher. At that time, no programming existed for care receivers other than basic interventions to meet needs for food, hygiene, medication for behavioral management, environmental safety, and structured routine. The general public did not know how to enhance the life quality of loved ones who had dementia and who lacked the cognitive abilities to engage in traditional activities. There was little, if any, information to help guide care givers. One wife was told by an examining physician that her husband had Alzheimer's disease and he recommended she take him home to die. Family members were merely educated regarding insidious disease processes, and left to stand by in grief as their loved ones drifted into the inevitable.

I began to explore various music therapy procedures that joined care receivers with their family members in music experiences that included singing with, dancing to, and listening to music. These appeared to provide unique potential for connection between family members and their loved ones, offering benefits for both care receivers and care givers. As this music therapy approach evolved, I designed specific protocols and conducted studies that resulted in a set of evidence-based outcomes.

Music therapy in clinical practice
for those with dementia

Definitions
The World Health Organization (2012) defines dementia as:
... a syndrome due to disease of the brain—usually of a chronic or progressive nature—in which there is disturbance of multiple higher cortical functions, including memory, thinking, orientation, comprehension, calculation, learning capacity, language, and judgment. Consciousness is not clouded. The impairments

of cognitive function are commonly accompanied, and occasionally preceded, by deterioration in emotional control, social behavior, or motivation. This syndrome occurs in a large number of conditions primarily or secondarily affecting the brain. (p. 7.)

With many types of dementia, Alzheimer's disease is the most common, comprising 60 to 70 percent of all people worldwide who have dementia (World Health Orgnization 2012). Lewy body disease and vascular dementia follow Alzheimer's disease as the next two most common causes of dementia in older adults (Armstrong 2012; Erkinjuntti and Gauthier 2009). While Lewy body dementia is identified by its combined characteristics of Alzheimer's disease and Parkinson's disease with some added perceptual deficits (Armstrong 2012), vascular dementia is a consequence of cerebrovascular disease and is one of the most preventable and treatable of all the dementias (Erkinjuntti and Gauthier 2009). In addition, fronto-temporal lobar degeneration causes dementia that can manifest in three ways, including (a) frontotemporal dementia that is characterized by personal and behavioral deviance; (b) semantic dementia that is marked by early changes in language function; and (c) progressive apparent non-fluent aphasia where speech is lost (Chauvire et al. 2007).

Music therapy is often used in dementia care to enhance the quality of life in those diagnosed with disease and their care givers. The American Music Therapy Association (2013) defines music therapy as "the clinical and evidence-based use of music interventions to accomplish individualized goals within a therapeutic relationship by a credentialed professional who has completed an approved music therapy program" (p. 1).

COMMON FEATURES OF DEMENTIA

While different types of dementia are associated with varying symptomatic markers, the loss of cognitive function is recognized as the principal feature of dementia. Even so, behavioral and psychological symptoms of dementia (BPSD), otherwise known as neuropsychiatric symptoms, accompany cognitive deficits regardless of the dementia subtype. BPSDs are inversely correlated with cognitive losses where BPSDs increase as cognitive function declines. These BPSDs are categorized by the International Psychogeriatrics Association (Finkel et al. 1996) as disturbed emotions, moods, perceptions, thoughts, motor activities, and altered personality traits that increase distress in both the person with dementia and the family care giver.

Behavioral and psychological symptoms of dementia are typically assessed by the *Neuropsychiatric Inventory* (NPI) which has well-established reliability and validity to determine components of agitation, aberrant motor behaviors, anxiety, apathy, depression, disinhibition, delusions, elation, hallucinations, irritability, and sleep or appetite changes (Cummings 1997). Of these the most prevalent in dementia are apathy, depression, irritability, agitation and anxiety. Fifty percent of those diagnosed manifest at least four symptoms simultaneously (Frisoni et al. 1999), even in the early stages of impairment (Monastero et al. 2009). Consequently, neuropsychiatric disturbances are a core feature of dementia and impede clinical outcomes (Meeks et al. 2007). Therefore, interventions that manage behavioral and psychological symptoms in dementia care are important to life quality (Katona et al. 2007).

Waning cognitive function and augmented behavioral and psychological symptoms of dementia contribute to the burden of care that directly influences the distress of care givers and care receivers. Associated misuse of drugs can frequently lead to long-term hospitalizations and associated high costs for care especially when nursing home admission is deemed necessary (Cerejeira et al. 2012). Family care givers are especially affected by their care receivers' agitation, aggression, irritability, and emotional lability, regardless of how frequent or severe the symptoms (Matsumoto et al. 2007). Yet, care givers identify psychotic symptoms, such as delusions and disruptive behaviors that include aggression and screaming, as those behaviors that impose the greatest burdens (Huang et al. 2012; Miyamoto et al. 2010; Rocca et al. 2010). Additional determinates of burden include the care giver's perspectives concerning life quality in the home, personal characteristics and the quality of the relationship between the care giver and the care receiver (Campbell et al. 2008). Consequently, burden is the principal reason for early admission to care facilities (Chan et al. 2003), and burden relief is important to life quality for both care givers and the care receivers wherever they reside.

Residential care

Admission to residential care for those with dementia usually occurs after the need for care exceeds the family care giver's resources, and is therefore an emotionally draining process. With admission, family members experience some liberation from day-to-day responsibilities; but, their loved ones continue to experience ongoing aberrant behaviors, agitation, delusions, depression, disinhibition, and irritability that shift in severity and frequency over time. Some symptoms are likely to abate, in one third of those admitted, after several months in residence (Bergh et al. 2011). Perhaps the predictable routine of the care facilities, reduced care giver stress, and a safe but least restrictive environment contributes to symptom reduction in some persons; however, most persons with dementia require interventions that provide symptom relief. Evidence indicates agitation is common among residents in long-term care for dementia even if other neuropsychiatric symptoms diminish over time (Wetzels et al. 2010). Agitation can result from sensory overstimulation, attitudes of care staff regarding difficult to manage behaviors, and the proportion of staff members to care receivers (Zuidema et al. 2010). Further, agitation to the point of aggression in nursing home placements increases with uses of psychotropic medications (Kunik et al. 2010). Evidence indicates that medications are not effective in managing agitation behaviors in dementia care; they can also lead to deleterious outcomes, including falls (Omelan 2006) that often result in serious injuries.

The duress of neuropsychiatric symptoms, inadequate medications for symptom management, and the portentous cognitive function losses in those with dementia severely blunts life quality for both care receivers and their care givers. Often families become distraught with their limited abilities to provide solace and comfort. When their loved ones no longer recognize them, are incapable of engaging in conversations, evade their visits by walking away, pull away from their touch, or strike out at them it can be heartbreaking. There is important need to develop non-pharmacological interventions that can provide relief from neuropsychiatric symptoms, and that can draw family members together to engage in satisfying interactions that foster their relationships.

SELECTED CLINICAL MUSIC THERAPY RESEARCH WITH CARE GIVERS AND CARE RECEIVERS

Clinical studies have provided evidence suggesting that individuals in mid- to late-stage dementia can actively participate in music, and that properly designed music therapy experiences function to re-establish verbal and nonverbal connections between care receivers and their care givers. The studies demonstrated two overall points. First, music therapy offers opportunities to engage positively with others throughout the dementia trajectory. Second, music therapy offers ways to compensate for some of the inexorable losses associated with the disease process. The evidence-based outcomes of selected studies about music therapy for care givers and care receivers include:

- Persons in the middle to late stages of dementia exhibit behaviors that require supervision to manage agitation. Music therapy may provide the structure to offer a safe, predictable environment in which persons can become actively engaged (Clair 1991a).
- Persons who have late-stage dementia actively engage in rhythmic playing with few prompts using drums, resulting in active participation for up to 30 consecutive minutes with minimal prompts (Clair and Bernstein 1990).
- Persons in late-stage dementia readily synchronize their drumming to play in time with a basic beat pattern. This synchronized playing occurs rapidly, within three to four rhythmic beats of the basic pattern. Some individuals in the late stage play the drum in double time and strike the drum around the periphery of the drum head, yet, they adhere to an ongoing rhythmic pattern. Synchronization is possible even when the disease is so progressed that the individual can no longer engage verbally with others, and when his or her procedural memories are so deteriorated he or she cannot complete simple activities of daily living such as brushing teeth, bathing, and dressing. Even with severe cognitive losses, persons musically interact with call/response patterns. These musical interactions symbolically represent the back and forth pattern of a verbal conversation. Sometimes the rhythmic response to the leader's call is an exact imitation of the leader's four-beat drumming pattern, and sometimes the response is a novel rhythmic pattern that is completed within the rhythmic time frame set by the leader (Clair et al. 1995).
- Persons in late-stage dementia do not actively choose their musical environment, nor do they actively demonstrate preference for the type of sensory input they receive through a particular music environment. They do not choose to turn music off or on, or note a preference for music as auditory stimulation as opposed to music as auditory combined with vibrotactile stimulation. Such music choices may not be cognitively possible in late-stage dementia. Care must be taken to consider best options for

providing music stimulation. An indicator for tolerance of particular music selections is whether persons stay in the room if mobile or have no agitation when music is played (Clair and Bernstein 1993).

- Music therapy for care givers and their spouse care receivers can enhance quality of life measures, including self-esteem and loneliness in the care givers (Clair et al. 1993).

- Background music, including music explicitly designed to elicit quiet and calm responses, is not effective in managing agitation in the dementia care residence, likely because individuals respond idiosyncratically to specific music selections (Clair and Bernstein 1994).

- Background music during task performance in persons with dementia may influence staff care givers to provide more prompts to engage when care receivers' familiar preferred background music is used. Therefore, the influence of background music may influence staff behaviors, which, in turn, affect care receivers' outcomes. It is possible that staff biases regarding care receivers' preferred music has greater effects on outcomes than the background music itself (Otto et al. 1999).

- Preferred music is not always known if family members are not aware and persons with late-stage dementia cannot express their preferences. A starting place for appropriate music selection is popular music of the young adult years, a preference indicated by older adults (Gibbons 1977).

- Singing and reading, when compared to sitting close by in silence, influence alert responses in persons with late-stage dementia; and, singing and reading are recommended for family care givers who desire to elicit alert responses from their care receivers. Often family care givers are not comfortable with their singing skills. They are just as likely to elicit responses from their care receivers while reading to them (Clair 1996).

- It is possible for persons in end stage dementia to respond vocally to live singing in music therapy, and to remain alert for up to one hour after the music therapy session ends (Clair 1991b).

- Family care givers, including spouses, are often uncertain during visits to special care units when their loved ones are in the later stages of dementia and are no longer verbally responsive; however, singing, rhythm playing with drums, and ballroom dancing offered by a music therapist are effective ways for care givers to actively engage with their loved ones (Clair and Ebberts 1997).

- Persons with dementia exhibit better adherence to an exercise program when it is enhanced with music than when it is conducted without music (Mathews et al. 2001).

- Family or friend care givers can quickly learn to implement singing, rhythm playing with drums or ballroom dancing during music therapy protocols to engage their loved ones; and, care givers trained by a music therapist are confident to continue using music engagements when the music therapist discontinues support (Clair 2002).

- Persons in mid-stage dementia are likely to respond immediately or not at all to prompts for music participation, a response pattern that does not change with repeated sessions over time. Consequently, initial assessments of music responses are essential to provide the best use of resources (Clair et al. 2005).

The contributions of these published studies are important to the development of effective music therapy interventions because they present evidence that persons in the middle to late stages dementia (a) can engage in active music making; (b) are successful even without previous music experiences; (c) are capable of learning how to play different rhythm patterns; (d) can sustain attention in active music making for up to 30 minutes at a time; and (e) are far more capable of interacting with others through music than previously thought. Further, this research demonstrates care givers can learn to use music to facilitate engagement with their care receivers.

The research process also revealed that spouses and family members were distressed when loved ones could not speak, wandered away, or did not recognize them. Some care receivers recoiled from affectionate gestures and touch, leaving care givers with a feeling of abandonment. Care givers appreciated music therapy interventions that offered opportunities for re-engagement with cherished family members. They often spoke with delight about how music therapy allowed them to glimpse loved ones as they once were, if only for a moment. Professional care givers expressed their amazement when music therapy interventions actively engaged their care receivers when other interventions were ineffective. Family members also valued demonstrations of decreased agitation, increased alertness and increased care receiver cooperation in treatment regimens following music therapy sessions.

These study outcomes embody a line of research designed (a) to inform music therapy clinical practice; and (b) to enhance life quality for care receivers and their family and/or professional care givers. Life quality is defined by the ability to function at the highest levels possible across cognitive, social, emotional, communication, motor, and physical domains. These functional levels for both care givers and care receivers directly affect independence, autonomy, comfort and the ability to meaningfully engage with others. This meaningful engagement facilitates a sense of belonging within families and within communities. As functions become impaired through the dementia disease process, music therapy interventions are used to enhance residual functioning, and to provide the best possible outcomes. Therefore, music therapy improves life quality as it improves functioning. Training care givers to use music empowers them to improve functioning within their care receivers and greatly adds to life quality for all concerned.

Some weaknesses can be observed within these studies. The research failed to report sufficient information for replication, and also lacked adequate details for inclusion in meta-analyses. Therefore, there is need to continue the quest for effective music therapy interventions in dementia care through rigorously designed research.

EVIDENCE-BASED PRACTICE IN MUSIC THERAPY

The origins of evidence-based music therapy practice lie in medical research and practice and have evolved to combine the following to make treatment decisions and plans: (a) Systematic reviews of the scientific literature, (b) practitioner experience and professional opinion, and (c) client preferences and values (Else and Wheeler 2010). The research literature for evidence-based practice falls into two types: Efficacy research with strong internal validity conducted in tightly controlled clinical trials where generalizability is limited, and effectiveness research with strong external validity conducted in clinical settings where outcomes are applicable to the "real world" but assumptions regarding causality are limited (Else and Wheeler 2010).

The preponderance of research in music therapy with persons who have dementia and their families falls into the category of effectiveness research. Yet, music therapy research is not extensive and is currently insufficient to support all treatment plans and decisions. There is an ongoing need to seek additional evidence to support music therapy practice through research.

Developing a Theoretical Framework for Music Therapy in Dementia Care

While it is generally accepted that music is beneficial for persons who have dementia, research has not clearly defined the functions of music and the efficacy of specific music therapy interventions in a full range of dementia populations. To advance the field of music therapy in dementia care it is essential to build well-designed research lines that can meet scholarly standards and can withstand the rigors of critical review. Such research begins with a strong theoretical framework.

A theoretical framework seeks to ground research and practice through established themes. These themes are derived through philosophical considerations, knowledge derived from previous research, and clinical practice experiences. The following proposed theoretical framework incorporates a wide range of factors that fall within two fundamental areas: Established research, including the neuroscience literature, and principles of practice gleaned from knowledge of experienced, credentialed music therapy professionals. The growing knowledge in these two areas makes theoretical framework development an enduring process in which theory informs clinical practice, clinical practice informs research and research outcomes yield evidence-based knowledge. New knowledge, in turn, enhances the development of the theoretical framework (Figure 20.1).

FIGURE 20.1 Theoretical framework development.

BUILDING THE THEORETICAL FRAMEWORK

A theoretical framework for music therapy in dementia care is formed around considerations of (a) population characteristics, (b) the need to restore or maintain function, and (c) an understanding of music as a facilitator for behavioral change. It is well-established that neuropsychiatric symptoms of dementia become more pronounced, and that cognitive functioning fades as dementia progresses. The most common of these neuropsychiatric symptoms include apathy, depression, irritability, agitation and anxiety (Frisoni et al. 1999). Evidence indicates music therapy is more effective than standard care to reduce delusions, agitation and apathy particularly in persons with severe dementia (Raglio et al. 2010). Further research shows that music therapy improves cognitive function (Bruer et al. 2007), and reduces behavioral and psychological symptoms of dementia (Ueda et al. 2013) making music therapy a powerful intervention for improved life quality for those who have dementia.

It is, therefore, important to consider implementing music therapy interventions to manage neuropsychiatric and cognitive characteristics when standard care fails to contribute adequately to life quality. Clinical experience indicates that the most effective interventions are designed through considerations of optimal arousal and principles of practice.

OPTIMAL AROUSAL: A CARDINAL TENET
FOR DEMENTIA CARE

Neuropsychiatric symptoms in dementia are linked to problem behaviors that tend to occur when (a) individuals become stressed, and (b) the stress compromises their residual abilities to cognitively process the stimuli around them (Hall and Buckwalter 1987; Cheung et al. 2011). Persons may react to this environmental stress with shifts in arousal. Arousal can be understood as the physiological and psychological state of being awake or reactive to stimuli; in dementia, it often manifests as under arousal or over arousal (Chen et al. 2011).

Under arousal is characterized by passive behaviors that range from non-engagement in an activity to complete withdrawal where individuals move away from others, close their eyes as if asleep, curl into a fetal position, or leave the room. It may seem these persons are apathetic or disinterested in stimuli around them when, in fact, they lack sufficient cognitive function to become aroused and attentive without an appropriate intervention.

Over arousal is likely to occur with the presentation of a complex stimulus or the simultaneous occurrence of multiple stimuli which become overwhelming. Over arousal is characterized by stress-triggered behaviors including pacing, wandering, verbal outbursts or screaming, physical aggression, inabilities to engage procedural memory for simple tasks, failure to follow simple directions, and more. Interestingly, over arousal can also be manifested as withdrawal from stimuli, perhaps in the attempt to escape stress.

The most effective music therapy interventions in dementia care begin with careful considerations of an individual's initial arousal state to which musical elements are matched to evoke musical responses. Therefore, rhythm, tempo, dynamics, duration, phrasing, and pitch of the music are matched to body movements, vocal sounds, facial expressions, and

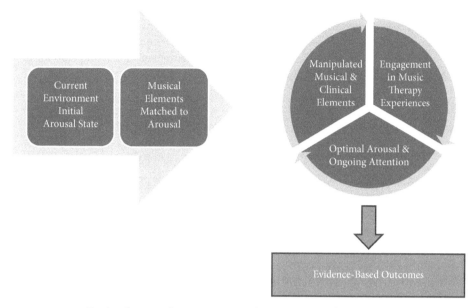

FIGURE 20.2 Optimal arousal, attention, and engagement leading to music therapy outcomes.

overall demeanor in order to musically reflect the individual's behaviors. Through musical reflection, the skillful music therapist shifts the individual's attention focus and elicits initial engagement responses. Building on initial responses the music therapist manipulates musical experiences that alter responses until optimal arousal is reached, a response state in which attention is facilitated to achieve best possible functioning.

Optimal arousal is maintained by ongoing assessment of an individual's responses throughout each music therapy intervention. With assessment information the music therapist continually modifies or maintains musical and clinical elements to achieve pre-determined goals. Consequently, optimal arousal is dynamic and integral to effectiveness of well-conceived music therapy interventions that are comprised of musical experiences specifically designed to achieve desired outcomes. These outcomes include (a) increased engagement in music and an absence of neuropsychiatric symptoms; (b) increased sustained, selective, and alternating attention which enhance procedural and working memories; and (c) improved verbal or non-verbal interactions with others. These outcomes transfer readily to situations outside of music therapy sessions to improve cognitive, social, and communication functioning that facilitate cooperation with care givers and improve life quality (Figure 20.2).

THEORETICAL PRINCIPLES FOR MUSIC THERAPY IN DEMENTIA CARE

A number of factors contribute to arousal, attention, engagement and desirable outcomes for those with dementia. Clinical practice and research have informed theoretical principles that are important to current music therapy interventions. Though these principles are integral to music therapy practice, they also are useful to music therapists who train care givers to use music with their care receivers. Ultimately, these principles contribute to functional outcomes that enhance life quality for those with dementia and those who care for them. These principles are discussed below.

Familiar/preferred music facilitates engagement

Familiar music tends to provide comfort through its predictability and is often identified as preferred music. Yet, not all familiar music is desired, since preferences depend on many other factors which can include but are not limited to personal taste, associations with past experiences, stimulative and sedative qualities, and the meaning of the music to the person.

Preferred music is used in music therapy interventions to expedite engagement and the selection of the best music depends on the intent for outcomes. It is possible that some preferred music may have adverse effects, especially when it leads to unexpected and undesirable responses, for example music intended for relaxation stimulates movement and dancing. For some music therapy interventions, such as relaxation, it is important to select unfamiliar music so that a relationship can be established between the new music and the desired outcomes. Best music choices for each music therapy intervention will ultimately depend upon each individual's responses to it.

Musical timbres affect responses to music for people who have dementia

Observation shows that differences in the timbres of music can affect behaviors of those who have dementia. This can happen whether or not the person likes a particular piece of music. For instance the broad spectrum of sound that is characteristic of some recorded music can trigger agitation and exacerbate uncooperative behaviors even when the song is an old favorite. A song is likely to have best results if it is presented with a sung melody or a simple played melody with sparse accompaniment, e.g. a singer or a flute player accompanied by a piano or not accompanied at all. The environment in which the music occurs can also affect a person's response to it. For instance, if the music is played in a small sized room (eight by10 foot or smaller) with walls covered with ceramic tiles, the sound can trigger agitation. At the same time individuals can become agitated when an environment is particularly busy with people coming and going, a television or radio is playing, people are talking, and perhaps other noises are occurring. Adding music to disturbing environments is not likely to provide calm. Instead, it is likely to push individuals past their tolerance thresholds to become more verbally or physically aggressive. If efforts are not made to decrease the sensory stimuli in such environments, acting out behaviors can continue to increase in intensity to the point of serious injury, e.g. someone is shoved, falls and breaks a hip. Therefore, awareness of how sounds affect individuals, including musical sounds, is essential to designing a comfortable environment in which those who have dementia can function at the highest level possible.

Stimulative and sedative music can be strong behavioral influences

Stimulative and sedative music characteristics relate directly to arousal and can increase or decrease participation levels with music. Stimulative music is commonly characterized by accented rhythms that may have syncopation, bright timbres, dynamic changes, variations in form, harmonic progressions that defy expectations, and melodies with large interval jumps. Stimulative music tends to evoke rhythmic motor movements such as toe tapping or hand clapping. Sedative music, on the other hand, is commonly characterized by non-accented and non-syncopated rhythms, gentle timbres, predictable form, little to no dynamic change, consistent forms and harmonies, and simple melodies. Sedative music tends to promote calmness and relaxation. Of concern is a possible paradoxical effect where music with sedative characteristics elicits outcomes opposite of those expected. (Clair and Memmott 2008).

Former experiences with music can be re-engaged

Experiences are linked with music when those experiences and certain music occur in contiguity (Gfeller 2002). Through repetition, the association strengthens until just listening to the music triggers multisensory memories. For example, slow dance music from the young adult years may trigger memories of a young dance partner to include smells of cologne and freshly shampooed hair, the touch of one cheek to the other, the sensation of encircled arms, romantic musings and love.

Music is powerful for recalling specific autobiographical information once it becomes associated with experiences, even after a dementia diagnosis. When persons with Alzheimer's disease were asked to recall memories from their pasts the content while exposed to their own chosen music was more specific, more emotional, more quickly retrieved, and required less executive processing than memories recalled during silence (El Haj et al. 2012).

The associations linked with music can have emotional valences[1] that are positive, negative, or neutral. Furthermore, persons who are depressed do not respond as strongly to positive valences as persons who are not depressed (Lepping 2013). Still all emotional responses to music depend upon each individual's experiences and, consequently, the same piece of music can affect various people differently. Interestingly, associations with music can shift over time, for example, music that a couple danced to in their early life together may bring tears of loneliness to the surviving spouse many years later.

Cautions for evoking negative associations with any piece of music are important. The associations can lead to adverse, distressful reactions that become difficult to manage, especially in persons with dementia who lack the cognitive and communication functions necessary to convey their discomfort. It is impossible to predict whether selected music will have positive or negative outcomes. Therefore, vigilance is essential. At the first sign of discomfort with a piece, the music must be stopped and another selection used in order to avoid undesirable reactions and distress.

Music can be an iconic representation of feelings

Music often has strong associations with emotions and serves to directly represent those emotions when words cannot be used to convey them (Gfeller 2002). Music that was emotional for someone at a younger age most likely continues the poignant relationship with feelings in later years. For instance, music that conveys feelings of love continues to convey it throughout a life time. Other music may express feelings of anger or frustration and may serve to communicate such feelings when the abilities to verbally articulate them are gone.

Emotion and arousal are changed by music

Music affects arousal and emotions as musical stimuli are processed in the brain (Thaut 2002, p. 12). Consequently, music experiences can be designed to promote arousal which influences alert responses. Once an individual is aroused by music, a skillful music therapist can employ a range of music experiences that facilitate change of emotions and ultimately affect mood. Positive changes in affect are essential to modifying behaviors (Thaut 2002, p. 21) and are critical in dementia care to manage the neuropsychiatric symptoms of persons with dementia.

Singing is soothing

Sung music has powerful influences to quiet and soothe persons across the life span from birth until death. Perhaps singing becomes strongly associated with calming from early childhood when lullabies are sung to bring comfort. When singing imitates a lullaby it is likely associated with feelings of safety and security that make it reassuring. Often persons with dementia who become distressed through their lack of ability to understand the environment calm quickly when soothing singing is introduced.

Singing cues facilitate understanding

As persons enter later stages of dementia spoken words become more and more difficult to understand. Individuals can become agitated or severely withdrawn during care givers' attempts to communicate verbally with them. As distress mounts cognitive function is further impeded. Sung cues, instead of spoken ones, often facilitate cooperation with less stress. Research evidence indicates that persons with dementia better understand care activities when care givers sing rather than provide verbal narration (Götell et al. 2002; 2009; Chatterton et al. 2010).

Sung instructions can ease distress, and can diminish confusion. Singing slows the presentation of verbal information that allows more time for cognitive processing. In addition, speech and singing are mediated by different neural networks and learning verbal content through song employs different neural networks than learning through spoken words (Thaut 2005, p. 84). Further, music regulates attention and arousal in the brain (Thaut 2005,

p. 83) and the metrical organization of music makes it easier to remember verbal material (Thaut 2005, p. 6). Therefore, the rhythmic organization of music that carries verbal information through sung lyrics may enhance understanding.

Facial expressions and tone of voice provide emotional input

Research demonstrates persons with frontotemporal dementia lose the ability to interpret emotions from facial expressions; yet, persons with Alzheimer's type dementia retain abilities to understand the emotional meaning of facial expressions (Neary et al. 2005). Further research demonstrates facial expressions of happiness are most sensitive and well preserved into the Alzheimer's disease process (Maki et al. 2013).

Clinical observations demonstrate persons with Alzheimer's type dementia also retain the ability to interpret meanings from tone of voice and demeanor. Consequently, gruff tones of voice, grimaced faces, and body language lead to distress in those who have Alzheimer's type dementia. Conversely, pleasant vocal tones with a corresponding facial expression and body language are interpreted positively. It seems persons who lose the ability to cognitively interpret words spoken to them derive information from other cues. Consequently, professional and family care givers who carefully monitor their non-verbal cues may enhance comfort levels in their care receivers which lead to better cooperation.

Active singing provides familiarity and comfort

Singing is readily accessible, comfortable, familiar, and engaging. Singing familiar songs, in particular, around persons with dementia often spontaneously engages them in the singing, particularly if the songs have lyrics that were learned by memory in early life, e.g. songs learned in school. Singing provides opportunities to "belong" with others in a familiar activity that carries over from times of full engagement in community life. Singing links those who have dementia with their families and friends after language losses make verbal interactions impossible. Furthermore, singing requires deep breathing to initiate and sustain vocal sounds and deep breathing is a precursor to physical relaxation. Therefore, singing engagement can be used to induce relaxation responses that quiet and calm those in distress.

Active rhythm playing provides predictability and certainty

Rhythm provides a framework for motor responses that are stimulated by auditory cues. The rhythm entrains responses so that all persons play in synchrony. Rhythmic entrainment follows a law of physics that states: When two bodies in nature move in close timing they adjust to move in synchrony because less energy is required to move in synchrony than in opposition (Hart 1990).

Auditory rhythmic cues can entrain motor responses without cognitive processing

Various researchers have shown that auditory rhythmic cures bypass higher order cognitive processing (e.g. Thaut 2005, p. 79). This entrainment makes it possible for persons with dementia to play percussion instruments rhythmically even into late stages of the disease process (Clair et al. 1995). Furthermore, rhythm facilitates successful participation in exercise programming (Mathews et al. 2001). Rhythm provides structure that is predictable, accessible, and entices participation. Through engagement in rhythmic participation, persons can interact non-verbally with others and have some sense that they belong as a part of a group.

A well-structured routine provides safety and well-being

In addition to the predictability and security provided through music participation, a well-structured routine adds to an individual's well-being. The consistency of such a routine reassures individuals and dissipates their stress as it supports their functional abilities. Routines can be implemented through structured schedules at the residence, and through protocols used in music therapy interventions.

THE STATE OF MUSIC THERAPY RESEARCH WITH THOSE WHO HAVE DEMENTIA

The body of literature concerning beneficial outcomes of music therapy in interventions for those with dementia is large and spans journals in several disciplines; however, critical reviews of the research belie the certainty of research outcomes due to inadequate research designs, failure to adequately describe music therapy interventions and general lack of scholarly rigor (Vink et al. 2004; Koger and Brotons 2000). Still, there is evidence to show that music therapy enables short-term improvements in mood and behaviors (McDermott et al. 2013) while it increases emotional expression, enhances speech fluency, and improves speech content (Brotons and Koger 2000). Furthermore, music therapy is effective in the non-pharmacological management of neuropsychiatric symptoms in persons who have dementia (Seitz et al. 2012). It decreases agitation and prevents medication increases that occur more often during standard care (Ridder et al. 2013). Preferred music may be particularly effective in agitation management (Sung and Chang 2005; Garland et al. 2007), mood change and socialization (Wall and Duffy 2010). Further evidence demonstrates improvements in cognitive functioning during music therapy that endure until the next morning after a music therapy session on the previous day (Bruer et al. 2007).

Positive emotional changes with music occur in those with Alzheimer's disease who retain emotional processing abilities with music far into the disease process (Drapeau et al. 2009; Gagnon et al. 2009; Omar et al. 2010); but, those who have dementia due to frontotemporal lobar degeneration cannot process musical emotions and facial expressions (Omar et al.

2011) which limits effectual applications of music with them. These individuals may, however, continue to respond to the rhythmic elements of music through rhythmic entrainment where motor movements become synchronized with auditory cuing, a process that incorporates little to no cognitive functioning (Tháut 2005 p. 142). These entrainment responses can be structured into rhythm playing experiences, promoting engagement in meaningful musical activity. Further, rhythm playing provides opportunities for verbal and non-verbal social interaction across dementia diagnoses and across stages of disease process.

Literature is replete with claims that music is pleasant and desirable to persons with dementia. However, one well-designed research study demonstrates that merely listening to recorded music was not pleasurable or interesting when compared to active engagement in social interactions for those diagnosed with dementia in residential care (Cohen-Mansfield et al. 2011.) In a follow-up study of pleasure experiences in persons with advanced dementia, persons with higher assessment scores for activities of daily living and communication had more pleasure with all types of social stimuli, self-identity stimuli, and music when compared to the control condition (Cohen-Mansfield et al. 2012). This research implies a negligible value of music listening if it is not selected according to individual preferences or is used without consideration of personal experiences. Yet, playing background music for large groups of people in common living spaces is a usual practice in many residential care facilities for older adults who have dementia. Music therapy students and practitioners are encouraged to present these findings to care providers where they work, and to suggest ways that music can be used more effectively.

THE FUTURE OF MUSIC THERAPY
IN DEMENTIA CARE

The future of music therapy in dementia care will be shaped through clinical research studies that clearly establish the effects of interventions on functional outcomes. These interventions must integrate assessed needs with functional treatment goals; they must also facilitate nonmusical outcomes through music experiences that can transfer to "real life" situations. Nonmusical outcomes include, but are not limited to, ameliorated symptoms of distress, attention through optimal arousal, improved mood, stress management and enhanced cognitive function that engages residual memory including procedural memory, and revived relationships with family members.

To have impact on the music therapy profession, future research must test clinical interventions and describe those interventions with sufficient detail for replication. The reporting guidelines for music interventions are articulated by Robb et al. (2011). These reporting guidelines include (a) the theoretical basis for the intervention; (b) detailed content regarding the music and how it is used; (c) delivery schedule; (d) description of the intervention; (e) assurance of treatment fidelity; (f) setting in which the music was used; and (g) the unit of delivery (p. 273).

Further, music therapy research designs of the future must be rigorous enough to withstand criticism, and must provide strong evidence-based outcomes. The literature is replete with arguments regarding hierarchies of evidence and research rigor as they relate to research designs and outcome implications.

Before an applied research study is designed to test a new intervention, it is necessary to conduct field work in a small sample of participants to develop a clinical protocol for that intervention. A protocol is defined as a step-by-step procedure that leads consistently to projected clinical treatment outcomes. A protocol is tested through repeated applications where ongoing evaluations and modifications are conducted for each applied procedural step and its placement within the sequence. The protocol is improved through investigating all modifications to produce the most desirable outcomes. Once projected outcomes become highly consistent with the initial set of participants, the protocol is realized. The resulting protocol design is ready for further study with a new sample of persons who fit within the population.

Even after field testing the protocol may not be suitable for a randomized control trial (RCT). While additional research is indicated to further document the effectiveness of music therapy with persons who have dementia, protocols for music therapy interventions are well-established and provide a firm foundation for further study. Great strides have been made to positively influence the life quality of care receivers and their care givers.

The passion for enhancing dementia care is strong and the desire to make a difference in quality of life lives on in music therapists around the world. Research studies designed with scholarly rigor, that yield high levels of evidence and include carefully described music therapy interventions, are indicated. These studies will afford the guidance music therapists need to advance the field in viable and efficacious services to those with dementia and their families.

NOTE

1. Emotional valence refers to the pleasure value of an emotion as provoking positive or negative experiences; where, for example sadness has negative valence, and happiness has positive valence. This does not mean sadness is a *negative emotion* but rather that it is valenced as belonging on the negative side of the emotional continuum because it can be upsetting to experience feelings of sadness.

REFERENCES

American Music Therapy Association. (2013). A definition of music therapy. Retrieved from: <http://www.musictherapy.org/>.

Armstrong, R.A. (2012). Visual signs and symptoms of dementia with Lewy bodies. *Clinical and Experimental Optometry* 95(6): 621–630. doi: 10.1111/j.1444-0938.2012.00770.x.

Bergh, S., Engedal, K., Røen, I., and Selbæk, G. (2011). The course of neuropsychiatric symptoms in patients with dementia in Norwegian nursing homes. *International Psychogeriatrics* 23: 1231–1239. doi: 10.1017/S1041610211001177.

Brotons, M. and Koger, S.M. (2000). The impact of music therapy on language functioning in dementia. *Journal of Music Therapy* 37(3): 183–195.

Bruer, R.A., Spitznagel, E., and Cloninger, C.R. (2007). The temporal limits of cognitive change from music therapy in elderly persons with dementia or dementia-like cognitive impairment: a randomized controlled trial. *Journal of Music therapy* 44(4): 308–328.

Campbell, P., Wright, J., Oyebode, J., Job, D., Crome, P., Bentham, P. et al. (2008). Determinants of burden in those who care for someone with dementia. *International Journal of Geriatric Psychiatry* 23: 1078–1085. doi: 10.1002/gps.2071.

Cerejeira, J., Lagarto, L., and Mukaetova-Ladinska, E.B. (2012). Behavioural and psychological symptoms of dementia. *Frontiers in Neurology* 3: 73. doi: 10.3389/fneur.2012.00073.

Chan, D.C., Kasper, J.D., Black, B.S., and Rabins, P.V. (2003). Presence of behavioral and psychological symptoms predicts nursing home placement in community-dwelling elders with cognitive impairment in univariate but not multivariate analysis. *Journal of Gerontology* 58: 548–554.

Chatterton, W., Baker, F., and Morgan, K. (2010). The singer or the singing: Who sings individually to persons with dementia and what are the effects? *American Journal of Alzheimer's Disease and Other Dementias* 25(8): 641–649. doi: 10.1177/1533317510385807.

Chauvire, V., Even, C., Thuile, J., Rouillon, F., and Guelfi, J.D. (2007). Frontotemporal dementia: A review. *Encéphale* 33(6): 933–940.

Chen, Y., Clair, A., and Nakamura, N. (2011). Life quality through music therapy over expanded life spans in dementia care. Presentation at the American Music Therapy Association Annual Conference, Atlanta, GA.

Cheung, D.S., Chien, W.T., Lai, C.K. (2011). Conceptual framework for cognitive function enhancement in people with dementia. *Journal of Clinical Nursing* 20(11–12): 1533–1541. doi: 10.1111/j.1365-2702.2010.03584.x.

Clair, A.A. (1991a). Rhythmic responses in elderly and their implications for music therapy practice. *Journal of the International Association of Music for the Handicapped* 6: 3–11.

Clair, A.A. (1991b). Music therapy for a severely regressed person with a probable diagnosis of Alzheimer's disease: A case study. In K. Bruscia (ed.), *Case studies in music therapy*, pp. 571–580. Phoenixville, PA: Barcelona Publishers.

Clair, A.A. (1996). Alert responses to singing stimuli in institutionalized persons with late stage dementia. *Journal of Music Therapy* 33(4): 234–247.

Clair, A.A. (2002). The effect of caregiver implemented music applications on mutual engagement in caregiver and care receiver couples with dementia. *American Journal of Alzheimer's Disease & Other Dementias* 17: 286–290.

Clair, A.A. and Bernstein, B. (1990). A preliminary study of music therapy programming for severely regressed persons with Alzheimer's type dementia. *Journal of Applied Gerontology* 9: 299–311.

Clair, A.A. and Bernstein, B. (1993). The preference for vibrotactile versus auditory stimuli in severely regressed persons with dementia of the Alzheimer's type compared with dementia due to ethanol abuse. *Music Therapy Perspectives* 11: 24–27.

Clair, A.A. and Bernstein, B. (1994). The effect of no music, stimulative music and sedative music on agitated behaviors in persons with severe dementia. *Activities, Adaptations, and Aging* 19: 61–70.

Clair, A.A. and Ebberts, A.G. (1997). The effects of music therapy on interactions between family caregivers and their care receivers with late stage dementia. *Journal of Music Therapy* 34(3): 148–164.

Clair, A.A. and Memmott, J. (2008). *Therapeutic uses of music with older adults*. Silver Spring, MD: American Music Therapy Association.

Clair, A.A., Tebb, S., and Bernstein, B. (1993). The effects of a socialization and music therapy intervention on self-esteem and loneliness in spouse caregivers of those diagnosed with dementia of the Alzheimer's type: A pilot study. *American Journal of Alzheimer's Care and Related Disorders and Research* January/February: 24–32.

Clair, A.A., Bernstein, B., and Johnson, G. (1995). Rhythmic characteristics in persons diagnosed with dementia, including those with probable Alzheimer's type. *Journal of Music Therapy* 32(2): 113–131.

Clair, A.A., Mathews, M., and Koslowski, K. (2005). Assessment of active music participation as an indication of subsequent music making engagement for persons with midstage dementia. *American Journal of Alzheimer's Disease and Other Dementias* 20(1): 37–40.

Cohen-Mansfield, J., Marx, M.S., Thein, K., and Dakheel-Ali, M. (2011). The impact of stimuli on affect in persons with dementia. *Journal of Clinical Psychiatry* 72(4): 480–486. doi: 10.4088/JCP.09m05694oli.

Cohen-Mansfield, J., Marx, M.S., Freedman, L.S., Murad, H., Thein, K., and Dakheel-Ali, M. (2012). What affects pleasure in persons with advanced stage dementia? *Psychiatric Research* 46(3): 402–406. doi: 10.1016/j.jpsychires.2011.12.003.

Cummings, J.L. (1997). The neuropsychiatric inventory assessing psychopathology in dementia patients. *Neurology* 48(5 Suppl 6), 10S–16S

Drapeau, J., Gosselin, N., Gagnon, L., Peretz, I., and Lorrain, D. (2009). Emotional recognition from face, voice, and music in dementia of the Alzheimer type. *Annals of the New York Academy of Science* 1169: 342–345. doi: 10.1111/j.1749-6632.2009.04768.x.

El Haj, M., Fasotti, L., and Allain, P. (2012). The involuntary nature of music-evoked autobiographical memories in Alzheimer's disease. *Consciousness and Cognition* 21(1): 238–246. doi: 10.1016/j.concog.2011.

Else, B. and Wheeler, B. (2010). Music therapy practice: relative perspectives in evidence-based reviews. *Nordic Journal of Music Therapy* 19(1): 29–50.

Erkinjuntti, T. and Gauthier, S. (2009). The concept of vascular cognitive impairment. *Frontiers of Neurology and Neuroscience* 24: 79–85. doi: 10.1159/000197886.

Finkel, S.L., Costa e Silva, J., Cohen, G., Miller, S., and Sartorius, N. (1996). Behavioral and psychological signs and symptoms for dementia: A consensus statement on current knowledge and implications for research and treatment. *Internal Psychogeriatrics* 8(Suppl. 3): 497–500.

Frisoni, G.B., Rozzini, L., Gozzetti, A., Binetti, G., Zanetti, O., Bianchetti, A. et al. (1999). Behavioral syndromes in Alzheimer's disease: Description and correlates. *Dementia and Geriatric Cognitive Disorders* 10: 130–138.

Gagnon, L., Peretz, I., and Fulop, T. (2009). Musical structural determinants of emotional judgments in dementia of the Alzheimer type. *Neuropsychology* 23: 90–97. doi: 10.1037/a0013790.

Garland, K., Beer, E., Eppingstall, B., and O'Conner, D.W. (2007). A comparison of two treatments of agitated behavior in nursing home residents with dementia: Simulated family presence and preferred music. *American Journal of Geriatric Psychiatry* 15(6): 514–521.

Gfeller, K. (2002). Music as communication. In: R.E. Unkefer and M.H. Thaut (eds), *Music therapy in the treatment of adults with mental disorders*, 2nd edn, pp. 42–59. St. Louis, MO: MMB Music, Inc.

Gibbons, A.C. (1977). Popular musical preferences of elderly persons. *Journal of Music Therapy* 14(4): 180–189.

Götell, E., Brown, S., and Ekman, S. L. (2002). Caregiver singing and background music in dementia care. *Western Journal of Nursing Research* 24(2): 195–216.

Götell, E., Brown, S., and Ekman, S.L. (2009). The influence of caregiver singing and background music on vocally expressed emotions and moods in dementia care. *International Journal of Nursing Studies* 46(4): 422–430.

Hall, G.R. and Buckwalter, K.C. (1987). Progressively lowered stress threshold: A conceptual model for care of adults with Alzheimer's disease. *Archives of Psychiatric Nursing* 1: 399–406.

Hart, M. (1990). *Drumming at the edge of magic*. New York, NY: Harper-Collins.

Huang, S.S., Lee, M.C., Liao, Y.C., Wang, W.F., and Lai, T.J. (2012). Caregiver burden associated with behavioral and psychological symptoms of dementia (BPSD) in Taiwanese elderly. *Archives of Gerontology and Geriatrics* 55(1): 55–59. doi: 10.1016/j.archger.2011.04.009.

Katona, C., Livingston, G., Cooper, C., Ames, D., Brodaty, H., and Chiu, E. (2007). International Psychogeriatric Association consensus statement on defining and measuring treatment benefits in dementia. *International Psychogeriatrics* 19: 345–354.

Koger, S.M. and Brotons, M. (2000). Music therapy for dementia symptoms. *Cochrane Database Systematic Review* 3, CD001121. Retrieved from: <http://www.ncbi.nlm.nih.gov/pubmed/10908486>.

Kunik, M.E., Snow, A.L., Davila, J.A., McNeese, T., Steele, A.B., Balasubramanyam, V. et al. (2010). Consequences of aggressive behavior in patients with dementia. *Journal of Neuropsychiatry and Clinical Neurosciences* 22: 40–47. doi: 10.1176/appi.neuropsych.22.1.40.

Lepping, R.C. (2013). Neural processing of emotional music and sounds in depression. Unpublished doctoral dissertation. The University of Kansas, Lawrence, KS.

Maki, Y., Yoshida, H., Yamaguchi, T., and Yamaguchi, H. (2013). Relative preservation of the recognition of positive facial expression "happiness" in Alzheimer disease. *International Psychogeriatrics* 25(1): 105–110. doi: 10.1017/S1041610212001482.

Matsumoto, N., Ikeda, M., Fukuhara, R., Shinagawa, S., Ishikawa, T., Mori, T. et al. (2007). Caregiver burden associated with behavioral and psychological symptoms of dementia in elderly people in the local community. *Dementia and Geriatric Cognitive Disorders* 23(4): 219–224.

McDermott, O., Crellin, N., Ridder, H.M., and Orrell, M. (2013). Music therapy in dementia: A narrative synthesis systematic review. *International Journal of Geriatric Psychiatry* 28(8): 781–794. doi: 10.1002/gps.3895.

Mathews, R.M., Clair, A.A., and Kosloski, K. (2001). Keeping the beat: Use of rhythmic music during exercise activities for the elderly with dementia. *American Journal of Alzheimer's Disease and Other Dementias* 16(6): 377–380.

Meeks, S., Young, C.M., and Looney, S.W. (2007). Activity participation and affect among nursing home residents: Support for a behavioural model of depression. *Aging & Mental Health*, 11(6): 751–760.

Monastero, R., Mangialasche, F., Camarda, C., Ercolani, S., and Camarda, R. (2009). A systematic review of neuropsychiatric symptoms in mild cognitive impairment. *Journal of Alzheimer's Disease* 18: 11–30. doi: 10.3233/JAD-2009-1120.

Miyamoto, Y., Tachimori, H., and Ito, H. (2010). Formal caregiver burden in dementia: impact of behavioral and psychological symptoms of dementia and activities of daily living. *Geriatric Nursing* 31: 246–253. doi: 10.1016/j.gerinurse.2010.01.002.

Neary, D., Snowden, J., and Mann, D. (2005). Frontotemporal dementia. *The Lancet Neurology* 4(11): 771–780.

Omar, R., Hailstone, J.C., Warren, J.E., Crutch, S.J., and Warren, J.D. (2010). The cognitive organization of music knowledge: A clinical analysis. *Brain* 133(Pt 4): 1200–1213.

Omar, R., Rohrer, J.D., Hailstone, J.C., and Warren, J.D. (2011). Structural neuroanatomy of face processing in frontotemporal lobar degeneration. *Journal of Neurology, Neurosurgery, and Psychiatry* 82(12): 1341–1343. doi: 10.1136/jnnp.2010.227983.

Omelan, C. (2006). Approach to managing behavioural disturbances in dementia. *Canadian Family Physician* 52(2): 191–199.

Otto, D., Cochran, V., Johnson, G., and Clair, A.A. (1999). The influence of background music on task engagement of frail, older persons in residential care. *Journal of Music Therapy* 36(3): 182–195.

Raglio, A., Oasi, O., Gianotti, M., Manzoni, V., Bolis, S., Ubezio, M.C. et al. (2010). Effects of music therapy on psychological symptoms and heart rate variability in patients with dementia: A pilot study. *Current Aging Science* 3(3): 242–246.

Rocca, P., Leotta, D., Liffredo, C., Mingrone, C., Sigaudo, M., Capellero, B. et al. (2010). Neuropsychiatric symptoms underlying caregiver stress and insight in Alzheimer's disease. *Dementia and Geriatric Cognitive Disorders* 30: 57–63. doi: 10.1159/000315513.

Ridder, H.M., Stige, B., Qvale, L.G., and Gold, C. (2013). Individual music therapy for agitation in dementia: An exploratory randomized controlled trial. *Aging and Mental Health* 17(6): 667–678. doi: 10.1080/13607863.2013.790926.

Robb, S.L., Burns, D.S., and Carpenter, J.S. (2011). Reporting guidelines for music-based interventions. *Journal of Health Psychology* 16(2): 342–352. doi: 10.1177/1359105310374781.

Seitz, D. P., Brisbin, S., Herrmann, N., Rapoport, M. J., Wilson, K., Gill, S. S. et al. (2012). Nonpharmacological interventions for neuropsychiatric symptoms of dementia in long term care: A systematic review. *Journal of the Medical Directors Association* 13(6): 503–506.

Sung, H.C. and Chang, A.M. (2005). Use of preferred music to decrease agitated behaviours in older people with dementia: A review of the literature. *Journal of Clinical Nursing* 14(9): 1133–1140.

Thaut, M. (2002.) Psychomusical foundations of music therapy. In: R.F. Unkefer and M.H. Thaut (eds), *Music Therapy in the Treatment of Adults with Mental Disorders*, pp. 2-69, 2nd edn. St. Louis, MO: MMB Music, Inc.

Thaut, M. (2005). *Rhythm, Music, and the Brain*. New York, NY: Routledge.

Ueda, T., Suzukamo, Y., Sato, M., and Izumi, S.I. (2013). Effects of music therapy on behavioral and psychological symptoms of dementia: A systematic review and meta-analysis. *Aging Research Reviews* 12(2): 628–641. doi: 10.1016/j.arr.2013.02.003.

Vink, A.C., Birks, J.S., Bruinsama, M.S., and Scholten, R.J. (2004). Music therapy for people with dementia. Cochrane Database Systematic Review (3): CD003477. Retrieved from: <http://www.ncbi.nlm.nih.gov/pubmed/15266489>.

Wall, M. and Duffy, A. (2010). The effects of music therapy for older people with dementia. *British Journal of Nursing* 19(2): 108–113.

Wetzels, R.B., Zuidema, S.U., de Jonghe, J.F., Verhey, F.R., and Koopmans R.T. (2010). Course of neuropsychiatric symptoms in residents with dementia in nursing homes over 2-year period. *The American Journal of Geriatric Psychiatry* 18: 1054–1065.

World Health Organization (2012). *Dementia: A public health priority*. Geneva, Switzerland: World Health Organization. Retrieved from: <http://www.who.int/mental_health/publications/dementia_report_2012/en/>.

Zuidema, S.U., de Jonghe, J.F., Verhey, F.R., and Koopmans, R.T. (2010). Environmental correlates of neuropsychiatric symptoms in nursing home patients with dementia. *International Journal of Geriatric Psychiatry* 25: 14–22. doi: 10.1002/gps.2292.

CHAPTER 21

....

MUSIC THERAPY
IN GRIEF AND MOURNING

....

CLARE O'CALLAGHAN AND NATASHA MICHAEL

INTRODUCTION

....

> I cry a lot to that song which is really odd, because it's a really fast pace ... I really
> love it. He sings about like the waves crashing down, the tears going down the face
> ... It's a good song to cry to. (19-year-old female with cancer.)
>
> O'Callaghan et al. 2012, p. 691

In traditional societies almost everyone participates in music making, usually within daily
life. Traditional ceremonial music often involves the supernatural and community participation to promote health and shared ways of dealing with loss and death. In Western more individualistic societies, music commonly signifies formalized vocal or instrumental sounds,
performed by people ascribed as *musicians* and heard by audiences (Dissanayake 2006) or
through technological transmission. Although music plays a diminishing role in *modern*
health care (Biesele and Davis-Floyd 1996) *everyday* music activities continue to help west-
erners deal with loss (DeNora 2012), notably through private use (O'Callaghan et al. 2013).
Music therapists are increasingly helping people to mourn and deal with grief. This chapter
describes music therapists' work with people mourning losses associated with life changing
or threatening conditions and bereavement, that is, loss through death. The term *mourning*
emphasizes the public expressions of grief, while the term *grief* focuses on the intrapsychic,
emotional experience of real, perceived, or anticipated loss. While there is overlap between
the terms, mourning is influenced by one's beliefs, cultural norms, and traditions (National
Cancer Institute 2012). Throughout this paper, music therapy illustrations will reinforce how
music therapists can enable *mourning music* in clinical and community contexts in which
people may struggle to find ways to helpfully mourn, where *mourning music* is "music listened to or composed to commemorate a death or loss, or otherwise used to express feelings
associated with grief and bereavement" (Stein 2004, p. 791).

WHAT IS MUSIC THERAPY AND ITS ROLE IN MOURNING?

Music therapy can be defined as the professionally informed and creative use of music in a therapeutic relationship with people identified as needing biopsychosocial or spiritual help, or who desire increased self-awareness, to further their life satisfaction and quality. Music therapists focus on the therapeutic process rather than musical products. Participants do not have to have a musical background to benefit (O'Callaghan 2010). Music therapy is distinguished from music thanatology which is the provision of "prescriptive music, using harp and voice at bedside" with the compassionate musician's presence (Cox and Roberts 2007, p. 80). In music therapy patients and/or families are invited to explore and choose from a range of music therapy methods and processes. This may encompass familiar music listening or performances, creative explorations with unfamiliar music, and guided usages of music (O'Callaghan 2010). More specific details are in Table 21.1.

Music therapy provides opportunities for participants to experience thoughts and feelings which, within the therapeutic relationship, can enable catharsis, support, reframing, and/or integration of the loss within one's altered identity and life. Imagery and music may also elicit symbolic or dream-type material which can enable non-verbal means of working through loss experiences. Elicited imagery can be further considered through verbal or art based modalities via which the loss maybe creatively encountered and mourned.

Bereavement theory acknowledges that dealing with profound loss can encompass an adaptive process of oscillating between confronting and avoiding grief tasks (Stroebe and Schut 1999).

Table 21.1 Music therapy processes and how they may provide therapeutic opportunities for mourning

General processes	Usages
Familiar music listening or performing by therapist and/or participant which encompasses loss themes and associated feelings	Music-based counseling
Lyrical analysis
Lyric substitution in familiar songs or instrumental music.
Music based life review, e.g., audio, visual and/or textual recordings of one's reminiscences and significant reflections; playlists of significant musical milestones.
Creative explorations with unfamiliar music	Song writing
Music improvisation
Guided usages of music	Relaxation and/or guided imagery inductions with music
Bonney Method of Guided Imagery and Music
Music-based legacy creation	Song compositions
Music-based audio-visual recordings
Music and esthetic experience	Therapeutic music lessons
Music appreciation
Environmental music therapy: music in institutional settings to promotes patient, visitor, and staff interaction and well-being (Aasgaard 1999)
Music performances/concerts involving patients and families

Arguably this also relates to people grieving non-death related losses. People who are mourning need opportunities to seek refuge from grief's intense, sometimes wrenching visceral states, and cognitive experiences. Music therapy relaxation, and other creative and accessible processes, can provide a refuge from distress associated with mourning. Music can enrich life and promote acceptance. One 23-year-old male with cancer said: "It might be the end but you know there's still a lot of good stuff going on…. you've got music there … if I die … this is still good now…. You realize that you can enjoy stuff and … at that moment it's good." (O'Callaghan et al. 2012, p. 692.)

OVERVIEW OF MOURNING WITHIN MUSIC THERAPY

> The song was more helpful than the empty words to the bereaved—probably the tune can mediate the emotions in more subtle ways than words and thus be more consoling.
>
> Saresma 2003, p. 612

Throughout music therapists' work there are opportunities to support patients and families dealing with life changing events, including developmental, mental health, oncological, and degenerative neurological conditions, or traumatic injuries. For example, parents often struggle when their child does not meet developmental milestones and need to adjust their expectations (Barnett et al. 2003). Music therapy sessions targeted at families with infants with a disability can promote parents' mental health and parent-child communication skills (Williams et al. 2012). In mental health settings Bright (1999) has used music therapy to support people mourning lost or damaged relationships, personal health, or a stillborn baby where "Familiar music … often helps to bring suppressed thoughts and feelings to the surface" (p. 488). The therapist can then offer counselling to assist adjustment when these feelings appear.

Within music improvisation, the music therapist and participant may play together on tuned[1] (e.g. keyboard, xylophone) or untuned (e.g. drums, rain sticks) instruments, and also vocalize. Participants can play improvised music to indicate how one feels. The premise is that clients creatively express aspects of themselves through the musical improvisation. Therapists' improvisations reflect or mirror and support the participants' music to affirm that the participants have been heard and are known. The shared musical explorations can be enjoyable, freeing, extend participants' creative musical play, which can transduce into new and potentially adaptive ways of apprehending the world.

Careful assessment of participants' reactions in music therapy is essential to enable helpful mourning experiences, that is, the feeling of support, relief, and strength to encounter loss related distress. People react to music therapy in myriad ways. Magee and Davidson (2004) examined the role of music therapy with six adults who had multiple sclerosis resulting in moderate to severe physical disabilities and mild to cognitive impairment. Participants were involved in a mean of ten individual music therapy sessions over six months. Data included participant interviews and the music therapists' reflections. Findings indicated that participants' attachment to pre-composed songs was one of the only constant relationships in their increasingly isolated lives. Improvisation could also be cathartic, improve mood, and affirm musical skill development. Participants mourned their illness related losses, while music therapy could still facilitate a reconstituted identity. Nonetheless, improvisation could also remind of former functional capacities (Magee and Davidson 2004). Constant reminders of loss when struggling with improvisation may be more distressing than helpful and another method may need to be offered if distress at functional losses is expressed or observable. Hence music therapists need to constantly assess and tailor sessions according to participants' abilities and preferences.

Adults with mental disorders have also used song writing to express, and likely mourn, losses (Grocke et al. 2009). For example, lyrics from a song writing group living with severe mental illnesses included, "Now he wanders alone, got no place to call home, ... he's so scared inside.... there's just no one he can lean on" (Grocke et al. 2009, p. 444). Song writing in music therapy can proceed in various ways, for example: (a) The participant (or group) considers a topic and then brainstorms lyrical ideas—the therapist may encourage their free association through offering prompts and questions; (b) the therapist and participant transforms the ideas into song lyrics; (c) the participant is invited to suggest musical elements (melody, harmony, etc.) or is offered musical choices; and (d) the song is recorded (O'Callaghan et al. 2009), preferably with participant involvement. Both the lyrics and melody can express one's mourning, for example a wailing tritone—a harsh sounding musical interval—was selected by one cancer patient for the lyric "helpless."

Participants with traumatic brain injury (TBI) have also used song writing to mourn and adjust. In a lyrical analysis of 82 songs written by people with TBI, participants expressed feelings related to pain, isolation, dependency, helplessness, anger, and poor self-image. Grief was related to loss of connections with important people and events in previous lives, as well as losses in family, workplace and social roles. Additionally changes in cognitive, communicative and physical functions, and identity and financial security were reflected (Baker et al. 2005). Music therapists can also help patients mourning such losses through assisting the patients' families to promote their life quality. This can include focusing on improving educational, social, and parenting skills, along with rehabilitation and stress reduction (Davis et al. 1999; Edwards 2011).

Music therapists increasingly support communities in mourning immediately following disaster, aiming to reduce isolation, and promote "normalcy" and positive experiences. For example, after the 2008 Sichuan earthquake in China, which killed approximately 70,000 people, a music therapy educator took three teams of music therapy students to provide music performances and activities to survivors and relief workers, and music classes for children returning to schools. Research which examined the educator's and students' reflections about this work revealed that earthquake survivors of all ages can benefit from activities offered by music therapy students through having opportunities to relax, reflect, emote, learn, exercise, socialize, and share positive times with families and local communities. Arguably the survivors and relief workers mourning devastating losses were helped because the music was an esthetic reminder of hope for improved lives (Gao et al. 2013).

MUSIC THERAPY, MOURNING, AND PALLIATIVE CARE

> The song brought comfort to my life, the song showed me the path back to life. The song helped me in my sorrow more than any words. And as death changes life, it also changed the message of that song.
>
> Sirpa, in Saresma 2003, p. 612

Palliative care is an approach that improves the quality of life of patients and their families experiencing life threatening illness. It aims to prevent and relieve suffering by treating physical, psychosocial, and spiritual problems, affirming life, and helping the family cope (World Health Organization 2008). There are numerous descriptions of how palliative care music therapists integrate mourning music into their work, that is, help patients,[2] and families express feelings related to advancing illness, grief, bereavement, and to commemorate loss (Dileo and Loewy 2005; Hilliard 2005; Magill 2009, Munro and Mount 1978; O'Callaghan 2010). The music therapist's focus is always on how mourning within music therapy can assist patients to have better quality moments, a peaceful and meaningful death, and support family members' coping. Music therapists may work in diverse ways with people with end-stage illnesses. For example some use more improvisational based work while others use more song writing, relaxation, familiar music, and/or verbal based techniques. All music therapists, nonetheless, are connected by a belief that music can assist with grief and mourning (Lee 1995).

Music therapists typically receive referrals from multidisciplinary team members, patients, their families, or through "case finding," that is, offering music therapy as time allows. As patients' conditions fluctuate, sessions are flexibly scheduled, vary from minutes to over an hour, and are offered on a one off basis or regularly. Patients may participate in individual or group-work music therapy in individual or multibed rooms, or in studios or day hospice settings. The first author usually takes an electric piano and sheet music which includes about 7000 pieces that she can immediately play. Many music therapy departments also incorporate extensive music libraries, audio equipment, and instruments which patients and families can borrow.

Patients who choose to have music therapy tend to select or create music that reflects memories, people, or feelings they want to connect with. Patients may then reflect on associated thoughts and feelings. Elicited memories often affirm a well-lived life, sometimes juxtaposed with sadness that these experiences will never be lived again. Identifications with loss related lyrics, and musicians perceived to have also experienced loss, can simultaneously enable expression and support for one's mourning. One patient in his forties, for example, said that "Let it be" (a song by the Beatles) would be his life anthem now that he was dying, and recalled a life of hard work, feeling unappreciated, and a lengthy illness thwarting travel plans. Arguably the musical refrain provided a vehicle for this patient to mourn and a coping tool for his diminishing sense of control over his degenerative illness. Hymns and songs that inspire strength may also offer comfort for patients and families dealing with loss. Sometimes however, patients acknowledge music that is too painful to hear: Music may then paradoxically become "a sacred conservatory" where the loss is displaced and silently preserved (Stein 2004, p. 794).

Therapeutic song writing can be used effectively in music therapy with people receiving cancer and palliative care treatments as patients and families can quickly express the essence of their feelings, thoughts, and messages in a contained manner, including those which are difficult to verbalize (Heath and Lings 2012; O'Callaghan et al. 2009). Patients with cognitive impairment can also be involved when therapists provide sufficient structure to help them to participate to their maximum potential. By offering multiple choices of lyrics, melodies, and harmonies to people with word finding and short-term memory difficulties song writing can be facilitated. The musical accompaniment can reinforce emotional meaning of the text and, because music is a mnemonic, patients and families can more easily remember the song. Repeatedly sounding these songs can also be cathartic and comforting. For example, before she died a mother said that she had heard her daughter repeatedly playing the song that she (the mother) had composed. The lyrics included: "Once I could give pleasure … now it's all gone … time's needed to adjust … discover and actualize all lying inside of me." It is plausible that the daughter used the song to comprehend and release grief associated with her mother's deterioration.

Music therapists have analyzed lyrics written in their palliative care sessions and used theory to substantiate speculated therapeutic outcomes. Analysis of 64 songs' lyrics written by 39 palliative care patients revealed adverse experiences associated with advanced illness in seventeen percent (eleven) of the songs, and grief related to missing family, home, and former life in eight percent (five songs) (O'Callaghan 1996). Another analysis of songs written by 27 cancer in-patients for their children uncovered descriptions of the parents' distress related to missing their children, anticipatory grief about leaving children, a desire that their children understand their need "to go," their hopes for the children, suggestions about who the children can turn to when they are not available, and how they can be remembered (O'Callaghan et al. 2009).

Patients can also set their lyrics to familiar songs or classical melodies. For example, one mother wanted to write a song for her four-year-old son to help him mourn and cope after she died. As his favorite song was "Twinkle Twinkle" she set her words to this melody, including, "Mum lives in a star she's always there for you, whenever you need me look up at the sky." It is suggested that therapeutic song writing offers parents a means of creating developmentally accessible ways to remain connected with their children during their illnesses, and supports the child's adaptive mourning if a parent dies, as positive reminders of the deceased help those left behind (Raphael 1984). This is particularly important work because there is little information about how health workers can support parents receiving palliative care and their children (Saldinger et al. 2004).

Bereaved children and adolescents have also composed songs expressing grief and loss, and lyric analyses of songs written by pediatric cancer patients uncovered themes which included hope, coping, family support, physical status, and humor (studies reviewed in O'Callaghan and Grocke 2009). This indicates that song writing can also help young people to mourn and deal with aversive treatment experiences. A meta-analysis of controlled studies examining the effectiveness of various methods for bereaved children and adolescents also found that music therapy was one of the most "promising treatment models" (Rosner et al. 2010, p. 99). Hilliard (2001) conducted a controlled trial examining grief therapy comprising eight music therapy sessions with bereaved children (n = 18). Techniques included singing, rap-writing, improvisation, drumming, lyrics analysis, song writing, and music listening. The focus of the therapeutic process was on identifying emotions, understanding grief and cognitive reframing. Music therapy group participants displayed significantly reduced grief symptoms and behavioral problems compared to the control group. McFerran et al. (2010) included responses of sixteen adolescents who had (mostly) experienced deaths of family members and attended group music therapy for support. Methods used in the study included song writing, musical improvisation, and song listening and discussion. Groups, which involved up to fourteen weekly sessions, gave participants helpful permission to grieve, release feelings, experience reduced stress, and/or reduce isolation.

MUSIC THERAPY, MOURNING, AND LEGACY WORK

Legacies can be tangible products that patients create in sessions for a specific purpose, and include patients' recorded song compositions prefaced with significant messages, as well as music-based life reviews whereby dying patients leave information and messages to those left behind (Hogan 1999). They may support the bereaved and also assist the creators to prepare for death. For example, after composing and recording a song for his two children a dying parent said, "I think they know that I love them, but now I know that they will always know."

Music therapy legacies can include both these tangible artifacts as well as session memories. These can also enable mourners to have comforting connections with the deceased (O'Callaghan et al. 2013). For example, in research examining the role of music and music therapy for bereaved caregivers of people who had died from cancer, one participant reflected on how music therapy sessions helped him to express messages to his wife which would have been otherwise difficult. Families' positive memories with dying patients can also help the bereaved (O'Callaghan 2013). This can be described as "preloss care" (Magill 2009). Given that one's relationship with the deceased affects how people cope in bereavement (Mancini et al. 2009), it follows that families' experiences of patients' advancing illnesses also influence how they grieve and mourn. Bad memories of patients' palliative care are associated with negative reactions while good care is associated with more positive reactions (Reid et al. 2006).

In music therapy, preloss care is evident when families request music for the palliative care patients which express lyrical messages or elicit memories which convey what they want the patient to feel and know. For example, songs requested from courtships can lead to shared "knowing" eye contact, touching, singing, and dancing. Such embodied memories can elicit emotions and connections that verbal memories likely cannot (DeNora 2012). The multiple messages which can be interpreted in music allow families and friends with shared music histories to experience unspoken and meaningful moments that no-one else can be privy to. These memories may be later relived in mourners' imaginations, shared discussions, and embodied expressions, including art and craftwork. One bereaved wife for example, knitted a sweater with images from memories of music therapy sessions shared with her husband before he died from motor neuron disease. Music therapy can thus help grieving family members mourn, reintegrate, and continue their bonds with the deceased through visual, kinesethic, and sound memories, and music-based activities (O'Callaghan et al. 2013). Memories of music therapy conducted with children can also give bereaved parents "something to hang on to" (Lindenfelser et al. 2008, p. 339).

Although music therapists aim to support mourning and assuage grief, it is plausible that a deceased person's legacy may intensify grief and distress associated with an unsatisfying relationship. Different attachment styles with the deceased variably affect grief reactions (Mancini et al. 2009). Therefore some family members may need to loosen or relinquish bonds with the deceased in order to adjust (Stroebe et al. 2010). Music therapists need to further examine the effect of legacies created by dying patients on those who will mourn them, and to consider that they may not always be appropriate. Similarly, patients may be disappointed with how their legacies are received. For example, a patient with advanced illness composed a song about his love for his wife, and hope for more happy times together.

However, the wife did not like the song. He later told the therapist that he had tried his best and "couldn't do anything else." The therapist offered support as the patient mourned the loss of hope for a better spousal relationship.

CONCLUSION

> I'd cry and cry and then I'd feel a bit better ... You almost know you're going to be in pain, so in a way you try not to (listen to son's funeral music) but then there's some days when you can't help it, because it's just a comfort.
>
> O'Callaghan et al. 2013

Mourning music connects people with emotions related to loss, memories, and images in a creative and contained time frame. Each time a piece of music is experienced, the perceiver "composes a new work" (McAdams 1984). Therefore, mourning music allows people to apprehend loss in altered forms, and potentially allows emotional release, self-soothing, new awareness, and strength to move onward. Throughout our communities, people use music in idiosyncratic ways for self-care. The above mentioned mother, for example, locked herself in her car to listen to her deceased son's music. Music therapists often work, however, with patients too physically, cognitively, developmentally, or mentally vulnerable to use words or music to effectively mourn, and are dealing with families struggling to develop or maintain connections with loved ones affected by serious conditions or trauma. Music therapy offered through a therapeutic relationship can help many of these patients and families through: Supporting cathartic release; being a vehicle for continuing and reworking bonds with who and what is mourned; helping the rebuilding of grief affected lives; affirming lifetime contributions; and legacy creation.

Grief and mourning reactions vary amongst individuals within and across social and cultural groups. Music therapists use varied, individualized, flexible, patient- and family-centered, and evidence-based approaches to help people mourn. Music usage to alleviate human loss is threaded throughout civilization. In modern health care, music therapists endeavour to continue this tradition, exploring and enabling opportunities for mourning music to promote individual and community coping and well-being.

NOTES

1. Tuned instrument improvisation can be easily introduced to many participants through the pentatonic scale: only playing black notes on a piano sound harmonious together.
2. Patients instead of participants is used in this section when music therapy is described with in-patients, day hospice patients, or people received home based palliative care services.

REFERENCES

Aasgaard, T. (1999). Music therapy as milieu in the hospice and paediatric oncology ward. In: D. Aldridge (ed.), *Music Therapy in Palliative Care: New Voices*, pp. 29–42. London: Jessica Kingsley Publishers.

Baker, F., Kennelly, J. and Tamplin, J. (2005). Themes with songs written by people with traumatic brain injury: Gender differences. *Journal of Music Therapy* 42(2): 111–122.

Barnett, D., Clements, M., Kaplan-Estrin, M., and Fialka, J. (2003). Building new dreams: Supporting parents' adaptation to their child with special needs. *Infant Young Child* 16(3): 184–200.

Biesele, M. and Davis-Floyd, R. (1996). Dying as a medical performance: The oncologist as charon. In: C. Laderman and M. Roseman (eds), *The Performance of Healing*, pp. 291–322. New York: Routledge.

Bright, R. (1999). Music therapy in grief resolution. *Bulletin of the Menninger Clinic* 63(4): 481–498.

Cox, H. and Roberts, P. (2007). From music to silence: An exploration of music-thanatology vigils at end of life. *Spirituality and Health International* 8(2): 80–91.

Davis, W.B., Gfeller, K.E. and Thaut, M.H.A. (1999). *An Introduction to Music Therapy Theory and Practice*, 2nd edn. Boston: McGraw-Hill Co Inc.

DeNora, T. (2012). Resounding the great divide: Theorising music in everyday life at the end of life. *Mortality* 17(2): 92–105.

Dileo, C. and Loewy, J. (eds). (2005). *Music Therapy at the End of Life*. Cherry Hill NJ: Jeffrey Books.

Dissanayake, E. (2006). Ritual and ritualization: Musical means of conveing and shaping emotion in humans and other animals. In: S. Brown and U. Voglsten (eds), *Music and Manipulation: on the Social Uses and Social Control of Music*, pp. 31–56. Oxford and New York: Berghahn Books.

Edwards, J. (ed.) (2011). Music Therapy in Parent-infant Bonding, pp. 191–207. Oxford: Oxford University Press.

Gao, T., O'Callaghan, C., Magill, L., Lin, S., Zhang, Ju., Zhang, Ji., et al. (2013). A music therapy educator and undergraduate students' perceptions of their music project's relevance for Sichuan earthquake survivors. *Nordic Journal of Music Therapy* 22(2): 107–130.

Grocke, D., Bloch, S., and Castle, D. (2009). The effect of group music therapy on quality of life for participants living with a severe and enduring mental lillness. *Journal of Music Therapy* 46(2): 90–104.

Heath, B. and Lings, J. (2012). Creative songwriting in therapy at the end of life and in bereavement. *Mortality* 17: 106–118.

Hilliard, R. (2001). The effects of music therapy-based bereavement groups on mood and behaviour of grieving children: A pilot study. *Journal of Music Therapy* 38: 291–306.

Hilliard, R. (2005). *Hospice and Palliative Care Music Therapy: A Guide to Program Development and Clinical Care*. Cherry Hill, Jeffrey Books.

Hogan B. (1999). Music therapy at the end of life: Searching for the rite of passage. In: D. Aldridge (ed.), *Music Therapy in Palliative Care: New Voices*, pp. 68–81, London: Jessica Kingsley Publishers.

Lee, C. (1995). *Lonely waters: Proceedings of the International Conference, Music Therapy in Palliative Care*. Oxford: Sobell Publications.

Lindenfelser, K., Grocke, D., and McFerran, K. (2008). Bereaved parents' experiences of music therapy with their terminally ill child. *Journal of Music Therapy* 35: 330–348.

Magee, W. and Davidson, J. (2004). Music therapy in multiple sclerosis: Results of a systematic qualitative analysis. *Music Therapy Perspectives* 22(1): 39–51.

Magill, L. (2009). Caregiver empowerment and music therapy: Through the eyes of bereaved caregivers of advanced cancer patients. *Journal of Palliative Care* 25: 68–75.

Mancini, A.D., Robinaugh, D.A., Shear, K. and Bonnana, D.A. (2009). Does attachment avoidance help people cope with loss? The moderating effects of relationship quality. *Journal of Clinical Psychology* 65(10): 1127–1136.

McAdams, S. (1984). The auditory image: A metaphor for musical and psychological research on auditory organization. *Advances in Psychology* 19: 289–323.

McFerran, K., O'Grady, L. and Roberts, M. (2010). Music therapy with bereaved teenagers: A mixed methods perspective. *Death Studies* 34: 541–565.

Munro, S. and Mount, B.M. (1978). Music therapy in palliative care. *Canadian Medical Association Journal* 119: 1029–1034.

National Cancer Institute (2012). Grief, bereavement, and coping with loss.<http://www.meb.uni-bonn.de/Cancernet/CDR0000062821.html>. Retrieved 7th January, 2013.

O'Callaghan, C. (1996). Lyrical themes in songs written by palliative care patients. *Journal of Music Therapy* 33(2): 74–92.

O'Callaghan, C. (2010). The contribution of music therapy to palliative medicine. In: G. Hanks, N. Cherny, N. Christakis, M. Fallon, S. Kaasa, and R. Portenoy (eds), *The Oxford Textbook of Palliative Medicine*, 4th edn., pp. 214–221. Oxford: Oxford University Press.

O'Callaghan, C. (2013). Music therapy preloss care through legacy creation. *Progress in Palliative Care* 21: 78–82.

O'Callaghan, C. and Grocke, D. (2009). Lyric analysis research in music therapy: Rationales, methods, and representations. *Arts in Psychotherapy* 36: 320–328.

O'Callaghan, C., Barry, P., and Thompson, K. (2012). "One of my friends": Music's relevance for adolescents and young adults with cancer. *Support Care Cancer* 20: 687–697.

O'Callaghan, C., O'Brien, E., Magill, L., and Ballinger, E. (2009). Resounding attachment: Cancer inpatients' song lyrics for their children in music therapy. *Support Care Cancer* 17(9): 1149–1157.

O'Callaghan, C., McDermott, F., Hudson, P., and Zalcberg, J. (2013). Sound continuing bonds with the deceased: The relevance of music, including preloss music therapy, for eight bereaved caregivers. *Death Studies* 37: 101–125.

Raphael, B. (1984). *The Anatomy of Bereavement*. Melbourne: Hutchinson & Co Ltd.

Reid, D., Field, D., and Relf, M. (2006). Adult bereavement in five English hospices: Participants, organisations and pre-bereavement support. *International Journal of Palliative Nursing* 12(7): 320–327.

Rosner, R., Kruse, J., and Hagl, M. (2010). A meta-analysis of interventions for bereaved children and adolescents. *Death Studies* 34(2): 99–136.

Saldinger, A., Cain, A., Porterfield, K., and Lohnes, K. (2004). Facilitating attachment between school-aged children and a dying parent. *Death Studies* 28: 915–940.

Saresma, T. (2003). "Art as a way to life": bereavement and the healing power of arts and writing. *Qualitative Inquiry* 9: 603–620.

Stein, A. (2004). Music, mourning, and consolation. *Journal of American Psychoanalytic Association* 52: 783–811.

Stroebe, M. and Schut, H. (1999). The dual process model of coping with bereavement: Rationale and description. *Death Studies* 23: 197–224.

Stroebe, M., Schut, H., and Boerner, K. (2010). Continuing bonds in adaptation to bereavement: Toward theoretical integration. *Clinical Psychology Review* 30(2): 259–268.

World Health Organization (2008). WHO definition of palliative care. <http://www.who.int/cancer/palliative/definition/en/>. Retrieved 13 October, 2012.

Williams, K.E., Berthelsen, D., Nicholson, J.M., Walker, S., and Abad, V. (2012). The effectiveness of a short-term group music therapy intervention for parents who have a child with a disability. *Journal of Music Therapy* 49: 23–44.

APPROACHES AND MODELS OF MUSIC THERAPY

CHAPTER 22

··

APPROACHES AND MODELS
OF MUSIC THERAPY

··

JANE EDWARDS

APPROACHES AND MODELS

··

THE development of music therapy internationally has been characterized by the founding of multiple *models* of practice, as well as the development of *approaches* that practitioners apply in their work. Inclusion criteria for the eleven models and approaches presented in the Oxford Handbook of Music Therapy are that each is taught as a major part of music therapy training in at least one programme in the English-speaking world, and that the model or approach has a presence in the published literature with at least one monograph or edited book outlining foundational theory, practice principles, and techniques. Additional criteria included that a trainer or researcher in the model or approach was available to write the material, and that training in the model or approach is offered at entry level to the profession. Some of the models and approaches included such as Developmental Music Therapy, are founded on principles that are integrated into many music therapists' practice whereas others, such as Nordoff-Robbins Music Therapy (Nordoff and Robbins 1977), require specialist qualifications in order to achieve recognition as an expert practitioner.

Some well-known models of music therapy, for example the Bonny Method of Guided Imagery and Music (BMGIM) (Bruscia and Grocke 2002), and Neurologic Music Therapy (NMT) (Thaut and Hoemberg 2014) have not been included in the approaches and models section of the Oxford Handbook of Music Therapy, although an overview of BMGIM is provided in a different section (Grocke this volume). One of the reasons these models are not included is that, as per the above criteria, this text is primarily aimed at the needs of students and new practitioners. BMGIM is a training process undertaken through completing a series of *levels* of competency (Bonny 2002). The introductory level of BMGIM is offered in some music therapy courses but most practitioners undertake further training in BMGIM after their accreditation as a music therapist. BMGIM training is also available to people who are not qualified as music therapists. NMT is also offered at the graduate level, and training for non-music therapists is available. An OUP Handbook has been dedicated to NMT (Thaut and Hoemberg 2014).

In consultation with the authors of the models and approaches section of the Oxford Handbook of Music Therapy (Edwards this volume), it was decided to use the terms *models*

Table 22.1 Models and approaches in music therapy.

Models	Approaches
Nordoff-Robbins music therapy	Feminist perspectives
The field of play	Psychodynamic music therapy
Community music therapy	Developmental music therapy
Resource-oriented music therapy	Anthroposophical music therapy
Culture-centered music therapy	
Aesthetic music therapy	
Vocal psychotherapy	

and *approaches* to describe the eleven traditions of practice represented even though some are perhaps best described as *perspectives*, for example the feminist approach. For the purposes of this chapter, a model can be considered unique to music therapy, and an approach is one in which an established tradition of therapeutic practice or theory outside of music therapy has been integrated within music therapy techniques and methods. Using this criteria the models and approaches chosen for this book are categorized in Table 22.1.

Each of the models and approaches emphasizes or illuminates an aspect of music therapy deemed to be important by the model's founders such as musical, sociocultural, relational, and behavioral, or cause-response dimensions; and all models and approaches reference and emphasize each of these factors in some way. The coherence of an approach or model is not particularly evident from descriptions of its techniques and methods—which are often similar across music practices in music therapy, education, and community arts—but rather can be seen in the way the approach or model explains the role of music, the role of the therapist, and the processes in the work.

In the remainder of the chapter an outline of key features of each of the models and approaches listed in Table 22.1 will be presented. For a more comprehensive reading of these, the relevant chapters in the Oxford Handbook of Music Therapy (Edwards this volume) should be consulted. Methods and techniques are not elaborated here and wider reading is needed to source the ways in which the models and approaches are enacted in practice.

NORDOFF-ROBBINS MUSIC THERAPY

Paul Nordoff and Clive Robbins began providing therapeutic music sessions for children in special education services in the late 1950s (Nordoff and Robbins 1977; Guerrero et al. this volume). Paul Nordoff was a composer for 25 years before he became a pioneer in the field of music therapy (De'Ath 2013). Clive Robbins was a special educator working with children with disabilities when they began their collaboration (Hadley 2003).

> Their partnership began in 1959 at Sunfield Children's Homes in Worcestershire, England, and they worked together for approximately 16 years in Europe and the United States. In 1975, formal training in Nordoff-Robbins music therapy began at the newly opened Nordoff-Robbins Music Therapy Centre in London. In the same year, Clive Robbins formed a new music

therapy team with his wife Carol Robbins (1942–1996). The Robbinses continued to develop and disseminate the Nordoff-Robbins approach to music therapy, and in 1990 established the Nordoff-Robbins Center for Music Therapy at New York University's Steinhardt School of Culture, Education, and Human Development.

(this volume)

A feature of the model is that it is primarily *music-centered* (Aigen 2014). Aigen has explained that "in music-centered music therapy, the mechanisms of music therapy process are located in the forces, experiences, processes, and structures of music" (Aigen 2014, p. 18). Many countries offer training based on the Nordoff-Robbins model, and training workshops for qualified practitioners from other approaches are also offered internationally.

THE FIELD OF PLAY

The field of play was developed by Carolyn Kenny (Kenny this volume), who is well known for her contribution and research in the area of indigenous studies as well as music therapy. She has described the field to which the title of the model refers as a:

> ... river that constantly flows beneath our various methods of practice, we can accept the grounded energy of the river, which flows without effort. Too often, we take the river for granted or forget about it entirely. This river of being holds the greatest gifts for our patients and clients because it is our presence, our being, and our very existence. If we accept this river, then we can do or try our work as part of a natural process in an ecology of being.

Kenny this volume

This ecology of practice is reliant on the practitioner accepting the importance of self-awareness, not just of one's psychological state including feelings and moods, but of the wider cultural and social context through which they have developed their values and world outlook. Practitioners must make an effort to understand the conscious and unconscious values they holds as a result of their developmental and cultural context because this is a key to being present to the real experience of others. It is important that therapists suspend their judgement as to what a human life should be like (Kenny 2003).

Valuing the need for therapists to engage their own potential and capacities provides a pathway to journeying with clients as they explore and attain their own potentiality. As Carroll (2010) has indicated in her reflection on the applicability of the field of play in music therapy education:

> We all have an inner drive to know and reach our potential. I envision inner drive as a spark that needs to be fuelled through meaningful activity that is goal-oriented, resource-rich, cul-turally sensitive and socially-mediated.

Carroll 2010, np

The field of play has applications for every music therapy practitioner even if they do not employ it as their primary model of practice. For the mature practitioner, revisiting the field of play can offer further riches through prompting consideration of the self and other in interaction towards integration.

COMMUNITY MUSIC THERAPY

Community music therapy seeks to honor and elaborate practices in music therapy that involve inclusive and collaborative interactions between practitioners and their clients. Stige (2002) has described the model as founded from multiple developments across four decades in Germany, Norway, and the UK. One of the founding reference points for community music therapy is *social music therapy*, developed by German pioneer Christoph Schwabe (Stige 2002) which emphasized communal rather than individualized human experience in society. Responding to the misperception that it is a model that refers to work in community or non-clinical contexts, Stige described *community* when referred to within community music therapy as "no longer being just a context to work *in* but also a context to work *with*" (Stige 2002, np).

Stige and Aarø (2011) have described how: "Community music therapy encourages musical participation and social inclusion, equitable access to resources, and collaborative efforts for health and wellbeing in contemporary societies" (p. 5). Some aspects of Community Music Therapy can be observed to represent dissatisfaction with music therapy traditions and practices; seeking to foster new and emergent practices (Stige 2002).

Some early proponents of community music therapy anticipated an adversarial relationship between the model and what was described as the *consensus model* of music therapy; that is, established contemporary music therapy practice. Minimal critique was afforded to the polarizing of community music therapy against this the *consensus model*. This perhaps slowed the understanding of community music therapy as offering a unifying clarion call to music therapists navigating new health care service contexts where music therapy models founded on older institutional and pathology-treatment perspectives were found wanting when new and dynamic perspectives entered mainstream health care.

RESOURCE-ORIENTED MUSIC THERAPY

Rolvsjord developed the resource-oriented approach to music therapy (Rolvsjord 2007, 2010). She described how:

> … engagement with these elaborations grew from recognition that a gap existed between the perspectives presented in the literature about music therapy in mental health, and my own practice of music therapy in this clinical context.
>
> Rolvsjord 2007

Her theoretical rationale for resource-oriented music therapy was informed from interdisciplinary perspectives including empowerment philosophy, the common factors approach, positive psychology, and current musicology (Rolvsjord 2010). She wrote:

> A resource-oriented approach can be described as: (1) Involving the nurturing of strengths, resources and potentials; (2) involving equal collaboration rather than intervention; (3) viewing the individual within their context; and (4) seeing music as a health resource.
>
> Rovsjord this volume

Resource-oriented music therapy focuses on positive health and the importance of positive emotions and experiences as part of therapeutic processes. This positivity is emphasized across a range of psychotherapeutic approaches (Seligman and Csikszentmihalyi 2014; Lopez et al. 2014). Perspectives from musicking (Small 1998), and sociology of music (DeNora 2000), also inform resource-oriented music therapy.

CULTURE-CENTERED MUSIC THERAPY

Brynjulf Stige developed culture-centered music therapy as a way to bring together existing ways of working in and thinking about music therapy practice (Stige this volume). His inspiration in developing this model was primarily the work of music therapists Carolyn Kenny and Even Ruud along with the influence of cultural psychology. He has suggested that culture is "the accumulation of customs and technologies enabling and regulating human coexistence" (Stige 2002, p. 38) using *accumulation* to recognize that culture always involves change and exchange. *Customs* is used to refer to activities and rituals as well as ways of thinking and feeling. The technologies referred to in this definition include physical apparatus' and symbolic tools such as language and music. One of the main ideas communicated by this definition, is that culture makes human life possible, in positive and negative ways:

> ... culture is what happens when people spend time together; they act and they interact, they produce artifacts and they use artifacts, and they do this as they make rules and break rules, if only to make new rules. Culture then is shaping people and shaped by people, in conscious and non-conscious ways, some of the latter being related to human nature...
>
> Stige 2002, p. 38

A key tenet of culture-centered music therapy is the idea of participation. That is, disabling structures within societies and communities, which can be attitudes or physical spaces, prevent participation. The role of music therapy is to consider how a person's opportunities can be enabled by music participation.

AESTHETIC MUSIC THERAPY

Aesthetic Music Therapy (AeMT) is considered a music-centered theory (Lee this volume). The model was developed by Colin Lee during the time he worked as a music therapist with people living with AIDS. Aigen (2005) has described that music-centered thinking in music therapy falls into two distinct categories: Therapists who consider music-centeredness central to their practice, for example, Nordoff-Robbins and AeMT, and those who consider music-centeredness as just one aspect of their practice, for example Community Music Therapy and Guided Imagery and Music. In the latter, words may be used to describe and interpret the musical phenomena, and in the former the music itself can be the means to understand the therapeutic process. Lee understands music-centered practice as relevant and being able to be adapted to all clinical approaches (this volume). Considering the intent within musical processes is the key, rather than focusing on specific clinical interventions with specific therapeutic goals as in some types of traditional music therapy practice.

AeMT considers clinical practice from a musicological, philosophical, and compositional perspective, reflecting on the musical dialogue between client and therapist as the main basis for assessment. Interpretation comes from an understanding of the musical structures. The development of clinical musicianship and musical science is at the heart of AeMT and includes an understanding of listening, esthetics, composition and the balance between musical and clinical forms. Understanding the building blocks of clinical-musical structures is essential to AeMT. AeMT promotes the view that the quality of music in therapy, whatever theoretical approach is in operation, is fundamental. AeMT does not advocate a dismantling of extra-musical theories, but rather, it proposes that the consideration of the esthetic quality of music as a way to further expand contemporary clinical theories.

VOCAL PSYCHOTHERAPY

Diane Austin developed vocal psychotherapy through her work in private practice in New York. As an accomplished jazz singer the voice was central to her experience of music therapy as a trainee, and subsequently in her work with clients. At the core of vocal psycho-therapy is the use of the voice and singing to explore the life world of the client as part of a therapeutic process. Vocal psychotherapy is indicated when poor vocal quality of speaking or singing is linked to recent trauma, or to neglectful and abusive childhood experiences.

The physical and psychological benefits of deep breathing are part of the foundation for the work undertaken in vocal psychotherapy. "Breath is the basis of life itself. Life begins and ends with a breath." (Austin this volume). The sounding of the voice is reliant upon breath. "As long as we are emotionally protective our breathing cannot be free ... the voice will depend on compensating strength in the throat and mouth muscles" (Linklater 1976, p. 12). The physiological and the psychological effects of breathing occur in reciprocity. Building awareness of the breath by loosening constriction of the throat, chest, or abdomen can realign the connection to feelings, and dramatically affect the quality of both the speaking and singing voice in a positive way (Austin 2008).

In vocal psychotherapy it is understood that deep breathing slows the heart rate and calms and nurtures the nervous system of the body. Making natural sounds and movements as well as toning (Keyes 1973) can increase awareness of the breath and bodily sensations while also providing an outlet for emotions through spontaneous vocal expressions. As the founder of vocal psychotherapy has noted: "Many clients are amazed by the sometimes childlike or primal sounds that emerge, intuitive and instinctual sounds that have been long repressed because there was no safe space in which to make them." (Austin this volume.)

FEMINIST PERSPECTIVES

The feminist approach in music therapy (Hadley and Hahna this volume) has been explained by many practitioners and theorists (for example, Baines 2013; Curtis 2012;

Edwards and Hadley 2007; Hadley 2006). In this approach the foundational principles of feminism are used to understand contexts of practice and the ways in which peoples' needs are defined and framed in such contexts. The development of various feminist movements arose from concerns about the social and political subjugation of women which at various times in history in the developed world have seen women paid less than men for the same work, lacking access to the vote, or being prevented from working or taking equal part in society in one or more ways. Therefore a common misconception is that only women can be feminists, but feminism is a way of perceiving the world and the needs of communities that can be productively shared and embraced by people of any gender who value the benefits of equality for all (Edwards and Hadley 2007).

Multiple perspectives exist within feminism. It is a broad theoretical and practical approach in which culture, race, politics and social class are critiqued and re-valued. A feminist sensibility promotes the idea that many groups in society, especially those marginalized by stigma relating to disease or disability, are severely disadvantaged in relation to dominant groups whose members conform to societal norms and have access to unseen privilege (McIntosh 1998). The music therapist working within the feminist approach is an activist and advocate for the groups with whom she or he works (Baines 2013). The role of music therapy is not simply to invite participation and to offer support to clients, but to also enable their emancipation (Hadley 2006).

PSYCHODYNAMIC MUSIC THERAPY

Psychodynamic music therapy is founded on psychoanalysis, which was originally developed by Sigmund Freud. His first psychoanalytic publication *Traumdeutung* (The Interpretation of Dreams) appeared in 1900. Since that time, psychoanalysis has undergone multiple differentiations, revisions, and developments (Metzner this volume). The basic underlying assumption in psychodynamic music therapy is the existence of dynamic processes in an unconscious mind, which has an influence on intrapsychic and interpersonal processes within and outside of the musical activity between the therapist and patient (Metzner this volume). The therapeutic relationship is distinguished by the attentiveness of the music therapist to his or her own reactions, feelings, fantasies, and ideas, known as countertransference, which are triggered by the patient's transference. Psychodynamic music therapy proposes that with the assistance of music, human beings can become aware of their inner states, and can communicate these through performed musical expression. From a psychoanalytic viewpoint, music is considered to portray meaning and to give the individual the feeling of being mirrored, accompanied, and even personally understood.

Clinical applications of psychodynamic music therapy are found mainly in mental health, psychosomatics, and in an adapted manner in special education. The research into practices and outcomes is primarily undertaken using qualitative methods. Training for competency in this work requires developing skills through learning theoretical and practice considerations and committing to personal therapy experiences in group and/or individual settings in order to understand therapeutic processes from an experiential perspective.

DEVELOPMENTAL MUSIC THERAPY

Developmental music therapy (DMT) has three main theoretical orientations: (1) Theories of stress, coping, and adaptation; (2) human life span development, including stage models of development, and musical milestones of development; and (3) ecological perspectives such as Bronfenbrenner's bioecological model of development (Bronfenbrenner 1995). DMT can be described as eclectic and opportunistic in terms of its wider theoretical breadth. Developmental perspectives can be found many descriptions of clinical work where clinicians use aspects of developmental theory to elaborate and explain the rationale for their practise (for example, Edwards 2005).

Edith Boxill termed her approach developmental music therapy (Boxill 1985), and hers is the strongest contribution to this approach within the field of music therapy. She developed her DMT ideas based on her extensive music therapy work with people who have developmental disabilities. By combining her professional experience along with humanistic ideas, and psychobiological insights Boxill showed how music making could develop sensitive and reciprocal contact between the client and therapist, as well as promoting the client's sense of self, other, and the environment.

ANTHROPOSOPHICAL MUSIC THERAPY

The founder of anthroposophy Rudolf Steiner (1861–1925) is probably best known in contemporary times as the founder of the Waldorf or Steiner schools. According to Uhrmacher:

> Anthroposophy can be thought of in two ways. First, it is a path of self-development for those who wish to follow Steiner's direction toward spiritual development and cognition. According to Steiner, through specific types of meditation, human beings can directly perceive the spirit world. Second, Anthroposophy is also the fruit from Steiner's ideas and methods. Biodynamic farming, Anthroposophic medicine, eurythmy, and Waldorf schools are a few of the results of Steiner's spiritual knowledge. People who embrace Steiner's ideas refer to themselves as Anthroposophists, and one may refer to them collectively as belonging to the Anthroposophical movement.
>
> Uhrmacher 1995, p. 402

Anthroposophical music therapy (AnMT) developed through Steiner's *curative education*, which was applied in therapeutic communities for people with disabilities established in many countries of the world (Intveen this volume). Training in AnMT is available in several countries including Germany and the USA (Intveen this volume).

AnMT is unique in its understanding of the way in which tonalities and in particular types of scales have an effect on the human organism. Additionally, the timbre and *character* of certain instruments is key to techniques that are applied in this approach. There are many instruments unique to AnMT such as the lyre and the choroi (Intveen has outlined these aspects of AnMT in a number of papers, for example, Intveen (2010), Intveen and Edwards (2012)).

CONCLUSION

As can be observed through the models and approaches described above, there are multiple ways that music therapy has developed as a field of practice. Each of the founders of the models and approaches above began their quest for describing and naming a type of work because there was a gap observed in the theory and framing of current practices. Some of these models and approaches will continue to develop and be expanded and some will likely lose favor or begin to decline in interest, either because they become increasingly similar to other approaches or because a newer iteration is elaborated with changed nomenclature that becomes popular. This is normal in the development of a field and should be welcomed. However, it is to be anticipated that critical responses to new ideas arise to help refine the field of music therapy, and to appraise its relevance and contribution to education, health care, and community services. At the same time being able to acknowledge the historical foundations of music therapy practice traditions is a key value in becoming a mature and maturing profession.

The challenge for music therapy practitioners is to found their work theoretically without being too dogmatic about a model or an approach, since dogmatism can limit new developments and thwart expressive and creative thinking. Nonetheless, just being able to apply the methods and techniques of music therapy does not a practitioner make. The foundation and guidance of theory strengthens understanding of processes in the work, and allows the practitioner to tolerate difficult moments, and challenges. Commitment to a theoretical framework allows thinking about *why* something is occurring, and it supports the practitioner to be patient, flexible and open when there is confusion or uncertainty about the ways in which a client or service user is describing their experiences, or when it is not clear what the therapist might be able to do or offer next.

Without theory music therapists only have their own limited experience to guide them. It could be argued that music therapists are then only as capable as any music enthusiast to be available and responsive to the needs to the people served through respectful collaboration in music therapy practice. Music therapy training requires learning about theory within the parameters of at least one model or approach, and this engagement must be thorough and intensive. Trainees may initially struggle with having to do so much thinking and analyzing of their own reactions and integration of key theoretical concepts in the first instance at a time when they want to improve their techniques and methods. Ultimately good enough training allows students to first comprehend, perhaps even somewhat self-consciously, and eventually internalize, the theoretical basis of their professional thinking in practice.

REFERENCES

Aigen, K. (2005). *Music-centered music therapy*. Gilsum, NH: Barcelona Publishers.

Aigen, K. (2014). Music-centered dimensions of Nordoff-Robbins Music Therapy. *Music Therapy Perspectives* 32(1): 18–29.

Austin, D.S. (2008). The theory and practice of vocal psychotherapy: Songs of the self. London: Jessica Kingsley Publishers.

Baines, S. (2013). Music therapy as an anti-oppressive practice. *The Arts in Psychotherapy* 40: 1–5.

Bonny, H.L. (2002). Body listening: A new way to review the GIM tapes. *Nordic Journal of Music Therapy* 11(2): 173–177.

Boxill, E.H. (1985). *Music Therapy for the Developmentally Disabled.* Texas: Pro-Ed Inc.

Bronfenbrenner, U. (1995). Developmental ecology through space and time: A future perspective. In: P. Mohen, G.H. Edler, and K. Luscher (eds), *Examining Lives in Context: Perspectives on the Ecology of Human Development*, pp. 619–647. Washington DC: American Psychological Association.

Bruscia, K.E. and Grocke, D.E. (eds). (2002). *Guided Imagery and Music: The Bonny Method and Beyond*, Vol. 1. Gilsum, NH: Barcelona Publishers.

Carroll, D. (2010). The Field of Play in music therapy education. In: *Voices: A World Forum for Music Therapy*, Vol. 10, No. 2.

Curtis, S.L. (2012). Music therapy and social justice: A personal journey. *The Arts in Psychotherapy* 39: 209–213.

De'Ath, L. (2013). "A sun among men": The EE Cummings songs of Paul Nordoff. *Journal of Singing* 69: 307.

DeNora, T. (2000). *Music in everyday life.* Cambridge: Cambridge University Press.

Edwards, J. (2005). The role of the music therapist in working with hospitalized children. *Music Therapy Perspectives* 23: 36–44.

Edwards, J. and Hadley, S. (2007). Expanding music therapy practice: Incorporating the feminist frame. *The Arts in Psychotherapy* 34: 199–207.

Hadley, S. (2003). Meaning making through Narrative Inquiry: Exploring the Life of Clive Robbins. *Nordic Journal of Music Therapy* 12(1): 33–53.

Hadley, S. (ed.). (2006). *Feminist Perspectives in Music Therapy.* Gilsum, NH: Barcelona Publishers.

Intveen, A. (2010). "The piano is a wooden box with false teeth"—Perspectives in anthroposophical music therapy as revealed through interviews with two expert practitioners. *The Arts in Psychotherapy* 37: 370–377.

Intveen, A. and Edwards, J. (2012). The history and basic tenets of anthroposophical music therapy. In: *Voices: A World Forum for Music Therapy* [Online], 12. Available: <https://normt.uib.no/index.php/voices/article/view/646/548> Accessed 22 June, 2012.

Kenny, C.B. (2003). Beyond this point there be dragons: Developing general theory in music therapy. In: *Voices: A World Forum for Music Therapy*, Vol. 3, No. 2.

Keyes, L.E. (1973). *Toning: The creative power of voice.* Los Angeles: DeVorss.

Linklater, K. (1976). *Freeing the Natural Voice.* London: Drama Publishers.

Lopez, S.J., Pedrotti, J.T., and Snyder, C.R. (2014). *Positive psychology: The scientific and practical explorations of human strengths.* London: Sage Publications.

McIntosh, P. (1998). White privilege: Unpacking the invisible knapsack. *Race, class, and gender in the United States: An integrated study* 4: 165–169.

Nordoff, P. and Robbins, C. (1977). *Creative Music Therapy: Individualized Treatment for the Handicapped Child.* New York: John Day Company.

Rolvsjord, R. (2007). *"Blackbirds Singing": Explorations of Resource-Oriented Music Therapy in Mental Health Care.* Unpublished Ph.D., Institut for Kommunikation, Aalborg Universitet, Aalborg.

Rolvsjord, R. (2010). *Resource-oriented music therapy in mental health care.* Gilsum, NH: Barcelona Publishers.

Seligman, M.E. and Csikszentmihalyi, M. (2014). Positive Psychology: An Introduction. In: *Flow and the Foundations of Positive Psychology*, pp. 279–298. Netherlands: Springer.

Small, C. (1998). *Musicking*. Hannover, NH: University Press of New England.

Stige, B. (2002). *Culture-Centered Music Therapy*. Gilsum, NH: Barcelona Publishers.

Stige, B. and Aarø, L.E. (2011). *Invitation to Community Music Therapy*. London: Routledge.

Thaut, M.H. and Hoemberg, V. (eds). (2014). *Handbook of Neurologic Music Therapy*. Oxford: Oxford University Press.

Uhrmacher, P.B. (1995). Uncommon schooling: A historical look at Rudolf Steiner, anthroposophy, and Waldorf education. *Curriculum Inquiry* 25(4): 381–406.

CHAPTER 23

FEMINIST PERSPECTIVES IN MUSIC THERAPY

SUSAN HADLEY AND NICOLE HAHNA

INTRODUCTION

THIS chapter presents an overview of the developments of feminist perspectives in music therapy. The history of feminism in music therapy is outlined with many of the key early proponents of the approach introduced. There are many different definitions of and approaches to feminism. In fact, a more inclusive term to encapsulate the diversity of thought in the field is *feminisms* (Enns 2004). The diversity of feminist perspectives within the theory and practice of therapy is an essential component in understanding its use within the clinical setting. As such, feminist therapy has often been described as a *lens* or a *framework*, instead of a single unifying approach. Although some authors do identify their approach as *feminist music therapy* many see feminism as one contributing perspective within their work. Therefore, for the purposes of this chapter, the term feminist informed music therapy will be used to honor the wide variety of practice and personal definitions within this approach.

Next, the basic tenets of feminism are described, which include the importance of valuing women's perspectives, egalitarianism, collaboration, mutuality, examining social constructs, examining the flow of power in relationships, examining discursive practices, representation, and empowerment. Drawing upon work by various music therapists, we examine how feminist music therapists have approached assessment, treatment, evaluation, research, ethics, supervision, and education. Finally, we outline areas that need to be further addressed in music therapy, based upon a feminist framework. Thus, we highlight inequities that exist in the field of music therapy, including gender inequities for women in the field, problematic aspects of how we define and understand the process of therapy and the therapeutic relationship, ways in which music perpetuates a culture's biases, and more liberatory research and educational practices.

HISTORICAL OVERVIEW

The incorporation of feminist perspectives in music therapy has, until recently, been limited. Elsewhere proposals as to why this has occurred have been presented (Hadley and Edwards

2004; Edwards and Hadley 2007). Although feminist approaches to music therapy have to date had limited representation, it is significant that feminism is now being included as a major approach within the field of music therapy practice and research (McFerran 2010; Abrams 2010, Bruscia 2012).

Since feminism is considered to be a grassroots movement, there is no single founder or unified approach to feminist informed music therapy. Instead, it operates as an emerging theory with multiple perspectives and sources of ideas. A number of key figures in the development of feminist informed music therapy can be identified chronologically. Heineman (1982) was one of the first music therapists to research gender role socialization and sex-role stereotypes. In her research she explored why there was an "underrepresentation of women in supervisory and administrative positions in the field of music therapy" (p. 20). Surveying 195 music therapists, Heineman found significant differences between men and women in four out of fifteen statements measuring career aspirations, and in two out of fifteen statements measuring perceived career success. She noted that gender difference found for each of these statements was consistent with societal stereotypes. Significantly more women than men agreed that their spouse's career took precedence over their own, that when they had children they would stop working or work part-time, that they did not expect to work until retirement age, and that they did not envision themselves supervising other music therapists (pp. 30–31). Heineman concluded:

> There are forces operating in our society which define rigid roles for both women and men. The same barriers which exist to prevent women from holding supervisory positions also exist to prevent men from being successful in a helping profession. It would seem that there is a need in our educational process to encourage individual achievement rather than sex-stereotypes roles.
>
> (Heineman 1982, p. 32)

In a similar study, Curtis (1990) surveyed 836 women music therapists with questions that examined role models, awareness of bias (in general and in their own work situations), the effects of gender-role stereotyping, and general satisfaction with the profession of music therapy. She found that "[t]he most prominent concerns ... were inadequate salary and lack of advancement opportunities, leisure time, time or money for continuing education, prestige, and professional recognition" (pp. 61–62). As a result of her research findings, Curtis expressed her hope that through open dialogue women would become more aware of how they experience gender bias and, when denying its existence, how they are contributing to its perpetuation. She expressed her desire that such dialogues will inspire women to become advocates for change.

Another music therapist who was comparatively early in engaging feminist theory was Baines (1992). She was one of the first music therapists to describe feminist therapy in detail. In her Masters thesis, she encouraged music therapists to use sociological and political perspectives to understand their work in order to become aware of sexist biases, to accept the clients' perceptions as the most valid, and to establish egalitarian relationships with their clients. Drawing on anti-racist and feminist thought, Baines noted that "feminist framing assists in building a more ethically sensitive practice that involves itself in the personal problems of the client as well as the social problems that often cause, exacerbate, or reinforce the oppression, disempowerment, and individual pain of the client" (p. 2). In this study, Baines examined the sociocultural and political implications of music therapy and envisioned the possibilities of it "as a force for positive global change in the coming century" (p. 3). This groundbreaking paper heralded the role of music therapy as a means toward social change.

Also drawing on the principles and practices of feminist therapy, Curtis (2000) developed a specific model of feminist informed music therapy for the empowerment of women, specifically for increasing the self-esteem of women who have been abused by their intimate male partners. Her model integrated principles and practices of existing feminist therapy with those of music therapy. In this model, she advocated the use of innovative techniques of feminist analysis of power and gender-role socialization through lyric analysis and song writing to work on goals such as increasing empowerment, increasing self-esteem, increasing independence, examining oppression, valuing women's experiences, and examining gender roles.

Around the turn of the century, several music therapy scholars were describing the significance of feminist theory on their perspectives. For example, Ruud (1998) described feminism as one of his main theoretical influences, and later discussed its influence in his thinking on relationality, empowerment, reflexivity, and other postmodern currents (Ruud 2010). Similarly, Rolvsjord (2010) used feminist theory to develop the *resource-oriented music therapy* model, which de-emphasized a medical, symptom-based approach to music therapy and encouraged client empowerment. Hadley and Edwards (Hadley and Edwards 2004; Edwards and Hadley 2007) have described the ways in which feminist perspectives can help music therapy as a profession openly to question and elucidate some of its own hidden assumptions.

Along with the growing body of literature about feminist perspectives in music therapy, there has been a growing concern about gender inequities within the profession of music therapy. Critiquing a claim by James (1985) of more parity between males and females publishing articles in the music therapy literature, Curtis (2000) urged music therapists to view James' conclusion in relation to the ratio found within music therapy since there are far fewer male music therapists and yet they are the lead authors for half of the published articles in music therapy. Edwards and Hadley (2007) further examined issues of gender inequities in music therapy in the United States in terms of educational attainment, average salaries, academic rank, employment positions, publishing rates, and positions on publishing boards.

Concerned with the lack of publications addressing feminist perspectives in music therapy, Hadley (2006a) invited a group of women music therapists to write about how they understood the relationship between feminism and music therapy. At the time of writing this chapter, this book is the only major text in music therapy that focuses on feminism and feminist perspectives in practice, teaching and research. In this book the reader can find some of the major themes of feminism elaborated. In particular, many of the authors showed how feminist theory is inextricably linked to their own life journey, including their spiritual and cultural traditions and experiences. A small selection of these chapters will be described in the section that follows.

The chapters in the first section are clustered around the sociological themes that they explored. Adrienne (2006) applied ideas of feminist sociologists to the field of music therapy envisioning a way of practicing music therapy which takes into account sociological and feminist values. McFerran and O'Grady (2006) explored the potential of community music therapy, practiced within a feminist worldview, to free itself and its agents from the oppressive potential of therapy, society, and the self. They suggested that the value of a feminist community music therapy is that it works with people within the context of their *gendered* social, cultural, and political environments. Kenny (2006) and Goldberg (2006) presented feminist perspectives which are tied in with spirituality, the former in terms of an indigenous ecological worldview and the latter related to an African Goddess tradition.

Kim (2006) described the centrality of Han (sorrow and anger that grows) in the lives of Korean women because of their oppressive life circumstances. She described the circumstances of traditional Korean women, and provided a brief overview of the feminist movement and feminist therapy in Korea. Kim also provided a brief overview of the role of music in healing and therapy in traditional Korean society, including shamanistic rituals and folk music of healing. Finally, she explored the suitability of music as a form of expression in therapy for Korean women and suggested various music therapy methods that would work well for a feminist orientation within Korean music therapy. Similarly, Lee (2006) explored feminist music therapy in Taiwan. She provided a brief overview of the role of music in healing in Taiwan, distinguishing between the indigenous, Chinese, and Western cultural traditions. Shamanism and folk medicine were prominent in the traditional approaches, and the role that women played in these rituals was central. In addition, Lee explored what would be required for the formation of feminist oriented music therapy in Taiwan.

The second section of the book includes chapters focused on feminist perspectives in clinical work and will be discussed below in the procedures section. The third section of the book focused on significant aspects of music therapy: discourse, music, music therapy techniques/approaches, and issues of representation. Rolvsjord (2006) examined the use and functions of the language we use in music therapy—how we talk and write about music, clients, pathology, the therapeutic relationship, and gender or relationships. A central theme in her chapter is focusing on gender politics within music therapy and the implications of this. Her work is inspired by postmodernist and poststructuralist feminist traditions, specifically the French feminist tradition, which focuses on language and power-relations in language.

Examining song selection for women's empowerment in music therapy, Jones (2006) suggested that it is crucial that we not only consider client preference, and the relevance of lyric content to client issues and treatment needs, but that we consider the significant impact of the larger environment/society on the welfare of our clients. She suggested that it is our responsibility as music therapists to become aware of the sexist subtext found in much of the popular music we use in music therapy sessions—both the overt and covert messages which contribute to the ways clients view themselves and/or their attitudes about and behaviors toward women.

Exploring issues of representation in our profession, Streeter (2006) explored the idea that the rise of capitalism has led to competitiveness which ultimately has led to the branding of various marketable products, including music therapy. She noted that we have now defined many separate approaches to music therapy, within which we separate out and name distinct techniques. This branding allows groups of practitioners access to a specific theoretical and therapeutic marketplace and allows students to shop around for a brand they like before starting a training course. However, it can also lead to protection of the brand and perhaps to a fundamentalism arising from the branding, which has the potential to impede the profession and diminish the possibility for positive social change.

Exploring issues of representation of women more generally, Edwards explored ways we can improve as music therapists, not only in terms of greater acknowledgement of the achievements of women music therapists, but also in terms of how clients' bodies are viewed by themselves or others. She also encouraged music therapists to examine the broader systemic issue of discourse regarding health and illness and how these are formed and framed by patriarchy, in our understandings of gender and sexuality. She further encouraged music therapists to examine how women are represented in music, and in hearing the voices of, and advocating for, those whose perspectives may have been discounted or silenced by the majority culture.

The chapters in the final section of the book focused on specific areas of training in music therapy: pedagogy, supervision, assessment, research, and ethics.

More recently, there have been several publications exploring feminism, pedagogy, and music therapy (Hahna and Schwantes 2011; Hahna 2011, 2013). In order to gain a more informed picture of the views and use of feminist pedagogy and feminist music therapy by music therapy educators in the United States, Hahna and Schwantes (2011) conducted a survey of music therapy educators to determine if they identified as feminist music therapists as well as if they utilized components of feminist pedagogy in teaching music therapy. A majority of participants reported using aspects of feminist pedagogy in their teaching (67 per cent) however only 46 per cent of respondents self-identified as feminist music therapists. For a more in-depth understanding of the use of feminist music therapy pedagogy, Hahna (2011) interviewed four music therapy educators about their lived experiences using a feminist music therapy pedagogical practice. The results of this study indicated that feminist theory was an integral philosophy for the music therapy educators interviewed, which manifested within the classroom, within themselves, and within their communities. A strong identity formation grounded in feminist theory as well as an intentional and personal sense of moral obligation towards social justice was a theme that was prevalent for all four of the music therapy educators interviewed. Viewed as a practice, feminist music therapy pedagogy "is a theory set into action—it is a living, breathing phenomena that the music therapy educator embodies through 'aspiration'" (p. 206).

Following the publication of the edited collection of work on feminist perspectives in music therapy (Hadley, 2006a), a number of perspectives were shared in reviews of the book. Nicol (2010) noted that the book is not one that will appeal to everybody. She described it as "discomforting and provocative" (p. 199). She also raised many of the controversial aspects inherent in the book, such as: Why are there no male writers? Why do we need this book? Am I feminist enough to contribute to it? O'Callaghan (2007) noted the irony "that a consequence of promoting feminist discourse in music therapy is that, arguably, a new hegemony is potentially formed" (p. 80). However, she went on to state that "the emphasis on reflexivity in this text, alongside an openness to the multiple lenses through which music therapy phenomena can be viewed, arguably creates a site where one's professional assumptions can be challenged, and subjugated knowledge uncovered" (p. 80).

Meadows (2008) pointed to what he saw as contradictions in the feminist book (Hadley 2006a) by contrasting the views of one author with the views of another. However, feminist theory is by no means a unified standpoint. As Bordo (2003) states, "contemporary feminism remains a diverse and pluralistic enterprise" (p. 216). In emphasizing "contradictions," Meadows actually highlighted one of the tenets of the book which was to provide a "diverse collection of feminist perspectives in music therapy. Meadows believed that the "'incongruities in perspectives' represented within this volume create problems in understanding some dimensions of feminist music therapy" (p. 43). By using the phrase "dimensions of feminist music therapy," he failed to understand that the authors were not espousing a single approach but rather diverse and pluralistic feminist perspectives.

In response to Dileo (2006), who highlighted her reservations about self-disclosure and social activism which are two of the ethical tenets of feminism, Daveson (2007) noted that "this reflection is a welcomed addition in the text, as often the authors seemed able to critique non-feminist viewpoints, but less frequently offered a critique of their own viewpoint when presenting their work" (p. 88). However, Baines (2007) suggested that:

> ... like all aspects of our behavior that impact our clients, the tenets of feminist practice must be completed judiciously. However, the significant rehabilitative effect of empowering one's clients through appropriate self-disclosure is profound. Concurrently, the goal of a safer more inclusive world for both us and our clients inherent in social activism are powerful reasons to move toward a full feminist philosophy of practice. As social barriers are replaced with inclusiveness, won't health and wellness, the fundamental goals of working within the health care establishment, blossom more readily?
>
> (Baines 2007, p. 127)

Another criticism often raised about feminism in music therapy, is that it is too narrow because the focus is only on women. This critique was raised by music therapy survey participants who did not identify as feminist (Hahna and Schwantes 2011). This perspective is valuable because it shows how, for many people, feminism has been learned as a concept that only concerns women whereas feminism actually functions as a critique, as well as a call for the overthrow, of the systemic oppression of the patriarchy which effects everyone. Also, this criticism does not take into account the importance of gender disparities in the music therapy profession, in music therapy discourse, in our clients' lives, and in society more generally. It also points to a more dichotomous understanding of gender as opposed to defining gender as a fluid construct with differences in terms of gender identity and/or expression.

Others, such as Pavlicevic (2007) have suggested that perhaps feminist perspectives are not only too limiting, but also have overlaps with other approaches to music therapy, such as humanism and community music therapy. While there are certainly overlaps, this does not diminish the significance of a specific feminist lens that can be used to view music therapy research, practice, and teaching. For example, humanism does not examine existing systems of oppression and the unequal distribution of power nor does it work towards ending all forms of oppression in a patriarchal society. In fact, it can be argued that the patriarchal understanding of the human is that which is white, male, heterosexual, middle-class, and able-bodied. The current authors do not understand patriarchy as only about the power differentials between men and women, but as critical race feminists suggest, patriarchy is reflected in all instances of the master-slave dynamic (Sajnani 2012). This can be seen in terms of not only gender, but race, class, religion, sexual identity, and ability. Given this, many third wave[1] feminists see the body, in all of its variations, as a site of political and social struggle.

In terms of community music therapy (CoMT), important critical work with a focus on issues of social justice is emerging in the literature. Some of this work has been specifically influenced by feminist theory, for example the work or McFerran and O'Grady (2006). Furthermore, Vaillancourt (2012), explored ways in which community music therapy can contribute to social justice, and suggested that:

... music therapists might need more guidance in pursuing this type of [social justice] work through CoMT. We may need, for example, to increase our knowledge about conflict resolution and social injustice. We could possibly integrate feminist music therapy into training to serve as a framework to address social justice.

(Vaillancourt 2012, p. 177)

Also focusing on an emerging trend of social justice work in music therapy, Curtis (2012) examined some important overlaps between feminist informed music therapy and community music therapy. Growing from her own personal story, she described feminist music therapy as being, by its very nature, a type of community therapy. She believes that it encompasses community music therapy, but also extends beyond its scope, by providing an "explicit feminist analysis of the community" (p. 212). For Curtis (2012):

Feminist music therapy provides a feminist understanding of the complex interaction of multiple oppressions of unjust societies, of power and privilege on one hand and of disempowerment and marginalization on the other. It requires more, however, than understanding, even more than healing the wounds caused by unjust societies; it requires no less than activism for the transformation of those societies.

(Curtis 2012, p. 12)

Growing out of her understanding and integration of ideas from feminist theory and critical analysis, Baines (2013) has exhorted the development and application of "anti-oppressive practices" in music therapy work with clients of all ages, backgrounds, and abilities. Anti-oppressive practice, as outlined by Baines, recognizes that "the power imbalances in our society affect us all" (p. 4). Anti-oppressive practice is "a way of addressing the 'problems' that our clients present within the context of their socio-political reality and resourcing both ourselves, and persons we serve to address social inequity toward the goal of creating a socially just future" (p. 4). Resonating with this stance, Hadley (2013) explored how we are shaped and positioned by dominant/subjugating narratives including patriarchy, Eurocentricism, heterosexism, capitalism, psychiatry/psychology, and medicine. She has explored the ways in which our understandings of ourselves and others are fundamentally shaped by such narratives. She suggested that creative arts therapists may be complicit with these dominant and/or subjugating narratives through our educational and research practices. Finally, she discussed the need for constant vigilance against such dominant/subjugating narratives in order to work towards anti-oppressive practice and social justice.

Basic tenets of feminism as applied to music therapy

There has been a steady increase in the music therapy literature that outlines the application of feminist principles in clinical work. For example, Estrella (2001), Stige (2001), and Dileo (2001) have all referred to aspects of feminist theory in describing how they developed their approaches to supervision. Day and Bruderer (2002) employed feminist principles when providing a space for agency and determination for women abused in childhood who were either pregnant or had young children. In this work, songwriting was utilized to give voice to the experiences of these women—their pain, distrust, anxiety, and their power and determination to live life differently. Chestnut (2004) explored family work in music therapy from a feminist perspective. According to Chestnut, "A feminist approach to family therapy not only empowers individuals but empowers the entire family to live peacefully and equally within itself, with others, and the world" (p. 21). Sharing about their work with women who had experienced intimate partner violence, Hahna (2004) examined the use of the Bonny Method of Guided Imagery and Music (GIM) from a feminist perspective focusing on empowerment, and York and Hearns (2005) incorporated feminist perspectives in their work with women survivors of abuse, which resulted in the development of a performance piece/ethnographic drama.

While there is always room for *diversity of practice* within feminisms, several common themes exist that unify feminist informed music therapists across philosophical and personally meaningful beliefs (Enns 2004, p. 10). These include: (a) believing that the personal is political[2]; (b) striving to create egalitarian relationships; (c) respecting and valuing a person's lived experiences[3]; (d) examining power differentials; (e) consciousness raising; (f) decentering; (g) examining social constructs; (h) valuing diversity and examining the intersection of various identity markers; and (i) working toward social justice (Enns 2004; Worell and Remer 2003). Empowerment is also a central concern, in terms of the process and product of feminist informed music therapy (Jones 2006; Rolvsjord 2004, 2010). While it is never possible to provide a completely equal relationship between two people, a feminist informed therapist analyzes the power imbalances within the therapeutic relationship and makes adjustments as needed:

> Feminist theory demands a critical analysis at the macro level regarding the socioeconomic, cultural, and political forces that impact a particular client, as well as at the micro level of the therapeutic relationship and experience....[making] moment-to-moment considerations within the encounter between therapist and client that provide opportunities not only to avoid the perpetuation of power-over injuries, but also to empower within the relationship itself by encouraging client authority and assertiveness.
>
> (Gentile et al. 2008, p. 73)

Adrienne (2006) and Curtis (2006) both delineated principles for a feminist informed approach in music therapy practice. Applying ideas of sociologists and feminist sociologists to the field of music therapy, Adrienne proposed four principles for a feminist informed music therapy. According to Adrienne, a feminist informed music therapist should: (a) be well trained in the social premises of music and challenge the social functions of music that unconsciously perpetuate gender oppression; (b) practice friendship in music; (c) understand that music out of a bonded community context is dissociative and disembodied; and, (d) work to make music free from the capitalist patriarchal paradigm of economic exchange. Another example of the application of feminist informed principles to music therapy is the work of Curtis (2006). Curtis utilized principles from feminist therapy to transform her practice of music therapy which included: (a) that the personal is political; (b) that interpersonal relationships are to be egalitarian; and, (c) that women's perspectives are to be valued.

Hadley (2006b) and Forinash (2006) both outline principles for feminist informed pedagogy and supervision respectively including openness, collaboration, mutuality, examining biases and assumptions, reflexivity, exploring multiple perspectives, examining authority, awareness of power differentials, advocacy, and activism. In Hadley's exploration of feminist informed pedagogy, she emphasized the importance of "safe-guarding the initial learning environment" to allow students to feel supported as they challenged their own, and society's, notions regarding constructs and identity markers (p. 399). Additionally, Hadley emphasized the importance of moving away from a tradi-tional classroom style, which assumes that the teacher is all knowing and that the student is an empty slate, towards a more collaborative and egalitarian system where the teachers and the students are learner/participants. Forinash explored ways in which the need for social action fits into the supervisory relationship. Regarding the need for advocacy in supervision, she states:

> We should not encourage our supervisees to adjust to the absurd sexist and racist encounters but rather question each instance of sexism and racism that we encounter. This applies not only to supervision and the supervisory relationship, but also to our encounters in the world. The personal is indeed political.

(Forinash 2006, p. 424)

Other authors have examined ways in which we can bring a feminist critique to the pro-fession of music therapy. Using a destabilizing discourse analysis, Rolvsjord (2006) dis-cussed the use of "mother" concepts in music therapy literature and how these contribute to the conservation of traditional expectations of gender roles. Other authors that have written about the importance of feminist critique of constructs, as covered in the previous section, include Edwards (2006) and Streeter (2006).

PROCEDURES USED IN FEMINIST-INFORMED MUSIC THERAPY

Feminist principles are realized through applying core techniques of demystification of all aspects of therapy which involves power analysis in terms of various aspects of a clients' life including the therapeutic relationship, as well as critically examining the socializa-tion process of becoming *male* or *female*. A feminist-informed approach to therapy also includes a critical examination of what society, in accordance with the medical model, defines as a *problem* (Rolvsjord 2010). This requires attention to the bias embedded within traditions of health care, including diagnostic procedures in relation to mental health issues (Enns 2004; Lafrance and McKenzie-Mohr 2013; Shuttleworth 2006; Worell and Remer 2003).

Assessment—Shuttleworth (2006) **has provided an overview of critical perspectives that therapists coming from a multicultural and/or feminist informed perspective have brought to aspects of the assessment process. These include systemic bias from assign-ment of diagnosis from the** *Diagnostic and Statistical Manual* (*DSM*, American Psychiatric Association 2013) and therapist bias in conducting the assessment. Some of the systemic and individual biases Shuttleworth noted included: (a) "language that is culture-bound, includ-ing terms of sexism, ethnocentrism, ageism, ableism, racism, classism, and heterosexism" (p. 432); (b) bias in the assessment towards the life experience of a particular cultural group with the use persons from the majority culture as the definition of "normal"; and (c) ways in which the therapist's beliefs can impact assessment and may lead to "misjudgment about the client" (p. 433). Therapists practicing from a multicultural or feminist informed perspective often advocate for the creation of culturally sensitive assessment tools and culturally responsive diagnoses to address the concerns highlighted by Shuttleworth regarding bias in the assessment process (Enns 2004; Hays 2008; Worell and Remer 2003). In fact, Lafrance and McKenzie-Mohr (2013) point to the *DSM*'s links to patriarchy, pointing out ways in which "the *DSM* can serve to oppress those on the margins of society, while bolstering professional and corporate interests" (p. 122).

Additionally, a feminist informed therapist can engage with the client to help them reframe their current "symptom" as a coping skill and see their "problem" from a systemic viewpoint, instead of solely an intrapsychic phenomenon. Lafrance and McKenzie-Mohr (2013) have argued that "the *DSM* submits persons to Westernized construction of pathology and focuses on the individual in isolation—an especially pernicious problem for those living in oppressive circumstances" (p. 123). Without understanding a client within the context of their culture, it becomes all too easy to blame marginalized persons as opposed to viewing their "symptoms" as a response to the injustice perpetrated upon them by an oppressive culture. For example, when working with a survivor of abuse that has been diagnosed with PTSD, a feminist informed music therapist might highlight the fact that client's experiencing of symptoms related to her abuse is a normal reaction to the experience of abuse, which is about control and oppression. The therapist might also highlight the client's ability to create coping strategies while in the abusive situation, and reframe the symptoms she is experiencing as something that was a key to her survival of the abuse but that is no longer needed as she has left the abusive situation. The therapist could further address systemic issues related to misogyny, helping the client to see ways in which our culture has narrowly defined gender roles and implicitly condones violence against women. A therapist working from a feminist informed model would also work to raise consciousness regarding the oppression of women and work to end violence against women in her own community and the society as a whole.

Treatment—In terms of treatment, feminist informed music therapists are concerned with all aspects of the therapy process and therapeutic relationship, with the aim of "applying the principles of feminist theory to the actual practice of therapy" which can prove to be quite challenging, especially when a feminist therapist is attempting to increase their awareness of personal biases and internalized patriarchy (Hart 2008, p. 9). An important critique from feminist informed therapists of the current health care system in the United States is the examination of who has access to therapy and/or health care, as these are often tied together, and who makes decisions regarding a client's eligibility for services, length of therapy, and/or the goals of therapy. In addition, feminist therapists examine the systemic and/or economic barriers many persons who would like to receive therapy but cannot afford to do so face. Yet another critique of treatment in the United States is the biomedical model as it has been applied to behavioral health which employs a reductionist view of treatment, based upon diagnosis, assessment, and presenting symptoms (Lafrance and McKenzie-Mohr 2013). Once a client has access to therapy, feminist informed therapists examine how language might serve as a barrier between the client and the therapist or perpetuate cycles of oppression (Adrienne 2006; Hart 2008). Finally, the movement towards a capitalistic, or consumer model, of mental health has been criticized by feminist therapists, such as Hart (2008):

> As therapists are increasingly defined as people who are hired to provide services, the sig-
> nificance of therapy as a personal relationship is diminished or rendered invisible … Feminist
> therapists see the alternative to this stance as a view of therapy in which the therapist makes
> a personal investment in both the person and the person's goals when the two decide to enter
> the therapy relationship together.

(Hart 2008, p. 25)

Other important aspects of feminist informed therapy used during the treatment phase include examining how individual problems are related to the social and political context of the person, challenging assumptions of gender constructs, valuing of diversity, reflexivity, giving voice to persons oppressed by the majority culture, viewing women as having agency, and empowering clients (Brabeck and Brown 1997; Enns 2004; Ballou et al. 2008; Rolvsjord 2010; Worell and Remer 2003). Lafrance and McKenzie-Mohr (2013) advocate for a combination of feminist and narrative therapies which "invites a liberatory process of co-authorship: one that emphasizes a collaborative and supportive working relationship, addresses context, and embraces the uniqueness of persons' lives" (p. 135).

Many feminist informed therapists emphasize the importance of being aware of their multiple cultural and social "locations" as an important consideration for clinical work. One such music therapist, Merrill (2006), described her work as a Caucasian music therapist working with a West Indian woman who was recovering from a cerebrovascular accident. The author was cognizant of her experiences as a white woman when working with this woman, who's racial and cultural experiences were foreign to so many of the staff working with her. Some of the more explicitly feminist features of Merrill's work were the significance she placed on reflexivity, her explorations of power and influence, her emphasis on advocacy, being action-oriented, and finding voice (both hers and her client's). Similarly, examining her work through multiple lenses, Purdon (2006) wrote about her clinical and community work in the area of violence against women, particularly with three teen girls who were abused. She described various lenses through which her understandings over her lifespan have been shaped: the "normal childhood" lens, the "traditional music therapist" lens, and the "feminist" informed lens.

Not only concerned with acknowledging multiple "locations" of the therapist and the client, feminist informed music therapists use a variety of techniques. These techniques are developed by the music therapist and are consistent with their experience and understanding of feminisms—there is not a definitive set of feminist informed therapy techniques. Many feminist informed music therapists emphasize collaboration as part of the treatment process, making treatment decisions with the client(s). For example, York (2006) fostered collaboration by encouraging the clients she worked with to share their poems and journals that they wrote outside of the music therapy sessions in a basket placed in the middle of the group circle. She took these entries and incorporated them into songs, which she shared with the group members, encouraging them to provide feedback.

O'Grady (2009) also emphasizes collaboration as a central tenet of feminist informed music therapy. In her research, she employed a grounded theory analysis to explain the therapeutic potentials of creating and performing music within the context of an

Australian maximum-security women's prison. The research involved seven women in prison who collaboratively created and performed a musical together with artists from a theatre company. She found that creating and performing music served as a bridge from the inside to the outside for these women: from physical and symbolic *inside* places to *outside* places; from private to public; from solitude to togetherness; from focus on self to others; and, from subjective to objective thought processes. Her feminist informed framing is seen in the way that she situates herself in the research and in how she understands the complexity of the women in prison. It is also seen in the non-hierarchical relationship with the women.

Feminist informed music therapists also value the experiences of women. Bradt (2006), for example, described her process working with women with chronic pain and how she came to value their experiences of their pain. She used vocal toning, breathing techniques, and vocal improvisation as music therapy techniques in order to help her clients to reconnect to their bodies, and to their emotions. Through music therapy, the women with whom she worked began to feel empowered and began to find their voices.

With the rise of Black feminist thought, Latina/Chicana feminism, Native American/ Indigenous feminism, Asian American feminism, Islamic feminism, and Queer theory/ Lesbian feminism, there has been as a challenge "to address more accurately the intersections of race, ethnicity, gender, class, sexual orientation, geography, language, ability, and a multitude of other social factors and roles" (Villaverde 2008, p. 55). We are beginning to see such critiques emerge in the feminist music therapy literature as well. Kenny (2006) and Goldberg (2006) have described their work utilizing theories from Native American and African traditions, respectively. Also, grounding their feminist informed approaches in non-Western theoretical traditions are Kim (2006) and Lee (2006), who explored Korean and Taiwanese concepts of healing and feminist concerns for women from these cultures. As feminist informed music therapy seeks to give voice to groups that have been marginalized, it becomes increasingly important to cultivate and honor music therapy discourse that addresses intersectionality so that the voices of feminist informed music therapy are diverse and rich.

Evaluation—In terms of music therapy evaluation, feminist informed music therapists look for ways to make the evaluation process collaborative between the therapist and the client. Hahna (2004) facilitated collaborative evaluation by "including the participant's statements and input as well as the researcher's clinical impressions" in documentation of GIM sessions (p. 61). The author made a point to, when possible, include the client in the documentation process and to show the client the notes written by the therapist for transparency. Additionally, "in all instances the participant's view was considered of equal importance to the researcher's [view] as the participant was the expert of her own story, session experience, and personal connection to the imagery" when evaluating important imagery, themes, and client progress over time (p. 61).

This is not to suggest, however, that the therapist does not contribute to the evaluation process. Instead, a feminist informed music therapist aspires to create an egalitarian relationship, which can be used for evaluation of the client's progress.

Feminist informed music therapists also attempt to conduct collaborative evaluations. Both the client and the therapist are seen as having expertise and are encouraged to bring this knowledge to all aspects of the therapeutic process, including evaluation. Feminist informed music therapists also make the evaluation process transparent. This can involve filling out paperwork with the client, often side-by-side, or showing the client reports that have been written by the therapist if the client was not present, as a type of member checking (Hahna 2004). This brings up issues pertaining to music therapy research and ethics, which will be discussed in the following section.

Research and ethics—Feminist researchers have critiqued all aspects of what is considered to be knowledge or research (Minnich 2005; Reinharz 1992). They have challenged the hierarchical aspects of research, the historically patriarchal roots of positivist research (as well as the institutions that continue to promote this), the exclusion of women as either participants in research or as researchers themselves, as well as the failure of patriarchal institutions to conduct research on issues that are central to women's lives. Wheeler (2006) provided an initial overview of feminist informed music therapy research. Rolvsjord and Hadley (forthcoming) have expanded further on feminist and transformative research as it pertains to music therapy. In many ways, feminist informed researchers have used their own research as "a strategic tool for activism and intervening in public and private inequity" (Villaverde 2008, p. 107) by exposing logocentrisim and androcentrism and designing research that is congruent with feminist theory and practice.

Feminist informed guidelines for ethics emphasize the need for feminist therapists to be socially active to end "all forms of oppression and privilege" (Ballou et al. 2008, p. 128). This may be difficult for music therapists that do not have a pre-existing feminist informed or social work background[4] to embrace, as this is not part of most music therapy training syllabi, nor is it listed as part of the codes of ethics for international music therapy organizations.

While ethics codes that emphasize feminist principles have not yet been fully incorporated into the music therapy codes of ethics (Dileo 2006; Wheeler 2006), Hahna (2010) has made a call for such inclusion for Bonny Method Guided Imagery and Music therapists. Examples of other codes of ethics that emphasize social action and feminist principles can be found at the Feminist Therapy Institute (as cited in Ballou et al. 2008).

CONCLUSION

Feminist informed music therapy is still developing and growing within the profession. There are many wonderful possibilities within this approach. We will conclude this chapter by outlining some areas that can be further addressed in music therapy as our critical consciousness as a profession is expanded and sensitized to issues in relationship to the need for inclusiveness, reflection on existing power disparities, and the subjugation of others embedded in the patriarchy.

Gender inequities in music therapy

There are many unsettling statistics in terms of gender inequities in music therapy. Statistics on the disproportionate numbers of males to females: (a) holding advanced degrees in music therapy; (b) holding positions in higher education; (c) authoring articles in peer reviewed journals; and, (d) holding editorial positions with music therapy journals have been outlined in previous publications (Hadley 2006b; Edwards and Hadley 2007), as have the dispropor-tionate salaries for males as compared to females. An examination of systems of privilege/oppression that contribute to such gender disparities in music therapy is encouraged in order to achieve equity in these and other areas of concern.

Understandings of music therapy

It is important to note that many current definitions of music therapy adhere to an illness or disability ideology. The view reflected is that there is a health "problem" that resides in an individual. This requires that the therapist engage in a hierarchical relationship with the cli-ent, *helping* the client by assessing their needs, providing an intervention of treatment, and then evaluating the client's progress. Rolvsjord (2010) critiques the unreflective use of the term *intervention* in music therapy discourse, a term "associated with military language," which "implies that someone from the outside is taking action" and notes that the use of this term is "problematic in a discourse emphasizing equality and mutuality" (pp. 22–23).

So, we need to ask ourselves, how does the way that we practice therapy reinforce patriar-chal systems? How do we see ourselves as experts? How do we understand the people with whom we work? How do we understand illness/health, disability/ability? What are the goals that drive us in our work? Who establishes these? How do we understand the therapeutic relationship? In what ways does our form of practicing music therapy function as a means to social conformity?

Power in and of music

A perpetuation of bias within music therapy, as argued by Adrienne (2006), is the fact that most music therapists have trained in a Western classical tradition, which is rooted in a patriarchal culture (McClary 1991). As music therapists we must raise our consciousness regarding this issue and the implications that covert and overt messages might have on both music therapists and the clients with whom we work. Additionally, Rolvsjord (2012) explores ways in which the voice can be gendered, discussing ways we "perform" gender in our society as well as cultural stereotypes related to music and gender, such as ideals related to gender-based vocal ranges, and the behavioral health effects this can have for a client when their singing voice does not fall into the stereotypical vocal range that is socially expected.

Gender and cultural biases are not just present in classical music—they exist also in the popular music. What kinds of popular music are taught in music therapy programs and from what cultures? How are we taught to analyze these in terms of perpetuation of social hierar-chies? Jones (2006) discussed the importance of consciously selecting songs for use in music therapy that do not perpetuate misogyny. She explored ways in which popular music has been dominated by male artists and also "perpetuates a negative message to and about women" (p. 335). Thus, a feminist critique of both the lyrics and the music, in terms of gender and cul-tural biases, is important when selecting songs for therapy, as is providing opportunities for song discussion focusing on power differentials, gender role constructions, and the glorifica-tion and/or justification for privilege and oppression. We need to explore ways that power relations are communicated in the music we use. How does music reinforce or destabilize gender politics, sexual politics, racial politics, and ability politics? How does music speak to social class? How does our use of music in therapy empower or disempower various groups?

Research approaches

Feminist research emphasizes that knowledge is situated and thus acknowledging one's standpoint as a researcher is important. Important methodological and discursive strategies central to feminist research include collaboration, awareness of power-relations, embracing multiple perspectives and illuminating perspectives of those who are disadvantaged, embracing the perspective of the "subject" of the research, questioning dominant/grand narratives, and critiquing discursive strategies which support systems which maintain unequal power relations. Feminist research broadly construed is founded on principles of critical theory, being both critical and emancipatory (Sarantakos 2005, p. 54). Feminist research as it pertains to music therapy is discussed in detail by Rolvsjord and Hadley in the third edition of Music Therapy Research (Wheeler, forthcoming).

Historically, randomized controlled trials have been "commonly accepted as the gold standard research design for evaluating the efficacy of health care interventions" (Bradt 2012, p. 120). However, a more liberatory approach to research, which is a core element in feminist research, is found in participatory action research. This kind of research "not only involves active lay participation in the research process, it also involves shared ownership of the research ... [and] it is aimed at solving problems as they are experienced by a group or community" (Stige 2002, p. 277). Furthermore, it is "linked to concerns about social justice and change" (Stige 2005, p. 404). Another research methodology that could be more widely used in the creative arts therapies is critical ethnography, which aims to reveal ideology, and to examine the historical, cultural, and social frameworks of the research participants (Madison 2011). Some important questions which can be addressed by feminist research include: In what ways do our approaches to research reinforce oppressive systems? How do we judge this? In what ways do the topics of our research contribute to empowerment, ones that challenge and decenter oppressive systems? Also, who is acknowledged for the intellectual capital for the dissemination of the research?

Inclusive curricula

In what ways is our curriculum inclusive of all voices? We need to explore ways to make our teaching practices more emancipatory, liberatory, or disruptive of the status quo and reduce ways in which they reinforce oppressive practices. This exploration must include an examination of the pedagogical styles we adopt. The need for curricular and pedagogical reform in music therapy is critical given the historical purpose of academe—to educate clergy. The historical pursuit of educating a select few, as distinguished by the laity or mass public, has led to the exclusion of minorities from the halls of higher education. It has also meant that the curriculum in higher education has been based upon the teachings of the Church (Lucas 1994), which may not be appropriate for the training of music therapy students to work with persons of diverse cultural backgrounds. Without using a liberatory pedagogy and critically examining the content of our curriculum, we must ask ourselves—what are we really teaching our students?

Music therapy can rightly celebrate its capacity to invite new dialogues and build up critical groups such as those developed by practitioners and scholars engaged in feminist informed music therapy. A field's flexibility and openness to new ideas is a guarantee of its future capacity and scope. Music therapy has shown increasing diversity and openness to new ideas. It is important that this growth continues, not with lone voices championing a single view, but with the collective expertise of music therapists worldwide coming together to offer a perspective, a critique, or even to question the value of feminist theory in their own lives, including professional, personal, spiritual, and cultural dimensions.

Notes

1. For additional information on waves of feminism, see Enns (2004), Rowe-Finbeiner (2004), and Villaverde (2008).
2. The term the "personal is political" was used in an article by Hanisch (1970/2000; 2006) to describe the political nature of the personal and public aspects of women's lives, with the word "political" referring to "power relationships, not the narrow sense of electoral politics" (2006, p. 1).
3. Feminist therapists encourage clients to give voice to their lived experience, their subjective world, and their diverse voices as part of the valuing of women and women's experiences (Minnich 2005; Worrell and Remer 2003).
4. The National Association for Social Work (NASW) in the United Sates lists social action in its ethics code. "Social workers should act to prevent and eliminate domination of, exploitation of, and discrimination against any person, group, or class on the basis of race, ethnicity, national origin, color, sex, sexual orientation, gender identity or expression, age, marital status, political belief, religion, immigration status, or mental or physical disability." (National Association of Social Workers 2008).

References

Abrams, B. (2010). Evidence-based music therapy practice: An integral understanding. *Journal of Music Therapy* 47(4): 351–79.

Adrienne, J. (2006). A feminist sociology of professional issues in music therapy. In: Susan Hadley (ed.) *Feminist Perspectives in Music Therapy*, pp. 41–62. Gilsum, NH: Barcelona Publishers.

American Psychiatric Association (2013). *Diagnostic and statistical manual of mental disorders* (5th edition). Washington, DC: Author.

Baines, S. (1992). *The sociological and political contexts of music therapy: A question of ethics.* (Unpublished master's thesis). New York University, New York, NY.

Baines, S. (2007). Review of *Feminist Perspectives in Music Therapy. Music Therapy Perspectives* 25(2): 125–127.

Baines, S. (2013). Music therapy as an anti-oppressive practice. *Arts in Psychotherapy* 40, 1–5.

Ballou, M., Hill, M., and West, C. (eds). (2008). *Feminist Therapy Theory and Practice: A Contemporary Perspective.* New York, NY: Springer.

Bordo, S. (2003). *Unbearable weight: Feminism, western culture, and the body* (10th anniversary edition). Berkeley, CA: University of California Press.

Brabeck, M. and Brown, L. (1997). Feminist theory and psychological practice. In: J. Worell and N.G. Johnson (eds), *Shaping the Future of Feminist Psychology: Education Research, and Practice*, pp. 15–35. Washington, DC: American Psychological Association.

Bradt, J. (2006). The voices of women suffering from pain. In: S. Hadley (ed.), *Feminist Perspectives in Music Therapy*, pp. 291–306. Gilsum, NH: Barcelona Publishers.

Bradt, J. (2012). Randomized controlled trials in music therapy: Guidelines for design and implementation. *Journal of Music Therapy* 49(2): 120–149.

Bruscia, K. (2012). *Readings in Music Therapy Theory*. Gilsum, NH: Barcelona Publishers.

Chestnut, M. (2004). *Family music therapy: Family work in music therapy from a feminist perspective*. (Unpublished master's thesis). New York University, New York, NY.

Curtis, S.L. (1990). Women's issues in music therapy. *Music Therapy Perspectives* 8, 61–66.

Curtis, S.L. (2000). Singing subversion, singing soul: Women's voices in feminist music therapy. (Doctoral dissertation, Concordia University, 1997). *Dissertation Abstracts International, Section A: Humanities and Social Sciences* 60(12): 4240.

Curtis, S.L. (2006). Feminist music therapy: Transforming theory, transforming lives. In: S. Hadley (ed.), *Feminist Perspectives in Music Therapy*, pp. 227–244. Gilsum, NH: Barcelona Publishers.

Curtis, S. (2012). Music therapy and social justice: A personal journey. *The Arts in Psychotherapy* 39(3): 209–213.

Daveson, B. (2007). Feminist Perspectives in Music Therapy [Book Review] [online]. Australian *Journal of Music Therapy* 18: 87–88.

Day, T. and Bruderer, H. (2002). *A Journey of Healing and Hope through Song*. Brisbane: Queensland Government.

Dileo, C. (2001). Ethical issues in supervision. In: M. Forinash (ed.), *Music Therapy Supervision*, pp. 19–38. Gilsum, NH: Barcelona Publishers.

Dileo, C. (2006). Feminist therapy ethics: Implications for music therapy. In: S. Hadley (ed.), *Feminist Perspectives in Music Therapy*, pp. 475–491. Gilsum, NH: Barcelona Publishers.

Edwards, J. (2006). A reflection on the role of informants from feminist theory in the field of music therapy. In: S. Hadley (ed.), *Feminist Perspectives in Music Therapy*, pp. 367–388. Gilsum, NH: Barcelona Publishers.

Edwards, J. and Hadley, S. (2007). Expanding music therapy practice: Incorporating the feminist frame. *The Arts in Psychotherapy* 34: 199–207.

Enns, C.Z. (2004). *Feminist Theories and Feminist Psychotherapies: Origins, Themes, and Diversity*, 2nd edition. Binghamton, NY: The Haworth Press.

Estrella, K. (2001). Multicultural approaches to music therapy supervision. In: M. Forinash (ed.), *Music Therapy Supervision*, pp. 39–65. Gilsum, NH: Barcelona Publishers.

Forinash, M. (2006). Feminist music therapy supervision. In: S. Hadley (ed.), *Feminist Perspectives in Music Therapy*, pp. 415–27. Gilsum, NH: Barcelona Publishers.

Gentile, L., Kisber, S., Suvak, J., and West, C. (2008). The practice of psychotherapy: Theory. In: M. Ballou, M. Hill, and C. West (eds), *Feminist therapy theory and practice: A contemporary view*, pp. 67–86. New York, NY: Springer.

Goldberg, F.S. (2006). Descent to the Goddess: A spiritual and psychological journey to the feminine. In: S. Hadley (ed.), *Feminist Perspectives in Music Therapy*, pp. 97–126. Gilsum, NH: Barcelona Publishers.

Hadley, S. (ed.). (2006a). *Feminist Perspectives in Music Therapy*. Gilsum, NH: Barcelona Publishers.

Hadley, S. (2006b). Developing a feminist pedagogical approach in music therapy. In: S. Hadley (ed.), *Feminist Perspectives in Music Therapy*, pp. 393–413. Gilsum, NH: Barcelona Publishers.

Hadley, S. (2013). Dominant Narratives: Complicity and the Need for Vigilance in the Creative Arts Therapies. *The Arts in Psychotherapy* 40(3): 373–381.

Hadley, S. and Edwards, J. (2004). Sorry for the silence: A contribution from feminist theory to the discourse(s) within music therapy. [Online] *Voices: A World Forum for Music Therapy*. Available at: <http://www.voices.no/mainissues/mi40003000152.html>.

Hahna, N. (2004). *Empowering women: A feminist perspective of the Bonny method of guided imagery and music and intimate partner violence* (Unpublished master's thesis). Radford University, Radford, VA.

Hahna, N. (2010). Exploring the possibilities of a feminist-informed ethics model. *Bonny Method Resources* 23(2): 4–5.

Hahna, N. (2011). Conversations from the classroom: Reflections on feminist music therapy pedagogy in teaching music therapy. *Dissertation Abstracts International: Section A. Humanities and Social Sciences* 72(07): 0413.

Hahna, N. (2013). Towards an emancipatory practice: Incorporating feminist pedagogy in the creative arts therapies. *The Arts in Psychotherapy* 40(3): 436–440. doi: 10.1016.j.aip.2013.05.002.

Hahna, N. and Schwantes, M. (2011). Feminist music therapy pedagogy: A survey of music therapy educators. *Journal of Music Therapy* 48(3): 289–316.

Hanisch, C. (2000). The personal is political. *Notes From the Second Year: Women's Liberation in 1970*. S. Firestone and A. Koedt (eds.). [Online] Available at: <http://www.carolhanisch.org/CHwritings/PersonalisPol.pdf>.

Hanisch, C. (2006). Introduction: The personal is political. *Notes From the Second Year: Women's Liberation in 1970*. S. Firestone and A. Koedt (eds.). [Online] Available at: <http://www.carolhanisch.org/CHwritings/PersonalisPol.pdf>.

Hart, M.M. (2008). The context of therapy: Application. In: *Feminist therapy theory and Practice: A contemporary perspective*, pp. 9–37. New York, NY: Springer.

Hays, P.A. (2008). *Addressing Cultural Complexities in Practice: Assessment, Diagnosis, and Therapy*, 2nd edition. Washington, DC: American Psychological Association.

Heineman, M. (1982). *A study of career aspirations and perceived career success in female and male registered music therapists*. Unpublished master's thesis, Florida State University, Tallahassee, FL.

James, M.R. (1985). Sources of articles published in the *Journal of Music Therapy*: The first twenty years, 1964–1983. *Journal of Music Therapy* 22(2): 87–94.

Jones, L. (2006). Critical reflections on song selections for women's empowerment in music therapy. In: S. Hadley (ed.), *Feminist Perspectives in Music Therapy*, pp. 329–354. Gilsum, NH: Barcelona Publishers.

Kenny, C.B. (2006). The earth is our mother: Reflections on the ecology of music therapy from a native perspective. In: S. Hadley (ed.), *Feminist Perspectives in Music Therapy*, pp. 63–96. Gilsum, NH: Barcelona Publishers.

Kim, S.-A. (2006). Feminism and music therapy in Korea. In: S. Hadley (ed.), *Feminist Perspectives in Music Therapy*, pp. 127–155. Gilsum, NH: Barcelona Publishers.

LaFrance, M.N. and McKenzie-Mohr, S. (2013). The *DSM* and its lure of legitimacy. *Feminism and Psychology* 23(1): 119–140. doi: 10.177/0959353512467974.

Lee, C.C.S. (2006). Women, power, music therapy: A feminist perspective on music therapy in Taiwan. In: S. Hadley (ed.), *Feminist Perspectives in Music Therapy*, pp. 157–181. Gilsum, NH: Barcelona Publishers.

Lucas, C.J. (1994). American higher education: A history. New York, NY: St. Martin's Press.

McClary, S. (1991). *Feminine Endings: Music, Gender, and Sexuality*. Minneapolis, MN: University of Minnesota Press.

McFerran, K. (2010). *Adolescents, Music and Music Therapy: Methods and Techniques for Clinicians, Educators and Students*. London, UK: Jessica Kingsley Publishers.

McFerran, K. and O'Grady, L. (2006). Birthing feminist community music therapy: The progeny of community music therapy practice and feminist therapy theory. In: S. Hadley (ed.), *Feminist perspectives in music therapy*, pp. 63–80. Gilsum, NH: Barcelona Publishers.

Madison, D.S. (2011). *Critical ethnography: Method, ethics, and performance* 2nd ed. London: Sage.

Meadows, A. (2008). Feminist perspectives in music therapy: An essay response to the book *Feminist Perspectives in Music Therapy*, edited by Susan Hadley, (Barcelona Publishers, 2006). *British Journal of Music Therapy* 22(1): 35–44.

Merrill, T. (2006). Power and voice in the institutional setting: A journey toward activating a feminist music therapy approach. In: S. Hadley (ed.), *Feminist Perspectives in Music Therapy*, pp. 187–204. Gilsum, NH: Barcelona Publishers.

Minnich, E.K. (2005). *Transforming Knowledge*. 2nd edition. Philadelphia, PA: Temple University Press.

National Association of Social Workers (2008). *Code of Ethics of the National Association of Social Workers*. [Online] Available at: <http://www.socialworkers.org/pubs/code/code.asp>.

Nicol, J.J. (2010). Review of *Feminist Perspectives in Music Therapy*. *Canadian Journal of Music Therapy* 16(1): 199–204.

O'Callaghan, C. (2007). Review of *Feminist Perspectives in Music Therapy*. *British Journal of Music Therapy* 21(2): 78–80.

O'Grady, L. (2009). The therapeutic potentials of creating and performing music with women in prison: A qualitative case study. (Unpublished doctoral dissertation). The University of Melbourne, Melbourne, Australia.

Pavlicevic, M. (2007). Review of *Feminist Perspectives in Music Therapy*. *Nordic Journal of Music Therapy*. [Online] Available at: <https://njmt.b.uib.no/2007/01/31/feminist-perspectives-in-music-therapy/>.

Purdon, C. (2006). Feminist music therapy with abused teen girls. In: S. Hadley (ed.), *Feminist Perspectives in Music Therapy*, pp. 205–226. Gilsum, NH: Barcelona Publishers.

Reinharz, S. (1992). *Feminist Methods in Social Research*. New York, NY: Oxford University Press.

Rolvsjord, R. (2004). Therapy as empowerment: Clinical and political implications of empowerment philosophy in mental health practices of music therapy. *Nordic Journal of Music Therapy* 13, 99–111.

Rolvsjord, R. (2006). Gender politics in music therapy discourse. In: S. Hadley (ed.), *Feminist Perspectives in Music Therapy*, pp. 311–327. Gilsum, NH: Barcelona Publishers.

Rolvsjord, R. (2010). *Resource-oriented Music Therapy in Mental Health Care*. Gilsum, NH: Barcelona Publishers.

Rolvsjord, R. (2012, May). *Disruptive voices: Singing, empowerment, and the performance of gender in music therapy*. Paper presented at the Gender, Health, and Creative Arts Therapies Conference, Montreal, Canada.

Rolvsjord, R. and Hadley, S. (forthcoming). Critical inquiries: Feminist perspectives and transformative research. In: B.L. Wheeler and K. Murphy (eds), *Music Therapy Research* (Third Edition). New Braunfels, TX: Barcelona Publishers.

Rowe-Finkbeiner, K. (2004). *The f word: Feminist in jeopardy—Women, politics, and the future*. Berkley, CA: Seal Press.

Ruud, E. (1998). *Music Therapy: Improvisation, Communication, and Culture*. Gilsum, NH: Barcelona Publishers.

Ruud, E. (2010). *Music Therapy: A Perspective from the Humanities*. Gilsum, NH: Barcelona Publishers.

Sajnani, N. (2012). Response/ability: Imagining a critical race feminist paradigm for the creative arts therapies. *The Arts in Psychotherapy* 39: 186–191.

Sarantakos, S. (2005). *Social Research*. Hampshire, Palgrave Macmillan.

Shuttleworth, S. (2006). Viewing music therapy assessment through a feminist therapy lense. In: S. Hadley (ed.), *Feminist Perspectives in Music Therapy*, pp. 429–450. Gilsum, NH: Barcelona Publishers.

Stige, B. (2001). The fostering of not-knowing barefoot supervisors. In: M. Forinash (ed.), *Music Therapy Supervision*, pp. 161–176. Gilsum, NH: Barcelona Publishers.

Stige, B. (2002). *Culture-centered Music Therapy*. Gilsum, NH: Barcelona Publishers.

Stige, B. (2005). Participatory action research. In: B. Wheeler (ed.), *Music therapy research*, second edition. Gilsum, NH: Barcelona Publishers.

Streeter, E. (2006). What are we doing to ourselves? The branding of music therapy in academia. In: S. Hadley (ed.), *Feminist Perspectives in Music Therapy*, pp. 355–366. Gilsum, NH: Barcelona Publishers.

Vaillancourt, G. (2012). Music therapy: A community approach to social justice. *The Arts in Psychotherapy* 39: 173–178.

Villaverde, L.E. (2008). *Feminist Theories and Education*. New York, NY: Peter Lang.

Wheeler, B. (2006). Feminist music therapy research. In: S. Hadley (ed.), *Feminist Perspectives in Music Therapy*, pp. 451–474. Gilsum, NH: Barcelona Publishers.

Worell, J. and Remer, P. (2003). *Feminist Perspectives in Therapy: Empowering Diverse Women*, 2nd edition. Hoboken, NJ: John Wiley and Sons.

York, E. (2006). Finding voice. Feminist music therapy and research with women survivors of domestic violence. In: S. Hadley (ed.), *Feminist Perspectives in Music therapy*, pp. 245–265. Gilsum, NH: Barcelona Publishers.

York, E. and Hearns, M. (2005, July 20). *A music therapy research protocol with women victims of intimate partner violence*. Paper presented at the 11th World Congress of Music Therapy, Brisbane, Australia.

CHAPTER 24

PSYCHODYNAMIC MUSIC THERAPY

SUSANNE METZNER

INTRODUCTION

THE basic underlying assumption in psychodynamic music therapy is the existence of, and dynamic processes in, an unconscious mind, which has an influence on intrapsychic and interpersonal processes within and outside of the musical activity between the therapist and patient. The therapeutic relationship is distinguished by the attentiveness of the music therapist to his or her own reactions, feelings, fantasies, and ideas, which are triggered by the patient's transference. Psychodynamic music therapy proposes that, with the assistance of music, human beings can become aware of their inner states, and can communicate these through performed musical expression. From a psychoanalytic viewpoint, music is considered to portray meaning and to give the individual the feeling of being mirrored, accompanied, and even personally understood.

The first psychodynamic music therapy practice can be traced to the late 1960s. Since that time, the theoretical framework has been fundamentally changed due to the findings of empirical research in areas such as infancy and neurophysiology. Contemporary psychodynamic music therapy integrates developmental theories, attachment theory, theories about affect regulation and mentalization, symbolic theories, psychotraumatology, and neuropsychoanalysis. Clinical applications of psychodynamic music therapy are found mainly in mental health, psychosomatics, and, in an adapted manner, in special education. The research into practices and outcomes is primarily undertaken using qualitative methods. Training for competency in this work requires developing skills through learning theoretical and practice considerations and undertaking personal therapy experiences in group and/or individual settings.

PSYCHOANALYTIC BACKGROUND

Psychodynamic music therapy is founded on psychoanalysis, which was originally developed by Sigmund Freud. His first psychoanalytic publication *Traumdeutung* (The

Interpretation of Dreams) appeared in 1900. Since that time, psychoanalysis has undergone manifold differentiations, revisions, and developments. Therefore, it is not usually a theoretical concept that is coherent and consistent in all of its components. Although it rests upon the basic assumption of the existence of the unconscious, the conditions under which it has developed specific characteristics and effects have been continually transformed.

Psychoanalysis has left traces in almost every socially relevant area of twentieth-century life and in everyday thinking of the Western world. Psychoanalysis is an integral part of contemporary discourse. Numerous disciplines of human and social science (such as psychology and psychiatry, neurology and neurobiology, sociology, anthropology, philosophy) and also art and literature, engage with psychoanalytic theory. It is these many interconnections and cross-references between psychoanalysis and other fields that partly accounts for its complexity. Although it has not been very common for the field of psychoanalysis to occupy itself with issues of music, more recently there have been some publications that consider psychoanalytic concepts (for example, Rose 2004). Conversely, it can be noted that musicians and musicologists seldom make references to psychoanalysis. In the light of this, psychoanalytic-oriented music therapy has a bridging function in reference to understanding musical processes as well as the significance of music in human life. Through reports of therapeutic work, knowledge has been gained about how the acoustic, dynamic, and rhythmic forms of vitality functions (Stern 2010) are interrelated with the physical, emotional, cognitive, and social processes for individuals living within specific socio-cultural contexts. From music therapy, psychoanalysis can learn how human emotions are articulated in music, and how, with the help of music, human beings can become aware of their inner states and can communicate these through musical expression.

Historical overview

Concepts of music therapy based on psychoanalytic theory began to develop in the late 1960s and appeared in specialized academic publications in the early 1970s, after the first international music therapy conventions[1]. This interest in psychoanalysis in music therapy evolved simultaneously in various European countries, consistently focusing in the area of adult psychiatry. This development can be observed in the context of major social developments including the changes in the concept of humanity following the two World Wars and the reform movement in psychiatry. Three points regarding this historical development of music therapy will be briefly mentioned here. Firstly, the previously strained relationship between psychiatry and psychotherapy was eased, and, starting in the 1960s, following the first pioneering publications, an increasing number of psychotherapeutic methods and techniques were developed, the majority of them based on psychoanalysis (Streeck and Dümpelmann 2005). Thus, psychoanalysts such as Harm Willms (1975) in Berlin and Raoul Schindler (Schumacher 2005, p. 14) in Vienna supported the conceptualization and implementation of music therapy in psychiatric hospitals. Secondly, in connection with social–psychological theoretical approaches and the first social–psychiatric experiments, a movement was founded in which the image of the mentally ill person was changed to one no longer helplessly at the mercy of his or her illness; this is what is now termed *empowerment*. Thirdly, developments in contemporary music culture at the beginning of the 1970s were fertile ground for the advancement of music therapy based on psychoanalysis. Greater freedom in composition, the inclusion of improvisation in performance, and the emphasis on communication through music were counter-movements to the constraints of the strict serial school. In Germany, Mauricio Kagel (Schwartz 2009) was the key representative of this New Music. These musical characteristics remain part of the psychodynamic music therapy approach until today.

With reference to the pioneers of music therapy who adopted a psychoanalytic approach, names such as Edith Lecourt in France, Mary Priestley in the UK (1975)[2], and Johannes Th. Eschen in Germany must be mentioned. However, I share the view of the historical musicologist, Manuela Schwartz (2004) that it is more correct to assume the existence of an entire network, in which theorists as well as practitioners, music therapists, psychoanalysts, and composers of different countries were involved and still are today. In the course of time, they have made quite different contributions to developments in psychoanalytic music therapy. Whereas some have provided for an expansion of the fields of application to wider populations such as child and adolescent therapy, trauma therapy, psychosomatics (for example, Jahn-Langenberg 2003; Langenberg et al. 1995), special education, mental disability care, geriatric psychiatry, and forensics (for example, Compton Dickinson et al. 2012), others have contributed substantively to the development of theories. The significance of the concept of potential space by D.W. Winnicott (1971; Odgen 1985) has become a common cross-national point of reference for music therapists who follow a psychodynamic approach (Niedecken 1988; Nolan 1989; Metzner 1999b; Sutton 2002); however, there are also concepts, such as *materialistic socialization theory*, that have not become popular outside of the country of origin. A. Lorenzer (1983) was a psychoanalyst of the so-called Frankfurt School, on whose ideas many German psychoanalytically-oriented music therapists have based their approach. At the same time, some psychoanalytic concepts such as counter-transference or Daniel Stern's theory of self-development have stimulated other, predominantly humanistic, models of music therapy. In turn, modern concepts such as mentalization theory (cf. Gergely 2000; Fonagy et al. 2002) are interlinked with cognitive therapy approaches.

The history of the terms used for music therapy with a psychoanalytic concept reveal some of the developments as well as the major issues of discussion. Whereas on the one hand, psychoanalytic psychotherapy can include music, giving the non-verbal processes space within the therapeutic relationship and creating a special emphasis, on the other, the method consists of musical work with the patient that reflects a psychoanalytical viewpoint. Depending on the perspective, the method is then called *analytical music therapy, psychoanalytic music therapy, analytically oriented/informed music therapy,* or *music therapy within a psychoanalytic framework.* Since, in the field of psychoanalysis, *psychodynamic therapy* has gained popularity as the umbrella term for various analytic and depth psychological approaches to therapy, the term *psychodynamic music therapy* is most commonly used in contemporary practice.

BASIC TENETS OF PSYCHOANALYTIC THEORY

Psychoanalysis can be seen as a method to gain insight into unconscious mental processes. It is also a method for the treatment of mental disorders; and further, it is a psychological theory of mental life and experiences which especially emphasizes the unconscious aspects of such processes. Epistemologically, psychoanalysis belongs to the field of hermeneutics. Epistemological interest is focused on the object to be observed. For example, the focus might be on such aspects as the actions and experiences of a person, a social form of life, a social development, or a work of art. It becomes possible to deduce underlying unconscious processes by observation and interpretation. In turn, the occupation with the object changes the manner of observation, the methodological approach, and theory formation. This dynamic process of reciprocal influence is of great significance for psychoanalytic therapy, but it is also quite a prominent topic in current discussions in the neurosciences in connection with research on the complex interactions of inner structures with the environment or within the neuronal networks (Northoff 2011).

Most psychoanalytic knowledge was originally gained in clinical practice. This has led to a psychodynamic understanding of dysfunction and of treatment. In traditional psychoanalytic theory formation, questions arose as to the internal processes that take place in humans, such as which desires, fears, convictions, and fantasies determine his or her actions, and which unresolved conflicts underlie psychological and functional disturbances. Only later, especially since the 1950s, has the interpersonal perspective been foregrounded in psychoanalysis. This approach deals with the influence of real relationships between humans on their well-being and need satisfaction[3]. Thus, the interpersonal perspective accentuates the dependency of subjective feelings and actions on the reactions and actions of other persons and the effects of one's own actions on their reactions. Social situations are examined in respect to how the concerned interaction partners react to the wishes and expectations of the respective other, how they react to one another, which effects the reciprocal reactions have, and, in turn, how this is reflected in their expectations, convictions, and behavioral dispositions. However, as late as the 1980s, psychoanalytic theory was predominantly influenced by drive psychology, object relations theory, and a concept of the ego, whose developmental task in therapy was to gain greater autonomy through insight in unconscious conflicts and to develop more mature defense structures.

Starting with the *intersubjective turn* that can be observed in Edmund Husserl's phenomenology of the 1920s and then flourished within the humanities during the following decades (Schütz and Luckmann 1975), and continuing with the results of empirical infant research from the beginning of the 1980s (Trevarthen 1979; Stern 1985), the growing experience in the treatment of severe mental disorders (Mentzos 1995), and, finally, the upsurge of neurobiological research (Schore 1994; Northoff 2011), a radical change occurred in psychoanalysis.

Psychodynamic theory today is impossible without a theoretical framework, which includes developmental theory, attachment theory, affect and mentalization theory, and psychotraumatology. The numerous empirical scientific studies that have been conducted in the last decades have confirmed psychoanalytical knowledge that severe disturbances in early parent–child relationships (in particular through separation traumata, emotional neglect, and child abuse) lead to a highly significant risk to develop psychopathological disorders over the entire life span.

The fact that early life experiences can have such dramatic effects is connected with the intersubjective nature of the human being, which makes him or her vulnerable to dysfunctional forms of early attachment relationships.[4] Thus, today's understanding of psychodynamic therapy in which disorders are understood to be due to failed or disturbed intersubjective processes can only take place in the form of a developmental process, through which self-regulatory skills are (re-)gained. In this regard, development is seen as a non-linear process, in the course of which events can be given a new meaning and can be integrated in a more mature psychic structure. The central question is which developmental steps are most conducive for the patient to overcome fears and to be able to have new interpersonal experiences.

Gergely and Unoka (2011, p. 874) proposed that subjective awareness of differentiated emotional self-states occurs mainly through social interaction and, from there, this awareness develops in a way that is specific for each individual. This process is understood as a developmental step that costs considerable effort: it requires the ability of the self to become aware of the internal emotional states of others and to recognize the mutual participation in such states. Further, due to the lifelong development of the human brain and neural plasticity, one can assume that, not just during childhood and adolescence but over the entire life span, human development is triggered both by biological factors and by interactions with the environment (Northoff 2011).

Thus, all modern theories of development should be understood as process models of interacting and mutually influencing systems of self and environment, in which the regulatory relationship between child and care giver is especially important during the early years. In particular, affect-regulating interactions, where positive affects are increased and negative affects are minimized, play a fundamental role not only for the development of the self but also for attachment behavior.

Whereas Bowlby's and Ainsworth's original work on attachment theory in the 1960s was shaped by an emphasis on cognition and behaviorism and was considered incompatible with the psychoanalytical concepts of those times, the current interest in emotional and physically rooted processes, in interactive regulation and early experience-dependent brain development, and in stress and unconscious relational transactions has led to a convergence of these two theoretical approaches in more recent times (Schore 1994)[5]. All of these developments inevitably led to changes in treatment techniques, and also influenced practices in psychodynamic music therapy. However, as works edited by Bruscia (1998) and Eschen (2002b) demonstrate, psychodynamic music therapy has not yet incorporated these changes, perhaps because of the rapid development of psychoanalytic concepts. Concurrently contemporary presentations of psychodynamic music therapy differ from each other. This diversity can be partly explained by the breadth and the heterogeneity of the field of psychoanalysis.

CLINICAL PRINCIPLES IN PSYCHODYNAMIC MUSIC THERAPY

The basic principle of treatment in psychodynamic music therapy consists of working through biographic experiences that are actualized in the musical and verbal interactions within a therapeutic relationship. According to psychoanalytic theory, deprivation, traumatic experiences, or disturbed development of object relations during early childhood are causally related to later psychiatric disorders. The symptoms that manifest are not considered deficits, but are seen as phenomena that have developed over a longer period of time and that have gained an unconscious meaning. Dysfunctional experiences can become audible in the musical experiencing and behavior of the patient, and in his or her musical relationships with the therapeutic process. From the perspective of psychoanalysis, therapeutic treatment can only take place within a therapeutic relationship where transference, counter-transference, and resistance are able to be considered (see Streeter 1999). In contrast to other therapeutic methods, psychoanalytic approaches welcome disturbances, or obstacles, in the relationship because, through these, the patient can become aware of and work through unconscious biographical experiences which can then lead to greater understanding and to change.

Depending on the severity of the disturbance and the resources of the patient, his or her current life situation, and the context of the music therapeutic treatment, the therapy focuses more in the present or concentrates on the past. The setting and the frequency of treatment are specified, and the therapist uses a more active or more silent intervention strategy. As relationship experiences from childhood can be revived in the counter-transference relationship, the therapist focuses on regressive processes (Balint 1968)[6], especially during musical interactions, in order to prevent the dissolution of ego-functions.

The technical principles of treatment in conducting psychodynamic psychotherapy, such as abstinence, a basically open and questioning therapeutic attitude as well as technique—for example, holding (Winnicott 1945), containment (Bion 1962; de Backer 1993), and mirroring (Kohut 1971; Shengold 1974; Winnicott 1971; Malin 2011)—clarification, affect identification, confrontation, and interpretation, are applied in psychodynamic music therapy both in talking with the patient and in the musical actions of the therapist (Niedecken 1988). Pedersen (2004) identified two listening perspectives that relate to different types of counter-transference, where the therapist either focuses on the musical play of the patient or pays more attention to his or her own emotional reactions to the music. Keeping these perspectives balanced is the basis of the therapeutic attitude of active listening whilst improvising with the patient.

The recent developments in psychoanalysis previously described, namely a treatment concept that is intersubjective, oriented toward development, and giving consideration to the non-verbal expressions of the patient, fits together well with psychodynamic music therapy, so that theoretical manoeuvring is no longer necessary to legitimate the musical relationship that develops between patient and therapist through their mutual activity. This is so because empirical research in the form of direct observation of interactions between infants and care givers—as well as between patients and therapists—has provided the insight that whenever the patient is not able to talk about his or her experiences with early care givers, he or she needs to re-enact them (McLaughlin 1992; Streeck 2000). By means of musical interactions between the therapist and the patient, music therapy can provide opportunities to act out interpersonal interactions that cannot be expressed through everyday language, such as merging, perpetuation, non-attunement, feeling overwhelmed, and so forth. In this respect, counter-transference is considered the most important agency of the therapist, using emotional reactions or arising fantasies to understand the relationship experiences of the patient and to guide the patient in making use of the past for development in the here and now. What is important are the questions as to how the patient (a) perceives, (b) tolerates, and (c) expresses affects, and if (d) the influence of affects can be accepted in relationships to others (cf. Fonagy et al. 2002; Dümpelmann 2004).

This is also relevant for the person who has a mental disorder and is experiencing affective states that are confusing or peculiar to him or her, and whose perception of self and environment is restricted. The prerequisite for a healing interpersonal experience is that his or her current internal states are *mirrored* or *reflected* externally, namely in contingent reactions of the social environment attuned to the patient. Fonagy et al. (2004) as well as Gergely and Watson (1996, 1999) have found that the empathetic affect-mirroring expressions of the primary care giver towards the infant and, identically, of the therapist towards the patient, fulfil their function only when they occur as altered variations of normal/regular motor patterns, in other words, in *"marked"* form. In the field of music therapy, Strehlow (2009) has established the relevance of marked mirroring also for the musical interaction between therapist and patient.

The formation of cognitive representation of emotions that occurs through social interaction creates the necessary preconditions for the individual to regain his or her mentalization ability—in other words, (a) to become aware of his or her own affective states through introspection, (b) to anticipate and evaluate his or her own instrumental and expressive behavioral tendencies induced by emotions, and (c) to modify these in a way that is more consistent with the environment. The goal of psychodynamic treatment aiming at personal development and emotional self-regulation is to enable the patient to deal more efficiently with emotionally-laden interpersonal situations and with long-term intimate relationships in the future.

It is possible to connect the intersubjective approach in psychoanalysis with group analytic therapy, which, especially in the in-patient treatment setting in mental health, accounts for a great share of the work done by music therapists. In group analytic music therapy (Lecourt 1993; Metzner 1999a; Ahonen-Erikäinen 2007), the focus is on triadic and multi-person relationships. It is the field where the subject and his or her objects, the conscious and the unconscious, the internal and the external world, work together through a dynamic characterized by mutuality in the formation of relations within the group. In the framework of this relational perspective, conflict and reconciliation become the object of a complex investigation. This investigation focuses on the effect of the subject's intrapsychic world and on the formation of relations with *objective others*, on one hand, and on the influence of social reality on the formation of the individual's internal object relations, on the other.

Foulkes, who developed the model of group analysis in the 1940s, assumed that there are four main therapeutic processes: mirroring, exchange, social integration, and activation of the collective unconscious (Foulkes 1948). An essential aspect of therapeutic change lies in people discovering what they can do for others (Foulkes and Anthony 1957). Tschuschke and Dies (1994) conducted an in-depth study of five therapeutic factors in group work: group cohesiveness, self-disclosure, feedback, interpersonal learning, and family re-enactment. In group analysis, destructive activities too are regarded as important starting points for creativity. Therefore, aspects such as power and hierarchy, destructive activities, the oppression or exclusion of group members by musical means must be addressed through the group music therapy processes (Metzner 2001).

Musical principles in psychodynamic music therapy

From a psychoanalytic viewpoint, music is the articulation of human experiences, and with the assistance of music, human beings can become aware of their inner states and can communicate through performed expression. Thus, Purdon (2002, pp. 106–111) distinguishes five different roles of music in psychodynamic therapy including "Music as bridge", "Music as safe place," and "Music as carrier of the client's story."

In clinical practice, there exists a broad spectrum of methods and playing techniques of music therapy. Generally, alternation between talking and mutual improvisation or listening to music are more or less the rule, but considering the fact that not all clients are capable of verbalization, the function of music, as well as how music is handled in therapy, is something which has to be developed by each patient and therapist anew. So, for example, there might be almost no talking in some sessions and. at another time. music is played only sporadically; mutual improvisations might take place without mutuality becoming a characteristic of the resulting music; a therapist may play for the patient or compositions are played from a recording and, at another time, pieces are rehearsed so that the distinction to music lessons becomes blurred; and, at one time, pieces of music that are the subject of conversation are not played whilst, at another time, music serves to maintain discretion.

Another method of psychodynamic music therapy is "psychodynamic movement," which was developed by Mary Priestley (Pedersen 2002a,b; Metzner 2009). This technique consists of a combination of improvised music and improvised movement in a group setting led by co-therapists. Within the free floating process of musical and movement improvisation, body sensations, affects, and fantasies are set free and have a cathartic effect. Unrevealed intrasubjective and interpersonal experiences are reflected in a group discussion afterwards.

Despite the manifold ways of using music in psychodynamic therapy, instrumental improvisation probably plays the biggest role (Scheiby 2002). In her study of the practice of analytic music therapy in the area of mental health care, Odell-Miller (2007) also concluded that instrumental improvisation is used particularly often with clients with psychosis or borderline disorders and is effective in comparison to receptive approaches.

One reason for the infrequent reference to the use of composed music in psychodynamic music therapy reports may be because patients with severe mental disorders are not able to make effective use of the potential space between the presentation and the presented (Metzner 2004). This does not hold for patients who have a more mature psychic structure, as shown by Clarkson and Geller (1996) in their psychoanalytic approach to guided imagery and music. Lecourt (1998) identifies differences in the degree of counter-transference in active and receptive music therapy.

Psychodynamic music therapy is not characterized by predefined functions of music or specific techniques. Rather, the means by which the musical material is processed between the therapist and patient, and how the connected interpersonal and intrapsychic processes are dealt with is key to the psychoanalytic foundations of the approach. To understand the musical processes in psychodynamic music therapy psychologically, the findings of preverbal interactions gained by infant research, psychoanalytic dream theory, and some metaphor or symbol theory[7] appear to be of particular relevance. On the basis of these assumptions, tonal expressions by the patient that sound inept or incorrect are considered to be potential messages and are answered musically by the therapist, but are not automatically brought into any rhythmic–harmonic order. Thus, psychodynamic music therapy is based on a broader understanding of music and, in particular, results from deep involvement with contemporary classical Western music.

Without this, improvisations in psychodynamic group music therapy, where the therapist often operates with only minimal structuring, could only be experienced as chaos. But, especially during group improvisations, polymorphic and diverse but simultaneously occurring mediatory processes are stimulated in a special way. The value of tangible practice, of spontaneous impulses and ideas should not be underestimated, because experiencing and provoking unusual sounds, interpreting and (re)constructing the external world lead to the transformation of the interpreting structures of the individual (Metzner 2005). The therapist especially needs competence in how to nestle oneself into situations and processes, to express and perform (mimetic aspects), to deal with extreme emotional and cognitive states (aesthetic aspects), and how to find, to hide, or to invent meaning (semiotic aspects) which are encouraged by musical improvisation. This is where the non-conformist power of improvisation psychodynamic in music therapy lies in general, and in group improvisations in particular.

APPLICATIONS AND CONTRAINDICATIONS

Psychodynamic music therapy is applicable within the entire spectrum of mental and psychosomatic disorders. This also includes mental distress that can occur for people in exceptional life situations, for example, those with an organic illness or after suffering a significant loss. The goals of treatment can, therefore, vary and it is not always intended that the aim of psychodynamic music therapy is to eliminate the cause of the disorder. In connection with rehabilitative measures, psychodynamic music therapy is indicated if it can help alleviate mental suffering, promote self-healing forces, and contribute to a largely independent lifestyle and the integration in a work and educational setting, according to the 15th Convention on the Rights of Persons with Disabilities (2006)[8].

Systematic research investigating failed therapy, or indeed other methods of music therapy, has not yet been conducted. Considerations about diagnosis-specific contraindications that Mary Priestley (1994, pp. 13–14) once formulated are considered obsolete today, as shown by the reports and research results of successful psychodynamic work in music therapy with acute psychotic (Metzner 2010), traumatized (Engelmann 2013), or mentally impaired persons (Becker 2002). Because of the variability of the settings, methods, and forms of intervention, from the viewpoint of psychodynamic music therapy, the idea of a diagnosis-specific contraindication is an assumption that is highly questionable. The therapist has many opportunities to adapt his or her concept to the needs or competencies of the patient.

ASSESSMENT

Before music therapy treatment can begin, it is necessary to make an assessment by conducting an initial interview from a psychodynamic perspective. Consideration is given to the patient's biography, including his or her musical experience, memories of the patient, as well as paying attention to transference and counter-transference in verbal and musical interactions. This generally leads to a psychodynamic hypothesis about the relationship between symptom formation and personality development with reference to the patient's biographical and social context. The major part of the diagnostic interview is usually performed with the multi-professional team. Operationalized forms of specific musical assessment have not yet been developed in the area of psychodynamic music therapy because one does not assume a direct relationship between symptomatology, the patient's subjective experiences, and treatment prerequisites on the one hand, and the musical expression of the patient on the other. Most music therapists who pursue a psychodynamic approach have developed their own individual strategy in order to assess aspects important for the music therapeutic procedure at the beginning of therapy. Apart from improvisation themes like "sounds that you like and sounds that you dislike", "starting with a dialogue", or "finding a path through an unknown terrain", most psychodynamic music therapists seem to invite the patient to freely improvise and to play whatever comes to his or her mind.

Evaluation and research

The evaluation of psychodynamic music therapy starts with a systematic documentation of the process of therapy. Furthermore, case supervision also accompanies the therapeutic process. In a model of Balint group work developed for music therapists (Strobel et al. 1988), free improvisation is integrated into the supervision, which is then guided by associations that arise in connection with the presented case.

Measures of quality assurance primarily serve to reflect upon the therapeutic relationship and to function as a control mechanism in reference to the subjectivity of the therapist. The results of such professional self-reflection are evident in editions of case studies (e.g. Bruscia 1998; Hadley 2003; Metzner 2007, 2013) which are suitable for qualitative synthesis.

As the choice of a research method follows the epistemological interest and the scientific question, existing models will be modified individually. Within the field of psychodynamic music therapy, the focus lies on the unconscious, so methods of hermeneutic or depth hermeneutic interpretation are of main interest. Psychodynamic music therapy research is generally oriented more toward complex interrelationships rather than outcomes in form of measureable improvement of individual symptoms. A randomized controlled effectiveness study, such as conducted by Erkkilä et al. (2011) of a psychoanalytically oriented concept of music therapy for the treatment of depression as primary diagnosis, is still something of a rarity. In contrast, qualitative studies predominate, most of them conducted in connection with dissertations; some examples are briefly mentioned here to identify the areas where research has been done so far. Applied research and theory-generating research are often interconnected. This also applies to studies concerning transference (Hannibal 2001) and counter-transference (Pedersen 2007) which have been conducted in the field of mental health.

Trondalen (2004) has examined the *special moments* occurring in the therapy with a patient diagnosed with anorexia. Strehlow (2013) investigated musical scenes with borderline patients and found typical interaction patterns. Storz (2002) has developed a model of short-term psychodynamic therapy, whereas Metzner (1999a, 2003) has analyzed triadic processes in group music therapy. Kunkel (2008) studied initial improvisations with psychotic patients and was able to identify the dominant interaction forms for this group of clients, whereas de Backer (2005) has analyzed and defined the musical phases within free improvisations over many sessions. Mahns (2004) examined processes of symbol formation in his work with children, whereas Dehm-Gauwerky (2006) identified processes of fragmentation as reflected in the music of patients with dementia. Wrogemann-Becker (2010) focused on musical interactions with blind children as a starting point to describe the distinctive features of ego development. Becker (2002) has conducted research in the field of music therapy with persons with profound and multiple disabilities. All of these psychodynamic music therapy research studies have applied methods of analysis from musicology including listening analysis, and notation, as well as methods of qualitative social and psychotherapy research—also in combination with each other.

With the help of musical notation, Niedecken (1988) and de Backer (2005) have illustrated how it is possible to make interpretations using in-depth hermeneutics. Langenberg et al. (1993) worked with narrative texts formulated by independent describers of musical improvisations created during music therapy. Metzner (2000) developed a guide for the in-depth hermeneutic analysis of group improvisations. Two phenomenologically-oriented analysis instruments (Trondalen 2007; Grocke 2007) are appropriate for the examination of musical processes in psychodynamic music therapy, the same as the Assessment of the Quality of Relationship (AQR) developed by Schumacher and Calvet (1999) on the basis of Stern's model for the observation of the quality of contact in music therapy with autistic persons.

Training

In addition to musical and methodological competencies, and the theoretical knowledge of psychoanalysis, the numerous decisions that have to be made by the therapist in psychodynamic music therapy make it necessary for him or her to reflect on their own inclinations and the risks related to the exercise of power within the relationship. In order to prevent the therapist's own conflicts, fears, or inhibitions from affecting the relationship negatively, it is important for the therapist to recognize and accept his or her own biases and limitations. For this reason, both systematic self-reflection of the therapist and supervision are indispensable in psychodynamic music therapy. The ability to tolerate one's own feelings and thoughts—including those that are undesirable or taboo—that arise within the context of a therapeutic relationship and to deal with them in a careful and constructive manner is acquired during the training period in music therapy. Furthermore, in the area of analytical music therapy, an inter-therapy (Priestley 1975; Eschen 2002a, p. 19) model has been developed, where three students in turn take on the roles of patient, therapist, and supervisor.

Psychodynamic music therapy is a component of various academic training programs for music therapists at masters level, especially in Europe. However, common standards with reference to theoretical and basic subjects do not yet exist. Further, due to the high costs, it is not possible to provide self-experience in music therapy to the necessary extent in every program. Because of these limitations, after finishing their degree, some qualified music therapists decide to complete postgraduate psychodynamic training programs for psychotherapists. The music therapy program at the University of Leuven Hogeschool voor Wetenschap en Kunst Lemmensinstituut (Belgium), directed by Jos De Backer and Jan van Camp, has a clearly psychodynamic orientation. A masters degree in analytical group music therapy can be acquired at the Université Paris Descartes (France)[9], headed by Edith Lecourt.

CASE STUDY

The following case study provides insights into the initial stage of psychodynamic music therapy with a patient who was admitted into a psychiatric clinic due to a recurring, severe depressive episode accompanied by stupor (ICD 10 F31.5). The findings of empirical research on music therapy for depression (Maratos et al. 2008; Erkkilä et al. 2011) and for severe mental disorders (Gold et al. 2009) support the assumption that improvement of symptoms for people presenting with this specific clinical picture can be expected. However, what the statistics do not provide are the clinical problems that must be tackled in the course of music therapy in each individual case. Many details must be considered in psychodynamic music therapy including biographic and memory data, but also the observations, feelings, reflections, and hypothesis formation by the therapist are important. Therefore, I have integrated some theoretical considerations in my case study.

Scene I: first meeting

The music therapist visited Mrs W., a 54-year-old patient, in her room on the ward. There she found Mrs W. lying fully clothed on her bed, awake but totally motionless, and said hello to her. From her facial expression and the sounds of her breathing it was not possible to tell if she was aware of the therapist's presence. Although the therapist could perceive the patient's feeling of tension and rigidness, she simultaneously felt that she was somewhat unable to empathize with her. She interpreted this as dissociation in counter-transference and saw this as a defense against overwhelming feelings such as fear, terror, powerlessness, and pain.

With the intention to neither overtax the patient by being too direct in an offer to communicate, nor to leave her all by herself, the therapist used preverbal expressive behavior of the patient as a starting point; she chose the calimba from the bag of various instruments that she had brought along with her and started to pluck the tines. The tones seem to be coming from a music box that was turning irregularly and much too slowly, so that one could not recognize the melody. The breathing sounds had stopped and the patient now had her eyes closed. The therapist did not know if the patient had fallen asleep as she quietly left the room.

Current situation and case history

A few days earlier, Mrs W. had been admitted to the psychiatric clinic because of a severe depressive episode accompanied, for the first time, by psychotic symptoms (stupor). Previously she had received a diagnosis of bipolar affective disorder (F31.5). Recently, she was no longer able to cope with the tasks of everyday living. She felt restless on the inside and as if she were paralyzed on the outside. She developed sleep problems and became increasingly silent. She was totally exhausted mentally and physically and—as she reported later during therapy—suffered from enormous psychological pressure and a feeling of guilt for something that could never be changed.

Mrs W. grew up with two brothers (+1 and –2 years) in a simple social environment. Her father was a construction worker and had a proclivity for alcohol. Although he was not violent when drunk, it was frightening for the children to see the changes in their father after drinking. Her mother experienced depression and took her own life when the patient was 13 years old. Although her strictly religious paternal grandmother took over the household, she did not develop a close relationship with her grandchildren. Further, nobody was permitted to talk about the mother's death. Although the facts are rather sparse, it is possible to suggest that these early relationship experiences were shaped by insufficient affective attunement between primary care givers and contributed to the difficulties of a child who became depressive later in life (see Green 1993; Reck et al. 2002).

After completing secondary school, the patient started vocational training as a bakery shop assistant, where she became pregnant as a consequence of sexual abuse by her employer. Her own attempts to terminate pregnancy caused life-threatening injuries, so that she, as a then 16-year-old patient, had to undergo emergency treatment. The patient completed her vocational training without her family finding out about the true reason for her hospitalization and without anything being addressed at the workplace. Her fear about communicating the sexual assault by her boss, and her willingness to continue her training there, bear testimony to the patient doing everything she could not to disturb her social environment.

On completion of her training, Mrs W. met her future husband whom she married after becoming pregnant again. The birth of her daughter, and of a son two years later, were both normal. Mrs W. stayed at home to take care of the children, was very ambitious about keeping her household in order, did not socialize very much, and did not pursue her own interests. In retrospect, however, the patient considered this the best time in her life, where everything was taken care of. From her self-report it is obvious that order, control, and a stable relationship made it possible for her to experience herself as self-assured, efficacious, and emotionally stable.

When both children, aged 9 and 11, went to camp during summer vacation, the patient, who was 32 years old at that time, followed them with the intention to make herself useful there. However, she behaved so strangely that the counselors sent her home. She arrived at home the next day and attracted negative attention as she upset an elderly neighbor, who was living alone, by talking with him in a sexually provocative way. From a psychodynamic viewpoint, through the separation from her children, the patient experienced an object loss that was traumatic for her[10] with consequences for the regulation of her sense of self and self-esteem as well as of her emotional self. In psychodynamic thinking, it is understood that she compensated for this loss (unconsciously) by using a manic defense by sexual means.

The social–psychiatric service who were notified about her situation supported her to choose to enter a psychiatric hospital. Upon admittance she was diagnosed according to ICD 10: manic episode—F30.1. After four weeks of in-patient treatment, the patient asked to be discharged so that she could take care of her children who had returned home from camp. Soon afterward, Mrs W. developed feelings of shame and social phobia as a consequence of the previous occurrences and was treated with medication by a practice-based psychiatrist.

However, the depressive symptomatology that had developed did not improve. Gaining weight as a side- effect of medication gave the patient the feeling of being unattractive and worthless; this she found confirmed when her husband sometimes became aggressive. However, buying a mobile home and spending time at a permanent motor camp together with close friends had a stabilizing effect on their marriage after some time.

After her daughter left home, once she had finished training as a nurse, the patient, who was 43 years old at the time, decompensated, showing all the main symptoms of a severe depressive episode (F31.4) as well as sleep disorders, feelings of guilt, thoughts of self-punishment, and suicidal ideation. She was given treatment, first on an in-patient, then on an out-patient basis in a psychiatric clinic for 22 weeks. The focus of the multi-professional treatment concept was the patient's extreme separation anxiety, which—from the viewpoint of self-theory and developmental theory (Stern 1985; Fonagy et al. 2002; Fonagy and Target 2003; Gergely and Unoka 2011)—is rooted in a structural disturbance and which can be traced back to insufficient availability, empathy, and affect regulation of early attachment figures as well as traumatizations (the death of her mother and the sexual assault by the employer). This led to a permanent fear held by the patient that she would be abandoned any time that she dared to express her autonomy and powerfulness (see Böker 2011, pp. 129).

In the following years, the patient remained relatively stable for a longer time; only after 10 years did she develop symptoms again in connection with a separation situation when her son, who had lived at home up until then, suddenly and unexpectedly decided to move out. Following the onset of another severe depressive episode accompanied by insomnia, feelings of loneliness and self-doubts, pain and feelings of numbness in her legs, the patient started to abuse alcohol, until her daughter took steps to have her hospitalized.

Beginning treatment: Indication and setting

The music therapy that is presented here is one element of a multi-professional in-patient program with a psychodynamic approach in combination with pharmacological treatment. The patient's symptoms, her muteness, and other signs of depersonalization suggest that an individual setting, where the focus is initially placed on the regulation of (body-) self/environment relationships and on attachment security, was warranted.

The music therapist decided upon a therapy setting with a high frequency of sessions, namely three times per week—each lasting 15 minutes—in the room of the patient. In consideration of the severity of the depressive episode, the therapist's primary goal was to provide *environmental care*, in the sense of Winnicott, and to accompany her empathetically, while simultaneously being alert for counter-transference, in particular in reference to the previously observed dissociation of sensual, emotional, and cognitive processes. The therapist brought a small selection of musical instruments to each session in order to discover the preferences of the patient and prepare her for the musical equipment she would encounter when eventually she came to the music therapy room. In these sessions there was not much talking; the instruments were looked at, touched, held, and briefly played. The therapist avoided asking any questions, and Mrs W. did not express herself any differently than before, continuing to utter brief breathing sounds. Often, the patient fixed an intense gaze on the therapist. This caused feelings of discomfort in the therapist, so she tried to shift the attention to other channels by suggesting an activity with the instruments. The therapeutic situation was dominated by the feeling of being cut off from the external as well as the internal world, but moments of tranquility were also experienced.

Scene II: Unsuccessful attunement processes

In the third week of treatment, the stupor receded, and Mrs W was able to come to the music therapy room for her ninth session. Instead of the small-sized instruments with which she was acquainted already, she spontaneously appeared interested in a pair of conga drums. The therapist encouraged her to try out the instrument. Mrs W. beat on the drums several times, surprisingly fast and loudly with the palms of her hands in a simultaneous but audibly asynchronous manner. In a way as if no echo, no pause should be allowed to occur, the therapist reacted immediately by striking the bass xylophone a couple of times but, because she was holding large felt mallets, the strikes turned out to be soundless. In the same forced manner as before, Mrs W. beat simultaneously but asynchronously on the congas and then looked at the therapist with a mixture of determination and approval-seeking. It was a difficult moment in the therapeutic relationship because the therapist neither wanted to confirm the patient's actions, that were obviously made with the intention to fulfil what she believed to be the expectations of the therapist, nor refuse the patient's justified wish to get approval for her initiative. Therefore, the therapist decided to focus the attention on the choice of instruments saying "From the big instruments standing around here, you have chosen an instrument of which we have two, a somewhat bigger one and a somewhat smaller one." Mrs W. gave her a silent glance that did not show if she agreed or not. The rest of the session, lasting 15 minutes, was spent locating the smaller instruments with which Mrs W. was already familiar.

Scene III: The discovery of the dead sound

Starting in the fourth week of treatment, music therapy consisted of two weekly sessions, each lasting 30 minutes, but only in the seventh week did the patient dare to take first steps out of her numbness, and for the first time she expressed an emotion in response to her perception of sounds. How did this come about?

Although the patient remained depressive and self-accusing on the ward, in movement and music therapy one could see changes in her motor skills. She had extended her playing technique on the congas by first loudly striking one conga several times with one hand and then the other conga with the other hand. In between, she also played with two hands again, but could not develop an alternating technique. From the viewpoint of music, the different pitches of the series of beats—dim dim dim dim, dum dum dum dum—carried the seed of a *call and response*. Due to the lack of phrasing, it was not possible for a structure to evolve, indicating that the patient still felt lack of orientation. Furthermore, this music did not appear to ask for any accompaniment; there was not much more for the therapist to do than discretely remain in the background, while playing ambient sounds, and to wait. From the viewpoint of treatment, there was some danger in this of leaving the patient alone.

In the sixteenth session that is described here, the therapist decided to express her feelings, saying that the playing of the patient sounded as if somebody "always has to fight her way through life." The patient first reacted with the usual lingering gaze, but then had the idea to select a mallet from the available beaters. She chose a large, very soft mallet and first tried it out on the bass xylophone, which apparently scared her, as she said "That sounds dead to me." The fact that she (a) had started to search, (b) described the sound that she has accidentally found in metaphorical terms, and (c) provided an affective connotation, indicated that she could feel the mutual resonance previously expressed by the therapist. If one interprets the patient's comment in a very broad way, one can say that she was frightened by her own emotional numbness, thus—understandably enough—reacting to a dead sound with fear.

The therapist reached for the other soft mallet and played a variation of the previous sequence of tones on the bass xylophone, saying afterwards "Yes, that sounds dead. As if it takes your breath away." With this offer of affect differentiation, she provided a starting point for mentalization. Patient and therapist played back and forth on this instrument several times; they mutually listened to the "dead" sound. The therapist mentioned that one could try out different mallets, but Mrs W. instead decided to play the congas with the mallet.

Scene IV: Face to face

Starting in the seventh week of treatment, the patient increasingly carried out daily chores on the ward, carefully supervised by the nursing staff and discussed in reference to its function as a coping strategy. On the weekends, Mrs W. was allowed home to see if she could master facets of everyday life, and she spent time with her husband on the camp site. Since she stayed in bed there longer than he saw fit, he became physically aggressive, with the consequence that Mrs W. returned to the ward with a black eye in the ninth week of treatment. Besides the necessity to think about involving the police, from a psychodynamic perspective, one can interpret this as the patient's attempt to delegate her aggression. So, in psychodynamic therapy, the therapist's intervention in real-life situations always has to be balanced with helping the patient to gain insight in her own involvement in these situations.

More and more, it had become clear that the patient blamed herself for her lethargy, and then found her husband's reaction understandable. The depressive state of the patient once again became worse. According to the patient, she felt "as if she were dead" inside. However, the fact that she was able to describe her current state with words was seen as an indication that she was making progress in treatment.

When one day she did not appear at lunchtime and could not be located on the clinic grounds, a nurse and the music therapist quickly decided to drive to Mrs W.'s apartment. There, they found the patient sitting on the grass in front of the house surrounded by a group of people. She had jumped out of the first floor window, which resulted in a sprained ankle. Again, from a psychodynamic viewpoint, in a patient diagnosed with bipolar disorder, this parasuicidal act would be interpreted as the manic component lying dormant in the depressive episode, which was already recognizable in the asynchronous percussive play of the patient.

In the next, twenty-fifth, music therapy session, Mrs W. came to the room limping and with a guilty facial expression, but with her mood clearly changed for the better. The therapist told the patient that she did not see it as an act of ingratitude, but as a panic reaction through which the patient had wanted to free herself. The therapist described how the patient's actions gave her a fright. In this way, she reflected the manic potential being defended under consideration of the psychodynamic assumption previously mentioned. Mrs W. reacted to this statement with visible relief. Then, they decided to play some music. It was difficult for the patient to stand up but she indicated that she would like to play the congas, so the therapist showed her how one can hold the instrument between one's legs and beat on the conga skin. The therapist took the other conga and sat down opposite the patient.

The atmosphere of the situation had now radically improved. The therapist should perhaps have felt relieved about this, but instead she started to feel angry. She followed the impulse to be the first to loudly and powerfully beat on the instrument. Mrs W. reacted in her habitual way of playing, slapping on the skins several times with both hands at the same time. This was followed by a solitary beat made by the therapist. The patient looked up, anticipated the next beat coming and grinned. "Now it's your turn" the therapist called to the patient after her third slap on the conga. The patient followed by pounding three times on the conga: right, left, right. She appeared somewhat inept while doing this, and the dynamic of her playing was less powerful than that of the therapist. In answer to the question of how she was feeling, the patient said that she could not say anything about that, but, in any case, she did not feel "as if I am dead." The therapist answered that sometimes it is necessary to let some time pass, before being able to integrate an intensive experience in one's inner world and to find an appropriate expression for this.

From the perspective of developmental theory, much happened in this twenty-fifth session. The therapist perceived an emotion in herself and spontaneously expressed it. If one understands this affect as counter-transference, then one can consider the strikes on the drum as the interpretation. This is confirmed in the fact that the patient was not only in a position to tolerate the emotions being expressed in the play of the therapist, but that she was spontaneously willing to participate in what was happening. The affect was held in the interaction. This way, the patient could free herself from how she had previously been playing and could now play in a manner that was partly imitating, partly varying, while at the same time experiencing her agency. Regarding the question about how she was feeling (and, indirectly also, after the evaluation of her actions), she neither manically heightened nor depressively dampened anything, but was able to relate to the implicit feeling for nothing definite that is grounded in physical processes. The therapist responded to this and deferred what had already been mutually felt but what did not yet exist to a later point in time. This triggered the process of representation of an interactive affect regulation. From a musical perspective, a space full of new opportunities developed, and joint improvisation could start in the following music therapy process.

LIMITATIONS, CONTROVERSIES, CONCLUSIONS

Points of criticism in connection with psychodynamic music therapy can be made from various perspectives. First, one must consider that psychoanalysis itself is a quite heterogeneous field, so that a common theoretical framework for psychodynamic music therapy is impossible to establish. As a consequence, vast differences can exist between different models, leading to critique from all sides. Second, it is important to note that—as already previously mentioned—even some newer publications have not yet integrated current developments in psychoanalysis and, consequently, some reservations about psychodynamic music therapy are based upon outdated conceptions.

The field of psychoanalysis could perhaps find fault with psychodynamic music therapy because, in most training programs, training analysis is much too short. In turn, music therapy could criticize the purely verbal psychodynamic methods of psychotherapy because they do not take enough consideration of non-verbal interactions. From the viewpoint of music psychology and music medicine, again one cannot deny the fact that psychodynamic music therapy has not paid sufficient attention to the physiological effects of sound, rhythm, and dynamics. On the other hand, supporters of psychodynamic music therapy would counter this with the argument that some areas of music medicine practice and research do not take into consideration the effects of music on mental representations of experiences.

There is no question that psychodynamic music therapy does not pay enough attention to processes of learning that occur during therapy, regarding these merely as side-effects. Further, resource-oriented music therapy argues that psychodynamic concepts are too strongly pathogenetically orientated and that the existing resources of patients are not fully recognized (for example, Rolvsjord 2010). This criticism is not really justified because no therapy can ignore the patient's competencies and self-regulatory skills. However, from a psychodynamic perspective, the reasons for restrictions in the quality of life of these persons and for the exhaustion of their coping mechanisms are the focus. A music therapy concept being strongly oriented toward a salutogenetic concept, could be looked at, from a psycho-dynamic perspective, as the denial of reasons for suffering and failure, and a rejection of the patient's subjective reality being founded in his or her biography.

Community music therapy also considers the approach as a measure that can have an influence on social injustices (for example, Stige 2003). In this connection, the question naturally comes up as to whether empowerment is the only method by which to exercise social criticism. For psychoanalysis, the social–political dimension has always been relevant since Sigmund Freud ([1930] 1975). It has focused on politically charged phenomena such as war, anti-Semitism, right-wing extremism, terrorism, and adolescent violence. However, with a couple of exceptions, a socio-critical position in music therapy publications appears to be a rarity. However, if psychodynamic music therapy is seen as a field where contemporary classical music has become very important, this builds a bridge that allows the artistic expression of social issues. This is in contrast to models of music therapy that are based on a rather classical–romantic or popular concept of music where music exists to support and encourage rather than to express every state of being, including conflicted and dissociated states. Psychodynamic music therapy therefore offers an important means by which musical relating can be understood in therapeutic practice.

NOTES

1. The first international meetings were held 1970–1973 in Lenk (Switzerland), Zagreb (Yugoslavia), and Berlin (Germany), and the first official international conference for music therapy took place in 1974 at University of Paris—Faculty of Medecine Pitié Salpêtrière in Paris—and was prepared by Edith Lecourt (F), Harm Willms (D), Darko Breitenfeld (HR), and Angela Fenwick (UK). Further information at: https://normt.uib.

no/index.php/voices/article/viewArticle/425/349 and https://normt.uib.no/index.php/voices/article/view/611/489

2. For overview see Darnley-Smith and Patey, 2003, pp. 24–30. A complete archive of personal/clinical diaries from Priestley and all extant audiotapes of her clinical work are situated at Temple University Philadelphia (http://www.temple.edu/musictherapy/home/dbs/amt_priestley.htm)

3. For an overview of theoretical developments see Greenberg and Mitchell (1983).

4. In this connection it is not important, if the intersubjectivity of the human being is considered primarily innate or as something that develops in the first few months of life. In particular, the discovery of mirror neurons has provided support for the idea of a primary intersubjectiveness, which Trevarthen already advocated in the 1970s. Daniel Stern, too, revised his original belief that intersubjectivity only starts after the age of nine months, and in his new introduction to *The interpersonal world of the infant* (Stern 2000: xx) he speaks of the existence of primary intersubjectivity almost from the very beginning of life. An overview of current research is presented in the contributions edited by Bråten (2007).

5. Edwards, 2011, has summarized recent developments of (not primarily psychoanalytic) attachment theory for music therapy.

6. For music therapy, and especially for psychotic patients, see de Backer (1996).

7. In particular, the differentiation between presentational and discursive symbolics by Langer (1942).

8. http://treaties.un.org/Pages/ViewDetails.aspx?src=TREATY&mtdsg_no=IV-15&chapter=4&lang=en

9. http://www.musicotherapie-afm.com/specialisation_mag.html

10. According to Agid et al. 1999, Barnes and Prosen 1985, and Crook and Elliot 1980, depressive patients experience two to three times more losses during childhood than healthy controls.

References

Agid, O. et al. (1999). Environment and vulnerability to major psychiatric illness: a case control study of early parental loss in major depression, bipolar disorder and schizophrenia. *Molecular Psychiatry* 4(2): 163–172.

Ahonen-Erikäinen, H. (2007). *Group Analytic Music Therapy*. Gilsum, USA: Barcelona Publishers.

Balint, M. (1968). *Basic Fault: Therapeutic Aspects of Regression*. London: Tavistock Publications.

Barnes, G.E. and Prosen, H. (1985). Parental death and depression. *Journal of Abnormal Psychology* 94: 64–69.

Becker, M. (2002). *Begegnung im Niemandsland. Musiktherapie mit Schwermehrfachbehinderten Menschen*. Weinheim: Beltz.

Bion, W.R. (1962). *Learning from Experience*. London: Heinemann.

Böker, H. (2011). *Psychotherapie der Depression*. Bern: Hans Huber.

Bråten, S. (ed.). (2007). *On being Moved: From Mirror Neurons to Empathy*. Philadelphia, Amsterdam: Benjamins.

Bruscia, K.E. (ed.) (1998). *The Dynamics of Music Psychotherapy*. Gilsum, USA: Barcelona Publishers.

Clarkson, G. and Geller, J.D. (1996). The bonny method from a psychoanalytic perspective: insights from working with a psychoanalytic psychotherapist in a guided imagery and music series. *The Arts in Psychotherapy* 23: 311–319.

Compton Dickinson, S., Odell-Miller, H., and Adlam, J. (eds). (2012). *Forensic music therapy. A treatment for men and women in secure hospital settings.* London/Philadelphia: Jessica Kingsley Publishers.

Crook, T. and Eliot J. (1980). Parental death during childhood and adult depression: a critical review of the literature. *Psychological Bulletin* 87: 252–259.

Darnley Smith, R. and Patey, H. (2003). *Music therapy.* London: Sage.

de Backer, J. (2005). *Music and psychosis. The transition from sensorial play to musical form by psychotic patients in a music therapy process.* PhD dissertation, Aalborg Universitet. Available at: http://old.musikterapi.aau.dk/forskerskolen_2006/phd-backer.htm (accessed 12 July 2012).

de Backer, J. (1996). Regression in music therapy with psychotic patients. *Nordisk Tidsskriftfor Musikkterapi* 5: 24–30.

de Backer, J. (1993). Containment in music therapy. In: T. Wigram and M. Heal (eds.), *Music therapy in health and education*, pp. 32–39. London/Philadelphia: Jessica Kingsley Publishers.

Dehm-Gauwerky, B. (2006). *Inszenierungen des sterbens—innere und äußere wirklichkeiten im Übergang. Eine psychoanalytische studie über den prozess des sterbens anhand der musiktherapeutischen praxis mit altersdementen menschen.* Marburg: Tectum Verlag.

Dümpelmann, M. (2004). Kontingenzerfahrungen und affektentwicklung—entwicklungspsychologische ansätze in der psychotherapie von psychosen. In: M.E. Ardjomandi (ed.). *Jahrbuch der gruppenanalyse*, pp. 169–178. Heidelberg: Mattes.

Edwards, J. (2011). The use of music therapy to promote attachment between parents and infants. *The Arts in Psychotherapy* 38: 190–195.

Engelmann, I. (2013). Mine alone is the land of my soul. In: S. Metzner (ed.). *Reflected sounds. Case studies from psychodynamic music therapy*, pp. 113–162. Giessen: Psychosozialverlag (English EPUB-edition of German original edition).

Erkkilä, J. et al. (2011). Individual music therapy for depression: randomised controlled trial. *British Journal of Psychiatry* 199(2): 132–139.

Eschen, J.Th. (2002a). Analytical music therapy—introduction. In: J.Th. Eschen (ed.) *Analytical music therapy*, pp. 17–33. London/Philadelphia: Jessica Kingsley Publishers.

Eschen, J.Th. (ed.). (2002b). *Analytical music therapy.* London/Philadelphia: Jessica Kingsley Publishers.

Fonagy, P. and Target, M. (2003). *Psychoanalytic theories—perspectives from developmental psychopathology.* London: Routledge, Chapman & Hall.

Fonagy, P., Gergely, G., and Jurist, E.L. (eds). (2004). *Affect regulation, mentalization and the development of the self.* New York: Karnac books.

Fonagy, P., Gergely, G., Jurist, E.L., and Target, M. (2002). *Affect regulation, mentalization and the development of the self.* New York: Other Press.

Foulkes, S.H. (1948). *Introduction to group analytic psychotherapy.* London: Heinemann.

Foulkes, S.H. and Anthony, E.J. (1957). *Group psychotherapy—the psychoanalytic approach.* London: Karnac.

Freud, S. (1900; 1989). *Die traumdeutung*, Frankfurt a. M.: Fischer Studienausgabe.

Freud, S. (1930; 1975). *Das unbehagen in der kultur.* Frankfurt a. M.: Fischer Studienausgabe.

Gergely, G. (2000). Reapproaching Mahler: new perspectives on normal autism, symbiosis, splitting and libidinal object constancy from cognitive developmental theory. *Journal of the American Psychoanalytic Association* 48: 1197–1228.

Gergely, G. and Unoka, Z. (2011). Bindung und mentalisierung beim menschen. Die entwicklung des affektiven selbst. *Psyche* 65: 862–890.

Gergely, G. and Watson, J. S. (1996). The social biofeedback theory of parental affect-mirroring: The development of emotional self awareness and self-control in infancy. International *Journal of Psycho-analysis* 77: 1181–1212.

Gergely, G. and Watson, J. S. (1999). Early social-emotional development: Contingency perception and the social-biofeedback model. In: P. Rochat (ed.). *Early Socialization*, pp. 101–136. Mahwah, NJ: Lawrence Erlbaum Associates Inc.

Gold, C., Solli, H.P., Kruger, V., and Lie, S.A. (2009). Dose–response relationship in music therapy for people with serious mental disorders: systematic review and meta-analysis. *Clinical Psychology Review* 29: 193–207.

Green, A. (1993). Die tote Mutter. *Psyche* 47: 205–240.

Greenberg, J. and Mitchell, S. (1983). *Object relations in psychoanalytic theory*. Cambridge, Massachusetts/London, England: Harvard University Press.

Grocke, D. (2007). A structural model of music analysis. In: T. Wosch and T. Wigram (eds), *Microanalysis in music therapy—methods, techniques and applications for clinicians, researchers, educators and students*, pp. 149–161. London/Philadelphia: Jessica Kingsley Publishers.

Hadley, S. (ed.) (2003). *Psychodynamic music therapy: case studies*. Gilsum, USA: Barcelona Publishers.

Hannibal, N. (2001). *Præverbal overføring i musikterapi—kvalitativ undersøgelse af overføringsprocesser i den musikalske interaktion. Udgivet på net* [The preverbal transference relationship in music therapy]. PhD dissertation, Aalborg University.

Jahn-Langenberg, M. (2003). Harmony and dissonance in conflict: psychoanalytically informed music therapy with a psychosomatic patient. In: S. Hadley (ed.), *Psychodynamic music therapy: case studies*, pp. 357–374. Gilsum, USA: Barcelona Publishers.

Kohut, H. (1971). *The analysis of the self*. New York: International Universities Press.

Kunkel, S. (2008). *Jenseits von jedem? Grundverhältnisse, beziehungsformen und interaktionsmuster im musiktherapeutischen erstkontakt mit schizophrenen patienten.* Doctoral Dissertation, Hochschule für Musik und Theater, Hamburg. Available at: http://ediss.sub. uni-hamburg.de/volltexte/2009/3954/ (Accessed 12 July 2012).

Langenberg, M., Frommer, J., and Tress, W. (1993). A qualitative research approach to analytical music therapy. *Music Therapy. Journal of the American Association for Music Therapy* 12: 59–84.

Langenberg, M., Frommer, J., and Tress, W. (1995). From isolation to bonding: a music therapy case study of a patient with chronic migraines. *The Arts in Psychotherapy* 22: 87–101.

Langer, S.K. (1942). *Philosophy in a new key: a study in the symbolism of reason, rite and art.* New York: New American Library of World Literature.

Lecourt, E. (1993). *Analyse de groupe et musicothérapie*. Paris: ESF Editeur.

Lecourt, E. (1998). The role of aesthetics in countertransference; a comparison of active versus receptive music therapy. In: K. Bruscia (ed.), *The dynamics of music psychotherapy*, pp. 137–159. Gilsum, USA: Barcelona Publishers.

Lorenzer, A. (1983). Sprache, lebenspraxis und szenisches verstehen in der psychoanalytischen therapie. *Psyche* 37: 97–115.

McLaughlin, J.T. (1992). Nonverbal behaviors in the analytic situation: the search for meaning in nonverbal cues. In: S. Kramer and S. Akthar (eds), *When the body speaks. Psychological meanings in kinetic clues*, pp. 132–161. Northvale, New Jersey/London: Jason Aronson Inc. Pub.

Mahns, W. (2004). *Symbolbildung in der analytischen Kindermusiktherapie: eine qualitative Studie über die Bedeutung der musikalischen Improvisation in der Musiktherapie mit Schulkindern*. Tübingen, Germany: Mohr Siebeck.

Malin, B.D. (2011). Kohut and Lacan: mirror opposites. *Psychoanalytic Inquiry* 31: 58–74.

Maratos, A.S., Gold, C., Wang, X., and Crawford, M.J. (2008). Music therapy for depression. *Cochrane Database of Systematic Reviews* 1: CD004517.

Mentzos, S. (ed.). (1995). *Psychose und konflikt. Zur theorie und praxis der analytischen psychotherapie psychotischer störungen*. Göttingen: Vandenhoeck & Ruprecht.

Metzner, S. (1999a). *Tabu und turbulenz. Musiktherapie mit psychiatrischen patienten*. Göttingen: Vandenhoeck & Ruprecht.

Metzner, S. (1999b). Psychoanalytically informed music therapy. In: T. Wigram and J. De Backer (eds), *Clinical applications of music therapy in psychiatry*, pp. 102–118. London: Jessica Kingsley Publishers.

Metzner, S. (2000). Ein traum: eine fremde sprache kennen, ohne sie zu verstehen. Zur evaluation von gruppen improvisationen. *Musiktherapeutische Umschau* 21: 234–247.

Metzner, S. (2001). Psychoanalytische musiktherapie. In: H.-H. Decker-Voigt (ed.), *Schulen der musiktherapie*. Ernst Reinhardt Verlag, München/Basel.

Metzner, S. (2003). The significance of triadic structures in clients undergoing therapy for psychosis in a psychiatric ward. In: S. Hadley (ed.), *Psychodynamic music therapy: case studies*, pp. 257–272. Gilsum, USA: Barcelona Publishers.

Metzner, S. (2004). Some thoughts on receptive music therapy from a psychoanalytic viewpoint. *Nordic Journal of Music Therapy* 13: 143–150.

Metzner, S. (2005). Following the tracks of the other. Therapeutic improvisations and the artistic perspective. *Nordic Journal of Music Therapy* 14: 155–163.

Metzner, S. (ed.) (2007). *Nachhall. musiktherapeutische fallstudien*. Giessen: Psychosozialverlag.

Metzner, S. (2009). Psychodynamic movement. In: H.H.-Decker-Voigt and E. Weymann (eds), *Lexikon musiktherapie*, pp. 191–192. Göttingen/Bern/Wien: Hogrefe.

Metzner, S. (2010). About being meant. Music therapy with an in-patient suffering from psychosis. *Nordic Journal of Music Therapy* 19: 133–150.

Metzner, S. (ed.) (2013). *Reflected sounds. Case studies from psychodynamic music therapy*. Giessen: Psychosozialverlag (English EPUB-edition of German original edition).

Niedecken, D. (1988). *Einsätze. Material und beziehungsfigur im musikalischen produzieren*. Hamburg: VSA-Verlag.

Nolan, P. (1989). Music as transitional object in the treatment of bulimia. *Music Therapy Perspectives* 6: 49–51.

Northoff, G. (2011). *Neuropsychoanalysis in practice—brain, self and objects*. Oxford: Oxford University Press.

Odell-Miller, H. (2007). *The practice of music therapy for adults with mental health problems: the relationship between diagnosis and clinical method*. PhD dissertation, Aalborg University. Available at: http://old.musikterapi.aau.dk/forskerskolen_2006/helen_odell-miller.htm (accessed 12 July 2012).

Odgen, T.H. (1985). On potential space. *International Journal of Psychoanalysis* 66: 129–141.

Pedersen, I.N. (2002a). Models and methods of music therapy: analytically oriented music therapy. In: T. Wigram, I.N. Pedersen, and L.O. Bonde (eds), *A comprehensive guide to music therapy*, pp. 121–125. London/Philadelphia: Jessica Kingsley Publishers.

Pedersen, I.N. (2002b). Psychodynamic movement—a basic training methodology for music therapists. In: J.Th. Eschen (ed.), *Analytical music therapy*, pp. 190–217. London/Philadelphia: Jessica Kingsley Publishers.

Pedersen, I.N. (2004). *Exploring and understanding the phenomenon of counter transference used as a clinical concept by music therapists working with musical improvisation in adult psychiatry*. PhD dissertation, Aalborg Universitet. Available at: http://old.musikterapi.aau.dk/forskerskolen_2006/i-n-pedersen.htm (accessed 12 July 2012).

Pedersen, I.N. (2007). *Countertransference in Music Therapy*. Unpublished PhD Dissertation. Aalborg University, Aalborg, Denmark.

Priestley, M. (1994). *Essays on analytical music therapy*. Phoenixville, PA: Barcelona Publishers.

Priestley, M. (1975). *Music therapy in action*. St. Louis, MO: MMB Music.

Purdon, C. (2002). The role of music in analytical music therapy. In: J.Th. Eschen (ed.) *Analytical music therapy*, pp. 104–114. London/Philadelphia: Jessica Kingsley Publishers.

Reck, C., Backenstrass, M., and Mundt, C. (2002). Depression und interaktive affektregulation. In: H. Böker and D. Hell (eds), *Therapie der affektiven störungen*, pp. 45–54. Stuttgart: Schattauer.

Rolvsjord, R. (2010). *Resource-oriented music therapy in mental health care*. Gilsum NH: Barcelona Publishers.

Rose, G. (2004). *Between couch and piano: psychoanalysis, music, art, and neuroscience*. Hove/New York: Brunner-Routledge.

Scheiby, B. (2002). Improvisation as a musical healing tool and life approach. In: J.Th. Eschen (ed.), *Analytical music therapy*, pp. 115–153. London/Philadelphia: Jessica Kingsley Publishers.

Schore, A. (1994). *Affect regulation and the origin of the self*. Mahweh, NJ: Erlbaum.

Schütz, A. and Luckmann T. (1975). *Strukturen der lebenswelt*. Neuwied: Luchterhand.

Schumacher, K. (2005). Zeitsprünge 1968—1994—2004. In: S. Metzner (ed.), *Faszination musiktherapie*, pp. 13–17. Lilienthal: Eres Edition Horst Schubert.

Schumacher, K. and Calvet, C. (1999). The AQR—an analysis system to evaluate the quality of relationship during music therapy. *Nordic Journal of Music Therapy* 8: 180–192.

Schwartz, M. (2004). Einzelne pioniere oder gewachsenes netzwerk?—Versuch einer historischen eingrenzung der geschichte der musiktherapie. Available at: http://www.musiktherapie.de/fileadmin/user_upload/medien/pdf/mu_downloads/schwartz_geschichte-mt.pdf (accessed 12 July 2012).

Schwartz, M. (2009). "Musik zum Öffnen." Kompositionen Mauricio Kagels im kontext musiktherapeutischer ansätze. In: H.-K. Jungheinrich (ed.), *Aufgehobene erschöpfung. Der komponist Mauricio Kagel*, pp. 89–110. Mainz: Schott Music.

Shengold, L. (1974). The metaphor of the mirror. *Journal of the American Psychoanalytic Association* 22: 97–115.

Stern, D.N. (1985; 2000). *The interpersonal world of the infant*. New York: Basic Books.

Stern, D.N. (2010). Forms of vitality. Exploring dynamic experience in psychology, the arts, psychotherapy, and development. Oxford: Oxford University Press.

Stige, B. (2003). *Elaborations toward a notion of community music therapy*. Dissertation, Department of Music and Theatre, Oslo.

Storz, D. (2002). Fokale musiktherapie. Entwicklung eines modells psychodynamisch musiktherapeutischer kurztherapie. Wiener Beiträge zur Musiktherapie Band 4. Wien: Edition Präsens.

Streeck, U. (2000). *Erinnern, agieren und inszenieren*. Göttingen: Vandenhoeck und Ruprecht.

Streeck, U. and Dümpelmann, M. (2005). Psychotherapie in der Psychiatrie. In: H. Böker (ed.), *Psychoanalyse und psychiatrie: geschichte, krankheitsmodelle und therapiepraxis*, pp. 250–263. Berlin/Heidelberg Springer.

Streeter, E. (1999). Definition and use of the musical transference relationship. In: T. Wigram, and J. De Backer (eds), *Clinical applications of music therapy in psychiatry*, pp. 84–101. London/Philadelphia: Jessica Kingsley Publishers.

Strehlow, G. (2009). Mentalisierung und ihr nutzen für die musiktherapie (Mentalisation and its benefits in music therapy). *Musiktherapeutische Umschau* 30: 89–101.

Strehlow, G. (2013). Mentalisierung und ihr Bezug zur Musiktherapie: Mentalization and its Relation to Music Therapy. *Musiktherapeutische Umschau* 34(2): 135–145.

Strobel, W., Loos, G., and Timmermann, T. (1988). Die musiktherapeutische Balint-Gruppenarbeit. *Musiktherapeutische Umschau* 9: 267–283.

Sutton, J. (2002). Preparing a potential space for a group of children with special needs. In: A. Davies and E. Richards (eds), *Music therapy and group work*, pp. 188–201. London/Philadelphia: Jessica Kingsley Publishers.

Trevarthen, C. (1979). Communication and cooperation in early infancy: A description of primary intersubjectivity. In: Bullowa, M. (ed.), *Before speech: the beginning of interpersonal communication*, pp. 321–347. New York: Cambridge University Press.

Trondalen, G. (2004). *Klingende relasjoner. En musikkterapistudie av "signifikante øyeblikk" i musikalsk samspill med unge mennesker med anoreksi*. [Vibrant interplay. A music therapy study of "significant moments" of musical interplay with young persons suffering from anorexia nervosa]. Unpublished Ph.D., The Norwegian Academy of Music, Oslo.

Trondalen, G. (2007). A phenomenologically inspired approach to microanalysis of improvisation in music therapy. In: T. Wosch and T. Wigram (eds), *Microanalysis in music therapy—methods, techniques and applications for clinicians, researchers, educators and students*, pp. 198–201. London/Philadelphia: Jessica Kingsley Publishers.

Tschuschke, V. and Dies, R.R. (1994). Intensive analysis of therapeutic factors and outcome in long-term inpatient groups. *International Journal of Group Psychotherapy* 44: 185–208.

Willms, H. (ed.) (1975). *Musiktherapie bei psychotischen erkrankungen*. Stuttgart: Gustav Fischer Verlag.

Winnicott, D.W. (1945). Primitive emotional development. In: D.W. Winnicott (1958) *Through paediatrics to psychoanalysis: collected papers*, pp. 145–156. London: Tavistock.

Winnicott, D.W. (1971). *Playing and reality*. Hove/New York: Brunner-Routledge.

Wrogemann-Becker, H. (2010). *Ich-entwicklung blinder kinder und die rolle der musiktherapie. Zur symbolbildung unter der bedingung von blindheit*. Doctoral dissertation, Hochschule für Musik und Theater, Hamburg. Available at: http://ediss.sub.uni-hamburg.de/volltexte/2010/4919/ (accessed 12 July 2012).

CHAPTER 25

THE FIELD OF PLAY
A Focus on Energy and the Ecology of Being and Playing

CAROLYN KENNY

THE BEGINNINGS

WHEN I was a young classical piano student, I obeyed the nuns who were my teachers. I practiced my scales over and over again, played single measures and longer phrases repeatedly until they reached perfection, memorized Bach, Beethoven, Schuman, and others. The nuns were strict teachers. So I learned to play well. I learned the value of repetition and discipline. But in quiet moments when no one was at home, I put aside the strict protocols and gave myself over to the intuitive spontaneity of improvisation.

Improvising created space for me to claim my uniqueness and my spirit. The piano was a play space in which I could move beyond discipline, protocols, imposed structures, and the expectation of others. It was an unconditional space that invited spontaneity and freedom. On days when I was happy, I played my happiness. On days when I was sad, my playing reflected this.

Then at age sixteen, I began to sing for the cancer patients at Our Lady of Perpetual Help Cancer Home in downtown Atlanta. Even though I was singing the elegant standards that the patients requested, my sense of play and spontaneity transferred to the patients. Now my singing/playing were influenced by the conditions of the patients, their suffering and laughter, their conditions of being. At that age, I had never heard of something called music therapy.

BEING A MUSIC THERAPIST

Many years later, after performing professional music therapy for two years with silent Debbie, who lived in a convalescent home and, at age 36, she spoke her first word. The word was *piano*. Indeed, we had been playing our sessions at the piano three times a week for two years. In the first two months, I played melodies to Debbie while she sat beside me at the piano with no response. Then I started adding my voice and creating lyrics in relation to Debbie, like "Debbie has bright blue eyes, clear as the sky." Sometimes when I sang to her, Debbie turned her head to face me while we sat together at the piano. We continued like this for many months. I would make up lyrics about the weather that day or the surrounding land or sing about the birds chirping outside. After about one year, Debbie started to make guttural sounds and humming to accompany me. In the second year, she lifted her one functioning hand to the piano and played random notes while I continued to play and sing. At this time, she started to laugh. But she had never spoken until one crystal moment when the nurses tried to roll her back to her room because she wasn't responding enough and because they had determined that other patients would be more responsive. She objected by finally finding her first word in spite of her traumatic brain and spinal cord injury. Things only improved from this first word of protest. Soon she was using her one functioning hand to "play" the piano and was trying to sing.

That night I reflected on the following question: Why did I keep going back to play music with Debbie for those years prior to the word "piano"? I realized that we were not only playing the piano but also playing "life." We were playing in the deepest sense. Then it came to me. I kept going back because of the beauty. Even though the work was often frustrating and difficult, still, it was beautiful. As well, Debbie was beautiful, even though her body was greatly disfigured. I saw and felt her spirit, which was very beautiful to me. I responded to her energy.

Because of my engagement in this music therapy work with Debbie and many other patients in that hospital and other contexts, I felt that I could no longer use language and terminology to describe our sessions that did not resonate on this very deep level with my experience in music therapy. So, another question was born. Can I find another language to describe the music therapy experience that honors this deep level of existence that we had found together in the musical encounter?

My journey to explore new ways to describe the music therapy experience is well documented in many texts with many words and thoughts spilling onto the pages about The field of play (Kenny 2006; Kenny 2014). But let me give you the essence.

> Music is an energy system. By this, I mean that the complexities of music begin with vibration that interacts and moves the whole human being—body, mind, heart, spirit, and soul.
>
> Music is a field of loving and creating when engaged by Music Therapists. By this I mean that the first intention in the practice of Music Therapy is not only empathy and compassion, but also love in the deepest sense. We work to design creative spaces then create new possibilities with our patients and clients.

The seven fields in the field of play

In the field of play there are seven energy fields that begin to overlap as the music therapist encounters and engages patients. The seven fields alternate between opening and closing fields as they mirror the ecological presence of both therapist and patient. The notion of ecology is used here as the basic human process in the sustaining of life—the opening and closing of the valves in the heart, the intake and outtake of breath, the ending of summer and beginning of fall, the waxing and waning of the moon, the ebb and flow of ocean waves. The nature of being is ecological. As a music therapist, I anticipate and embrace this alternating rhythm of opening and closing fields.

I imagine the music therapy experience as an interactive system with such an ebb and flow. When I began my journey of exploration in the mid 1970s, I had easy access to field theory, which was one contemporary idea within the spectrum of systems theories. Field theory made a lot of sense to me because it referenced an interactive energy system (Lewin 1951; McWhinney 1991). It is relational, dynamic, and never static. As well, field theory resonates deeply in indigenous (native) spiritual approaches (Kawagley 2006). The recognition of energy is largely a function of intuition—a highly sophisticated form of logic that brings all of the senses, feelings, and cognitive insights quickly to the surface in an integrated fashion. For the music therapist this means that there is an immediacy in recognizing energies that might be missed with an over emphasis on procedures and other external conditions that interfere with intuition thus missed opportunities. A music therapist might think that she cannot be over-burdened with things like an ecology of being that relates one not only to the conditions of the patient, but also to the conditions of the earth herself. However, Kawagley explains: "Much has been said of intuition as a way of knowing deriving from the unconscious mind, but in an interconnected world even the unconscious is attuned to the forces of nature." (2006, p. 32.) This is a tremendous resource for the patients and therapists. In indigenous ways of knowing, the experience and process of the patient/therapist also gives energy back to the earth. Once I asked the Musqueam Elder, Walker Stogan, why the Salish people held their winter ceremonial dances in the Winter. He said: "The people must dance in the winter to give energy back to the earth because in the winter, the earth's energy is low." (personal communication.)

Though the notion of ecology has been used by other music therapists (for example, Stige 2002) to describe human development, the use of this term has only related to the individual, social, and cultural contexts constructed theoretically by Urie Bronfenbrenner (1979) best known for his ecological systems theory. Thus the term is used as analogy instead of metaphor. The exchange of energy between humans and the Earth in Indigenous cultures is more metaphor than analogy. And as true metaphor, it is also literal. There is a continuous and dynamic interplay between ourselves and the earth in every situation.

I behold my experience with patients and clients in music therapy as an environment or ecology of being. In this environment, there are so many conditions that could be expressed through music. Often these conditions cannot be expressed in words. So music is a way to express very deep thoughts and feelings that words cannot often not express. It takes a clear and elegant focus on totality to really experience such depth. In order to achieve this focus, I could not focus solely/soulfully on behavior. And I also knew that it took a certain kind of consciousness that was not distracted by prescriptive lists and "how to do's" in music therapy.

THE ESTHETIC

When I had the realization that Debbie was a field of beauty, I understood that I was a field of beauty, too, and that all human beings are fields of beauty. This notion might seem absurd, romantic, or impractical to some—to define the human person as a field of beauty. But years later, years after I had completed my initial theoretical explorations to make new language about my experience in music therapy, I came across Ellen Dissanayake's book *Homo aestheticus* (1992). Dissanayake, a neo-Darwinian, had made an important scholarly contribution to the literature that coalesced with my own understanding of human nature. Dissanayake used notions like "making special," "empathy" and claimed the arts were so essential to being human that they defined us as a species (Dissanayake 2001, 1992). I had the realization that my understanding of the human person came from an ancient tribal understanding of our purpose in human life. Our purpose is to be beautiful in the profound sense, to create beauty, and to add beauty to our world from our essential nature as human beings.

The Navajo Blessing way also resonated with my perceptions of the music therapy encounter:

> With beauty before me, I walk
> With Beauty behind me, I walk
> With beauty above me, I walk
> With beauty below me, I walk
> From the East beauty has been restored
> From the South beauty has been restored
> From the West beauty has been restored
> From the North beauty has been restored
> From the zenith in the sky beauty has been restored
> From the nadir of the Earth beauty has been restored
> From all around me beauty has been restored.
>
> Witherspoon 1977, pp. 153–154; Kenny 2014, p. 99

As I recited this beautiful prayer, I understood that it was also describing "a field"—a field of beauty that surrounds us and is inside of us, and thus "is" the human person. To be blessed is to be surrounded by beauty that it imbues us with its essence. Therefore, each of us is a field of beauty.

> The aesthetic is a field of beauty that is the human person. This field contains all non-verbal cues, which are communicated by the person in being and acting and are perceived through the intuitive function. The aesthetic is an environment in which the conditions include the person's human tendencies, values, attitudes, memories of life experiences, and all elements that unite to create the whole and complete form of beauty, which is the person. Furthermore, each therapist and client is a complete and whole aesthetic. In and through the aesthetic domain, we express our human conditions. An aesthetic is what one carries and communicates into the world based on the choices—conscious and unconscious—the judgments on what one considers "beautiful." The aesthetic is an open space that is constantly evolving with the newness and playfulness of all things
>
> Kenny 2006

In order to perceive the patient as an esthetic, it is important for the therapist to pause and become attuned to "being," to "spirit." We put aside our lists of goals and objectives. We feel the energy and prepare ourselves to be receptive to the interaction of our two fields—the patient and the therapist. Or, in the case of groups, the energy of each person in the group and also the energy of the entire group as an esthetic phenomenon. So much of our work involves "doing." And we often forget to fall completely into just being. In a being state of consciousness, we have better access to the deeper areas of existence beyond words, explanations, and procedures—where the music lives. It is not that we do not value this aspect of ourselves. But we often tend to ignore its importance in favor of more transactional approaches to our work.

THE MUSICAL SPACE

A very special space evolves when the music therapist and patient begin to "play." Eventually, they find the totality of each other's esthetics and create a closed space in which their commonalities and differences blend into the sound. Perhaps their shared or contrasting conditions find each other in the music. This is a very intimate space and parallels Winnicott's notion of "transitional space" in early childhood. Everyone needs such an intimate space from time to time especially when one is traumatized, disabled, or suffering in any way (Winnicott 1971).

Music is an expressive medium. Whether consciously or unconsciously, the choices one makes in the musical interplay represent conditions in the musical space. The patient and therapist play and play until they establish a common set of human conditions as expressed in the music—a shared or contrasting tonality, rhythm, timbre, dynamic, or other elements in the musical encounter—leading tones, atonal patterns, call and response, rondo forms, and many others. Thus, the musical space is:

> ... a contained space. It is an intimate and private energy field created in the relationship between the therapist and client. It is a sacred space, a safe space, which becomes identified as home base, a territory that is well known and secure. Initial entry into this space is gained when participants are motivated to make the first sound, a creative gesture, a risk, and a self-motivated action from an intention to engage. The space is sealed off or contained when both participants have joined each other in these first silences and sounds. They get to know each other in the territory. In this energy field of musical begin and acting, the emerging process of delicate new beginnings in development is enacted in musical form.
>
> Kenny 2006

Often, because of the sharp focus and developing state of new consciousness, the therapist and client lose their awareness of people and sounds that are outside of this space and could play for a long time. We now know that music can encourage plasticity in the brain (Baker and Tamplin 2006; Baker and Roth 2004). As the playing continues, new spaces are created not only in the brain but also in the whole being. New possibilities arise in a secure field or setting. When safe space is determined, we want to bath in the presence of delicate and new beginnings.

THE FIELD OF PLAY

Play is one of the central experiences of human life (Huizinga 1949; Brown 2010). My understanding of the term play is dual. It means playing music, but also the more general sense of playing in life. One is more likely to access a sense of play when one feels secure. Music therapists work with so many people who are traumatized that a sense of play is far from their awareness. So many people coming to music therapy services are unable to imagine being playful. Once a patient feels secure in the musical space, then, a new field emerges—the field of play. This is not a stage or a level. It is a space with particular conditions and can happen anytime in the therapeutic encounter. The primary condition is safety. Once a patient feels safe in the musical space, they feel free to experiment with new forms in the musical encounter—new feelings, thoughts, expressions, and behaviors that are represented in the music. For example, a patient will move out of the known territory of a familiar tonality or rhythm to experiment with new and unfamiliar forms.

Sometimes new forms are presented by the therapist in her improvising. Sometimes new forms emerge out of the spontaneous imagination of the clients. Either way, they are incorporated into the musical play. So this space is an open space that receives new forms.

> The field of play is a space of experimentation, discovery, wonder, modeling, imitation in sound forms that express, represent, and communicate significant feelings, thoughts, attitudes, values, behavioral orientations, issues of growth, and change. It has the quality of surprise, playfulness, fluidity, and confidence.
>
> Kenny 2006

RITUAL

As a student in my graduate studies in Anthropology, I began my scholarly journey to learn about many things (Kenny and Stige 2002). As an indigenous scholar, ritual was a deeply held concept that I knew in a tacit way. My graduate thesis proposed that music provides a context for symbolic death and rebirth process, as a form of ritual. These processes are represented in the melody, harmony, rhythm, tone, texture, timbre, and other elements of music. The death and rebirth ritual in music also puts us in touch with the broader processes of our living earth. The human being is a bioregion, just like other bioregions on the Earth, with similar processes. Joyce Tillman also offers "the structures of the world" in her treatment of musicking (Boyce-Tillman 2009). The structure of death and rebirth of wholes and/or parts of us is such a structure. As human beings we mirror and embody the structures of the world. We are in constant motion with our death and rebirth.

All species perform rituals. Rituals are a very important way for living creatures to be in accord with the patterns of the universe. Since our early days as human beings we have created rituals around the cycles of the moon and stars, the patterns of the seasons, the rhythm of life itself (Kenny 2006).

Music has many ritual forms—ABA form, call and response form, and the many variations in tonality, rhythm, timbre, dynamics, and other elements that play with the materials of music—sound and silence. These musical rhythms represent our need and desire to structure our existence around some constants, some reliable benchmarks that remind us that we are connected.

> Rituals are repeatable forms that make space for innovation—an arena of forms, gestures, the constants, which provide a ground base for creativity and change. Musical rituals are created by sounds that are repeated over the course of one or more sessions. Ritual has a sacred quality, just as the musical space and interplay with our consciousness to create a feeling of existential

time so that all that can emerge, does emerge given the conditions in the field. It too, is contained and serves as another home base

Kenny 2006

A PARTICULAR STATE OF CONSCIOUSNESS

Rituals induce a particular state of consciousness. We know that repetitive rhythms shift consciousness into liminality (Rouget 1985, Boyce-Tillman 2009). Liminality opens up the space to dreams, creativity, and discovery. Being in liminal consciousness liberates us from norms, old patterns of behavior, thought, or feeling.

When we enter this type of consciousness, we are in a state of deep concentration and focused attention, yet deep relaxation. We have receptivity to new experiences, new forms, and new sound perceptions.

> A particular state of consciousness opens the fields to more input. It is a state of deep concentration and focused attention, yet deep relaxation. It allows receptivity to new experiences, new forms, and new perceptions in the movement toward wholeness. When one flies in the sound, a feeling of inner motivation can develop—an embodiment of newness and growth
>
> *Kenny 2006*

There is a paradox in the notion that as we move toward beauty, we move toward wholeness if we accept the premise that we are already whole. But this liminality in our patients and ourselves reminds us that we strive toward a more and more elegant and complex beauty and wholeness over time. In the particular state of consciousness, inspired by our experiences in music, we become elevated to new heights that challenge our limitations.

Debbie never imagined that she would speak or play again after her accident. Yet, she was motivated through our being together and through our musical encounters to crash through the boundaries of her seeming limitations. This type of crashing happens over and over again in the music whether it is through structured or spontaneously composed songs, as I shared with Debbie, or through open and spontaneous improvisation with patients in music psychotherapy.

POWER

Once a patient experiences the freedom and confidence in flight through liminality, she feels her sense of power and agency to taking charge. She has a renewed sense of confidence, which, of course, happens in expanding horizons throughout the process.

> Power is a cumulative energy that draws one into new possibilities in the arena of change. Power is experienced through a dialogue between inner motivation, strength, movement, and significant external resources in the existent field. Because of its need to accumulate energy power is enacted through contact with threshold points. There is a need, once again, as in the musical space, and ritual, for containment. Thresholds points begin to interact and at some

point, this energy field is too dense to be contained. When this point is reached, once again, there is a bursting forth into a new field/space

Kenny 2006

CREATIVE PROCESS

The new field is extraordinarily creative and, in fact, can be called the creative process. The process is the product. This is a very difficult position to accept because it flies in the face of our need to control the outcomes of our work. However, in my experience, as long as I give my full attention to the process, and am exquisitely aware of the being-ness and playfulness of my client and myself not only deepen our consciousness, but also many positive outcomes ensue. Some of these products are even on the lists of goals, objectives, and outcomes determined by a therapeutic team. However, the negative space in the lists of procedures and goals is extraordinarily important, just like the rests in a musical score, composition, or performance. The negative spaces sing, too. They make room for new things to happen—things which we cannot always predict.

> The creative process is the interplay of forms (sounds and silences), gestures, and relationships (in music and between therapists and patients) that, as a whole, constitute the context for a movement toward wholeness. If we make a commitment to creative process in the Field of Play, we enter a zone of existential being and acting, which is not product-oriented or consumer-oriented. In this space, we appreciate each emerging moment as the only moment in time; yet acknowledge the past with attention for possible future movement. This space is informed by love, the intelligence of the heart, and thus the knowledge of the self-organizing system. It assumes that given its creativity, a safe environment, and appropriate resources, after trauma, a person will naturally use the creative process to facilitate reorganization and re-integration.

Kenny 2006

CLINICAL EXPERIENCE

Alyce and I sat down beside each other at the piano. I asked her to play. Instead, she performed. Alyce was a highly trained and talented pianist who had actually forgotten how to be playful. Her mother brought her to music therapy because she had been bullied in school and refused to go back.

Though she was only thirteen years old, she had taken on the personality and human qualities of a seasoned performer. As I sat beside her, I felt the finely crafted façade that had stolen the playfulness. We worked together in music therapy once a week over a nine-month period. Over this time, she did learn to play. She found her vulnerability and her creativity, and slowly began to create trusting attachments through shared conditions in the music. She also wrote poems and crafted art with chalk pastels when we listened to the improvisations I had recorded of our shared playing at the piano. Later, she made a piece of art through these listenings that she titled, "Being Born Again through the Music."

By this time, my experiences with Debbie were history. I was so grateful that I had worked over the many years to develop my ideas about the field of play. As I sat and played improvisations with Alyce, my sensitivities to her energy in the liminal space of our music making were keen. It has been this way for a long time. Awareness is important. But language is, too (Whorf 1956; Tannen 1998). Once I had some words, a new language to describe my music therapy experience that had integrity because the words matched my experiences, I felt at home.

TRYING NOT TO TRY THE FIELD OF PLAY

Every professional practice starts with the being of the practitioner. The mantle of professionalism sometimes surrounds this deep and complex part of us with a fog of procedures and protocols demanded by transactional mandates. However, the primary relational influence we have with our patients and clients is our unspoken energy, our presence, and the way we communicate our own life conditions through the spaces we create for and with our clients. We are the music. And the music brings us into relationship with others—with their suffering and joys, their abilities and disabilities, their hopes and dreams.

The field of play is located at the source of being. It provides a refuge for existence and spaces for new growth. If you decide that spirit is a part of everything in the universe, you will feel it, see it, hear it all around you. It takes a great deal of faith to adopt and adapt the field of play. The boundaries are different every time. There are no concrete controls. There isn't a list of prescribed procedures. The only goal is to play. Edward Slingerland, a cognitive psychologist and a scholar in the field of Asian Studies refers to the art of spontaneity as "trying not to try"—difficult at best (2014).

However if we can imagine the field of play as the river that constantly flows beneath our various methods of practice, we can accept the grounded energy of the river, which flows without effort. Too often, we take the river for granted or forget about it entirely. This river of being holds the greatest gifts for our patients and clients because it is our presence, our being, and our very existence. If we accept this river, then we can do or try our work as part of a natural process in an ecology of being. This approach mirrors a very important Native American principle—the principle of non-interference. And I can't help but recall the many times I have seen the term "intervention," a kind of interference, used in music therapy literature. Maybe that's why I had to take this journey to find some new language and new concepts for my own practice. As Whorf (1956) reminds us—our language creates our thoughts creates our reality. Now that I have the field of play I feel liberated from the command and control of language that might inhibit me from the deep and rich human encounters that are available through music in music therapy.

REFERENCES

Baker, F. and Roth, E.A. (2004). Neuroplasticity and functional recovery: Training models and compensatory strategies in music therapy *Nordic Journal of Music Therapy* 13(1): 20–32.

Baker, F. and Tamplin, J. (2006). *Music Therapy Methods in Neurorehabilitation: A Clinician's Manual*. London: Jessica Kingsley Publishers.

Boyce-Tillman, J. (2009). The transformative qualities of a liminal space created by musicking. *Philosophy of Music Education Review* 17(2): 184–202.

Bronfenbrenner, U. (1979). *The Ecology of Human Development: Experiments by Nature and Design*. Cambridge, MA: Harvard University Press.

Brown, S. (2010). *Play: How it shapes the brain, opens the imagination, and invigorates the soul.* New York: Penguin Books.

Dissanayake, E. (2001). An ethological view of music and its relevance for music therapy. *Nordic Journal of Music Therapy* 10(2): 159–175.

Dissanayake, E. (1992). *Homo aestheticus: Where Art Comes From and Why*. New York: Free Press.

Huizinga, J. (1949). *Homo ludens*. London: Granada Publishing.

Kawagley, O. (2006). *A Yupiak Worldview: A Pathway to Ecology and Spirit.* Long Grove, IL: Waveland Press.

Kenny, C. (2006). *Music and Life in the Field of Play: An Anthology*. Gilsum NH: Barcelona Publishing.

Kenny, C. (2014). *The field of play: Ecology of being in Music Therapy, Voices: A world forum for Music Therapy* 14(1). <www.voices.no/index.php/voices/article/view/737/626>. Retrieved July 21, 2014.

Kenny, C. and Stige, B. (2002). *Contemporary Voices in Music Therapy: Communication, Culture, and Community*. Oslo: Unipub forlag.

Lewin, K. (1951). *Field Theory in Social Science: Selected Theoretical Papers*, edited by Dorwin Cartwright. Oxford, England: Harpers.

McWhinney, W. (1991). *Of Paradigms and Systems Theories*. Venice, CA: Enthusion, Inc.

Rouget, G. (1985). *Music and Trance: A Theory on the Relations between Music and Possession*. Chicago: University of Chicago Press.

Slingerland, E. (2014). *Trying not to Try: The Art and Science of Spontaneity*. New York: Crown Publishers.

Stige, B. (2002). *Culture-centered Music Therapy*. Gilsum, NH: Barcelona Publishers.

Tannen, D. (1998). *The Argument Culture: Moving from Debate to Dialogue*. New York: Random House Publishing Group.

Whorf, B.L. (1956). *Language, Thought, and Reality: Selected Writings of Benjamin Lee Whorf*. In: John B. Carroll (ed.). Cambridge: MIT Press.

Winnicott, D.W. (1971). *Playing and Reality*. London and New York: Routledge.

Witherspoon, G. (1977). *Language and Art in the Navajo Universe*. Ann Arbor, MI: University of Michigan Press.

CHAPTER 26

....

POISED IN THE CREATIVE NOW
Principles of Nordoff-Robbins Music Therapy

....

NINA GUERRERO, DAVID MARCUS,
AND ALAN TURRY

> Within the music child, and reachable through it, is the presence of the being
> child. In the assimilation of musical experience and the integration of musical
> activity, the being child indwells the music child as the organizing agent that gives
> the response or activity its integrity, its originality, its unique meaningfulness, its
> message of individual human presence.
>
> Nordoff and Robbins 2007, p. 17

INTRODUCTION

....

NORDOFF-ROBBINS music therapy was founded through the pioneering collaboration
between Paul Nordoff (1909–1977), an accomplished composer and pianist, and Clive Robbins
(1927–2011), an innovative special educator. Their partnership began in 1959 at Sunfield
Children's Homes in Worcestershire, England, and they worked together for approximately
16 years in Europe and the United States. In 1975, formal training in Nordoff-Robbins music
therapy began at the newly opened Nordoff-Robbins Music Therapy Centre in London. In the
same year, Clive Robbins formed a new music therapy team with his wife Carol Robbins (1942–
1996). The Robbinses continued to develop and disseminate the Nordoff-Robbins approach
to music therapy, and in 1990 established the Nordoff-Robbins Center for Music Therapy at
New York University's Steinhardt School of Culture, Education, and Human Development.

Today, this specialized approach is practiced throughout the world by music therapists working with a wide spectrum of clinical populations. Also known as *Creative Music
Therapy* (Nordoff and Robbins 1977/2007), it is considered to be the original music-centered approach within music therapy practice traditions (Aigen 2005), and has a rich

heritage with a highly developed model of practice. The work of Nordoff and Robbins emphasized interactive music-making with clients and "came about from a love of musical creation, musical expression, and musical experience" (Robbins 2011, p. 66). The theories about music as therapy that evolved were developed from their lived experiences of music in clinical situations. Throughout its history, the clinical techniques, training methods, and research within this model have all emerged from engagement with clinical work. Influences from a range of traditions of theory and practice related to music, philosophy, psychotherapy, health care, and education are evident, even while this music therapy approach has remained firmly rooted in close observation and analysis of the details of musical communication and interaction that occur within sessions. The core principles of Nordoff-Robbins music therapy reflect a continual endeavor to be informed and guided by the *creative now* of each clinical encounter.

MEETING THE *MUSIC CHILD*

The therapeutic potentials of Nordoff-Robbins music therapy lie in the development of interactive, inter-responsive musical relationships between therapist and client, and among clients in a group. The therapist creates musical forms utilizing dynamic forces inherent in the musical elements of tones, melody, rhythm, harmony, dynamics, tempo, and so forth. This process is intended to arouse and engage clients' musical sensitivities, and thereby promote their growth and development. Musical processes are viewed as the medium of therapeutic change. A basic premise is that musicality is a fundamental, universal human capacity. Nordoff and Robbins conceptualized this capacity as the *music child* which is inborn within each individual, embodying his or her creative core potential for growth and development, irrespective of disability or illness. According to their inaugural text *Creative Music Therapy* (originally published in 1977), the music child consists of "an organization of receptive, cognitive, and expressive capabilities that can become central to the organization of the personality" insofar as an individual "can be stimulated to use these capabilities with significant self-commitment" (2007, p. 4). By inviting the client into a co-active musical relationship, the therapist promotes and supports the client's optimal engagement through the therapeutic opportunities in the music-making process. As Nordoff-Robbins music therapy has expanded into a variety of settings over the past five decades—including mental health, work with older adults, and programs within medical settings—the concept of the music child remains central, invoking the power of creative engagement to access clients' capacities for resilience, flexibility, and adaptability throughout the lifespan.

Rather than follow a pre-determined protocol of musical activities, the therapist observes, intuits, and responds to the presence and actions of the client, and engages the client in spontaneous musical interactions. Such interaction is a process of continuous empirical assessment: The therapist listens keenly to the client's music-making as evidence of who the client is and the ways in which music might contribute to his or her development and well-being. An individual's music-making is thought to be of "uniquely personal significance" (Nordoff and Robbins 2007, p. 3), revealing the creative potential within, as well as exposing the limitations faced. The expressive qualities of one's music convey the extent of "flexibility

484 POISED IN THE CREATIVE NOW

and adaptability ... fluidity and motion" in one's emotional life, and thus one's capacity to be receptive and responsive to new experiences (Pavlicevic 1997, p. 116).

In accordance with the humanistic principle of self-actualization (Maslow 1982), the Nordoff-Robbins approach "utilizes music to harness the client's will, and recognizes that musical peak experiences can help clients transcend behavioral or dynamic patterns that impede self-enhancement" (Turry 2001, p. 351). As clients develop musically, they are considered to be discovering their core potentials. They are not only becoming more able to engage in music and express themselves musically; they are also becoming more fully themselves (Aigen 1998). By drawing a client into active musical collaboration, the therapist can build upon the client's impulses toward positive development, cultivating intrinsic motivation for interaction and expression rather than scripted responses to extrinsic demands. Clive Robbins referred to this process as working at the client's *developmental threshold*—intervening "to stimulate personal growth, develop self-confidence, ameliorate a painful or limiting condition, and invite him/her into experiences of healing support, liberation, and human companionship" (Robbins 2008).

COMMUNICATION AND INTERACTION THROUGH THE DYNAMIC FORM OF MUSIC

The Nordoff-Robbins approach addresses therapeutic goals through "in-depth utilization of the structural and expressive elements of both improvised and pre-composed music" (Guerrero and Turry 2012, p. 131). Tones and the relationships among them are regarded as temporal events and dynamic forces that vitally affect human experience. The therapist attempts to discern clients' evolving responses to aspects of the musical context, such as harmonic tension and resolution; varying melodic and harmonic intervals; consonance and dissonance; predictable tonal sequences and unexpected creative leaps; tempo and dynamic contrasts; steady pulse or rhythmic freedom; the use of the voice; and shifting textures of instrumental sound. In order to employ music effectively as a medium of communication and interaction, therapists in training learn to develop fluency and versatility in working with musical elements, tonalities, idioms, and styles.

Improvisation in this approach is often described as *compositional improvisation*, since therapists incorporate rhythmic structure, harmonic direction, and melodic motifs to create distinct musical forms which invite clients' response. As Turry and Marcus have explained (2003), "to the spontaneous expressive efforts of the clients, therapists bring a thorough grasp of the aesthetic principles by which such expression may be given form and context" (p. 201). In group sessions, therapists can improvise music that "makes the contributions of each member clearer to the others and enhances the possibilities for meaningful responsive interaction. The resultant counterpoint preserves each individual voice yet unites them in a common creative undertaking" (p. 201). Through such *aesthetic shaping*, the music can lead clients into heightened responsivity and interaction while embracing their present activity. In this way, clinical improvisation allows the therapist to work at each client's developmental threshold, "meeting her impulses, enhancing their communicative impact, and affirming her gains" while "providing a mobile repertoire of supportive, confirming, nourishing, and onward-leading musical experience" (Robbins 2008). Goals need not be pre-determined, but may be uncovered and addressed sequentially in the ongoing process of therapy.

Music therapists who have trained in the Nordoff-Robbins approach have attributed the therapeutic potency of music to the congruence between the dynamic, kinetic qualities of musical form and the qualities of human emotions and physiological functions (Pavlicevic 1997). Ansdell (1995) describes the "pulses and tones, tensions and resolutions, phrasing of actions, bursts of intensity, repetitions and developments" that characterize physiological processes, coordinating the components of each of the body's systems and coordinating these systems with each other (p. 8). Pavlicevic (1997) observes that "the ebb and flow, tensions and relaxations in music resemble the ebb and flow, tensions and relaxations of human feeling" (p. 32). Music does not capture emotions as static entities, but rather conveys the processes of their unfolding and transformation over time.

Pavlicevic has developed the concept of *dynamic form* which draws upon Daniel Stern's concept of *vitality affects*, encompassing such qualities as "surging, fading away, fleeting [or] drawn out" which may be found across various human activities and experiences (Pavlicevic 1997, p. 106). Dynamic form is a characterization of vitality affects in terms of musical elements, including rhythm, tempo, pitch contour, dynamics, and timbre. Through the dynamic form of an improvisation, qualities of expression are intimately linked with qualities of experience, rather than being "an *external* display of ... internal, categorical emotional states such as joy, anger, sadness, and so on" (p. 121). Thus, to the extent that a therapist responds musically to the dynamic form of her client's activity and presence, she is not merely "reading" or inferring qualities of the client's emotions; rather, she herself directly experiences these qualities. In this way, clinical improvisation creates an immediate "intersubjective experience for therapist and client," and offers the client "an experience of 'being known'" (p. 117).

The therapist endeavors to create music that *itself* understands the client (Nordoff, cited by Aigen 1996). Inherent in musical understanding is direct engagement; rather than merely "commenting on" what the client presents, the therapist is "being with the client" through musical attunement (Pavlicevic 1997, p. 152). Psychologists Mills and Crowley (1986) argue that "being with" a client—perhaps especially so with clients who have limited verbal communication—requires communication "at 'breathing' levels of awareness" (p. 97), attuning to subtle non-verbal cues such as breathing and posture, and thereby conveying to the client: "*I see it, I hear it, I experience it; I do understand what it's like to be in that position*" (p. 93). Such non-verbal cues may act as a vital force in shaping clinical improvisation in creative music therapy.

By joining readily in the client's spontaneous playing, movement, and vocalization, the therapist works to draw the client into increasingly reciprocal communicative interaction. What is most importantly communicated in this musical interaction is that each of them *is affected by* the presence and actions of the other. As in the early, pre-verbal development of communication between infants and their caregivers (Trevarthen et al. 1998), the interpersonal dynamics of shared attention, mirroring, and emotional attunement are paramount in the unfolding of musical communication between client and therapist. Just as caregivers nurture the growth of communication by making their actions contingent upon an infant's spontaneous facial expressions, movements, and sounds (Stern 1990), in clinical improvisation the therapist creates music that is contingent upon the client's spontaneous acts, placing these acts within a framework of musical exchange. The therapist attempts to "read" the communicative potential of the client's acts, and to offer a response which the client can recognize as such. In spite of conditions that may hinder the development of communication and relationship, the *potential* for this development is addressed as the therapist seeks to engage the client's "communicative consciousness" (Pavlicevic 1997, p. 103).

Musical communication in this therapeutic approach emerges through immersion in spontaneous interaction, rather than through direct instruction. This is analogous to the process that occurs in young children's natural acquisition of their native language. Collaborative improvisation serves as a means of immersing individuals in rich, spontaneous musical dialogue, thereby developing their musical communication in a naturalistic manner. In this musical dialogue, as Aigen (1996) has observed, the therapist seeks to create a meaningful aesthetic context which enhances the expressive significance of the client's actions. The "spontaneously and flexibly evolving structures" (p. 19) of creative music-making allow for learning through the repetition of familiar musical or verbal material in new contexts, and the presentation of new material in familiar contexts. As with the development of language in infancy, the development of musical communication does not occur through mere exposure to the communication medium, but rather through meaningfully structured engagement. Clients' growth in communication and interaction is intimately entwined in their overall development; it becomes part of their way of being, unlike behavioral change which is externally imposed.

Although the therapist will sometimes imitate the client's playing, the therapist works to create music that communicates her own experience of the client and of their relationship. The flexibility of this improvised music sparks the client's recognition of the therapist's separate, responsive presence, drawing the client into enhanced inter-responsiveness (Aigen 1998). In order for the client to perceive that he is being listened to, he must recognize the presence of the listener. Benjamin (1988) has described the analogous interaction in parent-infant communication. In vivid contrast to responses by mechanical objects, "the mother's response is both more attuned (it 'matches' the infant) and more unpredictable … mixing novelty with repetition … The combination of resonance and difference that the mother offers can open the way to a recognition that transcends mastery and mechanical response, a recognition that is based on *mutuality*" (Benjamin 1988, p. 26).

The infant's sense of agency and personal initiative develops in the context of this evolving recognition of others. Similarly, in therapy, a client may become more self-aware when provided with music that asserts the autonomous presence of the therapist rather than conforming to his immediate needs. As Aigen (1998) has described in his case study of Indu, an adolescent client of Nordoff and Robbins with cerebral palsy and developmental delays, "it is in [the] nonmeeting of his immediate needs that Indu becomes more aware of his self and his own desires; he thus experiences an enhanced motivation and ability to engage in actions which express his needs … " (p. 183). In this way, the client's intrinsic desire to communicate and interact is cultivated.

CREATIVE PROCESSES IN THERAPY

While the clinical use of improvisation is clearly advantageous to the therapist as a versatile tool for "searching out a means of contact" with a client (Robbins 1993, p. 13), it has a further profound benefit: It affords *the client* the opportunity to improvise, to "discover and explore both music and herself" (p. 13). Such creative activity supports the actualization of clients' capacities, making them "communicative and communicable" (Nordoff and Robbins 2007, p. 195). The therapeutic significance of creative engagement, as Maslow (1982) observes, lies in the fact that "capacities clamor to be used, and cease their clamor only when they *are* well used." In this respect, "capacities are also needs." The unused capacity "can become a disease center or atrophy, thus diminishing the person" (p. 201). During peak experience through immersion in creative activity, an individual's capacities are fully expressed. Whereas normally only "part of our capacities are used for action, and part are wasted on restraining these same capacities," at the peak of functioning "there is no waste" (p. 106). One is "able to listen" to oneself and to others "without contamination by expectations based on past situations … or hopes or apprehensions based on planning for the future." The result is "improvised … emergent and newly created" activity which is valued for its own sake (pp. 108–109).

The development of self, in a humanistic paradigm, involves the discovery of meaning in one's own experience. Creative engagement in music offers clients a forum for meaningful activity and interaction. As Robbins points out, for clients whose range of experience has been constrained by disabling conditions, "musical experience is so much more important because it is that much more meaningful in proportion" (cited by Aigen 1996, p. 16). By participating ever more fully in creative music-making, the client comes to experience himself, like music, "as a form that is continually being improvised in the world" (Ansdell 1995, p. 27), ever emerging and undergoing transformation. Such experience is congruent with the humanistic conception of the self as dynamic, a "continually changing constellation of potentialities, not a fixed quantity of traits" (Rogers 1961, p. 122). Therapy presents the client with an opportunity to discover "new aspects of himself in the flow of his experience" (p. 124), and collaborative improvisation allows the therapist to join the client in delving into this flow.

For both clients and therapists, creative musical interaction allows the integration of contrasting human faculties: rational and intuitive, cognitive and emotional, conscious and unconscious. Similarly, the effective use of play in therapy has been described as freeing both therapist and child "to use the whole personality" (Winnicott 1971, p. 54). Wholly immersed in creative activity together, both client and therapist may be affected in ways that lie beyond their immediate abilities to construe or construct. In the training courses he taught at the Nordoff-Robbins Center for Music Therapy at New York University (NYU), Clive Robbins devoted attention to the therapist's cultivation of creative freedom in musical interaction with clients. He developed a diagram entitled "Poised in the Creative Now" (Figure 26.1). This depicts the therapist embarking upon a session, and indicates the broad range of resources, both acquired and intrinsic, that the therapist can utilize in the creation of the music that drives the therapy process. These resources are dispersed equidistantly under six headings that surround the center of the diagram, which is designated as *Clinical Musicianship*. The lower half of the diagram lists abilities or qualities that are largely acquired through experience—musical experience, clinical experience, general clinical training, and knowledge of the particular case. The upper half of the diagram encompasses qualities that are more unlearned, but inherent, including *Intuition, Creative Freedom*, and *Expressive Spontaneity*.

The category of *Expressive Spontaneity* takes account of the therapist's own "musical self" or music child, as well as personal and artistic inspiration, which are essential ingredients in the creative process of therapy. The forces of *inspiration* and *intuition*, along with

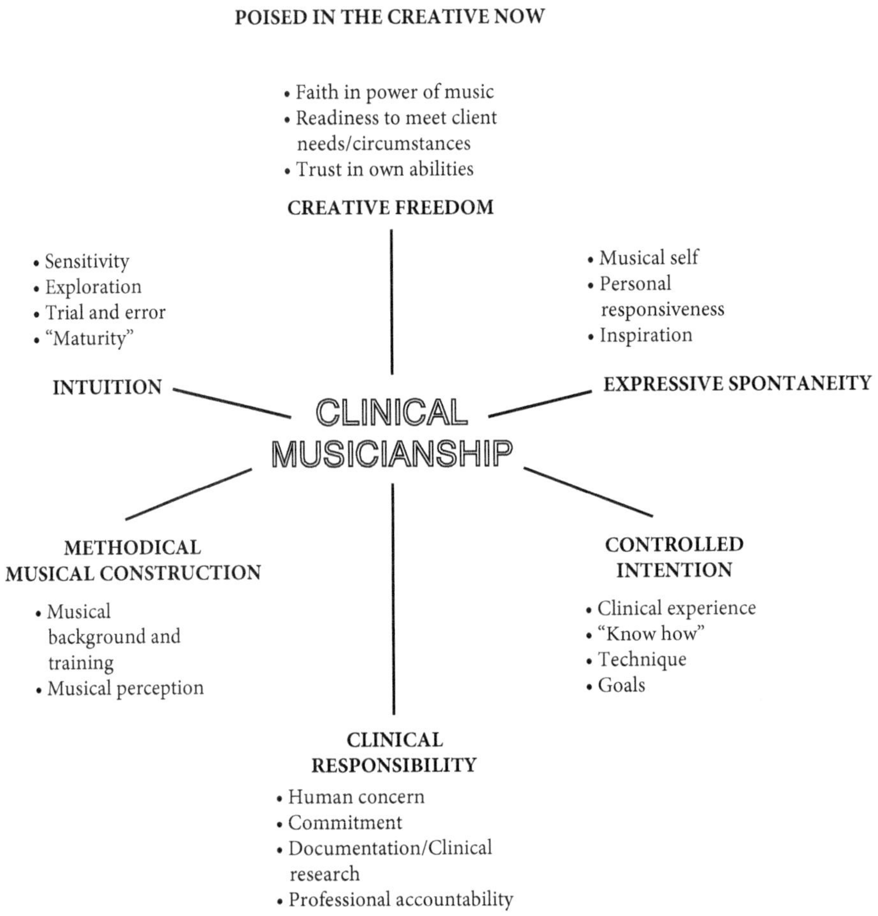

POISED IN THE CREATIVE NOW

- Faith in power of music
- Readiness to meet client needs/circumstances
- Trust in own abilities

CREATIVE FREEDOM

- Sensitivity
- Exploration
- Trial and error
- "Maturity"

- Musical self
- Personal responsiveness
- Inspiration

INTUITION

CLINICAL MUSICIANSHIP

EXPRESSIVE SPONTANEITY

METHODICAL MUSICAL CONSTRUCTION

- Musical background and training
- Musical perception

CONTROLLED INTENTION

- Clinical experience
- "Know how"
- Technique
- Goals

CLINICAL RESPONSIBILITY

- Human concern
- Commitment
- Documentation/Clinical research
- Professional accountability

FIGURE 26.1 Poised in the creative now.

imagination, had special significance in the anthroposophical teachings of Rudolf Steiner (1861–1925). These were considered pathways to the development of deeper awareness and knowledge (Steiner 1977, 1998). The founding and early development of Nordoff-Robbins music therapy were substantially influenced by these anthroposophical values and concepts (Robbins 2005).

The high value placed by anthroposophy on music and the arts in human experience is reflected in Robbins' writing (1993) about the historical context of music therapy:

> Throughout history, mankind has created music for self-expression, for socio-political and religious rituals, and for artistic and cultural experience. The inspirational processes and compositional techniques of music have been channeled into many social purposes … In creative music therapy, the same artistic processes that have produced and continue to produce the social repertoire of music are at work. One is aware of an equal artistic integrity in action, now clinically focused on meeting an individual human being's needs, whether adult or child. (p. 8)

From this perspective, the creative processes of music as an artistic medium are vital to its therapeutic efficacy. Hence, therapists are trained to make musical interventions "not only appropriately, but creatively" (p. 8), availing themselves of the unique expressive possibilities music offers. As Robbins argues, "we must remember that the power of music in therapy stems from the reality that music is an art, that music therapists are privileged to mediate this art to meet many areas of need and experience" (1993, p. 16).

By way of illustration, he describes the lyrical, tenderly expressive song *Wonderful* which he and Walter Stafford, a music therapist who trained at the Nordoff-Robbins Center, composed for their client Karyn, a nine-year-old girl with developmental delays and characteristics of autism (Robbins 1993, p. 17): "The song was truly inspired by Karyn in exactly the same process whereby a character in a libretto inspires a composer with a song or an aria. From session to session, as in a studio, there was a working through; ideas were tried and discarded, clearing the way toward the realization of a theme that had existential truth and definition" (p. 25). He similarly describes his and Carol Robbins's team work with Nicole, a child born in the 24th week of gestation who was four years old when she began therapy: "The improvisations for Nicole, for her piano playing and dancing, were directly inspired by the uniqueness of her being as manifested in the whole gestalt of her ongoing response. The living music reflected—lovingly imaged—the living child, moment by creative moment" (p. 25).

Empirical phenomenology

In Nordoff-Robbins music therapy, clinical improvisation is regarded as an empirical approach to treatment, since it requires therapists' keenly developed perception of and response to moment-by-moment developments in clients' expression and interaction. This *empirical phenomenology* (Ansdell 2012, p. 3) also characterizes the Nordoff-Robbins approach to research and theory development. The creative spontaneity of musical interactions during sessions is balanced by careful detailed observation which gathers evidence of clients' responses to therapeutic interventions. To this end, therapists make high-quality audio-video recordings of each session for review prior to the next session. While reviewing a session, they frequently pause to examine significant events, noting clients' responses and transcribing music considered important to remember for subsequent sessions. This method of close analysis—called *indexing*, as it generates a time-based index of significant moments in each session for future reference—is standard procedure in Nordoff-Robbins practice, originating in the intense care and focus with which Clive Robbins and Paul Nordoff conducted session analysis from the earliest days of their partnership. This has been described as embodying Goethe's concept of bringing love and devotion to the study of an object (Ansdell and Pavlicevic 2010). As the first editor of Goethe's scientific works, Steiner was strongly influenced by Goethe's principle of *saving the phenomena* in theory-building and research, which entails close, respectful observation of phenomena within their natural settings as opposed to reducing them to theoretical or numerical abstractions (Ansdell 2012, p. 3). In accordance with this principle, research within the Nordoff-Robbins tradition characteristically involves in-depth examination of courses of therapy, which is both *idiographic*—"attending to the individuality of each case, of each manifestation of the phenomenon," and *seriated*—"building a collection of exemplary cases for comparison and amplification" (Ansdell 2012, p. 3).

As music therapists collaborate with professionals from other fields to provide interventions and measure outcomes relevant to particular client populations, it is important to characterize the therapy process with the highest possible degree of specificity and completeness. The extensive archive of Nordoff-Robbins music therapy session recordings serves as an invaluable resource for the "musically specific research" (Robbins 1993, p. 16) that is indispensable for understanding the process and outcomes of music therapy. Such research is grounded in the premise that a client's responses to therapy are "intimately related to the kinds of musical experiences created, and to the musical techniques that [establish] her skills and experiences and then [extend] them" (p. 16). Robbins argued against reductive accounts of music therapy in which "the music is left faceless, anonymous … as if music itself didn't matter," as if "all music were the same, and all uses of music in therapy were equivalent" (p. 16). On the contrary, in the Nordoff-Robbins approach, it is in the intimate details of the music that the unfolding communication and relationship between client and therapist are manifested.

ASSESSMENT AND EVALUATION

Nordoff and Robbins developed a set of rating scales (Nordoff and Robbins 2007) that reflected their interdisciplinary collaboration with other professionals in a clinical setting, while maintaining the musical specificity of their approach to therapy. At the Day-Care Unit for Psychotic Children within the Department of Psychiatry in the School of Medicine at the University of Pennsylvania, working under a grant from the National Institute of Mental Health,[1] they utilized an existing assessment tool in clinical psychology, the Behavior Rating Instrument for Autistic Children (BRIAC—Ruttenberg et al. 1966), as a model for developing "instruments for evaluating musical and behavioral responses in individual improvisational music therapy" (2007, p. 367) within and across sessions. They drew upon two of the BRIAC scales—*Scale I: Nature and Degree of Relationship to an Adult as a Person*, and *Scale II: Communication*. As Nordoff and Robbins described, they applied these scales "to similar areas of behavior in music therapy, their terminology being at first interpretively modified to be relevant. Music therapy data were reviewed, subjected to comparative analysis, and progressively incorporated" (2007, p. 367).

The instruments that emerged from this process of adaptation were named *Scale I: Child-Therapist Relationship in Musical Activity* (later renamed *Child-Therapist Relationship in Coactive Musical Experience*), and *Scale II: Musical Communicativeness*. Nordoff and Robbins also created *Scale III: Musicing. Forms of Activity: Stages and Qualities of Engagement* based on an original scale devised by the Day-Care Unit research group for "assessing stages of mastery … to measure the emergence of a child's autonomous behavior" (2007, p. 368). Scale III was conceived as "the music therapy equivalent of this measure, as it delineated the degree and nature of a child's autonomy in terms of discrete areas of musical activity" (p. 368), including "separate hierarchic taxonomies for rhythmic and melodic forms, differentiated by their complexity" (Mahoney 2010, p. 24).

The clinical source material for the development of these scales consisted of Nordoff and Robbins's courses of improvisational music therapy with 52 children and adolescents ranging in age from three to 16 years, including 26 who showed behaviors characteristic of the autism spectrum, and others with a variety of developmental disabilities or severe emotional disturbance. Therapy sessions were audio recorded, and "a description of each child's musical and general behavior in every session was indexed to the recording" (Nordoff and Robbins 2007, p. 369). The scales were developed through detailed study of the session indexes. In the ensuing decades, the scales have been implemented in a variety of settings internationally by therapists trained in the Nordoff-Robbins approach. At the NYU Nordoff-Robbins Center, all three scales underwent extensive revision based on analysis of video recorded courses of therapy conducted at the Center (p. 369).

In addition to functioning as evaluation tools in Nordoff and Robbins's project at the children's psychiatric Day-Care Unit and in subsequent therapy programs, the scales "have served therapists ... as instruments of clinical perception" (Nordoff and Robbins 2007, p. 369), providing a developmental framework for describing a course of therapy. As such, the scales have been of particular utility in Nordoff-Robbins training programs. Scale I, the most widely used of the scales (Wigram et al. 2002), sets forth seven levels in the development of the client-therapist relationship, beginning with *unresponsiveness* or *active rejection* and progressing toward *stability and confidence in interpersonal musical relationship* (p. 374). In its higher stages of development, this relationship is characterized by mutuality and reciprocity in the joint creation of music. At each of its seven levels, the scale captures the dynamic interplay between qualities of *participation* and *resistiveness* in the unfolding of the therapeutic relationship (pp. 372–373).

CONCLUSION

In clinical practice and research within Nordoff-Robbins music therapy, human beings and music itself are addressed in a naturalistic context of creative interaction. Therapists meet clients as equal partners in collaborative improvisation, adapting flexibly and sensitively to clients' evolving participation. Therapists cultivate their own musical responsiveness so that they may engage clients as fully as possible in music-making, rather than imposing preconceived limits upon clients'—or their own—experience of the expressive and dynamic potentials of music. It is by generating and studying creative musical experiences of significant depth and scope that practitioners of this approach come to understand the ways in which music may contribute to human development, healing, and well-being.

Future generations of Nordoff-Robbins practitioners, trainers, and researchers will continue to build upon the legacy of Paul Nordoff and Clive Robbins. New studies and materials for teaching are being published to add to the existing body of training resources. Clinicians and trainers are providing a foundation upon which to develop research methodologies to assess clinical processes and outcomes. In turn, research on Nordoff-Robbins music therapy will continue to test and refine its theory and clinical practice. New areas of practice are emerging as Nordoff-Robbins clinicians enter into interdisciplinary collaborations within a variety of institutions.

Even as these new developments take place, the unique essential characteristic of the approach remains embedded—that musical structures in and of themselves are harnessed in improvisation-based practice that is rooted in music-centered theory. Techniques both to enhance creativity and to establish grounded scientific methods of enquiry continue to develop. Just as music holds qualities of both support and challenge for potential clinical encounters, the approach itself brings together the highest ideals of art and science.

NOTE

1. This was an award of $1 million obtained in 1962 for a five-year "Music Therapy Project for Psychotic Children under Seven," the first grant from the National Institutes of Health (NIH) for the study of music therapy.

REFERENCES

Aigen, K. (1996). *Being in music: Foundations of Nordoff-Robbins music therapy.* Nordoff-Robbins Music Therapy Monograph Series #1. St. Louis, MO: MMB Music.

Aigen, K. (1998). *Paths of Development in Nordoff-Robbins Music Therapy.* Gilsum, NH: Barcelona.

Aigen, K. (2005). *Music-centered Music Therapy.* Gilsum, NH: Barcelona.

Ansdell, G. (1995). *Music for Life: Aspects of Creative Music Therapy with Adult Clients.* London: Jessica Kingsley.

Ansdell, G. (2012). Steps toward an ecology of music therapy: A readers' guide to various theoretical wanderings 1990–2011. In: K. Bruscia (ed.), *Readings in Music Therapy Theory.* Gilsum, NH: Barcelona Publishers.

Ansdell, G. and Pavlicevic, M. (2010). Practicing "gentle empiricism": The Nordoff-Robbins research heritage. *Music Therapy Perspectives* 28(2): 131–138.

Benjamin, J. (1988). *The Bonds of Love.* New York: Pantheon.

Guerrero, N. and Turry, A. (2012). Nordoff-Robbins music therapy: An expressive and dynamic approach for young children on the autism spectrum. In: P. Kern and M. Humpal (eds), *Early Childhood Music Therapy and Autism Spectrum Disorders: Developing Potential in Young Children and their Families*, pp. 130–144. London: Jessica Kingsley.

Mahoney, J.F. (2010). Interrater agreement on the Nordoff-Robbins evaluation scale 1: Client-therapist relationship in musical activity. *Music and Medicine* 2(1): 23–28.

Maslow, A.H. (1982). *Toward a Psychology of Being*, 2nd edn. New York: Van Nostrand Reinhold.

Mills, J.C. and Crowley, R.J. (1986). *Therapeutic Metaphors for Children and the Child Within.* New York: Bruner/Mazel.

Nordoff, P. and Robbins, C. (2007). *Creative Music Therapy: A Guide to Fostering Clinical Musicianship*, 2nd edn. Gilsum, NH: Barcelona.

Pavlicevic, M. (1997). *Music Therapy in Context: Music, Meaning and Relationship.* London: Jessica Kingsley.

Robbins, C. (1993). The creative processes are universal. In: Margaret Heal and Tony Wigram (eds), *Music Therapy in Health and Education*, pp. 7–25. London: Jessica Kingsley.

Robbins, C. (2005). *A journey into creative music therapy.* Gilsum, NH: Barcelona Publishers.

Robbins, C. (2008). *Defining the Developmental Threshold.* Unpublished document, Nordoff-Robbins Center for Music Therapy, New York University.

Robbins, C. (2011). On the connections between the Nordoff-Robbins practice of Creative Music Therapy, Steiner's anthroposophy, Maslow's humanistic psychology, and other psychological and philosophical considerations. In: Nordoff-Robbins Center staff (eds), *Clinical Improvisation: Expanding Musical Resources*, pp. 64–68. Unpublished document, Nordoff-Robbins Center for Music Therapy, New York University.

Rogers, C.R. (1961). *On Becoming a Person*. Boston: Houghton Mifflin.

Ruttenberg, B., Dratman, M., Frankno, J., and Wenar, C. (1966). A behavior rating instrument for autistic children—BRIAC. *Journal of the Academy of Child Psychiatry* 5: 453–479.

Steiner, R. (1977). *Eurythmy as Visible Music*, 2nd edn. London: Rudolf Steiner Press.

Steiner, R. (1998). *Education for Special Needs: The Curative Education Course. Twelve Lectures by Rudolf Steiner*. London: Rudolf Steiner Press.

Stern, D. (1990). *Diary of a Baby: What your Child Sees, Feels, and Experiences*. New York: Basic Books.

Trevarthen, C., Aitken, K., Papoudi, D., and Robarts, J. (1998). *Children with Autism: Diagnosis and Intervention to Meet their Needs*, 2nd edn. London and Philadelphia: Jessica Kingsley Publishers.

Turry, A. (2001). Supervision in the Nordoff-Robbins music therapy training program. In: M. Forinash (ed.), *Music Therapy Supervision*, pp. 351–378. Gilsum, NH: Barcelona.

Turry, A. and Marcus, D. (2003). Using the Nordoff-Robbins approach to music therapy with adults diagnosed with autism. In: D.J. Wiener and L.K. Oxford (eds), *Action Therapy with Families and Groups*, pp. 197–228. Washington, DC: American Psychological Association.

Wigram, T., Nygaard, I., Pedersen, L., and Bonde, O. (2002). *A Comprehensive Guide to Music Therapy: Theory, Clinical Practice, Research, and Training*. London: Jessica Kingsley.

Winnicott, D.W. (1971). *Playing and Reality*. London: Routledge.

CHAPTER 27

RUDOLF STEINER AND THE DEVELOPMENT OF ANTHROPOSOPHICAL MUSIC THERAPY
A Historical Overview

ANDREA INTVEEN AND JOHN CLARK

THE foundations of anthroposophical music therapy lie in anthroposophy, a doctrine developed by the Austrian Rudolf Steiner (1861–1925). The term anthroposophy is derived from the Greek word "anthropos" meaning human being, and "sophia" meaning wisdom. It therefore means "the wisdom of the human being" (Bamford 2002, p. 8). Anthroposophy's origins can be traced to a range of philosophical traditions including Theosophy and Rosicrucianism (Bamford 2002).

Information about Steiner's life is available from numerous anthroposophical sources (for example Bamford 2002; Childs 1995; Lachman 2007; Lindenberg 1997; Wilkinson 2001), including also Steiner's own autobiography (Steiner 1928). Steiner grew up in a Roman Catholic family, and studied mathematics, natural history, and chemistry in Vienna. Reportedly, he also taught himself Latin and Greek and studied the works of the contemporary philosophers of his time, such as Fichte (Childs 1995). In 1883, at the age of twenty-two, Steiner was invited to edit Goethe's scientific writings for the "Deutsche Nationalliteratur" (Childs 1995), a collection of German literary writings leading up to the time of Goethe, which was edited by Joseph Kürschner (1853–1902) and contained 164 annotated volumes. In 1891 Steiner attained his Ph.D. at the University of Rostock in the North of Germany (Childs 1995). He is probably best known in contemporary times as the founder of the Waldorf or Steiner schools. Steiner was both interested and influential in the education of children with special needs within an anthroposophical context, but also acted in other areas, such as anthroposophical architecture, drama, painting, and poetry. Additionally, he created the movement art "eurythmy" (Bamford 2002).

Steiner was secretary of the German Theosophical Society for some time, and in 1913 he founded the Anthroposophical Society (Bamford 2002; Childs 1995). His most important writings include "The Philosophy of Freedom" (Steiner 1964) and "Occult science: An outline" (Steiner 2005). Together with Ita Wegmann, Rudolf Steiner created the foundations for anthroposophical medicine (Steiner and Wegmann 1996), which they proposed to be an extension of mainstream medicine. It includes herbal medicine as well as a specific anthroposophical approach of homeopathy (see Hamre et al. 2004, 2007) and serves as the foundation of the remedial and therapeutic impulse in anthroposophy, which also finds expression in the anthroposophical arts therapies, such as art therapy, eurythmy therapy, and music therapy (AnMt).

AnMt developed as a therapy practice in *curative education*, an interdisciplinary anthroposophical approach to remedial work with people with intellectual disabilities (König 1966). Music has always played a central role in anthroposophical communities which provide services for people with special needs, many of which were founded after 1924 (Beilharz 2004a). The "Sonnenhof" in Arlesheim, Switzerland is an anthroposophical community with a residential home and a special school for children, adolescents, and adults with special needs. In the late 1920s, some of the first attempts to apply music systematically and therapeutically were made at this site (Beilharz 2004a).

After 1950 AnMt was further developed by pioneering personalities such as Karl König, a doctor and curative educator who developed music therapy treatments for children with specific conditions and who also published his ideas (Beilharz 2004a; König 1966). Hans-Heinrich Engel and Hermann Pfrogner collaborated for several years and both were involved in a music therapy study circle in the Christophorus home in the Netherlands. This group's activities had a long-lasting influence on AnMt. It consisted of music therapists, doctors, curative educators, and musicians (Beilharz 2004a). Both Pfrogner and Engel investigated intervals, also in a cosmological context (Pfrogner 1978, 1981, 1986; Engel 1999). Engel (1999) explored Steiner's ideas of the existence of a link between musical elements, planets, and organs of the human organism.

THE FIRST TRAINING PROGRAMMES

The emergence of the first AnMt training courses profoundly influenced the approach's further development. From 1974 to 1981 a course was provided at the Christophorus Home in the Netherlands with Veronika Bay as one of its founders. Christoph-Andreas Lindenberg developed the music therapy foundations in Camphill (Beilharz 2004a) and later founded the Dorion School of Music Therapy in Pennsylvania, USA (Beilharz 2004a; Willig 2005), which still exists today.

Maria Schüppel founded the anthroposophical music therapy training course in Berlin at "Musiktherapeutische Arbeitsstätte" in 1963 and directed it until 1993 (Beilharz 2004a). Originally a composer and pianist, she combined her musical knowledge and experience with the anthroposophical view of the human being (Bissegger 2001). At the time of writing the training programme at "Musiktherapeutische Arbeitsstätte" is directed by Peter Fausch. Johanna Spalinger co-founded the music therapy training at the Orpheus School of Music Therapy near Bern in Switzerland (Beilharz 2004a) together with Marlise Maurer and Heinrich Schneider.

With the emergence of anthroposophical music therapy schools to train aspiring therapists, the number of skilled and specialized therapists increased while the applications of AnMt spread beyond the boundaries of curative education (Beilharz 2004a). The areas of expanded AnMt practice include, for example, pediatrics, internal medicine, psychiatry, palliative medicine (Felber et al. 2003), intensive care (Reinhold 1993), oncology, psychosomatics, neonatology, gynecology (Pütz 2008) and other areas of medical expertise.

CONTENTS OF ANMT TRAINING

The information for this section is gained from the course documentation from the training programme at "Musiktherapeutische Arbeitsstätte" in Berlin (2010). The courses at the "Dorion School of Music Therapy" in Glenmoore, Pennsylvania, United States and the "Orpheus-Schule für Musiktherapie" in Switzerland have similar contents, although there are also some variations in content and focus between the three programmes (Intveen 2011).

"Musiktherapeutische Arbeitsstätte" in Berlin offers a private course based on anthroposophical ideas and lasts for eight-and-a-half semesters. The training at the "Arbeitsstätte" strives to be a comprehensive interdisciplinary theoretical and practical course. The aim is to enable graduates to practice AnMt in all medical, educational, and social fields of application. The course is divided into three phases with the first phase consisting of a two-year-period of broader basic education. The second phase lasts fourteen months and encompasses practical music therapy education. Placements consist of two six-week-blocks in special education or clinical fields. Phase three is a mentored internship with supervision, which extends over a full year and during which extensive documentation has to be undertaken. This is followed by the final exams.

The theoretical subjects in the course include professional ethics, professional law, assessment and diagnostics, case conceptualization, treatment settings, and devising a treatment plan, as well as documentation and evaluation. Verbal techniques are part of the curriculum, as well as a large number of medical subjects, including embryology, anatomy, physiology, pathology, psychiatry, and gerontology. Furthermore, subjects such as pharmaceutics, development of the human being, pedagogy, and comparative music therapy are included. In addition to this, a number of psychological and psychotherapeutic subjects are taught, such as psychology, developmental psychology, and psychotherapy, as well as prevention and salutogenic concepts.

The practical subjects include application of therapy instruments, peer supervision, as well as experiential and biographical work. There is an individual training plan which includes individual lessons in singing, lyre, and in playing a bowed stringed instrument, but also some music theory subjects. An important part of the training consists of the students' own experience of musical phenomena. Graduates of the course qualify with a certificate in accordance with the guidelines of the Association for Anthroposophical Arts Therapies in Germany (AAArTiG) and the medical section of the independent academy for humanities at the Goetheanum in Dornach/Switzerland ["Freie Hochschule für Geisteswissenschaft am Goetheanum, Dornach/Schweiz, Medizinische Sektion"].

In comparing the contents of the different AnMt training courses with each other and with other, state-recognized and accredited training courses, it becomes apparent that the anthroposophical courses strive to incorporate both anthroposophical contents and aspects that would also be important in accredited, non-anthroposophical music therapy courses, such as professional ethics, research, experiential aspects, supervision, peer-supervision, etc. (Intveen 2011; Intveen and Edwards 2012). However, the website of the training course at

"Musiktherapeutische Arbeitsstäte" ("Musiktherapeutische Arbeitsstätte" 2010) creates the impression that the main guideline for AnMt training refers to the anthroposophical professional bodies and not the state authorities.

THE ANTHROPOSOPHICAL VIEW
OF THE HUMAN BEING

AnMt is closely connected to the principles of anthroposophical medicine and both are based on the anthroposophical view of the human being. In Steiner's writings, the latter is outlined in great detail (for example Steiner 1964, 1987, 1998, 2004). Anthroposophy has proposed a range of explanatory models of human nature. It would be beyond the scope of this book chapter to explain all of these. In order to understand some of the foundation concepts of AnMt, the *threefold* and *fourfold* models of the human being are important and will be described.

The fourfold human being

The anthroposophical model of the fourfold human describes the relationship between the physical parts and other, immaterial and spiritual aspects of the human being (Damen 2004). It is based on the idea that body, soul, and spirit are all part of human nature (Steiner 2004). Steiner proposed that the human being "consists of a physical body, an etheric body, an astral body, and an ego" (Steiner 1970, p. 121). These "bodies" or "members" are regarded as respectively connected to the mineral, plant, and animal kingdoms in nature, and through their connection with these bodies, the different kingdoms of nature are assumed to be represented in the human being (Felber 2003a,b; Steiner 2004). In the anthroposophical view, the *physical body* is linked to the mineral kingdom and constitutes the body that can be physically seen and touched (Felber 2003b; Gäch 2004). As an example, according to Gäch (2004) the mineral quality of the human being finds expression in the skeleton.

Bento claimed that in order to exist and not to fall into pieces, the physical body needs the help of the *etheric body*, which is of a "fluid nature" (Bento 2004, p. 13). The etheric body furthers the activity of life-building and formative forces (Felber 2003b). It is assumed to be connected to the plant kingdom (Felber 2003b; Gäch 2004) and to encompass the organic nature of the human being (Gäch 2004). The ether body is perceived to contain the human being's vitality, as well as deeply rooted habits and emotional imprinting, parts of the memory and the basis of a person's emotional constitution (Florschütz 2007).

Steiner considered the *astral body* as the finest of the four bodies, and it is here that human desires are located (Steiner 2004). The astral body is understood to contain all the different attributes of the soul (Kern 2007). From an anthroposophical viewpoint, the astral body is related to the human being's membership of the animal kingdom (Felber 2003b) in so far as instincts, desires, and drives are contained in it (Gäch 2004). It is regarded as the centre of emotional life (Felber 2003b). Practising music is seen as a pathway for accessing the astral body, since music's inherent structural principles are assumed to enhance and support the development of structural principles in humans (Gäch 2004).

In the anthroposophical understanding of the fourfold human being the ego is regarded as the core of the personality. Through it human beings perceive the laws of the outside world by way of thinking and thereby absorb part of the world's spiritual aspects (Kern 2007). While the other three bodies are connected to the mineral, plant and animal kingdom, the ego is linked to the sphere of the human being (Gäch 2004) and is characterized by the capacity for self-awareness, awareness of one's environment and of spirituality, as well as the ability to be active in a spiritual and creative way (Felber 2003b). Individuality is considered to be the ego's main characteristic (Gäch 2004). Steiner (2002) believed that the ego contains a person's ability to love. Anthroposophists advocate that the different parts of the fourfold human being are not separated from each other but interact with and support each other in their functions (for example Gäch 2004; Kern 2007).

The fourfold human being and musical elements

In AnMt musical experience is understood to be connected to the fourfold human being in distinctive ways. Damen (2004) proposed that music listening is an outward activity which is accompanied by an inner experience. This inner experience is linked with the physical body. When this inner experience has a vitalizing effect, it is considered that the ether body is involved. When feelings and emotions are elicited through musical experience then the astral body is assumed to be involved. If music listening leads to spiritual experiences, this is interpreted as an ego activity (Damen 2004).

Felber (2003a) suggested that the physical body finds musical expression in everything related to architectural principles in music, such as the solid structure provided by musical measure or the way chords are constituted. The ether body, related to the plant world, is seen as connected to anything in music which is of a plastic nature, such as rhythm or certain melodic shapes (Felber 2003a). The astral body is expressed musically in everything that is colorful in music or associated with light and warmth, like timbre or certain intervals. Musical form, as expressed in composition, is related to the ego principle (Felber 2003a).

THE FOURFOLD HUMAN BEING
AND MUSICAL INSTRUMENTS

Anthroposophists propose that the ego, astral body, ether body, and physical body are connected to the four elements fire, air, water, and earth (Reinhold 2003). The involvement of these four elements in processes associated with human constitution and human body fluids, as well as temperaments, is also found in humoral pathology based on Hippocratic ideas (Bujalkova et al. 2001). In the anthroposophical view, fire is related to the ego, air to the astral body, water to the ether body, and earth to the physical body (Reinhold 2003). Reinhold suggested that wind instruments are linked with the element of fire and with the ego, as tone production through blowing has a fiery quality and the player is engaged on an ego-related level. Light and airy sounds are created in plucking, which is perceived to be connected to the astral body (Reinhold 2003). Reinhold proposed that bowing can contain a watery, flowing quality and that this may suggest a connection between bowed instruments and the ether

Table 27.1 Connections between the fourfold human being, the four elements, musical instruments, and musical elements as suggested by Felber (2003a) and Reinhold (2003)

Ego	Astral Body	Ether Body	Physical Body
Fire	Air	Water	Earth
Wind Instruments	Plucked Instruments	Bowed Instruments	Percussion Instruments
Form Principle: Composition	Colour Principle: Timbre, Intervals	Plastic Principles: Rhythm, Melody	Architectural Principles: Measure, Chords

body. The solid character of the earth element is seen as linked to the physical body and to percussion instruments. However, the qualities attributed to musical instruments in AnMt are not static or fixed. For example, Reinhold (2003) argued that on one single instrument, such as the tenor chrotta, fiery, airy, watery and earthy music can be played. Besides that, the cultural and sometimes religious contexts into which musical instruments can be embedded is not denied in AnMt (Reinhold 2003). The connections between the fourfold human being and musical instruments are shown in Table 27.1.

The threefold human being and its connection with thinking, feeling, and willing

While the four members of the fourfold human being are perceived to provide an understanding of the structure of the human being in relation to nature, the model of the threefold human being offers insight into the fields of action in between these four members (Gäch 2004). In addition to the fourfoldness described above, in anthroposophy a threefoldness is presented as linked to the soul activities of thinking, feeling, and willing (Gäch 2004). These are understood to be respectively related to the upper (head), middle (chest), and lower (limbs) human being (Steiner 2004). These connections are shown in Table 27.2.

Steiner (2004) stressed that these systems do not have fixed boundaries but are interconnected. When considering the human being in accordance with the model of the threefold human being, a polarity between the head and the limb system, the upper and lower human being becomes apparent (Felber 2003a). The middle human being, which manifests in the chest or trunk part of the human body, is seen as the meeting place of these two polarities (Felber 2003a). The upper human being—with the head as its main manifestation—is interpreted as an expression of the world of ideas and sense perceptions (Felber 2003a). It is also described as a calming, cooling influence within the human organization (Felber 2003a; Gäch 2004; Reinhold 1996).

From an anthroposophical point of view, the lower human being finds a physical manifestation in the limbs and in the metabolism (Damen 2004; Felber 2003a; Gäch 2004). Its task is one of movement and activity (Felber 2003a; Gäch 2004), production of warmth and decomposition of substances (Gäch 2004).

The middle human is physically manifest in breathing and heartbeat (Felber 2003a). It is also called the "rhythmic system" (Damen 2004; Felber 2003a; Gäch 2004) and functions as a mediator between the head and the limb system (Felber 2003a; Gäch 2004). In

Table 27.2 Parts of the human organism and their connections to the soul qualities of thinking, feeling and willing (compare Steiner 2004)

Head	Chest	Abdomen/Limbs
Upper human being	Middle human being	Lower human being
Thinking	Feeling	Willing

anthroposophy, the three different parts of the human being are perceived to be linked to three different soul activities: thinking, feeling, and willing (Steiner 2004). Steiner (2004) suggested that the upper human being is connected to thinking, the lower human being to willing and the middle human being to feeling. In this context, will is seen as the human being's capacity to relate to the world through activity (Steiner 2004; Lievegoed 2005).

Lievegoed (2005) stated that feelings swing between polarities, such as sympathy and antipathy or love and hate, creating a pattern which resembles the rhythmic processes in the human being, such as inhalation and exhalation. These processes are interpreted as a reflection of the cosmic rhythms, which find expression—for example—in the change of the seasons (Lievegoed 2005).

The threefold human being and musical elements

In the anthroposophical view musical elements and the soul activities of thinking, feeling, and willing correspond to each other (Steiner 1970, 1980; Reinhold 1996). For example, melody is perceived to be related to thinking (Reinhold 1996; Gäch 2004), harmony is believed to be linked to feeling, and rhythm corresponds to willing (Steiner 1970, 1980; Gäch 2004; Reinhold 1996).

Rhythm in music is closely connected to movement and dance while movement is thought to distract from melody. The latter is identified with the calm quality of thinking (Reinhold 1996). Harmony is assumed to be located between melody and rhythm, and to connect them (Reinhold 1996). The major keys are considered more outgoing in character, the minor keys more inward. In the transition between major and minor, the polarities of human experience, such as opposing feelings, day and night, inhalation and exhalation, are expressed (Reinhold 1996). In AnMt, therapeutic significance is attributed to these ideas: It is assumed that through music with a strong rhythmical accentuation the will can be activated or that relaxation can occur in listening to a beautiful melody. From an AnMt point of view, pathological imbalances can thus be brought back into balance (Reinhold 1996).

The threefold human being and musical instruments

In AnMt, musical elements and instruments are regarded to have specific effects in accordance with the anthroposophical view of the human being (Reinhold 1996; Reinhold 2003; Beilharz 2004c). Steiner perceived wind instruments to be related to the upper, bowed instruments to the middle and percussion instruments to the lower human being (Steiner 1970, 1980). Reinhold (2003) proposed that when wind instruments are played, a feeling of calmness is produced in the player. Sound production is linked to the breath and movement

Table 27.3 Connections between the threefold human being, musical elements,
and instruments (Reinhold 2003; Steiner 1970, 1980)

Head	Chest	Abdomen/Limbs
Upper human being	Middle human being	Lower human being
Thinking	Feeling	Willing
Melody	Harmony	Rhythm
Wind Instruments	Stringed Instruments	Percussion Instruments

of the limbs is minimal in the process of playing (Reinhold 2003). This is assumed to indicate a connection with the upper human being.

In contrast to this, playing percussion instruments is directly connected to the movement of the limbs. The original link between the percussive element in music and dance is still observable, which suggests a connection with the soul activity of willing and with the lower human being (Reinhold 2003). The connection of stringed instruments with the middle human being shows in the way they are sometimes held near the chest area but also in the way they relate to harmony in music. The former is especially true for the lyre, children's harp and kantele (Reinhold 2003). The links between the parts of the threefold human being, musical elements and instruments are indicated below in Table 27.3.

BASIC TENETS OF ANMT

Musical and therapeutic specifics of AnMt

Some elements of AnMt are unique to the approach such as the use of specific musical elements, tonalities, and instruments. This section gives a brief overview of some of the musical and therapeutic features of AnMt. Reference to the avoidance of electronic media and electronic music in AnMt is also considered as it is a distinctive aspect of the approach.

In AnMt practice, conventional musical instruments are used, as well as specialized instruments designed for use in AnMt (Beilharz 2004b; Gevecke 2004; Kumpf 2004; Reinhold 1996, 2003). In addition to "traditional" Western scales and tonalities, scales and musical sequences indigenous to AnMt are applied in the therapeutic process, such as the mirrored planetary scales (von Lange 1968) or the Mercury Bath (Bissegger 2004; Intveen; 2010a,b). There are other sequences that are not included here, for instance the Tao sequence (Engel 1999; Pfrogner 1986) and the Breathing Melody (Intveen 2011).

Tonalities and sequences: The mirrored planetary scales and the Mercury Bath

The mirrored planetary scales

The mirrored planetary scales are particular tonal sequences that are used by some anthroposophical music therapists. It is beyond the scope of this chapter to give a detailed account of the complex and elaborate assumed cosmological connections between planetary tones, planetary scales, human organs, days of the week, and soul-related qualities, as described by Engel (1999). Therefore, only a partial summary of this complex subject will be presented. According to Engel (1999) and von Lange (1968) the different tones of the diatonic scale are connected to seven planets. Both authors agree that C is linked with Mars, D with Mercury, E with Jupiter, F with Venus, G with Saturn, A with the Sun, and B with the Moon. On each of these tones, planetary scales are built up, which differ in structure, quality, and in their ascending and descending forms. Chromatic changes in the descending scales cause changes in accidentals (von Lange 1968). This comes about through mirroring the intervals of the ascending scale in reverse order in the descending scales (Intveen 2010b).[1]

If, for example, in the ascending Mars scale, which contains the same notes as the C-Major scale and the Ionian mode, the first interval from C to D is a whole tone, the first interval in the descending scale is also a whole tone, from C down to B flat and so on (Intveen 2010b). None of the ascending scales have accidentals and thus they are outwardly identical to the ascending church modes (Intveen 2010b). The Mercury scale is Dorian and the only mirrored planetary scale with the same notes in the ascending and the descending scale (von Lange 1968). The other descending planetary scales contain different combinations of intervals and accidentals (Intveen 2010b; von Lange 1968). Sharpened notes in the descending scales are interpreted as bringing light into the scale while flattened notes are seen to add a more darkened, inward quality (von Lange 1968).

In AnMt, the *tone of the day* is sometimes used to mark the beginning and end of sessions (von Lange 1968). This is based on the idea that the days of the week are connected to planets (von Lange 1968). The tone which is assigned to the planet in question would then be the tone of the day connected to this planet. For example, the tone D is assumed to be connected to Mercury, which in turn is associated with Wednesday, which would make D the tone of the day for Wednesday. Von Lange (1968) suggested that musical activities used in AnMt treatment could be more effective if the tone of the day is introduced, so that a connection with the cosmic forces is created.

The Mercury Bath

The Mercury Bath is a sequence composed by Maria Schüppel (Bissegger 2004). Bissegger (2004) emphasized the Mercury Bath's light, sparkly and invigorating quality, which is due to the 7/8-measure and the constant change between major and minor. This sequence is based on the Mercury scale, starts and ends on the tone D, doesn't contain any accidentals and consists of arpeggiated ascending and descending major and minor triads, with major and minor alternating (Intveen 2010b). There is little reference to the Mercury Bath's therapeutic applications in the AnMt literature. Engel (1999) has implied therapeutic uses, which are only comprehensible to experienced anthroposophists. In-depth interviews with AnMt practitioners carried out by Intveen (2011) revealed that the Mercury Bath is regarded as a sequence that can be applied for a great range of people and symptoms and that the harmonizing effect of this sequence is perceived to come about by mixing up things and loosening tightened structures or any developments that may have stagnated.

Musical specifics: Use of specialized musical instruments

Instruments such as the lyre (Beilharz 2004b), bordune lyre (Tobiassen 2004), chrotta (Gevecke 2004), choroi flutes (Pedroli 2004), or Bleffert metal instruments (Kumpf 2004) are specific to AnMt and were developed within the model. Singing and therapeutic voice work is also quite important in AnMt. There is a particular approach to singing founded by Werbeck-Svärdström, who collaborated with Steiner for some time and aimed at *uncovering the voice* rather than building it up (Werbeck-Svärdström 1980). Reference to the subject of therapeutic singing is also made by Felber, Reinhold, and Stückert (Felber et al. 2003). As will be seen in this section, the instruments have been developed to offer solutions to medical or developmental problems. The idea that certain musical elements, tones, and ways of playing have certain therapeutic effects is relatively unique to AnMt in comparison with many other music therapy approaches.

Wind instruments

A range of wind instruments are used in AnMt. Some have been designed especially for use in AnMt while others such as the gemshorn, crumhorn, or alphorn (Reinhold 1996) exist outside of AnMt practice. This section of the chapter focuses on instruments created specifically within AnMt.

The copper flute and the Choroi flute

The copper flute is a wind instrument with a gentle timbre (Reinhold 1996). The pitch of the tones played is regulated by the strength of breath, and there are no finger holes. A minimal increase in intensity of breath is needed to change the pitch to the next highest tone in the overtone scale. Players therefore learn to increase the strength of their breathing gradually. This instrument is sometimes used for patients with respiratory conditions, such as asthma (Reinhold 1996).

Choroi flutes have a light, clear timbre (Reinhold 1996), their shape is cylindrical and the wood they are made from is only treated with oil (Reinhold 2003). Choroi flutes are available with diatonic and pentatonic tuning, and also as interval flutes with only one hole, which allows the player to play two notes, either a fourth or a fifth apart (Reinhold 2003). Pedroli (2004) remarked that the Choroi flute is easy to play but produces a musically satisfying tone. Reinhold (1996) advocated that the sensitive psyche of small children can be addressed with this instrument, as well as adults who—from an anthroposophical viewpoint—don't respond well to the *earthier* qualities in music, such as clients with anorexia.

Stringed instruments

The stringed instruments created within AnMt include the lyre (Beilharz 2004b) and chrotta (Reinhold 1996). Others, for example the bowed psaltery, have been adopted by AnMt and are used frequently in this context (Reinhold 1996; von Kries 2004). This section will focus on the stringed instruments built specifically for AnMt practice.

Bowed stringed instruments

The chrotta According to Reinhold (1996) the anthroposophical chrotta has been developed for therapeutic purposes, modelled on the ancient Celtic crwth, which was a bowed lyre (Gevecke 2004). The chrotta is described as having a warm, delicate timbre, and it is available in different pitches, depending on the size of the instrument (Reinhold 1996). The tenor chrotta, which is the one most often used in anthroposophical music therapy

(Reinhold 1996), is tuned like a cello (Reinhold 2003). It is held between the knees and usually played with a viol-bow (Gevecke 2004; Reinhold 1996) and a viol bow grip (Gevecke 2004). With reference to the anthroposophical model of the threefold human being the chrotta—as a bowed instrument—corresponds to the middle human being (Reinhold 1996). Reinhold has pointed out that, depending on how the instrument is played, the music produced can relate to the rhythm element in music, and therewith to the lower human being, when using pizzicato, or to the melody element and to the upper human being when bowing (Reinhold 2003).

There are specific ways in which the chrotta is played in AnMt, depending on the therapeutic indications and aims. For example, clients can bow the open strings while the left arm is moving along with the bowing right arm in a mirrored movement. This is perceived to have a strong connection to breathing and to the middle human being (Reinhold 1996; Gevecke 2004), both physically (Reinhold 1996) and emotionally (Gevecke 2004). According to Reinhold (1996) this exercise on the chrotta can be especially helpful for patients who suffer from breathing difficulties, for example due to asthma or lung cancer. It is assumed that through the relationship between the quasi-breathing bowing gesture combined with intensive listening, physical breathing is freed up. On the one hand, the breathing process is put into a musical context, and on the other the client is allowed to forget about the physical act of breathing by being preoccupied with playing, listening, and performing the mirrored arm movements (Reinhold 1996).

Reinhold (1996) has described that another way of using the chrotta therapeutically is for a client to place their feet on the instrument while the therapist bows. According to Reinhold (1996), the perception of the vibration of the low-pitched tones can restore impaired sensitivity, warmth, and blood flow in the legs. Gevecke (2004) stressed the generally warming qualities of the chrotta sound and its ability to envelop and to resolve tension, stiffness or hardening on a physical level, or anxiety and depression on an emotional level.

Plucked stringed instruments

The plucked stringed instruments used in AnMt are mostly descended from the lyre family. Lyres are available in different sizes, from quite small to big instruments, and this variety enables AnMt practitioners to use them as needed with patients with different constitutions (Reinhold 1996).

The lyre The modern anthroposophical lyre was designed by Edmund Pracht and Lothar Gärtner in 1926 (Beilharz 2004b). The ancient lyre goes back to about 3000 BC in Mesopotamia and also existed in ancient Greece as "lyra" or "kithara" and during Celtic times as "crwth" or "rotta" (Beilharz 2004b). Pracht's dissatisfaction with the piano's timbre and sound in connection with the purpose of highlighting the qualities of musical elements became an incentive to develop a different instrument. Lothar Gärtner took up some of Pracht's ideas, made some changes and founded his own lyre studio in Konstanz, Germany. Other lyre builders followed over time and today there are lyre builders all over the world building lyres of different shapes and sizes and with different sound qualities and pitch ranges (Beilharz 2004b).

For example, the solo lyre has a pitch range from c to d3 the large soprano lyre ranges from e to d3, the small soprano lyre from g to a2, the big alto lyre from E to f2 and the small alto lyre from G to a. The descant lyre encompasses the tones from g to C5. There are also tenor and bass lyres with tones reaching down to C or contra-A (Beilharz 2004b). Reinhold (2003) has suggested that the alto lyre is the one most commonly used in AnMt.

The timbre of the lyre is considered to be able to open up a space for listening while embracing the musical elements of melody, harmony, and rhythm (Reinhold 1996). Reinhold (1996) has suggested that the purity of the lyre tone can help listeners in perceiving the nature of musical phenomena and that a systematic application of musical elements then becomes possible through the use of the lyre in active and receptive therapy. In AnMt the lyre is considered an instrument which addresses the middle human being. Its sound is perceived to promote relaxation and to relieve symptoms of congested breathing, pain and tension. In AnMt the lyre is also advocated for use with clients in low awareness states (Reinhold 1996).

In addition to the above described chromatic lyres there are also instruments with diatonic or pentatonic tuning, or lyres that can be tuned as a chord, such as the kantele (Reinhold 1996) which has its origins as a traditional Finnish instrument belonging to the family of psalteries (Rahkonen 2007–2011). Another variation is the bordune lyre, which can be tuned in chords or open chords (Reinhold 1996). Its tuning is flexible and the pitch-range within which the strings can be tuned encompasses a fourth (Tobiassen 2004). The bordune lyre is considered an excellent group instrument and can also be used for song accompaniment (Tobiassen 2004).

Percussion instruments: The Bleffert metal instruments

"Conventional" percussion instruments, such as drums or maracas, are used in AnMt. However, there are also specialized anthroposophical percussion instruments made from forged metal, built by Manfred Bleffert. This group of instruments includes tamtam, cymbal, tubular bells, gongs, glockenspiel, small cymbals, and triangles. The seven different instrument groups relate to developmental processes in the human being. The order of those instruments is important, since from an anthroposophical point of view there is a specific developmental process leading from the tamtam to the triangle and vice versa (Kumpf 2004).

Many of the instruments Bleffert built originate in ancient instruments used in Asian cults, such as the tamtam, cymbal, or gong. Those archetypal versions of the present instruments were meant to help people to connect with divine forces. The metals the instruments are made from are iron, bronze, and copper. Many of the instruments described above are available in any of these metals (Kumpf 2004).

Concluding thoughts about the use of specified tonalities and instruments in AnMt

This overview of specialized instruments in AnMt shows that instrument use is closely connected to Steiner's view of the human being. Prescriptive use of musical elements becomes apparent in the way intervals, scales, and musical sequences are applied in this approach. However, there are limitations to this prescriptive aspect of AnMt. Although musical elements and instruments are sometimes applied in a prescriptive way, AnMt practitioners don't view themselves as musical "apothecaries" ["Musikapothekertum"] (Florschütz 2009). Therapeutic treatments composed and devised for individual clients are not intended to be generalized in a symptom-oriented way, or mimicked in music therapy treatment without considering individual patients' constitutions (Florschütz 2009).

Therapeutic specifics: Avoidance of electronic media

One of the characteristics of AnMt practice is the avoidance of electronic musical playback media. A number of anthroposophical authors have criticized the use of modern pop music and the use of electronic playback devices through which such music is heard, and have consequently dismissed the value of using popular music in music therapy (for example Engel 1999; Ruland 1992). According to Engel's anthroposophical perspective modern music has distinct and problematic characteristics. He described pop music as an evil counterpart to music therapy, which in his opinion contributes to minimizing peoples' consciousness by using excessive volume and mutilated melody sequences which are reduced to three to six bars. Engel proposed that hearing this music leads to the development of destructive tendencies in human beings (Engel 1999).

Ruland has argued that through recording music and playing it back electromagnetically, the physical qualities of the music are "frozen solid" (Ruland 1992, p. 116). He has proposed that purely electronic music deceptively creates the impression of being cosmic (Ruland 1992). He has claimed that after a period of listening to this kind of music, "There is a perceptible loss of vital strength and one feels as though one's soul had been hollowed out" (Ruland 1992, p. 117).

In other music therapy approaches outside of AnMt, such as the Bonny Method of Guided Imagery and Music (Bonny 2002) or Community Music Therapy (Rieger 2006) using recorded music or electronically amplified instruments, such as electric guitar or bass, is a foundation of music therapy practice (for example Bonny 2002; Rieger 2006; Trondalen 2010; McFerran 2010).

The therapeutic process in AnMt

The therapeutic process in AnMt consists of several stages, such as music therapy diagnosis, phrasing of the direction the treatment may take, devising a treatment plan, evaluation, and a music therapy report (Damen 2004). This is considered the *outer* process in AnMt (Damen 2004). AnMt practitioners also advocate the existence of an *inner* process, which consists of aspects such as the therapeutic relationship or rational and intuitive courses of action in creating a musical treatment (Damen 2004).

Referral, diagnosis, and development of therapeutic goals

This section of the chapter shows that AnMt has its own distinct procedures of referral, diagnosis, treatment design, and evaluation.

Referral

In anthroposophical clinics, schools, or homes, music therapy is often included in the overall treatment plan by a doctor, in collaboration with a therapeutic team (Reinhold 1996). In outpatient treatment, the doctor advises the patient to avail of music therapy, and if possible, the doctor refers patients to a music therapist he or she knows. The treatment plan is then discussed between physician and music therapist (Reinhold 1996). The general procedure for

AnMt is to be prescribed by a doctor and the medical diagnosis is the first step in the process of devising a music therapy treatment for a patient (Pütz 2008). This can either be a conventional or an anthroposophical medical diagnosis. From the primary medical diagnosis the indication for AnMt is deduced (Pütz 2008).

A referral to AnMt is not dependent on patients' previous musical experiences, but on the abilities and strengths which they should develop with the help of music (Reinhold 1996). Similarly, it is not essential whether or not a patient can express himself or herself adequately in music (Damen 2004). Music can help patients to listen to their own musical expressions and thereby gain valuable insights into their own state of being. This is seen as an integration process that can lead to therapeutically desired change (Damen 2004).

Diagnosis

During the diagnostic process in AnMt the models of the threefold and fourfold human being can help practitioners integrate a person's presenting symptoms into a larger context (Damen 2004). The first step after the medical diagnosis is clarification about other therapies applied, about the way clinical symptoms present, about biographic characteristics, previous experiences with music and about the client's healthy resources (Pütz 2008). Especially in these early stages of the diagnostic process, interdisciplinary cooperation is important (Damen 2004). The musical diagnosis phase then follows.

Pütz (2008) has described the musical diagnosis as a phenomenological perception of the client through the therapist. This includes paying attention to the patient's physical appearance, the presence of the patient's personality, how emotional aspects and vitality find expression, but also how the four members of the fourfold human being are revealed, as well as aspects connected with the patient's constitution and the temperament (Pütz 2008). These observations are intended to create an impression of the way the four members of the four-fold human being interact in a particular client (Damen 2004). This can provide the music therapist with ideas as to which musical elements might help the client (Damen 2004).

Continuous or process-oriented assessment serves as a quality control of the treatment and can give music therapists information on the degree to which therapeutic goals have been met and whether a client's musical behavior may have changed (Pütz 2008). In the process of musical diagnosis the therapist observes whether and how the patient listens, how he or she plays or sings, including musical parameters such as tempo, dynamics, or expression (Damen 2004; Pütz 2008). The instruments preferred by clients and their relationship to musical elements such as melody, harmony, and rhythm, are important aspects to be observed (Damen 2004; Pütz 2008). Other parameters of interest to the therapist during assessment include musical memory, musical receptiveness, comprehension of consonance and dissonance, or preference of high or low pitch or major and minor keys (Pütz 2008). Some extra-musical parameters are part of the initial diagnosis, such as the client's experiences in the musical process, aspects of the client-therapist relationship and the depth and frequency of breathing during the musical activities. It is then the music therapist's task to draw the essence from this holistic diagnostic process (Pütz 2008).

Development of therapeutic goals and objectives

Therapeutic goals in AnMt are developed using the initial diagnosis and the musical diagnosis as a starting point (Pütz 2008). Therapeutic aims and objectives are developed for each client and encompass medium-term goals and long-term objectives depending on the client's resources and symptoms. An important therapeutic objective mentioned in the AAArTiG[2] guidelines for anthroposophical arts therapies is the transfer of the client's ability for self regulation from the music therapy situation into everyday life (Pütz 2008). There are a number of possible therapeutic goals in AnMt. In the AAArTiG guidelines for anthroposophical arts therapies, a mobilization of resources on a holistic level is mentioned as a therapeutic goal, as well as a positive self-image, increase in self-esteem, ego strength, behavioral changes and increased self-regulation. Ultimately, AnMt aims to support clients' self-regulation on a spiritual, emotional, vegetative, and physical level (Pütz 2008).

RESEARCH

The development of anthroposophy as a doctrine, a spiritual path, and a practical way of life was marked by endeavors to create an alternative to the dominant views of Steiner's time, which were perceived to be *materialist* and *positivist* (Bamford 2002). Steiner aimed to develop an alternative science which included what he perceived as the realities of the spiritual world and which was rigorous at the same time (Bamford 2002). He was attracted to phenomenology as practised in Goethe's scientific approach, which includes, for example, the concept of *delicate empiricism* (Goethe 1977). Delicate empiricism is characterized by the researcher or observer becoming intimately identical with the phenomenon, which can lead to theory building in its own right (Goethe 1977; Pfau 2010). Delicate empiricism has also been described as a process of gaining a thorough understanding of a phenomenon which is based on direct experience through empathic observation (Seamon 1998).

Phenomenology, including the Goethean style, is viewed as "the exploration and description of phenomena, where *phenomena* are the things or experiences as human beings experience them" (Seamon 1998, para 3). It is a "science of beginnings that demands a thorough, in-depth study of the phenomenon, which must be seen and described as clearly as possible" (Seamon 1998, para 3). Its followers claim that phenomenology practised in this sense can be seen as a "rigorous empirical science" which is a research practice rather than a conceptual system (Simms 2010, p. 1).

In anthroposophy, Goethean phenomenological research is practised in various different contexts and the one most relevant for AnMt is the phenomenological exploration of musical elements, the results of which have an impact on the use of the same in AnMt. AnMt practitioners have undertaken phenomenological studies to explore the basic *gestures* and meanings of musical elements, such as intervals, harmonies or rhythms (Ruland 1990; Pfrogner 1981). Goethean phenomenological studies in connection with musical elements are carried out by anthroposophical music therapists with the aim of applying musical elements correctly and effectively in AnMt (Florschütz 2009; Felber and Spalinger 2003).

In phenomenological music studies as conducted by AnMt practitioners the musical parameters examined include individual tones (Felber and Spalinger 2003; Florschütz 2009), timbre of different materials or instruments (Florschütz 2009; Bissegger 2001), intervals, (Bissegger 2001; Florschütz 2009; Felber and Spalinger 2003), rhythms (Felber and Spalinger 2003; Bissegger 2001), scales (Bissegger 2001; Felber and Spalinger 2003; Florschütz 2009), measures, different kinds of musical form or harmonies (Bissegger 2001). Little is published about this topic and what is available (for example Felber and Spalinger 2003) does not meet the standards of scientific research articles, but describes the process and role of phenomenon studies.

The effectiveness of anthroposophical medical therapy, including AnMt, was presented through a study by anthroposophical physicians titled "Anthroposophic Medicine Outcomes Study" (AMOS) (Hamre et al. 2004). This four-year prospective cohort study, which was carried out in Germany in collaboration with a health insurance provider, indicated evidence for the effectiveness of anthroposophical medicine and anthroposophical creative arts therapies, including music therapy (Hamre et al. 2004). One hundred and forty-one medical practices in Germany providing anthroposophical-medical treatment participated in this study. 898 patients aged 1–75 years were referred to and treated for chronic diseases with methods related to anthroposophical medicine (AM). These include also AnMt, which is categorized as a component of anthroposophical art therapy (Treichler 1993; Hamre et al. 2004, 2007).

The study investigated patients' disease symptoms, health-related quality of life, treatment costs, adverse effects, therapy effectiveness (patient and doctor ratings), and satisfaction ratings (Hamre et al. 2004). Patient diseases included mental disorders, musculoskeletal problems, respiratory disorders, headache disorders, and others (Hamre et al. 2004). The researchers found that substantial improvements occurred in health-related quality of life and disease symptoms measures during the two-year follow-up (Hamre et al. 2004). Furthermore, a reduced number of hospital days was observed, which was connected to a cost reduction which outweighed the additional costs of providing AM therapies. Since the average duration of patients' diseases before participating in the study was at six-and-a-half years, the authors found this result encouraging (Hamre et al. 2004).

There are some more recent studies available in which aspects of AnMt are investigated. A study of neonatal music therapy (Teckenberg-Jansson et al. 2010, p. 1) compared the effects of music therapy as a dual treatment in combination with kangaroo care with kangaroo care only in terms of premature infants' physiological responses, such as heart rate, respiration, transcutaneous O2-saturation, and blood pressure. Measures were taken "before, during and after every therapy session" (Teckenberg-Jansson et al. 2010, p. 1). Kangaroo care was defined as "skin to skin contact with the caregiver" (Teckenberg-Jansson et al. 2010, p. 1). While the term AnMt was not mentioned, the music therapist who administered the treatment is an anthroposophically trained practitioner. In the music therapy sessions she sang accompanied by a ten string anthroposophical lyre in pentatonic tuning (Teckenberg-Jansson et al. 2010).

Results indicated that a repeated combination of kangaroo care with music therapy slowed down the pulse and respiration rates and increased transcutaneous O2-saturation. There was a significant effect on blood pressure in dual therapy compared to kangaroo care only. From these results, the authors concluded that "repeated combination of music therapy and kangaroo care may be more beneficial for preterm infants than KC alone in terms of certain physiological outcomes and parent self-reports" (Teckenberg-Jansson et al. 2010, p. 1).

Further research investigating the effects of AnMt is needed. The examination of AnMt as a "complete" treatment package, rather than investigation of single aspects, such as use of the lyre, may be indicated. Qualitative research methods or a mixed methods approach may offer a valid way of conducting research on the topic of AnMt (Intveen 2011).

CONCLUSION

The basic tenets and historical development of AnMt have been outlined in this chapter, including also an overview of some of the specialized anthroposophical instruments and musical sequences, as well as elements of the therapeutic process. A brief introduction into the subject of research in connection with AnMt was provided.

Due to its distinct protocols of assessment, referral, and evaluation, in combination with a long history of clinical practice, AnMt may be described as a valid music therapy model with a music-centered orientation (Intveen 2011). However, in communication with other music therapists, problematic aspects of the inclusion of AnMt into the pool of contemporary music therapy models have been raised. These include the lack of recognition of AnMt training courses by universities, and the lack of scientific proof for the anthroposophical ideas underpinning this practice (see also Intveen and Edwards 2012). For example, along with what Summer called *New Age* music healing traditions, AnMt has received criticism for building on cosmological connections that can easily be shown to have no scientific basis (Summer 1996). Similarly, the avoidance of electronic music and equipment may seem problematic to music therapists outside of the AnMt framework since clinical experience shows that especially in music therapy work with adolescents and young adults, the use of these media is often indicated. There have been accounts of successful band projects in community music therapy, which included the use of electronic devices (for example Rieger 2006). A number of authors have advocated that it is important to use music styles, such as rock music, rap, or hip-hop, (for example Ruud 1998, Hadley and Yancy 2012) that are meaningful to adolescents as they are connected to community and identity and further personal expression. The application of these musical styles in therapy programmes usually includes the use of electronic devices.

Further discussion with openness on all sides is needed in order to create a bridge of communication between AnMt practitioners and music therapists involved in practice, theory and research of contemporary music therapy models. Florschütz has proposed that the way AnMt practitioners view their approach as a discipline adjunct to anthroposophical medicine could be considered a countermovement to the efforts made by professional bodies for the music therapy profession to be recognized as an independent approach in Germany (Florschütz 2009). However, the German example, in which AnMt was part of a manifesto devised by representatives of the main music therapy approaches, shows the development of AnMt as being embedded in the general picture of main stream music therapy approaches (Ewers-Grewe et al. 2010).

NOTES

1. It should be noted that today's anthroposophists and AnMt practitioners are aware of the modern view of the planetary system, which includes the Earth and Uranus, excludes Earth's Moon and consists of eight planets orbiting around the Sun. However, in anthroposophical music therapy, the seven-planet-system is used on a more symbolic and spiritual-esoteric basis. Ruland has proposed that the seven-planet-system in AnMt is

based on the Ptolemaic view of the cosmos and could be understood as an expression of the limitations of human understanding at a given point of historical time, rather than as a theory founded in error.

2. Anthroposophical Association for Arts Therapies in Germany.

REFERENCES

Bamford, C. (2002). Introduction. In: Steiner, R. (ed.), *What is anthroposophy?*, pp. 1–32. Great Barrington, MA: SteinerBooks.

Beilharz, G. (2004a). Acht Jahrzehnte Musik in der anthroposophischen Heilpädagogik. Ein Blick auf Entwicklungslinien und Pioniergestalten. In: Beilharz, G. (ed.), *Musik in Pädagogik und Therapie*, pp. 79–90. Stuttgart: Verlag Freies Geistesleben.

Beilharz, G. (2004b). Die Leier. In: Beilharz, G. (ed.), *Musik in Pädagogik und Therapie*. Stuttgart: Verlag Freies Geistesleben.

Beilharz, G. (ed.) (2004c). *Musik in Pädagogik und Therapie*. Stuttgart: Verlag Freies Geistesleben.

Bento, W. (2004). *Lifting the veil of mental illness: An approach to anthroposophical psychology*. Great Barrington, MA: SteinerBooks.

Bissegger, M. (2001). Anthroposophische Musiktherapie. [Anthroposophic music therapy]. In: H.-H. Decker-Voigt (ed.), *Schulen der Musiktherapie*, pp. 357–386. Munich: Ernst Reinhardt GmbH & Co.

Bissegger, M. (2004). Die rezeptive Musiktherapie in der Anthroposophie. In: Frohne-Hagemann, I. (ed.), *Rezeptive Musiktherapie. Theorie und Praxis*, pp. 341–358. Wiesbaden, Germany: Reichert Verlag.

Bonny, H. (2002). *Music consciousness: The evolution of Guided Imagery and Music*. Gilsum, NH, USA: Barcelona Publishers.

Bujalkova, M., Straka, S., and Jureckova, A. (2001). Hippocrates' humoral pathology in nowaday's reflections. *Bratisl Lek Listy (Bratislava Medical Journal)* 102: 489–492.

Childs, G. (1995). *Rudolf Steiner: His life and work. An illustrated biography*. Edinburgh: Floris Books.

Damen, O. (2004). Wesenszüge anthroposophischer Musiktherapie. In: Beilharz, G. (ed.), *Musik in Pädagogik und Therapie*, pp. 265–283. Stuttgart: Verlag Freies Geistesleben.

Engel, H.-H. (1999). *Musikalische Anthropologie*. Dornach, Switzerland: Medizinische Sektion der Freien Hochschule für Geisteswissenschaft am Goetheanum.

Ewers-Grewe, B., Haase, U., Haesner, U., Haffa-Schmidt, U., Heidemann, J., Landes, G., et al. (2010). *Kasseler Thesen zur Musiktherapie* [Online]. Berlin: Deutsche Musiktherapeutische Gesellschaft online. Available: <http://www.musiktherapie.de/fileadmin/user_upload/medien/pdf/Kasseler_Thesen_zur_Musiktherapie.pdf>. [Accessed 22/06/ 2012].

Felber, R. (2003a). Elemente der Musiktherapie und ihre Beziehung zum Menschen. In: Felber, R., Reinhold, S., and Stückert, A. (eds), *Anthroposophische Kunsttherapie 3: Musiktherapie und Gesangstherapie* (2nd edition), pp. 24–35. Stuttgart: Urachhaus.

Felber, R. (2003b). Wo finden wir das Musikalische? In: Felber, R., Reinhold, S., and Stückert, A. (eds), *Anthroposophische Kunsttherapie 3: Musiktherapie und Gesangstherapie* (2nd edition), pp. 19–23. Stuttgart: Urachhaus.

Felber, R., Reinhold, S., and Stückert, A. (eds). (2003). *Anthroposophische Kunsttherapie 3: Musiktherapie und Gesangstherapie*. Stuttgart: Urachhaus.

Felber, R. and Spalinger, J. (2003). Bewusstes Erleben des Musikalischen—sogenannte "Phänomenstudien." In: Felber, R., Reinhold, S., and Stückert, A. (eds), *Anthroposophische Kunsttherapie 3: Musiktherapie und Gesangstherapie*, pp. 73–75. Stuttgart: Urachhaus.

Florschütz, T. (2007). Sinn and Sein. Aussagen Rudolf Steiners zum Phänomen des Unbewussten und deren Bedeutung für eine künstlerisch-psychotherapeutische Behandlungsmethodik auf anthroposophischer Grundlage—unter besonderer Berücksichtigung der Musiktherapie—Textuntersuchung, Konzeptentwurf und exemplarische Ausführungen zur psychotherapeutischen und musikpsychotherapeutischen Handhabe der imaginativen Selbstperspektivierung. Hamburg: Hochschule für Musik und Theater Hamburg.

Florschütz, T. (2009). Anthroposophische Musiktherapie. In: Decker-Voigt, H.-H. and Weymann, E. (eds), *Lexikon Musiktherapie,* 2nd revised and expanded edition, pp. 33–41 Göttingen: Hogrefe.

Gäch, A. (2004). Das anthroposophische Menschenbild. In: Beilharz, G. (ed.), *Musik in Pädadgogik und Therapie*, pp. 31–39. Stuttgart: Verlag Freies Geistesleben.

Gevecke, J. (2004). Die Chrotta. In: Beilharz, G. (ed.), *Musik in Pädagogik und Therapie*, pp. 190–197. Stuttgart: Verlag Freies Geistesleben.

Goethe, J.W.V. (1977). *Schriften zur Naturwissenschaft.* Stuttgart, Germany: Philipp Reclam jun.

Hadley, S. and Yancy, G. (eds). (2012). *Therapeutic uses of rap and hip-hop.* New York and London: Routledge.

Hamre, H.J., Becker-Witt, C., Glockmann, A., Ziegler, R., Willich, S.N., and Kiene, H. (2004). Anthroposophic therapies in chronic disease: The anthroposophic medicine outcomes study (AMOS). *European Journal of Medical Research* 9: 351–360.

Hamre, H.J., Witt, C.M., Glockmann, A., Ziegler, R., Willich, S.N., and Kiene, H. (2007). Anthroposophic art therapy in chronic disease: A four-year prospective cohort study. *Explore* 3: 365–371.

Intveen, A. (2010a). Music as therapy: The role of music in anthroposophical music therapy. *VIII European Music Therapy Congress; Evidence for Music Therapy Practice, Research and Education.* Cadiz/Spain.

Intveen, A. (2010b). "The piano is a wooden box with false teeth"—Perspectives in anthroposophical music therapy as revealed through interviews with two expert practitioners. *The Arts in Psychotherapy* 37: 370–377.

Intveen, A. (2011). *Discovering anthroposophical music therapy: An investigation of its origins and applications.* Ph.D. Doctoral thesis, University of Limerick.

Intveen, A. and Edwards, J. (2012). The history and basic tenets of anthroposophical music therapy. *Voices: A World Forum for Music Therapy* [Online], 12. Available: <https://normt.uib.no/index.php/voices/article/view/646/548> [Accessed 22/06/2012].

Kern, H. (2007). Analyse einer phänomenologischen Didaktik am Beispiel der Musik. Goethes Erkenntnisart als Ausgangspunkt didaktischer Überlegungen. Bielefeld: University of Bielefeld, Germany, Faculty of Pedagogics.

König, K. (1966). Music therapy in curative education. In: Pietzner, C. (ed.), *Aspects of curative education*, pp. 253–265. Aberdeen, Scotland: The Aberdeen University Press.

Kumpf, C. (2004). Die Metall-Klanginstrumente von Manfred Bleffert. In: Beilharz, G. (ed.), *Musik in Pädagogik und Therapie*, pp. 227–245. Stuttgart: Verlag Freies Geistesleben.

Lachman, G. (2007). *Rudolf Steiner: An introduction to his life and work.* London: Penguin.

Lindenberg, C. (1997). *Rudolf Steiner: Eine Biographie* (Vol. 1). Stuttgart: Freies Geistesleben.

Lievegoed, B.C.J. (2005). *Phases of childhood. Growing in body, soul and spirit.* Edinburgh: Floris Books.

McFerran, K. (2010). *Adolescents, Music and Music Therapy: Methods and Techniques for Clincians, Educators and Students*, London and Philadelphia: Jessica Kingsley Publishers.

Musiktherapeutische Arbeitsstätte [2010, Online]. Berlin: Musiktherapeutische Arbeitsstätte Berlin. Available: <http://www.musiktherapeutische-arbeitsstaette.de/index.php?open=home> [Accessed 14/10 2010].

Pedroli, T. (2004). Die Choroiflöte. In: Beilharz, G. (ed.), *Musik in Pädagogik und Therapie*, pp. 203–208. Stuttgart: Verlag Freies Geistesleben.

Pfau, T. (2010). "All is leaf": Difference, metamorphosis, and Goethe's phenomenology of knowledge. *Studies in Romanticism* 49: 3–41.

Pfrogner, H. (1978). *Die sieben Lebensprozesse*, Freiburg i.Br., Germany, Verlag Die Kommenden.

Pfrogner, H. (1981). *Lebendige Tonwelt. Zum Phänomen der Musik*. Munich: Langen-Mueller.

Pfrogner, H. (1986). *Tao. Ein Vermächtnis*. Schaffhausen: Novalis Verlag.

Pütz, H. (2008). *Leitlinie zu Behandlung mit anthroposophischer Kunsttherapie (BVAKT)* [Online]. Association for Anthroposophic Art Therapy in Germany. Available: <http://www.anthroposophische-kunsttherapie.de/pdf/2008_LL_BVAKT.pdf> [Accessed 25/02/2010].

Rahkonen, C. (2007–2011). Kantele. *Oxford Music Online. Grove Music Online*. Oxford: Oxford University Press.

Reinhold, S. (1993). Musiktherapie in der Intensivmedizin. In: M. Glöckler, J. Schürholz, and M. Walker (eds), *Anthroposophische Medizin: Ein Weg zum Patienten; Beiträge aus der Praxis anthroposophischer Ärzte, Therapeuten, Pflegender und Pharmazeuten*, pp. 93–100. Stuttgart: Verlag Freies Geistesleben.

Reinhold, S. (1996). *Anthroposophische Musiktherapie. Eine Hinführung*. Bad Liebenzell, Verein für Anthroposophisches Heilwesen e.V.

Reinhold, S. (2003). Die Instrumente in der Musiktherapie. In: Felber, R., Reinhold, S., and Stückert, A. (eds), *Anthroposophische Kunsttherapie 3: Musiktherapie und Gesangstherapie*, 2nd edition, pp. 45–57. Stuttgart: Urachhaus.

Rieger, G. (2006). Musiktherapie und Gemeinwesenarbeit. *Musiktherapeutische Umschau* 27: 235–244.

Ruland, H. (1990). *Musik als erlebte Menschenkunde*, Stuttgart and Kassel: Gustav Fischer Verlag and Bärenreiter Verlag.

Ruland, H. (1992). *Expanding tonal awareness. A musical exploration of the evolution of consciousness guided by the monochord*. London: Rudolf Steiner Press.

Ruud, E. (1998). *Music therapy: Improvisation, communication and culture*. Gilsum, NH: Barcelona Publishers.

Seamon, D. (1998). Goethe, nature and phenomenology. Goethe's way of science: A phenomenology of nature [Online]. Available: <http://www.arch.ksu.edu/seamon/book%20chapters/goethe_intro.htm>.

Simms, E.-M. (2010). Research that blows the mind: Phenomenological research methods in Husserl and Goethe. *Human Science Research Conference*. Seattle, WA, USA.

Steiner, R. (1928). *The story of my life*. London: The Anthroposophical Publishing Company.

Steiner, R. (1964). *The philosophy of freedom. The basis for a modern world conception*. London: Rudolf Steiner Press.

Steiner, R. (1970). The human being's experience of tone. In: Steiner, R. (ed.), *Art In the light of mystery wisdom*, pp. 118–137. London: Rudolf Steiner Press.

Steiner, R. (1980). *Das Tonerlebnis im Menschen*. Dornach, Switzerland: Rudolf Steiner Verlag.

Steiner, R. (1987). *The four temperaments*. Great Barrington, MA, USA: Anthroposophic Press.

Steiner, R. (1998). *Education for special needs. The curative education course. Twelve lectures by Rudolf Steiner*. London: Rudolf Steiner Press.

Steiner, R. (2002). *What is anthroposophy? Three perspectives on self-knowledge*. (C. Bamford and M. Spiegler, Trans.). Great Barrington, MA: SteinerBooks.

Steiner, R. (2004). *Study of man. Fourteen lectures by Rudolf Steiner*. London: Rudolf Steiner Press.

Steiner, R. (2005). *Occult science. An outline*. London: Rudolf Steiner Press.

Steiner, R. and Wegmann, I. (1996). *Extending practical medicine. Fundamental principles based on the science of the spirit*. London: Rudolf Steiner Press.

Summer, L. (1996). *Music: The New Age elixir*. Amherst, New York: Prometheus Books.

Teckenberg-Jansson, P., Huotilainen, M., Pölkki, T., Lipsanen, J., and Järvenpää, A.-L. (2010). Rapid effects of neonatal music therapy combined with kangaroo care on prematurely-born infants. *Nordic Journal of Music Therapy, iFirst*, 1–21.

Tobiassen, M. (2004). Die Choroi-Bordunleier. In: Beilharz, G. (ed.), *Musik in Pädagogik und Therapie*, pp. 463–474. Stuttgart: Verlag Freies Geistesleben.

Treichler, M. (1993). Die anthroposophischen Kunsttherapien. In: Glöckler, M., Schürholz, J., and Walker, M. (eds), *Anthroposophische Medizin Ein Weg zum Patienten; Beiträge aus der Praxis anthroposophischer Ärzte, Therapeuten, Pflegender und Pharmazeuten*, pp. 83–92. Stuttgart: Verlag Freies Geistesleben.

Trondalen, G. (2010). The flute and I: The Bonny Method of Guided Imagery and Music (GIM) with a young man. *Voices: A World Forum for Music Therapy* [Online], 10. Available: <https://normt.uib.no/index.php/voices/article/view/356/430>.

Von Kries, G. (2004). Streichpsalter. In: Beilharz, G. (ed.), *Musik in Pädagogik und Therapie*, pp. 198–202. Stuttgart: Verlag Freies Geistesleben.

Von Lange, A. (1968). *Mensch, Musik und Kosmos. Anregungen zu einer goetheanistischen Tonlehre*. Freiburg: Verlag die Kommenden.

Werbeck-Svärdström, V. (1980). *Uncovering the voice. The cleansing power of song*. London: Rudolf Steiner Press.

Wilkinson, R. (2001). *Rudolf Steiner: An Introduction to His Spiritual World-view, Anthroposophy*. Temple Lodge Publishing.

Willig, S. (2005). The Dorion school of music therapy—a personal journey. *Lilipoh* 10: 26–27.

CHAPTER 28

··

AESTHETIC MUSIC THERAPY

··

COLIN ANDREW LEE

'… simply the thing I am shall make me live.'

Michael Tippett: 'The Knot Garden' (1970)

PRELUDE

··

MOZART'S Requiem, KV 626, was written in part just before his death in 1791. At the age of thirty-six, Mozart spent the last fifteen days of his life bed-ridden and for the final few of these he was delirious (O'Shea 1990). He completed only part of the Requiem before his death. What he left, however, was music full of spiritual and aesthetic content that has survived not only as a masterpiece, but also as a work brimming with therapeutic potential. The Requiem was written under difficult personal circumstances. Not only did it portray the pain of loss, but also the joy of life. It is one of the finest examples of a work that reflects the intense values of the human condition.

To understand Mozart as a composer-music therapist in the context of the Requiem is to consider the clarity between music and human representation of life. Even if heard for the first time by a listener, the piece can transcend cultural and contextual barriers. It portrays not only the sacred, but also the secular affirmations of relationships and everyday life. As a music therapist who worked in end-of-life care for eight years, I always had Mozart's Requiem as a constant companion in my work. As I travelled the complex and often circuitous path of the therapeutic process, the Requiem influenced me as a therapist on many different levels: as a receptive experience, a stylistic core for improvisations, a means to facilitate the therapeutic relationship with clients, and an understanding of counter-transference. For me, Mozart's Requiem speaks to all that is reflective and spiritual in music. It's potential to influence my clinical practice and potentially the practice of other music-centered music therapists, both pragmatically and philosophically, cannot be underestimated.

Alfredo, a client with AIDS, came into the music therapy room quietly for his first session. He surveyed the piano and percussion instruments, and without speaking, began playing a large conga with both hands. Moving in large circular motions, he improvised slow, regular rhythmic phrases. Alfredo's musical presence and relationship to music was immediate. After listening to the quality and intent of his playing, I began to respond on the piano, matching his timbre and quality of play-ing with the opening phrases from the 'Introitus' of Mozart's Requiem. The music soon became symphonic with themes, counter-themes, development, and recapitulation, all based from the opening sequence of Mozart's music. There was a sense that the improvisation had been played before, that its form had always been in existence, and that we were merely acting as a conduit in bringing its presence to life. The compositionally influenced structures were a part of Alfredo's creative emotional unleashing. His rhythmical motives on the conga were extraordinary and the counter melodic lines of his xylophone playing, nothing more than miraculous. Alfredo's grasp of compositional structure was inspiring. I remember the final recapitulation with the greatest clarity. It was as if we had been building towards the main heroic theme throughout the improvi-sation. That it had been hinted at in the beginning, only coming to full fruition in the coda. The grandeur of the closing music, so closely akin to the grandeur of Mozart's Requiem, expressed a sense of longing yet exhilaration. The music left us both exhausted, yet alive. The depth of the silence that followed contained a level of awareness and relationship that was reflective of the intense improvisation we had just played, and which was to continue in our future work.

These heightened musical experiences occurred throughout my early years as a music therapist trained in the tradition of Nordoff-Robbins. I began to question these "moments of awakening." Rinpoche eloquently expressed the ability that such great works of art have to transcend our sense of reality:

> Who, really listening to the greatest masterpieces of Beethoven or Mozart, could deny that another dimension at times seems to be manifesting through their work?
>
> (Rinpoche 1992, p. 315)

What was it about the thematic core of Mozart's music that allowed the therapeutic rela-tionship and process to travel so dynamically? What were the links between improvisations influenced by seminal works such as these, and clinical outcome? It seemed their occur-rences often came when my musical role as a therapist was confident, when I had practiced themes and distillations from pre-composed music. The more musically sure I became, the more likely these "moments of awakening" would occur. Of course, the client's responses and disability/illness dictated the progression and outcome of therapy. Regardless of this, it became clear that the more musically assured I was, the more likely advances in therapy would be possible. I allowed great Classical composers such as Beethoven and Stravinsky, as well as those from Jazz (Keith Jarrett) and Popular Music (Elton John), to become my teachers—looking to their music to enrich and expand my resource palette.

History

In 1985, after completing The Nordoff-Robbins training course in London, I initially worked with adults with learning disabilities. It was during this time that I embraced the craft of clini-cal improvisation. Through detailed daily practicing, I formulated my own authentic voice, which then directly affected my ongoing work with clients. It was during this time that I began to understand the need to equally know epistemological theory and clinical musicianship.

In 1988, I gained the Music Therapy Charity's Research Fellowship, the purpose of which was to look at the affects of music therapy with people living with HIV/AIDS. After an extensive literature review and investigation of possible methodologies the research became balanced between the qualitative method of collaborative enquiry (Reason and Rowan 1981) and the more detailed discipline of music analysis (Cooke 1987). I began by conducting two music analysis pilot projects (Lee 1989, 1990) from my work in learning disabilities. Following these studies, the main Ph.D. research focused on investigating the balance between musical representations of living with HIV/AIDS, and how this impacted the therapeutic process (Lee 1992, 1995). Through collaboration with three individual clients and three outside observers (a musician, a psychotherapist, and a music therapist), critical passages from six improvisations were musically analyzed. The resulting infrastructures were then directly related to the aims of therapy and the client's perceptions on the validity of these links. The rigor of music analysis was compared with clinical interpretation and outcome. The final stages of the research suggested a possible method of analyzing clinical improvisations (Lee 2000).

Following my doctoral studies, I acquired the first established music therapy position in end-of-life care at the Sir Michael Sobell House Hospice, Oxford. Even though at that time improvisation was not considered a central clinical technique (Munro 1984), I continued to explore its use as a direct intervention especially in working with near-death clients. In 1998, I immigrated to North America to take up full-time teaching, initially at the University of the Pacific, California, followed by Berklee College of Music, Boston, and finally at Wilfrid Laurier University, Canada.

Working in a university environment, I was able to dedicate more time to conduct research. Changing my geographical environment, as well as my professional one, allowed me the freedom to explore detailed projects investigating further the discipline of clinical improvisation. Even though my central point of reference had always come from Nordoff-Robbins (Nordoff and Robbins 2007), I uncovered new ways of thinking that came from my experience as a composer and clinician. Contemporary, world, and fusion music began to directly affect my music-centered thinking. Investigating the literature in musicology and aesthetics opened new worlds of possibilities that dramatically affected my views on the future of music therapy. By analyzing the pre-composed music of Western composers and linking the compositional process to that of clinical improvisation new horizons opened that dramatically changed my ideas on the links between the process and outcome of clinical practice. These music-centered associations became a great source of inspiration that finally culminated in the conception of Aesthetic Music Therapy (AeMT) (Lee 2001, 2003a).

After twelve years of research, and reflection, this writing represents an attempt to articulate a theory of music therapy that balances music-centered thinking and the aims and objectives of the therapeutic process (Lee 2003a, b). As music therapy develops through the new millennium we must focus not only on the rigor of outcome, but also the inspirational qualities of music. The creative value of music and its spiritual mysteries are the hallmarks of what makes music therapy such a unique and powerful discipline. Music therapists should continue to explore and develop clinical musicianship alongside the non-musical evaluation of therapeutic intent. The quality of music in music therapy must equal knowledge in clinical articulation, if the profession is to remain equally based between the polarities of "art" and "science."

DEFINITION

My initial definition of AeMT came from the need to clarify the essence of my ongoing work in a single statement:

> AeMT considers music therapy from a musicological and compositional point of view. Looking at theories of music to inform theories of therapy, it proposes a new way of exploring clinical practice.
>
> (Lee 2003a, p. 1)

Defining any model of music therapy, either broadly or from a single theory, is fraught with complications (Bruscia 1998). How can one definition ever describe the dynamic between music and health? And yet, definitions are crucial if our practice is to be accepted as a credible contemporary profession. Definitions act as a catalyst to clarify and differentiate the principles and practice of the view of an individual or a collective.

Music therapy has historically aligned itself with non-musical theoretical traditions developed in the areas of psychology, psychotherapy, and medicine. The need to understand and validate therapeutic processes and outcomes within the parameters of non-musical disciplines has been essential for the development of professional identity. However, connections with the intra-theoretical research on musicology, aesthetics, philosophy, and ethnomusicology have remained largely unlinked. The need to achieve desired clinical outcomes has led, I believe, to the oversight of the importance of music itself, its construction, content, and aesthetic value. And yet, it is music that holds the essential core of what defines music therapy:

> Would a physician contemplate surgery if he or she did not know the intricate biological workings of the body? And yet music therapists use music with little knowledge of its structural makeup. We use music yet seem ignorant of its complexities. We interpret through extramusical theories in the hope that its intangibility may somehow become tangible. Yet until we examine the qualities of music itself, its biological structure, its outcome will remain a mystery.
>
> (Lee 2003a, p. xv)

By aligning clinical practice to music studies, music therapy can begin to appreciate the constructs of music itself. By researching musical process through formally designed musicological protocols, music therapists can realize a greater understanding of the balance between process and outcome.

One of the key elements in AeMT[1] is that whether the music is focused on Western art music or other world music genres, it is based on improvisation and improvised song that is centered on the client's music.

> By acknowledging a client's sounds and musical preferences, and engaging in improvised musical dialogues, the therapist imbeds meanings in sounds initiated by the client. Performing this on a regular basis eventually creates a structured system of sounds akin to a language. Every therapeutic relationship and language created in AeMT is unique, as it is based on the client's personality, needs, and reasons for being in therapy. Furthermore, each person involved in the therapeutic relationship will interpret the music differently, as musical improvisation is the mode of communication. What may mean everything to the client, may

mean little to the therapist, and vice versa. Accepting this uncertainty and working within this framework makes it possible for musical experiences to be shared but ultimately kept private.

(McGrath 2012)

AeMT is a music-centered theory. Music-centered thinking in music therapy has been described as falling into two distinct categories (Aigen 2005): one includes the therapists who consider music-centeredness central to their practice, for example, Nordoff-Robbins and AeMT, and the other is where music-centeredness is considered just one aspect of practice, for example in Community Music Therapy and Guided Imagery and Music [GIM]. Words may be used to describe and interpret the musical phenomena, or the music itself can be the means to understand the therapeutic process. Music-centered practice is not confined to one theoretical stance and can be adapted to all clinical approaches. It is a way of considering the intent within musical processes rather than a distinct approach to specific clinical interventions with specific therapeutic goals. The music therapist can therefore adapt a music-centered philosophy to such approaches in therapeutic practice as psychotherapy, medicine, humanism, behaviorism, and GIM.

AeMT considers clinical practice from a musicological, philosophical, and compositional perspective, reflecting on the musical dialogue between client and therapist as the main basis for assessment. Interpretation comes from an understanding of the musical structures and how they are balanced with the non-musical foci of aims and objectives. The development of clinical musicianship and musical science is at the heart of AeMT and includes an understanding of listening, aesthetics, composition, and the balance between musical and clinical forms. Understanding the building blocks of clinical-musical structures is essential to AeMT.

In AeMT, improvisation and songs are considered as anchors at either end of a continuum. An improvisation can lead into a song and a song can move into an improvisation. What connects the two are form and the emphasis on adapting music when working clinically. AeMT promotes the view that the quality of music in therapy, whatever theoretical approach is in operation, is fundamental. AeMT does not advocate a dismantling of extra-musical theories, but rather, it proposes for the consideration of aesthetic quality of music as a way to further expand contemporary clinical theories.

AeMT in Context

The growing literature on music therapy over many years has provided a broad spectrum of research that reflects the ever-growing interest for the therapeutic powers of music (Wigram 2004; Hadley and Yancy 2012; Stige et al. 2010). There is greater public awareness that music can be considered as a viable alternative to medications (Sankaran 2008). Current advances in medical technology have allowed for irrefutable documentation of successful outcomes in the utilization of music as a clinical modality (Wormit et al. 2012). Research has also emphasized how music connects communities and provides a better understanding of different cultures in our society (Stige and Aarø 2012).

An evident research gap in recent investigations is the lack of consideration for the essential qualities and content of music itself as equal to the context in which it is being used. To discuss music and therapy from a spiritual, emotional, and social perspective, one must take a leap of faith. One must believe that there are connections between music and health that make us part of a greater whole. What are the inspirational qualities of music that make it so inherently therapeutic? How can music therapy find a way to use music that is directed, yet allows its inherent creativity to transcend the empirical? What are the spiritual components of music that make it timeless and a necessary part of everyday living? AeMT acknowledges all of these questions, rejoicing in the essential qualities of music and its power to heal.

In his discussion on aesthetics Even Ruud wrote:

> We do not only need theories from sociology, psychology, and anthropology of music, but we also need the discourses from aesthetic theory as a basis for reflection about the aspects of art that defend the use of music in therapy.
>
> (Ruud 2010, p. 77)

He further argued that music-centered theories should not remain in isolation and should be contained within "contextual understandings of musical meaning" (p. 82).

When I first proposed AeMT as a new theory, I focused directly on compositional and improvisational considerations, investigating musical inspiration and its possible links to therapy (Lee 2003a, b). Even to this day, AeMT still remains a relatively young developing theory in the process of finding balance between outcome and process, therapy and art, context and community. This journey of discovery, which initially focused on the mystical qualities of music, began earlier with the publication of "Music at the Edge" (Lee 1996).

It was through my work with Francis[2] that I began to understand the crucial role of musical qualities to facilitate therapy. AeMT is due in no small part to the work with Francis and everything he shared with me as a client. He said:

> I think music has an overall power that is greater than the other art forms. It seems to me that it embraces the entire sphere of expression … music lifts everything on to a different plane of totality. Mind and soul are opened by music. I have this image of a sphere, and different forms of expression—in that somehow, music enfolds and encompasses the whole ball, lifting it to a different height.
>
> (Lee 1996, p. 140)

It was these transformative processes within music making that Francis and I shared together that inspired me to formulate a music-centered approach, which culminated in the creation of AeMT; an approach that to this day remains embedded among other important clinical approaches and that highlights the significance of the relationship between music and therapy.

Medical ethnomusicology

Medical Ethnomusicology is a recently established field that embraces many disciplines including health, healing, culture, spirituality, and the arts (Koen 2009). It is based on the belief that there are many possibilities in using music as an agent for healing. It includes many different theoretical models including the study of performance, religion, prayer, meditation, community, and education (Koen 2008). It challenges the idea that music medicine, neurology, and music therapy in general has used, for the most part, Western musical tradi-tions in their practice. This view of current practice is in part true although the profession is now looking beyond the barriers of established musical norms. AeMT has tried to address this limitation by providing clinical-musical scenarios from different world influences (Lee and Houde 2011). It is the mandate of AeMT to expand musical styles, thus paralleling the tenor that medical ethnomusicology has taken in recent years. AeMT promotes the view that music therapists need to embrace and become more inclusive of music from diverse cultures. Through community initiatives and the expansion of popular styles (Hadley and Yancy 2012), music therapy has begun to unravel the significance of cultural influence on the intrinsic features of music.

Rohrbacher's (2008) groundbreaking work linking ethnomusicology and music therapy has been an important contribution to creating new ways of thinking (Fachner 2007; Tucek 2006). His research has underscored the fact that clients come from different cultural back-grounds, and as such, have diverse musical needs. A music therapist's knowledge of each client's musical roots is vital. The music therapist's understanding of the qualities of music from a client's cultural perspective is paramount to the creation of an appropriate clinical response. Every therapeutic encounter is unique, as is every musical connection between therapist and client.

Philosophy of music

The approach of AeMT has direct associations with the theoretical contexts of philoso-phy (Kania 2011), humanism (Sharpe 2000), and aesthetics (Scruton 1997). Unfortunately, because the literature on these disciplines does not include any references to health or ther-apy, the relevance of their theoretical contexts have largely been ignored in music therapy. Despite the fact that there are hardly any studies linking music therapy to these fields, the dialogue about their theoretical contexts have revealed many truths about the emotional qualities of music itself. Developments in music, language, imagination, style, and ontol-ogy provide fruitful literature for music therapists to consider. Discourse on music, expres-sion theories, (Robinson 2011) and the arousal of emotions (Matravers 2011) are all relevant concepts that could be crucial for the understanding of how music affects the emotion of the listener, and therefore potentially the responses of a client. Budd queried, "What is the aes-thetic significance of the musical arousal of emotions by the emotional qualities of music?" (2011, p. 214). How does the aesthetic content of clinical music affect the arousal of emotions for both client and therapist? AeMT is based on the belief that the aesthetic significance of music is essential, and that the qualities of music fundamental to facilitating the emotional arousal necessary for therapeutic growth.

Music-thanatology

AeMT can also be placed in context with other music-centered spiritual practices. One such practice that is inextricably linked to AeMT is music-thanatology (Schroeder-Sheker 2001). Music thanatology is a palliative medical modality and has been offered as a standard com-ponent of supportive and end-of-life care in American hospitals and hospices since 1992.

The most important connection between them comes from the fact that AeMT primarily took its clinical roots from work with the dying. Even though AeMT is currently not confined to one client group, it was work in end-of-life care that formed the foundations of its theory (Lee 2005). Music-thanatology is a practice in the service of dying people and their families, primarily using harp and voice. It is receptive and based on the use of prescriptive music and contemplative musicianship. The science of prescriptive music is a process that attunes itself to the specific needs of the dying person. Musical interventions are precise and carefully graded;

> Student interns must learn how to deliver a single musical theme in many different ways, emphasizing wide-open fifths, or thirds, or seconds, or sevenths. They must learn how to use texture, consonance, and dissonance *clinically,* how to use major and minor scales, chromaticism, harmony, and rhythm *clinically.*
>
> (Schroeder-Sheker 2001, p. 57)

The musical connections with AeMT are strong. The use of tones and intervals–the knowledge of harmonies, scales, and rhythms as precise clinical interventions–all of these elements are central to both approaches. In this sense, clinical musicianship in AeMT can also be seen as prescriptive. In tandem with these practical links are the spiritual beliefs that music has the ability to transform the here-and-now of our conscious existence and transport us to an experience beyond our rational knowing. It is in the creative-emotional intersection between music and healing that music-thanatology and AeMT are allies.

Theory to practice

Developing musical resources

The practice of AeMT is based on the mastery of clinical musicianship (Nordoff and Robbins 2007) as an equal partner with the skills of assessment, outcome and process. Clinical musicianship is at the heart of AeMT because it provides the musical basis for the therapist to affect the therapeutic process (Lee and Houde 2011). By listening clinically and responding with precise musical interventions, the therapist is able to help guide the client through the therapeutic process. Clinical-musical resources are learned and developed through practice and the manipulation of musical elements to achieve therapeutic aims.

Central to developing clinical musicianship is the acquisition of musical resources (Lee and Houde 2011). Musical resources include all aspects of clinical music making, songs, community-based performances, improvisational themes, and detailed distillations from pre-composed music. Musical resources act as the building blocks for the therapist's musical knowledge. Resource building requires the ability to build repertoire, songs, and improvisational techniques that can be moulded to fit the aims and objectives of the therapeutic process. Acquiring an extensive range of musical resources should be one of the first aims an AeMT clinician becomes skilled in. Without a broad range of musical techniques it is impossible to develop the relationship necessary for successful clinical outcomes. In AeMT, it is advocated that the greater the musical skills the therapist develops, the more likely it is that the process of engagement with the client will find deeper levels of outcome.

The precision of clinical listening (Lee 2003a, b; Verney and Ansdell 2010) and musical response is based on a multi-complex set of procedures that must be adapted to the specific needs of the client. By acknowledging the sounds initiated by the client and their musical preference, and then engaging them in musical dialogue, the therapist embeds meaning in the musical form. Eventually this creates a structured system of sounds akin to any other language. In AeMT every therapeutic relationship will be unique based on the client's musical personality, needs, and reasons for being in therapy. Each person in the relationship (client and therapist) will interpret the musical language differently. The beauty of AeMT is accepting this uncertainty and being able to live in the space where musical meanings are shared.[3] Everyone's relationship to music will be different. What is constant is the understanding of musical structures, so that when therapists respond to clients, they do so with musical and therapeutic insight. Through the building of musical resources, the therapist can facilitate the client's position in the therapeutic alliance with greater precision and insight.

Improvisation

Improvisation, one of the main techniques used by music therapists, can be an elusive and misunderstood practice. Many therapists discuss the use of improvisation from a non-musical perspective, often choosing to emphasize outcome rather than focus on the quality of the music used (Wosch 2007). Very few therapists, however, stress the value of musical content and the inherent properties of music in the process. Clinical improvisation, as indeed improvisation itself, is complex (Brown 2011). Can improvised music have the same level of quality as a crafted composition? Is it possible to create coherently formed music that has the same structural depth as a pre-composed piece? Clinical improvisation is not only a reflection of the therapeutic relationship, but also the therapist's musical interpretation of the clinical process.

AeMT emphasizes knowing, understanding, and having available precise musical structures in response to the client's playing. The moment the client begins to play or sing is the moment of the initial contact. This may occur immediately or after the establishment of trust. It is at the moment of contact that the therapist must listen intently to the sounds being produced before playing. Therapists often respond musically too soon, often not taking the time to wait and listen to the quality and intent of the client's playing. The decision to respond musically should be based on various factors that define the objectives and boundaries of the process. It is often the initial moment of musical response that dictates the effectiveness of the process.

The pedagogy of improvisation is still in its infancy (Lee and Houde 2011; Nordoff and Robbins 2007; Wigram 2004). The theoretical and philosophical bias of the individual university or college program significantly influences the clinical improvisation training and experience of a novice music therapist. There is not one individual path that a music therapist can follow to acquire the technical and musical skills to become a competent clinical improviser. Certain clinical approaches advocate improvisation as central to their practice (Nordoff and Robbins 2007), while others place less emphasis on learning how to improvise (Thaut 2005). In AeMT whatever approach the therapist favors, improvisation is not an intrinsic gift, but a skill that must be learned and practiced with dedication and commitment.

Form

Central to creating an effective clinical improvisation is the ability to provide musical-clinical form. However, it is important to distinguish the difference between musical-art form from musical-clinical form. Musical-art form in contemporary improvisation is often free from consonant structures. The form is not dictated from the outside but rather created from within the organic development of the improvisation. Musical-clinical form in AeMT, on the other hand, relies on the utilization of consonant structures. Its form is significantly shaped by the extraneous influence of the client's needs. In AeMT, form must be provided from the outside to contextualize the client's expression, offering musical-clinical responses that depict the needs of the client and the therapeutic process. Musical direction and security are critical and must be reflected in the therapist's responses. The core of AeMT is the therapist's ability to contextualize the client's playing. The therapist must find a balance between the aims of therapy and the creative expression of the improvisation. Clinical improvisations can either be based on simple progressions or more thematically complex structures with interweaving themes and counter-themes. As the music is created moment-by-moment, the therapist must be able to recapitulate themes and motives, thus providing security and containment for the therapeutic relationship and ongoing objectives.

> Edgar, a client with Down's syndrome and moderate learning disability, was non-verbal yet musically creative and free. His improvisations were often symphonic in scope, yet also scattered and unfocused. The intent of my musical responses as therapist was to provide consonant structures in order for him to expand his musical and intellectual abilities, and place his musical expression in a coherent form that would allow communication. The music often took the structure and style of Stravinsky ballets. Themes from 'Petrushka' (1910 –1911) and 'The Rite of Spring' (1913) were incorporated as overall themes. The overriding tonal framework was colored with dissonance and highly complex syncopated rhythms. The energy and direction of his improvised compositions was addictive. Through continued expansion of his distinctive style and developing organic form, Edgar began to see his place within our shared musical dialogue. His playing became more structured and articulated—the musical communication between us subsequently becoming more sophisticated. Our work together culminated in an improvisation of epic symphonic form. Freedom and composition came together in a musical expression of therapeutic and musical cohesion, allowing Edgar the opportunity to fulfill his creative potential as a musician, composer, and human being.

Tone

The musical tone, as initiated by the client, is an occurrence that heralds the beginning of therapy. It exists as a reflection of the client and of the potential for the initial stages of melody and harmony. The tone becomes the essence of the therapist's interpretation and response. Its quality and emotional intent can hold the truth for the ensuing musical discourse. The tone can encapsulate the intensity of living. It can speak to the emotional content of the player and communicate to the therapist everything that is real and reflective of the client; "The single tone holds within itself—and so many compositions begin with a single tone—'the promise of the whole' that is to come. The whole experience." (Robbins and Robbins 1998, p. 43).

The therapist must therefore wait and listen intently before responding. The texture, timbre and intent of the opening tone must be treated with absolute respect. The therapist's response, moving to other tones, marks the beginning of melody, and subsequently, the creation of harmonic form. The peak from the tone can provide a musical opening that mirrors the client and their potential for musical-creative freedom.

> Susan, a client with profound, multiple learning and physical disabilities embraced music with every fiber of her being. In music, her disabilities became secondary to her desire to communicate musically and be a part of passionate improvisational creations. Her ability to grasp sticks was limited and required support from a co-therapist. Her voice, however, soared and allowed for a freedom of expression that was breathtaking. Improvisations would often begin with Susan playing, with assistance, a tone chime. The fundamental chosen tone became the essence of simple melodic themes leading to harmonic structures that reflected the emotional presence of Susan and the beauty of her singing and playing. Through her two-part contribution (tone chime and voice), and the therapist's response (piano and voice), a four-part discourse emerged that felt reminiscent of a late Beethoven string quartet. In these experiences, the fundamentals of tone, musical development, communication, and spirituality came together to represent the indispensable elements of AeMT.

Styles

Improvisational styles are defined as a set of musical idioms and conventions that can be identified as belonging to particular cultures or communities (Lee and Houde 2011). The term can also refer to a composer's unique approach within a style. A style can contain several idioms, which are a set of defining musical characteristics or components that work together. Styles do not exist in isolation. They often borrow elements or evolve directly from one another. One of the major aspects of evoking a style is considering *how* the music is to be played. This includes following the "rules" of instrumentation, tempo, timbre, form, timing, and other such conventions (Lee, 2013).

In AeMT, styles can be crucial in meeting the client's needs. Some clients verbally indicate a preferred style of music, but often therapists must take the initiative to determine the appropriate style to be used. It is important for the therapist to fully assess a client's musical tendencies and offer music that will fit their style. Styles can be thought of as having "personalities" which match or reflect the client's characteristics. Improvisational styles can provide a musical opening for the client to express both their emotional and practical needs, thus addressing more accurately the aims of the therapeutic process.

Acquiring a broad range of styles can take many years to accomplish. The therapist must be dedicated and believe in the inspirational qualities of music to heal. By consciously practicing musical elements that go to make up a specific style, the therapist will begin to hear and understand with greater clarity the elements of their growth as a clinical musician. By then taking formed musical ideas and molding them into the therapeutic dialogue, a greater awareness between client and therapist will emerge. The therapist can call upon either a precise element from a particular style, or use broader motives that add to the general improvisational color and direction of therapy.

> Christine, a client with profound learning disabilities was non-verbal and constantly restless. She would pace unevenly throughout every session and avoid contact with either the therapist

or co-therapist. Her resistant presence was that of a person without order or form. The main aim of work with Christine was to provide a musical environment that expressed and accepted her scattered presence, but that also acknowledged the possibility of coherence and structure. As the work developed, there came instances offering acknowledgement that allowed open, fleeting moments of communication. Stylistically, improvisations where based on contrasting musical ideas; syncopated music–Ravel, Alborada del Gracioso–to match her uneven gait, and the distillation of slow chord progressions–Prelude from J.S. Bach's Cello Suite No 1 (BWV 1007)–to promote relaxation. The final part of the session and goodbye song was developed and based on the "Interlude: Dawn", from Benjamin Britten's opera "Peter Grimes." Op.33. These distinct contrasting styles that were continued from session to session, acted as musical/ therapeutic 'leitmotivs' providing consistency and security. They were chosen because they reflected the opposing characteristics of Christine's presence. It was these musical themes and motives that provided the emotional/musical space for Christine to transcend her disability and eventually enter music making and further therapeutic goals.

The architectural tonic

The *Architectural Tonic* is a way of conceptualizing and thinking musically in a session. It is the identification of a tone that is introduced into a session and acts as the central focus for a single improvisation, complete session or series of sessions. The source of the architectural tonic can come from various sources: (a) as introduced by the client through vocalizations/ songs and/or tonal inferences from instrumental playing; (b) as introduced by the therapist in response to the client's playing and mood; and (c) as introduced as a part of the musical dialogue between client and therapist (Lee 2003a, b).

The architectural tonic can appear at the beginning of a session or at any point within the process. Once the tonic has been ascertained, all musical ideas will relate back to the fundamental tone. The architectural tonic acts as a musical pillar providing stability and coherence for the musical-therapeutic process (Lee and Houde 2011).

> Sessions with the Penderecki String Quartet (Ahonen and Lee 2011) were musically challenging, yet liberating. The quartet's repertoire included standard works from the classical and romantic periods, but they also specialized in contemporary music. As a therapist, I played every session from the piano. Every improvisation began with a stated tone normally initiated from a single player. Once the architectural tonic had been established, the improvisational/ compositional form became clear. It was the defining tone that provided both the musical core and emotional anchor for each improvisation. The session normally contained two to three improvisations. The architectural tonic influenced the whole session, each improvisation being related to the tonic, e.g. D (minor), A (middle eastern), D (major). Specific styles were also influenced by the architectural tonic, e.g. based on F, influenced from Bartok's String Quartet No IV (1928), 5th movement (Allegro molto).

New perspectives

Music therapy, for the most part, has been more focused on popular Western music and less influenced by culturally diverse musical traditions. Looking to influences from other cultures is a relatively recent phenomenon. With migration and the increasing significance of multiculturalism in societal norms, people bring with them music from their heritage. It is not uncommon for music therapists to encounter clients of different ethno-racial backgrounds. Music therapists cannot ignore the vast diversity of musical heritage clients bring to sessions. Adapting world music influences clinically is probably one the greatest challenges music therapists face in the 21st century. Clients must be able to express and explore their emotional needs within musical parameters where they feel safe. Therapists must therefore know many diverse musical landscapes that can be adapted to meet the needs of clients with reference to their culture:

> Incorporating world music into music therapy can be an exciting experience for client and therapist. Opening your ears to new sounds and experimenting with different instruments can create opportunities for the unexpected, which is often when growth can take place.
>
> (Lee and Houde 2011, p. 339)

To integrate music from a different world style, therapists must first immerse themselves in the authentic sounds of the specific culture the music emerges from. They must understand the context from where the music originates. It is not enough to take a generalized Western representation of a specific world style and consider that representation as authentic. The therapist must have knowledge of the musical temperament, its derivation, and the settings in which it is used. Using authentic instruments is also ideal if the intent is to offer a genuine sound. AeMT proposes that contemporary music therapy embrace and extend musical resources to include music from different and varied cultures. The following are just a few examples of new musical horizons that AeMT has embraced.

Bali—gamelan

Balinese music is based on the collective experience of community and the group process (Loth 2006). It is an ensemble that consists of a diversity of instruments: metallophones, xylophones, drums, gongs, flutes and strings, as well as voice. The term gamelan comes from the Javanese word *gamels* meaning "to strike." In Balinese music, there is no harmony. Instead, the musical dialogue is based on melody, rhythm and texture. There is a consistency in the tonal centre of each piece that provides musical stability. The transparency of musical invention offers a refreshing balance to the often dense musical structures of Western music.

Balinese music creates a musical environment that is greater than the sum of its parts:

> The gamelan was created for the community and intended for the average person. Unlike in the Western musical tradition, where music is highly exclusive, music in Bali is inclusive. Learning the gamelan structures and traditions are natural and introduced at a very young age. Every villager is invited and expected to participate in music-making because it is integrated and built into religion and ritual life.
>
> (Pun 2011, p. 80)

The musical experience of the whole, interactive learning and community are all key elements that could have direct links to group music therapy. In Balinese music, the texture and timbre of tuned percussion, deeply resonating gongs and ringing bronzes, provide a musical environment that is emotionally rich. It has a transformative quality that if offered with precision and insight, could prove invaluable as a future resource in clinical improvisation (Loth 2006).

India—ragas

Ragas are devoid of functional harmony. A raga is meditative in character, with each raga being chosen to depict a specific mood or atmosphere:

> Broadly speaking the word "raga" refers to a style of music belonging to the Indian classical system. From a literal perspective, the term "raga" translates to the word "colour" or "mood." It also refers to the ascending/descending scale and melodic framework used for improvisation.
>
> (Lee and Houde 2011, p. 315)

Indian music has a suspended and timeless quality. The drone, which accompanies each raga, provides a musical stability that is the foundation for its distinctive musical style.

Embedded in Indian music is an essence of the contemplative and spiritual. When listening to and exploring ragas, the therapist must be open to their ethereal and metaphysical essence, which has the potential to provide an emotional-musical connection for clients. As previously mentioned, developing resources in AeMT is a product of musical knowledge, learning and practice. Once familiarity of the music is attained, the opportunity for exploring emotional-musical connections can be exploited. Ragas must be heard and played with dignity and respect, listening to every tone and nuance that will allow for their true emotional nature to impact the therapeutic process.

Contemporary music

AeMT has long promoted an awareness and practical knowledge of present day music. The 21st century is a rich age of diverse musical trends. Tonality and atonality over the last hundred years has been stretched and contorted over a broad range of musical styles. The distinctions between classical, popular, and world music have now become somewhat blurred. With the recent explorations on the therapeutic value of popular music styles, especially Rap and Hip-Hop (Hadley and Yancy 2012), and the broadening of musical performances necessary for the development of community music therapy (Stige and Aarø 2012), music in therapy has expanded.

> The deep bass, street sounds, record noise, layers of samples, groove, and aggressive beats that are all part of the Hip-Hop aesthetic reflect the world in which … participants … live. This allows those sounds to penetrate and affect them in ways other sounds and musical aesthetics may not.
>
> (Lightstone 2012, p. 249)

Music therapy has developed its language from the foundations of popular tonal music. It is now crucial that the profession looks to broadening its horizons. Music therapy needs to be contemporary, both clinically and musically. By allowing present day musical trends to influence clinical practice, and by knowing the cultural make-up of diverse contemporary styles, music therapists can achieve a more balanced and current practice. AeMT embraces present day music and celebrates its ability to provide musical experiences that are truly reflective of clients and reflexive to their needs. J.S. Bach, Ravi Shankar, and Eminem, can all become equal partners in providing a musical path that will allow clients to experience musical richness and therapeutic potential.

MUSIC ANALYSIS

Music analysis is perhaps the most enigmatic aspect of research in music therapy. Acknowledging that music is the essential component, it would seem evident that music analysis should be crucial in music therapy research. We can articulate outcome within definable medical and psychological indices. The intricacies of process, however, are based on two more indefinable tandems: music and emotion (philosophy) and music and relationship (psychotherapy). Both of these do not fit easily within the strict boundaries of empirical research. What is it then, that music analysts are looking for when they embark on the detailed process of isolating musical infrastructures, and what uniform methodologies could be found to place their findings into more generalized results? Some essential questions are:

- Why is the music analysis of clinical improvisation important?
- How does one musically analyze?
- On what criteria does one choose musical extracts to analyze?
- What music analytic models does one adopt?
- How important is transcribing the music and what form of transcription does one use?
- How musically precise does one need to be in one's transcription?
- What clinical questions is one hoping to answer through music analysis?

Bonde (2005) has suggested three possible levels of focus for music research: *material properties* of music (stimulus or effect); *intentional properties* of music (description, analysis, and interpretation of meaning); or *musical processes* (interactions and relationships). In music analysis, all levels of focus are essential in producing meaningful results. Results from music analysis are only valid if they can be measure alongside the meaning of the therapeutic process, relationship and clinical aims. What is it that music researchers are hoping to gain by isolating and analyzing music (Ruud 2010)? What is achieved by separating the musical infrastructures of an improvisation? Is there a danger that music analysis may provide results that are too removed from the core of practice, and that the potential for over-interpretation may produce results that are insignificant (Erkkilä 2007)?

By deconstructing the musical elements of clinical improvisation, it is possible to find connections between micro-musical analyses and clinical outcomes. Music therapists often speak of the musical-therapeutic union when the client and therapist become one. It is these moments of union that can be isolated for detailed micro-musical analysis. Researching the musical constructs of tones, harmonies, rhythms, and timbres provides a musicological understanding of the dialogue between client and therapist. The results of the analysis can then be translated to the non-musical indices of clinical outcome. Connecting the musical process and clinical outcomes in this manner highlights the relationship between music and therapy. These results can also provide an armamentarium of musical interventions. Just as music itself cannot be exactly reproduced in every performance, its emotional and musical qualities can only hope to provide results that are specific to one setting. Through continued research, each small result of musical-clinical knowing can be added on to a greater body of knowledge that over time will begin to build a more concrete and proven science of musical and therapeutic data.

There are different ways to transcribe music. Bergstrom-Nielsen (1993) presents a detailed and creative form of transcription called "graphic notation." What is being analyzed in his approach is not the detail of specific musical elements, but rather the broader setting of improvisational feeling and shape. Each score is represented through an explanation of signs, which provides a framework for the ensuing analysis. Musical elements are transcribed and created through freely articulated representations of the music. Notations may include colorful artistic splashes, free creative diagrammatic representations, and human figures. The data produced through graphic notation is spontaneous and reflects the ever-shifting nature of clinical improvisation.

In AeMT, data is created through standard musical notation. Music notation can take many forms: from exact transcriptions with bar lines and time signatures to the freer structure of scores as developed in contemporary music by such figures as Cage, Stockhausen, and Schafer. The use of standard musical notation has been criticized for adhering to the "old musicology." The criticism being that by producing standardized transcriptions, the essential elements of anthropology and culture are inadvertently overlooked. However, the merits of standard musical notation as a basis for developing desired clinical outcomes in the therapeutic process cannot be ignored, and in fact may outweigh such negative appraisal. Only by standard musical notation can therapists critically examine in detail the fine relationships between the elements of music such as intervals, harmonic progressions, and rhythmic patterns that flow from the creativity of both client and therapist. In recent years, there has been a resurgence of attention to the value of standard musical notation (Strange 2012; Turry 2011), providing acknowledgment to its technical worth and lending more credence to its use (Streeter 2012).

AeMT AND INDIGENOUS MUSIC-CENTERED THEORY

The idea that music therapy needs to find a theory that is not dependent on outside disciplines has long been advocated and discussed (Aigen 2005, Daveson et al. 2008).[4] The position of music therapy as a field has made its quest for a congruous clinical theory and appropriate research challenging. In the pursuit of a theory indigenous to music therapy, its proponents raise certain questions. Does music therapy need a theory developed from within its own practice or is such a notion outdated and not in line with contemporary thinking? If music is to be considered as adjunct, then indeed this argument may be true. The counter-argument, however, is that until we establish a music-centered indigenous theory, music therapy will always remain biased towards the generation of desired outcomes. Music is the essential core, and without a clear understanding of its constructs, the emotional content and intricacies of musical creativity will be presumed a general concept. Music therapy is a complex inter-relational phenomenon. The microanalysis of music within an indigenous theoretical framework, as advocated in AeMT, will provide the platform that will raise the rigor in the understanding of the role of music in therapy.

How then might an indigenous music-centered theory be created? Is it possible to create a method of analysis that answers the complex boundaries of process and outcome? In formulating a theory that does not rely on allied fields, the question becomes: Can we comprehend the musical-clinical processes solely through the medium of music? The answer to this question lies in an understanding of the relationship between music, emotions and the clinical adaptation of musical elements. It is in the interface between music and its creative, humanistic make-up where the answers lie to formulating a theory that is truly music-centered and indigenous. The path to finding such an idealistic, yet pure response to music in therapy is still in its infancy. It requires a greater understanding of the science of music through the therapist's knowledge and practice of clinical musicianship. It also requires a method of response and assessment that is both precise yet open to the creative elements of improvisation, composition, and the dynamic forces of the client-therapist relationship in music.

AeMT, GENDER, AND IDENTITY

As I was beginning to develop AeMT as a theory, I also began to concomitantly explore its therapeutic relationship with human sexuality. Living as a gay man and working as a music therapist through the HIV/AIDS pandemic in the 1980s and 1990s, I began to understand the balance between strength and frailty in a community, which endured the trauma of potential annihilation while keeping its dignity in the face of loss and bereavement. For many clients with whom I worked, music became a medium for expression of creativity in the midst of pain and suffering. It was a time of bitterness and enlightenment. I pondered on my identity both as a gay man and a music therapist (Lee 2008), and more importantly, why it was relevant to be open about my sexuality in my work. My response to the HIV/AIDS crisis and my decision to embrace its challenge as a therapist was in part because I was gay. When the AIDS catastrophe hit, gay men had two choices: either to withdraw or become actively involved. For the first time in my career, I was forced to examine my own vulnerability and authenticity.

AIDS was initially associated with homosexuals and intravenous drug users. Gay men and drug addicts were disparaged, and victim blaming was very commonplace. There was little sympathy for those who acquired the virus, except possibly for hemophiliacs who were viewed as victims of contaminated transfusions. The world of HIV/AIDS care was chaotic. Entering it as a therapist, I felt like I was being immersed in a swirling vortex of pandemonium.

Having previously worked with clients with learning disabilities and mental health issues, I had developed a way of working that provided me with confidence and self-assurance. However, I was quick to discover that despite my accumulated knowledge and clinical experience, the therapeutic boundaries in HIV/AIDS care required me to implement drastic changes in my clinical approach and techniques. As I took my first tentative steps, merging the professional and personal domains of my persona, I wondered how best I might contribute to the seemingly insurmountable challenge of meeting the needs of clients living with HIV/AIDS.

As a music therapist, my work experience with HIV/AIDS clients became a catalyst for my quest to attain more authenticity in the field. My realization of needing to be true to my identity both as a gay man and clinical musician by heeding the call to work with clients who were living with HIV/AIDS served as an impetus to form a greater appreciation of the creativity, musicality, and musicianship of my clients. I began to recognize the fact that just as I needed to be genuine with who I am both as a person and as a professional, music therapy as a field needed to be more authentic by accepting the indisputable truth that the elements of music and the harmonious relationship that develops between client and therapist is in fact the crux to achieving success in therapy. This understanding became my inspiration and motivation to advocating for an indigenous, music-centered theory that was autonomous from the influence of allied disciplines. This understanding became integral to the foundations of AeMT as a theory.

Through the symphonic structures of improvisations, my music-centered practice rose to a new level—one that began to address the balance between composition and improvisation in a space that allowed the therapeutic process to become more fluent and creative. In AeMT and HIV/AIDS, the music-centered nature of the process invites the client into a dialogue that is ever-present and real. The sense of balance between the inspirational qualities of music and therapeutic intent, can rise to allow the client to truly fulfill their creative and personal potential.

AeMT and Paul Nordoff

Paul Nordoff (1909–1977) is one of the pioneering figures in music therapy, and he was also an established American art composer. It could be argued that Paul Nordoff was the first composer-music therapist and that his clinical improvisations were clearly an extension of his compositional thinking.

AeMT considers that composing and improvising are extensions of each other and that their use in therapy is chosen from a continuum of clinical and musical responses. Aspects of composing are inherently found in improvising and vice versa. What is important for the development of AeMT is the fact that clinical and art musicianship go hand-in-hand to produce music that is aesthetically valid yet therapeutically focused. When listening to Nordoff's compositions, it is easy to understand how he stepped so effortlessly into clinical improvisation. The rapturous qualities of his art music are evident in his clinical music. It is the essential aesthetic musical components of the Nordoff-Robbins approach that is responsible for its major contribution to field of music-centered music therapy.

The influence of Paul Nordoff on the development of AeMT is substantial. As a fellow composer-music therapist, I realized that the foundation of my development as a clinical improviser was greatly influenced by his musical thinking. Similar to Nordoff's experience, allowing music of great composers to directly affect my clinical and musical thinking became an inspirational aspect of my work. As I allowed myself to freely create as a composer-music therapist, the quality of my therapeutic acumen improved. I considered every session as the beginning of a new composition. Clinical symphonies, concertos, chamber works, sonatas and operas began to emerge. This was one of the most exciting and motivating periods of my career.

AeMT posits that music therapists should be inspired by the music they use. Without inspirational music, the therapeutic process potentially becomes dull and lifeless. Musical inspiration is not dependent on clinical theory or style of intervention, but rather how the therapist incorporates the musical elements being used. The simplest of musical ideas can be played with passionate intent or be directionless if not considered carefully. Thus, every musical statement and nuance becomes crucial in the intricacies of the musical-clinical process.

It is my hope that one day Paul Nordoff's stature as a composer becomes equal to that of his contributions to music therapy (De'Ath 2013). Through a greater understanding of the balance between his artistic and therapeutic creativity, it may be possible to further articulate the interface between clinical and aesthetic practice. It is this balance that is the ultimate aim of AeMT and its potential influence on present-day music therapy. Being a composer in music therapy is one of the most profound experiences a musician can have. The ability to create passionate musical forms in the service of clients is the ultimate aim of music therapy and is why music exists as a cultural and communal phenomenon. Even though Paul Nordoff is now considered a historical figure, the immediacy of his musical genius will always be relevant. His case studies and teaching on music (Nordoff and Robbins 2007) resound with accuracy and creative freedom that make his contribution to music therapy continually contemporary and current.

Coda

AeMT is built from my hope that music therapists can consider all that is musical in clinical practice. A fundamental thrust in AeMT is that practitioners value music and its qualities, and learn to adapt it to the therapeutic relationship with precision and creative freedom. The true core of music therapy must surely be one that balances artistic veracity with scientific validity. Just as Mozart was able to translate a sense of the divine in his Requiem, so should the therapist be able to create music that is not only clinically appropriate, but also aesthetically valid. Even when the most minimalist musical responses are required, the therapist should consider their response with dedication and care. It is through the creative immediacy of music that clients can translate their world into musical form. Through inspired music making, therapists can mirror the clients' playing and reveal to them new ways of being.

The building of tones, melodic lines, harmonic sequences, rhythmic patterns, and textures, all combine to create a musical force that is ultimately healing. In order to bring clients to a sophisticated musical space, therapists must learn the art of clinical musicianship. This ability is not easily mastered and takes years of dedicated focus and practice. However, there are lessons and treasures to be gained along the way. Therapists can begin to know music and their own inventiveness in a new light. Through the detailed learning of musical elements therapists can learn to re-evaluate their own relationship with music and know their clients in new and deeper ways.

AeMT embraces all that is musical, promoting a greater understanding of music and its elements in therapy. It incorporates all musical styles as relevant from western classical, popular, and jazz, to contemporary and world influences. Music cannot be thought of as a singular form, and as such, therapists need to know many different genres and styles. It is through the advanced knowledge of music that the therapist will be able to provide a sophisticated musical palette necessary for the client's growth. As contemporary music therapy begins to explore theories of community, gender, medicine, and ethnomusicology, indigenous music-centered theories such as AeMT must remain central to the practice (Lee 2003b). It is music that makes the practice of music therapy unique among all the allied health professions. Among the many philosophies and vocations that exist to serve the needs of its diverse clientele, AeMT celebrates the power of music to heal and the relationship that flourishes between client and therapist.

ACKNOWLEDGMENTS

To Monique McGrath for our ongoing discussions on AeMT, to Sara Pun for her advice on Balinese music, to Therese Schroeder-Sheker for her inspirational discussions on spirituality and music, and Renato Liboro for his unwavering love and support.

NOTES

1. Taken from writings with Monique McGrath as part of ongoing discussions and conversations on AeMT and ethnomusicology.
2. Francis, the name of the client as described in "Music at the Edge" (Lee 1996).
3. Taken from writings with Monique McGrath.
4. For further discussion please read Aigen (2005), pp. 29–34.

REFERENCES

Ahonen, H. and Lee C.A. (2011). The meta-musical experiences of a professional string quartet in music-centered psychotherapy. In: A. Meadows (ed.), *Developments in Music Therapy Practice: Case Study Perspectives*, pp. 518–542. Gilsum, NH: Barcelona Publishers.

Aigen, K. (2005). *Music-Centered Music Therapy*. Gilsum, NH: Barcelona Publishers.

Bergstrom-Nielsen, C. (1993). Graphic notation as a tool in describing and analyzing music therapy improvisations. *Music Therapy* 12: 40–58.

Bonde, L.O. (2005). Approaches to researching music. In: B. Wheeler (ed.), *Music Therapy Research*, pp. 489–525. Gilsum, NH: Barcelona Publishers.

Brown, L.B. (2011). Improvisation. In: T. Gracyk and A. Kania (eds), *The Routledge Companion to Philosophy and Music*, pp. 80–90. London and New York: Routledge.

Bruscia, K. (1998). *Defining Music Therapy* (2nd edition). Gilsum, NH: Barcelona Publishers.

Budd, M. (2011). Music's arousal of emotions. In: T. Gracyk and A. Kania (eds), *The Routledge Companion to Philosophy and Music*, pp. 233–242. London and New York: Routledge.

Cooke, N. (1987). *A Guide to Musical Analysis*. London: Dent.

Daveson, B., O'Callaghan, C., and Grocke, D. (2008). Indigenous music therapy theory building through grounded theory research: The developing indigenous theory framework. *The Arts in Psychotherapy* 35(4): 280–286.

De'Ath, L. (2013). "A sun among men"–The E.E. Cummings songs of Paul Nordoff. *Journal of Singing* (in press).

Erkkilä, J. (2007). Music therapy toolbox (MTTB)—An improvisation analysis tool for clinicians and researchers. In: T. Wosch and T. Wigram (eds), *Microanalysis in Music Therapy*, pp. 134–148. London and Philadelphia: Jessica Kingsley Publishers.

Fachner, J. (2007). Wanderer Between Worlds—Anthropological perspectives on healing rituals and music. Retrieved from: <http://www.wfmt.info/Musictherapyworld/modules/mmmagazine/showarticle.php?articletoshow=202>.

Hadley, S. and Yancy, G. (2012). *Therapeutic Uses of Rap and Hip-Hop*. London and New York: Routledge.

Kania, A. (2011). Definition. In: T. Gracyk and A. Kania (eds), *The Routledge Companion to Philosophy and Music*, pp. 3–13. London and New York: Routledge.

Koen, D. (2009). *Beyond the Roof of the World: Prayer, and Healing in the Pamir Mountains*. New York: Oxford University Press.

Koen, B. (2008). Music-prayer-meditation dynamics in healing. In: D. Koen, J. Lloyd, G. Bar, and K. Brummel-Smith (eds), *The Oxford Handbook of Medical Ethnomusicology*, pp. 93–120. New York: Oxford University Press.

Lee, C.A. (1989). Structural Analysis of Therapeutic Improvisatory Music. *Journal of British Music Therapy* 3(2): 11–19.

Lee, C.A. (1990). Structural Analysis of Post-tonal Therapeutic Improvisatory Music. *Journal of British Music Therapy* 4(1): 6–20.

Lee, C.A. (1992). *The Analysis of Therapeutic Improvisatory Music with People Living with the Virus HIV and AIDS*. Ph.D. thesis, City University, London.

Lee, C.A. (1995). The Analysis of Therapeutic Improvisatory Music. In: A. Gilroy and C. Lee (eds), *Art and Music: Therapy and Research*, pp. 35–50. London: Routledge.

Lee, C.A. (1996). *Music at the Edge: The Music Therapy Experiences of a Musician with AIDS*. London and New York: Routledge.

Lee, C.A. (2000). A Method of Analyzing Improvisations in Music Therapy. *Journal of Music Therapy* 37(2): 147–67.

Lee, C.A. (2001). The Supervision of Clinical Improvisation in Aesthetic Music Therapy: A music-centered approach. In: M. Farinas (ed.), *Music Therapy Supervision*, pp. 247–70. Gilsum, NH: Barcelona Publishers.

Lee, C.A. (2003a). *The Architecture of Aesthetic Music Therapy*. Gilsum, NH: Barcelona Publishers.

Lee, C.A. (2003b). Reflections on Working with a String Quartet in Aesthetic Music Therapy. (online) *Voices: A Forum for Music Therapy* 3(3), accessed May 6, 2010, at: https://voices.no/index.php/voices/article/viewArticle/132.

Lee, C.A. (2005). Living in Music. In: C. Dileo and J. Loewy (eds), *Music Therapy at the End of Life*, pp. 489–525. Cherry Hill, NJ: Jeffrey Books.

Lee, C.A. (2008). Reflections on Being a Music Therapist and a Gay Man. *Voices: A World Forum for Music Therapy* 8(3), accessed May 30th, 2012, at: <https://normt.uib.no/index.php/voices/article/view/415/339.html>.

Lee, C.A. (2013). Styles and the architectural tonic. In: K. Kirkland (ed.), *International Dictionary of Music Therapy*, p. 10. London: Routledge.

Lee, C.A. and Houde, M. (2011). *Improvising in Styles. A Workbook for Music Therapists, Educators and Musicians*. Gilsum, NH: Barcelona Publishers.

Lightstone, A. (2012). Yo, can ya flow! Research findings on hip-hop aesthetics and rap therapy in an urban youth shelter. In: S. Hadley and G. Yancy (eds), *Therapeutic Uses of Rap and Hip-Hop*, pp. 211–251. New York and London: Routledge.

Loth, H. (2006). How gamelan music has influenced me as a music therapist—A personal account. *Voices: A World Forum for Music Therapy* 6(1), accessed April 17th, 2012, at: <http://www.voices.no/mainissues/mi40006000201.html>.

Matravers, D. (2011). Arousal theories. In: T. Gracyk and A. Kania (eds), *Routledge Companion to Philosophy and Music*, pp. 212–222. London: Routledge.

McGrath, M. (2012). Taken from unpublished e-mail correspondence.

Munro, S. (1984). *Music Therapy in Palliative/Hospice Care*. St. Louis, MO: Magna Music, Baton Inc.

Nordoff, P. and Robbins, C. (2007). *Creative Music Therapy: A Guide to Fostering Clinical Musicianship*. Gilsum, NH: Barcelona Publishers.

O'Shea, J. (1990). *Music and Medicine. Medical Profiles of Great Composers*. London: J.M. Dent.

Pun, S. (2011). *Balinese Music and Music Therapy*, Master's thesis. Wilfrid Laurier University.

Reason, P. and Rowan, J. (eds). (1981). *Human Inquiry: A sourcebook of new paradigm research*. Chichester: Wiley.

Rinpoche, D. K. and Rinpoche, P. (1992). *The Heart Treasure of the Enlightened Ones*. Boston, MA: Shambhala Publications.

Robbins, C. and Robbins, C. (1998). *Healing Heritage: Paul Nordoff Exploring the Tonal Language of Music*. Gilsum, NH: Barcelona Publishers.

Robinson, K. (2011). *Out of Our Minds: Learning to be Creative*. New York: John Wiley & Sons.

Rohrbacher, M. (2008). The application of Hood's nine levels to the practice of music therapy. In: D. Koen, J. Lloyd, G. Barz, and K. Brummel-Smith (eds), *The Oxford Handbook of Medical Ethnomusicology*, pp. 265–307. Oxford: Oxford University Press.

Ruud, E. (2010). *Music Therapy: A Perspective from the Humanities*. Gilsum, NH: Barcelona Publishers.

Sankaran, R. (2008). Homeopathic Healing with Music. In: D. Koen, J. Lloyd, G. Barz, and K. Brummel-Smith (eds), *The Oxford Handbook of Medical Ethnomusicology*, pp. 393–409. Oxford University Press.

Schroeder-Sheker, T. (2001). *Transitus: A Blessed Death in a Modern World*. Missoula, MT: St Dunstan Press.

Scruton, R. (1997). *The Aesthetics of Music*. Oxford: Clarendon Press.

Sharpe, R.A. (2000). *Music and Humanism*. Oxford: Oxford University Press.

Stige, B., Ansdell, G., Elefant, C., and Pavlicevic, M. (2010). *Where Music Helps. Community Music Therapy in Action and Reflection* London and USA: Ashgate Publishing.

Stige, B. and Aarø, L.E. (2012). *Invitation to Community Music Therapy*. New York and London: Routledge.

Strange, J. (2012). Psychodynamically informed music therapy groups with teenagers with severe special needs in a college setting. In: J. Tomlinson, P. Derrington, and A. Oldfield (eds), *Music Therapy in Schools*, pp. 179–194. London and Philadelphia: Jessica Kingsley Publishers.

Streeter, E. (2012). Computer aided music therapy evaluation: Testing the music therapy logbook prototype 1 system. *The Arts in Psychotherapy* 39(1): 1–10.

Thaut, M. (2005). *Rhythm, music and the brain: Scientific foundations and clinical applications*. New York: Routledge.

Tucek, G. (2006). Traditional Oriental Music Therapy—A regulatory and relational approach. <http://wfmt.info/Musictherapyworld/modules/mmmagazine/issues/20060929134150/MTT7_3_October_ebook_1.pdf#page=124>.

Turry, A. (2011). *Between Music and Psychology*. Lambert Academic Publishing.

Verney, R. and Ansdell, G. (2010). *Conversations on Nordoff-Robbins Music Therapy.* Gilsum NH: Barcelona Publishers.

Wigram, T. (2004). *Improvisation: Methods and Techniques for Music Therapy Clinicians, Educators and Students.* London and Philadelphia: Jessica Kingsley Publishers.

Wormit A.F., Warth M., Koenig J., Hillecke T.K., and Bardenheuer H.J. (2012). Evaluating a Treatment Manual for Music Therapy in Adult Outpatient Oncology Care. *Music and Medicine* 4: 65–73.

Wosch, T. (2007). Measurement of Emotional Transitions in Clinical Improvisations with EQ 26.5. In: T. Wosch and T. Wigram (eds), *Microanalysis in Music Therapy.* London and Philadelphia: Jessica Kingsley Publishers.

CHAPTER 29

CULTURE-CENTERED MUSIC THERAPY

BRYNJULF STIGE

INTRODUCTION

CULTURE is not like a coat that you can take off before entering a music therapy session or situation. If you do not respect the culture of another person then you do not respect the person. Culture enables and restricts human life and development and Culture-Centered Music Therapy facilitates constructive and critical re-examination of practice, theory, and research in this light. More than a stimulus influencing human behavior, culture is considered a resource for action and an integral element in human interaction. People's physical, psychosocial, and spiritual needs are explored in relational and contextual terms. In Culture-Centered Music Therapy, human interdependence is not understood as a challenge to autonomy but rather as a basis for it. This combination of perspectives highlights the interaction between our internal and external worlds and between individual and community.

In this chapter I will first position Culture-Centered Music Therapy within the history of ideas in music therapy, with a focus on various notions of culture and on the developments that have made culture-centered a contemporary force within music therapy thought. I will then outline three tenets of the orientation, with a focus on culture as resource for self and society, music as situated activity, and music therapy as health musicking. Subsequently I will outline some implications for practice, theory, and research. Then I will present a case example exploring aspects of how music therapy can create space for social-musical participation. Finally I will sum up with some concluding points that also address possibilities for future development of Culture-Centered Music Therapy.

A caveat should be included at this point. Culture-Centered Music Therapy is used here as an umbrella term for description of a broad tradition within the discipline that highlights participation, action, and transactional development through music in and as culture (Stige 2002). Not all the authors I refer to in the chapter would use the selected label for description of their work. At the same time, in the music therapy literature the label *culture-centered* is at times used to refer to other more or less related ideas, such as the need for multicultural awareness in music therapy. This chapter seeks to provide clarity as to the use of the term, and how the culture-centered orientation has been developed and elaborated within music therapy.

A FIFTH FORCE IN THE HISTORY OF IDEAS
IN MUSIC THERAPY?

One of the tantalizing tasks in writing about Culture-Centered Music Therapy is clarification of the term culture itself. It is a broad, rich, and multifaceted term, both in our everyday conversations and in academic discourse. Some argue that this discredits the notion. Others acknowledge that the situation reflects the omnipresence and importance of culture in human life. One metaphor often used to communicate this, is that "when it comes to culture, we are fish in the water. We are not able to leave the river in order to take a distanced look at it" (Stige 2002, p. 16). This is not to suggest that reflexivity is not possible or desirable, only that we engage the lens of our own culture when thinking about our role and place in culture. Music sociologist Tia DeNora (2013) has developed a similar argument when she suggests that we can only see culture through the ways we point to it. This act of "pointing" sort of "performs" the culture that we want to describe. In consequence, our accounts not only reflect culture but also affect culture.

One of the important distinctions to make here is between the idea that culture is always present in human life and the idea that culture is all there is to human life. Culture-Centered Music Therapy is clearly subscribing to the first idea more than to the other. The basic idea is *not* that humans are products of cultural context. Instead, there is a search for more interactional and transactional perspectives on the relationships between individuals and their environments. And, as we will see, to talk about human culture without considering human nature is hardly productive in music therapy. How could we approach the question of defining culture, then? I have previously offered a definition suggesting that culture is "the accumulation of customs and technologies enabling and regulating human coexistence" (Stige 2002, p. 38). The term *accumulation* reminds us about how culture always involves change and exchange. The term *customs* refers to activities as well as ways of thinking and feeling. As used in this definition, technologies include physical tools such as instruments as well as symbolic tools such as language and music. One of the main ideas communicated by this definition, then, is that culture makes human life possible, in positive and negative ways:

> ... culture is what happens when people spend time together; they act and they interact, they produce artifacts and they use artifacts, and they do this as they make rules and break rules, if only to make new rules. Culture then is shaping people and shaped by people, in conscious and non-conscious ways, some of the latter being related to human nature as evolved in phylogeny
>
> (Stige 2002, p. 38).

A definition or a short description could not cover the continuously evolving complexity of human culture but it might be helpful when we want to highlight some aspects of relevance for music therapy discourse: The main mode of human existence is coexistence and as the human species has evolved, human life is unthinkable without culture. We must understand culture as an indispensable resource, then, but as with any resource, its value depends upon use in context. Culture not only enables human activity, it also regulates it in various ways. Some regulation is needed and helpful, but culture can also be repressive and destructive. Culture-Centered Music Therapy therefore encompasses cultural critique and self-reflection.

Culture has not been neglected in the music therapy literature but it has often been presented as an external factor or a given set of stimuli influencing people. A typical example is:

> Culture and society define music and determine how it is used. It is a basic premise in the field of music therapy that music of cultures other than one's own has little or no meaning (Gaston 1968) and that one will not respond to or participate in it
>
> (Gibbons 1977, as quoted in Davis, et al. 1999, p. 296)

This argument implies what we could call *cultural determinism*; the idea being that culture and society determine how people use music. In this way, culture is reduced to an external factor influencing us and there is not much space left for neither personal agency nor sociocultural change (see Stige 2003/2012, p. 143 ff. for further discussion). In contrast, the culture-centered tradition suggests a more ecological perspective, where culture is also related to possibilities for action. Two of the music therapy theorists who paved the way for this kind of thinking are Carolyn Kenny and Even Ruud. Both presented their doctoral dissertations in 1987 and both focused on theory development in ways that inform contemporary thinking within Culture-Centered Music Therapy.

In the thesis *The Field of Play*, Kenny (1987) presented a theoretical study of music therapy processes. She based the development of a theoretical model on her own clinical experience, a review of relevant literature, and a creative phenomenological and exploratory approach, including dialogue with a panel responding to a recording and theoretical description of a music therapy session. To describe the theory Kenny proposed is beyond the scope of this chapter, but to illuminate some of the premises she worked from is highly relevant. Kenny referred to music therapists such as Sears, Bonny, and Nordoff and Robbins who proposed the significance of "environment," "sound presence," and "landscape" (respectively) in music therapy processes. Kenny then took an *ecological* perspective in her understanding of relationships in these "fields," as evidenced by her references to a "whole systems perspective" and "expanding systems model."[1] This led her to propose relationships of reciprocal influence: "Does the person organize the music or does the music organize the person?" (Kenny 1987, p. 39). And: "The aesthetic is a field of beauty which is the human person.... The aesthetic is an environment ... " (Kenny 1987, p. 173). She then developed a contextual perspective where both music and humans are understood as relational systems, allowing for mutually constitutive processes, as exemplified by how she defines power in music therapy processes: "Power is that cumulative energy which draws one into new possibilities in the arena of change. Power is experienced through a dialogue between inner motivation, strength and movement and significant external resources in the existent field" (Kenny 1987, p. 176).

In the thesis *Music as Communication and Interaction*[2], Ruud (1987) also focused on theory development in music therapy, with the aim of developing theoretical language that contributes to the legitimacy of music therapy as a discipline within the humanities, in close relationship to systematic musicology. Again, the dissertation is much too long and rich in content for any summary of its contents and readers are directed to Ruud (1998) for developments of some of the ideas originally presented in the dissertation. Here I want to highlight how Ruud's notions of music, health, and therapy prefigured contemporary performative and transactional perspectives within Culture-Centered Music Therapy. I will illustrate this by clarifying aspects of the notion of music that Ruud developed in his thesis: In an interdisciplinary argument for an understanding of music as communicative activity, he explicitly linked this notion to the cultural historical theory tradition and stressed how human activity is situated historically and socially (Ruud 1987, p. 329).[3] Consequently, Ruud (1987, p. 331) described music both as human interaction in context and as a tool that enables use and action. His discussion of music in many ways prefigured notions that later have become influential in the interdisciplinary study of music, such as Small's (1998) notion of music as situated activity ("musicking") and DeNora's (1999; 2000) notion of music as resource for action.

Both Kenny and Ruud's contributions influenced my own first attempt of developing an elaborated perspective on music therapy as situated human activity (Stige 2002). I chose the term Culture-Centered Music Therapy to communicate this perspective and developed an argument about implications for practice, theory, and research that I will summarize and update in the present chapter. One significant theoretical context in 2002 was the "cultural turn" within interdisciplinary music studies, with obvious implications for music therapy (see e.g. Ansdell 2001). Today we might perhaps suggest that there has been a "cultural turn" in music therapy as well, as exemplified with recent developments such as Community Music Therapy (Pavlicevic and Ansdell 2004; Stige and Aarø 2012), feminist perspectives in music therapy (Edwards and Hadley 2007; Hadley and Edwards 2004; Hadley 2006), and resource-oriented music therapy (Rolvsjord 2010).

Bruscia has proposed that culture-centered perspectives should be seen in relation to the history of ideas in music therapy. He argues that music therapy, like psychology, has evolved through various "forces" of thought, if in a slightly different order:

> Our first force contributed discoveries about how music influences human behavior and the physical world. Our second force unearthed unconscious dimensions of music experience, and explored their implications for therapy. Our third and fourth forces explicated the role of music in self-actualization and spiritual development respectively.
>
> (Bruscia 2002, p. xv)

Bruscia then proceeds to suggest that culture-centeredness is the fifth force in music therapy:

> This will be the force that debunks many of our uncontextualized generalizations about the nature of music, therapy, and music therapy itself. This will be the force that reminds us that all interactions, musical and nonmusical, clinical and nonclinical, are situated within many larger, frequently overlooked frames of perception and communication. To be culture-centered is to be variously aware that there are frames of history, frames of environment, frames of ethnicity, frames of language, frames of belief and value, and the never-ending, shifting frames that evolve between individuals through moment-to-moment interaction.
>
> (Bruscia 2002, p. xv)

Theorists will probably disagree as to how to describe and categorize the history of ideas in music therapy, but Bruscia's argument about the need to relate culture-centered perspectives to this history is convincing. Only in this historical context will it be possible to discern if and how Culture-Centered Music Therapy contributes with new and fruitful perspectives.

As a conclusion to this section, I find it tempting to play with the term of "fifth force" and instead propose the idea of a "fifth possibility." In order to illustrate this point, I can refer to a model that Bruscia has been active in introducing to music therapy, namely the conceptual model of quadrants with the dimensions of individual/collective and interior/exterior, based on Wilber's evolutionary-developmental theory (see e.g. Bruscia 1998). The debate about the validity of Wilber's model is not what I want to focus on here, but its value as a heuristic tool of reflection. It would clearly be a mistake to think of Culture-Centered Music Therapy as a tradition that could be located in one of these quadrants (as say "collective interior"). Culture-Centered Music Therapy advocates a fifth possibility; it builds on traditions of thought that actively try to transcend the distinctions that these quadrants are based upon. The basic idea is ecological; the individual and the collective constitute each other reciprocally, and our internal and external worlds are in continuous interaction. This claim will become clearer as I now will outline some of the basic tenets of Culture-Centered Music Therapy.

BASIC TENETS IN CULTURE-CENTERED MUSIC THERAPY

We produce culture collectively through human interaction in context. This does not suggest that culture-centered perspectives are limited to the collective level of human existence. In fact, culture-centeredness has become increasingly relevant due to the individualism of modern societies.

> According to Nielsen (1993), the cultural individualism of modernity could be characterized through use of a "culturalization hypothesis," that is, a hypothesis that states that culture has become increasingly important in modern societies, as it provides the individuals with the tools they need in search of identity. Culture, which Nielsen links closely to meaning, is no longer linked directly to society and the immediate social context of the individual. Culture is differentiated from society; there is a "culturalization" of human life in which individuals have the possibility of engaging with several different cultural contexts in their identity projects.
>
> (Stige 2003/2012, p. 47)

"Social" and "cultural" are not interchangeable terms, then. It is more helpful to think of culture as a resource that enables and regulates interactions between the individual and the group. Culture-Centered Music Therapy is based on an ecological understanding of the relationship between humans and their surroundings. In this section I will outline three basic tenets, namely: (1) culture as resource for self and society; (2) music as situated activity; and (3) music therapy as health musicking.

Culture as resource for self and society

Culture is often understood as a force external to the individual. In Culture-Centered Music Therapy there is more of a focus on culture as a resource for the dynamic interplay between self and society. Individual agency is culturally constituted. People act and interact through use of cultural resources (Krüger and Stige, in press). This is not to say that culture cannot be restricting or repressive, but there is no way out beyond use of cultural resources. Self-regulation, critique, planning, and creative action all require internalization and appropriation of the tools and signs provided by culture (Gillespie and Zittoun 2010).

This resource-oriented notion of culture is different from the notion typically found in various "cross-cultural" approaches. The field of cross-cultural psychology, for instance, tends to treat culture as a characteristic of a social group, with the implication that individuals "belong to" a culture. This is the tradition of research where say "American culture" is compared to "Japanese culture." There are several problems with this tradition, often linked to the tendency to interpret culture as a stable and homogenous entity at group level (Valsiner 2007, pp. 22–25). The alternative that I find relevant for Culture-Centered Music Therapy is to see culture as more diversified and as continuously evolving. People take active part in these processes, as there is a dynamic interdependence among self systems and social systems (Markus and Hamedani 2010).

An analogy would be the development of parent-infant bonding. Infants are not products of their environment; they actively co-construct the relationships that constitute the context of their development (Edwards 2011). Of course, there are nuances to this. The metaphor of culture as external force influencing the individual is not always irrelevant. Edwards (2011, p. 8) provides an interesting example when she refers to a study revealing that German and French babies differ in the contour of their cries, even if their cries are recorded within five days of birth, because of the language to which they have been exposed by that age. This indicates that cultural influences begin in utero. But as Edwards's edited book so clearly illuminates, *participation in relationships* is central to human development. When we are born we start interacting with other people and embark on a journey of cultural learning in ways that go beyond influence. We are primed with the toolkit of communicative musicality. This enables immediate interactive participation through sound and movement (Malloch and Trevarthen 2009). In the process of human development we learn to use mediated tools and signs with language and music being two of the more important human sign systems. As we internalize sign systems we develop the capacity to reorganize signs in an endless number of ways. We develop tools for creative thinking and acting in communication with others.

Culture transcends the notion of external influence, then. The work of Indian born literary theorist Homi Bhabha (1994/2004) has contributed much to our understanding of identity as continuously evolving from active use of mixed influences. He uses the concept of "hybridity" to explore this. That there is a dynamic interdependence among self systems and various social systems is a notion Culture-Centered Music Therapy shares with a range of sociocultural theories, including cultural-historical activity theory and theories in cultural anthropology. I have previously developed this argument mainly with reference to cultural psychology (Stige 2002), where there is a rich and evolving literature on how culture and mind make up each other, over the history of communities and over the life course of the individual (Kitayama and Cohen 2007; Valsiner 2007).

Music as situated activity

The cultural study of music was pioneered by anthropologists and ethnomusicologists, with a focus on music *in* culture and music *as* culture (Merriam 1964) and gradually also on culture in music at a broader range of levels of analysis (Keil and Feld 1994). Today, the cultural study of music is central to a range of music disciplines (Clayton et al. 2011). Here I will focus on a notion I find particularly relevant for Culture-Centered Music Therapy, namely music as *situated activity*.

In the previous section I mentioned how Ruud's (1987, p. 331) discussion of music as communicative activity and interaction in context in some ways prefigured the notion that Small (1998) developed in his famous book *Musicking*. Small treats music as a verb, not as a noun:

> To music is to take part, in any capacity, in a musical performance, whether by performing, by listening, by rehearsing or practicing, by providing material for performance (what is called composing), or by dancing.
>
> (Small 1998, p. 9)

Small's (1998) concept of music as a verb invites a "performative turn" in our thinking about music (with a broad notion of performance, then, encompassing all situations where people make or use music). Small suggests that performances do not exist in order to present musical works but that musical works exist in order to enable performances. This is not a shocking suggestion to most music therapists, who are used to flexible use of musical repertoire in order to serve people and situations. More importantly, perhaps, Small's notion reminds us about how music and context are linked. Music as human activity is necessarily *situated activity*; it evolves in time in a certain place. The situated nature of musical activity suggests that we take the multilayered history of evolving events into consideration, with the three dimensions of phylogeny, cultural history, and ontogeny (phylogeny referring to the evolution of the human species and ontogeny to the development of the individual). The moment-to-moment experience of musicking involves use of resources developed in these three historical contexts (Stige 2002, pp. 79–109). For an elaboration of this idea, see Pavlicevic and Ansdell's (2009) discussion of how communicative musicality and collaborative musicking are related.

The notion of music as situated human activity is central to much contemporary thinking in music therapy, and authors such as Gary Ansdell (2014) and Ken Aigen (2014) have developed elaborated arguments about "how music helps" in ways that illuminate relationships between music-centered and culture-centered thinking in the discipline.

How, then, are the ideas of music as situated activity and music as resource related? The (mus)ecological notions of affordances and appropriation offer one way of understanding the relationships (see DeNora 2000). Music as resource offer possibilities for action and participation, through appropriation in a situation. Access and active *use* of available resources is what matters, not the resources in themselves.[4] In the next section I will use the notion of "health musicking" to discuss how music therapy can enable active use of available resources in musical activity.

Music therapy as health musicking

The performative notion of music as situated activity suggests that what music affords in relation to health and well-being grows out of the relationships established in each situation. I have previously proposed the following definition of music therapy to highlight this: "Music therapy as professional practice is situated health musicking in a planned process of collabo-ration between client and therapist" (Stige 2002, p. 200). With inspiration from a range of theoretical contributions, including Small's concept of musicking and DeNora's discussion of affordance and appropriation, I have used the notion of *health musicking* to communi-cate the idea that relationships between music and health are performed in context (Stige 2002; 2012).

The therapeutic setting is of course only one of many possible contexts, and the notion of health musicking therefore underlines the continuity between music therapy and other practices and consequently also the significance of collaboration across professions and between professionals and lay people. Bonde (here using the spelling "musicing") summa-rizes this aspect of the argument in the following way:

> In this way, health musicing can be understood as the common core of any use of music expe-riences to regulate emotional or relational states or to promote well-being, be it therapeutic or not, professionally assisted or self-made. Social science research in recent years has docu-mented some of the many ways in which music is used to promote health by "lay people" in their daily lives.
>
> (Bonde 2011, p. 121)

The notion of health musicking is based on a performative understanding of health, as devel-oped by Ruud (1979; 1998), Aldridge (1996; 2004), DeNora (2000; 2007) and others. This exemplifies the broader theme of how relationships between self and society develop, as dis-cussed above. In defining the notion of *health musicking* more specifically, I took inspiration from Burke's (1966) narrative theory on human action, where social interaction and com-munication is described in terms of the "dramatistic pentad" of act, scene, agent, agency, and purpose.

> Health musicking is characterized by careful assessment and appropriation of the health affordances of arena, agenda, agents, activities, and artifacts.
>
> (Stige 2002, p. 211)

In other words, health musicking could be understood as processes where various agents collaborate and negotiate in relation to the agendas, artefacts, and activities of any given arena. In a brief dictionary entry on "health musicking," Bonde has made distinctions that might be helpful in understanding the various aspects involved in health musicking, namely: (1) personal resources; (2) musical elements; and (3) various contextual aspects (Bonde 2013, p. 56). I will use these distinctions to explicate the interplay of aspects according to the culture-centered tenets I have outlined above: In culture-centered perspective, personal resources do not belong to the individual only, but arise from the dynamic interplay of self and society. Also, the agents that take part in health musicking might often try and increase their agency through the development of alliances. The musical elements that they can use in this process go beyond the traditional elements of sound to include musical activities and artefacts (instruments, songs, and so on); music emerges as resource for action. The various contextual aspects include the agenda (the goals and the rationale for the activity) and the arena (the setting, with its ecological relationships to other settings). These various aspects come into action and interaction partly because music is temporal; it requires musical activ-ity and it can happen concurrently with other activities and behavior. Consequently, music becomes integrated with other activities and processes at micro and macro levels of society (Clarke et al. 2010).

> Investigations of relationships between music and health could not be reduced to the study of the direct effect of musical parameters but must also include investigations of the use of musical and paramusical features of a situation. The term "paramusical" is used here as an alternative to "extramusical," to avoid the misleading impression that things are either 'totally' musical or not musical (Stige et al. 2010, p. 298). We need to understand the relationships between those phenomena that we perceive as specifically musical and those actions and activities that go with these, and as Korsyn (2003) reminds us, what we consider musical is not given but continuously constructed musically and discursively. When we listen to music, for instance, we do not just hear sounds and silences. Sometimes we can hear the arena of the music, such as when we hear the acoustics of a church as an element of choral singing or a noisy audience as part of the sound of a live recording. Perhaps we can hear aspects of the agenda also, as when someone sings to praise or please, to challenge or tease.
>
> (Stige 2012, pp. 185–186)

If in health musicking resources are mobilized in time, we need to understand how agency is made possible. In the example below, I will illustrate how this can happen and I will use the terms *participation* and *interaction rituals* to clarify this. Participation is key. This is a notion which is sometimes used to denote the act of "joining in." A broader notion which stresses how participation requests mutuality and enables change is highly relevant in a culture-centered perspective (Stige 2006). I will explore participation in and as interaction rituals. Sociologist Goffman (1967), who was inspired by the work of Durkheim (1912/1995), made the term interaction rituals well known through his studies of "face-to-face behavior." I will use the term as developed further by Collins (2004). These authors focus less on ritual as ceremony and formality and more on ritual as everyday activity of interpersonal inter-action. According to Collins (2004), interaction rituals arise when there are *mutual foci of attention* and *increased emotional energy* among participants. Repetition is not a defining feature of an interaction ritual, then, according to Collins. Nevertheless interaction rituals are quite often repeated, because they build *group membership* and *community*.

A CASE EXAMPLE: CREATING SPACE
FOR SOCIAL-MUSICAL PARTICIPATION

The case example I have chosen to include is developed from an ethnographic study of a festival for music and the arts in a rural county in Western Norway. Since 1988, this festival has established itself as an energizing yearly event, bringing about one hundred adults with intellectual disabilities and their helpers together. During the weekend the festival lasts, all participants (including helpers, instructors, and organizers) live together and create music and arts together. After three intense days of activity, processes and products merge in a final performance. The festival is organized by NFU, a Norwegian association for individuals with intellectual disabilities and their families, with the double aim of creating an inspiring cul-tural event and building an arena for cultural politics. The main goal in relation to the latter is to spur the development of inclusive cultural activities in local communities (Stige 2010).

I have included this case example in order to illuminate some of the arguments made above, such as how culture allows for dynamic interplay between self systems and social systems and also how health musicking can involve mobilization of resources through interaction rituals.

The example I will present is taken from a workshop simply called "Singing and Playing." There are roughly fifteen participants present, including some helpers. The participants with intellectual disabilities are all adults, with moderate intellectual disability and varying degrees of language skills. Here is a note describing one of my first observations of the workshop:

> As usual, the first song is a greeting song. One of the music therapists takes the lead and presents each participant to the group. When it comes to a female participant in her fifties, the music therapist sings her name and asks if she's here, as the lyrics of the song suggest. The woman answers loudly: "No, she ain't around today" and then laughs vigorously, as the music therapist and the rest of the group do too.
>
> Another participant, sitting in his wheel chair, looks like he's falling asleep. But when the song comes to him he's awake indeed. He sings, softly but lively, a whole verse of the song, beautifully performed. He sings to a young woman next to him, whom he knows well. The music therapist adjusts the volume and the tempo of the song to attune to his way of singing.

(Stige 2010, p. 120)

This little note includes two important observations: The workshops were usually organized around some kind of shared activity but there was simultaneously space for individual contributions that would change the quality of the music and the social interaction. I will explore this through a brief summary of three themes developed in the published case study, namely "Participation as self-presentation," "Participation as co-creation of social space," and "Participation as ritual negotiation" (Stige 2010, pp. 125–147).

Participation as self-presentation

As I have illuminated, a description of the participation in this workshop must account for different ways of taking part. Through participant observation, analysis of video recordings, and consultation with relevant literature, the qualitative case study of the workshop offered description of five different ways of taking part, which we could think of as five different "styles of self-presentation": (1) non-participation; (2) silent participation; (3) conventional participation; (4) adventurous participation; and (5) eccentric participation (Stige 2010, p. 130). I can briefly summarize the descriptions of each:

Non-participation involves "not being there," either by leaving or never arriving or by being there physically but showing no sign of being present psychologically and socially. *Silent participation* involves "being there but not taking part in the action". Participants give the impression of being mentally and socially present, through watching and listening. *Conventional participation* involves "joining in and performing" what is expected in the situation. This, then, includes synchronization with others in the situation and it includes taking one of the roles available, through say singing, playing, dancing, or conducting. *Adventurous participation* differs from conventional participation in that the contribution of the individual is "standing out." The contribution deviates from what is expected in ways that require active adjustment by the other people present. *Eccentric participation* is more dramatic than adventurous participation and "goes across" what is happening in the group: "It will usually either establish a new center of mutual attention and action or it will break up the existing structures. In the first case, leadership is challenged. In the second case the coherence of the group is challenged" (Stige 2010, pp. 130–131).

The above should not be thought of as a list of discrete categories, but as a description of the repertoire of possibilities for participation in a workshop like this:

> Non-participation, for instance, may gradually be transformed into silent participation which again may turn into conventional participation. Elaborated conventional participation at some point becomes adventurous, and if escalated further may turn into eccentric participation. The process is not necessarily linear, however. As we have seen, silent participation may at times turn into say adventurous participation. And eccentric participation, at the extreme, may turn into non-participation. Together the forms of participation represent a repertoire of possibilities.
>
> (Stige 2010, p. 132)

Participatory contexts vary considerably when it comes to the range of possibilities for participation, depending on the etiquette, so to say. In the workshop I studied, there seemed not to be too much pressure in the direction of conventional participation but space for a range of ways of taking part. In order to understand this process, we need a notion of participation as co-creation of social space.

Participation as co-creation of social space

From observing the music therapists in action I could see how they worked hard to try and establish situations where each participant could take part in his or her way. This was performed through careful selection of musical material, sensitive musical-emotional attunement to each person, responsive and respectful use of humor, and also willingness to be flexible in relation to roles. This list of therapeutic actions—probably quite recognizable for most music therapists—indicates that the idea of participation as self-presentation needs to be expanded. The five categories I presented above highlight the self-presentation of each participant but they do not illuminate the interaction that surrounds and contains this. We need language that enables us to talk about and explore how the moments are *co-created*.

> One central observation made is that most music therapists in most sessions of the festival were willing to let scripts go, activities go, and even their roles as leaders of the group go, as long as there was mutual focus of attention and emotional entrainment in the group. Examples even include moments of "musical mutiny," where the music therapists accepted that one participant abruptly introduced a new song in the middle of another activity, as long as this new song was taken up by the others in the group. In situations where eccentric contributions were not taken up by the group, the music therapists would take a more active role in re-establishing a focus of attention and action…
>
> This way of describing the workshops reveals that what may look very different at first glance, such as e.g. silent participation and adventurous participation, may contribute in comparable ways in a given situation, if our focus is not just various self-presentations, but the co-creation of social space. If the self-presentation of therapists and other "helpers" is just as

crucial to examine as that of the participants, we need to understand more of the collaborative dimension of participation.

(Stige 2010, p. 133)

According to Collins, central ingredients of interaction rituals include bodily co-presence, mutual focus of attention, and shared mood (Collins, 2004, pp. 47–101). In a music therapy workshop as the one described here, *bodily co-presence* is established at two levels. The group is seated in a semicircle and therefore visibly present for each other in a clear way. Also, the structure of activities is often arranged so that there is space for attention to one participant at the time. *Mutual focus of attention* is established in *social-musical* ways. When activities address one person at a time, for instance, there is space for this person to get engaged. At the same time, the activity and the group's attention is drawn to the person's participation in the musical activity. Let us now turn to the next point in Collins's list of interaction ritual ingredients, namely the establishment of shared mood. Collins (2004, p. 92) describes inter-action rituals as "emotion transformers" that, for instance, can turn negative emotions into positive ones. In the case of this workshop, it was particularly obvious how emotions were transformed during the sequences where each person's participation was in focus. Some participants would be careful and introduce a sort wary delicacy into the interaction. With John, it was a completely different story:

> John sat patiently, but with visible eagerness, waiting for his turn. When the music therapist came to his verse, the song and the situation was immediately transformed. John grabbed the hands of the music therapist and initiated a rocking movement and an acceleration of the speed of the song. The music therapist attuned her contribution by increasing the volume of her singing and the situation was energized considerably.
>
> With use of the categories developed in the previous section we could call John's contribution *adventurous*, but we must also pay attention to how others in the situation attune to the adventure. In this case the music therapist allowed the adventure, perhaps to some degree anticipated it, and accommodated quite actively. Both were adjusting their participation in relation to each other. And it did not stop with increased speed and volume of the song and rocking movements from where John was sitting on the chair. All of a sudden he stood up and hugged the music therapist warmly and enthusiastically, and for a long time.

(Stige 2010, p. 137)

This little sequence exemplifies how the participants in the workshop co-construct a social space that is inclusive; with room for improvisation and unexpected episodes. The interaction produces *social spaciousness* where many different personal and spontaneous contributions are welcome.

> The broad range of possible styles of self-presentations in music described earlier therefore does not necessarily imply fragmented situations with a series of individual foci so that things fall apart. If integrated in interaction rituals, these various styles of self-presentation may become part of the co-creation of a more inclusive social space. *Participatory spaciousness* implies that there is room for unity beyond uniformity.

(Stige 2010, p. 138).

The fact that participatory spaciousness is created does not suggest that there are no conflicts or that mechanisms of power do not apply, as we will soon see.

Participation as ritual negotiation

So far I have described interaction rituals that seem to be able to combine each individual's need for spaciousness with the group's need for mutual focus and attention. Of course this is not the whole story. All possibilities were not always equal. I will use processes of *ritual intensification* and the issue of *situational stratification* to clarify this. Ritual intensification is partly what interaction rituals are about. Durkheim (1912/1995, p. 217) used the metaphor of "electricity" to describe how a ritual can create an extraordinary degree of exaltation. Shared emotions often intensify when expressed through rhythmic entrainment and music therapists should be well qualified to work effectively with interaction rituals. They need, however, to be conscious about the issue of situational stratification:

> ... there is a tradition for sophisticated work with rhythmic entrainment in music therapy, e.g. through the improvisational approach pioneered by Nordoff and Robbins. This approach involves musicing where the therapist's music imitates and incorporates the sounds and rhythms of the client. If performed with respect and sensitivity, this could lead to an affective change that makes the client more willing to enter into musical collaboration and eventually a therapeutic relationship ... The music therapists working in this particular *Cultural Festival* all worked in a tradition informed by this approach. In the group situation, imitation of and synchronization with each individual's contributions were supplemented by even more intensifying strategies. Individual and dyadic improvisations were typically interspersed with sequences of community singing, often with rhythmic movements, which obviously intensified the situation. Also, the music therapist would sometimes enthusiastically exaggerate his or her response to the participant's contribution, through "amplified" mimics and/ or sounds...
>
> These forms of ritual intensification seemed to be used in order to help participants to move from one form of participation to another, say from silent participation to conventional participation. Or it was used to intensify the participation within one form (in direction of more elaborate and expressive conventional participation, for instance). Quite often these strategies of ritual intensification worked. Clients were encouraged to take part and to take part with more emotional energy. There is, however, a therapeutic dilemma to be discussed in relation to this: If the music therapists are very active in intensifying a ritual, they also run the risk of putting themselves in the centre of action and attention, which according to interaction ritual theory could have negative effects for other participants with more limited expressive resources.
>
> (Stige 2010, pp. 139–140)

As Collins (2004, pp. 102–140) explains, "energy stars" may use a ritual to "charge their batteries" of emotional energy. Participants who find themselves in subordinate roles may experience the same ritual as an energy drainer, however. The value of the music therapists' willingness to accept and acknowledge adventurous and eccentric participation is put in perspective by this. These forms of participation challenge the established order of the music therapist as the "sociometric star." Adventurous and eccentric participation might be valuable because they decenter the therapist and put other participants in focus. Because the social space was co-created, the music therapists never "abdicated," however, they were always part of the (inter)action.

SOME IMPLICATIONS FOR PRACTICE, THEORY, AND RESEARCH

This example includes ways of working that are recognizable for many music therapists. Culture-Centered Music Therapy is not a new approach or model but a theoretical orientation with relevance for several fields of practice. While the notion of ritual is central in the selected example, my point here is not to discuss rituals in music therapy as such, even though that might have been interesting.[5] What is offered above is a theoretically informed description of how participants in music therapy negotiate their interaction through use of cultural resources, even when human interaction seems to be most spontaneous and unscripted. The example illuminates, for instance, how human individuality is closely linked to co-created social space.

As I described in the section on basic tenets, Culture-Centered Music Therapy is an orientation that highlights mobilization of resources through health musicking. Interaction rituals, then, exemplify the dynamic interplay between self and society, which of course happens at many levels; the dyad, the small group, the broader community, and so on. I will describe some general implications for the field. One place to start is to examine implications for how we define music therapy. Take the appendix to Bruscia's (1998) *Defining Music Therapy*; it includes more than sixty definitions. Most of them implicitly or explicitly focus on change in the individual client. The tenets I have discussed above suggest a broader horizon. The definition of music therapy proposed by Even Ruud provides us with a perspective that is pertinent to Culture-Centered Music Therapy. This definition was published in Norwegian several decades ago (Ruud 1979) but it is not included in Bruscia's appendix, as it was not published in English at the time he wrote his book. In a later book in English Ruud (1998, pp. 51–52) presented a translation of his seemingly simple definition where he suggests that music therapy is an effort to *increase possibilities for action*. What makes this proposal valuable for our understanding of Culture-Centered Music Therapy is that Ruud grounds his definition on a sociological critique of the medical model. The "medical model" (understood as a generalized way of understanding pathology and not a perspective specific to medicine) suggests that therapy focuses on the diagnosis and treatment of the health problems of an individual. Ruud promotes an alternative view which acknowledges that problems can have social and cultural origins and pathways:

> This is why I came up with the idea of defining music therapy as an effort to "increase the possibilities for action." To increase a person's possibilities for action would mean not only to empower her but also to alleviate—through changing the context of music therapy—some of the material or psychological forces that keep her in a handicapped role.
>
> (Ruud, 1998, pp. 51–52)

This definition and Ruud's comments indicate implications for music therapy practice that are compatible with the tenets outlined above. As I have argued, specific principles for practice must be developed in context. However, the acronym of PREPARE—developed for description of some features that to varying degree seem to characterize Community Music

Therapy—might illustrate some possible implications. The PREPARE acronym summarizes the following qualities of practice: P—Participatory, R—Resource-oriented, E—Ecological, P—Performative, A—Activist, R—Reflective, and E—Ethics-driven (Stige and Aarø 2012, pp. 18–24). Details on the various qualities are given in the chapter on Community Music Therapy in this Handbook. The tenets I have presented in this chapter suggest that very many of these qualities are relevant for development of culture-centered practice in a range of contexts, for instance in neuro-rehabilitation, education, or mental health (whether or not the music therapist opts to identify the practice as Community Music Therapy). In a case study of culture-centered music therapy in a mental health setting, I have tried to clarify how practice informed by culture-centered perspectives will typically be relational and contextual, where the clients' use of the activities and relationships offered in music therapy can be combined with creative use of the possibilities and challenges of everyday life (Stige 2011).[6]

Implications for the discipline of music therapy can be identified both in relation to theory and research. If human resources and challenges are linked to the three dimensions of phylogeny, cultural history, and ontogeny, as I have argued in this chapter, Culture-Centered Music Therapy is necessarily interdisciplinary in nature. If humans have a biological disposition for taking interest in social interaction and shared meaning-making, this suggests that as soon as we are born we start on a trajectory of cultural learning, which includes—of course—musical participation. Music therapy developed according to culture-centered principles, then, does not suggest a narrow focus on culture. Culture is a resource that enables human interaction and we can use it as a lens for the study of the wellbeing of individuals and communities. Implications for research obviously include use of ethnography and participatory action research), as these are research methods very well suited for exploration of human interaction in context, but there is no reason why say research informed by neuroscience should not be relevant too, if we take into consideration "the mutually attuned and coordinated bodies of which the brain is a part" (Voestermans and Baerveldt in 2000, as quoted in Stige 2002, p. 34).

CONCLUDING POINTS

The interdisciplinary nature of Culture-Centered Music Therapy might raise the question if it is an entirely new perspective or an integrative perspective on music therapy. Bruscia addresses this question in the following way:

> One of the lessons we are learning as a profession is that one new idea does not necessarily replace or surpass previous ideas; rather, each new idea enters into an already existing culture of ideas, where all ideas begin to interact. Thus, when a new idea is introduced, the entire culture is fertilized: existing ideas are influenced by the new idea, and the new idea is influenced by its integration into the existing culture. Thus, culture-centered thinking does not replace or surpass the behavioral, psychodynamic, humanistic, or transpersonal forces of thought; rather, it catalyzes them to be more culture-sensitive; in return, the established forces challenge culture-centered thinkers to somehow integrate existing values into their thinking. The developmental process is more holistic than linear, so that there is a place for every idea of continuing relevance.
>
> (Bruscia 2002, p. xvi)

I find Bruscia's argument thought-provoking and challenging. There are tensions and contradictions in contemporary music therapy, not only defined by the various theoretical perspectives available but also by the relationships between practice and academia, between
music therapy as art and music therapy as science, and so on. To make "place for every idea"
is not possible, yet a highly relevant invitation. One of the contributions of Culture-Centered
Music Therapy could be to suggest new cultural metaphors for the complex mixing of ideas
that music therapists seem to be doomed to deal with. If we take the huge epistemological
differences between various theories and practices seriously, metaphors that suggest smooth
blending of ideas seem less illustrative than metaphors that acknowledge tensions and conflicts. Cultural theory can provide us with the metaphor of hybridity, for instance, and this
is probably a helpful way of understanding the necessary mixing of ideas in music therapy
(Bunt and Stige 2014). For cultural theorist Bhabha (1994/2004), hybridity is dissidence
and ambivalence; it is the active confrontation of forces that define our identity as fixed.
Hybridity involves mixing various cultural elements in the face of hegemony. It enables creative rethinking of established principles and it provides a space of negotiation and articulation of new meanings. Culture-Centered Music Therapy's contribution could be to help us
take steps in this direction.

NOTES

1. Kenny (1985) had previously published an article exploring the relevance of such perspectives for music therapy.
2. My translation of the original title in Norwegian: "Musikk som kommunikasjon og
   samhandling."
3. The cultural historical theory tradition was pioneered by Russian scholars such as
   Vygotsky and Leontiev in the early 20th century and is highly influential on contemporary sociocultural theory. Ruud's main reference to this tradition was the work of the
   Norwegian social theorist Regi Enerstvedt (1977).
4. See Gillespie and Zittoun (2010) for a more general discussion on use of cultural resources.
5. See for instance Kenny (2014) for reflections on the roles of rituals in music therapy.
6. See Rolvsjord and Stige (2015) for a clarification of various concepts of context in music
   therapy.

REFERENCES

Aigen, K. (2014). *The Study of Music Therapy. Current Issues and Concepts*. New York: Routledge.
Aldridge, D. (1996). *Music Therapy Research and Practice in Medicine. From Out of the Silence.*
   London: Jessica Kingsley Publishers.
Aldridge, D. (2004). *Health, the Individual and Integrated Medicine*. London: Jessica Kingsley
   Publishers.
Ansdell, G. (2001). Musicology: Misunderstood guest at the music therapy feast? In: Aldridge,
   D., DiFranco, G., Ruud, E., and Wigram, T., *Music Therapy in Europe*, pp. 17–33. Rome:
   Ismez.
Ansdell, G. (2014). *How Music Helps—in Music Therapy and Everyday Life*, Farnham,
   UK: Ashgate.

Bhabha, H.K. (1994/2004). *The Location of Culture*, New York: Routledge.

Bonde, L.O. (2011). Health musicing—music therapy or music and health? A model, empirical examples and personal reflections. *Music and Arts in Action* 3(2): 120–140.

Bonde, L.O. (2013). Health musicking. In: K. Kirkland (ed.), *International Dictionary of Music Therapy*, p. 56. New York: Routledge.

Bruscia, K. (1998). *Defining Music Therapy* (2nd edition). Gilsum, NH: Barcelona Publishers.

Bruscia, K. (2002) Foreword. In: B. Stige, *Culture-Centered Music Therapy*, pp. 3–13. Gilsum, NH: Barcelona Publishers.

Bunt, L. and Stige, B. (2014). *Music Therapy—An Art Beyond Words* (2nd edition). London: Routledge.

Burke, K. (1966). *Language as Symbolic Action: Essays on Life, Literature, and Method*. California: University of California Press.

Clarke, E., Dibben, N., and Pitts, S. (2010). *Music and Mind in Everyday Life*. New York: Oxford University Press.

Clayton, M., Herbert, T., and Middleton, R. (eds). (2011). *The Cultural Study of Music. A Critical Introduction* (2nd edition). New York: Routledge.

Collins, R. (2004). *Interaction Ritual Chains*. Princeton, NJ: Princeton University Press.

Davis, W.B., Gfeller, K.E., and Thaut, M.H. (1999). *An Introduction to Music Therapy. Theory and Practice* (2nd edition). Dubuque, IA: WCB/McGraw-Hill.

DeNora, T. (1999). Music as a technology of the self. *Poetics* 27: 31–56.

DeNora, T. (2000). *Music in Everyday Life*. Cambridge, UK: Cambridge University Press.

DeNora, T. (2007). Health and music in everyday life—A theory of practice. *Psyke & Logos* 28(1): 17.

DeNora, T. (2013). *The Music Asylum: Defining Wellbeing through Music in Everyday Life*. Farnham, UK: Ashgate.

Durkheim, E. (1912/1995). *The Elementary Forms of Religious Life* (translated by Karen E. Fields). New York: The Free Press.

Edwards, J. (2011). Music therapy and parent-infant bonding. In: Edwards, J. (ed.), *Music Therapy and Parent-Infant Bonding*, pp. 4–20. New York: Oxford University Press.

Edwards, J. and Hadley, S. (2007). Expanding music therapy practice: Incorporating the feminist frame. *The Arts in psychotherapy* 34(3): 199–207.

Enerstvedt, R. (1977). *Mennesket i et fylogenetisk og ontogenetisk perspektiv* [Humans in a Phylogenetic and Ontogenetic Perspective]. Oslo, Norway: Forlaget Ny Dag.

Gillespie, A. and Zittoun, T. (2010). Using resources: conceptualizing the mediation and reflective use of tools and signs. *Culture & Psychology* 16(1): 37–62.

Goffman, E. (1967). *Interaction Ritual. Essays on Face-to-Face Behavior*. New York: Anchor Books.

Hadley, S. (ed.) (2006). *Feminist Perspectives in Music Therapy*. Gilsum, NH: Barcelona Publishers.

Hadley, S. and Edwards, J. (2004). Sorry for the silence: A contribution from feminist theory to the discourse(s) within music therapy. *Voices: A World Forum For Music Therapy* 4(2). Retrieved May 5, 2013, from: <https://normt.uib.no/index.php/voices/article/view/177/136>.

Keil, C. and Feld, S. (1994). *Music Grooves*. Chicago: The University of Chicago Press.

Kenny, C.B. (1985). Music: A whole systems approach. *Music Therapy* 5(1): 3–11.

Kenny, C.B. (1987). *The Field of Play. Theoretical Study of Music Therapy Process*. Doctoral dissertation, The Fielding Institute. UMI Order Number 8802367.

Kenny, C. (2014). The Field of Play: An ecology of being in music therapy. *Voices: A World Forum For Music Therapy* 14(1). Retrieved from: <https://voices.no/index.php/voices/article/view/737>.

Kitayama, S. and Cohen, D. (eds). (2007). *Handbook of Cultural Psychology.* New York: Guilford Press.

Krüger, V. and Stige, B. (in press). Music as a structuring resource: A perspective from community music therapy. In: Klempe, H. (ed.), *Cultural Psychology of Music Experiences.* Charlotte, NC: IAP: Information Age Publications.

Malloch, S. and Trevarthen, C. (eds). (2009). *Communicative Musicality.* Oxford: Oxford University Press.

Markus, H.R. and Hamedani, M.G. (2010). Sociocultural psychology: the dynamic interdependence among self systems and social systems. In: Kitayama, S. and Cohen, D. (eds), *Handbook of Cultural Psychology,* pp. 3–39. New York: Guilford Press.

Merriam, A. P. (1964). *The Anthropology of Music.* Evanston, IL: Northwestern University Press.

Nielsen, H.K. (1993). *Kultur og modernitet* [Culture and Modernity]. Aarhus, Denmark: Aarhus University Press.

Pavlicevic, M. and Ansdell, G. (eds). (2004). *Community Music Therapy.* Jessica Kingsley Publishers.

Pavlicevic, M. and Ansdell, G. (2009). Between communicative musicality and collaborative musicing. In: Malloch, S. and Trevarthen, C. (eds), *Communicative Musicality,* pp. 357–376. Oxford: Oxford University Press.

Rolvsjord, R. (2010). *Resource-Oriented Music Therapy in Mental Health Care.* Gilsum, NH: Barcelona Publishers.

Rolvsjord, R. and Stige, B. (2015). Concepts of context in music therapy. *Nordic Journal of Music Therapy* 24(1): 44–66.

Ruud, E. (1979). *Musikkterapi* [Music Therapy]. *Musikk i Skolen* [Music in Schools, 4/1979], pp. 34–5.

Ruud, E. (1987). *Musikk som kommunikasjon og samhandling. Teoretiske perspektiv på musikkterapien.* [Music as Communication and Interaction. Theoretical Perspectives on Music Therapy.] Doctoral dissertation, University of Oslo.

Ruud, E. (1998). *Music Therapy: Improvisation, Communication and Culture.* Gilsum, NH: Barcelona Publishers.

Small, C. (1998). *Musicking. The Meanings of Performing and Listening.* Hanover, NH: Wesleyan University Press.

Stige, B. (2002). *Culture-Centered Music Therapy.* Gilsum, NH: Barcelona Publishers.

Stige, B. (2006). Toward a notion of participation in music therapy. *Nordic Journal of Music Therapy* 15(2): 121–38.

Stige, B. (2010). Musical participation, social space and everyday ritual. In: Stige, B., Ansdell, G., Elefant, C., and Pavlicevic, M. (eds), *Where Music Helps. Community Music Therapy in Action and Reflection,* pp. 125–127. Aldershot, UK: Ashgate Publishing Limited.

Stige, B. (2003/2012). *Elaborations toward a Notion of Community Music Therapy.* Gilsum, NH: Barcelona Publishers.

Stige, B. (2011). The doors and windows of the dressing room: Culture-Centered Music Therapy in a mental health setting. In: Meadows, T. (ed.), *Developments in Music Therapy Practice: Case Examples,* pp. 316–33. Gilsum, NH: Barcelona Publishers.

Stige, B. (2012). Health musicking: a perspective on music and health as action and perfor-
    mance. In: MacDonald, Raymond, Gunter Kreutz, and Laura Mitchell (eds), *Music, Health
    and Wellbeing*, pp. 183–95. New York: Oxford University Press.

Stige, B. and Aarø, L. E. (2012). *Invitation to Community Music Therapy*. New York: Routledge.

Stige, B., Ansdell, G., Elefant, C, and Pavlicevic, M. (2010). Conclusion: When things take shape
    in relation to music: Towards an ecological perspective on music's help. In: Stige, B., Ansdell,
    G., Elefant, C., and Pavlicevic, M. (eds), *Where Music Helps. Community Music Therapy in
    Action and Reflection*, pp. 277–308. Farnham, UK: Ashgate.

Valsiner, J. (2007). *Culture in Minds and Societies: Foundations of Cultural Psychology*.
    New Delhi: Sage Publications India.

....

CHAPTER 30

RESOURCE-ORIENTED PERSPECTIVES IN MUSIC THERAPY

....

RANDI ROLVSJORD

INTRODUCTION

....

Tracing the roots of resource-oriented perspectives

As an articulated and specific approach resource-oriented music therapy is a recent contributor to the discipline of music therapy. Although notions of "resource-orientation" and "resource-oriented music therapy" have been widely used in the oral discourses in Europe, it has appeared in only a peripheral way in written texts about music therapy. Since the millennium shift, the concept of resource-oriented music therapy has been more elaborated, and is now frequently used in the international discourse in music therapy. Roots can also be traced back historically to different countries, schools, and traditions in music therapy, and be linked to the broader and interdisciplinary discourse and political movements within health and health care.

William W. Sears (1996/1968[1]) was an early author in the field of music therapy who made explicit reference to the music therapeutic process relevant to resource-oriented approaches. In the classic article "Processes in Music Therapy," he proposed a classification of experiences offered to the individual in a music situation in music therapy: "Experience within structure," "Experience in self-organization," and "Experiences in relating to others" (Sears 1996, p. 34). Each classification consists of a set of constructs that define an explicit relationship between music and the individual's behavior: that is, the ways of engaging with music in which the client is involved. Sears highlighted aspects of music therapy concerned with social skills and social acceptance, of self-acceptance, enhancement of esteem by others, as well as aspects of learning skills and compensating for physical or mental limitations (Sears 1996/1968). Sears' classifications highlight several resource-oriented aspects and represent an historical trace for more current perspectives that focus on resources and strengths rather than on symptom reduction and elimination of pathology. In the classical text Sears emphasised that his classifications are not connected to specific traditions in music therapy or specific psychological schools. Thus as an historical source, we might suggest that this text documents the general tendency in music therapy to include resource-oriented aspects as a regular part of practice.

However, there are also aspects related to specific traditions in music therapy that must be emphasized as involving articulations and emphasis of aspects that could be recognized as strengths-oriented or resource-oriented. The focus within the early humanistic psychology on self-actualization (Maslow) and client-directed perspectives (Rodgers), was central to the early developments of the Nordoff-Robbins tradition (Nordoff and Robbins 1977; Ruud 1980). Resource-oriented aspects of the Nordoff-Robbins approach are also identified by Garred (2006) who has linked aspects of resource-orientation to the music-based practice of Creative Music Therapy (Garred 2006, p. 253). It would however be too simplified to conclude a direct line from the Nordoff-Robbins tradition in music therapy to the current resource-oriented perspectives. The term resource-oriented has in other texts been used to describe features of psychoanalytically informed practice (Bonde et al. 2001[2]; Trondalen 2004). Humanistic perspectives that imply levels of resource-orientation also informed the Viennese School of music therapy (Mössler 2011), as well as other humanistic or existential perspectives such as the work of Carolyn Kenny (1982). Perspectives from humanistic psychology in specific and the humanistic values in general obviously represents a continuous historical trace for resource-orientation in music therapy from the early 1960-ties, up to today. Even Ruud's book *Music therapy: A Perspective from the Humanities* (Ruud 2010) is a recent example of this trace.

In the more recent history of the discipline of music therapy, some theoretical perspectives have anticipated the more explicit conceptualizations of resource-oriented music therapy. Of specific relevance are perspectives that connected the therapeutic practice in music therapy to aspects of *positive health*, such as *quality of life* and *health promotion*. Ruud's (1990) definition of music therapy as "an effort to increase possibilities for action"[3] (Ruud 1990, p. 24; Ruud 1998, p. 52), can be considered one of the strongest proposals of a therapeutic strategy involved with positive health rather than illness or pathology. With Ruud's texts about music therapy and quality of life (Ruud 1997a, 1998) the concept of health and therapy was linked to a salutogenic orientation (Antonovsky 1979, 1987). Similarly, with Bruscia's revised definition of music therapy (Bruscia 1998), the salutogenic perspective informed the shift from *achieving health* to *promoting health* which has contributed to the articulation of strategies for health promotion in music therapy. Salutogenic perspectives have also been discussed by Stige (2002) and Aasgaard (2002).

Another specific theoretical conceptualization that will be emphasized here is the understanding of *music as a health resource*. Music as a health resource is a theoretical notion that points towards the flexibility and potentials for varied uses of music in relation to a broad understanding of health promotion. Kenny (1982) envisioned *music as a resource-pool* (Kenny 1982), representing a multiplicity of potentials of use for clients. Such potentials were further explored and structured in her holographic model in *The Field of Play* (Kenny 1989). Further, based in his research in music and identity, Ruud (1997a) identified four categories, ways in which musical involvement can be a health resource linked to the idea of quality of life (Ruud 1997a, 1997b, 1998): awareness of feelings (or vitality), agency, belonging and

meaning (Ruud 1998). Aigen (2005) developed a music-centered approach that also emphasis development of musical strengths and relationship to music. Ideas of music as a health
resource, has been further integrated and investigated in theoretical contributions in music
therapy that link to current perspectives in musicology and music sociology with specific
emphasis of research in the use of music in everyday life. Concepts of *health musicking*[4] has
been elaborated and linked to possibilities for resource-mobilization (Ansdell and DeNora
2012; DeNora 2007; Pavlicevic and Ansdell 2009; Stige 2002, 2012).

Finally resource-oriented perspectives are linked to contextual perspectives[5]. Several
authors have contributed to the growing awareness of cultural aspects and the culturally and
historically situatedness of music, human beings, and music therapy. That is, to perspectives
that understand individuals, health and illness and therapy in historical and cultural contexts. Historical and anthropological perspectives were presented by Ruud (1990, 1998), and
contextual perspectives can also be traced back to the tradition of Schwabe and his work
on *Regulative Musiktherapie* and on *Sozialmusiktherapie* (Stige 2003; Schwabe 2005; Ruud
2005). With the elaborations of Community music therapy which has rapidly evolved since
the millennium shift (i.e. Ansdell 2002; Pavlicevic and Ansdell 2004; Stige 2002, 2003; Stige
and Aarø 2012), the implications of contextual perspectives to the practice of music therapy
has been addressed, providing a new understanding of music therapy practices in community settings.

Towards a conceptualization of resource-oriented music therapy

Since the millennium, the conceptualization of resource-oriented perspectives in music
therapy has been more explicitly used and discussed in the literature. The German music
therapist Christoph Schwabe (2000/2005) was the first to offer an elaboration of the concept of resource-oriented music therapy[6]. Schwabe however describes his elaborations of the
concept of resource-oriented music therapy as a continuous development since 1960 where
resource-oriented thinking gradually gained more importance (Schwabe 2005). The English
translation of Schwabe's article was published at the same time as my own first elaborations
of a resource-oriented approach (Rolvsjord 2004; Rolvsjord et al., 2005a,b).

In his article Schwabe connects the salutogenic potentials of music therapy to ontological
aspects of music which he describes in terms of the dual character of music as both object
and action (Schwabe 2005, p. 52). Schwabe's perspective is further informed by German
psychology and psychotherapy theory and research, such as Victor Frankl and the more
recent contributions concerned with resource-activation in psychotherapy by Klaus Grawe[7].
Schwabe (2000/2005) has explored resource-orientation as a general and implicit aspect of
music therapy, and suggests that resource-orientation might be an integrative element of different traditions and schools in music therapy (Schwabe 2005, p. 49).

In despite of his focus on implicit resource-oriented aspects in music therapy, Schwabe,
however emphasise that resource-orientation is more than "bringing in some friendly
impulses into therapy" (Schwabe 2005, p. 49). Thus, he also proposes some possible practical implications as to nurture the possibilities of the resource-oriented music therapy.
Schwabe (2005, p. 52) raises a strong critique to the "pharmacological music therapy" and

"effectence-motivated" music therapy by which clients become passive consumers. Rather, he emphasizes the self-healing forces related to the clients' active involvement with music:

> Above all, the most important aspect in this concept is the activity of the patients. They are not reduced to passive consumers of effectance-oriented treatments, but they are active partners in the therapy process.
>
> (Schwabe 2005, p. 52)

Schwabe outlines three aspects of resource-orientation: the first aspect outlined is the activation of self-healing forces. Schwabe emphasizes however, that the mobilization of healing forces in the patient is not sufficient. Thus, the second aspect is concerned the dealing with the external reality and involves "enabling the patient to establish a direct, constructive, and active contact with their surrounding reality" (Schwabe 2005, p. 50). Finally, as a third aspect he emphasizes the concept of humanity, with regard to the therapists focus on potentials rather than on deficits (Schwabe 2005, p. 50). This latter concept underlines the importance of the therapist attitude and values regarding the client as a human being and a person with both strengths and limitations.

ELABORATIONS OF A RESOURCE-ORIENTED APPROACH

My own work offers a more explicit elaboration of a resource-oriented approach to music therapy (Rolvsjord 2007, 2010) in the field of mental health care. I had experienced a gap existed between the perspectives presented in the literature about music therapy in mental health, and my own practice of music therapy[8] in this clinical context (Rolvsjord 2007). In *Resource-oriented music therapy in mental health care* (Rolvsjord 2010) I build up a theoretical rationale for resource-oriented music therapy informed by an interdisciplinary theoretical discourse. The theoretical perspectives adopted draw on multiple perspectives in an interdisciplinary field of theory and research that emphasize different aspects concerned with resource-orientation including empowerment philosophy, common factors approach, positive psychology, and current musicology. Perspectives from the empowerment philosophy are concerned with the interaction and interdependency between individual and community regarding health issues, and emphasize aspects of enablement, control, and participation (Dalton et al. 2001, Sprague and Hayes 2000). With a contextual model in psychotherapy (common factors approach) the "context" of multiple factors that works in psychotherapy is described, with emphasis on the client factors and the therapeutic relationship (Wampold 2001; Duncan et al. 2010). Perspectives related to the movement or discourse of Positive psychology (Seligman and Csikszentmihalyi 2000; Snyder and Lopez 2002) accentuates aspects concerned with positive health and the importance of positive emotions and positive experiences as part of therapeutic processes. Finally theoretical frames are connected with current culturally informed perspectives from musicology and music sociology, pointing toward an understanding of music that emphasizes the culturally situated active engagement (i.e. Small 1998; DeNora 2000).

The theoretical elaboration of the approach (Rolvsjord 2007, 2010) does not offer a definition of resource-oriented music therapy, but instead articulates four characteristics, or descriptors. A resource-oriented approach can be described as: (1) involving the nurturing of strengths, resources and potentials; (2) involving equal collaboration rather than intervention; (3) viewing the individual within their context; and (4) seeing music as a health resource (Rolvsjord 2010, p. 73ff). Thus, the resultant resource-oriented approach involves a flexible and collaborative use of music as a health resource, and highlights strengths and resources that individuals has and/or can access. User involvement and client's self-determination and agency in the therapeutic process are emphasized. Relational aspects are explored with regard to the emphasis on user-involvement, and described in terms of equal collaborations, negotiations, and mutuality.

As already demonstrated, the concept of resource-oriented music therapy interacts with similar approaches in an interdisciplinary landscape. In this landscape where descriptions of strengths perspectives, client-centered approaches and positive therapy are offered, the term resource-oriented should be clarified as this might illuminate the contextual dimensions of the resource-oriented music therapy approach. The term resources is associated with economics, but is also used in sociology in a broader sense (Rolvsjord 2010). The concept of resources implies more than personal strengths or talents, such as musical skills, it also includes "objects" the individual can access and use in her/his efforts towards health promotion and a better life. Thus, the concepts of resources point towards the contextual dimensions and thus link the therapeutic endeavor to a cultural, political, and economic reality (Rolvsjord et al. 2005a).

Implicit in my elaborations of a resource-oriented approach (Rolvsjord 2007, 2010) there is a strong critique of "medical models"[9] in the field of mental health care in general as well as in music therapy specifically. One of the clearest implications of this is the emphasis of the client's contributions to the therapeutic process. Ideas about the importance of specific techniques and therapist-led interventions are challenged, and I have emphasized the *client's craft*. The client's craft is described both in terms of competence and efforts in using music in everyday life, and competence and efforts regarding the therapy sessions and therapeutic process (Rolvsjord 2006, 2010, 2013, 2014). However, the aligned construct of the *therapist's craft* is also offered emphasizing the significance of the therapist, both in terms of the meaning of the therapist's "being" as well as "her/his doing" (Rolvsjord 2010). The therapist is considered to be, and acting as, an authentic person in the collaborations with the client, not primarily as an intervening expert. *How* the therapist is doing what she does is considered as important as *what* she is doing. The constructs of client's craft and therapist's craft may be useful in order to understand the importance of equal relationship and the concept of collaborations between client and therapist. A good relationship in therapy is not an intervention (something that the therapist does), but is something evolving and unfolding between two human beings, both two persons with strengths and weaknesses. The active involvement of both the client and the therapist is emphasized and described in terms of interactions, mutuality, authenticity, and democratic negotiations (Rolvsjord 2010, p. 214ff).

In spite of the focus on client involvement, some guidelines for the music therapists were developed (Rolvsjord et al. 2005a; Rolvsjord 2010). These guidelines describe principles of actions and were originally elaborated as a flexible manual for the use of controlling therapist treatment fidelity in a randomized controlled trial (Gold et al. 2005). However, with regard to the emphasis of the client's crafts and the relationship, it would be more adjacent to see these guidelines as a reflective tool (Mössler et al. 2011), rather than a manual. The principles were developed with regard to the more general characteristics of a resource-oriented approach, and thus can be seen as concretizations of *performed attitudes* rather than interventions. The therapeutic principles (Rolvsjord et al. 2005a) were organized in four categories[10]: (1) unique and essential; (2) essential but not unique; (3) acceptable, but not necessary; and (4) not acceptable. This structure was used in order to highlight the similarities and differences to other music therapy models (Rolvsjord et al. 2005a, p. 23).

1. **Unique and essential therapeutic principles**
   1.1 Focusing on the client's strengths and potentials.
   1.2 Recognizing the client's competence related to her/his therapeutic process.
   1.3 Collaborating with the client concerning goals of therapy and methods of working.
   1.4 Acknowledging the client's musical identity.
   1.5 Being emotionally involved in music.
   1.6 Fostering positive emotions.

2. **Essential but not unique therapeutic principles**
   2.1 Engaging the client in musical interplay (such as musical improvisation, creating songs, playing pre-composed music or listening to music).
   2.2 Acknowledging and encouraging musical skills and potentials.
   2.3 Reflecting verbally on music and musical interplay.
   2.4 Listening and interacting empathically.
   2.5 Tuning into the client's musical expressions.
   2.6 Collaborating with the client concerning the length and termination of the therapy process.

3. **Acceptable but not necessary therapeutic principles**
   3.1 Teaching instruments/music.
   3.2 Sharing one's own experiences.
   3.3 Presenting/performing music with the client outside the therapy setting.
   3.4 Providing therapeutic rationale.
   3.5 Having music as the primary goal of therapy.
   3.6 Reflecting verbally and musically on problems.

4. **Not acceptable—proscribed therapeutic principles**
   4.1 Neglecting the client's strengths and potentials.
   4.2 Having a strong focus on pathology.
   4.3 Avoiding emerging problems and negative emotions.
   4.4 Directing in a non-collaborative style.[11]

The complete set of principles should illuminate the collaborative and contextual aspect of the approach, and concretize dimensions of potential strength and resource foci, such as the client's musical identity and musical skills. The principles should guide the whole process of therapy, including assessment and evaluations. Reflecting the multiple possibilities and affordances of music as a health resource, the principles do not give any guidelines as to what type of musical interaction and/or musical activities that are warranted. This challenges the therapist to be flexible and to make considerations of how to work and what to do together with the client. The principles are explained in depth in an appendix to the article (Rolvsjord et al. 2005b) and in Rolvsjord (2010).

CASE MATERIALS

Rolvsjord (2010) presents two case studies. The cases of the therapeutic collaborations with two young women are explored through the multiple angles of the client's story, the therapist's story and a researcher's reflections. Mössler et al. (2011), presents four case vignettes that focuses on therapists' use of the principles in the flexible manual for resource-oriented music therapy. A case report by Solli (2008) in the context of acute mental health care, focus on potential resources mobilized in improvizations within a rock music idiom in the collaborations with a young man suffering from psychoses. Although described as client-centered and culture-centered, Stige (2011) presents a case study which highlight aspects of user-involvement and that illuminate the possibility and potentials of a contextual approach within individual therapy.

To give an example of a resource-oriented approach, I will revisit a case report about the collaborations in music therapy with Sophie[12] (Rolvsjord 2001). The case report was written some years before I had started my elaborations of resource-oriented music therapy. However, the work with Sophie was indeed a very formative experience that informed the elaborations of a resource-oriented perspective. Thus, the case highlights some basic features of resource-oriented music therapy. From the initial introductions to the case report, two basic aspects of what the collaborations with Sophie can teach us are articulated. First, the client's ability and competence in making the therapy work for her, and second, the importance of engaging with activities that provides potentials for development of resources, in this case to learn to play the piano:

> In telling this story, I hope to demonstrate how a client grasps the possibilities of what music involves, despite her traumatic experiences and difficulties in coping with her life. Watching her way of using songs to communicate with me, and to work with important incidents and relations, filled me with deep admiration and respect. In this clinical perspective I will point to how learning musical skills can provide a space for psychotherapeutic music therapy work, and how such didactic aspects in therapy can be an important supplement of other therapeutic treatments.
>
> (Rolvsjord 2001, p. 77)

The case report *Sophie learns to play the piano* (Rolvsjord 2001) describes the therapeutic collaborations with a 17-year-old girl. She had been admitted to a mental health institution after a period of extensive self-harm and a suicide attempt after a traumatic incidence. The music therapy collaborations lasted for one-and-a-half years, with regular weekly sessions. I will quote the first part from the original case presentation, and then present a short summary of the rest of the therapeutic process as presented by Rolvsjord (2001). The first three sessions are presented as follows:

> The first time I met Sophie she was hardly looking at me at all. She seemed extremely shy and she obviously lacked self-confidence. As I have already mentioned, another patient had

forwarded Sophie's wish to learn to play the piano. In our first session she was looking down to the floor, occasionally gazing at me and at the piano. Her face was hidden behind her long hair, but I could see that she was listening to me, and she was communicating with a careful nodding that made her hair slightly sway from side to side. I presented her with different instruments, but I could see that she was only interested in the piano. I told her that I had seen her looking at the piano and asked if she wanted to play this instrument. "Can you teach me how to play", she said in a silent voice. These were the only words she spoke in this session. I told her that I certainly would, but also told her that since this was music therapy she could use the sessions to speak with me about anything she would like to in full confidence.

She would not play today, but nodded when I asked her if she would like me to play the piano for her. I had a songbook on the piano, and I asked her to choose a song that she would like to hear. She looked through the whole book, stopped for some seconds at one special song. She started again and stopped at the same song. "Do you want me to play that song?" She confirmed her choice by nodding. I played and sang the song "Crying in the rain" (Greenfeld/King) for her[13].

In the next session she was encouraged to sit by my side at the piano. She was looking in the songbook, and found the song "Don't cry for me Argentina" (Lloyd Webber). I showed her the chords on the piano, and I could see that she was recognizing them. She smiled when I confirmed that I could see that she was familiar with some of the chords. "Are there any chords that you do not know", I asked, and she pointed to one single chord. The chords were drawn on a schematic picture of the piano keys. At the end of the session she asked if she could bring the schematic picture of the chords with her to practice. But still she did not dare to play with me.

In the third session she takes the final step into the musical space (to use Kenny's (1989) term). The session started in the corridor where she was juggling with some balls. In the music therapy room, I grabbed the xylophone, and invited her to play a little more with the balls. Then I improvised to her juggling, and tried to mirror the intensity of her play. Every time she lost a ball to the floor, this was reflected in the music. It seemed to me that she was really enjoying this game, and so did I. The playful atmosphere following this ball game made it possible for me to encourage her to sit by the piano in a humoristic way: "It is difficult to play the piano sitting that far away", I stated. Responding to this, she tumbled on to the piano stool, and unintentionally touched one of the piano keys, so that it sounded. I struck the piano keys and stated that we had started to make music together. She chose the song introduced in our first session, "crying in the rain", and asked me to sing when she played the chords on the piano. I completed the musical arrangement by singing and playing the bass guitar.

(Rolvsjord 2001, pp. 79–80)

In the sessions that followed Sophie continued to bring songs, and after a while I (the therapist) noticed some reoccurring themes in the song lyrics. Gradually I became more and more convinced that Sophie's choices of songs were not incidental but indeed communicative. Consequently I started to bring some of the themes into the verbal exchanges as to recognize the importance these themes might have for Sophie. After a while I also suggested to write a song. To get started I had suggested some words to be part of the song, and later I composed our first song based on words approved by Sophie. After this Sophie contributed to our song-creations by suggesting words that could be included. After some sessions that had focused on songwriting, Sophie brought a pre-composed song with the title "afraid of strong words." This initiated a pause in the process of songwriting and a refocus on developing skills at the piano. The therapy ended with songs of goodbye when I had to take leave from work (Rolvsjord 2001).

The story of Sophie and her efforts towards learning to play the piano might illumine some of the central aspects of resource-oriented music therapy that I will outline in the following: clients' contributions in the therapeutic process, therapists efforts, collaborations, and contextual dimensions.

How does the client contribute to the therapeutic process? One facet of this, that we can see, is the initiative that Sophie takes of telling a fellow patient that she would like to play the piano. Although indirectly, by doing this, she takes an initiative towards starting with music therapy. Implicit in this initiative, we may also presume Sophie to have some knowledge and competence about what sort of activity or engagement that could be motivating and or useful in some sense or another for her. The next example our story outlines, is her initiative in the first session. Although she is clearly struggling to take part in the communication, she is able to use her eyes to communicate her wish to play the piano to the music therapist. In the following sessions she starts to use the music therapy sessions and the musical activity learning to play the piano as a possibility to communicate some of her pains and sorrows through her song choices.

So what is the therapist doing? In the initial sessions, she is acknowledging the client's wish to learn to play the piano, but at the same time displaying other possibilities of musicking, as to point to other possible ways of using music as a health resource. This is crucial to the initial assessments. The episode with the juggling balls may be an example of the therapist being engaged and unfolding her own playfulness, thus being authentic in her meeting and engagement in music. The same can be said about the songwriting process, where the therapist is actively involved and actively take part in the creative work. Finally, we can also say that the case exemplify the possibility of recognizing the pains and difficult emotions the client presents through her songs, but at the same time is trying to grasp possibilities to also stimulate positive emotions such as with the cheerful episode of the juggling balls.

The relational aspects are closely connected to the previous aspects. The collaborations between the therapist and the client demonstrate active involvement from both parts. There are limited explicit verbal exchange between the therapist and client concerning the ways of working and the goals of therapy, but we can still see some examples of mutuality in general and in decision-making processes. Both take initiatives, and both are demonstrating a commitment in their musical engagement.

A final characteristic of a resource-oriented approach that I will discuss in relation to this case is the contextual. Indeed the contextual dimension of individual therapy sessions in a medical institution like this can be questioned. However, we might recognize a contextual awareness through the focus on learning to play the piano, an activity that is acknowledged in many social groups and communities. Further we might point to the use of songs and choices of music that recognized Sophie's musical and cultural competence and identity.

RESEARCH RELATED TO THE RESOURCE-ORIENTED APPROACH

In the field of mental health care, a randomized controlled trial (RCT) studying the effectiveness of resource-oriented music therapy on clients with low motivation has been completed

(Gold et al. 2013). This pragmatic trial included 144 participants with a primary non-organic mental disorder (diagnoses by criteria of ICD-10, F1-F6), and additionally met the definitions of the criteria low motivation. The intervention was described as resource-oriented music therapy, guided by the principles described by Rolvsjord et al. (2005a,b). Music therapy was provided for the clients in bi-weekly session over a period of three months. The results of the study were generally positive in favor of music therapy when compared to the control (treatment as usual). Significant results were found with regard to the negative symptoms (which was the primary outcome), as well as for effects of functioning, clinical global impressions, social avoidance through music and vitality. Interestingly, it was also noted that the attendance rates in the study for the participants receiving music therapy were very good, indicating that "music therapy might help to keep clients in contact with psychiatry" (Gold et al. 2013, p. 327).

In relation to the mentioned RCT two studies focused on the application and implementation of the therapeutic principles in singular cases included in the before mentioned RCT. Asperheim (2009) explored the implementation of therapeutic principles observed through video analysis of single sessions, and Mössler et al. (2011) explored the application of therapeutic principles in therapeutic processes of four clients and four therapists situated in different clinical sites that participated in the RCT. Mössler et al. discuss the clinical relevance related to their experiences with the application of the resource-oriented principles with regard to the establishment of the therapeutic relationship, and in terms of long- and short-term care. They emphasize the principles as a guide that "provided essential therapeutic attitudes to get in contact with the clients" as well as to maintain a solid relationship (Mössler et al. 2011, p. 87). Based on their experiences they had also found the principles useful both for clients in short-term and long-term care (Mössler et al. 2011).

Clients' experiences in resource-oriented music therapy were explored by Rolvsjord (2007, 2010). This qualitative case study investigated two young female clients' experiences through in-depth interviews. Rolvsjord identified four main themes that were characteristic of the clients' experience: (1) regaining rights to music; (2) musical mastery and enablement; (3) voicing trauma and negative emotions; (4) experiences of positive emotions; and (5) negotiations of resources and problems. The stories of the two clients' experiences with music therapy focused to different degrees on these themes, although all the five themes occurred as part of both women's experiences with resource-oriented music therapy (Rolvsjord 2007, 2010). The case studies documented the importance positive emotions and experiences of mastery and enablement can have in a therapeutic process. The study also demonstrated a potential continuum of focus on resources and strengths and focus on problems and illness (Rolvsjord et al. 2005a), where resource-orientation is not opposing the possibility to also use music therapy to work with problems. One of the case studies, with the client named Emma, also pointed towards the confrontational aspects of resource-orientation, and documented the interaction between the focus on strengths and focus on problems in a therapeutic process.

Some recent studies also report research of music therapy that combines resource-oriented approach with other context/client specific perspectives. Lindenfelser et al. (2012) studied music therapy in paediatric palliative care informed by strengths/resource-oriented perspectives and family centered perspectives. Shih (2011) develops a stabilization music therapy model for music therapy in crisis interventions after trauma, and described the process of intervention after the China Sichuan earthquake.

THE CURRENT INTERDISCIPLINARY CONTEXT OF RESOURCE-ORIENTED PERSPECTIVES

As an emerging perspective and approach resource-oriented music therapy is connected to, informed and inspired, by several movements and fields of discourse in an interdisciplinary landscape. The theoretical elaborations of Rolvsjord (2004, 2006, 2007, 2010) and of Schwabe (2000/2005) include some of these perspectives. As resource-oriented perspectives is also in constant elaborations in the interdisciplinary discourse of health and health care, there are a number of possible perspectives that might contribute to the elaboration of resource-oriented perspectives in music therapy. In the following I will review some of the contributions in music therapy that contribute to such a broadened *context* of resource-oriented perspectives[14].

Since the millennium, the movement of *positive psychology* has been a very fast-growing branch of psychological theory, research and practice, critical to the preoccupation of treatment of pathology in psychology (Seligman and Csikszentmihalyi 2000). Positive psychology focuses on positive health and quality of life, and is occupied with themes such as human flourishing, well-being, happiness, hope, self-esteem, and positive emotions (Snyder and Lopez 2002). Positive psychology is one of the perspectives informing the resource-oriented music therapy approach presented by Rolvsjord (2010). Ruud (2010) also connects perspectives in positive psychology to resource-orientation in music therapy, and also suggesting musicking as a relevant area of interest for positive psychology. Further, he draw links from perspectives on positive emotions to the relevance of the Bonny Method of Guided Imagery and Music (BMGIM) emphasizing potentials in BMGIM with regard to personal strengths, resilience, and wellness (Ruud 2010, p. 96). Baker and Ballantyne (2013) build on to perspectives on positive psychology in their study of the impact of group songwriting and performing on perceptions of quality of life and social wellbeing of older adults living in a community of retirees. The study explores experiences of the pleasant life, the engaged life, and the meaningful life. The authors conclude that the engagement in the music therapy group had "contributed to promoting a life in happiness" (Baker and Ballantyne 2013, p. 14).

A concept that has evolved in the discourse of positive psychology is *resilience*, by Pasiali (2012) discusses the possibilities of fostering resilience of children and their families in music therapy. In her paper she is examining various music therapy interventions in terms of their potentials within a resilience framework. Pasiali is advocating a resource-oriented framework to assist the development of resilience (Pasiali 2012, p. 44), and emphasizes the need to address preventive interventions in multiple contexts of the families (Pasiali 2012, p. 50).

The *recovery movement* is another current discourse, in the field of mental health, that strongly emphasize resource-orientation, and that has recently been introduced in the music therapy literature. Perspectives on recovery focus on the possibilities for coping and living with mental illness, and emphasize the personal efforts and everyday life context as crucial to the process of recovery (Davidson et al. 2010; Slade 2009). Chhina (2004) introduces recovery perspectives in her discussion of the role of music therapy in psychosocial rehabilitation, and point towards a person-centered and consumer orientated model of music therapy that focus on the client's strengths. More recently several texts point towards similarities between the recovery perspectives and resource-oriented music therapy (Grocke et al. (2008); McCaffrey et al. 2011; Solli and Rolvsjord 2015; Solli et al. 2013). The research on music therapy in recovery include qualitative studies of users' experiences (Solli and Rolvsjord 2015), as well as case studies and case reports that identify possible roles of music therapy in recovery (Solli 2009; Solli 2014; McCaffrey et al. 2011). A qualitative study by Kooiji (2009) identifies themes of recovery in songs written in music therapy, exploring the client's own experiences of their life with illness as they are expressed in song lyrics.

Another important interdisciplinary perspective, which is clearly linked to resource-orientation and strengths perspectives, is the empowerment philosophy. The philosophy of empowerment is basic to the resource-oriented approach presented by Rolvsjord (2004, 2010), and is also a core concept related to the recovery movement. The concept of empowerment is linked to a philosophy connected to democratic and humanistic values, and can be traced back to the civil rights movements in the 1960s. The concept and philosophy of empowerment in music therapy has been discussed in several texts (Daveson 2001; Procter 2001; Rolvsjord 2004). Empowerment perspectives are also frequently represented in the discourse of community music therapy (Procter 2001; Stige and Aarø 2012; Pavlicevic and Ansdell 2004), and central to feminist therapy approaches (Curtis 1996, 2006; York 2006; Hadley 2006). User-participation and/or consumer directed music therapy services in a community project are explored by Baines (2003). The project is further explored in a study of Baines and Danko (2010), focusing on the consumers experiences with the consumer-directed program.

In the field of music therapy, the movement of community music therapy represents a perspective with many similarities to the resource-oriented approach presented in this chapter. Resource-orientation was identified as one of the key features of community music therapy based in a synthesis of eight case studies of community music therapy projects in four different countries (Stige et al. 2010). Stige and Aarø (2012), present a modified formulation based in the findings from the previous mentioned studies (Stige et al. 2010) of qualities that characterize community music therapy structured through the acronym PREPARE: Participatory, Resource-oriented, Ecological, Performative, Activist, Reflective, and Ethics-driven. Stige and Aarø (2012) link the resource-oriented quality to welfare and equality, and by this emphasizing the political and contextual aspects of resources.

In the context of community music therapy there are several texts that explore processes regarded with the mobilization of resources for marginalized groups[15]. Here I will mention some texts that in particular contribute to an understanding of social resources. Procter (2006, 2011) explores possibilities for mobilization of *social capital* in music therapy. Social capital is a concept from sociology that might contribute to elaborate the concept of resource-orientation. Procter's explorations of a concept of music therapy as a mobilization of musical-capital, which is described in terms of a pre-social-capital (Procter 2004, 2006, 2011) contributes to an understanding of the bridge between music therapy and everyday life contexts. Krüger and Stige (2015) explore the concept of music as a *structuring resource*, which similarly might contribute to the understanding of how resources mobilized in the context of music therapy might be transferred to everyday life contexts. Finally I will mention Ansdell and DeNora (2012) and Ansdell (2014) who explores "musical-social-resources" in the cultivation of musical *flourishing* and *well-being*.

Ansdell (2014) and Ansdell and DeNora's (2012) discussions are also examples of the increasing amount of texts in music therapy that link up with the fast growing interdisciplinary field of *music and health* (MacDonald et al. 2012). According to MacDonald et al. (2012b) music and health is theme shared by several fields of practice which they lists as: music therapy, community music, music education, and everyday uses of music (MacDonald et al. 2012b, p. 8). This broad range of music and health practices offers various perspectives that contribute to the understanding of music as a health resource in various contexts ranging from music therapy in medical institutions, to the non-institutionalized and individual uses of music in everyday life contexts.

SOME CONSIDERATIONS AND DILEMMAS

In this last section of this chapter I will try to sum up the chapter by outlining some dilemmas and controversies that the literature concerning resource-oriented music therapy articulates. The first dilemma I will address are concerned with the status of resource-oriented music therapy. Is resource-oriented music therapy to be understood as an approach or as a more general feature of music therapy? There seems to be a tension between the conceptualizations of Scwhabe (2000/2005) who conceptualize resource-oriented music therapy as a general and potentially integrative element with regard to the different models and traditions in music therapy, and my own elaborations on the concept of a more specific resource-oriented approach (Rolvsjord 2010).

As this chapter has illuminated, resource-oriented perspectives are linked to a broad interdisciplinary field of theory, research, and practices. With this as a background, at the present stage it would be most precise to understand resource-oriented music therapy as being both a specific approach and a general aspect of music therapy that are present in various music therapy models. It must be underlined at this point that even conceptualized as a specific *approach*, resource-oriented music therapy does not imply formal and structural features frequently associated with music therapy *models* such as educational programs. However, Rolvsjord (2010) emphasizes that as an approach resource-oriented music therapy "imply more than adding some friendly elements to existing models" (Rolvsjord 2010, p. 11). A resource-oriented approach can indeed be regarded as in tension with, if not, conflicting with traditional approaches that aligns with the medical model. In order to counteract the strong presence of the medical model in therapy culture, a conscious choice of working resource-oriented is recommended (Rolvsjord 2010, p. 198).

Even though resource-oriented aspects has been noted in both Nordoff-Robbins tradition (Garred 2006) and analytical oriented music therapy (Bonde et al. 2001; Pedersen 2014[16]), resource-oriented features of other approaches or models in music therapy are perhaps most clearly articulated in community music therapy (Stige et al. 2010; Stige and Aarø 2012). Stige et al. (2010) acknowledges the similarities between the resource-oriented features of community music therapy with characteristics of the resource-oriented approach and state that:

> We acknowledge these similarities and think that they demonstrate how community music therapy may be developed in dialogue with other practices of and perspectives on music

therapy. The resource-oriented feature of community music therapy of course also resonates with the developments in other related disciplines, such as recent research on efficacy and positive emotions in psychology and on social capital in social studies.

(Stige et al. 2010, p. 283)

Following the argumentation from Stige et al. (2010), we may understand resource-orientation as a recent theme, or a movement shared within a broad landscape of discourses in psychology, sociology, medicine, social work. Thus, there is a broad landscape of perspectives linked to several disciplines and various practices that has emphasized this dimension of resource-orientation. Similarly to what Stige et al. (2010) says about the resource-orientation feature of music therapy, it can be said that the focus on collaboration and contextual aspects highlighted in community music therapy are also central to resource-oriented music therapy.

Community music therapy and resource-oriented music therapy could be understood as "siblings" in the landscape of music therapy approaches. However, they accentuate differently their similar processes and features. At a practice level the differences might be clearer: Community music therapy projects usually happen in community contexts and it usually focus on group work and performances and describe change on collective levels. Throughout this text we have seen many examples of resource-oriented music therapy in the traditional medical contexts of health institutions, although there should be highly relevant for resource-oriented music therapy to also explore the non-medical/non-institutionalized contexts. Further, resource-oriented music therapy has focused on the individual in context, and the individual in interaction with the context, and thus most frequently described change at an individual level. This however is obviously a very simplistic explanation. It is probably more useful to conceive practices along an individual-community continuum which includes interactions across contexts (Rolvsjord and Stige 2015). Consequently there is a need to develop therapeutic practices along such a continuum.

In conclusion

Resource-oriented music therapy is a perspective that aligns with a broad interdisciplinary context of theory and practices. There seems to be a growing awareness in the discourse of music therapy about the relevance of mobilization of resources. As an approach, resource-oriented music therapy has been most clearly elaborated in the context of mental health care. There is obviously a need to explore the relevance and the practices of resource-oriented music therapy in other contexts of health promotion and health care.

Notes

1. This article was first published in E.T. Gaston's (1968) book "Music in therapy".
2. There is an English version of the book: Wigram et al. (2002). A Comprehensive Guide to Music Therapy, but the term resource-oriented is only used in the Danish version.
3. The definition was formulated in Norwegian in 1990. Here I refer Ruud's own translation (Ruud 1998).

4. The concept of musicking (Small 1998) and Gibson's concept of affordance and appropriations which are known to music therapists via the work of DeNora (2000) has been crucial in the developments of this understanding in music therapy.
5. See Rolvsjord and Stige (2015) for a discussion of contextual perspectives in music therapy.
6. Schwabe's article "Wachstumsförderung versus Musikalische Psychospekulation. Ressourcenorientierte Musiktherapie" published in 2000, is available in an English translation (2005). Further exploration of the German notion of *ressourcenorientierte musikterapie* is available for readers who understand German.
7. Grawe's work on resource-activation and mechanisms of change is well introduced in english articles (Grawe 1997; Gassmann and Grawe 2006).
8. Being "brought up" in the Norwegian tradition of music therapy I had learned to foster experiences of mastery and to build upon the clients' strengths and musical identity.
9. For clarifications of the concept of a medical model see Wampold (2001). For relevant discussions in music therapy see also Ansdell (2002) and the concept of consensus model in music therapy.
10. The structure was suggested by Waltz et al. (1993).
11. Reproduced from Research Rigour and Therapeutic Flexibility: Rationale for a Therapy Manual Developed for a Randomized Controlled Trial, Randi Rolvsjord, Christian Gold, Brynjulf Stige, Nordic Journal of Music Therapy, ©2005, Taylor & Francis, with permission. Reprinted by permission of the publisher (Taylor & Francis Ltd, <http://www.tandf.co.uk/journals>).
12. This case report was originally published in Nordic Journal of Music Therapy.
13. Song lyrics are taken out from the quote here.
14. A similar *family* of perspectives are identified as "anti-oppressive practices" in music therapy by Baines (2013).
15. See Stige and Aarø (2012) for a more comprehensive review on this.
16. Pedersen (2014) critique the Resource-oriented approach as elaborated by Rolvsjord, Gold and Stige (2005b) and suggests a combination of salutogenic and pathogenic perspectives that varies across different phases of the therapeutic process.

References

Aasgaard, T. (2002). *Song creations by children with cancer—Process and meaning.* Unpublished Ph.D. Thesis, Institute of Music and Music therapy, Aalborg University.
Ansdell, G. (2002). Community music therapy and the winds of change—A Discussion Paper. *Voices: A World Forum for Music Therapy* 2(2). https://voices.no/index.php/voices/article/view/83/65. doi: 10.15845/voices.v2i2.83
Ansdell, G. (2014). *How music helps in music therapy and everyday life.* Surrey: Ashgate Publishing Limited.
Ansdell, G. and DeNora, T. (2012). Musical flourishing: Community music therapy, controversy, and the cultivation of wellbeing. In MacDonald, R., Kreutz, G., and Mitchell, L. (eds), *Music, health, and wellbeing*, pp. 97–113. Oxford: Oxford University Press.
Aigen, Ke. (2005). *Music-centered music therapy.* Gilsum, NH: Barcelona Publishers.
Antonovsky, A. (1979). *Health, stress and coping.* London: Jossey-Bass Publishers.
Antonovsky, A. (1987). *Unraveling the mystery of health. How people manage stress and stay well.* London: Jossey-Bass Publishers.

Asperheim, L. (2009). Implementering av terapeutiske prinsipp for ressursorientert musik-kterapi: Ei kvalitativ analyse av enkeltstående timar. [Implementation of therapeutic principles for resource-oriented music therapy: A Qualitative analysis of singular sessions]. Unpublished master thesis, University of Bergen.

Baines, S. (2003). A consumer-directed and partnered community mental health music therapy program. *Voices: A World Forum for Music Therapy*, 3(3). Available from: <https://voices.no.no/index.php/voices/article/view/137/113>.

Baines, S. (2013). Music therapy as an anti-oppressive practice. *The Arts in Psychotherapy* 40: 1–5. doi: 10.1016/j.aip.2012.09.003.

Baines, S. and Danko, G. (2010). Community mental health music therapy: A consumer-initiated song-based paradigm. *Canadian Journal of Music Therapy* 16(1): 148–191.

Baker, F. A. and Ballantyne, J. (2013). "You've got to accentuate the positive": Group songwriting to promote a life of enjoyment, engagement and meaning in aging Australians. *Nordic Journal of Music Therapy* 22(1): 7–24. doi: 10.1080/08098131.2012.678372

Bonde, L.O., Pedersen, I. and Wigram, T. (2001). *Når ord ikke slår til*. [When Words Fails]. Århus: Forlaget Klim.

Bruscia, K.E. (1998). *Defining music therapy*. Gelsim, NH: Barcelona Publishers.

Chhina, C. (2004). Music therapy and psychosocial rehabilitation: Towards a person-centered music therapy model. *Canadian Journal of Music Therapy* 11(1): 8–30.

Curtis, S.L. (1996). *Singing Subversions, Singing Soul: Women's Voices in Feminist Music Therapy*. Theses for the Degree of Doctor of Philosophy. Concordia University, Montreal, Quebec.

Curtis, S. (2006). Feminist music therapy: Transforming theory, transforming lives. In: S. Hadley (ed.), *Feminist perspectives in music therapy*, pp. 227–244. Gilsum, NH: Barcelona Publishers.

Dalton, J.H., Elias, M.J., and Wandersman, A. (2001). *Community Psychology. Linking Individuals and Communities*. London: Wadsworth (Thomson Learning).

Daveson, B.A. (2001). Empowerment: An intrinsic process and consequence of music therapy practise. *The Australian Journal of Music Therapy* 12: 29–37.

Davidson, L., Rakfeldt, J. and Strauss, J. (2010). *The roots of the recovery movement in psychiatry*. Chichester, West Sussex: John Wiley and Sons Ltd. doi: 10.1002/9780470682999

DeNora, T. (2000). *Music in everyday life*. Cambridge: Cambridge University Press. doi: 10.1002/9780470682999

DeNora, T. (2007). Health and music in everyday life—A theory of practice. *Psyche and Logos* 28(1): 271–287.

Duncan, B.L., Miller, S.D., Wampold, B.E. and Hubble, M.A. (2010). *The heart and soul of change*. Second edition. Washington: American Psychological Association.

Garred, R. (2006). *Music as therapy. A dialogical perspective*. Gilsum, NH: Barcelona Publishers.

Gassmann, D. and Grawe, K. (2006). General change mechanisms: The relation between problem activation and resource-activation in successful and unsuccessful Therapeutic Interactions. *Clinical Psychology and Psychotherapy* 13: 1–11. doi: 10.1186/1471-244X-5-39

Gaston, E. Thayer (1968). *Music in Therapy*. New York: Macmillan.

Gold, C., Rolvsjord, R., and Stige, B. (2005). Resource-oriented music therapy for psychiatric patients with low therapy motivation: Protocol for a randomised controlled trial [NCT00137189] *BMC Psychiatry* 5: 39. doi: 10.1186/1471-244X-5-39

Gold, C., Mössler, K., Grocke, D., Heldal, T.O., Tjemsland, L., Aarre, T., … and Rolvsjord, R. (2013). Individual music therapy for mental health care clients with low therapy motivation:

Multicentre randomised controlled trial. *Psychotherapy and psychosomatics* 82(5): 319–331. doi: 10.1159/000348452

Grawe, K. (1997). Research-informed psychotherapy. *Psychotherapy Research* 7(1): 1–19. doi: 10.1080/10503309712331331843

Grocke, D. Bloch, S., and Castle, D. (2008). Is there a role for music therapy in the care of the severely mentally ill. *Australasian Psychiatry* 16(6): 442–445. doi: 10.1080/08098131.2014.890242

Hadley, S. (ed.) (2006). *Feminist perspectives in music therapy.* Gilsum, NH: Barcelona Publishers.

Kenny, C.B. (1982). *The mythic artery. The magic of music therapy.* Atascadero, California: Ridgeview Publishing Company.

Kenny, C. B. (1989). *The field of play. A guide to the theory and practice of music therapy.* Atascadero, California: Ridgeview Publishing Company.

Kooij, C.V. (2009). Recovery themes in songs written by adults living with serious mental illnesses. *Canadian Journal of Music Therapy* 15(1): 37–58.

Krüger, V. and Stige, B. (2015). Between rights and realities–music as a structuring resource in child welfare everyday life: a qualitative study. *Nordic Journal of Music Therapy* 24(2): 99–122. doi: 10.1080/08098131.2014.890242

Lindenfelser, K.J., Hense, C., and McFerran, K. (2012). Music therapy in pediatric palliative care: Family-centered care to enhance quality of life. *American Journal of Hospice and Palliative Medicine* 29(3): 219–226. doi: 10.1177/1049909111429327

MacDonald, R., Kreutz, G., and Mitchell, L. (eds). (2012). *Music, health and wellbeing.* New York, NY: Oxford University Press. doi: 10.1093/acprof:oso/9780199586974.003.0001

MacDonald, R., Kreutz, G., and Mitchell, L. (2012b). What is music, health and wellbeing and why is it important? In: R. MacDonald, G. Kreutz, and L. Mitchell (eds), *Music, health and wellbeing,* pp. 3–11. New York, NY: Oxford University Press. doi: 10.1093/acprof:oso/9780199586974.001.0001

McCaffrey, T., Edwards, J., and Fannon, D. (2011). Is there a role for music therapy in the recovery approach in mental health? *The Arts in Psychotherapy* 38: 185–189. doi: 10.1016/j.aip.2011.04.006

Mössler, K. (2011). "I am a psychotherapeutically oriented music therapist": Theory construction and its influence on professional identity formation under the example of the Viennese school of music therapy. *Nordic Journal of Music Therapy* 20(2): 155–184. doi: 10.1080/08098131.2011.571276

Mössler, K., Fuchs, K., Helsal, T.O., Karterud, I.M., Kenner, J., Næsheim, S., and Gold, C. (2011). The clinical application and relevance of resource-oriented principles in music therapy within an international multicentre study in psychiatry. *British Journal of Music Therapy* 25(1): 72–91. doi: 10.1080/08098131003768115

Nordoff, P. and Robbins, C. (1977). *Creative music therapy.* New York: John Day and Co.

Pasiali, V. (2012). Resilience, music therapy and human adaptation: nurturing young children and families. *Nordic Journal of Music Therapy* 21(1): 36–56. doi: 10.1080/08098131.2011.571276

Pavlicevic, M. and Ansdell, G. (2004). *Community music therapy.* London: Jessica Kingsley Publishers.

Pavlicevic, M. and Ansdell, G. (2009). Between communicative musicality and collaborative musicing: A perspective from community music therapy. In: S. Malloch, and C. Trevarthen (eds), *Communicative Musicality,* pp. 357–376. Oxford: Oxford University Press.

Pedersen, I. N. (2014). Music therapy in psychiatry today: Do we need specialization based on the reduction of diagnosis-specific symptoms or on the overall development of resources? Or do we need both? *Nordic Journal of Music Therapy* 23(2): 173–194. doi: 10.1080/08098131.2013.790917

Procter, S. (2001). Empowering and enabling—Music therapy in non-medical mental health provision. *Voices: A World Forum for Music Therapy* 1(2), available from: <https://normt.uib. no/index.php/voices/article/view/58/46>.

Procter, S. (2004). Playing politics: Community music therapy and the therapeutic redistribution of musical capital for mental health. In: M. Pavlicevic and G. Ansdell (eds), *Community music therapy*, pp. 214–230. London: Jessica Kingsley.

Procter, S. (2006). What are we playing at? Social capital and music therapy. In: R. Edwards, J. Franklin, and J. Holland (eds), *Assessing Social Capital: Concept, Policy and Practice*, pp. 146–162. Newcastle: Cambridge Scholars Press.

Procter, S. (2011). Reparative musicking: Thinking on the usefulness of social capital theory within music therapy. *Nordic Journal of Music Therapy* 20(3): 242–262. doi: 10.1080/08098131.2010.489998

Rolvsjord, R. (2001). Sophie learns to play the piano. A case study exploring the dialectics between didactic and psychotherapeutic music therapy practices. *Nordic Journal of Music Therapy* 10(1): 11–85. doi: 10.1080/08098130109478020

Rolvsjord, R. (2004). Therapy as empowerment. Clinical and political implications of empowerment philosophy in mental health practises of music therapy. *Nordic Journal of Music Therapy* 13(2): 99–111. doi: 10.1080/08098130409478107

Rolvsjord, R. (2006). Whose power of music? A Discussion on music and power-relations in music therapy. *British Journal of Music Therapy* 20(1): 5–12.

Rolvsjord, R. (2007). *"Blackbirds Singing": Explorations of resource-oriented music therapy in mental health care.* Unpublished doctoral dissertation, Institute for Communication and Psychology, Aalborg University.

Rolvsjord, R. (2010). *Resource-oriented music therapy in mental health care.* Gilsum, NH: Barcelona Publishers.

Rolvsjord, R. (2013). Music therapy in everyday life: With the organ as the third therapist. In: L.O. Bonde, E. Ruud, M. Skånland, and G. Trondalen (eds), *Music and health narratives*, pp. 201–220. Oslo, Norway: NMH-publikasjoner 2013. Skriftserie fra Senter for musikk og helse.

Rolvsjord, R. (2014). What clients do to make music therapy work: A qualitative multiple case study in adult mental health care. *Nordic Journal of Music Therapy.* doi: 10.1080/08098131.2014.964753

Rolvsjord, R., Gold, C., and Stige, B. (2005a). Research rigour and therapeutic flexibility: Rationale for a therapy manual developed for a randomised controlled trial. *Nordic Journal of Music Therapy* 14(1): 15–32. doi: 10.1080/08098130509478122

Rolvsjord, R., Gold, C., and Stige, B. (2005b). Therapeutic principles for resource-oriented music therapy: A contextual approach to the field of mental health. Appendix to the article Research Rigour and Therapeutic Flexibility by R. Rolvsjord, C. Gold, and B. Stige, published in *Nordic Journal of Music Therapy* MT 14(1) 2005 Retrieved July 1, 2005, from <http:// www.njmt.no/appendrolvsjord141.html>.

Rolvsjord, R. and Stige, B. (2015). Concepts of context in music therapy. *Nordic Journal of Music Therapy* 24(1): 44–66. doi: 10.1080/08098131.2013.861502

Ruud, E. (1980). *Music therapy and its relationship to current treatment theories.* St. Louis: Magnamusic-Baton.

Ruud, E. (1990). *Musikk som kommunikasjon og samhandling.* [Music as communication and interaction] Oslo: Solum forlag.

Ruud, E. (1997a). Music and the quality of life. *Nordic Journal of Music Therapy* 6(2): 86–97. doi: 10.1080/08098139709477902

Ruud, E. (1997b). Music and identity. *Nordic Journal of Music Therapy* 6(1): 3–13. doi: 10.1080/08098139709477889

Ruud, E. (1998). *Music therapy. Improvisation, communication and culture.* Gilsum, NH: Barcelona Publishers.

Ruud, E. (2005). Introduction to Christoph Schwabe: resource-oriented music therapy. The development of a concept. *Nordic Journal of Music Therapy* 14(1): 47–48. doi: 10.1080/08098139709477889

Ruud, E. (2010). *Music Therapy: A Perspective from the humanities.* Gilsum, NH: Barcelona Publishers.

Schwabe, C. (2000). Wachstumsförderung versus musikalische psychospekulation. ressourcenorientierte musiktherapie. In: C. Schwabe and I. Stein (eds), Ressourcenorientierte musiktherapie, pp. 158–165. *Crossener Schriften zur Musiktherapie. Band XII.*

Schwabe, C. (2005). Resource-oriented music therapy—The development of a concept. *Nordic Journal of Music Therapy* 14(1): 49–56. doi: 10.1080/08098139709477889

Sears, W.W. (1996). Processes in music therapy. *Nordic Journal of Music Therapy* 5(1): 33–42. doi: 10.1080/08098139609477865

Seligman, M. and Csikszentmihalyi, M. (2000). Positive psychology. An introduction. *American psychologist* 55(1): 5–14. doi: 10.1037/0003-066X.55.1.5

Shih, J.H.T. (2011). Stabilization music therapy model and process: 512 China Sichuan earthquake crisis intervention, Part 1 of 2. *Music and Medicine* 3(2): 84–88. doi: 10.1177/1943862110378108

Slade, M. (2009). *Personal recovery and mental Illness.* New York: Cambridge University Press. doi: 10.1017/CBO9780511581649

Small, C. (1998). *Musicking. The meanings of performing and listening.* Middeltown, Connecticut: Wesleyan University Press.

Snyder, C.R. and Lopez, S.J. (eds). (2002). *Handbook of positive psychology.* Oxford: Oxford University Press.

Solli, H.P. (2008). "Shut up and play!" Improvisational use of popular music for a man with Schizofrenia. *Nordic Journal of Music Therapy* 17(19): 67–77. doi: 10.1080/08098130809478197

Solli, H.P. (2009). Musikkterapi som integrert del av standard behandling I psykisk helsevern. [Music therapy as integrated part of standard care in mental health care]. In: E. Ruud, (ed.), *Musikk i psykisk helsearbeid med barn og unge* [Music in mental health care with children and adolescence], pp. 15–36. Skriftserie fra Senter for Musikkterapi Oslo: NMH Publikasjoner. doi: 10.1093/jmt/50.4.244

Solli, H.P., Rolvsjord, R., and Borg, M. (2013). Toward understanding music therapy as a recovery-oriented practice within mental health care: A meta-synthesis of service users' experiences. *Journal of Music Therapy* 50(4): 244–273.

Solli, H. P. and Rolvsjord, R. (2015). "The Opposite of Treatment": A qualitative study of how patients diagnosed with psychosis experience music therapy. *Nordic Journal of Music Therapy* 24(1): 67–92. doi: 10.1080/08098131.2014.890639

Solli, H.P. (2014). Battling illness with wellness: A qualitative case study of a young rapper's experiences with music therapy. *Nordic Journal of Music Therapy.* doi: 10.1080/08098131.2014.907334

Sprague, J. and Hayes, J. (2000). Self-determination and empowerment: A feminist standpoint analyses of talk about disability. *American Journal of Community Psychology* 28(5): 671–695. doi: 10.1023/A:1005197704441

Stige, B. (2002). *Culture-centered music therapy*. Gilsum, NH: Barcelona Publishers.

Stige, B. (2003). Elaborations *towards a notion of community music therapy*. Oslo: Unipub forlag.

Stige, B. (2011). The doors and windows of the dressing room: Culture-centered music therapy in a mental health setting. In: A. Meadows (ed.). *Development in music therapy practice: Case study perspectives*. Gilsum, NH: Barcelona Publishers.

Stige, B. (2012). Health musicking: A perspective on music and health as action and performance. In: R. MacDonald, G. Kreutz, and L. Mitchell (eds), *Music, health and wellbeing*, pp. 184–95. New York, NY: Oxford University Press. doi: 10.1093/acprof: oso/9780199586974.003.0014

Stige, B., Ansdell, G., Elefant, C., and Pavlicevic, M. (2010). *Where music helps: Community music therapy in action and reflection*. Aldershot, UK: Ashgate.

Stige, B. and Aarø, L.E. (2012). *Invitation to community music therapy*. New York: Routledge.

Trondalen, G. (2004). *Klingende relasjoner. En musikkterapistudie av "signifikante øyeblikk" I musikalsk samspill med unge mennesker med anoreksi*. [Sounding relations. A music therapy study of significant moments in musical interplay with young people with anorexia]. Oslo: Norges Musikkhøgskole.

Waltz, J., Addis, M.E., Koerner, K., and Jacobson, N.S. (1993). Testing the integrity of a psychotherapy protocol: assessment of adherence and competence. *Journal of Consulting and Clinical Psychology* 61(4): 620–630. doi: 10.1037/0022-006X.61.4.620

Wampold, B. E. (2001). *The great psychotherapy debate: Models, methods, and findings*. Mahwah, NJ: Lawrence Erlbaum Associates Publishers.

Wigram, T., Pedersen, I., and Bonde, L.O. (2002). *A comprehensive guide to music therapy*. London: Jessica Kingsley Publisher Ltd.

York, E. (2006). Finding voice: Feminist music therapy and research with women survivors of domestic violence. In: S. Hadley (ed.), *Feminist perspectives in music therapy*, pp. 245–66. Gilsum, NH: Barcelona Publisher.

CHAPTER 31

DEVELOPMENTAL MUSIC THERAPY

JANE EDWARDS AND JASON NOONE

Music therapy is normalizing, it is socializing, it is humanizing, in a word it is music therapy for living

Boxill 1985, p. 21

We music therapists have as our therapeutic agent a universal means of human expression, MUSIC!

Boxill 1997, p. 9

INTRODUCTION

DEVELOPMENTAL music therapy provides the integration of multiple theoretical perspectives through which practitioners and researchers seek to understand the context in which the challenges faced by the client and their family or social network are experienced and enacted. The model draws on three main theoretical orientations: (1) Theories of stress, coping, and adaption; (2) Human life span development including stage models;[1] (3) Ecological perspectives such as Bronfenbrenner's bioecological model of development, along with cultural and family theories. DMT can be described as eclectic and opportunistic in terms of its wider theoretical breadth. That is, where an approach from outside the field of music therapy has resonances with these three theoretical pillars it can be incorporated into the developmental practitioner's approach, for example narrative therapy (White and Epston 1990). Boxill is the music therapist who most consistently termed her approach developmental music therapy (Boxill 1989). The traces of developmental perspectives can also be found in many descriptions of clinical work where clinicians use developmental theory, or aspects therein, to elaborate and explain the rationale for their practice.

The main ways in which music therapists incorporate the developmental music therapy model when working with individuals and families is by considering the life stage of the individual or group/family, in relation to the social and cultural context in which the individual and group operate.

STRESS AND COPING

This brief review is intended to orient novice readers to key concepts in the field of stress, coping, and adaptation. Wider reading and training is recommended in order to be able to use these concepts proficiently in professional practice.

Throughout each stage of the life span every human experiences stress. Adjustment to stress is called coping. At different stages of life we cope in different ways (Skinner et al. 2003). For example, consider the scenario in which baby Emma while snoozing in her cot at home is frightened by the noise of a loud bang outside, startles and starts to cry. Her Mum also hears the bang followed by her baby's frightened wail. Although initially alarmed she realizes that a rubbish bin in the yard has been blown over by the wind. She moves towards the cot, reassures Emma with a cuddle and soothing vocalization, and equilibrium is restored evidenced by Emma drifting off to a deep sleep. This simple scenario of parental responsiveness to infant stress is enacted over and over throughout the world every day.

Through the course of human development the ability to manage stress is at first developed in collaboration with at least one loving and sensitive care giver. Then, through childhood and adolescence the ability to increasingly successfully self-regulate to manage stress develops.

The attachment experiences of closeness and bondedness in the earliest relationships of human life lays down biological and neurological strengths to help manage psychological and social stress throughout the life course. Stress reactivity, or responsivity, is a term used to indicate the extent to which a person is vulnerable to experiencing a stress reaction when confronted with a stressor. Positive and consistent emotional support and psychological safety in the early years provides a foundation for lower stress reactivity throughout life (Nachmias et al. 1996). That is, responses to stressors are not as intense and potentially problematic for people with lower stress reactivity. Rather than a simple linear process of interaction, the actions, reactions, and communications between infants and their care givers belong in a myriad of intention with reference to experiences of self and others. Trevarthen (2009) has provided multiple rich elaborations of these interactions between adults and infants through microanalysis of these collaborative acts. His resultant formulation of the theory of intersubjectivity based on this analysis provides,

> ... understanding [about] the emotional "moral" regulations of human community, the feelings of relatedness to one another and to meaning that determine the sense each individual has of self-worth, and the "personal narrative history" each discovers in relation with recognized others
>
> Trevarthen 2009, p. 509

Through the early years the infant depends on external support to develop the capacity for managing their internal state. Stern (2001) indicated that it is not imperative that the interactions between the care giver and the infant are *perfect*; the skill of being able to *repair derailments* within the regulatory process between care giver and infant positively influences infant coping (Stern 2009, p. 9).

Returning to the story of baby Emma, consider the same scenario but this time her mother is on the phone dealing with a family crisis involving her nephew when the loud bang is heard. Instead of hanging up immediately when she hears Emma's frightened cry she takes some time to reassure the caller, and promises to call back soon. By the time she moves towards her baby, lifts her out of the cot and starts to reassure her, Emma is highly distressed. It takes quite some time of rocking and comforting for Emma to calm down and begin to coo happily. No damage is done. However, in the same scenario where a care giver is unavailable or unable to give the baby the emotional support they need when distressed, and this happens consistently, eventually baby Emma will experience immense distress but will not cry or vocalize to indicate this stress. As she develops and matures through childhood, adolescence, and adulthood, her neuro-hormonal system will be unable to respond to stress in ways that promote clear thinking and calm behavior.

The complex scenario of the too intrusive parent or care giver is also acknowledged as problematic (Barnett et al. 2008). For example, if the care giver cannot tolerate the baby's distress and becomes angry with the baby, or too insistent that their crying stop the baby can become frightened of the care giver and will stop looking to him or her for comfort. Experiencing this type of constant threat in infancy causes the developing child to acquire habits of responding that disallow calm and fun filled play. As Perry (2009) has explained "The brain will 'reset'—acting as if the individual is under persistent threat" (p. 244) even when there is no obvious external threat present.

Stressful or traumatic experiences in early life can also cause lifelong harm through triggering dysregulation of the immune system (Fagundes et al. 2013). Fagundes et al. observed that the reasons that children who had experienced extreme stress as children were more vulnerable to physical illness in later life is that they "(a) are more psychologically and physiological sensitive to stress, and (b) have fewer social and psychological resources available to help them cope with stress." (Fagundes et al. 2013, p. 11).

As infants rapidly develop experiencing multiple stimuli for the first time in their lives it is acknowledged that:

> ... the organizing, sensitive brain of an infant or young child is more malleable to experience than a mature brain. While experience may alter the behavior of an adult, experience literally provides the organizing framework for an infant and child.
>
> Perry 2009, p. 245

During infancy and childhood the brain and its functions develop rapidly. The developing brain is dependent on receiving the right kinds of stimulation that can shape and support emotional regulation and maturation. As Perry explained:

> The brain is organized in a hierarchical fashion with four main anatomically distinct regions: Brainstem, diencephalon, limbic system, and cortex. During development the brain organizes itself from the bottom up, from the least (brainstem) to the most complex (limbic, cortical) areas. While significantly interconnected, each of these regions mediates distinct functions, with the lower, structurally simpler areas mediating basic regulatory functions and the highest, most complex structures (cortical) mediating the most complex functions.
>
> Perry 2009, p. 241–242

During early life the infant brain develops rapidly. Interpersonal and intrapsychic regulation are crucial to a healthy start to life, and these processes are interdependent (Beebe and Lachmann 1998). In infancy and early childhood, "Patterned, repetitive activities shape the brain in patterned ways, while chaotic experiences create chaotic dysfunctional organization." (Perry 2009, p. 252). A key factor in development relevant for music therapy practice is the development during infancy of the capacity for synchrony (Feldman 2007). This is a concept nuanced more specifically than the concepts of *responsiveness* or *sensitivity* (Feldman 2007). As Feldman has explained:

> Synchrony describes the intricate 'dance' that occurs during short, intense, playful interactions; builds on familiarity with the partner's behavioral repertoire and interaction rhythms; and depicts the underlying temporal structure of highly aroused moments of interpersonal exchange that are clearly separated from the stream of daily life.
>
> Feldman 2007, p. 329

Importantly for music therapy practice it is important to remember that around two months of age "gaze synchrony—the co-occurrence of social gaze between parent and child—becomes the most pronounced form of synchrony and provides an organizing framework for the emergence of coordinated behavior in other modalities, such as co-vocalization and the matching of affective states" (Feldman and Eidelman 2007, p. 291). Therefore encouraging face to face interactions between care givers and infants in music therapy sessions can support the development of many other satisfying interactive processes.

When the ability to respond to stress normatively is disrupted or forms inadequately, an individual can become vulnerable to mental health difficulties throughout their life (Schore 2001). Therefore music therapy programmes which are aimed at facilitating the successful mutual co-regulation of parent and infant equilibrium aim to prevent future psychological problems, and buffer the parent or care giver and infant from the harm caused by unsatisfying and mis-regulated interactions. Music therapists have demonstrated this in various contexts including with children who are hospitalised for illness or injury (Edwards and Kennelly 2011; Robb 2000).

Through childhood, adolescence, and adult life the capacity to manage stress is key to optimal mental health when coping with adversity (Aldwin 2012). Music is used in everyday life as a stress buffer, and increasingly healthcare services are interested in finding ways to optimize music use in supporting health and healing. Although there are caveats that accompany this claim, music has been shown in many studies to decrease stress and to strengthen the human immune response (Fancourt et al. 2013). The goal of music therapy with children and their families is to establish structure and patterning that results in greater capacity for self-regulation, that is, the ability to for the individual to self-soothe and manage stress.

During adolescence there is a greater vulnerability to stress through needing to adjust to rapid physiological and hormonal changes, which also involves encountering multiple experiences for the first time. One or both parents can play an important role in buffering stress, although parents can also induce stress for the adolescent when they are unable to nurture their child's need for greater independence (Betts et al. 2009). Having one person outside of the family network who is a confidante is key to successful coping through the drama of adolescence, and clinicians are encouraged to screen for risk by asking adolescent clients whether they have someone outside of the family in whom they can confide (McNairn et al.

2004). This life stage involves experimentation and some experiments do not have positive consequences. The ability to manage the consequences of ones actions, and integrate the learning from these, to take forward into adult life is important.

HUMAN LIFE SPAN DEVELOPMENT

The human life span is lengthy in comparison to many other mammals, with a long period of early immaturity where rapid physical, cognitive, and social development occurs. Human development is enacted through a series of stages of capacity from infancy then childhood, adolescence, adulthood, and older adulthood. The infant skull is not fully formed to allow the brain quadruple in size during the first four years of life (Dissanayake 2008). The human baby cannot speak, walk, nor manipulate objects meaning they are highly dependent on care giver support for their survival. The newborn infant is therefore primed for experiences of attachment and closeness, in order to foster intimacy with care givers who become *attached* to the child with the ability to hold the infant's needs in mind and where necessary place these needs ahead of their own. Dissanayake (2008) proposed that human infants and care givers have developed complex vocal interactions, described as *proto-music,* as a means by which this closeness could be developed. The highly musical interactions between care givers and infants was observed in microanalysis of these interactions in research conducted by Malloch and Trevarthen (2009). They described this interaction as *communicative musicality* as it has both musical structures and communicative intent. The high pitch and exaggerated prosody of these utterances has interested linguists over decades, and evidence for the universality of this way of interacting between infants and care givers has been found (Bryant and Barrett 2007).

Prior to the development of speech, the human infant learns a great deal about emotions, non-verbal communication, and interpersonal intimacy. They learn through interactions with care givers and other adults as well as siblings and children in their social, care, and familial environments. As they do not speak, and for much of their early development do not understand speech, they receive communication in multimodal form through closeness with at least one care giver (Stern 2010).

> What does the baby have to learn in these first 12–18 months (before they can speak)? The list includes what you do with your eyes when with another, how long to hold a mutual gaze, what turn-off head movements work, and with whom, how close you should let the other come to you ... how to read body positions ... how to enter into turn taking when vocalizing with another ... how to joke around, negotiate escalate, back off ... make friends, and so on.
>
> Stern 2010, p. 110–111

Stern (2000) described how the ability to relate and communicate with others occurs through a series of developmental phases of intrapsychic and interpersonal capacity in infancy which have various *domains.* These include the "emergent self" from birth until two months, "Core self" from two to six months, the "subjective self" that emerges in the period from seven to fifteen months, the "verbal self" at fifteen to eighteen months, and then the "narrative self" at around three to three-and-a-half years (Stern 2000, p. xxv).

Many models have been proposed as to how children develop after infancy through to adolescence. The well-known stage models of the twentieth century include Freud's psychosexual stages of development (Freud 1979), Piaget's proposition of the process of cognitive development (Piaget 1999), Erikson's stages of psychosocial development (Erikson and Erikson 1998), and Kohlberg's schema of moral development (Kohlberg 1981). Each of these models has been used, most commonly in the fields of psychology and education, to understand how children develop, and in turn to advise how practitioners might optimize children's learning, development, and adaptation to stress. Each of the models has received extensive critique and review of its current place in how to think about the complexity of children's development (e.g. Slee and Shute 2014) which is beyond the scope of this chapter.

The exact time period of a person's life in which they are considered adolescent varies between cultures, and from individual to individual. Some consider that there are multiple stages to adolescence including a final stage which begins at age 18 and continues to the age of 25 years (Arnone 2014). Although the onset of pubertal change could be considered the commencement of the life stage of adolescence, if a girl growing up in the developed world starts menstruating at eleven years old she will not necessarily be at the social age of adolescence. Similarly someone the same age struggling with gender identity may be hesitant to enter the psychological and social storm of adolescence and might try to retain their childhood status for as long as possible. A young man at age 22 who has left his home of origin and is living with his partner and two young children might occupy a different social and role space developmentally than a 22-year-old university student who lives at home with his parents. Therefore, human chronological age needs to be calibrated against developmental and social age when accepting music therapy referrals for children, adolescents, and young adults.

ECOLOGICAL PERSPECTIVES ABOUT DEVELOPMENT

Bronfenbrenner promoted the idea that every person needs to be considered as a developing being within a context of influences. He proposed a nested model of environmental influences on the individual and family. This model allows thinking about the individual's development within the social and environmental context of their world. Each of the rings of the micro, meso, macro, and exo system can be thought of as "a set of nested structures, each inside the next, like a set of Russian dolls" (Bronfenbrenner 1979, p. 22).[2]

Bronfenbrenner's model is described as having the dimensions of "person-process-context" (Bronfenbrenner 1995, p. 622) with the requirement that *time* also be considered. He also described how *proximal processes* (Bronfenbrenner and Evans 2000) influence how the individual operates within their social and familial context (Figure 31.1).

These are the reciprocal ways that development occurs within a process that involves time, as well as between persons in interaction as follows:

> ... throughout the life course, human development takes place through processes of progressively more complex reciprocal interaction between an active, evolving biopsychological human organism and the persons, objects, and symbols in its immediate external

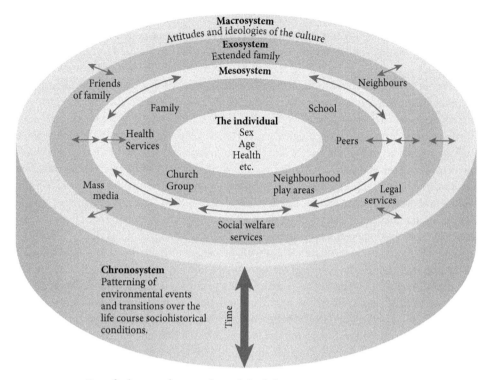

FIGURE 31.1 Bronfenbrenner's nested model of the environment

Reproduced from J.M. Bowes and A. Hayes (eds), *Children, Families and Communities: Contexts and Consequences*
© 1997, Oxford University Press, with permission from Oxford University Press.

environment ... Examples of enduring patterns of proximal process are found in feeding or
comforting a baby, playing with a young child, child-child activities, group or solitary play,
reading, learning new skills, athletic activities, problem solving, caring for others in distress,
making plans, performing complex tasks, and acquiring new knowledge and know-how.

Bronfenbrenner and Morris 2006, p. 797

The *microsystem* is the localized setting where the individual's everyday interactions occur.
For a child this can include day care or school, the family setting, the social setting of play
with other children, and religious or cultural settings where their family is engaged.

The *mesosystem* involves relations between microsystems. For example, if their parents
are in conflict with school authorities children may experience stress.

The *exosystem* is a part of environmental influences revealed when decisions are made
in another setting in which the individual does not have an active role influences what the
individual experiences in the microsystem. For example the local government services may
decide to renovate the park closest to a child's home meaning that for some months the child
does not have access to open play spaces. Another example of an environmental influence
within the exosystem is the health care services. For example, a mother needing regular dialysis might need to travel a long distance to hospital three times per week. This may disrupt
everyday family life for herself and her young children.

The *macrosystem* refers to the culture in which individuals live. This includes the behavior patterns, and beliefs of a group of people that are passed between generations. Some of these beliefs can be found in children's stories, or fables that are told and re-told throughout history.

The *chronosystem* involves the patterning of environmental events and transitions over the life course with reference to the sociohistorical conditions. For example a child growing up in the turmoil of war will have a very different life course than a child who is growing up in a country that has enjoyed decades of peace.

When considering the bioecological model of development in music therapy practice each individual as well as the family and the wider network needs to be considered within the context of their cultural, social, and historical time period when referrals are received. For example, if working in a hospital setting the music therapist may be referred a young child who is very withdrawn. On meeting the child at bedside the music therapist notices that the father does not speak to either the therapist or his child, and does not look towards either the therapist when she is speaking nor at his son when the music therapist is show-ing him the guitar and instruments and starting to sing a song she thinks he might know. In discussion with the team it is agreed that the father's non-responsiveness is of concern, and that it would help if he were able to be more available for his child. The music therapist asks the father whether he would like to record some songs that he can leave with his son if for any reason he needs to leave the bedside. Initially they agree to choose some songs from a playlist but after the father reveals that he played guitar in a wedding band for many years the music therapist begins recording him playing along with her while she sings and plays guitar. Eventually he sings and plays without her, recording song after song. In the opportunities for brief discussion between recordings of the songs the music therapist becomes aware of the father's feelings of helplessness and guilt at the accident that brought his son to the hospital for treatment. A few days later the music therapist reads in the notes that father and son were observed to be playing with some toys together which allowed the staff to take a blood test without any protest from the child. The next time she is on the ward she notes that the father is playing a guitar that is kept at the ward station, and some other children are joining him and his son in an impromptu singsong.

When families are referred who have a different cultural or social background than that of the music therapist it is important to keep in mind that ones' own chronological time might not resonate with theirs. For example, where a family have fled a war situation or have come from a situation of living year on year with uncertainty about their future in a refugee camp their ideas about the future, or about the past, about personal safety, about religious and political freedom might be very different to that of the therapist. Life for the person referred and their family members may have been lived in abject poverty and isolation or in a com-petitive and grasping survival mode. In taking a developmental perspective, it is important to make time to understand the circumstances of the client, and to make space to be aware of any customs or religious practices that may be essential to their identity and well-being.

MUSICAL STAGES OF DEVELOPMENT

The infant's musical capacities develop alongside their rapidly progressing motor, lan-guage, and social development in the early years. Musical skill acquisition has a regular developmental sequence (Hargreaves 1986; Briggs 1991). Briggs used an extensive literature base of studies of music in the early years to propose a phased model charting this development in the four areas of capacity, (1) auditory, (2) vocal/tonal, (3) rhythmic, and (4) cognitive. Infants first use their musical abilities in listening and vocalizing during the "reflex phase" from birth to nine months. They then develop skills in being able to copy musical phrases and learn snatches of songs during the "intention phase" until around eighteen months. The next eighteen months of the "control phase" shows rapid development of the ability to control musical elements and in the final "integration phase" children are able to learn a music instrument, and rapidly learn songs, rhymes, rhythms, and chants (Briggs 1991).

As with language abilities, perception and reception develop first and then the ability to perform musical tasks including singing and use of instruments (Miyamoto 2007). Loewy (1995) elaborated the musical stages of speech development in a study of the pre-verbal skills in infancy and the relationship of these to music therapy work with clients who are not able to speak. As the infant's hearing, vocalizations, and their musical perceptual system are well developed it is important to consider the ways in which musical interactions can offer opportunities for infants' developmental growth, especially where psychological, physical, or communicative skills may need additional supports to mature optimally.

Music therapists use this knowledge in their assessment of children's needs, in particular noting that for many children who are developmentally delayed in areas such as language or coordination their musical skills can be at a normal stage of development for their chronological age. Where this is observed it can offer an opportunity to use music as a means to develop skills in other areas. Boxill (1985) used a range of developmental theories and her experience of practice techniques to propose a developmental music therapy model; particularly to support the use of music therapy with people who are multiply disabled. The second part of the chapter describes her contribution to developmental music therapy.

EDITH BOXILL'S DEVELOPMENTAL MUSIC THERAPY

Edith Boxill based her approach to developmental music therapy on her extensive music therapy work with people who have developmental disabilities. By combining a strong personal perspective along with Humanistic ideas, clinical observations, and psychobiological insights Boxill showed how music making could develop sensitive and reciprocal contact between the client and therapist, as well as promoting a sense of self, other, and the environment. This section of the chapter provides a summary of Boxill's developmental music therapy model with reference to her key works published in a paper in 1981, a book published in the 1990s, and a co-authored text in 2007, updated from the original 1985 text.

Boxill's DMT model "encompasses a broad spectrum of musical experiences designed to enhance all domains of functioning—motoric, communicative, cognitive, affective and social" (Boxill 1985, p. 15). Used therapeutically, music facilitates direct contact, promoting the development of a strong client-therapist relationship. This in turn allows for the facilitation of expression and learning in all domains of functioning. Access to positive, successful and pleasurable experiences is also made possible (Boxill and Chase 2007). Boxill's DMT is grounded in humanistic psychotherapeutic theory, emphasizing the importance of self-regulation of needs and wants, intrinsic learning, and human relationships.

Boxill's approach to music therapy is holistic with the intent of "exploring responses to music on various levels of human experience" (Boxill and Chase 2007, p. 21). Central to this approach is the development of self through musical relating (Boxill 1997; Boxill and Chase 2007) which includes the *Continuum of Awareness*. Understanding the needs of people who are multiply disabled requires consideration of their functioning in a holistic manner. That is, difficulties in one particular domain of functioning can have effects on other domains. In parallel, therapeutic benefits in one area of a client's life can positively affect the capacities of the whole person. The role of the music therapist is to facilitate the intrinsic motivation of the client within the therapeutic relationship to self-actualize and transcend the limitations of disabling conditions.

Where clients have underdeveloped skills in relating and interaction Boxill proposed a developmental approach in music therapy using clinical improvisation strategies with a view to "awakening, heightening, and expanding awareness" (Boxill 1985, p. 75). A central concept is the *continuum of awareness* (Boxill 1985) a process whereby the therapist assesses, acknowledges, and then works with the client's responsiveness with the goal of bringing them into the continuum of awareness. This process aims to encourage the client's ability to discriminate between self and other, in particular between the self and the therapist. Three strategies form the basis of this approach as follows:

1. *Reflection*—the musical mirroring of the here-and-now client.
2. *Identification*—the symbolic representation, in musical forms of the here-and-now client and therapist.
3. *Our Contact Song*—composed or improvised song that serves as an affirmation of the client-therapist relationship (Boxill 1981).

As an advocate of music therapy as a *primary treatment modality* for people with disabilities (Boxill and Chase 2007), Boxill consistently promoted music therapy's capacity to offer "opportunities for personal development and humanness, opening paths for expression and learning" (Boxill and Chase 2007, p. 18). Music is an alternative form of contact to verbal communication which can facilitate contact "on multidimensional organismic levels" (Boxill and Chase 2007, p. 18). This in turn assists the acquisition of living skills. In addition, music therapy offers a normalizing effect, making it a particularly useful therapy for people with disabilities who are described as "isolated from the stream of life" (Boxill and Chase 2007, p. 18).

Engagement in music therapy can increase awareness of self, other, and the environment. This awareness can improve functioning, well-being, and independence for the person who is living with a disability (Boxill and Chase 2007). Music therapy has a broad scope for addressing psychosocial, physical, and emotional issues in an interdisciplinary manner supplementing and reinforcing other disciplines "while implementing its own program" (Boxill 1985, p. 16).

Developmental perspectives

Developmental growth in the domains of physical, social, emotional, communication, musical, and adaptive functioning is considered in a holistic manner within Boxill's model.

"Domains of functioning are inextricably interwoven. Human development proceeds simultaneously in the various domains and involves interaction among the many areas of functioning. Constitutional and environmental influences affect this interaction in both average and atypical development" (Boxill and Chase 2007, p. 36). The music therapist must also be aware that development in each domain can be uneven "resulting in marked discrepancies between functioning levels in different domains" (Boxill and Chase 2007, p. 36). Developmental disability is considered to occur where motor skills, adaptive skills, communication skills, and social skills are not acquired, or "do not progress at a typical rate" (Boxill and Chase 2007, p. 36). Difficulties in one domain of functioning may interfere with the acquisition of skills in another, with motor and communication difficulties emphasized by Boxill (1985) as causing greatest potential disruption to a person's capacity for awareness and relating. A music therapist is required to be familiar with the developmental, maturational, organic, sensory, social/emotional, cognitive, and motoric aspects of a disorder in any particular domain as well as its effects on other domains.

THE CONTINUUM OF AWARENESS

Adapted from a concept originating with the founder of Gestalt Therapy F. Perls (1973), a continuum of awareness is the "creative process of using music functionally as a tool of consciousness to awaken, heighten, and expand awareness of self, other, and the environment" (Boxill and Chase 2007, p. 98). The client and therapist actively participate in a process of intrinsic learning that leads to action (Boxill and Chase 2007). The emphasis of this process is on "self-motivation, interpersonal, and interpersonal integration, and autonomy" (Boxill and Chase 2007, p. 98).

The fundamental goal of DMT is the development of a sense of self, which Boxill perceived as *critical need* for those with developmental disabilities (Boxill and Chase 2007), although she always maintained that DMT could be applied to all people seeking therapeutic support (Boxill 1997). The music therapy process can stimulate awareness, promote communication and participation and ultimately afford "personal fulfilment and wholeness" (Boxill and Chase 2007, p. 99)—all of which are considered to develop a person's sense of self within this model.

CYCLE OF AWARENESS

The more specific theoretical basis for Boxill's approach to using music to promote consciousness or awareness is the cycle of awareness (Zinker 1977; cited in Boxill 1985) which moves from awareness to excitement to contact. This psychophysiological process of self-regulation (Perls 1974, cited in Boxill 1985) is set in motion initially by sensorial experiences. Sensations lead to first to awareness, and then to the development of a figure-ground relationship. This awareness leads to "the mobilization of energy which leads to contact in a psychological and/or physiological sense" (Boxill and Chase 2007, p. 99). This facilitates the fulfilment of a need or want through some sort of action or behavior (Boxill 1985). The cycle begins again when the focus shifts to a new sensation, or point of awareness.

The shift from one cycle to another typically moves with a natural rhythm and can help to bring about integration and self-awareness. This is a liberating force that enables people to take responsibility for their own actions, to make their own choices (Boxill 1985). However, disruptions to this cycle arising from perceptual distortions or imbalance between sensory or motoric systems may lead to an imbalance between sensing and doing (Boxill 1985). In the case of developmental delay or disability:

> ... for idiopathic, organic, congenital or psychological reasons, awareness is severely defi-
> cient ... The inability to be aware of experiencing is manifest in lack of purpose, and resultant
> misused, misdirected unused, unoriented energy.
>
> Boxill and Chase 2007, p. 100

Intrinsic learning

Boxill described intrinsic learning as "internalized changes in awareness" (1985, p. 73). In DMT this capacity for intrinsic learning is developed through operationalizing the contin-uum of awareness. Through music therapy interactions the clients experiences "increasing levels of awareness of self, others, the environment, and the self in relation to others and the environment" (Boxill and Chase 2007, p. 101). This learning is connected to an individual's fundamental needs (Boxill 1985) and stimulates "a sense of self that can lead to the desire for adaptive behavior and purposeful functioning" (Boxill and Chase 2007, p. 101). This involves "being aware ... being in contact with one's holistic field ... having sensory, emotional, cog-nitive and energetic support of the psychobiological being" (Boxill and Chase 2007, p. 101). Initiating an individual into conditions of conscious awareness "—the ability to direct atten-tion, pay attention, and focus energy—can lead to increasing degrees of sensory perception, responsiveness, expressivity, higher forms of functioning and full realization of the person's potential" (Boxill and Chase 2007, pp. 101–102).

Musical foundations of intrinsic learning

Intrinsic learning can be addressed and developed through musical experiences and expres-sion. Singing, chanting, instrument playing, and music-movement can "promote function-ing and learning on many levels of mind-body awareness" (Boxill and Chase 2007, p. 102). In music therapy, these experiences can help a client to develop awareness and self-control in order to acquire a skill or to decrease behaviors that interfere with daily life (Boxill 1985). Skills are not treated in a linear fashion as "treatment focuses on improving functioning holistically in that intrinsic learning and change nurture the total being as a specific skill in any one domain is attained" (Boxill and Chase 2007, p. 102). In addressing a goal, work "is therefore within the horizontal, vertical, and circular dimensions of a continuum." Areas of functioning or development, such as motor skills or language "may be at different stages yet be worked on simultaneously" (Boxill and Chase 2007, p. 102). Change is considered to occur through the client's developing awareness of self and of the total environment (Boxill 1985). The degree of progress in the "ability to perceive, encode, assimilate, and act on what has been perceived is relative to the person's level of functioning, physical condition, degree of motivation generated, and the creative pathways used to help the person achieve change" (Boxill 1985, p. 79). Essentially, musical sensory experiences activate the person internally, setting in motion the cycle of awareness that leads to external action (Boxill 1985). Over the course of a music therapy intervention the person's responsiveness to musical stimuli increases (Boxill 1985). Thus, when "progress from simple to more complex musical experiences and activities takes place, transfer to forms of higher functioning can result." (Boxill and Chase 2007, p. 102).

IMPROVISATIONAL STRATEGIES IN DMT

Boxill developed three main clinical improvisation strategies for music therapy intervention "with a view to awakening, heightening, and expanding awareness" in people with developmental disabilities of any age or functioning level (1985, p. 75). These are *reflection, identification*, and *Our Contact Song*.

Reflection: This is "the mirroring and matching in musical and non-musical forms of the here-and-now client" (Boxill 1985, p. 75). This strategy/technique adapts Roger's psychotherapeutic technique into a music therapy context. This involves immediate playback of person's vocal, instrumental and physical behaviors, given musical form by the music therapist. As an expression of unconditional positive regard for the client, this technique helps to establish a strong therapeutic relationship (Boxill 1985). The therapist "stays absolutely in the present, co-existing and co-experiencing with the client, avoiding interpretations that might be subjective projections or misconstrued readings of what is occurring" (Boxill and Chase 2007, p. 105).

Identification: This involves the "symbolic representation, in musical forms (both vocal and instrumental), of the here-and-now client and therapist" (Boxill 1985, p. 75). This strategy is often used simultaneously with reflection to awaken and continuously raise awareness in individuals who are unaware of their experiencing, or are unable to communicate what they are experiencing (Boxill 1985). Improvised songs or rhythmic chants are used to feed back the "here-and-now person and what is happening in the environment" (Boxill and Chase 2007, p. 106), identifying who they (and the therapist) are, and what they and the therapist are doing in order to heighten awareness of self, other, and the environment (Boxill 1985). Where a person is non-verbal "the therapist becomes the alter ego, bringing meaning and focus to the experience to heighten the person's level of awareness while clients with verbal ability are encourage to engage in this process by singing or changing along" (Boxill 1985). Boxill (1997) likened the multi-modal responses of reflection and identification to the empathic quality of parent-infant interactions in early infancy which she described as "finding ways to make contact with another human being on the simplest, most elementary non-verbal levels" (p. 68). Reflection and identification are used to facilitate musical contact. This ultimately leads to musical explorations that deepen the therapeutic relationship, and to the discovery of *Our Contact Song* (Boxill 1985).

Our Contact Song: This is a composed or improvised song affirms the client-therapist relationship that is the catalyst for the first reciprocal expression initiated by the client and signifying the awareness of the existence of another (Boxill 1985). Arising from the client's interests, strengths, behaviors, and difficulties, the song may "come to the therapist intuitively; it may be consciously chosen by the therapist or 'clued in' by the client" (Boxill and Chase 2007, p. 109). Whether composed or improvised, it should lend itself to improvisational changes or adaptations in order to serve the therapeutic relationship and attain various goals and objectives (Boxill 1985).

The aim of these strategies is to "bring what is happening into the client's awareness and mobilize organismic energy (physical, mental, and emotional) for action" (Boxill and Chase 2007, p. 105). As part of a therapeutic process, the therapist must build "a pattern of small successes, giving direct reinforcement, and identifying the client's accomplishments in ways that can be received understood and assimilated" (Boxill and Chase 2007, p. 111). In this way, momentum for addressing goals and objectives is created (Boxill and Chase 2007). Through the use on clinical improvisation and adapted music, the therapist uses or redirects anything the client may bring—"mannerisms, symptoms, behaviors, sounds, idiosyncratic vocalizations, verbalizations, feelings, emotions, moods" to co-exist, co-experience with the client. Boxill described that:

> ... this acknowledgement of the person is designed to stimulate sensations that effect a shift in the client's perception of self in relation to the environment, a shift from a state of confluence to one of existing and making contact as a separate being.
>
> Boxill and Chase 2007, p. 111

This model of therapy conceptualizes treatment as a process—"an opening up and eventual deepening of awareness through a growing capacity for adaptive musical and non-musical behaviors; it is the opening up of pathways for developing the mind-body unity that lays the groundwork for intrinsic learning" (Boxill and Chase 2007, p. 116). Facilitating and maintaining the experiential nature of participation and relatedness is considered more important than adherence to a predetermined procedure (Boxill 1985). This model "does not abolish form but encompasses it" (Boxill and Chase 2007, p. 116).

> This emphasis on treatment as *process* requires that the therapist has empathic understanding of the inner organic flow in its many forms: Impulses, pulsations, connections, mood changes, feeling states—energy that generates musical as well as non-musical expression and behavior. Whatever the particular dynamic of the moment may be, the therapist co-exists and interexperiences with the client.
>
> Boxill and Chase 2007, p. 116

Ultimately, to be in process with a client means "to be in synchrony, in rhythm with that person" (Boxill and Chase 2007, p. 116).

Conclusion

Understanding and applying the tenets of developmental theory is a cornerstone of professional music therapy practice whether or not a practitioner describes their music therapy approach within DMT parameters. Theories of stress and coping help music therapists to understand mechanisms and processes of change for clients across the life span who are referred within diverse treatment contexts. Stage models of development offer insights into critical windows of development and the tasks required. Ecological perspectives help practitioners to keep the wider context in mind, including the effects of familial, cultural, and social environments on individuals' well-being. Within music therapy research and practice many publications attest to the centrality of developmental theories to inform a range of approaches. Edith Boxill stands out as a key advocate of a developmental approach within music therapy practice.

Boxill's model of music therapy embraces a humanistic perspective where the fundamental goal is the development of a sense of self through meaningful contact within a therapeutic relationship; facilitated through the continuum of awareness. For music therapists, understanding the developmental issues that may hinder self-actualization as well as understanding the relationship between musical experience and the various domains of functioning are crucial in providing effective therapy. Other approaches such as Orff music therapy (Orff 1980; Voigt 1999), and Nordoff-Robbins' music therapy (1971) also combine person-centered concepts with developmental insights, and a focus on the sensitive and responsive use of clinical improvisation techniques (Aigen 1996).

Edith Boxill's writings offer a personal, philosophical, and empathic perspective along with strong practical and methodological suggestions for developing flexible, appropriate and accountable music therapy programmes. Ultimately, however, her description of her role in music therapy as a *witness* to the efforts of her clients towards self-realization is inspiring in its humility and a fine example to music therapists of how values, training, experience, and therapeutic rigor can combine to give the best possible support to clients (Boxill 1981).

Developmental music therapy offers insights into the lifeworld of individual clients and service users by considering their needs within the context of their developing lives with reference to all of the influences on their psychological health and well-being. Additionally, DMT promotes the goal of integrating family networks within music therapy work, moving away from traditions of working with a sole child while the parent waits elsewhere during the session. Understanding cultural and environmental contexts of influence on clients allows a richer and more nuanced interaction during music therapy sessions. All human beings are developing in context through time. DMT promotes the honoring and exploration of this process.

NOTES

1. Increasingly referred to as *developmental science* (Bronfenbrenner and Evans 2000).
2. Graduates from the University of Melbourne through the 1980s and 1990s will remember that Professor Dorothy Scott actually brought a Matroyshka to her lectures to demonstrate this.

REFERENCES

Aigen, K. (1996). *Being in Music: Foundations of Nordoff-Robbins Music Therapy*. St. Louis: MMB, Music Inc.
Aldwin, C. (2012). Stress and coping across the lifespan. In: Susan Folkman (ed.), *The Oxford Handbook of Stress, Health, and Coping*. Oxford: Oxford University Press.

Arnone, J. (2014). Adolescents may be older than we think: Today 25 is the new 18, or is it? *International Journal of Celiac Disease* 2(2): 47–48.

Barnett, M.A., Deng, M., Mills-Koonce, W.R., Willoughby, M., and Cox, M. (2008). Interdependence of parenting of mothers and fathers of infants. *Journal of Family Psychology* 22(4): 561.

Beebe, B. and Lachmann, F. (1998). Co-constructing inner and relational processes: Self and mutual regulation in infant research and adult treatment. *Psychoanalytic Psychology* 15: 480–516.

Betts, J., Gullone, E., and Allen, J.S. (2009). An examination of emotion regulation, temperament, and parenting style as potential predictors of adolescent depression risk status: A correlational study. *British Journal of Developmental Psychology* 27(2): 473–485.

Boxill, E.H. (1981). A continuum of awareness: music therapy with the developmentally handicapped. *Music Therapy* 1(1): 16–22.

Boxill, E.H. (1985). *Music Therapy for the Developmentally Disabled.* Texas: Pro-Ed Inc.

Boxill, E.H. (1989). *Music therapy for living: The principle of normalization embodied in music therapy.* St Louis, MO: MMB Music.

Boxill, E.H. (1997). *The Miracle of Music Therapy.* New Hampshire: Barcelona.

Boxill, E.H. and Chase, K. (2007). *Music Therapy for Developmental Disabilities.* Texas: Pro-Ed Inc.

Briggs, C.A. (1991). A model for understanding musical development. *Music Therapy* 10(1): 1–21.

Bronfenbrenner, U. (1979). *The Ecology of Human Development.* Harvard MA: Harvard University Press.

Bronfenbrenner, U. (1995). Developmental ecology through space and time: A future perspective. In: L P. Mohen, G.H. Edler, and K. Luscher (eds), *Examining Lives in Context: Perspectives on the Ecology of Human Development*, pp. 619–647. Washington DC: American Psychological Association.

Bronfenbrenner, U. and Evans, G.W. (2000). Developmental science in the 21st century: Emerging questions, theoretical models, research designs and empirical findings. *Social Development* 9(1): 115–125.

Bronfenbrenner, U. and Morris, P.A. (2006). The bioecological model of human development. In: W. Damon, R.M. Lerner, and N. Eisenberg (eds), *Handbook of Child Psychology*, pp. 793–827. New York: Wiley.

Bryant, G.A. and Barrett, H.C. (2007). Recognizing intentions in infant-directed speech evidence for universals. *Psychological Science* 18(8): 746–751.

Dissanayake, E. (2008). If music is the food of love, what about survival and reproductive success? *Musicae Scientiae* 12(1 suppl.): 169–195.

Edwards, J. and Kennelly, J. (2011). Music Therapy for children in hospital care: A stress and coping framework for practice. In: A. Meadows (ed.), *Developments in Music Therapy Practice: Case Study Perspectives*, pp. 150–165. Gilsum, NH: Barcelona Publishers.

Erikson, E.H. and Erikson, J.M. (1998). *The Life Cycle Completed* (extended version). New York: W.W. Norton and Company.

Fagundes, C.P., Glaser, R., and Kiecolt-Glaser, J.K. (2013). Stressful early life experiences and immune dysregulation across the lifespan. *Brain, Behavior, and Immunity* 27: 8–12.

Fancourt, D., Ockelford, A., and Belai, A. (2013). The psychoneuroimmunological effects of music: A systematic review. *Brain, Behavior, and Immunity* 36: 15–26.

Feldman, R. (2007). Parent–infant synchrony and the construction of shared timing: Physiological precursors, developmental outcomes, and risk conditions. *Journal of Child Psychology and Psychiatry* 48(3–4): 329–354.

Feldman, R. and Eidelman, A.I. (2007). Maternal postpartum behavior and the emergence of infant–mother and infant–father synchrony in preterm and full-term infants: The role of neonatal vagal tone. *Developmental psychobiology* 49(3): 290–302.

Freud, S. (1979). *On sexuality: Three Essays on the Theory of Sexuality, and Other Works*. A. Richards (ed.). London: Penguin.

Hargreaves, D.J. (1986). *The developmental psychology of music*. Cambridge: Cambridge University Press.

Kohlberg, L. (1981). *The philosophy of moral development: Moral Stages and the Idea of Justice* (Essays on moral development, Vol. 1). San Fancisco: Harper and Row.

Loewy, J.V. (1995). The musical stages of speech: A developmental model of pre-verbal sound making. *Music Therapy* 13(1): 47–73.

Malloch, S. and Trevarthen, C. (eds). (2009). *Communicative musicality: Exploring the basis of human companionship*. Oxford: Oxford University Press.

McNairn, J.D., Cavanaugh, R.M., Jr and Rosenbaum, P.F. (2004). Lack of a confidant: An important marker for getting depressed or upset easily and having thoughts of self-harm in adolescents. *Journal of Adolescent Health* 34(2): 138–139.

Miyamoto, K.A. (2007). Musical characteristics of preschool-age students: A review of literature. *Update: Applications of Research in Music Education* 26(1): 26–40.

Nachmias, M., Gunnar, M., Mangelsdorf, S., Parritz, R.H., and Buss, K. (1996). Behavioral inhibition and stress reactivity: The moderating role of attachment security. *Child Development* 67(2): 508–522.

Orff, G. (1980). *The Orff Music Therapy*. Translated by Margaret Murray. New York: Schott Music Corporation.

Perls, F. (1973). *The Gestalt Approach and Eye Witness to Therapy*. Palo Alto, CA: Science and Behavior Books.

Perry, B.D. (2009). Examining child maltreatment through a neurodevelopmental lens: Clinical applications of the neurosequential model of therapeutics. *Journal of Loss and Trauma* 14(4): 240–255.

Piaget, J. (1999). The stages of the intellectual development of the child. In: A. Slater and D. Muir (eds), *The Blackwell Reader in Developmental Psychology*. London: Blackwell.

Robb, S.L. (2000). The effect of therapeutic music interventions on the behavior of hospitalized children in isolation: Developing a contextual support model of music therapy. *Journal of Music Therapy* 37(2): 118–146.

Schore, A. (2001). The effects of early relational trauma on right brain development, affect attunement, and infant mental health. *Infant Mental Health Journal* 22: 201–269.

Slee, P.T. and Shute, R. (2014). *Child Development: Thinking About Theories Texts in Developmental Psychology*. London: Routledge.

Skinner, E.A., Edge, K., Altman, J., and Sherwood, H. (2003). Searching for the structure of coping: A review and critique of category systems for classifying ways of coping. *Psychological Bulletin* 129: 216–269.

Stern, D.N. (2001). Face-To-Face Play: Its Temporal Structure as Predictor af Socioaffective Development. *Monographs of the Society for Research in Child Development* 66(2): 144–149.

Stern, D.N. (2010). *Forms of Vitality: Exploring Dynamic Experience in Psychology, the Arts, Psychotherapy, and Development*. Oxford: Oxford University Press.

Stern, D.N. (2009). *The First Relationship: Infant and Mother*. Harvard, MA: Harvard University Press.

Stern, D. (2000). *The Interpersonal World of the Infant: A View from Psychoanalysis and Developmental Psychology*, 2nd edn. New York: Karnac Books.

Trevarthen, C. (2009). The intersubjective psychobiology of human meaning: Learning of culture depends on interest for co-operative practical work–and affection for the joyful art of
good company. *Psychoanalytic Dialogues* 19(5): 507–518.

Voigt, M. (1999). Orff music therapy with multiple-handicapped children. In: T. Wigram
and J. de Backer (eds), *Clinical Applications of Music Therapy in Developmental Disability,
Paediatrics and Neurology*, pp. 166–182. London: Jessica Kingsley.

White, M. and Epston, D. (1990). *Narrative Means to Therapeutic Ends*. New York: W.W.
Norton and Company.

Zinker, J. (1977). *Creative process in Gestalt therapy*. Oxford: Brunner/Mazel.

CHAPTER 32

COMMUNITY MUSIC THERAPY

GARY ANSDELL AND BRYNJULF STIGE

INTRODUCTION

Is Community Music Therapy[1] a model, a theory, a method, or "just" a practical approach? We will suggest it's none of these, or indeed a unified or easily definable thing at all. As such CoMT is perhaps best characterized as a *movement*—a relatively unexpected yet rapidly-assembled alignment of international music therapists motivated to rethink aspects of the practice, theory, and professional identity of music therapy. Characterizing CoMT as a "social movement" (Barnes 1995) helps explain the particular pattern of its emergence and development, and the varying reactions to it. It also indicates how the movement critically refracts dimensions of the practice, discipline, and profession of international music therapy more generally in its late-modern phase—showing how it is adapting to the demands and opportunities of globalization, cultural plurality, economic crisis, and the restructuring and revisioning of health and social care services. In its short history CoMT has functioned variously as an inspiration for broader and more flexible practice, as a critique of traditional theory, as a platform for exploring fresh interdisciplinary theory, and as an instigator of inter-professional dialogue and dispute.

This chapter will attempt an overview of this wide and complex territory, orientating readers to the key events, arguments, and practices of this international movement. We will suggest that its timely appearance serves as an early indication of where music therapy can and perhaps should go next in order to adapt to and serve best the human musical needs and rights of our changing and challenged times.

EMERGENCE AND (NON)DEFINITION

Most previous developments in music therapy have tended to emerge through single (or duo) pioneers who were located in single national traditions. CoMT presents both continuity and contrast to this pattern. Brynjulf Stige (2003/2012) has shown how the "roots and routes" that prepared CoMT were fostered firstly in independent national sites, but came together in a uniquely late-modern way, exemplified by its first collective international appearance and performance at the 10th World Congress of Music Therapy in Oxford, UK in July 2002[2].

> What is this thing, "community music therapy"? Who needs another name? Who are they? How dare they! So went the high-table gossip at the Oxford Congress. The organizers had planned a 'community track' to address the professional marginalization of this aspect within the previous twenty years. Serendipitously, Ansdell's (2002) online article "Community Music Therapy and the Winds of Change" was published a month before the congress on the year-old English-language music therapy online journal, Voices <www.voices.no>—which for the first time had reached a more international readership and stoked both interest and controversy. Mercedes Pavlicevic hosted a lively panel-group at Oxford, where people variously said that CoMT was obvious, confusing, misguided, new, old, not music therapy, unnecessary, revolutionary, traditional, professional suicide, and professional salvation, as well as "a big British balloon."

Why this range of divergent and contested opinion? A little history and context can show how these reactions and interpretations epitomized the complex pattern of international music therapy as it approached a new period of change and development. As Stige has shown (2003/2012), CoMT is far from new or innovative in one sense. Its roots and ancestors can be seen in traditional healing practices, "community music" and music education traditions, and within many national traditions of music therapy such as Britain, Germany, Scandinavia, United States, South America, Australia, South Africa, Canada, and Japan.

Several key pioneers of music therapy show social and community dimensions within their early work: Florence Tyson (1968) and Edith Hillman Boxill (1985) in America; Juliette Alvin (1968), Mary Priestley (1975), Nordoff and Robbins (1965/2004, 1971/1983, 1977/2007) in America and Britain; Carolyn Kenny (1982) in Canada; even Ruud (1980, 1987/1990, 1998) in Norway; Chistoph Schwabe (Schwabe and Haase 1998) in East Germany[3]. These pioneers, and the traditions they founded, initially worked flexibly across a continuum between individualized work in discrete settings and more public and socially-oriented work. Some of these pioneers also developed theoretical approaches that included sociocultural perspectives for music therapy, attempting to broaden the prevailing tendency to psychologize or medicalize it in search of institutional support and legitimation. Traditions such as (much of) the Scandinavian and Australian practices developed and advocated broad-based and flexible approaches throughout the period 1970–2000. But mostly the international music therapy discourse and practice narrowed during the period 1980–2000 under the pressures of insitutionalization, rationalization, and medicalization; following the lead of more influential psychotherapeutic theories and norms in defining and modelling health and treatment individually and *internally*, and censoring as *unprofessional* some of the common music therapy practices such as performance or other forms of social and cultural work using music. Ironically, one of the factors behind the development of CoMT in Britain and some other European countries was that by the late 1990s some practitioners were frustrated at having to *hide* their broader context-relevant practices because these did not fit with then current theoretical and professional norms (Ansdell 2002, 2004). They described their relief at *coming out* as more flexible musician therapists through their identification with the CoMT movement, feeling that they could legitimately justify the range of activities they engaged with in their professional practice such as individual sessions, small groups, choirs, and rock bands, as belonging to the remit of music therapy work.

So whilst the varying appearances of CoMT seemed simultaneous in the early 2000s, this was partly an illusion. Each *node* had developed separately according to slightly differing national circumstances and pressures, and then became internationally visible through the sudden collective networking of these separate nodes as the performed expression of an international *zeitgeist*. The *second generation* of music therapists who were again working in broader ways in the late 1980s–1990s were also gradually mounting a gentle revolt against then current restrictive practices, disciplinary and professional norms and theories.

When further international networking began during 2002, transmission of these ideas happened relatively rapidly through a burst of practical reporting and scholarly writing in a series of books, doctoral studies and articles, mostly in English (Stige and Aarø 2012). These include: the first doctoral thesis on CoMT (Stige 2003/2012); a book *Community Music Therapy* (Pavlicevic and Ansdell 2004); a five-year international research project reported in the volume *Where Music Helps: Community Music Therapy in Action and Reflection* (Stige et al. 2010); the first textbook, *Invitation to Community Music Therapy* (Stige and Aarø 2012); a substantial profile in an influential interdisciplinary compendium, *Music, Health, and Wellbeing* (MacDonald et al. 2012); inclusion in the *Oxford Companion to Music Education* (Aigen 2012), and mention as a major *cross-current* to community music in the first major study of this area (Higgins 2012).

Whilst this wide-ranging recognition of CoMT has been relatively rapid, it is worth asking whether it adds anything to the earlier and still extant traditions of socially and culturally oriented music therapies. In simple terms, yes; CoMT has added a focal rallying-point for a maturing international movement that can align in new ways because of information technology, such as the VOICES web-journal and other international media in English. These media platforms can provide opportunities to mutually respond to shared professional and intellectual opportunities and challenges. There is also an important element of discontinuity between first-generation community-oriented approaches to music therapy and the newer CoMT discourse. This relates to how CoMT focuses on contemporary professional contexts and on new disciplinary cross-fertlilizations concerning music, sociality, and health. A common misunderstanding is that CoMT is simply *adding community*, putting traditional clinical music therapy practices and ideas into community settings as a response to de-institutionalization. But CoMT has a more radical and creative agenda than this: which is to rethink and re-practice music therapy from a contemporary ecological and sociocultural stance, and to take seriously the idea that music therapy can also work as health promotion and social activism as well as giving *individual attention* in the classic therapeutic sense. The aim was never to replace individual music therapy, but rather to re-connect it again to possibilities of broader musical-social opportunities. CoMT therefore aims to be a "joined-up music therapy" that works flexibly *across* the individual-communal continuum. This does, however, suggest a more radical questioning of whether music therapy can ever sit entirely comfortably within an individualist and medical pathology-centered treatment and evaluation framework.

An interesting tension was palpable in the early years of CoMT in relation to its definition. For some it was simply *not* music therapy, whilst others saw it as expanding or violating the conventional boundaries of music therapy. A few commentators (Ruud 2004) picked on the use of performance as its key defining characteristic, a view in turn resisted by others for both practical and theoretical reasons. But overall, and to the frustration of many, the early advocates of CoMT resisted the invitation to define it overmuch, with formulations such as CoMT is an "anti-model that encourages therapists to resist one-size-fits-all-anywhere models (of any kind) and instead to follow where the needs of clients, contexts and music leads" (Ansdell 2003). Bruscia provided a definition of CoMT in his text *Defining Music Therapy* (1998, p. 237) anticipating what was soon to flourish. Stige's doctoral survey (2003/2012, p. 426) suggested a pragmatic three-level description of CoMT as a tri-partite phenomenon operating as: (i) an area of professional practice, (ii) an emerging sub-discipline, and, (iii) an emerging professional specialty.

The resistance to premature definition was partly a political response to increasingly restrictive definitions of music therapy. Under the mantle of medical and positivist frames, music therapy in its mid-life developmental phase (1980–2000) had increasingly defined itself and its practices and techniques abstractly and independently of local and cultural circumstances. But one of CoMT's central tenets was that making music for health and well-being aims is not abstract but particular, local, circumstantial, cultural, plural and unique. So to over-define what CoMT is, or could be, *anywhere* and for *anyone* would be a contradiction in terms. It was considered instead that a *fuzzy definition* would be more honest and helpful, one that left space for local and particular clarification and exemplification in action. Another consideration was the more political one: *who* defines—experts, or participants? Whose voices are we listening to when we ask what music therapy is—to whom, where, when, and why?

It could be said that a question and not an answer gives the clearest response to those anxious to define the issues, dilemmas, aims, principles, and practices of CoMT. The crystallizing question was asked by Knut, a man with a learning disability in rural Norway in 1983. This arose spontaneously during the work of Brynjulf Stige and Ingunn Byrkjedal, and has subsequently become known as "Knut's question:"

> "Can I too play in the marching band?" Knut asks two young music therapists who have come to run conventional music therapy in a local music school (a different venue from where Knut and his friends live). On the wall of the music room are pictures of the respected local marching band, with their shiny instruments and smart uniforms. Knut identifies with them, and asks whether he and his friends will be able to play with them too? The two music therapists choose to take this question very seriously—on practical, theoretical, and political levels[4]. They expand the aims and possibilities of their music therapy project to address Knut's question—and it informs Brynjulf Stige's development of CoMT over the next thirty years. For Knut's question is at root about issues of inclusion, social justice, cultural resources, and their equitable access, aesthetics, health and well-being as being more than individual, and the possibilities of musical and social action that music therapy can either open up or fail to see or acknowledge. Knut's question importantly goes beyond considerations such as his individual "pathology," problems and limitations, and also of the aims of traditional models of therapy as healing or adjustment to society. Rather it opens up a challenging but crucial area about the relationship between music therapy and human value and needs in relation to human rights, inclusion, social and cultural health and, overall, justice.

A compromise has been established in relation to the ongoing demand for, and resistance to, definition. This is to outline various orientating principles, features, characteristics, aims, and qualities of CoMT. These help discussion of practices, ideas, and dilemmas in relation to the work without over-prescribing, limiting, or imposing abstract and non-local factors—or, importantly, suggesting that a single feature is defining. For example, in an early article "Community Music Therapy and the Winds of Change" Ansdell (2002) suggested that CoMT poses a series of critical questions that challenged the then current "consensus model" of music therapy both in practice and theory in relation to the following key areas—which are addressed to a music therapist critically considering their stance in a specific setting where music therapy might help:

- **Identities and roles**: *who am I* as a music therapist? What am I expected to *do*?
- **Sites and boundaries**: *where* do I work as a music therapist? Where are the limits to this work? What are the limits on *what* I do there?
- **Aims and means**: *what* am I trying to do as a music therapist, and *why*? *How* do I go about achieving these aims?
- **Assumptions and attitudes:** on what theoretical assumptions do I base all of the above? How do these ideas affect my attitude towards both people and music?

In relation to the emerging practices of CoMT, Ansdell's suggestion was that a transition was implied for all four domains. The overall answer to the questions was towards music-therapeutic practices that were more flexible, context-sensitive, and multiple.

Stige and Aarø (2012, pp. 18–24) give a further way of orientating a music therapist's reflections through the acronym PREPARE, which positively characterizes CoMT through a series of *qualities*:

- P = **participatory**—optimal musical participation is fostered for all, blending professional and lay expertise where possible; aiming towards democratic musical collaborations.
- R = **resource-oriented**—musical collaboration helps mobilize material, social, and cultural resources for people and places, empowering and enabling.
- E = **ecological**—music therapy practice needs to explicitly consider the nested and multiple ecological relationships between people, groups, musical things and places (seen both in their physical and sociocultural aspects).
- P = **performative**—human development, health promotion, and restoration is seen to have a key performative aspect that collaborative musical performance can mobilize. Musicking 'performs' the multiple ecological relationships a person is nested within.[5]
- A = **activist**—a natural part of a CoMT agenda is social change, on however modest a scale, because the personal, social, and political are not theoretically or practically separated. CoMT is an invitation for music therapy to become more socially conscious and involved.
- R = **reflective**—action is balanced by reflection, but not just by therapists. The participatory and democratic ethos of CoMT attempts to include all participants in ongoing reflective dialogue about aims, needs, evaluation, and understanding of work.
- E = **ethics-driven**—the ethical foundation of CoMT is negotiated and navigated in context, but is based on universal principles which try to link human needs, rights and possibilities, e.g. freedom, equality, respect, solidarity, justice.

The important point in this scheme is that no *single* quality or feature is exclusive or sequentially necessary, but that most are needed in some combination (though the blend will be locally and situationally determined). The PREPARE scheme could be held up against any example of music therapy practice and it will at least be possible to see whether there is a basic sympathy with the principles, processes and values of CoMT, even if a practitioner may not call or want to call it such explicitly. Equally, using the scheme will reveal which practices or models conflict substantially with this orientation.

A more positive broad-based definition is suggested by Stige and Aarø (2012), that "Community music therapy encourages musical participation and social inclusion, equitable access to resources, and collaborative efforts for health and well-being in contemporary societies" (p. 5). The next section will look at the flexibility and invention with which individual practitioners achieve this within very different physical, social and cultural contexts—but through work that has clear family resemblances.

PRACTICE

The approach to the identity and definition presented in the previous section copes well with the seeming paradox that as a practice CoMT necessarily works locally (according to needs, possibilities and cultural factors) but can also be recognized and identified with globally. Additionally, CoMT is not primarily theory or research-led, but mostly shapes-up locally in reference to exemplary precedents that have inspired or given a practitioner "permission" to go beyond traditional practices and limits in order to respond musically and imaginatively to the immediate needs of their context. To explore this pattern of practice we shall present two main illustrative examples in this section that were thoroughly researched by us, through ethnographically informed case studies (Stige et al. 2010).

Scrap metal[6]

Music therapist Stuart Wood tells the audience gathered on a summer night in a church near London: "Tonight's music is unique. You have not heard it anywhere before, and you will never hear it again. You may hear something extraordinary take place". The Scrap Metal concert is the culmination of an unusual Community Music Therapy project for a group of people with neurological problems, their friends and family. The audience both witnesses and participates in the event, which consists of prepared and spontaneous pieces improvised by an ensemble who play instruments made from things found in a scrap-yard—including a car bonnet, typewriter, "strung sink," bicycle wheel, and three buckets. The music is partly inspired by the spirit of John Cage and others, a "musical happening" that characterizes how sounds and people can be together, here and now.

This event has been extremely carefully prepared over a three months period by Stuart and the participants. It grew organically out of an earlier phase of this project, which had begun within a medical facility for people rehabilitating from acquired brain injury. The exploratory project was called "From Therapy to Community" (Wood et al. 2004) and had three progressive stages, progressively helping people "outwards" through musical pathways that could include 1:1 music therapy, various musical groups and learning-focused musical workshops that linked patients' rehabilitation needs with their musical preferences, and finally to performance in the community[7]. A professional motivation for the project had been the question "What comes after conventional hospital-based treatment?" When people returned home their challenges and aims rapidly became psychosocial ones: to find a place and identity within their local community, to adjust to life, to find personal strengths and access the resources of the community to support them. Could music and music therapy still help?

The seed for the Scrap Metal concert had been one patient's spontaneous comment within an individual MT with Stuart, when she said "I feel like I'm on the scrap-heap." Other patients in a group had resonated with the idea, and this led to her rehabilitation community enacting this idea and powerful symbol, and transforming it into a creative and public performance. They made a visit to a scrap-yard and turned scrap into musical instruments with the help of an expert metal-worker. They invited family, colleagues, and other musicians in the local network to be collaborators in a series of workshops which explored the musical potential of the "found objects," then prepared a set of improvisations that could form a public concert.

The workshops culminated in a concert in the church that summer evening. People described it as a transformative ritual for everyone. Distinctions between groups of people became unimportant as the musical event took over. After the concert a member of the audience tells Stuart "this is music as it should be." It was at once an aesthetic, social, and political success.

The Senior choir[8]

In a rural Norwegian town a group of older people gather weekly to sing, travelling as much as 60km from surrounding isolated areas to attend the Thursday rehearsal. Their conductor Solgunn Knardal is a music therapist. The participants range from 70–90 years old, and their health is as various as you'd expect from such a group (though only one lives in an institution, and is still able to belong to the choir despite her advanced dementia). The choir is foremost a cultural activity, and the members are certainly not defined as a "client group" or solely in relation to their health needs. They are primarily there to sing, though when asked why they attend they also link their participation to their health and well-being, on an individual and social level. There's also an activist twist to the group when they talk about how their performances prove to other (younger) people that they can still effectively contribute to social life. During the rehearsal they work hard to learn the songs. Their conductor Solgunn effortlessly combines her role of amateur choir conductor with the more therapeutic role of motivator, mediator, and manager. Her sensitivity and awareness as a music therapist comes especially into play in how she balances the musical-social strengths and challenges of this particular group. But it's also clear how there's mutual support within the group, a quality of ongoing social collaboration that helps make the choir work for everyone.

This evening the choir starts singing a humorous love song they know well called "Viss du var ei båre" ("If you were a wave"). There is joy and power in the air and they sing as if they are really surfing on the wave that they are singing about. They sing almost like they are a bunch of youngsters, falling in love for the first time.

So why is this group associated with "music therapy" at all? And is it significant that they are helped by a music therapist? Yes and no. Rather than a therapeutic group, perhaps the best description of the Senior Choir would be a "community of practice," where the social, educational, and artistic functions organically combine to endorse well-being and music. The ongoing satisfaction and success of the choir depends on the challenges of their age and health being recognized and sensitively navigated around. As a music therapist Solgunn is well-equipped to do this—trained as she is to think about the varying relationships between musicking, health, illness, and the politics of inclusion and exclusion. At varying levels—as skilled choir conductor, and as sensitive music therapist—she helps keep the choir singing and performing. And this process in turn arguably helps keep the singers healthy and happy in what could be a very challenging time of their lives. When Brynjulf Stige researches this group of singers they tell him about their love of singing, the help it gives them, how they think about each other and the choir as a whole. "When I sing," one member tells him, "then the sounds of the song carry me." Another simply says "When I sing, then I am not so alone."

The choir could be seen as providing an opportunity for cultivating care: not just from experts to patients, but also the development of a culture of mutual care between all choir participants—blending self-care, mutual care, and expert care. All of this happens relatively naturally and unselfconsciously as part of singing in a choir …

Can these two projects really be described as music therapy? If so, are they primarily treatment, rehabilitation, health promotion, or illness prevention? For whom? These questions provide a focus for some of the difficulties that CoMT brings for conventional or traditional definitions of *practice* and *outcome*. But this *problem* only emerges when the point of orientation is a traditional medical one—where problems come first, and when the treatment framework is individualistic, mechanistic, and curative. The two projects above do not look much like conventional music therapy if we think of the usual sequence in practice of (i) assessment of problems (ii) treatment of problems with targeted interventions, followed by, (iii) evaluation of outcomes. In relation to *Scrap Metal* and the *Senior Choir* the following questions also emerge:

- *Who* is the client? (Who has the 'problem', where, and when?)
- *Who* has the solution? What is it?
- *Where* is the intervention targeted?
- *How* is the benefit related to the intervention?
- *Who* is helped? (*Where* is helped? *When* is helped?)

The dilemmas that these traditional medical and therapeutic questions bring up suggests that a different relationship between music, people, community, illness, health, and well-being needs to be entertained when exploring CoMT in practice—one that is more pluralistic, holistic, and ecological.

Such an understanding emerges through the vignettes in how the following key features stand out in relation to both (themes which echo the characterizing qualities of the PREPARE acronym quoted above):

1. Attention is given across the individual-communal continuum, not losing the value of individual musical experiences and work, but going beyond an individualistic view.
2. A whole context is worked with, and worked within. You see a progressive movement "out-and-around" as musical connections help people bond and bridge socially, and as the effects of musicking ripple-out amongst the surrounding physical and symbolic community.

3. The projects are motivated and sustained by people's *musical* commitment, and the democratic musical collaboration between a wide variety of people (who vary in their health status, musical skill, and professional training and identity).
4. Performance is a central but not exclusive or defining vehicle for the work—giving people chance to perform their music *and* health, and to be witnessed by others as "musically healthy" (albeit often medically "ill").
5. Health and well-being are seen as social and cultural (rather than just biological or psychological)—and as performed in contexts of time, space, and occasion. Musical work happens alongside (and is often complementary) to medical or health work.
6. The projects are expert-guided and "assured," but not expert-led.
7. The projects are associated with ideas of music as therapeutic (in a broad sense of being beneficial for health and well-being) but not always either recognized or defined as "music therapy" as conventionally defined or understood.
8. The projects aim to foster *musical community* in as natural a way as is possible. They offer helpful ways for people to belong together, collaborate, show hospitality and celebrate collective identity, creativity, and vitality. These human needs and rights contribute directly to health promotion and illness prevention.

Underlying these particular features that are shared by most CoMT practice we suggest is a guiding principle, a set of orientating values, and some characteristic processes.

The "music centered principle" expresses the simple fact that music and musicking come first for all participants (including therapists). Problems, pathology, or limits always come second. People primarily want to make music for music's sake, and this involves a commitment to musicking together. Therapeutic, social or health gains can certainly flow from this, but are not necessarily directly attributable to it. If we ask "What do people need?" (even in some relatively extreme human situations) the answer is "to still make music." To a varying extent all participants share responsibility for musical access, hospitality, facilitation, and fruitful development of the musicking. Music therapists, as relative experts, sometimes guide or assure the safety and satisfactoriness of such work, but they seldom completely lead or determine it—the musicking is seen to have its own directions and needs that are determined by the particular constellation of people, resources and circumstances. This principle and attitude derives especially from the Nordoff-Robbins tradition of music therapy, but it can also be seen in other approaches (Aigen 2005). It contrasts sharply to music therapy practices where pathology, theories about pathology, and expert-led treatment come first, musicking second. When music comes first, anyone involved in CoMT finds themselves following where music leads—which is sometimes surprising, but usually helpful.

Built on this music-centered principle (either consciously or by default) are a set of core values that seem naturally to flow from such creative, democratic, and locally-situated musicking. The values both characterize what we *do* want (and often what sensitive musicking is serving to compensate for in a situation), and correct for, or compensate for what we *don't* want:

- *Freedom*—musicking at its best can afford freedom-*from* limitations, freedom-*to* do and be different things, and freedom-*within* the specific medium of music. Musical freedom is personal, relational, and political. It involves participation, liberation, and the balancing of individuality with social interdependence.

- *Equality*—musicking at its best affords fair play and fair share of resources, attention, connection and inclusion. Musicking brings people in from the margins, and promotes opportunity. Musical equality addresses issues of social justice.
- *Respect*—musicking at its best affords hearing and acting-towards others with respect. Hearing another person as whole, as beautiful, as gifted is to recognize them fully, to bestow personhood and dignity upon them. Musical respect fosters collaborative respect-in-action.
- *Solidarity*—musicking at its best fosters shared identity, group cohesion, a sense of hospitality, belonging, and purpose. Musical solidarity fosters and supports shared needs and rights.

As with any statement of values, there is necessarily a level of idealism and an attempt at universality. But this is tempered by how in specific local circumstances and occasions there will inevitably also be conflict and dispute concerning values. We present the four values above as orientations to practices that are relational, ecological, and negotiable. Importantly, such negotiation of the core values can happen in-and-through musical-social processes as imagined and carried-out in their local circumstances (see Ansdell 2010a, pp. 181–182 on respect; Stige and Aarø 2012, pp. 175–201 on these four values). These core values are directed not just to *human needs*, but also to *human rights*. Taking seriously the connection between needs and rights is part of the expanded frame of thinking about music therapy practice that CoMT promotes, seeing how the connections between individual and social health is rightly a political concern, if only at a local level.

A final aspect of CoMT practice is how the music-centered principle and the over-arching values show through local and pragmatic processes, formats, practicalities, and ethics. In contrast with more defined music therapy approaches, it's somewhat difficult to characterize this level, for the simple reason that CoMT is plural, variable and locally-tailored—or as Stige and Aarø (2012) comment, "In community music therapy it is not possible to explore the question of how music helps independently of the question of where music helps" (p. 230).

Stige and Aarø (2012) suggest three main types of practice in CoMT: *routes, projects,* and *programs.* The *Scrap Metal* project organically followed a client's own *musical route* from an individual session and its inspiration to include more people and end up in a public performance. Knut's question about playing in the marching band led to a formal *project* that followed an agenda and was a time-limited endeavor. The *Senior Choir* is a more conventionally structured and ongoing *programme* of activity. These three categories are not exclusive, or indeed comprehensive, but they do all share a further over-arching characteristic of CoMT process: they are all *participatory* and *reflective.* Linking with the principle and values mentioned earlier, all CoMT processes attempt to involve everyone in democratic processes to decide *what to do, how to do it (musically and otherwise), how it's going* and *what to do next.* Both human and musical processes are innately directional, orientating, and leading forwards, encouraging change. CoMT processes are ultimately "movement in the direction of health, well-being, and social-musical change" (Stige and Aarø 2012, p. 208).

How such a direction is achieved through musical means in CoMT is various and plural. Its pragmatic and locally-determined process has been usefully represented by Stuart Wood's (2006) "matrix" practice framework (see Figure 32.1).

This presents a flexible and multiple "menu" of possible *formats* of music therapy work, and of the multiple potential routes through it. Traditional music therapy arranges a few

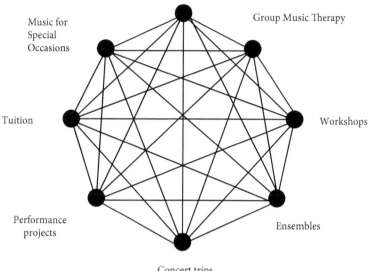

Individual Music Therapy

Music for
Special
Occasions

Group Music Therapy

Tuition

Workshops

Performance
projects

Ensembles

Concert trips

FIGURE 32.1 Matrix of Music Therapy Formats.

chosen formats in a hierarchy privileging individual work and small group work as "proper therapy" and proscribes other musical-relational formats, such as learning instruments, workshops, music for occasions, performances, as "not therapy." Wood presents in contrast the whole repertoire of ways of people making music together as potential *affordances* for music therapy work with an individual or community. They offer different possibilities for different situations, and different routes. The matrix model follows the music-centered principle, in that *any* form of musical experience is potentially helpful—but without imposing a standard or hierarchical sequence of process. It also illustrates the point that CoMT is potentially able to accommodate steps in an individual client's development *and* attend to how this interfaces with the interdependent musical resources and potentials of a broader community.

Such variability of process clearly has implications for other aspects of professional practice, but again these aspects have led to illuminating thinking that has challenged dogma and encouraged reflective pragmatism. CoMT has replaced the traditional therapeutic norms and rules of boundaries with a notion of "safe flexibility," where boundaries of time, place, and person are reflected on situationally and pragmatically. Professional ethics takes the same turn: instead of "you must not" it is a case of "in this place, time, situation is it wise to/ not wise to ... ?" Ethics are human, negotiated, and contextual, not institutional or theoretical. Often CoMT projects bring difficult human and organizational predicaments, but this is part of the territory, and the negotiation of conflict and misunderstanding a necessary and fruitful process.

A final aspect of process is the reflection on whether the work is successful or useful. Traditionally (and especially within the medical model) such questions are part of a system of evaluation, outcome research and debates on efficacy and effectiveness. CoMT practices and attitudes tend to problematize each of these. Who is a project successful for? In what, and in whose, terms? When does the work end? Who decides on its value? Outside of the medical model's mapping of assessment, treatment and evaluation it's often not so easy to answer such questions directly and singularly. In CoMT work aims, processes and outcomes can be multiple and distributed over time, space and person—and as such are non-linear, continuous and cyclical. To focus on just one simple example in relation to this: when should members of the *Senior Choir* stop attending? As Stige and Aarø suggest, "people come to a band or a choir week after week; they do not leave because they feel better but stay because they feel good" (2012, p. 229). This may create practical problems for funding, but it per- haps represents a more realistic reality of how music helps in many situations, and how we can promote and defend this in terms of the resources society is willing to devote to musi- cal routes to health promotion and rehabilitation. The development of the argument over evaluation and outcome in relation to CoMT is in its early days, but it could contribute to a broader debate on the overlap between arts, therapy, and public health.

DISCIPLINE

As a discipline CoMT can be seen to be developing a particular body of knowledge about the connections between people, music, health, illness, community, society, and therapy. One of CoMT's contributions to the broader discipline of music therapy has been to question what theory can and should do in relation to practice. As Ansdell and DeNora (2012) wrote in relation to CoMT: "what is required is not a theory that specifically directs or explains practice 'non-musically', but one which can orientate practice within a broader theoretical territory in which flexible musical-social practice can 'explain itself' without being reduced to the instrumentalization of a single theory of any type" (p. 106). CoMT has functioned as a "Trojan paradigm" (Ansdell 2014b) smuggling in a more sociocultural and ecological orien- tation into a theoretical landscape that had increasingly limited its view of people and music to individualist and *internalist* psychological or physiological parameters. The newer ecolog- ical view that CoMT has promoted helps thinking about the broader issues that are increas- ingly relevant to a music therapist's current professional work such as the sociocultural nature of illness, recovery, and well-being—and how musicking is naturally part of this. This turn aligns well with parallel theoretical shifts in other disciplines such as music education, community music, music psychology, musicology, and in many health-based disciplines.

As the various forms of practice have emerged so too has new theory—both inductively from practice, and as result of well-chosen abductions from current interdisciplinary theory that has presented a good "match" for, and further illumination of, practice. In this process CoMT has developed a new conversation with several perspectives from the humanities and social sciences that conventional music therapy had not previously tapped and which in some cases has been a mutually creative venture. A new body of knowledge is gradually accumulating within CoMT that is serving the broader music therapy discipline by provid- ing alternate and complementary perspectives on music, health, therapy, and community.

In 2003 the Norwegian Research Council funded a major study to explore Community Music Therapy—in practice, and in theory. The study facilitated collaboration between four international centers, exploring how a range of projects—in Norway, South Africa, Israel, and England—could help with the theoretical elaboration of CoMT. As with the practice of CoMT, the results of this study reflected both continuity and innovation in relation to music therapy theory. Each research participant brought a particular theoretical contribution (which often reflected an ongoing interdisciplinary dialogue that they were involved with) and the group together worked over a four-year period to synthesize perspectives in search of a more inclusive theoretical view of CoMT. The resulting book—*Where Music Helps* (Stige et al., 2010)—brings together perspectives from current music studies, psychobiology, community psychology, music sociology, and the sociology of health and illness. This theoretical expedition proved fruitful.

CoMT has encouraged a rethinking of three key interdependent dimensions of relevance to contemporary music therapy: (i) health and well-being, (ii) community, music, and therapy, (iii) music and musicking. We will tackle each of these individually to begin with (though in the space available we will only be able to give a brief outline of these complex areas[9]).

Rethinking health and well-being

A mainstream biomedical/psychological framework cannot serve as an adequate primary guide to the rationale, processes, and outcomes of the broader family of CoMT practices because of its underlying individualist, "internalist," and reductionist tendencies. The medical model attempts to locate and define illness or disease (or disability, impairment, abnormality), to treat and ideally cure it. Its focus is individual, its diagnoses aim to be objective and causal, and its solutions mechanical and precisely targeted at negative symptoms. It necessarily focuses on what is wrong or lacking, and tends to define health in binary terms—as "present" or "absent." As powerful and necessary as medical science will always remain, it is increasingly seen not to be a sufficient singular approach to health overall. A few simple questions can highlight this; for example if we ask *when* are we healthy? And *where?* This introduces occasion and situation into health, and suggests how it may vary across parameters that are not solely material or biological (Ansdell and DeNora 2012). Further, if someone says that they feel healthiest when they are singing despite the fact that their chronic objective symptoms do not change, how does this inflect what "being healthy" means? The particular problem of understanding "mental health" are particularly illuminating when considering the limitations of the medical and organic model of health (Bentall 2010). The reality of health is perhaps better understood as multidimensional—there is no "one form" of health that exists outside of a relational, social and cultural context.

CoMT practices and attitudes do not sit easily with an exclusively medical model of health. The CoMT movement has turned instead to alternatives such as the "ecological model" (Bronfenbrenner 1979) which links health with social, cultural, and political factors. These factors often negatively influence health—through poor physical and social environments, the impact of injustice or deprivation, or through how stigmatizing social attitudes and lack of support create and emphasize disability and exclusion. But considered positively, physical, and cultural resources, social processes and attitudes can be powerfully mobilized to support and develop health. Increasingly the word and concept *well-being* is used to indicate those aspects of health that exist beyond biological functioning, or normative views of an ideal life. Instead, "well-being" promotes how "health" and "illness" are not necessarily opposites, but exist on an ever-shifting continuum. It emphasizes individual and collective human flourishing, whatever people's objective health status is. It concentrates on *qualities* of living, on *when* and *how* and *where* we feel well, satisfied, fulfilled, or transcend ourselves (even perhaps when we are seriously ill, or dying). We need, that is, a more performative picture of "being well" that emerges when there is an optimal arrangement of relational, social and spiritual dimensions. We do not "have" well-being, but it emerges *between* us and the people, things, events, and processes of our lives.

CoMT focuses on how music helps well-being in this sense, how it helps create *musical flourishing*[10] (Ansdell and DeNora 2012)—an ecological state that includes "performing health," coping-in-a-situation, or finding wellness for a while whilst involved in musicking. These are important achievements in situations where health challenges are chronic, not acute; where contextual factors seem intractable; where hope is a key necessary ingredient for change; where mutual care a more realistic path than cure.

The rethinking of health CoMT engages with looks beyond the narrow definition of health as the absence of disease, or indeed of any sense of normative physical, mental, or social functioning. Instead it understands health and well-being as an emergent phenomenon and a *situated process* within a complex ecology of relational, social, and spiritual dimensions. Well-being is an experiential quality of *being-well-in-a-situation*; one which is necessarily mediated by social, cultural, and political factors: *who* we are with; *when* things come together; *what* resources we have access to; and *how* we are seen and treated by others. Both health and well-being can be seen to emerge from the creative couplings between people, practices, and modes of experience.

Consequently, as Stige and Aarø write, "the purpose of community music therapy is not primarily healing and treatment but the promotion of health in the widest possible meaning of the word" (2012, p. 59). Stige (2002; 2012) has suggested the concept of "health musicking" to convey this project—an idea that could also apply across other activities that use music as part of rehabilitation, prevention and promotion, and which CoMT often collaborates with as part of a broader agenda of situated help. "Musical well-being" encapsulates how music often helps by capturing health as it flies.

Rethinking community, music, and therapy

Most traditional music therapy has based its practice on individualized treatment, and its theory on relational or group theories from psychology. Emerging CoMT practices necessitated theorizing also about community, culture, and society, and rethinking the relationships between individual, community, music, health, and therapy. Fortunately, the latest perspectives from disciplines such as community psychology, the sociology of health, anthropology, community music theory, social work, and health promotion have helped this rethinking.

The conceptual shift has been away from a tendency to polarize individuality/society and towards the more ecological conception of an individual-communal continuum that we all continually travel across, and within which our lives are naturally nested at a variety of interdependent levels. Human potential, problems, and challenges take shape within this social and material ecology, leading to the stance that a community is potentially something that needs working *with*, and not just within. Increasingly theory and research in a variety of disciplines has shown how health and well-being are not primarily individual properties, but are intimately related to context, and to the basic social needs to participate, be connected, belong, be respected, share experiences and rituals, cooperate and collaborate, and have the opportunity to practice mutual care and recognition, hospitality and conviviality. Loss of any of these basic needs through illness, disability, deprivation, oppression, or any other circumstance leads to a substantial threat to health and well-being—both for individuals and for communities as a whole. Isolation, and loss of social identity and social connections have been shown to seriously undermine health[11].

"Community" is admittedly a broad and ambivalent concept that has its problems and critics (Esposito 2010; Higgins 2012).[12] But it serves well in characterizing a non-individualist sense of people sharing things in common, belonging and acting-together in some way in a particular location and context, and of this togetherness having a particular quality. Within CoMT the word and concept "community" is used in a variety of senses:

- *communities of place* where people live together locally;
- *communities of identity* where belonging rests on shared characteristics, beliefs or interests;
- *communities of circumstance* where people live temporarily together because of illness, imprisonment, migration, or extreme event;
- *communities of practice* where people build belonging through shared projects or rituals.

When music therapists work in broader ways they often discover how these categories overlap or complexify, but are potential practical and conceptual sites where music can help through strengthening the sense of belonging and cultivating shared experience, identity, inclusion, or more public forms of activism.

Working musically both in and with communities shows-up some of the recognized "mechanisms" or rituals of social and community life, and these have gradually become part of the evolving theoretical discourse of CoMT. The social phenomenology of music itself shows how musical togetherness and grouping is possible in the first place through how music works (Ansdell 2014a). Concepts from social, anthropological, and political discourses have been fruitfully applied to CoMT projects and their theorization. In particular: social networks and support, social capital, empowerment, social exclusion/inclusion, social rituals and performances, hospitality, and *communitas* (Stige 2002; Krüger 2004, 2012; Ansdell 2010b; Jampel 2006, 2011; Storsve et al. 2010; O'Grady 2009; Procter 2004, 2006; Curtis and Mercado 2004; Vaillancourt 2009; Oosthuizen 2006; Ruud 2010; Rolvsjord 2010; Soshensky 2011). None of these theories intend to form a single conceptual base for CoMT, but each serves in the role of providing a *sensitizing theory*, revealing ways in which music therapy can engage and potentially enhance community experience and well-being through: (1) creating contacts, relationships, and networks, (2) furthering respect, reciprocity, and mutual care, (3) decreasing isolation, disconnection, and exclusion.

As stated in the previous section, such work is not necessarily targeted at the level of individual improvement or cure. Rather, it addresses what can help maintain, or partially restore, a level of individual and community health and well-being. CoMT is multi-dimensional involvement, not just a "social intervention." It is a way of reaching the essential flow of social life that transcends the individual/community binary. At this level CoMT can also make a recognizable contribution to health promotion and illness prevention (areas that traditional music therapy clearly has an impact on, but has not acknowledged or theorised enough previously). The theoretical rethinking cued by CoMT has re-emphasized that it is not possible to address health and well-being fully without addressing aspects of community, justice, and equity. "Therapy" is therefore understood in a broad sense, and perhaps in a way closer to the original Greek *therapeutes*—the guide who walks besides and attends to those in need, rather than the expert healer with superior knowledge who intervenes but cannot accompany the person for long.

Rethinking music and musicking

The underlying music-centered principle of CoMT necessitates a suitable theory of people, music, and well-being to support the approach. Fortunately, a radical rethinking of music in relation to personal and social life has proved highly relevant and inspiring for CoMT (Ansdell 2004, 2010a,b; Ruud 2010). This shift has coming from a synthesis of the insights from the "new musicology," anthropological studies of cross-cultural and sub-cultural musics and practices, popular music studies, social psychology of music, music education, and music sociology. Together this has brought a reorientation towards understanding and studying music-in-*action,* or *musicking* (Small 1998; Elliott 1995) in relation to people, context, and culture. This has functioned as a "correction" to how traditional music theory reified musical objects and largely omitted their contexts of performance, use and meaning (Cook 1998, 2012).

Traditional approaches to music therapy have been heavily influenced by the way classical musicological discourse theorized music as an abstract object (or set of part-objects such as frequencies, melodies, rhythms) that people contemplate, use or research. A second influence came from the more scientific view of first-generation music psychology that viewed music as a stimulus, a direct physical influence that "does" things to people in a relatively passive way. Only relatively recently has a third, more performative and ecological way of thinking about people and music emerged which suggests how music (as *musicking*) is better thought of as something more interactive, context-dependent, plural, and distributed—a dynamic web of connectedness happening between musical people, musical things, and musical situations[13]. As the music educationalist Margaret Barrett writes: "Ecological thinking might be viewed as a striving for connectedness, for the establishment of a relationship of the self to the interconnecting systems in which we live and work: cognitive, emotional, social, cultural, physical" (2012, p. 209). In this way CoMT is a striving for human musical connectedness, in the service of human flourishing. In this service there is a clear continuity between where, when and how music helps in music therapy, and in everyday life (Ansdell 2014a).

Ecological models of music and musicking have been outlined by Small (1998), Clarke (2005), Windsor (2012), DeNora (2011a), and Barrett (2012) in relation to the authors' various professional fields. All share in common the need to recognize and theorize how music works within and amongst the multiple physical and social relationships we live in and through. Ecological modelling gives an effective theoretical platform for exploring the range of "music and health ecologies" that become visible through music therapy practice (Ansdell 2014a). Such an ecological model also allows a range of diverse theory and research in music studies to be incorporated. This includes theorizing music as the essence of relational and social life (Sawyer 2003; McPherson et al. 2012; Pitts 2012; Cook 2012; DeNora

2011a,b), and the development of theoretical models linking musicality (as a psychobiologi-cal platform) to the sociocultural dimensions of musicianship and musicking: "communica-tive musicality" (Malloch and Trevarthen 2009) and "collaborative musicking" (Pavlicevic and Ansdell, 2009).

Two key ideas related to an ecological model of musicking have been especially important for CoMT. These logically follow on from each other. Firstly, the concept pairing of *musi-cal affordances/musical appropriations* was developed in the music sociology of Tia DeNora (2000, 2003, 2011a). A "musical affordance" is what a particular musical property, process, or situation offers or makes possible—but only insofar as our perceptual and cultural capac-ity can pick this up (i.e. it is personal and situational not general and abstract). Likewise, a "musical appropriation" is a person's unique and active "taking" and working-with what's offered by such a musical property or situation. DeNora's theory is of music resolutely *in action*, underpinned by the new sociology's insistence that cultural material is not just a *reflective* material (of social or psychological reality) but is an active constituent in building and maintaining our psychosocial life together. We can therefore only know what a musical affordance is by participating in, or directly witnessing its action consequences for a particu-lar person or situation.

This leads to a second key concept that goes beyond the traditional binary of "musi-cal/extramusical." The theory of musical affordance/appropriation suggests how seem-ingly "non-musical other things" (such as movements, emotions, communications, identities, public events) take shape in relation to seemingly "purely musical things" (sound-ing forms and their performances). But these benefits are neither exactly musical nor "non/ extra-musical"—that is, "outside" of the musical. The term *"para-*musical" has been sug-gested as an appropriate term for this latter "go-with" class of phenomena (Stige et al. 2010, pp. 297–299). "Para" as a prefix suggests "besides," "alongside," on the border, or connect-ing through or between. The realm of the para-musical therefore indicates the full range of the "more-than-musical" phenomena—be these physical or mental, individual, relational, social, or political phenomena. In this model, music is far from being a physical stimulus leading to predictable outcomes. It "'acts,' rather, only 'in concert' with the material, cultural, and social environments in which it is located" (DeNora 2003, p. 157) – where the musical and para-musical can seldom be separated.

CoMT and research

Together the three basic areas of theoretical rethinking outlined above give a more ecological understanding of music and health that then serves as a framework both for practice-based reflection and for more systematic research-based inquiry. The research agenda of CoMT takes a constructivist and ecological starting-point—in terms of why research is done, where, when, and how. It attempts to stay true to the principles, values, and practice orienta-tions of CoMT outlined in earlier sections. Stige and Aarø (2012, p. 235) suggest thinking of "research-related practice" rather than "research-based practice" in relation to CoMT. As such, studies so far have taken a perspective that could be characterized as predominantly qualitative, ethnographic, participatory, and activist—qualities that demonstrate how "we also do research because we want to change a situation, not only because we want to describe, explain, or evaluate it" (Stige and Aarø 2012, p. 237).

The research agenda in CoMT is in its early days, but a research-base in the discipline is steadily accumulating. CoMT research is not intended primarily to direct or justify practice by providing direct causal evidence for health benefits of musicking. Its research perspective instead problematizes this approach, and explores alternative perspectives for demonstrating the relevance, value, and accountability of music therapy practice (Ansdell and DeNora, forthcoming; DeNora 2013; Stige and Aarø 2012).

PROFESSION

> When I first heard of CoMT I thought "that's the very *last* thing we need now!" Here we are struggling to keep the professional reputation of music therapy; to persuade the medical insurances to pay for it; to convince interdisciplinary colleagues that it is a distinct area of practice that is grounded in evidence-based research and professional ethics. And my first impression was that CoMT seemed to work against all of these! But now I'm beginning to see that it's not so simple as this—music therapy survives and prospers by adapting and rethinking itself too—not just defending itself in traditional ways.[14]

As a profession, music therapy can be understood as a community of practitioner-scholars with a recognized education that qualifies them for a skilled role, with obligations and rights in relation to clients, colleagues, other professions, and the public (Stige 2003/2012, p. 221). Obviously, the members of a profession do not all meet each other personally, so the community is imaginary in many respects. It evolves around arenas of communication, such as professional journals and conferences. Usually a culture of commitment and identity develops. This is not to suggest that there cannot be controversies. Certainly, CoMT is part of controversies at several levels within the profession of music therapy. Here, then, we want to examine what we could learn from the controversies about profession and professionalization that CoMT has sparked, or perhaps just illuminated.

Music therapy in the "system of professions"

One context to consider here is Abbott's (1988) theory of the "system of professions." Abbott used the term *jurisdiction* to describe how (disciplined) practice and profession are related. The jurisdiction defines the "territory" under the authority of each profession. Professionalization, then, can be understood as the fight for monopoly; each profession strives for authorized monopoly of judgment for an area of original responsibility. Abbot underlines that this is only one possible strategy. There are several types of jurisdiction. Only full jurisdiction involves control over a territory, as described above. There are alternative strategies such as subordination, division of labor (according to specific competencies), and intellectual jurisdiction (superior knowledge in a field of competition). Given these distinctions, it seems clear that CoMT is incompatible with strategies of professionalization that involve striving for full jurisdiction or for subordination to the medical profession. It is not equally clear that CoMT is incompatible with division of labor or intellectual jurisdiction. Whatever appraisal one might have of this, we find it more realistic to consider CoMT in the light of re-professionalization than de-professionalization.

When Abbott (1988) used the phrase *system of professions,* he highlighted how professions compete against one another for access to funds and even access to the beneficiaries of service, the clients. The moves of one profession affect the opportunities of other professional groups. For instance, if one group attempts to increase its market value by keeping its numbers low, this might create space for other groups to enter areas that the first profession ignores. The image that comes to mind is that of a game where colleagues within a profession become team mates who work together in order to win over the other teams. If some team mates start looking in different directions, then, the majority might feel that these people are not being helpful to the cause. They are perhaps even creating problems for the profession's possibilities of succeeding. An example of how such professional forces can be seen in action is shown by how the British music therapy profession has responded defensively to CoMT (Barrington 2005, 2008; Ansdell and Pavlicevic 2008; Procter 2008).

If and when the competition between professions becomes too obvious to the public, there are usually criticisms suggesting that the professionals are too self-preoccupied. Abbott (1988) claims, however, that the competition should not be understood in the light of power dynamics only. Professions are subjected to a range of contradictory pressures and he argues that naïve notions of idealistic servers of clients and community should not be replaced by cynical critique suggesting that the professions are just serving their own interests. If we relate this to music therapy, we probably do well in considering the possibility that CoMT is not always a selfless radical practice; it might also be a response to changes in society that open up new possibilities for creating interesting jobs for music therapists. Therefore, traditional professional issues such as identity, education, and ethics are not made irrelevant by CoMT. On the contrary, CoMT illuminates the relevance of rethinking these issues continuously.

Identity and flexibility

CoMT's relevance in contemporary societies relates to the increasing request for participatory and empowering practices focusing on people's resources in everyday contexts. The emergence of CoMT is one possible response to this, with a particular focus on music's social and communal possibilities. This implies a contextualized transformation of music therapy, and it is not possible to identify one specific professional identity that could be said to be essential for CoMT practices. What seems to be shared is a readiness to negotiate roles and identities (Stige and Aarø 2012, p. 272). Procter (2008) uses the term *reflexive adaptability* to describe what he considers a necessity and an ideal in this situation. As music therapists we should always be willing to reconsider our professional role in relation to the changing needs of a situation, but this flexibility should be informed by values and knowledge tested in dialogue, it should not be automatic or superficial. According to this argument, CoMT is not a fanciful invention that requires flexibility from the music therapist. Rather, it is a movement that reflects developments in society, when interpreted in ways that value empowerment and participation.

When it comes to rewards, the situation is highly complex. Perhaps some of the music therapists that have been inspired by CoMT are idealists more interested in the rewards of engaged musicianship, activism, and mutual collaboration than in the rewards of professional status and stability. A whole profession could not be idealistic in this way, but instead of thinking of those advocating CoMT as threats we could review how they contribute to keeping the profession at the edge, searching for the productive dynamics of hybridity. Instead of thinking of music therapy as an established health profession, music therapists could also keep alive a creative interplay between their identities as musicians and as health workers. Instead of just focusing on the problems of the individual, they could also work for social change and nurture resources at individual as well as communal levels. Throughout the chapter we have described theoretical and political-ethical arguments that support the relevance of this line of thinking. The question a practicing music therapist might ask is: is there anybody around me supporting this too? It is hard to change the world all by yourself.

Again, the national and political contexts vary considerably. In some countries there are systems of reimbursement that mainly focus on individualized health care services, so that music therapists wanting to work more broadly need to look for NGO's or other organizations trying to establish alternatives. In other countries, public health programs and social change initiatives trying to challenge health inequities are actively supported by government authorities, so that music therapists might be able to find a place for their work within these contexts. In either case, CoMT shows how there are alternatives to the idea of a specialized position within an established hierarchy of professions; music therapists could also develop their professional identity within situated partnerships (Stige and Aarø 2012, pp. 274–278).

Competencies, training, and education

Any reconsideration of roles and responsibilities require relevant competencies. The culturally situated practice of CoMT is no exception. With Adrienne (2006), we must ask what skills and theories music therapists need in order to develop situated and collaborative practice. Aigen (2012) suggests that music therapists need to learn how to navigate in a landscape where several professions have overlapping roles. Vaillancourt (2009) advocates the integration of practical and reflective components with the purpose of developing deeper understanding of oppression. As mentioned above, Stige and Aarø (2012, pp. 274–278) suggest that we need to educate music therapists to engage in flexible partnerships. Eventually, several of these suggestions could also be linked with concerns about equality and diversity when it comes to access to professional training. For instance: from which ethnic groups and socioeconomic classes do we recruit our students? Such questions are far from insignificant in relation to the visions that inform CoMT.

Issues of competencies and education are of course closely linked to the questions discussed above; to what kind of training leads to the recognition that music therapy as a profession strives for in society. In countries where music therapy is state-registered as an allied health profession, there might for instance be pressures in the direction of including substantial information about various disorders and their therapeutics in the training of music therapists. This could hardly harm? It depends. Given the complexities of CoMT practice, we need to review whether music therapy educations set aside enough time and space for the specific competencies this kind of practice requires:

> To practice community music therapy involves working with varied situations where the safety and possibilities of both individual and group should be managed. There will be intergroup processes to deal [with] as well as a broader ecology, including deliberations with the

public and/or the involved partnerships. All this should evolve around solid social-musical work, respecting the often diverse cultural backgrounds and preferences of participants. It is not obvious that this practice requires less competency and skills than individualized music therapy where you work with one client at the time or perhaps a small group in the safe environment of the music therapy room

(Stige and Aarø 2012, p. 280)

At least four alternatives are able to be imagined concerning training in CoMT: first, aspects of CoMT could be integrated as topics within various subjects of existing educations. Second, CoMT could be developed as a separate subject within existing education programmes. Third, separate education courses in CoMT could be established, and, fourth, continuing education courses could be established for practitioners that already have a degree in music therapy. As Stige and Aarø (2012, p. 279) note, there is currently little research to support a description of what the most common alternative is in various countries or a reflection about the advantages and disadvantages of each alternative. What seems clear is that to the degree the education and supervision of music therapists is transformed by CoMT, it will prepare candidates for a professional role where the notion of expertise is transformed too. The idea of individual expertise allowing interventions to proceed from the therapist is complemented by the idea of expertise in partnership, where helpful involvement emerges from within a community of practice.

Professional ethics in the context of collaboration

In CoMT boundaries of time and space are often flexible. In a general reflection about developments in late modern societies, Bauman (1993) suggests that as "walls" fall down ethical dilemmas pop up. If CoMT involves emancipation from some established standards of practice, it does not mean that ethics loses its topicality. Instead, ethical issues become crucial in new ways and must be dealt with in new ways.

Stige and Aarø (2012, pp. 281–285) have developed a notion of "participatory ethics" for CoMT, where norms such as *exclusivity* (the avoidance of dual relationships) are replaced by more adaptable norms, such as *collaborative reflexivity* (the willingness to consider one's position and influence carefully and to develop these considerations through communication and collaboration). There is in many countries a need to revisit existing ethical guidelines, then, if they are based upon the traditions of individualized practice in clinical contexts (Aigen 2004). Participatory ethics involve a transformation of our understanding of professional responsibility:

Ethical performance includes a range of actions, from showing respect in interpersonal dialogues to showing engagement in relation to situations of social injustice. … we could say that ethical performance involves showing respect in a context where solidarity is nurtured by the acknowledgement of other people's rights to freedom and equality

(Stige and Aarø 2012, p. 284)

If we link back to the concerns about music therapy in the "system of professions" described earlier in this section, we can see that the movement of CoMT requests less of a competitive edge between professions and more of a collaborative ethos. This is of course an idealistic description. We need to examine in context what practical and political conditions could enable such a transition.

CONCLUSION AND PROSPECTS

We suggest that CoMT has attempted a practical and theoretical re-imagining and re-orientating of contemporary music therapy based on the following key commitments:

- a critical response to *individualism* in attitudes towards therapy, health and well-being, that has led to considering how music can help both people *and* places; personal problems *and* their associated psycho-sociocultural ecologies; individuals *and* communities; personal problems *and* public concerns.
- A practical and theoretical defence of the notion that musicking is performative, and that it helps link together the individual-communal continuum; and that this largely non-verbal performative dimension is as therapeutically important as is its ability to sometimes afford symbolic representation and reflection.
- An attempt to bring about a better relationship between the possibilities of specialist music therapy and the broader scope of "health musicking" and music in everyday life practices. This can forge a more productive link between professional and lay expertise.
- To relate human needs to a wider perspective on human rights—emphasizing that "musical justice" is often rightly part of a music therapist's agenda. CoMT is a musical call for the universal values of social justice, human potential, and mutual care.

This agenda is showing signs of gradually influencing the diverse international community of music therapy. As such, some would say that CoMT has perhaps already served its function as a movement—things *have* changed in people's attitudes, ideas and practices in relation to how music, and the specialist help that music therapists are able to give, can contribute to our troubled world. However, there are few reasons to expect that a critical response to individualism and an over-reliance on the medical model will become irrelevant any time soon. We might need to replace the idea of linear progress with that of endless circular struggles between individualized and socialized health strategies, professional and lay autonomy, and so on. Exploring how "community," "music" and "therapy" make sense together—in practice and in theory—will continue to be a necessary and fruitful enterprise.

NOTES

1. "CoMT" henceforth. The title is found both capitalized and uncapitalized in the literature.
2. See the online journal *Voices: A World Forum for Music Therapy* (<www.voices.no>), 12(2) (2012) for accounts of the 10th World Congress.
3. Scwhabe's work in this area was developed in East Germany in the 1970s and 1980s, while the reference here is to a book published (with Ulrike Haase as co-author) after the unification of the two German states.
4. For the details of this case see Stige (2003/2012, p. 20 ff. and Chapter 6).

5. The term "musicking," music understood as situated activity, is discussed later in the chapter, in the section on how CoMT's invites rethinking of the discipline.

6. The complete study of this case can be found in Stige et al. (2010), Chapter 11: "Can everything become music? *Scrap Metal* in Southern England."

7. The *musical pathways* scheme has been effectively described in Wood's (2006) *musical matrix* model which is explored in a later section.

8. The complete study of this case can be found in Stige et al. (2010), Chapter 17: "Caring for music: the *Senior Choir* in Sandane, Norway."

9. More comprehensive treatments of each can be found in: Aasgaard (2004); Ansdell and Pavlicevic (2005); Pavlicevic and Ansdell (2009); Stige and Aarø (2012); Stige et al. (2010); Ansdell and DeNora (2012); DeNora (2013); Ansdell (2014).

10. "Flourishing" is the best translation of Aristotle's holistic concept *eudaimonia*, which lies at the root of contemporary thinking about wellbeing (Vernon, 2008; Ansdell and DeNora, 2012).

11. See Stige and Aarø (2012), Chapter 4, "Community and Social Resources" for a summary of the research on this area as relevant to discussion of CoMT.

12. For a critical discussion of the notion of "community" in CoMT, see Baines (2013).

13. Stige (2002, pp. 211–213) suggests a mnemonic for identifying and thinking-about the interdependent dimensions of a musical ecology, using "5 As": Arena; Agenda; Agents; Activity; Artefacts. In a given occasion of musicking how are these five dimensions interacting—for better or worse? How together do they create meaning and effects?

14. This statement (2012) from a music therapist in Germany is typical of the professional response to CoMT in the last decade.

References

Aasgaard, Trygve (2004). A Pied Piper among White Coats and Infusion Pumps: Community Music Therapy in a Paediatric Hospital Setting. In: M. Pavlicevic and G. Ansdell (eds), *Community Music Therapy*, pp. 147–166. London: Jessica Kingsley Publishers.

Abbott, Andrew (1988). *The System of Professions. An Essay on the Division of Expert Labor.* Chicago: The University of Chicago Press.

Adrienne, Jennifer (2006). A Feminist Sociology of Professional Issues in Music Therapy. In: S. Hadley (ed.), *Feminist Perspectives in Music Therapy*, pp. 41–62. Gilsum, NH: Barcelona Publishers.

Aigen, Kenneth (2004). Conversations on Creating Community: Performance as Music Therapy in New York City. In: M. Pavlicevic and G. Ansdell (eds), *Community Music Therapy*, pp. 186–213. London: Jessica Kingsley Publishers.

Aigen, Kenneth (2005). *Music-Centered Music Therapy.* Gilsum, NH: Barcelona Publishers.

Aigen, Kenneth (2012). Community Music Therapy. In: G. McPherson and G. Welch (eds), *Oxford Handbook of Music Education*, pp. 138–54. New York: Oxford University Press.

Alvin, Juliette (1968). Changing Patterns in Music Therapy—The Mental Patient and Community Care in England. In: G.E. Thayer (ed.), *Music in Therapy*, pp. 389–393. New York: Macmillan Publishing.

Ansdell, Gary (2002). Community Music Therapy and the Winds of Change—A Discussion Paper. *Voices: A World Forum for Music Therapy*. Retrieved January 12, 2013, from: <https://normt.uib.no/index.php/voices/article/view/83/65>.

Ansdell, Gary (2003). The Stories We Tell—Some Meta-Theoretical Reflections on Music Therapy. *Nordic Journal of Music Therapy* 12(2): 152–159.

Ansdell, Gary (2004). Rethinking Music and Community: Theoretical Perspectives in Support of Community Music Therapy. In: M. Pavlicevic and G. Ansdell (eds), *Community Music Therapy*, pp. 65–90. London: Jessica Kingsley Publishers.

Ansdell, Gary (2010a). Belonging through Musicing: Explorations of Musical Community. In: B. Stige, G. Ansdell, C. Elefant, and M. Pavlicevic (eds), *Where Music Helps. Community Music Therapy in Action and Reflection*, pp. 41–62. Aldershot, UK: Ashgate Publishing Limited.

Ansdell, Gary (2010b). Where Performing Helps: Processes and Affordances of Performance in Community Music Therapy. In: B. Stige, G. Ansdell, C. Elefant, and M. Pavlicevic (eds), *Where Music Helps. Community Music Therapy in Action and Reflection*, pp. 161–188. Aldershot, UK: Ashgate Publishing.

Ansdell, Gary (2014a). *How Music Helps: In Music Therapy and Everyday Life*. Farnham: Ashgate Publishers.

Ansdell, Gary (2014b). Revisiting 'Community music therapy and the winds of change'(2002): an original article and a retrospective evaluation. *International Journal of Community Music* 7(1): 11–45.

Ansdell, Gary and DeNora, Tia (2012). Musical flourishing: Community Music Therapy, Controversy, and the cultivation of wellbeing. In: R. MacDonald, G. Kreutz, and L. Mitchell (eds), *Music, Health and Wellbeing*. Oxford: Oxford University Press.

Ansdell, Gary and DeNora, Tia (forthcoming). *Musical Pathways for Mental Health*. Farnham: Ashgate Publishers.

Ansdell, Gary and Pavlicevic, Mercédès (2005). Musical Companionship, Musical Community: Music Therapy and the Process and Values of Musical Communication. In: D. Miell, R. MacDonald, and D. Hargreaves (eds), *Musical Communication*, pp. 193–213. Oxford: Oxford University Press.

Ansdell, Gary and Pavlicevic, Mercédès (2008). Responding to the Challenge: Between Boundaries and Borders (Response to Alison Barrington). *British Journal of Music Therapy* 22(2): 73–76.

Baines, Sue (2013). Music therapy as an Anti-Oppressive Practice. *The Arts in Psychotherapy* 40: 1–5.

Barnes, Barry (1995). *The Elements of Social Theory*. London: UCL Press.

Barrett, Margaret (2012). Troubling the creative imaginary: Some possibilities of ecological thinking for music and learning. In: D. Hargreaves, D. Miell, and R. MacDonald (eds), *Musical Imaginations*, pp. 206–219. Oxford: Oxford University Press.

Barrington, Alison (2005). Music Therapy: A Study in Professionalisation. Unpublished doctoral dissertation. Durham, UK: University of Durham, Department of Music.

Barrington, Alison (2008). Challenging the Profession. *British Journal of Music Therapy* 22(2): 65–72.

Bauman, Zymunt (1993). *Postmodern Ethics*. Oxford: Blackwell.

Bentall, Richard, P. (2010). *Doctoring the Mind: Why Psychiatric Treatments Fail*. London: Penguin.

Boxill, Edith Hillman (1985). *Music Therapy for the Developmentally Disabled*. Maryland: An Aspen Publication.

Bronfenbrenner, Urie (1979). *The Ecology of Human Development. Experiments by Nature and Design*. Cambridge, MA: Harvard University Press.

Bruscia, Kenneth (1998). *Defining Music Therapy* (second edition). Gilsum, NH: Barcelona Publishers.

Clarke, Eric (2005). *Ways of Listening: An Ecological Approach to the Perception of Musical Meaning*. Oxford: Oxford University Press.

Cook, Nicholas (1998). *Music. A Very Short Introduction*. New York: Oxford University Press.

Cook, Nicholas (2012). Beyond Creativity? In: D. Hargreaves, D. Miell, and R. MacDonald (eds), *Musical Imaginations*, pp. 451–459. Oxford: Oxford University Press.

Curtis, Sandra L. and Mercado, Chelsey, S. (2004). Community Music Therapy for Citizens with Developmental Disabilities. *Voices: A World Forum for Music Therapy*. Retrieved February 24, 2011, from: <https://normt.uib.no/index.php/voices/article/view/185/144>.

DeNora, Tia (2000). *Music in Everyday Life*. Cambridge: Cambridge University Press.

DeNora, Tia (2003). *After Adorno. Rethinking Music Sociology*. Cambridge: Cambridge University Press.

DeNora, Tia (2011a). *Music-in-Action: Selected Essays in Sonic Ecology*. Aldershot: Ashgate.

DeNora, Tia (2011b). Practical consciousness and social relation in *MusEcological* perspective. In: D. Clarke and E. Clarke (eds), *Music and Consciousness: Philosophical, Psychological and Cultural Perspectives*, pp. 309–325. Oxford: Oxford University Press.

DeNora, Tia (2013). *Music Asylums: Wellbeing Through Music in Everyday Life*. Farnham: Ashgate.

Elliott, David, J. (1995). *Music Matters. A New Philosophy of Music Education*. New York: Oxford University Press.

Esposito, Roberto (2010). *Communitas: The Origin and Destiny of Community*. Stanford: Stanford University Press.

Higgins, Lee (2012). *Community Music: In Practice and in Theory*. Oxford: Oxford University Press.

Jampel, Peter (2006). Performance in music therapy with mentally ill adults. Doctoral dissertation, New York University.

Jampel, Peter (2011). Performance in Music Therapy: Experiences in Five Dimensions. *Voices: A World Forum for Music Therapy* 11(1). https://voices.no/index.php/voices/article/view/275

Kenny, Carolyn B. (1982). *The Mythic Artery. The Magic of Music Therapy*. Atascadero, CA: Ridgeview Publishing Company.

Krüger, Viggo (2004). Læring gjennom deltagelse i et rockeband. Et instrumentelt case studie om situert læring i musikkterapi [Learning through Participation in a Rock Band. An Instrumental Case Study on Situated Learning in Music Therapy]. Unpublished master thesis. Oslo/Sandane, Norway: Norwegian Academy of Music /Sogn og Fjordane University College.

Krüger, Viggo (2012). Musikk—fortelling—fellesskap. Musikkterapi i en barnevernsinstitusjon [Music—Narrative—Community. Music Therapy in a Children's Welfare Institution]. Unpublished Doctoral Dissertation. Bergen, Norway: The Grieg Academy, University of Bergen.

MacDonald, Raymond, Kreutz, Gunter, and Mitchell, Laura (eds). (2012). *Music, Health and Wellbeing*. New York: Oxford University Press.

Malloch, Stephen and Trevarthen, Colwyn (eds). (2009). *Communicative Musicality. Exploring the Basis of Human Companionship*. Oxford, UK: Oxford University Press.

McPherson, Gary, Davidson, Jane, and Faulkner, Robert (2012). *Music in Our Lives: Rethinking Musical Ability, Development and Identity*. Oxford: Oxford University Press.

Nordoff, Paul and Robbins, Clive (1965/2004). *Therapy in Music for Handicapped Children.* Gilsum, NH: Barcelona Publishers.

Nordoff, Paul and Robbins, Clive (1971/1983). *Music Therapy in Special Education.* Saint Louis, MO: Magna-Music Baton.

Nordoff, Paul and Robbins, Clive (1977/2007). *Creative Music Therapy.* Gilsum, NH: Barcelona Publishers.

O'Grady, Lucy (2009). The Therapeutic Potentials of Creating and Performing Music with Women in Prison: A Qualitative Case Study. Unpublished Doctoral Dissertation. Melbourne: University of Melbourne, Faculty of Music.

Oosthuizen, Helen (2006). Diversity and Community: Finding and Forming a South African Music Therapy. *Voices: A World Forum for Music Therapy.* Retrieved February 19, 2011, from: <https://normt.uib.no/index.php/voices/article/view/277/202>.

Pavlicevic, Mercédès and Ansdell, Gary (eds). (2004). *Community Music Therapy.* London: Jessica Kingsley Publishers.

Pavlicevic, Mercédès and Ansdell, Gary (2009). Between Communicative Musicality and Collaborative Musicing. In: S. Malloch and C. Trevarthen (eds), *Communicative Musicality.* Oxford: Oxford University Press.

Pitts, Stephanie (2012). *Chances and Choices: Exploring the Impact of Music Education.* Oxford: Oxford University Press.

Priestley, M. (1975). *Music Therapy in Action.* London: St Martin's Press.

Procter, Simon (2004). Playing Politics: Community Music Therapy and the Therapeutic Redistribution of Musical Capital for Mental Health. In: M. Pavlicevic and G. Ansdell (eds), *Community Music Therapy.* London: Jessica Kingsley Publishers.

Procter, Simon (2006). What are we Playing at? Social Capital and Music Therapy. In: R. Edwards, J. Franklin, and J. Holland (eds), *Assessing Social Capital: Concept, Policy and Practice.* Cambridge: Scholars Press.

Procter, Simon (2008). Premising the Challenge (Response to Alison Barrington). *British Journal of Music Therapy* 22(2): 77–82.

Rolvsjord, Randi (2010). *Resource-Oriented Music Therapy in Mental Health Care.* Gilsum, NH: Barcelona Publishers.

Ruud, Even (1980). *Hva er musikkterapi?* [What is Music Therapy?] Oslo, Norway: Gyldendal.

Ruud, Even (1987/1990). *Musikk som kommunikasjon og samhandling. Teoretiske perspektiver på musikkterapien.* [Music as Communication and Interaction. Theoretical Perspectives on Music Therapy.] Oslo, Norway: Solum.

Ruud, Even (1998). *Music Therapy: Improvisation, Communication and Culture.* Gilsum, NH: Barcelona Publishers.

Ruud, Even (2004). Defining Community Music Therapy. [Contribution to Moderated Discussions] *Voices: A World Forum for Music Therapy.* Retrieved January 16, 2006, from: <http://www.voices.no/discussions/discm4_07.html>.

Ruud, Even (2010). *Music Therapy: A Perspective from the Humanities.* Gilsum, NH: Barcelona Publishers.

Sawyer, Keith (2003). *Group Creativity: Music, Theater, Collaboration.* New Jersey: Lawrence Erlbaum.

Schwabe, Christoph and Ulrike Haase (1998). *Die Sozialmusiktherapie (SMT)* [Social Music Therapy]. Wetzdorf, Germany: Akademie für angewandte Musiktherapie Crossen.

Small, Christopher (1998). *Musicking. The Meanings of Performing and Listening.* Hanover, NH: Wesleyan University Press.

Soshensky, Rick (2011). Everybody is a star: Recording, performing, and Community Music Therapy. *Music Therapy Perspectives* 29: 23–30.

Stige, Brynjulf (2002). *Culture-Centered Music Therapy.* Gilsum, NH: Barcelona Publishers.

Stige, Brynjulf (2003/2012). *Elaborations Towards a Notion of Community Music Therapy.* Gilsum, NH: Barcelona Publishers.

Stige, Brynjulf (2012). Health Musicking. In: R. MacDonald, G. Kreutz, and L. Mitchell (eds), *Music, Health and Wellbeing.* New York: Oxford University Press.

Stige, Brynjulf and Aarø, Leif Edvard (2012). *Invitation to Community Music Therapy.* New York: Routledge.

Stige, Brynjulf, Ansdell, Gary, Elefant, Cochavit, and Pavlicevic, Mercédès (2010). *Where Music Helps. Community Music Therapy in Action and Reflection.* Farnham, UK: Ashgate Publishing.

Storsve, Vegar, Westby, Inger, A., and Ruud, Even (2010). Hope and Recognition. A Music Project among Youth in a Palestinian Refugee Camp. *Voices: A World Forum for Music Therapy.* Retrieved February 21, 2011, from: <https://normt.uib.no/index.php/voices/article/view/158/246.>.

Tyson, Florence (1968). The Community Music Therapy Center. In: G.E. Thayer (ed.), *Music in Therapy*, pp. 382–388. New York: Macmillan Publishing.

Vaillancourt, Guylaine (2009). Mentoring Apprentice Music Therapists for Peace and Social Justice through Community Music Therapy: An Arts-Based Study. Dissertation submitted to the Ph.D. in Leadership and Change Program. Santa Barbara, CA: Antioch University.

Vernon, Mark (2008). *Wellbeing.* Stocksfield: Acumen.

Windsor, Luke (2012). Music and affordances, *Musicae Scientiae* 16(1): 102–120.

Wood, Stuart (2006). "The Matrix": A Model of Community Music Therapy Processes. *Voices: A World Forum for Music Therapy.* Retrieved February 19, 2011, from: <https://normt.uib.no/index.php/voices/article/view/279/204>.

Wood, S., Verney, R. and Atkinson, J. (2004). From therapy to community: Making music in neurological rehabilitation. In: M. Pavlicevic and G. Ansdell (eds), *Community music therapy*, pp. 48–65. London: Jessica Kingsley Publishers.

CHAPTER 33

VOCAL PSYCHOTHERAPY
Discovering Yourself through the Voice

DIANE AUSTIN

INTRODUCTION

VOCAL psychotherapy is based on the premise that the voice is a primary instrument in music therapy. When we sing, our voices and our bodies become the instruments by which music is formed and sounded. We are intimately connected to the source of the sound and the vibrations. We make the music, we are immersed in the music, and we are the music. As we breathe deeply to sustain the tones we create our heart rate slows down and our nervous system is calmed. Our voices resonate inward to help us connect to our bodies and express our emotions as they resonate outward to help us connect to others. Singing can provide clients with an opportunity to express the inexpressible, to give a voice to all the parts that long to be heard, and join them in a song of integration.

The human voice is the most versatile of all instruments in that its resonances can be continuously changed by movements of the larynx, jaw, tongue, and lips (Jourdain 1997). Singing is also a neuromuscular activity and muscular patterns are closely linked to psychological patterns and emotional response (Newham 1994). Vocal psychotherapy is based on the idea that when we sing internally resonating vibrations break up and release blockages of energy, releasing feelings and allowing a natural flow of vitality and a state of equilibrium to return to the body. These benefits are particularly relevant to clients who have *frozen* or numbed off areas in the body that hold traumatic experience.

THE VOCAL CONNECTION BETWEEN PARENTS AND INFANTS

The voice is a primary source of connection between caregivers and infants. During gestation, the human fetus receives musical stimulation from sound vibrations transmitted through the amniotic fluid (Ilari and Polka 2006). The sounds we hear in the womb, the rhythm of our mother's heartbeat, the flow of her breathing, and the nuances of her voice directly stimulate the cortex (Minson 1992). This stimulation provides nourishment that is critical to the development of the brain and the central nervous system (Minson 1992; Storr 1992; Tomatis 2005).

Babies prefer their mothers' voice singing compared to speaking (Nakata and Trehub 2004). The mother too is attuned to her child's sounds and learns to distinguish the nuances of the different sounds and the needs they convey. In a mutual, co-created dance of sounds and movements, mother and baby feel a sense of oneness. The infant feels safe and begins to trust the mother and the mother receives sensory reassurance that will help her understand and answer her child's messages (Miller 1997). Somewhere between the third and fourth month, infants produce sounds that resemble singing. At about six months of age, babies enter the "lall-ing" period and move their lips and tongue rhythmically making sounds like "la-la-la" (Loewy 2004). During this stage babies are not necessarily communicating messages, they are simply enjoying the pleasurable sensation of repeating simple syllables.

From a very early age babies recognize the sound of their caregivers' voices. The mother's voice is like a cord that connects the child to its life source and provides the positive intrauterine and post-birth experiences so essential to the child's ability to bond with others. The vocal interaction in speech and song between mother, father, other caregivers, and the child, and the reliability and continuity of this reciprocated sound is critical to the child's developing sense of self. This sound connection is an auditory reflection of the emotional and psychological relationship between the parent and the child (Malloch and Trevarthen 2009; Newham 1994).

BREATH

At the core of Vocal psychotherapy is the use of the voice and singing to make clinical interventions that move the therapeutic process forward. The physical and psychological benefits of deep breathing are always a part of any vocal intervention. Breath is the basis of life itself. Life begins and ends with a breath. "As long as we are emotionally protective our breathing cannot be free ... the voice will depend on compensating strength in the throat and mouth muscles" (Linklater 1976, p. 12). There is reciprocity between the physiological and the psychological effects of breathing. Cutting off the breath by constricting the throat, chest, or abdomen can sever the connection to feelings and dramatically affect the quality of both the speaking and singing voice (Austin 2008). Vocal psychotherapy is indicated when poor vocal quality of speaking or singing is linked to recent trauma, or to neglectful and abusive childhood experiences.

Deep breathing slows the heart rate and calms and nurtures the nervous system. Making natural sounds and movements and toning (Keyes 1973, 2008) can increase awareness of the breath and bodily sensations while also providing an outlet for emotions and spontaneous vocal expression. For instance, before singing a song or vocally improvising, I will ask clients to inhale and exhale several times. On the last few exhalations I will suggest they allow a moan, groan, or any sound at all to emerge. This usually increases the duration of the exhalation and relaxes and prolongs the inhalation leaving the client feeling more embodied and present. Many clients are amazed by the sometimes childlike or primal sounds that emerge, intuitive and instinctual sounds that have been long repressed because there was no safe space in which to make them.

Songs

Do you remember the first song you ever heard? Perhaps you remember who sang it to you. What do you feel when you think of it or hear it played? Is there a song that reminds you of your mother or father? Your first love? Your high school graduation? When you hear or sing these songs do they bring up memories of who you were with? How you were feeling? There are songs that are significant because we played and sang them over and over again when we were happy or sad, or because they reflected what we were feeling at different points in our lives. They help us remember people, places, and things that were important to us.

Clients often reveal the issues that are prominent in their lives by the songs they choose to sing or listen to in sessions. When clients choose a song to listen to or sing in the presence of the therapist, they are often telling a great deal about their emotional, psychological, or spiritual state. They could also be revealing something about the transference that is, the feelings they have about the therapist which are related to their past history of significant emotional connection with others. They are revealing something they cannot say either because they aren't consciously aware of it, they don't have the words to say it, or they do not feel safe enough to talk about it. But they are disclosing thoughts and feelings, nonetheless through the title and lyrics of songs. Many times these are thoughts and feelings they want the therapist to listen to and understand through empathizing. As an example of this is a client whose first song was about a man made of cellophane. When we discussed the lyrics, she realized that she always felt like she was made of cellophane, that people could look right through her and they did. She felt invisible in her family, because her brother received all the attention and it felt to her that no one noticed her. This theme was now reoccurring in her life and realizing the origins of this wound helped us to work together towards resolution.

Songs offer a safe container with a beginning, middle and end, a familiar structure. The song chosen to listen to or to sing, is known to the client and therefore predictable, so there is a greater sense of control over the music. The structure inherent in a song offers containment for emotional material that may emerge. The repeated singing of a song can help clients work through the feelings or issues the song evokes. Significant songs can also reinforce qualities or ideals clients want to internalize. These kinds of songs can be inspiring and provide a resource for those who need it.

Dvorkin (1991) has discussed the use of songs as *transitional objects*. Winnicott (1971) developed the idea of the transitional object; objects such as a special toy or blanket that the child uses in the course of emotional separation from the primary caregiver that substitute for the adult and relieve stress, especially at bedtime. These special objects can counteract feelings of loss and abandonment and "preserve the illusion of a loving, comforting and soothing mother" (Moore and Fine 1990, p. 207).

I have often made recordings for clients of the two of us singing one of their favorite songs or improvisations. Some clients prefer it if I sing alone so they can listen to their recordings to help manage their anxiety when I am away or they are on vacation. One client found it helpful to listen to a recording of the two of us singing lullabies. She needed to listen to the lullabies every night. We had just begun working together and hearing my voice each night helped her build a sense of safety and security about our work together.

Clients do not always realize the symbolic meaning of the song or why it is important to them until we listen to it, or sing it together. An example of this is when Julie brought in the sheet music to "I Can't Make You Love Me." She said it was about her last boyfriend who broke up with her unexpectedly. She was still trying to accept that it was over. When we sang the song together it was a very emotional experience for her. Afterwards we talked about the lyrics and I asked her for associations. She said she felt abandoned by him. I asked if she had ever felt this way before; which is a classic question. She replied, "I don't know ... I guess I felt this same kind of loss with another guy I really liked but it didn't work out either." We talked some more and I questioned her about other feelings of loss she had experienced. Then I suggested we sing the song again and see if any other images or feelings emerged. By the end of the session Julie made a connection to how she felt when her parents divorced. She was only nine years old at the time and was very close to her father. He remarried shortly afterwards, started another family and moved to another state when she was thirteen. She saw him infrequently after he moved. It was an immense loss for her. She had told me the details of the divorce before but only in a matter-of-fact way. This time she was crying, demonstrating that she was connected to the effect this experience had on her life and how it had especially affected her capacity to feel safe in relationships.

VOCAL IMPROVISATION

Improvisation comes from a natural impulse to play and experiment. When that impulse is allowed free expression through vocal and musical play, spontaneity is released (Spolin 1986). Spontaneity plays a dynamic role in most forms of psychotherapy. When clients are able to be spontaneous they can allow for the natural flow of impulses and can express themselves from an authentic center of being. Healing can occur because clients can discover and connect with their true voices. They can experience themselves freed from the tyranny of *shoulds* and *oughts*. Instead they can access and express genuine feelings, thereby opening a channel to the true self.

Vocal improvisation is a creative process and "is potentially in and of itself an agent of change, a transforming experience for both client and therapist" (Turry 2001, p. 352). Improvising vocally requires both therapist and client to become comfortable with the process of not knowing, not knowing what sounds, words or feelings are waiting in the wings of the unconscious and what they may reveal about the participants. There is a sense of flowing with time and our evolving consciousness and a feeling of being enlivened when we can create our own form (music, sounds, words) instead of *con-forming*; that is, duplicating someone else's way of being or acting. When we are improvising vocally we are in the moment, present to ourselves, the music and our accompanying feelings and sensations. We are also moving toward the future and the creation of something that has not yet come into being and the sounds, melodies and words we improvise, trigger feelings, memories, and associations from the past (Austin 1996; Turry 1998).

Researchers at Johns Hopkins University's Peabody Institute discovered that when jazz musicians improvise, their brains turn off the neural areas responsible for self-censoring and inhibition, and the areas responsible for self-expression are activated (Limb and Braun

2008). The research was motivated by the scientists' curiosity about the almost trance-like states jazz musicians enter to create their unique and personal improvisations and the connection between these states and the brain. They found that a region of the brain known as the dorsolateral prefrontal cortex slows down activity during improvisation. This area is linked to self-censoring and planned actions. At the same time, researchers saw increased activity in the medial prefrontal cortex, an area of the brain linked with self-expression and creativity. They used the findings to suggest that this type of brain activity might be active during other types of improvisational behavior fundamental to social life for musicians and non-artists. They further suggested that this type of creativity allowed humans to advance as a species (Limb and Braun 2008).

I believe that a facilitating musical environment can support anybody to sing and/or improvise vocally. A safe place and a trusting relationship, combined with musical forms that engage the clients' sensibilities and musical interests can enable clients to take musical risks and call forth the creativity that is essential to the individuation process. If they can face the unknown and take risks sounding and singing, chances are they will eventually transfer this ability to the rest of their lives.

VOCAL HOLDING TECHNIQUES

Vocal Holding Techniques are used within a method of vocal improvisation I have been developing and refining since 1994 (Austin 1996; 2001; 2004; 2006; 2008). I often improvise with clients using these techniques. Vocal holding techniques involve the intentional use of two chords in combination with the therapist's voice in order to create a consistent and stable musical environment that facilitates improvised singing within the client therapist relationship. This method provides a reliable, safe structure for the client who is afraid of, or unused to, improvising.

This improvisational structure is usually limited to two chords in order to establish a predictable, secure musical and psychological container that will enable clients to relinquish some of the mind's conscious control, to be engaged with their bodies, and to allow their spontaneous selves to emerge. The simplicity of the music and the hypnotic repetition of the two chords, combined with the rocking rhythmic motion and the singing of single syllables can produce a trance-like altered state and easy access to the world of the unconscious. The steady, consistent harmonic underpinning, the rhythmic grounding and the therapist's singing encourage and support the client's vocalization. Within this strong yet flexible musical container the client can explore new ways of being, experience the freedom of play and creative self-expression, and allow feelings and images to emerge (Austin 1996; 2001; 2008). The client's voice, feelings, and emerging aspects of the self are all held within this musical matrix.

Vocal holding techniques also support a connection to self and other and can be used to promote a therapeutic regression in which unconscious feelings, sensations, memories, and associations can be accessed, processed, and integrated. As a client Joseph said, "At first it was not easy to sing in therapy. Although I loved music, I feared my voice and the tunes that might emerge. I was afraid it would make me too vulnerable and unprotected. But I sang, and the little child that emerged felt safe. He was held by the piano chords and your voice. The child felt free."

These unconscious experiences are directly related to parts of the self that have been split off and suspended in time due to traumatic occurrences. When contacted and communicated with, these younger parts can be reunited with the ego and the vital energy they contain can be made available to the present day personality. Developmental arrests can be repaired and a more complete sense of self can be attained.

This method is especially useful in working through developmental injuries and arrests due to traumatic ruptures in the parent-child relationship and/or empathic failures at crucial developmental junctures. Vocal holding techniques are not meant to be a prescription or recipe and are not necessarily used in the order that follows. For the sake of clarity, I will describe the process as it appears to complement the developmental stages. As with any therapeutic intervention, however, the client's history, diagnosis, transference reactions, and unique personality and needs should determine the approach taken to accomplish therapeutic goals. For example, in initial sessions with Sara, she indicated that she felt more comfortable when improvising with words. It wasn't until the second year of working together that she started to find singing without words comforting and lullaby-like. At this point in the therapy she had begun to work on early childhood issues, so the musical change reflected her psychological state and needs.

In the initial "vocal holding" phase the client and I sing in *unison*. Singing together on the same notes can promote the emergence of a symbiosis-like transference and countertransference. This is important for clients who never had a satisfactory experience of merging with an emotionally present, attuned mother. Through a replication of early mother-child relatedness, these clients can eventually internalize a stable sense of self and then gradually renegotiate the stages of separation and individuation. Sometimes the improvised vocalizations that emerge that are reminiscent of a three- to six-month-old child's babbling.

Singing in unison can be soothing. This is useful when clients need comforting or closure at the end of a session that has been highly emotional. It is also a way to encourage clients to improvise. They may feel safer because they are not alone or exposed and they can draw on the therapist's voice for support.

Mirroring occurs when a client sings her own melodic line and I respond by repeating the client's melody back to her. I often used mirroring with Linda to support her in finding, strengthening and staying grounded in her authentic voice (for example when she felt frightened to confront her mother). Mirroring also helped her to hear and accept new parts of her personality, like the happy child, when they emerged. This musical reflection provides encouragement and validation for the client's experiences.

Grounding, when I sing the tone or root of the chords, provides a base for clients' vocalizations. They can improvise freely and return to our *home base* whenever they want to check in again. One client referred to the grounding tones as *touch tones*. This musical process is reminiscent of a typical pattern of interaction between the child and the maternal figure that occurs when the child begins to move away from the mother to explore the environment. In the ideal situation, the mother stays in contact with the child and supports and encourages her increased efforts to individuate; otherwise the stages of separation-individuation become associated with abandonment. Linda expressed it this way: "I felt like I had all the time and space I needed. I could move away from you and you wouldn't get angry or try to hold me back, like my mother would or leave me alone in the room crying if I disagreed with her. I could do whatever I wanted to, take as long as I wanted to get out what I wanted to get out and go as far out as I wanted to but if I wanted to return I could … you never shut the door … you never left … the music never left."

Vocal holding techniques are introduced into the music psychotherapy session in various ways. With clients who are especially anxious about improvising but want to try, I might explain this method in detail. Usually, however, I give a minimal description or simply ask: "Would you like to try singing about this (person, situation, feeling, etc.)? I then ask clients if they want two or more chords. They sometimes choose the exact chords or give a general description ("something minor"), but if they have little or no knowledge of chord structure or need help finding the sound they want, I might play examples of different chord combinations (major, minor, suspended, etc.) and ask for their preference. Occasionally, clients will describe a mood or feeling they would like to evoke and together we search for and find the fitting chords (Austin 1996). The clients may also suggest a rhythm that fits the sound they want.

We begin by breathing together. As previously described, deep breathing is critical in focusing, relaxing, and grounding clients in their bodies. Breathing together begins the process of vocal attunement that continues as the therapist attempts to match the client's vocal quality, dynamics, tempo, and phrasing. Being present to clients as an empathically attuned companion may also involve matching their physical movements (for example, rocking together) and making eye contact. Eye contact can reinforce the intimacy engendered by singing together but may be too intense an experience for some clients, and even distracting for others.

CASE EXAMPLE: VICKY

Vicky, a twenty-eight year old professional cellist, sought out music psychotherapy for what she believed was a psychosomatic illness. Approximately two years ago, after a successful performance, she awoke to find she could not move her right hand. Since that episode, she had been suffering from periodic pain in both her right hand and arm that was seriously affecting her ability to practice and perform. Vicky had been to the best doctors and physical therapists, who found nothing wrong with her. She felt she was losing her "musical self" and she was now convinced the problem was not in her body but in her mind. She was very ashamed of acknowledging this.

Vicky described her family as "normal." Both her parents were high achieving professionals. She had a brother three years younger who still lived at home. Initially, Vicky was reluctant to discuss her family and only wanted to talk about her music and her physical ailment. She appeared to be very bright, serious, and responsible, a person driven to constantly achieve, and pursued by a harsh perfectionistic inner critic. She seemed to live more in her thoughts than in her body. She spoke very quickly in a high pitched, monotone voice seldom taking a deep breath or leaving any space for feelings to emerge. I sensed a great deal of anxiety and fragility underneath her confident manner.

Vicky was interested in her dreams and usually brought at least one to each session. The majority of these were archetypal "trauma dreams" (Kalsched 1996) with images of car crashes, wounded animals, and dismembered bodies. I felt the dreams were providing us with a picture of what was happening to Vicky intrapsychically, of the severe split between her mind and her instinctual self.

As the therapy progressed, Vicky came more into focus as a "parentified child" (Miller 1981) who took care of her emotionally immature and unavailable parents by "holding herself together" and relinquishing her needs and neglecting her young, emotional self in the process. Her music was the one area of her life in which she felt free to express her feelings. Listening to Vicky describe her situation and hearing the desperation in her voice, I was reminded of my senior year of high school when I developed vocal nodes. I remembered how devastated I felt. Like Vicky, I depended on my music, in my case singing, to provide an outlet for feelings that were otherwise too difficult and frightening to express.

I had the sense that Vicky's psychosomatic symptoms were related to the shame and guilt she felt acknowledging her feelings and the problems within her family; where it was acceptable to complain about physical problems but not emotional ones. Intuitively, I felt that her hand was carrying all her unresolved grief and rage. Vicky's dreams provided information about her unconscious processes but her associations to the material remained on an intellectual level. I felt we needed to access the feelings connected to the dream images. I often use music to work with dreams. Since music and dreams speak a similar language (symbolic), and both directly access the unconscious, it is as if no translation is necessary for the music to resonate in the heart of the dream image and release its affective component.

I thought singing would be an effective way of working with Vicky because as she was not identified as a singer, there was no performance pressure associated with singing. By singing together her hands would not need to be involved, offering a potentially conflict free area to explore. Vicky had enjoyed singing in choirs during her school years but had never improvised using her voice before. During one session I introduced her to vocal holding techniques and when we stopped singing she said, "I felt a chill, like a ghost came into me … I've always been two people, one is independent and rational; the other is all energy and emotion … it's like they came together for a minute." Vocal holding techniques are especially useful when working with dissociative defenses and the kind of mind-body splits so prevalent in traumatized clients (Austin 1998, 1999). The two parts that Vicky experienced coming together during the singing symbolized a moment of integration that would have to be repeated over and over again to be resolved.

The session that follows took place during our third month of working together. Vicky had just returned from a weekend with her parents. When I asked her how things went she said: "Fine, but my hand started hurting again when I was practicing Sunday." When I inquired further about her interactions with her family and any feelings she had experienced during the weekend, she was vague and changed the subject. She was speaking very fast and in an excited manner but with little real affect. She kept changing topics. I had the thought "a moving target is hard to hit" that she was defending against delving too deeply into any subject. At one point she mentioned a past dream she'd had and I asked her if she'd had any dreams this weekend. She reported the following: "I am at the airport and I'm all excited watching the planes taking off. A plane takes off right in front of me but then turns to the right suddenly and crashes into a building. The plane goes up in flames and I start yelling for help. Men come out of the airport with stretchers and I go with them. There are people badly burned lying on the ground. Then I see a baby. I'm not sure if it's alive or dead. It's all shriveled up."

Instead of asking Vicky for her associations to the dream and/or offering any interpretations, I asked if she would like to try exploring the dream in the music, using two chords and singing. She agreed and came to the piano to sit beside me. I suggested either singing the overall feeling of the dream or an image that felt particularly meaningful to her. She wanted to focus on the image of the baby. I asked her what chords she would like and she said she wasn't sure. I played different combinations for her and she settled on A minor 9 to F major 9. We began by breathing together several times. Breathing helps the client and the therapist, release excess anxiety, get grounded in his/her body. Breathing together is the beginning of the process of vocal attunement. It also serves as a transition state between speaking and singing.

I played slowly and softly in the middle register of the piano. The tempo, dynamics, repetitious rocking rhythm, and the chord voicings which were suspended 9ths that resolved along with occasional arpeggios seemed to support her voice and create a feeling state that complemented the dream. I liked this music. It felt both soothing to me yet conveyed a particular kind of sadness mixed with longing.

She began singing "ah-h-h," holding the tone—stretching it out. The tone she chose and the open sound suggested a willingness to explore her feelings. I joined her immediately and we started singing in unison. She seemed comfortable with the unison, as if taking in my support and gathering strength by merging or joining with me before beginning to move on her own. She slowly began a descending melodic line, which I mirrored and then harmonized with and then we returned to unison. Her singing voice was softer, breathier and had a more feeling, receptive quality than the music of her speaking voice, which was usually monotone, fast and staccato. At moments, her singing sounded frail and vulnerable to me and seemed to give voice to her young, wounded feminine self. At one point she began an ascending melodic line and I remember thinking she needed a firm grounding base to support this upward movement. I held a low tone while she ascended. I had an image of a little bird whose spirit had been broken but who kept trying to get off the ground. I believed the baby in the dream was her young, feeling self that was suspended somewhere between life and death.

This belief was grounded in experience both professional but also personal. I had spent many years in psychotherapy working to reclaim and integrate the young dissociated feeling parts of myself. The image of the shriveled up baby filled me with sadness and compassion.

Vicky's singing became dissonant at one point alternating between the flat five and the fifth of A minor 9, and then alternating between the dominant seventh and the seventh of F major. She may have been influenced by my use of suspended 9ths to create tension and resolution. I was playing whole steps to produce this effect, whereas she was singing half steps and creating even more tension by alternately singing tri-tones. I wondered if the music was reflecting her pain but perhaps also her ambivalence about living. The music built and then diminished in volume and intensity as she sang descending and ascending melodic lines. I alternated between unison and harmony sometimes mirroring and overlapping into unison and harmony again. The music felt sad to me and filled with yearning. We "pulsed" together in unison and harmony. The volume and intensity increased as we ascended up the scale. I felt connected to her. I noticed when singing she utilized a vocal range of over an octave, a contrast with the fairly monotone range she spoke in. We descended again and her voice grew soft. I began playing in the high register of the piano and arpeggiating the notes in what sounded like the chimes of a music box. She changed from "ah-h" to "hm-m-m-"; a more closed sound which seemed more regressive and perhaps protective. I joined her singing. I saw that she was rocking back and forth and I matched her movement. The singing grew softer and we breathed together and came to a close. We sat in silence for a few moments when the music ended.

I then asked her what she was experiencing. She said, "It's like we were waking up that dead baby." She began crying and continued "everyone thinks I'm the happy one and my life should be so good ... I feel sad for my brother and my mother, I worry about her." Vicky began to talk more openly about her family and how they affected her. Her father emerged as a self-centered person with severe mood swings who could be verbally abusive at times and more loving at other times. Over the weekend he had been extremely critical of her playing and told her she should give up the cello and pursue another career. At the end of the session, I reflected how unsafe she must have felt growing up with such an unpredictable parent and how difficult it has to be to express herself in such a critical atmosphere. I believe the "vocal holding" created a nurturing safe environment that enabled Vicky to dialogue with her unconscious so that she could retrieve a piece of what had been lost to her, an image from the depths and the feelings connecting her to the part of herself contained within the image.

This session was at times difficult for me. I could easily empathize with aspects of Vicky, her perfectionism and the accompanying performance anxiety, the successful persona and the fragile child underneath. I attempted to use my feelings of countertransference (my response to her transference) to understand and connect with her. I was also aware of the danger of over-identifying with Vicky and losing my therapeutic stance and with it the ability to be fully present to Vicky and her experience. I reminded myself that although we had some similar wounds we were different people at different stages in the healing process. Deep breathing also helped me to tune into my own feelings stay grounded in my body and maintain my boundaries.[1]

FREE ASSOCIATIVE SINGING

Free associative singing is the term I use to describe a technique that can be implemented when words enter the vocal holding process. It is similar to the technique of free association (Freud 1977) in that clients are encouraged to verbalize whatever comes into their head with the expectation that by doing so, they will come into contact with unconscious images, memories and associated feelings. It differs from Freud's technique in that the client is singing instead of speaking, but more significantly, the therapist is also singing and contributing to the musical stream of consciousness by making active verbal and musical interventions. The accompaniment is a two-chord holding pattern or repetitive riff, and along with my singing contains the client's process. The emphasis now is not only on "holding" the client's emerging self and psychic contents but on creating momentum through the music and the lyrics that will propel the improvisation and the therapeutic process forward.

The progression to words and the more active role I take on generally promote a greater differentiation between the client and myself. When I begin questioning, reframing, and adding my own words to the improvisational dyad, the transference and countertransference can become much more complex. The client may experience me not only in a supportive mother role, but in other roles as well including as representing figures from the client's interpersonal and intrapsychic world.

In its simplest form "free associative singing" involves clients singing a word or phrase and my mirroring or repeating the words and melody back to them. We always start with deep breathing and sometimes ease into this new stage by first singing without words. The vocal holding techniques of singing in unison, harmonizing and grounding add additional and various kinds of support and containment. I begin the process of vocal attunement by breathing in unison with the client. As we sing together I attempt to match the client's vocal quality, timbre, dynamics, tempo, and phrasing. With the movement to words there is often a need for more variation in the music. The two chords remain the basis for the musical improvisation but changes in the client's feeling states and emotional intensity often require a broader musical palette. Variations in dynamics, tempo, voicings, arpeggiation, rhythm, accents, rests, alternate chord substitutions, and chord extensions (adding 7ths, 9ths, 11ths, 13ths) enable me to reflect and support the client's experience. In this way, I use not only my voice and the lyrics but also the music to deepen the vocal improvisation and the therapeutic process.

Throughout the improvisation I continually make critical decisions about when, how, and what to sing with the client. This is especially true when I move beyond simply mirroring the client's lyrics and music and begin to vocally provide empathic reflection, make gentle interpretations by singing thoughts and feelings clients may be having but are not yet voicing, and use repetition to emphasize important words and help the clients digest the meaning in the words. Critical to the effectiveness of this method is the use of the "double" (Moreno 1994). The "double" is the inner voice of the client. The therapist sings as the "double" in the first person using "I." Drawing on induced countertransference, empathy, and intuition as well as knowledge of the client's history, I give voice to feelings and thoughts the client may be experiencing but is not yet singing, perhaps because the feelings and thoughts are uncomfortable, unconscious, or the client has no words for, or ability to conceptualize the experience. When the doubling is not accurate it still moves the process along as clients can change the words to fit their truth. When it is accurate, it provides clients with an experience of being truly seen and understood.

As free associative singing can be very effective in eliciting a therapeutic regression and connecting with repressed or dissociated feelings, it is a powerful technique that requires advanced training. For the beginning vocal psychotherapist, there are simpler adaptations that can be used. For instance, the subject being sung about can be limited to categories that offer more structure such as: I need … I wish … or I can. The therapist joins in the singing and repeats the lyrics back to the clients using the vocal holding techniques of singing in unison, harmonizing and grounding to add additional and various kinds of support.

CASE EXAMPLE: KRISTEN

The following example demonstrates the effectiveness of free associative singing with a young woman dealing with unprocessed grief related to her father's death. Kristen is a 26-year-old counseling student. She came to therapy to deal with a depression that was sometimes highly debilitating and had led to suicidal ideation. Her father died five years ago and she lived with her mother, whom she described as controlling and intrusive. She told me "I feel like I have to hide who I really am … So I'm good and I'm quiet and that's how I feel safe." Kristen had been in verbal psychotherapy for several years, and felt that her intellectual defenses inhibited her ability to access the feelings surrounding her core issues. She often felt moved when listening to music or singing and although she had no previous training in music, she was hopeful that this new way of working could be a way to connect to her true self.

During the first year of music psychotherapy, we dealt mainly with her inability to separate from her mother and her role as her mother's caretaker. The following session took place during our second year of working together. We had been discussing her father's death, its effect on her and the fact that she had never been able to grieve her loss. We decided to work in the music and she picked two minor chords for accompaniment. We began as we always did, with deep breathing while I played the piano and left space for Kristen to begin singing.

CLIENT (C): I remember (she sings softly)
THERAPIST (T): I remember (I repeat the melody and lyrics and match her vocal quality)
C: you were lying in the bed (she sings in a soft, slow monotone)
T: you were lying in the bed (I match her vocal quality, tempo, and dynamics)
C: mom was sitting in the chair
T: mom was sitting in the chair
C: she was crying
T: she was crying
C: but I couldn't cry (she sings louder and with more feeling)
C AND T: but I couldn't cry (I sing harmony with her and her voice swells)
C: I had to be strong
T: I had to be strong (I sense her anger)
C AND T: I had to be strong! (we sing in unison loudly)
T: she needed me to lean on (I know she's referring to her mother)
C: to lean on
T: to lean on (her mother has always looked to her for mothering)
C: I shut down (softer and staccato)
T: I shut down (I match her volume and phrasing)
C: there was no place to put my feelings
T: (I join in on) put my feelings
T: so I never got to feel them (I make a suggestion)
C: I never got to feel them (I begin to feel sad)
T: and I never got to cry (I use my countertransference to make this intervention)
C: and I never got to cry (she starts to cry softly)
C: (continues to cry, then sings) he told me, "I'll see you tomorrow"
T: (I join her and sing in unison with her) I'll see you tomorrow
C: but he lied
C AND T TOGETHER: but he lied! (we sing loud and angrily)
C: and I never got to say "I love you"
T: I love you (I feel her sadness)
C: I love you (she sings softly, tears streaming down her face)

C AND T TOGETHER: I love you (*I feel empathy as I harmonize with her*)

C: now there's just an empty hole where my feelings used to be

T: oo oo oo oo oo oo oo, hmm hmm hmm hmm (*I sing this refrain several times while she cries. The melody is reminiscent of a lullaby*)

C: now it's time to let you go (*I join in and we sing in unison*)

C: now it's time to say goodbye (*she sings softly and slowly*)

T: now it's time to say goodbye (*I match her dynamics and tempo*)

C: goodbye

T: goodbye (*I feel sad*)

C: goodbye (*crying quietly*)

C AND T TOGETHER: goodbye (*we sing in harmony until the note fades away*).

When we finished singing, Kristen said she felt a release, relief and lighter. I felt she had been carrying this grief for a long time and that it was a contributing factor to her depression. This free associative singing created a facilitating environment where she could express and process her feelings about her father's death and begin to bring some closure to this loss.

Conclusion

As I developed this approach I conducted research for a doctoral thesis (Austin 2004). I used a qualitative method of data gathering and data analysis that incorporated narrative forms and arts based explorations with three clients from my private practice. The findings highlighted the unique integration of music and words that occur in my approach. Because of the way I view singing in vocal psychotherapy and because I primarily work with singing improvised music and lyrics, my work is simultaneously, as Bruscia (1998) has described, both music *in* therapy and music *as* therapy. The music is doing something necessary and the words are doing something necessary. Music and lyrics are the catalyst for therapeutic growth; they open the doors to the unconscious and provide a container for in-depth processing to occur.

As I listen to the client's music and lyrics I am gathering and processing the information I receive. This information informs my interventions. The client responds or reacts and I listen in order to assess the effectiveness of the intervention. I gather more information by tuning in to the client and myself and processing what I hear. I may then change or expand the intervention to make it more effective, or I may form a new intervention.

My doctoral research revealed that the vast majority of my interventions were motivated by moments of disconnect in the client or between the client and myself. It follows that my intentions were primarily concerned with enabling the clients to connect to or to deepen the connection to themselves, including their feelings, memories, sensations, images, and parts of the self that contain these resources, and also to me. Singing is invaluable in this process as it connects body, mind and spirit, thinking and feeling, different parts of the self, and self and other.

The combination of singing music and lyrics and having the comfort and flexibility to move and flow from one *language* to another, gave me more avenues of access to the clients so that I could reach them at whatever developmental stage they were working through. The lyrics and musical interventions overlapped and supported each other. Over time, singing nonverbally and singing with lyrics within the context of the therapeutic relationship, helped the clients connect with, relate to and gradually begin to integrate encapsulated parts of the self that had been rejected, lost, or hidden away. The stream of sound, sensation, feelings and energy exchanged between the client and the therapist in the music, the words and the silence, provided the clients with an opportunity to have a corrective emotional experience and to renegotiate crucial junctures when the relationship with the primary caretaker was ruptured. Making sounds, singing nonverbally and improvising music and lyrics worked together to weave a connection, a bridge back to the self.

NOTE

1. The complete improvisation is available at <www.dianeaustin.com>.

REFERENCES

Austin, D. S. (1996). The role of improvised music in psychodynamic music therapy with adults. *Music Therapy* 14(1): 29–43.
Austin, D. (1998). When the psyche sings: Transference and countertransference In improvised singing with individual adults. In: K.E. Bruscia (ed.), *The dynamics of Music psychotherapy*, pp. 315–344. Gilsum, NH: Barcelona Publishers.
Austin, D. (1999). Vocal improvisation in analytically oriented music therapy with adults. In: T. Wigram and J. De Backer (eds), *Clinical Applications of Music Therapy in Psychiatry*, pp. 113–150. London: Jessica Kingsley.
Austin, D. (2001). In search of the self: The use of vocal holding techniques with adults traumatized as children. *Music Therapy Perspectives* 19(1): 22–30.
Austin, D. (2004). *When words sing and music speaks: A qualitative study of in depth music psychotherapy with adults*. Doctoral dissertation, New York University, School of Education.
Austin, D. (2006). Songs of the self: Vocal psychotherapy for adults traumatized as children. In: L. Carey (ed.), *Expressive and creative arts methods for trauma survivors*, pp. 133–52. London: Jessica Kingsley Publishers.
Austin, D. (2008). *The theory and practice of Vocal Psychotherapy*. London: Jessica Kingsley Publishers.
Bruscia, K.E. (ed.). (1998). *The dynamics of music psychotherapy*. Gilsum, NH: Barcelona Publishers.
Dvorkin, J. (1991). Individual music therapy for an adolescent with borderline personality disorder: An object relations approach. In: K. Bruscia (ed.), *Case studies in music therapy*, pp. 251–68. Gilsum, NH: Barcelona Publishers.
Freud, S. (1977). *Introductory lectures on psychoanalysis* (Vol. 1). London: WW Norton & Company.
Ilari, B. and Polka, L. (2006). Music cognition in early infancy: Infants' preferences and long-term memory for Ravel. *International Journal of Music Education* 24(1): 7–20.
Jourdain, R. (1997). *Music, the brain, and ecstasy: How music captures our imagination*. New York: William Morrow.

Kalsched, D. (1996). *The inner world of trauma: Archetypal defenses of the personal spirit.* London: Routledge.

Keyes, L.E. (1973). *Toning: The creative power of voice.* Camarillo, CA: DeVorss.

• Keyes, L.E. (2008). Toning: The creative and healing power of the voice. Camarillo, CA: DeVorss.

Limb, C.J. and Braun, A.R. (2008). Neural substrates of spontaneous musical performance: An fMRI study of jazz improvisation. *PLoS One* 3(2): e1679.

• Linklater, K. (1976). *Freeing the natural voice.* New York: Drama Book Publishers.

Loewy, J. (2004). Integrating music, language and the voice in music therapy. In: Voices: A World forum for Music therapy (Vol. 4, No. 1). Retrieved from: <https://voices.no/index.php/voices/article/viewArticle/140>.

Malloch, S. and Trevarthen, C. (2009). *Communicative musicality: Exploring the basis of human companionship.* Oxford: Oxford University Press.

Miller, A. (1981). *The drama of the gifted child.* New York: Basic Books.

Miller, A. (1997). *Banished knowledge.* New York: Anchor Press.

Minson, R. (1992). *A sonic birth. Music and Miracles.* Wheaton, IL: Quest Books.

Moore, B.E. and Fine, B.D. (eds). (1990). *Psychoanalytic terms and concepts.* New Haven: Yale University Press.

Moreno, J.D. (1994). *Psychodramatic moral philosophy and ethics. Psychodrama since Moreno.* London: Routledge.

Nakata, T. and Trehub, S.E. (2004). Infants' responsiveness to maternal speech and singing. *Infant Behavior and Development* 27(4): 455–64.

Newham, P. (1994). *The singing cure: An introduction to voice movement therapy.* Boston: Shambhala.

Spolin, V. (1986). *Theater games for the classroom: A teacher's handbook.* Evanston, IL: Northwestern University Press.

Storr, A. (1992). *Music and the mind.* New York: The Free Press.

Tomatis, A. (2005). *The ear and the voice.* Lanham, MD: Scarecrow Press.

Turry, A. (1998). Transference and countertransference in Nordoff-Robbins music therapy. In: K. Brusica (ed.), *The dynamics of music psychotherapy*, pp. 161–212. Gilsum, NH: Barcelona Publishers.

Turry, A. (2001). Supervision in the Nordoff-Robbins music therapy training program. In: M. Forinash (ed.), *Music therapy supervision*, pp. 351–78. Gilsum, NH: Barcelona Publishers.

Winnicott, D.W. (1971). *Playing and reality.* London: Psychology Press.

SECTION THREE

MUSIC THERAPY METHODS

CHAPTER 34

···

METHODS AND TECHNIQUES

···

JANE EDWARDS

INTRODUCTION

···

THIS chapter provides a brief overview of methods and techniques in music therapy. Methods and techniques in music therapy are primarily music based and are descriptors of the ways in which the therapist and service user or client engage in musical experiences. Bruscia (1998) identified four main music therapy methods: Receptive, Recreative, Creative, and Improvisation. These are based on improvisational, compositional, and music listening opportunities that music therapists engage with clients. Music therapists can use music-based techniques with any combination of acoustic, electric, or electronic instrumentation, and opportunities to sing and vocalize are also offered.

The ways in which music therapists use music techniques has affinity with methods used by practitioners in community music, music educators, and music and medicine. The main difference in the use of the methods between these disciplines is the theoretical basis for the work. Theory provides a practitioner with a way to think and reflect, and to have other ways of seeing what is happening in the work rather than what seems to be the most obvious at first consideration. Anyone with musical skills can play music for or even with another person; a person who is tired, in pain, or has a chronic illness or disability. Music therapy is distinguished from other music-based offerings in health care by both the training of the clinician, and the use of theoretical thinking to guide the use of techniques and principles in making helpful responses to needs with which the client presents. The relating that occurs when working with clients is a powerful therapeutic agent in the process. Understanding and using methods and techniques appropriately is essential but so is understanding reactions and interactions in the dynamic interpersonal space between the therapist and the client.

MUSIC THERAPY METHODS, TECHNIQUES, AND PROCEDURES

···

A music therapy *method* is a pithy shorthand descriptor for the way the music therapist and client interact musically. Bruscia (1998) has categorized these ways of interacting as improvisation, creative (composition), receptive (listening), and re-creative. Many music therapists have also described music performance as a method (for example, O'Brien 2006;

Soshensky 2011). *Techniques* are the more specific ways that music is used within the method and include; song singing, song writing, music listening and music relaxation techniques, musical improvisation, learning an instrument, and many other musical processes and interactions.

Procedures in music therapy are descriptions of how the process of engaging clients musically through methods and techniques is undertaken. Usually the procedure will involve what is said, what is played, whether the therapist demonstrates any of the options presented, whether the therapist plays or doesn't play, and how the techniques are applied. The procedure may indicate how techniques can be used in group and individual therapy contexts. As music therapy is a client-led relational therapy these procedures are rarely developed into protocols which are procedures which must be followed specifically. Procedures operate as guidelines and suggestions for how music therapy methods and techniques can be used in practice. As this chapter focuses on methods and techniques readers should source case material about music therapy practice (for example, Hadley 2003; Meadows 2011) to learn more about procedures.

MUSIC THERAPY TECHNIQUES

A technique is a process by which music use is specified within a music therapy method. For example the creative method includes the technique of song writing. As accomplished musicians many music therapists use music outside of their music therapy work in creative ways. As musicians they will usually practice and perform regularly. They may also use their skills to write songs, for example for family members on special occasions, and may lead group singing in religious, social, or family gatherings. The difference in using these techniques within music therapy is that the musical processes are not intended to solely entertain, to unify groups, or to give pleasure but are intended to contribute towards the development of the client's skills or capacities or to offer relief from pain or distress. The engaging and uplifting capacities of music must be skilfully used to ensure optimal outcomes especially as many clients referred to music therapy services are highly vulnerable through injury, illness, or other distressing experiences. The esthetic of the musical presentation of the therapist is essential also. Attention to vocal tone and quality when vocalizing or singing, the sound quality of the instruments used or offered to the client, the capacity of the instruments to *hold* or reflect strong feelings are all within the remit of the music therapists' responsibilities when providing opportunities to create and share musical experiences.

Song writing

The use of song writing in music therapy has been documented for decades in music therapy practices across many countries where the profession is well developed including the USA (Schmidt 1983) and Australia (O'Callaghan 1990). Within the use of song writing in music therapy practice a number of further granulated techniques can be used such as song parody (Edwards 1998; Robb 2003), fill-in-the-blanks (Schmidt 1983), and co-writing of songs about client generated themes (O'Callaghan 1995; Robb 2003).

In song parody the therapist uses an existing song melody and works with the client's choice of words to reflect a mood, a situation, or to describe current personal events. Fill-in-the-blanks, also known as the *cloze* procedure (Freed 1987) is a technique where the therapist provides some of the lyrics and encourages the client to fill in the words that are missing. For example, the therapist may compose a song but leave out key words allowing the client to share their responses.

> I am here today to share ____
> Sometimes it's ____ but I am ____
> I want to thank ____ and tell him/her/them ____
> I am ready for ____ and everything is ____

Some therapists write songs for clients or use clients' texts to compose songs (for example Aasgaard 2000). More typically therapists work alongside people in a process by which clients tell their story through song. For example, O'Callaghan (1996) described a procedure for songwriting with people referred to music therapy. She described a song writing *paradigm* involving eleven steps in song creation with patients with whom she worked. Some of these steps include the selection of a topic by the patient, and their choice of key after being played options by the music therapist.

Improvisational techniques

Some practitioners in music therapy use improvisation as the primary basis of musical interaction in music therapy. For example, the British Association for Music Therapy emphasizes the use of improvisation in their definition:

> Music therapy is a psychological therapy which uses the unique qualities of music as a means of interaction between therapist and client. Attentive listening on the part of the therapist is combined with shared musical improvisation using instruments and voices so that people can communicate in their own musical language, whatever their level of ability.
>
> British Association for Music Therapy website: <http://www.bamt.org/music-therapy.html>

However, many music therapists around the world also use improvisation of some kind in their practice even if it is not their primary method. The ways improvisation is used can depend on the model or orientation of the practitioner, and also the training they have completed.

Improvised instrumental music can support children or adults who are pain or experiencing uncomfortable or distressing medical procedures (Edwards and Kennelly 2011). In mental health services improvised music in group therapy can facilitate the experience of community among people receiving in-patient care, and can support and address needs for self-expression (de l'Etoile 2002; Ansdell and Meehan 2010). Service user accounts of participation in music therapy indicate that musical improvisation offers a way to develop and extend their existing positive relationship with music (Ansdell and Meehan 2010).

Techniques and procedures used within improvisation in music therapy vary according to whether music therapy is being offered a part of a group process or in an individual session context. Many techniques have been described and refined in relation to the music therapist's contribution within musical improvisation (see for example, Bruscia 1987; Wigram 2004) including mirroring, holding, reflecting, and grounding.

Music composition

Songwriting is one type of music composition. Additionally music therapists can work with clients to create instrumental works for performance (Noone 2008), or devise musical accompaniments for movies or slide shows created by the client. Music technology is used by many music therapists to support the musical creation process (Magee 2006; Noone 2008). In a charming vignette O'Callaghan et al. (2007) described a child receiving radiotherapy treatment who began composing piano pieces after attending music therapy and proudly brought them in to perform for team members.

CONCLUSION

Music therapists use the engaging and emotionally reflective qualities of music to help people who have additional needs whether psychological, physical, or spiritual. The methods and techniques used in music therapy do not stand apart from the theoretical rationale supporting the work with clients. The methods and techniques have parity with those used in other areas of professional music making such as music education, community music, and music and medicine. Music therapy practitioners and students are challenged to consider the theoretical basis of their use of music to ensure that rationales and proposed mechanisms of change can be described to others. Sometimes in training students can be keen on learning as much about methods and techniques as possible; the *how to* of practice. Care must be taken that this eager learning is not used as a way to look and sound like a music therapist. It is also through observing, thinking, and reflecting about processes that have occurred throughout sessions that the work becomes therapeutic. Questioning the underpinning rationale for techniques used is needed rather than only focussing how many techniques there are and how to use them. Theoretical principles guiding the practitioners use of music, whether music based (Aigen 2005) or from related psychological therapies (Hilliard 2001), are the key to ethical and effective practice.

REFERENCES

Aasgaard, T. (2000). An ecology of love: Aspects of music therapy in the pediatric oncology environment. *Journal of Palliative Care* 17(3): 177–181.
Aigen, K. (2005). *Music-centered Music Therapy*. Gilsum, NH: Barcelona Publishers.
Ansdell, G. and Meehan, J. (2010). "Some Light at the End of the Tunnel" Exploring Users' Evidence for the Effectiveness of Music Therapy in Adult Mental Health Settings. *Music and Medicine* 2(1): 29–40.
Bruscia, K. (1987). Improvisational models of music therapy. Springfield, IL: Charles C Thomas.
Bruscia, K.E. (1998). *Defining Music Therapy*. Gilsum, NH: Barcelona Publishers.
de l'Etoile, S.K. (2002). The effectiveness of music therapy in group psychotherapy for adults with mental illness. *The Arts in Psychotherapy* 29(2): 69–78.
Edwards, J. (1998). Music therapy for children with severe burn injury. *Music Therapy Perspectives* 16(1): 21–26.

Edwards, J. and Kennelly, J. (2011). Music Therapy for children in hospital care: A stress and coping framework for practice. In: Anthony Meadows (ed.), *Developments in Music Therapy Practice: Case Study Perspectives*, pp. 150–165. Gilsum, NH: Barcelona.

Freed, B.S. (1987). Songwriting with the chemically dependent. *Music Therapy Perspectives* 4(1): 13–18.

Hadley, S. (ed.) (2003). *Psychodynamic Music Therapy: Case Studies*. Gilsum, NH: Barcelona Publishers.

Hilliard, R.E. (2001). The use of cognitive-behavioral music therapy in the treatment of women with eating disorders. *Music Therapy Perspectives* 19(2): 109–113.

Magee, W.L. (2006). Electronic technologies in clinical music therapy: A survey of practice and attitudes. *Technology and Disability* 18(3): 139–146.

Meadows, A. (ed.). (2011). *Developments in Music Therapy Practice: Case Study Perspectives*. Gilsum, NH: Barcelona Publishers.

Noone, J. (2008). Developing a music therapy programme within a person centred planning framework. *Voices: A World Forum for Music Therapy*, v. 8, n. 3, np ISSN 1504-1611. Available at: <https://voices.no/index.php/voices/article/view/420>.

O'Brien, E. (2006). Opera therapy: Creating and performing a new work with cancer patients and professional singers. *Nordic Journal of Music Therapy* 15(1): 82–96.

O'Callaghan, C.C. (1990). Music therapy skills used in songwriting within a palliative care setting. *The Australian Journal of Music Therapy* 1(1): 15–22.

O'Callaghan, C.C. (1995). Songs written by palliative care patients in music therapy. *Lonely waters*, pp. 31–40. Oxford: Sobell Publications.

O'Callaghan, C.C. (1996). Lyrical themes in songs written by palliative care patients. *Journal of Music Therapy* 33(2): 74–92.

O'Callaghan, C.C., Sexton, M., and Wheeler, G. (2007). Music therapy as a non-pharmacological anxiolytic for paediatric radiotherapy patients. *Australasian Radiology* 51(2): 159–162.

Robb, S.L. (2003). Designing music therapy interventions for hospitalized children and adolescents using a contextual support model of music therapy. *Music Therapy Perspectives* 21(1): 27–40.

Schmidt, J.A. (1983). Songwriting as a therapeutic procedure. *Music Therapy Perspectives* 1(2): 4–7.

Soshensky, R. (2011). Everybody is a star: Recording, performing, and community music therapy. *Music Therapy Perspectives* 29(1): 23–30.

Wigram, T. (2004). *Improvisation: Methods and Techniques for Music Therapy Clinicians, Educators, and Students*. London: Jessica Kingsley Publishers.

CHAPTER 35

SONGWRITING TECHNIQUES IN MUSIC THERAPY PRACTICE

TRYGVE AASGAARD
AND STINE C. BLICHFELDT ÆRØ

INTRODUCTION

"SONGWRITING" refers to the ways in which music therapists help clients to create their own songs (Baker and Wigram 2005; Baker et al. 2008, 2009). Naming these practices "therapeutic songwriting" is one way of emphasizing the particular goals and settings in music therapy where the predominant focus is on potential relationships between the musical processes and the health and well-being of the client or group.

Music therapists use a variety of techniques, which may also have different therapeutic goals. Several other aspects of the song are equally interesting as the creative musical and literary elements such as the health status of the client(s)/patient(s) during the creative process, where the song related activities take place, forms of cooperation, artifacts, performances, and potential audiences. If songwriting has a justified place in the music therapist's repertory of skills, there has to be a concern about what song making means to the songwriter as well as the relationships between this intervention and various health parameters of the client/s. There is possibly no such a thing as a song; just like *music*, a *song* cannot easily be reduced to a single variable or factor. Like all other therapies, music therapy takes place within a certain context, which also influences any song-related experience or effect.

DISTINCTIONS AND DEFINITIONS

Songwriting in music therapy has been defined by Baker and Wigram (2005) as: "The process of creating, notating and/or recording lyrics and music by the client or clients and therapist within a therapeutic relationship to address psychosocial, emotional, cognitive and communication needs of the client" (p. 16). This definition covers any stage and element of the creative process until a potential performance. Performance-related activities, including listening and rehearsing, in a definition of songwriting might also be included in comtemporary music therapy practices.

A song is a musical *work of art*: a text or poem is sung or a vocal composition created, with or without accompaniment and as a form of musicking (Small 1998), where the work of art does not exist over and above its performance. Works of art are particular culturally emergent or culturally produced entities that are embedded in various human contexts. The fundamental nature and meaning of "a song" lie not in the song object, but "[...] in action, in what people do" (Small 1998, p. 8).

To make, to remember, and to perform a *song* is not dependent on recording the text or music. In cultures dependent on oral traditions, songs may be remembered and used for centuries without ever being written down. This is also the case in industrialized cultures: Children—alone or in a group—may spontaneously make small songs or chants which are recalled or recreated on purely an oral level. Hospitalized children and their family members sometimes develop personal songs, often based on well-known, old melodies (Aasgaard 2002). When these are only recorded in the memory of the participants, the degree of privacy and intimacy increases. In such cases, the label "songwriting" may be somewhat misleading. Words like to "create" or "compose" are often seen in descriptions of how a song is made, but terms like "song creations" or "song compositions" are not commonly used in music therapy literature.

It is not always easy to define exactly what can be named "a song"—or not. A final song product can be the preliminary end stage of improvisatory activities. Recording an instrumental/vocal improvisation makes it easy to transform the various sounds to notes and written words. Many therapists find this material helpful as documentation and to gain a better understanding of on the processes ocurring in a session. Who decides when improvisation activities result in a song product or composition? Such decisions have probably more to do with people than the parameters of the musical material The close relationship between composing and improvising was reflected in the comprehensive guide to improvisational music therapy where examples of songwriting and story making were related to models of improvisation (Bruscia 1987). When music therapists highlight excerpts from clinical improvisation for listening purposes, the musical material enters a grey-zone between process and product, but such improvisations are usually not named *songs*. Melody and lyrics are usually present in a song; however, many children will call any melody or piece of music, a *song*, while lyrics alone do not qualify the category of song. A specific song's life after its creation is, however, dependent on certain musical/textual elements, which can be repeated in some form or another.

THE DEVELOPMENT OF SONGWRITING
IN MUSIC THERAPY

The topic and method of assisting clients to compose their own songs, has a far shorter history in music therapy practice than other methods such as improvisation or composing songs *for* various groups of clients. There are several possible factors that have been decisive for the relatively "late" interest for this topic. Song and instrumental *improvisation* has (had) a particularly strong position in many psychotherapeutically-orientated music therapy curricula and practices. From this position, processes in music therapy-related activities have perhaps been focused more than any product (e.g. "a song").

Dorothy Crocker in Texas, USA, was one of the first music therapists writing about her clients' self-made songs. In the early 1950's she inspired children who were at that time described as *emotionally maladjusted* to compose. She assisted them creating their own opera; with a dramatic plot about a *mean mother* which was the theme suggested by a seven-year-old girl (Crocker 1952). In Europe and Australia, the first literary contributions in this field appeared in the early 1990's (Griessmeier 1990; Griessmeier and Bossinger 1994; O'Callaghan 1990).

The first arenas for music therapy related songwriting recorded in the literature were within music therapy programmes in mental health institutions (Ruppenthal 1965; Castellano 1969; Ficken 1976). Johnson (1981) introduced *songwriting* to groups of socially disadvantaged or young people in trouble with the law. Gfeller (1987) developed a method of *songwriting in group* for people with reading or written language difficulties. Freed (1987) presented songwriting for chemically dependent adults, based on the Twelve-Step recovery program of Alcoholics Anonymous and Narcotics Anonymous. Other populations reported as using music therapy related song creations are pediatric burn patients (Rudenberg and Royka 1989; Loveszy 1991; Robb 1996; Edwards 1998), young adults with traumatic injuries (Amir 1990; Hadley 1996), patients with chronic degenerative illnesses (Magee 1999; Salmon 1995), developmentally disabled patients (Fischer 1991), forensic patients (Fulford 2002) and children with cancer (O'Callaghan and Jordan 2011). O'Callaghan has also published several articles on various themes related to songwriting within adult palliative care including "music therapy skills" (1990), "lyrical themes" (1996), and "therapeutic opportunities" (1997). Mayers (1995) described the use of songwriting with children who had experienced trauma.

In 2002, Trygve Aasgaard defended the first doctoral thesis on this theme, *Song creations by children with cancer—process and meaning*. This is a multiple instrumental case study of the "lifestories" of nineteen songs, and where the song-related activities and products are interpreted in a role perspective. In 2005, Felicity Baker and Tony Wigram edited the first textbook on this theme, *Songwriting. Methods, Techniques and Clinical Applications for Music Therapy Clinicians, Educators and Students*. Ten chapters provide in-depth information about songwriting with clients through the lifespan within the clinical fields of special education, mental health, oncology, neurology, and hospice/palliative care. Baker and Wigram highlight the different clinicians' specific goals, methods, techniques, and what happens to the songs after they have been created. In 2008–2009, the *Nordic Journal of Music Therapy* published, in two parts, the first worldwide, comprehensive survey on songwriting practices in music therapy, Therapeutic Songwriting in Music Therapy, based on data obtained from 477 music therapists in 29 countries (Baker et al. 2008, 2009). The survey, based on responses to a 21-question online survey, shows that 419 of the 477 participants included songwriting in their professional work and that music therapy related songwriting (reflective of the body of literature) is primarily practiced in Australia, New Zealand, USA, Canada, UK, and Norway.

Therapeutic goals. Many people of all ages in ordinary daily life, create tunes, write songs, add new lyrics to an old melody, or sing a song they already know. They can usually do so because they want to do it or some occasion requires it. They do not have to give a reason or explain *why*. In settings where music therapy is offered, it is actually not different; the music therapist may assist any client in the songwriting process without an elaborated goal. Humans want to make music because we are humans. When we are sick or dependent on care and treatment, however, we sometimes need some extra help to accomplish various purposes. Music therapists are skilled professionals who can help people in many ways through musical interactions and the relationships that subsequently form.

At times, songwriting, like many other therapeutic interventions, commences with definite expected outcomes, but ends with rather unexpected results. Goals may also be added or changed through the entire creative process. Because the making and performance of one's own song is a many sided activity and experience, the music therapist usually initiates or assists in the songwriting process with several simultaneous therapeutic goals, more or less linked to specific health issues, like a particular life-situation, disease, symptom, or conditions of treatment. In Baker et al.'s survey from 2008, goals of songwriting interventions were compared between different diagnostic groups: psychiatry (n = 103), developmental disability (n = 89), autistic spectrum disorder (n = 61), oncology (n = 51), dementia (n = 36), neurorehabilitation (n = 26), and other clinical areas (n = 53). This survey shows that very similar goals may, at times, be relevant in very different areas of practice. The most common goals of intervention in oncology and nevrorehabilitation were "validating experiences" and "externalize thought, fantasies, and emotions," while "choice and decision-making" was the most common goal in songwriting with clients suffering from dementia and clients with developmental disability.

In the psychiatric field the most common goals were "externalize thought, fantasies, and emotions" and "gain insight or clarify thoughts and feelings." "Telling the client's story" was a goal for songwriting in several diagnostic groups, while "language, speech, and/or conversational skills" and "develop cognitive skills" were solely related to clients with developmental disability or autistic spectrum disorder. Songwriting with the aim of "sending messages to significant others" were only reported from oncology. According to Baker et al., "When compared with the literature, these highly endorsed goal areas are relatively similar" (p. 115). Songwriting is also used for diagnostic purposes, enhancement of spirituality and with other goals not specified in the table because they are applied relatively seldom.

The method of songwriting. When a client is being assisted in the process of making a song, one is not dependent on any predetermined strategies or techniques. Literature on songwriting varies considerably in as to how songs are created, and many case reports only provide implicit reference to methods and techniques focusing instead on the outcomes, or the song itself and its lyrics. Some music therapists present elaborated procedures with definite steps or stages, others follow the intiative of the clients, the majority, however, have developed some kind of system, which seems to function with different clients.

Songwriting is most commonly a part of individual therapy, but songs can also be created in cooperation with families (Aasgaard 2002, 2005) or through group-work with clients, e.g. in various mental health/social programmes and geriatric in- or out-patient care (Day et al. 2009; Klein and Silverman 2012; Silverman and Leonard 2012). Group approaches in songwriting are most often dependent on structure and, eventually, set goals for each session.

The multi-stage methods are perhaps most helpful in group settings and for clients who have little initiative and few ideas when it comes to creating and putting together essential musical and literary elements that finally constitute "a song." A music therapist must, however, be prepared to adapt to clients who, from the very start of the creative process, have clear opinions about which (well-known) melody they want to use, who have already made lyrics or a poem which they think could be part of a song, or who find it quite natural to engage in text and musical matters simultaneously. We will here consider two different main approaches of assisting clients in songwriting.

METHODS BASED ON SPECIFIC STEPS OR STAGES

O'Callaghan, presented an eleven step protocol for songwriting based on experiences from 64 song projects with individual, dyads, or groups of patients (O'Callaghan 1996). This approach was developed in palliative care settings over many years with the aim to facilitate the patients' songwriting, with variations according to their physical and/or cognitive abilities (O'Callaghan 1996).

1. Offer Songwriting
2. Choose a topic
3. Brainstorm
4. The ideas that emerged were grouped into related areas, usually by the therapist, in what was to become a chorus or verses
5. Offer major or minor keys
6. Choose rhythmical features
7. Find the preferred style of mood
8. Melody: usually the patient was given the choice of two melodic fragments for each line of the song
9. Choosing accompaniment—only a few patients were involved in this
10. Naming the song (title)
11. After the song was written up, the therapist or, if possible, the patients recorded it

After seven years of music therapy practice with cancer patients aged between 17 and 85 years, Emma O'Brian developed what was called "Guiding Original Lyrics and Music" (GOLM), which bears many similarities with O'Callaghan's eleven steps, e.g. with the music therapist offering the patient musical examples from which to chose (O'Brien 2005). This five step method also starts with exploring ideas and themes, then grouping ideas into a song structure and, based on the patient's desired style, the song is being constructed in sections, it gets a melody, and, according to the author, a "secondary reframing of lyrics influenced by the melody" before melody and accompaniment are added (O'Brian 2005, p. 184).

Robert E. Krout (2005) proposed the songwriting process could be undertaken in ten steps, starting with determining " [...] focus of song by examining the clinical need" (step 1), and, finally, adding "additional accompaniment and stylistic features to make a song unique" (step 10). Throughout the creative process the therapist has the major responsibility for the various artistic choices, and the author rightly admits: "A disadvantage of the above approach might be that as the song is pre-composed by the therapist, it does not involve the clients (in this case the teenagers) in the song creation process" (Krout 2005, p. 223). The examples from O'Callaghan, O'Brien, and Krout indicate that some methods of songwriting are able to accomplish a song product even with patients with very few contributions as to the various song ideas and elements. However, if most elements of a song are accomplished through asking the client/patient to choose between two options given by the therapist, one must be aware of potential problems as to how far a therapist ought to influence the creative process and product while being aware also of the capacities and abilities of the client.

People who have Traumatic Brain Injury (TBI) often have several emotional, cognitive, and communication impairments. When communication skills are severely reduced, highly structured interventions are inevitable in the often long, slow, and painful way forward to a more normal life. In Australia, Felicity Baker has developed a protocol for songwriting with persons with TBI, where a major aim is to "[…] help them to be more proficient when conversing with others" (Baker 2005, p. 137). Prior to the onset of all forms of therapy within the comprehensive interdisciplinary treatment program, music therapy included, clearly observable potential outcomes must be formulated and sanctioned. Baker presents various pre-set goals, such as "To work on generating three new and related ideas (for insertion into a song) with minimum prompting." One way of assisting the patients in the process of developing ideas for lyrics, is a structured conversation based on the "wh" questions which may help to explore a specific topic in different directions. Baker exemplifies this by a row of suggested questions a patient may ask himself if the topic is (his favorite take-away restaurant).

If the patient is unable to communicate verbally, the music therapist has the opportunity to apply various alternative modes of communication to assist in creating lyrics such as alphabet boards, electronic talkers, or sign language, etc. In such cases the creative process can be slow and time-consuming. Baker underlines that when a patient definitely is not able to express thoughts and feelings adequately through words, songwriting may even be contraindicated (Baker 2005, p. 142).

Music making is facilitated when using an electronic keyboard with many built-in accompaniment styles. Baker also uses this instrument to explore the patient's musical preferences. She presents fifteen different harmonic progressions useful in constructing songs. These progressions are played several times for the patient to find out which of them is especially appealing (Baker 2005, p. 144). Chord progressions may be made within a system of two bars, like C—B♭, played again and again, or in a system of four or even eight bars (with one chord in each bar): C or C maj—A min—D min7—G7—E min7—A min—F—G7.

GUIDING PRINCIPLES AS ALTERNATIVE
TO STEP-WISE METHODS

If a music therapist wants to apply a "non-directive" or "less-directive" approach, we present an alternative that is not step-wise, but rather a loose framework of guidelines and some basic questions the music therapist ought to ask to her/himself throughout the periods when a song is being initiated, composed, and/or performed. This approach contains no specific starting or finishing point, because patients can enter the songwriting process in so many different ways. Patients may initially bring with them to music therapy one or more texts they have already made, or, on their own, produce material for, or the actual lyrics within few days. Some start a song project with visions of where the song should be performed and how the groove should sound.

The most crucial question that should continuously be kept in mind by the music therapist is: What does the patient want? Secondly: What is the patient able to accomplish without much assistance? The music therapist can tell what she/he may help with, such as collaborating with making a melody, arrangement, accompaniment, or with producing artefacts, such as sheet music with notes and lyrics, a CD or a video. We believe, however, that the music therapist should resist the temptation to "take over" the making of lyrics, and never persuade the patient to choose a particular theme. This attitude may certainly result in fewer finished songs, but gives a certain guarantee for authenticity, if this is understood as being an important factor in songwriting. The following guidelines (Table 35.1) are based on our experiences of assisting hospitalized young adults, youths, and children with neurological or heart/lung diseases, cancer, or serious mental health problems (Aasgaard 2004, 2005; Ærø and Aasgaard 2011). They may be helpful in guiding songwriting processes in cooperation with any individual patient.

Table 35.1 Guidelines for Songwriting

Lyrics	Music	Performance
✓ Give the patient sufficient time to write or to find her/his own words. Don't push!	✓ Common improvising or "playing" with musical elements often initiates decision-making as to what kind of music/style the song shall have. Even small rhythmical/melodic or harmonic fragments from patients may be a point of departure for further music making.	✓ Some songs are too private to be performed to others (simply having made the song may be enough).
✓ Check out if the patient wants to make a completely new song or re-write or change words in an old text.		✓ A good accompanist may "lift" a simple song from sounding ordinary to sounding excellent. Patients and relatives (etc.) usually highly appreciate this.
✓ Allow the patient to choose theme(s). Lyrics do not need to be autobiographical. Sick people do not necessarily want to make songs about sickness or personal problems.		✓ In institutions, the music therapist may promote different arenas for presenting songs to others. The music therapist may help with the making of song artefacts.
✓ Indicating a specific groove/ beat may boost verbal processing.	✓ A chosen groove (rhythmic pattern and bass-line) may be established before the actual making of a melody.	
✓ A well-known melody may provide a safe starting point for lyrical "exercises."	✓ When the music therapist is planning how to make an arrangement, the most important question is, "Who is going to perform the song?"	✓ It is advisable to engage patient/relatives in conversations about the future "life" of tangible products, like a song recording, and to ensure practices where the song product is being used according to professional and ethical standards.
✓ Repeating a lyric phrase can be an effective structuring element.		
✓ For whatever reason, be careful not to "improve" the patient's suggested lyrics more than strictly necessary.	✓ When (if) recording the song, reflect on what is most important: authenticity or a polished/professional result.	

Inspired by the empowerment philosophy, Randi Rolvsjord has presented a guide for songwriting, that consistently focuses the clients' competencies related to their therapeutic process of change, aiming at nurturing and developing recourses through musical collaboration (Rolvsjord 2005, 2010). As she wrote:

> The process of songwriting may take between one and three sessions, which includes some homework for the therapist, client, or both. I always transcribe the song onto manuscript paper, and make a recording of the song the client can take away with her/him. The musical notation (melody, chords, and lyrics) is sometimes important in assisting the client in learning to play the song and also makes it possible for other people to play the song. In addition it creates a concrete musical product, which can be stored and retrieved at a later date
>
> (Rolvsjord 2005, p. 100).

In the book, *Resource-Oriented Music Therapy in Mental Health Care* (2010), Rolvsjord presented eleven songs and their creative histories; songs made by two young women in their twenties. The first sessions with "Maria" are marked by different musical activities, like "[...] singing, improvising, and trying out different instruments, so as to show her some of the possibilities she had" (p. 89). Maria, diagnosed with Borderline Personality Disorder, impulsive type (F. 10.1, ICD-10), has a long history of self-mutilation and overdoses. She comes to music therapy because of her interest for music, and the therapust discovers that Maria has a beautiful singing voice. During the eighth music therapy session, Maria stated that she now wants to sing, not the usual popular songs she has been singing till now, but something else. This becomes the starting point for creating her own song in cooperation with the music therapist. The following quotation shows a songwriting process that is perhaps more improvisatory than predetermined, but with a music therapist who is pushing the song activities gently forwards:

CLINICAL EXAMPLE 1

In the rest of the session, we started to write a song. She suggested words and sentences that could be included: "I feel broken," "I need some time to heal," "I feel like a bird with a broken wing," "when I am ready to fly," "then I can start to live again," "pain," "darkness," "sorrow," "hope." "I do want a song with some hope," she said. "I want to get on with my life, you know." At the end of the session, we started to sing another precomposed song. [...] She asked me to show her the chords on the piano, as she wanted to accompany herself.

From session 12:[...] The progress with the song we started to write in session 8 slowed down. Maria wanted to sing and to learn more on the piano, but hesitated to work more with the songwriting because, as she said, it led her into thinking some destructive thoughts. In spite of this, I made a proposal for one verse and a chorus on the basis of the sentences and words she had suggested in session 8. In the 12th session, I presented this to her. She started immediately to work with a second verse because she thought the song was too short, and by the end of the session we had finished the song

Rolvsjord 2010, pp. 94–95

This account is quite far from an example of an unproblematic process of songwriting, but it demonstrates how the creative activities of songwriting mingle with other musical interactions over time. This patient is consistently ambivalent to her oeuvre: she may want to sing it, she makes a second voice to the song, and she learns how to play an accompaniment on the piano, but soon after, she tells that the song makes her sick, and during the next 24 sessions, her interest or capability for musical activities varies dramatically in accordance with her mental and physical status.

Songwriting is far from always being a straightforward, linear event, and in some settings it can be unrealistic to plan the sessions ahead. Reasons for this can relate to the clients' changing health condition or administrative decisions as to *where* the client is at different times.

EXAMPLES OF LYRIC CREATION TECHNIQUES

With the patients who are unlikely to be able to make a complete poem or lyrics, such as very young children, there is an option to demonstrate to the patient how she/he may substitute some existing words in a popular song with ones own. Just filling in one or two words in a ready-made song, is perhaps in a grey-zone of songwriting, but "Fill-in-the-Blank" may be very effective as a way of enjoyable musical communication where the young child easily can express thoughts and feelings: "I really like (to) …., but I don't like (to) …. " (Robb 1996).

In many cases, the creation of rhyming lyric patterns is regarded as a "must" for a good poem or song text. At times this is more important for the songwriter than creating logically meaningful lyrics; the music therapist must principally never try to interfere with the patient's rhyming choices but can make suggestions if the patient is frustrated that they cannot think of a rhyme.

> **CLINICAL EXAMPLE 2**
>
> One morning in the isolation unit of a Norwegian pediatric oncology ward, an eight-year-old girl writes two song texts. Her father gives the music therapist the small sheets of paper and explains that "Mary" wants musical arrangements and recordings to be made as soon as possible. Because of a very sore mouth she is not able to sing herself this time. Both songs are to be given to her primary nurse in the hospital she stayed before bone marrow transplantation became necessary. One text has few rhymes, but is probably a quite accurate account of all the nice things the nurse does for Mary: comforting her when she has much pain, reading for her and stays with her to make her sleep. The other text is full of rhyming words, but clearly nonsense "meanings," telling that Mary and her nurse are "pulling out our teeth" and "skipping rope with our feet." However, both songs were seemingly equally important to the young patient.

Song Parody or Song Augmentation (Edwards 1998) indicates use of "[…] the music of a pre-composed song whereby the lyrics of the original song are completely replaced by client-generated lyrics" (Baker et al. 2005, p. 124). At times, the songwriter keeps some central words from the original text, and by this, mixes old and new elements that may harmonize or be highly contrasting. An example of the latter is the following account of the blending of a most innocent well-known children's song with new words describing a very critical stage in the girl's period of treatment:

> **CLINICAL EXAMPLE 3**
>
> One morning, a seven-year-old girl, suffering from aplastic anemia, surprises the music therapist with a song she has made herself, and, according to the mother: without any help from others. Ten days earlier, she received bone marrow (stem-cells) from her big sister, and since that date, the isolation room has been her permanent address. Now she is eagerly waiting for her body to produce new, healthy blood corpuscles. "Hannah" has given the Norwegian version of Ba, ba, black sheep, have you any wool? an

> almost quite new text. This time, she is not asking for wool, but begging her own blood corpuscles to be more prolific. They answer, "yes," on the sole condition that Hannah promises keeping up her high spirits.
>
> As to "songwriting": Hannah creates the new lyrics without one word being written down. Everyone in the family soon learns the song by heart—and the blood corpuscles luckily follow Hannah's request!

Song Parody is also a potentially meaningful starting point for songwriting with adult clients. McCaffrey et al. (2011) described the applicaion of music therapy in a mental health service in Ireland. The theoretical focus for their work is a recovery approach focusing on "[…] a meaningful life beyond the limitations of illness and symptomatology" (p. 185). Clinical work by Tríona McCaffrey described in the paper included work with a 40-year-old Kevin who was dignosed with paranoid schizophrenia. Kevin chose his favorite singer, Bob Marley, and a song that he liked. Together the music therapist and Kevin created a song parody based on his choice of words through which Kevin was able to reveal aspects of his personal experience and inner life.

> *The sun is shining today*
> *Yet in my heart I'm grey*
> *The sun is shining today*
> *Yet in my heart I'm grey*
> *In my youth my life goes by*
> *And so I lay down and sigh*
> *Things are looking better*
> *Then it begins to rain*
> *No more sunshine for us*
>
> Reprinted from McCaffrey et al. (2011).

Music creation techniques

Melody and rhythm

For some clients, the creation of a melody comes naturally along with the text making. The music therapist must be able to hold on to musical elements as they develop, to remember melodic phrases, and—if necessary—to add structure to the emerging song, for example, by repeating some parts or keeping the tune in pitch. Even though there is a high degree of skill to creating an accomplished melody, most people are able to hum fragments of melodic themes, motifs or rhythmic figures that an be included in the song. When the client is very quiet or withdrawn, even the smallest fragment can provide a useful spark, such as the way she/he is saying a certain word or tapping fingers on the table. The occurrence of musical fragments can be facilitated through improvising, commencing call—response activities or through exploring different instruments (see Figure 35.1). O'Brien (2005, p. 198) uses a type

FIGURE 35.1 You are the most handsome boy in the school.

of melodic shorthand that she finds useful in assisting her to recall melodies that have been created within a session. In the following song example, *Love at first sight*, a melodic short-hand may look like this (see bar 8 and 9):

The client, a 13-year-old Norwegian girl, who wanted to write in English, made a musical motif while improvising on the keyboard (a rhythmic figure starting in bar 17). This frag-ment is then repeated and used as a recurring theme throughout the song.

This motif also functions as a "hook"[1] that forms the identity of the song. It must be remembered that also pauses are central elements in many good melodies. A well-placed pause can be an outstanding ingredient in a "hook." At times, lyrics call for "mickey-mousing": the melody is synchronized, mirrored, or parallel to the content of the lyrics. This is originally a film technique that synchronizes the accompanying music with the actions on screen.

Harmonic features and arrangement

Finding the right harmonics often goes hand in hand with the creation of the melody. Usually we go for a recognizable structure and "sound" that suit the client's ears, but at the same time are unique. Many songs' musical framework is based on verse and refrain, such as ABAB. A bridge may be added, resulting in a slightly more complex form, such as ABABCAB. The harmonic progressions are chosen among common chords related to the main key. The client's ability to play an accompanying instrument can also be a chosen frame for which chords to use.

Some clients also appreciate to be involved in making variations in the arrangement. Parts of the song may be modulated. This can be achieved through surprising beats, sounds or pauses, or orchestrating the song in different ways. A good musical arranger will be sensitive to the capabilities of the performing artist.

Very often though, we find that what is simple, is also the best. A single bass-line may act as an independent counterpoint that emphasizes the main melody. A single, repeated note may create suspension and keep being interesting for a long time when it is being accompanied by changing chords. For example, there is a D in all the following chords: Dm—F6—G—Fm6—Asus—Bb—C9—D.

A girl, six years of age, made the melody of "Sally comes and goes" while she was playing a xylophone. It appears like an altered C-major scale well suited to be played on this partic-ular instrument. The succeeding nonsense text is addressed to a beloved nurse; the words follow the rhythmic, repeated pattern of the melody. As the melody moves "upwards," the bass goes "down" and when the direction of the melody turns, this is mirrored in the bass-line.

The music therapist is a catalyst of songs where the process is dependent on a trusted relationship with the client. Every new relationship and context will probably mark the musical ideas from the therapist. And—like the researcher who is evaluating her/his own biases before commencing on a new project—the music therapist needs to be aware of own strengths and weaknesses as a co-composer/arranger and, eventually, take action to improve skills and knowledge.

Love ar first sight

ELECTRONIC MUSIC TECHNOLOGY IN SONGWRITING

During the last decades most young people have become familiar with the use of new technology; a field where many established music therapists have much to learn from the younger generation—also when they are our patients. Literature and research on the uses of new technology inevitably come some time after established practices. Today many music therapists develop new techniques and methods in this field, and exploration of how this differs from established music therapy techniques has been undertaken (Magee and Burland 2008).

Sally comes and Sally goes

09.06.11

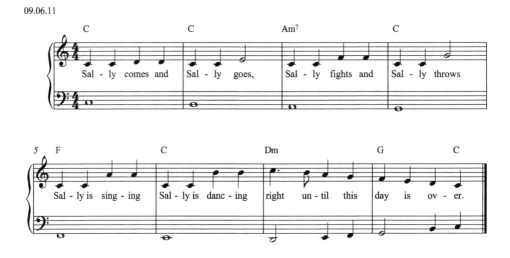

Electronic music technology rovides a number of potentially useful tools for various aspects of songwriting. Most clients, having reached a certain age, are now using laptops, Mp3 players, iPads, or advanced mobile phones in their daily life, and this technological familiarity may potentially facilitate entering the creative process of making a song. However, does the new technology also expand our creative possibilities of making music? Is it more effective as to obtaining speedy results? Even if that is true, is it a danger that technology takes over the creative process too much?

We have experienced that electronic equipment often serves as an intervening object between the client and the therapist. Simply exploring and "experimenting" with electronic and technical music devices, such as loops and apps, may be a pleasant and non-threatening way to start a song creation process, and practitioners of acoustic music can also certainly benefit from the multitude of possibilities related to multi-track recording.

The following pages contain examples and descriptions of some products that have been tried out and found useful. However, this very field of practice is where "learning by doing" is probably more useful than the best of written suggestions and manuals.

APPS

One finds many apps for iPad and androids designed for musical exploration. Many of them are limited in terms of creative or musical possibilities. Some of the most useful can make different types of loops based on the sounds available in the program. Some apps provide elements better suitable for improvising rather than composing, e.g. Bloom or Soundrop. Nodebeat (pentatonic) and Beatwawe are examples of programs that allow users to use different keys and tempo, and can easily be combined with acoustic instruments. An iPad can be convenient to use with people who have disabilities, or children even as young as one to two years of age.

LOOPS

There are several loop programs to find for both PC and Mac. Examples of free download programs for PC: ACID Pro and Magix Music Maker Basic. When it comes to Macintosh computers they are all delivered with the program Garageband installed. This is the program used in the following two examples. Out of a bank of loops, the client picks out rhythms, sounds and riffs, drags them one by one into the mixers, and builds up a musical environment. Some clients also learn the basics of mastering, such as fading in and out or muting a track for a period. The loops can easily be combined with acoustic elements through recording a voice or an instrument on a separate track.

CLINICAL EXAMPLE 5

Today's music therapy group at the hospital school engages two girls and two boys, all about 8–10 years old. They are going to make a song about summer, and will use a laptop to make the accompaniment. Our Garageband-group is divided in two parts: one working with the loops with the music therapist, the other group making text and rhymes together with the schoolteacher. After a while the groups switches, and by the end of the hour they have got 90 seconds of music and a written page of words describing their best summer memories. Together with the therapist, they identify a refrain, which everyone learns to sing. No one dare to start the rap-sequence, so the music therapist does the rap on the first acoustic-recorded track. One by one, the children get headphones on (so they can hear what is recorded already), and do their version of the refrain on yet another track. In the end they have five tracks with the children singing the refrain, a rap performed by the therapist, and the undergoing musical mix they all made together. The final lyrics are printed out and given to each child.

For more advanced musicians, a tool like Loopstation is a good alternative. Loopstation has no pre-set loops, but the user may create and record her/his own loops in various ways.

Skype—videoconferencing software

Skype is the most popular voice communication service in the world providing audio and video connection between to computers through internet. In 2011 Baker and Krout carried out a study of collaborative peer lyric writing between music therapy students in USA and Australia. The songwriting sessions were based on an eleven step protocol (adapted from Krout 2005)—some conducted with face to face dyads, other sessions applying the videoconferencing Skype software. Tools provided were pen and paper, keyboard, and guitar. The authors state that they had anticipated that "[…] the Skype context may interrupt the flow of self reflection and dialogue between the students during the songwriting sessions, however this was not the case" (p. 84). The students themselves claimed that the Skype mode of cooperating, where rather strict turn taking is a necessity, helped them to be more effective and that this way of creating a song together actually was quite engaging.

Baker and Krout (2009) have also explored how songwriting via Skype functions in long-distance clinical heath care. Today, various modes of telecommunication between health practitioners and clients/patients are developing rapidly within many fields of medical and mental health services. This pilot research project (a single controlled case study) dealt with Skype-based songwriting with "Harry," a 15-year old boy diagnosed with Asperger's Syndrome. Video footage of the two face-to-face sessions and two Skype sessions were compared as to interaction between the boy and the music therapist, and analyzed in the light of written reflections from the participants focusing similarities and differences and likes and dislikes related to the two settings for songwriting. Findings showed that Harry voiced more disagreements with the music therapist during a Skype session than during the face-to-face settings. Harry also played his guitar more in the Skype sessions. This may indicate that Harry experienced an increased level of confidence to contribute when "distance" was created between client and therapist. Eye contact was substantially greater during all the Skype video segments analyzed and there were more occurrences of smiling and laughing during the Skype sessions, suggesting higher levels of engagement (Baker and Krout 2009, p. 10).

Recording

Multi-track recording programs are now available for almost any laptop and are often standard equipment for Macs. What was only wishful thinking few years ago, is now reality for all people who are interested in music-making and recording: a light-weight portable studio. To master the basics of this software is relatively simple. A multi-track recording program may be used as an ordinary recorder directly through the laptop´s built-in microphone. Some music therapists prefer a laptop with an external soundcard with extra microphone(s) or "in-lines." A "live recording" requires basically not more than a single recording track, but if one wants to control specific elements of acoustic sounds (e.g. different instruments), several tracks are needed.

The vast possibilities of multi-track recordings allow the therapist to facilitate a process where the client works with her/his music-material over time, just like in a recording studio. This can be a tool in the creative process as well; the client listens to the product many times, gets new ideas, can discuss and express opinions and reactions, perform changes in the arrangement, etc. If the client has got problems with following a steady beat or finding the right pitch, the therapist can record a "helping-track" that later can be erased.

Examples of multi-track programs:

- Audacity (free download)
- Garageband
- Pro Tools (professional)
- Cuebase (professional)

CLINICAL EXAMPLE 6

Nathalie is 13 years and has severe diabetes. Several times a week her blood has to be "washed" in the dialysis machine. The dialysis treatment requires that she is "stuck in bed" for three or four hours, but during this period she often gets a session with the music therapist. Nathalie has got a Mac of her own, and wants to learn how to use Garageband. We start with creating a mix of loops: Nathalie chooses two drum rhythms, a bass-riff, and a picking guitar, and is spending some time deciding which instrument to come first, duration of the composition and the balance between the tracks. When this is done, it´s time to add an acoustic track. Now Nathalie wants to play bongos to give her mix even more "spice." With the headphones on, she starts recording, but after 30 seconds, the dialyses machine starts to beep! The strong beeping is inevitably also being recorded—the machine has, however, a quite a cool sound and a distinct rhythm. Afterwards, Nathalie listens to the mix a few times and decides to keep it that way—with the beeping integrated. The tune is being called "Dialyses."

Hand-recorder. A hand-recorder is easy to carry and can be placed almost anywhere. It is very useful for rehearsing or making a quick musical draft during the creation of a song, just to remember it on the go. Because of the small size, the client might pay less attention to a hand-recorder than to a recording laptop.

The recordings are sorted in files and folders and the hand-recorder is compatible with multi-track programs. After recording, the memory-card from the hand-recorder is plugged directly into the laptop where it can be opened as a file in a multi-track program. The composer/arranger may continue the creative process from there: mixing, adding tracks, or burning a CD.

Some therapists prefer professional multi-track recording software like Pro Tools or Cuebase. These programs provide studio-quality of the recorded soundtracks; to get a "full effect" one has to line up a sound card and a professional microphone. Such programs have got no loop functions integrated, but they are compatible with loop-programs to be bought (ex. Reason). In order to decide which is the most convenient way to progess, it is important for the music therapist to identify her/his needs and interests:

- Do you have time, space and interests enough to learn how to use it properly?
- How often do you need it for your clients; would it be better renting a studio every now and then?
- How important is the sound quality versus the importance of simplicity in your daily life as a therapist?

SHARING

When the song is recorded and saved on the computer, it can be burned on a CD. In Garageband, there is an option to burn a song directly, or send it to iTunes. One folder here keeps several songs until one reach the required tracks for completing a planned CD. The recorded song can also be saved as an Mp3 file and transferred to an iPod.

The many possibilities for sharing soundtracks from a computer are well-known: YouTube, Facebook, and other social networking services. Presentations of soundtracks can be combined with photos, video, or PowerPoint—all potential tools in the creative as well as the therapeutic process. The music therapist should, however, be very aware of the vulnerability of clients sharing their products of self-expression. Internet safety must always be on the agenda when the use of computers is involved. Particularly, when working with young people and children, the music therapist is also responsible for informing the clients (and often parents) with knowledge about potential outcomes of using the internet for presenting and sharing intellectual property. A song used as an appropriate "visiting card" in a period of life marked by illness, hospitalization, treatment, and the concomitant self-expression, might, at other times, be understood and appreciated very differently.

An artefact like a CD is indeed something different from an Mp3 file; a CD cover may convey messages just as much as musical elements or lyrics. In addition, it can also be touched, it can be a cool present, and it can be a keepsake with a long life.

> **CLINICAL EXAMPLE 7**
>
> Nina is in the middle of making another song for her CD-project. She wants to sing and the therapist will accompany on guitar. The two voices are recorded on one track. The laptop-recorder is placed right between the two of them, and after three takes they have a version they like. (It is smart always to keep several versions before one of them is chosen.) Nina wants to add some rhythms to her song, and with headphones on she plays some percussion instruments, recorded on one track after another. Later the soundtracks are mixed and balanced before the file is sent to iTunes where all her songs lie in a folder waiting to be burned on a CD. The plan is to finish the CD before Christmas so that many members of her family each can get one copy.

SCORES

If the therapist does have a program for writing scores, she can give her client very professional-looking hand-outs of the creative products. Many clients are proud to receive a full score which opens up for later performances with new artists. The most common professional programs are Sibelius, Finale, and Capella, but it is not difficult to find free music notation software, like MC Musiceditor, Crescendo, or MuseScore.

POTENTIAL ISSUES IN TECHNOLOGY-BASED SONGWRITING

When using technological devices, the therapist must be aware of the possibility of altered communication patterns with the client, whose attention towards the screen may overshadow face-to-face human communication. Technological problems can definitely occupy both the client's and the therapist's minds even more than when dealing with acoustic instruments. Staying behind a screen is also a form of protection from facing other people directly. The potential anonymity of internet networks boosts some people's courage for the good or bad, a fact that must be acknowledged by all music therapists with songwriting in their repertoires.

PERFORMANCE AND THE AFTERLIFE OF SONGS

The first accounts of songwriting in music therapy paid little attention to performance (Aasgaard 2005). As long as the professional interests are restricted to what is going on in the therapy room—the very music therapy session—and the (musical) relationships between the client and the therapist, the idea of performance does not easily fit a conception of what inside or outside of music therapy. Indeed, some clients we have met insist that they do not want therapy, just a little help to make a song. Writing songs is a regular activity in many peoples' lives but in therapy we must take care to understand why we are using songwriting, and how we think it is helping clients.

In the late 1990s, a new focus on performance aspects of music therapy was forwarded through concepts like "health performance" (Aldridge 1996) and the development of theoretical perspectives named "ecological practices" (Bruscia 1998), "music-environmental-therapy" (Aasgaard 1999), and "community music therapy" (Ansdell 2002) (Stige 2002). An interest for relationships between performance and songwriting was evident in Aasgaard's study (2002, 2005) of nineteen cases of songs made by patients in pediatric oncology settings. These songs were performed not only from beds in isolation rooms, but also during sing-songs in public areas of the hospital, in national TV transmissions, and in schools, homes, or even other hospitals far away from the patient—when CDs were sent to classmates and different friends as gifts.

In Baker et al.'s (2009) comprehensive research project on current songwriting practices and literature in music therapy, one question answered by the 419 participants who employ songwriting in their work is, "What happens to the song"? Dependent on different clinical groups, between 29 and 80% of the songs have been given to wider audience and between 17 and 33% have been performed to wider audience (p. 46).

What then is regarded as the most important element in a song made by a patient, assisted by a music therapist? The following story presents a music therapist with a dominating pre-understanding that lyrics matter most, but who is taught by a young songwriter that actions means more than words!

CLINICAL EXAMPLE 8

The first time I receive a song text from a young cancer patient, I am slightly disappointed. "Roy" has written nothing but a short nonsense verse. Although the text has a nice rhythm and funny rhymes, it expresses no sickness or hospital experiences. The "Animal-Nonsense-Poem," as the boy has named it, reveals no particular problems or concerns and could have been written by many bright, healthy, "normal" eight-year-old kids.... The music therapy literature on children with cancer I have read at the time, reported solely about "meaningful," autobiographical texts created by patients, often in company with the music therapist. However, I give the boy's poem a melody as requested. The next day we tape-record the new song—the patient singing (beautifully) and me playing the keyboard.

During the following weeks the song can be heard performed live at the sing-song ("The Musical Hour") in the entrance hall of the pediatric department. Roy and other patients are singing together with parents, hospital staff, and students. According to his changing physical strength, the song maker is standing, sitting, or lying—but he is always close to the grand piano and the music therapist. He looks immensely proud when his song is being performed. On one occasion, I sing the song in a children's programme on the radio. No name, hospital, or diagnosis is mentioned; but after having heard the programme, the father tells his son, "Now, you have become a famous guy." After this, the boy's confidence seems to boost every time his creative song-skills are focused on. "My OWN song will be played," he once explains to an older boy who is not sure if he wants to take part in "The Musical Hour." Roy suffers from Acute Myelogenic Leukaemia. For long periods he is seriously affected by nausea and fatigue. A student nurse who visits Roy's home one year after the successful completion of the intensive medical treatment reports that the written version of the song (text, melody, and chords) can be seen framed on the wall in the sitting room.

Aasgaard 2002, p. 1

The songs' fate beyond the music therapy room is now included in many accounts about songwriting. Emma Davies (2005) reports from a Child and Family Psychiatric Unit: "The very act of 'performing' the song in front of a video camera or tape recorder can be a huge achievement for some children who have struggled with low self-confidence for a long time" (p. 52). Davis also ascertains that it can be meaningful and a positive experience for some of these families when the child plays recordings with her/his own songs for various audiences. Such acts often focus talents and achievements rather than problems and failures. Many songs seemingly act as visiting cards with information about the healthy sides of patients with otherwise substantial health challenges:

CLINICAL EXAMPLE 9

On one occasion "Sara," a 14-year-old patient, instructs the 20 choir members to sing her own Spice Girls inspired song: Dance is Something for All Generations. It's only Limited by your Imagination. The girl, diagnosed with anorexia nervosa, shows the singers how to perform the chorus of the song while she receives her liquid "supper" through a naso-gastric tube! As a composer she is probably much more advanced than any choir-member, and for some minutes this rather shy, "difficult," seriously ill, and talented girl makes her therapists and carers sing after her pipe

Aasgaard 2004, p. 151

Usually songwriting results in products like sheet music or audio/video recordings. Some music therapists, like Wolfgang Köster (1997) and Emma O'Brien (2004), have also produced professional anthologies of patients' songs to reach the wider public. Can this, however, also be meaningful for the clients? Joke Bradt (2009) describes why the making of a CD was so important in Jane Golden's songwriting project with "at-risk" youth in a section of Philadelphia that is marked by great poverty and high crime rates:

> At the end of the 14-week songwriting cycle, a CD is created and a CD release party is organized in the community. The creation of the CD and its release party—which has attracted a good amount of media attention—has proven to be equally important as the songwriting process to the children. Sharing their songs with the larger community truly makes these kids believe that their voices are being heard and their messages are getting out there,
>
> Bradt 2009

Who is the owner of the "art-product," and how can we ensure that the future use of a song, stemming from music therapy activities, is conducted within high ethical and legal standards? Cherie Baxter and Clare O'Callaghan (2010) discuss these questions and give several different descriptions of how music therapy products can be used including "[...] suggestions for supporting patients making decisions about their products' future usages, when appropriate" (p. 2).

Some organizations have consent forms which therapists use when negotiating with patients (or their guardians) about their personal uses of the patients' products including research, professional recordings, and/or public dissemination. For example, O'Brien (2005) utilized a release form in order to gain permission to professionally record patients' songs for public distribution. Baxter used a "Consent for Sharing Music Materials" form to request permission for the use of the product(s) for education and/or research (Baxter and O'Callaghan 2010, pp. 7–8).

The many questions related to the status and (future) use of artistic products brought forward in music therapy settings must be addressed by all clinicians and also be reflected in any music therapy training program. Even if it is impossible to provide general rules, the clinician has a responsibility for knowing what (not) to do with song products after the client is discharged from music therapy or after the client's death.

OUTCOMES

Important outcomes for music therapy sessions can include clinical events, functional status, pain, and quality of life (Pino et al. 2012). The expanding literature on songwriting reports that people with various health challenges express that songwriting can be enjoyable and meaningful. In some cases, it is perhaps "sufficiently" meaningful to experience something that is, just, enjoyable. But can engaging in songwriting change anything in a client's life other than temporarily adding pleasurable experiences?

Emma O'Brien (1999/2005) interviewed eight adult cancer patients about their experiences from songwriting and "song sharing" (where patients played their songs to each other). Through open-ended questionnaires, the following themes were identified:

- Songwriting in music therapy was a pleasurable experience.
- Songwriting acted as a record for significant time in a patient's life.
- Songwriting was helpful in clarifying a patient's thoughts.
- Songwriting was a unique experience not usually expected in the hospital environment.
- Songwriting facilitated a positive experience of self-expression.
- Songwriting was a calming experience.
- Songwriting was an easy process, despite illness.

Several of the nineteen case studies of songs by children with cancer (Aasgaard 2002, 2005) document that the role of being a songwriter was experienced and acted by the child/youth many months after the actual song creative activities. Their common achievement of making *cool* songs was acknowledged by medical staff, classmates, and family, and became a part of the young patients' stories of being seriously ill and hospitalized.

Songwriting has been used as a therapeutic intervention for mothers who have experienced childhood abuse. Toni Day, Felicity Baker, and Yvonne Darlington (2009) conducted in-depth interviews with five women who had participated in a group programme with songwriting. All participants reflected positively on the process of creating their own songs and four of them continued to engage with their song creations when the sessions had concluded. One of the women described sharing the CD with friends and family as easier than trying to explain her experiences in this way:

> It's easier to play a CD to someone than try and explain it … some people get really emotional. I don't think some people understand as much as other people do. For some people it brings out a lot of their memories. Even if it's not the same memories, it could be similar things that happened. Some people just enjoy to listen to it (p. 145).

Hong and Choi (2011) conducted a study of songwriting oriented activities aiming at improving cognitive functions of elderly people with dementia. This is one of the very few effect studies with a control group relating to songwriting. The experimental group underwent a songwriting program consisting of sixteen weekly one hour sessions. A Korean version of the Mini Mental State Examination (MMSE) was applied to assess the cognitive function of the subjects. The results showed that the MMSE-K score of the experimental group increased by 3.8 points (26.0%) from 14.6 to 18.4 (p = 0.001) after intervention. In the control group, the MMSE-K scores decreased a little by 0.87 (5.8%) from 15.00 to 14.13 (p = 0.014) (Hong and Choi 2011, p. 221).

Conclusion

Songwriting in music therapy practice encompasses various techniques of assisting clients, children, adults, or elderly people, individually or in groups, to create lyrics and music and to perform and/or record their own songs. The most common clinical areas for songwriting today are psychiatry, autistic sprctrum disorder, developmental disability, oncology, dementia, and neurorehabilitation. Frequent therapeutic goals are related to validating experiences, externalizing thought, fantasies, and emotions or to develop cognitive skills. Specific goals, however, may not always be clearly defined before the creative process. Songwriting is often based on methods with defined steps or stages. This chapter also presents a less directive approach based on a loose framework of guidelines. Electronic music technology is becoming increasingly more appreciated and useful in songwriting. Clients' own advanced mobile phones or iPads, etc., often expand the creative possibilities, and "apps," "loops," "Skype," and simple multi-track programs may also be used by the client when the music therapist is not present. When using technological devices, the therapist must be aware of potential altered communication patterns with the client, and internet safety must always be on the agenda when the use of computers is involved. Research on outcomes from songwriting in music therapy practice is still in its infancy, but expansion from the sick-role, if only momentary, and various aspects of helath performance seem to be common experiences while cognitive function may improve as to elderly people with dementia. Songwriting seems often to be related to pleasure and enjoyable social communication by clients and is, without doubt, also perceived as a most *meaningful* activity by young or old persons with different health challenges.

NOTE

1. A "hook" is a repetitive, short phrase (a lyrical line and/or melodic riff) used in popular music to catch the ear of the listener and make the song memorable.

REFERENCES

Aasgaard, T. (1999). Music Therapy as Milieu in the Hospice and Paediatric Oncology Ward. In: D. Aldridge (ed.), *Music Therapy in Palliative Care. New Voices*, pp. 59–67. London: Jessica Kingsley Publishers.

Aasgaard, T. (2002). *Song Creations by Children with Cancer—Process and Meaning*. PhD, Aalborg University. Available at: vbn.aau.dk/files/195251818/trygve_aasgaard_thesis_150909.pdf [Accessed 20.03.2013].

Aasgaard, T. (2004). A Pied Piper among White Coats and Infusion Pumps: Community Music Therapy in a Paediatric Hospital Setting. In: M. Pavlicevic and G. Ansdell (eds), *Community Music Therapy*, pp. 147–166. London: Jesica Kingsley Publishers.

Aasgaard, T. (2005). Assisting Children with Malignant Blood Disease to Create and Perform their Own Songs. In: F. Baker and T. Wigram (eds), *Songwriting: Methods, Techniques and Clinical Applications for Music Therapy Clinicians, Educators and Students*, pp. 154–179. London: Jessica Kingsley Publishers.

Aldridge, D. (1996). *Music Therapy Research and Practice in Medicine: from out of the Silence*. London: Jessica Kingsley Publishers.

Ansdell, G. (2002). Community Music Therapy and The Winds of Change. *Voices: A World Forum for Music Therapy* 2 (2). Available at: <https://normt.uib.no/index.php/voices/article/viewArticle/83/65> [Accessed 14.04.2013].

Amir, D. (1990). A Song Is Born: Discovering Meaning in Improvised Songs through a Phenomenological Analysis of Two Music therapy Sessions with a Traumatic Spinal- cord Injured Young Adult. *Music Therapy* 9(1): 62–81.

Ærø, S.C.B. and Aasgaard, T. (2011). Musikkterapeut på en sykehusavdeling for barn: helse-fremmende arbeid for både pasient og miljø. In: K. Stensæt and L.O. Bonde (eds), *Musikk, helse, identitet*, pp. 141–160. Oslo: NMH publikasjoner, 3.

Baker, F. (2005). Working with Impairments in Pragmatics through Songwriting following Traumatic Brain Injury. In: F. Baker and T. Wigram (eds), *Songwriting: Methods, Techniques and Clinical Applications for Music therapy Clinicians, Educators and Students*, pp. 134–154. London: Jessica Kingsley Publishers.

Baker, F. and Krout, R. (2009). Songwriting via Skype: An online music therapy intervention to enhance social skills in an adolescent diagnosed with Asperger's Syndrome. *British Journal of Music Therapy* 23(2): 3–14.

Baker, F. and Krout, R. (2011). Collaborative peer lyric writing during music therapy training: a tool for facilitating students' reflections about clinical practicum experiences. *Nordic Journal of Music Therapy* 20(1): 62–89.

Baker, F. and Wigram, T. (eds). (2005). *Songwriting: Methods, Techniques and Clinical Applications for Music Therapy Clinicians, Educators and Students*. London: Jessica Kingsley Publishers.

Baker, F., Kennelly, J., and Tamplin, J. (2005). Songwriting to Explore Identity Change and Sense of Self-concept Following Traumatic Brain Injury. In: F. Baker and T. Wigram (eds), *Songwriting: Methods, Techniques and Clinical Applications for Music Therapy Clinicians, Educators and Students*, pp. 116–133. London: Jessica Kingsley Publishers.

Baker, F., Wigram, T., Stott, D., and McFerran, K. (2008). Therapeutic Songwriting in Music Therapy. Part I: Who are the Therapists, Who are the Clients, and Why is Songwriting Used? *Nordic Journal of Music Therapy* 17(2): 105–123.

Baker, F., Wigram, T., Stott, D., and McFerran, K. (2009). Therapeutic Songwriting in Music Therapy. Part II. *Nordic Journal of Music Therapy* 18(1): 32–56.

Baxter, C. and O'Callaghan, C. (2010). Decisions about the future use of music therapy: Products created by palliative care patients. *Australian Journal of Music Therapy* 21: 2–20.

Bradt, J. (2009). Hope is Change. *Voices: A World Forum for Music Therapy*. Available from: <http://testvoices.uib.no/?q=colbradt090309> [Accessed 19.04. 2013].

Bruscia. K. (1987). *Improvisational Models of Music Therapy*. Springfield, IL: Charles C. Thomas.

Bruscia, K. (1998). *Defining Music Therapy. Second Edition*. Gilsum, NH: Barcelona Publishers.

Castellano, J.A. (1969). Music Composition in a Music Therapy Program. *Journal of Music Therapy* 6(1): 12–14.

Crocker, D. (1952). Techniques in the use of music as therapy for the emotionally maladjusted child. *Music Therapy* 2: 175–180.

Davies, E. (2005). You ask Me Why I'm Singing: Song-creating with Children at a Child and Family Psychiatric Unit. In: F. Baker and T. Wigram (eds), *Songwriting: Methods, Techniques and Clinical Applications for Music Therapy Clinicians, Educators and Students*, pp. 24–44. London: Jessica Kingsley Publishers.

Day, T., Baker, F., and Darlington, Y. (2009). Experiences of song writing in a group programme for mothers who had experienced childhood abuse. *Nordic Journal of Music Therapy* 18(2): 133–149.

Edwards, J. (1998). Music Therapy for Children with Severe Burn Injury. *Music Therapy Perspectives* 16: 21–26.

Ficken, T. (1976). The Use of Songwriting in a Psychiatric Setting. *Journal of Music Therapy* 13(4): 163–172.

Fischer, R. (1991). Original Song Drawings in the Treatment of a Developmental Disabled, Autistic Young Man. In: K. Bruscia (ed.), *Case Studies in Music Therapy*, pp. 359–371. Gilsum, NH: Barcelona Publishers.

Freed, B.S. (1987). Songwriting with the Chemically Dependent. *Music Therapy Perspectives* 4: 13–18.

Fulford, M. (2002). Overview of a music therapy program at a maximum security unit of a state psychiatric facility. *Music Therapy Perspectives* 20(2), 112–116.

Gfeller, K. (1987). Songwriting as a Tool for Reading and Language Remediation. *Music Therapy* 6(2): 28–38.

Griessmaier, B. (1990). Bin ich's oder bin ich's nicht? *Musiktherapeutische Umschau*, 11(1): 37–56.

Griessmeier, B. and Bossinger, W. (1994). *Musiktherapie mit Krebskranken Kindern.* Stuttgart: Gustav Fischer Verlag.

Hadley, S.J. (1996). A rationale for the use of songs with children undergoing bone marrow transplantation. *The Australian Journal of Music Therapy* 7: 16–27.

Hong, I.S. and Choi, M.J. (2011). Songwriting oriented activities improve the cognitive functions of the aged with dementia. *The Arts in Psychotherapy* 38: 221–228.

Johnson, E.R. (1981). The role of objective and concrete feedback in self-concept treatment of juvenile delinquents in music therapy. *Journal of Music Therapy* 18(3): 137–147.

Klein, C.M. and Silverman, M.J. (2012). With Love From Me to Me: Using Songwriting to Teach Coping Skills to Caregivers of Those With Alzheimer's and Other Dementias. *Journal of Creativity in Mental Health* 7(2): 153–164.

Köster, W. (1997). "When sunshine gets cold" [CD].

Krout, R.E. (2005). The Music Therapist as Singer-songwriter: Applications with Bereaved Teenagers. In: F. Baker and T. Wigram (eds), *Songwriting: Methods, Techniques and Clinical Applications for Music Therapy Clinicians, Educators and Students*, pp. 206–223. London: Jessica Kingsley Publishers.

Loveszy, R. (1991). The use of Latin Music, Puppetry, and Visualization in Reducing the Physical and Emotional Pain of a Child with Severe Burns. In: K. Bruscia (ed.), *Case Studies in Music Therapy*, pp. 153–162. Gilsum, NH: Barcelona Publishers.

McCaffrey, T., Edwards, J., and Fannon, D. (2011). Is there a role for music therapy in the recovery approach in mental health? *The Arts in Psychotherapy* 38: 185–189.

Magee, W. (1999). Music Therapy in Chronic Degenerative Illness: Reflecting the Dynamic Sense of Self. In: D. Aldridge (ed.), *Music Therapy in Palliative Care. New Voices*, pp. 82–94. London: Jessica Kingsley Publishers.

Magee, W.L. and Burland, K. (2008). An Exploratory Study of the Use of Electronic Music Technologies in Clinical Music Therapy. *Nordic Journal of Music Therapy* 17(2): 124–141.

Mayers, K.S. (1995). Songwriting as a way to decrease anxiety and distress in traumatized children. *The Arts in Psychotherapy* 22(5): 495–498.

O'Brien, E. K. (1999). Cancer patients' evaluation of a music therapy program in a public adult hospital. *MusicMedicine*, 3, 285–300.

O'Brien, E. (2004). "Living soul", www.mh.org.au/livingsoul [CD].

O'Brien, E. (2005). Songwriting with Adult Patients in Oncology and Clinical Haematology Wards. In: F. Baker and T. Wigram (eds), *Songwriting: Methods, Techniques and Clinical Applications for Music therapy Clinicians, Educators and Students*, pp. 180–205. London: Jessica Kingsley Publishers.

O'Callaghan, C.C. (1990). Music Therapy Skills Used in Songwriting within a Palliative Care Setting. *The Australian Journal of Music Therapy* 1: 15–22.

O'Callaghan, C.C. (1996). Lyrical Themes in Songs Written by Palliative Care Patients. *Journal of Music Therapy* 33(2): 74–92.

O'Callaghan, C.C. (1997). Therapeutic Opportunities Associated with the Music When Using Song Writing in Palliative Care. *Music Therapy Perspectives* 15: 32–38.

O'Callaghan, C., and Jordan, B. (2011). Music therapy supports parent-infant attachments touched by life threatening cancer. In: J. Edwards (Ed). *Music Therapy and Parent-Infant Bonding*, pp. 191–208. Oxford: Oxford University Press.

Pino, C., Boutron, I., and Ravaud, P. (2012). Outcomes in Registred, Ongoing Randomized Controlled Trials of Patient Education. *PLoS ONE* 7(8): e42934.

Robb, S.L. (1996). Techniques in Song Writing: Restoring Emotional and Physical Well Being in Adolescents who have been Traumatically Injured. *Music Therapy Perspectives* 14: 30–37.

Rolvsjord, R. (2005). Collaborations on Songwriting with Clients with Mental Health Problems. In: F. Baker and T. Wigram (eds), *Songwriting: Methods, Techniques and Clinical Applications for Music therapy Clinicians, Educators and Students*, pp. 97–115. London: Jessica Kingsley Publishers.

Rolvsjord, R. (2010). *Resource-Oriented Music Therapy in Mental Health Care*. Gilsum, NH: Barcelona Publishers.

Rudenberg, M.T. and Royka, A.M. (1989). Promoting Psychosocial Adjustment in Pediatric Burn Patients through Music Therapy and Child Life Therapy. *Music Therapy Perspectives* 7: 40–43.

Ruppenthal, W. (1965). "Scribbling" in Music Therapy. *Journal of Music Therapy* 2(1): 8–10.

Salmon, D. (1995). Music and emotion in palliative care; accessing inner resources. In: C. Lee (ed.), *Lonely Waters: Proceedings of the International Conference Music Therapy in Palliative Care. Oxford, 1994*. Oxford: Sobell Publications.

Silverman, M.J. and Leonard, J. (2012). Effects of active music therapy interventions on attendance in people with severe mental illnesses: Two pilot studies. *Arts in Psychotherapy* 39(5): 390–396.

Small, C. (1998). *Musicking: The Meanings of Performing and Listening*. Middletown, CT: Wesleyan University Press.

Stige, B. (2002). *Culture-centered Music Therapy*. Gilsum, NH: Barcelona Publishers.

CHAPTER 36

GROUP MUSIC THERAPY RECONSIDERED

Of Musics, Contexts, and Discourses

MERCEDES PAVLICEVIC

It appears that there is no single, objective description of the appropriate social or scholarly category in which to locate music therapy, partly due to its hybrid nature, combining skills and knowledge from the two domains of music and of health.

Aigen 2005, p. 19

Psychology cannot provide a complete explanation of Group creativity; we need a group level of analysis, and we need to incorporate methods and concepts from sociology, communication, and organizational behaviour

Sawyer 2003, p. 13

To maintain a definitive non-musical meaning of the client's musical expression is to censor the autonomous voice of the client and constrict her individual agency. Therefore it is critical to reflect on musical structure in music therapy, but it is equally critical to reflect on what keeps those structures afloat.

Epp 2007, p. 17

When a group is improvising together, the unpredictability of each person's contribution implies that the performance is collaborative.

Seddon 2005, p. 48

A substantial literary canon on music therapy *individual* work between a music therapist and client (sometimes called one-on-one work) has created a wealth of knowledge about music therapy models, theories, techniques, and research. This knowledge base is emblematized by the *case study* report (Bruscia 1991; Meadows 2011). In contrast, group music therapy, while acknowledged professionally as a powerful therapeutic format, remains relatively undocumented and untheorized. This historical scarcity is puzzling, given that music therapists do group work in a range of formats as part of their service delivery in schools, care homes, health centers, hospitals, cafes, and community centers.

Parts of the problem are well-known, and concern the entire discipline. Music therapy is a hybrid discipline: neither situated discretely in musical, health, or social discourses or practices, but in shifting and complicated combinations of any of these. There is not a single music therapy practice—group or individual—neither is there a convenient or *grand* theoretical frame of reference. The link between music therapy theory and practice can be unpredictable, shifted by time and place. Finally, it must be acknowledged that groups—in and out of music therapy—are complex organisms: neither stable, nor necessarily unified, nor the result of individuals assembling of "more than two" persons in time and place and activity.

Rather than searching for one satisfying or explanatory group discourse—which might well be a spurious enterprise—this chapter attempts a broadening of discourse for music therapy group work, and begins by examining some descriptive conventions. A very brief biographical professional sweep is followed by a commentary on four contemporary group texts. Three group music therapy vignettes provide a prism for discursive foraging and improvising, drawn mostly from contemporary music therapy writings; and the chapter concludes with reflections on how a contemporary group music therapy discourse(s) might continually emerge.

In search of biographies:
Praxes and pioneers

The received music therapy canon has historically—until the turn of the millennium—positioned music therapy's social-political engagements and interests in the background—as though music therapists worked within socio-cultural vacuums. In contrast, accounts of music healing practices, from fields of anthropology/ethnomusicology, have always situated practices in the midst of, and as part of, everyday economic, religious, musical, medical, and political currents of their time and place (Gouk 2000; Horden 2000; Koen 2008). However, a more recent reframing of the founding music therapy accounts, by music therapist Brynjulf Stige and sociologist Leif Aaro (Stige and Aaro 2012), (re)embeds the work and ideas of music therapy pioneers as part of their contemporary historical, social, political, economic, and geographical milieus. Thus, Florence Tyson established the Community Music Therapy Center in New York in the 1950s (Tyson 1968) as part of a broad based development of Community-based centers; while Carolyn Kenny (1982) privileged rituals and myths in response to overly medical-behavioral emphases in practices. Christoph Schwabe (1987), writing and working within an East German tradition that predated the unification of Germany founded "Social Music Therapy" on his experiences and understandings of the individual and society mutually constituting one another. While in the UK, community music therapy emerged at the turn of the millennium in response to a discrepancy between narrowing disciplinary discourses and broadening practices; and in South Africa a distinctive praxis has responded to political instability and inequality with an emphasis on musical-social activism. Another contemporary text, by music therapists Trondalen and Bonde (2012), focuses explicitly on theoretical influences of music therapy models, also historically situated. Trondalen and Bonde cover Bonny's Guided Imagery in Music, informed by psychotherapy; Analytically Oriented Music Therapy by psychoanalysis; Nordoff and Robbins Creative Music Therapy, by anthroposophy and humanistic psychology, Cognitive Behavioral Music Therapy by behaviorism, and so on. Theories, it would seem, are of their time, place, and persons, and shift accordingly. In the 1980s, Even Ruud (1980, 1988) alerted music therapists to the relationship between practices and "the prevailing treatment theories" of the day—be these explicitly acknowledged by pioneers and practitioners, or not. More recently, music therapist Simon Procter (2008) considers the complexities of the "fit" and "drift" between powerful and legitimating theoretical narratives, and practitioners' quotidian enactments of a practice that responds to the changing and shifting needs of their working environments.

These biographical/historical snapshots of music therapy praxes already hint at music therapy navigating closely the intellectual, social and political currents of their time and place—whether or not they are described as such at the time of their geneses.

Given the temporal, contextual and fluid nature of music therapy discourses, it may be useful at this point to draw from Ken Aigen's (2005) work to consider how music therapists make links between theory and practice. His taxonomy considers the disciplinary origins of theories that inform music therapy thinking, and how music therapy scholars have translated, transplanted these—or not.

Recontextualized theory, he writes: "... seeks to describe and explain music therapy processes and phenomena in the terms of other disciplines such as psychoanalysis, neurology, or behavioural learning theory" (Aigen 2005, p. 23). The danger, he suggests, is one of reductionism, and of privileging the constructs of other theories over those of music therapy (and at times, it would seem, replacing music therapy). *Bridging Theory* establishes connections between terms and constructs from different disciplines, combining these with those specific to music therapy. He cites his own explorations of Keil's participatory discrepancies, within the context of music therapy improvisation: seeking to bridge between these, rather than reframe music therapy within other theories. *Indigenous Theory* he describes as original and specific to music therapy—based on the understanding that like all disciplines, music therapy also uses theory imported from other domains. Practice-based, indigenous theory explains phenomena unique to it. While Nordoff and Robbins' *Music Child* explains Nordoff Robbins practice, (with theoretical resonances from anthroposophy and the humanistic psychology), it is questionable whether indigenous theory is useful outside the discipline.

Thus far, we have explored the transient, situated nature of a range of music therapy models—of their time and place, theoretically, culturally, and politically. Where does this leave group music therapy discourse? Might its paucity also be the result of historical—cultural preferences—and absences? And how might understanding socio-cultural music therapy praxes help to redress this paucity?

The next section casts a brief glance at four contemporary group music therapy texts not because they represent the entire canon, but because they offer a discursive range—although, to reiterate, entire books on group work are few.

WITH SOME EXCEPTIONS: CURRENT TEXTS

Texts on group music therapy can be broadly clustered under those offering practical resources for practitioners, and those that privilege explaining and theorizing group work. Tom Plach's *The Creative use of music in Group Therapy* (1996) and Chris Achenbach's *Creative*

Music in Groupwork (1997) offer practical group musical resources and techniques, with suggestions of "extra-musical" functions of various activities; for example, warm up, finding a voice, self-expression, making contact, recovering from separations, and so forth. In addition to strategies for *doing* and *thinking about* the function of group work, Pavlicevic's (2003) *Groups in Music: Strategies from Music Therapy* offers various theoretical strategies for making sense of both the musical enactments and their functions, informed—at times implicitly—by bridging and recontextualized theories (from music, psychology, music therapy)—and by theories that are explicitly "group" focused. Davies and Richard's edited text *Sound Company* (2002), discusses group music therapy work within the psychoanalytic tradition, with influences of group analytic theories of Foulkes, Bion, and Yalom. A substantial range of group work is presented and discussed: with adults and children in a range of educational, health, clinic settings, and with a range of needs; as well as group work in supervision, and with music therapy students. Group work is described as offering opportunities for experiencing different kinds of simultaneous roles, relationships, and transferences, and different combinations of self-and-others. Larger groups offer opportunities for "spending time together," and for persons to experience themselves through contributing to the group. However, the distinctive phenomenological nature of the *group* remains elusive. Some chapters use dyadic terminology, and predominantly draw from psychological theories with a dyadic emphasis. This suggests the complexities of identifying and describing the essence and nature of groups and group work, even where group models (e.g. Foulkes' Group Matrix) might offer a supportive discursive resource.

In her empirical research on music therapy groups, music therapist Katrina Skewes (2002) reviewed group improvisations in music therapy by interviewing prominent international practitioners. While the questions are framed within group practices, the responses are surprising. The explicitly group responses have been highlighted.

> What is unique about music as therapy in groups?
>   An opportunity to work through issues in a different way; is different to words; can be safer than words; **transcends psychological individual experiences**; create a musical portrait of the individual; creates interactive entity—"the **representation of the group** at a moment in time"
>
> *(Skewes 2002, p. 50).*

> What outcomes do music therapy group improvisations facilitate?
>   Playing spontaneously, listening to the music of others, playing in a communicative way; flexibility in playing, awareness of relationship between self and the musical making meaningful music together.

> What are the characteristics of the music therapist leading group improvisations?
>   The ability to create a musical environment; creativity; intuition.

> On Musical Listening:
>   Music therapists listen to the musical qualities of the playing; salience is more relevant than interpreting musical elements; change and variation are significant indicators; playing together in time can mean many things.

> On Listening to the dynamics of the group
>   Music therapists juggle the dynamics of the group; the individual within the group; the group sound.

Apart from a few explicitly "group" oriented comments, some of which resonate with descriptions in *Sound Company*, many responses could be reframed as comments about individual music therapy work. Again, this suggests the difficulty that occurs when pinpointing the distinctive nature of group work in music therapy.

This brief overview of texts about group work in music therapy hints at the complexity of navigating between group music therapy experiences, enactments, activities, descriptions, explanations, and theories; and of the variable distances between any of these. While practitioners are skilled at the complexities of group practice, growing a group discourse is a complicated business. The next part of this chapter builds on these complexities and instabilities. Three brief vignettes serve as platforms for discursive improvisations. The commentaries on each of the vignettes draw, in the main, from contemporary music therapy texts. While each of the three commentaries may seem discursively exclusive to respective vignettes, that is not the intention. The discrete nature of the commentaries (the first is a social-musical discourse; the second is music-centered, and the third is on group improvisation) is simply a focusing tool, and indeed, any of these could be exchanged and melded together—rather like a group improvisation.

Foraging and improvising: Broadening instability

VIGNETTE 1—THE COMMUNITY CHOIR AT CHRISTMAS

M will leave her daughter behind for the performance, she says, as she needs a night off and wants to enjoy herself.... J has become the choir mascot, with her infallible sense of timing and pitch. S always ensures there's a bean bag, soft toys, and some hand instruments, while M has liquid bubbles in case her 15-year-old daughter becomes too agitated. E is to conduct us for David Bowie's "Space Odyssey," and sings the splendid solo line of "will you tell my wife I love her very much" which brings lumps to everyone's throat each time he does it. N and F practice the guitar chords together: N tells F that she'll "hide" behind him for the trickier chords. S is ensconced with the basses, while P, the choir leader, is amongst the altos, switching to the higher tune when needed. We're all bringing nibbles and drinks, and will gather at 6pm to set up chairs and eats before our guests (two each allotted) arrive—most of them live around the corner from this busy Metropolitan music therapy Center. This is our choir, preparing for our Christmas performance. We all live, work and shop in the neighborhood, and since joining, recognize one another in the streets and on public transport, and we're pretty clear that when we sang at the Camden Roundhouse for the last day of the 2012 Olympics London torch relay we were the very best of the four choirs (whatever they might have thought). We're ready to start and the hall is filled with children, teenagers, grandparents, siblings; tables heave with food and drink. We're off.

VIGNETTE 2—GROUP MUSIC THERAPY IMPROVISATION AND THE FOCUS GROUP

Four young adults with severe learning disabilities and two music therapists seem to be having a musical banter. At least, that's how the focus group of parents and professionals describe the video clip we're all watching as part of a small practitioner research focus group. On the video there are pauses, silences, sudden drum beats, giggles, a repeated three-note ostinato by the music therapist on the viola, then a vocal sound, a repeated sudden drum beat, more giggling, someone shakes a bell... the therapist at the

> piano offers some light harmonies with more rests.... The focus group discussants comment: it's like a group conversation, like teenagers hanging out, lots of silences, a bit of a mutter here, yeah, giggle, silence, another yeah—and more.... hardly a swing band in full flow....

VIGNETTE 3—THE GROUP: A MUSICAL CATASTROPHE

Three children are enjoying themselves, running, skipping, jumping, rolling on the floor, and hiding behind the piano, shouting, laughing, chattering.... The improvised music is strident and dispersed, reflecting the children's spiritedness, and the sparsest moments of what might pass for shared musicking swiftly vanish behind more exuberant leaping. For almost thirty seconds, the music therapist and T, hiding under the piano, engage in a spirited and quiet vocal duet, disrupted when H arrives and bangs chord clusters onto the piano. The pace is relentless and in between what feels like car crash improvisation, the two music therapists can only wonder what the special needs teacher, observing behind the one-way mirror, must be thinking of all this. In a follow-up phone conversation, the teacher is ecstatic; these are children who in the classroom and playground are inert, isolated—and she had no idea that T could sing, while H is normally painfully shy and P slow to engage in anything.

Vignette 1 presents a broad social-musical narrative that situates the choir event within the melee of culinary, logistical, economic, musical, and social resources; the description reads like a Music *Souk:* food, wine, singers, and songs to be displayed and exchanged, in ordered and chaotic extravagance. This narrative resonates with Small's notion of *musicking* (1998): that music is never alone, never separate from the relationships that it reflects and generates between people, between people and places (this building in north London) and (in this instance) festivities and season (a chilly midwinter's night).

This narrative resonates with current Community Music Therapy texts, influenced by contemporary studies in anthropology, sociology, community psychology, and cultural studies, and by community-oriented practices and theories (see Trondalen and Ole Bonde 2012). These texts assemble the ecological socio-cultural-musical fabrics of music therapy work, reaching out well beyond the "medical" or "educational" models, to consider social models of music, health, and well-being (Ansdell 2002; Pavlicevic and Ansdell 2004; Pavlicevic 2006; Stige 2002; Stige and Aaro 2012; Stige et al. 2010). Within such frames, theories of social capital social empowerment and social action (Edwards 2007; Procter 2006) help to contextualize a distinctive discourse. Two examples are helpful here. Gary Ansdell 's reflections (2010) on public group performances by people with medical/health needs—as part of a four nation study on Community Music Therapy (Stige et al. 2010); and Stige's characterizing of *Health Musicking* (2012). Ansdell's commentary on the two public performances conveys not only the sense of social belonging, pride in collective participation and sharing, the sense of musical commitment in the performance, but also proposes that this public social musical event offers opportunities for redistributing and animating the resources and skills latent in the locality. This broader narrative, with its Resource-Oriented music therapy resonances (Rolvsjord 2004, 2010), has a hint of social activism. It suggests a more even distribution of resources and skills than those implicitly conveyed in music therapy literature, (for example, with the music therapist in "expert helper" role). Ansdell is at pains to insist that such public events belong within music therapy practice rather than on its margins, with their professional origins in Nordoff and Robbins early public performances with children (Nordoff and Robbins 1975). Here, the performers are witnessed—both as individuals (soloists) and as a group—not as persons in need or on the margins of society, or "expert" music therapist-choir leader, but with reconstituted heath identities of skilled, efficient, supportive, cooperative, leading soloist, drummer, guitarist, pianist, listeners, and more. Musicking, we know, reconfigures our identities (Ansdell 2010; MacDonald et al. 2002).

The collective and individual resources and identities seem to be interchangeable, and improvised, defined through enacting choir-specific roles and responsibilities. While the choir leader may orchestrate the music in the longer-term, this is inseparable from the shared reservoir of songs, talented singers, guitarists and drummers and cooks that feature at that festival, and these in turn seem inseparable from the descriptions of the spacious and easily accessible, pleasant and free local rehearsal space, and local residents who open their home for the after-party.

Stige's *Health Musicking* (Stige 2003, 2012), offers another discursive prism for musical health performance; framing music therapy as a health event, with five affordances: The *arenas*—the site in which the choir event happens, as well as the ethos of this music therapy center that supports, allows for, and promotes such a reciprocally enhancing local musical event; the (at times implicit) *agendas*—of trust, mutual respect, musical friendships, social reciprocities and support, valuing making music together—having fun and celebrating together; the *agents*—whose skills, resources, will are enacted and embodied through participatory events; the *activities* themselves (cooking, drinking, singing, gossiping), and the *artefacts*—instruments, the well-lit space, songs, recipes, cultural traditions, and so on.

This kind of broadened discursive frame for Vignette 1 suggests a "social practice," that can be explained as a participatory ritual, generating, and sustaining social health and well-being, as fostering social collaborations, and generating shared values, meaning and understandings—all of which are key to ensuring social bonding (Dissanayake 2001, 2009; Rogoff 2003; Stern 2004).

Let us now consider Vignette 2.

In contrast to the musical melee of Vignette 1, Vignette 2 offers a "traditional" music therapy group scenario, ongoing over weeks if not months, within a closed space with (we imagine) few interruptions, as described in many more general music therapy texts (Bunt and Hoskyns 2002; Darnley-Smith and Patey 2003; Wigram et al. 2002). Participants' disability delineates their group membership, in keeping with medical model, psychological and special needs discourses. The roles in the vignette are formally identified as those of "music therapist" and "clients," and there is little in this narrative that signals the practice's broader socio-cultural context and networks—which of course, doesn't negate their presence (it is the vignette itself that is the focus here).

This is an ambiguous narrative: it frames the musicking event both directly and through the comments of focus group observers. These add a discursive resonance: how do observers, unschooled in music therapy discourse, decode the group's enactments? How do they translate musicking into "yeah yeah," "hanging out," and "having a banter"? How do musical acts come to be seen and explained as non-musical acts?

Emerging from Nordoff Robbins improvisational practice, Ken Aigen's (2005) music-centered framework understands participative *musicking* as the locus of therapeutic work (in contrast to approaches that use music as an adjunct or trigger to therapeutic work through other media, such as words, medical treatment, or art[1]). Music-centered theory (indigenous theory?)—explains participatory shared *musicking* not as separate from, but as embodying the *extra-musical*, while paradoxically also retaining the focus of the musical experience in music therapy praxis (Ansdell 2014; Epp 2007; Stige et al. 2010). Drawing from sociologist Tia DeNora's (2011) descriptions of how musical affordances depend on the perception that the musical and the extra-musical (e.g. feelings, movements) have something in common: that the musical incorporates aspects of the extra-musical, the notion of the *para-musical* (Stige et al. 2010) helps to frame the group improvisation in the Vignette as *embodied* social banter, *embodied* hanging out, with notions of shared meaning and understandings being enacted through participative musicking. By according musical qualities both within *explicitly* musical enactments, and people's everyday skills, resources, roles, and relationships, music-centered theory, helps to explain the musicalizing of shared experiences during, alongside and beyond music therapy, while also retaining the focus on the explicitly musical phenomena that forms part of these experiences. Such explanations have some discursive resonances with Pavlicevic's work (1991, 1997, 2000) on *Dynamic Form*, based on extensive close study of dyadic music therapy improvisation and drawing from a psychological discourse of non-verbal communication literature. Her work made an empirical case for dyadic music therapy improvisation and human relationship being a unified musical-emotional event. Neither exclusively musical nor exclusively emotional, but as both and as one concurrently, either one could be a portal for experiencing and describing the other. The musical–paramusical continuum described here helps to explain why, in the vignette narrative, unschooled observers instantly identify what the group improvisation might be about.

There is, however, a subtle professional—political point being made by the narrative, which is to do with professional accountability of music therapy practices. Rather than restricting the narrative to describing the group improvisation's impact on participants' social collaboration, social skills, behaviors, etc., the observers' (para-musical) comments mirror the musicking event as this is happening. This is more than a temporal trick, and subverts more conventional music therapy "impact" accounts. Such accounts often implicitly "justify" practice by suggesting a subsequent connection between musicking and people's lives beyond the musicking. That "instrumental" frame positions musicking as acting upon that which is separate from it, and subsequent to it. This separating of music from the extra-musical (whether behavior, language skills, social milieu) risks undermining the "*musicking heartbeat*" of music-centered theory, which offer powerful discourses for continuity of people's experiences before, during, and beyond "the music therapy session," however socially hermetic the portrayal of this event might be.

While this commentary on Vignette 2 offers a broadening discursive frame for music therapy praxis, the commentary on Vignette 3 explores groups as a distinctive phenomenon, hopefully approaching a group discourse more explicitly.

First, some maths. The vignette hints at constant dynamic clustering and separating of different combinations of dyads, trios, solos, and the splintering into five disconnected individuals. Although this differs from the more sedate gatherings of Vignettes 1 and 2, this disorder prompts fundamental questions: when is a collection of persons assembled for a common task in a common space a group? When is this collection NOT a group? When is "a collection of different combinations of persons" a group—or not? How are they similar or different? Can a group be not a group at the same time? If group music therapy is characterized by more than two (one therapist and one client), then how does a threesome of two music therapists and one client differ from that of two clients and one therapist, and from one parent

+ one baby +one therapist? And in a larger ensemble (Vignette 1)—how do the fluctuating roles and tasks (solo/accompanying/conducting/supporting/listening/arranging cushions/cooking) interfere—or enhance—what and how a group might be understood? And when might a dyad be a group?

These complicating questions are too easily side-stepped by neat representations of group music therapy in dyadic speak: the therapist(s) and the group; the choir and the conductor; the soloist and the ensemble. This is unsurprising given music therapy's historical reliance on (Western) psychological theories, themselves embedded in notions of the "self" as individual (the *psy* complex), with corresponding emphases on the dyad as the therapeutic unit (see Pavlicevic and Ansdell 2009).

Drawing from their music therapy group experiences, music therapists Pavlicevic and Ansdell (2009) developed the notion of *Collaborative Musicing*. Their music-centered framing of group music therapy events was influenced by cultural theorist Keith Sawyer's jazz improvisation group studies (more of this later), as well as the work by a range of scholars and practitioners in Malloch and Trevarthen's broad ranging text entitled *Communicative Musicality* (2009). *Collaborative Musicing* was also a two-fold expansion of Pavlicevic's *Dynamic Form* (2007), from explicitly dyadic to explicitly group focused, and from the explicitly musical-emotional focus to a broader bio-social-musical framing of music therapy improvisation. In *Collaborative Musicing,* the practitioners ambitiously attempted to synthesize group musicing in music therapy within a broader ecological frame, that sought to convey people's ongoing dynamic and reciprocal participation in social-cultural events and resources, already signalled by Stige's *Culture Centered Music Therapy* (2002).

Collaborative Musicing framed Pavlicevic's micro-study of music therapy group improvisations, considered in particular the improvising groups' topographies and choreographies (Pavlicevic 2010, 2011, 2012). These portray ongoing, at times split second, grouping and regrouping of any combination of clusters and subclusters during a shared—if not always single—improvisational musical "stream." The notion of "Magic Moments" conveys optimal collaborative moments as intrapersonal as well as inter-personal and supra-personal animation through one common temporal musical stream; and the author suggests that in those moments the "group" becomes one supra-subjective musicking organism. These descriptions parallel Keith Sawyer's extensive studies of improvising groups—in jazz, theatre, organizations, and business—(Sawyer 2000, 2003, 2005, 2007), that describe improvising groups as having distinctive properties: not simply more than the sum of their parts, but that transcend the properties of its individual members.

What and how might any of these concepts contribute to a group music therapy discourse?

I suggest that as a temporary first step to shifting towards a group phenomenological frame we begin by freeing ourselves of role labels (e.g., therapists, clients, choir members, audience, or observers). Such as their culturally sanctioned roles may well interfere with this discursive endeavor, and for this next exploration, I label all persons simply as "musicians." This is not to subvert or render invisible the roles and tasks that music therapists—or clients—enact in group work! This would be counter-productive to growing a discourse on group music therapy, given music therapists' specialist training, and the epistemological foundations for their work. However, for the purposes of exploring the group musical phenomenon afresh, professional labels and roles may distract from allowing the musical phenomenon to offer insights.

In the vignette, as in studies alluded to, we might consider that all the improvising musicians seem to both retain their sense of separateness while also experiencing "groupness." This, Sawyer describes as "a working together that is beyond individual and dyads" (2003, p. 365). In the vignette, however, exasperatingly for those two musicians (who happen to be music therapists), there seems to be no "together"; no apparent agreement or coordination of enactments, at least on the narrative surface, and apparently no musical structuring that can "hold" the ongoing grouping and re-grouping, despite the musicians' best intentions. However, on imaginatively entering through the narrative into the room, we might hear and see something rather more complex. We might see and hear one shared enactment, both musical and para-musical (i.e. shouting, running, jumping, singing, playing the piano, kicking), that is propelled by all, and whose quality is that of multiple disruptions, fragmentations of genre, multiple pulses, meters, and fragments of rhythms. Even if the group musicking seems rather distant from Sawyer's descriptions of jazz musicians using musical genres that are mutually agreed upon, conventional and idiosyncratic, with effortless split-second timing, we might reframe this musical "catastrophe" as a single enacted emergent, however chaotic and apparently incoherent, with the help of Sawyer's work on *Collaborative Emergence*. This clarifies the emergent nature of group systems (whether ordered or not): where individual contributions and actions cannot account for the group actions (or improvisation); and where there is no pre-structured plan or leader guiding the group. *Collaborative emergence* explains the group improvisation properties as transcending those of its (musicians) individuals: the whole, then, is not only the sum of its parts but also has distinctive properties. The group flow (however disrupted and dispersed in the vignette) in turn inspires the musicians to play and do things that they wouldn't do on their own. It both belongs to, and is beyond each of the musicians in the vignette. Cultural anthropologist Barbara Rogoff (2003) insists that such collectively produced and collectively experienced enactments are a critical part of, and cannot be separated from, individual and dyadic experiences of what and how it means to be a meaning-making human.

To return to group music therapy discourse, with its corresponding identities of therapists and clients or patients. It would seem that when, for therapeutic reasons, the client's (or therapist's) actions need discrete commentaries (e.g. for clinical reports on clients), such commentaries might need parallel descriptions of the group as one collective musicking system—with insistence on musical hierarchies and characteristics. However (to link to the commentary on Vignette 1), a convincing account needs to encompass the social-cultural structures within which such enactments happen. The musical and para-musical; the social-cultural supports and reciprocities; the mutual supports and trust that are invited, elicited, and enacted through group improvisation in music therapy; that as practitioners we understand to be part of generating, contributing to, shaping and drawing from, social-musical capital (Procter 2006).

FINAL DISCURSIVE IMPROVISATIONS

This chapter began by problematizing an asymmetry: music therapists do far more group work than is suggested by the writings in the music therapy literature. Various contemporary group music therapy texts, considered here, seem to point to the potential for further development and refinement. They appear to confirm what practitioners know well: that describing group music therapy is a complicated business, and risks drawing from reductive discursive frames embedded in dyadic psychological theories. Besides, many texts seem to ignore the social cultural worlds of which such practices form a part. Three vignette narratives, portraying improvisational group music therapy in action, presented an assortment of group practices. Discursive foraging was restricted (with small exceptions) to those contemporary music therapy texts that are, for the most part, under-represented in the general music therapy canon. Each of the three discursive improvisations considered a distinctive theoretical angle: socio-cultural perspectives; a music-centered discourse with a dual purpose, one for insisting that the musical and para-musical be considered simultaneously, and the second for considering these as part of a broader ecological framing. The third discourse possibly came the closest to considering the group as a distinctive phenomenon.

It is this statement that now needs some dismantling.

If, to borrow liberally from anthropologist Barbara Rogoff (2003), we all need a lifetime of enabling situations and shared opportunities and endeavors to constantly revise, expand, stretch our separate, common and shared humanity, then ecological opportunities, social (in this instance, group) priorities and relationships cannot be neatly removed from experiences of individual creativity and initiative. For music therapists, a group therapeutic endeavor offers just such shared and enabling situations, for all musicians, whatever their socially sanctioned identities outside group improvisations. A number of papers on improvisation (including Alterhaug 2004; Sawyer 2000, 2003; Seddon 2005) overlap with one another and with group music therapy improvisation on musicking and para-musicking fundamentals. In his description of "golden moments" Bjorn Alterhaug (2004) parallels music therapy's "Magic Moments" touched on earlier. He describes jazz musicians' existential need for striving towards such moments; and he sees musicians' need for agreement and mutual consent as points of departure for creative interactions—both in music and in everyday life. He describes group improvisations as offering contrasts to hierarchical and pyramidal group structures (think orchestras), offering instead fluid possibilities for distributing and rotating tasks (of leader, soloist, dictator, revolutionary, pretender, usurper, supporter, chorus).

Group descriptors such as Alterhaug's (he draws substantially from Sawyer's work) help to broaden music therapy discourses: for example, the notion of group mutual support could be theorized and described as more than psychological and behavioral. For music therapy praxes, these broadening and shifting discourses may help us to clarify how such lived musical and para-musical group experiences have the potential to become part of enactments with other persons, in other contexts. From a scientific, positivist perspective, this has yet to be convincingly "proved"; but from a broader discursive viewpoint, this lack of *proof* doesn't negate the continuity of people's lived musicking experiences.

This chapter has implicitly suggested that developing a convincing and broad ranging group discourse needs to begin with the practice, and that such developments need to be unembarrassed to revisit essential questions: what and when is the group? What is the nature of *musicking* in group music therapy? What is the nature of group improvisation in music therapy? What are the differences and similarities between dyadic, triadic, quartets, larger ensembles in music therapy (and do these matter?) How might music therapists best represent a collection of people with an astonishing variation of physical, mental, and social capacities and limitations who at times mutually enact sophisticated, flexible, shared social musical synchronicities? How might music therapists theorize such peak synchronicities—that may well challenge notions of what it means to have a "disorder," a "disability," and to be in "distress"?

Given music therapists' professional responsibilities for accounting for their work, and given that Group *musicking* seems to offer endless variety of social-musical psychological experiences, it would seem that this work demands a correspondingly flexible and elaborate discourse.

I conclude with a telling scenario, drawn from the context that spawned Vignette 2. In a modest qualitative study exploring how music therapy engaged with the needs of young adults with severe learning difficulties, parents and professionals familiar with services catering for this population were interviewed. In focus groups they watched films of—as it transpired—mostly group work. Analysis of discussion transcripts revealed four surprising continua of needs. These were surprising less because of the contents of each continuum, but because the four didn't seem to relate neatly to one another. These were: (a) personal/primary needs—arising within the person from the effects of the disability; such as in the areas of perceptual, language, motor, and health needs; (b) needs arising from engagements with others, ranging from dyadic engagements with family members, carers, peers (communicative, emotional expressive, relational); (c) needs arising from difficult environments, unaware social attitudes (self-esteem, self-value); (d) needs arising from flashpoints: generally temporary and triggered by, for example, life transitions and other acute stressors (Pavlicevic et al. 2013).

Many of the needs seemed to be situational: observers' descriptions of young adults' needs appeared and disappeared in their accounts, depending on those young adults' life context and resources available. In addition, the group improvisations videos were portals for considering each and all of young adults' needs, both within, during, and beyond group musicking. The musical and para-musical meanings of the group musicking examples seemed clear—and obvious—to the observers; and a broader socio-economic-cultural context seemed to be a given, underpinning all discussions. For the researchers, the four continua seemed to defy developmental or participatory conventions, and would not "fit" a neat, continuous narrative. In reporting we agreed to leave these as they were: open-ended and open to multiple interpretations and improvisations of meaning.

In concluding, a possibility presents itself; that is, to consider groups not as separate from other aspects of music therapy work, but as part of a broader discourse—hence the trick question: when is a duet a group?, and when might an individual be a group? This, perhaps, is the point of this discussion. That music therapy work—whether in duos, trios, small or large ensembles—be treated as an assembling of comprehensive practices, needing situated, comprehensive discursive elaborations. I suggest some caveats, however: that group work is a distinctive and hugely complex phenomenon and risks being minimized by the importing of principles from dyadic work; that dyadically based psychological theories do not easily convert to groups; that psychological theories alone are insufficient if music therapists are committed to broader social-cultural representations of the interwoven-ness of music therapy with everyday life; that to broaden any and all music therapy discourse music therapists need to forage well beyond traditional territory—as adventurous colleagues in this volume have been doing for some time; and as the three commentaries have attempted. The discursive complexities of group work need to be retained rather than resolved. By exploring an expanded group music therapy discourse, it is hoped that this chapter contributes to what really matters: collaboratively improvised emergent praxes that enrich and deepen people's musical experiences in any and all kinds of music therapy.

NOTE

1. See Bruscia's distinction between music *as* therapy and music *in* therapy.

REFERENCES

Achenbach, C. (1997). *Creative Music in Groupwork*. Bicester: Winslow Press Ltd.

Aigen, K. (2005). *Music-Centered Music Therapy*. Gilsum, NH: Barcelona Publishers.

Alterhaug, B. (2004). Improvisation on a triple theme: Creativity, jazz improvisation and communication. *Studia Musicologica Norvegica* 30: 97–118.

Ansdell, G. (2002). Community music therapy and the winds of change. *Voices: A World Forum for Music Therapy* 2(2). Retrieved from: *<https://normt.uib.no/index.php/voices/article/viewArticle/83/65>*.

Ansdell, G. (2010). Reflection: Where performing helps: Processes and affordances of performance in community music therapy. In: B. Stige, G. Ansdell, C. Elefant, and M. Pavlicevic (eds), *Where Music Helps: Community Music Therapy in Action and Reflection*, pp. 161–186. Aldershot: Ashgate.

Ansdell, G. (2014). *How Music Helps: In Music Therapy and Everyday Life*. Farnham: Ashgate.

Bruscia, K. (ed.). (1991). *Case Studies in Music Therapy*. Gilsum, NH: Barcelona Publishers.

Bunt, L. and Hoskyns, S. (2002). *The Handbook of Music Therapy*. Hove, East Sussex: Brunner-Routledge.

Darnley-Smith, R. and Patey, H.M. (2003). *Music therapy*. London: Sage.

Davies, A. and Richards, E. (eds). (2002). *Music Therapy and Group Work*. London: Jessica Kingsley.

DeNora, T. (2011). *Music-in-action: Selected Essays in Sonic Ecology*. Farnham: Ashgate.

Dissanayake, E. (2001). An ethological view of music and its relevance to music therapy. *Nordic Journal of Music Therapy* 10: 159–175. DOI: 10.1080/08098130109478029.

Dissanayake, E. (2009). Bodies swayed to music: The temporal arts as integral to ceremonial ritual. In: S. Malloch and C. Trevarthen (eds), *Communicative Musicality: Exploring the Basis of Human Companionship*, pp. 533–544. Oxford: Oxford University Press.

Edwards, J. (ed.). (2007). *Music: Promoting Health and Creating Community in Healthcare Contexts*. Newcastle: Cambridge Scholars.

Epp, E. (2007). Locating the autonomous voice: Self-expression in music-centered music therapy. *Voices: A World Forum for Music Therapy* 7(1). Retrieved from: *<https://normt.uib.no/index.php/voices/article/viewArticle/463/372>*.

Gouk, P. (ed.). (2000). *Musical Healing in Cultural Contexts*. Aldershot: Ashgate.

Horden, P. (2000). *Music as Medicine: The History of Music Therapy since Antiquity*. Aldershot: Ashgate.

Kenny, C. (1982). *The Mythic Artery. The Magic of Music Therapy*. Atascadero, CA: Ridgeview.

Koen, B. (ed.). (2008). *The Oxford Handbook of Medical Ethnomusicology*. Oxford: Oxford University Press.

MacDonald, R., Hargreaves, D., and Miell, D. (eds). (2002). *Musical Identities*. Oxford: Oxford University Press.

Malloch, S. and Trevarthen, C. (eds). (2009). *Communicative Musicality: Exploring the Basis of Human Companionship*. Oxford: Oxford University Press.

Meadows, A., Ed. (2011). *Developments in Music Therapy Practice: Case Study Perspectives*. Gilsum, NH: Barcelona Publishers.

Nordoff, P. and Robbins, C. (1975). *Music Therapy in Special Education*. London: MacDonald and Evans.

Pavlicevic, M. (1991). *Music in communication: Improvisation in music therapy*. Unpublished doctoral dissertation, University of Edinburgh.

Pavlicevic, M. (1997). *Music Therapy in Context*. London: Jessica Kingsley.

Pavlicevic, M. (2000). Improvisation in music therapy: Human communication in sound. *Journal of Music Therapy* XXXVII(4): 269–285.

Pavlicevic, M. (2003). *Groups in Music: Strategies from Music Therapy*. London: Jessica Kingsley.

Pavlicevic, M. (2006). Worksongs, playsongs: Communication, collaboration, culture and community. *Australian Journal of Music Therapy* 17: 85–99.

Pavlicevic, M. (2007). The Music Interaction Rating Scale (Schizophrenia) (MIR(S)): micro-analysis of co-improvisation in music therapy with adults suffering from chronic schizophrenia. In: T. Wosch and T. Wigram (eds), *Microanalysis in Music Therapy*. London: Jessica Kingsley.

Pavlicevic, M. (2010). Reflection: Let the music work: Optimal moments of collaborative musicing. In: B. Stige, G. Ansdell, C. Elefant, and M. Pavlicevic (eds), *Where Music Helps: Community Music Therapy in Action and Reflection*, pp. 99–112. Aldershot: Ashgate.

Pavlicevic, M. (2011). Just don't do it: A group's micro journey into music and life. In: A. Meadows (ed.), *Developments in Music Therapy Practice: Case Study Perspectives*, pp. 268–279. Gilsum, NH: Barcelona Publishers.

Pavlicevic, M. (2012). Between beats: Group music therapy transforming people and places. In: R. MacDonald, G. Kreutz, and L. Mitchell (eds), *Music, Health, and Well-being*, pp. 195–212. Oxford: Oxford University Press.

Pavlicevic, M. and Ansdell, G. (eds). (2004). *Community Music Therapy*. London: Jessica Kingsley.

Pavlicevic, M. and Ansdell, G. (2009). Between communicative musicality and collaborative musicing: A perspective from community music therapy. In: S. Malloch and C. Trevarthen (eds), *Communicative Musicality: Exploring the Basis of Human Companionship*, pp. 357–376. Oxford: Oxford University Press.

Pavlicevic, M., O'Neil, N., Powell, H., Jones, O., and Sampathianaki, E. (2013). Making music, making friends: Long-term music therapy with young adults with severe learning disabilities. *Journal of Intellectual Disabilities*, DOI: 10.1177/1744629513511354.

Plach, T. (1996). *The Creative use of Music in Group Therapy*. Springfield, IL: Charles C. Thomas.

Procter, S. (2006). What are we playing at? Social capital and music therapy. In: R. Edwards, J. Franklin, and J. Holland (eds), *Assessing Social Capital: Concept, Policy, and Practice*, pp. 146–162. Newcastle: Cambridge Scholars Press.

Procter, S. (2008). Premising the challenge. *British Journal of Music Therapy* 22: 77–82.

Rogoff, B. (2003). *The Cultural Nature of Human Development*. Oxford: Oxford University Press.

Rolvsjord, R. (2004). Therapy as empowerment: Clinical and political implications of empowerment philosophy in mental health practices of music therapy. *Nordic Journal of Music Therapy* 13: 99–111. DOI: 10.1080/08098130409478107.

Rolvsjord, R. (2010). *Resource-oriented Music Therapy in Mental Healthcare*. Gilsum, NH: Barcelona Publishers.

Ruud, E. (1980). *Music Therapy and its Relationship to Current Treatment Theories*. St Louis, MO: Magna-Music Baton.

Ruud, E. (1988). Music therapy: health profession or cultural movement? *Music Therapy* 7: 34–37.

Sawyer, R.K. (2000). Improvisational cultures: Collaborative emergence and creativity in improvisation. *Mind, Culture, and Activity* 7: 180–185. DOI: 10.1207/S15327884MCA0703_05.

Sawyer, R.K. (2003). *Group Creativity: Music, Theater, Collaboration*. London: New Erlbaum.

Sawyer, R.K. (2005). Music and Conversation. In: D. Miell, R.A.R. MacDonald, and D.J. Hargreave (eds), *Musical Communication*, pp. 45–60. Oxford: Oxford University Press.

Sawyer, R.K. (2007). *Group Genius: The Creative Power of Collaboration*. New York, NY: Basic Books.

Schwabe, C. (1987). Regulative Musiktherapie. Leipzig: Veb Georg Thieme.

Seddon, F.A. (2005). Modes of communication during jazz improvisation. *British Journal of Music Education* 22: 47–61. DOI: 10.1017/S0265051704005984.

Skewes, K. (2002). A review of current practice in group music therapy improvisations. *British Journal of Music Therapy* 16: 26–55.

Small, C. (1998). *Musicking: The Meanings of Performing and Listening*. Hanover and London: Wesleyan University Press.

Stern, D. (2004). *The Present Moment in Psychotherapy and Everyday Life*. New York, NY: Norton.

Stige, B. (2002). *Culture-centered Music Therapy*. Gilsum, NH: Barcelona Publishers.

Stige, B. (2003). *Elaborations Towards a Notion of Community Music Therapy*. Oslo: Unipub AS.

Stige, B. (2012). Health musicking: A perspective on music and health as action and performance. In: R. MacDonald, G. Kreutz, and L. Mitchell (eds), *Music, Health, and Well-being*, pp. 183–195. Oxford: Oxford University Press.

Stige, B. and Aaro, L.E. (2012). *Invitation to Community Music Therapy*. Abingdon: Routledge.

Stige, B., Ansdell, G., Elefant, C., and Pavlicevic, M. (2010). *Where Music Helps: Community Music Therapy in Action and Reflection*. Aldershot: Ashgate.

Trondalen, G. and Bonde, L.O. (2012). Music therapy: Models and interventions. In: R. Macdonald, G. Kreutz, and L. Mitchell (eds), *Music, Health, and Well-being*, pp. 40–62. Oxford: Oxford University Press.

Tyson, F. (1968). The Community Music Therapy Center. In: G.E. Thayer (ed.), *Music in Therapy*, pp. 382–388. New York: MacMillan.

Wigram, T., Pederson, I., and Bonde, L. (2002). *A Comprehensive Guide to Music Therapy: Theory, Clinical Practice, Research and Training*. London: Jessica Kingsley.

CHAPTER 37

RECEPTIVE MUSIC THERAPY

DENISE GROCKE

LISTENING TO MUSIC

LISTENING to music is an everyday experience for most people. DeNora (2000) and others have written extensively about music in everyday life, and the increasing ease of access to music via i-Pods, MP3 players, and other digital media. Studies have shown that we listen to music many hours a day and in varying contexts. Numerous studies have also investigated why people listen to music and the effect on mood. Over a 20-year period the Swedish psychologist Gabrielsson (2011) collected 1354 statements from members of the public about strong experiences while listening to music (SEM). The thematic analysis of these responses found seven main themes: that strong experiences while listening to music were hard to describe and were unique; Physical reactions including (1) tears (in 24 percent of responses) more so in women than men, (2) thrills, chills, shivers (ten percent), and piloerection (goose bumps) in five percent. Other reactions were muscle tension or relaxation, warmth (perspiration), palpitation of the heart, changed breathing, and a lump in the throat. Changed perceptions of time were recorded in 35 percent of responses, including experiences of being absorbed in the sound, so that the world around disappears; that time stands still, or does not exist; and that the experience was contained in a single "now" (moment). These responses parallel the intentions of mindfulness practice (described below). Ten percent of responses referred to images spontaneously evoked by the music: That music evoked inner images, such as nature, people, situations, events, dreams of another life, or of something different and better. Listeners imagined themselves performing the music, and sometimes SEM elicited an inner music, it came for no apparent reason, and sounded as clear as live music. With regard to feelings and emotions, responses included:

- Intense/powerful feelings, included overwhelming waves of feeling (15 percent).
- Positive feelings (72 percent).
- Negative feelings (23 percent).
- Different feelings (mixed, conflicting, changed) (13 percent).
- Using music to affect one's mood; that music becomes a resource (10 percent).

Of the 72 percent reporting positive feelings, these were further delineated as (in part):

- Joy, happiness, bliss (38.8 percent).
- Enjoyment, delight, sweetness, and beauty (27.3 percent).
- Peace, calm, harmony, stillness (11.1 percent).

Interestingly negative feelings included melancholy, unhappiness, and sadness in 8.6 percent of the responses. It is evident from these results that music evokes strong responses, even when a facilitating person (in the form of the therapist) is not present. The purpose of this chapter is to report on receptive music therapy approaches, where the music therapist facilitates some of the experience described above to improve clients' health and well-being.

WHAT ARE RECEPTIVE METHODS IN MUSIC THERAPY?

Receptive methods in music therapy include those approaches in which:

> … the client listens to music and responds to the experience silently, verbally or in another modality (e.g. art, dance). The music used may be live… or commercial recordings of music literature in various styles (e.g. classical, rock, jazz, country, spiritual, new age). The listening experience may be focused on physical, emotional, intellectual, aesthetic, or spiritual aspects of the music and the client's responses are designed according to the therapeutic purpose of the experience
>
> Bruscia 1998a, pp. 120–121

Bruscia (1998a) goes on to identify clinical goals in receptive music therapy as to:

1 Promote receptivity
2 Evoke specific body responses
3 Stimulate or relax the person
4 Develop auditory/motor skills
5 Evoke affective states and experiences
6 Explore ideas and thoughts of others
7 Facilitate memory, reminiscence, and regression
8 Evoke imagery and fantasies
9 Connect the listener to a community or sociocultural group
10 Stimulate peak and spiritual experiences (Bruscia 1998a, p. 121)

Receptive methods are not new to music therapy, although the term "receptive" is relatively new. Previously, methods where the client listened to music (either live or recorded) were referred to as "passive," however, with the knowledge of current research that indicates extensive involvement of physiological and affective systems of the body when listening to music, it is clear that responses, whether intentional or not, are more than passive.

Music therapists are not the only professionals who choose recorded music or improvise music live to engage clients in receptive experiences. Other professionals, particularly nursing staff in hospitals, also offer music to their patients. Dileo and Bradt (2005) clarify the difference between the use of recorded music by medical personnel and music therapists. They defined "music medicine" as a description for practices in which there are passive music listening interventions of pre-recorded music, implemented by medical personnel, whereas music therapy entails a qualified music therapist implementing an *in-person* treatment intervention using music therapy methods (Dileo and Bradt 2005, p. 9). Further, the interpersonal relationship between the patient and music therapist is maintained throughout the listening experience as the music therapist remains with the patient, however medical personnel generally do not remain with the patient during the listening experience.

There are many types of receptive music therapy approaches (Grocke and Wigram 2007) however this chapter will focus on three:

- Music-assisted relaxation for children and adults in different clinical settings
- Music and imagery
- Guided Imagery and Music (Bonny Method)

Each of these will be outlined according to salient features of the approach, and research that underpins evidence for effectiveness.

MUSIC-ASSISTED RELAXATION FOR CHILDREN AND ADULTS

In the early years of the development of music therapy, studies into the effect of music on the physiology of the body were prolific. Research studies from the 1970s and 1980s used sedative and stimulative music selections to measure the effect on physiological systems of the body, particularly heart rate, respiration rate and amplitude, and galvanic skin conductance (see review in Hodges and Sebald 2011, and Krout 2007). Music therapists began to explore the diverse responses of clients to different types of music, and recognized that music that was familiar to the client, and in the preferred style or genre was the most effective (Saperston 1999). Individualized music programs for clients in different contexts were developed—for women in labor (Clark et al. 1981; Hanser and O'Connell 1983), patients experiencing stress (Hanser 1985; Scartelli 1989) and anxiety pre-surgery (Spintge 1999), or in intensive care (Bonny 1983).

SALIENT FEATURES OF MUSIC-ASSISTED RELAXATION FOR CHILDREN AND ADULTS

Music-assisted relaxation is important in a variety of contexts where children and adults may experience stress, including hospitalization, in schools, or in the workplace. In addition, music-assisted relaxation that can be self-administered may be an important way of that people who are experiencing anxiety or pain can be supported.

Principles of music-assisted relaxation

1 Context. A quiet environment is conducive to listening to music, preferably with dimmed lighting and comfortable mat or chair on which to recline.

2 Voice quality of the therapist. Voice quality is crucial to facilitate relaxation in a client/patient. The therapist's voice tone should be warm, the volume soft (but loud enough to be heard), pitch should be mid-range, the dynamics of the spoken voice quite flat, and the pacing in time with client's breath (Grocke and Wigram 2007, p. 62 and p. 92).

3 Breath. A music-assisted relaxation normally begins with suggestions for deepening and slowing the breathing pattern of the client/patient. The therapist may audibly model slower breathing, however too much attention to regulating breathing may increase anxiety for some patients, particularly if he/she suffers from asthma, or has difficulty breathing because of a medical apparatus. Edwards (1999) uses the simple phrase "nice slow breathing" when working with children (p. 73).

4 Closed eyes. Music-assisted relaxation is enhanced if the client/patient can block out visual distractions by closing their eyes. Young children however may not be comfortable closing their eyes, and may prefer to relax with eyes open.

5 Relaxation inductions. A wide variety of relaxation inductions are in use, ranging from short inductions, often based on the client being aware of their breath, to more extended inductions including Progressive Muscle Relaxation (PMR, Jacobsen 1938), autogenic, autogenic with color (Grocke and Wigram 2007 pp. 97–107), mindfulness (Grocke and Van Dort 2013), and others developed by the practitioner.

6 Enhancing relaxation with a visualization. Listening to music in a relaxed state can be assisted by introducing a non-threatening image, such as a favorite place, or a place in nature. Children may enjoy hearing a story as part of the music and relaxation session, whereas for older children making a choice is important as a means of empowering him/her, and they may bring to mind the image of a favorite place. Directed imagery scripts can also be used (see Naparstek 1995; Standley 1991a) and are effective to help children sleep (Grocke and Wigram 2007, pp. 73–76).

7 Choice of music. The most effective music for relaxation is music that is liked by the client/patient. Preference for music is established from early adolescence, and asking the client about the type of music he/she enjoys is important to the effectiveness of the intervention. In a situation where a client/patient is unable to speak, or unable to indicate a choice, music is chosen by the therapist (see further discussion on therapist-chosen versus research-indicated music, below). Music suitable for relaxation has identifiable features:
   * Stable tempo
   * Stable or gradual change in: Volume, rhythm, timbre, pitch or harmony
   * Consistent texture
   * Consonant harmonies, and predictable modulations and cadences
   * Predictable melodic line, and repetition
   * Predictable structure and form
   * Gentle timbre
   * Few or gradual changes in dynamics (Wigram et al. (2002)).

Using the parameters outlined above, the therapist may choose instrumental music that matches the elements in tempo and form. Alternatively, music therapists may provide music for relaxation by playing music live. Music that is predictable enables the client/patient to fully relaxed and feel supported by the music and the presence of the therapist. Choice of genre is important, particularly for adolescents, who may prefer soft rock music, or meditative music.

THEORETICAL FRAMEWORKS IN MUSIC-ASSISTED RELAXATION RESEARCH

Numerous studies have investigated the effect of music-assisted relaxation for children and adult clients. The intention and benefits include the reduction of pain, fear, anxiety and distress, and enhanced mood, relaxation and positive experience, or a combination of these goals. Common theoretical frameworks that underpin these studies are presented below and include (1) Gate Control Theory (Melzack and Wall 1965; Melzack and Katz 2004), (2) entrainment (Rider 1985), (3) mental escape from the stressful environment (Loewy 1997), and (4) mindfulness (Kabat-Zinn 2005, and Nhat Hanh 1976).

The *Gate Control Theory* of pain (Melzack and Wall 1965) proposes that an auditory stimulus, such as music, acts to divert attention away from the experience of pain, by activating different areas of the brain required for processing auditory information. In a review of research studies of music therapy as procedural support for invasive medical procedures, Ghetti (2012) found that the Gate Control theory was the most commonly mentioned theory in these studies, although Melzack and Katz' (2004) theory of the body-self neuromatrix goes further to address the inter-related areas of the brain that are involved in pain perception and pain behavior. Ghetti (2012) stated that:

> Music therapy as procedural support may modify the various cognitive and emotional inputs to the neuromatrix by influencing attention, levels of anxiety, and meaning of the experience, as well as by impacting emotional responses through activation of the limbic system
>
> (p. 30).

In medical settings, *entrainment* (Rider 1985) has been used in the control of anxiety and pain. Initially the level of anxiety/pain is matched in the music, adopting the "iso" principle (meaning "the same") (Altschuler 1948). Gradually the dynamics can be reduced (e.g. slower tempo, gradual lessening of harsh timbres) until the patient's physiological parameters are reduced, thereby enhancing relaxation. Music that meets the features of "sedative" music (above) can induce deeper breathing that in turn controls symptoms of anxiety (rapid, shallow breathing and hypervigilance to stimuli), so that anxiety is reduced.

The reduction of anxiety pre-surgery has also shown reduction in the amount of analgesic used post-surgery (Spintge 1999), and reduced number of complications post-surgery. Other outcome studies have shown effectiveness of music in reducing distress in pediatric patients prior to surgical procedures (Robb et al. 1995), and to regulate breathing (Snyder Cowan 1991), particularly in children who have asthma.

A third perspective in support of providing music in stressful environments, is music listening and relaxation as a means of *mental escape* from the environment (Loewy 1997), to provide opportunities for creative thinking and fantasy, and to engage the imagination

(Snyder Cowan 1991). Visualizations (defined as static images used as a focus for relaxation), imagery scripts, and imagery sequences are used to enhance, deepen and prolong the relaxation (Grocke and Wigram 2007), and to allow the child or adult to mentally leave the stressful environment and imagine a more preferred environment, such as a favorite place (see further discussion in sections below).

Mindfulness. Intentional and focussed listening to music may enhance a mindful awareness of a person's physical, emotional, esthetic or spiritual life. Nhat Hanh (1976) suggests that mindfulness of the mind requires an attentiveness to observe and recognize feelings and thoughts in the moment. A central feature is to cultivate an attitude of letting go, or non-attachment, to accept what is in the moment without judgment (Kabat-Zinn 2005). While relaxation allows a stilling of the mind, carefully chosen music elongates the sense of being in the moment and allows an individual to be fully present (Grocke and Van Dort 2013).

RESEARCH STUDIES

A large body of literature exists on music and relaxation, and the effects on anxiety, fear and pain, including pediatric patients (Nolan 1997); pediatric burns patients (Barker 1991; Bishop et al. 1996; Edwards 2005; Robb et al. 1995); in cardiac rehabilitation (Mandel et al. 2010; Schou 2008); broncoscopy patients (Metzler and Berman 1991); chemotherapy-induced anxiety (Lin et al. 2011); other medical conditions (Saperston 1999), residential aged care (Short 2007); insomnia in older people (Ziv et al. 2008); and a stressful call center (Smith 2008).

Cochrane reviews on the effect of music interventions on mechanically ventilated patients (Bradt et al. 2010), coronary heart disease (Bradt and Dileo 2009) and cancer patients (Bradt et al. 2011) have all found evidence for music listening in decreasing physiological effects of anxiety, particularly in reducing heart rate and respiration rate.

Different types of relaxation inductions are used in these studies, and in Robb's (2000) study of state-trait anxiety she incorporated music-assisted progressive muscle relaxation (PMR), PMR alone, music listening, and silence as discrete groups. The participants were 60 university students. Although there was no significant difference between the four groups on the Speilberger State-Trait Anxiety Inventory, music-assisted PMR elicited the greatest level of change.

Who chooses the music?

One of the salient features of music-assisted relaxation is the choice of music, and often research studies provide paucity of information about the selection of music, who makes the choice, and the details of performance/recording (Robb et al. 2011; Wigram et al. 2002). This criticism was addressed in a landmark meta-analysis of systematically reviewed studies (Pelletier 2004) where music was used to decrease arousal due to stress. Twenty-two studies were identified as meeting inclusion criteria for meta-analysis. Six techniques were used across these studies including (1) passive listening (with instructions to just listen), (2) Guided Imagery and Music (described below), (3) vibrotactile stimulation via a couch that transmits sound in high density vibration, (4) PMR, (5) autogenic training, and (6) combinations of breathing, PMR, autogenic and/or imagery. A large effect size (d = + .6711) was found for music combined with relaxation techniques in reducing arousal. There were differences between the effects of certain relaxation inductions, where verbal suggestion (autogenic) with music had the greatest effect on level of stress. Interesting results were found with regard to the choice of music however. Interventions in which the choice of music was based on evidence in research studies were more effective than music chosen by the participants.

Pelletier (2004) has argued that the findings indicate that participant-preferred music may be too stimulating, rather than relaxing. Furthermore, individual interventions were found to be more effective than group listening interventions. Research-supported music selections for relaxation based music listening incorporate the following musical elements; slow tempo, low pitch, primarily stringed instruments, regular rhythmic patterns, no extreme changes in dynamics and no lyrics.

Music and imagery

Definition of music and imagery and rationale for use

Music and imagery approaches are used when the client/patient listens to music in a relaxed state, and imagery is either scripted or read by the researcher/clinician, or the imagery is spontaneously evoked in response to the music. The client may experience the imagery in silence, or in some methods, may engage with the therapist in dialogue about the imagery being experienced (as in the Bonny Method of Guided Imagery and Music) (Bonny 2002; Bruscia and Grocke 2002). Music and imagery is practiced in groups and with individual clients.

The combination of music and imagery has also been used to ameliorate pain within various clinical applications: In childbirth (Geden et al. 1989), in the control of stress (Rider 1985) in reducing anxiety prior to surgery (Naparstek 1995; Reilly 1996; Robb et al. 1995), and following surgery (Locsin 1981); in debridement procedures with children with severe burn injury (Edwards 1995), in pediatric music therapy (Edwards 1999), and with clients who have post-traumatic stress disorder (Blake 1994).

Imagery is most often understood as visual imagery, such as a scene that can be brought to mind easily (at the seaside, in the mountains, sitting beside a still lake, a favorite pet, or a favorite room at home). Samuels and Samuels (1975) explain that images may be memories that are indelibly imprinted in the brain and can be accessed at times to reduce stress, anxiety, pain, and sleeplessness. Other imagery experiences in adult clients can include somatic imagery (where changes are felt within the body), altered auditory experiences (where the client hears the music in a special way, as in Gabrielsson's study of SEM), abstract imagery (such as geometrical shapes, or colors), symbolic shapes (such as a cross or tunnel), and images of a significant person in the client's life (Grocke 1999, p. 15).

The function of the imagery is similar to that of music: As a distraction from pain, as a focus for the mind, or as a mental escape from a stressful environment. Imagery scripts (Naparstek 1995; Standley 1991b) may direct the imagery for a client/patient, however imagery that is self-evoked allows for special images, memories or persons to appear. Often the image is a memory of a person, place or event that has occurred in the person's life (Grocke 1999). In addition, music that is personally significant has strong associations to events in the person's life, thus imagery and music co-exist in memory.

Music choice

Music to stimulate imagery has different features than music for relaxation. Table 37.1 lists the distinguishing features of music for relaxation and to stimulate imagery.

Table 37.1 Comparison of the elements of music for relaxation and imagery.

Music for relaxation	Music for imagery
Tempo is consistent and steady	Tempo may vary
Tempo is slow	Tempo is predominantly slow, but there may be contrasting sections of faster music
Either duple or triple time, as long as it remains consistent	Fluctuations between duple and triple time may stimulate imagery
Melodic line may be predictable, with a rounded shape, and small range of intervals (often in step-wise progression). The phrases of the melody may match the intake and exhale of breath	Melodic line may include leaps and wide intervals. It might be unpredictable in places to stimulate imagery
Harmonic structure is typically tonal and consonant, with predictable sequence of chords, or suspended harmonies that resolve	Harmonic structure may have more variance, sometimes with dissonance
Instrumentation is likely to include strings and woodwinds, and exclude brass and percussion	Instrumentation may include various instruments including brass and percussion, although they are likely to be unobtrusive
Predominantly legato, however some effective music features legato melody line with pizzicato bass line	Combination of legato, staccato/pizzicato, marcato and other forms of stress and emphasis
Few dynamic changes	Larger dynamic changes, but not sudden or frightening
Repetition is a key feature	Repetition is less important—variation is needed to stimulate imagery
Texture likely to be consistent—could be thin or thick texture, but it is mostly consistent	Texture is likely to change from thin to thick
Supportive bass line	Bass line may vary between supportive and not
Predictable in melodic, rhythmic and harmonic features	Less predictable in melodic, rhythmic and harmonic features

Reproduced from Denise Grocke and Tony Wigram, *Receptive Methods in Music Therapy*, London: Jessica Kingsley Publishers, p. 46 © Jessica Kingsley Publishers, 2007.

OVERVIEW OF RESEARCH ON MUSIC AND IMAGERY

McKinney (1990) researched the effect of listening to a piece of classical music (Vaughan-Williams' Prelude *Rhosymedre,* orchestrated version), on spontaneous imagery. The participants in the study were two groups of college students, 81 in total. One group was given a relaxation induction, then left in silence to create images in their mind, the second group was given a relaxation induction followed by the music, with instructions to allow images to come to mind. The results indicated that music had no effect on the number of senses, types of imagery, vividness of the imagery, activity of the imagery, or percentage of time engaged in imagery. The music condition however significantly increased the intensity of the feelings experienced (p = .003).

A key element of the effectiveness of music and imagery as a therapeutic method is the creativity capacity of the participant to create imagery. McKinney and Tims (1995) used the Creative Imagination Scale to assign participants as either high imagers or low imagers. Two different pieces of music were used in the study, and both pieces of music increased the vividness and activity of the imagery for the high imagers, but not for the low imagers, the latter being more likely to experience feelings of relaxation with the music, rather than visual imagery. This study has implications for the use of music and imagery within clinical practice, particularly for hospitalized patients, where additional factors such as medication, tiredness, and levels of pain may impact the production of imagery.

GUIDED IMAGERY AND MUSIC (BONNY METHOD)

Guided Imagery and Music (Bonny Method) is a specialized form of receptive music therapy in which the client experiences music-evoked imagery in a deeply relaxed state (an altered state of consciousness), and imagery experiences are relayed verbally to the therapist who engages in dialogue to enhance the listener's experience. Guided Imagery and Music (hereafter GIM) was developed by Dr Helen Bonny in the 1970s (Bonny 1978a,b, 2002), and the method now bears her name. Typically there are four segments to a Bonny Method GIM session:

1 A pre-music discussion (often referred to as a prelude), during which the therapist and client discuss issues and concerns for the client, and then determine a focus for the music and imagery component.
2 A relaxation induction for the client, who may be lying on a relaxation mat, or in a reclining chair. The relaxation induction is of sufficient length for the client to be deeply relaxed. The focus image, pre-determined in the pre-music discussion, may be given to bridge the relaxation experience to the music.
3 The GIM component, comprising a music program chosen by the therapist from a vast array of programs currently available, or spontaneously programmed by the therapist in the moment. Bonny created 18 music programs of 30–45 minutes in length, and additional programs have been developed by GIM practitioners. The music programs

may be designed in various ways—a movement of a concerto may be placed alongside a work of a different composer for example. The central tenant of the music program is its contour, and therapeutic intention. Music programs may:

- Follow an affective contour, comprising an introductory selection of music to stimulate imagery, e.g. a work of an impressionist composer such as Debussy or Ravel; followed by a "deeper" selection in which the music may suggest a deeper emotion, so that a theme from the client's imagery may be explored from different perspectives; and at the end of the music program a more grounded piece of music, such as a work from the Baroque period to bring the client's imagery to a close.
- Comprise music that includes challenging selections of music, referred to as a "working" program (Bonny 1978b).
- Be designed to match emotion, such as grieving, affect release (for anger) (Bonny 1978b).
- Enhance spirituality, such as expanded awareness, peak experience (Bonny 1978b).

While the music is playing, imagery evoked by responses to the music is verbally relayed to the therapist, who makes verbal interventions to facilitate a deepening of the client's experience. Interventions are non-directive, and commonly help the client's narrative, e.g. "what is happening for you now?", "how does that feel for you?" Interventions are made with an awareness of the music, indeed the music is often referred to as "co-therapist" (Goldberg 1995).

4 As the music program comes to the end, the therapist reduces the number of verbal interventions as a deliberate means to help the client draw the imagery to a close. The closing selection of music also assists with this transition, often having a simple repetitive melodic line that is positive in mood. There is a period of post-music integration, which may include a drawn mandala (a circle is placed in the center of a sheet of paper for reference, and clients are encouraged to drawn anything to represent the music and imagery experience). The therapist then engages the client in a discussion of the session, beginning with the question "what stands out for you from the session?" The therapist does not interpret the imagery, although may suggest the client reflects on the meaning of the imagery.

GIM is practiced with individual clients in a series of sessions. Contraindications for GIM include clients/patients who are not able to benefit from the symbolic nature of the therapy, or those who are confused, or non-verbal, or those who are unable to return from a deeply relaxed state (Summer 1988).

OVERVIEW OF RESEARCH STUDIES IN GIM

Since the 1990s, studies have provided evidence for the effectiveness of GIM in enhancing health, and reducing symptoms in illness.

One of the first studies, conducted by McKinney et al. (1995), investigated the effect of GIM on levels of depression and beta-endorphin levels in eight healthy subjects, who were randomly assigned to either the experimental condition (GIM) or a wait-list control condition. The participants in the experimental group had a series of six weekly GIM sessions. The Profile of Mood States (POMS) was completed by the participants pre-post the series of GIM sessions, or the waiting period for the control group. Lower scores on depression were found in the experimental group compared to participants in the control condition, however there were no significant differences between the groups on levels of beta-endorphin activity.

A second study targeted levels of stress as measured by cortisol level (McKinney et al. 1997), taken before and after a series of six fortnightly GIM sessions and again at six-week follow-up. Healthy participants (n = 28) were randomly assigned into either the experimental condition (six GIM) sessions, or the control group. The control group was wait-listed—they had GIM sessions once the data had been collected. Mood was assessed on the POMS (Profile of Mood States), and blood samples measured cortisol levels. Those in the GIM group showed reduced total mood disturbance, depression, fatigue, and lower cortisol levels, and these indicators were still significantly reduced seven weeks after the end of the study demonstrating the long-term effects of the therapy.

Studies of GIM and patients with psychiatric conditions

A Swedish team of psychiatrists used the Hopkins Symptom Checklist-90 to measure psychiatric status in patients receiving GIM (Wrangsjö and Körlin 1995). Participants were fourteen adults (aged 19–63), 10 of who were rated as healthy and four who had mild to moderate psychiatric disturbance. Participants had a varying number of GIM sessions, depending on the individual's need. At the end of the GIM series participants showed a decrease in psychiatric symptoms (measured by HSCL-90) and interpersonal problems, and a significant increase in the participants' experience of life as more meaningful and coherent (measured by Antonovsky's Sense of Coherence Scale).

In a further study, Körlin and Wrangsjö (2002) grouped 30 participants into two groups based on scores on the Hopkins Symptom Checklist-90: functional (n = 20) and dysfunctional (n = 10). Following a series of GIM sessions, six of the ten people in the dysfunctional group improved sufficiently to be re-grouped into the functional group. For the total scores (n = 30), Körlin and Wrangsjö found significant improvement particularly in areas that are typically hard to treat, such as managing anger. They argued that GIM is effective because it draws on the person's inner resourcefulness to face issues, rather than in verbal therapies where the client relies on the therapist for guidance.

GIM has also been used in treating patients with posttraumatic stress disorder (PTSD) (Blake and Bishop 1994; Maack 2012). In Maack's (2012) mixed methods controlled trial, GIM was compared with Psychodynamic Imaginative Trauma Therapy (PITT). The GIM intervention was adapted for the clients, as is required for those who have been traumatized. There were 34 participants in each group; participants in the GIM condition showed significantly greater improvement in symptoms of complex PTSD, dissociation and quality of life, when compared to PITT, and the control condition. In addition, the improved scores were maintained at follow-up, indicating that the gains in therapy remained stable.

In a qualitative study, group GIM was chosen to activate "restitutional" factors in patients with severe mental illness (Moe 2002; Moe et al. 2000). The GIM intervention was adapted to the patients' presenting psychiatric state and sessions were directed toward instilling and enhancing resilience.

Medical conditions—hypertension

One of the earliest controlled studies in GIM was conducted by McDonald (1990) who examined the effect of GIM versus verbal therapy on hyper-tension. Participants (n = 30, aged 21–75) were assigned to one of three groups: Group 1 received six individual GIM sessions, Group 2 received six verbal therapy sessions, and Group 3 was a control condition. Blood pressure was measured prior to the sessions, weekly throughout the treatment phase, at the end of the therapy session, and again six weeks after the end of the sessions. The mean systolic and diastolic measures were used as data. Those in the GIM condition had significantly lower diastolic as well as systolic blood pressure than those in the other groups. Diastolic blood pressure reduced during the series of GIM sessions, whereas systolic blood pressure (which responds more slowly) reduced in the weeks *after* treatment.

A semiotic study of GIM following complex cardiac surgery

Semiotics is a study of the symbolic meaning of words, and Short et al. (2013) studied the written transcripts of GIM sessions given to six clients who had undergone complex cardiac surgery. She analyzed transcripts of sessions for semiotic meanings. Text from 31 GIM sessions was used in the analysis. Five grand themes emerged: (1) Looking through the frame, (2) feeling the impact, (3) spiraling into the unexpected, (4) sublime plateau, and (5) rehearsing new steps. Short looked for meaning in the words of clients relative to their life story. For example under theme 5, one participant in the imagery tried to unzip the fastener across the chest, a symbolic reference to the metal clips used to hold the rib cage together following cardiac surgery. Another person mentally played a game of golf, imagining the difficulties he might encounter. Findings indicated that semiotic analysis had the capacity to integrate all aspects of the GIM therapeutic session and deliver a depth of experiential meaning relevant to the therapeutic management of clients' post-surgical recovery.

Rheumatoid arthritis

Rheumatoid arthritis is one of the autoimmune diseases that is typically difficult to treat, with fluctuating symptoms, including high levels of pain (Grocke 2003). Jacobi and Eisenberg (2001/2) investigated the efficacy of ten individual GIM sessions on medical measures of 27 participants, including erythrocyte sedimentation rate (ESR, an indicator of disease status), walking speed, joint count and perception of pain intensity, and general psychological status including mood, symptoms of distress/anxiety and "ways of coping." Statistically significant results were found on lower levels of psychological distress, subjective experience of pain, walking speed, and joint count. Disease status was unaffected by GIM, and the authors argued that a longer period of treatment would be required for changes to occur in disease indicators.

Cancer

Two studies have investigated individual GIM sessions for cancer patients. Burns (2001) investigated the effect of GIM on mood (measured on the Profile of Mood States) and quality of life (measured on the QOL-CA scales) of eight cancer patients, 4 in the treatment group, and 4 in the wait-list control. After ten individual GIM sessions participants in the treatment group showed significantly better scores on mood and quality of life, when compared to the group who were waiting. In addition, mood and QOL-CA scores continued to improve after the post-test.

Bonde (2004) studied the effect of GIM on women recovering from breast cancer. Six women received 10 individual GIM sessions and anxiety and depression were measured pre-post on the Hospital Anxiety and Depression Scale (HADS), quality of life (EORTC-QLQ-30), and Antonovsky's Sense of Coherence Scale (SOC). Although there was no control group, results showed significantly reduced anxiety scores from pre-test to follow-up (week 17) for the five of the six women, and there was a large effect size. Depression was reduced for two of the six women but not at a significant level. Scores on the EORTC-QOQ-30 indicated increased level of function and quality of life, and a decrease in symptoms, but not at a significant level. The women in the study were also interviewed about their experiences of the GIM therapy. They reported that the imagery related to global aspects of their life such as self-understanding, and healing experiences (Bonde 2007).

Depression

A phenomenological study (Lin et al. 2010) described pivotal moments and changes in patients with depression. The study conducted in Taiwan interviewed five patients after each received eight GIM sessions. The forty transcripts were analyzed and coded into themes using a phenomenological process. These were: (1) Pushing aside a barrier, (2) gaining new insight, and (3) moving forward. Meaningful moments were coded as releasing mind-body rigidity, awareness and inspiration, acceptance and inner transformation.

Clients on stress leave from work

Beck (2012) adapted the Bonny Method of Guided Imagery and Music in her study of people on stress leave from work. Six modified GIM sessions were provided to 20 participants in a wait-list randomized controlled trial. Questionnaires included scales measuring perceived stress, mood, sleep quality, depression, anxiety, well-being, and a post-traumatic stress disorder (PTSD) scale. In addition, saliva samples were taken at baseline, pre-therapy, post-therapy, and at follow-up. Significant results were found on psychological variables of mood, sleep quality, anxiety, well-being, and physical symptoms, with high effect sizes (0.73–1.37, Cohen's *d*). A significant decrease in cortisol indicated reduced stress (medium effect size: 0.43). Significant results were seen for those participants who were in the early stages of stress leave, compared to those who had longer periods of leave. A qualitative analysis of interview data indicated fourteen themes, including specific imagery relative to the body, renegotiation of traumatic situations with work colleagues and family members leading to greater insight. Body imagery was mostly associated with sensorial effects (gut feelings), pain relief, and awareness of psychological patterns linked to pain.

Modes of consciousness

Bruscia's (1998b) heuristic study of clients living with the AIDS virus began with the clinician author reflecting on the therapeutic process, and through reflexivity, explored modes of consciousness during a GIM session. He delineated different worlds of consciousness that he entered into (as therapist) during a GIM session: The client's world, the therapist's personal world, and the therapist's therapist world. He identified four levels of experiencing (as a therapist):

1 A sensory level whereby the therapist senses what is happening for the client through his own body.
2 Affectively, where the therapist can identify feelings and emotions that are aroused by what is taking place for the client.
3 Reflectively, where the therapist tries to integrate meaning out of the sensory and effective experiences.
4 Intuitively, a level of spontaneous response to what is occurring for the client. Bruscia then demonstrated these worlds and levels of experiencing by presenting an extraordinary GIM session in which the client experienced himself being stoned to death. Bruscia's own reflection is captured in these words:

> It is very difficult to describe what Tom (the client) and I were experiencing in those last few moments of the man's death. Both of our voices were cracking: Our words fell into the same rhythm and tonality; and our bodies seemed filled with the tension and expectation
>
> (1998b p. 504).

Transpersonal experiences in GIM

Qualitative studies have also explored the depth of meaning in GIM. Lewis (1998–1999) studied the transpersonal matrix, in which she reviewed 128 GIM session transcripts, and categorized the imagery experiences described in the transcripts. Eight themes/categories emerged from the analysis. Transpersonal experiences involved:

1 Body changes
2 Past life imagery
3 Imagery of light and energy

4 Deep positive emotion
5 Archetypal or spiritual figures appeared in the imagery
6 Insights of wisdom
7 Unitive experience with the world

Lewis then related these to Wilber's (1986) spectrum of consciousness. All categories fell in levels 5–9, with none below 5, indicating all experiences were in the higher realms of consciousness. Lewis also ranked the music programs according to transpersonal experiences of the clients.

Phenomenological studies

Client experiences of music were explored through a phenomenological lens to narrate client's positive and negative experiences with the music in GIM and describe similarities and differences (Abbott 2004). Twelve participants were interviewed (nine female, three male). Four participants had up to 24 GIM sessions, six had 25–49 sessions and two had more than 90 sessions. Negative experiences with music were challenging but were often turning points in their therapy. They occurred when the music was incongruent with their experience, or had an undesirable or uncomfortable effect on them, which they tried to accommodate by using strategies to help. One was to reject the music, another to openly relate it to the imagery. Positive experiences on the other hand were seen as desirable, helpful, or supportive.

Pivotal moments in GIM

Another phenomenological study was Grocke's (1999) exploration of pivotal moments in GIM. Data for this study was derived from:

1 Interviews with clients about pivotal moments in their GIM experience.
2 Interviews with the therapists about their perceptions of those moments identified by the clients as being pivotal.
3 Analyzing the music that underpinned the clients' pivotal moments.

Seven clients volunteered to participate in the study, three male and four female. The leading interview question was: "Looking back over all the GIM sessions you have had, does one stand out for you as being pivotal? The participant was then asked to amplify on that experience—what was it like? Further questions were asked in order to collect descriptions of the experience relative to the research questions. From the seven client interviews, twenty themes emerged. Pivotal moments were (in part):

1 Remembered and described in vivid detail.
2 They were emotional and embodied experiences.
3 They impacted on the person's life.

4 Clients had insight into the meaning of the pivotal moment.

5 The effect was lasting.

6 The therapist's presence, or interventions, or silences were important to the pivotal experience.

7 The pivotal experience often followed unpleasant feelings or images which were uncomfortable, unpleasant or horrible.

Two GIM therapists were interviewed about their experience of witnessing the pivotal moments of their clients. From the therapists interviews fourteen themes emerged, and these were (in part):

- The therapists remembered the session identified by their clients as pivotal and also identified other sessions which they thought were pivotal.
- The client's pivotal experience was an emotional experience for the therapist and the therapists anticipated pivotal moments occurring.
- The therapists noted observable changes in the client's body language during a pivotal experience and intentionally intervened to facilitate the pivotal moment, but they were often silent during the precise moment.
- The therapist may intentionally intervene to facilitate a moment which may be pivotal.
- The therapist may feel time is suspended during a pivotal moment.

Using the Structural Model of Musical Analysis (Grocke 1999, 2007) an analysis of the music that underpinned the pivotal moment in GIM across the participants' experience found that the music prolonged the moment or provide momentum for it. Typically, the music was composed in a structured form with repetition of themes. It was predominantly slow in speed, predictable in melodic, harmonic and rhythmic elements, and featured dialogue between instruments.

Music studies

Studies of the effect of music in GIM

Two studies have focused on analyzing the salient features of music in generating imagery. Summer (2009) incorporated a music-centered GIM session using modification to traditional GIM: (1) Repeated selections of music—instead of a music program comprised of different pieces, the music program included repeated hearings of the same piece; and (2) music-centered guiding—instead of verbal interventions that focus primarily on imagery, the interventions focused primarily on the music. Four music therapist participants were able to use this process of deep listening as a means to listen to their internal world. Each participant's music experience was separated into music episodes that showed a successively changing listening attitude and hence, a changed relational capacity towards the music that deepened during the music program. For two participants there was a tendency to approach music listening from an analytical perspective, yet both were able to let go of this perspective to deepen their music listening stance throughout the GIM session.

The effect of music on shifts in imagery

Marr (2000) studied the effect of music on changes and shifts in imagery. She conducted a series of six sessions with four clients and recorded the music and imagery segment. The session in which the music program titled "Grieving" (Keiser Mardis) was used was selected for analysis. Marr wrote the imagery narrative across the score of the music for each of the music selections of the Grieving program, and looked for shifts in imagery related to what was occurring in the music. She used the Structural Model of Musical Analysis (Grocke 1999, 2007) to compare those events and found that imagery was evident when the music showed predictable rhythms, harmonic structure, and long and symmetrical melodic phrasing. In passages with rapid changes in tonality, dynamic range, rhythmic pulse and melodic fragmentation, imagery tended to be sparse with long, silent pauses in imagery reporting. Furthermore, tension and resolution that occurred in the music was matched in the imagery sequences. Images expanded with high pitches and light timbres and texture in the music, while they became embodied with low pitch and descending melodic lines. The use of solo instruments often matched somatic and kinesthetic imagery in specific parts of the body and, when used in dialogue, allowed several aspects of an image to be examined.

EEG studies

Developments in neurobiology and neuroscience have inspired several studies using EEG recording to graph changes in brain wave activity while engaged in GIM. Lem (1995) graphed EEG tracings of 27 participants listening to one selection of GIM music (Pierne's *Concertstücke for Harp and Orchestra*). The participants listened to the music without dialogue, and reported imagery at the conclusion of the music. Lem created an intensity spectrograph of the Pierne's *Concertstücke for Harp and Orchestra*, and provided averages for the graphed brainwave activity of the 27 participants. There were different graphs for posterior and anterior views. He laid these averaged graphs of brain activity across the spectrograph of the music, and explored relationships between the music and brain activity. Brain activity increased during moments of sudden and unexpected changes, such as the very soft harp cadenza towards the end of the piece. Lem explained that this finding has implications for how GIM therapists might guide clients, in particular, that changes in the music may be sufficient to stimulate new imagery and that guiding may interfere with this process.

An ambitious study of neurophenomenology used mixed methods to graph brain wave activity during GIM sessions (with verbal dialogue), and interface these results with qualitative interviews of the clients, using phenomenological analysis. Hunt (2011) adapted the traditional form of verbal interventions used by GIM therapists, instead using directed interventions representing six types of experience: Affect, Body, Interaction, Kinesthetic, Memories, and Visual, pre-recorded over two different classical musical pieces selected from the GIM repertoire. Four participants demonstrated distinctive reported imagery and brain wave activity, and a comparison across cases showed that: (1) The altered state of consciousness (ASC) involves both physical relaxation and ongoing focus on the imagery experience; (2) imagery generates brain activity in the same regions that would process information from similar real-life experiences; (3) beta and gamma frequencies played a significant role in how participants maintained an ASC and made meaning out of the imagery.

Merging neurobiological advances with psychotherapy is both exciting and challenging as the two paradigms do not seem immediately congruent, however as research into the neuroscience of the brain is directed to music, so too does future research appear the richer. The "discovery" of mirror neurons (Siegel 2007) has offered new ways to think about the was music therapy and GIM work, in that imagery indelibly imprinted on the brain might be used to positively influence coping strategies for those undertaking GIM as a form of psychotherapy.

IMPLICATIONS FOR THE FUTURE

One of the major criticisms of receptive music research is that researchers commonly under-report details about the music stimulus. In response to this criticism Robb et al. (2011) have developed guidelines for music-based interventions, and appropriate mechanisms for reporting under the CONSORT and TREND requirements. The list of improvements to reporting music interventions is lengthy, but those that apply to receptive music therapy include: (1) Clearer theoretical conceptualization to substantiate the choice of music interventions, (2) precise details of the music intervention and description of procedures for tailoring the intervention to individual's needs, (3) specifics of who chose the music, and better distinction and clearer rationale for therapist-chosen, and participant-chosen music selections, (4) describing the music's overall structure (i.e. form, elements, instrumental timbre) and details of the recording used (artist, length of the selection), as performances vary in quality, speed, and interpretation, (5) when using recorded music specify playback equipment and placement of headphones/speakers; who controls the volume, and decibel level, and (6) report number of sessions, session duration and session frequency including practice sessions. Adopting this set of recommendations will advance future research in receptive music therapy, and inevitably awaken new areas for collaborative studies.

REFERENCES

Abbott, E. (2004). Client experiences with the music in the Bonny Method of Guided Imagery and Music. In: A. Meadows (ed.), *Qualitative Inquiries in Music Therapy*, 2nd edn., pp. 36–61. Gilsum, NH: Barcelona Publishers.

Altschuler, I.M. (1948). A psychiatrist's experience with music as a therapeutic agent. In: D.M. Schullian and M. Schoen (eds), *Music and Medicine*, pp. 250–275. Freeport, New York: Books for Libraries Press.

Barker, L. (1991). The use of music and relaxation techniques to reduce pain of burn patients during daily debridement. In: C. Dileo Maranto (ed.), *Applications of Music in Medicine*, pp. 123–140. Washington: National Association for Music Therapy.

Beck, B. (2012). Guided Imagery and Music (GIM) with adults on sick leave suffering from work-related stress. A mixed methods experimental study. Doctoral dissertation, Aalborg University: Denmark.

Bishop, B., Christenberry, A., Robb, S., and Rundenberg, M. (1996). Music therapy and child life interventions with pediatric burn patients. In: M.A. Froehlich (ed.), *Music Therapy with Hospitalised Children*, pp. 87–108. Cherry Hill. NJ: Jeffrey Books.

Blake, R.L. (1994). Vietnam veterans with post traumatic stress disorder: Findings from a music and imagery project. *Journal of the Association for Music and Imagery* 3: 5–18.

Blake, R. and Bishop, S. (1994). The Bonny Method of Guided Imagery and Music (GIM) in the treatment of post-traumatic stress disorder (PTSD) with adults in a psychiatric setting. *Music Therapy Perspectives* 12 (2): 125–129.

Bonde, L-O. (2004). The Bonny Method of Guided Imagery and Music (BMGIM) with cancer survivors. Doctoral dissertation. Aalborg University: Denmark.

Bonde, L-O. (2007). Imagery, metaphor and perceived outcomes in six cancer survivors' BMGIM therapy. In: A. Meadows (ed.), *Qualitative Inquiries in Music Therapy*, 3rd edn., pp. 132–164, Gilsum, NH: Barcelona Publishers.

Bonny, H.L. (1978a). *Facilitating GIM sessions. GIM Monograph no.1.* Baltimore MD: ICM Books.

Bonny, H.L. (1978b). *The role of taped music programs in the GIM process. GIM Monograph no. 2.* Baltimore MD: ICM Books.

Bonny, H. (1983). Music listening for intensive coronary care units. A pilot project. *Music Therapy* 3: 4–16.

Bonny, H. (2002). *Music Consciousness: The evolution of Guided Imagery and Music.* Gilsum, NH: Barcelona publishers.

Bradt, J. and Dileo, C. (2009). Music for stress and anxiety reduction in coronary heart disease patients. *Cochrane Database of Systematic Reviews* 2009, Issue 2. Art. No. CD006577. doi: 10.1002/14651858.CD006577.pub2.

Bradt, J., Dileo, C., and Grocke, D. (2010). Music interventions for mechanically ventilated patients. *Cochrane Database of Systematic Reviews* 2010, Issue 12. Art. No. CD006902. doi: 10.1002/14651858.CD006902.pub2.

Bradt, J., Dileo C., Grocke, D., and Magill, L. (2011). Music interventions for improving psychological and physical outcomes in cancer patients. *Cochrane Database of Systematic Reviews* 2011, Issue 8 Art No: CD006911. doi: 10.1002/14651858.CD006911.pub2.

Bruscia, K. (1998a). *Defining Music Therapy. Second Edition.* Gilsum, NH: Barcelona Publishers.

Bruscia, K. (ed.) (1998b). *The Dynamics of Music Psychotherapy.* Gilsum, NH: Barcelona Publishers.

Bruscia, K. and Grocke, D. (eds). (2002). *Guided Imagery and Music (GIM): the Bonny Method and beyond.* Gilsum, NH: Barcelona Publishers.

Burns, D.S. (2001). The effect of the Bonny Method of Guided Imagery and Music on the mood and life quality of cancer patients. *Journal of Music Therapy* XXXVIII(1): 51–65.

Clark, M., McCorkle, R., and Williams, S. (1981). Music therapy-assisted labour and delivery. *Journal of Music Therapy* 18: 88–100.

DeNora, T. (2000). *Music in Everyday Life.* Cambridge: Cambridge University Press.

Dileo, C. and Bradt, J. (2005). *Medical Music Therapy: A Meta-analysis and Agenda for Future Research.* Cherry Hill, NJ: Jeffrey Books.

Edwards, J. (1995). "You are singing beautifully": music therapy and the debridement bath. *The Arts in Psychotherapy* 22(1): 53–55.

Edwards, J. (1999). Anxiety management in paediatric music therapy. In: C. Dileo (ed.), *Music Therapy and Medicine: Theoretical and Clinical Applications*, pp. 69–76. Washington: American Music Therapy Association.

Edwards, J. (2005). A reflection on the music therapist's role in developing a program in a children's hospital. *Music Therapy Perspectives* 23: 36–44.

Gabrielsson, A. (2011). Strong experiences with music. In: P.N. Juslin and J.A. Sloboda. *Handbook of Music and Emotion: Theory, Research, Applications*. Oxford: Oxford University Press.

Geden, E.A., Lower, M., Beattie, S., and Beck, N. (1989). Effects of music and imagery on physiologic and self-report of analogue labor pain. *Nursing Research* 38: 37–41.

Ghetti, C. (2012). Music therapy as procedural support for invasive medical procedures: toward the development of music therapy theory. *Nordic Journal of Music Therapy* 21(1): 3–35.

Goldberg, F. (1995). The Bonny Method of Guided Imagery and Music. In: T. Wigram, B. Saperston, and R. West (eds), *The Art and Science of Music Therapy: A Handbook*, p. 115. Switzerland: Harwood Academic.

Grocke, D. (1999). A phenomenological study of pivotal moments in Guided Imagery and Music. Doctoral dissertation. The University of Melbourne: Australia. <http://repository.unimelb.edu.au/10187/461>.

Grocke, D. (2003). Healing an inflamed body: the Bonny Method of GIM in treating rheumatoid arthritis. In: S. Hadley (ed.), *Psychodynamic Music Therapy*, pp. 389–401. Gilsum, NH: Barcelona Publishers.

Grocke, D. (2007). A structural model of music analysis. In: T. Wosch and T. Wigram (eds), *Microanalysis in Music Therapy*, pp. 149–161. London: Jessica Kingsley Publishers.

Grocke, D. and Van Dort, C. (2013). Music, imagery and mindfulness in substance dependency and personal growth. In: L. Rappaport (ed.), *Mindfulness and Arts Therapies*, pp. 117–128. London: Jessica Kingsley.

Grocke, D. and Wigram, T. (2007). *Receptive Methods in Music Therapy*. London: Jessica Kingsley Publishers.

Hanser, S. (1985). Music therapy and stress reduction research. *Journal of Music Therapy* 22 (4): 193–206.

Hanser, S. and O'Connell, A. (1983). The effect of music on relaxation of expectant mothers during labor. *Journal of Music Therapy* 29: 50–58.

Hodges, D.A. and Sebald, D.C. (2011). *Music in the Human Experience*. New York: Routledge.

Hunt, A. (2011). A neurophenomenological description of the Guided Imagery and Music experience. Doctoral dissertation, Philadelphia: Temple University.

Jacobi, E. and Eisenberg, J. (2001/2). The efficacy of the Bonny Method of Guided Imagery and Music in the treatment of Rheumatoid Arthritis. *Journal of the Association for Music and Imagery* 8: 57–74.

Jacobson, E. (1938). *Progressive Relaxation: A Physiological and Clinical Investigation of Muscular States and their Significance in Psychology and Medical Practice*. Chicago, IL: University of Chicago Press.

Kabat-Zinn, J. (2005). *Coming to our Senses*. New York: Hyperion.

Körlin, D. and Wrangsjö, B. (2002). Treatment effects of GIM therapy. *Nordic Journal of Music Therapy* 11(1): 3–15.

Krout, R. (2007). Music listening to facilitate relaxation and promote wellness: Integrated aspects of our neurophysiological response to music. *The Arts in Psychotherapy* 34: 134–141.

Lem, A. (1995). An integrated profile of brain-wave activity and structural variability of music in the study of music and imagery experiences in vivo. Unpublished Master's thesis, The University of Melbourne.

Lewis, K. (1998–1999). The Bonny method of guided imagery and music: Matrix for transpersonal experience. *Journal of the Association for Music and Imagery* 6: 63–85.

Lin, M-F., Hsu, M-C., Chang, H-J., Hsu, Y-Y., Chou M-H., and Crawford, P. (2010). Pivotal moments and changes in the Bonny Method of Guided Imagery and Music for patients with depression. *Journal of Clinical Nursing* 19: 1139–1148.

Lin, M-F., Hseih, Y-J., Hsu, Y-Y., Fetzer, S., and Hsu, M-C. (2011). A randomized controlled trial of the effect of music therapy and verbal relaxation in chemotherapy-induced anxiety. *Journal of Clinical Nursing* 20(7/8): 988–999.

Locsin, R. G. (1981). The effect of music on the pain of selected post-operative patients. *Journal of Advanced Nursing* 6(1): 19–25.

Loewy, J. (ed.) (1997). *Music Therapy and Pediatric Pain.* Cherry Hill, NJ: Jeffrey Books.

Maack, C. (2012). Outcomes and processes of the Bonny Method of Guided Imagery and Music (GIM) and its adaptations, and Psychodynamic Imaginative Trauma therapy (PITT) for women with complex PTSD. PhD dissertation, Aalborg University, Denmark.

Mandel, S.E., Hanser, S.B., and Ryan, J. (2010). Effects of a music-assisted relaxation and imagery compact disc recording on health-related outcomes in cardiac rehabilitation. *Music therapy perspectives* 28(1): 11–21.

Marr, J. (2000). The effects of music on imagery sequence in the Bonny Method of Guided Imagery and Music (GIM). Unpublished Master's thesis, The University of Melbourne, Australia.

McDonald, R. (1990). The efficacy of Guided Imagery and Music as a strategy of self-concept and blood pressure change among adults with essential hypertension. Doctoral dissertation, Minneapolis, MN, Walden University.

McKinney, C. (1990). The effect of music on imagery. *Journal of Music Therapy* 27(101): 34–46.

McKinney, C.H. and Tims, F.C. (1995). Differential effects of selected classical music on the imagery of high versus low imagers: Two studies. *Journal of Music Therapy* 32(1): 22–45.

McKinney, C., Antoni, M. H., Kumar, A., and Kumar, M. (1995). The effects of Guided Imagery and Music on depression and beta-endorphin levels in healthy adults: A pilot study. *Journal of the Association for Music and Imagery* 4: 67–78.

McKinney, C., Antoni, M., Kumar, M., Tims, F., and McCabe, P. (1997). Effects of guided imagery and music (GIM) therapy on mood and cortisol in healthy adults. *Health Psychology* 16(4): 390–400.

Melzack, R. and Katz, J. (2004). The gate control theory: reaching for the brain. In: T. Hadjistavroploulos and K.D. Craig (eds), *Pain: Psychological Perspectives*, pp. 13–34. Mahwah, NJ: Lawrence Erlbaum Associates.

Melzack, R. and Wall, P.D. (1965). Pain mechanisms: A new theory. *Science* 150: 971–979.

Metzler, R., and Berman, T. (1991). The effects of sedative music on the anxiety of bronchoscopy patients. In: C. Maranto (ed.), *Applications of Music in Medicine*, pp. 163–178. Washington, D.C.: The National Association for Music Therapy.

Moe, T. (2002). Restitutional factors in receptive group music therapy inspired by GIM. *Nordic Journal of Music Therapy* 11(2): 152–166.

Moe, T., Roesen, A., and Raben, H. (2000). Restitutional factors in group music therapy with psychiatric patients based on a modification of Guided Imagery and Music (GIM). *Nordic Journal of Music Therapy* 9(2): 36–50.

Naparstek, B. (1995). *Staying Well with Guided Imagery.* London: Thorsons.

Nhat Hanh, T. (1976). *The Miracle of Mindfulness.* Boston: Beacon Press.

Nolan, P. (1997). Music therapy in the pediatric pain experience: theory, practice and research at Allegheny University of Health Sciences. In: J. Loewy (ed.), *Music Therapy and Pediatric Pain*, pp. 57–68. Cherry Hill. NJ: Jeffrey Books.

Pelletier, C. (2004). The effect of music in decreasing arousal due to stress: a meta-analysis. *Journal of Music Therapy* XLI (3): 192–214.

Reilly, M. (1996). Relaxation, imagery and music as adjunct therapy to narcotic analgesia in the perioperative period. In: R. Rebollo Pratt and R. Spintge (eds), *Music Medicine*, Vol. 2, pp. 206–217. St Louis, MO: MMB.

Rider, M. (1985). Entrainment mechanisms are involved in pain reduction, muscle relaxation and music-mediated imagery. *Journal of Music Therapy* 22(1): 46–58.

Robb, S.L. (2000). Music-assisted progressive muscle relaxation, progressive musical relaxation, music listening, and silence. A comparison of relaxation techniques. *Journal of Music Therapy* 37(1): 2–21.

Robb, S.L., Burns, D.S., and Carpenter, J.S. (2011). Reporting guidelines for music-based interventions. *Journal of Health Psychology* 16(2): 342–352. doi: 10.1177/1359105310374781.

Robb, S., Nichols, R., Rutan, R., Bishop, B., and Parker, J. (1995). The effects of music assisted relaxation on preoperative anxiety. *Journal of Music Therapy*, XXXII(1): 2–22.

Samuels M.S. and Samuels N. (1975). *Seeing with the Mind's Eye*. New York: Random House.

Saperston, B. (1999). Music-based individualised relaxation training in medical settings. In: C. Dileo (ed.), *Music Therapy and Medicine: Theoretical and Clinical Applications*, pp. 41–51. Silver Spring, MD: American Music Therapy Association.

Scartelli, J. (1989). *Music and Self-management Methods*. St Louis. MMB.

Schou, K. (2008). Music therapy for post operative cardiac patients: a randomized controlled trial evaluating guided relaxation with music and music listening in anxiety, pain and mood. Doctoral dissertation, University of Aalborg, Denmark.

Siegel, D. (2007). *The Mindful Brain*. New York: Norton.

Short, A. (2007). Theme and variations on quietness: relaxation-focussed music and imagery in aged care. *Australian Journal of Music Therapy* (18): 39–61.

Short, A., Gibb, H., Fildes, J., & Holmes, C. (2013). Exploring the role of music therapy in cardiac rehabilitation after cardiothoracic surgery: a qualitative study using the Bonny method of guided imagery and music. *Journal of Cardiovascular Nursing*, 28(6): E74–E81.

Smith, M. (2008). The effects of a single music relaxation session on state anxiety levels of adults in a workplace environment. *Australian Journal of Music Therapy* 19: 45–66.

Spintge, R. (1999). Music Medicine: Applications, standards and definitions. In: R.R. Pratt and D. Grocke (eds), *MusicMedicine 3: MusicMedicine and Music Therapy: Expanding horizons*, pp. 3–11. Melbourne: Faculty of Music, University of Melbourne.

Standley, J. (1991a). *Music Techniques in Therapy, Counselling and Special Education*. St Louis: MMB.

Standley, J. (1991b). The effect of vibrotactile and auditory stimuli on perception of comfort, heart rate and peripheral finger temperature. *Journal of Music Therapy* 28(3): 120–134.

Summer, L. (1988). *Guided Imagery and Music in the Institutional Setting*. St Louis: MMB.

Summer, L. (2009). *Client Perspectives on the Music Experience in Music-centered Guided Imagery and Music*. Doctoral dissertation, University of Aalborg, Denmark.

Snyder Cowan, D. (1991). Music therapy in the surgical arena. *Music Therapy Perspectives* 9(1): 42–45.

Wigram, T., Pedersen, I., and Bonde, L-O. (2002). *A Comprehensive Guide to Music Therapy*. London: Jessica Kingsley.

Wilber, K. (1986). The spectrum of development. In: K. Wilber, J. Engler, and D.P Brown (eds), *Transformations of Consciousness*, pp. 65–105. Boston: Shambhala.

Wrangsjö, B. and Körlin, D. (1995). Guided Imagery and Music (GIM) as a psychotherapeutic method in psychiatry. *Journal of the Association for Music & Imagery* 4: 79–92.

Ziv, N., Rotem, T., Arnon, Z., and Haimov, I. (2008). The effect of music relaxation versus progressive muscular relaxation on insomnia in older people and their relationship to personality traits. *Journal of Music Therapy* 45(3): pp. 360–380.

MUSIC THERAPY RESEARCH

···

CHAPTER 38

MUSIC THERAPY RESEARCH
Context, Methodology, and Current and Future Developments

···

JANE EDWARDS

INTRODUCTION

···

RESEARCH is the process by which new knowledge is developed, existing knowledge is extended, and new theoretical frameworks are founded. In health care, research provides evidence for effective ways of working with patients or clients to achieve positive change; maintaining or improving optimal health and well-being. Research methods in health and education are characterized by a guiding research question or hypothesis, a theoretical or epistemological[1] orientation adopted by the researcher, a data source, and a selected method of data collection and analysis that is agreed in advance of the research commencing. All research is bound by an ethical code which is assured by approval from an Institutional Review Board, or an ethics committee. This process confirms that the processes of the research will cause no harm or discomfort to the participants, and will add value to existing knowledge.

Music therapy research is usually undertaken within the context of a university with outreach to recruit patients or students in health care or education. Initially music therapy in the university sector was built up through training programmes that were developed and delivered by people with professional experience in developing and leading music therapy services in education and health care. As higher education institutions across the world have become increasingly invested in all academic staff being research active including attaining PhDs and regularly applying for competitive research funding this has influenced the landscape of music therapy within the higher education environment. Increasingly it is unusual to find a course leader who does not either have a PhD or is working towards a PhD. Full-time permanent academic positions across the university context internationally usually require that the person has a PhD and a substantial body of work that has contributed to knowledge development in their specialist field.

TRADITIONS OF RESEARCH IN MUSIC THERAPY

In the fledgling years of music therapy research a commitment to quantitative methods within a strict positivist epistemology can be observed, especially in research publications within the USA. This was partly because of the influence of behavior modification as a technique in therapy practice (Madsen et al. 1968). Modifying behavior that could be observed and measured was the goal of music therapy. Many researchers used randomized controlled trials (RCT) to examine the effects of music therapy on behaviors of clients. RCTs are studies in which participants are randomly assigned to either a music therapy treatment group, or to a control group which does not receive the treatment. The RCT is considered a *gold standard* within medical research (Greenhalgh 2014). It is a highly effective method by which to test the effects and benefit of pharmacological medications. It can also show treatment outcomes when groups are compared where one group receives a treatment and another group, matched with the treatment group, do not (see Robb and Burns, this volume). Because of the alignment of music therapy with allied health, and the delivery of many music therapy services within medical contexts, the use of the RCT has been common in music therapy research (Bradt 2012).

The most important historical development in this type of research was the introduction of randomization, where participants or *subjects* are randomly assigned to one of the groups, whether treatment, control, or placebo (see Robb and Burns, this volume). This random allocation to groups minimizes bias and increases the likelihood that the results of the research will be trustworthy.

In the later part of the twentieth century music therapy research reports using new methods entered the published literature, and references to new methods can be observed (for example, Aigen 1993; Amir 1993a,b; Comeau 1991; Forinash 1992; Forinash and Gonzalez 1989; Langenberg et al. 1993). The early years of qualitative methods followed along the same route as other allied health research where *qualitative inquiry* or *qualitative research* became a commonly used descriptor (Edwards 2012). Although qualitative is a useful description for many research methods it is not in and of itself a method. Distinctions between methods and epistemologies within qualitative traditions have not always been well defined in music therapy research reports (Aigen 2008), and also in other allied health research writings (Carter and Little 2007). In the maturation of music therapy research a wider range of methods and traditions have been engaged, and knowledge about different methods has become more elaborated and differentiated. It is now agreed that all methods have an underlying epistemology, and in using qualitative method research it is essential to be able to state ones position in relation to the theory of knowledge creation to which one subscribes (Edwards 2012). Frequently used qualitative research methods in music therapy are grounded theory (see Daveson this volume; O'Callaghan 1996b; 2012), and phenomenology (Ghetti this volume).

An important distinction between research methods is whether they use *inductive* or *deductive* processes. Inductive refers to the way in which the researcher allows the information to be induced from the data during analysis (O'Callaghan and McDermott 2004; O'Callaghan 1996a). The researcher looks closely at the data, usually text or arts based, and reflects on the materials allowing meanings to emerge. Research which is *deductive* uses a pre-defined criteria to examine the data. For example, looking for particular incidences of a word in text or measuring a baseline behavior then providing treatment and following up with a further measure. Deductive might also refer to research in which the themes to be examined are decided in advance even when a qualitative method is used.

Research is published in journals following a process of anonymous peer review. A paper is submitted to just one journal and then the editor sends an anonymized version of the paper for review to at least two professionals with expertise in the area of the paper's content. The reviewers read the paper and provide feedback to the editor about their opinion of the paper. Reviewers can recommend the paper should be published, or they can request revisions, or they can recommend that the paper be rejected. It is not unusual that articles are rejected. It can be because the editor or reviewers do not think the topic of the paper is relevant to the journal, or there can be issues of quality with the research that deem it unsuitable for publication. Many researchers make revisions to rejected papers and then submit them to another journal. It is unacceptable to submit to more than one journal at a time, and authors must sign a declaration at submission that the work has not been published elsewhere or been submitted for review to another journal.

Peer reviewed articles appear in the following English language journals of music therapy: *Australian Journal of Music Therapy, British Journal of Music Therapy, Canadian Journal of Music Therapy, Journal of Music Therapy, Music Therapy Perspectives, Nordic Journal of Music Therapy*, the *New Zealand Journal of Music Therapy*, and *Voices*. There are also related journals which publish music therapy research papers including: *Psychology of Music, Music and Medicine*, and *The Arts in Psychotherapy*. Music therapy research also appears in medical and therapy journals (for example, Loewy et al. 2013, O'Callaghan et al. 2014). Therefore when students are researching projects or writing papers are encouraged to search the journal literature as well as reading relevant books and book chapters.

Trends in music therapy research

In this part of the chapter three trends in music therapy research will be discussed: (1) music therapy and evidence-based medicine, (2) arts-based research, and (3) mechanisms of change in music therapy.

Music therapy and evidence-based medicine

A number of music therapists have considered the ways that the profession can respond to the imperative of evidence-based medicine (EBM). EBM can be traced back to the 1960s but it more formally entered the lexicon of health care practice through the 1990s (Smith and Rennie 2014). As a PhD researcher in a department of Paediatrics and Child Health in the 1990s the author observed firsthand the shift in thinking about practice and services that occurred when EBM began to be a main point of interest for researchers, not just in medicine but also through nursing and allied health departments. In order to consider the implications for music therapy she gave a series of presentations which were then worked into scholarly papers for publication. After initial rejection some of the ideas were eventually published (Edwards 2005, 2004, 2002). Since that time others have also written about EBM and music therapy (for example Abrams 2010, and Standley 2012).

Rather than relying on the outcome of a single RCT to develop new practices in health care, EBM proposed an evidence hierarchy founded on single cases (weak evidence) through to meta-analyses (strong evidence). In a meta-analysis the research findings from a number of studies with patients who have similar characteristics are analyzed statistically to show whether the changes that have occurred across all of the studies are convincing enough to warrant inclusion of the treatment in standard care. Dileo and Bradt concluded that "Overall, EBP [practice] intends to assure that patient treatment is safe, effective, and cost-effective."(2009, p. 170)

Abrams has positioned evidence-based music therapy having multiple benefits for the profession:

> The virtues of an integral understanding of evidence-based music therapy practice are numerous. It can help promote clarity of the different roles, purposes, strengths, and limits of each domain of evidence. It provides accountability to core values, standards of integrity, and standards of rigor, all internally consistent within a given perspective in any given instance. Moreover, it encourages an awareness of the applicability and relevance of evidence to clinical work in any given case.
>
> Abrams 2010, p. 374

Earlier conceptualizations of EBM pointed out that music therapists are often referred clients or patients for whom other therapeutic supports or treatments have not been effective (Edwards 2005). Therefore because of the complexity of the client's situation and their unique needs traditional processes of matching of clients in control and treatment groups in the traditional RCT might not be possible.

Concepts used in *evidence* are now turning towards music therapy participants' views to be a better accessed and utilized form of evidence (for example, Ansdell and Meehan 2010). Although initially this author's concerns about EBM focused on inappropriate application by managers to limit innovation and cut services, in practice EBM has some but not complete influence on service leaders' decisions to support or close programmes. At the same time it has produced an outstanding number of music therapy meta-analyses published in the most important medical evidence database in the world, the Cochrane Library (for example Mössler et al. 2011).

Arts-based research

> The arts are increasingly being used in health care and related research to learn about the experiences of care workers and recipients, to gain access to marginalized voices, and to communicate research findings to a wider audience.
>
> Ledger and Edwards 2011, p. 313

Arts-based research is a movement that has developed internationally with minimal input from creative arts therapists. Ledger and Edwards (2011) provided a number of examples in which music therapists appeared reluctant to describe their research methods as *arts based*. This reluctance was hypothesized as emerging from anxiety about seeming scientific enough, especially when conducting research in health and medical contexts.

As artistic processes within music are central to music therapy practice, the use of music making or other creative arts processes could be considered compatible with the goals of music therapy inquiry. It is therefore puzzling why arts based processes are not more widely used in music therapy research.

Arts-based research was included in the main research textbook to date in music therapy (Wheeler 2005). Dianne Austin and Michele Forinash make a distinction between arts based research and the studies that have analyzed music created in music therapy sessions. They have shown that the arts can be used at every step in the research process to develop rich and expressive findings. Arts-based research is explained as offering a valuable way to gain insights that might not otherwise be discoverable (Austin and Forinash 2005).

Mechanisms of change in music therapy

Research contributes to knowledge about change, but researchers also have a responsibility to theorize why the change occurs. Research relevant to music therapy from the fields of psychology and neuroscience are key to understanding the mechanisms of change in music therapy. For example, music therapy relies on the evocative potentials of music to develop a way of relating between the therapist and the client that is helpful in meeting the client's needs and contributing to their well-being. Some of these evocative capacities include the ability of music to influence affect. In order to be able to interact and support clients in a way that is helpful and informed, understanding how music influences emotional states is key. Music therapists have extensive experience and expertise in observation of musical responses. As an experienced music therapy practitioner the following mechanism as to how emotional response to music might occur makes sense to the author. Julin and Västfjäll have proposed that when humans listen to music all of the following psychological processes happen, not separately but concurrently, and this is why an emotional response occurs:

> (1) brain stem reflexes, (2) evaluative conditioning, (3) emotional contagion, (4) visual imagery, (5) episodic memory, and (6) musical expectancy.
>
> Juslin and Västfjäll 2008, p. 563

Their proposition is interesting for music therapy practitioners to engage in order to understand the instantaneous aspects of response over which an individual has no control, and to confirm that there is no one piece of music that has the same effect on every listener. However, many psychological theories such as these that are relevant to music therapy are silent on the core interpersonal and relational aspects of music therapy. Therefore neuropsychological and physiological theories need to be accessed in order to further understanding of music therapy as a relational practice.

Developing theories about brain growth indicate that infant brains develop in collaboration and interaction with other brains (Schore 2010). Loving, predictable responsiveness from the adult care giver is essential for an infant's healthy start in life. The failure of the infant-parental bond to coalesce and attachment to be formed is disastrous for the child's ongoing development. This can occur because of maltreatment and/or neglect, or because of demands on the carer's own resources result in them being unavailable to the infant's needs.

This has lifelong consequences on development, particularly the skills needed for social interaction with others, and the resilience to deal with stressful experiences and events. Neurosequential modelling proposes that the infant brain develops in stages.

> The brain is organized in a hierarchical fashion with four main anatomically distinct regions: brainstem, diencephalon, limbic system, and cortex. During development the brain organizes itself from the bottom up, from the least (brainstem) to the most complex (limbic, cortical) areas. While significantly interconnected, each of these regions mediates distinct functions, with the lower, structurally simpler areas mediating basic regulatory functions and the highest, most complex structures (cortical) mediating the most complex functions. Each of these main regions develops, organizes, and becomes fully functional at different times during childhood...
>
> Perry 2009, p. 243

This theory is important for music therapy because it provides information to explain why children who have not developed self-regulatory processes due to severe early relational trauma, for example what Perry described as the "overanxious, impulsive, dysregulated child" (p. 243), might behave differently in the regulating *holding* environment of music therapy where predictable structure can contain and support the child's actions and spontaneity (for relevant case examples, see Drake 2011).

The therapeutic opportunities in music therapy lie not only in the client's responses to music but equally and sometimes more importantly in the therapist-client relating. Porges' Polyvagal Theory is so named because it associates two physiological systems with feelings of safety and security and explains how these function in interpersonal relating. These are:

> (a) the commonly known fight-or-flight system that is associated with activation of the sympathetic nervous system... and (b) a less-known system of immobilization and dissociation that is associated with activation of a phylogenetically more ancient vagal pathway.
>
> Geller and Porges 2014, p. 180

Using the Polyvagal Theory (Porges 2011) Geller and Porges (2014) have illuminated *therapeutic presence* as a salient factor reliant on neurophysiological processes by which safety, security, and trust are experienced in the therapeutic relationship. Given that many people who seek or are referred to psychological services have experienced a breakdown of their capacity to cope, or to relate successfully with others, the ability to provide safety and security in the interpersonal space is crucial to providing opportunities for capacity building towards growth and change.

> Expert therapists have reported that the experience of therapeutic presence involves concurrently (a) being *grounded* and in contact with one's integrated and healthy self; (b) being open, receptive to, and *immersed* in what is poignant in the moment; and (c) having a larger sense of spaciousness and *expansion* of awareness and perception. This grounded, immersed, and expanded awareness also occurs with (d) the intention of being *with and for* the client in service of their healing process. By being grounded, immersed, and spacious, with the intention of being with and for the other, the therapist invites the client into a deeper and shared state of relational therapeutic presence.
>
> Geller and Porges 2014, p. 180

Polyvagal theory has contributed to the development of new ways of working as well as supporting existing practices in music therapy. As Loewy (2011) noted:

> ... [Polyvagal Theory] contributes to the theoretical justification for the role that music therapy can play in activating neural circuits that regulate reactivity. Porges' rationale for and description of feeding and rocking as primal attachment behaviors which influence vagal afferent pathways is an essential contributor to the current thinking about the importance of the quality of care in the first stage of life. Music therapy practices that activate somatomotor components which trigger visceral change influence attachment practices which are critically important in the early years.
>
> Loewy 2011, p. 182

The relational dimensions of music therapy practice are underpinned by multiple psychobiological principles including those encapsulated in *communicative musicality* initially developed by Stephen Malloch in his postdoctoral work at Edinburgh University, which was then further elaborated (Malloch and Trevarthen 2009). Malloch and Trevarthen (2009) documented how the development of the theory and observation of the presence of communicative musicality occurred through many decades of research in the last century. Importantly multiple theorists and researchers from a range of fields, whether during field observations or in laboratory based experimental work, noted the expressive, dance and song like interactions between infants and the adults who share loving relationships with them. These multiple perspectives result in the conclusion that:

> ... we are evolved to know, think, communicate, create new things and care for one another in movement—through a sense of being in rhythmic time with motives and in tune with feelings to share the energy and harmony of meaning and of relating.
>
> Malloch and Trevarthen 2009, p. 8

CONTEXTS FOR RESEARCH

All research conducted with service users in music therapy involves a context. This may be a single site such as a school or a hospital (see Colwell, this volume), or multiple sites. It may involve a service such as an oncology department, or additionally it may involve participants who access multiple services, for example children with cerebral palsy. Each context differs as to how service users or students can be approached to be involved in the research, and who will act as formal or informal gate-keepers. Researchers planning projects need to factor in how the people who will contribute to managing the data collection of the project will be sorced, and how these potential gate-keepers will assist in managing the recruitment and involvement of service users. Often people who are crucial to the research such as gate-keepers receive little acknowledgement either in research reports, or in international publications. This can make it difficult for novice researchers to understand how crucial they are to conducting research which relies on data collection from service users or students (Porter et al. 2014).

Clinicians working within a service are often the referring point for participation in a music therapy project. The clinician can decide whether a person who meets the criteria for the project is able to manage the requirements of the project participation, and would potentially benefit from being a research participant. Clinicians are protective of their clients or patients. Therefore the researcher must take care to ensure that the clinician has confidence in the researcher and the research processes, that participants will not be taxed or made demands of in any problematic way. The gatekeeper may also be encoraged to note that the client may end up receiving music therapy, and that this participation may be highly enjoyable and potentially therapeutically beneficial.

One contextual dimension that has received limited attention in the literature is the role of the researcher and how this differs from the role of music therapist. Ledger (2010a) has reflected on her experiences as a music therapy researcher undertaking an ethnographic research project in a hospital that was developing a new music therapy service. She wrote:

> Returning to the familiar setting of a hospital brought to the fore a set of previously held positions and behaviors. I needed to manage not only the boundary between researcher and music therapist but also the boundaries between researcher and colleague, researcher and friend, and experienced music therapist and student. These boundaries needed to be negotiated and renegotiated throughout the duration of my ethnography. There were times when it was helpful to cross boundaries in order to build rapport and to show appreciation to the staff who contributed to my research. However, there were also times when I needed to establish clear boundaries and to reiterate my research intentions.
>
> Ledger 2010a, p. 300

Ledger's further reflection reveals some of the dilemmas that can arise when conducting qualitative methods research (Ledger 2010b). Unlike other types of research where one might collect data through testing or questionnaires, ethnography involves participation and observation. Being aware of the need to manage and negotiate role identity is an important part of undertaking this work.

THE FUTURE OF MUSIC THERAPY RESEARCH

As music therapy matures and grows as a field of practice it is developing its depth and breadth of research engagement. Contemporary research is immensely inspiring, especially for increasingly sounding the voices of service users (Ansdell and Meehan 2010; Solli et al. 2013), and the careful development of research procedures which ensure the complexity of musical experiences are not lost in the need for research rigor (Erkkilä et al. 2011). The development of greater sophistication in mixed methods research (see Erkkilä, this volume) will ensure that the outcomes of psychological testing or observation of the therapist will not be privileged over the lived experience of participants. The increasing harnessing of the capacities of technology in conducting systematic evaluation of music therapy services show promising developments (Streeter et al. 2012). More robust theoretical engagement with neuroscience and psychophysiology (for example Loewy 2011) and social theories (Baines 2013) will ensure that music therapy has strong theoretical bones upon which the flesh and sinew of competent practice can continue to grow.

NOTE

1. Epistemology refers to theory of knowledge. All research has an epistemological foundation whether or not it is made explicit. For further information see Edwards (2012).

REFERENCES

Abrams, B. (2010). Evidence-Based Music Therapy Practice: An Integral Understanding.
Journal of Music Therapy 47(4): 351–379.

Aigen, K. (1993). The music therapist as qualitative researcher. *Music Therapy* 12(1): 16–39.

Aigen, K. (2008). An analysis of qualitative music therapy research reports 1987–2006: Articles
and book chapters. *The Arts in Psychotherapy* 35: 251–261.

Amir, D. (1993a). Research in music therapy: Quantitative or qualitative? *Nordisk Tidsskrift for
Musikkterapi* 2(2): 3–10.

Amir, D. (1993b). Moments of insight in the music therapy experience. *Music Therapy*
12(1): 85–100.

Ansdell, G. and Meehan, J. (2010). "Some Light at the End of the Tunnel" Exploring Users'
Evidence for the Effectiveness of Music Therapy in Adult Mental Health Settings. *Music and
Medicine* 2(1): 29–40.

Austin, D. and Forinash, M. (2005). Arts-based research. In: B.L. Wheeler (ed.), *Music Therapy
Research*, 2nd edn, pp. 458–471. Gilsum, NH: Barcelona.

Baines, S. (2013). Music therapy as an anti-oppressive practice. *The Arts in Psychotherapy*
40(1): 1–5.

Bradt, J. (2012). Randomized controlled trials in music therapy: Guidelines for design and
implementation. *Journal of Music Therapy* 49: 120–149.

Carter, S. and Little, M. (2007). Justifying knowledge, justifying method, taking
action: Epistemologies, methodologies, and methods in qualitative research. *Qualitative
Health Research* 17: 1316–1328.

Comeau, P. (1991). *A phenomenological investigation of being effective as a music therapist.*
Doctoral dissertation, Temple University, Esther Boyer College of Music.

Dileo, C. and Bradt, J. (2009). On creating the discipline, profession, and evidence in the field
of arts and healthcare. *Arts & Health* 1(2): 168–182.

Drake, T. (2011). Becoming in tune: The use of music therapy to assist the developing bond
between traumatized children and their new adoptive parents. In: J. Edwards (ed.), *Music
Therapy and Parent-infant Bonding*, pp. 22–41. Oxford: Oxford University Press.

Edwards, J. (2002). Using the Evidence Based Medicine framework to support music therapy
posts in health care settings. *British Journal of Music Therapy* 16: 29–34.

Edwards, J. (2004). Can music therapy in medical contexts ever be evidenced-based? *Music
Therapy Today* V(4): 1–16.

Edwards, J. (2005). Possibilities and problems for evidence based practice in music therapy. *The
Arts in Psychotherapy* 32: 293–301.

Edwards, J. (2012). We need to talk about epistemology: Orientations, meaning, and interpretation within music therapy research. *Journal of Music Therapy* 49: 372–394.

Erkkilä, J., Punkanen, M., Fachner, J., Ala-Ruona, E., Pöntiö, I., Tervaniemi, M., et al. (2011).
Individual music therapy for depression: randomised controlled trial. *The British Journal of
Psychiatry* 199(2): 132–139.

Forinash, M. (1992). A phenomenological analysis of Nordoff-Robbins approach to music therapy: The lived experience of clinical improvisation. *Music Therapy* 11(1): 120–141.

Forinash, M. and Gonzalez, D. (1989). A phenomenological perspective of music therapy. *Music Therapy* 8(1): 35–46.

Geller, S.M. and Porges, S.W. (2014). Therapeutic presence: Neurophysiological mechanisms mediating feeling safe in therapeutic relationships. *Journal of Psychotherapy Integration* 24(3): 178.

Greenhalgh, T. (2014). *How to Read a Paper: The Basics of Evidence-based Medicine*. John Wiley & Sons.

Juslin, P.N. and Västfjäll, D. (2008). Emotional responses to music: The need to consider underlying mechanisms. *Behavioral and Brain Sciences* 31(05): 559–575.

Langenberg, M., Frommer, J., and Tress, W. (1993). A qualitative research approach to analytical music therapy. *Music Therapy* 12(1): 59–84.

Ledger, A. (2010a). Exploring multiple identities as a health care ethnographer. *International Journal of Qualitative Methods* 9(3): 291–304.

Ledger, A.J. (2010b). Am I a founder or am I a fraud? Music therapists' experiences of developing services in healthcare organizations. Doctoral thesis, University of Limerick, Ireland.

Ledger, A. and Edwards, J. (2011). Arts-based research practices in music therapy research: Existing and potential developments. *The Arts in Psychotherapy* 38: 312–317.

Loewy, J.V. (2011). Music therapy for hospitalized infants and their parents. In: J. Edwards (ed.), *Music Therapy and Parent-infant Bonding*, pp. 179–90. Oxford: Oxford University Press.

Loewy, J., Stewart, K., Dassler, A. M., Telsey, A., and Homel, P. (2013). The effects of music therapy on vital signs, feeding, and sleep in premature infants. *Pediatrics* 131(5): 902–918.

Madsen, C.K., Cotter, V., and Madsen, C.H. Jr (1968). A behavioral approach to music therapy. *Journal of Music Therapy* 5(3): 69–71.

Malloch, S. and Trevarthen, C. (eds). (2009). *Communicative Musicality: Exploring the Basis of Human Companionship*. Oxford: Oxford University Press.

Mössler K., Chen X., Heldal T.O., and Gold C. (2011). Music therapy for people with schizophrenia and schizophrenia-like disorders. Cochrane Database of Systematic Reviews, Issue 12. Art. No.: CD004025. DOI: 10.1002/14651858.CD004025.pub3.

O'Callaghan, C. (1996a). The relative merits of qualitative and quantitative research approaches in music therapy. *Australian Journal of Music Therapy* 7: 28–36.

O'Callaghan, C.C. (1996b). Lyrical themes in songs written by palliative care patients. *Journal of Music Therapy* 33(2): 74–92.

O'Callaghan, C. (2012). Grounded theory in music therapy research. *Journal of Music Therapy* 49(3): 236–277.

O'Callaghan, C. and McDermott, F. (2004). Music therapy's relevance in a cancer hospital researched through a constructivist lens. *Journal of Music Therapy* 41(2): 151–85.

O'Callaghan, C.C., McDermott, F., Michael, N., Daveson, B.A., Hudson, P.L., and Zalcberg, J.R. (2014). "A quiet still voice that just touches": music's relevance for adults living with life-threatening cancer diagnoses. *Supportive Care in Cancer* 22(4): 1037–1047.

Perry, B.D. (2009). Examining child maltreatment through a neurodevelopmental lens: Clinical applications of the neurosequential model of therapeutics. *Journal of Loss and Trauma* 14(4): 240–255.

Porges, S.W. (2011). *The Polyvagal Theory: Neurophysiological Foundations of Emotions, Attachment, Communication, and Self-regulation*. New York: Norton and Company.

Porter, S., McConnell, T., Lynn, F., McLaughlin, K., Cardwell, C., and Holmes, V. (2014). Recruiting participants for randomized controlled trials of music therapy: a practical illustration. *Journal of Music Therapy* 51(4): 355–381.

Schore, A. (2010). Relational trauma and the developing right brain: The neurobiology of broken attachment bonds. In: T. Baradon (ed.), *Relational Trauma in Infancy: Psychoanalytic, Attachment and Neuropsychological Contributions to Parent–Infant Psychotherapy*, pp. 19–47. New York: Routledge/Taylor & Francis Group.

Smith, R. and Rennie, D. (2014). Evidence-based medicine—an oral history. *JAMA* 311(4): 365–367.

Solli, H.P., Rolvsjord, R., and Borg, M. (2013). Toward understanding music therapy as a recovery-oriented practice within mental health care: A meta-synthesis of service users' experiences. *Journal of Music Therapy* 50(4): 244–273.

Standley, J.M. (2012). A discussion of evidence-based music therapy to facilitate feeding skills of premature infants: The power of contingent music. *The Arts in Psychotherapy* 39(5): 379–382.

Streeter, E., Davies, M.E., Reiss, J.D., Hunt, A., Caley, R., and Roberts, C. (2012). Computer aided music therapy evaluation: Testing the Music Therapy Logbook prototype 1 system. *The Arts in Psychotherapy* 39(1): 1–10.

Wheeler, B.L. (ed.) (2005). *Music Therapy Research*, 2nd edn. Gilsum, NH: Barcelona.

....

CHAPTER 39

MUSIC THERAPY RESEARCH
An Overview

....

BARBARA L. WHEELER

Music therapy is a diverse field and music therapy research increasingly reflects that diversity. Many methods and approaches are used to examine the various facets of music therapy practice and theory. This chapter provides an overview of music therapy research, and provides basic information about how research is conducted in this field.

Music therapy research is similar to research in other disciplines, but it has some unique aspects. It has the same definition and purposes, as described below, and most of the research methods that are employed are similar to those in other fields of health research. The focus on music is distinctive from most other types of health research. When the music, the therapist, and the client are included in the research process and outcomes a unique perspective is gained.

DEFINITION OF RESEARCH

....

Bruscia (1995b) has defined research as "a systematic, self-monitored inquiry which leads to a discovery or new insight which, when documented and disseminated, contributes to or modifies existing knowledge or practice" (p. 21). Gfeller (1995) described research as "a disciplined or systematic inquiry" (p. 29). She has also pointed to the importance of the definition proposed by Phelps et al. (2005) that research is "a carefully organized procedure that can result in the discovery of new knowledge, the substantiation of previously held concepts, the rejection of false tenets, and the formal presentation of data collected" (p. 3).

QUESTIONS AND TYPES OF RESEARCH

....

Research comes from the questions of the researcher or research team. Once the question is developed and refined a research method or approach is chosen because of its suitability to answer the question. While some people begin their research with a particular research method in mind, it is more usual to begin with the question and to let the question determine the method. Some basic examples of questions that lead to research designs are presented here.

Quantitative research

Descriptive

We might ask, "How does X influence our client during the process of therapy?" where X could be variations in the tempo, volume, tonality, or another aspect of an improvisation; type of instrument used; or things that are happening in the client's life outside of music therapy. Examples of descriptive research in music therapy could include studies that are based on surveys and questionnaires, single subject designs that rely on numerical data to determine the results, and studies of groups of people that use quantitative measures of outcomes but do not include a control group for comparison.

Experimental Research

We might ask, "Does X treatment work better than Y treatment?" X and Y could be music therapy and movement therapy or music therapy in combination with physical therapy versus music therapy alone. In experimental research, two or more treatment conditions are compared and participants are randomly assigned to conditions so that no variables outside of those that are being tested vary among conditions. Although it is not possible to achieve strict control outside of a laboratory, these designs do as much as possible to control all factors. These are standard experimental designs that answer questions about the effectiveness of music therapy and are often requested by those who determine what therapy should be supported or paid for.

Qualitative research

In qualitative research, we might ask, "What do clients experience in music therapy?" Qualitative research examines how phenomena are experienced and constructed through description, analysis, and interpretation. It relies upon words, music, sounds, or pictures to report the results and can help us learn more about aspects of the therapeutic setting. Qualitative research encompasses a wide range of methods, some of which grew out of phenomenology, existentialism, and hermeneutics in the social sciences. It looks for meaning and understanding and allows phenomena to unfold over time.

EXAMPLES OF MUSIC THERAPY RESEARCH

The following sections provide an overview of music therapy research with reference to a variety of methods. Examples have been selected to represent good research using each design, and encompassing a variety of topics. Although most studies are selected to represent a single method, studies can frequently employ several methods.

Quantitative research

Experimental research, including randomized control trials; exploratory trials; meta-analysis; survey research; quantitative single-case designs, including applied behavior analysis; and longitudinal research are examples of quantitative research and will be discussed here.

Experimental research/randomized control trials

A number of randomized control trials are currently available on various aspects of music therapy. The *Journal of Music Therapy* and the *Nordic Journal of Music Therapy* require authors to follow the CONSORT (Consolidated Standards of Reporting Trials) Statement (Schulz et al. 2010), which provides guidelines for reporting randomized control trials (RCTs) and insures that the reported information is transparent. In a RCT, participants are randomly assigned to conditions, with random assignment meaning that each person has an equal opportunity of being assigned to each condition. This controls for confounding variables by insuring that the conditions or groups are equivalent.

Examples of RCTs include two studies by Ghetti. In one (Ghetti 2011), of active music engagement with emotional-approach coping to improve well-being in liver and kidney transplant recipients, she evaluated the impact of music therapy under two conditions to which the patients were randomly assigned. One group received music therapy with an emphasis on emotional-approach coping, which uses emotional expression, awareness, and understanding to facilitate coping with significant life stressors, and the other group received music therapy without the emphasis on emotional-approach coping. In another RCT, Ghetti (2013) evaluated the use of music therapy emphasizing emotional-approach coping on preprocedural anxiety in adults receiving cardiac catheterization. Another RCT by Gattino et al. (2011) examined the effects of relational music therapy plus routine clinical activities compared with routine clinical activities alone on communication of children with autism.

Exploratory trials or studies

Exploratory trials (Medical Research Council 2000) or exploratory studies allow the researcher to gather information on how an intervention works but without including random assignment to conditions. Some of these, sometimes called quasi-experimental designs (Shadish et al. 2002), are similar to experimental designs such as the RCT but participants are not randomly assigned to groups.

One example is a study by Bensimon and Gilboa (2010), who studied Musical Presentation (MP), a therapeutic tool in which members of a group present themselves through musical pieces of their choice in and receive feedback from their peers, with the aim of increasing their sense of purpose in life and self-consciousness. Rather than randomly assigning participants to experimental and control groups, the researchers assigned them to the groups based on the times at which they were available.

Nayak et al. (2000) investigated the use of music therapy as an aid in improving mood and social interaction among people who have had traumatic brain injuries or strokes. Although the original intention was to randomly assign participants to the different groups that included an experimental group who received music therapy, a control group who received art therapy, and a control group receiving standard care, this goal was not achieved due to problems finding enough participants who met the criteria and were willing to participate. The completed study compared music therapy to standard treatment, but the condition to which participants were assigned was based on their availability rather than random assignment. Without randomization of participants the study design is considered to be much weaker because of the risk of bias.

In another type of exploratory study, data are collected but there is no control condition. The information gathered can help to determine whether the intervention can be carried out as planned. Studies of this type are often shared in professional journals. It is important that those writing them make it clear that, because they do not include any type of control, it is impossible to say what caused the effects that are seen. These studies are similar if not identical to what many clinicians do when they collect data on their work about how their clients respond or change during and after therapy. It is important for those involved with these designs to be aware of the limitations of such designs, and also to consider the similarities with data collected in regular clinical work.

Two studies of the *Sing and Grow* program for young children and their parents in Australia used pre-experimental designs. Nicholson et al. (2008) assessed the impact of a 10-week program for marginalized parents and their children in promoting positive parenting and child development. Williams et al. (2012) explored the impact on parental well-being, parenting behaviors, and child development for parents of children with disabilities and their children. Another example is of a music therapy program for women coping with breast cancer (Wheeler et al. 2010), while a fourth is the evaluation of a music therapy protocol to enhance swallowing training for people who have had strokes and have dysphagia (Kim 2010). In all four studies, data were gathered on targeted responses at several points and an evaluation of changes was made, but none of them included a control group. The findings of such studies can be used to develop more robust experimental procedures for future studies.

Meta-analysis

In a meta-analysis the researcher calculates a standard effect size[1] for each study, giving an indication of the size and variability of the phenomenon under investigation and allowing the studies to then be compared among themselves across all measures and variables. Meta-analyses have provided important information on the efficacy of music and music therapy in medicine. Standley (2000) conducted the first of these in 1986 and subsequently updated it several times. Standley (2002) later performed meta-analyses on the effectiveness of music therapy with premature infants in neonatal intensive care units and of music versus no music conditions during medical treatment of pediatric patients (Standley and Whipple 2003).

Dileo and Bradt (2005) completed a meta-analysis of 184 studies involving music in medical treatment. They included all studies that had been conducted with a control group that did not receive music. They included 47 dependent variables. The effects of music and music therapy were reported for each dependent variable, grouped according to 11 medical specialty areas: premature infants, fetal responses to music, pediatrics, obstetrics/gynecology, cardiology/intensive care, oncology and terminal illness, general hospital, surgery, rehabilitation, dementia, and dentistry.

Additional meta-analyses that have been conducted include an analysis of music education and music therapy objectives (Standley 1996), dementia (Koger et al. 1999), symptoms of psychosis (Silverman 2003), children and adolescents with autism (Whipple 2004), children and adolescents with psychopathology (Gold et al. 2004), stress reduction (Pelletier 2004), neurologic rehabilitation of upper and lower limbs (Chandra 2005), endoscopy procedures (Rudin et al. 2007), and several aspects of the treatment of people with Parkinson's disease (de Dreu et al. 2012). Meta-analyses are also part of some Cochrane reviews, discussed elsewhere in this chapter.

Survey research

Survey research refers to:

> the selection of a relatively large sample of people from a pre-determined population (the "population of interest"; this is the wider group of people in whom the researcher is interested in a particular study), followed by the collection of a relatively small amount of date from those individuals. The researcher therefore uses information from a sample of individuals to make some inference about the wider population.
>
> Kelley et al. 2003

Wigram (2005) divided music therapy survey research into three categories: (a) surveys of journals, (b) clinical surveys, and (c) surveys of training methods.

Surveys of journals, books, and other printed of web-based texts categorize the research and other articles according to the purpose of the survey. They can alert the profession to strengths and weaknesses, provide insight into where the research is happening, and determine how research is divided among clinical fields. Recent examples of this type of survey research include an analysis of music therapy journal articles by Brooks (2003) and analyses by Aigen of journals and books (2008a) and dissertations (2008b). Roberts and McFerran (2008) utilized both quantitative and qualitative methods for a content analysis of how music therapy was reported in Australian print media over a 10-year period.

Clinical surveys consider aspects of clinical practice, attitudes from both professionals and clients, and information about where people work. Examples include such diverse topics as: a survey of the use of aided augmentative and alternative communication during music therapy sessions with persons with autism spectrum disorders (Gadberry 2011); a survey of repertoire and music therapy approaches employed by Australian music therapists in working with older adults from culturally and linguistically diverse groups (Baker and Grocke 2009); and a survey of the expectations of cancer and cardiac hospitalized cancer and cardiac patients regarding the medical and psychotherapeutic benefits of music therapy (Bruscia et al. 2009). In an extension of traditional survey methods, Vega (2010) surveyed music therapists and also gave them a personality test and a test of burnout to examine possible relationships between personality, burnout level, longevity, and demographic variables among professional music therapists.

Surveys of training methods seek to learn more about music therapy practice, the experiences and attitudes of music therapy students, to assess the effectiveness of clinical training, and to explore competency requirements for music therapists. Researchers have sought information on a variety of topics. Stewart (2000) surveyed music therapists from the United Kingdom to assess personal qualities of music therapists, working models, support networks, and job satisfaction. Young (2009) surveyed music therapy internship directors to examine the extent to which multicultural issues were being addressed in internships in the United States and Canada; Gardstrom and Jackson (2011) surveyed music therapy program coordinators for information on personal therapy for undergraduate students; and Hahna and Schwantes (2011) surveyed music therapy educators regarding their views and use of feminist pedagogy and feminist music therapy.

Quantitative single-case designs and applied behavior analysis

Yin (2009) defines a case study as "an empirical inquiry that investigates a contemporary phenomenon in depth and within its real-life context, especially when the boundaries between phenomenon and context are not clearly evident" (p. 18). Smeijsters (2005) developed music therapy applications of case studies as single-case designs. Examples of quantitative single-case designs include a study of a preschooler with vision impairment in which the authors looked at the child's participation through several different playground adaptations that include musical stations and staff interactions (Kern and Wolery 2001); an examination of how girls with Rett syndrome make song choices (Elefant 2002, 2005); and a study of the emotional development of a client as reflected in improvisations (Smeijsters 2005; Wosch and Frommer 2002). Each of these studies used evaluation measurements and either a single case or a series of single cases to gather information.

Applied behavior analysis (Hanser 2005) can be considered a type of single-case design that includes specific designs and techniques, including reversal and multiple baseline designs. These designs are applied in behavioral research to test a hypothesis about the behavior of a single individual or group, examine the effect of a particular strategy, or examine intra-subject changes over time under different conditions. Wlodarczyk (2007) used a reversal design to examine the effect of music therapy on the spirituality of people in an in-patient hospice unit. Using a multiple baseline design, de Mers et al. (2009) looked at the effects of music therapy on challenging behaviors of young children in a special education setting. These designs have been used frequently in music therapy, as evidenced by Gregory's (2002) finding of 96 examples of this design in an analysis of four decades of the *Journal of Music Therapy*.

Longitudinal research

Longitudinal research provides information over a period of time (Ledger and Baker, 2005). According to Menard (2002), longitudinal research is when: (a) data are collected for each individual unit for two or more distinct time periods; (b) the units are the same from one time period to the next; and (c) the analysis of collected data involves some comparison of data between or among time periods. The most commonly used longitudinal designs

are: (a) repeated cross-sectional studies what are carried out regularly, each time using a
different sample (or primarily different sample); (b) prospective (panel) studies that collect
information from the same people repeatedly over a period of time (the preferred type); and
(c) retrospective studies in which people are asked to remember and reconstruct events and
aspects of their lives (Ruspini 2002). Several methods may be combined.

An example of a longitudinal study in music therapy is Ledger and Baker's (2007) investigation of the long-term effects of group music therapy on agitation levels of nursing home
residents with Alzheimer's disease. They tested residents at five time points over a year.
Although they found short-term reductions in agitation for those who received weekly
music therapy sessions, these positive effects did not continue over the year. Another
example is Dingle et al.'s (2013) exploration of the personal experiences of choir members with various mental, physical, and intellectual disabilities in relation to their wellbeing using the *interpretative phenomenological analysis* method developed by Smith (2004).
Interviews with participants occurred at the inception of the choir, after six months, and
after 12 months. This study is an example of a longitudinal study employing a qualitative
research method.

Mixed methods research

Mixed methods research uses a range of research methods. This allows diverse perspectives,
methods, and data to generate the information that is desired (Bradt et al. 2013b; Creswell
and Clark 2011). These methods are relatively new and in their very early stages of development and expertise in music therapy research. Issues in combining methods occur on pragmatic and philosophical/paradigmatic levels and are the subject of numerous discussions
and debates (K. Bruscia, personal communication, June 26, 2012; Johnson and Onwuegbuzie
2004; Teddlie and Tashakkori 2003).

Examples of mixed methods research in music therapy include a study by Grocke et al.
(2009) in which they studied the effect of group music therapy on quality of life and social
anxiety for people who had a severe and enduring mental illness. Quantitative data were
gathered through several scales that measured the dependent variables, and qualitative data
were gathered through focus group interviews and an analysis of lyric themes. Barry et al.
(2010) studied the effects of creating a music CD on pediatric oncology patients' distress
and coping during their initial radiation therapy treatment. They collected numeric and textual data for quantitative and qualitative analyses. Ridder (2005; Ridder and Aldridge 2005)
combined quantitative (including physiological measurements) and qualitative approaches,
using therapeutic singing, in case studies of individuals with frontotemporal dementia.

Qualitative research

Qualitative research is a broad term used to describe:

> the varieties of social inquiry that have their intellectual roots in hermeneutics, phenomeno-
> logical sociology, and the *Verstehen* tradition. Many scholars use the phrase *qualitative inquiry*
> as a blanket designation for all forms of social inquiry that rely primarily on qualitative data

(i.e. data in the form of words)... To call a research activity *qualitative* inquiry may broadly mean that it aims at understanding the meaning of human action

Schwandt 2007, pp. 247–248.

Tesch (1990) listed 46 terms used to describe different types of research that is broadly considered as qualitative research in the social sciences. The terms include: action research, case study, clinical research, collaborative inquiry, content analysis, dialogical research, conversation analysis, Delphi study, descriptive research, discourse analysis, ecological psychology, ethnography, ethnomethodology, experiential psychology, field study, focus group research, grounded theory, hermeneutics, heuristic research, holistic ethnography, imaginal psychology, interpretive interactionism, life history study, naturalistic inquiry, oral history, participant observation, phenomenography, phenomenology, qualitative evaluation, symbolic interactionism, and transcendental realism (p. 58).

Interest in qualitative research in music therapy began in the mid-1980s, when some music therapists started to consider the limitations of quantitative research in capturing important aspects of the music therapy experience (Wheeler and Kenny, 2005). All around the world music therapists started to explore the use of qualitative methods in their research. In the US, Aigen (1991) set the stage for the consideration of qualitative inquiry by music therapists in his doctoral dissertation, *The Roots of Music Therapy: Towards an Indigenous Research Paradigm*, as he considered historical influences on music therapy research from the philosophy and theory of science and critiqued what he called *the received view* from a position of process, clinical realities, creativity, and research methodologies (Wheeler and Kenny 2005). In Australia in the early 1990s, O'Callaghan was researching the experience of palliative care patients using grounded theory method and content analysis by examining the text of their songs created in music therapy (O'Callaghan 1996). Earlier in the US, Forinash (1992) used phenomenology to consider the experience of improvisation in Nordoff-Robbins music therapy sessions. In Germany at the same time Langenberg (Langenberg et al. 1992) and her colleagues used hermeneutic inquiry to understand which aspects of the therapeutic process were helpful for the client. The First International Symposium for Qualitative Research in Music Therapy was held in 1994, offering music therapists who were using qualitative methods in their research an opportunity to share and collaborate (Langenberg et al. 1996). This symposium was followed by similar gatherings, continuing until 2007.

Since the mid-1990s the number of qualitative studies has increased (see Aigen 2008a,b). This chapter will focus on some of the qualitative research methods that have been used by music therapists.

Many qualitative studies use *naturalistic inquiry* (Aigen 2005; Ely et al. 1991; Lincoln and Guba 1985), with the research being carried out in the settings that researchers want to understand, with the researcher's self experience and observation as the primary vehicle for data-gathering and analysis. Although naturalistic inquiry is sometimes considered to be a type of qualitative research (Aigen 2005), it is regarded in this chapter as a way of approaching the research and gathering information/data.

Phenomenological inquiry

Phenomenology is defined as: "A philosophy or method of inquiry based on the premise that reality consists of objects and events as they are perceived or understood in human consciousness and not of anything independent of human consciousness" (*American Heritage Dictionary* 2000/2009). Forinash and Grocke (2005) stated that "phenomenologists examine what is called the *lived experience*. This refers to experiences that we, as humans, have in relation to any event that we experience" (p. 321). Phenomenological inquiry is a frequently used method for music therapy researchers, probably because many of the questions of interest to music therapists are about people's experiences. *Reflexive phenomenology* is a term used by Colaizzi (Tesch 1990) for a form of phenomenology where the researcher uses his or her own experience as data. This is contrasted with empirical phenomenology, where data are gathered from others.

Examples of phenomenological inquiry in music therapy include Comeau's (2004) examination of how music therapists experienced times of being effective and ineffective in their work; Cooper's (2010) study of clinical-musical responses of Nordoff-Robbins music therapists during the process of clinical improvisation, which had a similar topic and some similar methods to an earlier phenomenological study of the lived experience of clinical improvisation by Nordoff-Robbins music therapists (Forinash 1992); and Gardstrom's (2004) study using descriptive phenomenology, as well as hermeneutic inquiry, to explore the experience of clinical improvisation with troubled adolescents.

Hermeneutic inquiry

Hermeneutics refers to the "art, theory, and philosophy of interpreting the meaning of an object" (Schwandt 2001, p. 115). The hermeneutic circle involves a constant analytic movement between the phenomena of interest and the structures (theories) developed in order to better understand the phenomenon. Theories are therefore tentative and evaluated against the data, further refined, and then reapplied to the data. The goal of hermeneutic research is to engage deeply in the circle of understanding in order to develop insightful and plausible interpretations of events.

Langenberg and her colleagues (Langenberg 1988; Langenberg et al. 1992, 1993) developed a psycho-analytically based method using what is called the *resonator function* to help observers gain access to the hidden meaning of an improvisation through a series of steps in which they listen to and respond to an improvisation by a client. Their system involves having a number of observers listen to a recording of a music therapy session and write down descriptions of the improvisation. They then follow a number of steps to compare and interpret the information and, finally, analyze the results in a process of hermeneutic circling in relation to clinical data from the client's case history.

Rolvsjord (2007, 2010) applied hermeneutic research to her study of a resource-oriented approach to music therapy, which intends to amplify the client's strengths rather than to focus on reparation of symptoms or difficulties. Rolvsjord states:

> According to the hermeneutic research tradition, understanding is arrived at through a process of dialogue between the researchers horizon and the texts that are studied. In my study, understanding and knowledge were generated through a similar reflexive and dialogical process between the empirical data and theory. This strategy for discovery has been labeled [by Alvesson and Sköldberg 2000] abduction.
>
> Rolvsjord 2007, p. 50

Others who have used hermeneutic inquiry in music therapy research include Bonde (2005), who employed a hermeneutic framework for understanding Bonny Method of Guided Imagery and Music (BMGIM) sessions; Gardstrom (2004), who used phenomenological and hermeneutic inquiry to investigate meaning in clinical music improvisation with troubled adolescents; Luce (2008), who studied music therapy students' epistemological development and how that influences their education and clinical training; and Jackson (2010), who explored responses to client anger in music therapy by examining cases, as units of data, through a process of hermeneutic phenomenological reflection.

Grounded theory

Grounded theory is defined as:

> a general approach of comparative analysis linked with data collection that uses a systematically applied set of methods to generate an inductive theory about a substantive area with the purpose of discovering theory from data. The researcher focuses on one area of study, gathers data from a variety of sources, and analyzes the data using coding and theoretical sampling procedure.
>
> Amir 2005

O'Callaghan (2012) presents a number of considerations and applications of grounded theory in music therapy.

Examples of grounded theory studies in music therapy include numerous studies by O'Callaghan, including one of the perceptions of a Chinese music therapy educator and students' perceptions of their music project's relevance for Sichuan earthquake survivors (Gao et al. 2013); another on the effect of music therapy on oncologic staff bystanders (O'Callaghan and Magill 2009); and one of the relevance of music for pediatric cancer patients (O'Callaghan et al. 2011). Amir (1996; see also Amir 1992) studied how music therapists and music therapy clients experienced meaningful moments in the music therapy process; while a study by Bonde (2007) in which he used a grounded theory procedure to investigate how cancer survivors described the experience and perceived outcome of therapy using BMGIM.

First-person research

First-person research is defined by Bruscia (2005b) as "any method in which researchers or participants gather data from themselves, using processes such as introspection, retrospection, self-perception, self-observation, self-reflection, self-inquiry, and so forth" (p. 379). One of the most well known types of first-person research is heuristic research (Moustakas 1990), in which a person studies his or her own responses as a way of understanding a phenomena. Bruscia suggests that the following situations may occur in first-person research: the researcher studies self, the researcher studies self and participants, participants study themselves, and co-researchers study themselves.

Examples of first-person research include a study by Bruscia (1995a) of his shifts in awareness/consciousness as he guided a Guided Imagery with Music (GIM) session and a study by Wheeler (1999) of the various sources of pleasure experienced in working with children with severe disabilities. The study of flute improvising by Schenstead (2012), described as a heuristic arts-based self-study (under arts-based research, below), is also an example of first-person research.

Participatory action research

Participatory action research is defined by Stige (2005b) as "… situated research advocating the primacy of the voices and goals of the participants themselves." Stige lists four of the dimensions central to this tradition: (a) active lay participation in the research process; (b) empowerment of participants and sociocultural change as part of the research agenda; (c) linkage of theory, practice, and research; and (d) application of a broad conception of knowledge when evaluating research processes and outcomes.

Baines (2000) reported on a pilot study for a program to "develop a cost effective group music therapy program that prioritized the requests of the consumers as the process for development, thereby readily incorporating consumer concerns and hopefully meeting consumer needs" (p. 54). A survey to assess the program was jointly developed by staff and consumers (clients), thus incorporating elements of participatory action research. A later report (Baines and Danko 2010) provided follow-up survey data supplemented by information from interviews with consumers.

Elefant's (2010) research suggests the importance of considering empowerment and social change when designing research so as not to risk ignoring critical voices among participants and thus contributing to preserving the status quo. The participatory action research project, with individuals who were part of a choir for people with severe physical disabilities, was a way of helping them to make their voices heard.

There are varied examples of action or participatory action research in the music therapy literature. One is Stige's (2002, Chapter 4) research with Upbeat, a group of people with mental challenges who were involved in a collaborative process to develop a more inclusive life in the community. Another is by Baker (2007), who used action research to evaluate a problem-based learning activity with students who were doing their first year of clinical training, emphasizing developing clinical reasoning skills. McFerran and Hunt (2008) used an action research process in a program to help adolescents cope with grief and loss in several situations. Rickson (2009) worked collaboratively with team members to facilitate their use of music with children who have special education needs and included action research in her consulting.

Ethnography and ethnographically informed research

Stige (2005a) stated: "Ethnography may be understood as a scholarly approach to the study of culture as lived, experienced, and expressed by a person or a group of people" (p. 392). There is an increasing amount of ethnographically informed research in music therapy.

Ledger (2010a) conducted an ethnographic study of service development in a health care organization. The ethnographic work revealed the inherent complexity of the researcher roles as she shifted between the identities of researcher, therapist, friend, and student while doing this research (Ledger 2010b).

Most of the case studies in the book about Community Music Therapy, *Where Music Helps* (Stige et al. 2010), are ethnographically informed music therapy research exploring how the effects of music and musicking are linked to human interaction in context. Ansdell (2010) explored what happens with a group of people in West London who get together to create and perform music. Pavlicevic (2010) documented the rich ethnographic context in and around a children's choir in South Africa. Stige (2010) studied participation in a festival that was started by music therapists several decades ago. In each of these cases, the researcher employed ethnographic research methods to study the people, the events, and the process of collaborative music making.

Arts-based research

Austin and Forinash (2005) have defined arts-based inquiry as "a research method in which the arts play a primary role in any or all of the steps of the research method. Art forms such as poetry, music, visual art, drama, and dance are essential to the research process itself and central in formulating the research question, generating data, analyzing data, and presenting the research results" (p. 458). Only a small number of arts-based research studies have been done in music therapy. Ledger and Edwards (2011) reviewed the arts based research conducted in music therapy and queried why music therapists have not engaged more enthusiastically in arts-based research. They suggested that music therapy researchers may be reluctant to adopt arts-based research practices due to a desire to insure that music therapy research is accepted as scientific and scholarly among other health care research. They also wondered whether music therapists may have used arts creation within their research approaches but have not highlighted this for various reasons, some of which might be related to the quest for recognition as a scientific and scholarly discipline.

Schenstead (2012) conducted a heuristic arts-based self-study through which she took an in-depth look at the intricacies of the personal improvisational process using her primary instrument, the flute. She improvised on stories and poetry that she had written and wrote about her experiences in a journal that became the main source of data. The journal was analyzed using an arts-based method and the findings took on the form of a performance piece in which she perform the stages of my process using a synthesis of poetry, artwork, music, and personal reflections. A final meta-reflection of the entire project presents a philosophy explaining the dynamics of the intrapersonal relationship.

Vaillancourt (2009, 2011) used arts-based research to create an apprenticeship music therapy model. In the first phase of the research, a research group met for five sessions, using "discussions, instrumental and vocal improvizations, adapted group sessions of the Bonny Method of Guided Imagery and Music (BMGIM), mandala drawing, collective and individual writing, and poetry" to deepen their reflections on their mentoring needs. In the second phase, Vaillancourt used a phenomenological approach to investigate the lifeworlds of the participants regarding their work together, using the artistic data from the previous work together to structure the interview questions. The results of the study, the emerging themes and essences of the participants' experiences, were reported through narratives and music, art, and poetry.

EVIDENCE-BASED PRACTICE AND MUSIC THERAPY

Evidence-based practice (EBP) is defined as "conscientious, explicit, and judicious use of current best evidence in making decisions about care of individual patients. The practice of evidence-based medicine means integrating individual clinical expertise with the best available external clinical evidence from systematic research" (Sackett et al. 1996, p. 71). EBP represents the combined use of (a) systematic reviews of the scientific literature, (b) practitioner experience and opinion, and (c) patient/client preferences and values for making clinical decisions and treatment/intervention planning.

EBP has received increased attention in music therapy as it has become apparent that by meeting the standards of EBP music therapy increases the opportunity to be accepted and funded. This is not without controversy and the issues surrounding the implementation of the evidence-based approach to music therapy have been elaborated (Abrams 2010; Edwards 2005b) The Cochrane Library and Cochrane reviews are an important source of information on EBP, and a number of Cochrane reviews have been done in music therapy, with the largest number in recent years.

The Cochrane Database of Systematic Reviews (<www.cochrane.org>) includes numerous reviews of various health care interventions. Cochrane reviews have been undertaken on music therapy for people with acquired brain injury (Bradt et al. 2010b), autistism spectrum disorder (Geretsegger et al. 2014), dementia (Vink et al. 2013), depression (Maratos et al. 2008), end-of-life care (Bradt and Dileo 2010), and for schizophrenia and schizophrenia-like disorders (Mössler et al. 2011); music during Caeserian section (Laopaiboon et al. 2009), for mechanically ventilated patients (Bradt et al. 2010a), improving psychological and physical outcomes in cancer patients (Bradt et al. 2011), preoperative anxiety (Bradt et al. 2013a), and stress and anxiety reduction in coronary heart disease (Bradt and Dileo 2009); and for singing for children and adults with cystic fibrosis (Irons et al. 2010).

Other types of research

Research on music

Bonde (2005) suggests that researching music includes "any method within music therapy in which researchers gather data concerning the relationship between music—improvised or composed, recorded or performed live—and client experiences and behavior" (p. 489) and that "the focus may be on material properties of music (stimulus or effect); on intentional properties of music (description, analysis, and interpretation of meaning); or on musical processes (interactions and relationships)" (p. 489). These may include studies of nonmusical or musical responses.

Studies that focuses on *nonmusical responses* include one by Elefant (2002, 2005), who used a single case multiple baseline, time series, within-subjects design to investigate whether songs in music therapy intervention could enhance the communication skills of seven girls with Rett syndrome. Ridder's research (2005; Ridder and Aldridge 2005) studied the use of therapeutic singing with individuals with frontotemporal dementia. This is presented under *mixed methods research*. They also viewed nonmusical responses, as do the examples of RCTs by Ghetti (2011; 2013) and Gattino et al. (2011); the exploratory studies by Bensimon and Gilboa (2010); Nayak et al. (2000); Williams et al. (2012); Wheeler et al. (2010); and Kim (2010) among others. The fact that so many examples of research on nonmusical responses have been presented in this chapter highlights that a great deal of music therapy research has focused on nonmusical responses or outcomes by music therapists.

There are also numerous examples of research on *musical responses*. The work on the *resonator function*, described under hermeneutic inquiry (Langenberg 1988; Langenberg et al. 1992, 1993), helped observers gain access to the hidden meaning of an improvisation. Bergstrøm-Nielsen (1993, 1999, 2010) developed a graphic notation as a tool for music therapists in notating and analyzing improvisations. Turry (2010) analyzed the relationship between words and music in clinically improvised songs with a woman with whom he had music therapy sessions for a number of years. Additional studies of musical responses that have been cited earlier in this chapter are by Cooper (2010), Forinash (1992), and Gardstrom (2004).

Historical research

Historical research is defined as "the systematic study of the past practices, materials, institutions, and people involved in therapeutic applications of music" (Solomon and Heller 1982). Historical research is a way of preserving the history of music therapy that people in the future will know of what led to that point. Historical research topics cover a wide range.

Several studies of music therapy pioneers, including Ira Maximillian Altshuler (Davis 2003), Willem van de Wall (Clair and Heller 1989), and James Leonard Corning (Davis 2012), have been published. Historical uses of music in hospitals, and the development of the profession of music therapy for hospital patients has been researched (e.g. Edwards 2007, 2008; Taylor 1981). Reschke-Hernández (2011) examined the history of music therapy treatment interventions for children with autism.

Kim (2009) conducted an "Historical Investigation Regarding the Perception of Music Therapy Among Korean Medical Professionals as Seen in Medical Journal Articles," which combines historical research with survey methods. In a narrative inquiry, Hadley (2001) explored connections between historical information and other aspects of Mary Priestley's life and work. She conducted a similar study of the life of Clive Robbins (Hadley 2003).

Philosophical inquiry and theory development

Bruscia (2005a) has said that a "theory is way of thinking about what we do or what we know" (p. 540) and that philosophy and theory "have the same aim: understanding." Bruscia also suggested that "they relate to practice and research in the same way" and that "both involve thinking activities, such as reflection, reasoning, criticism, speculation, and intuition" (p. 541).

Theory development has always been a part of the research work in music therapy. Sears (1968) suggested three processes in music therapy: experience within structure, experience in self-organization, and experience in relating to others, still provides a basis for the thinking of many about what music therapy does. Kenny (1989, 2006) organized her ideas into a formal theory and found a language to reflect her understanding of the music therapy process in what she termed *The Field of Play*.

Music therapy theory has continued to develop. Working to develop theory for the music therapy as procedural support for invasive medical procedures, Ghetti (2012) used qualitative document analysis to examine the literature in this field. She integrated findings from 19 primary sources to formulate a theoretically grounded working model. Robb (2012) suggests that music therapy research is moving from being outcomes-based to theory-based and that the attention that is now being paid to theory "offers one way to advance our understanding of the complex interactions between music, clients, and the education or health care environment" (p. 5).

In adaptations of theoretical research, Hadley (1999) compared philosophical premises underlying two approaches to music therapy, Creative Music Therapy, developed by Nordoff and Robbins (2007), and Analytical Music Therapy, developed by Priestley (1994). Mössler (2011) combined the development of theory and historical research as she examined the influence of theory construction on the formation of professional identity as it occurs in the Viennese School of Music Therapy.

Abrams (2011) has proposed that music is a temporal-aesthetic way of being. He proposed that music can be conceptualized as a phenomenon that transcends the concrete, physical medium of sound. In Abrams's theory, while music may be expressed *through* sound, its essence is located in the ways that human thought, feeling, and action unfold aesthetically in time, allowing the music in music therapy to be not merely a means for promoting *non-musical* health but also a particular dimension of human health itself, manifesting as the temporal-aesthetic component of each health domain typically targeted within music therapy work.

Research publications

Eight music therapy journals are published regularly in English, many by music therapy associations of their countries, and include varying amounts of research. In order of the dates on which they commenced publication (and which are listed), they are: *Journal of Music Therapy* 1964 (US); *Canadian Journal of Music Therapy* 1973; *Music Therapy Perspectives* 1982 (US); *British Journal of Music Therapy* 1987; *Australian Journal of Music Therapy* 1990; *Nordic Journal of Music Therapy* 1992 (representing all of the Nordic countries and now an international journal); *New Zealand Journal of Music Therapy* 1994; and *Voices: A Worldwide Forum for Music Therapy* 2001 (on-line: <www.voices.no>).

In addition to these journals published in English, the German journal, *Musiktherapeutische Umshcau,* has been published since 1980 and plays an important role in the development of German music therapy and thus music therapy internationally. *Music Therapy: Journal of the American Association for Music Therapy* was published from 1981–1996. *The Arts in Psychotherapy,* an international journal that covers all of the arts therapies, has been in publication since 1973, and includes a substantial amount of music therapy research. The *Journal of the Association of Music and Imagery (AMI)*, published since 1992, focuses on the Bonny Method of Guided Imagery and Music (BMGIM), which is closely related to music therapy. *Music and Medicine: An Interdisciplinary Journal*, published since 2009, includes current practices of music and medicine, including music therapy. Finally, many music therapy studies are published in journals of related disciplines.

Several people have reviewed music therapy research in the past decade, primarily through analyses of journal articles. Brooks (2003) examined 1521 articles from nine music therapy journals over a 37-year period, looking for trends and types of article and comparing them across journals. She tallied the numbers of research articles classified in the categories of quantitative, qualitative, clinical, historical, philosophical/theoretical, and professional.[2]

The number of articles published in each of these journals is, of course, related to the length of time that the journal has been published and the number of issues a year. Brooks found quantitative research articles to be the predominant category across all journals, with 542 articles. She found 55 historical articles and 136 philosophical/theoretical articles.

Edwards (2005a) reviewed eight journals for content and trends, and also examined the number of articles from one journal that were referenced in other journals. This was in order to reveal the extent to which music therapists showed awareness of each others work across the international community. To examine how many articles from one journal were cited by authors writing in other journals, she reviewed papers from the *Journal of Music Therapy (JMT)* from 1964–2003 and the *British Journal of Music Therapy (BJMT)* from 1995–2003. She found no papers from either the *New Zealand Journal of Music Therapy or the Canadian Journal of Music Therapy* to have been cited in *JMT* during the publication period reviewed. Citations from the *BJMT* appeared in eight papers in JMT, five of which were authored by music therapists from countries outside the United States. The lack of awareness and citation of authors from other countries is a concern for the internationalization of the discipline of music therapy.

Aigen examined qualitative articles and chapters (2008a) and qualitative dissertations (2008b) published from 1987–2006. He found 92 articles and book chapters, 55 doctoral studies, and six books to have been published during that period. In the period from 1987–1990, two articles and chapters and two dissertations (or doctoral theses) were published; from 1991–1994, five articles and chapters and seven dissertations; from 1995–1998, 20 articles and chapters and seven dissertations; from 1999–2002, 31 articles and chapters and 13 dissertations; and from 2003–2006, 34 articles and chapters and 23 dissertations. This clearly represents a large increase in qualitative research in music therapy, beginning in the mid-1990s.

Issues and problems

As music therapists work to meet the demands of evidence-based practice, making it clear that RCTs need to be conducted to determine the efficacy of music therapy, there is much discussion about several areas. One of these is whether too much emphasis is being placed on RCTs. Many music therapists feel that the work that they do cannot be adequately investigated using RCTs and other quantitative approaches. Edwards (2005b) indicated some of these concerns and the ways they can be addresses in medical music therapy, and her suggestions can apply beyond medical areas. Bradt (2012) has emphasized that RCTs are not the only type of investigation that should be done about music therapy processes and outcomes. She wrote, "It is of great importance to the field of music therapy that multiple types of evidence contribute to its knowledge base and that the dialogue of clinical effectiveness is not dominated by the biomedical hierarchical model of evidence-based practice (EBP) in which meta-analytic reviews and randomized controlled trials reign" (p. 121).

Another discussion is about how well the requirements for rigorous control in conducting RCTs can match with what actually occurs in a music therapy session. As Bradt (2012) says, "One of the major concerns expressed by music therapists about the use of RCTs is the claim that the treatments used in RCTs suffer so severely from the required standardization that they become irrelevant to clinical practice" (p. 136). One way to address this concern is to use a treatment manual, which contains guidelines for the treatment approach being investigated but does not provide a rigid set of procedures to use. Rolvsjord et al. (2005), who developed a manual for an RCT investigating resource oriented music therapy, say:

> Our pragmatic solution... has been to produce a manual with open descriptions of principles that emphasize contextual and collaborative aspects. The manual thus focuses upon underlying assumptions and values informing a contextual approach to resource-oriented music therapy, rather than describing specific actions, techniques, or procedures. In this way we hope to have avoided that the manualization should limit the possibilities for each therapeutic process to be tailored to match the individual client. We also think that the principles, if practiced with competence and not only adherence, have left enough space for the collaborative therapeutic process to develop relatively freely.
>
> (p. 28)

Another issue is the quality of music therapy research. As research has been reviewed for Cochrane Reviews and the quality evaluated on a number of criteria, it has become apparent that many music therapy studies are not of high enough quality to be included. Bradt (2012) said, "Reviews of the music therapy research literature indicate a need for increased scientific rigor in the design and conduct of RCTs" (p. 146). "It is important that music therapists contributing to our evidence base through RCT research are prepared to design trials that meet current methodological standards and, equally important, are able to respond appropriately to those design aspects (e.g. blinding of the participants) that are not feasible in music therapy research" (p. 121).

The positive side of this is that it providing guidance for music therapy researchers in raising the quality of the studies, leading to more studies that meet criteria for inclusion. This applies primarily to RCTs, and it seems that the number of RCTs about music therapy research is increasing.

Another problem in experimental research in music therapy is enrolling enough participants for the research study, which generally requires a certain number of participants who meet the inclusion criteria for the study. Since many music therapy procedures require multiple sessions, the number of available participants can be further limited. One of the solutions for this problem is for researchers from several facilities to collaborate so that the research includes participants from several institutions. This was done, for example, in two hospitals with a study of the effects of music therapy for mood disturbance during hospitalization for autologous stem cell transplantation (Cassileth et al. 2003), a multi-site study of the effects of parent-preferred melodies and entrained live rhythm and breath sounds on babies in neonatal intensive care units (Loewy et al. 2013), and a multi-site study of the effects of active music engagement on children with cancer (Robb et al. 2008) as well as a more recent study further investigating a therapeutic music video intervention (Robb et al. 2014). Increasing international cooperation is making international multi-site studies possible, as exemplified by a study of improvisational music therapy's effectiveness for children with autism spectrum disorders that aims to enroll 300 participants recruited from nine different countries (Geretsegger et al. 2012; International Standard Randomized Controlled Trial Number Register 2013) and one of individual music therapy for mental health care clients with low therapy motivation that enrolled 144 adults from three countries (Gold et al. 2013).

Challenges to music therapy research that are not specific to RCTs have to do with whether music therapy clinicians and others use the research that has been done. This has been an ongoing challenge for music therapy research (see Wheeler 2005, p. 6). Waldon (2015) surveyed US music therapists for information on the extent to which they engage in research-related activities or whether they perceive barriers to integrating research into clinical. He found differences in how research is utilized as well as perceived barriers between music therapist whose primary job role is research and those in clinical positions. He says that "this suggests a divide between those generating knowledge about the profession (researchers and academicians) and those responsible for delivering treatment (clincians). Furthermore, reported utilization varies as a function of work setting (e.g. between rehabilitation/medical settings and others)" (p. 1). There are also questions about how qualitative research, an important portion of current music therapy research, is related to the demands of evidence-based practice. One way that this is being addressed is through synthesis of qualitative research, which combines and integrates qualitative research that addresses a similar topic, question or population (Hannes and Lockwood 2012; Sandelowski and Barroso 2007).

Along with the challenges confronting music therapy research and researchers, there is a great deal of development and extension work that builds the profession and increases our knowledge within the profession as well as our visibility to others. Music therapy research draws from various traditions of inquiry, selecting the method as relevant to the questions being asked, and doing it with increasingly high quality. All of this brings music therapy closer to achieving an integral connection between theory, clinical practice, and research that Gaston (1968) suggested should form a tripod, each necessary in order for the other to stand.

Notes

1. An effect size is the difference between means in standardized units, or the number of standard deviations by which the means differ.
2. Since the focus of this chapter is music therapy research, clinical and professional articles are not included in this summary, although they were part of Brooks' (2003) analysis.

References

Abrams, B. (2010). Evidence-based music therapy practice: An integral understanding. *Journal of Music Therapy* 47(4): 351–379.

Abrams, B. (2011). Understanding music as a temporal-aesthetic way of being: Implications for a general theory of music therapy. *The Arts in Psychotherapy* 38: 114–119.

Aigen, K. (1991). The roots of music therapy: Towards an indigenous research paradigm. (Doctoral Dissertation, New York University, 1990). *Dissertation Abstracts International* 52(6): 1933A. (UMI No. DEY91-34717.)

Aigen, K. (2005). Naturalistic inquiry. In: B.L. Wheeler (ed.), *Music Therapy Research*, 2nd ed., pp. 352–364. Gilsum, NH: Barcelona Publishers.

Aigen, K. (2008a). An analysis of qualitative music therapy research reports 1987–2006: Articles and book chapters. *The Arts in Psychotherapy* 35: 251–261.

Aigen, K. (2008b). An analysis of qualitative music therapy research reports1987–2006: Doctoral studies. *The Arts in Psychotherapy* 35: 307–319.

Alvesson, M. and Sköldberg, K. (2000). *Reflexive methodology: New Vistas for Qualitative Research*. London: Sage.

American Heritage® Dictionary of the English Language, 4th ed., 2000/2009. Boston: Houghton Mifflin Company.

Amir, D. (1992). Awakening and expanding the self: Meaningful moments in the music therapy process as experienced and described by music therapists and music therapy clients. (Doctoral dissertation, New York University, 1992). *Dissertation Abstracts International* 53(8): 4361B.

Amir, D. (1996). Experiencing music therapy: Meaningful moments in the music therapy process. In: M. Langenberg, K. Aigen, and J. Frommer (eds), *Qualitative Music Therapy Research: Beginning Dialogues*, pp. 109–130. Gilsum, NH: Barcelona Publishers.

Amir, D. (2005). Grounded theory. In: B.L. Wheeler (ed.), *Music Therapy Research*, 2nd ed., pp. 365–378. Gilsum, NH: Barcelona Publishers.

Ansdell, G. (2010). Belonging through musicing: explorations of musical community. In: B. Stige, G. Ansdell, C. Elefant, and M. Pavlicevic, *Where Music Helps: Community Music Therapy in Action and Reflection*, pp. 41–62. Aldershot, UK: Ashgate.

Austin, D. and Forinash, M. (2005). Arts-based research. In: B.L. Wheeler (ed.), *Music Therapy Research*, 2nd ed., pp. 458–471. Gilsum, NH: Barcelona Publishers.

Baines, S. (2000). A consumer-directed and partnered community mental health music therapy program: Program development and evaluation. *Canadian Journal of Music Therapy* 7(1): 51–70.

Baines, S. and Danko, G. (2010). Community mental health music therapy: A consumer-initiated song-based paradigm. *Canadian Journal of Music Therapy* 16(1): 148–191.

Baker, F. (2007). Enhancing the clinical reasoning skills of music therapy students through problem based learning: An action research project. *Nordic Journal of Music Therapy* 16(1): 27–41. doi: 10.1080/08098130709478171.

Baker, F. and Grocke, D. (2009). Challenges of working with people aged 60–75 years from culturally and linguistically diverse groups: Repertoire and music therapy approaches employed by Australian music therapists. *Australian Journal of Music Therapy* 20: 30–55.

Barry, P., O'Callaghan, C., Wheeler, G., and Grocke, D. (2010). Music therapy CD creation for initial pediatric radiation therapy: A mixed methods analysis. *Journal of Music Therapy* 47(3): 233–263.

Bensimon, M. and Gilboa, A. (2010). The music of my life: The impact of the Musical Presentation on the sense of purpose in life and on self-consciousness. *The Arts in Psychotherapy* 37: 172–178.

Bergstrøm-Nielsen, C. (1993). Graphic notation as a tool in describing and analyzing music therapy improvisations. *Music Therapy* 12: 40–58.

Bergstrøm-Nielsen, C. (1999). The music of Edward, session one, as graphic notation. *Nordic Journal of Music Therapy* 8: 96–99.

Bergstrøm-Nielsen, C. (2010). Graphic notation—The simple sketch and beyond. *Nordic Journal of Music Therapy* 19(2): 162–177. doi: 10.1080/08098131.2010.497227.

Bonde, L.O. (2005). *The Bonny Method of Guided Imagery and Music (BMGIM) with cancer survivors. A psychological study with focus on the influence of BMGIM on mood and quality of life*. Unpublished PhD Thesis, Aalborg University, Aalborg, Denmark.

Bonde, L.O. (2007). Imagery, metaphor, and perceived outcome in six cancer survivors' Bonny Method of Guided Imagery and Music (BMGIM) therapy. *Qualitative Inquiries in Music Therapy* 3: 132–164.

Bradt, J. (2012). Randomized controlled trials in music therapy: Guidelines for design and implementation. *Journal of Music Therapy* 49(2): 120–149.

Bradt, J. and Dileo, C. (2009). Music for stress and anxiety reduction in coronary heart disease patients. *Cochrane Database of Systematic Reviews*, Issue 2. Art. No.: CD006577. doi: 10.1002/14651858.CD006577.pub2.

Bradt, J. and Dileo, C. (2010). Music therapy for end-of-life care. *Cochrane Database of Systematic Reviews*, Issue 1. Art. No.: CD007169., doi: 10.1002/14651858.CD007169.pub2.

Bradt, J., Dileo, C., and Grocke, D. (2010a). Music interventions for mechanically ventilated patients. *Cochrane Database of Systematic Reviews*, Issue 12. Art. No.: CD006902. doi: 10.1002/14651858.CD006902.pub2.

Bradt., J., Magee, W.L., Dileo, C., Wheeler, B.L., and McGilloway, E. (2010b). Music therapy for adults with acquired brain injury. *Cochrane Database of Systematic Reviews*, Issue 7. Art. No.: CD006787. doi:10.1002/14651858.CD006787.pub2.

Bradt, J., Dileo, C., Grocke, D., and Magill, L. (2011). Music interventions for improving psychological and physical outcomes in cancer patients. *Cochrane Database of Systematic Reviews*, Issue 8. Art. No.: CD006911. doi: 10.1002/14651858.CD006911.pub2.

Bradt, J., Dileo, C., and Shim, M. (2013a). Music interventions for preoperative anxiety. *Cochrane Database of Systematic Reviews*, Issue 6. Art. No.: CD006908. doi: 10.1002/14651858. CD006908.pub2.

Bradt, J., Burns, D.S., and Creswell, J.W. (2013b). Mixed methods research in music therapy research. *Journal of Music Therapy* 50(2): 123–148.

Brooks, D. (2003). A history of music therapy journal articles published in the English language. *Journal of Music Therapy* 40: 151–168.

Bruscia, K.E. (1995a). Modes of consciousness in Guided Imagery and Music (GIM): A therapist's experience of the guiding process. In: C.B. Kenny (ed.), *Listening, Playing, Creating: Essays on the Power of Sound*, pp. 165–197. Albany, NY: State University of New York Press.

Bruscia, K.E. (1995b). The boundaries of music therapy research. In: B.L. Wheeler (ed.), *Music Therapy Research: Quantitative and Qualitative Perspectives*, pp. 17–27. Gilsum, NH: Barcelona Publishers.

Bruscia, K.E. (2005a). Developing theory. In: B.L. Wheeler (ed.), *Music Therapy Research*, 2nd ed., pp. 540–551. Gilsum, NH: Barcelona Publishers.

Bruscia, K.E. (2005b). First-person research. In: B.L. Wheeler (ed.), *Music Therapy Research*, 2nd ed., pp. 379–391. Gilsum, NH: Barcelona Publishers.

Bruscia, K., Dileo, D., Shultis, C., and Dennery, K. (2009). Expectations of hospitalized cancer and cardiac patients regarding the medical and psychotherapeutic benefits of music therapy. *The Arts in Psychotherapy* 36: 239–244.

Cassileth, B.R., Vickers, A.J., and Magill, L.A. (2003). Music therapy for mood disturbance during hospitalization for autologous stem cell transplantation: A randomized controlled trial. *Cancer* 98(12): 2723–2739.

Chandra, P. (2005). *The effect of sound stimuli on neurologic rehabilitation of upper and lower limbs: A meta analysis.* Unpublished master's thesis, Florida State University, Tallahassee, FL. Retrieved from: <http://etd.lib.fsu.edu/theses/available/etd-07112005-131201/>.

Clair, A. and Heller, G. (1989). Willem van de Wall: Organizer and innovator in music educa-tion and music therapy. *Journal of Research in Music Education* 37(3): 165–178.

Comeau, P. (2004). A phenomenological investigation of being effective as a music therapist. *Qualitative Inquiries in Music Therapy* 1: 19–35.

Cooper, M. (2010). Clinical-musical responses of Nordoff-Robbins music therapists: The pro-cess of clinical improvisation. *Qualitative Inquiries in Music Therapy* 5: 86–115.

Creswell, J.W. and Clark, V.L.P. (2011). *Designing and Conducting Mixed Methods Research*, 2nd ed. Los Angeles: Sage.

Davis, W. (2003). Ira Maximilian Altshuler: Psychiatrist and pioneer music therapist. *Journal of Music Therapy* 40(3): 247–263.

Davis, W. (2012). The first systematic experimentation in music therapy: The genius of James Leonard Corning. *Journal of Music Therapy* 49(1): 102–117.

de Dreu, M.J., van der Wilk, A.S., Poppe, E., Kwakkel, G., and van Wegen, E.E. (2012). Rehabilitation, exercise therapy and music in patients with Parkinson's dis-ease: A meta-analysis of the effects of music-based movement therapy on walking ability, balance and quality of life. *Parkinsonism Related Disorders* 18, Suppl. 1: S114–S119.

de Mers, C.L., Tincani, M., Van Norman, R.K., Higgins, K. (2009). Effects of music therapy on young children's challenging behaviors: A case study. *Music Therapy Perspectives* 27(2): 88–96.

Dileo, C. and Bradt, J. (eds). (2005). *Music Therapy and Medicine: a Meta-Analysis of The Literature According to Medical Specialty.* Cherry Hill, NJ: Jeffrey Books.

Dingle, G.A., Brander, C., Ballantyne, J., and Baker, F.A. (2013). "To be heard": The social and mental health benefits of choir singing for disadvantaged adults. *Psychology of Music* 41(4): 405–421. doi:10.1177/0305735611430081.

Edwards, J. (2005a). Developments and issues in music therapy research. In: B.L. Wheeler (ed.), *Music Therapy Research*, 2nd ed., pp. 20–32. Gilsum, NH: Barcelona Publishers.

Edwards, J. (2005b). Possibilities and problems for evidence based practice in music therapy. *The Arts in Psychotherapy* 32: 293–301.

Edwards, J. (2007). Antecedents of contemporary uses for music in healthcare contexts: The 1890s to the 1940s. In: J. Edwards (ed.), *Music: Promoting Health and Creating Community in Healthcare Contexts*, pp. 181–202. Newcastle Upon Tyne: Cambridge Scholars.

Edwards, J. (2008). The use of music in healthcare contexts: A select review of writings from the 1890s to the 1940s. *Voices: A World Forum for Music Therapy*, 8(2). <https://voices.no/index.php/voices/article/view/428/352>.

Elefant, C. (2002). *Enhancing communication in girls with Rett syndrome through songs in music therapy.* Unpublished doctoral dissertation, Aalborg University, Aalborg, Denmark.

Elefant, C. (2005). The use of single case designs in testing a specific hypothesis. In: D. Aldridge (ed.), *Case Study Designs in Music Therapy*, pp. 145–162. London: Jessica Kingsley Publishers.

Elefant, C. (2010). Giving Voice: Participatory action research with a marginalized group. In: B. Stige, G. Ansdell, C. Elefant, and M. Pavlicevic, *Where Music Helps: Community Music Therapy in Action and Reflection*, pp. 199–215. Aldershot, UK: Ashgate Publishing.

Ely, M., Anzul, M., Friedman, T., Garner, D., and Steinmetz, A. M. (1991). *Circles within Circles: Doing Qualitative Research.* London: The Falmer Press.

Forinash, M. (1992). A phenomenological analysis of Nordoff-Robbins approach to music therapy: The lived experience of clinical improvisation. *Music Therapy*, 11, 120–141.

Forinash, M., and Grocke, D. (2005). Phenomenological inquiry. In: B. L. Wheeler (ed.), *Music therapy research*, 2nd ed., pp. 321–334. Gilsum, NH: Barcelona Publishers.

Gadberry, A.L. (2011). A survey of the use of aided augmentative and alternative communication during music therapy sessions with persons with autism spectrum disorders. *Journal of
Music Therapy* 48(1): 74–89.

Gao, T., O'Callaghan, C., Magill, L., Lin, S., Zhang, Junhan, Zhang, Jingwen, Yu, J., and Shi, Z.
(2013). A music therapy educator and undergraduate students' perceptions of their music
project's relevance for Sichuan earthquake survivors. *Nordic Journal of Music Therapy*
22(2): 107–130. doi: 10.1080/08098131.2012.691106.

Gardstrom, S. (2004). An investigation of meaning in clinical music improvisation with troubled adolescents. *Qualitative Inquiries in Music Therapy* 1: 77–160.

Gardstrom, S.C. and Jackson, N.A. (2011). Personal therapy for undergraduate music therapy
students: A survey of AMTA program coordinators. *Journal of Music Therapy* 48(2): 226–255.

Gaston, E.T. (1968). *Music in Therapy*. New York: Macmillan.

Gattino, G.S., Riesgo, R.D.S., Longo, D., Leite, J.C.L., and Faccini, L.S. (2011). Effects of relational music therapy on communication of children with autism: A randomized controlled
study. *Nordic Journal of Music Therapy* 20(2): 142–154. doi:10.1080/08098131.2011.566933.

Geretsegger, M., Holck, U., and Gold, C. (2012). Randomised controlled trial of improvisational music therapy's effectiveness for children with autism spectrum disorders (TIME-A):
Study protocol. *BMC Pediatrics*, 12:2. doi:10.1186/1471-2431-12-2.

Geretsegger, M., Elefant, C., Mössler, K.A., and Gold, C. (2014). Music therapy for people
with autism spectrum disorder. *Cochrane Database of Systematic Reviews*, Issue 6. Art. No.:
CD004381. doi: 10.1002/14651858.CD004381.pub3

Gfeller, K. (1995). The status of music therapy research. In: B.L. Wheeler (ed.), *Music Therapy
Research: Quantitative and Qualitative Perspectives*, pp. 29–63. Gilsum, NH: Barcelona
Publishers.

Ghetti, C. (2011). Active music engagement with emotional-approach coping to improve
well-being in liver and kidney transplant recipients. *Journal of Music Therapy* 48(4): 463–485.

Ghetti, C. (2012). Music therapy as procedural support for invasive medical procedures: Toward
the development of music therapy theory. *Nordic Journal of Music Therapy* 21(1): 3–35.

Ghetti, C. (2013). Effect of music therapy with emotional-approach coping on preprocedural
anxiety in cardiac catheterization: A randomized controlled trial. *Journal of Music Therapy*
50(2): 93–122.

Gold, C., Voracek, M., and Wigram, T. (2004). Effects of music therapy for children and adolescents with psychopathology: A meta-analysis. *Journal of Child Psychology and Psychiatry
and Allied Disciplines* 45: 1054–1063.

Gold, C., Mössler, K., Grocke, D., Heldal, T. O., Tjemsland, L., Aarre, T.,... Rolvsjord, R.
(2013). Individual music therapy for mental health care clients with low therapy motivation: Multi-centre randomised controlled trial. *Psychotherapy and Psychosomatics*
82(5): 319–331. doi: 10.1159/000348452.

Gregory, D. (2002). Four decades of music therapy behavioral research designs: A content
analysis of *Journal of Music Therapy* articles. *Journal of Music Therapy* 39(1): 56–71.

Grocke, D., Bloch, S., and Castle, D. (2009). The effect of group music therapy on quality of life
for participants living with a severe and enduring mental illness. *Journal of Music Therapy*
46(2): 90–104.

Hadley, S. (1999). A comparative analysis of the philosophical premises underlying Creative
Music Therapy and Analytical Music Therapy. *Australian Journal of Music Therapy* 10: 3–19.

Hadley, S. (2001). Exploring relationships between Mary Priestley's life and work. *Nordic
Journal of Music Therapy* 10: 116–131.

Hadley, S. (2003). Meaning making through narrative inquiry: Exploring the life of Clive Robbins. *Nordic Journal of Music Therapy* 12(1): 33–53.

Hahna, N.D. and Schwantes, M. (2011). Feminist music therapy pedagogy: A survey of music therapy educators. *Journal of Music Therapy* 48(3): 289–316.

Hannes, K. and Lockwood, C. (2012). *Synthesizing Qualitative Research: Choosing the Right Approach*. West Sussex, UK: John Wiley and Sons.

Hanser, S.B. (2005). Applied behavior analysis. In: B.L. Wheeler (ed.), *Music Therapy Research*, 2nd ed., pp. 306–317. Gilsum, NH: Barcelona Publishers.

International Standard Randomised Controlled Trial Number (ISRCTN) Register. (2013). <http://www.controlled-trials.com/ISRCTN78923965>.

Irons, J.Y., Kenny, D.T., and Chan, A.B. (2010). Singing for children and adults with cystic fibrosis. *Cochrane Database of Systematic Reviews*, Issue 5. Art. No.: CD008036. doi: 10.1002/14651858.CD008036.pub2.

Jackson, N.A. (2010). Models of response to client anger in music therapy. *The Arts in Psychotherapy* 37: 46–55.

Johnson, R.B. and Onwuegbuzie, A.J. (2004). Mixed methods research: A research paradigm whose time has come. *Educational Researcher* 33(7): 14–26.

Kelley, K., Clark, B., Brown, V., and Sitzia, J. (2003). Good practice in the conduct and reporting of survey research. *International Journal for Quality in Health Care* 15(3): 261–266.

Kenny, C. (1989). *The Field of Play: A Guide for the Theory and Practice of Music Therapy*. Atascadero, CA: Ridgeview Publishing Co.

Kenny, C. (2006). The Field of Play. In: C. Kenny (ed.), *Music and Life in the Field of Play: An Anthology*, pp. 80–122. Gilsum, NH: Barcelona Publishers.

Kern, P. and Wolery, M. (2001). Participation of a preschooler with visual impairments on the playground: Effects of musical adaptations and staff development. *Journal of Music Therapy* 38: 149–164.

Kim, S.J. (2009). Historical investigation regarding the perception of music therapy among Korean medical professionals as seen in medical journal articles. *Music Therapy Perspectives* 27(2): 122–129.

Kim, S.J. (2010). Music therapy protocol development to enhance swallowing training for stroke patients with dysphagia. *Journal of Music Therapy* 47(2): 102–119.

Koger, S.M., Chapin, K., and Brotons, M. (1999). Is music therapy an effective intervention for dementia? A meta-analytic review of literature. *Journal of Music Therapy* 36: 2–15.

Langenberg, M. (1988). Vom Handeln zum Be-Handeln. Darstellung besonderer Merkmale der musiktherapeutischen Behandlungssituation im Zusammenhang mit der freien Improvisation [From "dealing" to treating: Music therapy—Specific characteristics in the context of free improvisation]. Heidelberger *Schriften zur Musiktherapie*, Band 3. Heidelberg: Herausgegeben von der Stiftung Rehabilitation.

Langenberg, M., Frommer, J., and Tress, W. (1992). Qualitative Methodik zur Beschreibung und Interpretation musiktherapeutischer Behandlungswerke [Qualitative method of describing and interpreting works created in music therapy treatment]. *Musiktherapeutische Umschau* 13: 258–278.

Langenberg, M., Frommer, J., and Tress, W. (1993). A qualitative approach to Analytical Music Therapy. *Music Therapy* 12: 59–84.

Langenberg, M., Aigen, K., and Frommer, J. (eds). (1996). *Qualitative Music Therapy Research: Beginning Dialogues*. Gilsum, NH: Barcelona Publishers.

Laopaiboon, M., Lumbiganon, P., Martis, R., Vatanasapt, P., and Somjaivong, B. (2009). Music during caesarean section under regional anaesthesia for improving maternal and infant outcomes. *Cochrane Database of Systematic Reviews*, Issue 2. Art. No.: CD006914. doi: 10.1002/14651858.CD006914.pub2.

Ledger, A. J. (2010a). *Am I a founder or am I a fraud? Music therapists' experiences of developing services in healthcare organizations.* Unpublished doctoral thesis, University of Limerick, Ireland.

Ledger, A. (2010b). Exploring multiple identities as a health care ethnographer. *International Journal of Qualitative Methods* 9(3): 291–304.

Ledger, A. and Baker, F. (2005). Longitudinal research designs in music therapy: recommendations from a study of people with dementia. *Australian Journal of Music Therapy* 16: 88–103.

Ledger, A. and Baker, F. (2007). An investigation of long-term effects of group music therapy on agitation levels of people with Alzheimer's disease. *Aging and Mental Health* 11(3): 330–338.

Ledger, A. and Edwards, J. (2011). Arts-based research practices in music therapy research: Existing and potential developments. *The Arts in Psychotherapy* 38: 312–317.

Lincoln, Y.S. and Guba, E.G. (1985). *Naturalistic Inquiry.* Newbury Park, CA: Sage.

Loewy, J., Stewart, K., Dassler, A-M., Telsey, A., and Homel, P. (2013). The effects of music therapy on vital signs, feeding, and sleep in premature infants. *Pediatrics* 131: 902–918. doi: 10.1542/peds 2012-1367.

Luce, D.W. (2008). Epistemological development and collaborative learning: A hermeneutic analysis of music therapy students' experience. *Journal of Music Therapy* 45(1): 21–51.

Maratos, A., Gold, C., Wang, X., and Crawford, M. (2008). Music therapy for depression. *Cochrane Database of Systematic Reviews*, Issue 1. Art. No.: CD004517. doi: 10.1002/14651858. CD004517.pub2.

McFerran, K. and Hunt, M. (2008). Learning from experiences in action: Music in schools to promote healthy coping with grief and loss. *Educational Action Research* 16(1): 43–54.

Medical Research Council (2000). *A framework for development and evaluation of RCTs for complex interventions to improve health.* London: Medical Research Council.

Menard, S. (2002). *Longitudinal Research*, 2nd ed. Newbury Park, CA: Sage.

Mössler, K. (2011). "I am a psychotherapeutically oriented music therapist": Theory construction and its influence on professional identity formation under the example of the Viennese School of Music Therapy. *Nordic Journal of Music Therapy* 20(2): 155–184.

Mössler, K., Chen, X., Heldal, T.O., and Gold, C. (2011). Music therapy for people with schizophrenia and schizophrenia-like disorders. *Cochrane Database of Systematic Reviews*, Issue 12. Art. No.: CD004025. doi: 10.1002/14651858.CD004025.pub3.

Moustakas, C.E. (1990). *Heuristic research: Design, Methodology, and Applications.* Thousand Oaks, CA: Sage.

Nayak, S., Wheeler, B.L., Shiflett, S.C., and Agostinelli, S. (2000). The effect of music therapy on mood and social interaction among individuals with acute traumatic brain injury and stroke. *Rehabilitation Psychology* 45: 274–283.

Nicholson, J.M., Berthelsen, D., Abad, V., Williams, K., and Bradley, J. (2008). Impact of music therapy to promote positive parenting and child development. *Journal of Health Psychology* 13: 226–238.

Nordoff, P. and Robbins, C. (2007). *Creative Music Therapy: A Guide to Fostering Clinical Musicianship.* Gilsum, NH: Barcelona Publishers.

O'Callaghan, C. (1996). Lyrical themes in songs written by palliative care patients. *Journal of Music Therapy* 33: 74–92.

O'Callaghan, C. (2012). Grounded theory in music therapy research. *Journal of Music Therapy* 49(3): 236–277.

O'Callaghan, C. and Magill, L. (2009). Effect of music therapy on oncologic staff bystanders: A substantive grounded theory. *Palliative and Supportive Care* 7: 219–228. doi:10.1017/S1478951509000285.

O'Callaghan, C., Baron, A., Barry, P., and Dun, B. (2011). Music's relevance for pediatric cancer patients: A constructivist and mosaic research approach. *Supportive Care in Cancer* 19(6): 779–788. doi: 10.1007/s00520-010-0879-9.

Pavlicevic, M. (2010). Let the Music Work: Optimal Moments of Collaborative Musicing. In B. Stige, G. Ansdell, C. Elefant, and M. Pavlicevic, *Where music helps: Community Music Therapy in action and reflection*, pp. 99–112. Aldershot, UK: Ashgate.

Pelletier, C. L. (2004). The effect of music on decreasing arousal due to stress: A meta-analysis. *Journal of Music Therapy* 41(3): 192–214.

Phelps, R. P., Sadoff, R. H., Warburton, E. C., and Ferrara, L. (2005). *A Guide to Research in Music Education* (5th ed.). Lanham, MD: Scarecrow Press.

Priestley, M. (1994). *Essays on Analytical Music Therapy*. Gilsum, NH: Barcelona Publishers.

Reschke-Hernández, A.E. (2011). History of music therapy treatment interventions for children with autism. *Journal of Music Therapy* 48(2): 169–207.

Rickson, D. (2009). Researching one's own clinical practice: Managing multiple roles in an action research project. *Voices: A World Forum for Music Therapy*. <https://normt.uib.no/index.php/voices/article/viewArticle/364/287>.

Ridder, H.M.O. (2005). Music therapy with the elderly: Complementary data as a rich approach to understanding communication. In: D. Aldridge (ed.), *Case Study Designs in Music Therapy*, pp. 191–209. London: Jessica Kingsley Publishers.

Ridder, H.M.O. and Aldridge, D. (2005). Individual music therapy with persons with fronto-temporal dementia: Singing dialogue. *Nordic Journal of Music Therapy* 14: 91–106.

Robb, S.L. (2012). Gratitude for a complex profession: The importance of theory-based research in music therapy. *Journal of Music Therapy* 49(1): 2–6.

Robb, S.L., Clair, A.A., Watanabe, M., Monahan, P.O., Azzouz, F., Stouffer, J.W. et al. (2008). Non-randomized controlled trial of the active music engagement (AME) intervention on children with cancer. *Psycho-Oncology* 17: 699–708.

Robb, S.L., Burns, D.S., Stegenga, K.A., Haut, P.R., Monahan, P.O., Meza, J.,… Haase, J. E. (2014). Randomized clinical trial of therapeutic music video intervention for resilience outcomes in adolescents/young adults undergoing hematopoietic stem cell transplant: A report from the Children's Oncology Group. *Cancer* 120(6), 909–917.

Roberts, M. and McFerran, K. (2008). Music therapy in Australian print media: A content analysis. *Australian Journal of Music Therapy* 19: 27–42.

Rolvsjord, R. (2007). *"Blackbirds singing": An exploratory study*. Unpublished PhD Thesis, Aalborg University, Aalborg, Denmark.

Rolvsjord, R. (2010). *Resource-Oriented Music Therapy in Mental Health Care*. Gilsum, NH: Barcelona Publishers.

Rolvsjord, R., Gold, C., and Stige, B. (2005). Research rigour and therapeutic flexibility: Rationale for a therapy manual developed for a randomized controlled trial. *Nordic Journal of Music Therapy* 14(1): 15–32.

Rudin, D., Kiss, A., Wetz, R.V., and Sottile, V.M. (2007). Music in the endoscopy suite: a meta-analysis of randomized controlled studies. *Endoscopy* 39(6): 507–510.

Ruspini, E. (2002). *Introduction to Longitudinal Research*. New York: Routledge.

Sackett, D.L., Rosenberg, W.M.C., Gray, J.A.M., Haynes, R.B., and Richardson, W.D. (1996, Jan. 13). Evidence based medicine: What it is and what it isn't. *British Medical Journal* 312: 71–72.

Sandelowski, M. and Barroso, J. (2007) *Handbook for Synthesising Qualitative Research*. New York: Springer.

Schenstead, A.R. (2012). The timelessness of arts-based research: Looking back upon a heuristic self-study and the arts-based reflexivity data analysis method. *Voices: A World Forum for Music Therapy*, 12(1). <https://normt.uib.no/index.php/voices/article/view/589/514>.

Schulz, K.F., Altman, D.G., and Moher, D. (2010). CONSORT 2010 Statement: Updated guidelines for reporting parallel group randomised trials. *BMC Medicine* 8(18). doi:10.1186/1741-7015-8-18.

Schwandt, T.A. (2001). *Dictionary of Qualitative Inquiry*, 2nd ed. Thousand Oaks, CA: Sage.

Schwandt, T.A. (2007). *The Sage Dictionary of Qualitative Inquiry*. Thousand Oaks, CA: Sage.

Sears, W. (1968). Processes in music therapy. In: E.T. Gaston (ed.), *Music in Therapy*, pp. 30–44. New York: Macmillan.

Shadish, W.R., Cook, T.D., and Campbell, D.T. (2002). *Experimental and Quasi- experimental Designs for Generalized Causal Inference*. Boston, MA: Houghton Mifflin.

Silverman, M.J. (2003). The influence of music on the symptoms of psychosis: A meta-analysis. *Journal of Music Therapy* 40: 27–40.

Smeijsters, H. (2005). Quantitative single-case designs. In: B.L. Wheeler (ed.), *Music Therapy Research*, 2nd ed., pp. 293–305. Gilsum, NH: Barcelona Publishers.

Smith, J.A. (2004). Reflecting on the development of interpretative phenomenological analysis and its contribution to qualitative research in psychology. *Qualitative Research in Psychology* 1(1): 39–54.

Solomon, A., and Heller, G.N. (1982). Historical research in music therapy: An important avenue for studying the profession. *Journal of Music Therapy* 19: 161–178.

Standley, J.M. (1996). A meta-analysis on the effects of music as reinforcement for education/ therapy objectives. *Journal of Research in Music Education* 44: 105–133.

Standley, J.M. (2000). Music research in medical treatment. In: *Effectiveness of Music Therapy Procedures: Documentation of Research and Clinical Practice*, 3rd ed., pp. 1–64. Silver Spring, MD: American Music Therapy Association.

Standley, J.M. (2002). A meta-analysis of the efficacy of music therapy for premature infants. *Journal of Pediatric Nursing* 17(2): 107–13.

Standley, J.M. and Whipple, J. (2003). Music therapy for premature infants in the neonatal intensive care unit: Health and developmental benefits. In: S.L. Robb (ed.), *Music Therapy in Pediatric Healthcare: Research and Evidence-based Practice*, pp. 1–30. Silver Spring, MD: American Music Therapy Association.

Stewart, D. (2000). The state of the UK music therapy profession: Personal qualities, working models, support networks and job satisfaction. *British Journal of Music Therapy* 14(1): 13–31.

Stige, B. (2002). *Culture-Centered Music Therapy*. Gilsum, NH: Barcelona Publishers.

Stige, B. (2005a). Ethnography and ethnographically informed research. In: B.L. Wheeler (ed.), *Music Therapy Research*, 2nd ed., pp. 392–403. Gilsum, NH: Barcelona Publishers.

Stige, B. (2005b). Participatory action research. In: B.L. Wheeler (ed.), *Music Therapy Research*, 2nd ed., pp. 404–415. Gilsum, NH: Barcelona Publishers.

Stige, B. (2010). Musical participation, social space, and everyday ritual. Aldershot, UK: Ashgate Publishing. In: B. Stige, G. Ansdell, C. Elefant, and M. Pavlicevic, *Where Music Helps: Community Music Therapy in Action and Reflection*, pp. 115–147. Aldershot, UK: Ashgate.

Stige, B., Ansdell, G., Elefant, C., and Pavlicevic, M. (2010). *Where Music Helps: Community Music Therapy in Action and Reflection*. Aldershot, UK: Ashgate Publishing.

Taylor, D. (1981). Music in general hospital treatment from 1900 to 1950. *Journal of Music Therapy* 18(2): 62–73.

Teddlie, C. and Tashakkori, A. (2003). Major issues and controversies in the use of mixed methods in the social and behavioral sciences. In: A. Tashakkori and C. Teddlie (eds), *Handbook of Mixed Methods in Social and Behavioral Research*, pp. 3–50. Thousand Oaks, CA: Sage.

Tesch, R. (1990). *Qualitative Research: Analysis Types and Software Tools*. New York: The Falmer Press.

Turry, A. (2010). Integrating musical and psychotherapeutic thinking: Research on the relationship between words and music in clinically improvised songs. *Qualitative Inquiries in Music Therapy* 5: 116–172.

Vaillancourt, G. (2009). *Mentoring apprentice music therapists for peace and social justice through Community Music Therapy: An arts-based study*. Unpublished dissertation, Antioch University, Leadership and Change. <http://aura.antioch.edu/cgi/viewcontent.cgi?article=1007andcontext=etds>.

Vaillancourt, G. (2011). Creating an apprenticeship music therapy model through arts-based research. *Voices: A World Forum for Music Therapy* 11(1). <https://normt.uib.no/index.php/voices/article/view/341/446>.

Vega, V. (2010). Personality, burnout, and longevity among professional music therapists. *Journal of Music Therapy* 47(2): 155–179.

Vink, A.C., Bruinsma, M.S., and Scholten, R.J.P.M. (2013). Music therapy for people with dementia. *Cochrane Database of Systematic Reviews*, 2004, Issue 3, Art. No.: CD003477. doi: 10.1002/14651858.CD003477.pub2.

Waldon, E. (2015). Music Therapists' research activity and utilization barriers: A survey of the membership. *Journal of Music Therapy*, 52(1), 168–194. doi:10.1093/jmt/thv001

Wheeler, B.L. (1999). Experiencing pleasure in working with severely disabled children. *Journal of Music Therapy* 36: 56–80.

Wheeler, B.L. (2005). Overview of music therapy research. In: B.L. Wheeler (ed.), *Music Therapy Research*, 2nd ed., pp. 3–19. Gilsum, NH: Barcelona Publishers.

Wheeler, B.L., and Kenny, C. (2005). Principles of qualitative research. In: B.L. Wheeler (ed.), *Music Therapy Research*, 2nd ed., pp. 59–71. Gilsum, NH: Barcelona Publishers.

Wheeler, B.L., Weissbecker, I., Elwafi, P.R., and Salvador, C. (2010). The Susan G. Komen Music Therapy Initiative: Music therapy for women with breast cancer. *International Journal of Integrative Oncology* 3(1): 7–17.

Whipple, J. (2004). Music in intervention for children and adolescents with autism: A meta-analysis. *Journal of Music Therapy* 41: 90–106.

Wigram, T. (2005). Survey research. In: B.L. Wheeler (ed.), *Music Therapy Research*, 2nd ed., pp. 272–281. Gilsum, NH: Barcelona Publishers.

Williams, K.E., Berthelsen, D., Nicholson, J.M., Walker, S., and Abad, V. (2012). The effectiveness of a short-term group music therapy intervention for parents who have a child with a disability. *Journal of Music Therapy* 49: 23–44.

Wlodarczyk, N. (2007). The effect of music therapy on the spirituality of persons in an in-patient hospice unit as measured by self-report. *Journal of Music Therapy* 44(2): 113–122.

Wosch, T. and Frommer, J. (2002). Emotionsveränderungen in musiktherapeutische Improvisationen [Emotional changes in music therapeutic improvisations]. *Zeitschrift für Musik-, Tanz- und Kunsttherapie* 13: 107–114.

Yin, R.K. (2009). Case Study research: Design and Methods (4th ed.). Thousand Oaks, CA: Sage.

Young, L. (2009). Multicultural issues encountered in the supervision of music therapy internships in the United States and Canada. *The Arts in Psychotherapy* 36: 191–201.

....

CHAPTER 40

CHARTING THE TERRAIN OF GROUNDED THEORY RESEARCH IN MUSIC THERAPY

Where We've Been and Where We Have the Potential to Go

....

BARBARA A. DAVESON

THE DISCOVERY OF GROUNDED THEORY: IN THE BEGINNING ...

....

IN the 1960s two sociologists, Barney Glaser and Anselm Strauss, collaborated in a study of death and dying in hospitals (Charmaz 2006).

Grounded theory was discovered through their collaboration. Throughout their research they focused on their data in relation to their area of inquiry, and also on how they approached analysis. They explored analytical ideas and actively exchanged and examined how they approached and completed analysis. They delivered their research about dying in hospitals (Glaser and Strauss 1965), and they developed a systematic methodology that a global community of social scientists and music therapists use for research to this day. They called this methodology grounded theory, and it was first published in 1967 in their foundation text titled "The Discovery of Grounded Theory" (Glaser and Strauss 1967).

The culture at the time of the discovery of grounded theory: The modernist phase of qualitative research

Grounded theory was discovered at a time when quantitative research dominated. The dominant culture meant that the division between theory, and research was growing.

Research was primarily seen as a way to test theory. For example, research was used to test a research hypothesis rather than being used as a means to aid theory construction (Charmaz 2006).

Denzin and Lincoln have referred to phase of qualitative research development between the Second World War and the 1970s as the *modernist phase*. It was a time in which multiple qualitative traditions developed in rigorous ways. The production of texts, which formalized qualitative research traditions, were common throughout the modernist phase (Denzin and Lincoln 2003). Grounded theory aimed to integrate the strengths of the quantitative approach into the qualitative tradition (Walker and Myrick 2006). Through the use of a systematic and rigorous approach to data collection and analysis, it was shown how theory could be developed from data (Glaser and Strauss 1967). Grounded theory therefore offered an alternative to the dominant research approach of the time.

Today, grounded theory is viewed as an exceptional example of a qualitative research methodology that was discovered in the modernist phase of qualitative research. The methodology incorporates an emphasis on inductive reasoning and its foundations rest with symbolic interactionism and pragmatist philosophy. Symbolic interactionism views reality as social, which is developed through interactions with others (Vidich and Lyman 2003). Pragmatic philosophy aims to link theory with practice (Greenwood and Levin 2003). Grounded theory has been described as one of the more systematic approaches to qualitative research.

WHAT IS GROUNDED THEORY?

If the artist does not perfect a new vision in his process of doing, he acts mechanically and repeats some old model fixed like a blueprint in his mind.

John Dewey, *Art as Experience*, 1934, p. 50

Grounded theory methodology has evolved in many ways since it was discovered. Strauss, who is now deceased, developed his approach with Juliet Corbin, a nurse by background. Up until his death Strauss continued to believe in the value of theory and its importance to the development of any professional body of knowledge. Strauss believed that complexity was important and that any research method that aimed to examine social and social psychological processes should examine, analyze, and integrate some of this complexity (Charmaz 2006; Walker and Myrick 2006). Through their collaborations, Strauss and Corbin developed precise methods, procedures, and techniques, which are now used widely around the world (Corbin and Strauss 2008; Strauss and Corbin 1990; Strauss and Corbin 1998).

Since Strauss' death, Juliet Corbin has continued to publish on grounded theory research. Corbin, similar to Kathy Charmaz, another pioneer in grounded theory, describes herself as a constructivist grounded theorist even though she acknowledges that the foundations of grounded theory rest with symbolic interactionism and pragmatic philosophy. Kathy Charmaz, a student of Strauss (Sbaraini et al. 2011) proposed a distinction between *objectivist grounded theory* and *constructivist grounded theory*. Charmaz's and Corbin's work is popular and used extensively as a basis for grounded theory research studies.

Another student of Strauss, Adele Clarke, developed a further approach to grounded theory. This is a postmodern approach called *situational analysis*. It requires the researcher to map the data so that the area of inquiry can be situated within a unit of analysis. This unit of analysis may, for example, involve culture, society, and temporality. The situated nature of the inquiry then, in part, becomes the object of the study (Clarke 2005). Another type of grounded theory is being developed by one of Strauss' colleagues Leonard Schaztman. This type is called *dimensional analysis* (Sbaraini et al. 2011).

Each evolution of grounded theory has helped modernize and/or extend the original methodology. Even though this evolution has been helpful it has also complicated the field grounded theory (O'Connor et al. 2008). Many questions can arise regarding what constitutes grounded theory as so many developments have occurred since it was first discovered.

Today, grounded theory has become an umbrella term to refer to a collection of different approaches that involve "... systematic, yet flexible guidelines for collecting and analyzing qualitative data to construct theories 'grounded' in the data themselves ..." (Charmaz 2006, p. 2). The evolution of different types of grounded theory has resulted in a "family of methods" (Bryant and Charmaz 2007, p. 11). But, in essence, grounded theory is an empirical approach to research that relies on the use of distinct analytic methods (Clarke 2005). Many different terms to describe grounded theory research are evident in music therapy, including modified versions of grounded theory (Amir 1992a; Daveson and O'Callaghan 2012; Edwards and Kennelly 2002; O'Callaghan 1996) and versions that involve the entire grounded theory process ultimately resulting in theory. These are sometimes called complete, pure, or full-version grounded theory studies or simply grounded theory research (Daveson et al. 2008). In qualitative studies outside of the field of music therapy it is not uncommon for researchers to explain that their study drew upon the principles of grounded theory. These types of studies integrate methods or aspects of methodology from other research approaches. In other words, they may have completed a hybrid study.

THE FOUR KEY COMPONENTS OF GROUNDED THEORY RESEARCH

Within qualitative circles there has been some debate about what is required of a study for it to be called grounded theory (Morse et al. 2009). This discussion has begun to take place within the field of music therapy (Daveson et al. 2008). Some researchers maintain that certain characteristics are required in a grounded theory research study and prefer to draw distinctions between the various types of grounded theory studies (Daveson et al. 2008). Others are content to call any type of study that uses grounded theory methods or techniques (Amir 2005a). It is important to acknowledge this diversity. Nonetheless there are a number of key elements that are usually evident within grounded theory research. These elements include: (1) inductive reasoning, (2) evidence of constant comparison, (3) theoretical saturation, and (4) theoretical sampling. The next part of the chapter will provide information about each of these elements.

Inductive reasoning forms part of grounded theory

Grounded theory is mostly used as a qualitative methodology and most approaches to grounded theory rely primarily on inductive reasoning. Inductive reasoning involves a process whereby the findings emerge from the data (Patton 2002). Admittedly, there are elements of deductive reasoning involved in grounded theory research. However, deductive reasoning usually follows inductive reasoning in grounded theory research. For example, an element of deduction is required to establish relationships between categories that emerge from the data. But the process of establishing categories can only take place after an inductive process of discovering or constructing the concepts that lie within the data has been completed. This type of inductive analysis is quite different from a deductive approach to analysis. A deductive approach to analysis might involve, for example, the use of a pre-established coding framework to apply to the data (or to use to search through the data to find elements that fit the framework).

Grounded theory involves constant comparisons

Analysis is the interplay between researchers and data. It is both science and art

Strauss and Corbin 1998, p. 13

Constant comparison lies at the heart of grounded theory research. For this reason, grounded theory research is sometimes called the constant comparison method. From the moment researchers have data to analyze they compare what is within the data in order to develop research findings. This is primarily achieved through asking questions (Charmaz 2006; Corbin and Strauss 2008; Strauss and Corbin 1990; Strauss and Corbin 1998). For example, how does this data compare with the data from the previous interview? How does this concept compare with that concept? As grounded theory aims to compare social and or social psychological processes, comparing incident with incident and event with event is central to the research process. This focus helps the methodology remain true to its roots of symbolic interactionism with its focus on social action (Clarke 2005).

During the process of constant comparison, concepts found to be conceptually similar are grouped together into a higher-level descriptive concept, which is labelled a category or theme. Comparison is essential to analysis as it helps differentiate one category from another category. These comparisons help define the categories and ultimately produce your theory, if theory construction is your intention (Corbin and Strauss 2008; Strauss and Corbin 1990; Strauss and Corbin 1998). Music therapy grounded theory outputs do not always have to be theory, they can also include: grounded descriptive statements or a collection of categories, or a conceptual order of your findings (Daveson et al. 2008).

Making theoretical comparisons assist researchers in developing a definition or understanding of some phenomenon by looking at the property and dimensional level that is inherent within the category. What is significant about theoretical comparisons is that it forces the researcher to think about the property and dimensional level and not just at the specifics of the codes, or the raw data. Theoretical comparisons move the researcher away from description into the more abstract and therefore into the realm of theory development (Corbin and Strauss 2008).

The development of properties and dimensional ranges forms part of the constant comparison process. A property is a characteristic or attribute of a category. For example, a property of the category "reliving memories through songs" might be "vividness." The property of "vividness" can vary. In grounded theory research this variation is referred to as the dimensional range of the property. An example of the dimensional range of "vividness" may be "very vivid through to not at all vivid." Another property of the category titled "reliving memories through songs" might be "feelings of interconnectedness." These feelings of interconnectedness might vary between being "close" feelings of interconnectedness through to "distant/absent" feelings of interconnectedness. Within music therapy, some authors have used the terms properties and dimensional ranges to report on this information (Daveson 2006a; Edwards and Kennelly 2002). The term value ranges has also been used in music therapy, but not very frequently (Magee and Davidson 2004a). Others have included this information in their findings without use any of these terms (O'Callaghan 2001).

Theoretical saturation: When to stop collecting data and when to stop analysis

> *... variations can always be discovered*
>
> Corbin and Strauss 2008, p. 263

Theoretical saturation is another key component of grounded theory, and the definition of theoretical saturation in relation to grounded theory research has developed over time (e.g. Strauss and Corbin 1998, 1990). Early definitions of theoretical saturation focussed heavily on the need for the constant collection of data to support emerging findings (Strauss and Corbin 1990). Subsequent versions of theoretical saturation explained that theoretical saturation was only ever reached to a certain degree and within the constraints of what was possible in the research project (Strauss and Corbin 1998). Most recently, Corbin and Strauss define theoretical saturation as "... the point in analysis when all categories are well developed in terms of properties, dimensions and variations. Further data gathering and analysis will add little new to the conceptualization, though variations can always be discovered." (Corbin and Strauss 2008, p. 263).

Theoretical saturation is a construct that underpins grounded theory research. It is a key quality indicator of any grounded theory study and helps distinguish between whether a modified grounded theory or a pure grounded theory study has been completed. Theoretical saturation helps researchers in knowing when to stop collecting data and when to stop analysis. Theoretical saturation can be achieved to a degree in any research study (Strauss and Corbin 1998). In the interests of quality outputs the indicators for saturation in each study should be reported upon in publications.

Theoretical sampling: The sampling that underpins the data collection process

Data collection proceeds on the basis of theoretical sampling in grounded theory research, and this underscores the entire process of grounded theory research. It is a special type of sampling that ensures that data that can help develop theory will be collected (Strauss and Corbin 1990; Strauss and Corbin 1998). Theoretical sampling continues to be used until no new or relevant data emerges in relation to the categories that have been found. The categories must be densely developed or established before theoretical sampling can stop. The research findings should contain variation and the relationships between the categories need to be well-articulated (Strauss and Corbin 1990, p. 188). Theoretical sampling is sometimes preceded by purposive sampling (Sbaraini et al. 2011). Purposive sampling is sampling that is based on particular characteristics of a population that are of interest to the research (Rice and Ezzy 1999). For example, a researcher may begin sampling based on the characteristics of certain music therapy participants (purposive sampling). This type of sampling will be followed by sampling based on the emerging findings related to the phenomena being examined (theoretical sampling).

THE NUTS AND BOLTS OF COMPLETING GROUNDED THEORY RESEARCH

The process of how to complete a grounded theory study evolves as the research continues. Allowing the research process to evolve is to be expected as data collection is based upon theoretical sampling. Authors have described six grounded theory research steps: (1) start with an open beginning and research questions; (2) seek and gain ethics approval and consider ethical dimensions; (3) commence purposive sampling before proceeding to use theoretical sampling where possible; (4) begin data analysis; (5) continue onto theoretical sampling after purposive sampling, ongoing data analysis, and modifying data collection procedures (e.g. interviews) based on the data collected and analyzed so far; and (6) map concepts, theoretical memo writing, and refine concepts (Sbaraini et al. 2011). The steps involved in Strauss and Corbin's type of grounded theory can be condensed even further into three stages, as illustrated in Figure 40.1: (1) identifying concepts, (2) relating categories, (3) integrating and refining theory. These steps do not occur sequentially but rather they overlap and ultimately the research process is guided by your data.

Stage one: Identifying concepts

The researcher identifies concepts through a process of open coding in stage one. A code is as an abstract representation of phenomenon from within the data, as illustrated in panel one. The terms "concepts" and "codes" can be used interchangeably. Open coding is a process of dissecting and opening up the data. Open coding involves a microscopic or detailed examination of what is contained within the data. Open coding is aided through line-by-line analysis, and the researcher must remain open to what is within the data. In music therapy, there are many examples of open coding (Amir 2005b; Edwards and Kennelly 2002; Magee and Davidson 2004b; O'Grady and McFerran 2007a). Open coding helps identify properties and dimensional ranges inherent within the data.

Analytical devices to help identify concepts through open coding have been identified, including: asking questions; making comparisons between what's contained in the data; considering meanings of single or strings of words contained within the data; working with and using metaphors to represent the data; and searching for negative cases (Corbin and Strauss 2008).

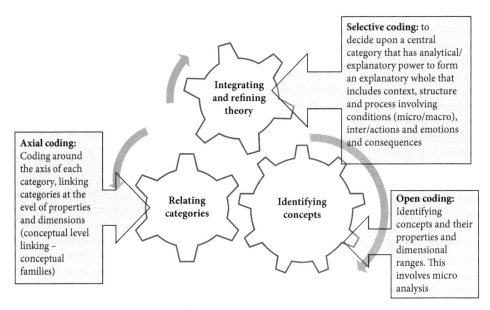

FIGURE 40.1 The three stages of grounded theory.

Panel one: Example of open coding of interview data

Research question: How is songwriting used within music therapy by family members who provide care to patients?

Caregiver interview data: ... *once I became involved in writing the song with the therapist I started to lose track of time and I started to forget about the drudgery of the hospital day. My husband started by listening to the words and our melodies, but after a little while he helped by singing our new words—it made me remember how I used to feel when we would sing to each other when we first started going out—we were very close then.*

Open codes: [removed from the everyday] [change in perception of time] [remembering feelings of closeness with patient/partner]

Stage two: Relating categories

The data starts to be reassembled through a process of axial coding after the data has been dissected and opened up through open coding. As the name suggests, axial coding involves the metaphorical rotation of the codes on their axis to help obtain different views and positions. Property and dimensional range information continues to be developed through this process, and information about social processes and structures are uncovered. Relationships between the different codes start to emerge. This stage leads onto the third stage where a major category is identified and developed (Corbin and Strauss 2008; Strauss and Corbin 1990; Strauss and Corbin 1998). Examples of axial coding can be found within music therapy (Amir 2005b; Daveson 2006a; O'Grady and McFerran 2007a). Analytical devices that help with axial coding, includes searching for and discovering contradictions within the data; using diagrams to visually depict emerging findings and relationships between categories;

writing memos (or accounts of the researcher's thoughts and analysis); summarizing emerging findings; laying out properties and their dimensions to compare them; relating categories and subcategories through statements; and looking for cues for the core category(/s) (Strauss and Corbin 1998).

Stage three: Integrating and refining theory

The emerging theory is refined and the categories identified earlier are integrated in stage three. This process is enabled through the use of selective coding which involves the researcher integrating categories along a dimensional level to form a theory. Relational statements that began to emerge in stage two are consolidated and developed further in stage three (Strauss and Corbin 1990; Strauss and Corbin 1998). So far most grounded theory studies have stopped short of theory development, however there are examples of theory construction from grounded theory research in music therapy (Daveson 2006a; O'Callaghan 2001). There are several analytical devices available to help with integrating and refining the development theory, including writing a storyline to depict the developing theory; drawing integrative diagrams about the findings; reviewing and sorting memos; reviewing the data and findings for internal consistency and logic; filling in poorly developed categories; trimming the developing theory in order to remove extraneous detail and incorporating variation into the theory (Corbin and Strauss 2008). Another more substantial analytical tool is called the paradigm, which has been described in detail by Corbin and Strauss. This involves establishing causal conditions, the corresponding phenomena, identifying contextual information, intervening conditions, actions and interaction strategies and the consequences (Corbin and Strauss 2008; Strauss and Corbin 1990; Strauss and Corbin 1998).

VARIATIONS ON A THEME: STAND-ALONE, NESTED OR EMBEDDED; MODIFIED, HYBRID OR PURE GROUNDED THEORY RESEARCH IN MUSIC THERAPY

> ... any definition of research ... is grounded in beliefs of the researcher as to what is a legitimate objective of study, the relationship between the knower and the known, the nature of causality, and what is meant by truth in research ... and an understanding of these questions will deepen music therapists' understanding of research and its meaning.
>
> Wheeler 2005, p. 3

Modified, pure, or hybrid studies

Within music therapy, there have been discussions regarding the variations of grounded theory. These variations include, modified grounded theory studies that stop short of theory development while involving the use of a systematic approach to grounded theory, and complete, pure, or full-version grounded theory studies which result in formal or substantive theory (Daveson 2008). A more recent and less commonly used variation in music therapy is the hybrid grounded theory study. This third variation of grounded theory research is not uncommon outside of the field of music therapy. Hybrid grounded theory studies are studies that draw upon the principles of grounded theory or one or some of the elements of grounded theory alongside elements from other methodologies, such as ethnography or narrative analysis. In contrast, a modified grounded theory may stay closer to the procedures inherent within grounded theory.

Nested or embedded grounded theory within mixed methods research

An application of grounded theory that is yet to be used in music therapy is the use of grounded theory within mixed methods research. This application may involve the nesting or embedding of a modified grounded theory study within a quantitative study, for example a randomized controlled trial. Plano Clarke explains that when qualitative studies are nested within quantitative studies they have little influence on the study; they simply sit alongside each other. In contrast, interaction between the designs occurs when a study is embedded within another study (Plano Clark et al. 2013). There is scope for modified grounded theory studies to be embedded or nested within another study. Also, there is scope for a quantitative study to be embedded within a grounded theory research design. Grounded theory therefore has several potential applications within mixed methods research which are yet to be explored and adopted within music therapy.

Grounded theory research outputs

Grounded theory study designs allow for various outputs. There are three potential outcomes of grounded theory studies. Modified grounded theory studies can result in a grounded descriptive statement, which is a statement about the categories or themes that have emerged from the study. A grounded descriptive statement can be presented as a collection of categories or themes or as a narrative regarding the categories or themes. A conceptual order outcome can also result from a modified grounded theory study. Conceptual order studies involve the use of open and axial, the development of relational statements, properties, and dimensional ranges. However, theory is not discovered or constructed when a conceptual order output results as the ontology (beliefs) that underpinned the research did not allow for theory to be developed or theoretical saturation was not attained. Substantive and formal theory indigenous to music therapy can result from complete or pure grounded theory studies as the entire process of grounded theory is used. This means that a major category is identified from within the data and relational statements between all of the categories have been developed (Daveson 2008). Hybrid studies have numerous potential outputs. As the use of hybrid studies is a fairly recent innovation, the scope of these outputs is yet to be fully known.

Should we identify different variations or call it all grounded theory?

Distinguishing between the type of grounded theory design that was used and the output that was produced is helpful when it comes to appraising the research that was conducted. Transparency is a quality indicator of qualitative research and transparency in relation to reporting on research design, conduct, and findings will aid the appraisal of the research. This in turn helps with the delivery of rigorous research (Daveson et al. 2008). Clearly reporting research designs will help advance the practice and service delivery of music therapy through research-led developments. Also, the use of the distinctions between modified, hybrid, and full version (pure or complete) grounded theory studies, can aid with the development of a clear understanding between the precursors to theory (descriptions, models, grounded descriptive statements, conceptual ordering), the differences between precursors to theory, and what constitutes theory. This information is useful to the development of the profession of music therapy and useful to theory construction within music therapy. A programmatic approach like this will also aid the development and evaluation of music therapy interventions. Clearly-reported and well-designed studies are also more likely to be included in narrative synthesis studies, which aim to synthesize the findings from a number of different studies, including qualitative studies, in order to summarize the evidence in relation to a particular area of treatment or clinical practice. The inclusion of music therapy research in these studies will help with the recognition of the value of music therapy interventions in health, education, medical and community contexts. Good quality research, using pre-established criteria usually from outside of the field of music therapy, will therefore help the profession grow.

A SCOPING EXERCISE OF GROUNDED THEORY RESEARCH IN MUSIC THERAPY

Grounded theory research is relatively common in music therapy. The findings from a scoping exercise of the music therapy literature are reported here to provide an indication of the types of studies that have been completed, the countries where the research has been conducted, and the fields where the studies took place. Grounded theory doctoral and postdoctoral research dissertations known to the author are also referenced here.

Search strategy

The database and electronic journal search that was used to find the studies was undertaken on July 2, 2012. Two databases were searched. The International Index for Music Periodical (IIMP) (full text), a music journal resource with more than half a million indexed articles was searched. IIMP contains the: Journal of Music Therapy (1990–1996; 1998; 2002–2012);

the Australian Journal of Music Therapy (2005 onwards 2011); Music Therapy Perspectives (2004 onwards); Canadian Journal of Music Therapy (2004 onwards excluding 2005); Canadian Music Educator (2002 onwards); The New Zealand Journal of Music Therapy (2010 onwards). The search terms used for IIMP were ("grounded theory" AND "music therapy") in all fields and text. For the IIMP records, the title, abstract and methods section (if included) were reviewed to screen papers for eligibility. The Taylor and Francis database contains the NJMT (1992 onwards) and this was also searched. The search term used with the Taylor and Francis database was "grounded theory" within the abstract only. Papers that were primary studies involving grounded theory music therapy research and ones that used the terms "grounded theory" or "constant comparison" within the title, abstract and or methods sections were included. Duplicates, opinion pieces, and book reviews were excluded. Only records published in English were included.

Thirty-five records were identified in the IIMP and the Taylor and Francis database. Thirty papers were identified in IIMP. Nine records in the IIMP were the inclusion criteria: Ahonen-Eerikainen et al. 2007; Amir 2005c; Daveson and O'Callaghan 2011; Donnell 2007; Magee and Davidson 2004a; O'Callaghan and McDermott 2004; O'Callaghan and Hiscock 2007; O'Grady and McFerran 2007b; Snow et al. 2008. Five records were identified in the Taylor and Francis database and four papers fulfilled the inclusion criteria: Edwards and Kennelly 2004; Eha et al. 2004; Magee and Burland 2008; O'Grady and McFerran 2007a.

The majority of the papers found involved research completed in Australia: Daveson and O'Callaghan 2011; Edwards and Kennelly 2004; O'Callaghan and McDermott 2004; O'Callaghan and Hiscock 2007; O'Grady and McFerran 2007b; O'Grady and McFerran 2007a. Other countries represented were the US (Amir 2005c), Canada: Ahonen-Eerikainen et al. 2007; Donnell 2007; Snow et al. 2008, England: Magee and Davidson 2004a; Magee and Burland 2008, and Estonia (Eha et al. 2004).

In addition, three music therapy grounded theory doctoral and post-doctoral research dissertations (known to the author) are available (Amir 1992b; Daveson 2006b; O'Callaghan 2001). The first grounded theory dissertation completed was authored by Amir in 1992 (Amir 1992b). This was followed in 2000 by Edwards in her PhD, which included one grounded theory study among other studies of music therapy for hospitalized children was completed (Edwards 2000). A full grounded theory dissertation was completed the next year, but it wasn't recognized as such by the author at the time (O'Callaghan 2001), and then five years later a third dissertation was completed. This dissertation involved two grounded theory studies; one modified grounded theory study and one complete grounded theory study (Daveson 2006b). There are also examples of grounded theory studies completed as part of a Masters degree studies and corresponding publications (O'Grady and McFerran 2007a).

Grounded theory has been used in various fields that music therapists work in, including for example palliative care and oncology (O'Callaghan and McDermott 2004), rehabilitation (Edwards J and Kennelly J, 2004; Magee and Davidson 2004a), the community (O'Grady and McFerran 2007a), and with adolescents in educational environments (Eha et al. 2004; Magee and Davidson 2004a). Three studies cut across different fields of practice (Amir 2005c; Daveson 2006b; Daveson and O'Callaghan 2011).

The majority of the studies involved collecting data from adults however two studies involved collecting data from children and or adolescents (Edwards and Kennelly 2004; Eha et al. 2004). Both music therapy participants and therapists have been approached for data for grounded theory studies. Music therapy grounded theory publications span a period of 20 years and this history of grounded theory research in music therapy includes hybrid (Donnell 2007), modified (Edwards and Kennelly 2004), and full-version (complete or pure) grounded theory studies (Daveson 2006a; O'Callaghan 2001). In essence, there has been a rapid increase in the number of grounded theory studies in music therapy since the turn of the twentieth century.

THE POTENTIALITY OF GROUNDED THEORY TO HELP ADVANCE MUSIC THERAPY

Let us "... render our implicit knowledge more public ..."

Aigen 1991, p. 377

Grounded theory has potential to advance the field of music therapy. Grounded theory studies can help reveal important findings about social processes, actions, interactions, and mechanisms within music therapy. Grounded theory can help us to inquire about what happens within music therapy and how processes unfold, and how people interact within these situations. Importantly, grounded theory can provide us with the opportunity to construct theories that are indigenous to music therapy, rather than theories that are reliant on data or assumptions better situated within other practices (Daveson et al. 2008). This is the case as grounded theory findings can be inductively derived from music therapy participants' and therapists' lived experiences within music therapy. This means that the experiences, process and interactions that occur within music therapy can be represented through grounded theory research. Importantly, diverse types of data can be analyzed in grounded theory studies to ensure that a comprehensive representation of music therapy phenomena. For example, observational, video, audio, drawings, diaries, memoirs, journals, autobiographies, and other text-based data such as newspaper clippings can all be used as data in grounded theory studies (Corbin and Strauss 2008). Grounded theory has the potential to allow for the construction of indigenous music therapy theory as it helps fulfil the requirements that Aigen identified as important to indigenous theory construction (Aigen 1991; Aigen 2005) including, for example, an examination of what occurs in music therapy including the music and an exploration of the therapeutic relationship and its interactions with treatment and outcome.

A CRITIQUE OF THE GROUNDED THEORY METHODOLOGY: STRENGTHS AND WEAKNESSES

Grounded theory is becoming more frequently used as a qualitative research methodology within the field of medicine (Sbaraini et al. 2011) and also within music therapy. The methodology though has both strengths and weaknesses. Certain approaches to grounded theory also have inherent strengths and weaknesses. Seven strengths and four weaknesses are identified here.

The strengths of grounded theory

First, methodological clarity is a strength associated with grounded theory research. Clear guidelines regarding how to start and stop analysis and how to proceed with analysis are included in Corbin and Strauss' book about grounded theory (Corbin and Strauss 2008). Clarity in reporting is required for this strength to be optimized.

Second, within grounded theory, systematic approaches to analysis are balanced by a need for creativity and flexibility. This flexibility and creativity avoids a rigid approach to analytical treatment and minimizes the risk of findings being imposed upon the data, rather than being induced from the data. Flexibility and creativity forms part of music therapy practice and this is a strength that music therapists can bring to the grounded theory research process.

Third, grounded theory research has a strong, established history which integrates diverse approaches. Grounded theory has developed and changed since its first discovery in 1967. There are at least five different approaches to grounded theory that can be found within the qualitative literature (Sbaraini et al. 2011). This diversity affords researchers with choice and can help researchers in selecting the grounded theory approach that best fits their area of inquiry, for example, constructivist or situational analysis. There are a growing number of examples of music therapy grounded theory studies that draw upon these different approaches. An emerging discourse about grounded theory research in music therapy is also apparent, and this may be helpful to researchers (Amir 2005a; Daveson 2006b; Daveson et al. 2008).

Four, the analytical devices inherent to grounded theory help ensure good qualitative research. For example, the use of memos and illustrative diagrams helps researchers to be transparent in their analysis and this aids credibility. Using these techniques aids reflexivity, which is a quality indicator of qualitative research.

Five, there is a grounded theory community and resources available to help researchers conduct grounded theory research. These resources include grounded theory institutes, blogs, and training videos available free on the internet (e.g. <http://allaboutgroundedtheory.blogspot.com/2011_01_01_archive.html>; <http://www.groundedtheory.com/>). Six, there are good examples of music therapy grounded theory research and therefore there are grounded theory skills and expertise to draw upon within the music therapy community. Edwards noted that there are a number of universities and institutions that are supporting the development of the research capabilities within the music therapy profession around the world (Edwards 2005). This may assist with additional modified, hybrid, and full-versions of music therapy grounded theory studies being completed in the future, including those that are firmly grounded within a relevant paradigmatic frame. Seven, there are good examples of grounded theory studies from within fields that music therapists work within, including within palliative care (e.g. Hack et al. 2010) and rehabilitation (e.g. Levack et al. 2011).

Weaknesses

First, grounded theory has been critiqued negatively for its hierarchical approach to theory development, and ambiguity regarding the techniques involved for the construction of theory in the latter stages of the research process (Wasserman et al. 2009). However, these ambiguities were mostly been addressed by Corbin and Strauss' third edition of the handbook on grounded theory (Corbin and Strauss 2008).

Second, methodological variation has led to confusion and lack of clarity regarding the academic standards required for grounded theory research. A challenge for the field of music therapy is to agree upon ways to describe and evaluate grounded theory research. Agreeing upon reporting standards will help mobilize our expertise within the profession and help with consistency regarding the presentation of findings. Within qualitative research in general there is a much debate and confusion regarding what constitutes grounded theory and this has made it difficult to assess the quality of some published studies. Researchers may be reluctant to draw upon studies whose quality cannot be ascertained. The absence of standards of grounded theory research in music therapy may jeopardize the chance of music therapy research being valued or used outside of our field. This is an important consideration in light of the limited funds to support health and social care interventions, and the growing use of narrative synthesis studies in order to summarize the available evidence for funders, managers, and clinicians. That shared, there are many established ways of evaluating the quality of qualitative research studies, such as the consolidated criteria for reporting qualitative research (COREQ) (Tong et al. 2007).

Third, on a practical level the extent of analysis and data collection required for a grounded theory study that results in formal or substantive theory may be prohibitive for smaller studies. When discussing grounded theory in music therapy Amir (Amir 2005a) asked two questions: "First, why are there so few grounded theory studies in music therapy? And second, why do we almost never see a full application of the grounded theory approach?" (p. 370). It is true that there are few examples of complete, pure, or full grounded theory studies that have resulted in theory in music therapy. However within music therapy, there are now examples of music therapy grounded theory research that has resulted in both substantive (O'Callaghan 2001) and formal theory (Daveson 2006b). Admittedly, both of these studies were completed as part of PhD research programmes. Nevertheless, they demonstrate that theory development from grounded theory is feasible within music therapy.

Four, there are some strands of grounded theory that suggest that a literature review to underpin the study is not required in the early stages of the research, and this may pose problems for ethics committees as the rationale to support the study is not demonstrated to support the need for the study. Also, avoiding reviewing the literature may not be helpful to research students who are about to embark on a research study. Reviewing and critically appraising research is an important core competency for any researcher, and a firm grasp of the literature will help develop robust research questions and study designs. Furthermore, reviewing the literature first will ensure that time and money isn't wasted on completing research that may be irrelevant or not required.

The need for critical appraisal of grounded theory research

Appraising the quality of the study

With the increased use of qualitative research and the possibility for qualitative studies to be included in narrative synthesis reviews it is becoming increasingly important to evaluate the quality of grounded theory research. There are a number of different approaches that can be applied to critiquing qualitative research in general and these can also be used to critique grounded theory research. For example, a check-list approach can be used to ensure that the correct procedures and methods have been included. Approaching the study from a procedural or methods perspective can be critiqued as a positivist way of approaching the critical appraisal of qualitative research as it is underpinned by a deductive approach to identifying what methods or procedures were or weren't used in the research. A different approach is to determine whether or not the research aligns with the ontology or paradigm that underscored the research (Edwards 2012), including studies informed by a-theoretical paradigms. Taking an approach that looks at the research ontology (underpinning beliefs) ensures that the values and beliefs that the researchers bring to the research are also examined. Examining the research just from a methods and procedural point of view potentially disregards the ways in which research is shaped and determined by the researcher. As there are strengths and weakness in both approaches researchers are encouraged to combine these approaches when critically appraising grounded theory research. This can be achieved through appraising the methodological/procedural, interpretive and theoretical rigor (Rice and Ezzy 1999).

The methodological/procedural rigor pertains to how the research was conducted by the researcher, for example whether or not open coding was used and whether it was followed by axial coding. When critiquing the methodological/procedural rigor one might ask "was a systematic and self-conscious research design used, and can the description of the methods stand alone" (Mays and Pope 2000)? Did the procedures used by the researcher match the description of the study that was provided?

Interpretive rigor examines how the understandings of the events and actions within the framework and worldview of those who were engaged in the research were represented. For example, this might include considering whether the views of the music therapy research participants were adequately sampled and represented in the study, and whether the findings adequately conveyed these views.

Theoretical rigor examines whether or not the theory and concepts chosen for the study align with the research strategy and with the goals of the research. For example, did the definitions of theoretical saturation used correspond with the study design and output (Rice and Ezzy 1999)? Did the quality indicators match the ontology that underpinned the study (Moran-Ellis et al. 2006)?

Appraising the theory

Evaluating the theory that results from grounded theory is also important. When Glaser and Strauss first published their grounded theory methodology, they indicated that the goal of grounded theory was to discover a theory that had grab, a theory that fits the data, and that works in the real world (Glaser and Strauss 1967). A grounded theory can also be evaluated in relation to its conceptual density, its durability over time and its modifiability, and importantly it can be evaluated in relation to its explanatory power (Glaser and Strauss 1967; Glaser 1978; Glaser 1992). In relation to qualitative health service research, Popay and colleagues wrote that we should aim to make "logical generalizations to a class of phenomena rather than probabilistic generalizations to a population" (Popay et al. 2008, p. 348). When we apply this to theory that results from grounded theory research it means that we should aim to be able to compare findings about our research topic (phenomena) to other areas. So for example, if we develop a theory about theme-based improvisation with adolescents we should also be able to see how the findings about these experiences relate to improvisatory experiences with other groups or settings. Note we aren't aiming to make predictions from theory constructed from grounded theory studies however we should be able to make plausible conclusions about what improvisation might be like with comparable cohorts and settings. To do this the theory should be conceptually dense, it needs to work in the real world, it needs to be durable and it needs to have enough explanatory power. These qualities rely on the key components of grounded theory: theoretical sampling and theoretical saturation. This means it's useful to examine whether they used theoretical sampling and saturation, and whether what they described also transpired in terms of research implementation.

Finally, a useful question to ask to help critique qualitative research in general is "What claims are being made for the generalizability of the findings to either other bodies of knowledge or to other populations or groups?" (Popay et al. 1998, p. 348). This question can also be asked of grounded theory research that claims to have developed theory.

WHAT THE FUTURE HOLDS FOR GROUNDED THEORY AND MUSIC THERAPY

After its discovery in the 1960s by Glaser and Strauss, the first grounded theory study to be conducted in music therapy was completed by Dorit Amir in 1992. This was followed by a rapid increase after the turn of the century of music therapy grounded theory research in all of its forms, i.e. modified, hybrid, and full-version/pure study designs. Over the last 20 years, the evolutions and variations of grounded theory have been both a blessing and a curse for music therapy. A blessing in that the use of grounded theory has allowed for an exploration of various study designs and innovation within the field, and a curse in that each variation makes it more difficult to be clear about what constitutes grounded theory research in music therapy. Variation also means it is more difficult to agree upon a set of design and reporting standards to help evaluate and advance research-led developments.

Music therapists face two challenges regarding grounded theory in music therapy. First, we have the challenge of continuing to create and to be innovative with the methodology while not sacrificing the quality and rigor of the methodology. Achieving this challenge will help with the recognition of music therapy research and will lead to improved clinical care for patients and families, and funding for services. Second, we need to optimize the potential of grounded theory to construct/discover theory that is indigenous to music therapy. Achieving this will allow us to make logical generalizations to a class of music therapy phenomena and help establish the profession. Anselm Strauss believed in the value of theory and its importance to the development of any professional body of knowledge until the day he died. Music therapy research abounds with descriptive accounts and while these are useful it is time to fully optimize the potentiality that grounded theory holds for music therapy in order to create music therapy indigenous theory with adequate explanatory power supported by sufficient methodological, interpretive, and theoretical rigor.

REFERENCES

Ahonen-Eerikainen, H., Rippin, K., Sibille, N., Koch, R., and Dalby, D.M. (2007). "Not bad for an old 85-year-old!" The qualitative analysis of the role of music, therapeutic benefits and group therapeutic factors of the St Joseph's Alzheimer's adult day program music therapy group. *Canadian Journal of Music Therapy 13*: 37–62.

Aigen, K. (1991). *The roots of music therapy: towards an indigenous research paradigm*. Doctoral thesis, New York University, New York.

Aigen, K. (2005). Philosophical inquiry. In: B. Wheeler (ed.), *Music Therapy Research*, 2nd edn, pp. 540–551. Gilsum, NH: Barcelona publishers.

Amir, D. (1992a). *Awakening and expanding the self: meaningful moments in the music therapy process as experienced and described by music therapists and music therapy clients*. New York University, New York.

Amir, D. (1992b). *Awakening and expanding the self: meaningful moments in the music therapy process as experienced and described by music therapists and music therapy clients*. Doctoral thesis, New York University, New York.

Amir, D. (2005a). Grounded theory. In: B. Wheeler (ed.), *Music Therapy Research* (2nd edn, pp. 365–378. Gilsum NH: Barcelona publishers.

Amir, D. (2005b). Musical humour in improvisational music therapy. *The Australian Journal of Music Therapy 16*: 3–24.

Bryant, A. and Charmaz, K. (2007). Introduction. In: L.H. Bryant and K. Charmaz (eds), *The SAGE Handbook of Grounded Theory*, pp. 1–28. Los Angeles: SAGE.

Charmaz, K. (2006). *Constructing Grounded Theory: a Practical Guide through Qualitative Analysis*. London: SAGE.

Clarke, A.E. (2005). *Situational Analysis. Grounded Theory after the Postmodern Turn*. Thousand Oaks, California: Sage.

Corbin, J. and Strauss, A. (2008). *Basics of Qualitative Research*, 3rd edn. London: Sage Publications.

Corbin, J.M. and Strauss, A.L. (2008). *Basics of Qualitative Research: Techniques and Procedures for Developing Grounded Theory*. London: Sage.

Daveson, B.A. (2006a). *A grounded theory study of music therapists' and clients' experiences and descriptions of temporality within music therapy*. University of Melbourne, Australia.

Daveson, B.A. (2006b). *Grounded theory study of music therapists' and clients' experiences and descriptions of temporality with music therapy*. PhD thesis, University of Melbourne, Australia.

Daveson, B.A. and O'Callaghan, C. (2011). Investigating the dimension of time: findings from a modified grounded theory study about clients' experiences and descriptions of temporality or time within music therapy. *Journal of Music Therapy 48*: 28–54.

Daveson, B. and O'Callaghan, C. (2012). Investigating the dimension of time: findings from a modified grounded theory study about clients' experiences and descriptions of temporality or time within music therapy. *Journal of Music Therapy 48*: 28–54.

Daveson, B.A., O'Callaghan, C., and Grocke, D. (2008). Indigenous music therapy theory building through grounded theory research: the developing indigenous theory framework. *The Arts in Psychotherapy 35*: 280–286.

Denzin, N.K. and Lincoln, Y.S. (2003). Introduction: the discipline and practice of qualitative research. In: N.K. Denzin and Y.S. Lincoln (eds), *The Landscape of Qualitative Research: Theories and Issues*, 2nd edn, pp. 1–46. London: Sage.

Dewey, J. (1934). Art as experience. New York: Minton Balch.

Donnell, N.E. (2007). Messages through the music: musical dialogue as a means of communicative contact. *Canadian Journal of Music Therapy* 13: 74–102.

Edwards, J. (2000). Developing a platform to inform music therapy research with hospitalised children. PhD thesis, University of Queensland.

Edwards, J. (2005). Developments and issues in music therapy research. In: B. Wheeler (ed.), *Music Therapy Research*, 2nd edn, pp. 20–32. Gilsum, NH: Barcelona.

Edwards, J. (2012). We need to talk about epistemology: Orientations, meaning, and interpretation within music therapy research. *Journal of Music Therapy* 49: 372–394.

Edwards, J. and Kennelly, J. (2002). Music therapy in paediatric rehabilitation: the application of modified grounded theory to identify categories of techniques used by a music therapist. *Nordic Journal of Music Therapy* 13: 112–126.

Edwards, J. and Kennelly, J. (2004). Music Therapy in Paediatric Rehabilitation. *Nordic Journal of Music Therapy*, 13: 112–126.

Eha, R., Ratnik, M., Tamm, E., and Zilensk, H. (2004). The Experience of Vibroacoustic Therapy in the Therapeutic Intervention of Adolescent Girls. *Nordic Journal of Music Therapy* 13: 33–46.

Glaser, B.G. (1978). *Theoretical Sensitivity: Advances in the Methodology of Grounded Theory.* Mill Valley, CA: Sociology press.

Glaser, B.G. (1992). *Basics of Grounded Theory Analysis: Emergence vs. Forcing.* Mill Valley, CA: Sociology press.

Glaser, B.G. and Strauss, A.L. (1965). *The Awareness of Dying.* Chicago: Aldine.

Glaser, B.G. and Strauss, A.L. (1967). *The Discovery of Grounded Theory: Strategies for Qualitative Research.* Chicago: Aldine.

Greenwood, D.J. and Levin, M. (2003). Reconstructing the relationships between universities and society through action research. In: N.K. Denzin and Y.S. Lincoln (eds), *The Landscape of Qualitative Research: Theories and Issues*, 2nd edn, pp. 131–166. London: Sage.

Hack, T.F., McClement, S.E., Chochinov, H.M., Cann, B.J., Hassard, T.H., Kristjanson, L.J., et al. (2010). Learning from dying patients during their final days: life reflections gleaned from dignity therapy. *Palliative Medicine* 24(7): 715–723.

Magee, W.L. and Burland, K. (2008). An Exploratory Study of the Use of Electronic Music Technologies in Clinical Music Therapy. *Nordic Journal of Music Therapy* 17: 124–141.

Magee, W.L. and Burland, K. (2008). An exploratory study of the use of electronic music technologies in clinical music therapy. *Nordic Journal of Music Therapy* 17: 124–141.

Magee, W.L. and Davidson, J.W. (2004a). Music therapy in multiple sclerosis: results of a systematic qualitative analysis. *Music Therapy Perspectives* 22: 39–51.

Magee, W.L. and Davidson, J.W. (2004b). Singing in therapy: monitoring disease process in chronic degenerative illness. *British Journal of Music Therapy* 18: 65–77.

Mays, N. and Pope, C. (2000). Assessing quality in qualitative research. *British Medical Journal* 320: 50–52.

Moran-Ellis, J., Alexander, V.D., Cronin, A., Dickinson, M., Fielding, J., Sleney, J., et al. (2006). Triangulation and integration: processes, claims and implications. *Qualitative Research* 6: 45–59.

Morse, J.M., Stern, P.N., Corbin, J., Bowers, B., Charmaz, K., and Clarke, A.E. (2009). *Developing Grounded Theory: The Second Generation.* Walnut Creek, CA, USA: Left Coast Press.

O'Callaghan, C. (1996). Lyrical themes in songs written by palliative care patients. *Music Therapy* 33: 74–92.

O'Callaghan, C. (2001). *Music therapy's relevance in a cancer hospital researched through a constructivist lens*. PhD thesis, Department of Social Work and Faculty of Music, University of Melbourne, Victoria, Australia.

O'Callaghan, C. and Hiscock, R. (2007). Inerpretive subgroup analysis extends modified grounded theory research findings in oncologic music therapy. *Journal of Music Therapy* 44: 256–281.

O'Callaghan, C. and McDermott, F. (2004). Music therapy's relevance in a cancer hospital researched through a constructivist lens. *Journal of Music Therapy* 41: 151–185.

O'Connor, M.K., Netting, F.E., and Thomas, N.L. (2008). Grounded theory: managing the challenge for those facing Institutional Review Board oversight. *Qualitative Inquiry* 14: 28–45.

O'Grady, L. and McFerran, K. (2007a). Community Music Therapy and Its Relationship to Community Music: Where Does It End? *Nordic Journal of Music Therapy* 16: 14–26.

O'Grady, L. and McFerran, K. (2007b). Uniting the work of community musicians and music therapists through the health-care continuum: a grounded theory analysis. *The Australian Journal of Music Therapy* 18: 62–86.

Patton, M.Q. (2002). *Qualitative Research and Evaluation Methods*. Thousand Oaks, California: Sage.

Plano Clark, V.L., Schumacher, K., West, C., Edrington, J., Dunn, L.B., Harzstark, A., Melisko, M., Rabow, M.W., Swift, P.S., and Miaskowski, C. (2013). Practices for embedding an interpretive qualitative approach within a randomized clinical trial. *Journal of Mixed Methods Research* 7(3): 219–242.

Rice, P.L. and Ezzy, D. (1999). *Qualitative Research Methods: A Health Focus*. Oxford: Oxford University Press.

Sbaraini, A., Carter, S.M., Wendell Evans, R., and Blinkhorn, A. (2011). How to do a grounded theory study: a worked example of a study of dental practices. *BMC Medical Research Methodololgy* 11: 1–10.

Snow, S., Snow, S., and D'Amico, M. (2008). Interdisciplinary research through community music therapy and performance ethnography. *Canadian Journal of Music Therapy* 14: 30–46.

Strauss, A. and Corbin, J. (1990). *Basics of Qualitative Research*. London: Sage.

Strauss, A. and Corbin, J. (1998). *Basics of Qualitative Research: Techniques for Procedures for Developing Grounded Theory*, 2nd edn. London: Sage.

Tong, A., Sainsbury, P., and Craig, J. (2007). Consolidated criteria for reporting qualitative research (COREQ): a 32-item checklist for interviews and focus groups. *International Journal for Quality in Health Care* 19(6): 349–357.

Vidich, A.J. and Lyman, S.M. (2003). Qualitative methods: their history in sociology and anthropology. In: N.K. Denzin and Y.S. Lincoln (eds), *The Landscape of Qualitative Research: Theories and Issues*, 2nd edn, pp. 55–129. London: Sage.

Walker, D. and Myrick, F. (2006). Grounded theory: an exploration of process and procedure. *Qualitative Health Research* 16: 547–559.

Wasserman, J.A., Clair, J.M., and Wilson, K.L. (2009). Problematics of grounded theory: innovations for developing an increasingly rigorous qualitative method. *Qualitative Research* 9: 355–381.

Wheeler, B. (2005). Introduction: overview of music therapy research. In: B. Wheeler (ed.), *Music Therapy Research*, 2nd edn, pp. 1–9. Gilsum, NH: Barcelona.

CHAPTER 41

....

PHENOMENOLOGICAL RESEARCH IN MUSIC THERAPY

....

CLAIRE M. GHETTI

INTRODUCTION

THROUGH the procedures of phenomenological research music therapists seek to understand and articulate the complicated, situated meanings inherent in the music therapy process. Systematic inquiry may reveal the *science* of music therapy, but uncovering and explicating the *art* of the discipline allows communication of the more ineffable elements of music therapy. It is the position of these creative elements within a subjective setting that makes the discipline of music therapy unique, but at the same time challenging to research and to explain. There is a demand for research methodologies that are responsive to the foundational and unique elements of the music therapy process, and that can accommodate the participant's subjective, conscious experience of music therapy phenomena. As phenomenological research unites aspects of the range of research traditions from the sciences and the humanities (Finlay 2009) and captures subjective experience of phenomena, it is a desirable approach for music therapists.

Before embarking on a course of phenomenological inquiry, it is important that music therapy researchers understand the philosophical assumptions underlying their chosen methodology. If a researcher engages in research without an express understanding of the underlying philosophical foundations, the research is at risk for lacking clarity and grounding in areas of purpose, method, and outcomes (Lopez and Willis 2004). Comprehension of phenomenological research begins with an examination of the philosophical foundations from which this form of research arose.

FOUNDATIONS OF PHENOMENOLOGICAL RESEARCH

Definitions

The term *phenomenon* is derived from the Greek word *phainesthai* meaning "to flare up, to show itself, to appear" (Moustakas 1994, p. 26). A phenomenon, therefore, is that which is brought to light by the senses, the manifestation of one's experience of an object or event. Phenomena involve objects, events, thoughts, decisions, feelings, etc., as they appear in our consciousness (Husserl 1927). The term *phenomenology* may be used to describe a philosophy (e.g. Husserl 1927), a theoretical perspective that informs several research methodologies, or a specific research methodology (e.g. Giorgi 1975). Even within the sphere of phenomenology as research methodology there are variations, including descriptive phenomenology and hermeneutic phenomenology.

In order to fully appreciate the theoretical assumptions and framework underlying phenomenological research and its utility in the field of music therapy, one must acknowledge the philosophical roots of this approach. Descriptive and hermeneutic forms of phenomenological research trace their development back to the works of various philosophers, including Husserl, Heidegger, Gadamer, and Merleau-Ponty.

Phenomenological philosophy

The German philosopher Edmund Husserl (1859–1938) is often referred to as the founder of phenomenology. He sought to discover the primary elements of human experience (Smith et al. 2009), and adopted a philosophy of *radical criticism* in reaction to the dominance of empirical science at the turn of the 20th century (Crotty 1998, p. 71). Husserl viewed personal experience as a form of primary knowledge, whereas he conceived of empirical science as secondary and dependent upon *first-order* personal experience (Smith et al. 2009). Husserl was critical of attempts to apply methods of empirical science to the study of psychology, asserting that humans do not merely respond objectively to stimuli, but instead respond to their own understandings of such stimuli (Laverty 2003).

Husserl founded his approach on considerations about how humans might use a rigorous process of inquiry to become aware of their own experience of certain phenomena, through a process that could unveil the essential elements of that experience. Furthermore, Husserl felt that the essential elements of lived experience could potentially transcend the limits of individual experience and provide some level of insight for others, too (Smith et al. 2009). Husserl's phenomenology was transcendental in nature, meaning that he was concerned with "consciousness as such" and not human consciousness, in particular (Giorgi 2012). He prompted phenomenologists to *go back to the things themselves* in order to uncover the conscious aspects of experience. The aim of this process was to understand these experiences as they were revealed, and to avoid seeing them through the veil of preconceptions, or become concerned with fitting them into previously existing schemata. For Husserl, phenomenology involved extracting oneself from simply living within everyday experience, to reflect back upon what it is like to have that experience:

> Focusing our experiencing gaze on our own psychic life necessarily takes place as reflection, as a turning about of a glance which had previously been directed elsewhere.
>
> Husserl 1927, p. 3

In turning one's gaze back upon experience, one can begin to examine one's own perceptions of the objects encountered in the world (Smith et al. 2009).

Husserl's approach allowed the capture of subjective forms of human experience as they appeared in consciousness (Husserl 1927). As a philosopher, his methods remained in the conceptual realm. He was primarily interested in people's forms of awareness, perception and consciousness as they manifest through individual psychological processes (Smith et al. 2009). Husserl acknowledged the role of the intersubjective, especially within the process of gaining insight about oneself and in the formation of subjective perceptions of reality (Moustakas 1994). One of his main contributions was to establish and promote an appreciation for the importance of examining human experience and the perception of that lived experience (Smith et al. 2009).

Following Husserl's foundational path making, Heidegger, Gadamer, and Merleau-Ponty all uniquely contributed to the conceptualization of humans as inextricably embedded within a world of relationships and subjectivity (Finlay 2008; Laverty 2003; Smith et al. 2009). Though he denied being an existentialist, philosopher and student of Husserl, Martin Heidegger (1889–1976) is associated with phenomenology becoming existentialist in purpose and in orientation (Crotty 1998). Heidegger diverged from Husserl's transcendental phenomenology and is often credited for laying the foundation for hermeneutic and existential forms of phenomenological philosophy (Smith et al. 2009). Heidegger placed emphasis on the concept of *Dasein* ("there-being"), the quality of *being* specific to being human, and felt that *being-in-the-world* was always contextual, perspectival, and temporal (Giorgi and Giorgi 2008; Smith et al. 2009). Thus, Heidegger was uncertain if knowledge could exist independent of interpretation, and he gave importance to the meaning that individuals make out of their lived worlds (Finlay 2008; Smith et al. 2009). As such, Heidegger supported an interpretivist theoretical perspective, a viewpoint congruent with hermeneutics (Giorgi and Giorgi 2008).

Phenomenological research

Phenomenological research methodologies developed from a desire to capture detailed description and reveal the underlying meanings of human experience. Such an approach lay in stark contrast to the empirical attempts to control, manipulate, and predict factors related to human experience that were prevalent in the early 20th century (Laverty 2003). Philosophers such as Husserl recognized that humans engage in complex relationships with the world around them and experience that world in a subjective way. Empirical sciences tended to miss the embedded, contextual meanings of experience, and therefore, researchers sought to develop methodologies that could accommodate the subjective and intersubjective realities of human experience. Thus, phenomenological research is an outgrowth of an underlying constructionist epistemology (sometimes referred to as constructivist), and stands in opposition to objectivist epistemology (Crotty 1998).

There are multiple approaches to conducting phenomenological research; however, most approaches include a focus on detailed description, the use of phenomenological reduction, a search for the essence of an experience, and a concern for the intentional relationships between people and situations (Giorgi 1997). The two most commonly encountered variants include descriptive phenomenology and hermeneutic[1] phenomenology. The aims, underlying assumptions, methods, and application of outcomes vary depending upon whether the methodology is descriptive or hermeneutic in nature, as will be discussed in more detail below. Despite the differences, several elements are common to both forms of phenomenology.

Aims of phenomenological research

The goal of phenomenological research is to make implicit meanings explicit to allow for a fuller understanding of lived experience. Thus, underlying meanings of experience are brought to light and transformed into a more general, less situation-specific level (Giorgi and Giorgi 2008). The outcome of phenomenological research is richly described contextual examples of the phenomenon that reveal the underlying psychological essence of that phenomenon (Giorgi and Giorgi 2008). In contrast to research with objectivist roots that might seek to test a hypothesis or a specific theory, because phenomenological research operates from a constructionist epistemology, its aims are to promote discovery and description.

Descriptive and hermeneutic phenomenological methodologies share an overall emphasis on describing and interpreting how people make sense of their experiences when such experiences are brought into consciousness (Patton 2002). This meaning making is important both on the level of the individual, and on the level of an essential essence of the experience that might share commonalities with others' experiences. Phenomenological research, therefore, focuses on exploring how people experience a phenomenon including, "how they perceive it, describe it, feel about it, judge it, remember it, make sense of it, and talk about it with others" (Patton 2002, p. 104).

Data collected during phenomenological research are often retrospective descriptions of experience, obtained from participants through the use of semi-structured, in-depth interviews. However, it is possible to gain on-going descriptions from participants over time, or to use an external observer's descriptions of a subject's experience. Alternatively, interactions and behaviors could be videotaped and subsequently analyzed to capture the essence of an experience, or participants may view video of themselves and discuss the experience as they watch it unfold on tape (Giorgi and Giorgi 2008).

Key principles

Intentionality

Husserl, like his teacher Franz Brentano, adopted a concept originating from Scholastic philosophy, that of *intentionality*. Intentionality was a critical concept within phenomenological philosophy and referred to the internal experience of being conscious of a phenomenon or object (Moustakas 1994). How one perceives an object depends upon one's mindset, one's location, and the context within which one encounters that object (Willig 2008). Consciousness is directed toward the world surrounding an object, whether it is a real world or an imaginary world (Giorgi and Giorgi 2008). Each act of intentionality consists of a *noema*, or the experience of an object, and a *noesis*, or the real, self-evident object (Moustakas 1994). Intentionality comprises the noema-noesis relationship, with textual (noematic) aspects of the phenomenon paired with structural (noetic) aspects to enable the uncovering of underlying meanings (Moustakas 1994).

Intersubjectivity

Phenomenology recognizes that humans are engaged in the world through a complexity of multiple, overlapping relationships to that world. Researchers within this perspective acknowledge the role of the intersubjective, and seek to capture thick descriptions of such interconnected subjective experience (Moustakas 1994).

Epoche, bracketing, and phenomenological reduction

The terms *epoche, bracketing*, and *phenomenological reduction* represent related, but philosophically distinct concepts, though they are commonly used interchangeably in the research literature (Bednall 2006; Gearing 2004; LeVasseur 2003). All three concepts "refer to a reflective process by which opinion and prejudice are suspended to focus attention on what is essential in the phenomena" (LeVasseur 2003, p. 411). Husserl's conceptualization of *bracketing* and of various forms of *reduction* evolved over the course of his writings, though at the core they represent crucial self-meditative processes that enable essences of the phenomenon under investigation to be revealed (Finlay 2008; Gearing 2004). When these philosophical concepts are applied within research, they reflect the epistemological, ontological and theoretical assumptions of the researcher, and vary in their form accordingly (Gearing 2004).

Phenomenology calls for the researcher to reflect upon and suspend her current conceptions and assumptions regarding a phenomenon, in order to engage with it in a fresh manner, remaining open to what emerges in the process (Crotty 1998). Husserl considered this purging of prior assumptions held within the natural attitude the *epoche*, a necessary process that enables the perception of a phenomenon's essence (LeVasseur 2003). The researcher undertakes systematic efforts to identify and temporarily set aside previous knowledge, beliefs and assumptions of a phenomenon in order to be open and receptive to participants' descriptions of their own lived experience (Moustakas 1994). It is from an on-going process of *epoche* that the researcher adopts a *phenomenological attitude*. This is:

> ... the process of retaining an empathic openness to the world while reflexively identifying and restraining pre-understandings so as to engage phenomena in themselves. Past knowledge is both restricted and used to interrogate the meanings that come to be, in order for the researcher to be more fully open to the research encounter.
>
> Finlay 2008, p. 29

Once a researcher achieves a shift to the phenomenological attitude, she engages in *bracketing*, which consists of a flexible process to suspend assumptions and preconceptions:

> Bracketing, as in a mathematical equation, suspends certain components by placing them outside the brackets, which then facilitates a focusing in on the phenomenon within the brackets.
>
> Gearing 2004, p. 1430

The researcher's theoretical perspective impacts how she approaches, understands, and analyzes the process of bracketing.

Gearing (2004) proposes a typology of bracketing wherein the research focus, research questions, and the researcher's theoretical perspective govern the form of bracketing chosen. Philosophically distinct forms of bracketing have arisen from positivist, postpositivist, interpretivist, constructivist, and postmodern theoretical perspectives; and may be classified as ideal bracketing, descriptive bracketing, existential bracketing, analytic bracketing, reflexive bracketing, and pragmatic bracketing (Gearing 2004). Aside from ideal bracketing, which represents a hypothetical philosophical ideal aimed at eliminating all internal and external suppositions, most forms of bracketing acknowledge the relational and reflexive[2] nature of the process in which the researcher influences the phenomenon and vice versa (Finlay 2008; Gearing 2004).

Bracketing remains a relevant concept for both descriptive and hermeneutic forms of phenomenology though the way the researcher approaches bracketing will match the epistemological foundations and theoretical assumptions of the chosen research approach. Descriptive bracketing represents a research-oriented application of Husserl's concept of *phenomenological reduction*. When using descriptive bracketing, the researcher aims to:

> ... set clearly aside the vast majority of their [*sic*] personal suppositions and to hold in abeyance most external suppositions, thereby allowing the researcher to focus in and describe the pure essences of the phenomenon.
>
> Gearing 2004, p. 1448

The researcher attempts to set aside most of her personal assumptions, but also realizes that it may be impossible to suspend various social or cultural suppositions (Gearing 2004). The researcher may undertake this process of bracketing by noting various beliefs underlying the study and:

> ... by writing a list of the expectations the researcher has, even in point form to begin with. The list includes assumptions that are drawn from the researcher's clinical experience, reading the literature, and other pressures on the outcomes of their investigation.
>
> McFerran and Grocke 2007, p. 275

Descriptive bracketing reflects a theoretical perspective ranging from postpositivism to interpretivism, and corresponds with descriptive forms of phenomenology. Once the researcher has engaged in descriptive bracketing, and has enabled the essence of the phenomenon to emerge, she reintegrates the bracketed material for purposes of interpreting and understanding its relation to the phenomenon (Gearing 2004).

In contrast, researchers who employ reflexive bracketing assert that it is impossible to suspend personal assumptions and suppositions during the research process. Instead, such researchers reflect upon and identify their assumptions, and acknowledge the influence of beliefs and suppositions on the phenomenon (Gearing 2004). Cultural and social influences are viewed as being inseparable from the researcher and from the phenomenon, and are worthy of study. Intersubjectivity is acknowledged and the researcher's own subjectivity is valued and used during the research process:

> The challenge is for the researcher to simultaneously embody contradictory stances of being "scientifically removed from," "open to" and "aware of" while also interacting with research participants in the midst of their own experiencing.
>
> Finlay 2008, p. 3

Reflexive bracketing is consistent with the assumptions of theoretical perspectives ranging from constructivism to postmodernism, and is congruent with the philosophy of hermeneutic phenomenology. Researchers often initiate reflexive bracketing while designing and preparing their research, modify the reflexive narrative throughout the research process, and reintegrate insights gleaned from bracketing during the data analysis phase. Regardless of the particular form of bracketing used, when a researcher engages in this process, she may be more likely to realize new aspects or dimensions of the experience as revealed in the data (Giorgi and Giorgi 2008).

Imaginative variation

Moustakas (1994) views phenomenological reduction as enabling the textural (noematic) description of the essence of a phenomenon. After textural descriptions of the phenomenon have been derived, a third step involves demarking the structural essences of the experience through the process of imaginative variation (Moustakas 1994). Imaginative variation involves imaginatively removing features of a phenomenon one by one to identify aspects that are essential to the phenomenon versus those that are not. Through this process the researcher parses out the essential essences of an experience to make explicit the underlying structures that contribute to the formation of those essences.

Particular methods

Certain research methods are commonly encountered in phenomenological research, including the use of purposive sampling to obtain participants and in-depth interviews to obtain data.

Purposive sampling

The manner in which potential participants are identified and invited to partake in a phenomenological study is consistent with the theoretical assumptions of this form of research. Since phenomenological research seeks to explore the lived experience of various phenomena, participants are often selected *purposively* to assure that they possess lived experience of the phenomena (Patton 2002). Potential participants may be identified through personal contacts, by secondary contacts or gatekeepers, or by referral from other participants (Smith et al. 2009). The researcher may either rely on the inclusion criteria to assure that participants have experienced the phenomenon of interest, or may use the first questions within the interview to ensure that the experience of the participants is relevant. Phenomenological researchers engage in detailed description and analysis of the lived experiences of their participants, and most studies have small sample sizes.

In-depth interviews

Phenomenological researchers commonly utilize in-depth interviews to obtain a rich description of the lived experience of a chosen phenomenon. Researchers use semi-structured interviews with open-ended questions to enable participants to reflect upon their experiences from multiple perspectives. The researchers aim for *thick description* of this phenomenon, capturing a nuanced and contextualized description of the experience. Researchers may choose to subtly redirect participants or request expansion of their descriptions throughout the course of the interview, to enable more detailed description (Racette 2004).

Descriptive phenomenology

True to its name, descriptive phenomenology aims to richly describe a phenomenon of interest, while staying faithful to the true nature and surrounding context of that phenomenon (Giorgi and Giorgi 2008). The descriptive approach to phenomenology is directly related to Husserlian thought, and is exemplified in the methods of Giorgi (1975/ 1985), Colaizzi (1978), and Moustakas (1994). Husserl considered interpretation as a specific form of description, and thus descriptive phenomenologists employ interpretation only in the service of providing a more accurate description of the underlying structures of an experience (Giorgi and Giorgi 2008; Moustakas 1994). Descriptive phenomenology is used to determine what an experience means to someone who has undergone it, and to identify any underlying structures or essences of that experience that might hold true for others (Moustakas 1994). Identifying these universal essences, also known as eidetic structures, enables one to capture the true nature of the phenomenon and thus marks the ultimate goal of descriptive phenomenology (Finlay 2009; Lopez and Willis 2004).

Researchers who partake in descriptive phenomenology believe in the importance of *descriptive bracketing* to identify and suspend one's prior knowledge and preconceptions and enable a fresh understanding of the essences of an experience (Gearing 2004; Lopez and Willis 2004; Willig 2008). Purists in this approach even suggest that researchers avoid engaging in a detailed review of literature prior to embarking on their study, in order to avoid being influenced by the existing literature (Streubert and Carpenter 1999).

Giorgi (1989, 2012) has contributed one of the more popular and systematic approaches to psychological descriptive phenomenology. Steps of Giorgi's (2012) process are listed in Table 41.1 for reference. In order to uncover a general, more universal essence of a phenomenon, descriptive phenomenological researchers may be advised to aim for a sample size of three or more participants (Giorgi 2008). Within Giorgi's steps, the researcher creates transformations of the raw data, repeating this transformation process multiple times until she achieves a clear synthesis of the data that reveals the underlying psychological aspects of the experience (Giorgi and Giorgi 2008). The structure is obtained by analyzing the transformed data to identify which elements are essential to a full understanding of the experience. Depending upon the variability of the full data set, a single structure may be adequate to explain all of the data, or multiple structures may be required (Giorgi and Giorgi 2008).

Hermeneutic phenomenology

Hermeneutic phenomenology, elsewhere referred to as interpretative phenomenology, is derived from the work of hermeneutic philosophers, including Heidegger, Gadamer, and Ricoeur (Finlay 2009; Giorgi and Giorgi 2008). Hermeneutics involves the interpretation of texts in such a way that enables a more "correct" and contextually-appropriate understanding (Moustakas 1994). Heidegger viewed interpretation as primary, with description being a

Table 41.1 Steps of Psychological Descriptive Phenomenological Analysis. Data from Giorgi (2012)

Pre-requisite:	Adopting an attitude of phenomenological reduction and being sensitive to a psychological perspective
Step (1)	Reading the entire transcription to obtain a sense of the whole
Step (2)	Re-reading the transcript and inserting a mark each time there is a transition in meaning to enable the creation of *meaning units*[1]
Step (3)	Maintaining the wording of the participant, but transforming the data to make explicit the underlying psychological value of the experience
Step (4)	Reviewing the psychological description of the experience and using free imaginative variation to identify the essential structure of the experience
Step (5)	Using the essential structure to better understand the raw data

[1] Meaning units are created based on the researcher's perspective, and thus may vary from researcher to researcher (Giorgi 2012). How the researcher transforms the meaning units, and not the length or exact nature of the meaning units, is most important (Giorgi and Giorgi 2008).

specific type of interpretation (Giorgi and Giorgi 2008), and thus in hermeneutic phenomenology, all description is viewed as a form of interpretation (Willig 2008). Giorgi (2012) views description as a process of relating the "given" of a certain lived experience, while interpretation involves assuming a *non-given factor* that helps to explain what is given within a certain experience. Hermeneutic phenomenologists move beyond description itself, and adopt certain interpretative assumptions that help explain the data (Giorgi 2012).

The hermeneutical form of phenomenological analysis incorporates interpretation akin to that which happens as part of the process of hermeneutics. Interpretative phenomenology makes use of the *hermeneutic circle* in which one reasons from a whole to parts, and from parts to a whole, in order to move back and forth between presupposition and interpretation (Willig 2008). In hermeneutic phenomenology the "reflective-interpretative process includes not only a description of the experience as it appears in consciousness, but also an analysis and astute interpretation of the underlying conditions, historically and aesthetically, that account for the experience" (Moustakas 1994, p. 10).

Hermeneutic phenomenologists assert that certain personal and cultural assumptions cannot be meaningfully suspended during the process of bracketing. Instead, they may use a process of *reflexive bracketing* to become more self-aware of suppositions that may influence the research. Researchers identify their pre-existing beliefs and assumptions and note how these beliefs impact or are impacted by the research process (Lopez and Willis 2004). Thus, researchers alternate between examining their own assumptions and re-visiting their participants' experiences with a fresh perspective, though the ultimate focus remains centered on the participants' experiences of the phenomenon (Finlay 2009). Meanings that are derived during interpretative research are necessarily co-constitutional in nature; they represent a mix of meanings formed by the participant and by the researcher, embedded within their respective contexts (Lopez and Willis 2004).

An additional difference between hermeneutic and descriptive phenomenology is that the former may employ a specific theoretical orientation or framework during the design, analysis or interpretation of a study (Lopez and Willis 2004). Such a theoretical framework serves to focus the study, make theoretical assumptions explicit, and help guide decision-making throughout the research process (Lopez and Willis 2004).

Examples of hermeneutic forms of phenomenological inquiry include van Manen (1990) and Interpretative Phenomenological Analysis (Smith 2004; Smith et al. 2009). Van Manen (1990) has argued that interpretation must be used when researchers attempt to describe elements such as artwork, music, or other forms of nonverbal expression. Thus, hermeneutic forms of phenomenology may be particularly useful in disciplines that include art forms, such as music therapy.

Interpretative Phenomenological Analysis (IPA)

One form of hermeneutic phenomenology that originated in the field of psychology is Interpretative Phenomenological Analysis (IPA) (Smith 2004; Smith and Eatough 2006; Smith et al. 2009). IPA explores how individuals make sense of major life experiences, and such studies often focus on specific poignant or significant experiences within a person's overall lived experience (Smith et al. 2009). Strongly linked to hermeneutic traditions, IPA recognizes the integral role of the researcher in the interpretative process (Finlay 2009). IPA researchers take part in a *double hermeneutic* since participants make sense of their experiences and the researcher, in turn, interprets the participants' meaning-making to gain a fuller understanding of the experience (Smith et al. 2009). Researchers are encouraged to discuss their assumptions and beliefs as they influence the research. IPA research typically uses small, homogenous samples, and examines convergence and divergence within the sample. Data are typically collected through semi-structured interviews, transcripts are analyzed by case before moving to cross-case analysis, and the researcher transforms the data through "analytic interpretation" into a narrative account (Smith et al. 2009).

Other phenomenological approaches

Researchers may adopt a phenomenological orientation or employ phenomenological methods in other forms of research that do not have description or interpretation as their core aims. Similarly, researchers may combine phenomenological analysis along with other forms of analysis to blend methodologies, such as in phenomenological narrative inquiry. Neurophenomenology is a contemporary methodology that combines phenomenological data of participants' experiences of a phenomenon with neurological data taken during that same experience. Varela (1996) pioneered the approach of neurophenomenology, and Hunt (2011) applied the methodology to the field of music therapy. Bruscia (2005) describes several other phenomenological approaches used within the context of first-person research that have direct application to music therapy research.

PHENOMENOLOGICAL MUSIC THERAPY RESEARCH

The second half of this chapter consists of a representative, but by no means exhaustive, sampling of phenomenological music therapy studies. Music therapy researchers have used phenomenological methodologies and methods in various ways to examine an array of experiences. Phenomenology has revealed clients' experience of music therapy (e.g. Grocke 1999; Hogan 1999; Hunt 2011; Rykov 2006; Skewes 2001), caregivers' experience of music therapy (e.g. Lindenfelser et al. 2008); music therapists' experience of music therapy (e.g. Forinash 1990, 1992; Forinash and Gonzalez 1989), music therapists' experience of effectiveness (Comeau 1991, 2004), music therapists' experience of musical countertransference (Dillard 2006) and of spirituality (Marom 2004); music therapy students' experience of a peer support group (Milgram-Luterman 2000) or of clinical practicum (Wheeler 2002) or cross-cultural supervision (Kim 2008), and music therapy educators' experience of feminist music therapy pedagogy (Hahna 2011), among other topics. A summary of representative studies in the area of phenomenological music therapy is included in Table 41.2. The following sections will describe ground-breaking phenomenological music therapy studies, and will explore unique applications of phenomenological methodologies within the current research landscape.

Music phenomenology

Before discussing applications of phenomenological research in music therapy, it is appropriate to acknowledge the field of music phenomenology and its contributions to research practice in music therapy. The field of music phenomenology enjoyed a flurry of development during the first part of the 20th century owing to the work of several German scholars. In the 1960s and 1970s, English translations of important works by Heidegger (*Being and Time*) and Merleau-Ponty (*Phenomenology of Perception*) gave rise to an interest in applying phenomenology to the field of musicology (Christensen 2012). In particular, musicologist and music theorist Lawrence Ferrara set forth a method for the phenomenological analysis of music that music therapy researchers have frequently adapted.

Consistent with a constructionist epistemology, Ferrara acknowledged that the meaning a music analyst ascribes to a piece of music is impacted by the analyst's orientation to that piece of music. He placed emphasis on analyzing the syntactical, semantic, and what he labeled "ontological" meanings of the music, in order to uncover the "human element in music" (Ferrara 1984, p. 357). The element of humanness is present within the music as it is composed, and as it is subsequently interpreted during analysis (Ferrara 1984). Ferrara's procedure for phenomenological analysis of music involves six steps, as described below in Table 41.3.

Music therapy researchers have found Ferrara's method to be relevant as it aims for embedded and reflexive understanding of an art form such as music. A comprehensive doctoral dissertation by Erik Christensen (2012) provides further discussion of key contributors to the field of music phenomenology.

Early phenomenological research in the field of music therapy

A critical exchange of ideas occurred between European and Scandinavian music therapists and those from North America in the early 1980s. Music therapy scholars and other contemporaries from European and Scandinavian countries shared knowledge of phenomenological traditions at a symposium titled "Music in the Life of Man" which was held at New York

Table 41.2 Selected Phenomenological Music Therapy Studies

Author/s	Year	Type of Source	Methodology	Methods	Participant Population	Phenomena of Interest	Comments
Racette	2004/1989	Journal article based on author's master's thesis	Phenomenological methods modeled after Colaizzi (1978), Giorgi (1970), and others	Interviews	8 adults (non-clinical) who had listened to music when upset	Listening to music when upset	Racette (1989) marks an early example of the application of phenomenological research to music therapy
Forinash and Gonzalez	1989	Journal article	Authors' 7-step music therapy adaptation of Ferrara's (1984) method of phenomenological analysis of music	Case study, Narrative	2 music therapists who worked with clients at the end of life	Therapists' perspective of music therapy during a client's process of active dying	Developed this approach out of a desire to more accurately describe the essence of clinical music therapy phenomena
Amir	1990	Journal article	Forinash and Gonzalez's (1989) 7-step adaptation of Ferrara's (1984) method of phenomenological analysis of music	Observation, analysis of audio and video recordings, interviews of patient and therapist	A young adult 10 months post spinal cord injury; music therapist	Therapist and client perspectives of the use of improvised song during music therapy	
Forinash	1990	Doctoral dissertation	Author's adaptation of Giorgi's (1975) method of phenomenological analysis	Case studies, audio recordings, transcription, process notes	10 terminally ill adults who received music therapy	Experience of music therapy for people who are terminally ill	Adapted Giorgi (1975) to enable exploration of the therapist–client relationship, and recognize music as a dynamic force

Comeau	1991/2004	Master's thesis and related journal article	Adapted and combined methods by Colaizzi (1978), Giorgi (1975), Racette (1989), and others	Two-part interviews	11 experienced music therapists (who served diverse client populations and used diverse MT approaches)	Experience of being effective versus ineffective as a music therapist	Method of analysis was stipulated in advance, but was flexible to revision as needed depending upon how data was emerging
Forinash	1992	Journal article	Phenomenological methods adapted from Giorgi (1984) and Forinash (1990)	Review of videotaped clinical sessions, interviews	8 music therapists in their first year of Nordoff–Robbins clinical training	Experience of engaging in Nordoff–Robbins clinical improvisation	
Grocke	1999	Doctoral dissertation	Combination of methods used by Giorgi (1975) and Colaizzi (1978)	Interviews with clients, music therapists and phenomenological musical analysis	7 adult clients who had received GIM sessions and their 2 music therapists	Client and therapist experience of pivotal moments in GIM music therapy sessions	Unique three-layered approach including analysis of client and therapist experiences of the same GIM sessions, and analysis of the music used during those sessions
Hogan	1999/1997	Published proceedings based on author's master's thesis	Descriptive phenomenological methods	Interviews with clients	9 adult clients who were terminally ill with cancer diagnoses	Client experiences of music therapy when terminally ill	Triangulated data collection

(Continued)

Table 41.2 continued

Author/s	Year	Type of Source	Methodology	Methods	Participant Population	Phenomena of Interest	Comments
Milgram–Luterman	2000	Doctoral dissertation	Hermeneutic phenomenological methods along with methods related to symbolic interactionism	Observations, interviews with student participants, participant journals, researcher log, interviews with professor	Senior undergraduate music therapy students and the group facilitator/ researcher	Student experience of a peer support group; music therapist facilitator experience of said group	
Skewes	2001	Doctoral dissertation	Methods modeled after Giorgi (1975); plus author's adaptation of Arnason's (1998) narrative description as basis for understanding musical data	Interviews, musical analysis	6 bereaved adolescents and their improvised music	Experience of group music therapy designed specifically for bereaved adolescents	Two-part study: 1) experiences of the participants; 2) phenomenological musical analysis of the group's improvised music
Wheeler	2002	Journal article	Origin of methods not specifically stated, but representative of descriptive phenomenological methods	Interviews	8 undergraduate students who were enrolled in music therapy practicum	Experiences and concerns of music therapy students engaged in clinical practicum	Students interviewed 3 times over the course of 1 year

Author/s	Year	Type of Source	Methodology	Methods	Participant Population	Phenomena of Interest	Comments
Gardstrom	2004	Journal article	Descriptive phenomenological methods; phenomenological music analysis	Music analysis, interviews, field notes, chart review	6 adolescents with severe behavioral and emotional disturbances, in partial hospitalization programs	Experience of clinical improvisation with adolescents with severe behavioral and emotional disturbances, from both adolescents' and therapist's perspective	Used Bruscia's (1987) Improvisation Assessment Profiles as part of music analysis
Marom	2004	Journal article based on author's master's thesis	Descriptive phenomenological methods as described by Forinash (1995) and Smeijsters (1997)	Interviews	10 experienced music therapists from a variety of clinical orientations	Experience of spirituality in music therapy from the therapist's perspective	
Dillard	2006	Journal article	Modified version of Giorgi's (1975) method for analyzing individual transcripts, plus cross-case analysis	Interviews	8 psychodynamically-oriented music therapists from the United States	Therapist experience of musical countertransference	"Impartial observer" to review trustworthiness of data
Gadberry	2006	Master's thesis	Colaizzi's (1978) descriptive phenomenological methods	Analysis of session videotapes, therapist session notes, therapist reflective journals, interview with mother and play therapist's written responses to questions	Seven-year-old boy with autism, his play therapist and his mother	Experience of music therapy and play therapy co-treatment for a boy with autism from parent's and therapists' perspectives	Triangulation of data sources; member checking

(Continued)

Table 41.2 continued

Author/s	Year	Type of Source	Methodology	Methods	Participant Population	Phenomena of Interest	Comments
Rykov	2006, 2007, 2008	Dissertation and related journal articles	Hermeneutic phenomenological methods influenced by van Manen; Arts-informed research	Intuitive analysis of data, arts-informed dissemination of results	10 adults with cancer	Experience of an 8-week music therapy cancer support group	Represented results through music, images, and poetry
Kim	2008	Journal article	Combination of methods by Giorgi (1985), Racette (1989) and Comeau (1991)	Interviews (with prepping of participants)	7 music therapists (from 3 different cultural backgrounds) who had experienced cross-cultural supervision	Supervisee's experience of being misunderstood and understood during cross-cultural music therapy supervision	Prepped participants to recall experiences in advance of the interview
Lindenfelser, Grocke, and McFerran	2008	Journal article (based on the first author's master's thesis)	Combination of methods by Giorgi (1975), Colaizzi (1978), and Moustakas (1994)	Interviews	7 bereaved mothers who had experienced music therapy with their terminally ill children	Bereaved parents' experience of music therapy with terminally ill child	
Muller	2008	Journal article	Descriptive phenomenological methods	Interviews	8 music therapists who experienced "being present" during 1:1 sessions with adult clients	Therapists' experiences of being present to their adult clients during 1:1 sessions	Formation of narrative "synopses" of each participant's experience

Clements-Cortés	2009, 2011	Doctoral dissertation and related journal article	Descriptive phenomenology that included aspects of case study research, narrative inquiry, and arts-based research	Interviews, session transcripts, music content, field notes, formal MT assessments, artwork created by researcher, artwork created by participants	4 adults with prognosis less than 6 months, receiving palliative care as in-patients, and two of their spouses	Participant, spouse and researcher/therapist experiences of relationship completion as facilitated by music therapy	Researcher created "artistic pieces" in reaction to the MT process, verified these with participants and used them to augment research dissemination
Ghetti	2011	Journal article	Predominantly methods of IPA as described by Smith and Eatough (2006) with adaptation to create distilled essences per participant modeled after Forinash and Grocke (2005) and others	Interviews	8 dual-certified music therapists/child life specialists with at least 3 years of pediatric MT experience since dual certification	Experience of being dual-certified in music therapy and child life, and the meaning of that lived experience	Organized by convergent and divergent experiences; no attempt to force one shared distilled essence of experience
Hahna	2011	Doctoral dissertation	Phenomenological methods of Giorgi (1975) and feminist methodology	Interviews, analytic memos and music lyrics	4 music therapy educators teaching music therapy at undergraduate and/or graduate levels	Feminist music therapy pedagogy as experienced by music therapy educators	Used member checking, triangulation of data and inter-rater reliability

(Continued)

Table 41.2 continued

Author/s	Year	Type of Source	Methodology	Methods	Participant Population	Phenomena of Interest	Comments
Hsiao	2011	Journal article	Phenomenological methods based on Moustakas' (1994) modification of the Stevick–Colaizzi–Keen method	Interviews	10 female music therapists who trained in the U.S., and returned to their countries of origin after graduating	Experience of reentry transition when returning to country of origin after completing music therapy training in the United States	Used purposive sampling with "maximum variation"; for trustworthiness, used partial external audit of data analysis and member checking
Hunt	2011	Doctoral dissertation	Neurophenomenological methods of Varela (1996)	Interviews, EEG coherence analysis	4 adults who underwent a single Bonny Method GIM session	Subjective and objective experience of a GIM session	Worked with an EEG lab and related experts to obtain and analyze the EEG data
Jónsdóttir	2011	Doctoral dissertation	Hermeneutic phenomenological analysis (not specifically IPA in the style of Smith)	Interviews (group and individual), questionnaires, participant diaries, transcriptions of music therapy sessions, researcher's reflective notes	7 mothers of children (aged 0–5 years) with special needs	Experience of musicking (with emphasis on songwriting) as part of 10 sessions of "music-caring" led by music therapist	Researcher as "participant observer"; triangulation of data sources
Jackson and Gardstrom	2012	Journal article	Generic form of qualitative content analysis with phenomenological intent	Participant journals, survey	9 female undergraduate music therapy students (from 2 universities in the U.S.)	Experience of being a "client" in short-term group music therapy	Mixed forms of data collection; researchers as interveners and analysts

Pothoulaki et al.	2012	Journal article	Interpretative Phenomenological Analysis	Interviews	9 adults with cancer diagnoses, attending out-patient services	Psychological processes involved in an improvisational music therapy program for adults with cancer	Provided an intervention (improvisational music therapy) and used IPA to examine
Young	2012	Journal article	Phenomenological methods based on Colaizzi (1978), Giorgi (1985) and others	Interviews	8 music therapists who had undergone GIM therapy	Client's experience of the postlude discussion phase in GIM	Also examined participants' reflections and observations related to their lived experiences of postlude discussion

Table 41.3 Steps of Phenomenological Analysis of Music. Data from Ferrara (1984)

Step (1)	Listening 'openly' to a piece, allowing any kind of meaning to arise (syntactical, semantic, or ontological), and describing that listening
Step (2)	Listening for textural form (*syntactical* meanings) and describing those meanings, while trying to bracket out semantic and ontological meanings
Step (3)	Listening for *semantic* meanings and describing such meanings
Step (4)	Listening for *ontological* meanings and describing such meanings
Step (5)	Engaging again in open listening and integrating the syntactical, semantic and ontological meanings through description

University in 1982 (Forinash and Grocke 2005). This exchange prompted music therapists working in the United States to contemplate the appropriateness of the use of phenomenological methods to study the complexity of musical experiences (Forinash and Grocke 2005). Music therapists were particularly drawn to the potential of phenomenology to enable the exploration and description of complex and subjective experiences related to the experiencing of music (Racette 2004). Carolyn Kenny presented a session entitled, *Phenomenological Research: A Promise for the Healing Arts* in 1983 at the Canadian Association for Music Therapy conference, in which she discussed the implications of using phenomenological research in the study of music therapy and other creative arts therapies (Forinash and Grocke 2005).

Around this time, Ruud (1987) and Kenny (1987) authored doctoral dissertations that were groundbreaking in their use of phenomenological methodology for the study of music therapy. Ruud (1987) was the first to adapt Ferrara's method of phenomenological analysis of music to render it appropriate for the analysis of musical improvisation. Ruud suggested the insertion of structural, semantic, and pragmatic levels of analysis in place of Ferrara's syntactical, semantic, and ontological levels (Christensen 2012). Ruud valued the interrelationships between participants within an improvisation over the precise musical form or syntax, and he proposed that pragmatic issues of meaning and therapeutic effect should be emphasized within the analysis (Christensen 2012).

In her dissertation entitled, "The Field of Play: A Theoretical Study of Music Therapy Process" (1987), Kenny used the phenomenological method of free imaginative variation to uncover essential essences of the music therapy process. The essences she identified were then modified by professionals from related areas of practice, for example art therapy, applied music, and philosophy, expanding the context of their meaning, and making the essences meaningful to professionals from different orientations.

In addition to Ruud, several other researchers found Ferrara's (1984) method to be a helpful starting point for the phenomenological analysis of music-centered forms of music therapy. Forinash and Gonzalez (1989) adapted Ferrara's method for the field of music therapy, and their approach has been subsequently adopted or modified by numerous other music therapy researchers. Forinash and Gonzalez (1989) expanded Ferrara's method to include seven steps:

1. Describing the client's background including psychosocial history.
2. Describing the course of the actual music therapy session.

3. Analyzing musical elements within the session (syntax).
4. Describing the sounds produced by the client, therapist, and environment ("sound as such").
5. Describing any referential meaning within the music of the session (semantics).
6. Considering and describing the perspective and meaning the client brings to the session from his/her own "lifeworld."
7. Evaluating in a "meta-critical" way the data collected in the preceding steps.

Forinash and Gonzalez (1989) illustrated this seven-step process by examining a single music therapy session with a woman at the end of life, and analyzing the clinical experience through a phenomenological lens. The ultimate aim of their approach was to capture a broader picture of the phenomenon of music therapy used with clients at the end of life by bringing all of the various subtle aspects of the experience into awareness, so that music therapists might be better prepared to assist their clients during the process of active dying.

Kasayka (1991) used Forinash and Gonzalez's (1989) adaptation of Ferrara to examine Bonny Method of Guided Imagery and Music (BMGIM) sessions. The client experienced imagery while listening to the five musical pieces making up the *Peak Experience* program. Kasayka then aligned the client's sequences of imagery with descriptions of the music occurring at the time of the imagery, and then commented on interrelations between the two (Forinash and Grocke 2005). Amir (1990) also adopted Forinash and Gonzalez's (1989) method to examine the use of music therapy with a young adult who had experienced a significant spinal cord injury. Using this methodology, Amir was able to describe and understand the various dimensions of meaning of the young man's improvised song within music therapy sessions. Amir observed music therapy sessions, reviewed audio and video data from the sessions, and interviewed the client and therapist to gain multiple perspectives on the client's experience.

Early researchers in phenomenological music therapy also found ways to apply the methods of Amedeo Giorgi and Paul Colaizzi of the Duquesne University school of phenomenology to music therapy research. Racette (1989, 2004) adopted methods by Colaizzi (1978) and Giorgi (1970) when authoring a master's thesis regarding eight adults' experiences of listening to music when upset. After grouping key statements, Racette prepared a synopsis of each participant's experience, compared all synopses to create an *essential description* containing elements common to all participants, and paired participant quotations with each common characteristic of the essential description to create an *illustrated description*.

In her doctoral dissertation, Forinash (1990) moved away from Ferrara's (1984) approach and instead adapted Giorgi's (1975) methods to identify the essences of music therapy with people approaching the end of life. She recorded and transcribed music therapy sessions, wrote process notes, bracketed her personal experiences related to the phenomenon, transformed transcripts and process notes into "meaning units" and those in turn into essences of the experience, and integrated and synthesized the essences into a description of the underlying structure of the phenomenon to enable the creation of a comprehensive description of the phenomenon.

Similarly, Comeau (1991, 2004) adapted and combined methods from Colaizzi (1978), Giorgi (1975), Racette (1989), and others in his master's thesis that examined eleven music therapists' experiences of being effective and ineffective with clients. Comeau created essences of each individual participant's experiences of effectiveness and ineffectiveness and then made comparisons across participants. Through the process of comparison, Comeau identified five main themes across participants and was able to discover several pertinent indicators of therapeutic effectiveness and ineffectiveness.

As phenomenological music therapy research became more prevalent, and researchers more experienced in such methods, they began to explore variations in method. Forinash (1992) examined the therapist's experience of engaging in Nordoff-Robbins clinical improvisation by interviewing eight music therapists who were completing their first year of NRMT training. Forinash included an interesting variation to assist in contextualizing the participants' responses. The standard practice of videotaping all clinical sessions at the NRMT clinic at New York University allowed the researcher to ask participants to select a videotape of a session in which they had improvised. The researcher and the participant reviewed the selected videotape together and the researcher inquired as to the participant's experience of clinical improvisation as it unfolded during that particular session. Forinash found that when participants reflected back upon their experience of clinical improvisation during a single session, they often connected with their own musical histories and life experiences beyond the context of the session, and these related experiences were brought to life in the session. The study enabled Forinash to identify factors whose further exploration could enrich future clinical training in this particular approach, for example, the identified "profound sense of facing the unknown in clinical improvisation" and the related sense of vulnerability (Forinash 1992, p. 138).

Grocke (1999) also adopted methods from Giorgi and Colaizzi in her doctoral dissertation of pivotal moments in the Bonny Method of Guided Imagery and Music. She interviewed seven clients and asked them to recall a session that had been pivotal, one that stood out "as distinctive or unique" (p. 69). In an expansion of the method, Grocke then interviewed the BMGIM therapists who had facilitated the pivotal sessions with the interviewed clients. She asked therapists about their memories and experiences of the pivotal sessions, and used the same methods of phenomenological analysis on transcripts of therapist interviews. Grocke then embarked on a third phase of the study, which involved creating a phenomenological description of the music that was used during the pivotal sessions. In the musical analysis, Grocke grouped significant musical "points of change" into musical meaning units. Taking full advantage of the detailed description and analysis inherent in phenomenological methods, Grocke then paired descriptions of the imagery experiences alongside descriptions of the music to tease out which aspects of the music might have stimulated particular imagery. Grocke's final distilled essence of pivotal moments in GIM reflected a combination of the essences from the seven clients, two music therapists, and the phenomenological descriptions of the music.

Phenomenological music therapy in the 21st century

As the field of music therapy ushered in a new millennium, interest in non-positivist forms of research that capture the multifaceted and subjective nature of music therapy experiences has continued to grow. Music therapy researchers have continued to mold and modify phenomenological methods to enable the exploration of complex and nuanced phenomena. Researchers have applied phenomenological analysis to lived experience as captured in interview transcripts, as well as to actual musical material, such as clinical improvisations (Skewes

2001). The expansion of methods has resulted in a more diverse research base that continues to evolve as theory, research practice, and technology develop. Several themes have emerged from the expansion of phenomenological music therapy research in the 21st century.

New perspectives

Phenomenological research has enabled the appreciation of music therapy phenomena from multiple perspectives. Researchers have explored parental and caregiver perspectives on the experience of music therapy (Clements-Cortés 2009, 2011; Gadberry 2006; Jónsdóttir 2011; Lindenfelser et al. 2008). Lindenfelser et al. (2008) were able to uncover common experiences among seven mothers whose terminally ill children had received music therapy prior to their death. Using descriptive phenomenological methods, the researchers created a cohesive global essence that encapsulated the overall experiences of the women, while still including experiences that were unique to certain mothers using their own language to do so. Similarly, Jónsdóttir (2011) acknowledged the stressors that mothers of children with special needs face and wondered if a process of music-based therapeutic support would help such mothers move through issues of loss and grief to improve their ability to cope. She provided ten, weekly *music-caring* sessions that used musicking (Small 2011), especially the process of songwriting, to provide an emotionally supportive and empathetic group context for the mothers. Jónsdóttir used a hermeneutic form of phenomenological analysis to examine the mothers' experience of *music-caring*, and found that essential aspects included: the group, musicking, songwriting, the recorded CD, the therapist, "me and my time," process and personal change, and the containing/mediating function of the participants' diary. In particular, Jónsdóttir described the essence of the mothers' musicking:

> Musicking brought joy and beauty, change and possibilities, as well as the relaxing, welcoming and caring atmosphere. Musicking together brought closeness, supported empathetic listening, and an empowered awareness of emotions by facilitating and deepening emotion expression.
>
> Jónsdóttir 2011, p. 369

Jónsdóttir concluded that the process of music-caring provided a resource for the mothers that enabled them to address their multidimensional needs.

Music therapy researchers have also expanded their inquiries into the therapist's experience of music therapy. Dillard (2006) explored the inner processes of psychodynamically-oriented music therapists reflecting on the experience of musical countertransference. Dillard used descriptive phenomenology methods, and as a result of the analysis she was able to expand upon her previous definition of musical countertransference to more accurately reflect the lived experience of the music therapists who participated. Muller (2008) examined music therapists' experiences of being present to their clients. Through the use of descriptive phenomenology, Muller explored how eight experienced music therapists who practiced from psychodynamic, existential-humanistic, or transpersonal orientations defined *being present* as a music therapist and how they perceived this state of being. Muller was able to explore the phenomenon and develop insight into the interactions between client, therapist and music that are involved in being present.

Marom (2004) explored the nature of spiritual moments in music therapy from the therapist's perspective. She purposefully sought experienced music therapists from a variety of clinical orientations. After interviewing ten music therapists, she followed descriptive phenomenological procedures, but also included several narrative stories that directly arose from the participants' data and helped illustrate certain meaning units. She analyzed across participants to identify recurrent themes, and formed a single cohesive description of the overall experience. Marom identified a conceptualization of spirituality grounded in her participants' experiences:

> Together the therapists portrayed spirituality as a dynamic force that at once reaches inward to touch the greatest depth of the human soul and outward to form powerful transpersonal connections with others and with God.
>
> Marom 2004, p. 65

She concluded that music therapists felt prepared to handle and incorporate spiritual experiences when they arose in sessions. At such moments, the therapists experienced intense emotions, but were able to continue in their particular roles within the session and were able to help clients transition back to reality once the spiritual experience had ended.

Hsiao (2011) was interested in the perspective of international music therapy students who had graduated from programs in the United States and then returned to their countries of origin. She used descriptive phenomenology to explore the experience of ten female graduates upon returning to their culture of origin, what it was like to try to establish music therapy careers in those countries of origin, and what types of circumstances impacted those experiences. In keeping with a phenomenological approach in the style of Husserl, Hsiao answered all of the interview questions herself in order to identify and bracket her own past experience of being an international student trained in the United States. Hsiao used peer researchers as part of a partial external audit of data analysis to promote trustworthiness, and she verified themes and descriptions with participants as part of the process of *member checking*. Hsiao related the study outcomes to existing theory and pointed out where her data varied. For example, she identified that the shift from student to professional, and the stark contrast between the professional development of music therapy in the US versus in countries of origin complicated the participants' experience of reentry transition. By synthesizing the outcomes of her data, Hsiao was able to make helpful recommendations for music therapy academic programs in the US, and for international students who plan to return to their countries of origin.

In addition to the therapist's perspective of music therapy, researchers have also addressed the supervisee's perspective of music therapy training. Kim (2008) explored the impact of cultural differences between supervisee and supervisor in the process of music therapy clinical supervision. Kim defined cross-cultural supervision as occurring when the supervisee and supervisor identify as members of two different ethnic, racial or cultural groups. She postulated that such differences might cause overt or implicit obstacles within the supervision process, thereby impacting effectiveness. She adapted Comeau's (1991) procedures for interviewing in which participants were asked to

> ... look back at what they had experienced in supervision, relive the experience moment by moment, and then describe it in as much detail as possible.
>
> Kim 2008, p. 10

Kim used descriptive phenomenology to examine seven supervisees' experiences of being misunderstood and being understood during the course of cross-cultural music therapy supervision. Kim concluded that pre-existing cultural differences between supervisee and supervisor will likely enter the supervisory experience, that issues related to power and authority can become intensified, and that supervisors' unresolved issues related to culture may negatively impact the relationship. Kim identified key elements for supervisors to consider when engaging in cross-cultural supervision.

Stemming from a desire to understand the impact of personal music therapy on students' development as music therapists, music therapy educators have studied undergraduate students' experience of engaging in short-term group music therapy (Jackson and Gardstrom 2012). Jackson and Gardstrom (2012) used qualitative content analysis to examine what knowledge students gain about themselves and others while undergoing group music therapy, and what they find most meaningful about the experience. Nine female junior and senior undergraduate music therapy students at two universities elected to take part in a series of music therapy groups led by the educator/researcher from the opposite university. Three, two-hour sessions were held approximately two weeks apart and consisted of a variety of music interventions as well as the use of other creative arts and verbal processing. The researchers gathered data through participants' personal journals as well as an online summary at the study conclusion. The researchers enlisted the assistance of an external qualitative researcher to verify the appropriateness of the descriptive codes they had formed, and paired codes with illustrative statements from the raw data. Participants most often wrote about personal insights gained during the process of group music therapy, yet the concluding survey indicated that gaining an increased sense of empathy toward the client was the most important part of the experience for them. The researchers concluded that self-awareness and effective therapeutic relationships within music therapy settings are related, and worthy of addressing in academic training.

Triangulation

Phenomenological researchers aim for richness and depth in their study of phenomena. Triangulation enables increased breadth or depth in the research process by diversifying data sources, employing multiple data analysts, using a variety of methods to address the research question, or examining the data through the lens of multiple theories or perspectives (Patton 2002). Several contemporary phenomenological music therapy researchers have used triangulation of data sources to enrich their descriptions of phenomena (e.g. Clements-Cortés 2009, 2011; Gadberry 2006; Jónsdóttir 2011; Milgram-Luterman 2000) or have used triangulation of data collectors (Hogan 1999). Milgram-Luterman (2000) conducted a phenomenological study of a music therapy peer support group as her doctoral dissertation. She sought to explore the inclusion of personal growth experiences, via a peer support group, within an undergraduate music therapy program. Milgram-Luterman used elements of a hermeneutic phenomenological approach to understand and interpret the experiences of undergraduate members of a music therapy peer support group, as well as her own experiences as facilitator/researcher. She gathered data from observations of meetings, participant interviews, participant journals, researcher logs, clinical supervisor feedback and interviews with a professor teaching the related core courses. Collecting data from multiple sources allowed her to apply the theory of symbolic interactionism to examine the verbal, non-verbal, and musical interactions between group members, and develop a broader perspective of the experience.

Clements-Cortés (2009, 2011) included aspects of case study research and narrative inquiry in her phenomenological analysis of the experience of relationship completion during the process of music therapy for four adults receiving palliative care as inpatients. The research included perspectives from the participants, spouses, and the researcher/therapist, and encompassed numerous sources of data: music used in music therapy sessions, content of discussions that occurred during sessions, researcher's field notes, medical chart notes, formal written music therapy assessment, transcriptions of recorded music therapy sessions, transcripts of semi-structured interviews with participants and spouses, artwork created by the participants, and artwork/creative pieces made by the researcher/therapist. From the voluminous data gathered from multiple sources, Clements-Cortés formed detailed case studies for each participant, which enabled the identification of themes per participant, and then engaged in cross-case analysis to identify global themes. Cross-case analysis resulted in the identification of six global themes common to all participants: love, loss, gratitude, growth/transformation, courage/strength, and saying good-bye. All of these aspects were integral parts of the process of relationship completion.

In her study of mothers of young children with special needs, Jónsdóttir (2011) included data from multiple sources. Data were comprised of: a questionnaire regarding general information about the participants, a questionnaire completed prior to the first group session, written diaries kept by the participants throughout the course of the study, transcriptions of session content, transcription of the group interview, transcriptions of the individual interviews, and researcher's reflective notes. Similarly, in her study of the experience of music therapy and play therapy co-treatment with a boy with autism, Gadberry (2006) gathered multiple forms of data. Sources of data included: videotapes of co-treatment sessions, transcriptions of co-treatment sessions, therapists' session notes, therapists' reflective journals, transcript from an audiotaped interview with client's mother, and the play therapist's written responses to a series of questions.

Inclusion of music analysis

With a desire to develop upon more indigenous forms of music therapy research, several researchers have included analysis of client or therapist music as part of the phenomenological analysis. As did Grocke (1999), Skewes (2001) added an additional source of data to her study of bereaved adolescents engaging in group music therapy sessions by applying phenomenological methods to analyze music material. Skewes viewed the improvised music material as representing participants' experiences as they evolved in the sessions. She used a process of phenomenological distillation to transform the music improvisations into narrative form, and had these narratives verified by experts. Once final verified narratives were formed, Skewes examined the narratives for meaning. Musical analysis included both descriptive and interpretative phases.

Gardstrom (2004) found Bruscia's (1987) Improvisation Assessment Profiles to be useful in analyzing the intramusical and intermusical relationships occurring in improvisations created by the therapist/researcher and the adolescents with severe behavioral and emotional disturbances with whom she worked. Gardstrom sought to understand the meaning of clinical music improvisation for this group of adolescents. She engaged six male and female adolescents who were attending partial hospitalization programs in five individual sessions of music therapy consisting of clinical improvisation and verbal processing. Sources of data included analysis of the music improvisations, interview transcripts, researcher's field notes, researcher's reflexive journal, information from chart reviews and staff interviews, and transcripts of concluding interviews. Through the process of analysis, the researcher was able to compare and contrast the ways that participants and the therapist drew meaning from the experience of improvisation. A primary finding of this study was that clinical improvisation was not always perceived of, or identified, as meaningful for both client and therapist.

Other researchers have included music material in their phenomenological analyses, including song lyrics and music used in sessions (Clements-Cortés 2009, 2011) and transcriptions of music therapy sessions (Gadberry 2006; Jónsdóttir 2011).

Reflexivity and introspection

In addition to seeking data from multiple sources, including from participants and from the music, researchers have also examined reflexivity within the research process. Phenomenological researchers, and those engaging in hermeneutic forms of phenomenology in particular, are aware of their impact on the processes and outcomes of research. Wheeler (2002) brought herself into the examination of undergraduate music therapy students' experience of clinical practica. She sought to understand how student perspectives varied from her own, and employed a longitudinal format to study students' perceptions at three points across the span of an academic year. Unique to this study was that the longitudinal approach allowed Wheeler to ask participants in subsequent interviews what they recalled about the first interview and how their experiences changed over time. Wheeler reflected upon the multiplicity of roles she took in this study, and encouraged participants to express how, if at all, their responses were influenced by the fact that she was also at times their practicum class teacher or supervisor. Wheeler examined her own experience of the research phenomenon within the discussion section and concludes:

> This research has allowed me to learn about my students' experiences in a manner that would not normally be available to me as a faculty member. This has been a real privilege. Although I know that I will never be able to totally understand things from a student's viewpoint, nor will I probably ever hear that viewpoint completely candidly, I believe that I approached this while doing the study.
>
> Wheeler 2002, p. 303

Wheeler compared her perspectives and assumptions to those revealed by her students, and pointed out areas where she has grown as a faculty member and supervisor as a result of this research.

Young (2012) also asked her participants to reflect upon their lived experiences, and in turn, she made interpretations about the psychological meanings underlying their experiences and their reflections. Young interviewed eight music therapists who had received GIM therapy to determine their experiences of the postlude discussion component of GIM sessions, and to solicit their reflections and observations on those experiences. Participants were asked to reflect upon postlude discussion sessions that were helpful and memorable versus those that were not. Participants' experiences varied greatly, but provided insight into the impact of the postlude discussion phase on clients and on their therapeutic progress.

Arts-based approaches in research

Acknowledging the artistic nature of music therapy, some researchers have embraced the use of arts-based approaches as a form of data collection or to convey the outcomes of their phenomenological studies. Clements-Cortés (2009, 2011) used client artwork and her own creation of artistic pieces during the course of her study of music therapy for relationship completion for adults at the end of life. The researcher/therapist constructed creative pieces in the form of poems or love letters following the interview phase that were inspired by her work with her four participants. These pieces offered an additional reflection on the experience of the participants and the researcher/therapist, and engaging in the process helped the researcher deepen her understanding of the participants' experiences. Furthermore, the researcher/therapist gave the artistic pieces to the participants to seek verification, and if the pieces were found to be reflective of the participant's experience, participants were encouraged to keep the creations as part of disseminating the results of the research.

Rykov (2006, 2007, 2008) used hermeneutic phenomenology (influenced by van Manen) to explore the meaning of a music therapy support group for ten adult cancer survivors. The data she collected included transcriptions of individual and group meetings, journal entries, session evaluation forms, music, images, and descriptive statistics. Rykov used an arts-based approach to represent and disseminate the results of her research through use of images (Rykov 2008), "melodic-poetic transcription" (Rykov 2007), poetry, and music (Rykov 2006). These arts-based expressive forms helped Rykov represent the complexity and multidimensionality of the phenomenon of interest.

Recent methodological developments

Music therapy researchers continue to search to find ways to adequately address the complex and subjective nature of music therapy. Researchers recognize that a single form of research methodology can rarely capture all aspects of a phenomenon. Contemporary methodologies are being developed that bridge subjective and objective examination of a phenomenon, and have direct application to music therapy.

Music neurophenomenology

Through her doctoral dissertation, Hunt (2011) aimed to study the experience of BMGIM in order to examine evidence that might explain a mind-body connection during the experience of guided imagery and music. She adopted Varela's (1996) neurophenomenological approach to correlate participants' subjective descriptions of their GIM experiences with electroencephalographic (EEG) data of those experiences. Four participants partook in a single GIM session in which the imagery script emphasized affect, body, interaction, kinesthetic, memories and visual kinds of imagery experiences. Subsequently, participants described their experiences to the researcher while watching a video playback of the session. An outside consultant completed "coherence analyses" on the EEG data. Hunt then synthesized the EEG and phenomenological data per participant, and used cross-case analysis to identify patterns of experience and brain response. Participants displayed unique correlations of subjective experience to brain response, though the researcher was able to draw conclusions based on the identification of several elements common across participants.

Interpretative Phenomenological Analysis

Though music therapy researchers have previously incorporated interpretative elements in their phenomenological analyses, the use of IPA is gaining popularity as a means to explore psychological processes underlying music therapy phenomena (Pothoulaki et al. 2012). Ghetti (2011) found IPA to be useful in enabling a detailed description of the experience of being dual-certified in music therapy and child life, and in interpreting the meaning of such lived experience. Ghetti followed procedures for IPA as described by Smith and Eatough (2006), though she modified the descriptive phase to create a distilled essence of each participant's experience of being dual-certified. Such modifications are permissible and appropriate under the flexible guidelines of IPA (Smith 2004; Smith and Eatough 2006). After analyzing the data by case and creating a distilled essence for each of her eight participants, Ghetti completed a cross-case analysis to identify themes that converged and diverged among participants. Ghetti found that the lived experiences of dual certified clinicians reflected two main overarching themes of identity and flexibility, where flexibility manifested in several areas including theoretical orientation, professional role, and clinical approaches. Furthermore, the nine resulting "superordinate" themes mostly related to "issues surrounding the formation and substance of professional identity" (p. 328).

Pothoulaki et al. (2012) provided an improvisational music therapy group for adults with cancer, and then used IPA to explore the psychological processes involved in such a group. The primary investigator was a psychologist, and a music therapist helped develop and implement the co-led music therapy treatment sessions. The authors chose IPA due to its appropriate fit with the field of health psychology, which examines issues of wellness and illness. The authors felt that IPA would enable a deeper level of analysis and comprehension of participants' experiences of a music therapy group and the psychological processes underlying such experiences. They sought to move beyond the determination of the efficacy of music therapy in this context, and instead consider the *psychological value* of engaging in such a therapy. The intervention consisted of twice-weekly semi-structured group music therapy sessions in a style consistent with the Nordoff Robbins music therapy approach. Sessions were co-led by a music therapist and a psychologist and concluded with verbal processing related to the musical experience. Researchers analyzed the data per case to identify emergent themes, and then engaged in cross-case analysis. Recurrent themes that arose in the analysis were reflective of aspects related to illness and psychological well-being and to social aspects of the group experience. Themes were linked to the situatedness of the data, and:

> … all the identified themes derived from the experience of participants in the music therapy sessions as this experience was perceived and filtered through "the eyes" of their current reality as an inseparable part of their existence: cancer.
>
> Pothoulaki et al. 2012, p. 65

The researchers concluded that music therapy created a means for creative expression, helped to form and unify the group, and provided unique therapeutic benefits due to the possibility for non-verbal expression.

Considerations for phenomenological research

Since the process of data analysis in phenomenological research is inherently subjective, and because the process may be flexible and responsive to changing needs during the course of the study, it is important for researchers to be transparent in reporting their methods and to engage in measures that will improve trustworthiness. The researcher may need to modify some aspects of the methods as the research progresses, in order to accommodate needs and preferences of participants and to assure that the phenomenon of interest is captured most completely (Gardstrom 2004). Thus, phenomenological methods may at times serve as a guide that remains somewhat flexible to the adaptation of methods depending upon how themes emerge during the process of analysis (Comeau 1991, 2004). Researchers may employ external research consultants to conduct regular auditing or oversight of the data collection and interviewing process to help assure that the researcher's biases are not contributing to the unintentional leading of participants in a certain direction (Gardstrom 2004).

In addition to issues of transparency and trustworthiness, another factor that arises in phenomenological research is the often-disproportionate percentage of time spent on data analysis. McFerran and Hunt (2008) discuss the often-disproportionate human contact to data analysis ratio. McFerran states that during the course of her doctoral dissertation research, she interacted with participants throughout a 10-week intervention, interviewed each one of them once, but then spent two years analyzing their interview and musical data. The desire to have participants engaged in more aspects of the research process led her to subsequently adopt participant action research as a means to expand upon themes that arose in her dissertation research.

Additional resources

It is beyond the scope of this chapter to provide detailed instruction on the step-by-step implementation of phenomenological music therapy research. Readers are encouraged to review studies of interest that have been described herein, for examples of specific methodological approaches. McFerran and Grocke (2007) have provided a systematic and thorough description of a seven-step phenomenological analysis rooted in Husserlian philosophy and the methods of the Duquesne School of Empirical Phenomenology (as exemplified by Giorgi [1975]) that may be considered a form of microanalysis when applied to music therapy interview data. The authors include two stages of imaginative variation, consistent with Moustakas (1990), and describe the creation of individual distilled essences for each participant. Readers intending to engage in phenomenological research are encouraged to select methods that are congruent with their philosophical and theoretical orientations, and are well-matched to answer their research questions.

Summary

Phenomenology offers particular advantages as a research methodology as it allows for a contextual understanding of the complex, lived realities of the individuals who engage in therapy (Lopez and Willis 2004). As music therapy researchers, we may join van Manen in using phenomenology to "involve the voice in an original singing of the world" (1990, p. 13), and to include artistic dimensions of music therapy in all aspects of the research process. It is likely that researchers will develop creative new variants that will spur the continued expansion of phenomenological methodology well into the future.

NOTES

1. Alternatively referred to as 'interpretative' phenomenology or 'interpretive' phenomenology (Finlay 2009).
2. The concept of *reflexivity* may be described as 'thoughtful, self-aware evaluation of the intersubjective dynamics between the researcher and researched... [which] involves critical self-reflection of how researcher's background, assumptions, positioning and behaviour impacts on the research process' (Finlay 2008, p. 3).

REFERENCES

Amir, D. (1990). A song is born: Discovering meaning in improvised songs through a phenomenological analysis of two music therapy sessions with a traumatic spinal-cord injured young adult. *Music Therapy* 9(1): 62–81.

Arnason, C. (1998). The experience of music therapists in an improvisational music therapy group. Unpublished Doctoral Thesis, New York University, New York, USA.

Bednall, J. (2006). Epoch and bracketing within the phenomenological paradigm. *Issues in Educational Research* 16(2): 123–138.

Bruscia, K. (1987). *Improvisational Models of Music Therapy*. Springfield, IL: Charles C. Thomas.

Bruscia, K. (2005). First-person research. In: B. Wheeler (ed.), *Music Therapy Research*, 2nd ed., pp. 379–391. Gilsum, NH: Barcelona Publishers.

Christensen, E. (2012). Music listening, music therapy, phenomenology and neuroscience. Doctoral dissertation. Aalborg University, Denmark.

Clements-Cortés, A. (2009). Episodes of relationship completion through song in palliative care. Doctoral dissertation. University of Toronto, Canada.

Clements-Cortés, A. (2011). Portraits of music therapy in facilitating relationship completion at the end of life. *Music and Medicine* 3(1): 31–39.

Colaizzi, P.F. (1978). Psychological research as the phenomenologist views it. In: R.S. Valle and M. King (eds), *Existential-phenomenological Alternatives for Psychology*, pp. 48–71. New York: Oxford University Press.

Comeau, P. (1991). A phenomenological investigation of being effective as a music therapist. Master's thesis. Temple University, Philadelphia, PA.

Comeau, P. (2004). A phenomenological investigation of being effective as a music therapist. *Qualitative Inquiries in Music Therapy* 1: 19–35.

Crotty, M. (1998). *The Foundations of Social Research: Meaning and Perspectives in the Research Process*. Thousand Oaks, CA: Sage Publications.

Dillard, L.M. (2006). Musical countertransference experiences of music therapists: A phenomenological study. *The Arts in Psychotherapy* 33(3): 208–217.

Ferrara, L. (1984). Phenomenology as a tool for musical analysis. *The Musical Quarterly* 70(3): 355–373.

Finlay, L. (2008). A dance between the reduction and reflexivity: Explicating the 'phenomenological psychological attitude'. *Journal of Phenomenological Psychology* 39: 1–32.

Finlay, L. (2009). Debating phenomenological research methods. *Phenomenology & Practice* 3(1): 6–25.

Forinash, M. (1990). *A phenomenology of music therapy with the terminally ill*. Doctoral dissertation. New York University.

Forinash, M. (1992). A phenomenological analysis of Nordoff-Robbins approach to music therapy: The lived experience of clinical improvisation. *Music Therapy* 11(1): 120–141.

Forinash, M. (1995). Phenomenological research. In: B. L. Wheeler (ed.), *Music therapy research: Quantitative and qualitative perspectives*, pp. 368–387. Gilsum, NH: Barcelona.

Forinash, M. and Gonzalez, D. (1989). A phenomenological perspective of music therapy. *Music Therapy* 8(1): 35–46.

Forinash, M. and Grocke, D. (2005). Phenomenological inquiry. In: Wheeler, B. (ed.) *Music therapy research*, 2nd ed., pp. 321–334. Gilsum, NH: Barcelona Publishers.

Gadberry, A. (2006). *A phenomenological study of the co-treatment of music therapy and play therapy with a boy diagnosed with autism*. Master's thesis. Texas Woman's University.

Gardstrom, S.C. (2004). An investigation of meaning in clinical music improvisation with troubled adolescents. *Qualitative Inquiries in Music Therapy* 1(4): 77–160.

Gearing, R.E. (2004). Bracketing in research: A typology. *Qualitative Health Research* 14(10): 1429–1452.

Ghetti, C.M. (2011). Clinical practice of dual-certified music therapists/child life specialists: A phenomenological study. *Journal of Music Therapy* 48(3): 317–345.

Giorgi, A. (1970). *Psychology as a Human Science: A Phenomenologically Based Approach*. New York: Harper and Row.

Giorgi, A. (1975). An application of phenomenological method in psychology. In: Giorgi, A., Fischer, C., and Murray, E. (eds), *Duquesne Studies in Phenomenological Psychology: Volume II*, pp. 72–79. Pittsburgh, PA: Duquesne University Press.

Giorgi, A. (ed.) (1985). *Phenomenology and Psychological Research*. Pittsburgh, PA: Duquesne University Press.

Giorgi, A. (1989). One type of analysis of descriptive data: Procedures involved in following a phenomenological method. *Methods* 1: 39–61.

Giorgi, A. (1997). The theory, practice, and evaluation of the phenomenological method as a qualitative research procedure. *Journal of Phenomenological Psychology* 28(2): 235–260.

Giorgi, A. (2008). Concerning a serious misunderstanding of the essence of the phenomenological method in psychology. *Journal of Phenomenological Psychology* 39: 33–58.

Giorgi, A. (2012). The Descriptive Phenomenological Psychological Method. *Journal of Phenomenological Psychology* 43: 3–12.

Giorgi, A. and Giorgi, B. (2008). Phenomenology. In: J.A. Smith (ed.), *Qualitative Psychology: A Practical Guide to Research Methods*, 2nd ed., pp. 26–52. Los Angeles: Sage Publications.

Grocke, D.E. (1999). *A phenomenological study of pivotal moments in guided imagery and music therapy*. Doctoral dissertation. University of Melbourne, Australia.

Hahna, N.D. (2011). Conversations from the classroom: Reflections on feminist music therapy pedagogy in teaching music therapy. Doctoral dissertation. Lesley University, Cambridge, MA.

Hogan, B. (1999). The experience of music therapy for terminally ill patients: A phenomenological research project. *MusicMedicine* 3: 242–252.

Hsiao, F. (2011). From the ideal to the real world: A phenomenological inquiry into student sojourners' reentry adaptation. *Journal of Music Therapy* 48(4): 420–439.

Hunt, A. (2011). A neurophenomenological description of the Guided Imagery and Music experience. Doctoral dissertation. Temple University, Philadelphia, PA.

Husserl, E. (1927). Phenomenology. For *Encyclopedia Britannica*. [Revised translation by R. Palmer.]

Jackson, N.A. and Gardstrom, S.C. (2012). Undergraduate music therapy students' experiences as clients in short-term group music therapy. *Music Therapy Perspectives* 30(1): 65–82.

Jónsdóttir, V. (2011). Music-caring within the framework of early intervention: The lived experience of a group of mothers of young children with special needs, participating in a music therapy group. Doctoral dissertation. Aalborg University, Denmark.

Kasayka, R. E. (1991). To meet and match the moment of hope: Transpersonal elements of the Guided Imagery and Music experience. Doctoral dissertation. New York University.

Kenny, C. (1987). The field of play: A theoretical study of music therapy process. Doctoral dissertation. The Fielding Institute, California.

Kim, S.A. (2008). The supervisee's experience in cross-cultural music therapy supervision. *Qualitative Inquiries in Music Therapy* 4: 1–44.

Laverty, S.M. (2003). Hermeneutic phenomenology and phenomenology: A comparison of historical and methodological considerations. *International Journal of Qualitative Methods* 2(3): 1–29.

LeVasseur, J.J. (2003). The problem of bracketing in phenomenology. *Qualitative Health Research* 13(3): 408–420.

Lindenfelser, K.J., Grocke, D., and McFerran, K. (2008). Bereaved parents' experiences of music therapy with their terminally ill child. *Journal of Music Therapy* 45(3): 330–348.

Lopez, K.A. and Willis, D.G. (2004). Descriptive versus interpretive phenomenology: Their contributions to nursing knowledge. *Qualitative Health Research* 14(5): 726–735.

Marom, M.K. (2004). Spiritual moments in music therapy: A qualitative study of the music therapist's experience. *Qualitative Inquiries in Music Therapy* 1: 37–76.

McFerran, K. and Grocke, D. (2007). Understanding music therapy experiences through interviewing: A phenomenological microanalysis. In: T. Wosch and T. Wigram (eds), *Microanalysis in Music Therapy: Methods, Techniques and Applications for Clinicians, Researchers, Educators, and Students*, pp. 273–284. Philadelphia: Jessica Kingsley Publishers.

McFerran, K. and Hunt, M. (2008). Learning from experiences in action: Music in schools to promote healthy coping with grief and loss. *Educational Action Research* 16(1): 43–54.

Milgram-Luterman, J. (2000). A phenomenological study of a music therapy peer support group for senior music therapy students. Doctoral dissertation. Michigan State University.

Moustakas, C. (1990). *Heuristic research: Design, methodology, and applications*. Sage Publications.

Moustakas, C. (1994). *Phenomenological Research Methods*. Thousand Oaks, CA: Sage.

Muller, B.J. (2008). A phenomenological investigation of the music therapist's experience of being present to clients. *Qualitative Inquires in Music Therapy* 4(3): 1–40.

Patton, M.Q. (2002). *Qualitative Research and Evaluation Methods*. 3rd ed. Thousand Oaks, CA: Sage Publications, Inc.

Pothoulaki, M., MacDonald, R., and Flowers, P. (2012). An interpretative phenomenological analysis of an improvisational music therapy program for cancer patients. *Journal of Music Therapy* 49(1): 45–67.

Racette, K. (1989). A phenomenological analysis of the experience of listening to music when upset. Master's thesis. Temple University.

Racette, K. (2004). A phenomenological analysis of the experience of listening to music when upset. *Qualitative Inquiries in Music Therapy* 1: 1–17.

Ruud, E. (1987). *Musikk som kommunikasjon og samhandling. Teoretiske perspektiv på musik-kterapien.* [Music as communication and interaction. Theoretical perspectives on music therapy.] Doctoral dissertation. University of Oslo.

Rykov, M.H. (2006). *Music at a time like this.* Doctoral dissertation. Ontario Institute for Studies in Education of the University of Toronto.

Rykov, M.H. (2007). Melodic-poetic representation: Research sings. *Canadian Journal of Music Therapy* 13(2): 160–170.

Rykov, M.H. (2008). Experiencing music therapy cancer support. *Journal of Health Psychology* 13(2): 190–200.

Skewes, K. (2001). The experience of group music therapy for six bereaved adolescents. Doctoral dissertation. University of Melbourne, Australia.

Small, C. (2011). *Musicking: The meanings of performing and listening.* Connecticut, USA: Wesleyan University Press.

Smeijsters, H. (1997). *Multiple perspectives: A guide to qualitative research in music therapy.* Gilsum, NH: Barcelona.

Smith, J.A. (2004). Reflecting on the development of interpretative phenomenological analysis and its contribution to qualitative research in psychology. *Qualitative Research in Psychology* 1: 39–54.

Smith, J.A. and Eatough, V. (2006). Interpretative phenomenological analysis. In: G.M. Breakwell, S. Hammond, C. Fife-Schaw, and J.A. Smith (eds), *Research Methods in Psychology*, 3rd ed., pp. 322–341. London: Sage.

Smith, J.A., Flowers, P., and Larkin, M. (2009). *Interpretative Phenomenological Analysis: Theory, Method and Research.* Thousand Oaks, CA: Sage Publications.

Streubert, H.J. and Carpenter, D.R. (1999). *Qualitative Research in Nursing: Advancing the Humanistic Imperative*, 2nd ed. Philadelphia: Lippincott.

van Manen, M. (1990). *Researching Lived Experience: Human Science for an Action Sensitive Psychology.* New York: SUNY Press.

Varela, F.J. (1996). Neurophenomenology: A methodological remedy for the hard problem. *Journal of Consciousness Studies* 3(4): 330–349.

Wheeler, B.L. (2002). Experiences and concerns of students during music therapy practice. *Journal of Music Therapy* 39(4): 274–304.

Willig, C. (2008). *Introducing Qualitative Research in Psychology: Adventures in Theory and Method*, 2nd ed. New York: Open University Press.

Young, L. (2012). Client experiences in postlude discussions in Guided Imagery and Music (GIM). *Qualitative Inquiries in Music Therapy* 7: 33–70.

CHAPTER 42

RANDOMIZED CONTROLLED TRIALS IN MUSIC THERAPY

SHERI L. ROBB AND DEBRA S. BURNS

DEFINITION AND PRINCIPLES OF RANDOMIZED CONTROLLED TRIALS

RANDOMIZED controlled trials (RCTs) are experiments that compare two or more groups of participants, and participants are assigned to groups based on chance. Groups include an experimental intervention group that is being compared to a treatment as usual, a low dose or attention control condition, and/or a comparative treatment group. The purpose of randomization is to equalize groups on both known and unknown characteristics that may influence the outcome (i.e. dependent variable) and the effectiveness of the intervention (i.e. independent variable). The terms "randomization" and "controlled" refer to the practice of structuring experiments in ways that minimize the influence of outside factors on the experimental results (Shadish et al. 2002).

Historically, RCTs were favored over non-randomized designs because they were considered the only design that could infer causation. In music therapy research, RCTs are designed to examine whether music therapy interventions caused desired effects on targeted outcomes, thus providing evidence for intervention effectiveness. While RCTs continue to be the "gold standard" for providing evidence of efficacy or effectiveness, alternative designs that are equally rigorous are gaining favor for reasons that will be explained later in this chapter (Kessler and Glasgow 2011).

Prior to describing how to lay the groundwork for RCT studies, their design characteristics, and limitations, it is important to first understand what criteria must be met in order to infer causality. Causality is the relationship between two events and is defined by five principles: temporal order, covariation, contiguity, congruity, and ruling out all other plausible causes for observed effects (Cook and Campbell 1979; Shadish et al. 2002; Sidani and Braden 2011).

CRITERIA FOR INFERRING CAUSALITY

Temporal order is the first and possibly the most common sense principle required to infer causality. This principle simply requires that, in order for a researcher to say the intervention caused changes in the outcome, the changes in the outcome (i.e. dependent variable) must occur after the intervention (i.e. independent variable). The main implication for research design is that to account for the principle of temporal order, the researcher must measure the dependent variable before *and* after the independent variable, so that changes in the dependent variable can be examined (Sidani and Braden 2011).

For example, in a study that examined the effect of a music therapy intervention on pre-procedural anxiety in patients awaiting cardiac catheterization, Ghetti (2013) measured dependent variables at baseline (i.e. before the intervention) and post-intervention (Ghetti 2013). This allowed the investigator to examine whether participant scores on dependent variables changed after receiving the intervention. In the absence of baseline measures, the investigator would not have been able to establish *temporal order*; in other words, she would not have known if the differences observed after the intervention were due to the intervention or already present before the participants experienced the study condition.

The second principle, **covariation**, suggests that, in order to infer causation, a group must be observed for changes in outcome after an intervention while being simultaneously observed for changes in outcome with no intervention. This, of course, is impossible to implement. Therefore, in order to conclude that an intervention is responsible for change observed in targeted outcomes, two equivalent groups are compared after the intervention. To be able to infer causation, only the group receiving the intervention would demonstrate changes in outcomes (Sidani and Braden 2011).

In theory, randomization equalizes groups on known and unknown characteristics such as gender, age, or other demographic factors. Randomization can increase the likelihood that the groups are equivalent except for receipt of the independent variable; however, the addition of pretest or baseline measures provides the opportunity to test and confirm group equivalence on known characteristics. For example, using statistical analyses, Ghetti (2013) was able to establish that there were no significant between group differences for each of the dependent variables (i.e. outcome measures) and for gender or age at baseline (Ghetti 2013). In other words, the investigator was able to establish that her groups were equivalent at baseline.

In cases where groups are not equivalent at baseline, pretest measures can provide a statistical way, by using covariates, to equalize groups prior to analysis if randomization does not work. For example, in their two-group RCT study, Robb and colleagues (2014) found that the intervention group reported significantly more religious activity participation than the control group at baseline (Robb et al. 2014). This allowed the investigators to statistically adjust for this difference prior to conducting between group comparisons post-intervention. In the absence of baseline measures, these investigators may have erroneously concluded that the intervention increased scores for religious activity, when those differences actually existed before the participants received the intervention.

Contiguity, the third principle required to infer causation, speaks to the immediacy of changes in the outcome relative to intervention timing. It is assumed that if the intervention is effective in influencing the targeted outcomes, those outcomes would change fairly close in proximity to the delivery of the intervention. Any latent changes leaves room for causal explanations other than the intervention. This principle influences timing of measurement administration, also referred to as data collection (Sidani and Braden 2011).

In addition to the principle of contiguity, it is important to use theory and existing evidence to support and inform decisions about when outcome measures should be administered. For example, Ghetti (2013) was interested in testing an intervention to manage pre-procedural anxiety which is an acute response to an immediate situation (Ghetti 2013). The decision to measure anxiety-related outcomes immediately post-intervention was consistent with the nature of acute distress, and the principle of contiguity. However, some investigators may have an intervention that is designed to impact immediate outcomes that are then expected to influence more latent outcomes. For example, an investigator may hypothesize that significant reductions in repeated procedural distress during cancer treatment (an immediate outcome) may lead to lower incidence of traumatic stress symptoms after treatment ends (a latent outcome). In this case, the investigator would measure distress after the procedural support intervention, but would also measure traumatic stress symptoms at the conclusion of the patient's cancer treatment.

Another necessity for inferring causality is the principle of **congruity**, or that the magnitude of the change in the outcome is congruent with the strength of the intervention. One way to guarantee that congruity occurs is to make sure that the outcomes being targeted by the intervention are meaningfully related to the problem or phenomena of interest. Although one might expect a music distraction intervention to have strong intervention effects for pain during a brief procedure, such as venipuncture, one would not expect it to have strong intervention effects on chronic, neuropathic pain because the mechanisms underlying each type of pain are different. It is not logical to expect strong intervention effects from atheoretical interventions; therefore, theoretical frameworks that define the problem and identify relevant outcomes help explain the role and structure of the music intervention including appropriate frequency and duration (Burns 2012).

Finally, in order to infer causality, **all other possible causes must be ruled out**. In 2004, the Treatment Fidelity Workgroup of the National Institutes of Health (NIH) Behavior Change Consortium (BCC) published recommendations to encourage consistent incorporation of treatment fidelity strategies into behavioral intervention research (Bellg et al. 2004). When testing a music intervention, the primary goal of treatment fidelity is to increase our ability to say, with scientific confidence, that any changes in outcomes were attributable to the intervention and nothing else. Given that various factors can contribute to changes in outcomes, such as patient characteristics, music therapist characteristics, music, or setting, it is important to use a range of methodological strategies and procedures to help control or counteract the impact of these factors on the outcomes or to make sure they happen equally across groups (Campbell and Standley 1963; Shadish et al. 2002; Sidani and Braden 2011). Bellg and colleagues (2004) offered a full discussion of the NIH BCC recommendations (Bellg et al. 2004). In addition, several authors have published manuscripts describing successful implementation of BCC treatment fidelity recommendations, using their own clinical trials to offer an illustrative, working model (Breitenstein et al. 2010; Carpenter et al. 2013; Resnick et al. 2005; Robb et al. 2011).

LAYING THE GROUNDWORK FOR EFFICACY AND EFFECTIVENESS TRIALS

Before describing the research process and related randomized designs, it is important to define what efficacy and effectiveness mean and how they are different from one another. Efficacy trials, sometimes referred to as explanatory trials, are designed to test hypotheses for the purpose of determining whether or not an intervention is beneficial under ideal circumstances

(Schwartz and Lellouch 2009; Thorpe et al. 2009). Effectiveness trials, also known as pragmatic trials, are designed to determine the effects of the intervention within the environment in which it will be implemented (Thorpe et al. 2009). Efficacy (explanatory) and effectiveness (pragmatic) trials are two ends of a continuum determined by the amount of controls put in place for intervention delivery, therapist training, comparison conditions, and outcome measurement. Generally, efficacy trials have an extreme amount of control and inflexibility in terms of intervention delivery, therapist training, and amount of follow-up. On the other hand, pragmatic trials are less structured in intervention delivery and therapist training, and measurement is often collected from the medical/education record and not specific research measures.

Music therapy interventions are consistent with the Medical Research Council's (MRC) definition of complex interventions because they often contain several interacting components, require clinical expertise for delivery, address multiple outcomes, and are usually tailored to the recipient (Craig et al. 2008). This complexity contributes to challenges in evaluating intervention effects and resulted in the MRC developing a framework to help researchers adopt appropriate methods. Best practice requires a systematic approach that does not begin with an efficacy trial—instead, the journey begins with intervention development studies where investigators use the best available evidence and theory to inform intervention design.

There has been increased criticism of the application of phased, drug evaluation models to behavioral intervention research (Craig et al. 2008; Glasgow et al. 2003); but, for illustrative purposes, it can be helpful to think about intervention development and testing in terms of a staged approach. Here, we reference the initial three stages for systematic intervention development and evaluation as described by the MRC (Craig et al. 2008), including definitions and examples from our own research on the Therapeutic Music Video (TMV) intervention, indicating where RCT design studies are most likely to occur. Interested readers are also referred to work by the *Sing & Grow* research team, wherein the investigators conducted and published a series of developmental and pilot studies that informed a subsequent effectiveness trial (Williams et al. 2012), as well as to preliminary pilot work by Ellerkamp and Goldbeck (2008) that led to a subsequent RCT pilot of a multimodal music therapy intervention for children with anxiety disorders (Goldbeck and Ellerkamp 2012).

Phase 1: Development. In this stage of intervention development, investigators begin by identifying the evidence base through systematic reviews, by developing theory, and/or by modeling the process and outcomes. Early studies that laid the foundation for the TMV intervention included:

1) development of the Contextual Support Model of Music Therapy (Robb 2000) which informed TMV intervention content/design
2) examination of anxiety and depressive symptoms in response to TMV and control conditions (Robb and Ebberts 2003a)
3) content analysis of patient-generated songs (Robb and Ebberts 2003b) which revealed the need for more relevant outcome measures. Specifically, themes from patient songs were consistent with protective/risk factors identified in Haase's Resilience in Illness Model (RIM), resulting in the adoption of the RIM as the measurement model for future studies (Haase et al. 2013).

Although developmental studies do not always use an RCT design, they are essential in laying the groundwork for subsequent stages of intervention testing where a RCT study may be deemed appropriate.

Phase 2: Feasibility/pilot testing. Primary aims for feasibility and pilot studies are to test the feasibility and acceptability of study conditions and procedures, examine recruitment/retention strategies and rates, and generate preliminary data to cautiously examine outcomes and inform sample size for subsequent efficacy trials (Conn et al. 2010; Leon et al. 2011; Thabane et al. 2010). Qualitative methods are often used to understand and evaluate acceptability of study conditions and measures, and to identify potential barriers to recruitment. Quantitative methods, including, but not limited to, RCT designs, are often used but the primary emphasis is on examining whether aspects of the design are feasible and acceptable once applied in a real-world setting. For example, Burns and colleagues (2009) conducted a study that examined feasibility and preliminary effects of the TMV intervention (Burns et al. 2009). Rates of consent, session completion, and questionnaire completion supported feasibility. More specifically, a consent rate of 63% was considered acceptable and could be used to inform study enrollment estimates for subsequent studies; low attrition rates indicated that once enrolled, study participants would likely complete; high completion rates for intervention and control condition sessions/activities indicated that the intervention could be delivered as designed and was well tolerated by patients undergoing intensive treatment.

Finally, measures at all three time points were completed by participants who were actively on study, with minimal missing data. The team also reported effect sizes (ES) and examined trends in outcomes to explore whether the TMV had any impact on targeted outcomes. These preliminary data suggested change was occurring in the desired direction and that further studies examining efficacy were warranted.

Phase 3: Evaluation studies. Aims for evaluation studies focus on assessing intervention efficacy but may also examine change processes or cost effectiveness. Evaluation or efficacy studies are not limited to the RCT. Investigators must select a study design that aligns with their research questions and circumstances under which the study will be conducted. For example, Robb and colleagues conducted a multi-site RCT examining TMV efficacy for adolescents/young adults undergoing stem cell transplant for cancer (Robb et al. 2014). This study is a good example of a parallel group RCT design, which will be described later in this chapter.

Randomization methods and designs

Methods of randomization

Randomizing research participants to intervention or comparison/control groups helps to assure that the groups are equal in terms of size and constitution at the beginning of the study, so that the only difference is the intervention or study condition each group receives. This enables the investigator to argue that any differences observed at the end of the study can be attributed to group assignment. The use of random group assignment means that each participant has the same chance of receiving any of the study conditions, and allocation should be carried out using procedures to insure that participants and investigators do not know in advance what group condition will be assigned.

The three most common types of randomization include simple randomization, block randomization, and stratified randomization (Wang and Bakhai 2006). **Simple randomization** occurs when a participant's group of assignment is generated at random without regard to previous or future participant group assignments. This type of randomization can be illustrated using a coin toss—where a toss of "heads" would mean assignment to the treatment group and "tails" would mean assignment to the control group. Each time the outcome is unpredictable (or random), but it can result in imbalanced assignment across the two groups, especially in smaller trials.

Block randomization equalizes the number of participants assigned to each group. The block size should be at least two times the number of groups in the study. For example, in a two-group randomized trial, the block size should be at least four participants. In order to implement block randomization, the research must first determine the number of blocks needed to cover the sample size, list all possible assignment orders within each block, and then generate a random number code for each block. For example, a study with two study conditions (A and B) and a block size of four, the possible treatment allocations within each block would be as follows: 1) AABB; 2) BBAA; 3) ABAB; 4) BABA; 5) ABBA; and 6) BABB.

Block randomization is useful if recruitment is slow, if there is a possibility that the study may be stopped early for safety or efficacy reasons, and/or if patient care changes substantially during the study period (Wang and Bakhai 2006). The weakness of block randomization is that the order of randomization may be predictable, depending on the number of randomizations within each block. Using the previous example, since there are four randomizations within a single block, group assignment for participants in the final or last two positions of the group would be predictable (e.g. BAB?; BB??). To address the risk for selection bias, it is recommended that investigators not reveal the blocking mechanism to study personnel who are enrolling participants and that investigators use random block sizes.

Stratified randomization is a form of block randomization, but it includes balancing on a baseline variable that is deemed theoretically important to the study. For example, the Stories and Music for Adolescent/Young Adult Resilience during Transplant (SMART) trial enrolled adolescents/young adults aged 11–24 years (Robb et al. 2014). Given developmental differences across this age span, the investigators considered age to be an important and potentially confounding variable. In order to yield intervention and low-dose control groups that were comparable in age, the randomization of participants was stratified on three age groups (11–13, 14–17, and 18–24 years). Had the investigators not used stratified randomization, the distribution of age across condition may have been unbalanced and produced group differences that were due to age/development rather than group condition.

Methods for generating group assignment or a randomization schedule include using a random numbers table, a computer-generated list of random numbers, or a flip of a coin. In addition to generating the group assignment schedule, investigators must also identify strategies to ensure allocation concealment—meaning those persons responsible for recruiting participants into the study have no prior knowledge about what groups the participants will be assigned to. Without allocation concealment, there is a great risk for biased enrollment.

Methods to ensure allocation concealment include use of central randomization, where a member of the study team not involved in participant recruitment is responsible for generating and revealing randomization status. A second method is the use of sequentially numbered, opaque sealed envelopes. The envelopes contain the group assignment of participants based on the randomization schedule, and are prepared by someone not involved in recruitment of study participants (Bradt 2012).

Types of randomized designs

While the most common RCT design is the **parallel group design**, there are two additional randomized designs that can provide the researcher with an opportunity to ask additional questions beyond whether or not a music therapy intervention was effective in bringing about desired changes. These additional options include the **crossover** and **factorial** designs. We will discuss each design and include a relevant music therapy study example.

The **parallel group design**, while basic, can vary by the timing of pre-testing, randomization, and the number of groups. These designs compare two or more groups to determine the impact of an intervention or independent variable. Participants can be randomized before or after pre-testing, after which the intervention and/or comparison condition is introduced. Post-testing can occur immediately after the intervention period and a follow-up, distal measurement (longitudinal designs) can be added to test for stability of results (see Figure 42.1).

In a study by Robb and colleagues (2014), the investigators used a parallel two- group RCT design to examine efficacy of a therapeutic music video intervention for adolescents/young adults undergoing stem cell transplant for cancer (Robb et al. 2014). Study participants completed baseline measures within 30 days of admission to the hospital unit, and were then immediately randomized to the intervention or low-dose control group. Then both groups received six sessions, two times per week during the acute phase of their stem cell transplant. Follow-up measures were taken after session 6, which was immediately post-intervention (i.e. Time 2), and again at 100 days post-transplant (i.e. Time 3). A study flow diagram (Figure 42.2) illustrates the timing of randomization, pre-testing (or baseline) measures, and subsequent measurement periods (Time 2 and Time 3 measures).

At times, it may not be possible to randomize individuals or groups of individuals to study conditions as is done in a parallel group design. Four situations in which randomization may not be possible include:

1) the population of interest is small and would not result in a large enough sample to examine between-group differences,

$$O \quad R \quad X_A \quad O \quad O$$

$$O \quad R \quad X_B \quad O \quad O$$

FIGURE 42.1 Parallel group design

Abbreviations: O = assessment; R = randomization; X_A = treatment A; X_B = treatment B

2) assignment to a control or usual care condition would be unacceptable to study participants,
3) the treatment delivery model at the participating agency exposes participants to all aspects of the treatment under investigation, or
4) the denial of treatment (i.e. assignment to a control condition) is considered unethical.

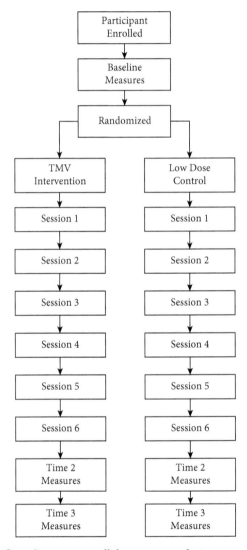

FIGURE 42.2 Study flow diagram, parallel two-group design

In these situations, the **crossover design** is an alternative that provides for both within- and between-group analyses by allowing participants to serve as their own controls.

The simplest version of this design is the two-period crossover design where, following baseline assessment, participants are randomly assigned to start with either treatment A or B in the first period, followed by assessment; then, they cross over to the alternative treatment in the succeeding second period, followed by a final round of assessment. Sometimes, investigators will schedule an interval of time between treatment conditions, to mitigate or "wash out" any possible carry-over effects from the first study condition (see Figure 42.3). This design is most suitable when treatments under investigation offer short-term relief and no carry-over is anticipated, treatments have a short duration, and participants are willing and able to experience both treatment conditions.

$$O \quad R \quad X_A \quad O \quad X_B \quad O$$

$$O \quad R \quad X_B \quad O \quad X_A \quad O$$

FIGURE 42.3 Two-period, crossover design

Abbreviations: R = randomization; O = assessment; X_A = treatment A; X_B = treatment B

Tan and colleagues (2010) used a two-period, crossover design to study effects of a two-phased music therapy intervention, compared with a no treatment control group, on measures of pain, anxiety, and muscle tension during burn debridement (Tan et al. 2010). The study was conducted over a two-day period, with participants serving as their own controls. Participants were randomized to receive the music therapy intervention on either the first or second day of the study. On treatment condition days, participants received a two-phased music therapy intervention that included music-based imagery (MBI) before and after dressing changes, and music alternate engagement (MAE) during dressing changes. On control condition days, participants engaged in routine patient activities and did not receive any of the music-based interventions. Measures were taken at seven different time points during the debridement process, and the timing of measurements was identical across conditions. Figure 42.4 illustrates the timing of randomization measurement (i.e. data collections). Note that patients were randomized to receive the intervention on either study day 1 or study day 2—this is where crossover occurred.

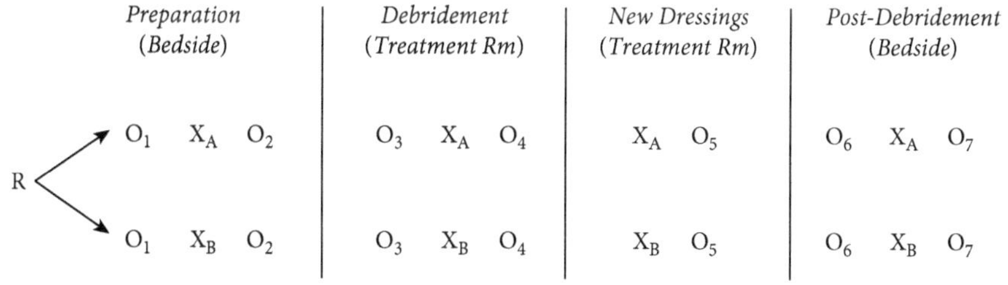

Preparation (Bedside)	Debridement (Treatment Rm)	New Dressings (Treatment Rm)	Post-Debridement (Bedside)
O_1 X_A O_2	O_3 X_A O_4	X_A O_5	O_6 X_A O_7
O_1 X_B O_2	O_3 X_B O_4	X_B O_5	O_6 X_B O_7

R

FIGURE 42.4 Study flow diagram, crossover design

A primary advantage of the crossover design is that by having participants serve as their own controls, variability is reduced, minimizing the required sample size needed to achieve adequate power. For example, in the study by Tan and colleagues (2010), the investigators conducted an interim analysis to obtain a more accurate sample size estimate (Tan et al. 2010). On the basis of the analysis, it was determined that a sample size of 29 participants would allow the investigators to detect a clinically significant reduction of pain (of at least 20%) with a power of 0.8 and a type 1 error of .05. In contrast, had the investigators used a parallel design to address the same questions, the sample size needed to detect a moderate effect size (.5) at an alpha = .05 and power at 0.8 would have been 192 participants. Another benefit of the crossover design is that investigators can examine efficacy without denying treatment to any group, and the design also functions to counterbalance and assess order effect. In the Tan study (2010), because the order of intervention and control conditions was randomized, the participants had an equal chance to receive music on the first day. Because study participants experience all treatment conditions, potential disadvantages of the design include an increase in the duration of study conditions, and potential carry-over effects can add complexity to statistical analysis and interpretation.

Factorial designs are useful because, in addition to examining the effect of an independent variable on a specified outcome, they allow the investigator to examine the effects of two or more independent variables and any subsequent interaction. For example, McKinney and colleagues (1997) used a between-subjects factorial design to test the effect of imagery, music, and the combination of music and imagery on plasma beta-endorphins (McKinney et al. 1997). In this study, the two independent variables were music (music vs. no music) and imagery (imagery vs. no imagery). Because the study used a between-subjects design, participants were randomly assigned to one of four groups (see Table 42.1). In factorial designs, each independent variable is grouped by itself and then, the two are grouped together. This results in a 2x2 factorial design. The statistical test determines the effect of each independent variable and then, the interaction (or combination) on the outcome.

When looking at numbers and the multiplication sign in factorial design descriptions (i.e. 2x2), each of the numbers represents an independent variable and the value of the number represents the number of levels of the independent variable. The McKinney study represents a 2x2 factorial design because it looked at two independent variables (music and imagery), and each variable had two levels (music vs. no music; imagery vs. no imagery). In a 3x2 factorial design, there would be two independent variables, one with three levels and one with two levels. For example, a study examining musical genre (jazz vs. classical vs. country) and imagery (imagery vs. no imagery) on mood states would represent a 3x2 factorial design.

Table 42.1 Example of a 2x2 factorial design

	Music	No Music
Imagery	Music + Imagery	Imagery Only
No Imagery	Music Only	No Music or Imagery

Theoretically, an infinite number of factors or independent variables could be tested, but in order to have an adequately powered study, the sample size needs to increase by approximately 15 participants for each variable. Therefore, a 2x2 factorial design with one outcome variable will require approximately 60 participants.

Limitations of the RCT design

While the RCT is considered the "gold standard" to infer causality and provide information about the effectiveness of interventions, there is a growing understanding about the limitations of RCTs when attempting to use research protocols in clinical practice. The ability to infer causality within an RCT is accomplished through clearly defining and randomizing the sample, as well as standardizing the setting, treatment protocol (intervention), and control or comparison condition (Sidani and Braden 2011). These practices, which increase the confidence that the outcomes are a result of the study intervention, create barriers to successfully integrating the intervention into clinical practice.

The strict inclusion and exclusion criteria used to define eligible participants who will consent for a study creates a homogeneous sample within the study, but often does not represent clinical populations that are more heterogeneous. The highly defined patient population also does not help answer the question of "what, with whom, and when?" Furthermore, in an effort to reduce threats to external validity, many RCTs take place in well-controlled settings (e.g. a lab, a hospital room, a small isolated classroom) which do not always represent the variety of clinical practice settings.

Interventions tested within the context of an RCT are also well controlled and usually defined by a protocol and/or a study manual. Treatment protocols provide step by step procedures for the delivery of interventions. The procedures ensure that there is a high level of fidelity in the delivery of the treatment, including standardizing the dose, timing, content, and qualifications of the music therapist. However, protocols do not take into account variation in patient characteristics and preferences, or therapist expertise.

ALTERNATIVE DESIGNS TO THE RANDOMIZED CONTROLLED TRIAL

While RCTs are the most rigorous trials to infer causality, there are both pragmatic and methodological concerns that may cause researchers to consider alternative designs. The control needed to insure internal validity within an RCT creates difficulties in terms of external validity. For example, stringent inclusion/exclusion criteria limits generalizability to other populations, so clinicians cannot really infer from the results that the intervention tested will work for their specific clinical population. Another important issue is whether or not it is ethical to randomize participants to an intervention that may not be helpful or to a no treatment control group.

There has been increased interest in the use of alternative designs to overcome common criticisms of the RCT. Alternative designs can answer similar, and at times more clinically meaningful questions, but in a more efficient and ecological manner. Three examples of alternative designs include the practical clinical trial (Estabrooks et al. 2014), preference trial designs (Torgerson and Sibbald 1998), and propensity score methodology (West et al. 2008). In brief, **practical trials** have similar characteristics to randomized designs (and may indeed be a randomized trial), but involve use of a more representative, heterogeneous sample of patients and therapists, and provide multiple outcomes that address both clinical and policy issues. **Preference trials** rely on patients' preference for group assignment—that is, they can choose the group to which they are assigned. And, **propensity score methodology** is a retrospective research design that mimics a randomized trial by creating probability scores regression analysis to control for known covariates. Researchers can then test the effectiveness of an intervention with data that already exists. Designs traditionally considered for single-subject studies, such as multiple baseline or interrupted time series, can also be used as alternatives to randomized trials (Glasgow et al. 2005). Finally, mixed methods designs provide the perspectives of quantitative and qualitative methodologies to obtain a more complete description of the benefits of music-based interventions (Bradt et al. 2013).

Summary

The RCT has historically been the "gold standard" for determining efficacy or effectiveness of music therapy interventions. The rationale for using RCTs has been based on design characteristics that allow the inference of causality. More recent thinking, however, acknowledges the limitations of RCTs, including their generalizability and rapid translation to clinical practice. Alternatives to RCTs maintain design characteristics that allow causality to be examined but also address more imperative policy and clinical implementation questions. The RCT remains one design option that warrants careful consideration, keeping in mind its relative strengths and limitations.

References

Bellg, A.J. et al. (2004). Enhancing treatment fidelity in health behavior change studies: best practices and recommendations from the NIH Behavior Change Consortium. *Health Psychology* 23(5): 443–451. doi: 10.1037/0278-6133.23.5.443 2004-18051-001 [pii]

Bradt, J. (2012). Randomized controlled trials in music therapy: guidelines for design and implementation. *Journal of Music Therapy* 49(2): 120–149.

Bradt, J., Burns, D.S., and Creswell, J.W. (2013). Mixed methods research in music therapy research. *Journal of Music Therapy* 50(2): 123–148.

Breitenstein, S.M., Fogg, L., Garvey, C., Hill, C., Resnick, B., and Gross, D. (2010). Measuring implementation fidelity in a community-based parenting intervention. *Nursing Research* 59(3): 158–165. doi: 10.1097/NNR.0b013e3181dbb2e2

Burns, D.S. (2012). Theoretical rationale for music selection in oncology intervention research: an integrative review. *Journal of Music Therapy* 49(1): 7–22.

Burns, D.S., Robb, S.L., and Haase, J.E. (2009). Exploring the feasibility of a therapeutic music video intervention in adolescents and young adults during stem-cell transplantation. *Cancer Nursing* 32(5): E8–E16. doi: 10.1097/NCC.0b013e3181a4802c

Campbell, D.T. and Standley, J.C. (1963). *Experimental and quasi-experimental designs for research*. Chicago: Rand McNally & Company.

Carpenter, J.S. et al. (2013). Strategies used and data obtained during treatment fidelity monitoring. *Nursing Research* 62(1): 59–65.

Conn, V.S., Algase, D.L., Rawl, S.M., Zerwic, J.J., and Wyman, J.F. (2010). Publishing pilot intervention work. *Western Journal of Nursing Research* 32(8): 994–1010.

Cook, T.D. and Campbell, D.T. (1979). *Quasi-experimentation: design and analysis issues for field settings*. Boston: Houghton Mifflin.

Craig, P. et al. (2008). Developing and evaluating complex interventions: the new Medical Research Council guidance. *British Medical Journal* 337: a1655. doi: 10.1136/bmj.a1655

Ellerkamp, T., and Goldbeck, L. (2008). Musiktherapie für ängstliche Kinder. *Musiktherapeutische Umschau* 29(1): 26–33.

Estabrooks, P., Almeida, F., and Galaviz, K. (2014). Reach Effectiveness Adoption Implementation Maintenence (RE-AIM). Retrieved March 10, 2014, from <URL>http://www.re-aim.org/index.html

Ghetti, C.M. (2013). Effect of music therapy with emotional-approach coping on preprocedural anxiety in cardiac catheterization: a randomized controlled trial. *Journal of Music Therapy* 50(2): 93–122.

Glasgow, R.E., Lichtenstein, E., and Marcus, A.C. (2003). Why don't we see more translation of health promotion research to practice? Rethinking the efficacy-to-effectiveness transition. *American Journal of Public Health* 93(8): 1261–1267.

Glasgow, R.E., Magid, D.J., Beck, A., Ritzwoller, D., and Estabrooks, P.A. (2005). Practical clinical trials for translating research to practice: design and measurement recommendations. *Medical Care* 43(6): 551–557.

Goldbeck, L. and Ellerkamp, T. (2012). A randomized controlled trial of multimodal music therapy for children with anxiety disorders. *Journal of Music Therapy* 49(4): 395–413.

Haase, J.E., Kintner, E.K., Monahan, P.O., and Robb, S.L. (2013). The Resilience in Illness model, part 1: exploratory evaluation in adolescents and young adults with cancer. *Cancer Nursing*. doi: 10.1097/NCC.0b013e31828941bb

Kessler, R. and Glasgow, R.E. (2011). A proposal to speed translation of healthcare research into practice: dramatic change is needed. *American Journal of Preventive Medicine* 40(6): 637–644. doi: 10.1016/j.amepre.2011.02.023

Leon, A.C., Davis, L.L., and Kraemer, H.C. (2011). The role and interpretation of pilot studies in clinical research. *Journal of Psychiatric Research* 45(5): 626–629. doi: 10.1016/j.jpsychires.2010.10.008

McKinney, C.H., Tims, F.C., Kumar, A.M., and Kumar, M. (1997). The effect of selected classical music and spontaneous imagery on plasma beta-endorphin. *Journal of Behavioral Medicine* 20(1): 85–99.

Resnick, B. et al. (2005). Treatment fidelity in behavior change research: a case example. *Nursing Research* 54(2): 139–143. doi: 00006199-200503000-00010 [pii]

Robb, S.L. (2000). The effect of therapeutic music interventions on the behavior of hospitalized children in isolation: developing a contextual support model of music therapy. *Journal of Music Therapy* 37(2): 118–146.

Robb, S.L. and Ebberts, A.G. (2003a). Songwriting and digital video production interventions for pediatric patients undergoing bone marrow transplantation, part I: an analysis of depression and anxiety levels according to phase of treatment. *Journal of Pediatric Oncology Nursing* 20(1): 2–15. doi: 10.1053/jpon.2003.3

Robb, S.L. and Ebberts, A.G. (2003b). Songwriting and digital video production interventions for pediatric patients undergoing bone marrow transplantation, part II: an analysis of patient-generated songs and patient perceptions regarding intervention efficacy. *Journal of Pediatric Oncology Nursing* 20(1): 16–25. doi: 10.1053/jpon.2003.4

Robb, S.L., Burns, D.S., Docherty, S.L., and Haase, J.E. (2011). Ensuring treatment fidelity in a multi-site behavioral intervention study: implementing NIH Behavior Change Consortium recommendations in the SMART trial. *Psychooncology* 20(11): 1193–1201. doi: 10.1002/pon.1845

Robb, S.L. et al. (2014). Randomized clinical trial of therapeutic music video intervention for resilience outcomes in adolescents/young adults undergoing hematopoietic stem cell transplant: a report from the Children's Oncology Group. *Cancer* 120(6): 909–917. doi: 10.1002/cncr.28355

Schwartz, D. and Lellouch, J. (2009). Explanatory and pragmatic attitudes in therapeutical trials. *Journal of Clinical Epidemiology* 62(5): 499–505. doi: 10.1016/j.jclinepi.2009.01.012

Shadish, W.R., Cook, T.D. and Campbell, D.T. (2002). *Experimental and quasi-experimental designs for generalized causal inference*. Boston: Houghton Mifflin.

Sidani, S. and Braden, C.J. (2011). *Design, evaluation, and translation of nurse interventions*. West Sussex, UK: John Wiley & Sons, Inc.

Tan, X., Yowler, C.J., Super, D.M., and Fratianne, R.B. (2010). The efficacy of music therapy protocols for decreasing pain, anxiety, and muscle tension levels during burn dressing changes: a prospective randomized crossover trial. *Journal of Burn Care and Research* 31(4): 590–597. doi: 10.1097/BCR.0b013e3181e4d71b

Thabane, L. et al. (2010). A tutorial on pilot studies: the what, why and how. *BMC Medical Research Methodology* 10: 1. doi: 10.1186/1471-2288-10-1

Thorpe, K.E. et al. (2009). A pragmatic-explanatory continuum indicator summary (PRECIS): a tool to help trial designers. *Canadian Medical Association Journal* 180(10): E47–E57. doi: 10.1503/cmaj.090523

Torgerson, D.J. and Sibbald, B. (1998). Understanding controlled trials. What is a patient preference trial? *British Medical Journal* 316(7128): 360.

Wang, D. and Bakhai, A. (2006). *Clinical trials: a practical guide to design, analysis, and reporting*. London: Remedica.

West, S.G. et al. (2008). Alternatives to the randomized controlled trial. *American Journal of Public Health* 98(8): 1359–1366. doi: 10.2105/AJPH.2007.124446

Williams, K.E., Berthelsen, D., Nicholson, J.M., Walker, S., and Abad, V. (2012). The effectiveness of a short-term group music therapy intervention for parents who have a child with a disability. *Journal of Music Therapy* 49(1): 23–44.

CHAPTER 43

··

MIXED METHODS RESEARCH IN MUSIC THERAPY

··

JAAKKO ERKKILÄ

INTRODUCTION

OVER the past decades, ideas about the most relevant research for music therapy have changed many times. This is probably because health care-related disciplines, such as music therapy, are not only influenced by scholars' ideas and preferences but also society and societal decision makers. For example, in the early 1990s, qualitative research methodology was the primary focus for music therapy scholars, especially in Europe and Scandinavia. Important books on qualitative methodology (e.g. Langenberg et al. 1996; Smeijsters 1997) were published and researcher networks were established to build capacity to pursue a qualitative research strategy. It was strongly believed that reductionist ways of looking at the complex clinical processes in music therapy could only lead to poor understanding; ultimately failing to uncover unique music therapy phenomena.

The above conclusion is easy to understand when considering some of the essential concepts and techniques of music therapy which involve highly abstract phenomena such as feelings and emotions and non-verbal perceptions and processes. Counter-transference, for example, is a psychoanalytic concept with specific meaning. Within music therapy it has undergone unique reformulation to include specific music based interactions (Bruscia 1998; Priestley 1994). As counter-transference is difficult, if not impossible, to measure or quantify; many scholars agree that the most relevant way to investigate music therapeutic counter-transference is to apply a qualitative research strategy where it is possible to gain insight into some of the profound, intrasubjective, and highly interpretative features and contents of the phenomenon of the experiences of the client and the therapist in music therapy practice. This kind of research is understood to improve the profession in terms of clinical methods and training, and it also improves our knowledge about the characteristics of different client populations.

Since the early twenty-first century, quantitative research strategies in music therapy—and in therapy research in general—have been extended and elaborated. It is evident that music therapy research is strongly affected by societal requirements, in particular by any research developments in the medical field. The kind of research independency our profession had in near past is not as evident anymore. A major reason for this is the relatively new practice of medicine called evidence-based medicine (EBM). The term was first introduced in the medical literature in 1990s (Evidence-Based Medicine Working Group 1992) and was largely influenced by a book *Effectiveness and Efficiency: Random Reflections on Health Services* written by Archie Cochrane (Cochrane 1972) who was a Scottish epidemiologist. Honoring his name, Cochrane Centers and a network called the Cochrane Collaboration have been established for collecting and sharing information on the best practices of medicine. In a relatively short time the importance of quantitative research strategy in medical and related research has increased. It is so because EBM movement advocates large samples, strict methodologies—such as randomized control trials (RCT)—and objective, standardized outcome measures as the highest degree of evidence. Although EBM recognizes other types of research—such as single case studies, or expert opinion supported by qualitative methodologies—the adherence to levels of evidence within a hierarchical structure makes these types of evidence *weaker* within the EBM system. In the EBM hierarchy, opinion and case material are placed at the bottom of the pyramid of evidence while results from RCTs and meta-analysis are at the top. What has happened in health care systems in many countries, unfortunately, is that without the so called *hard evidence*, usually associated with RCTs, a clinical approach is not considered to be evidence-based. Thus, in order to remain in the mainstream health care system, music therapy research has followed the trends of the medical field, which currently means adaptation to the EBM framework. Some critical discussion about whether this dominance of EBM can be accommodated in music therapy has occurred (e.g. Abrams 2010; Edwards 2005).

Another major reason for the influence of outside forces within music therapy research is because of the ongoing development of the professional recognition of music therapy. Most music therapy trainings are now located in universities. At the same time music therapy clinicians have increased their full-time work opportunities within the official health care system rather than working in short-term hourly paid projects. The growing professional recognition of music therapy has meant a decrease in independence, increasing the influence of wider forces to maintain the status and recognition of the profession.

Both qualitative and quantitative strategies have their benefits for better understanding the essence, mechanisms, and effect of music therapy. Qualitative methods allow deep exploration of abstract and complex phenomena, resulting in our understanding them in a unique way. Sometimes qualitative research process is described as a procedure where a complex phenomenon is broken down into smallest possible pieces and then put together again, such as in Grounded Theory method (see Strauss and Corbin 1990). This offers a way to understand the construct of the phenomenon as well as causes and consequences within it. Such research work is highly intensive and typically only a small number of cases are investigated. This is because the research is intensive, and uses huge numbers of words in procedures of analysis. The eventual understanding attained through qualitative method is highly different from the generalized outcomes that result when quantitative methods are used. Therefore qualitative strategies could be suggested as serving the experts within the field, such as music therapy clinicians. Further understanding of the profound and complex phenomena encountered in professional work with clients is the aim of every clinician. It is through this understanding that developing as a clinician becomes possible. On the other hand the decision makers responsible for the use of common resources in health and education services are not so interested in the content of our work but rather need to know the effectiveness of it. They are not interested in knowing about the individual client experience but rather want to know whether we can generalize the effect over a diagnostic population and whether we can show the effect based on standardized, interdisciplinary outcome measures such as those used in other areas of health care research.

When using quantitative strategy, generalization is possible. That is, as long as appropriate procedures are used, and the sample size is sufficiently large to be able to address the research questions, the results of any study can be understood to be applicable to any other people who are similar to the study participants. If it is found after post and follow-up test comparison between an experiment and control group that those clients who received music therapy improved significantly in terms of certain, relevant outcome measures, most of the work is done. Furthermore, if the scientific community accepts this work and it is able to be published in an esteemed journal you can share the news with your colleagues, and celebrate the success with sparkling wine. Additionally, your study might even improve the status of music therapy in the medical field.

Music therapy has been increasingly researched within the positivist paradigm using quantitative methods such as the randomized controlled trial (RCT). However, many questions about what happens in music therapy, and why, still remain. For instance, many forms of therapy have been demonstrated to be effective in accordance with EBM standards. This may give a driver's license for a therapy technique but the effectiveness of the technique does not tell much about its uniqueness. It also does not assist in understanding much about the difference between techniques—the difference between cognitive analytic therapy and improvisational music psychotherapy, for instance. In other words, from a sociopolitical perspective a successful RCT is an excellent achievement but the question often remains, how much the study actually increases clinical understanding and development of the profession.

Let me give an example. I was leading a research team who recently completed a RCT on improvisational music therapy for depression (Erkkilä et al. 2011). The study was successful in terms of design and results and was published in a highly regarded psychiatric journal. The results speak positively for music therapy as an effective treatment for depression. It is one of the contributions to music therapy and depression research, which probably in near future will be saturated enough to list music therapy as an effective form of treatment. In other words, music therapy is now *proven* to be an effective treatment for depression. But these studies do not tell much about the uniqueness of music therapy, or the mechanisms of change as to how the therapy works. More research, possibly qualitative, should be made in order to answer these questions. In the editorial of the report of the study it was stated:

> Clinical trials inevitably focus on the outcomes of interventions rather than the process through which these outcomes may be achieved. Further research using mixed methods is needed if a better understanding of the active ingredients of music therapy that enhance patient outcomes is to be reached.
>
> (Maratos et al. 2011, p. 93)

A mix of qualitative and quantitative strategies is needed in order to better understand why patients improve. It sounds simple but is it simple to mix research strategies? After all, for some scholars mixing qualitative and quantitative strategies is considered totally impossible (for example, Sandelowski 2001).

MIXED METHODS RESEARCH, WHAT IS IT?

After Tashakkori and Creswell (2007) mixed methods may be defined as "research in which the investigator collects and analyses data, integrates the findings and draws inferences using both qualitative and quantitative approaches or methods in a single study" (p. 4). Researchers in social sciences are tempted to turn to mixed methods when the phenomena under investigation are diverse and because methods from the quantitative and qualitative traditions, have their own unique strengths, as stated above.

In music therapy research, quantitative methods are often employed for group comparison purposes. The functionality of a clinical method in a client group can be investigated by dividing subjects into two groups where only one of the groups (the experimental group) is offered music therapy and the second one acts as a control group. Here, a *control* group means that the subjects in it participate in the same tests—typically baseline, post, and follow-up tests—at the same time points but instead of participating in music therapy the subjects only receive standard care, for instance. This kind of design benefits from having as many subjects as possible in each of the groups. When all the subjects undergo the same tests consisting of the same outcome measures, comparing the test results between the groups gives a relatively authentic answer whether or not music therapy was more effective than the standard care only. This simplistic example of quantitative research strategy in music therapy research raises questions about the benefits and shortcomings of a single research strategy. An undeniable benefit is that research such as this sheds light on the overall effectiveness of music therapy. On the other hand, not much can be discerned about why a music therapy was found to be effective or not. In particular, if subjects in music therapy group improve significantly better than those in control group, it is very important to know which specific factors in music therapy create the effect. It is here that the mixed methods approach enters the picture offering the opportunity to look at all of the factors that could contribute to the change for participants more closely.

When the overall effect is already known, a researcher can then use a qualitative research strategy to involve a single subject, or few subjects, from the data for further exploration of the ingredients of the effect. Unlike quantitative strategies, a qualitative researcher is free to use purposive sampling; that is, seeking a participant who represents a certain aspect of interest for further investigation. This qualitative concept refers to a sampling strategy where a researcher selects a case from a larger data set based on the representativeness of the case within a class under interest. This is also called paradigmatic case sampling (Given 2008). A researcher can choose a subject from the group of those clients who responded well to music therapy by purposefully searching for a client best representing a class called *good treatment response*. In this client's therapy process many of the typical features of the good treatment response class can be clearly seen and his/her process is generally similar to other participants from a class representativeness point of view. This way a researcher may gain deeper understanding of the unique mechanisms of music therapy (qualitative understanding), which explains the effect which was initially found (quantitative understanding).

However, it can be difficult to represent an entire mixed methods study in a single research paper. Sometimes researchers have to publish their quantitative and qualitative results separately due to tight rules about methods of research as well as the traditions of a journal. Furthermore, journal articles always have limitations for length. Reporting an empirical, quantitative study usually allows no space for qualitative reflection; which tends to be wordy. Different epistemological foundations of quantitative and qualitative strategies sometimes cause problems as well. Some scholars consider that these two approaches are mutually exclusive (see Sandelowski 2001). One problem in combining the approaches is that many who have been trained and enculturated to use quantitative methods cannot necessarily comprehend the qualitative research report. Some scholars see it as loose and undisciplined—even methodologically weak (see Castro et al. 2010). However, mixed methods methodology has continued to develop and many of the known problems have been addressed (Bradt et al. 2013).

DIFFERENT TYPES OF MIXED METHODS RESEARCH

Researchers to date have developed different understandings of mixed method studies, and there is no current consensus as to what MMR should be. Since Doyle (2009) there have been ongoing attempts to completely integrate the two approaches, quantitative and qualitative, but the definition of mixed methods will change over time as this research approach continues to grow.

When planning a mixed methods research study one should make decisions on: (1) timing of the quantitative and qualitative methods; (2) on weighting of the quantitative and qualitative methods; and (3) on mixing of the qualitative and quantitative methods (Creswell 1994; Creswell and Clark 2007). Alternatives for timing are *concurrent* and *sequential* timing, alternatives for weighting are *equal* and *unequal* weight, and alternatives for mixing are *merging* the data (during analysis and interpretation), *embedding* the data and *connecting* the data.

One can also decide whether to conduct partially or fully mixed methods research. When taking timing and status of the approaches into account, the alternatives are (Leech and Onwuegbuzie 2009):

(1) Partially mixed concurrent equal status design.
(2) Partially mixed concurrent dominant status design.
(3) Partially mixed sequential equal status design.
(4) Partially mixed sequential dominant status design.
(5) Fully mixed concurrent equal status design.
(6) Fully mixed concurrent dominant status design.

One of the most elaborated mixed methods research models is called integrative mixed methods model (IMM). The model, created by Castro et al. (2010) gives a dominant role to a qualitative approach at the beginning, with the quantitative approach entering the picture later on in data analysis. The research consists of procedural steps that are: (a) creating focus questions, (b) extracting response codes, (c) creating thematic categories, (d) dimensionalizing the thematic category via scale coding, (e) qualitative-quantitative data analysis, and (f) creating story lines. In this model the frequency of certain themes is associated with importance and explanatory power. In other words, the more a certain theme appears in informants' verbal descriptions, the more important role it has in defining the phenomenon under investigation. The relationship between the themes can be investigated with quantitative methods such as correlation and explorative factor analysis.

From a qualitative point of view the IMM is rather *daring*. One of the fundamental differences between research approaches is their conception of scientific truth. An inexplicable exception within results in quantitative research is often treated as an *outlier* and is removed from the data analysis, but in qualitative thinking *outliers,* which may offer divergent perspectives on the results, are considered equally important and sometimes are examined more closely than perspectives which are more homogeneous. Similarly, in qualitative research an individual, unique experience is as important as the experiences that are common among the informants. In other words, using quantification as a criteria for defining the importance of a phenomenon is not a principle easy to share among qualitative researchers. An individual qualitative case study, for instance, can produce a profound and detailed description of a phenomenon under investigation (see, for example, Solli 2014). The researcher aims to represent the individual's unique experience. Any findings presented may be relevant to some people who have a similar experience but the results are not intended to represent any more than one person's perspective. Rather than generalizing across the population the qualitative researcher promotes naturalistic generalization which is a process where insight is gained by reflecting on the details and descriptions presented in a series of case studies (Melrose 2009). As researchers recognize similarities in case studies that fit to their own experiences then conclusions or even generalizations—with some reservations—can be made.

In clinical music therapy such models as IMM offer interesting possibilities. When researching an individual music therapy process consisting of a number of sessions, the frequency and timing of certain clinical themes within the process may give valuable information on essential aspects of the client's difficulties. This kind of analysis may also have value in relation to other clients with similar problems.

MIXED METHODS MUSIC THERAPY RESEARCH

The ingredients of clinical music therapy are numerous consisting of various highly abstract factors such as: music and the meaning; treatment theory; models, methods, and techniques of music therapy, as well as all the aspects of a human beings way of feeling, expressing, and interacting. It is no wonder then that music therapy is challenging to research, or that qualitative approach, which has the capacity to investigate complex phenomena, has had an important role in music therapy research. The quantitative approach is often experienced as too reductionist for music therapy research though the pressure is high to use it, in particular along with the march of EBM in health care research, including psychotherapy research. Bonde (2007) considers mixed methods useful in music therapy research because the approach combines methodologies such as descriptive statistics, phenomenological descriptions, and hermeneutic interpretations. This can be an advantage in providing information to the multidisciplinary team. For example, he has referred to the way in which qualitative music therapy studies can sometimes have no credibility among the medical professionals in cancer care (Bonde 2007).

In the next section some music therapy mixed methods studies are presented. A distinction is made between the studies where a single research report is based on mixed methods, and where a larger-scale research project uses mixed methods but publishes quantitative and qualitative results as separate reports.

MT research reports with mixed methods

An exploratory randomized controlled trial was conducted on group music therapy for post-traumatic stress disorders (Carr et al. 2012). In addition to quantitative measures data consisted of video recordings, process notes, and exit interviews. These are typical data types within qualitative analysis. Qualitative content analysis focused for instance on patient experiences of music therapy to better understand subjective experiences. The authors stated that the mixed methods design helped providing a rich account of music therapy not only as a tolerable and enjoyable personal experience, but also as a feasible and effective clinical intervention.

Sometimes in music therapy trials it happens that no significant difference between the control and experiment groups can be found on any outcome measures. This may be due to research related factors such as the sample being too small, or inappropriate outcome measures. Of course it can also be that the therapy did not work. If non-significant results are based on research-related factors, a qualitative approach can help in describing the possible benefits of music therapy based on, for instance, the clients' experiences. Although this will not lead to generalization for other people who are experiencing the same difficulties as the clients in the study, it may be of importance for planning later studies on the topic.

In another mixed methods study Silverman (2010) investigated the perceptions of music therapy interventions from inpatients with severe mental illness. A quantitative approach was utilized for evaluating helpfulness and enjoyable of music therapy interventions. A likert scale (1 = low, 7 = high) was used for measuring these. Qualitative data was derived from three open questions: (1) please explain the session in which you participated: what did you do? (2) Please explain what you thought the purpose of the session was, and (3) please make any comments about the session. In this study, neither of the approaches had a dominant role and the design was based on a concurrent strategy for the data collection and analysis.

A study by Bonde (2005) about the Bonny Method of Guided Imagery and Music (BMGIM) with cancer survivors is based on advanced mixed methods model. All the data was collected at the same time, quantitative approach was given less priority, and it also addressed different question than the dominant method (qualitative). The main research question was "what is the influence of ten individual BMGIM sessions on mood and quality of life in cancer survivors?" Quantitative data was derived from standardized questionnaires that were analyzed by statistical methods. Qualitative data was based on session data (transcripts, music, drawings) and analyzed by grounded theory and hermeneutic analysis methods. The last stage was a synthesis of the two approaches aka mixed methods analysis. Bonde suggests that there are advantages and disadvantages in mixed methods approach based on his experience. For instance, mixed methods gives a voice for participants and makes the study more communicative among those professionals who do not accept pure qualitative research reports as evidence. On the other hand, mixed methods as such do not help much if there are problems in successfully applying the approach (for instance, the sample size is too small). Bonde also points out the possible problems concerning the style of the mixed methods research reports and editors' and reviewers' criticism with regard the design that may cause difficulties in getting the results published.

In large-scale music therapy research projects, such as randomized controlled trials (RCT) with a high numbers of participants, it is typical to gather diverse data suitable both for quantitative and qualitative analysis. When planning a study, researchers first create a publication plan in awareness of the fact that quantitative results often have to be published separately as independent publications. Thus, a research project can consist of several publications.

MT research projects with mixed methods (multiple publications)

Due to publication principles of journals and to the substantial amount of data, large-scale mixed methods research projects tend to release several publications. Qualitative and quantitative results can be published separately, for instance. This typically improves the possibilities to get the results published because mixed methods publication channels are limited. Publishing results separately and dividing them into main–and sub-publications can be appropriate also from temporal point of view. Researchers and research projects need publications and the academic community and the profession benefit from publishing the results as soon as possible. The only possibility to connect all the results to one mixed methods study would probably be a monograph of some kind. However, in some scientific communities such as universities the journal literature is considered of higher value and researchers must take account of the metrics that are used to evaluate their contribution. This is in order to keep their jobs, to attain further research funding, and to retain momentum for their study and ideas.

The effect of improvisational music therapy for depression was examined through the implementation of an RCT (Erkkilä et al. 2011). The quantitative approach had a dominant role in that study and quantitative data analysis was carried out first (sequential approach). However, qualitative data, such as therapists' notes and video and audio recordings of the sessions, was gathered as well. The reason for this was researchers' awareness of limited interpretative power of quantitative results in the case that the experimental group of clients receiving improvisational music therapy improved significantly in one or more outcome measure. Ultimately it was shown that the experimental group improved significantly better that the control group. They were less depressed and anxious, had better general functioning, and better treatment response in the primary outcome measure of depression than the control group. The question then arose, what *mechanisms of change* (see Maratos et al. 2011) were behind these findings. Thus, a need to examine the treatment process in detail using a qualitative approach was obvious. This combination of quantitative and qualitative approaches where qualitative methods are employed for further explaining what has been found is one of the typical applications of mixed methods research. In mixed methods literature this practice is called embedded design (Caracelli and Greene 1997) of which the embedded experimental model (Creswell and Clark 2007), where priority is given to the quantitative methodology, is the most common variant (Doyle 2009).

In the study by Erkkilä et al. the questions such as *how clinical improvisation is connected to emotional processing and recovery in the treatment of depression* and *how improvising affect processing of the client's illness* remained unanswered in the main publication where only the quantitative results were reported. In a master's thesis (Koski-Helfenstein 2011) a phenomenological analysis was employed for answering these further questions using improvisations and discussions between the client and the therapist as the data. The author found that clinical improvisation was connected to expression and recognizing of emotions connected to the depressive disorder. Through musical images the client comes into contact and awareness of emotional material on pre-conscious level within the act of improvisation. The process helps the client in meaning formation and stimulates verbal expression. This can often be seen as lively and profound post improvisational conversations between the client and the therapist (Koski-Helfenstein 2011).

CONCLUSIONS

Mixed methods research design means mixing the methodologies in a study, even quantitative and qualitative research strategies that sometimes are thought to be fundamentally different and impossible to connect. In music therapy research, and in psychotherapy research in general, both quantitative and qualitative approaches have undeniable benefits. Many music therapy scholars represent the view where the two approaches are not mutually exclusive but complementary. Music therapy as a profession is also forced to be tolerant in regard with the research strategies because there is a social expectation that music therapy research should show evidence of effects and change, not only the experiences of the participants. The dominance of evidence-based medicine in health care and its influence on the health research field is one of those factors that in many countries has influenced the imperative to use quantitative approaches. RCTs seem to have dominance over other methodologies in offering convincing evidence of a useful treatment model.

One reason for the growth of mixed methods in therapy research probably rises from the need to gain deeper understanding on the specific, or even unique mechanisms of a treatment, not only on the effect as such. Developing a clinical method also requires profound, experience based knowledge and understanding of complex, multilayered, causal processes. Here, a client and therapist perspective, to name some, enters the picture. Gaining a deep understanding of a complex phenomenon often requires utilization of qualitative methods.

The mixed methods approach in research highlights some problems in reconciling two fundamentally different approaches. The starting point of quantitative approach always is a strict combination of procedures consisting of careful planning of the research questions, design, hypotheses, data gathering, analysis, and reporting. Even research reports are typically briefed in details allowing not much flexibility and the principle called IMRD (introduction, methods, results, discussion) is an expected format. Thus, quantitative approach demonstrates methodological strength. Criticisms are therefore not in relation to methodology but rather the inability of this type of research to be able to answer complex, multifaceted, phenomenological, and existential questions. Contrary to this, the qualitative approach is often questioned as to methodological processes which are often emergent from the data which is analyzed usually with reference to an open, simple, question.

Differences between research approaches occurs because of different understandings of scientific truth where detailed methodological procedures are easily seen leading to reductionism. In other words, detailed procedures are seen as preventing other possible procedures and therefore as an incomplete or reductionist understanding of the phenomenon under investigation. It is then very much dependent on the qualitative researcher's personal skills, talents, and research experience to do convincing qualitative research. The methodological freedom in qualitative research is not available to the quantitative researcher. Understandably, this state of affairs leads to greater variation in quality of qualitative research than quantitative. Therefore, when mixing approaches, it is important to pay attention to the quality of analysis no matter what approach it is in question. Yet another difference between the two approaches is that once a quantitative researcher has undertaken the basic planning work correctly, the analysis as such is a rather mechanical, even quick process. Doing qualitative analysis, in contrast, is always time-consuming and far from the routine technical work of other research procedures. It is therefore also vulnerable to human errors and influence.

Integrative models, such as the IMM (see above), is one way to improve the quality of mixed methods. When mixed methods research becomes more common in music therapy it is probable that more models will be introduced where issues such as integration and balance of the approaches are in particular addressed. A possible problem in this development may be to find publication channels for the studies. High ranking medical journals, for instance, usually have fixed standards for research reports. Therefore, it may take some time until mixed methods strategy becomes standardized enough to really be accepted for these journals. Music therapy as a health care profession is also dependent on publishing in medical journals and therefore has to keep doors open to different, also traditional, researching, and reporting strategies. On the other hand, mixed methods have much to offer to music therapy. Journals in music therapy and related areas such as psychotherapy can be more open to mixed methods research papers.

In terms of larger music therapy research projects, a good starting point is to first carefully evaluate which research approaches and data will best answer the research questions. If both quantitative and qualitative approaches become appropriate, the team can create an innovative publication plan where many aspects, including scientific, professional, societal, and political, are addressed. In particular, if there is a need to boost qualitative findings, or just make them more attractive for those readers who do not appreciate qualitative strategy as such. It still may be worth of considering the possibility of publishing pure quantitative results (e.g. on a RCT) separately in an esteemed journal with a good impact factor.

References

Abrams, B. (2010). Evidence-based music therapy practice: An integral understanding. *Journal of Music Therapy* 47(4): 351–379.

Bonde, L.O. (2005). *The bonny method of guided imagery and music (BMGIM) with cancer survivors. A psychosocial study with focus on the influence of BMGIM on mood and quality of life* (Doctoral thesis). Aalborg: Department of music and music therapy, Aalborg University.

Bonde, L.O. (2007). Using multiple methods in music therapy health care research. Reflections on using multiple methods in a research project about receptive music therapy with cancer survivors. In: J. Edwards (ed.), *Music: Promoting Health and Creating Community in Healthcare Contexts*, pp. 105–122. Cambridge: Cambridge Scholars Press.

Bradt, J., Burns, D.S., and Creswell, J.W. (2013). Mixed Methods Research in Music Therapy Research. *Journal of Music Therapy* 50(2): 123–148.

Bruscia, K.E. (1998). *The Dynamics of Music Psychotherapy*. Gilsum, NH: Barcelona Publishers.

Caracelli, V.J. and Greene, J.C. (1997). Crafting mixed-method evaluation designs. *New Directions for Program Evaluation* 74: 19–32.

Carr, C., d'Ardenne, P., Sloboda, A., Scott, C., Wang, D., and Priebe, S. (2012). Group music therapy for patients with persistent post-traumatic stress disorder—an exploratory randomized controlled trial with mixed methods evaluation. *Psychology and Psychotherapy: Theory, Research and Practice* 85: 179–202.

Castro, F.G., Kellison, J.G., Boyd, S.J., and Kopak, A. (2010). A methodology for conducting integrative mixed methods research and data analyses. *Journal of Mixed Methods Research* 4(4): 342–360.

Cochrane, A. (1972). *Effectiveness and efficiency. Random reflections on health services.* London: Nuffield provincial hospitals trust, 1972. London: Nuffield Provincial Hospitals Trust.

Creswell, J.W. (1994). *Research Design: Qualitative and Quantitative Approaches*. Thousand Oaks, CA: Sage.

Creswell, J.W. and Clark, P. (2007). *Designing and Conducting Mixed Methods Research.* Thousand Oaks, CA: Sage.

Doyle, L. (2009). An overview of mixed methods research. *Journal of Research in Nursing* 14(2): 175–185.

Edwards, J. (2005). Possibilities and problems for evidence based practice in music therapy. *The Arts in Psychotherapy* 32: 293–301.

Erkkilä, J., Punkanen, M., Fachner, J., Ala-Ruona, E., Pöntiö, I., Tervaniemi, M. et al. (2011). Individual music therapy for depression: Randomised controlled trial. *British Journal of Psychiatry* 199: 132–139.

Evidence-Based Medicine Working Group (1992). Evidence-based medicine working group. Evidence-based medicine. A new approach to teaching the practice of medicine. 268(17): 2420–2425.

Given, L.M. (2008). Purposive sampling. *The Sage Encyclopedia of Qualitative Research Methods*, pp. 697–698. Thousand Oaks, CA: Sage.

Koski-Helfenstein, R. (2011). Kliinisen improvisaation käynnistämä emotionaalinen prosessointi musiikkiterapiassa masennuksen hoidossa. [Emotional processing stimulated by clinical improvisation in music therapy for depression.] Master's thesis. Department of Music, University of Jyväskylä, Finland.

Langenberg, M., Aigen, K., and Frommer, J. (1996). *Qualitative Music Therapy Research: Beginning Dialogues*. Gilsum, NH: Barcelona Publishers.

Leech, N.L. and Onwuegbuzie, A.J. (2009). A typology of mixed methods research designs. *Quality and Quantity* 43: 265–275.

Maratos, A., Crawford, M.J., and Procter, S. (2011). Music therapy for depression: It seems to work, but how? *The British Journal of Psychiatry* 199: 92–93.

Melrose, S. (2009). Naturalistic generalization. In: A.J. Mills, G. Durepos, and E. Wiebe (eds), *Encyclopedia of Case Study Research*, pp. 599–601. Thousand Oaks, CA: Sage.

Priestley, M. (1994). *Essays on Analytical Music Therapy*. Gilsum, NH: Barcelona Publishers.

Sandelowski, M. (2001). Combining qualitative and quantitative sampling, data collection and analysis techniques in mixed method studies research. *Nursing and Health Sciences* 23: 246–255.

Silverman, M.J. (2010). Perceptions of music therapy interventions from inpatients with severe mental illness: A mixed-methods approach. *Tha Arts in Psychotherapy* 37: 264–268.

Smeijsters, H. (1997). *Multiple Perspectives: A Guide to Qualitative Research in Music Therapy*. Gilsum, NH: Barcelona Publishers.

Solli, H.P. (2014). Battling illness with wellness: a qualitative case study of a young rapper's experiences with music therapy. *Nordic Journal of Music Therapy*, (online ahead-of-print).

Strauss, A.L. and Corbin, J. (1990). *Basics of Qualitative Research: Grounded Theory Procedures and Techniques*. Thousand Oaks, CA: Sage.

Tashakkori, A., and Croswell, J.W. (2007). Editorial: The new era of mixed methods. *Journal of Mixed Methods Research* 1: 3–7.

CHAPTER 44

....

RESEARCHING MUSIC THERAPY IN MEDICAL SETTINGS

....

CYNTHIA M. COLWELL

INTRODUCTION

....

MEDICAL Music Therapy uses evidence-based therapeutic music interventions to address physical, emotional, cognitive, social, behavioral, and related psychosocial and physiological needs of individuals in medical settings ranging from the birthing center to the neonatal intensive care unit (NICU) through pediatrics, cancer care, general medical/surgical, and rehabilitation for older adults. Medical settings can include general hospitals, children's hospitals, and rehabilitation facilities and can include both in-patient and out-patient services. Within these facilities, medical music therapists can be found facilitating treatment interventions on every unit (AMTA Fact Sheet).

It is important for readers to be aware of the distinction between music medicine1, which typically uses recorded music facilitated by medical personnel where the music is the primary agent of change, and medical music therapy, in which music interventions are facilitated by a trained and qualified music therapist (Dileo 2006). In music therapy the relationship or rapport between the therapist and patient is considered a key ingredient of the therapeutic benefit attained.

This chapter provides an overview of a sampling of medical music therapy research in hospital settings for adult patients. Additionally, considerations for music therapy research in hospital settings are presented. The hospital setting is a unique context for research. Planning and collaboration is key to patient recruitment, retention, and study completion.

The medical treatment context is an especially challenging place in which to conduct music therapy research. On the one hand, there are many patients who, although ill 'have time opportunities and willingness to participate in a study of how music therapy affects them. On the other hand, there are patients who might be compromised by their illness, injury, or treatment, or who are in pain, anxious or vulnerable in some other way and therefore less open to being approached for study participation. Requesting permission for involvement directly from patients or from family members can be potentially intrusive and needs to be managed carefully. Proposing to play music with or for patients or engaging them in active music making can possibly be challenging to nursing and other treatment routines, and sometimes is viewed as a non-essential part of treatment and care. Committees with responsibility for approving research in hospitals have to weigh whether the benefits of the research outweigh any risks. These risks primarily concern patient safety but can include consideration of the burden on the patient and/or family to read additional documentation and provide signatures, and the effort required from staff for their potential roles in facilitating the music therapy study.

WHERE MUSIC THERAPY RESEARCH
HAS BEEN CONDUCTED

The next part of this chapter shows some of the areas of hospital care where music therapy research has been conducted. A review of representative research conducted in each area is presented.

Adult oncology

Music therapy in oncology settings functions to enhance quality of life of both cancer patients and their caregivers (Hanser 2006; Kruse 2003; Standley 1992). The focus is on improving quality of life while reducing symptoms associated with the disease and treatment (Bellamy and Willard 1993; Magill 2006; Porchet-Munro 1988; Weber et al. 1997). Targeted outcomes can include promoting self-expression through music, using music to improve mood and reduce stress, facilitating group music interactions for social outcomes, and stimulating physical and emotional well-being (Richardson et al. 2008). A variety of studies observed patients' perceptions and acceptance of music therapy services, compared standard nursing care to music therapy interventions, or examined the impact of diverse music therapy interventions on psychological and/or physiological measures.

Burns et al. (2005) were interested in determining which of two different types of music therapy interventions, music making or music listening, that cancer patients would prefer. Music making is considered interactive while music listening is considered more receptive. The researchers were interested in examining personal factors (anxiety, affect, fatigue, and coping) and perceptions about music therapy and how they might impact patients' preferences. Most of the participants indicated that they would be interested in participating in music therapy with 68% selecting music listening, 17% selecting music making, and 15% expressing a lack of interest. Those participants who selected music listening had more anxiety and higher negative affect. Participants who had higher Seeking Social Support scores, a coping strategy, were more likely to choose participating in some type of music therapy intervention than not. When examining the impact of patients' views of benefits, barriers, and confidence in participating in music interventions, some interesting but not unexpected results were reported. Patients who preferred music listening felt there were fewer barriers and more benefits from this receptive approach than those not interested in music therapy.

Neither those in the interactive or receptive preference group had more confidence that they could participate in music making than those not interested in participation but the individuals who would participate had more confidence in their ability to participate in the receptive intervention than the group not interested in participating.

O'Callaghan (2001) was also interested in understanding participants' experiences of music therapy in a cancer hospital. Information was gathered from open-ended questions posed to patients, visitors and staff and included the researcher's perception of the program's relevance. The researcher's approach was through thematic analysis of this information based on grounded theory. Grounded theory, an inductive data analysis paradigm, starts with data collection from which key codes are pulled from the text. Codes are grouped in categories that are further delineated into themes that form the basis for theory. Seven themes emerged from the analysis and included such foci as "music therapy or music can be associated with increased well-being, self-awareness, and self-expression" (p. 158). Using the similar data analysis paradigm, O'Callaghan and McDermott (2004) sought to determine the relevance of music therapy in a cancer hospital as viewed by patients, visitors, staff, and researchers. They defined relevance as what did the music therapy do and did it help? Comparable themes were evident and included patient views including "cancer and its treatment is physically enduring but MT can elicit shifts in physical awareness through altering sensory and somatic experience, or through motivating movement" (p. 164) or staff views including "many staff think that at least patients experience MT positive—emotionally, physically, spiritually or socially—as it helps them to negotiate their illness, including 'time out from it,' and to connect with people and times past" (p. 170). In a follow-up study, O'Callaghan (2007) examined the relationships between specific patient characteristics and responses from patients on a questionnaire about their music therapy experiences. A variety of themes were developed from the participants' responses. Results included the following: the number of sessions did not seem to impact reported experiences, males stated more positive affective responses and were more likely to return the questionnaire, but less likely to actually participate in sessions. Female respondents provided more description of memories and were more analytical of how music therapy helped them during treatment. Middle-aged patients viewed the experiences as bringing people together, while older patients focused more on the response to evoke memories.

From a unique perspective, O'Callaghan and Colegrove (1998) were interested in examining the introduction approach of music therapy students to oncology patients in cancer treatment. Verbal approaches were analyzed and the relationships among these approaches, the level of observed pain/physical comfort of the patient and the choice to engage in music therapy were analyzed. Patients were more likely to participate in live music therapy if (a) they heard music therapy sessions happening in the environment prior to their introduction, (b) their musical preferences were solicited, (c) live music was offered prior to any mention of music therapy, and (d) patients exhibited a moderate level of discomfort. Patients tended to initially refuse if (a) musical preferences were not solicited, (b) music therapy was explained, and (c) they were either experiencing no discomfort or significant discomfort.

A myriad of music therapy studies have examined music-based interventions on treatment outcomes across diverse domains. Common outcomes include pain and anxiety reduction, mood state enhancement, physiological measures deemed appropriate, and overall quality of life. Hanser et al. (2006) examined the effect of music therapy on psychological function, qualify of life, and physiologic stress arousal of women with metastatic breast cancer. Music therapy was compared with standard oncology supportive care. The music therapy intervention consisted of three sessions occurring all on one day during their chemotherapy infusion treatment with live music, improvisation, and songwriting occurring at each of the three sessions. While no difference between conditions were noted, there were significant differences after the MT sessions when examining relaxation, comfort, happiness, and heart rate.

Ferrer (2007) examined the impact of familiar live music on the anxiety levels of patients undergoing chemotherapy treatments. Standard care was the control condition compared with 20 minutes of familiar live music on anxiety, heart rate, blood pressure and fatigue, worry, fear, comfort, and relaxation. Results of the live music intervention indicated decreased anxiety, fear, and fatigue, and improved relaxation. Live music presented by the music therapist was singing with guitar accompaniment, patient-preferred music with the verbal encouragement to sing along as comfortable.

Comparing listening to music with music improvisation, Burns et al. (2001) wanted to determine the impact on psychological (well-being, relaxation, tension, energy) and physiological data (salivary immunoglobulin A [sIgA] and cortisol). All participants experienced listening (recorded or live), instrumental improvisation, and a follow-up focus group where they were asked to compare these experiences. Results indicated that those in both the listening to recorded music and listening to live music had increased well-being and decreased tension and energy. During the improvisation intervention, well-being and energy increased while tension decreased. Listening to music increased the levels of sIgA but did not elicit a change following improvisation.

Waldon (2001) also compared two formats of group music therapy with adult oncology patients, one considered making music and one considered responding to music. Making was defined as songwriting and improvisation while responding was defined as lyric analysis, relaxation, and imagery. Both treatment interventions had an impact on improving mood states but neither seemed to impact group cohesion.

Music imagery has been independently investigated as a treatment intervention for individuals with a cancer diagnosis. In 2001, Burns examined the impact of music imagery on the mood and live quality of cancer patients and found that the Bonny Method of Guided Imagery and Music more positively impacted the mood and quality of life scores of cancer patients after the sessions and at a delayed data point than those not receiving similar interventions. Later, Burns et al. (2008), compared music imagery to standard care on positive and negative affects, fatigue, and anxiety. Music imagery consisted of the therapist educating participants on how to use music imagery and then followed up with experiential imagery. Appropriate equipment was supplied to participants for follow-up independent music imagery experiences. Results indicated that music imagery is a feasible treatment intervention as indicated by rate of consent, percentage of completed sessions and measurement tools. No significant differences were found between interventions except with participants who reported higher levels of distress as they seemed to have lower anxiety after music imagery than those in standard care. Similarly in 2010, Gimeno wanted to compare imagery with music (New Age genre) and imagery on inducing relaxation (reduced heart rate) and reducing nausea and emesis of cancer patient undergoing chemotherapy. As with Burns et al. (2008), at-home music listening for relaxation was encouraged. Results indicated a decrease in heart rate and frequency of nausea and emesis for both conditions.

In addition to chemotherapy, oncology patients may have bone marrow and stem cell transplantation (Boldt 1996; Cassileth et al. 2003) or radiation therapy (Clark et al. 2006; Chorna 2010; O'Callaghan et al. 2012) as part of a treatment regimen for cancer. Patients undergoing stem cell transplantation can experience significant psychological distress that can adversely affect their mood (Cassileth et al. 2003). Music therapy was compared with standard care on patient's mood as assessed by the Profile of Mood States. Patients in the music therapy intervention experienced significantly lower scores on the Anxiety/Depression scale and on the total mood disturbance score when compared with controls.

Radiation therapy (RT) may be used in conjunction with or in lieu of chemotherapy and/or surgical options. Clark and his associates (2006) used preferred music to reduce emotional distress and fatigue and pain during this treatment regimen. The music therapy treatment intervention was recorded music listening and results indicated that depression, fatigue, and pain were not impacted by music therapy but anxiety and treatment-related distress were lower yet there was a decline in this impact across the RT regimen perhaps indicating the need for more frequency of listening interventions. Chorna (2010) also used music therapy (live preferred music) to reduce anxiety in patients during radiation. Results indicated lower procedural anxiety for the music therapy group especially during the first treatment delivery. O'Callaghan et al. (2012) also examined self-selected music on patient's anxiety during the initial radiation treatment. Results indicated a decrease in anxiety for both the treatment and control interventions with no different between conditions which may have been impacted by the relatively low pre-treatment anxiety reported. Participants in the music intervention were more likely to want music in future treatment sessions and reported that they felt more supported and distracted and that the treatment session seemed to go more quickly.

Both patients and families of oncology patients can experience anxiety, depression, and alteration of quality of life. Cermak (2005) examined the effect of music therapy and songwriting on these outcomes. These interactive sessions included songwriting about the patient and family (group one) or live preferred music and counseling (group two). Group one had two sessions, one to focus on material for songwriting, the second to write, record, and perform the song. Group two had one session focusing on preferred music listening and counseling. Measures taken one week after the session indicated that those in the songwriting group had higher Quality of Life Scores than the listening/counseling group.

Coming from a different outcome perspective, researchers have examined the impact of music on oncology staff. Canga et al. (2012) examined the impact of environmental music therapy on the needs of those in the waiting room or the actual chemotherapy infusion suite. Environmental music therapy was defined as live instrumental music performed by music therapists and determined by physical space, environmental noise, and preferences of those in the environment. Results of this pilot study using a six-question questionnaire and noted informal comments revealed that staff felt the music was influential in altering the environment and that volume was appropriate. O'Callaghan and Magill (2009) were interested in the impact of music therapy on oncology staff who informally observe music therapy interventions with patients. In a two-part study, the researchers first asked staff to complete a questionnaire on the relevance of music therapy for patients, next they interviewed a different sample of nursing and medical staff to determine the personal impact of these types of informal observations of music therapy treatment interventions. Perceptions of the staff as indicated on the questionnaire were that there were emotional, cognitive, and team cohesion effects that potentially resulted in improved patient care. Self-reported impacts reported through the interviews indicated similar personal benefits and improved patient care. Three potential detriments were noted: audibility of the music, initial concern about the viability of the treatment, and potential impact on productivity due to reduced pace as a result of staff relaxation as a byproduct of the intervention.

Obstetrics and gynecological

Women's health issues in both the obstetric and gynecological realms have been subject to research using music therapy to impact various treatment outcomes. In obstetrics, studies have indicated a reduction in anxiety, pain, and length of labor when music is paired with traditional Lamaze exercises (Codding 1982; Hanser et al. 1983; Winslow 1986). In gynecology, music reduced pain following in-office procedures (Davis 1992), and surgery for OB-GYN patients (Locsin 1981), and decreased narcotic ingestion for a patient with advanced endometriosis (Colwell 1997).

In 1990, Cathy McKinney summarized the literature available at that time and discussed the impact of music therapy on various psychological factors active during pregnancy and childbirth and discussed how music listening has been found to reduce pain, promote relaxation, and stimulate paced breathing. Included in this summarization was a study in the early 1980s that described the clinical path of using music during labor and delivery (Clark et al. 1981). Patients preselected music with the guidance of a music therapist and this music was used in pre-delivery training sessions and then during the actual labor and delivery process. The impact of this training and subsequent use of music in the presence of the therapist was compared with standard care on patients' self-reported perceptions and memories of the labor and delivery process. Outcomes seemed to indicate use of music impacted the success of the birth experience. A subsequent document by the lead author (Clark 1986) provided a practical guide for Music Therapy-Assisted Childbirth.

Elizabeth Collins Cook completed an updated systematic categorization of the literature targeting the use of music and music therapy during pregnancy in 2012. Her premise was that maternal emotional and physiological stress and anxiety should be examined due to their potential detrimental impact on the mother and developing fetus. Cook states that the literature supports the use of music listening and music therapy alone or with other interventions on prenatal stress and anxiety but further indicates that the relationship with the music therapist may be critical for long term positive effects. Her hope is that the results of her review will initiate resurgence in music therapy in prenatal care.

As in other medical fields, nurses are facilitating studies labeled as music therapy in the obstetrics milieu. Shu-Chen Chang of Taiwan and nursing colleagues examined the impact of music on various physiological and psychological measures of pregnant woman. Initially in 2005, Chant and Chen studied the effect of music on physiologic measures, anxiety, and satisfaction during Cesarean delivery. Standard care was compared to preferred-music listening and results indicated that those listening to music had significantly lower anxiety and higher self-reported satisfaction during the Cesarean birthing process. Chang et al. (2008) further examined the effect of music on the stress, anxiety, and depression of pregnant woman in Taiwan. Those patients listening to music had reduced perceived stress, state stress, and depression compared to those in the control group who only indicated a decrease in perceived stress. In a later study, Liu et al. (2010) used a similar music protocol for women during labor to reduce pain and anxiety. When compared to standard care, women in the latent stage of labor reported lower pain and anxiety.

The use of music therapy to decrease pain and anxiety during labor and delivery is often described anecdotally as well as empirically in the literature (Browning 2000; Gonzalez 1989). Browning (2001) targeted using music in assisting relaxation and breaking the "fear-tension-pain syndrome" of mothers during childbirth. When comparing outcomes of participants using traditional breathing and relaxation techniques with those who also engaged in music therapy sessions, no difference between the groups in relation to medication ingestion were noted. Significant differences between participants groups were noted with the music therapy participants reporting improved relaxation in the hours immediately preceding childbirth and more personal control during the labor process.

Pregnancy can be very stressful for any woman but due to the age and circumstances of teenagers, there can be increased levels during adolescent pregnancy. The use of a music and relaxation intervention was compared to no intervention on the state and trait anxiety of adolescents during the third trimester of pregnancy (Liebman and McClaren 1991). No significant differences were found when comparing the two groups, yet the researchers discussed the impact of the grouping and differing levels of anxiety on the pretest as potentially impacting these intervention effects.

The use of music therapy in early labor was compared to standard care on the outcomes of fetal heart rate, strength of uterine contraction and self-perception of pain and fatigue (Fulton 2005). Music listening was the therapeutic intervention and consisted of patient-preferred live music presented by the music therapist once the uterine contractions were five minutes or less apart. Results indicated a reduction in self-reported pain and fatigue for participants in the music listening condition.

Following delivery, the process of mother and child establishing the breastfeeding routine can be anxiety producing for both individuals (Procelli 2005). Mothers who received music therapy prior to breastfeeding attempts were observed to have less anxiety-related behaviors and more behaviors that demonstrated comfort and relaxation. Mothers corroborated these results with self-reported feelings of relaxation and decreased anxiety. Behavioral states of the babies did not differ between the music therapy and control groups.

General medical/surgical

An early reference to the use of music in modern medical settings is that of dentistry (Cherry and Pallin 1948). While not within what the reader might think of as a typical "medical setting" it is important to mention as one of the building blocks of music therapy in the general medical model (Standley 1986). Comparable to some of the uses of music by nurses in a passive listening intervention, some of the research in dentistry using music for pain and anxiety, is also not always facilitated by music therapists (Aitken et al. 2002; Klassen et al. 2008) but has found some positive outcomes for dental patients and builds the foundation for future work targeting pain and anxiety in in-patient medical environments. General medical/surgical is a somewhat inclusive term for medical units that meet the needs of a variety of patient groups including but not limited to transplant, cardiac care, internal medicine, gastrointestinal, and surgeries due to a variety of causes.

Ghetti (2011) examined active music engagement (AME) with emotional-approach coping to improve well-being in liver and kidney transplant recipients. She compared the impact of three groups, AME, AME with emotional-approach coping (EAC), and a control group on affective states, pain, coping self-efficacy, hospital satisfaction, and willingness to and length of ambulation. Results indicated that those in the AME with EAC has significant increases in positive affect while AME alone led to significant decreases in pain. Both of the music therapy groups seemed to decrease negative affect that can be an indicator of perceived stress/anxiety.

Music therapy has also been used with patients with a variety of cardiac issues (Hanser 2013; Hanser and Mandel 2005) often targeting stress responses. Hanser, Mandel and research colleagues have examined the effect of music therapy in cardiac rehabilitation. In their first study in 2007, Mandel, Hanser, Secic, and Davis, defined music therapy as music experiences, counseling, and Music-Assisted Relaxation and Imagery. In combination with cardiac rehabilitation, this group was compared to a cardiac rehabilitation only group with results indicating a decrease in systolic blood pressure for the music therapy group. In a follow up study (Mandel et al. 2010), researchers evaluated the impact of a music-assisted relaxation and imagery CD on outcomes of patients in cardiac rehabilitation. A significant decrease in systolic blood pressure was again reported with additional impact on state anxiety and stress.

Expanding on her work on a transplant unit, Ghetti (2013) again using the addition of emotional-approach coping as a strategy, randomly placed cardiac catheterization patients into three treatment interventions, standard care control group, music therapy with emotional-approach coping or a talk-based emotional-approach coping group to examine the impact on positive affective states and physiological measures in adults prior to the procedure. After only a single music therapy session, participants exhibited an increased positive affect over those in the talk-based or standard care groups. There was a decreased negative affect for all participants regardless of group with no differences in physiological measures of heart rate, respiratory rate, or oxygen saturation.

As patients process the personal ramifications of cardiac rehabilitation post cardiothoracic surgery, Short et al. (2013) had six individuals participate in weekly Bonny method guided imagery sessions. The themes associated with the recovery process developed from these imagery experiences included patients' physical changes, adjustment after surgery, and anticipated lifestyle post surgery. Both cardiac and cancer patients were surveyed asking them to offer their opinions about the efficacy of music therapy for its medical and psychotherapeutic benefits (Bruscia et al. 2009). Various music activities and styles were presented and the researchers were interested in comparing the results based on the patient health diagnosis and music background. Results indicated that both oncology and cardiac patients felt the expected benefits of music therapy were as a social and recreation activity, to relieve stress or anxiety, to find spiritual support or inspiration, for emotional support and comfort, to enjoy music more fully, to examine and express feelings, to communicate to loved ones, to think about one's life, to find greater hope and meaning in life, and to ward off feelings of isolation and loneliness. Cancer patients indicated statistically higher benefits than cardiac patients in many of these areas. Both diagnostic groups rated listening to music as the most effective type of music therapy intervention and spiritual/religious music the most effective style of music to be used.

Mechanical ventilation is a medical technique to replace spontaneous breathing and is used to provide breathing assistance but is not curative of disease. Taking someone off of ventilation is obviously the desired outcome although the weaning process is highly stress inducing. Using sedation to reduce anxiety during this process can be contraindicated due to the side effects of sedation that can impact the respiratory system. Hunter et al. (2010) examined the impact of music therapy on anxiety, days to wean, and patient and nurse satisfaction. Significant differences in heart and respiratory rates indicated patient relaxation across the session that supports the feasibility of music as a treatment modality during this process. Treatment sessions were designed for each patient and consisted of singing, playing and improvisation, songwriting, lyric discussion and music-assisted relaxation and imagery. In a more recent study targeting anxiety and sedative exposure of ICU patients using ventilation, researchers (Chlan et al. 2013), compared patient-directed music intervention with two non music-based treatments, the use of noise-abating headphones or standard care. Patients in the music listening intervention had a greater reduction in anxiety and intensity of sedation compared with standard care but not with patients wearing the headphones. A significant reduction in sedation frequency was found between those in the music intervention and both non music-based groups.

Surgery is a significant cause of stress, anxiety, and pain. Stress can have an impact on coping strategies and physiological responses (Miluk-Kolasa et al. 1996). Gooding and medical colleagues at the University of Kentucky completed a review of the literature examining anxiety and pain in relation to surgery (Gooding et al. 2012). Although some mixed results and need for further research are evident, their findings indicate that music interventions can reduce anxiety, pain, and sedative intake. Most of the studies involve passive music listening with an indication that researcher-selected music may be more impactful as they have the expertise to choose literature with music elements that support altering these therapeutic outcomes including stable rhythms, smooth melodic lines, and consistent tempos and dynamics.

In contrast to the more prevalent music listening strategies, Walworth et al. (2008) facilitated live music therapy sessions with patients undergoing elective brain surgery in an attempt to reduce anxiety and stress while improving patients' perception of the situation, induce relaxation, reduce medication administration and decrease overall length of stay. These sessions were held prior to the surgery and each subsequent post-surgical day of admission and were compared to routine medical care. Results indicated significant change in anxiety, perception of hospitalization experience, relaxation, and stress.

In consideration of the unique aspects of surgical implications related to a cancer diagnosis, Chaput-McGovern and Silverman (2012) were interested in the music therapy immediate and sustained treatment gains on relaxation, pain, anxiety, nausea, and perception of the patient-preferred live music therapy experience. There were significant positive immediate gains from pre- to post-intervention measures yet no significant difference between post-intervention and follow-up measure indicating maintenance of results in this pilot study.

Not only do patients experience anxiety related to surgical procedures, but loved ones who are relegated to the waiting room can experience significant levels of stress as well. Jarred (2003) examined the impact of live music on self-reported anxiety levels. Three treatment groups included a direct music group (songs requested for 20 minutes of live music), an indirect music group (present in the same room but were not offered an opportunity for music choice), and a control group that received no music. Outcomes included self-reported anxiety, stress, worry, relaxation, and enjoyment levels on Visual Analog Scales. Results indicated no differences in anxiety, stress, or worry but there was a difference in relaxation levels between the music groups and control group. Participants in the direct group where live music was presented described more enjoyment than the indirect group. In a similar stressful situation, patients admitted through the Emergency Room often experience significant amounts of pain and anxiety. Negrete (2011) used live music to decrease pain and anxiety and improve quality of life in the unique ER setting. Results indicated that those who participated in live music had a significant decrease in pain and an increase in comfort. Live music included listening to patient preferred music or continuous instrumental music with verbal instructions for relaxation and breathing.

DEVELOPING MUSIC THERAPY RESEARCH IN MEDICAL SETTINGS

As evident in the above examples of research, in spite of the small number of music therapy practitioners internationally there is a strong tradition of music therapy research studies in medical contexts. In this next section of the chapter, the ways in which research can be carried out in a medical context, including some potential pitfalls and challenges, is presented for consideration when planning and conducting research.

Guiding question or hypothesis

A research question typically grows out of clinical practice and the desire to understand the impact of music-based interventions. Consideration of the epistemological approach and subsequent theoretical perspective will help determine the research methodology, relevant research to review, and the decision of a research design and methods. The acronym PICO (Richardson et al. 1995) is often used in evidence-based medical practice when designing clinical research. P stands for the population, I for intervention, C for comparison group, and O for outcome. This has been more recently adapted (Aveyard and Sharp 2009) in an attempt to be inclusive of a more qualitative stance with P representing people or perspective, I for issue, C for context/setting, and O for opinions/attitudes. While not all-encompassing, these assists can guide the researcher to consider the components needed to plan and conduct a research study. Depending on the perspective chosen, the research will either have a guiding question or one or more hypotheses.

Choice of epistemology

Music therapy research is increasingly being described as grouped in three categories of research: (1) objectivist, (2) constructivist, and (3) mixed methods (O'Callaghan

2009; O'Callaghan and McDermott 2004). Choosing the epistemological position is part of the researcher's dilemma pertaining to what is the question behind the research (Edwards 2012). The objectivist approach is aligned with positivism and typically uses experimental designs to address a predetermined hypothesis. Positivism is a branch of science that concentrates on knowledge as developed from logical and mathematical outcomes as empirical evidence that can be observed and measured and as such these underlying "truths" develop theory. The constructivist approach views that knowledge and meaning is created during the interaction between experiences and ideas and takes a more reflexive stance in its methodology and analyses. These can take the form of grounded theory, ethnography, or discourse analysis. Mixed methods research supports both paradigms regarding how knowledge may be created within a single study (Bradt et al. 2013). It allows the researcher to generalize from the targeted sample to a population but also develop a deeper, contextual understanding of the phenomenon being examined. Mixed methods consist of both quantitative and qualitative data within a single study. The data can be gathered simultaneously or sequentially (Creswell and Clark 2011).

Planning the research

As described, planning the research begins with formulating the guiding question or hypothesis while concurrently determining the epistemological position best suited to answer the question(s). This shapes the methodology and the specific methods the researcher uses in the study (Crotty 1998). Logistically, researchers must ponder numerous issues during the design and approval process with a sample presented for consideration that may vary based on clinician/researcher, methodology, or facility.

Choice of population

Study implementation may fail because of population or cohort issues. Researchers ideally should have had clinical experience working with the population in the past so possess the clinical wisdom of effective treatment interventions with specific populations and in particular medical settings. This insight can lead the clinical researcher to better understand and address issues around asking appropriate research questions, creating feasible designs and successfully obtaining consent, participation, and retention in a research study. Where small numbers of highly diverse patients are admitted somewhat irregularly to a unit or ward the choice of research method must be able to accommodate small numbers or the choice of diverse populations within the sample, potentially low uptake of participation in the research, and anticipation of momentum issues in the research as gathering an adequate sample can be time intensive. Although challenging to some starting out on a research career, it is sometimes more productive and effective to start researching with populations that are admitted regularly in the hospital context in which the research is to take place. Gaining information about admissions over the past two years can help to point to a population that is well represented as a means to determining feasibility of specific music-based interventions.

Institution Review Board/Human Subjects Consent

While there is variability regarding the processes for obtaining permission to conduct research in medical settings at different facilities nationally and internationally, safeguards are typically put into place to protect the patient(s). The intent of an Institutional Review Board (IRB) is solely to protect the rights and welfare of the patient(s). They examine the process for consent to participate in a proposed research study and evaluate the intended benefits and potential risks to the patient and whether or not the benefits outweigh the risks. At times, a music therapy researcher working with an IRB will discover the opportunity for education and advocacy for the profession as the committee may have questions about music therapy before they can make a determination on the proposed study. Researchers must be aware that professional jargon common to clinicians/researchers may not be familiar terminology (i.e., music-assisted relaxation, active music engagement, guided imagery with music) to an IRB not well versed in this area and as such further check backs may be needed before approval is granted.

Relevant research

Numerous research studies with the term "music therapy" in their titles or in the description of intervention strategies have been conducted and yet on close reading one can find that a qualified music therapist was not involved in the implementation of the research. While these can be published in esteemed and informative publications, it is important that the reader be aware that medical personnel rather than music therapists may have implemented these music-based interventions; typically receptive music listening. In addition, as researchers are reviewing relevant research and developing supported methodological approaches or designing music-based intervention strategies, it is essential to find publications that are based in a supported theoretical framework (Burns 2012; Hanson-Abromeit 2015; Robb 2012) and are transparent in their intervention reporting (Robb et al. 2011).

Music therapy interventions/research environment

Commonly in medical settings is patient admission may be transient. Patients may be in over night for observation, anticipate a short stay following the delivery of a baby, be termed a "frequent flyer" due to a chronic health condition, or require an extended stay due to rehabilitation after a stroke or cardiac episode. Therefore, a patient may be available to a clinician/researcher for only a one-time encounter or for an extended period of continuity with varying session frequency. Depending upon this variability, the setting or intended research question, the choice of a single versus more extended session focus may have to be anticipated with the study design and implementation.

Conducting the research

As in the planning of research in medical settings, the actual facilitation or conducting of research in this milieu has inherent challenges that can alter intended completion. As in any naturalistic environment, the setting, the individuals, and the therapeutic medium are all potential variables that can impact the outcomes of the research.

Treatment interruptions

When facilitating a music-based intervention for a patient as a clinician in a medical setting, it is not uncommon to anticipate treatment interruptions. Treatment interruptions may be medically or socially related. Visitors, phone calls, medical personnel visits, scheduled and unscheduled medical interventions or tests all function to delay, postpone, or cancel the session. Continuity often depends upon the desires of the patient or the urgency of the medical needs. When these interruptions occur during a research project, carefully controlled variables such as duration of a session, verbal processing following songwriting, or completion of a clinical measure may not be able to be completed as planned thus altering the validity of the process. Precautions may need to be taken to ask the patient to consider requesting to not be disturbed during this time, choosing a time-frame in consultation with ward staff that will be the least likely to involve medical interventions, or designing a study that can handle the flexibility of such interruptions, or has a short intervention time.

Patient, family, and staff influence

As part of the informed consent process required of the IRB, the intent of the study is disclosed to the patient. This can cause the patient to want to "help" the researcher be successful in the research endeavor and may impact the responses or participation of the patient. It may be necessary for the researcher to offer services before discussing a potential research study or the facility may require direct discussion of the consent process prior to any therapeutic engagement is initiated to maximize control and decision making of the patient. Family members can have a similar or a contrasting reaction if they do not see the necessity of the research project or fear its impact on the physical and emotional health of their loved one. On occasion, a family member can persuade or dissuade a patient's participation in a research project. Staff can also influence the research process either positively or negatively. They may intervene without understanding the necessary controls of the study, or may provide undue influence on the patient. Research collaboration with staff members can help alleviate their concerns when they are intimately familiar with the process and invested in its success. Prior experience with the patient must also be considered when the researcher is conducting a study. Rapport is a key element of a therapeutic intervention and the establishing of a previous relationship for some study participants but not others can impact research outcomes. Prior experience with music therapy as a treatment modality may also impact participant's desire to consent or maintain participation in the research project.

Ethical considerations

If a therapist also works clinically with this potentially vulnerable population, ethical issues needs to be considered. When implementing music-based interventions, music therapists address levels of a priori assessed needs of the patient but are also responsive to the verbal and non-verbal behaviors that indicate the required directionality of the treatment intervention. In a research venue, depending upon the methodology chosen, it is not always appropriate for a researcher to alter the process in a responsive fashion as it may invalidate the research measures. Randomized controlled studies that use a control group or a wait-list control group are considered an excellent comparative group against an examined treatment intervention, but the ethical issue of withholding or delaying a potentially beneficial treatment can impact how the study will be approved, designed, consented and/or conducted.

CONCLUSION

This chapter provides but a sampling of the wealth of diverse research being completed in a myriad of medical settings. Individuals interested in conducting research in such settings are encouraged to become familiar with relevant research, specifically examining intervention reporting, the therapeutic function of the music elements in these interventions, and subsequent treatment outcomes through varied research epistemological approaches. The clinical wisdom of the researcher is vital to the process of planning and conducting research in medical settings and as such clinicians are encouraged to base their research inquiries from within their own clinical practice experience.

NOTE

1. This term also appears in some literature as MusicMedicine because of the German origins of some of the literature about the use of music in medical settings (Spintge 1999).

REFERENCES

Aitken, J.C., Wilson, S., Coury, D., and Moursi, A.M. (2002). The effect of music distraction on pain, anxiety and behavior in pediatric dental patients. *Pediatric Dentistry* 24(2): 114–118.

Aveyard, H. and Sharp, P. (2009). *A Beginner's Guide to Evidence Based Practice in Health and Social Care* 1st ed. Maidenhead, UK: Open University Press.

American Music Therapy Association (AMTA). AMTA Fact Sheet: *Music Therapy and Medicine*. Retrieved at: <http://www.musictherapy.org/assets/1/7/MT_Medicine_2006.pdf>.

Bellamy, M.A. and Willard, P.B. (1993). Music therapy: An integral component of the oncology experience. *International Journal of Arts Medicine* 2(1): 14–19.

Boldt, S. (1996). The effects of music therapy on motivation, psychological well being, physical comfort and exercise endurance in bone marrow transplant patients. *Journal of Music Therapy* 33: 164–188.

Bradt, J., Burns, D.S., and Creswell, J.W. (2013). Mixed methods research in music therapy research. *Journal of Music Therapy* 50(2): 123–148.

Browning, C.A. (2000). Using music during childbirth. *Birth and the Family Journal* 27(4): 272–276.

Browning, C.A. (2001). Music therapy in childbirth: Research in practice. *Music Therapy Perspectives* 19(2): 74–81.

Bruscia, K., Dileo, C., Shultis, C., and Dennery, K. (2009). Expectations of hospitalized cancer and cardiac patients regarding the medical and psychotherapeutic benefits of music therapy. *The Arts in Psychotherapy* 36(4): 239–244.

Burns, D.S. (2001). The effect of the Bonny Method of Guided Imagery and Music on the mood and life quality of cancer patients. *Journal of Music Therapy* 38: 51–65.

Burns, D.S. (2012). Theoretical rationale for music selection in oncology intervention research: An integrative review. *Journal of Music Therapy* 49: 7–22.

Burns, S.J.I., Harbuz, M.S., Hucklebridge, F., and Bunt, L. (2001). A pilot study into the therapeutic effects of music therapy at a cancer help center. *Alternative Therapies in Health and Medicine* 7(1): 48–56.

Burns, D.S., Sledge, R.B., Fuller, L.A., Daggy, J.K., and Monahan, P.O. (2005). Cancer patients' interest and preferences for music therapy. *Journal of Music Therapy* 42(3): 185–199.

Burns, D.S., Azzouz, F., Sledge, R., Rutledge, C., Hincher, K. Monahan, P., and Cripe, L.D. (2008). Music imagery for adults with acute leukemia in protective environments: A feasibility study. *Supportive Care in Cancer* 16: 507–513.

Canga, B., Hahm, C.L., Lucido, D., Grossbard, M.L., and Loewy, J.V. (2012). Environmental music therapy: A pilot study on the effects of music therapy in a chemotherapy influsion suite. *Music and Medicine* 4: 221–230.

Cassileth, B., Vickets, A., and Magill, L. (2003). Music therapy for mood disturbance during hospitalization for autologous stem cell transplantation. *Cancer* 98: 2723–2729.

Cermak, A.M. (2005). The effect of music therapy and songwriting on anxiety, depression and quality of life in cancer patients and their families as measured by self-report. Unpublished Master's Thesis, Florida State University, *Electronic Theses, Treatises and Dissertations*. Paper 3981.

Chang, M.Y., Chen, C.H., and Huang, K.F. (2008). Effects of music therapy on psychological health of woman during pregnancy. *Journal of Clinical Nursing* 17(19): 2580–2587.

Chang, S. and Chen, C. (2005). Effects of music therapy on women's physiologic measures, anxiety, and satisfaction during cesarean delivery. *Research in Nursing and Health* 28: 453–461.

Chaput-McGovern, J. and Silverman, M. (2012). Effects of music therapy with patients on a post-surgical oncology unit: A pilot study determining maintenance of immediate gains. *The Arts in Psychotherapy* 29(5): 417–422.

Cherry, H. and Pallin, I. (1948). Music as a supplement in nitrous oxide-oxygen anesthesia. *Anesthesiology* 9(4): 391–399.

Chlan, L., Weinert, C.R., Heiderscheit, A., Tracy, M.F., Skaar, D.J., Guttornson, J.L., and Savik, K. (2013). Effects of patient-directed music intervention on anxiety and sedative exposure in critically-ill patients receiving mechanical ventilator support: A randomized clinical trial. *Journal of the American Medical Association* 309(22): 2335–2344.

Chorna, O. (2010). The effect of music therapy on patients' anxiety and perception during radiation oncology simulation and treatment. *Electronic Theses, Treatises and Dissertations*. Paper 3754.

Clark, M. (1986). Music therapy-assisted childbirth: A practical guide. *Music Therapy Perspectives* 3: 34–41.

Clark, M., McCorkle, R., and Williams, S. (1981). Music therapy-assisted labor and delivery. *Journal of Music Therapy* 18: 88–100.

Clark, M., Isaacks Downton, G., Wells, N., Redlin-Frazier, S., Eck, C., Hepworth, J.T., and Chakravarthy, B. (2006). Use of preferred music to reduce emotional distress and symptom activity during radiation therapy. *Journal of Music Therapy* 63: 247–265.

Codding, P. (1982). An exploration of the uses of music in the birthing process. Unpublished Master's Thesis, The Florida State University, Tallahassee, FL.

Collins, E.C. (2012). *The use of music and music therapy to reduce stress and anxiety during pregnancy: A systematic categorization of the literature.* Unpublished masters thesis, Drexel University.

Colwell, C.M. (1997). Music as a distraction and relaxation to reduce chronic pain and narcotic ingestion: A case study. *Music Therapy Perspectives* 15(1): 24–31.

Creswell, J.W. and Plano Clark, V.L. (2011). *Designing and conducting mixed methods research,* 2nd ed. Thousand Oaks, CA: Sage Publications, Inc.

Crotty, M. (1998). *The Foundations of Social Research.* Thousand Oaks, CA: Sage Publications, Inc.

Davis, C.A. (1992). The effects of music and basic relaxation instruction on pain and anxiety of women undergoing in-office gynecological procedures. *Journal of Music Therapy* 29: 202–216.

Dileo, C. (2006). Effects of music and music therapy on medical patients: A meta-analysis of the research and implications for the future. *Journal of the Society of Integrative Oncology* 4(2): 67–70.

Edwards, J. (2012). We need to talk about epistemology: Orientations, meaning, and interpretation within music therapy research. *Journal of Music Therapy* 49: 372–394.

Ferrer, A.J. (2007). The effect of live music on decreasing anxiety in patients undergoing chemotherapy treatment. *Journal of Music Therapy* 44: 242–255.

Fulton, K. (2005). The effects of music therapy on physiological measures, perceived pain, and perceived fatigue of women in early labor. *Electronic Theses, Treatises and Dissertations.* Paper 4376.

Ghetti, C. (2011). Active music engagement with emotional-approach coping to improve well-being in liver and kidney transplant recipients. *Journal of Music Therapy* 48: 463–485.

Ghetti, C. (2013). Effect of music therapy with emotional-approach coping on pre-procedural anxiety in cardiac catheterization. *Journal of Music Therapy* 50: 93–122.

Gimeno, M.M. (2010). The effect of music and imagery to induce relaxation and reduce nausea and emesis in patients with cancer undergoing chemotherapy treatment. *Music and Medicine* 2(3): 174–181.

Gonzalez, C.E. (1989). The music therapy-assisted childbirth program: A study evaluation. *Journal of Prenatal and Perinatal Psychology and Health* 4: 111–124.

Gooding, L., Swezey, S., and Zwischenberger, J.B. (2012). Using music interventions in perioperative care. *Southern Medical Journal* 105(9): 486–490.

Hanser, S. (2006). Music therapy in adult oncology: Research issues. *Journal of the Society for Integrated Oncology* 4(2): 62–66.

Hanser, S.B. (2013). Music therapy in cardiac healthcare: Current issues in research. *Cardiology in Review* 22(1): 37–42.

Hanser, S.B. and Mandel, S.E. (2005). The effects of music therapy in cardiac healthcare. *Cardiology in Review* 13: 18–23.

Hanser, S., Larson, S.D., and O'Connell, S.A. (1983). The effect of music on relaxation of expectant mothers during labor. *Journal of Music Therapy* 22: 50–58.

Hanser, S.B., Bauer-Wu, S., Kubicek, L., Healey, M., Manola, J., Hernandez, M., and Bunnell, C. (2006). Effects of a music therapy intervention on quality of life and distress in women with metastatic breast cancer. *Journal of the Society of Integrative Oncology* 4(3): 116–124.

Hanson-Abromeit, D. (2015). A Conceptual Methodology to Define the Therapeutic Function of Music. *Music Therapy Perspectives* 33(1): 14–27.

Hunter, B., Oliva, R., Sahler, O., Gaisser, D., Salipante, D., and Arezina, C. (2010). Music therapy as an adjunctive treatment in the management of stress for patients being weaned from mechanical ventilation. *Journal of Music Therapy* 47: 198–219.

Jarred, J.D. (2003). The effect of live music on anxiety levels of persons waiting in a surgical waiting room as measured by self-report. Unpublished master's thesis, Florida State University. *Electronic Theses, Treatises and Dissertations.* Paper 3550.

Klassen, J.A., Liang, Y., Tjosvold, L., Klassen, T.P., and Hartling, L. (2008). Music for pain and anxiety in children undergoing medical procedures: A systematic review of randomized controlled trials. *Ambulatory Pediatrics* 8: 117–128.

Kruse, J. (2003). Music therapy in United States cancer settings: Recent trends in practice. *Music Therapy Perspectives* 21(2): 89–98.

Liebman, S.S. and MacLaren, A. (1991). The effects of music and relaxation on third trimester anxiety in adolescent pregnancy. *Journal of Music Therapy* 28(2): 89–100.

Liu, Y.H., Chang, M.Y., and Chen, C.H. (2010). Effects of music therapy on labour pain and anxiety in Taiwanese first-time mothers. *Journal of Clinical Nursing* 19(7–8): 1065–1072.

Locsin (1981). The effect of music on the pain of selected post-operative patients. *Journal of Advanced Nursing* 6: 19–25.

Magill, L. (2006). Role of music therapy in integrative oncology. *Journal of the Society of Integrative Oncology* 4(2): 79–81.

Mandel, S.E., Hanser, S.B., Secic, M., and Davis, B.A. (2007). Effects of music therapy on health-related outcomes in cardiac rehabilitation: A randomized controlled trial. *Journal of Music Therapy* 44: 176–197.

Mandel, S.E., Hanser, S.B., and Ryan, L.J. (2010). Effects of a music-assisted relaxation and imagery compact disc recording on health-related outcomes in cardiac rehabilitation. *Music Therapy Perspectives* 28: 11–21.

McKinney, C.M. (1990). Music therapy in obstetrics: A review. *Music Therapy Perspectives* 8: 57–60.

Miluk-Kolasa, B., Matejek, M., and Stupnicki, R. (1996). The effects of music listening on changes in selected physiological parameters in adult pre-surgical patients. *Journal of Music Therapy* 33: 208–218.

Negrete, B.J. (2011). The use of music therapy in the emergency room for pain and anxiety management. Unpublished master's thesis, Florida State University. *Electronic Theses, Treatises and Dissertations.* Paper 2693.

O'Callaghan, C. (2001). Bringing music to life: A study of music therapy and palliative care experiences in a cancer hospital. *Journal of Palliative Care* 17(3): 155–160.

O'Callaghan, C. (2007). Interpretive subgroup analysis extends modified grounded theory research findings in oncologic music therapy. *Journal of Music Therapy* 44: 256–261.

O'Callaghan, C. (2009). Objectivist and constructivist music therapy research in oncology and palliative care: An overview and reflection. *Music and Medicine* 1(1): 41–60.

O'Callaghan, C. and Colegrove, V. (1998). Effect of the music therapy introduction when engaging hospitalized cancer patients. *Music Therapy Perspectives* 16(2): 67–74.

O'Callaghan, C. and Magill, L. (2009). Effect of music therapy on oncologic staff bystanders: A substantive grounded theory. *Palliative and Supportive Care* 7: 219–228.

O'Callaghan, C. and McDermott, F. (2004). Music therapy's relevance in a cancer hospital researched through a constructivist lens. *Journal of Music Therapy* 41: 151–185.

O'Callaghan, C., Sproston, M., Wilkinson, K., Willis, D., Milner, A., Grocke, D., and Wheeler, G. (2012). Effect of self-selected music on adults' anxiety and subjective experiences during initial radiotherapy treatment: A randomized control trial. *Journal of Medical Imaging and Radiation Oncology* 56(4): 473–477.

Porchet-Munro, S. (1988). Music therapy in support of cancer patients. *Recent Results in Cancer Research* 108: 289–294.

Procelli, D.E. (2005). The effects of music therapy and relaxation prior to breastfeeding on the anxiety of new mothers and the behavior states of their infants during feeding. *Electronic Theses, Treatises and Dissertations*. Paper 463. <http://diginole.lib.fsu.edu/etd/463>.

Richardson, W.S., Wilson, M.C., Nishikawa, J., and Hayward, R.S. (1995). The well-built clinical Question: A key to evidence-based decisions. *American College of Physicians Journal Club* 123(3): A12–A13.

Richardson, M.M., Babiak-Vazquez, A.E., and Frenkel, M.A. (2008). Music therapy in a comprehensive cancer center. *Journal of the Society for Integrative Oncology* 6(2): 76–81.

Robb, S.L. (2012). Gratitude for a complex profession: The importance of theory-based research in music therapy. *Journal of Music Therapy* 49 (1): 2–6.

Robb, S.L., Burns, D.S., and Carpenter, J.S. (2011). Reporting guidelines for music-based interventions. *Music and Medicine* 3: 271–279.

Short, A., Gibb, H., Fildes, J., and Holmes, C. (2013). Exploring the role of music therapy in cardiac rehabilitation after cardiothoracic surgery: A qualitative study using the Bonny Method of Guided Imagery and Music. *Journal of Cardiovascular Nursing* 28(6): E74–E81.

Spintge, R. (1999). MusicMedicine: Applications, standards, and definitions. *MusicMedicine* 3: 3–11.

Standley, J. (1986). Music research in medical/dental treatment: Meta-analysis and clinical applications. *Journal of Music Therapy* 23(2): 56–122.

Standley, J. (1992). Clinical applications of music and chemotherapy: The effects on nausea and emesis. *Music Therapy Perspectives* 10(1): 27–35.

Waldon, E. (2001). The effects of group music therapy on mood states ad cohesiveness in adult oncology patients. *Journal of Music Therapy* 38: 212–238.

Walworth, D., Rumana, C.S., Nguyen, J., and Jarred, J. (2008). Effects of live music therapy sessions on quality of life indicators, medications administered and hospital length of stay for patients undergoing elective surgical procedures for brain. *Journal of Music Therapy* 45: 349–359.

Weber, S., Nuessler, V., and Wilmanns, W. (1997). A pilot study on the influence of receptive music listening on cancer patients during chemotherapy. *International Journal of Arts Medicine* 5(2): 27–35.

Winslow, G. (1986). Music therapy in the treatment of anxiety in high-risk mothers. *Music Therapy Perspectives* 3: 29–33.

MUSIC THERAPY TRAINING AND PROFESSIONAL ISSUES

CHAPTER 45

TRAINING, EDUCATION, AND PROFESSIONAL ISSUES IN MUSIC THERAPY

JANE EDWARDS

In many ways, we are very fortunate to be music therapists. The significance of the work we do, of the music we make with clients, and of "stepping into their souls and hearts" in music therapy will indeed help us in our final chapters to know that we have made our mark.

Cheryl Dileo 2013

INTRODUCTION

MUSIC therapy is continually increasing in recognition and profile internationally, its research evidence base is expanding and consolidating, and theoretical maturity is beginning to emerge. This is an exciting time to be part of the music therapy profession. Choosing music therapy as a career can be challenging, daunting, and exciting. Working with music every day, contributing to positive change in peoples' lives, and having regular opportunities to share and collaborate with other practitioners through teamwork and participation in national and international conferences are some of the aspects that make music therapy a fantastic job.

Becoming a practitioner in music therapy occurs at multiple levels. At an individual level the student's processes and learning are part of this *becoming*. At an interpersonal level the interactions between students as a group and in collaboration with their educators and clinical supervisors shape and frame the development of professional competencies. At a wider systemic level the values and processes of training are influenced by the provider institution which is usually a university, and the department in which the music therapy training programme is housed (Edwards 2013). This systemic level also includes the external regulator such as state or national accreditation structures and the requirements of the relevant professional body.

The practicing music therapist works within a system that includes contact with co-workers, clients, carers, and families, and within institutions or structures that are informed or maintained by policy, legal, and financial frameworks. This chapter provides an overview of topics relevant to training and professional practice in music therapy. Self-development as a trainee and also as a practitioner are discussed along with issues arising around the topics of regulation of the profession internationally, issues in developing new posts, and features of working as a music therapist in an allied health team.

Training

Professional training is a form of education in which theoretical learning and practical application of methods and techniques are combined. Becoming a music therapy practitioner involves a process of learning that requires understanding the functions of music and the processes of therapy alongside the practical *doing* of music therapy through experiential learning in student placements where observing and leading on-site music therapy occurs with individuals and groups. Perhaps the most important learning as a student involves the *un*-learning of ineffective ways of helping such as giving *good* advice to clients, or using music that is liked or easily learned by the trainee but is either not known or not appreciated by the client or their carers. Students often need to be patient with themselves during training as it takes time to learn the skills of active listening and empathy, and to develop an appreciation of the dynamic processes that can occur between the therapist and the client, family, or group. The creativity and flexibility that music therapy requires is difficult to learn within the short space of time of a course, and therefore in many courses prerequisite knowledge, and the testing of skills in auditions and interviews form part of the entry requirements for being admitted.

Every country differs in the training processes and requirements to be qualified and/or credentialed. Regions within countries can also have different routes to training. In Europe most training is at postgraduate level, but many other countries and regions have undergraduate training programmes. It is uncertain whether providing training only at postgraduate level supports the recognition of music therapy as a profession (Register 2013), but in Europe the first country to achieve state recognition, the UK, has only ever provided accredited music therapy training at postgraduate level.

The process of training at postgraduate level is often quite different from students' experiences in undergraduate degrees. Usually music therapy students spend a great deal of their on-campus course time together as they are scheduled to attend the same classes. Groups or cohorts are often between 15 and 25 in number, or sometimes even fewer, which can create a feeling of closeness and interdependency that is quite distinct from larger undergraduate programmes in which students study different combinations of subjects. In the experience of more than two decades as a music therapy course director, the author can attest that groups can experience supportive closeness and usually continue to enjoy contact throughout their professional lives. However, sometimes group members can find being in a small, close group difficult. It is especially challenging for some group members when one or more students are not progressing well (Edwards 2014). Usually there are processes within the course to support the group when difficulties arise. One of these is the experiential group which is a supportive process by which students can interact in a confidential space with a qualified facilitator.

Experiential learning

Experiential learning in music therapy can be offered in a range of ways in training courses. Group experiences that are intended to be *therapy-like* can be facilitated by a trained professional not otherwise associated with the course. Individual psychotherapy, or experiential group work is required in order that students can develop an understanding of what occurs in individual and group therapy processes. As presented elsewhere in terms of therapy training, the author has advised that:

> Many programmes use a combination of requirements by which the student undertakes self learning; including regular individual psychotherapy with a person not associated with the course programme, and/or experiential group work provided within the structured course timetable, optimally provided by a person not associated with trainee assessment.
>
> Edwards 2013, p. 216

Students work in confidential groups with a qualified therapist who is paid by, but is usually not otherwise associated with, the training programme. They can use this experience to learn the processes of therapy such as negotiating, focusing on themes that arise, listening actively, responding empathically, and facilitating group processes in a supportive way. Such experiences can give students the opportunity to better understand how it may feel for a client to be part of a group. Getting stuck, finding it frustrating, and spending time working out what is happening can be common interactions in group therapy. It is therefore invaluable for students to be able to have a safe experience of learning how these processes can work.

Personal development is not the primary goal of therapy training but through engaging new study topics, and undertaking fieldwork placements students have multiple opportunities to develop greater empathy for others. Communication skills are developed, theoretical knowledge is deepened, and additional music skills are extended through regular practicing (Wheeler et al. 2005). Courses which require personal development work through individual and group processes, such as mandated individual psychotherapy and experiential group work, fulfil obligations to ensure that graduates have the best possible chance of being effective while also withstanding the stressors of future practice. By exploring their motivations for wanting to study music therapy students have the chance to develop greater insight into their expectations of therapeutic work, and their strengths and weaknesses. This process might sometimes evoke unwelcome and yet necessary thoughts and memories which need to be considered and integrated to better understand the effects of client experiences on the therapist.

New posts

Upon graduation music therapists can work with people throughout the life span, and in a variety of settings. Many music therapists will be the first person in that role in the organization, sometimes working in a new position that they helped create. This is a unique aspect of music therapy and one which has received relatively limited attention in the music therapy literature. The author has held many posts where she was the first music therapist, for example in a nursing home, and in a children's hospital (Edwards 2005), and has been described as a *veteran* of start-up work (Ledger 2015). Working in a new post requires the regular adjustment to learning the procedures required of the organization but also the need to shape and build the service so that it can grow and be sustainable over time. As Ledger has recounted:

> When a music therapist enters a health care or educational institution, s/he typically joins a team of established professionals. Often existing team members have been working together for a long period of time, have long-established ways of working, and additionally have never worked with a music therapist before. Many music therapists have described the need to demonstrate the value of music therapy, to educate others about possible spaces for music therapy, and to determine the ways in which music therapy could best fit into the team.
>
> Ledger 2015

Even if the music therapist is appointed to an existing post managers and colleagues who are new to the organization may never have worked with a qualified music therapist previously. In every stage of music therapy work education and information need to be crafted to the capacities of co-workers to understand and support the music therapy service.

Teams

Most music therapists working in health or education services will be part of an identified service team. In private practice music therapists interact with the workers who have referred clients and so they are sometimes required to engage with planning and reporting responsibilities with the client's wider care team. Interprofessional collaboration between music therapists and other allied health professionals has been documented, including with speech and language professionals (Geist et al. 2008; Hamilton, Cross, and Kennelly 2001), nurses (Canga et al. 2012), and physiotherapists (O'Kelly and Koffman 2007).

Statutory recognition

Music therapists have dedicated immense time and effort to attaining professional recognition (Register 2013; Waller and Guthrie 2013). Some countries and regions have facilitated the development and growth of the profession of music therapy through attaining government recognition. This recognition affords parity with other professional groups in allied health, and allows the protection of the title of music therapist. Many countries and regions where this has not been attained have still managed to develop training courses, professional associations, and regulatory procedures by which music therapists can be credentialed and work professionally in education and health care (De Backer et al. 2014).

Self-care

The allied health literature contains frequent references to the burden of caring. Terms such as *burn out, compassion fatigue, secondary stress disorder*, and *compassion stress* point to the costs of caring for others (Radey and Figley 2007). Music therapy reports have also indicated the potential for occupational burnout (for example, Fowler 2006; Vega 2010). Many practitioners experiencing giving selflessly to others as inherently satisfying. However, many clients referred for therapy will be intensely distressed, at least to some extent. Interacting with people who are stressed and distressed can be wearying work especially in relational therapies such as music therapy. Relational therapies require the therapist to be emotionally present, empathetic, and be able to think and process their thoughts while being supportive to the client (Teyber and Teyber 2014). Stress can also occur even when interactions with clients are mutually appreciated. Management issues, organizational change, team member interactions, and disruptions or changes to facilities such as treatment rooms or equipment availability can often be beyond the control of the individual worker. These kinds of work stresses can distract from quality work with clients, be disruptive, and cause anxiety. Self-care can act as a buffer to the stress and strain of working life as a therapist. Integrating self-care strategies into the working week is important rather than only engaging strategies when stress has become overwhelming (Skovholt and Trotter-Mathison 2014).

Building a strong future in music therapy

Music therapy is constantly evolving to take into consideration new opportunities in developing the range and scope of practice. Music therapy is relevant to the whole human life span from in utero through to the final hours and moments of breath. Trainees who successfully graduate emerge as practitioners committed to lifelong learning about themselves, their clients, and the profession. Many music therapists dedicate time and effort to serving the professional associations on committees or in leadership roles. Some music therapists develop the skills to supervise students on placement, or to provide professional supervision to colleagues (Daveson and Kennelly 2011). Further research through higher degrees is a pathway that many music therapists are able to choose in contemporary times. For some of these graduates, professional university-based careers await, or further clinical leadership opportunities can be taken in a wide range of education and health care services. It is the contribution of every single music therapist across the world that builds and grows the profession to be strong and fruitful for the current times and for the future.

References

Canga, B., Hahm, C.L., Lucido, D., Grossbard, M.L., and Loewy, J.V. (2012). Environmental music therapy: A pilot study on the effects of music therapy in a chemotherapy infusion suite. *Music and Medicine* 4(4): 221–230.

Daveson, B. and Kennelly, J. (2011). Reflections regarding Australian music therapy supervision: Guidance and recommendations for establishing internal and external supervisory arrangements aided by cross-national reflection. *Australian Journal of Music Therapy* 22: 24.

De Backer, J., Nöcker-Ribeupierre, M., and Sutton, J. (2014). Music therapy in Europe. In Jos De Backer and Julie Sutton (eds), *The music in music therapy: Psychodynamic music therapy in Europe: clinical, theoretical and research approaches*, pp. 24–36. London: Jessica Kingsley Publishers.

Dileo, C. (2013). Life can only be understood backwards; But it must be lived forward. *Voices: A World Forum for Music Therapy* 13(1).

Edwards, J. (2005). The role of the music therapist in working with hospitalized children. *Music Therapy Perspectives* 23: 36–44.

Edwards, J. (2013). Examining the role and functions of self-development in healthcare therapy trainings: A review of the literature with a modest proposal for the use of learning agreements. *European Journal of Psychotherapy & Counselling* 15(3): 214–232.

Edwards, J. (2014). Facilitating the highly bonded cohort: Should more be done to anticipate and reduce the potential for hyper-cohesiveness and deindividuation in therapy training cohorts in universities? *European Journal of Psychotherapy & Counselling* 16: 114–126.

Fowler, K.L. (2006). The relations between personality characteristics, work environment, and the professional well-being of music therapists. *Journal of Music Therapy* 43(3): 174–197.

Geist, K., McCarthy, J., Rodgers-Smith, A., and Porter, J. (2008). Integrating Music Therapy Services and Speech-Language Therapy Services for Children with Severe Communication Impairments: A Co-Treatment Model. *Journal of Instructional Psychology* 35(4): 311–316.

Hamilton, L., Cross, J., and Kennelly, J. (2001). The interface of music therapy and speech pathology in the rehabilitation of children with acquired brain injury. *Australian Journal of Music Therapy* 12: 13.

Ledger, A. (2015). Developing new posts in music therapy. In: J Edwards (ed.), *Oxford Handbook of Music Therapy*. Oxford: Oxford University Press.

O'Kelly, J. and Koffman, J. (2007). Multidisciplinary perspectives of music therapy in adult palliative care. *Palliative Medicine* 21(3): 235–241.

Radey, M. and Figley, C. R. (2007). The social psychology of compassion. *Clinical Social Work Journal* 35(3): 207–214.

Register, D. (2013). Professional recognition of music therapy: Past, present, and future. *Music Therapy Perspectives* 31(2): 159–165.

Skovholt, T.M. and Trotter-Mathison, M.J. (2014). *The Resilient Practitioner: Burnout Prevention and Self-care Strategies for Counselors, Therapists, Teachers, and Health Professionals*. London: Routledge.

Teyber, E. and Teyber, F.M. (2014). Working with the process dimension in relational therapies: Guidelines for clinical training. *Psychotherapy* 51(3): 334–341.

Vega, V.P. (2010). Personality, burnout, and longevity among professional music therapists. *Journal of Music Therapy* 47(2): 155–179.

Waller, D. and Guthrie, M. (2013). The sociology of regulation: The case of psychotherapy and counselling and the experience of the arts therapies. *British Journal of Guidance and Counselling* 41(1): 4–13.

Wheeler, B.L., Shultis, C.L., and Polen, D. (2005). *Clinical Training Guide for the Student Music Therapist*. Gilsum, NH: Barcelona Publishers.

CHAPTER 46

....

MUSIC THERAPY
TRAINING REQUIREMENTS

....

SUZANNE B. HANSER

"Only the educated are free." Epictetus, *The Discourses*

INTRODUCTION

....

THIS chapter presents a summary of the skills and competencies expected of the trained music therapist. It focuses on the standards and guidelines established in the USA since the establishment of the first course in 1919 and the first professional association in 1950. It details the standards that have emerged after almost 100 years of music therapy training in America, and includes the current status of training practices in the English-speaking countries of the world. To begin this effort, the author interviewed a small group of eighteen music therapy educators in order to sample current thinking in the field. Through this process, an intricate web of philosophical approaches, scientific values, and musical abilities were revealed that are woven into the education of the music therapist in every institution of higher learning. Thus the education and training of music therapists is not without controversy, given the depth and breadth of the services they provide, and the diversity of ideologies that undergird their practice. As a result, this chapter is not intended to provide a comprehensive understanding of education and training, but instead to: (a) Present the challenges experienced in training provision; (b) provide some perspectives about training provision; and (c) detail standards, guidelines, and competencies that have been devised by professional organizations.

PERSPECTIVES FROM SEASONED MUSIC THERAPY EDUCATORS

The first part of this chapter presents responses from eighteen music therapy educators who were asked to reflect on what they consider are the most important aspects of training provision in music therapy. The current President of the International Association for Music and Medicine, Dr Jane Edwards, has summarized some of the issues in training thus:

> Music therapy training is like the pieces of a puzzle we hand to the students. The most important aspect of the training is the integration of these pieces to create a coherent, integrated whole. Each student's self-development is key to this process and there is no one right way to achieve the capacities of a useful practitioner. However, I really believe from over 20 years' experience of teaching music therapy that for our students, this integration occurs with dedication, reflection, openness, reading, practicing, and keeping an inquiring attitude while engaging in all that a course demands of one.

Her perspective was echoed by responses from music therapy educators throughout the world, in their own words, and through the lenses of their own educational values. The sampling of educators' opinions that were shared with this author in preparation for this chapter revealed an extraordinary wealth of expectations and range of thinking. Certainly, this is due to the diverse nature of the practice of music therapy, but it also reflects vastly opposing beliefs regarding the most important element in the training of a music therapist. This is precisely the question that was posed to a selection of educators from around the world, who also train in English. The following are their responses to complete the phrase: "The most important element in training a music therapist is:"

> From Barbara Hesser, New York University:
>   … the development of skills for and knowledge about music psychotherapy, supervised clinical experience and self-growth experiences through music. It is the combination of all these elements which makes a good music psychotherapist. Though all are important, I want to emphasize the importance of a student experiencing the power of music therapy for themselves and coming to understand how music can be used in their own transformation and healing. Without this felt experience, it is my belief that their music therapy work will not be as deep or effective as is possible.

Professor Hesser believes that engaging in one's own personal music therapy is the best means to becoming a music therapist. Her graduate program prepares music psychotherapists who are capable of providing insight-oriented music therapy.

> From Sheri Robb, Indiana University:
>   I am not sure I can identify the single most important element in training music therapists. I believe each student has their own unique strengths and areas for growth, which ultimately informs what they will need during training. But I believe every music therapist will benefit by developing their skills in the areas of clinical observation, critical thinking, and communication—working to synthesize information to inform the interventions/treatment they will provide to each individual patient. I firmly believe that one never finishes their education and training, so instilling a passion for lifelong learning and discovery, as well as developing

a heart for service will help to ensure that music therapists will continue to grow throughout their career and find ways to share their unique talents to help advance the profession.

From James Robertson, Queen Margaret University, Scotland:
    The most important element in training a music therapist is to respect the individuality of each student and to consider teaching as a learning process from which we all can grow.

Professors Robb and Robertson both attended to the learning process as the critical element of the teaching process, and spoke to what the individual student brings in becoming a music therapist.

From Jayne Standley, The Florida State University:
    … teaching the application of evidence-based music therapy literature for innovative clinical applications.

Professor Standley emphasized the need for the music therapist to be up-to-date regarding the literature, implying a need to understand research in multiple disciplines. She also revealed the value of innovation—a skill beyond imitating the models that have been demonstrated in course work, but bringing a new way of implementing knowledge and skills clinically.

From Diane Austen, New York University:
    … being emotionally present with the students.

From Robert Krout, Southern Methodist University:
    … the ability and willingness of educators and clinical supervisors to engage and mentor student music therapists in all areas relating to the discipline and profession, not just to merely share a knowledge base.

From Elizabeth Coombs, University of Wales:
    … facilitating the development of an internal supervisor. Once training is over, and the student is a qualified therapist, the availability of this resource is core to the development of a unique music therapy persona that will ensure a high standard of clinical practice.

Professors Austen, Krout, and Coombs saw the nature of the teacher/student relationship as a source of learning, perhaps a prerequisite for effective teaching/learning to take place. They would probably agree that a tripod of mentor, supervisor as role model, and the internalized teacher are the necessary trainers of a music therapist.

From Even Ruud, University of Oslo:
    … musical empathy.

Professor Ruud put it simply, yet the concept, "musical empathy" is not simple to define in terms of tasks that demonstrate the profound connection through music that is at the core of this principle, and obviously a core definition of music therapy, according to Even Ruud.

From Ron Borczon, California State University at Northridge:
    … making sure that the student is grounded in who s/he is as a person. This combined with strong musical skills are the basic building blocks from which the educational process can develop.

This "grounding," or deep knowing, demands a degree of maturity and life experience that must develop both within and outside of the classroom environment. It is a wise and evolved teacher who can nurture the student's progress in this arena, while also teaching very specific musical skills.

> From Mary Adamek, University of Iowa:
> … developing the best possible music skills and musicality, and continue this development throughout our careers. High level musicianship paired with strong therapeutic skills creates a foundation for effective music therapy interventions leading to positive outcomes.

Musicianship is the key strength here, and its link to effective treatment expresses Professor Adamek's value that the true goal of building musical skills and musicality is to provide the best outcomes of therapy.

> From Tessa Watson, University of Roehampton:
> … helping each student to engage deeply with the training process, to develop a reflective stance where they can observe and meet the needs of their clients, and use their music within a therapeutic relationship… to help students to be able to provide some coherent evaluation of this process.

Reflective learning is essential to the reciprocal relationship between teacher and student, and this implies that a healthy working relationship akin to the therapeutic alliance become established.

> From Lars Ole Bonde, Aalborg University:
> … the training of awareness, leading to the integration of musical presence and self reflexivity.

Perhaps two of the most difficult abilities to teach, "self-awareness and self-reflexivity," stand strong in Professor Bonde's answer.

> From Barbara Wheeler, University of Louisville:
> … integrating what one can learn from the "literature" with clinical work is most important. Of course, we want our students to be the best clinicians that they can be, and I think that the way to do this is for them to build their clinical skills on what they have learned in the classroom, largely from reading, discussing, and integrating the music therapy literature: theoretical, "practical," and research.

Professor Wheeler offered a hint of how the educator can truly integrate knowledge and skills, by emphasizing the importance of applying learning from the classroom directly into the clinical setting.

> From Colin Lee, Wilfrid Laurier University:
> … the knowledge and acquisition of clinical musicianship. Clinical musicianship requires a musicological and clinical understanding of the elements that define the therapeutic relationship. Clinical musicianship requires an understanding of the balance between the processes of musical creation, and the outcome of aims and objectives. Through a series of rigorous music-centered courses the students learns to adapt their artistic musicianship directly for the therapeutic needs of the client(s). Clinical musicianship and music-centered practice can be applied to all theories and models of music therapy.

Professor Lee emphasized "clinical musicianship" as the nucleus for growing musicianship, therapeutic relationship, and insight into the client's needs. This approach centers the student in the work with the expectation that the necessary knowledge and skills will spiral outward from this experience.

> From Brynjuif Stige, University of Bergen:
> … to open up for dialogues and reflections that help us embrace that we never will know for sure what the most important element is. This will shift from student to student over time and the best we can achieve is to nurture the capacity to stay open for new learning and new possibilities as the situations we are part of evolve.

This existentially-oriented approach acknowledges that within the complexities of learning and practicing music therapy, the openness to new ideas is the critical feature of the learning process.

> From Mary Ellen Wylie, University of Evansville:
> … feedback that is given for the obvious gains as well as the subtle changes that a student music therapist makes because they always appreciate knowing you are aware of their efforts.

Professor Wylie addressed the process of change and the importance of feedback along the way.

> Barbara Crowe, Arizona State University:
> … instilling a passion for music and its potential to benefit people.

Professor Crowe is aware of the need for fervor and dedication to the field of music therapy that is necessary in order to be successful.

These responses represent a wide range of perspectives and values that the educator brings to the training of music therapy students. Now the question must be asked, "How can a student be trained in all of the above, plus meet the established skills and competencies required by professional agencies?" Indeed, how does one train practitioners to do all that these professors and colleagues suggest and also:

- Serve individuals and groups?
- Gain knowledge of needs throughout the life span?
- Learn how to treat individuals, from severely impaired to well, from physically challenged to mentally sound?
- Meet the needs of any individual who seeks therapy for any number of conditions, diagnoses, or educational deficits?
- Provide multiple levels of care, from recreational to insight-oriented music therapy?
- Develop self-awareness and insight sufficient to be a successful therapist?
- Master skills in therapeutic process and musicianship, and then, as Dr Edwards recommends, to integrate all aspects of this learning effectively?

Fortunately, music therapists are masters at discovering and devising creative solutions to problems. Karen Goodman (2011) provides an account of the many pedagogical techniques applied by music therapy educators. Beyond the standard lecture format, learning occurs through collaborative, experiential, and music-centered experiences. These include such diverse activities as: Roundtable, structured controversy, thinking-aloud paired problem solving, role playing, experiential self-inquiry, music therapy training groups, video-recorded feedback, performing music therapy plays, and using instructional technology. Goodman offers helpful advice on the admissions process, advisement, curriculum design, teaching and evaluation techniques, reading and writing assignments, use of presentations, and the assessment and evaluation of learning. Tony Wigram (2009) is particularly astute regarding the special relationship between professor and doctoral students, and emphasizes how this alliance enhances the process of learning and discovery.

MUSIC THERAPY SUPERVISION

As a clinical practice, music therapy must be taught in the clinic as well as the classroom. To guide the process, there are two excellent texts on the subject of music therapy supervision: *Music Therapy Supervision* by Michele Forinash (2001) and *Supervision of Music Therapy: A Theoretical and Practical Handbook* by Helen Odell-Miller and Eleanor Richards (2009).

Forinash illuminates approaches and strategies that are unique to each of the contributing authors in her edited volume. She presents theoretical underpinnings of diverse methodologies, including the background literature, ethics, and multicultural issues surrounding supervision. She presents models of preprofessional and professional supervision, as well as that in special advanced institutes, like Analytical Music Therapy, the Bonny Method of Guided Imagery and Music, and Nordoff-Robbins Music Therapy.

Helen Odell-Miller and Eleanor Richards (2009) impart a case approach to supervision, with contributions from many scholars of music therapy. Contributors discuss issues in early training and adults with learning disabilities, an integrated development model of supervision, triangulation and other issues of supervision in forensic psychiatry, unconscious growth and emerging identify of the therapist, process of supervision in the psychiatric setting, personal and organizational factors in the supervisory relationship, supervision of clinical work with children, boundaries, and key elements in a good working relationship between student and music therapy researcher at the doctoral level. In her chapter, Odell-Miller (2009) discusses the evolution of ideas and practices, including the development of a supervision scheme, which includes experiential work and cross-training approaches, as approved by the Association of Professional Music Therapists in the UK (APMT 1990, 2008). These integrate musical and non-musical dimensions of the work as a music therapist. Bunt and Hoskyns (2002) reflect on the humanistic perspective of music therapy supervision. They also recommend applying the best music therapy practices to the supervision process by using musical interactions and musical improvisation, e.g., asking the supervisee to improvise around the feelings of a client or playing like the client.

> Supervision in music therapy is an interactive process between a practitioner and a more experienced colleague, concentrating on musical, practical, and dynamic issues. There is a mutual shared interest in the work with the central emphasis on the practitioner becoming more effective in working with clients. Through the establishment of a clear fame of meetings, the supervisor facilitates open and honest articulation of material arising from the work. The process takes place within a context that is both supportive and critically reflective (p. 262).

Barbara Wheeler (2000) surveyed music therapy educators in the USA about their practices of supervising undergraduate clinical practice. She found that while educators have a common goal to provide students with a variety of client populations and services, and agree on the general means of accomplishing these goals, they differ widely in the expected tasks and responsibilities, qualifications of the site supervisor, their compensation, and the relationship between class and clinical site. Perhaps one of the more creative approaches to supervision is articulated in an article by Felicity Baker and Robert Krout (2011). These noted educators asked their students in pre-internship clinical practice to compose songs collaboratively, using self-reflection of their practicum experiences for the content. Their lyrics were rich with insight, specifically in areas of personal growth, which included: Developing an awareness of own abilities/thoughts, looking after the self, using helpful self-talk, conflict of imposter vs. authenticity, and questioning the self. Categories of positive responses included: Expressing positive music therapy experiences with clients, the rewards o doing music therapy, and offering gratitude for the client. Barbara Wheeler and Cindy Williams (2012) asked students to keep journals about their practicum experiences, notating their responses to their clients and also their supervisors. The authors recommend this process to inform instructors about the impact of these potentially emotionally-charged first clinical encounters.

In the US, there is a standardized training for clinical training directors, and an approval process both for establishing a clinical training site as an internship, and becoming qualified as a supervisor (see <www.musictherapy.org>). At the Fourth European Congress of Music Therapy in Leuven, Belgium in 1998, delegates from Denmark, Sweden, Italy, Germany, and other countries forged an international collaboration leading to the first training for music therapy supervisors across Europe. It took place at the Royal Swedish Academy of Music, facilitated by Ingrid Hammerlund (2001).

THE ORIGINS OF MUSIC THERAPY TRAINING

The first known college curriculum for music therapy was actually established under the term, "musicotherapy" at Columbia University in New York City, in 1919 (Literary Digest 1919). This was well in advance of curricular guidelines, which were approved by the National Association for Music Therapy (NAMT) in 1952, two years after NAMT came into being. For a more thorough understanding of the development of music therapy training, Shannon de l'Etoile offers an excellent history of education and training in the *Journal of Music Therapy* (2000). Jane Edwards (2008) has described the advent of music therapy in the medical arena, including how early "musico-therapists" and "music therapeutists" received their training.

Music therapy training in English-speaking countries around the world

World Federation of Music Therapy (WFMT)

In 1999, just prior to the World Congress of Music Therapy in Washington, DC, Denise Erdonmez Grocke, Chair of the WFMT Commission on Education, Training, and Accreditation, convened a group of fifteen music therapy educators from nine countries.

This Symposium brought forth a set of guidelines for music therapy education and training that could pertain to training programs around the world. The intention of the symposium was to develop model guidelines, to address various levels of training, and to establish a forum for debate and discussion. The outgrowth of this meeting was the following:

> The practice of music therapy requires an intensive program of study and supervised clinical training through an institution of higher education over an extended period of time.
>
> Intensive studies shall consist of:
>   Musical skills and knowledge;
>   biological, psychological, and social studies; and
>   music therapy knowledge and skills.
> Clinical training shall consist of:
>   Supervised field experiences in various areas of music therapy;
>   a program of study may be general or specialized.
> A general program of study shall cover:
>   Active and receptive methods of music therapy;
>   applications of music therapy with a wide variety of populations and in various settings;
>   different philosophical and theoretical orientations;
>   ethical principles and research; and
>   existing models of music therapy practice.
>   A specialized program may focus on one or more specific models or orientations.
>
> The program should promote the student's personal growth and professional development. It may be basic or advanced depending upon the depth and breadth of training, the system of education, the standards of practice, and the credential or qualification granted to the graduate. The most appropriate level may be determined partially by the educational system of the country.
>
> The program of study is one which:
>   has a set curriculum;
>   includes required reading;
>   is offered on a regular basis, usually each year;
>   requires that the students are assessed and evaluated through various forms of examination;
>   is recognized in the country by the appropriate professional organization or government agency;
>   and is periodically evaluated for quality of teaching.
>
> The program should stipulate criteria for the selection of students. Selection should be based on an assessment of music skill, academic qualification, and suitability of personal qualities.
>
> The music therapy program should be taught by a person appropriately educated and trained in music therapy who has substantial clinical experience in various aspects of the field. Similarly, clinical training should be supervised by an experienced music therapist. The training institution should provide and maintain appropriate academic and technological resources

Wheeler and Grocke 2001, p. 67

Currently, the World Federation of Music Therapy remains a valuable resource for examining the evolving field of music therapy around the globe; see <www.musictherapyworld.net>.

MUSIC THERAPY EDUCATION IN THE UNITED STATES

The profession has grown to encompass 69 AMTA-approved training programs in the USA in 2013. This has come after extensive dialogue and effort devoted to curricular issues in the USA. In their analysis of a survey to music therapy educators in 2000, Groene and Pembrook provide a timeline that includes the evolution of curriculum revision and competency formulation. It is summarized in Table 46.1 to demonstrate how discussions and survey research with professionals have shaped current guidelines for education and training.

In the USA, professional organizations like the American Music Therapy Association (AMTA) and the Certification Board for Music Therapists (CBMT) have taken on standards for education and training as part of their mission. AMTA is the national, professional organization representing the field of music therapy. From its website, <www.musictherapy.org>, comes the following statement regarding education and training:

> The education of a music therapist is unique among college degree programs because it not only allows a thorough study of music, but encourages examination of one's self as

Table 46.1 Timeline of curriculum and competency developments for music therapy training in the USA

1946	Van de Wall reported a survey of music in institutions
1950	The National Association for Music Therapy was formed with minimum standards for curriculum developed two years later
1956	19 clinical training directors were surveyed with students' functional music skills indicated as needing more training and development
1971	The American Association for Music Therapy is founded
1975	AAMT develops competencies for practice which are published in 1978
1980	Numerous surveys of music therapy practitioners are undertaken to determine the most important competencies for the field.
1982	In the largest survey to date in music therapy, music therapists (N=466) were surveyed by Lathom (1982) to examine professional and training needs.
1985	The first national board certification exam is held
1987–88	Various steps are undertaken toward the development of competency standards.
1996	The unification agreement between AAMT and NAMT to form the AMTA is passed by both organizations and a 3 year transition period commences
1997	CBMT survey of 27% of all those holding certification as a music therapist (N=707). Advanced degree was mooted but the majority did not think it would be helpful for skills or professional advancement.
1998	Draft competency standards are developed and approved by the AMTA Commission on Education and Clinical Training
1999	November, AMTA Assembly of Delegates approved the competency standards

NB: this information is summarized from an extensive timeline developed by Groene and Pembrook (2000) well as others. Students may begin their study on the undergraduate or graduate level. The entry-level curriculum includes clinical coursework and extended internship requirements in an approved mental health, special education, or health care facility. Upon successfully completing academic and clinical training, and subsequently passing the national examination administered by the independent Certification Board for Music Therapists, the graduate acquires the credential, Music Therapist-Board Certified (MT-BC).

The approved curriculum is designed to impart entry level competencies in three main areas: Musical Foundations, Clinical Foundations, and Music Therapy Foundations and Principles as specified in the AMTA Professional Competencies. Entry level study includes practical application of music therapy procedures and techniques learned in the classroom through required fieldwork in facilities serving individuals with disabilities in the community and/or on-campus clinics. Students learn to assess the needs of clients, develop and implement treatment plans, and evaluate and document clinical changes.

Individuals who have a baccalaureate degree may elect to complete the degree equivalency program in music therapy offered by most AMTA-approved universities. Under this program, the student completes only the coursework necessary for equivalent music therapy training without necessarily earning a second baccalaureate degree. Some schools may require that the student's initial degree be in music.

Graduate programs in music therapy examine, with greater breadth and depth, issues relevant to the clinical, professional, and academic preparation of music therapists, usually in combination with established methods of research inquiry. Selected universities offer doctoral study in music therapy, some of which include coursework in music therapy in combination with doctoral study in related areas.

Adapted from A Career in Music Therapy, Copyright © 1998–2014,
American Music Therapy Association.

In 2010, AMTA revised its Standards for Education and Clinical Training. This extensive document appears in Appendix I. Excerpts of the preamble to this document are presented here:

The American Music Therapy Association, Inc., aims to establish and maintain competency-based standards for all three levels of education (bachelor's, master's, and doctoral), with guidelines for the various curricular structures appropriate to different degrees, as defined by the National Association of Schools of Music (NASM). Using this competency-based system, the Association formulates competency objectives or learning outcomes for the various degree programs, based on what knowledge, skills, and abilities are needed by music therapists to work in various capacities in the field. Academic institutions should take primary responsibility for designing, providing, and overseeing the full range of learning experiences needed by students to acquire these competencies, including the necessary clinical training.

A bachelor's degree program should be designed to impart professional level competencies as specified in the *AMTA Professional Competencies*, while also meeting the curricular design outlined by NASM. Since education and clinical training form an integrated continuum for student learning at the professional level, academic institutions should take responsibility not only for academic components of the degree, but also for the full range of clinical training experiences needed by students to achieve competency objectives for the degree. This would include developing and overseeing student placements for both pre-internship and internship training.

A master's degree program should be designed to impart selected and specified advanced competencies, drawn from the *AMTA Advanced Competencies*, which would provide breadth and depth beyond the *AMTA Professional Competencies* that are required for entrance into the music therapy profession. At this level the degree should address the practice of music therapy wherein the music therapist applies and integrates a comprehensive synthesis of theories, research, treatment knowledge, musicianship, clinical skills, and personal awareness to address client needs. The curricular design would be appropriate to the degree title, per agreement between AMTA and NASM.

The doctoral degree should be designed to impart advanced competence in research, theory development, clinical practice, supervision, college teaching, and/or clinical administration, depending upon the title and purpose of the program. AMTA will work with NASM in the delineation of the doctoral degree in music therapy.

Academic institutions and internship sites should take primary responsibility for assuring the quality of their programs, jointly and/or separately. This is accomplished by regular, competency-based evaluations of their programs and graduates by faculty, supervisors, and/or students. The Association will assure the quality of education and clinical training through its approval standards and review procedures. The Association encourages diversity among institutions and programs and respects the operational integrity within academic and clinical training programs.

In implementing these standards, the Association shares the beliefs that education and clinical training are not separate processes, but reflect a continuum of music therapy education; that education and clinical training must be competency based at all levels; that education and clinical training must be student centered; and that education and clinical training must exist in a perspective of continuous change to remain current. The Association also believes in the importance of music as central to music therapy and that music study must be at the core of education and clinical training.

These standards must be viewed along with the Association's *Professional Competencies, Advanced Competencies, Standards of Clinical Practice, Advisory on Levels of Practice in Music Therapy, Code of Ethics, Policies and Procedures for Academic Program Approval,* and *National Roster Internship Guidelines.*

Reproduced from *AMTA Standards for Education and Clinical Training*,
Copyright © 1998–2014, American Music Therapy Association.

As is evident, AMTA also committed to a competency-based model for curriculum. The skills and competencies required of the professional music therapist are found in Appendix II. They cover the following 25 general areas:

A. MUSIC FOUNDATIONS
    1. Music Theory and History
    2. Composition and Arranging Skills
    3. Major Performance Medium Skills
    4. Keyboard Skills
    5. Guitar Skills
    6. Voice Skills
    7. Percussion Skills
    8. Non-symphonic Instrumental Skills
    9. Improvisation Skills
    10. Conducting Skills
    11. Movement Skills

B. CLINICAL FOUNDATIONS
    12. Exceptionality
    13. Principles of Therapy
    14. The Therapeutic Relationship

C. MUSIC THERAPY
  15. Foundations and Principles
  16. Client Assessment
  17. Treatment Planning
  18. Therapy Implementation
  19. Therapy Evaluation
  20. Documentation
  21. Termination/Discharge Planning
  22. Professional Role/Ethics
  23. Interdisciplinary Collaboration
  24. Supervision and Administration
  25. Research Methods

Adapted from *AMTA Professional Competencies*, Copyright © 1998–2014, American Music Therapy Association.

In 2005, AMTA's Assembly of Delegates approved a working document developed by their Education and Training Advisory Board, titled *Advisory on Levels of Practice in Music Therapy*. This policy articulates two levels of practice within the music therapy profession, based on the belief that trends and evolving needs of the profession must be reflected in its curriculum, and that these expanding requirements may be above and beyond the undergraduate education, with its competencies above. The preamble of this paper distinguishes between the two levels, and goes on to present the history and development of the separation:

> Professional Level of Practice: Based on the AMTA *Professional Competencies* acquired with a baccalaureate degree in music therapy or its equivalent, which leads to entrance into the profession and Board Certification in Music Therapy.
>
> Advanced Level of Practice: Based on the AMTA *Advanced Competencies*, which is defined as the practice of music therapy wherein the music therapist applies and integrates a comprehensive synthesis of theories, research, treatment knowledge, musicianship, clinical skills, and personal awareness to address client needs. A music therapist at an Advanced Level of Practice has at least a bachelor's degree or its equivalent in music therapy, a current professional designation or credential in music therapy (i.e. ACMT, CMT, MT-BC, or RMT), professional experience, and further education and/or training (e.g. receiving clinical supervision, a graduate degree, and/or advanced training). It is anticipated that in the future music therapists at the Advanced Level of Practice will hold at least a master's degree in music therapy that includes advanced clinical education. The advanced music therapist demonstrates comprehensive understanding of foundations and principles of music, music therapy, treatment, and management in clinical, educational, research, and/or administrative settings.
>
> Following the adoption of the *Advisory on Levels of Practice in Music Therapy*, AMTA appointed a Task Force on Advanced Competencies, which was charged with developing competencies for the Advanced Level of Practice as outlined in the Advisory. The Advisory describes four domains for the Advanced Level of Practice: Professional Growth, Musical Development, Personal Growth and Development, and Integrative Clinical Experience. The general headings and subheadings of the proposed Advanced Competencies have been reorganized to provide a better understanding of the context of these competencies, not only within the music therapy profession, but also beyond it for other constituencies. It is acknowledged that the advanced music therapist may not demonstrate competence in each of the areas of the *Advanced Competencies*, but would instead demonstrate acquisition of the majority of

these competencies, with most, if not all, in the area(s) of his/her practice (e.g. clinical, supervisory, academic, research).

The *Advanced Competencies* provide guidelines for academia, both in regards to qualifications for university/college faculty and in setting standards for master's degree programs in music therapy. The AMTA *Standards for Education and Clinical Training* specify standards for academic faculty employed full-time at a college or university with primary responsibilities for teaching music therapy and/or directing a music therapy program at the undergraduate or graduate level. Such qualifications for faculty require a music therapist practicing at an Advanced Level of Practice. The AMTA *Standards for Master's Degrees* state that "the purpose of the master's degree programs in music therapy is to impart advanced competencies, as specified in the AMTA *Advanced Competencies*. These degree programs provide breadth and depth beyond the AMTA *Professional Competencies* required for entrance into the music therapy profession." The *Advanced Competencies* will also serve to guide the development of standards for the doctoral degree in music therapy, which shall focus on advanced competence in research, theory development, clinical practice, supervision, college teaching, and/or clinical administration.

The *Advanced Competencies* also provide guidelines for the Advanced Level of Practice in clinical, supervisory, administrative and research settings, as well as in government relations work dealing with such issues as state licensures and employment practices. Music therapists with master's degrees and other professional requirements are being granted state licensures in the creative arts therapies (music therapy) and related disciplines in some states.

Reproduced from *AMTA Advanced Competencies*, Copyright © 1998–2014, American Music Therapy Association.

Much discussion and debate has been generated since the adoption of this as a work in progress. Currently, arguments for the Master's degree as the entry level requirement for the profession are being posited, and AMTA has established a special advisory group to examine the feasibility of such a curricular change. The initial document was designed as a vision for the future of the field, and its implications have yet to be determined within the context of American music therapy education.

Meanwhile, the CBMT has served as an agency that is independent of the AMTA, to credential music therapists. The following is from their website: <http://www.cbmt.org/fact-sheets/mt-bc-fact-sheet/>:

The credential Music Therapist-Board Certified (MT-BC) is granted by the Certification Board for Music Therapists (CBMT) to identify music therapists who have demonstrated the knowledge, skills and abilities necessary to practice music therapy at the current level of the profession. The purpose of board certification in music therapy is to provide an objective national standard that can be used as a measure of professionalism by interested agencies, groups, and individuals.

The Certification Board for Music Therapists administers a written objective examination, based on a nationwide music therapy practice analysis that is regularly reviewed and updated to reflect current clinical practice. Both the practice analysis and the examination are developed using guidelines issued by the Equal Employment Opportunity Commission, and the American Psychological Association's standards for test validation. Once Board Certified, a Music Therapist must recertify every five years. The purpose of recertification is to encourage the MT-BC to maintain skills and to continue professional growth and development. The Board Certification program is accredited by the National Commission for Certifying Agencies (NCCA). NCCA approval signifies that the CBMT adheres to the established criteria and standards set by the Commission.

Reproduced from *MT-BC Fact Sheet* © The Certification Board for Music-Therapists, 2011.

Today, over 5600 music therapists hold the credential, Music Therapist-Board Certified (MT-BC) granted by the Certification Board for Music Therapists. This credential reflects the certificants' willingness to participate in an independently administered national certification program that undergoes a rigorous review every five years in order to maintain its accreditation. This accreditation review by NCCA serves as the means by which CBMT strives to maintain the highest standards possible in the construction and administration of its national examination and recertification programs, ultimately designed to reflect current music therapy practice for the benefit of the consumer. Also, because of its success, CBMT is regarded as a leader in the credentialing field, particularly for professions with around 5000 practitioners.

The vision of national certification as expressed by the profession of music therapy took shape as CBMT became fully accredited by the NCCA in 1986 (then known as the National Commission for Health Certifying Agencies) with the second administration of the national examination. The Recertification Program was initiated in 1988 to maintain full accreditation. Today, by remaining in compliance with the accreditation standards established by the NCCA, CBMT demonstrates to MT-BC's, employers, government agencies, payers, courts, and professional organizations that:

1. CBMT's MT-BC program has been reviewed and meets certification standards set by an impartial, objective commission whose primary focus is competency assurance and protection of the consumer, and
2. CBMT programs meet or exceed the same standards licensing boards use in test development and administration.

Reproduced from *Accreditation* © The Certification Board for Music-Therapists, 2011.

CBMT developed its policies and procedures in compliance with other national agencies in the USA that establish ethical guidelines for credentialing professionals. On its website: <http://www.cbmt.org/about-cbmt/accreditation/>.
CBMT discusses its history and development:

ICE is the Institute for Credentialing Excellence. Based in Washington, D.C., ICE is a membership organization that provides a forum for all types of practitioners and organizations interested in competency assurance and certification. ICE is the only national organization that focuses on certification of practitioners in a variety of professions and occupations. Its members include certification organizations, professional associations, employers, educators, test development companies and consultants, state licensing boards, federal agencies, and consumer groups. Through its annual educational conferences and workshops, ICE provides access to expertise in certification, licensure and testing, as well as information about the state-of-the-art in the credentialing arena.

The CBMT's involvement with ICE, formerly NOCA, and NCCA began in 1980 when the National Association for Music Therapy (NAMT) joined as an affiliate member. At the time, NAMT's Certification Committee explored the establishment of a certification program for the profession of music therapy. It was recognized that NOCA/NCCA was the leading authority on certification in the country with the only objective standards for national certification organizations. In 1980, NCCA was called the National Commission for Health Certifying Agencies (NCHCA). The health was dropped in 1987 as it became clear that the accreditation standards applied to all professions and occupations, not just those that are health-related. ICE, formerly NOCA, has members whose groups are in all kinds of professions and occupations.

When the CBMT was created in 1983 to be the independent credentialing body for Music Therapists, CBMT became a member organization of NOCA. CBMT's certification program was accredited in 1986 upon its initial application to the Commission. The CBMT's accreditation is renewed every five years, most recently in 2006. Among ICE members, formerly NOCA members, the CBMT is recognized as having a quality certification program that is a leader in the field, particularly among professions with around 5000 practitioners.

Adapted from *Accreditation* © The Certification Board for Music-Therapists, 2011.

The CBMT Recertification Program, initiated in 1988, is designed to provide certificants with guidelines to assist them in remaining competent with current practice and further enhancing their knowledge in the profession of music therapy. The recertification program contributes to the professional development of the MT-BC through a program of continuing education, professional development and professional service opportunities… To support CBMT's commitment of ensuring the competence of the certificant and protecting the public, certification must be renewed every five years with the accrual of 100 recertification credits or by re-taking the examination.

Reproduced from *The Recertification Program* © The Certification Board for
Music-Therapists, 2011.

The Certification Board Examination is based on the CBMT Scope of Practice. This document can be found in Appendix III. Details on gaining admission to the Music Therapy Board Certification Examination are detailed at <http://www.cbmt.org/about-certification/the-recertification-program/>:

Candidates for Music Therapy Board Certification must have successfully completed the academic and clinical training requirements for music therapy, or their equivalent as established by the American Music Therapy Association. To be eligible to sit for the music therapy board certification examination, these requirements must be completed by the examination administration date.

If the candidate is a current MT-BC taking the music therapy board certification examination to fulfill recertification requirements, the MT-BC must be in the fourth year of his/her recertification cycle and have paid all maintenance fees through the fourth year, including any applicable late fees.

Reproduced from *Eligibility Requirements* © The Certification Board for
Music-Therapists, 2011.

As stated above, in order to maintain the MT-BC credential, music therapists must renew their status by taking the examination or completing the required continuing education. They must fulfill these recertification requirements through providing documentation every five years. Requirements for taking the examination are found in <http://www.cbmt.org/examination/eligibility-requirements/> and recertification requirements are found in <http://www.cbmt.org/recertification/recertification-credit-option/>:

Certificants may pursue recertification by accruing 100 recertification credits during the five-year recertification cycle.
   Certificants accrue recertification credits in the following ways:
1. Completing graduate coursework in areas related to the CBMT Scope of Practice
2. Attending educational programs, such as workshops, courses and trainings, etc.

3. Designing and completing individualized self-study programs, or completing standardized self-study programs
4. Attending short educational events, such as in-services and conference presentations
5. Attending regional and national music therapy conferences
6. Conducting professional programs such as publishing, presenting workshops, completing a thesis or dissertation, etc.
7. Contributing service to music therapy organizations and external organizations
8. Providing supervision in internship or pre-internship settings

Adapted from *Recertification Credit Option* © The Certification Board for
Music-Therapists, 2011.

Current issues for educators, as reported by Groene and Pembrooke (2000), include the expanding use of technology in music therapy practice, and thus, the need to incorporate training in the latest technologies for prospective music therapists. These have yet to be incorporated in either the competencies or the Board Certification Examination.

Music therapy education in the United Kingdom

The professional association for music therapy in the United Kingdom is the British Association for Music Therapy (BAMT), established in 2011 in a merger between the British Society for Music Therapy (BSMT) and the Association of Professional Music Therapists (APMT). The latter developed a registry of music therapists, with 612 professional members, as of 2009. Thanks to extensive advocacy efforts, music therapy is a well-established allied health profession, recognized as one of the Arts Therapies by the Health Professions Council (HPC). This means that only those registered with the HPC are entitled to use the title, *music therapist*. Standards for education and training may be found in: <http://www.hpc-uk.org/assets/documents/1000295EStandardsofeducationandtraining-fromSeptember2009.pdf http://www.hpc-uk.org/assets/documents/100004FBStandards_of_Proficiency_Arts_Therapists.pdf>

The first course of training in the UK was founded in 1968 at the Guildhall School of Music in London, developed by Juliette Alvin. There are currently seven colleges accredited in the United Kingdom to offer Master's level training in music therapy, including Guildhall School of Music and Drama, Nordoff-Robbins Centres in London and Edinburgh, University of Surrey, University of the West of England, Anglia Polytechnic University, and the Welsh College of Music and Drama. A registry of accredited courses can be found in: <http://www.hpc-uk.org/education/programmes/register/index.asp?EducationProviderID=all&StudyLevel=all&ModeOfStudyID=all&professionID=1&Submit.x=39&Submit.y=17>

Music therapy education in South Africa

The University of Pretoria is currently the only music therapy training course in South Africa. It was developed by Dr Mercedes Pavlicevic, and later approved by the Health

Professions Council of South Africa, in 1999, as a two-year graduate course of study. There exist strong ties amongst the arts therapies in the country, having formed the South African Network of Arts Therapies Organization in 1997.

Music therapy education in the Republic of Ireland

There is one music therapy training currently in the Republic of Ireland at the University of Limerick. The course is a two-year full-time Master's program which enrolled its first students in September 1998. The course was developed through a process of consultation with 3 international music therapy experts: Professor Kaja Jensen (USA), Professor Tony Wigram (UK/Denmark), and Professor Leslie Bunt (UK). The course aims to meet international competencies for practice. Graduates have been able to work in the UK after registration with the Health and Care Professions Council, and to gain registration status in Canada and Australia. Music therapy is not a recognized profession in the Irish health services, and music therapy graduates often work on short-term contract in service provider roles. The inaugural course director was Dr Wendy Magee. Dr Jane Edwards has served as the course director since 1999.

The Irish Association of Creative Arts Therapists is the professional body for music therapists in Ireland. It has founded a working group for recognition of the Creative Arts Therapies in Ireland.

Music therapy education in Canada

Seven universities are the sites of music therapy training programs leading to the MTA credential, as accredited music therapists. The Accreditation Review Board oversees the granting of the MTA, and has continuing education requirements that are much like those of the CBMT in the USA. Capilano College was the first to be approved by the Canadian Association for Music Therapy (CAMT) in 1977. Currently, other programs of study are offered at Acadia University, Canadian Mennonite University, Université du Québec a Montréal, University of Windsor, and Wilfrid Laurier University. Concordia University offers a curriculum similar to the equivalency certificate program in the USA.

The Health Professions Act (http://www.bclaws.ca/civix/document/id/complete/statreg/96183_01) regulates the profession of music therapy along with other counseling professionals.

Music therapy education in Australia

Music therapy has a distinguished history in Australia. The International Society for Musical Therapeutics (ISMT) was established in Sydney as a branch of the organization in New York

City in 1922 (or 1924, according to the autobiography of Esther Kahn). Post-World War II, the association was no longer viable, but some years later, the Red Cross Music Therapy Service began to play a part in the development of music therapy services and education. The Australian Music Therapy Association was established as a formal entity in 1975, and developed specific accreditation requirements for validation of curricula and the training music therapists, leading to candidates receiving the Registered Music Therapist (RMT) credential. More information can be found at: <http://www.austmta.org.au/about/our-history>.

The first approved course was founded at the University of Melbourne, under the leadership of Dr Denise (Erdonmez) Grocke. Three other programs have been accredited since that time: University of Queensland (to close in 2015), University of Technology, Sydney (closed), and University of Western Sydney.

CURRENT ISSUES WORLDWIDE

Health care and education trends

It is clear that new developments in health care, special education, and prevention/wellness are dramatically changing the environment in which music therapists are trained and practice. The evidence base for music therapy and other interventions is expanding, and the provision of quality services is becoming increasingly complicated. New paradigms, like integrative medicine and psychoneuroimmunology (Hanser 2009), are marking the geography of therapeutic services with new treatment delivery models and techniques. In this climate, the music therapist must not only be well-trained in those skills and competencies that are specific to music therapy, but also able to work within a complex and quickly shifting delivery system. The ease of communication across the globe is facilitating the flow of information which means there are more data to interpret and technical knowledge to learn. Music therapists must also be competent advocates for the unique services that they provide in order to remain competitive in a vast marketplace of services. For example, the Bureau of Labor Statistics in the USA (2011) cites the growing population of elders as justification for a greatly enhanced number of practitioners in health care and social assistance. This is a positive challenge for the profession and a strong rationale for training more music therapists to meet the demand.

Technology

New technologies are not only transforming the way people communicate, do business and socialize, but they are affecting the way in which music therapy services are provided. The educational community has been slow to respond to the need for reformation of curricula in this area. Magee and Burland (2008) lay out a model for the utilization of electronic music technologies, especially for individuals who have complex needs. Mihailidis et al. (2010) developed an arts therapy computer application from the ground up, by surveying arts therapists in English-speaking countries regarding the requirements for a potentially successful tool that would engage people with dementia. The range and scope of technological applications are growing rapidly, but music therapists may not be ready to take advantage of the new software and hardware.

It appears that there is a lack of adequate training and preparation for music therapists to apply many of these technologies. A survey by Magee (2006), updated by Hahna et al. (2012), found a substantial number of barriers to the use of new technologies. In Hahna et al.'s study, 600 respondents to a questionnaire from the US, Canada, Australia, and the UK identified a significant need for better preparation. While music therapists reported using a great variety of technological advances, in general, they have little formal training. In fact, the sources of their education in technology were self-taught, peers, music therapy conferences, university, then technology seminar, and other, in rank order. More and more colleges have courses devoted to music and music therapy technology, and include specialized training institutes, yet there is currently no requirement by an accreditation body for competency in music therapy technology. Magee (2013) points out that while more courses are offered in music technologies, the specific clinical uses and contraindications are not necessarily emphasized to the degree that they should be. As technology gains greater prominence in the work of the music therapist, these issues will become even more important.

Levels of practice

In the USA, the entry level music therapist must have: (1) Earned at least a Bachelor's degree or its equivalent from a program approved by AMTA; (2) obtained the skills, competencies, and supervised clinical experience articulated by the CBMT; and (3) passed the Certification Board Examination. In order to become more aligned with other allied health care professions and music therapy requirements around the world, AMTA is now considering advancing the level of entry into the profession to the Master's degree. The rigorous requirements for becoming a competent music therapy professional, including the approved clinical training, already necessitates more than the customary four years to complete. However, requiring graduate study has been a controversial topic for many reasons, one of which involves the massive changes in current undergraduate curricula that would be required for all AMTA-approved programs. The expanding knowledge base and access to knowledge may ultimately necessitate this critical curricular change. Currently, town meetings, task forces, and special committees are gathering data and considering recommendations to AMTA's Assembly, its policy-making body.

The need for personal therapy

Gardstrom and Jackson (2011) surveyed program directors of AMTA-approved music therapy curricula to determine their policies and expectations regarding personal therapy for the music therapist in training. Of those responding, 14 percent replied that they require some kind of personal therapy for their students; 32 percent encourage personal therapy in the form of verbal therapy (73 percent of this subgroup) and music therapy (46 percent of this subgroup). In the USA, there are legal and ethical issues surrounding whether therapy can be required, and economic considerations relative to the cost of procuring therapy services. However, the philosophical background of a particular course of study will determine whether personal therapy is considered necessary or relevant. For example, psychoanalytic and psychodynamic approaches view personal therapy as essential to the process of becoming a therapist, while cognitive behavioral approaches that call for a more balanced alliance between therapist and client may question its importance altogether. At the time of preparing this chapter personal therapy is required in music therapy courses in the UK and Ireland. The need for further research to support the efficacy and value of personal therapy has been proposed (Edwards 2013).

Multicultural training

In a 1988 issue of the *Journal of Music Therapy*, Joseph Moreno declared that music therapists must have basic working knowledge of basic genres of music from around the world. Recognizing the need for greater understanding of world cultures, the editor of *Music Therapy Perspectives* asked Moreno to contribute a regular column, entitled "International Perspectives," which he did, from 1990 to 1994. In 1995, Manal Toppozada surveyed professional music therapists, and found that 78.2 percent recommended multicultural training for music therapy students. The methods of providing that education, however, were extremely diverse. In Darrow and Molloy's research (1998), music therapists emphasized the importance of understanding the cultures of their clients, and expressed frustration when they did not have an understanding of their clients' cultural backgrounds. However, only four out of the twenty-five colleges they randomly selected for review actually required a course in multicultural music therapy. A more recent survey of music therapy training directors in the USA (Bies 2011) identified only one music therapy course devoted specially to teach cultural topics. Yet 50 percent of the educators rated their programs as "very effective" or "effective" in teaching their music therapy students cultural issues. One challenge for half of the respondent colleges was a lack of cultural diversity in the local clientele. While respondents stated that there was a dearth of teaching materials available, there are some interesting texts, notably *Culture-Centered Music Therapy* by Brunjuif Stige (2002).

Karen Estrella (2001) speaks to the unique position of the music therapy clinical supervisor in being a gatekeeper and advocate for the profession, and also a role model as a fully competent music therapist. She emphasizes the responsibility of the supervisor not only to demonstrate and facilitate cultural competence amongst peers, students, and clients, but also to the administration of the facility. The role of the supervisor, however, is fraught with challenges because, among other issues, the "power" ascribed to the supervisor creates a sensitive culture all on its own.

Mutliculturalism does not only refer to race and class, but also gender. A culture receiving much attention is that of the lesbian, gay, bisexual, and transsexual (GLBT) community. In the past several National Conferences of the American Music Therapy Association, sessions have been devoted to the topic, and there are commentaries on *Voices: A World Forum for Music Therapy* (<https://normt.uib.no/index.php/>) voices about the unique needs and contributions of people who identify as belonging within the GLBT community. Clearly, there will be more to come in the definition, research, development, and implementation of systematic training for multicultural music therapy.

THE FUTURE

The future of music therapy will be guided by its education and training, and the values that music therapy educators hold regarding the most important elements for preparing the prospective music therapist. They have immense responsibility for ensuring that music therapists of the future are competent to provide the best services possible. This is, perhaps, the greatest challenge of all.

REFERENCES

APMT (1990). *Supervision criteria*. London: Association of Professional Music Therapists.

APMT (2008). Clinical supervision: Information and guidance document. London: Association of Professional Music Therapists.

Baker, F. and Krout, R.E. (2011). Collaborative peer lyric writing during music therapy training: A tool for facilitating students' reflections about clinical practicum experiences. *Nordic Journal of Music Therapy* 20(1): 62–89.

Bies, A.H. (2011). *Effectiveness of Music Therapy Education in Addressing Multicultural Competencies: Survey of Music Therapy Program Directors*. Unpublished master's thesis. Athens, OH: Ohio University.

Bunt, L. and Hoskyns, S. (2002). *The Handbook of Music Therapy*. London: Brunner Routledge.

Bureau of Labor Statistics. (2011). *Occupational Outlook Handbook*, 2010–2011 edition. Retrieved July 17, 2011 from <http://www.bls.gov/oco/oco2003.htm>.

"Columbia University to heal wounded by music," *The Literary Digest* 60 (January-March 1919).

Darrow, A.A.A. and Molloy, D. (1998). Multicultural perspectives in music therapy: An examination of the literature, educational curricula, and clinical practices in culturally diverse cities of the United States. *Music Therapy Perspectives* 16(1): 27–32.

de l'Etoile, S. (2000). The history of the undergraduate curriculum in music therapy. *Journal of Music Therapy* 37(1), 51–74.

Edwards, J. (2008). The use of music in healthcare contexts: A select review of writings from the 1890s to the 1940s. *Voices: A World Forum for Music Therapy*, 8(2). <http://voices.no/index.php/voices/article/view/Article/428>. Accessed on December 28, 2012.

Edwards, J. (2013). Examining the role and functions of self-development in healthcare therapy trainings: A review of the literature with a modest proposal for the use of learning agreements. *European Journal of Psychotherapy & Counselling* 15(3): 214–232.

Estrella, K. (2001). Multicultural approaches to music therapy supervision. In: M. Forinash, (ed.), *Music Therapy Supervision*. Gilsum, NH: Barcelona Press.

Forinash, M. (2001). *Music Therapy Supervision*. Gilsum, NH: Barcelona Press.

Gardstrom, S.C., and Jackson, N.A. (2011). Personal therapy for undergraduate music therapy students: A survey of AMTA program coordinators. *Journal of Music Therapy* 48(2): 226–255.

Goodman, K.D. (2011). *Music therapy education and training: From theory to practice*. Springfield, IL: Charles C. Thomas.

Groene, R.W. and Pembrook, R.G. (2000). Curricular issues in music therapy: A survey of collegiate faculty. *Music Therapy Perspectives* 18(2): 92–102.

Hahna, N.D., Hadley, S., Miller, V.H., and Bonaventura, M. (2012). Music technology usage in music therapy: A survey of practice. *The Arts in Psychotherapy* 39(5): 456–464.

Hammerlund, I. (2001). *A music therapy supervision training for supervisors.* Naples, Italy: European Congress of Music Therapy.

Hanser, S.B. (2009). From ancient to integrative medicine: Models for music therapy. *Music and Medicine* 1(2): 87–96.

Magee, W.L. (2006). Electronic technologies in clinical music therapy: A survey of practice and attitudes. *Technology and Disability* 18(3): 139–146.

Magee, W.L. (2013). Indications and contra-indications for using music technology with clinical populations: When to use and when not to use. In: W. L. Magee (ed.), *Music technology in therapeutic and health settings*, pp. 83-107. London: Jessica Kingsley Publishers.

Magee, W.L. and Burland, K. (2008). An exploratory study of the use of electronic music technologies in clinical music therapy. *Nordic Journal of Music Therapy* 17(2): 124–141.

Mihailidis, A., Eng, P., Blunsden, S., Boger, J., Richards, B., Zutis, K. et al. (2010). Towards the development of a technology for art therapy and dementia: Definition of needs and design constraints. *Arts in Psychotherapy* 37: 293–300.

Moreno, J. (1988). Multicultural music therapy: The world music connection. *Journal of Music Therapy* 25(1): 17–27.

Odell-Miller, H. (2009). The history and background of supervision in music therapy. In: H. Odell-Miller and E. Richards (eds), *Supervision of music therapy: A theoretical and practical handbook*, pp. 5–22. London: Routledge.

Odell-Miller, H. and Richards, E. (2009). *Supervision of music therapy: A theoretical and practical handbook*. London: Routledge.

Stige, B. (2002). *Culture-centered music therapy*. Gilsum, NH: Barcelona Publisher.

Toppozada, M.R. (1995). Multicultural Training for music therapists: An examination of current issues based on a national survey of professional music therapists. *Journal of Music Therapy* 32(2): 65–90.

Wheeler, B.L. (2000). Music therapy practicum practices: A survey of music therapy educators. *Journal of Music Therapy* 37: 286–311.

Wheeler, B.L. and Grocke, D.E. (2001). Report from the World Federation of Music Therapy commission on education, training, and accreditation education symposium. *Music Therapy Perspectives* 19(1): 63–67.

Wheeler, B.L. and Williams, C. (2012). Students' thoughts and feelings about music therapy practicum supervision. *Nordic Journal of Music Therapy* 21(2): 111–132.

Wigram, T. (2009). Supervision of PhD doctoral research. In: H. Odell-Miller and E. Richards (eds), *Supervision of music therapy: A theoretical and practical handbook*, pp. 173–191 London: Routledge.

CHAPTER 47

....

DEVELOPING NEW POSTS
IN MUSIC THERAPY

....

ALISON LEDGER

INTRODUCTION

....

Is it me, or is that a look of contempt?
Do I pay too close attention?
Do I try too hard to win respect
For my brand new intervention?

Should we focus on the work itself?
Keep our heads down to the ground?
But then there'll be no-one to represent,
We won't even make a sound.

Motivation comes from patient time,
It's my heart that keeps me here,
But it cannot beat forever,
I have to think of my career.

As I stick up my two fingers
To the sceptics in this place
I wonder, is it worth it?
Do my efforts go to waste?[1]

Ledger 2010, p. 300–301

THIS chapter provides an overview of the skills and strategies used by music therapists to develop new posts. Examples from the music therapy literature and doctoral research (Ledger 2010) are presented to illustrate some of the common issues encountered by music therapists when they create new work and enter established health care teams. Interdisciplinary perspectives from the field of management and from studies which have examined the introduction of other health care roles are included. These sources help to explain music therapists' experiences, and offer a means to identify and even classify strategies for developing music therapy posts. However, all of the literature from within and outside music therapy indicates that start up work is rarely straightforward and requires processes of adaptation and reflection in context. The process of organizational change has been observed to be fluid, dynamic, and unpredictable and in most cases, successful change takes time (Dawson 2003; Shanley 2007). This chapter emphasizes the importance of considering the specific start up context and the critical need for music therapy training and supervision to support the development of new posts in music therapy.

Around the globe, qualified music therapists are working hard to develop new posts. As music therapy is a relatively new health care profession, music therapists are regularly required to create new positions, to be the first to introduce the idea of music therapy to managers and professionals, to demonstrate the value of music therapy for health and well-being, and to give time and effort to securing their positions in the organizations where they are employed. As music therapy grows and develops worldwide, music therapists are also increasingly moving into new and exciting areas of practice, such as parent-infant bonding and disaster relief.

Since most, if not all music therapists undertake some form of service development in their everyday working lives, further reflection about the skill-set music therapists need to develop new posts is warranted. Some music therapists have described the strategies they have used to build programmes in hospital settings (Edwards 2005; Loewy 2001, 2007) and there is a growing literature about inter-professional work in music therapy (for examples see O'Kelly and Koffman 2007; Twyford and Watson 2008), but research about the processes through which music therapy posts become accepted and established is only in its infancy.

Music therapists' experiences
of developing new posts

As music therapy becomes better established worldwide, music therapists are beginning to reflect on their experiences of developing new posts. Revealing accounts of the challenges of music therapy development work have been published (Miles 2007; Konieczna 2009). Konieczna (2009) indicated that she experienced a lack of supervision and felt a burden of responsibility to prove her worth as she developed a music therapy programme in a residential facility for children in Poland. References to the challenges of developing new posts can also be found in *Voices' Country of the Month* feature, where authors inform readers about the development of music therapy in their respective countries. Recent *Country of the Month* postings have referred to challenges such as limited resources, cultural differences (Kowaleski 2011), misunderstandings about music therapy, a lack of professional support, and the need to advocate for music therapy when developing new posts (Kavaliova-Moussi 2012). Similar challenges are reported in the publications of national music therapy associations (Browne et al. 2007; Cosgrove 2005). For example, Bernadette Whyte referred to the demands of "selling" music therapy and "fighting [her] corner" when developing sessional, part-time, or temporary music therapy positions in Ireland (Browne et al. 2007, p. 15).

Jane Edwards (2005) provided one of the most detailed reflections on the development of a music therapy post. Challenges she experienced when developing a pediatric music therapy programme included fitting music therapy into a medical context, distinguishing music therapy from existing uses of music, and the unpredictable nature of the work. Edwards indicated that it took time for her to determine suitable roles for music therapy, to gain access to patients, and to demonstrate the value of music therapy in a hospital setting. She recalled how the role of the music therapist needed to be "emergent and responsive" (p. 43) to patients' and staff members' needs.

Joanne Loewy (2001) described how she founded a music therapy programme in a New York hospital in pediatrics and then expanded the programme to other areas of the hospital. Important steps in this expansion included establishing a need for music therapy and illustrating its effectiveness. Loewy described how being a pioneer in music therapy "takes efforts" (p. 4), particularly when there are "antagonists" (p. 9) within a hospital team. From her perspective, not all music therapists possess a flair for instituting programmes, and there is a critical need for further training in grant writing and "program building" in music therapy (p. 5).

Music therapists' experiences of developing new services in health care organizations were the subject of my doctoral study at the University of Limerick, Ireland (Ledger 2010), supervised by Jane Edwards who is a veteran of successful start up work. I explored the service development experiences of twelve music therapists from Australia, Canada, Ireland, the United Kingdom, and the United States, through a combination of narrative inquiry, arts-based research, and ethnographic fieldwork. This study included the collection of stories from experienced music therapy service developers about their early experiences, as well as observation of the introduction of a new music therapy service in a hospital in Ireland. I observed that music therapy participants conveyed strong feelings of isolation, insecurity, and uncertainty in relation to their service development experiences and recounted challenges such as role ambiguity and resistance from other workers. A review of literature published in the areas of change management and the implementation of new health care roles revealed that music therapists encounter similar challenges to other workers who have tried to introduce changes to existing services. This literature provided an additional source of ideas for ways in which music therapists can develop new posts successfully.

The existing music therapy service development literature has indicated that developing new posts is inherently challenging. In my experience, music therapists tend to view these challenges as something unique to their profession and frequently respond to challenges and blockages as if they are personally intended. My wider reading suggests that similar obstacles are reported by workers who have introduced new approaches, systems, and practices in the commercial sector and in other areas of health care work (Dawson 2003; Dulaney and Stanley 2005; Shanley 2007).

In the field of management, change is viewed as a highly challenging process that requires major shifts in workers' practices, values, identities, and roles (Dawson 2003; Deegan et al. 2004). According to theorists such as Lewin, the process of change involves breaking down long-established traditions and ways of working, recognising the need for change, and enacting and incorporating a change into a new system (Cartwright 1951). Attempts at change can also be subject to strong restraining forces, such as firmly-held values, past experiences, time or resource constraints (Cartwright 1951; Dulaney and Stanley 2005). From a change management perspective, music therapists should expect to encounter challenges when they introduce new posts to established health care teams. Greater exposure to change management ideas may encourage practitioners to anticipate challenges and to engage strategies for overcoming obstacles to music therapy development.

THE INITIAL START-UP OF A POST

Although there is a growing literature to support the application of music therapy in a wide range of settings, there is comparatively little literature which provides information about the ways in which music therapists have started their posts. Edwards (2005) described how she gained entry to the Royal Children's Hospital in Brisbane, Australia, after visiting several possible sites where she could offer supervised training for music therapy students. The personal connections of a retired music therapist led Edwards to make contact with a surgeon at the children's hospital, who facilitated an opportunity to give a Grand Round presentation to practitioners and administrators. In Edwards' recollection, the Grand Round presentation left a strong impression on a Clinical Nurse Consultant from the pediatric burns unit, and music therapy commenced in the burns unit soon after. Edwards' is a relatively rare account of service development, and provides useful clues as to the ways in which music therapy posts can be established.

Some music therapy posts have been established when practitioners have managed to distinguish their practice from other types of interventions provided by professional musicians, community musicians, complementary and alternative medicine (CAM) practitioners, and other creative arts therapists. In a survey of 67 cancer care managers, Daykin and Bunt (2006) found that managers did not make clear distinctions between various types of music interventions and they proposed that "the specific contribution of the professional music therapist is not necessarily well understood" (p. 411). Daykin and Bunt suggested that it may be beneficial for music therapists to emphasize their unique contribution if they wish to introduce a position in a place where music is already available. However, not all music therapists agree that there is a need to delineate clear boundaries between music therapy and other music practices (Ansdell and Pavlicevic 2008; Hartley 2008). For instance, Moss (2008) has reported successful implementation of a combination of music therapy, live music performance, and recorded music in her role as a qualified music therapist working as a hospital arts officer in Ireland. Moss' experience suggests that it may not always be necessary for a music therapist to mark out an exclusive role, but rather to select the most appropriate way of working with music according to patient need (Moss 2007). I experienced a similar need to remain flexible about how music could be implemented when developing a music therapy programme for families in schools (Ledger 2011).

There is also some evidence that music therapists have gained posts through demonstrating the financial benefits of music therapy. Hilliard (2004) identified insufficient funds as a primary reason why music therapists were not employed in US hospices. Based on his survey research with hospice administrators, he emphasized that music therapists need to educate administrators about potential funding sources and the financial benefits of adding a music therapy programme. This may become increasingly important in an international climate of growing economic concern.

Music therapists who participated in the doctoral research I undertook indicated that the creation of music therapy posts can sometimes be aided by a fortunate or serendipitous alliance. Several music therapists explained how a prior relationship with an influential person had facilitated their acceptance. Influential people included managers and workers who had the power to introduce music therapy to other members of staff. When

I observed the introduction of a new music therapy service in a hospital, it was the medical consultant who was perceived to be the most influential in getting music therapy started. Hospital staff explained that the medical consultant held considerable power over hospital decision-makers, due to traditional hierarchies within medicine. Fortunately the consultant had seen music therapy introduced successfully elsewhere and staff believed that it was his strong support that had facilitated the introduction of music therapy.

The critical role of "gatekeepers" in admitting entry to organizations is an aspect which is emphasized in literature on organizational change and in studies of change implementation in hospital settings (Cartwright 1951; Dulaney and Stanley 2005). For example, Dulaney and Stanley (2005) described how the introduction of a new structured treatment approach was facilitated by the sponsorship and support of a medical director, an administrator, a physician, a nurse, and a range of other influential staff. Their work showed how gatekeepers can exist both within formal and informal power structures of a health care organization. Staff members may exert considerable influence despite little formal power, "by virtue of their longevity on a unit, or their clinical expertise, or their close relationship with those who have formal power" (Dulaney and Stanley 2005, p. 164). To date, there has been little reflection on or examination as to the locations of power in relation to the introduction of music therapy services. This is an important area for future reflection and research.

From the sparse information available about music therapy start up, it is not possible to establish clear causal links between influential factors. It is likely that successful start up depends on a complex range of context-based factors, and the key to gaining entry in one practice setting may not necessarily open the door in another. Furthermore, the development of new posts may be strongly influenced by power dynamics within the organization, and a music therapist's relationships with other workers. This becomes even more evident when the music therapist's entry into an established professional team is considered.

ENTERING AN ESTABLISHED TEAM

When a music therapist enters a health care or educational institution, s/he typically joins a team of established professionals. Often existing team members have been working together for a long period of time, have long-established ways of working, and additionally have never worked with a music therapist before. Many music therapists have described the need to demonstrate the value of music therapy, to educate others about possible spaces for music therapy, and to determine the ways in which music therapy could best fit into the team (Ledger 2010; Loewy 2001; Silverman and Chaput 2011).

Management researchers have proposed that workers can fit into teams in either supplementary or complementary ways (Guan et al. 2011; Kristof-Brown et al. 2005). Sometimes a worker's goals and values match those of the team, other times a worker fills a gap in the existing team (Kristof-Brown et al. 2005). In the music therapy literature, there is evidence to suggest that music therapists fit into their teams in both supplementary and complementary ways. Some music therapists have described how they have strived to fit in with existing health care approaches or systems, such as a medical model of evidence and treatment (Edwards 2005), imperatives to deliver measurable outcomes, or existing reporting mechanisms (Ledger 2010). Other music therapists have described how they have identified a way for music therapy to fill an unmet need or niche (Ledger 2010; Loewy 2001, 2007). For example, Loewy described how she recognized a role for music therapy when she discovered her hospital was in need of a less expensive sedation intervention which included caregivers and involved less risk (Loewy et al. 2005).

When a music therapist joins an existing team, s/he enters a space which was previously the domain of other professionals. In order to work effectively, a music therapist may be looking to secure financial resources, a therapy room and desk, time with patients, and a place in professional team meetings. The development of a music therapy post could therefore be understood as a threat to other workers' established territory. Other professionals may need to make room for the music therapist, which may lead to rivalry and tensions. Recent literature related to inter-professional work in music therapy has highlighted the potential for conflict, resistance, and territorialism when a new music therapy service is being introduced (Darsie 2009; Hobson 2006; Twyford and Watson 2008). Other professionals may be reluctant to acknowledge roles for music therapy which they believe to be within their own areas of expertise (Choi 1997; Darsie 2009), or wary of new approaches that they regard as unfamiliar or different (Miller 2008; Neale 2010; O'Kelly and Koffman 2007). In highly stressful practice environments, there is also a potential for workers to become envious of a music therapist who they perceive to be evading difficult work (Miller 2008; Neale 2010).

Inter-professional tension is a phenomenon which is widely reported in the health care literature. Though effective inter-professional work is promoted as an ideal, it has been described as difficult to achieve in practice due to diversity in health care approaches, historical differences, power dynamics between the health care professions, and poor communication between health care staff (Atwal and Caldwell 2005; Gotlib Conn et al. 2009; Hall 2005). Researchers have found that health care professionals show resistance to inter-professional work when they perceive that their scope of practice is being intruded upon (Hall 2005; Kvarnström 2008). In a recent evaluation of an inter-professional education initiative, Baker et al. (2011) observed that workers in similar health care professions engaged in "elbowing behavior" (p. 102), to set boundaries, carve out professional niches, and defend the uniqueness of their professions. It is also highly likely that health care workers retreat to their own professional cultures at times of instability and change (Brown et al. 2000; Hall 2005). It is therefore unsurprising that music therapists can encounter resistance when they are developing new posts and entering established health care teams. Understanding the possible origins of this resistance may be useful for bypassing or lessening its impacts on the successful development of music therapy services.

Music therapists have reported that their practice approaches are misunderstood by members of inter-professional teams (Loewy 2001; Magee and Andrews 2007). Magee and Andrews (2007) identified a lack of role understanding as one of the main barriers to music therapy's inclusion in multidisciplinary neurorehabilitation teams. They observed that it was uncommon for patients to be referred to music therapy for physical needs, despite research evidence which indicated a useful role for music therapy in gait training. In a study of palliative care team members' perceptions of music therapy, O'Kelly and Koffman (2007) found that nurse interviewees expressed fears about the emotional effects of music therapy and held an expectation that creative ability was required. One of the music therapists who participated in my doctoral research indicated that she had been misperceived as "something diversional or entertainment," and other respondents reflected that it took time for other team members to understand the role of the music therapist. These experiences indicate that misperceptions about music therapy are commonly encountered in start up, and explaining and demonstrating music therapy are important parts of the music therapist's role.

It may be reassuring for current and future music therapists to know that other health care workers report that their role and work are misunderstood. In the wider health care literature, there are countless examples of workers who feel that their roles are poorly understood, including doctors, nurses, occupational therapists, and other allied health staff (Moore et al. 2006; Pellatt 2005; Suter et al. 2009). Pellatt (2005) observed a "knowing paradox" in her study of inter-professional roles within a rehabilitation team, whereby health professionals believed that they understood others' contributions to the team, yet perceived that they were misunderstood in return. Studies of the implementation of new health care roles have also highlighted the potential for role ambiguity when a new profession is introduced to a team of more established professionals (Arving and Holmström 2011; Cummings et al. 2003; Lindblad et al. 2010). In a study of the introduction of advanced nurse practitioners (ANPs), interviewees reported divergent understandings of the ANP role and there was "a trend toward uncertainty regarding the role" (Cummings et al. 2003, p. 141). Lack of role clarity was perceived to lead to underutilization of ANPs, including limited ANP involvement in education and research activities. ANPs also experienced limited access to patients, as medical residents tried to manage all but the most stable of patients. A similar situation was reported in a study of newly appointed dual diagnosis workers (McLaughlin et al. 2008). One dual diagnosis worker described how opportunities to demonstrate the value of her work were limited, as she was only referred the patients that "nobody else wants to work with" (p. 300).

Studies of new role bearers' experiences have revealed a need for improved role understanding in teams (Arving and Holmström 2011; Cummings et al. 2003; Lindblad et al. 2010). New music therapists may therefore benefit from initiating role discussions with other members of the team or proposing that time be provided for role explanations within team meetings. At the same time, it may be important for music therapists to recognize that team members' roles are neither fixed nor stable. Croker et al. (2012) have likened the health care team to a cycling peloton, in which members jostle for positions and move dynamically towards a shared destination. In their view, incoming team members need to be "responsive to, become part of and, in turn, subtly shape the *form* and *feel* of the team" (p. 16). Studies of the implementation of new health care roles have also demonstrated how professional roles shift over time and in relation to other health care team members (Bridges and Meyer 2007; O'Connor 2006). These studies further emphasize a need for music therapists to adopt flexible and collaborative approaches when introducing new posts.

While there is some evidence that music therapists have reflected on the challenges of joining an established team, there is also literature which suggests that the introduction of music therapy can have positive benefits for existing team members. O'Callaghan and Magill (2009) found that staff who witnessed music therapy reported feeling "part of a team providing good patient care" (p. 226), and other staff members have benefited from team building activities facilitated by a music therapist (Hilliard 2006; Loewy 2001). Likewise, health care staff interviewed during my hospital-based fieldwork reported that positive collaborative experiences with the music therapist had encouraged them to pursue collaborative work with other colleagues for the first time.

In summary, literature on person-group fit, inter-professional work, and new role bearers' experiences encourages us to think more about the impact the introduction of a music therapy post has on other workers. The effects of music therapy on clients and their families have become increasingly established in the past decades. Including the effects of music therapy on staff can enrich out professional perspective and provide an avenue for further professional growth.

The path of music therapy development

Development takes patience,
It won't happen overnight.
You might never feel "established"
So just work towards "alright".

Ledger 2010, p. 302

Once a music therapist gains entry into an organization or institution, s/he may anticipate continued growth in music therapy over time. However, published accounts of music therapy service development suggest that it is rare that music therapy posts grow in a predictable, linear fashion (Edwards 2005; Ledger 2010; Loewy 2001).

Participants in my research recalled setbacks in the development of their music therapy posts and reported that the amount of music therapy increased and decreased due to unpredictable factors. They portrayed music therapy as a service which was highly sensitive to changes in the economic climate, changes in policy, and also powerfully effected by turnover of staff. One participant described how her music therapy service had switched between periods of growth, regression, and recovery. She recalled needing to backtrack repeatedly when she was allocated four different managers in the short space of five months. Each time a new manager was appointed, she perceived that she need to re-introduce music therapy and wait for staff to become comfortable again, before promoting or requesting further music therapy development. In her view, changes in staff had delayed her efforts to expand the music therapy service to other areas of the hospital.

I'm now being watched by the manager's eye
Perhaps I need to hold on til this moment's gone by,
Before I make another step to further my position,
Before the staff are comfortable to make the right decision
To allow me the space, to fulfil my potential,
To build on opportunities as much as I am able.
Until that time, I'll play it safe, I'll hold the status quo,
I'll wait until the climate's right for MT's place to grow.

Ledger 2010, p. 303

Setbacks can be experienced as frustrating when a music therapist is passionately working to develop a new post (Ledger 2010). Therefore, it may be helpful for music therapists to know that other workers experience setbacks when introducing change. Commentators on change in the commercial sector have increasingly drawn attention to the complex path of change initiatives (Dawson 2003; Styhre 2002). Studies of change in hospital organizations have found that change rarely happens smoothly, and the process of change is often hindered by cultural and contextual factors (Braithwaite 2006; Dulaney and Stanley 2005; Shanley 2007). For example, Braithwaite's (2006) research on the introduction of clinical directorates in Australia found that attempts at changing management structures were hampered by existing hierarchies and routines. Despite initiatives to reduce professional tribalism and to bring different professions together, old structuring behaviors continued. Nurses talked to nurses, doctors talked to doctors, and positions were formed behind the scenes rather than through the newly introduced systems.

Another study that explored cultural factors and change implementation was Viitanen and Piirainen's (2003) action research study of a physiotherapy development in a Finnish hospital. Through the process of implementing an education programme involving critical reflection, Viitanen and Piirainen learned about the hospital's underlying values and cultures. Although the hospital communicated a message that education was desirable, it became evident that only certain types of education were acceptable. Knowledge dissemination and procedural instruction were perceived to be appropriate, whereas critical reflection was not. Though frequently powerful, health care cultures may not always be immediately apparent and can remain hidden until a change is introduced.

Time may be a critical factor in the transition to any new health care role. Schwartz et al. (2011) interviewed ten nurses who had recently started work in a mental health hospital and found that it took nurses time to gain confidence, to establish credibility, and to secure the trust of other workers. Nurses described how they initially adopted a passive role in order to develop their understandings of the work environment, the patient population, and the health care team. Watching and listening to other team members was crucial for observing the functions and dynamics of the team and for "learning how to fit in" (p. 156). New nurses perceived that they needed to prove themselves and build on past successes before they could take on a more active role. The transition from novice to trusted team member did not happen overnight.

From the rich narratives I collected in my research, it was clear that developing a music therapy post requires considerable time and persistence. Music therapists reported that it had taken them time to secure the necessary funding and resources to develop their posts, to gain acceptance and to build trust with managers and other health care workers, to gain access to patients, to find a role for music therapy, and to establish music therapy as an integral part of the organization. The length of time taken to establish a music therapy post varied greatly from setting to setting, and ranged from several months to even years.

SERVICE DEVELOPMENT STRATEGIES

Am I a founder or am I a fraud?
Forging my way through this baffling place,
Struggling daily to make some headway,
Working hard to impress, doing all to save face.

I'm like a lone salesman, my profession's on sale,
I think I'd rather sell doughnuts.

Ledger 2010, p. 298

In the course of my doctoral research, I became aware that music therapists felt unsure of what it was that they needed to do to develop their posts successfully. Music therapists expressed uncertainty as to whether they should provide in-service presentations to staff, which other professionals they should align themselves to, whether they should get involved in promotional activities, and whether or not they should restrict their focus to the music therapy work and allow the benefits to speak for themselves. Detailed exploration of the music therapists' experiences indicated that the processes surrounding music therapy development were highly complex. No straightforward recommendations emerged and it is likely that the preferred service development approach depends on the particular context in which a music therapist is employed. However, some general principles were garnered from management literature and from existing accounts of music therapy service development. These general principles included identifying opportunities for development, communicating and collaborating with other workers, and appointing change agents to assist with the development of a new music therapy post.

Identifying opportunities for development

For many of the music therapists in my study, there seemed to be a *right time* for developing a music therapy post. Music therapy participants recalled that they had made progress when there was money available, once staff had witnessed the benefits of music therapy, or when other team members were observed to be ready for further change. Specific times when developments were achieved included a period after a successful student placement, a time when managers were particularly satisfied with the music therapy service, and a time when other allied health professionals were also being employed. The music therapists' stories indicated that they were highly skilled at identifying these opportunities for change.

In the broader health care literature, Dulaney and Stanley (2005) stated that successful change begins with careful assessment of an organization's readiness for change. It may be profitable for a music therapist to examine an organization's history of adopting changes and to explore the ways that recent changes have unfolded. In addition, it may be especially crucial for a music therapist to detect cultures at work in the particular organization where they are employed. In health care organizations, traditions can be powerful and a music therapist may need to be aware of strong historical forces. Music therapists in my study reflected that it had taken time for them to gain an understanding of their organizations. They recalled learning about organizational cultures and values through observation and through meeting with managers and other health care staff. They also explained how they needed to build a history and track record of their own before pushing for further development.

Along with identifying opportunities, it may be important for music therapists to recognize when it is unlikely that further development will be achieved. This was particularly evident in one of the service development stories I collected. The music therapist had aspirations to expand her service to other areas in the hospital but decided it was not yet time to push for additional change. There had been a number of staff changes and she perceived that she needed to show staff that she understood their culture and needs before pushing for further music therapy development. Loewy (2001) has suggested that music therapists should only develop posts in areas where they can be supported to grow and flourish. Sometimes a music therapist may need to concede that the obstacles to music therapy growth are insurmountable, and then withdraw to develop music therapy elsewhere.

> Should I stay or should I go?
> Can't go on fighting any more
> I think I could do better and
> I'm tired of this war.
> > Ledger 2010, p. 298

Communicating and collaborating with other workers

In studies of organizational change in hospitals, communication and collaboration are presented as the keys to successful change (Deegan et al. 2004; Dulaney and Stanley 2005; Wynne 2004). Researchers have proposed that workers are more likely to accept and sustain changes if they are involved in the change process and have opportunities to raise their concerns (Deegan et al. 2004; Kirchner et al. 2012). There is evidence to suggest that music therapists are equally aware of this need to communicate and collaborate when introducing a new approach to workers. Literature on music therapy and inter-professional work has emphasized a need for music therapists to educate others about their roles (Magee and Andrews 2007; O'Kelly and Koffman 2007). Professional practice and training guidelines include inter-professional collaboration as a core component of music therapy practice and training (American Music Therapy Association 2008; Australian Music Therapy Association 2004; Copley et al. 2007; Health Professions Council 2007). However, best practice in teaching inter-professional work and programme building is yet to be established.

Two survey studies have indicated that formal inservicing can be an effective way of communicating the benefits of music therapy to other workers (Darsie 2009; Silverman and Chaput 2011). In both of these studies, health care workers showed increased awareness of the potential applications of music therapy after attending a music therapy in-service. Music therapy in-services have included information such as definitions of music therapy, training requirements for music therapists, music therapy goals and treatment processes, and research outcomes which support a role for music therapy. Additionally, music therapists have indicated that video excerpts of music therapy sessions can be particularly effective in educating staff about music therapy aims and applications (Darsie 2009; Loewy 2001). In planning a music therapy in-service, music therapists may wish to consider other workers' interests, and to prepare for the possibility that education about music therapy might not always be well-received. Tríona McCaffrey identified a potential for music therapists to be perceived as condescending when "preaching" about music therapy (Ledger 2010, p. 204) and Silverman and Chaput (2011) indicated that music therapists should emphasize that the introduction of music therapy will not detract from others' work.

Music therapists have further highlighted the importance of engaging other workers in collaborative work when developing new posts (for examples see Hobson 2006; O'Kelly and Koffman 2007; Twyford and Watson 2008). In a ground-breaking text about music therapy and integrated team working, Twyford and Watson (2008) presented inter-professional collaboration as a way in which music therapists can clarify professional roles and boundaries, convey the importance of music therapy, learn from others, and gain support from other staff. In summarizing the core themes of their book, Twyford and Watson indicated that working with others may be especially important for music therapists who are striving to consolidate their roles. This was reinforced by the music therapists in my study, who held a perception that it was more beneficial to show others music therapy than to try and explain it. Almost all of the music therapists in my study recalled situations in which they had invited staff to observe or assist in music therapy sessions. When staff members worked with a music therapist in sessions, they witnessed the benefits of music therapy for themselves, heard positive feedback from patients or family members, and were assisted to carry out their own treatment procedures. The music therapists perceived that it was often a powerful learning experience for workers to see patients smiling, laughing, singing, or crying in music therapy sessions, particularly when a patient's progress in other therapies was slow. Magee (2005) has similarly observed that music therapy can engender hope for a team who are caring for patients with complex illnesses or disabilities.

Edwards (2005) explained how her role needed to be "emergent and responsive" (p. 43) when she developed music therapy in a children's hospital. Music therapists in my study equally stressed a need to respond to others when developing music therapy posts. Several explained how they had listened to others in order to develop a post that was responsive to the culture of the organization and the needs of patients, families, and staff. They reported learning about the needs of their organization through observation, through formal discussions and team meetings, and by spending time with other staff over meals. Through listening to others, music therapists came to develop roles for music therapy which they had not anticipated, or which they had previously regarded as beyond their scope of practice. For example, several music therapists described how they had become involved in other music activities within their organizations, such as a Christmas concert or a similar community event. These activities were understood as more than entertainment, or a chance to demonstrate their music skills. Instead, they offered music therapists further opportunities to communicate and collaborate in a slightly different context.

As mentioned earlier in this chapter, it may be particularly important for music therapists to build relationships with gatekeepers who have the power to advance music therapy's position within the organization. Music therapists in my study emphasized the importance of building relationships with managers and financial decision-makers in particular, and Edwards has since described how the development of her post was facilitated by the support of key staff members who were held in high esteem (Ledger et al. 2013). Loewy (2001) described how she included statements from key gatekeepers in the creation of promotional videos about music therapy, thereby educating them about music therapy while giving them an important role in communicating the benefits of music therapy to the rest of the organization. This is a valuable example of a way in which collaboration may lead to greater access and acceptance in the team.

> To survive depends on who you know.
> A contact can be key
> To being taken seriously,
> To who you get to see.
>
> Ledger 2010, p. 301

Appointing change agents

In my practice and research experience, music therapists tend to view the development of music therapy posts as their sole responsibility (Ledger 2010). Perhaps this is because we believe that we are the only ones who can truly understand our profession, or because we strongly identify with the role of a lone pioneer. Music therapy literature contains countless stories of music therapists bravely forging their own way, including biographies of early music therapy pioneers (for examples see Hadley 2003; Howard 2009; Neugebauer 2010). It may even be the "up and coming" nature of music therapy that attracts many of us to this work. As music therapists, we are afforded many opportunities to be creative, to innovate, and to work independently. However, if we only learn how to work as lone pioneers, we will potentially miss valuable opportunities to involve others in the development of music therapy services.

The image of the music therapist as a successful pioneer is contrary to understandings of successful change initiatives which appear in management literature. Management academics have emphasized the importance of appointing a team of change agents when a change is introduced (Dawson 2003; Kirchner et al. 2012). In change initiatives, a steering group is often appointed to plan and implement organizational change, to educate others about the change, to garner support from various workers, to evaluate and communicate change outcomes, and to help each other to persist when the change process becomes arduous (Deegan et al. 2004; Dulaney and Stanley 2005). In hospital organizations, steering groups usually involve a range of people with different agendas, including both managers and health professionals (Deegan et al. 2004; Dulaney and Stanley 2005). In the current era of heightened accountability, there is also increased pressure on professionals to include patients and community members in the development and implementation of services (Boyle and Harris 2009; Christie 2011).

Loewy (2001) has revealed the potential for other workers to become "allies" (p. 5) in the development of music therapy posts. However, none of the music therapists in my study mentioned the formation of a formal steering group to guide the development of their posts. Furthermore, when I undertook fieldwork to observe the introduction of a music therapy post, I noted that the introduction of a new recreational therapy post received much stronger support than music therapy. During my interview with a hospital manager, it became apparent that the introduction of the recreational therapy post was being led by a committee of clinicians, managers, and administrators.

Music therapists may benefit from requesting that a steering group be established to oversee and support the development of future posts. A music therapy steering group could be comprised of a range of relevant stakeholders, including management, financial, human resources, and public relations personnel, other professionals, patients or clients, and family members. They may not need to meet regularly but can be updated through email, and consulted and/or acknowledged at key points in the development of the music therapy service.

Recommendations

This section contains recommendations for music therapists, managers, and other workers, and music therapy educators based on the available literature and research on music therapy service development.

Recommendations for music therapists

Literature from management, inter-professional work and learning, and music therapy fields indicates that the introduction of new practices can be met with resistance from other workers. Music therapists have recalled feeling unwelcome and intimidated when introducing music therapy to others and have often met antagonists along the way (Ledger 2010; Loewy 2001). Music therapists should therefore expect some resistance when they are developing a post and put strategies in place to deal with any resistance they experience. Music therapists in my study reported that it had been helpful for them to talk with more experienced service developers, which suggests that professional supervision can help in supporting music therapists in the development phase. Supervisors play a valuable role in assisting music therapists to cope with the demands and disappointments of music therapy start up, to inter-pret colleagues' behavior and consider what might be threatening or difficult for them, and to manage their reactions to complex issues.

As many of us work independently as sole music therapy practitioners, we may not always look for help from others when developing new work. However, literature from the field of management emphasizes an important role for others when a change is being introduced. In any organization, there may be gatekeepers who have the power to admit or refuse entry to new practices (Cartwright 1951; Dulaney and Stanley 2005). Music therapists may therefore benefit from identifying the key people in their organizations who can support them to develop a music therapy post. In my research, it was clear that others had played key roles in helping the music therapists to advocate for music therapy, to obtain necessary funding, to gain access to patients, and to build networks with other staff.

As I read the stories of experienced music therapy service developers, it was evident that the music therapists were passionate about music therapy and held strong beliefs about the benefits of music therapy for patients, family members, other workers, and the wider organization. As music therapy development appears to take time, music therapists may need to be patient and persistent in their development work. They may also need to be alert to opportunities for developing music therapy further. It is recognized that music therapists need to be sensitive, thoughtful, and responsive in their work with clients (Australian Music Therapy Association 2004; Health Professions Council 2007). My research indicates that these qualities are also needed for development work. Music therapists have commonly described how they have developed their roles in response to others' needs and been sensitive to the culture of their organizations when developing new work (Edwards 2005; Ledger 2010; Loewy 2001; 2007).

Recommendations for managers and other workers

Literature related to music therapy development has revealed several ways in which others can support the development of a music therapy service. Other workers have come to recognize the benefits of music therapy after observing music therapy sessions and through working closely with music therapists (Ledger 2010; Twyford and Watson 2008). Several studies have indicated that music therapy has benefits for staff as well as for clients and their families (Hilliard 2006; Magee 2005; O'Callaghan and Magill 2009). It is therefore recommended that other workers avail of invitations to observe and assist in music therapy sessions and seek opportunities to collaborate with music therapists. Other workers can help a music therapist to determine an appropriate role, by sharing their ideas for ways that music therapy could fit into the team.

Music therapists in my study reported that they were unsure what they needed to do to develop music therapy successfully. Managers can help by sharing information about financial matters and the organization's values and cultures. Music therapists may then be clearer about what is needed for music therapy to become better established. Managers should also be aware of the demands of music therapy start up and put resources in place to support new music therapists. For example, the formation of steering groups of staff, client, and community representatives may lessen the burden on music therapists to develop their services alone. Managers can facilitate the formation of a steering group by identifying local champions and rewarding those who help to promote change at all levels within the organization (Kirchner et al. 2012). If workers are allocated time to participate in steering groups, this may further motivate their involvement and show that music therapy is an organizational priority. There is also a critical role for managers in ensuring that new music therapists can receive adequate professional supervision.

Recommendations for music therapy educators

When I began my research on music therapy service development, I assumed that music therapists experience a unique set of challenges when developing new posts. Through wider reading, I discovered that the process of change is almost always regarded as challenging and that music therapists aren't the only professionals to feel misunderstood. Music therapists may come to feel less isolated if they realize that other professionals encounter similar challenges. It is therefore recommended that music therapists in training receive further education about change management, including the strategies and conditions that may be necessary for successful change. This type of training could also be offered to practitioners as part of continuing professional development processes. At all levels of music therapy training, guest presenters could include information about how their services were developed.

CONCLUSION

We are only just beginning to understand the complex processes that surround the development of music therapy posts and to develop a literature that reflects this understanding. What we know is that many music therapists will be the first employee in role, and the first music therapist that many of their new colleagues will have met. It can be challenging to introduce music therapy to more established workers, to secure funding and resources, to gain acceptance from inter-professional team members, to determine a role for music therapy, and for music therapy to become an integral part of a health care or education organization. These aspects of music therapy development take time. Published accounts indicate that the development of music therapy posts can be facilitated or restricted by a range of complex forces, such as historical factors, power dynamics, organizational cultures, and a music therapist's relationships with other workers (Edwards 2005; Ledger 2010; Loewy 2001, 2007). It is therefore likely that the best approach for developing posts is highly dependent on the music therapist's particular organizational context. For this reason, only general recommendations for music therapists, managers and other workers, and music therapy educators are offered to readers of this chapter. Music therapists are best advised to learn as much as possible about the context, through listening to others who have successfully navigated the terrain.

NOTE

1. The poems included in this chapter were written by the author in response to narratives provided by music therapists about their service development experiences (Ledger 2010).

REFERENCES

American Music Therapy Association (2008). *AMTA professional competencies*. Available at: <http://www.musictherapy.org/about/competencies/>.

Ansdell, G. and Pavlicevic, M. (2008). Responding to the challenge: Between boundaries and borders. *British Journal of Music Therapy* 22(2): 73–76.

Arving, C. and Holmström, I. (2011). Creating a new profession in cancer nursing? Experiences of working as a psychosocial nurse in cancer care. *Journal of Clinical Nursing* 20: 2939–2947.

Atwal, A. and Caldwell, K. (2005). Do all health and social care professionals interact equally: a study of interactions in multidisciplinary teams in the United Kingdom. *Scandinavian Journal of Caring Sciences* 19(3): 268–273.

Australian Music Therapy Association. (2004). *Competency standards in music therapy*. Available at: <http://www.austmta.org.au/system/files/Competency%20standards.Overseas%20trained%20music%20therapists.Aug2013.doc>.

Baker, L., Egan-Lee, E., Martimianakis, M.A., and Reeves, S. (2011). Relationships of power: Implications for interprofessional education. *Journal of Interprofessional Care* 25: 98–104.

Boyle, D. and Harris, M. (2009). *The Challenge of Co-production*. London: Nesta. Available at: <http://www.nesta.org.uk/library/documents/Co-production-report.pdf>.

Braithwaite, J. (2006). An empirical assessment of social structural and cultural change in clinical directorates. *Health Care Analysis* 14: 185–193.

Bridges, J. and Meyer, J. (2007). Policy on new workforce roles: A discussion paper. *International Journal of Nursing Studies* 44(4): 635–644.

Brown, B., Crawford, P., and Darongkamas, J. (2000). Blurred roles and permeable boundaries: the experience of multidisciplinary working in community mental health. *Health and Social Care in the Community* 8(6): 425–435.

Browne, A., Lloyd, M., and Whyte, B. (2007). Out of the blue. *Journal of the Irish Association of Creative Arts Therapies* 1: 14–16.

Cartwright, D. (ed.). (1951). *Field Theory in Social Science: Selected Theoretical Papers by Kurt Lewin*. New York: Harper & Row.

Choi, B. (1997). Professional and patient attitudes about the relevance of music therapy as a treatment modality in NAMT approved psychiatric hospitals. *Journal of Music Therapy* 34: 277–292.

Christie, C. (2011). *Commission on the future delivery of public services*. Scotland: Public Services Commission. Available at: <http://www.scotland.gov.uk/Resource/Doc/352649/0118638.pdf>.

Copley, J.A., Allison, H.D., Hill, A.E., Moran, M.C., Tait, J.A., and Day, T. (2007). Making interprofessional education real: A university clinic model. *Australian Health Review* 31(3): 351–357.

Cosgrove, J. (2005). Conception to delivery. *Journal of the Irish Association of Creative Arts Therapies* 20–27.

Croker, A., Trede, F., and Higgs, J. (2012). Collaboration: What is it like?—Phenomenological interpretation of the experience of collaborating within rehabilitation teams. *Journal of Interprofessional Care* 26: 13–20.

Cummings, G.G., Fraser, K., and Tarlier, D.S. (2003). Implementing advanced nurse practitioner roles in acute care: An evaluation of organizational change. *Journal of Nursing Administration* 33(3): 139–145.

Darsie, E. (2009). Interdisciplinary team members' perceptions of the role of music therapy in a pediatric outpatient clinic. *Music Therapy Perspectives* 27(1): 48–54.

Dawson, P. (2003). *Understanding Organizational Change: The Contemporary Experience of People at Work*. London: Sage.

Daykin, N. and Bunt, L. (2006). Music and healing in cancer care: A survey of supportive care providers. *The Arts in Psychotherapy* 33: 402–413.

Deegan, C., Watson, A., Nestor, G., Conlon, C., and Connaughton, F. (2004). Managing change initiatives in clinical areas. *Nursing Management* 12(4): 24–29.

Dulaney, P. and Stanley, K. M. (2005). Accomplishing change in treatment strategies. *Journal of Addictions Nursing* 16(4): 163–167.

Edwards, J. (2005). A reflection on the music therapist's role in developing a program in a children's hospital. *Music Therapy Perspectives* 23(1): 36–44.

Gotlib Conn, L., Lingard, L., Reeves, S., Miller, K., Russell, A., and Zwarenstein, M. (2009). Communication channels in general internal medicine: A description of baseline patterns for improved interprofessional collaboration. *Qualitative Health Research* 19(7): 943–953.

Guan, Y., Deng, H., Risavy, S.D., Harris Bond, M., and Li, F. (2011). Supplementary fit, complementary fit, and work-related outcomes: The role of self-construal. *Applied Psychology, An International Review* 60(2): 286–310.

Hadley, S. (2003). Meaning making through narrative inquiry: Exploring the life of Clive Robbins. *Nordic Journal of Music Therapy* 12(1): 33–53.

Hall, P. (2005). Interprofessional teamwork: Professional cultures as barriers. *Journal of Interprofessional Care* 19(Supp 1): 188–196.

Hartley, N. (2008). The arts in health and social care—is music therapy fit for purpose? *British Journal of Music Therapy* 22(2): 88–96.

Health Professions Council. (2007). *Standards of proficiency—arts therapists*. Available at: <http://www.hpc-uk.org/assets/documents/100004FBStandards_of_Proficiency_Arts_Therapists.pdf>.

Hilliard, R.E. (2004). Hospice administrators' knowledge of music therapy: A comparative analysis of surveys. *Music Therapy Perspectives* 22(2): 104–108.

Hilliard, R.E. (2006). The effect of music therapy on compassion fatigue and team building of professional hospice caregivers. *The Arts in Psychotherapy* 33(5): 395–401.

Hobson, M.R. (2006). The collaboration of music therapy and speech-language pathology in the treatment of neurogenic communication disorders: Part II-collaborative strategies and scope of practice. *Music Therapy Perspectives* 24(2): 66–72.

Howard, M. (2009). An interview with two pioneers of Canadian music therapy: Carolyn Kenny and Nancy McMaster. *Voices: A World Forum for Music Therapy* 9(2). https://normt. uib.no/index.php/voices/article/view/351/275

Kavaliova-Moussi, A. (2012). Music Therapy in Bahrain. *Voices: A World Forum for Music Therapy*, [Online]. Available at: <https://voices.no/community/?q=country-of-the-month/ 2012-music-therapy-bahrain>.

Kirchner, J.E., Parker, L.E., Bonner, L.M., Fickel, J.J., Yano, E.M., and Ritchie, M. (2012). Roles of managers, frontline staff and local champions, in implementing quality improvement: stakeholders' perspectives. *Journal of Evaluation in Clinical Practice* 18: 63–69.

Konieczna, L. (2009). Building the first music therapy programme: A reflection on new music therapy in new place. *Voices: A World Forum for Music Therapy* 9(3). https://voices.no/index. php/voices/article/view/55.

Kowaleski, J.B. (2011). Music Therapy in Antigua and Barbuda: Two Music Therapists, One Small Island. *Voices Resources*. Retrieved January 08, 2015, from https://voices. no/community/?q=country-of-the-month/2011-music-therapy-antigua-and-barbu da-two-music-therapists-one-small-island.

Kristof-Brown, A.L., Zimmerman, R.D., and Johnson, E.C. (2005). Consequences of individuals' fit at work: A meta-analysis of person-job, person-organization, person-group, and person-supervisor fit. *Personnel Psychology* 58: 281–342.

Kvarnström, S. (2008). Difficulties in collaboration: A critical incident study of interprofessional healthcare teamwork. *Journal of Interprofessional Care* 22(2): 191–203.

Ledger, A.J. (2010). *Am I a founder or am I a fraud? Music therapists' experiences of developing services in healthcare organizations.* Unpublished doctoral thesis, University of Limerick, Ireland.

Ledger, A. (2011). Extending group music therapy to families in schools: A reflection on practical and professional aspects. In: J. Edwards (ed.), *Music Therapy and Parent-Infant Bonding*, pp. 127–140. Oxford: Oxford University Press.

Ledger, A., Edwards, J., and Morley, M. (2013). A change management perspective on the introduction of music therapy to interprofessional teams. *Journal of Health Organization and Management* 27(6): 714–732.

Lindblad, E., Hallman, E., Gillsjö, Lindblad, U., and Fagerström, L. (2010). Experiences of the new role of advanced practice nurses in Swedish primary health care—A qualitative study. *International Journal of Nursing Practice* 16: 69–74.

Loewy, J.V. (2001). Building bridges in team centred care. *The Australian Journal of Music Therapy* 12: 3–12.

Loewy, J. (2007). Developing music therapy programs in medical practice and healthcare communities. In: J. Edwards (ed.), *Music: Promoting health and creating community in healthcare contexts*, pp. 17–28. Newcastle: Cambridge Scholars.

Loewy, J., Hallan, C., Friedman, E., and Martinez, C. (2005). Sleep/Sedation in children undergoing EEG testing: A comparison of chloral hydrate and music therapy. *Journal of Perianesthesia Nursing* 20(5): 323–331.

Magee, W.L. (2005). Music therapy with patients in low awareness states: Approaches to assessment and treatment in multidisciplinary care. *Neuropsychological Rehabilitation* 15(3/4): 522–536.

Magee, W.L. and Andrews, K. (2007). Multi-disciplinary perceptions of music therapy in complex neuro-rehabilitation. *International Journal of Therapy and Rehabilitation* 14(2): 70–75.

McLaughlin, D.F., Sines, D., and Long, A. (2008). An investigation into the aspirations and experiences of newly appointed dual diagnosis workers. *Journal of Psychiatric and Mental Health Nursing* 15(4): 296–305.

Miller, C. (2008). Music therapy and collaborative working in adult mental health: Creative connections and destructive splits. In: K. Twyford and T. Watson (eds), *Integrated Team Working: Music Therapy as Part of Transdisciplinary and Collaborative Approaches*, pp. 124–153. London: Jessica Kingsley.

Miles, L. (2007). A life of music therapy: Working together and in isolation. *Voices: A World Forum for Music Therapy* 7(3). https://voices.no/index.php/voices/article/view/552.

Moore, K., Cruickshank, M., and Haas, M. (2006). Job satisfaction in occupational therapy: A qualitative investigation in urban Australia. *Australian Occupational Therapy Journal* 53: 18–26.

Moss, H. (2007). Integrating models of music therapy into acute hospitals: An Irish perspective. In: J. Edwards (ed.), *Music: Promoting Health and Creating Community in Healthcare Contexts*, pp. 29–51. Newcastle: Cambridge Scholars.

Moss, H. (2008). Reflections on music therapy and arts in health. *British Journal of Music Therapy* 22(2): 83–87.

Neale, L. (2010). Organisational anxiety, envy, and defences: In and out of the music therapy room. *British Journal of Music Therapy* 24: 42–49.

Neugebauer, C. (2010). Mary Rudenberg, music therapist pioneer. *Voices: A World Forum for Music Therapy* 10(1). https://voices.no/index.php/voices/article/view/323/235.

O'Callaghan, C. and Magill, L. (2009). Effect of music therapy on oncologic staff bystanders: A substantive grounded theory. *Palliative and Supportive Care* 7: 219–228.

O'Connor, H. (2006). Primary care mental health workers: a narrative of the search for identity. *Primary Care Mental Health* 4(2): 93–98.

O'Kelly, J. and Koffman, J. (2007). Multidisciplinary perspectives of music therapy in adult palliative care. *Palliative Medicine* 21: 235–241.

Pellatt, G.C. (2005). Perceptions of interprofessional roles within the spinal cord injury rehabilitation team. *International Journal of Therapy and Rehabilitation* 12(4): 143–150.

Schwartz, L., Wright, D., and Lavoie-Tremblay, M. (2011). New nurses' experience of their role within interprofessional health care teams in mental health. *Archives of Psychiatric Nursing* 25(3): 153–163.

Shanley, C. (2007). Management of change for nurses: lessons from the discipline of organizational studies. *Journal of Nursing Management* 15: 538–546.

Silverman, M.J. and Chaput, J. (2011). The effect of a music therapy in-service on perceptions of oncology nursing staff. *Music Therapy Perspectives* 29(1): 74–77.

Styhre, A. (2002). Non-linear change in organizations: organization change management informed by complexity theory. *Leadership & Organization Development Journal* 23(6): 343–351.

Suter, E., Arndt, J., Arthur, N., Parboosingh, J., Taylor, E., and Deutschlander, S. (2009). Role understanding and effective communication as core competencies for collaborative practice. *Journal of Interprofessional Care* 23(1): 41–51.

Twyford, K. and Watson, T. (eds). (2008). *Integrated Team Working: Music Therapy as Part of Transdisciplinary and Collaborative Approaches*. London: Jessica Kingsley.

Viitanen, E. and Piirainen, A. (2003). Reflection on work culture: the key to success. *Reflective Practice* 4(2): 179–192.

Wynne, R. (2004). Ten Australian ICU nurses' perceptions of organizational restructuring. *Australian Critical Care: Official Journal of the Confederation of Australian Critical Care Nurses* 17(1): 16–24.

CHAPTER 48

....

COLLABORATING
A Role for Music Therapy within Interprofessional Teams and Beyond

....

KAREN TWYFORD

INTRODUCTION

....

COLLABORATION, as a human behavior, inherently involves motivation to share knowledge, learn, and problem solve with others (Reeves et al. 2010). Increasingly, and most notably since the turn of this century, collaboration between professionals and organizations is called for universally and particularly so within health, education, and social care sectors. Collaboration on a variety of levels and with differing collaborative partners has historically been important for music therapists for personal and professional reasons, and for the evolution of the profession itself.

For many music therapists, the interprofessional team provides a collaborative source of professional sustenance and personal stimulus. For some, team membership, whether in health, social care, or in education, is a necessity, offering employment stability, and networking opportunities. For others the team provides a means to advance and consolidate a professional identity. Effective teamworking is increasingly considered vital for successful outcomes for clients, professionals, and advancement of the profession of music therapy itself (Twyford and Watson 2008). However, while many benefits may be realized, teamworking can be challenging.

Professional collaboration at a variety of levels and for a range of reasons forms an integral part of teamworking. For this reason, understanding the concept of teamworking, the terminology which surrounds it and how music therapists function within interprofessional teams is valuable, not only to music therapists but also the profession of music therapy. The following pages draw on literature from both music therapy and other related areas to explore the concept of interprofessional teamworking, the impact for music therapists, levels of interprofessional teamworking, and what is needed to improve strategies for the future. This chapter is based on work undertaken for a prior text where music therapists and other health care professionals described their experiences of working within teams where music therapy services were provided (Twyford and Watson 2008).[1] The goal of this chapter is to provide a relevant understanding of the current situation for the profession of music therapy.

INTERPROFESSIONAL TEAMS

> Good quality care depends upon professions working together in interprofessional teams
>
> Reeves et al. 2010, p. 1

Interprofessional working, and most notably the concept of teams and teamwork within health and social care, has received increased attention over the last 30 years and particularly since the turn of the twenty-first century. Worldwide, professional associations and regulatory bodies are increasingly calling for members to work effectively in interprofessional teams. The reason being, that teams are considered to offer a combination of skills and coordination of services with the potential to provide efficient and enhanced continuity of care for particular client populations. Individually, professionals will possess differing concepts of what "team" means, however essentially a successful team relies on solid team configuration and composition where each member has a clear understanding of what teamworking entails and where this is a collective responsibility to achieve shared aims and objectives, and clear structure. Writers who explore these issues include Brill (1976); Cartmill et al. (2011); Miller et al. (2001); Ovretveit (1993); Sines and Barr (1998); West and Slater (1996) and Gilbert et al. (2010).

Team typologies

As the notion of and necessity for teamworking increases in health and social care, and education a variety of team structures are defined in the literature, each essentially distinguished by the level of collaboration that occurs within them (Brill 1976; Miller et al. 2001; Ovretveit 1993; Sines and Barr 1998). A variety of team model typologies are detailed in health and social care, and education literature over recent times (Cameron et al. 2009; Miller et al. 2001; Reeves et al. 2010), however multidisciplinary, interdisciplinary, and transdisciplinary are perhaps the most widely recognized and referenced terms, particularly within the music therapy literature.

The typologies *multidisciplinary, interdisciplinary*, and *transdisciplinary* indicate the varied levels of collaboration in existence within each respective model. *Multidisciplinary* refers to teams made up of a variety of professionals but who practice autonomously, where work is coordinated for purely functional and logistical purposes but without team focus; *interdisciplinary* refers to teams of varying professionals who work collaboratively to coordinate planning to provide a more holistic service delivery; and *transdisciplinary* where a high degree of collaborative working is evident and results in shared aims, information, tasks, and responsibility. In a transdisciplinary model the potential of teamworking is realized as workers seek the experience of others and gain greater awareness and appreciation of other professionals with whom they work and which in turn influences their own work. In essence, a transdisciplinary model enables a swift and fluid interplay between team members, largely due to the release of stereotyped roles and role perceptions, hierarchical relationships, and exclusive professional jargon.

Studies within health care teams have revealed that teamwork and team effectiveness are increasingly higher in teams working within interdisciplinary and transdisciplinary team approaches, as opposed to multidisciplinary models (Cartmill et al. 2011; Körner 2010). Successful transdisciplinary teams are determined by a number of contributing factors which include, client population, particularly those with complex needs who require an integrated approach involving physical, psychological, and social levels of care; opportunities for communication with colleagues; and most importantly an organizational structure that supports transdisciplinary teamwork (Cartmill et al. 2011).

These varied typologies have explained the phenomena of interprofessional work at different levels; however Reeves et al. (2010) argue further that the descriptions in general use are linear and should in fact be viewed pragmatically as teamwork in practice is complex. The authors propose that previous use of the terms *team* and *teamwork* have been used generically. They offer a contingency approach to categorize teamworking where key elements in a continuum create a more realistic picture of teamwork, in which teams are matched for the purpose that they are intended to serve, dependent on particular needs, contextual influences and available resources. In this approach different forms of interprofessional work exist and identified as, teamworking, collaboration, coordination, and networking. These types of interprofessional work can be compared with other traditional typologies, whereby teamwork relates to transdisciplinary; collaboration to interdisciplinary; and coordination to multidisciplinary.

With these thoughts in mind, ultimately it is *how* professionals work together that is a major factor affecting the coordination and delivery of services. Therefore the concept of *teamwork* or *transdisciplinary* teaming is a powerful tool for dealing with fragmentation (O'Connor and Walls 2004); shared responsibility and strengthening of staff relationships though a process of team building (Chapman and Ware 1999); reducing the diagnostic and intervention burden on any one discipline (Moran Finello 2011); and demonstrating improved attendance, increased capacity within a service offered and reduced waiting times for a service (Bell et al. 2009).

AN UNDERSTANDING OF TEAMWORKING

> The levels of cooperation, coordination and collaboration characterizing the relationships between professions in delivering patient-centered care
>
> Definition of teamworking, The Interprofessional Education Collaborative
> Expert Panel 2011, p. 2

Effective teamworking requires effort and is not without its challenges (Brill 1976; Galvin and McCarthy 1994; Reeves et al. 2010; Twyford and Watson 2008; West and Slater 1996). Team success requires tasks which are clearly defined and motivating overall in addition to synthesis and integration of skills and knowledge to stimulate team members. Additionally, effective teamworking requires an awareness of the diverse purposes required for different forms of integrated working (Cameron et al. 2009). According to Reeves et al. (2010) teamworking comprises five key elements, including shared team identity; clear team roles, tasks, and goals; interdependence between team members; integrations between work practices; and shared commitment and responsibilities.

Engeström (2008) describes the coordinating of activities of interprofessional teamwork as *knotworking*, a key concept of activity theory, where the separate threads of professional activity are continuously tied, untied and retied to create "knotworking knots" of combined care. These "knots" are modified depending on the activity itself and the individuals involved. Collaboration between working partners is of vital importance in the phenomenon of knotworking.

Further, Reeves et al. (2010) detail interprofessional teamwork within a framework which includes separate yet interconnected factors including relational, processual, organizational, and contextual domains. Relational factors affect relationships shared by professionals such as professional power, heirarchy, socialization and team composition, roles and processes. Historically the professionalization of professions has impacted on a profession's place in team hierarchy, where some hold a dominant position, for example medicine. However, protectionist attitudes can result from this process as professions guard the areas of knowledge and expertise that they have acquired and may have prejudice about the abilities and knowledge of other professionals (Klinar et al. 2012; Reeves et al. 2010).

Processual factors of interprofessional teamworking affect how the work of the team is carried out across different workplace situations, for example, time and space. Having co-located office space is an important facilitator for informal team communication between professionals (Cartmill et al. 2011). Contextual factors involve the broader social, political, and economic landscape in which the team is placed and lastly, organizational factors affect the local organizational environment in which the interprofessional team operates (Reeves et al. 2010). Underlying organizational support will provide the backbone and structure to enable teams to function effectively (Cartmill et al. 2011) and are an integral component to successful team approaches (Engeström 2008).

Individuals in teams

Whilst a team is a way of coordinating each person's efforts to create a final collective result, individual team members can make influential professional and personal contributions through their professional knowledge, expertise, skills, and personal characteristics (Twyford and Watson 2008). Individuals join teams for a variety of personal and professional reasons, they may see the value of doing so to cooperate and coordinate for professional or client interest, and/or for the social-emotional and competence-related benefits of teamworking (Allen and Hecht 2004). The team setting can provide some professionals with employment opportunities for the majority if not the entirety of their working career. An effective team member therefore requires considerable key skills to function or integrate within the team, and contribute to overall team success. Factors include personal commitment, team commitment, maturity, self-discipline, flexibility, willingness and ability to listen, learn, and share from others, an acceptance of other's differences, and self objectivity in relation to others (Cartmill et al. 2011; Reeves et al. 2010; Twyford and Watson 2008).

MUSIC THERAPY IN THE INTERPROFESSIONAL TEAM

The interprofessional team has been historically important to music therapists for a variety of professional and personal reasons (Eisler 1993; Hills et al. 2000; Moss 1999; Odell Miller

2002; Priestley 1993; Sutton 2002). This has been particularly so for music therapists who are setting up new positions or for those in geographical or professional isolation (O'Hagan et al. 2004; Rickson 2010; Twyford 2009). The team itself has provided a environment for music therapists to establish an identity, and for the discipline to be valued, understood, and accepted by other professionals, however music therapists have had to work hard to achieve this (Eisler 1993; Lee and Baker 1997; Odell Miller 2002; Wigram 2000), and workplace training to inform other professionals about music therapy has proved useful (Jacobs 2000; Jacobs and Lincoln 2003).

The need for a common terminology

Teamworking at different levels within teams is predominantly referred to as *multidisciplinary, interdisciplinary*, and *transdisciplinary* within music therapy literature from the United Kingdom, Australia, United States of America, and New Zealand (Hobson 2006; Kennelly et al. 2001; Krout 2004; Lee and Baker 1997; O'Hagan et al. 2004; Register 2002; Rickson 2010a; Twyford 2004a, 2008; Twyford and Watson 2008; Wheeler 2003). Additionally, Krout (2004) proposes a *synerdisciplinary* model. However, recent research from Spring (2010) suggests that the profession of music therapy may be behind the times with its use of teamworking terms, particularly in relation to health care, where the term *interprofessional* is increasingly prevalent.

Spring's survey of music therapy program directors at AMTA approved institutions in the United States of America revealed that confusion exists regarding the definitions and use of collaborative terminology and that "collaborative terms are used interchangeably, and are not always clearly defined or understood" (Spring 2010, p. 54). Spring's findings indicate that the term collaboration may be the most commonly used and understood term as it refers to the joint work between two disciplines and may encompass various collaborative models including multidisciplinary, interdisciplinary, transdisciplinary, and co-treatment. Further, Spring recommends that adequate familiarity with the terms, definitions, and models regarding collaboration as consistent with the literature in other health care disciplines is important for music therapists and music therapy educators as the use of common terminology may "naturally lead to the development of a common language for collaboration within the music therapy profession and among related disciplines" (Spring 2010, p. 60).

There is a diverse range of music therapy models in existence worldwide. Each of these is influenced by differing theoretical orientations, and for this reason music therapists may choose to implement and adapt different models of working depending on the client group with which they work (Ahonen-Eerikainen 2003). Professional collaboration will exist at some level regardless of specific treatment models and will be most successful and effective when all professionals involved maintain a system of shared belief about overall patient care and treatment (Hobson 2006). Ultimately, if work is undertaken from a basis of music itself and the uniqueness of what it can offer, then goals and methods used will be representative of musical belief, professional roles, and client relationship and provide a meaningful therapy experience (Brown 1999; Meadows 1997). It can therefore be assumed that the personality of the therapist involved and the nature and culture of the working environment will to a certain extent determine the level of collaborative work undertaken (Twyford and Watson 2008). In essence, team type is irrelevant and rather it is individual professional commitment to, and support for collaboration which will ensure its success and effectiveness.

COLLABORATION: THE WHAT, WHY, AND HOW?

Reeves et al. define collaboration as "an active and ongoing partnership, often between people from diverse backgrounds, who work together to solve problems or provide services" (2010, p. xii). Collaboration at an inter-agency and interprofessional level within health, social care, and education has been an increasingly prominent issue of recent times (Barrington 2003; Department of Health, 2001, 2004, 2007; Government of Western Australia 2007; Macadam and Rodgers 1997; Ministry of Education 2006). Relevant health and social care, education, and music therapy literature provides a comprehensive understanding of collaboration as it relates to the interprofessional team and what this means for music therapists.

The rationale for collaboration

Barr et al. state that "[a]ll teamwork is collaboration, but not all collaboration is teamwork" (2008, p. 4), and this has important implications for music therapists. It is integral to the growth and development of the profession that successful collaboration is understood and that healthy collaborative relationships be built with others (Heiderscheit and Jackson 2011; Register 2002).

There is a case for collaboration when it promotes quality public health, improves clinical care, and meets regulatory requirements; when it provides personal development and satisfaction, equips and enables others, promotes social inclusion, and organizational development; and where it is responds to the economic market regarding choice and demand, and utilization of resources (Meads et al. 2008).

Collaborative working offers opportunities for creativity and innovation, and provides professional, political, and personal benefits (Twyford and Watson 2008). Additionally, collaboration enables best use of existing facilities and creates new opportunities for those involved (Hattersley 1995; Macadam and Rodgers 1997; West and Slater 1996). When collaborative working is clearly planned and with specific purpose, the coordination of appropriate, holistic input enables more cohesive and efficient services for clients and continuity of their care (Durham 2002; Robben et al. 2012; Twyford 2004b; Twyford and Watson 2008; Watson et al. 2004).

On a professional level for music therapists, working collaboratively provides a greater understanding of the professional roles of others and the way in which roles relate to each other (Twyford and Watson 2008; Watson and Vickers 2002), and promotes openness and support for those in isolated positions (Twyford and Watson 2008). The sharing of different perspectives and skills within the team is a great benefit of collaborative work (Watson 2002), particularly as it provides other professionals firsthand experience and greater understanding of music therapy. The experiential nature of collaborative work can provide professional emotional support during times of stress and difficult phases in clinical work. Personally, collaborative working can be stimulating, refreshing, complementary, and enriching for the different professionals involved (Walsh Stewart 2002; Finlay et al. 2001). Additionally it can provide a sense of identity and belonging, both central teamworking factors which assist professionals to cope with the emotional impact of their work (Twyford and Watson 2008).

McCarthy et al. (2008) in their survey of board certified music therapists ascertained that a large amount of collaboration takes place between music therapists and speech-language pathologists, with three-quarters of music therapists indicating that they have worked with speech-language pathologists at some point in their career. Their study identified a number of benefits and challenges for collaboration between the two disciplines which consolidated existing evidence. Hobson (2006 and 2006a) explored the realities of music therapists and speech-language pathologists working collaboratively in relation to the treatment of neurogenic communication disorders and ascertains that optimal application of either discipline actually requires effective collaboration between the two. Hobson stressed that professionals from both disciplines should fully understand each other's scopes of practice to ensure that each party recognizes which aspects of treatment might be best treated by one or other professional in a less integrated approach, or where a fully integrated partnership may be preferable.

In an attempt to better understand how music therapists collaborate, Heiderscheit and Jackson (2011) surveyed board certified music therapists to determine what typified successful collaborations, as well as the challenges faced and the unexpected outcomes of collaboration. The results of their study identify three defined levels of music therapy collaboration, which include functional, creative, and innovative. Functional collaboration involves music therapists working with others to achieve specific goals, using a planned process. Creative collaboration also involves joint working between music therapists and others towards specific goals, however in this classification the goal is achieved through an emerging creative process which utilizes new and unique knowledge and talents. Innovative collaboration is where music therapists and others work together with no planned outcomes or process in what can be described as a journey of discovery and a shared desire to discover and learn together (Heiderscheit and Jackson 2011). Interestingly, preliminary results to the study suggest the majority of music therapists working collaboratively are doing so for self-promotional purposes to increase other professionals understanding of music therapy or to create employment (N. Jackson, personal communication, February 27, 2013).

Ingredients for successful collaboration

Fundamentally, successful collaboration requires interest, belief and commitment by all team members (Cameron et al. 2009; Moran Finello 2011) and will be enabled when there is mutual support, respect, and an understanding of each other's professional skills, roles, and relationships within the team (Miller 2008; Twyford and Watson 2008). Other contributing factors include willingness to harmonize one's own ideas and activities with those of others; a preparedness for expansion of professional roles and potential loss of autonomy (Barrington 2008; Cameron et al. 2009; Hobson 2006; Vyt 2008); and on a personal level the ability to put one's ego aside (Moran Finello 2011).

As previously mentioned organizational structures are important (Barrington 2008; Cameron et al. 2009) and factors such as lack of funding and resources, cooperation between agencies, and administrative support for collaborative approaches can impede collaborative efforts (Moran Finello 2011). Creation of a team identity is crucial and complex issues such as self-esteem, self-image, and status need to be considered by organizations (Twyford and Watson 2008). Maintaining regular team meetings is one way to address practical issues such as time in collaborative working, as is sharing of records. Additionally, collaborative work necessitates a clear rationale including specific aims and objectives in order to ensure its effectiveness (Twyford and Watson 2008). However, ultimately, there is no simple formula for successful collaboration, instead "it involves trial and error, persistence, open-mindedness, willingness to go beyond typical professional expectations, and understanding and acceptance of scope of practice" (Hobson 2006, p. 72).

Potential challenges to collaboration

A number of personal, professional, and organizational factors can and do impede successful collaboration and may include such as aspects as personality, poor communication skills, individual dominance, status, hierarchy, and gender effects (Twyford and Watson 2008). Issues of conflict with colleagues is inevitable when working collaboratively and therefore predetermined mechanisms to handle these tensions are essential and should be established at the outset of the work (Moran Finello 2011; Twyford and Watson 2008). Additionally, time is documented as a key obstructing factor to collaboration; however the question is whether time can be *made* or *found*, and perhaps a flexible attitude towards this dilemma is required.

Hobson (2006), a music therapist, warns that "when professionals bring vastly different perspectives or perceptions related to the goals and values of treatment, collaborative efforts may be weakened" (p. 68). Collaboration can therefore be difficult to achieve due to separateness in professional development (Barrington 2008; West and Slater 1996) and inherent individual identification with particular social/professional groups (Hean et al. 2006). Further, Gundlach et al. (2006) argue that team identification (the extent to which an individual team member perceives a sense of "oneness" with a workplace team), meta-perception accuracy (the correctness of one's assumptions of how others view their behaviors) and team identity, influence the relationship between individualism-collectivism and team performance. These authors speculate that it is in fact task interdependence that controls the relationship between individualism-collectivism and team identification because individuals must rely on other team members for information, resources, and support.

To avoid potential risks and barriers to successful collaboration, collaborative partners should therefore seek to understand scopes of practice, training issues, and professional standards of respective disciplines involved (Cartmill et al. 2011; Hobson 2006; Moran Finello 2011), clarity about roles and expectations will also be important (Cameron et al. 2009; Hobson 2006). Hobson also states that "in order for collaboration to be effective, territorialism must be minimized, cross-disciplinary communication must be fostered, and each professional must stay within ethical guidelines with regard to competency" (p. 70). Establishing and sustaining good working relationships with other professionals who are likeminded about collaborating, being prepared for changes in role, ensuring that roles are shared and not dictated and remaining consistent in collaboration even when things seem uncertain are ways to minimize territorialism and protectionist attitudes. Most importantly, client care is paramount and less emphasis should be placed on professional image (Hobson 2006).

Further understanding of the complexity of collaborative working and the challenges it presents may be drawn from a psychoanalytic perspective. In an influential case study describing how anxiety can function to disrupt successful teams Menzies (1960) discussed the unavoidable processes of denial, splitting, and projection defence mechanisms in teamworking and their potential impacts on collaboration and cooperation between team members. A denial defence may involve professionals continually rejecting viewpoints or arguments of others; splitting, where "good" and "bad" actions are separated; and projection; where a professional ascribes their own personal attributes, thoughts, or emotions onto other professionals. Perhaps the most powerful dynamic in teamworking is splitting, due to the highly personal nature of it, that is, it relates to competence, intelligence, ethics, and morality; it can be hostile due to its highly defensive and blaming characteristics; co-workers can become emotionally involved and take sides against others; and it often involves projection (Eddy 2012). In turn this complicates an individual's ability to confront and address workplace challenges and anxieties. Splits can be activated within teams when working conditions are intense and when some staff only work with patients within time-boundaried sessions and are viewed by others as providing special services (Miller 2008).

These internal defence systems have manifested as socially and culturally acceptable and perhaps become inherent within organizational structures. Ultimately, when there is inadequate training and support for teams from an organizational perspective the quality of team function will be impaired and envy, rivalry, stress, splitting, and "burn out" may result for team members (Kerr et al. 2007; Miller 2008). A study by Hills et al. (2000), detailed these types of issues and identified five sources of pressure for music therapists employed in multidisciplinary teams which included a lack of understanding of the profession from others, organizational issues, heavy workload, clinical issues, and conflict with work colleagues. Hedderly (2008), a music therapist, states that "supervision and staff support forums are central to assisting the team with this playing of ideas, where alternative perspectives can be exchanged and processes such as splitting and merging can be observed and reflected upon, in order that a coherent approach can be developed"(p. 141).

Unconscious team defences can and do occur to distance team members, particularly where there is a lack of understanding and difficulty with integrating the emotional material of clients contributed from therapies such as music therapy (Miller 2008). As such team members may categorize the music therapist as something more familiar for example a music teacher, in order to eradicate feelings of not knowing or understanding. Additionally, conscious and unconscious internal conflicts stemming from childhood will affect workplace experiences and performance for individuals and also impact on roles and working relationships with other professionals. As such transference and countertransference in the workplace is inevitable. Additionally, team members may experience psychological regressive behavior as being part of a group, particularly if they sense a loss of power and/or autonomy, a loss of stability and predictability, and are uncertain or ambiguous towards authority and task. This in turn can be destructive within the team, perpetuating anxieties and activating internal defence systems (Diamond and Allcorn 2003). Unless team members possess the capacity to modify or abandon innate defence mechanisms and develop more appropriate methods professionals may actually revert to uni-professional approaches when working in highly stressful situations (Menzies 1960).

MUSIC THERAPY AS PART OF THE COLLABORATIVE WEB WITHIN HEALTH, SOCIAL CARE, AND EDUCATION

> I have always sought out transdisciplinary working, initially due to working in isolation and increasingly as I have seen its value to clients and to mutual understanding amongst professionals. The process of merging skills, ways of working, insight and experience has sometimes felt like a journey from separate parts into one entity and has been well worth the effort.
>
> Tyas in Twyford and Watson 2008

Historically, the music therapy literature has indicated that collaborative partnerships between music therapists and other professionals has existed where commonalities or parallels between models were evident, for example joint working with speech language therapists and physiotherapists (Bonny 1997; Kennelly et al. 2001; Summer 1997). The text *Integrated Teamworking; Music Therapy as part of Transdisciplinary and Collaborative Approaches* (Twyford and Watson 2008) provides extensive examples of music therapists working with other health care and education professionals, and family members. Throughout the various chapters reasons for collaborating; ways in which it is approached and implemented; and the experience of being involved with others in the process of clinical work are explored. The first chapter involves interventions with children (Twyford 2008) and explores collaborative work undertaken in schools, mental health, and hospital settings, using case studies to examine diverse collaborative approaches in the areas of assessment and treatment. Collaborative working practices within the area of adult learning disability offers a comprehensive understanding of work in this area and reasons for utilizing these approaches. This clinical area in particular has a long history of professionals working in collaboration with families and carers as well as fellow professionals, in which part of their involvement with the client may be to provide support, advice, and training to carers. Miller (2008) examines interprofessional and interagency collaboration within adult mental health service provision, which are considered central to the effective provision of mental health care, particularly in the UK. Miller stresses the need for support resources to identify, understand, and work with dynamics and unconscious processes that originate in mental health work and the necessity for collaborative work and in this setting. Collaborative work with adults who have neuro-disability stemming from acquired conditions is the focus of Magee's chapter (2008). Collaborative working is identified as important for music therapists working in this relatively new area of music therapy clinical practice, particularly due to the complex combination of client's needs which are challenging for the team as a whole. Magee discusses the differences in working models and the flexibility required of the therapist to work as an integral part of the treatment team. Freeman (2008a) explores the benefits and challenges of collaborative working with the elderly population. She notes that most collaboration takes place outside of clinical sessions with professionals, family members and carers, although joint working within the clinical space can occur for time limited projects. Freeman also considers collaboration with interpreters as co-therapists, to address clients' need for reciprocal verbal understanding and to ensure that client's full access to therapy is facilitated. The final chapter by Barrington (2008) considers the broader context of teamwork in relation to historical and organizational factors and the ways in which the music therapy profession has engaged with the concept of teamwork.

The following paragraphs share relevant and recent examples of collaborative partnerships involving music therapists, illustrating the ways in which they value the importance of the team and teamworking. Increasing evidence of diverse and increasingly creative partnerships suggests music therapists collaborate for a number of purposes which can include enabling client communication; promoting movement and functional skills; strengthening the creative process; promoting emotional well-being; empowering others; providing a meta-perspective; and developing research partnerships.

Enabling client communication

Collaborative interventions involving music therapy and speech language therapy are one of the most widely documented partnerships (Bower and Shoemark 2009; Hill 2005; Kennelly et al. 2001; Walsh Stewart 2002). The non-verbal and pre-verbal qualities of music can assist in establishing the essential components for language as they include motivation, awareness of self and others, and listening and attention skills. Further the prosodic elements of music can be effective in promoting interpersonal relationships (Bower and Shoemark 2009). Empirical evidence highlights the parallels between both musical and spoken language which provides valid reasons for the two professions to work together.

Twyford and Parkhouse (2008) detail varied collaborative approaches developed for use with children and young adults with severe to profound and multiple learning difficulties and also autism, in a special school setting in the UK. Their work integrates music therapy and speech language therapy within a variety of formats including structured, where activities are pre-planned and based on a theme; semi-structured, where an underlying theme provides a focus for more loosely planned activities; and unstructured, dynamic sessions which are guided by a child's emotional and communicative state. The authors describe their changing professional roles as static, shared, and fluid as each format requires and note that these approaches enable skill sharing and appreciation of each other's role.

A collaborative case study by Geist et al. (2008) provides a further example involving children detailing the integration of music therapy with pre-existing speech-language services for a four-year-old child diagnosed with global developmental delay in a preschool setting. The authors followed a planned intervention procedure consisting of assessment of current communication needs and skills; assessment of child's potential within music therapy; team meetings to target and select priority communication goals; planning, implementation, and evaluation of collaborative music therapy/speech-language therapy classroom based intervention. Results of the study indicated increased engagement and social validity in the classroom after therapies were integrated, which could be attributed to the repetitive and augmentative opportunities that music provided in which to practice communication goals.

Watson and Germany (2008) describe a group which addresses issues of communication and interaction for clients with severe learning disabilities situated within a community team for adults with learning disabilities in London. Germany, a speech language therapist, discusses her role with this particular client group and reflects on ways in which working jointly with a music therapist can be useful. In particular Germany notes the challenge of working with clients who are emotionally not ready to learn new skills that are identified for them, and acknowledges the potential for including a music therapist to help the client develop and gain maximum benefit from speech language therapy interventions. In working together, Watson, the music therapist in this partnership notes that there was "a richness of therapeutic input that isn't found when working alone" (2008a, p. 115).

Lindeck and Pundole (2008) shared their collaborative group work project at the Royal Hospital for Neuro-disability, London with head-injured adults which integrates speech and language therapy and music therapy. Following a review of patient needs on the ward, the therapists set out to facilitate a change of focus from an impairment-based medical model to a social model of intervention. The project intended to optimize service provision, promote a carry-over of previously practised patient skills, provide a more motivating forum for patients and maximize use of their preserved neuro-pathways. The patients identified for the group had varying skill levels, and for this reason the authors implemented a combination of music and drama techniques to provide opportunities for each patient to participate to the best of their abilities.

A case study by Bower and Shoemark (2009), both music therapists, detailed work undertaken with a pediatric patient with an acquired brain injury, emerging from coma and post-traumatic amnesia. The intervention involved a combination of clinical music therapy and co-facilitated music therapy/speech pathology sessions which were effective in enhancing the social capacity of the patient. Techniques including therapeutic song singing, rhythmic speech cueing, and music improvisation were implemented. The collaborative intervention was effective in promoting improved verbal intelligibility, sustained appropriate participation in the sessions, and improved language and comprehension skills. The authors ascertained that music provided "a familiar and predictable structure to support and encourage appropriate interpersonal responses and an increase in interpersonal interaction..." (p. 70).

Promoting movement and functional skills

Collaboration between music therapists and physiotherapists is also historically well documented in the music therapy literature. Worldwide, authors have highlighted the value of this particular partnership, and illustrated ways in which music, when appropriately planned and delivered, can provide a stimulative, supportive, and predictive framework in which movement can be organized; address movement goals; enhance sensory, perceptual, and motor skills; and promote emotional well-being for children and adult client populations (Bunt 1994; Elefant and Lotan 1998; Grasso et al. 1999; Hooper et al. 2004; Meadows 1997, 2002; Turnbull and Robinson 1990; Wigram 1992). More recent examples are found in the area of adult learning disabilities and neurorehabilitation.

Watson (2008b), in her case example describes the evolution of a music therapy and physiotherapy group for people with profound and multiple learning disabilities accessing specialist health services in the UK. In addition to the music therapist and physiotherapist, the group also included two physiotherapy assistants and day center support workers. Watson notes that a set basic structure was implemented and became more relaxed as the work progressed and the therapists/assistants became more competent in their understanding of each other's techniques and gained greater confidence in improvising with music. Staff roles were initially static and developed over the course of the work, with the role of the leader becoming more fluid between therapists over time. Watson notes that evaluation of the work was crucial to its success, not only because client progress and benefits could be observed, but that it was a useful tool to justify the high numbers of staff and resources required for the work. The combined use of sound, touch, and movement yielded significant results for the clients and also the staff involved.

Music therapy integrated with occupational therapy services provides a forum for clients to develop their functional skills in a creative way. Millman (2008), a music therapist, provides an example of this partnership as part of her work with Jefferson, an occupational therapist, in a neurorehabilitation setting, within a brain injury rehabilitation ward. In the case, Millman discusses work with a young woman, which was initiated by Jefferson due to the woman's physical status. Music technology was incorporated into the joint work to offer a creative means for the woman to practice her developing functional skills. The therapists also anticipated that the woman would achieve a high level of individual control within music therapy and which could then be generalized to other areas of her life. Initially, Jefferson played a supportive and facilitative role, where he responded to and supported client initiated movement. Over time his role became more observational as the woman gained independence, and then concluded as the sessions moved from joint to one-to-one music therapy sessions. While in this case professionals maintained clearly defined roles, it does provide an example of overlapping team goals, such as communication, cognition, or physical status, which can be addressed through joint working.

Strengthening the creative process

Increasingly creative collaborations involving music therapy and arts therapies across the client category spectrum are documented in the literature. Therapists involved in these partnerships note the potential for all professionals involved to explore new territories and gain inspiration, whilst also reinforcing confidence and strength in their own modality (Brightman and Ridlington-White 2005).

Travaglia and Treefoot (2010) detail their collaborative initiative involving music therapy and dance and movement therapy, with a young teenage client diagnosed with global developmental delay. The therapists describe their approach which involved a small number of face-to-face meetings over a defined period of time, whereby they were able to share information and video, and jointly reflect and discuss client need and progress in each respective discipline. Travaglia and Treefoot note that this collaboration enabled a greater insight into each other's work and also promoted a deeper understanding and more holistic view of the client, which they believe in turn increased their own professional effectiveness.

The Bridge Project initiated by Tyas, a music therapist, Souster, a drama therapist, and de Sousa, a dance movement therapist, (2008) was set up to provide therapeutic support for adults with a learning disability who were moving from an established hospital setting into the community. The project also assisted clients in processing feelings related to loss of mobility, fragile health, and bereavement, and utilized a storyline to structure the sessions and provide focus. The therapists detail a fluid partnership and note an openness between therapists to take on one another's roles, which allowed for experimentation and exploration of different media in the sessions. De Sousa stated of the experience that "providing all these specialist mediums within one session created a container of strength and variation that the clients seemed to benefit from. This container seemed to get stronger and stronger the longer that we worked together" (2008, p. 121).

Miller, a music therapist and Guarnieri, a drama therapist (2008), provide another example of collaborative working, which in this case was situated in a low secure ward within a forensic psychiatric service. This collaboration commenced in response to the observed difficulties patients were having in making links with others and engaging in creative processes. The therapists detail a fluid partnership where no one therapist was burdened with having the leading role, and a free setting for the clients to utilize. Miller and Guarnieri note that it was necessary for the two therapists to take time to learn more about each other's approaches and develop a shared theoretical stance in order to overcome potential difficulties in linking the two modalities. In addition to this the authors describe how their ability to respond non-judgementally to each other's engagement in each other's media and had a shared interest in their group members communications within the group promoted an open creative space for both the therapists and also the patients.

One last illustration of a creative partnership involves music therapy and poetry therapy with substance abuse clients in an outpatient treatment center. Kaufman, a poet and psychiatrist and Goodman, a music therapist (2009) describe a collaborative process involving a number of stages. In this creative process, the clients are initially presented with poems for reflection and discussion. Clients then create their own poems and are offered the opportunity to have their poem set to music, with the assistance of the music therapist. The process of creating music for each poem occurs at a number of progressive songwriting levels where the client becomes increasingly involved their own music making. Whilst Kaufman and Goodman indicate the potential for this type of creative partnership they pose a number of considerations for future work of this kind.

Promoting emotional well-being

One of the guiding philosophies of all music therapy interventions is to optimize quality of life, promote positive change and improve emotional and spiritual health and well-being for clients and patients across the broad spectrum of care. A number of unique and specialized collaborative examples demonstrate the ways that music can be used to support the complex needs of the team, clients, and family members.

Music and attuned movement therapy is a method developed by music therapists Fearn and O'Connor (2008) working with children with profound physical, learning, health, and emotional difficulties. Their work evolved over time at the Cheyne Day Centre, where a fully integrated service of education, therapy, and health care is offered. In this approach the two music therapists work closely with another consistent team professional; which may include teachers, physiotherapists, occupational therapists, speech and language therapists, nursery nurses or classroom assistants; and a child. The co-therapist acts as a movement facilitator for the child, providing a powerful and holistic intervention. The music therapist uses improvised music to mirror, reflect, attune and contain the child's musical, physical, and emotional responses. The double feedback experienced by the child as a result of the combined approach evidently hastens the child's awareness of self and self in relation to others, promoting full engagement and enabling the child to reach their full potential.

Music therapists have noted the positive impact a collaborative approach has for other team members working together in hospital settings, in that it can humanize clinical relationships and also provide emotional support in what can sometimes be a difficult working environment (Aasgaard 2000; Petersen 2005). O'Neill (2008) emphasizes the importance of working collaboratively with the team in the hospital setting, particularly in relation to her work with children with acute life-threatening physical health conditions. She discusses the importance of attending weekly psychosocial team meetings to share information and discussion regarding children and families, and for her own emotional stability. O'Neill notes her reasons for seeking collaborative working includes alleviating professional and personal isolation and to enable opportunities to reflect at a deeper level in what is a hectic and fast paced environment.

In addition to supporting the goals of the wider professional team, music therapy in the hospital setting can provide emotional support and opportunities for self-expression for patients and also their families (Edwards 1999; Edwards and Kennelly 2004). Magill, a music therapist and Berenson, a reflexologist (2008) describe a collaborative initiative for hospitalized advanced stage cancer patients and their families. The combination of therapies provides a multifaceted experience aims to promote reduced anxiety, pain, and isolation, enable access to levels of awareness and help to increase responsiveness. The approach is relationship focused to facilitate communication between patients, family members, and staff, and provide the potential for a more peaceful dying experience for those involved. The therapists detail a dynamic and fluid approach, where therapists respond instinctively using their own specific individual skills in relation to client and family need.

Darnley-Smith (2008) provides another example of working collaboratively within the hospital setting with clients of all ages with mental health problems. In this case Darnley-Smith illustrates how involvement of a close family member in music therapy, in this case the husband of an elderly lady with Alzheimer's disease, achieves richer and more informed clinical work. During the process of the work, which was a situation of grief and loss, the husband was able to bring positive contributions into the sessions which involved the couple's shared history. Darnley-Smith discusses the ensuing relationship which developed and which enabled life review and some form of closure for the husband as his wife's life was ending.

From a different perspective, Bolger (2012) describes her role as part of a psychosocial team involved in an Asia-Pacific wide international development program. Bolger describes her close work with her Bangladeshi colleague and co-worker to implement a women's music group in a refuge for destitute women and children in rural Bangladesh. The colleagues used a strategy of supportive facilitation to promote leadership skills amongst the women. Bolger noted that ongoing collaboration was crucial to the establishment and ongoing development of the music group, particularly in relation to practical support and culturally relevant and appropriate goals and systems for the work.

Work in the area of mental health

Music therapists working within mental health settings also advocate for the necessity of close collaboration between team members, and in particular those that refer to the service. Collaborating with other professionals in mental health work promotes close working relationships, provides continuity for individuals and family once therapy concludes and also assists in integrating the therapy into the wider-support network that is offered by the service (Molyneux 2005).

An example from Molyneux (2008b) illustrates how collaboration between a music therapist and clinical psychologist was implemented to develop a healthy attachment within a sibling group, within a child and adolescent mental health team. Additionally, each professional played a central task to support the inclusion of additional family members into the work. Professionals undertook separate roles in the joint work, that is one facilitated and one observed/reflected on what was taking place. However, together they provided a therapeutic alliance in which they could comment on what was taking place and model ways to do things differently which may include more appropriate patterns of behavior and interactions.

Sloboda (2008) describes her collaborative work with ward staff in a small psychiatric unit as fruitful. Unit staff sought and valued a range of therapeutic input and Sloboda found that co-working with members of the nursing team provided a vital communicative link to the wider team, in that they could share and highlight the patient's experiences. The specific skills and distinct roles of the nursing staff facilitated a particular quality of relationship with patients, which was distinct from those formed with the music therapist. As such nursing staff could model engagement for patients, and also provide a containing function which may involve encouraging patients to play or demonstrating ways to play.

Further, a case by Freeman (2008b) illustrates collaboration both within the multidisciplinary team, but also in the wider context of the community, demonstrating the necessity for team members to operate closely together at all times in order for clients' best interests to be achieved. The work was placed in a residential continuing care ward for older people with severe and enduring functional mental health problems, and considered the ways in which music and spirituality can offer connection. The case focused on the responses from one session and the subsequent collaborative web established which involve team members and religious communities with the express purpose of facilitating clients' spiritual needs.

Work in the area of learning disability

Collaborative working in the area of adult learning disability provides opportunities for new perspectives and wider expertise and thinking, particularly where the work is difficult and involves events which may give rise to transferences and projections from clients necessitating supervision to address challenges (Watson 2008a). An example from Radoje, a music therapist, Betteridge and Zivor, both psychologists (2008) illustrates collaborative work within a multidisciplinary community team for adults with learning disabilities, involving a man with Down's syndrome, with a history of self-harm. Radoje, who initiated the joint work, discusses how she prepared her co-therapists, with musical skills to enable them to participate fully in the music making within the joint sessions. Roles were clearly defined with the music therapist taking a leading and more containing musical role, whilst co-therapists used the percussion instruments to respond to other aspects of the client's music. Regular discussion and peer supervision was vital as was individual and joint supervision to support the work and to think together about the splitting that occurred during sessions. The therapists concluded that future collaborative working of this kind required specific planning to address potential challenges and should "be more structured in terms of responsibilities and expectations, aims of therapy and clearly defined roles, employ standardized baseline measures for both the psycho-emotional state of client, and the effectiveness of professional collaboration, and incorporate more practise for the non music therapist on musical instruments" (2008, p. 111).

Collaborating to empower others

Over recent years music therapists have broadened the collaborative networks in which they work. Music therapists have worked collaboratively for a number of reasons including addressing specific client need, gaining a greater understanding of professional roles and providing experiential insight. However, perhaps in keeping with the principles of community music therapy work, music therapists are increasingly describing ways in which they work to empower others to use music confidently and independently, following a period of involvement within music therapy. The literature provides examples of music therapists working collaboratively with parents, teachers, and peers, and also within international development work.

Parents and care givers

Music therapists are increasingly answering the call for family-centered practice as part of health care, early intervention, and education strategies (Molyneux 2005; Shoemark and Dearn 2008; Williams et al. 2012; Woodward 2004, 2008). Family-centered care promotes empowerment for parents in advocating and caring for their infant or child, focusing on children's strengths rather than weaknesses and providing confidence that progress might generalize to other settings (Woodward 2004). Music therapy can be used with parents to address attachment issues and to promote closeness and bonding (Abad and Williams 2006; Molyneux 2005). In early intervention, music therapists work closely with parents using music and songs to promote positive parent-child interactions, parental responsiveness, parenting self-efficacy in addition to children's skill development (Williams et al. 2012).

Shoemark and Dearn, both music therapists, describe their working approach in neonatal care (2008) which is focused around the family and not just the child. Parents are an active part of planning, decision making, and provision of their child's care in this approach. The authors ascertain that a productive partnership with parents requires that the music therapist must possess five essential character traits to ensure success, including poise, approachability and personability, consistency of character, and an ability to maintain boundaries. In addition to these traits, music therapists must provide a consistent service, earn the trust of parents, be prepared to provide a service regardless of status or location of the infant, and be able to resource the family to sustain the work independently.

Woodward (2008) describes an example of collaboration between music therapist and mother which highlights the importance of collaborating with parents and illustrates how this type of partnership can afford new insight, understanding and opportunities to everyone involved. The work involved a child with autism, and Woodward noted that in collaborating with the mother it was important that strategies were developed jointly, to enable confidence in the parent rather than coming from an "expert" point of view which might undermine an already vulnerable parent. Woodward described how the collaborations between music therapist and mother enabled the mother to try out new things, which even involved taking emotional risks. Collaborating with the parent created opportunities for joint thinking to see things from a different perspective; a containing environment where the mother could explore new ways of interacting with her son; and lastly an opportunity for the child, who was particularly insular, to develop a new relationship, with the music therapist.

Teachers and peers in mainstream education

A review of international literature reveals increasing documentation regarding collaborative and consultative peer and teacher-mediated strategies to facilitate educational and therapeutic goals for young children and students with special educational needs (Caltabiano 2010; Chou 2008; Hooper 2002; Hughes et al. 1990; Humpal 1991; Kern 2004; Kern and Aldridge 2006; Pecoraro Esperson 2006; Rickson 2010a; Rickson and Twyford 2011, Twyford and Rickson 2013). Music therapists implementing collaborative strategies note that collaboration and consultation used within mainstream education contexts provides more holistic and comprehensive interventions and treatments and service continuity (Kern 2004; Rickson 2010; Twyford 2012).

In her study, Kern (2004) ascertained that peer-mediated and teacher-mediated interventions can result in greater positive peer interactions and meaningful play during short periods of structured musical activities in preschool playgrounds between young children with autism and their typically developing peers. She noted that integral to this process is training and consultation with peers and staff which involves modelling, explaining, methods for cueing, engaging using song or words, prompting, supporting, following, and responding. Further, Caltabiano (2010) determined that peer and teacher-mediated interventions facilitated the development and acquisition of specific social skills in students with autism spectrum disorders. Caltabiano's study illustrated that children with autism spectrum disorders were more socially responsive when peer and/or teacher modelling was implemented and that peers and teachers could be taught skills such as peer initiating, questioning, prompting, modelling, and proximity.

A study by the author of this chapter (Twyford 2012) revealed benefits for inclusive music therapy work involving identified children with special educational needs, their peers and school staff in mainstream school settings. The model utilized peer- and teacher-mediated strategies to promote peer relationships and skill development. The music therapist modelled implementation of structured and improvised music activities and interaction skills for peers and staff to generalize and implement in an ongoing way, when her involvement concluded. Post-intervention questionnaire findings indicated that peers and staff involved in the work noted personal skill development; greater self-learning; an increase in self-confidence to use music with the identified child; improved relationships and friendships.

Rickson (2010a) researched how a music therapist consultant is able to empower special education team members to use specially planned music experiences to assist children with very high needs to meet individual developmental or academic goals. A Music Therapy School Consultation protocol was developed as part of the research which entailed a focused, time-defined process of non-linear stages each comprising a number of carefully planned activities and strategies. Rickson noted that in assisting team members to commence using music in their day to day work with students that she needed to support them to "reframe their understanding of music from something that people trained and/or experienced create, to a communicative act that is natural and accessible for all" (p. 60, 2010a). When working collaboratively in this way it is important that music therapists build upon what team members are already doing and not overwhelm them with what music therapists can do. Strategies need to be accessible, meaningful, time-efficient, and cost-effective.

International development

Coombes (2011) writes about her work with Project Bethlehem in the West Bank where she worked with SOS Village and School Staff to empower them to use music therapeutically with children and students. She noted that working creatively and therapeutically benefited not only the children participating in the work, but also the staff teams. Staff noted the project provided them with opportunities to explore new ways of working with the children.

Providing a meta-perspective

While many collaborative partnerships are formed with a specific creative or functional premise, others are created with the potential of providing a meta-perspective for the professionals involved, or the organizations in which they work. Molyneux (2008a), a music therapist, details her collaborative work with a consultant in child and adolescent psychiatry and an occupational therapist. In this example music therapy is integrated within a multi-disciplinary team assessment process for families referred to Child and Adolescent Mental Health Services (CAMHS). While each professional carries out assessments within their own respective discipline, team members also work in both generic key worker roles to provide a multifaceted approach which reduces the potential for professional isolation. Further, Twyford, a music therapist, Parkhouse, a speech and language therapist, and Murphy, a physiotherapist (2008), describe their process of dynamic transdisciplinary assessments for children with complex needs. This partnership was formed to understand children's responses in a more comprehensive and experiential way and to reduce unnecessary continuous assessments, professional misinterpretation of responses, and discussion and liaison time.

Hedderly (2008) discusses team functioning from a psychoanalytically informed perspective in relation to her group work with adults with a diagnosis of borderline personality disorder. She notes the potential for defensive cohesion or fragmentation within teamworking, where clients' difficulties with separating out and managing difference can be mirrored.

Hedderly cautions the need for the music therapist to have a clear identity and role in this work and stresses the need for strong staff cohesion to understand and manage the powerful emotional material that arises in the work. An organizational meta-perspective relating to team functioning, which may involve intense supervision and feedback meetings, will be instrumental to ensure that a service is coherent, interdependent, and principally helpful.

Collaborating in research

Increasing evidence is found in the music therapy literature of collaborative research projects involving music therapists and other professions. Often a shared professional and academic interest has been generated to realize the potential of music therapy with a variety of client groups. Ansdell et al. (2010) describe a qualitative-phenemenological study in which a group of three music therapists, a music psychologist, and a psychiatrist drew out descriptions and interpretations of clinical events from a single case of a woman with a psychotic illness. The intention of the study was to raise interprofessional awareness and understanding of music therapy's ability to assist this client group and to begin to formulate provisional theories. Further, Snow et al. (2008), a music therapist, drama therapist, and researcher combined social sciences with creative arts methodologies including community music therapy and critical performance ethnography (ethnodrama) processes to develop a "musical ethnodrama" with adults with developmental disabilities. The intention of the study was to change audience perspectives regarding perceptions of people with developmental disabilities, as well as to provide opportunities to effect therapeutic changes within the performers themselves.

Interprofessional education: Experiential learning to improve collaboration

> Interprofessional Education occurs when two or more professions learn with, from and about each other to improve collaboration and the quality of care.
>
> Centre for the Advancement of Interprofessional Education (CAIPE), 2002

Interprofessional education (IPE) as defined above has been on the agenda as an important component of primary health care since 1978 (World Health Organization 2010). Since this time the subject has gained increased interest as the need to improve collaborative practices and the quality of care provided by professionals working together has been realized (Australasian Interprofessional Practice and Education Network 2013; Barr and Low 2012; Barr et al. 2005; Brooks and Thistlethwaite 2012; Centre For The Advancement Of Interprofessional Education 2013; Klinar et al. 2012; Pollard et al. 2004; Reeves et al. 2008; Robben et al. 2012; Zwarenstein et al. 2007, 2009). Two Cochrane reviews have revealed that interprofessional education could offer ways to improve collaboration and patient care. (Reeves et al. 2008) and that the impact of practice-based interventions designed to adjust interprofessional collaboration can improve health care processes and outcomes

(Zwarenstein et al. 2009), however results could not be generalized due to the limited number of studies meeting selection criteria in each review. Various frameworks, for example the Creating an Interprofessional Workforce Framework (CIWF) in the UK (DOH 2007) and programmes such as The SCRIPT Programme—Structuring Communication Relationships for Interprofessional Teamwork (Zwarenstein et al. 2007) have been developed to assist with interprofessional collaboration and education.

The question remains however as to how prepared new graduates really are for working collaboratively when entering the workforce. For this reason interprofessional education needs to be an integral part of all health and social care courses (Barr and Low 2012). While health care profession students do share common core values, knowledge, and skills, they typically train in isolation, forming exclusive professional identities. Some professional organizations are recognizing that their professionals are increasingly working more collaboratively within teams at different levels, however caution is expressed, particularly for new graduates who may be unrealistically expected to function in integrated and interdependent health care teams (Klinar et al. 2012; Speech Pathology Australia 2009). Students involved in profession specific training will usually rate their own communication and teamwork skills positively, and are generally positive towards interprofessional learning, however attitudes regarding interprofessional interaction and collaborative working can be negative (Pollard et al. 2004). Evidence suggests that pre-qualifying IPE, which may include themes, modules, or placements, provides introductory or short-term outcomes, such as a change of attitudes and acquisition of knowledge (Barr et al. 2005) and that the use of combined classroom and clinical placements are the most effective setting for teaching professional collaboration skills which will be sustained over time (Morison and Jenkins 2007).

Maintaining interprofessional practice requires education and learning to become an integral part of the work environment. As such learning opportunities should occur both internally and externally to promote and improve continued collaboration between professionals (Cartmill et al. 2011) and to benefit organizational and service delivery (Barr et al. 2005). This could be achieved through interprofessional educational seminars and workshops, where different health care professionals are brought together to exchange experiences and learn what roles they may play in the team (Klinar et al. 2012; Robben et al. 2012). Additionally, these types of team development programmes have the potential to assist teams in developing more integrated levels of collaborative working (Körner 2010). On a personal level, technology provides increasing access for professionals to accrue updated profession specific and also interprofessional knowledge (Vyt 2008). Social networking, websites, journals, and ebooks are accessible to all professionals and can promote interprofessional awareness and understanding.

Interprofessional learning should be designed to encourage flexible working across organizational and professional boundaries (Barr and Low 2012). As such general core competencies for interprofessional collaborative practice may be useful where professional competencies in health care are defined as "Integrated enactment of knowledge, skills, and values/attitudes that define the domains of work of a particular health profession applied in specific care contexts" and interprofessional competencies in health care are "Integrated enactment of knowledge, skills, and values/attitudes that define working together across the professions, with other health care workers, and with patients, along with families and communities, as appropriate to improve health outcomes in specific care contexts" (The Interprofessional Education Collaborative Expert Panel 2011) p. 2). The desired principles of interprofessional competencies should therefore be patient-centered; community and population-oriented; relationship-focused; process-orientated; linked to activities, strategies and assessments appropriate to the learner; integrated across the learning continuum; sensitive to context and applicable across practice settings; provided in a common and meaningful language across professions; and lastly outcome-driven (The Interprofessional Education Collaborative Expert Panel 2011).

Implications for the music therapy profession

> Successful interprofessional learning can develop students' ability to communicate and work with other professionals, potentially improving the environment for service users and professionals.
>
> Health Professions Council 2009, p. 40

Music therapy is valued by most teams in which it is situated, however some music therapists suggest there is often a lack of understanding of the role the music therapist plays by health care staff (Hillmer 2007; Magee and Andrews 2007; O'Kelly and Koffman 2007), and why referrals should be made to the service (Wigram et al. 2002). While the benefits of music therapy are recognized for specific populations, it is however possible that team members may be missing components and layers to their understanding, which may require the development of a language to communicate the effectiveness of the work to a wider audience (Moss 1999), however particularly in relation to the psychotherapeutic value of music therapy (Leong 2011). For this reason increased exposure to the discipline may yield a higher referral rate and greater confidence in and attitude towards the profession (Hillmer 2007). Ultimately, the interprofessional team can have substantial impact on music therapy program development, public awareness, and professional recognition and growth (Leong 2011).

Collaboration with other professionals is identified as a core competency in most music therapy standards of practice (Castle Purvis 2010; Spring 2010) and a pre-registration professional requirement of The Allied Health Professions, UK (2009). However the concept may be made easier if the required knowledge, values, and skills were nurtured in initial training before professional attitudes and stereotypes are established. As already discussed, opposition and negative perceptions amongst team members can result from ingrained ideologies and working cultures (Twyford and Watson 2008). By engaging in interprofessional education initiatives before professional identity is solidified, Castle Purvis (2010), argues that issues of professional tribalism may be reduced. Additional benefits will mean that music therapy graduates will be confident in articulating their role, purpose, and the potential of music therapy as an allied health profession, to other practitioners. While most major training institutions indicate that collaboration with other professionals is addressed within university training programs, it is however questionable what levels of competency are actually achieved (Castle Purvis 2010; Spring 2010).

The necessity for interprofessional education at pre-graduate level has been discussed by music therapists over recent years (Castle Purvis 2010; Magee 2008; Spring 2010), with suggestions that music therapists are not adequately prepared for working collaboratively during music therapy training. The first review of its kind to consider interprofessional education and implications for music therapy highlights that many models already exist in university health care training across Canada, however music therapy courses do not currently access this (Castle Purvis 2010). It is vital therefore that "interprofessional education should play a significant role in music therapy education to better prepare for effective teamwork in clinical practice, and to work toward improving client outcomes." (Castle Purvis 2010, p. 95).

In the interim, continued explanation and research to promote a greater understanding of music therapy should be documented in both music therapy and also other professional journals (McCarthy et al. 2008; Olofsson and Fossum 2009). Evidence suggests that music therapists are already realizing the value of this notion particularly where work is collaborative (Geist et al. 2008; Leaning and Watson 2006; Magill and Berenson 2008; O'Kelly and Koffman 2007).

Conclusion

A boat doesn't go forward if each one is rowing their own way.

Swahili proverb

Collaboration for many music therapists has been and will continue to be essential. Recent worldwide governmental directives, will continue to encourage professionals to utilize the team to realize comprehensive care which considers all professionals, the client and their family and carers. Music therapy, as a profession is placed opportunely in the collective professional collaborative web. Effective collaboration requires the ability to relate, an inherent principle of our profession which can positively impact personal, professional, and organizational levels of teamworking. The evolution and consolidation of the profession of music therapy over the last fifty years has seen worldwide development of increasingly varied models and creative applications of clinical interventions with extensive client populations within the health, social, and education sectors. As a result, music therapists are evidently expanding their working practices with a diversity of professions in a variety of situations and can offer considerable worth and knowledge to interprofessional teams.

Essentially, clinicians can and should learn from each other. However, to collaborate at any professional level, there needs to be a common purpose; professionals prepared to work together; processes to enable success, and perhaps above all commitment, energy, openness to change, and honesty from all parties involved. For music therapists, collaborating with others provides rich learning experiences and the opportunity to convey the importance and efficacy of our work. The opportunity to bring together different areas of expertise allows skills and perspectives to be combined in order to meet client's needs more effectively and comprehensively. Effective collaboration will ultimately ensure that client care is steered forward collectively towards positive and beneficial outcomes.

Note

1. Permission for this chapter which summarizes aspects of the original manuscript *Integrated Team Working: Music Therapy as part of Transdisciplinary and Collaborative*

Approaches, Twyford, K. and Watson, T. (eds) (2008) has been granted from Jessica Kingsley Publishers, and coeditor Tessa Watson.

REFERENCES

Aasgaard, T. (2000). An ecology of love: aspects of music therapy in the pediatric oncology environment. *Journal of Palliative Care* 17(3): 177–181.

Abad, V. and Williams, K. (2006). Early intervention music therapy for adolescent mothers and their children. *British Journal of Music Therapy* 20(1): 31–38.

Ahonen-Eerikainen, H. (2003). Musical dialogue and other working methods of music therapists and forms of music therapy for children. In: L. Kossolapow, S. Scobie, and D. Waller (eds), *Arts-therapies-communication: On the way to a Regional European Arts Therapy*, Vol. 2, pp. 61–68. New Brunswick: Transaction Publishers.

Allen, N.J. and Hecht, T. (2004). The "romance of teams": Toward an understanding of its psychological underpinnings and implications. *Journal of Occupational and Organizational Psychology* 77: 439–461.

Ansdell, G., Davidson, J., Magee, W.L., Meehan, J., and Procter, S. (2010). From "This f***ing life" to "that's better" . . . in four minutes: An interdisciplinary study of music therapy's "present moments" and their potential for affect modulation. *Nordic Journal of Music Therapy* 12(1): 3–28.

Australasian Interprofessional Practice and Education Network (2013). Viewed 14 March 2013. <http://www.aippen.net/>.

Barrington, A. (2003). Multi-professional teamwork, in possession of author.

Barrington, A. (2008). Collaboration: The bigger picture. In: K. Twyford and T. Watson (eds), *Integrated Team Working: Music Therapy as part of Transdisciplinary and Collaborative Approaches*, pp. 203–213. London: Jessica Kingsley Publishers.

Barr, H. and Low, H. (2012). *Interprofessional education in pre-registration courses. A CAIPE guide for commissioners and regulators of education*. Viewed 14 February 2013. <http://www.caipe.org.uk/silo/files/caipe-guide-for-commissioners-nd-regulators-of-eduction-.pdf>.

Barr, H., Freeth, D., Hammick, M., Koppel, I., and Reeves, S. (2005). *The evidence base and recommendations for interprofessional education in health and social care*. Viewed 8 February 2013. <http://www.health.heacademy.ac.uk/doc/resources/Evidence08.pdf/>.

Barr, H., Koppel, I., Reeves, S., Hammick, M., and Freeth, D. (2008). *Effective interprofessional education: Argument, assumption and evidence (Promoting partnership for health)*. Viewed 14 February 2013. <http://reader.eblib.com.au/(S(ci202gsmwdxaa1swqgusakuv))/Reader.aspx?p=351098ando=277andu=CSLIBM1590081Dandt=1364813066andh=3A8A0E1714DAD179155FEACCB1F00E8A2D1E9662ands=7952663andut=902andpg=1andr=imgandc=-1andpat=n#>.

Bell, A., Corfield, M., Davies, J., and Richardson, N. (2009). Collaborative transdisciplinary intervention in early years: Putting theory into practice. *Child: Care, Health and Development* 36(1): 142–148. DOI: 10.1111/j.1365-2214.2009.01027.x.

Bolger, L. (2012). Music therapy and international development in action and reflection: A case study of a women's music group in rural Bangladesh. *The Australian Journal of Music Therapy* 23: 22–40.

Bonny, H. (1997). The state of the art of music therapy. *The Arts in Psychotherapy* 24(1): 65–73.

Bower, J. and Shoemark, H. (2009). Music therapy to promote interpersonal interactions in early paediatric neurorehabilitation, *The Australian Journal of Music Therapy* 20: 59–75.

Brightman, A. and Ridlington-White, H. (2005). Co-therapy within arts therapy: Splits and opposites—the healing journey. *BSMT/APMT Annual Conference Proceedings.* London: BSMT Publications.

Brill, N.I. (1976). *Teamwork: Working together in the Human Services* Philadelphia: JB Lippincott Company.

Brooks, V. and Thistlethwaite, J. (2012) Working and learning across professional boundaries. *British Journal of Educational Studies* 60(4): 403–420. DOI: org/10.1080/00071005.2012.729 665.

Brown, S. (1999). Some thoughts on music, therapy, and music therapy. *British Journal of Music Therapy* 13(2): 63–71.

Bunt, L. (1994). *Music Therapy: An Art Beyond Words.* London: Routledge.

Caltabiano, A. (2010). The impact of music therapy on the social behaviours of children with autism in a structured outdoor inclusive setting. BA thesis, University of Sydney, Australia. Viewed 8 February 2013. <http://ses.library.usyd.edu.au/bitstream/2123/6442/1/Caltabiano%202010.pdf>.

Cameron, C., Moss, P., Owen, C., Petrie, P., Potts, P., Simon, A., and Wigfall, V. (2009). *Working together in extended schools and children's centres: A study of inter-professional activity in England and Sweden.* Viewed 8 February 2013. <https://www.education.gov.uk/publications/standard/publicationDetail/Page1/DCSF-RBX-09-10>.

Cartmill, C., Soklaridis, S., and Cassidy, J.D. (2011). Transdisciplinary teamwork: The experience of clinicians at a functional restoration program. *Journal of Occupational Rehabilitation* 21: 1–8. DOI: 10.1007/s10926-010-9247-3.

Castle Purvis, T. (2010). Interprofessional education in mental health: Implications for music therapy. *Canadian Journal of Music Therapy—Revue canadienne de musicothérapie* 16(1): 95–116.

Centre for the Advancement of Interprofessional Education (CAIPE) (2002). *Interprofessional education—A definition.* Viewed 14 March 2013. <http:www.caipe.org.uk>.

Centre for the Advancement of Interprofessional Education (CAIPE) (2013). *Interprofessional education—A definition.* Viewed 14 March 2013. <http://www.caipe.org.uk/>.

Chapman, L. and Ware, J. (1999). Challenging traditional roles and perceptions: Using a transdisciplinary approach in an inclusive mainstream school. *Support for Learning* 14(3): 104–109.

Chou, Y. (2008). The effect of music therapy and peer-mediated interventions on social communicative responses of children with autism spectrum disorders. MA dissertation, University of Georgia, USA. Viewed 8 February 2013. <http://kuscholarworks.ku.edu/dspace/bitstream/1808/4435/1/umi-ku-2707_1.pdf>.

Coombes, E. (2011). Project Bethlehem—Training educators and health workers in the therapeutic use of music in the West Bank. *Voices: A World Forum for Music Therapy* 11(1). Viewed 22 February 2013. <https://voices.no/index.php/voices/article/viewArticle/291/445>.

Darnley-Smith, R. (2008). Music therapy with an elderly couple. In: K. Twyford and T. Watson (eds), *Integrated Team Working: Music Therapy as part of Transdisciplinary and Collaborative Approaches,* pp. 188–194. London: Jessica Kingsley Publishers.

Department of Health (2007). *Creating an interprofessional workforce: An education and training framework for health and social care in England.* Viewed 14 February 2013. <http://www.caipe.org.uk/resources/creating-an-interprofessional-workforce-framework/>.

Department of Health (2004). *National service framework for children, young people and maternity services: Disabled children and young people and those with complex needs*. Viewed 14 February 2013. <https://www.education.gov.uk/publications/standard/_arc_Healthanddisabilities/Page4/DH-40496>.

Department of Health (2001). *Valuing people: A new strategy for learning disability for the 21st Century*. Viewed 14 February 2013. <http://webarchive.nationalarchives.gov.uk/+/www.dh.gov.uk/en/Publicationsandstatistics/Publications/PublicationsPolicyAndGuidance/DH_4009374>.

Diamond, M. and Allcorn, S. (2003). The cornerstone of psychoanalytic organizational analysis: Psychological reality, transference and countertransference in the workplace. *Human Relations* 56(4): 491–514.

Durham, C. (2002). Music therapy and neurology. In: L. Bunt and S. Hoskyn (eds), *The Handbook of Music Therapy*. London: Brunner-Routledge.

Eddy, B. (2012). The "splitting" dynamic. Viewed 8 February 2013. <http://www.highconflict-institute.com/articles/mediation-a-negotiation-articles/78-hci-articles/published-articles/139-splitting-at-work>.

Edwards, J. (1999). Music therapy with children hospitalised for severe injury or illness. *British Journal of Music Therapy* 13(1): 21–27.

Edwards, J. and Kennelly, J. (2004). Music therapy in paediatric rehabilitation. *Nordic Journal of Music Therapy* 13(2): 112–126.

Eisler, J. (1993). Stretto -Music therapy in the context of the multidisciplinary team: Establishing a place in the multidisciplinary team. *Journal of British Music Therapy* 7(1): 23–24.

Elefant, C. and Lotan, M. (1998) *Rett syndrome a transdiciplinary approach: Music and physical therapy intervention. Music therapy—A dialogue: Proceedings of the Fourth European Music Therapy Congress*. Viewed 22 February 2013. <http://www.musictherapyworld.net/WFMT/Publication_Center.html>.

Engeström, Y. (2008). *Teams to Knots: Studies of Collaboration and Learning at Work*. Viewed 14 March 2013. <http://reader.eblib.com.au/(S(0ofmoxpkospixodyodh3lctj))/Reader.aspx?p=343513and0=277andu=CSLIBM1590081Dandt=1364815748andh=3D0oF1561585 4E84D6E23760860A6E42FEFBEDADands=7952663andut=902andpg=1andr=imgand c=1andpat=n#>.

Fearn, M.C. and O'Connor, R. (2008). Collaborative working at the Cheyne day centre, London. In: K. Twyford and T. Watson (eds), *Integrated Team Working: Music Therapy as part of Transdisciplinary and Collaborative Approaches*, pp. 55–61. London: Jessica Kingsley Publishers.

Finlay, C., Bruce, H., Magee, W.L., Farrelly, S., and McKenzie, S. (2001). How I use music in therapy. *Speech Therapy in Practice* Autumn: 30–35.

Freeman, A. (2008a). The elderly. In K. Twyford and T. Watson (eds), *Integrated Team Working: Music Therapy as part of Transdisciplinary and Collaborative approaches*, pp. 179–202. London: Jessica Kingsley Publishers.

Freeman, A. (2008b). Groupwork, the team and spirituality. In: K. Twyford and T. Watson (eds), *Integrated Team Working: Music Therapy as part of Transdisciplinary and Collaborative Approaches*, pp. 195–230. London: Jessica Kingsley Publishers.

Galvin, S. and McCarthy, S. (1994). Multi-disciplinary community teams: Clinging to the wreckage. *Journal of Mental Health* 3: 157–166.

Geist, K., McCarthy, J., Rodgers-Smith, A., and Porter, J. (2008). Integrating music therapy services and speech-language therapy services for children with severe communication impairments: A co-treatment model. *Journal of Instructional Psychology* 35(4): 311–316.

Gilbert, H.V., Yan, J., and Hoffman, S.J. (2010). A WHO Report: Framework for Action on Interprofessional Education and Collaborative Practice. *Journal of Allied*

Health 39(1): 196–197. Viewed 15 March 2013. <http://scholar.harvard.edu/files/hoffman/files/18_-_jah_-_overview_of_who_framework_for_action_on_ipe_and_cp_2010_gilbert-yan-hoffman.pdf>.

Government of Western Australia (2007). *Health networks—Collaborative health care planning for the whole community, overview and guidelines.* Viewed 14 March 2013. <http://www.healthnetworks.health.wa.gov.au/publications/>.

Grasso, M., Allison, D.J., Button, B.M., and Sawyer, S.M. (1999). Music and physiotherapy: Evaluation of a program developed for caregivers of infants and toddlers with cystic fibrosis. In: R. Rebollo Pratt and D. Erdonmez Grocke (eds), *MusicMedicine3—MusicMedicine and Music Therapy: Expanding Horizons,* Faculty of Music, The University of Melbourne, Parkville.

Gundlach, M., Zivnuska, S. and Stoner, J. (2006). Understanding the relationship between individualism-collectivism and team performance through an integration of social identity theory and the social relations model. *Human Relations* 59(12): 1603–1632.

Hattersley, J. (1995). The survival of collaboration and co-operation. In: N. Malin (ed.), *Services for People with Learning Disabilities.* London: Routledge.

Health Professions Council (2009). *Standards of education and training guidance.* Health Professions Council London. Viewed 8 February 2013. <http://www.hpc-uk.org/assets/documents/1000295FStandardsofeducationandtrainingguidance-fromSeptember2009.pdf>.

Hean, S., Macleod Clark, J., Adams, K., Humphris, D., and Lathlean, J. (2006). Being seen by others as we see ourselves: The congruence between the ingroup and outgroup perceptions of health and social care students. *Learning in Health and Social Care* 5: 10–22.

Hedderly, P. (2008). A team approach: The rewards and challenges of collaborative working within a personality disorder treatment service. In: K. Twyford and T. Watson (eds), *Integrated Team Working: Music Therapy as part of Transdisciplinary and Collaborative Approaches,* pp. 136–140. London: Jessica Kingsley Publishers.

Heiderscheit, A. and Jackson, N. (2011). Discovering together: Music therapy collaboration. *Proceedings of the 13th WFMT World Congress of Music Therapy,* July 5–9 2011, Seoul, Korea, pp. 88–89. Viewed 15 February 2012. <http://www.musictherapytoday.wfmt.info/Music_Therapy_Today/MTT__Special_Issue_files/MTT_Congress%20Proceedings_Rev.7-31-2011.pdf>.

Hill, C. (2005). Bridge Over Troubled Waters? A study of music therapy and speech and language therapy in combined practice. MA dissertation, Nordoff Robbins Music Therapy Centre London, City University, London.

Hillmer, M.G. (2007). Survey of nurses' attitudes and perceptions toward music therapy in the hospital setting. MA thesis, University of Kansas.

Hills, B., Norman, I., and Forster, L. (2000). A study of burnout and multidisciplinary team-working amongst professional music therapists. *British Journal of Music Therapy* 14(1): 32–40.

Hobson, M. (2006). The collaboration of music therapy and speech-language pathology in the treatment of neurogenic communication disorders: Part I—diagnosis, therapist roles and rationale for music. *Music Therapy Perspectives* 24(2): 58–65.

Hobson, M. (2006a). The collaboration of music therapy and speech-language pathology in the treatment of neurogenic communication disorders: Part II—collaborative strategies and scope of practice. *Music Therapy Perspectives* 24(2): 66–72.

Hooper, J. (2002). Using music to develop peer interaction: An examination of the response of two subjects with a learning disability. *British Journal of Learning Disabilities* 30(4): 166–170.

Hooper, J., McManus, A., and McIntyre, A. (2004). Exploring the link between music therapy and sensory integration: An individual case study. *British Journal of Music Therapy* 18(1): 15–23.

Hughes, J., Robbins, B., McKenzie, B., and Robb, S. (1990). Integrating exceptional and nonexceptional young children through music play: A pilot program. *Music Therapy Perspectives* 8: 52–56.

Humpal, M.E. (1991). The effects of an integrated early childhood music program on social interaction among children with handicaps and their typical peers. *Journal of Music Therapy* 33(1): 19–33.

Interprofessional Education Collaborative Expert Panel (2011). *Core competencies for interprofessional collaborative practice: Report of an expert panel.* Interprofessional Education Collaborative, Washington DC. Viewed 14 March 2013. <http://www.aacn.nche.edu/education-resources/ipecreport.pdf>.

Jacobs, A. (2000). An investigation into the perception of music therapy in a service for adults with learning disabilities—The way forward. MA dissertation. Viewed 14 April 2013. <http://www.anglia.ac.uk/ruskin/en/home/faculties/alss/deps/mpa/r_c/music_therapy_research/dissertations/anna_jacobs.html>.

Jacobs, A. and Lincoln, S. (2003). Swimming against the Flow: What is the Role of the Arts Therapies in Multidisciplinary Teamworking? Paper presented at Nordic Music Therapy Conference in Bergen, May 2003.

Kaufman, D.L. and Goodman, K.D. (2009). *The use of music therapy as a complement to poetry therapy.* Viewed 8 February 2013. <http://www.inter-disciplinary.net/wp-content/uploads/2009/06/music-and-poetry.pdf>.

Kennelly, J., Hamilton, L., and Cross, J. (2001). The interface of music therapy and speech pathology in the rehabilitation of children with acquired brain injury. *The Australian Journal of Music Therapy* 12: 13–20.

Kern, P. (2004). Using a music therapy collaborative consultative approach for the inclusion of young children with autism in a childcare program. PhD dissertation, Universität Witten/Herdecke, Witten, Germany.

Kern, P. and Aldridge, D. (2006). Using embedded music therapy interventions to support outdoor play of young children with autism in an inclusive community-based child care program. *Journal of Music Therapy* 43(4): 270–294.

Kerr, I.B., Dent-Brown, K., and Parry, G.D. (2007). Psychotherapy and mental health teams. *International Review of Psychiatry* 19(1): 63–80.

Klinar, I., Ferhatovic, L., Banozic, A., Raguz, M., Kostic, S., Sapunar, D., and Puljak, L. (2012). Physicians' attitudes about interprofessional treatment of chronic pain: Family physicians are considered the most important collaborators. *Scandinavian Journal of Caring Sciences.* DOI: 10.1111/j.1471-6712.2012.01039.x.

Körner, M. (2010). Interprofessional teamwork in medical rehabilitation: A comparison of multidisciplinary and interdisciplinary team approach. *Clinical Rehabilitation* 24: 745–755.

Krout, R E. (2004). A synerdisciplinary music therapy treatment team approach for hospice and palliative care. *Australian Journal of Music Therapy* 15: 33–45.

Leaning, B. and Watson, T. (2006). From the inside looking out: An intensive interaction group for people with profound and multiple learning disabilities. *British Journal of Learning Disabilities* 34(2): 103–109.

Lee, K. and Baker, F. (1997). Towards integrating a holistic rehabilitation system: The implications for music therapy. *The Australian Journal of Music Therapy* 8: 30–37.

Leong, D. (2011). Team members' process of understanding music therapy: Exploring interdisciplinary team perspectives. MA thesis, Wilfrid Laurier University, Ontario.

Lindeck, J. and Pundole, A. (2008). "Express yourself!" In: K. Twyford and T. Watson (eds), *Integrated Team Working: Music Therapy as part of Transdisciplinary and Collaborative Approaches*, pp. 168–187. London: Jessica Kingsley Publishers.

Macadam, M. and Rodgers, J. (1997). The multi-disciplinary and multi-agency approach. In: J. O'Hara and A. Sperlinger (eds), *Adults with Learning Disabilities. A Practical Approach for Health Professionals*. Chichester: John Wiley and Sons.

Magee, W. (2008). Team working to meet complex needs with acquired neurological conditions. In: K. Twyford and T. Watson (eds), *Integrated Team Working: Music Therapy as part of Transdisciplinary and Collaborative Approaches*, pp. 154–178 London: Jessica Kingsley Publishers.

Magee, W.L. and Andrews, K. (2007). Multi-disciplinary perceptions of music therapy in complex neuro-rehabilitation. *International Journal of Therapy and Rehabilitation* 14(2): 70–74.

Magill, L. and Berenson, S. (2008). The conjoint use of music therapy and reflexology with hospitalized advanced stage cancer patients and their families. *Palliative and Supportive Care* 6(3): 289–296.

McCarthy, J., Geist, K., Zojwala, R., and Schock, M.Z. (2008). A survey of music therapists' work with speech-language pathologists and experiences with augmentative and alternative communication. *Journal of Music Therapy* 45(4): 405–426.

Meadows, A. (1997). Music therapy for children with severe and profound multiple disabilities: A review of literature. *The Australian Journal of Music Therapy* 8: 3–17.

Meadows, A. (2002). Approaches to music and movement for children with severe and profound multiple disabilities. *The Australian Journal of Music Therapy* 13: 17–27.

Meads, G., Ashcroft, J., Barr, H., Scott, R., and Wild, A. (2008). *The Case for Interprofessional Collaboration: In Health and Social Care (Promoting Partnership for Health)*. Hoboken, NJ: Wiley-Blackwell.

Menzies, I. (1960). A case-study in the functioning of social systems as a defence against anxiety: A report on a study of the nursing service of a general hospital. *Human Relations* 13: 95–121. DOI: 10.1177/001872676001300201. Viewed 13 March 2013. <http://hum.sagepub.com/cgi/content/refs/13/2/95>.

Miller, C. (2008). Music therapy and collaborative working in adult mental health: Creative connections and destructive splits. In: K. Twyford and T. Watson (eds), *Integrated Team Working: Music Therapy as part of Transdisciplinary and Collaborative Approaches*, pp. 124–153. London: Jessica Kingsley Publishers.

Miller, C. and Guarnieri, M. (2008). Integrating two different disciplines: A music and drama-therapy group. In: K. Twyford and T. Watson (eds), *Integrated Team Working: Music Therapy as part of Transdisciplinary and Collaborative Approaches*, pp. 146–162. London: Jessica Kingsley Publishers.

Miller, C., Freeman, M., and Ross, N. (2001). *Interprofessional Practice in Health and Social Care: Challenging the Shared Learning Agenda*. London: Arnold.

Millman, R. (2008). Music therapy within the multidisciplinary team: Different approaches—shared goals. In: K. Twyford and T. Watson (eds), *Integrated Team Working: Music Therapy as part of Transdisciplinary and Collaborative approaches*, pp. 163–167. London: Jessica Kingsley Publishers, London.

Ministry of Education (2006). *Specialist services standards*. Ministry of Education, Wellington.

Molyneux, C. (2005). Music therapy as a short term intervention with individuals and families in a child and adolescent mental health service. *British Journal of Music Therapy* 19(2): 59–66.

Molyneux, C. (2008a). Music therapy as part of a multidisciplinary family assessment process. In: K. Twyford and T. Watson (eds), *Integrated Team Working: Music Therapy as part of Transdisciplinary and Collaborative Approaches*, pp. 42–47. London: Jessica Kingsley Publishers, London.

Molyneux, C. (2008b). The Stone family. In: K. Twyford and T. Watson (eds), *Integrated Team Working: Music Therapy as part of Transdisciplinary and Collaborative Approaches,* pp. 74–79. London: Jessica Kingsley Publishers, London.

Morison, S., and Jenkins, J. (2007). Sustained effects of interprofessional shared learning on student attitudes to communication and team working depend on shared learning opportunities on clinical placement as well as in the classroom. *Medical Teacher* 29(5): 450–456.

Moss, H. (1999). Creating a new music therapy post: An evidence-based research project. *British Journal of Music Therapy* 13(2): 49–58.

Moran Finello, K. (2011). Collaboration in the assessment and diagnosis of preschoolers: Challenges and opportunities. *Psychology in the Schools* 48(5): 442–453. Wiley Periodicals. DOI: 10.1002/pits.20566.

O'Connor, M. and Walls, M. (2004). Building blocks to best practice—Introducing an integrated holistic model of early intervention with children and families. *Proceedings of a CECDE Conference on Defining, Assessing and Supporting Quality in Early Childhood Care and Education,* Dublin Castle. Viewed 14 February 2013. <http//www.cecde.ie/gaeilge/pdf/Questions%20of%20Quality/Walls.pdf>.

O'Hagan, S., Allen, D., Bennett, M., Bridgman, A., Lumsden, K., and Wallace, L. (2004). Transdisciplinary teamwork improves care: Five disciplines combine skills to assist people with intellectual disabilities. *Annual Journal of the New Zealand Society for Music Therapy* 2: 50–57.

O'Kelly, J. and Koffman, J. (2007). Multidisciplinary perspectives of music therapy in adult palliative care. *Palliative Medicine* 21(3): 235–241.

O'Neill, N. (2008). Collaborative working in an acute paediatric hospital. In: K. Twyford and T. Watson (eds), *Integrated Team Working: Music Therapy as part of Transdisciplinary and Collaborative Approaches*, pp. 68–73. London: Jessica Kingsley Publishers, London.

Odell Miller, H. (2002). Music narratives in music therapy treatment for dementia. In: L. Bunt and S. Hoskyns (eds), *The Handbook of Music Therapy*. London: Brunner-Routledge.

Olofsson, A. and Fossum, B. (2009). Perspectives on music therapy in adult cancer care: A hermeneutic study. *Oncology Nursing Forum* 36(4): E223–E231.

Ovretveit, J. (1993). *Co-ordinating Community Care*. Buckingham: Open University Press.

Pecoraro Esperson, P. (2006). The pleasure of being "differently able": Integration through music therapy in primary schools. *Music Therapy Today* (Online) 7(2): 413–429. Viewed, 22 February 2013. <http://musictherapyworld.net>.

Petersen, E. M. (2005, November). Music therapy and oncology at the National Institute of Cancer. In: *Voices: A World Forum for Music Therapy* (Vol. 5, No. 3). Available athttps://normt.uib.no/index.php/voices/article/view/234/178.

Pollard, K., Miers, M., and Gilchrist, M. (2004). Collaborative learning for collaborative working? Initial findings from a longitudinal study of health and social care students. *Health and Social Care in the Community* 12(4): 346–358.

Priestley, M. (1993). Music therapy in the multidisciplinary team, in Stretto: Music Therapy in the context of the multidisciplinary team. *Journal of British Music Therapy* 7(1): 26–27.

Radoje, M., Betteridge, S., and Zivor, M. (2008). Music therapy and psychology: A joint approach. In: K. Twyford and T. Watson (eds), *Integrated Team Working: Music Therapy as part of Transdisciplinary and Collaborative Approaches,* pp. 107–111. London: Jessica Kingsley Publishers, London.

Reeves, S., Zwarenstein, M., Goldman, J., Barr, H., Freeth, D., Hammick, M., and Koppel, I. (2008). Interprofessional education: Effects on professional practice and health care outcomes. *Cochrane Database of Systematic Reviews,* Issue 1. Art. No.: CD002213. DOI: 10.1002/14651858.CD002213.pub2.

Reeves, S., Lewin, S., Espin, S., and Zwarenstein, M. (2010). *Promoting Partnership for Health: Interprofessional Teamwork for Health and Social Care.* Chichester: Wiley-Blackwell Publishing Limited.

Register, D. (2002). Collaboration and consultation: A survey of board certified music therapists. *Journal of Music Therapy* 4: 305–321.

Rickson, D. (2010). Music therapy school consultation: A literature review. *New Zealand Journal of Music Therapy* 8: 59–91.

Rickson, D. (2010a). The development of a music therapy school consultation protocol for students with high or very high special education needs. PhD dissertation, New Zealand School of Music, Wellington.

Rickson, D. and Twyford, K. (2011). Music therapy consultation in a New Zealand School: Staff members' perceptions of outcomes. *New Zealand Journal of Music Therapy* 9: 61–85.

Robben, S., Perry, M., Van Nieuwenhuijzen, L., Van Achterberg, T., Olde Rikkert, M., Schers, H. et al. (2012). Impact of interprofessional education on collaboration attitudes, skills, and behaviour among primary care professionals. *Journal of Continuing Education in the Health Professions* 32(3): 196–204. DOI: 10.1002/chp.

Shoemark, H., and Dearn, T. (2008). Keeping parents at the centre of family centred music therapy with hospitalised infants. *Australian Journal of Music Therapy* 19: 3–24.

Sines, D. and Barr, O. (1998). Professions in teams. In: T. Thompson and P. Mathias (eds), *Standards and Learning Disability.* Balliere: Tindall.

Sloboda, A. (2008). Co-working music therapy with other disciplines: Co-working a music therapy group with nursing staff. In: K. Twyford and T. Watson (eds), *Integrated Team Working: Music Therapy as part of Transdisciplinary and Collaborative Approaches,* pp. 141–145. London: Jessica Kingsley Publishers, London.

Snow, S., Snow, S., and D'Amico, M. (2008). Interdisciplinary research through community music therapy and performance ethnography. Recherche interdisciplinaire: musicothérapie communautaire et ethnographie de la performance. *Canadian Journal of Music Therapy* 14(1): 30–46.

The Speech Pathology Association of Australia (2009). *Transdisciplinary practice position statement.* Viewed 8th February 2013. <http://www.speechpathologyaustralia.org.au/library/Transdisciplinary%20Practice.pdf>.

Spring, E. (2010). The interdisciplinary collaborative competency in music therapy: Terminology, definitions, and teaching approaches. MA thesis, College of Fine Arts of Ohio University, Ohio.

Summer, L. (1997). Considering the future of music therapy. *The Arts in Psychotherapy* 24(1): 75–80.

Sutton, J. (2002). Survival in the workplace: The strength and vulnerability of the music therapy practitioner. *British Journal of Music Therapy* 16(2): 62–64.

Travaglia, R. and Treefoot, A. (2010). Exploring the dance and music dialogue: Collaboration between music therapy and dance movement therapy in Aotearoa/New Zealand. *New Zealand Journal of Music Therapy* 8: 34–58.

Turnbull, D. and Robinson, M. (1990). Music and movement as therapy for primary language and learning disordered children. *The Australian Journal of Music Therapy* 1: 45–49.

Twyford, K. (2004a). New directions: An investigation into music therapy as part of a collaborative multidisciplinary approach. MA dissertation, University of Surrey, Roehampton.

Twyford, K. (2004b). From multidisciplinary to interdisciplinary: An investigation into collaborative approaches in music therapy practice. *Proceedings from the BSMT/APMT Annual Conference- Changes; Exploring Clinical, Professional and Global Perspectives*, pp. 65–73. London: BSMT Publications.

Twyford, K. (2008). Collaborative and transdisciplinary approaches with children. In: K. Twyford and T. Watson (eds), *Integrated Team Working: Music Therapy as part of Transdisciplinary and Collaborative Approaches*, pp. 31–90. London: Jessica Kingsley Publishers, London.

Twyford, K. (2009). Finding a niche: Establishing a role for music therapy within the Ministry of Education, Special Education NZ. *New Zealand Journal of Music Therapy* 7: 6–31.

Twyford, K. (2012). Getting to know you: Peer and staff perceptions of involvement in inclusive music therapy groups with students with special educational needs in mainstream school settings. New Zealand Journal of Music Therapy 10: 39–73.

Twyford, K. and Parkhouse, C. (2008). Collaborative working in a special needs setting. In: K. Twyford and T. Watson (eds), *Integrated Team Working: Music Therapy as part of Transdisciplinary and Collaborative Approaches*, pp. 62–67. London: Jessica Kingsley Publishers, London.

Twyford, K. and Rickson, D. (2013). In their element! Student responses to the work of a music therapist in music therapy school consultation. *Music Therapy Perspectives* 31(2): 127–136. DOI: 10.1093/mtp/31.2.127.

Twyford, K. and Watson, T. (2008). *Integrated Team Working: Music Therapy as part of Transdisciplinary and Collaborative Approaches*. London: Jessica Kingsley Publishers.

Twyford, K., Parkhouse, C., and Murphy, J. (2008). Transdisciplinary assessments with children with complex needs. In: K. Twyford and T. Watson (eds), *Integrated Team Working: Music Therapy as part of Transdisciplinary and Collaborative Approaches*, pp. 48–54. London: Jessica Kingsley Publishers, London.

Tyas, R., Souster, J., and de Sousa, C. (2008). Building bridges: Joint working with drama, music and dance movement therapy. In: K. Twyford and T. Watson (eds), *Integrated Team Working: Music Therapy as part of Transdisciplinary and Collaborative Approaches*, pp. 117–135. London: Jessica Kingsley Publishers, London.

Vyt, A. (2008). Interprofessional and transdisciplinary teamwork in health care. *DiabetesMetabolism Research and Reviews* 24(1): S106–S109. DOI: 10.1002/dmrr.835.

Walsh, R. and Stewart, R. (2002). Combined efforts: Increasing social-emotional communication with children with autistic spectrum disorder using psychodynamic music therapy and division TEACCH communication programme. In A. Davies and E. Richards (eds), *Music Therapy and Group Work*. London: Jessica Kingsley Publishers.

Watson, T. (2002). Music therapy with adults with learning disabilities. In: L. Bunt and S. Hoskyns (eds), *The Handbook of Music Therapy*. London: Brunner-Routledge.

Watson, T. (2008a). Collaboration in music therapy with adults with learning disabilities. In: K. Twyford and T. Watson (eds), *Integrated Team Working: Music Therapy as part of*

Transdisciplinary and Collaborative Approaches, pp. 91–123. London: Jessica Kingsley Publishers, London.

Watson, S. (2008b). A music therapy and physiotherapy group. In: K. Twyford and T. Watson (eds), *Integrated Team Working: Music Therapy as part of Transdisciplinary and Collaborative Approaches*, pp. 101–106. London: Jessica Kingsley Publishers, London.

Watson, T. and Germany, A. (2008). A music and communication group. In: K. Twyford and T. Watson (eds), *Integrated Team Working: Music Therapy as part of Transdisciplinary and Collaborative approaches*, pp. 112–116. London: Jessica Kingsley Publishers, London.

Watson, T. and Vickers, L. (2002). A music and art therapy group for people with learning disabilities. In: A. Davies and E. Richards (eds), *Music Therapy and Group Work*. London: Jessica Kingsley Publishers.

Watson, T., Bragg, A., and Jeffcote, N. (2004). Working together -Integrated multi- disciplinary practice with women. In: N. Jeffcote and T. Watson (eds), *Working Therapeutically with Women in Secure Mental Health Settings*, pp. 91–107. London: Jessica Kingsley Publishers.

West, M. and Slater, J. (1996). *The Effectiveness of Teamworking in Primary Healthcare*. London: Health Education Authority.

Wheeler, B. (2003). The interdisciplinary music therapist. *Voices: A World Forum for Music Therapy*. Viewed 14 April 2013. <http://www.voices.no/?q=fortnightly-columns/2003-interdisciplinary-music-therapist>.

Wigram, T. (1992). Aspects of music therapy relating to physical disability. *The Australian Journal of Music Therapy* 3: 3–15.

Wigram, T. (2000). (interviewed by H. Loth). Historical perspectives interview series. *British Journal of Music Therapy* 14(1): 5–12.

Wigram, T., Pedersen, I.N., and Bonde, L.O. (2002). *A Comprehensive Guide to Music Therapy: Theory, Clinical Practice, Research and Training*. Philadelphia: Jessica Kingsley Publishers.

Williams, K.E., Berthelsen, D., Nicholson, J., Walker, S., and Abad, V. (2012). The effectiveness of a short-term group music therapy intervention for parents who have a child with a disability. *Journal of Music Therapy* 49(1): 23–44.

Woodward, A. (2004). Music therapy for autistic children and their families: A creative spectrum. *British Journal of Music Therapy* 18(1): 8–14.

Woodward, A. (2008). Martha and Rio: Collaborative working with a parent and child. In: K. Twyford and T. Watson (eds), *Integrated Team Working: Music Therapy as part of Transdisciplinary and Collaborative Approaches,* pp. 80–100. London: Jessica Kingsley Publishers, London.

World Health Organization (WHO) (2010). *Framework for action on interprofessional education and collaborative practice*. World Health Organization, Geneva. Viewed 14 March 2013. <http://www.who.int/hrh/resources/framework_action/en/>.

Zwarenstein, M., Goldman, J., and Reeves, S. (2009). Interprofessional collaboration: Effects of practice-based interventions on professional practice and healthcare outcomes (Review). *The Cochrane Collaboration*. Hoboken, NJ: John Wiley and Sons, Ltd.

Zwarenstein, M., Reeves, S., Russell, A., Kenaszchuk, C., Gotlib Conn, L., Miller, K.L. et al. (2007). Structuring communication relationships for interprofessional teamwork (SCRIPT): a cluster randomized controlled trial. DOI: 10.1186/1745-6215-8-23. Viewed 22 February 2013. <http://www.trialsjournal.com/content/8/1/23>.

CHAPTER 49

....

RECOGNITION OF MUSIC THERAPY IN EUROPE

....

MONIKA NÖCKER-RIBAUPIERRE

INTRODUCTION
....

MUSIC therapy has continued to become established as a professional discipline through the last twentieth and early twenty-first century. The era of pioneering music therapy founders has come to an end along with uncontrolled and unrestricted professional activity by music therapists. This now makes way for greater regulation and accreditation by governmental processes. This regulation allows for greater scrutiny of effective practice and greater security of tenure and employment for music therapy professionals.

In Europe, Austria, and the United Kingdom were the early pioneers of music therapy; establishing professional associations and training programmes in the 1950s (Ansdell et al. 2002; Gold 2003). East Germany, Germany, and the Nordic countries followed closely from these initial developments (Aasgaard and Trondalen 2004; Wosch 2003). In 1990, a visionary group of music therapists[1] established a forum for the development of the profession in music therapy in Europe: the European Music Therapy Confederation (EMTC). The aim of this group was to provide Europe-wide communication and cooperation in the field of music therapy. In 2005 the EMTC achieved the status of an officially acknowledged professional body: EMTC AISBL (*Association Internationale Sans But Lucratif* or International Non-Profit Organization).

In 1997, The Bologna Treaty[2] formulated changes for the European academic system. This agreement stipulated that all second level European University degrees were to become either Bachelor or Master degrees. This process was to be completed by 2009. The Bologna Treaty aimed to establish a common and comparable system of higher education and research for academic training. On this basis, the EU regulates professions and thus ensures mobility. That is, a student from one European country can undertake a semester of study in a comparable course in another European country and receive credit for the study completed. All academic music therapy training courses have had to adapt their curricula to these requirements. Privately run training courses which are not qualified to dispense university degrees have committed themselves to adhere to clearly defined minimal standards in relation to music therapy training.

FORMAL RECOGNITION: A PROCESS AND A GOAL

Gaining formal recognition for the profession of music therapy in Europe was initially the major priority for the EMTC. The founding members of the EMTC expected to be supported by the EU in order to gain official and statutory recognition within the European Union. However, the prior rejection of recognition of alternative therapies by the EC in 1995 forced the EMTC to consider other options for their mission. To seek clarity on the situation, the former EMTC core board[3] met with the Heads of Unit, European Commission, Internal Market, for regulated professions and for mutual education system in Brussels.[4] Their message was that if the EMTC opted for official recognition of music therapy within the EC, this would involve at least 20 years' of further campaign work in addition to hefty bureaucratic requirements. They strongly recommended that the EMTC continue to work on developing a professional foundation and establishing high standards for the qualified music therapist. The EMTC could thus avoid danger of potential future over-regulation. This led the General Assembly of the EMTC to structure the EMTC professionally to define high level requirements for inclusion of individual practitioners onto a European Music Therapy Register (EMTR).

THE PRESENT SITUATION

Europe at the end of 2012, there were 5103 members registered in 40 professional associations. As some countries do not have an official register of music therapists, the actual number may be higher. As heterogeneous as the numbers of professionals appear, from four in Bulgaria to about 1500 in Germany, so are the numbers of the professional associations. Associations vary in number from one in the UK, Norway, Finland, Ireland, and some Eastern countries, to seven in Spain.

The professional and legal environment of music therapy in Europe varies between countries. Different prerequisites, requirements, and rules regulating the practice of music therapy in different jurisdictions. Working as a music therapist is closely connected with the professional recognition as an independent health profession, which in turn is related to the status of the training programs and national quality standards. Presently, only three countries have a law regulating the practice of music therapy. In the majority of the EMTC member countries anyone can "train" as a "music therapist" and work as a "music therapist" or use music therapy methods or elements in other health care and alternative medical professions, in music education, and in social work. This is the situation in most European countries and is exactly why EMTC was formed, and what it seeks to address and change.

Professional acknowledgement and recognition is thus of prime importance for individual music therapists as well as for professional associations, supported and safeguarded by the EMTC. To assure and safeguard the quality, to increase national possibilities for recognition, the EMTC formulated standards for the European Music Therapy Register EMTR. This Register includes only BA and MA degrees. It has been functioning since 2012.[5]

RECOGNITION:
STATUTORY—ACADEMIC—PROFESSIONAL

Recognition is by definition the state or quality of being recognized or acknowledged.

In order to obtain information about the different situation of recognition in the countries, the following questionnaire was sent out to the EMTC delegates.

- How many music therapists are working in your country?
- Is music therapist a protected title in your country?

If protected: by whom?

- Do you have a (national) definition of music therapy? If yes, please cite
- Who guarantees the professional quality: The Law/Health System

Professional associations/or

- If music therapy is recognized, is there any registration procedure? Are there requirements for *continuing professional development CPD*?
- Most important: how would you describe the recognition of music therapy in your country?

The details leading to this survey are of course limited to the information received from the country delegates. In fact, there is such a wide difference in all the answers are that this summary can only provide an overview in the broadest sense. It can sum up some similarities and differences in order to provide an idea of the extent of this heterogeneity of the profession.

As music therapy work is yet to be standardized and regulated in most European countries, in many countries people are doing this work without recognition of their credentials. These professionals are mostly known by recognized titles in the institutions that they work for.

For our profession, I propose to distinguish between statutory recognition, and academic recognition: recognition in specific health care, clinical, and social areas, recognition at the academic level, and professional recognition (registered in national associations).

The professional associations are eager to establish one step after the other. Over and beyond academic recognition, this involves the definition of music therapy as a prerequisite for any protection of the title, the development of a national register of qualified music therapists to assure the quality including requirements for continuing professional development CPD, and the proof of efficacy with evidence-based research.

A major effort must be directed to discussions to convince the legal authorities of the importance of official recognition.

This is not so easy because there are some upcoming difficulties and requirements in accordance with national regulations of the health system.

Some examples: In Germany the status of psychotherapy was revised in accordance with new regulations of psychotherapy profession in 2000, which excluded many therapeutic methods, also music therapy. In France there is recognition of music therapy only for psychologists who have followed music therapy studies.[6] There is now government regulation of psychotherapy and music therapy does not meet the conditions. Therefore it is no longer legally possible to use the term "psychotherapy" when speaking of music therapy.

In 1992, the Norwegian Government approved music therapists to be able to hold professional appointments within *special education schools*, but the title is not protected. In 2010, the MA training institutions in Bergen and Oslo (Norway), the Trade Union for Music Therapists, and the Norwegian Association for Music Therapy, sent an application to the Health Directory to apply for an authorization for music therapists. Such an authorization means a change of the Law, respectively § 48/1, to include music therapy—they are still waiting.

In their efforts to reach statutory recognition, and as the UK has done with success, some countries are working in conjunction with all of the arts therapies: Czech Republic, Germany, Hungary, Ireland, and Luxembourg. On the other hand, some countries are still integrated in the arts therapies like The Netherlands, Estonia, Poland, and Slovenia, while others are working with the Psychotherapy Law like Bulgaria, and Finland.

These examples demonstrate that the way to statutory recognition is characterized by many requirements and years of endless efforts. There are however, possibilities and many examples of "recognition" on a "lower" non-statutory level to increase the acceptance within the academic and clinical world, and to work clinically, in institutions or in private practice.

STATUTORY RECOGNITION

Three countries in Europe have achieved statutory recognition: the UK in 1999 and Austria and Latvia in 2009. These countries are noted for being the first places in which music therapy was developed; in Austria (Gold 2003; Mossler, 2008) and UK, and then in Latvia (Lagzdina 2009). Music therapy has been officially recognized as a health profession in the UK with statutory recognition of the Arts Therapies by the Health and Care Professions Council (HCPC) since an act of parliament in 1997. Music therapists working in the UK have to be registered with HCPC, with the umbrella title of *Arts Therapist*. The regulation of the profession took a number of years of extensive work in the UK (Bunt and Hoskyns 2013).

There are formulated standards of proficiency:

- Standards for the same modules in the training courses (titled Standards of Education and Training).
- Standards of ethics: documentation, monitoring, and training.
- Standards of proficiency: profession specific standards.
- Standards for registration follow a very stringent procedure, including requirements for Continued Professional Development CPD.[7]

Whenever a profession renews its registration—every two years—2.5% of the profession is audited and has to send a full CPD profile to show that they meet these standards. Music therapists and other arts therapists are part of the reviewing team.[8]

For individual registration: The HCPC has five standards for CPD which all registered music therapists must meet, and a log of CPD should be completed every year: to show the evidence of what the therapist had learned. The use of a private insurance is recommended.

There is a growing recognition of music therapy in the UK. State regulation has brought with it greater status within the allied health professions in the National Health Service. However, understanding and recognition of the value of music therapy varies regionally and also within the statutory providers of health, education and social care.

It has been the role of the professional association (BAMT) to develop means of improving recognition and promoting music therapy through a new organization, new website, social media, and the introduction of a National Music Therapy Week held every two years.[9]

The statutory recognition in Austria dates from July 1, 2009. The autonomous Music Therapy Law is partly influenced by thy Psychotherapeutic Law. Since then the official status of music therapy in Austria one of "an independent scientific-creative and expressive-therapeutic method." After having successfully completed the Austrian university training courses (Vienna/MA or Krems/BA and MA) the new music therapist can be registered according to his/her academic level BA or MA. Immediately after recognition, the music therapist must follow the CPD requirements as formulated by the Ministry of Health. The responsibility in working with patients is determined according the level of training: music therapists on BA level are entitled to work with co-responsibility in clinical settings, on MA level independently in private practice—according to the title "co-responsible music therapist" for BA and "responsible music therapist" for MA. Music therapists in Austria can now have their own professional identity without sharing the Law with any other profession and without any interference from outside profession.[10]

In both countries this success has taken 20 years of continued and hard work. The UK law regulating allied health professions including all of the arts therapies is applied under section 60 of the Health Act 1999 and came into force on 12 February 2002 (see also Karkou et al., 2011). The Austrian Law governing the protection of title for music therapy does not include other arts therapies.

Since 2009 music therapy is recognized and protected by the Ministry for Health in Latvia. The profession was recognized in the adoption of Occupation Regulations and Standards of Profession by the Ministry of Education of Latvia along with the other areas of art, dance movement, and drama therapy. As the Latvian music therapists started their first training course in 2001 and their professional association in 2005, this is excellent progress for such a small population of only 23 music therapists.

According to this law, music therapists are enabled to work in health care and provide social care in educational institutions. The music therapist can work independently in state, municipal, non-governmental, or commercial organizations. The music therapy association confirmed certification and re-certification regulations and well as a reformed code of ethics. Certification of the first music therapists by the Association of Professional Organizations of Medical Professionals has occurred. This includes requirements for certification for regular practice and for supervision over the first two years following graduation.

The registration of music therapy technology in the list of health care technologies held by the Ministry of Health of Latvia was a significant step. Now, music therapy is recommended for rehabilitation.[11]

RECOGNITION AT THE ACADEMIC LEVEL

Since the early 2000s, the northern and middle European countries and some southern European countries have modeled their university training curricula according to BA and MA requirements. These training courses are accredited by national academic accreditation committees. A survey of accredited training courses from 2005 showed 60 official programs throughout Europe: 19 in the South, 23 in the Middle and 19 in the North. 30 courses were at MA level, with 12 at BA level. Additionally, there are increasing numbers of universities providing PhD level music therapy research training.[12] As these training courses are officially accredited at this level, they have reached academic recognition in the respective countries. The quality and the accreditation of training courses on these levels generates music therapeutic identity.

Music therapy has greater academic recognition in countries where music training courses are accredited by governmental authorities. In the following countries, although there is an absence of government accreditation, academic recognition does exist. This is the case in Belgium, Czech Republic, Denmark, Estonia, Finland, France, Germany, Norway, Portugal, Serbia, Spain, Switzerland, and The Netherlands—Cyprus and Greece are developing this capacity.

A side-effect of the academic registration together with increasing scientific research studies is that music therapy, in some countries, is now presented and implemented in some countries into different health care areas and in medical treatment guidelines.

PROFESSIONAL RECOGNITION—RECOGNITION IN HEALTH CARE AND SOCIAL AREAS

All other European countries are striving for statutory recognition. Because the profession is not recognized nor protected by any specific law, the music therapy associations are working to establish some type of national sovereign and self-regulatory recognition. They all include the EMTC code of ethics with or without national additions. Some countries have their own definition of music therapy, some have adapted the WFMT definition (1996),[13] and some have no definition.

In nearly all European countries, the professional associations follow the Bologna Treaty with its requirements for standards based on BA and MA level. They formulate their own quality standards and with this their individual requirements for recognition. Some of countries are working on Continuing Professional Development (CPD) as a prerequisite for their national register. Examples are Belgium, Czech Republic, Germany, Italy, Luxembourg, The Netherlands, Serbia, and Switzerland.

Few countries have a national title, defined and protected by the respective professional associations: in Germany the title "music therapist DMtG," in Luxembourg "music therapist GML," in Serbia the title "music therapist AMTS," in Switzerland the title "music therapist SFMT." Their registration standards follow the EMTC standards, and they require CPD.

The development of national registers is established or in progress in several countries: Czech Republic, France, Germany, Italy (by individual associations), Luxembourg, Serbia, Switzerland, and the Netherlands. The registration is connected with the agreed and signed Code of Ethics in accordance with that of the EMTC. To assure the quality, the frame for the developing national registration is provided through the two academic levels.

In some countries, music therapists are partly recognized as their contribution is explicitly recommended or acknowledged in specific clinical areas as the following examples attest.

Although in Denmark music therapy is not acknowledged as a health care profession, it is an important supplement in health care. In Finland music therapists have a "semi-official" position as music therapy is reimbursed as medical rehabilitation of patients with severe disabilities and rehabilitative psychotherapy in various institutions or private practice. In Germany, music therapy in conjunction with the art therapies is integrated into the health care treatment guidelines of dementia care, eating disorders, attention disorders, pain, and depression.

In Lithuania music therapy is recommended for the work with special needs (autism, cochlea implant, intellectual impairment) and in conjunction with the arts therapies integrated in psychic health centers. In Norway music therapy is partly recognized for psychosis, in Poland for psychiatry, whereas in Serbia music therapy is recommended for all psychiatric disorders. According to their National Guidelines for Health and Medical Care and Social Services, in Sweden music therapy is recommended for the treatment for individuals with schizophrenia, and since June 2013 (by the National Board of Health and Welfare) as treatment within palliative care. In The Netherlands music therapy is recommended for dementia and neurological rehabilitation.

The status of professional recognition can be seen as either individually recognized and registered as trained music therapist by the national professional organization and/or in being accepted as music therapist in special clinical or institutional care areas. These possibilities seem to enhance the professional acceptance because in all European countries music therapists are working in clinical or social/educational settings. Of course, these settings are limited but specified and acknowledged by the respective authorities. Increasing national and international research, including research reviews, meta-analysis and the Cochrane Library, will help to expand these areas and to support the different recognition processes.

Conclusion

Music therapy as a profession was developed from the late 1950s onwards by highly qualified individual music therapists. The profession was and is still based on a range of philosophies, theories, and methods that were developed in the different countries according to their pioneers, their cultural background and their professional identity. As the EMTC was founded, the various associations and their delegates in many countries had to learn to become familiar with this manifold richness offered for the therapeutic work with clients.

The music therapy community is rapidly expanding with its academic and scientific research, publications, embedded in a worldwide network. Thus music therapy is on the way to obtain acknowledgement in the health care area around the world and thus to achieve the goal of legal recognition. In Europe, three countries are in this favorable position, and an increasing number of countries are following steps to be integrated into the national, social, and health systems. For the majority of the European countries, there remains much work ahead in order to be able to work as freely and with the same protection as in the UK, Austria, and in Latvia.

Notes

1. Tony Wigram, Helen Odell-Miller, Gianluigi di Franco, and Patxi del Campo.
2. Convention on the recognition of qualifications concerning higher education in the European region.(The European Treaty Series, n°165, Council of Europe—UNESCO joint Convention), Lisbon, 11 April 1997.
3. Jos De Backer, Monika Nöcker-Ribaupierre, Julie Sutton.
4. Pamela Brumpter-Coret and Corinne Guidicelli.
5. <www.emtc-eu/register>.
6. Information by Adrienne Lerner, VP EMTC and Nicole Duperret, F delegate.
7. <http://www.hpc-uk.org/apply/>.
8. <http://www.hpc-uk.org/registrants/cpd/>. Statutory instruments 2007 No 2781—Professional Qualifications—The European Communities (Recognition of Professional Qualifications)—Regulations 2007. Crown copyright 2007—Printed and published in the UK by The Stationery Office Limited—under the authority and superintendence of Carol Tullo, Controller of Her Majesty's Stationery Office and Queen's Printer of Acts of Parliament.1398 10/2007 171398T 19585.
9. Information by Helen Loth and Tessa Watson, UK delegate.
10. <https://www.google.com.au/#q=musiktherapiegesetz.pdf>. Information by Elena Fitzthum, AU delegate.
11. Information by Mirdza Paipare, LI delegate.
12. Since 2012 in the EMTC website there are 88 training course: including private training courses from South and Middle Europe.
13. See EMTC website.

References

Aasgaard, T. and Trondalen, G. (2004). Music Therapy in Norway. *Voices Resources.* Retrieved March 18, 2014, from: <http://testvoices.uib.no/community/?q=country/monthnorway_july2004>.

Ansdell, G., Bunt, L., and Hartley, N. (2002). Music Therapy in the United Kingdom. *Voices Resources.* Retrieved March 20, 2014, from: <http://testvoices.uib.no/community/?q=country-of-the-month/2002-music-therapy-united-kingdom>.

Bunt, L. and Hoskyns, S. (2013). Setting the scene. In: L. Bunt and S. Hoskyns (eds), *The Handbook of Music Therapy*, pp. 9–26. London: Routledge.

De Backer, J., Nöcker-Ribaupierre, M., and Sutton, J. (2014). The identity and professionalization of European music therapy, with an overview and history of the European Music Therapy Confederation. In: J. De Backer and J. Sutton (eds), *The Music in Music Therapy. Psychodynamic Music Therapy in Europe*, pp. 24–36. Jessica Kingsley Publishers: London.

Gold, C. (2003). Music Therapy in Austria. *Voices Resources*. Retrieved January 10, 2015, from http://testvoices.uib.no/community/?q=country-of-the-month/2003-music-therapy-austria.

Karkou, V., Martinsone, K., Nazarova, N., and Vaverniece, I. (2011). Art therapy in the post-modern world: Findings from a comparative study across the UK, Russia and Latvia. *The Arts in Psychotherapy* 38(2): 86–95.

Lagzdina, V. (2009). Music Therapy—One of the Newest Professions in Latvia. *Voices: A World Forum for Music Therapy*. Retrieved June 11, 2013, from: <http://testvoices.uib.no/?q=country/monthlatvia_january2009>.

Mössler, K. (2008). Update on Music Therapy in Austria. *Voices Resources*. Retrieved January 11, 2015, from http://testvoices.uib.no/community/?q=country-of-the-month/2008-update-music-therapy-austria.

Wosch, T. (2003). Music Therapy in Germany. *Voices Resources*. Retrieved March 17, 2014, from: <http://testvoices.uib.no/community/?q=country/monthgermany_march2003>.

··

CHAPTER 50

SELF-CARE IN MUSIC THERAPY
The Art of Balancing

··

GRO TRONDALEN

INTRODUCTION

··

THIS chapter addresses self-care for qualified music therapists. The key to self-care is nurturing oneself, giving love, caring, compassion, recognition, support, and openness. It means *giving* to yourself and also *receiving* caring and support from others, not least through the means of music. This is a chapter reflecting on a variety of issues that may afford and affect ways of taking care of oneself with the aim of raising the music therapist's awareness and reflection of how to take care and develop in her[1] daily work and/or in periods of time out, or sabbaticals.

Such a reflexive focus keeps the music therapist in mind but other helping professionals might also be inspired by the content which might also offer them ideas for self-care to prevent *burnout, compassion fatigue*, or *compassion stress*. Approaching self-care for music therapists has to be *context sensitive* in regards to both personal dispositions and the professional setting. Talking about self-care for music therapists; biology (i.e. physical aspects), psychological issues (mental state, existential being), and context (work setting and home/social context) are to be connected and taken into consideration.

Firstly, the text outlines a theoretical matrix. Then a paragraph on needs and resources linked to *wear and tear* for the music therapist follows. Thereafter, a section focusing *self-care* related to the music therapist's different contexts and roles: music therapist, musician, teacher, and researcher. Self-experience and supervision are also evident within a chapter on self-care for music therapists. The text closes with a discussion along with some closing comments.

A THEORETICAL MATRIX

··

Music therapists have the most interesting, wonderful, and demanding profession. The therapist meets and works together with a variety of people: all through the means of music.

However, such a relational profession comes with a price: the music therapist is using her own self to communicate, observe, and support a healing process in the music therapy process. Offering oneself in such a process and journey requires many skills, not least, an awareness in the present moment and consecutively the ability to offer *good enough* input at the right moment. This calls for an intuitive approach in the here and now and at the same time a reflective mind that is able to sort out and think about "what's really going on here?"

Such a position requires an integration of different roles, such as connecting the musician, the intuitive and reflective therapist, and often in addition, the skills to perform research about clinical practice. The music therapist is also a person with a private life, be it as a mother, partner, daughter, caretaker, etc. that influences her mental and physical status. Some music therapists have even more roles, as they are teachers at educational institutions, which might include supervision, teaching, and most often an obligation to conduct research and to publish. All of these roles influence and constitute the professional music therapist (Trondalen 2004a). It is no wonder that the music therapist's self-care is not always well managed, when being overwhelmed by never-ending demands.

From a methodological point of view, it is not an easy task to investigate self-care or personal well-being, as neither research methodology nor theoretical interpretations are neutral. There can be a body-mind split, connoting something that is divided. Another aspect is that the research methodology requires asking certain questions about, for example, hardiness, self-efficacy, and control which actually guides the subjects to see themselves within the frame of these restricted terms (Kvalem 2011). This eventually may affect the persons' perspective.

At the very core of this chapter is the notion of *self-care* which is directly linked to personal health and well-being. The theologian Sigurdson (2008) suggests that health arises from the relationship *between* our physical/mental condition and our sense of existential well-being. Health ought not to be understood as a category but as a continuum, wherein bodily functioning profoundly influences our mental state of being and vice versa, not least when stress and illness take over. Besides, the existential aspect of health is linked to human existence, including its cultural, political, reflective, religious and social dimensions. Therefore, health is seen as a positive relation between the dimensions of physical/mental and existential well-being, which may be understood as a way of finding meaning and fulfilment by *being-in-the-world*.

The reflections above also elucidate the concept of health, as opposed to *ill health* (Boyd 2000, p. 9), in an interesting way. A music therapist may have many constraints linked to stress or a long-term physical disease and/or a personal experience of illness, and still experience *good health*. An additional way of approaching health is to state health as an experience (Ruud 2008). Such a view includes health as both a *resource* and an act of *participation*, of which is affected by life itself throughout a life span, and is consequently in constant change. Furthermore, Schei, with reference to the philosopher van Hooft, points out that human beings must process their circumstances and experiences by applying their self-awareness within a narrative structure (van Hooft in Schei 2009). We have a fundamental need to create a sense of coherence in life via a higher philosophy of existence and accordingly, the lack or loss of health can be experienced as a threat to our existential being. Approaching health in such a broad way provides a context within which our cultures are conditioned by history and given meaning through discourse (Schei 2009; Zosso 2010; Trondalen 2013).

NEEDS AND RESOURCES

The qualified music therapist is included in the large group of helping professions who are burdened with some *costs* of caring. Caring for others as music therapists or as music therapy faculty involves putting our own needs aside and relating to the life world of the client. It could require us to tune in to his life in general, or one traumatic event, or to listen to and support his struggle with a chronic illness. We must be patient and sensitive while at the same time managing demanding psychological and educational material.

Mental health is a balancing act that may be affected by different factors such as genes, traumas, by private pressures and by the stress of working. Encountering stress experiences day after day may lead to frustration, emotional exhaustion, depersonalization, or burn-out. Compassion fatigue and compassion stress exist, and contribute to the realization that perfection does not exist (Figley 2002; Richardson-Delgado 2006; Montello 2000; Gerbert 2010). Such *wear and tear* on music therapists is called a number of names such as stress, burnout, post traumatic stress disorder (PTSD), and secondary traumatic stress reaction (STDS). These terms are sometimes used interchangeably with compassion fatigue (Figley 2002) and chronic fatigue syndrome. These phenomena are linked to physical, emotional, and mental exhaustion (see Figure 50.1).

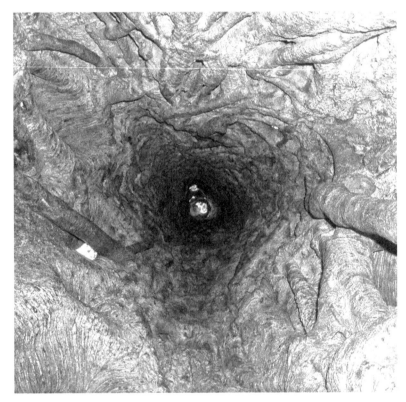

FIGURE 50.1 Empty inner space. (Inside a tree in the rainforest, stranglehold by lianas.)

Burnout is defined as an "acute disorder or reaction characterized by exhaustion resulting from overwork, with anxiety, fatigue, insomnia, depression, and impairment in work performance" (Colman 2003, p. 105). *Burnout* is not a recognized disorder in the DSM-V although it is accepted in the ICD-10 as a "State of vital exhaustion" (Z73.0) and can be found under "Problems related to life-management difficulty" (Z73). Significant reductions in non-verbal memory and auditory and visual attention have been found for people suffering from burnout (Sandström et al. 2005). Symptoms include negative emotions where the person appears to be angry, frustrated, stuck, or bored (Brooks 2013).

Post traumatic stress disorder (PTSD) is recognized in both DSM-V and ICD-10. It is a severe anxiety disorder that can develop after exposure to any event resulting in psychological trauma. Very often the traumatic event is repeatedly experienced in the here and now. PTSD is less frequent and more enduring than the more commonly seen post traumatic stress (also known as acute stress response).[2] Formal diagnostic criteria, both (DSM-V, 2013), and (ICD-10, 2010) require that the symptoms for PTSD last more than one month and cause significant impairment in social, occupational, or other important areas of functioning. Secondary traumatic stress reaction (STSD) is linked to knowing about a traumatic event experienced by a significant other, and the stress stemming from helping, or wanting to help this person. STSD, a function of bearing witness to the suffering of others, has been termed "compassion fatigue" (Figley 2002). In contrast to burnout, compassion fatigue "is associated with a sense of helplessness and confusion [...] and is highly treatable once workers recognize it and act accordingly" (p. 1436). Chronic fatigue syndrome (CFS) also called ME, is sometimes mentioned as a controversial disorder characterized by persistent or recurrent fatigue, and must occur for at least six months after (and not before) the onset of the disorder. CFS might be followed by or perhaps caused by a viral infection (Colman 2003). Music therapists must watch out for signs and symptoms of exhaustion, and to find ways to manage and seek support when they are experiencing difficulties.

A survey of burnout and multidisciplinary team-working amongst professional music therapists in the UK (n = 151), found that members of multidisciplinary teams had higher levels of personal accomplishment, but they were found to have similar levels of emotional exhaustion and depersonalization as compared to those working independently (Hills et al. 2000). A study examining the possible relationship between personality, burnout level, longevity, and demography variables among professional music therapists based in the US (n = 137) was carried out through questionnaires and tests (Vega 2010). Results showed that the personality traits most descriptive of the music therapist were "emotional sensitivity, reasoning, apprehension, warmth, openness to change, self-reliance, extraversion, anxiety, abstractness, rule-consciousness, and self control" (p. 173). It is interesting to notice that only anxiety and sensitivity were both predictive of burnout and these were highly characteristic of the music therapists participating in the study. In addition, the probability score (i.e. logistic regression) showed that highest degree earned is significantly (p>.000) predictive of longevity.

A study of German female qualified music therapists and burnout indicated certain risk factors related to the music therapy profession (Glomb 2007). Amongst these job specific strains are; challenges in regulating closeness/distance while working musically with the client, participating in teams with others who are not recognizing and not familiar to the field of music therapy, poor institutional working conditions, lack of professional recognition/

authorization at a national level (i.e. influencing economic factors and the conditions of employment), in addition to uncertain professional identity as a music therapist. However, the latter aspect was also reported in the opposite way; a typical resource was the strong identification end emotional bonding the music therapist had to her profession. Other resources were linked to the experience of success in the treatment of the client and the joy and fulfilment of dealing with the music itself. The study also suggests some aspect to prevent burnout and increase job satisfaction. Amongst these are, the importance of choosing the profession deliberately, choosing working places suitable to personal disposition and strengths, reasonable working conditions, engagement in team working, performing further education, self-experience and supervision (p. 369).

Figley (2002) demonstrated that psychotherapists who work with people who have chronic illness tend to disregard their own needs when focusing on the need of their clients.[3] Figley has proposed an ecological model to manage, treat, prevent and mitigate compassion fatigue in the therapist. The model advises: (a) a comprehensive review of compassion fatigue for educational purposes, (b) to desensitize the therapist to traumatic stressors, (c) searching for a right dosage of exposure, and (d) assessing and enhancing social support.

In her PhD study exploring burnout and renewal amongst music therapy faculty Richardson-Delgado (2006) found that music therapy faculty experienced significantly less burnout than the normative sample as measured by the Maslach Burnout Inventory (MBI). Her findings showed that music therapy faculty use music as a way to combat stress and help with the renewal process (see Figure 50.2).

FIGURE 50.2 Bridging.

SELF-CARE

....

Self-care is obviously an important issue to be addressed for music therapists. Compassion stress is part of the normal process of working with humans who have additional needs (Hanser and Mandel 2010). There are many offers of dealing with self-care and self-development difficulties. Some advice provides easy going *quick fix* solutions through, for example, online social networking services and micro blogging, while other recommendations are based on clinical expertise and empirical research (for the latter, see, for example, Brooks 2013; Clark and Waldman 2013; Hanser and Mandel 2010). However, music therapists are such a diverse group in which interests, personality and contexts differ from person to person. What might be optimal self-care for one person does not necessarily constitute self-care for another. The music therapist may, as previously mentioned, have different roles such as clinician, musician, researcher, partner, supervisor, mentor, or teacher. Accordingly, self-care has to be linked to the individual's context.

As a music therapist

The music therapist has undergone a specialized training and has a specific responsibility as a therapist in a music therapy session. However, she is not alone in such a relationship. On the contrary, this author's basic assumption is that the relating experience itself is the driving force of human development and growth. Such a theoretical philosophy is fundamentally dyadic recognising communication as a relational process (Stern 1985/2000; Trondalen 2004b; Stensæth and Trondalen 2012).

"Being a music therapist takes heart, passion, compassion and commitment to follow it through" (Richardson-Delgado 2006, p. 89). It is not uncommon to hear from music therapists: "I am so tired of clients. I feel I am completely drained after the sessions." On the one hand, it is mentally demanding and time consuming to do music therapy sessions. On the other hand, the author might wonder if the music therapist herself sometimes misses the potential nurturing of *being present* with another person in the session. Allowing for joint *nurturing* in a music therapy session is focusing on the affordances of the *relating experience through music* itself. Music as a relating experience to oneself and another can be understood as a way of "being-in-the-world," where playing serves as a promotion of well-being and performing of personal identity. From a philosophical point of view, the human being is understood as *homo communicans*, with an inherent humanity able to share experiences and actions. Such an exchange allows for recognition and partaking in one another's life at an existential level. Accordingly, a humanistic-existential perspective may be interpreted as self-care also in the music therapy session per se, both for the client and the therapist (Trondalen 2008, 2004b).

The relationship between the client and the therapist is of vital importance. I. Yalom has suggested the term *Fellow Travelers* (2001/2002) as a description of a joint, but not identical, relationship. From a philosophical point of view, this indicates a subject-subject position, as opposed to the client being an *object* that is treated in therapy. Being a fellow traveller does not however, allow the music therapist to disclaim responsibility for understanding and monitoring the therapeutic process. It does, however, abolish the "distinctions between *them* (the afflicted) and *us* (the healers): 'we are all in this together'" (p. 8). From this follows an attention towards what emerges *between* the equal human beings, as the relationship is seen as the basis of development and growth (Trondalen 2011a; Johns 1993). Accordingly, a relating experience through music presents itself both as a process of dialoguing (frame and medium) and an agent (non-referral); ultimately promoting health and well-being.

An intersubjective perspective offers an interesting way of being with one another in the therapy space. In a musical improvisation, for example, object and subject positions are constantly changing and being negotiated (Ruud 1998). Listening to each other, joining in with similar, however not identical chords and rhythms, requires a position where listening, following and contributing are taken. In clinical practice, the music therapist's choices of methodology and procedures in the session is informed by the immediate affectively attuned awareness, with its inherent tacit knowledge (empathy, professional skills, experience, and intuition), which is perceived and performed in the here-and-now (Trondalen and Skårderud 2007). Such a therapeutic attitude is rooted in intuition, and it can be understood as a lived performance of an immediate and creative mobilization of the total and unified experience the music therapist possesses (Trondalen 2013). Playing together, creating songs, singing and talking together, all constitutes the power of the present moment, and may actually constitute self-care for the music therapist herself.

While engaging with each other at a genuine level, the therapist may realize she is being vitalized in the relationship as well. An experienced therapist once told me her *secret* of working a lifetime in music therapy:

> I'm not rushing through the day in spite of the daily pressured time schedule. I am trying to be *really present* in every meeting with the client. If I should rush from one to another, I would never experience and gain the profit of being a fellow traveller. I don't want to miss the opportunity to be surprised by the client. Surprised by *how* he is managing his life through sickness and constrain. *Presence* in the moment, allows for wonderful ways of being enlightened, touched, encouraged, and nurtured, and following, the relating experience becomes a source of inspiration and self-care also for me as a music therapist.

Being present in the relating experience through music, simultaneously includes an exchange of musical ideas and gestures, for example the beat, the key, and dynamic expression, and an awareness of how it *feels* to be with the other person at an existential level. It is also important to recognize *how* the musical interaction moves along, rather than only the themes/phrases in the music or the musical actions as such. From a philosophical point of view, such a sharing of a joint experience allows the therapist to feel recognized within the musical relationship, even if the client does not have musical training.

As a musician

Music and musicianship is essential to a music therapist.[4] As such, music is not only essential to the music therapy profession but is at the music therapist's very core: "Music isn't something that I do; it's something that I am." (Richardson-Delgado 2006, p. 84). When this is the case, it might be terrifying when the joy of music making or listening to the music is decreasing due to feeling emotionally and mentally drained.

Research evidence and publications referring to music therapy with music therapists to approach burnout are of limited quantity. One of the reasons is that music therapists are included in general research studies investigating music treatment in relation to their *medical* condition, for example, *Music for stress and anxiety reduction in coronary heart disease patients* (Bradt and Dileo 2009). Treatment of music therapists is often a *hidden* practice, as they are included in bigger studies of health professionals, and therefore do not report themselves as receiving treatment adapted for their special needs, such as burnout. Often music therapists do not want anyone to know they are having problems, and are reluctant to participate in research which might lead to possible identification. The author assumes this is due to the fact that recognition may not only influence the music therapist at a personal level, but also have an effect on a professional career as a performing musician/music therapist.

The flutist J. Buller (2002) described what it is like to be an injured musician: "It's painful; it's as if my familiar self and world has died" (p. 22). When the music therapist or a musician tends to lose her connections to familiar events and experiences in her life, illness and trauma basically pose a threat to her existential being. It is, however, the author's basic assumption that it *is* worthwhile to promote positive musical experiences to support positive emotions and an improved quality of life, which in turn can also influence medical conditions like exhaustion and burnout.

C. McKinney et al. (1997) studied the effect of *receptive music therapy*, i.e. Guided Imagery and Music (GIM) on mood and cortisol in healthy adults. Such changes in hormonal regulation may have health implications for chronic stress, from which musicians and music therapists can suffer a great deal. The Australian music therapist R. Martin (2007) studied the effect of a series Guided Music Imagery (GMI) sessions on music performance anxiety (MPA). The results showed a trend towards reduction in MPA and indicated that GMI may be useful in reducing MPA. A qualitative study explored short term GIM with ten European musicians. The study points out that the musicians used the music as "nurturing" in a way that supported personal strength and promoted well-being (Trondalen 2015). While a case study with a male *musician/music therapist* shows how GIM can promote a "hero's journey" and affect personal life and work performance (Trondalen 2010).

Also *expressive* approaches to burnout and traumatic stress in music therapists are of vital importance. Examples from case studies with musicians provide useful insight to music therapists challenging emotional and physical draining. A case study of a female jazz pianist plagued with a false-self personality constellation and symptoms of post traumatic stress disorder shows how she was able to use instrumental and vocal improvisation to deal with her struggles and discover her purpose in life (Montello 2003). Other case studies confirm positive development, while providing useful ideas and theoretical interpretations of music therapy with musicians, be it in private or institutional settings (Timmermann 1983; Austin 2006; Decker-Vogt 2012). It is noteworthy to metioned improvisation in connection to burnout. Improvisation is both a method, a technique, and a creative resource in itself. The improvisation, per se, includes all kinds of expressions and serves as a source of creativity and communication at all levels (Alterhaug 2004).

In spite of documented health challenges at a physical and mental level, music therapists go on playing. This may be because the problem is also the solution. Though music performance makes many demands and takes its toll, as the title "Mich macht krank, was ich liebe" [What I love makes me ill] (Decker-Vogt 2012) indicates, musicians/music therapists benefit from music as a means of self-care, when using *music* to regulate emotions and develop new strength. Another aspect is related to the music therapist's theoretical orientation, which may change over time. Such a point is made by the music therapist Igary (2004) as he tells his story of how his professional and personal identity was reconstructed and renewed, through the encoutner with new theories in music therapy.

It may be that music therapists are especially suited to understand challenges that music therapist and musicians face, as the music therapist can recall her own musical—and music therapy—training with the pressure to excel in the different settings. These experiences are vitally important to empathically understand and offer a unique form of treatment for the music therapist which can be based on interviews and actual playing as therapy (Quentzel and Loewy 2012a,b).

As a teacher and researcher

Many music therapists who are working as teachers and researchers at universities and colleges are heavily burdened with committees, staff and student meetings, research budgets, student's issues, and work overload. Some also do clinical work in an official institution or in a private clinic in addition to their academic obligations. Encountering pressure day after day, may lead to frustration, emotional exhaustion, depersonalization, burnout, compassion fatigue or compassion stress. Nevertheless, J.M. Richardson-Delgado (2006), indicated that music therapy faculty experienced significantly less burnout than the normative sample on the Maslach Burnout Inventory, MBI, and that music therapy faculty possess resources that other professionals might not, such as the ability to find rejuvenation through music.

Another positive factor found was that music therapy faculty had specific professional training that helped them combat stress and burnout, as the music therapy curriculum contains a great deal of training in stress management. Music therapy faculty with higher educational status had lower burnout ratings and emotional exhaustion (2006). This may be due to the fact that researchers find performing research as life fulfilling, interesting and even fun. Doing research allows for an in depth investigation of clinical, theoretical, and philosophical levels of music therapy, of which in turn can lead to an depth knowledge promoting personal, clinical, and scientific integration (Trondalen 2004a). Additionally, many researchers have a stronger passion for working scientifically than doing clinical work.

However, the findings that higher educational status results in lower burnout ratings and emotional exhaustion are contradictory to what other researchers have suggested. Individuals with higher educational levels may be more prone to burnout because they may have higher career expectations and may be disappointed when those expectations are not met (Malach-Pines and Yaife-Yanai 2001).

All music therapy faculty members, who were interviewed, reported that they listened to music to help with stress reduction (Richardson-Delgado 2006). Faculty also mentioned that they composed music, played music with fellow musicians, and in their own homes, or performed music in order to relieve stress. One interviewee said: "I think that we forget as music therapists to take care of our own music and take of ourselves through music ... you know, it's the whole reason we got into this thing in the first place." (p. 84). Music was not only essential to their profession but also to their personal core. Universities should provide retreats and stress management training for their faculty that incorporates music. Hiring a music therapist to conduct those retreats will help the faculty understand how to use music for renewal (p. 98). It seems as if educational institutions may overlook the power of music to decrease levels of burnout.

One way of promoting personal self-care can be to make a private collection of music; a *medicine chest* of music for different purposes. This may include personal improvisational recording and performances by others. Also during long-term research processes, it can be useful to use music to contain the different stages within the process. The music approach can be composing, playing, or listening aiming at keeping focused or acquiring new creative ideas, while still nurturing oneself through music.

A study of elementary school teachers, performed by Cheek et al. (2003) indicated that there is an increased tendency to burnout among music educators and this is influenced by environmental and demographic variables. Music therapy techniques (i.e. re-creational) seem to provide useful intervention for music teachers' burnout—and it is possible this could be beneficial for music therapy faculty. The researchers found that experimental group subjects who received instruction regarding the use of music listing for stress reduction, and were required to select and listen to music recordings that were *meaningful* to them, reported significant lower levels of burnout symptoms than control group subjects (2003). This is similar to the findings from Batt-Rawden's PhD study *Music and Health Promotion: The role and significance of music and musicking in everyday life for the long-term ill* (2007) (see Figure 50.3).

Self-experience

The artist Elisabeth Bjørnsen Werp has an artwork named "Persona." It is made with tempera[5] on wood. Firstly, she paints the motif on the canvas. Thereafter, she hides the motif with different layers of tempera, ashes, soil, and iron. The next step in the creative process is to scrape off layers by layers in a way that enlighten the motif itself. In the end, it seems as if only the essential qualities of what was originally painted are visible for the observer.

Transferring this concept to music therapy and the process of self-care, one might think of the process of self-care as similar to the phase of uncovering done by the artist. The subject of investigation, the music therapist, unveils different layers in her personal history and explores phenomena in her own psych and personal life story, for example together with a GIM therapist (see, for example, Trondalen 2010, 2004a, 2009/2010). To be able to work as a music therapist, as a lifelong love story, self exploration and supervision is of vital importance. As therapists, a personal competency linking personality, temper, and existential orientation is needed.

Such an exploration of a personal narrative involves among others, life stories linked to close family, relations, group belonging, values, and ideological thinking. From a self-care point of view, this author suggests to focus an "I-narrative," more closely a "progressive narrative." Such a progressive narrative, aims exploring challenges and possibilities (Engedal 2003) striving at joining different parts of a "multi-narrative" of which a life consists. In short, an investigation of the emerging person, rooted in her own experiences and present elucidation. This part is linked to how she reconciles herself to her private soulscape, her personal development, and how this affects her in the present *meeting* with the client.[6] A present awareness includes both an encounter with herself and her history, *and* with the client in

FIGURE 50.3 Sources from my inner self.

music therapy. Accordingly, self development and self-care are evident to grow and develop as a music therapist.

There are different ways of performing self-care within the frame of self-experience through music. One expressive way can be playing out a *Musical Life Panorama* (MLP) (Frohne-Hagemann 1998, p. 104):

> The MLP works with the emotional meaning of experiences, events, and memories that are connected with music in one's biography and it can be used in a verbal form (talking about music) and in an active form (conducting improvisation).

The self-experience may be individually performed, in a dyad, or shared in a group. A musical biography can identify significant moments in a music therapist's life story where music played a significant role and elucidate personal pro and cons of musical preferences and styles and serve as a *musical memory album*. Another idea is to work out a musical *coat of arms*: a symbol unique to the individual music therapist, and to her family, her profession, essential characteristics in her music therapy approach etc. Such a musical artifact can serve as a concrete way of performing identity (profession, heritage) and support identity as a music therapy (Trondalen 2004a).

At a meta-theoretical level, these tasks serve as a reinforcement of the musician's personal sense of well-being and existential coherence as they connect personal, transpersonal, and social spaces (Ruud 1997; Antonovsky 1987). These spaces arise from and support one's personal and professional *identity* as a music therapist.

SUPERVISION

Supervision through music therapy is an important part of the self-care process. A variety of music therapy methods can be introduced in the supervision setting, and played out and explored verbally afterwards together with an experienced supervisor. These methods can be receptive music therapy, improvisational music therapy (instruments and/or voice), re-creative music therapy (singing and playing), or compositional music therapy. Some music therapists want to do a special type of music therapy, namely the individual *Bonny Method of Guided Imagery and Music, GIM* (Bonny 1999/2000) for supervision purposes, as the model offers a multilayered modality for investigating professional issues. A time-limited approach to supervision can be useful, investigating a limited area of topics (see, for example, Trondalen 2009/2010). A verbal dialogue with her fellow traveler, who has had a similar, albeit not identical experience, enables the music therapist supervisee to explore the lived experience within a relational context, affording support to her link between inner and outer life.

Through GIM the supervisee often discovers themes affecting her job performance, as was the case with Susan (female, music therapist, 37 years old). Susan was listening to the GIM program *Relationship*:[7]

> The music—lots of strength in it—the deep music—[allow yourself to recognize that strength]—my strength hasn't acquired the place it should have—it's so sad—[allow yourself to give the strength enough space in the music]—it is about daring to believe in the strength in the basso—[stay with the music]—I am a part of something bigger than myself—it's the music ... old man with authority—I wonder what he has to say?—[would you like to move closer to him?]—he's sitting down; a wise man in front of me—[does he have something to say to you?]—Something about "daring to stand up and believe in myself"—[can you treasure that message?]—ambivalence—but yes.

Susan termed the drawing ("mandala") that she made after the music journey "Transformation." It was hard for Susan to believe she was good enough in her daily music therapy job. She struggled. Susan came into contact with different categories of experiences in GIM (Grocke 1999, p. 15). She connected to the deep tones in the music, relating to her inner strength, while exploring her personal ambivalence of believing in herself. This is similar to suggestions from Pines and Aronson (1988) saying that debilitating feelings of helplessness begin to decrease when an individual begins to take responsibility for effecting a change in a difficult situation.

The verbal conversation focused on Susan's inner self as a house, with people coming and going into most of her inner rooms. She found it hard to reserve a place for herself within her personal *soulscape*. Due to the ambiguity of the music, the client was able to appropriate the music in her own way. Through a restored sense of her emotional self, Susan seemed to experience that relational experiences in GIM offered an exploration of new and beneficial ways of relating. This in turn was transferred (as an analogy) to her daily life. Through music listening, verbal processing, and drawing Susan gained personal strength and increased self-efficacy, which supported her professional and personal development in the form of a renewed identity as a professional music therapist.

The GIM process seemed to support Susan by fostering her creative health resources through musical and verbal dialogue. Such an approach downplays pathological aspects of a person's life (cf. burnout) in favor of healthy dimensions, in order to allow for self-actualization and search for meaning within a relational context.[8] Expressed differently, Susan seemed to recognize herself, including both her vulnerability and strength as a performing music therapist in her professional setting. Such recognition at an existential level promotes autonomy and relation, hence assisting different dimensions of health (Schibby 1993; Sigurdson 2008).

Music therapists can also join a *music therapy group* for supervision and self-experience. This process can strengthen personal identity (self in relation to others) as well as deepen the group process. Songs, for example, can be used to unite and bring people together, integrating groups through a variety of themes and issues. The lyrics and thoughts expressed therein can inspire both the individual and the group of music therapists (Loewy 2002). There are many ways of preventing illness and promoting well-being for music therapists as caregivers, ranging from attending music therapy oneself to participating in music activities for joy and recreation. The project *Caring for the Caregiver* training as part of the New York City Music Therapy Relief Project offers useful ideas on how to take care of oneself as a caregiver (Loewy and Hara 2007).[9]

Richardson-Delgade (2006) found that several music therapy faculty interviewees noted the role of supervision, in terms of mentoring programs in helping faculty to cope with these stress factors. Especially one faculty member described the mentoring program for new faculty provided at his/her campus (p. 98):

> As second year faculty members, we, all of us, were given the opportunity to hook up with a seasoned veteran, and meet with that person however often we wanted to throughout the year. I have continued that relationship with the mentor that I had last year. [The mentor is a] wonderful person. And that helps.

It is also important that employers can offer a range of different programs and initiatives to promote health and well-being to the faculty staff. Examples are flexible working arrangements in the form of part-time, casual, and telecommuting work.

Some music therapists seek *pastoral counseling* also through music, as they are longing for greater insight as a need in their daily life, or as caregivers working, for example, within a palliative end-of-life setting. In Richardson-Delgade's study (2006), many faculty members also mentioned meditation or prayer as part of their daily activities. One faculty member

FIGURE 50.4 A work-life balance. Rauland, Norway.

said (p. 86): "I also pray. I mean its [*sic.*] part of my religious belief and so, when I'm feeling stressed and like I can't handle things I pray about it." Hence, music therapists are working towards integration of physical, mental, and existential dimensions of life as a necessary way of self-care, to be able to support others during their life journeys (see Figure 50.4).

Discussion

The art of balancing

Work-life balance is a concept including proper prioritizing between "work" (career and ambition) and "lifestyle" (health, pleasure, leisure, family, and spiritual development/media-tion).[10] An imbalance may lead to an empty inside and the feeling of burnout (see Figure 50.1). A work-life balance has to be appraised and updated every day as there are huge negative consequences of an imbalance.

Many music therapists have a multifaceted working career as clinicians, teachers, researchers, supervisors, and mentors. For a music therapist it is important to choose jobs due to disposition, genes, strength, and personal drives. An informative job description may prevent confusion and different expectations both for the employers and the employee. Some jobs offer teamwork opportunities. This is useful, especially if the team is support-ive and recognizes music therapy as a useful treatment. High (enough) degree of education, courses for further education, mentor program, supervision, and supportive employer can be experienced as self-care, promoting personal accomplishment and preventing exhaus-tion. Institutions that train musicians and music therapists should offer health promotion and wellness courses to the students and the professionals (Ginsborg et al. 2009; Manchester 2007). These actions may strengthen a professional identity and combat stress reactions.

Significant others like familial sources of support, empowering peers and friends play an indispensible role in every person's life. The music therapist herself needs to be aware of how her personal history and drives influence in the present meeting with a student or a client, and allow for development and growth at a personal level; empowering the inner soulscape. Music therapy together with an experienced supervisor/music therapist is a valuable way of approaching self experience: personal inspection, recollection, and retention.

Similar to her instrument, the music therapist's body needs to be *tuned*. This implies a necessary variation between working (doing) and resting (being), good nutrition, getting enough sleep, a healthy lifestyle, and maintaining a good physical condition (Spahn 2009) with a special focus on breathing exercises, as *breathing* is connected to life itself. Promoting cultivation of both inner muscles for stabilization and outer layers for moving the limbs are also important, as good coordination will help body stability and balance while fending off for example shoulders and neck strains for a music therapist (Sparre 2009; Fadnes and Leira 2006). Today, brain research and neuroscience continues to expose the connections between inner muscles, basic physiological processes, and mental function, particularly in the context of slow movement, which also seems to promote an increased intake of oxygen.[11] In particular, the limbic system and thalamus—"the brain's neurophysiological Me"—provide a "link between the cortex and the brain stem, which might have a central role in connecting emotional tonus and mood" (Myskja and Lindbæk 2000, p. 1184). It thus appears that the cognitive neuron networks are very important to the adequate regulation of our emotions (Blood 1999; Plessen and Kabricheva 2010). When a music therapist displays mental and physical symptoms of exhaustion and burnout: the body is talking.

A wellness approach: Music as self-care

There are many ways of approaching healing forces in a day-to-day activity such as: walking, running, breathing, singing and chanting, songwriting, playing and improvising on instrument are some. For ideas, procedures and techniques to use music as self-care (see, for example, Brooks 2013; Clark and Waldman 2013; Hanser and Mandel 2010; Mandel 1996; Trondalen 2013).

Supporting creative health resources in an aesthetic practice as music therapy in modern society can be linked to "an assemblage of activities designed to promote health and prevent sickness" (Aldridge 2004, p. 37), rather than a focus on personal health management in response to sickness. Health becomes a creative performance linked to personal values and cultural norms. Accordingly, health is understood through *experience* rather than the objective measurement of bodily functions.

This implies that the music therapist downplays pathological aspects in favor of healthy dimensions, in order to allow for self-care, self-actualization and the search for meaning. Such a humanistic perspective on focusing resources still takes the music therapist's illness (bio-medical perspective) into consideration however, in a *dialogical* way by focusing positive creative resources to cope with a variety of constraints such as burn out, exhaustion, PTSD, etc. Following, a growing interest in a departure from a key focus on diagnosis, in favor of a *wellness model* for illness prevention for musicians and music therapists. Such an interest focuses on resources and strengths, while emphasizing health promotion and preventive actions (Cockey 2000; Rolvsjord 2010; Spahn 2009; Ruud 2008).

However, it must not be said music therapists should avoid, or not take psychological or medical treatments into consideration when struggling with burnout and exhaustion. It is however, interesting to look closer to the language being used. An example is for example if "performance anxiety" is termed "occupational stresses or pathology" (Martin 2007, p. 31). Health, including physical, mental, and existential dimensions can be understood as a *resource* everybody has, and manage in different ways within a variety of contexts (Trondalen 2013).

Maranto (1992) suggests a rationale for *the uses of music* to treat, for example performance anxiety in musicians. This author would like to suggest a similar treatment to a music therapist who is struggling with burnout and related issues. This is due to the fact that music is safe, non-invasive, accessible, stigma-free treatment for stress and performance anxiety in musicians, and it is an approach that may positively contribute to their lifestyles (p. 280). C. Maranto also draws attention to the musician's belief system, as she points out that musician, and in my view not least music therapist, are aware of the music's influence on them personally and on their lives (p. 279). Music may support the music therapist's inner life, and strengthen personal development in a way that promotes self-care for the music therapist.

Summing up

This chapter has focused self-care for qualified music therapists, reflecting on a variety of issues that may afford and affect ways of taking care of oneself. It aims at raising the music therapist's awareness and reflection focusing her different roles as music therapist, musician, teacher, and researcher in a mixture of contexts. She is presented with tools of self-care like self-experiences and supervision. A key focus has been on *music* as source of inspiration in a variety of settings. The author would like to support for the music therapist to walk, dance, paint, sing, play, express, give thanks, feel, laugh, walk, pray, meditate, listen, imagine, and enjoy—to nurture herself to be able to nurture others—and not least as a necessary and wonderful part of *Life* itself.

Epilogue

I have been walking in my life's landscape as a music therapist, a clinician, a researcher, a teacher, a mother, a wife, a grandmother, a supervisor, and a colleague. All the time I have used music in self-experience and supervision, and in my private space.

I have been privileged as a *fellow traveler* to many music therapists, clients, students, teachers, supervisors, colleagues, and researchers. We have been sharing dreams and values and the power of music.

I am always reminded of this: All human being are always more—*semper major*—always more than personal narratives and observation. What we perform in life, be it musically, biologically, socially, or spiritually, does not disclose the depths in our existence.

Notes

1. In this text the music therapist is termed "she," and the student/client "he."
2. For a review of the history, definition, and development of the classification of trauma and traumatic stress, see Loewy and Hara (2007).
3. For prevalence of STS and STDS in psychotherapists working with patients with chronic illnesses, see, for example, Figley (2002).
4. Useful information on research and ideas for music therapy with musicians, see Trondalen (2013).
5. Tempera is a permanent fast-drying painting medium consisting of colored pigment mixed with a water-soluble binder medium, usually pigments dispersed in an emulsion miscible with water, typically egg yolk (Oxford Dictionary).
6. This is not least important due to being able to recognize and handle phenomena that psychodynamic theory terms (counter) transference and projective identification.
7. The GIM program *Relationship -M* includes: Chopin *1st Piano Concerto (Romance)*, Rachmaninoff *2nd Symphony (Adagio)*, Resphigi *Fountains of Rome (Valle Guilia and Villa Medici)*. See Bonny (1978) and Bruscia and Grocke (2002), Appendix B.
8. For an introduction to *Resource-oriented music therapy* see Rolvsjord, R. (2010).
9. Also the text *Caring for Caregivers* can provide useful ideas for support and self-caring actions (Daveson 2013).
10. <http://en.wikipedia.org/wiki/Work%E2%80%93life_balance>.
11. This may be one of the reasons why many music therapists make use of mindfulness techniques, slow movement techniques/methods such as Alexander, Pilates, Feldenkreis, Taji, Qigong, and so on.

References

Aldridge, D. (2004). *Health, the Individual, and Integrated Medicine. Revisiting an Aesthetic of Health Care*. London: Jessica Kingsley Publishers.

Alterhaug, B. (2004). Improvisation on a triple theme: Creativity, Jazz Improvisation and Communication. *Studia Musicologica Norvegica* 30: 97–118.

Antonovsky, A. (1987). *Unraveling the Mystery of Health. How People Manage Stress and Stay Well*. San Franscisco: Jossey-Bass Publishers.

Austin, D. (2006). Songs of Self: Vocal Psychotherapy for Adults Traumatized as Children. In: L. Carey (ed.), pp. 133–151. *Expressive and Creative Arts Methods for Trauma Suvivors*. London: Jessica Kingsley.

Batt-Rawden, K.B. (2007). Music and Health Promotion: The role and significance of music and musicking in everyday life for the long-term ill. Unpublished PhD, University of Exeter.

Blood, E.J. (1999). Emotional Responses to Pleasant and Unpleasant Music Correlate with Activity in Paralimbic Brain Regions. *Nature Neuroscience* 2(4): 382–387.

Bonny, H.L. (1978). *The Role of Taped Music Programs in the GIM Process: Theory and product. GIM Monograph # 2*. Baltimore, Maryland: ICM Books.

Bonny, H.L. (1999/2000). Facilitating Guided Imagery and Music (GIM) sessions. In: L. Summer (ed.), *Music Consciousness, The Evolution of Guided Imagery and Music*, pp. 269–298. Gilsum, NH: Barcelona Publishers.

Boyd, K.E. (2000). Disease, illness, sickness, health, healing and wholeness: exploring some elusive concepts. *Medical Humanities* 26: 9–17.

Bradt, J. and Dileo, C. (2009). Music for stress and anxiety reduction in coronary heart disease patients. *Cochrane Database of Systematic Reviews*, April. 15(2): CD006577. doi: 10.1002/14651858.CD006577.pub2

Brooks, D.M. (2013). Professional Burnout. In: L. Eyre (ed.), *Guidelines for Music Therapy Practice in Mental Health of Adolescents and Adults*. Gilsum, NH: Barcelona.

Bruscia, K.E. and Grocke, D.E. (eds). (2002). *Guided Imagery and Music: The Bonny Method and Beyond*. Gilsum, NH: Barcelona Publishers.

Buller, J. (2002). What Is It Like to Be an Injured Musician? *Candian Music Educatior* 43: 20–23.

Cheek, J.R., Bradley, L.J., Parr, G., and Lan, W. (2003). Using Music Therapy Techniques to Treat Teacher Burn Out. *Journal of Mental Health Conseling* 25: 204–217.

Cockey, L. (2000). Annotated Bibliography on Musicians Wellness. *American Music Teacher* 49: 54–62.

Colman, A.M. (2003). *A Dictionary of Psychology*. New York/Oxford: Oxford University Press.

Daveson, B.A. (2013). Caring for Caregivers. In: J. Allan (ed.), *Guidelines for Music Therapy Practice in Adult Medical Care*. Gilsum, NH: Barcelona.

Decker-Vogt, H.-H. (2012). "Mich macht krank, was ich liebe." In: H.-H. Decker-Vogt (ed.), *Zwischen Tönen und Wörten. Ein Reader mit Aufsätzen, reden und Interviews*, pp. 67–112. Wiesbaden: Reichelt Verlag.

DSM-V (2013). *Diagnostic and Statistical Manual of Mental Disorders*. American Psychiatric Association.

Engedal, L.G. (2003). Mange fortellinger—et liv. Momenter til belysning av narrativ teori. *Tidsskrift for sjelesorg* 23: 165–179.

Fadnes, B. and Leira, K. (2006). *Balansekoden—om samspillet mellom kroppslig og mental balance*. Oslo: Universitetsforlaget.

Figley, C.R. (2002). Compassion Fatigue: Psychotherapists' Chronic Lack of Self Care. *Psychotherapy in Practice* 58: 1433–1441.

Frohne-Hagemann, I. (1998). The "Musical Life Panorama." A facilitating method in the field of clinical and sociocultural music therapy. *Nordic Journal of Music Therapy* 7: 104–112.

Gerbert, F. (2010). Wenn Arbeit krank macht. Burn-out—das Leiden einer modernen Gesellschaft. Warum die Zahl der Ausgebrannten wächst. *Focus* 10: 92–103.

Ginsborg, J., Kreutz, G., Thomas, M., and Illiamon, A. (2009). Healthy Behaviors in Music and Non-music Performance Students. *Health Education* 109: 242–258.

Glomb, S. (2007). Berufsspezifische Belastungen und Burnout bei Musiktherapeutinnen. *Musiktherapeutische Umschau* 28: 365–369.

Grocke, D.E. (1999). A Phenomenological Study of Pivotal Moments in Guided Imagery and Music Therapy. PhD, Faculty of Music. University of Melbourne, Victoria, Australia.

Hanser, S.B. and Mandel, S.E. (2010). *Manage Your Stress and Pain Through Music*, Boston: Berklee Press.

Hills, B., Norman, I., and Forster, L. (2000). A Study of Burnout and Multidiciplinary Team-Working amongst Professional Music Therapists. *British Journal of Music Therapy* 14: 32–40.

ICD-10 (2010). International Statistical Classification of Diseases and Related Health Problems, 10th Revision.

Igary, Y. (2004). "Music Therapy is Changing" and So Am I: Reconstructing the Identity of A Music Therapist. *Voices: The World Forum for Music Therapy* 4.

Johns, U. (1993). Intersubjektivitet som grunnlag for utvikling. *Spesialpedagogikk* 3: 41–46.

Kvalem, I.L. (2011). *Health Psychology*. New York, University of Oslo: McGraw-Hill Education.

Loewy, J.V. (2002). Song sensation: How fragile we are. In J.V. Loewy and A.F., Hara (eds), *Caring for the Caregiver: The use of music and music therapy in grief and trauma*, pp. 33–42. Silver Spring: The American Music Therapy Association, Inc.

Loewy, J.V. and Hara, A.F. (eds). (2007). *Caring for the Caregiver: The Use of Music and Music Therapy in Grief and Trauma*, 2nd ed. Silver Spring: The American Music Therapy Association, Inc.

Malach-Pines, A. and Yaife-Yanai, O. (2001). Unconscious Determinants of Career Choice and Burnout: Theoretical model and counseling strategy. *Journal of Employment Counseling* 38: 170–184.

Manchester, R. (2007). Health Promotion Courses for Music Students. *Medical Problems of Performing Artists* March: 26–29.

Mandel, S.E. (1996). Music for Wellness: Music Therapy for Sress Management in Rehabilitation Program. *Music Therapy Perspectives* 14: 38–43.

Maranto, C.D. (1992). Music Therapy in the Treatment of Performance Anxiety in Musicians. In R. Spintge and R. Droh (eds). *MusicMedicine*, pp. 273–283. St Louis: MMB.

Martin, R. (2007). The Effect of a Series of Short GIM Sessions on Music Performance Anxiety. Master in Music Therapy, Music Therapy Department. Melbourne, University of Melbourne.

McKinney, C., Antoni, M.H., Kumar, M., Tims, F.C., et. al. (1997). Effects of Guided Imagery and Music (GIM) Therapy on Mood and Cortisol in Healthy Adults. *Health Psychology* 16: 390–400.

Montello, L. (2000). The Perils of Perfectionism. *International Muscian* XCIX(8): 14–15.

Montello, L. (2003). Protect This Child: Psychodynamic music therapy with a gifted musician. In: S. Hadley (ed.), *Psychodynamic Music Therapy: Case Studies*, pp. 299–318. Gilsum, NH: Barcelona Publishers.

Myskja, A. and Lindbæk, M. (2000). Hvordan virker musikk på menneskekroppen? *Tidsskrift for Norsk Lægeforening* 10: 1182–1185.

Oxford Dictionary. "Tempera." Downloaded 10 February 2013: <http://oxforddictionaries. com/definition/english/tempera?q=tempera>.

Pines, A. and Aronson, E. (1988). *Career burnout: Causes and cures*. New York: The Free Press.

Plessen, K.J. and Kabricheva, G. (2010). Hjernen og følelser—fra barn til voksen. *Tidsskrift for den norske legeforening* 130: 932–935.

Quentzel, S. and Loewy, J. (2012a). An Integrative Bio-Psycho-Musical Assessment Model for the Treatment of Musicians: Part I—A Continuum of Support. *Music and Medicine* 2: 117–120.

Quentzel, S. and Loewy, J. (2012b). An Integrative Bio-Psycho-Musical Assessment Model for the Treatment of Musicians: Part II—Intake and Assessment. *Music and Medicine* 2: 121–125.

Richardson-Delgado, J.M. (2006). Exploring Burnout and Renewal Among Music Therapy. PhD Thesis, Faculty of Psychology, Capella University.

Rolvsjord, R. (2010). *Resource Oriented Music Therapy in Mental Health Care*. Gilsum, NH: Barcelona publishers.

Ruud, E. (1997). Music and Identity. *Nordic Journal of Music Therapy* 6: 3–13.

Ruud, E. (1998). Improvisation as a liminal experience. In: E. Ruud (ed.), *Music Therapy: Improvisation, Communication and Culture*. Gilsum, NH: Barcelona Publishers.

Ruud, E. (2008). Et humanistisk perspektiv på musikkterapien. In: G. Trondalen and E. Ruud (eds), *Musikkterapi et fag i utvikling. Musikkterapifaget gjennom 30 år: en antologi*.

NMH-publikasjoner 2008:4, Skriftserie fra Senter for musikk og helse, Oslo: Norges musikkhøgskole.

Sandström, A., Rhodin, I.N., Lundberg, M., Olsson, T., and Nybergl, L. (2005). Impaired cognitive performance in patients with chronic burnout syndrome. *Biological Psychology* 69: 271–279.

Schei, E. (2009). Helsebegrepet—selvet og cellen. In: E, Ruud (ed.), *Musikk i psykisk helsearbeid for barn og unge*. NMH-publikasjoner 2009:5, Skriftserie fra Senter for musikk og helse, Oslo: Norges musikkhøgskole.

Schibby, A.L.L. (1993). The Role of "Recognition" in the Resolution of a specific Interpersonal Dilemme. *Journal of Phenomena Psychology* 24: 175–189.

Sigurdson, O. (2008). Vil du bli frisk? In: G. Bjursell and L.V. Westerhäll (eds), *Kulturen och hälsen. Essäer om sambandet mellan kulturens yttringar och hälsans tillstånd*, pp. 189–218. Stockholm: Santérus Förlag.

Spahn, C. (2009). Gesundheit für Musiker: Vermittlung von Gesundheitskompetenzen im Musikstudium (Health for Musicians: Imparting Health Competency in Music Education). *Das Orchester—Zeitschrift für Orchesterkultur und Rundfunk-Chorwesen* 57: 27–29.

Sparre, M. (2009). *Balansenøkler. Om å balansere kroppen og livet*. Oslo: Tropos forlag.

Stensæth, K. and Trondalen, G. (2012). Dialogue on Intersubjectitvity: Interview with Stein Bråten and Colwyn Trevarthen. *Voices*. 4. Downloaded 5 January 2013: <https://voices.no/index.php/voices/article/view/682/568>.

Stern, D.N. (1985/2000). *The Interpersonal World of the Infant. A View from Psychoanalysis & Developmental Psychology*. New York: Basic Books.

Timmermann, T. (1983). Einzelmusiktherapie mit einem Suchtkranken Rockmusiker. *Musiktherapeutische Umschau* 4: 39–50.

Trondalen, G. (2004a). Jakten på det integrerte menneske. En studie av 30-GIM reiser med fokus på symboler og bilder. Final Project BMGIM training. *København: Dansk Institut for GIM Uddannelse*.

Trondalen, G. (2004b). *Klingende relasjoner. En musikkterapistudie av "signifikante øyeblikk" i musikalsk samspill med unge mennesker med anoreksi*. PhD, NMH-publikasjoner 2004:3, Oslo: Norges musikkhøgskole.

Trondalen, G. (2008). Musikkterapi—et relasjonelt perspektiv. In: G. Trondalen and E. Ruud (eds), *Perspektiver på musikk og helse. 30 år med norsk musikkterapi*. NMH-publikasjoner 2008:3, Skriftserie fra Senter for musikk og helse, Oslo: Norges musikkhøgskole.

Trondalen, G. (2009/2010). Exploring The Rucksack Of Sadness: Focused, Time-Limited Bonny Method of Guided Imagery and Music with a Female Executive. *Journal of Association for Music and Imagery* 12: 1–20.

Trondalen, G. (2010). The Flute and I: The Bonny Method of Guided Imagery and Music with a Young Man. *Voices: The World Forum for Music Therapy*, 4. A special issue dedicated to the life and work of Helen Bonny. Downloaded November 15 2013: <https://voices.no/index.php/voices/article/view/356/430>.

Trondalen, G. (2011a). Music Is About Feelings: Music Therapy with a Young Man Suffering From Anorexia Nervosa. In: A. Meadows (ed.), *Developments in Music Therapy Practice: Case Study Perspectives*, pp. 234–252. Gilsum, NH: Barcelona.

Trondalen, G. (2015). Resource-oriented Bonny Method og Guided Imagery and Music (R-oGIM) as a Health Resource for Musicians. Nordisk tidskrift for musikkterapi—*Nordic Journal of Music Therapy*, 205–240. doi: http://dx.doi.org10.1080/08098131.2014.987804

Trondalen, G. (2013). Music Therapy for Musicians. In L. Eyre (ed.), *Guidelines for Music Therapy Practice in Mental Health of Adolescents and Adults*. Gilsum, NH: Barcelona.

Trondalen, G. and Skårderud, F. (2007). Playing With Affects. And the importance of "affect attunement." *Nordic Journal of Music Therapy* 16: 100–111.

Vega, V.P. (2010). Personality, Burnout, and Longevity among Professional Music Therapists. *Journal of Music Therapy* 47: 155–179.

Waldman, J., and Clark, M.F. (2013). *Stand Flower Shine: Caring for the Woman Within.* Monkton, Maryland: Piney Creek Studio.

Yalom, I.D. (2001/2002). *The Gift of Therapy. Reflections on being a Therapist.* London: Judy Piatkus Ltd.

Zosso, A. (2010). Intéressons-nous aux musiciens! Étude qualitative sur leurs représentations de la santé. *Kinésithérapie la Revue* 98: 42–44.

AUTHOR INDEX

Subject Index